FISKE GUIDE TO COLLEGES 2015

FISKE GUIDE TO COLLEGES 2015

EDWARD B. FISKE

**former Education Editor of
the *New York Times***

**with Shawn Logue
and
the *Fiske Guide to Colleges* staff**

Published by Sourcebooks, Inc.
P.O. Box 4410
Naperville, Illinois 60567-4410
(630) 961-3900
Fax: (630) 961-2168
www.sourcebooks.com

Thirty-First Edition

**Your comments and corrections
are welcome. Please send them to:**

Fiske Guide to Colleges
Fax: (603) 835-7859
Email: editor@fiskeguide.com

Printed and bound in the United States of America.

DR 10 9 8 7 6 5 4 3 2

To Sunny

Contents

Index by State and Country

The colleges in this guide are listed alphabetically and cross-referenced for your convenience. Below is a list of the selected colleges grouped by state. Following this listing, you will find a second listing in which the colleges are categorized by the yearly cost of attending each school.

Index by Price

	PUBLIC	PRIVATE
$$$$	$13,001–$17,200	$45,001–$50,000
$$$	$10,001–$13,000	$42,001–$45,000
$$	$8,001–$10,000	$37,001–$42,000
$	Less than $8,000	Less than $37,000

Price categories are based on current tuition and fees and do not include room, board, transportation, and other expenses.

PUBLIC COLLEGES AND UNIVERSITIES

PRIVATE COLLEGES AND UNIVERSITIES

The Best Buys of 2015

Following is a list of 44 colleges and universities that qualify as Best Buys based on the quality of their academic offerings in relation to the cost of attendance.
(See page xviii for an explanation of how Best Buys were identified.)

Public

Arizona State University
University of Edinburgh (UK)*
The Evergreen State College
University of Florida
Indiana University
University of Iowa
Iowa State University
University of Mary Washington
University of Maryland Baltimore County
New College of Florida
University of North Carolina Asheville
University of North Carolina at Chapel Hill
North Carolina State University
Ohio University
Purdue University
University of St. Andrews (UK)*
SUNY–University at Buffalo
SUNY–College at Geneseo
University of Texas at Austin
University of Toronto (Can)*
Trinity College Dublin (Ire)*
University of Wisconsin–Madison

Private

Adelphi University
Alfred University
Austin College
Baylor University
Brigham Young University
California Institute of Technology
Cooper Union
Deep Springs College
Elon University
Goucher College
Morehouse College
Mount Holyoke College
Olin College of Engineering
Rice University
College of St. Benedict and St. John's University
University of the South (Sewanee)
Southwestern University
Spelman College
Syracuse University
Trinity University (TX)
Warren Wilson College
Xavier University of Louisiana

*These colleges are public institutions, but Americans and other non-Europeans should compare them in cost and academic quality to top U.S. privates.

Introduction

FISKE GUIDE TO COLLEGES—AND HOW TO USE IT

The 2015 edition of the *Fiske Guide to Colleges* is a revised and updated version of a book that has been a bestseller since it first appeared over three decades ago and is universally regarded as the definitive college guide of its type. Features of the new edition include:

- Updated write-ups on more than 300 of the country's best and most interesting colleges and universities

- A list of schools that no longer require the SAT or ACT of all applicants

- A "Sizing-Yourself-Up" questionnaire that will help you figure out what kind of school is best for you

- "A Guide for Preprofessionals," which lists colleges and universities strong in nine preprofessional areas

- A list of schools with strong programs for students with learning disabilities

- Designation of the 44 schools that constitute this year's Best Buys

- Statistical summaries that give you the numbers you need, but spare you those that you do not

- Authoritative rankings of each institution by academics, social life, and quality of life

- The unique "If You Apply To" feature, which summarizes vital information about each college's admission policies—including deadlines and essay topics

- A section on top Canadian, British, and Irish universities that offer first-rate academics and are easily the equivalent of the flagship public institutions and elite privates in the U.S.—but much less expensive than the latter

Picking the right college—one that will coincide with your particular needs, goals, interests, talents, and personality—is one of the most important decisions any young person will ever make. It is also a major investment. Tuition and fees alone now run at least $8,000 at a typical public university and close to $37,000 at a typical private college, and the overall tab at the most selective and expensive schools tops $50,000. Obviously, a major investment like that should be approached with as much information as possible.

That's where the *Fiske Guide to Colleges* fits in. It is a tool to help you make the most intelligent educational investment you can.

WHAT IS THE *FISKE GUIDE TO COLLEGES*?

Fiske Guide to Colleges mirrors a process familiar to any college-bound student and his or her family. If you are wondering whether to consider a particular college, it is logical to seek out friends or acquaintances who go there and ask them to tell you about their experiences. We have done exactly that—but on a far broader and more systematic basis than any individual or family could do alone.

In using the *Fiske Guide*, some special features should be kept in mind:

- The guide is **selective**. We have not tried to cover all four-year colleges and universities. Rather, we have taken more than 300 of the best and most interesting institutions in the nation—the ones that students most want to know about—and written descriptive essays of 1,000 to 2,500 words about each of them.

- Since choosing a college is a matter of making a calculated and informed judgment, this guide is also **subjective**. It makes judgments about the strengths and weaknesses of each institution, and it contains a unique set of ratings of each college or university on the basis of academic strength, social life, and overall quality of life. No institution is a good fit for every student. The underlying assumption of the *Fiske Guide* is that each of the colleges chosen for inclusion is the right place for some students but not a good bet for others. Like finding the right husband or wife, college admissions is a matching process. You know your own interests and needs; the *Fiske Guide* will tell you something about those needs that each college seems to serve best.

- Finally, the *Fiske Guide* is **systematic**. Each write-up is carefully constructed to cover specific topics—from the academic climate and the makeup of the student body to the social scene—in a systematic order. This means that you can easily take a specific topic, such as the level of academic pressure or the role of fraternities and sororities on campus, and trace it through all of the colleges that interest you.

HOW THE COLLEGES WERE SELECTED

How do you single out "the best and most interesting" of the more than 2,200 four-year colleges in the United States? Obviously, many fine institutions are not included. Space limitations simply require that some hard decisions be made.

The selection was done with several broad principles in mind, beginning with academic quality. Depending on how you define the term, there are about 175 "selective" colleges and universities in the nation, and by and large these constitute the best institutions academically. All of these are included in the *Fiske Guide*. In addition, an effort was made to achieve geographic diversity and a balance of public and private schools. Special efforts were made to include a good selection of four types of institutions that seem to be enjoying special popularity at present: engineering and technical schools, those with a religious emphasis, those with an environmental focus, and those located along the Sunbelt, where the cost of education is considerably less than at their Northern counterparts.

Finally, in a few cases we exercised the journalist's prerogative of writing about schools that are simply interesting. The tiny College of the Atlantic, for example, would hardly qualify on the basis of a superior academic program or national significance, but it offers an unusual and fascinating brand of liberal arts within the context of environmental studies. Likewise, Deep Springs College, the only two-year school in the *Fiske Guide*, is a unique institution of intrinsic interest.

HOW THE *FISKE GUIDE* WAS COMPILED

Each college or university selected for inclusion in the *Fiske Guide to Colleges* was sent a questionnaire to be filled out and returned online. This questionnaire covered topics ranging from their perception of the institution's mission to the demographics of the student body. Administrators were also asked to recruit a cross section of students to complete another electronic questionnaire with questions relating to what it is like to be a student at their particular college or university.

The questions for students, all open-ended and requiring short essays as responses, covered a series of topics ranging from the accessibility of professors and the quality of housing and dining facilities to the type of nightlife and weekend entertainment available in the area. By and large, students responded enthusiastically to the challenge we offered them. The quality of the information in the write-ups is a tribute to their diligence and openness. American college students, we learned, are a candid lot. They are proud of their institutions, but also critical—in the positive sense of the word.

Other sources of information were also employed. Administrators were invited to send us any in-house research or other documents that would contribute to an understanding of the institution, and they were invited to comment on their write-up in the last edition. Also, staff members have visited many of the colleges, and in some cases, additional information was solicited through published materials, such as the Common Data Set, telephone interviews, and other contacts with students and administrators.

The information from these various questionnaires was then incorporated into write-ups by staff members under the editorial direction of Edward B. Fiske, former education editor of the *New York Times*.

THE FORMAT

Each essay covers certain broad subjects in roughly the same order. They are as follows:

Academics	**Housing**
Campus setting	**Food**
Student body	**Social life**
Financial aid	**Extracurricular activities**

Certain topics are covered in all of the essays. The sections on academics, for example, always discuss the departments (or, in the case of large universities, schools) that are particularly strong or weak, while the sections on housing contain information on whether the dorms are co-ed or single sex and how students get the rooms they want. Other topics, however, such as class size, the need for a car, or the number of volumes in the library, are mentioned only if they constitute a particular strength or weakness at that institution.

We paid particular attention to the effect of the 21-year-old drinking age on campus life. Also, we noted efforts that schools' administrations have been making to change or improve the social and residential life on campuses through such measures as creating learning communities, restricting fraternities, and constructing new recreational facilities.

BEST BUYS

One of the lesser-known facts of life about higher education in the U.S. is that price and quality do not always go hand in hand. The college or university with the jumbo price tag may or may not offer a better education than the institution across town with much lower tuition. The relationship between the cost paid by the consumer and the quality of the education is affected by factors ranging from the size of an institution's endowment to calculations by college officials about what the market will bear.

In the face of today's skyrocketing tuition rates, students and families in all economic circumstances are looking for ways to get the best value for their education dollar. Fortunately, there are some bargains to be found in higher education; it just takes a bit of shopping around with a little guidance along the way. The *Fiske Guide* has an "Index by Price" that groups public and private institutions into four price categories, from inexpensive to very expensive. We also go one step further and suggest a number of schools that offer outstanding academics with relatively modest prices. This year we have designated 44 such institutions—22 public and 22 private—as Best Buys. Look for the Best Buy graphic next to the college name. (A list of all 2015 Best Buys appears on page xv.)

Most of our Best Buys fall into the inexpensive or moderate price category, and most have four- or five-star academic ratings. But there are bargains to be found among all levels and types of institutions. For example, some of the best values in American higher education are public colleges and universities that have remained relatively small and offer the smaller classes and personalized approach to academics that are typically found only in expensive private liberal arts colleges. Several of these are included as Best Buys.

STATISTICS

At the beginning of each write-up are basic statistics about the college or university—the ones that are relevant to applicants. These include the address, type of location (urban, small town, rural, etc.), enrollment, male/female ratio, SAT or ACT score ranges of the middle 50 percent of the students, percentage of students receiving need-based financial aid, relative cost, percentage of students who procure loans, average debt incurred by students, whether or not the institution has a chapter of Phi Beta Kappa, the number of students who apply and the percentage of those who are accepted, the percentage of accepted students who enroll, the number of freshmen who graduate within six years, and the number of freshmen who return for their sophomore year. For convenience, we include the telephone number of the admissions office, the school's website, and email and mailing addresses.

Unlike some guides, we have intentionally not published figures on the student/faculty ratio because colleges use different—and often self-serving—methods to calculate the ratio, thus making this particular statistic virtually meaningless.

Within the statistics, you will sometimes encounter the letters "N/A." In most cases, this means that the statistic was not available. In other cases, however, such as schools that do not require standardized tests, it means "not applicable." The write-up should make it clear which meaning is the relevant one.

We have included information on whether the school has a chapter of Phi Beta Kappa because this academic honorary society is a sign of broad intellectual distinction. Keep in mind, though, that even the very best engineering schools, because of their relatively narrow focus, do not usually qualify under the society's standards.

Tuition and fees are constantly increasing at American colleges, but for the most part, the cost of various institutions in relation to one another does not change. Rather than put in specific cost figures that would immediately become out of date, we have classified colleges into four groups ranging from inexpensive ($) to very expensive ($$$$) based on estimated costs of tuition and fees for the 2014–2015 academic year. The results for each college can be found in the "Index by Price" on pages xii–xiv. Separate scales were used for public and private institutions, and the ratings for the public institutions are based on the cost for residents of the state; out-of-staters should expect to pay more. If a public institution has a particularly low or high surcharge for out-of-staters, this is noted in the essay. The categories are defined as follows:

	PUBLIC	PRIVATE
$$$$	$13,001–$17,200	$45,001–$50,000
$$$	$10,001–$13,000	$42,001–$45,000
$$	$8,001–$10,000	$37,001–$42,000
$	Less than $8,000	Less than $37,000

SAT AND ACT SCORES

A special word needs to be said about standardized test scores. Some publications follow the practice of giving the median or average score registered by entering freshmen. Such figures, however, are easily misinterpreted as thresholds rather than averages. Many applicants forget that if a school reports average SAT–Critical Reading scores of 500, this means that, by definition, about half of the students scored below this number and half scored above. An applicant with a 480 would still have lots of company.

To avoid such confusion, we report the range of scores of the middle half of freshmen—or, to put it another way, the scores achieved by those in the 25th and 75th percentiles. For example, that college where the SAT–Critical Reading average was 500 might have a range of 440 to 560. So if you scored within this range, you would have joined the middle 50 percent of last year's freshmen. If your score was above 560, you would have been in the top quarter and could probably look forward to a relatively easy time; if it was below 440, you would have been struggling along with the bottom quarter of students.

Keep in mind that score ranges (and averages, for that matter) are misleading at the growing number of colleges that no longer require test scores from all applicants (see the section on SAT and ACT Optional Schools on pages xxxv–xxxvi). The ranges given for these colleges typically represent the range of scores of students who choose to submit their test scores, although they are not required to do so.

Unfortunately, another problem that arises with SAT and ACT scores is that, in their zeal to make themselves look good in a competitive market, some colleges and universities have been known to be less than honest in the numbers they release. They inflate their scores by not counting certain categories of students at the low end of the scale, such as athletes, certain types of transfer students, or students admitted under affirmative action programs. Some colleges have gone to such extremes as reporting the relatively high math scores of foreign students, but not their relatively low verbal scores. Aside from the sheer dishonesty of such practices, they can also be misleading. A student whose own scores are below the 25th percentile of a particular institution needs to know whether his profile matches that of the lower quarter of the student body as a whole, or whether there is an unreported pool of students with lower scores.

Even when dealing with a range rather than a single score, keep in mind that standardized tests are an imprecise measure of academic ability, and comparisons of scores that differ by less than 50 or 60 points on a scale of 200 to 800 have little meaning. According to the laws of statistics, there is one chance in three that the 550 that arrived in the little envelope from ETS should really be at least 580 or no more than 520. On the other hand, median scores offer some indication of your chances to get into a particular institution and the intellectual level of the company you will be keeping—or, if you prefer, competing against. Remember, too, that the most competitive schools have the largest and most sophisticated admissions staffs and are well aware of the limitations of standardized tests. A strong high school average or achievement in a field such as music will usually counteract the negative effects of modest SAT or ACT scores.

SCHOLARSHIP INFORMATION

Since the first edition of the *Fiske Guide to Colleges* appeared, the problems of financing college have become increasingly critical, mainly because of the rising cost of education and a shift from grants to loans as the basis for financial aid packages.

In response to these developments, many colleges and universities have begun to devise their own plans to help students pay for college. These range from subsidized loan programs to merit scholarships that are awarded without reference to financial need. Most of these programs are aimed at retaining the middle class. The last year or so has seen a number of both public and private universities substituting grants for loans and even eliminating tuition for low- and many middle-income students.

Some colleges advertise that they are "need-blind" in their admissions, meaning that they accept or reject applicants without reference to their financial situation and then guarantee to meet the "demonstrated need" of all students whom they accept. Others say they are need-blind in their admissions decisions, but do not guarantee to provide the financial aid required of all those who are accepted. Still others agree to meet the demonstrated need of all students, but they package their offers so that students they really want receive a higher percentage of their aid in the form of outright grants and a lower proportion in repayable loans.

"Demonstrated need" is itself a slippery term. In theory, the figure is determined when students and families fill out a needs-analysis form, which leads to an estimate of how much the family can afford to pay. Demonstrated need is then calculated by subtracting that figure from the cost at a particular institution. In practice, however, various colleges make their own adjustments to the standard figure.

Students and parents should not assume that their family's six-figure annual income automatically disqualifies them from some kind of subsidized financial aid. In cases of doubt, they should fill out a needs-analysis form to determine their eligibility. Whether they qualify or not, they are also eligible for a variety of awards made without regard to financial need.

Inasmuch as need-based awards are universal at the colleges in this guide, the awards generally singled out for special mention in the write-ups in the *Fiske Guide to Colleges* are the merit scholarships. We have not mentioned awards of a purely local nature—restricted to residents of a particular county, for example—but all college applicants should search out these awards through their guidance offices and the bulletins of the colleges that are of interest to them. Similarly, we have not duplicated the information on federally guaranteed loan programs that is readily available through both high school and college counseling offices, but we cite novel and often less expensive variants of the federal loan programs that are offered by individual colleges.

For more information on the ever-changing financial aid scene, we suggest that you consult the companion book to this guide, the *Fiske Guide to Getting Into the Right College.*

STUDENT LOANS AND AVERAGE DEBT RATING

In today's academic climate it is common for students and/or their families to borrow funds to assist with paying tuition and other college expenses. Therefore, a potentially useful piece of information is the proportion of students at each school who find it necessary to procure loans to finance their education. The student loan percentage considers any loan program used by students at any time during their tenure at an institution. Included are institutional, state, Federal Perkins, Federal Direct Subsidized and Unsubsidized student loans, Federal Family Education Loans, and private loans certified by an institution, excluding parent loans. To ensure the most accurate information, schools submitted this data for students comprising their last graduating class. When available, this data was confirmed using the Common Data Set.

For a variety of reasons, the average debt carried by graduating seniors varies greatly from college to college as well as from student to student. Nevertheless, when considering a particular school, many prospective students will find it useful to know how much debt is typically incurred by students at that school. Thus the 2015 *Fiske Guide* lists the Average Debt Rating (ADR) for each school as reported in each institution's Common Data

Set. The ADR is based on the average cumulative amount of principal borrowed per undergraduate at each college or university during their tenure as a student. Using $25,300 as the median we have organized the schools into four categories from low average debt ($) to high average debt ($$$$). Both public and private institutions were rated using the same criteria.

DEBT RATING	AVERAGE PER UNDERGRADUATE CUMULATIVE PRINCIPAL BORROWED
$$$$	More than $30,300
$$$	$25,301–$30,300
$$	$21,301–$25,300
$	Less than $21,300

RATINGS

Much of the fierce controversy that greeted the first edition of the *Fiske Guide to Colleges* over three decades ago revolved around its unique system of rating colleges in three areas: academics, social life, and quality of life. In each case, the ratings are done on a system of one to five, with three considered normal for colleges included in the *Fiske Guide*. If a college receives a rating higher or lower than three in any category, the reasons should be apparent from the narrative description of that college.

Students and parents should keep in mind that these ratings are obviously general in nature and inherently subjective. No complex institution can be described in terms of a single number or other symbol, and different people will have different views of how various institutions should be rated in the three categories. They should not be viewed as either precise or infallible judgments about any given college. On the other hand, the ratings are a helpful tool in using this book. The core of the *Fiske Guide* is the essays on each of the colleges, and the ratings represent a summary—an index, if you will—of these write-ups. Our hope is that each student, having decided on the kind of configuration that suits his or her needs, will then thumb through the book looking for other institutions with a similar set of ratings. The three categories, defined as follows, are academics, social life, and quality of life.

Academics ✍

This is a judgment about the overall academic climate of the institution, including its reputation in the academic world, the quality of the faculty, the level of teaching and research, the academic ability of students, the quality of libraries and other facilities, and the level of academic seriousness among students and faculty members.

Although the same basic criteria have been applied to all institutions, it should be evident that an outstanding small liberal arts college will by definition differ significantly from an outstanding major public university. No one would expect the former to have massive library facilities, but one would look for a high-quality faculty that combines research with a good deal of attention to the individual needs of students. Likewise, public universities, because of their implicit commitment to serving a broad cross section of society, might have a broader range of curriculum offerings but somewhat lower average SAT scores than a large private counterpart. Readers may find the ratings most useful when comparing colleges and universities of the same type.

In general, an academics rating of three pens suggests that the institution is a solid one that easily meets the criteria for inclusion in a guide devoted to the top 10 percent of colleges and universities in the nation.

An academics rating of four pens suggests that the institution is above average even by these standards and that it has some particularly distinguishing academic feature, such as especially rich course offerings or an especially serious academic atmosphere.

A rating of five pens for academics indicates that the college or university is among the handful of top institutions of its type in the nation on a broad variety of criteria. Those in the private sector will normally attract students with combined SAT scores of at least 1300 on Critical Reading and Math, and those in the public sector are invariably magnets for the top students in their states. All can be assumed to have outstanding faculties and other academic resources.

In response to the suggestion that the range of colleges within a single category has been too broad, we have introduced some half-steps into the ratings.

Social Life ☎

This is primarily a judgment about the amount of social life that is readily available. A rating of three telephones suggests a typical college social life, while four telephones means that students devote an above-average amount of time to socializing. It can be assumed that a college with a rating of five is something of a party school, which may or may not detract from the academic quality. Colleges with a rating below three have some impediment to a strong social life, such as geographic isolation, a high percentage of commuting students, or a disproportionate number of nerds who never leave the library. Once again, the reason should be evident from the write-up.

Quality of Life ★

This category grew out of the fact that schools with good academic credentials and plenty of social life may not, for one reason or another, be particularly wholesome places to spend four years. The term "quality of life" is one that has gained currency in social science circles, and, in most cases, the rating for a particular college will be similar to the academic and/or social ratings. The reader, though, should be alert to exceptions to this pattern. A liberal arts college, for example, might attract bright students who study hard during the week and party hard on weekends, and thus earn high ratings for academics and social life. If the academic pressure is cut-throat rather than constructive, though, and the social system is manipulative of women, this college might get an apparently anomalous two stars for quality of life. By contrast, a small college with modest academic programs and relatively few organized social opportunities might have developed a strong sense of supportive community, have a beautiful campus, and be located near a wonderful city—and thus be rated four stars for quality of life. As in the other categories, the reason can be found in the essay to which the ratings point.

OVERLAPS

Most colleges and universities operate within fairly defined "niche markets." That is, they compete for students against other institutions with whom they share important characteristics, such as academic quality, size, geographic location, and the overall tone and style of campus life. Not surprisingly, students who apply to College X also tend to apply to the other institutions in its particular niche. For example, "alternative" colleges such as Bard, Bennington, Hampshire, Marlboro, Oberlin, Reed, and Sarah Lawrence share many common applications, as do those with an evangelical flavor, such as Calvin, Hope, and Wheaton (IL).

As a service to readers, we ask each school to give us the names of the eight colleges with which they share the most common applications, and these are listed in the "Overlaps" section at the end of each write-up. We encourage students who know they are interested in a particular institution to check out the schools with which it competes—and perhaps then check out the "overlaps of the overlaps." This method of systematic browsing should yield a list of 15 or 20 schools that, based on the behavior of thousands of past applicants, would constitute a good starting point for the college search.

IF YOU APPLY TO

An extremely helpful feature is the "If You Apply To" section at the end of each write-up. This is designed for students who become seriously interested in a particular college and want to know more specifics about what it takes to get in.

This section begins with the deadlines for early admissions or early decision (if the college has such a program), regular admissions, and financial aid. If the college operates on a rolling-admissions basis—making decisions as the applications are received—this is indicated.

Many colleges require a fee in order to apply to their institution. This section includes any application fees that may be required. If there is no application fee, or if a school offers a discounted fee for online applications, this information is indicated as well.

Colleges have widely varying policies regarding interviews, both on campus and with alumni, so we indicate whether each of these is required, recommended, or optional. We also indicate whether reports from the person doing the interview are used in evaluating students or whether, as in many cases, the interview is seen only as a means of conveying information about the institution and answering applicants' questions. You are within your rights to ask the admissions office to explain how they view interviews.

This section also describes what standardized tests—SAT, ACT, or Subject—are required, and whether applicants are asked to write one or more essays. In the latter case, the topics are given.

CONSORTIA

Many colleges expand the range of their offerings by banding together with other institutions to offer unusual programs that they could not support on their own. These options range from foreign study programs around the world to semesters at sea, and keeping such arrangements in mind is a way of expanding the list of institutions that might meet your particular interests and needs. The final section of the *Fiske Guide* describes 12 of these consortia and lists the member institutions.

MOVING FORWARD

Students will find the *Fiske Guide* useful at various points in the college selection process—from deciding whether to visit a particular campus to selecting among institutions that have accepted them. To make it easy to find a particular college, the write-ups are arranged in alphabetical order in the indexes. An "Index by State and Country" and the "Index by Price" can be found on pages ix and xii, respectively.

While most people are not likely to start reading at Adelphi and keep going until they reach Yale (though some tell us they do), we encourage you to browse. This country has an enormously rich and varied network of colleges and universities, and there are dozens of institutions out there that can meet the needs of any particular student. Too many students approach the college selection process wearing blinders, limiting their sights to local institutions, the pet schools of their parents or guidance counselors, or ones they know only by possibly outdated reputations.

But applicants need not be bound by such limitations. Once you have decided on the type of school you think you want—a small liberal arts college, an engineering school, or whatever—we hope you will thumb through the book looking for similar institutions that might not have occurred to you. As already noted, one way to do this is to look at the overlaps of schools you like and then check out those schools' overlaps. Many students have found this worthwhile, and quite frankly, we view the widening of students' horizons about American higher education as one of the most important purposes of this book. Perhaps the most gratifying remark we hear comes when a student tells us, as many have, that she is attending a school that she first heard about while browsing through the *Fiske Guide to Colleges*.

Picking a college is a tricky business. But given the current buyer's market, there is no reason why you should not be able to find the right one. That's what the *Fiske Guide to Colleges* is designed to help you do. Happy college hunting.

Sizing Yourself Up

The college search is a game of matchmaking. You have interests and needs; the colleges have programs to meet those needs. If all goes according to plan, you'll find the right one and live happily ever after——or at least for four years. It ought to be simple, but today's admissions process resembles a high-stakes obstacle course.

Many colleges are more interested in making a sale than they are in making a match. Under intense competitive pressure, many won't hesitate to sell you a bill of goods if they can get their hands on your tuition dollars. Guidance counselors generally mean well, but they are often under duress from principals and trustees to steer students toward prestigious schools regardless of whether the fit is right. Your friends won't be shy with advice on where to go, but their knowledge is generally limited to a small group of hot colleges that everyone is talking about. National publications rake in millions by playing on the public's fascination with rankings, but a close look at their criteria reveals distinctions without a difference.

Before you find yourself spinning headlong on this merry-go-round, take a step back. This is your life and your college career. What are you looking for in a college? Think hard and don't answer right away. Before you throw yourself and your life history on the mercy of college admissions officers, you need to take some time to objectively and honestly evaluate your needs, likes and dislikes, strengths and weaknesses. What do you have to offer a college? What can a college do for you? Unlike the high school selection process, which is usually predetermined by your parents' property lines, income level, or religious affiliation, picking a college isn't a procedure you can brush off on dear ol' Mom and Dad. You have to take some initiative. You're the best judge of how well each school fits your personal needs and academic goals.

We encourage you to view the college selection process as the first semester in your higher education. Life's transitions often call for extra energy and focus. The college search is no exception. For the first time, you'll be contemplating a life away from home that can unfold in any direction you choose. Visions of majors and careers will dance in your head as you sample various institutions of higher learning, each with hundreds of millions of dollars in academic resources; it is hard to imagine a better hands-on seminar in research and matchmaking than the college search. The main impact, however, will be measured by what you learn about yourself. Piqued by new worlds of learning and tested by the competition of the admissions process, you'll be pushed as never before to show your accomplishments, clarify your interests, and chart a course for the future. More than one parent has watched in amazement as an erstwhile teenager suddenly emerged as an adult during the course of a college tour. Be ready when your time comes.

DEVELOP YOUR CRITERIA

One strategy is to begin the search with a personal inventory of your own strengths and weaknesses and your "wish list" for a college. This method tends to work well for compulsive list-makers and other highly organized people. What sorts of things are you especially good at? Do you have a list of skills or interests that you would like to explore further? What sort of personality are you looking for in a college? Mainstream? Conservative? Offbeat? What about extracurriculars? If you are really into riding horses, you might include a strong equestrian program in your criteria. The main problem won't be thinking of qualities to look for—you could probably name dozens— but rather figuring out what criteria should play a defining role in your search. Serious students should think carefully about the intellectual climate they are seeking. At some schools, students routinely stay up until 3:00 a.m. talking about topics like the value of deconstructing literary texts or the pros and cons of free trade. These same students would be viewed as geeks or weirdos on less cosmopolitan campuses. Athletes should take a hard look at whether they really want to play college ball and, if so, whether they want to go for an athletic scholarship or play at the less-pressured Division III level. Either way, intercollegiate sports require a huge time commitment.

Young women have an opportunity all to themselves—the chance to study at a women's college. The *Fiske Guide* profiles a dozen such campuses, a vastly underappreciated resource on today's higher education scene. With small classes and strong encouragement from faculty, students at women's colleges move on to graduate study in significantly higher numbers than their counterparts at co-ed schools, especially in the natural sciences. Males seeking an all-male experience will find two options in the *Fiske Guide*: Hampden–Sydney College and Wabash College.

Students with a firm career goal will want to look for a course of study that matches their needs. If you want to major in aerospace engineering, your search will be limited to schools that have the program. Outside of specialized areas like this, many applicants overestimate the importance of their anticipated major in choosing a college. If you're interested in a liberal arts field, your expected major should probably have little to do with your college selection. A big purpose of college is to develop interests and set goals. Most students change their intentions regarding a major at least two or three times before graduation, and once out in the working world, they often end up in jobs bearing no relation to their academic specialty. Even those with a firm career goal may not need as much specialization as they think at the undergraduate level. If you want to be a lawyer, don't worry yourself looking for something labeled "prelaw." Follow your interests, get the best liberal arts education available, and then apply to law school.

Naturally, it is never a bad idea to check out the department(s) of any likely major, and occasionally your choice of major will suggest a direction for your search. If you're really into national politics, it may make sense to look at some schools in or near Washington, D.C. If you think you're interested in a relatively specialized field, say, oceanography, then be sure to look for some colleges that are a good match for you and also have programs in oceanography. But for the most part, rumors about top-ranked departments in this or that should be no more than a tie-breaker between schools you like for more important reasons. There are good professors (and bad ones) in any department. You'll have plenty of time to figure out who is who once you've enrolled. Being undecided about your career path as a senior in high school is often a sign of intelligence. Don't feel bad if you have absolutely no idea what you're going to do when you "grow up." One of the reasons you'll be paying megabucks to the college of your choice is the prospect that it will open some new doors for you and expand your horizons. Instead of worrying about particular departments, try to keep the focus on big-picture items, such as: What's the academic climate? How big are the freshman classes? Do I like it here? and Are these my kind of people?

KEEP AN OPEN MIND

The biggest mistake of beginning applicants is hyperchoosiness. At the extreme is the "perfect-school syndrome," which comes in two basic forms.

In one category are the applicants who refuse to consider any school that doesn't have every little thing they want in a college. If you're one who begins the process with a detailed picture of Perfect U. in mind, you may want to remember the oft-quoted advice, "Two out of three ain't bad." If a college seems to have most of the qualities you seek, give it a chance. You may come to realize that some things you thought were absolutely essential are really not that crucial after all.

The other strain of perfect-school syndrome is the applicant who gets stuck on a "dream" school at the beginning and then won't look anywhere else. With those 2,200 four-year colleges out there (not counting those in Canada and Great Britain), it is just a bit silly to insist that only one will meet your needs. Having a first choice is OK, but the whole purpose of the search is to consider new options and uncover new possibilities. A student who has only one dream school—especially if it is a highly selective one—could be headed for disappointment.

As you begin the college search, don't expect any quick revelations. The answers will unfold in due time. Our advice? Be patient. Set priorities. Keep an open mind. Reexamine priorities. Again, be patient.

To get the ball rolling, move on to the Sizing-Yourself-Up Survey.

FISKE'S SIZING-YOURSELF-UP SURVEY

With apologies to Socrates, knowing thyself is easier said than done. Most high school students can analyze a differential equation or a Shakespearean play with the greatest of ease, but when it comes to cataloging their own strengths, weaknesses, likes, and dislikes, many draw a blank. But self-knowledge is crucial to the matching process at the heart of a successful college search. The 30-item survey on page xxvi offers a simple way to get a handle on some crucial issues in college selection—and what sort of college may fit your preferences.

In the space beside each statement, rate your feelings on a scale of 1 to 10, with 10 = Strongly Agree, 1 = Strongly Disagree, and 5 = Not Sure/Don't Have Strong Feelings. (For instance, a rating of 7 would mean that you agree with the statement, but that the issue is a lower priority than those you rated 8, 9, or 10.) After you're done, read on to "Grading Yourself" to find out what it all means.

FISKE'S SIZING-YOURSELF-UP SURVEY

Size

_____ 1. I enjoy participating in many activities.

_____ 2. I would like to have a prominent place in my community.

_____ 3. Individual attention from teachers is important to me.

_____ 4. I learn best when I can speak out in class and ask questions.

_____ 5. I am undecided about what I will study.

_____ 6. I want to earn a Ph.D. in my chosen field of study.

_____ 7. I learn best by listening and writing down what I hear.

_____ 8. I would like to be in a place where I can be anonymous if I choose.

_____ 9. I prefer devoting my time to one or two activities rather than many.

_____ 10. I want to attend a college that most people have heard of.

_____ 11. I am interested in a career-oriented major.

_____ 12. I like to be on my own.

Location

_____ 13. I prefer a college in a warm or hot climate.

_____ 14. I prefer a college in a cool or cold climate.

_____ 15. I want to be near the mountains.

_____ 16. I want to be near a lake or ocean.

_____ 17. I prefer to attend a college in a particular state or region.

_____ 18. I prefer to attend a college near my family.

_____ 19. I want city life within walking distance of my campus.

_____ 20. I want city life within driving distance of my campus.

_____ 21. I want my campus to be surrounded by natural beauty.

Academics and Extracurriculars

_____ 22. I like to be surrounded by people who are freethinkers and nonconformists.

_____ 23. I like the idea of joining a fraternity or sorority.

_____ 24. I like rubbing shoulders with people who are bright and talented.

_____ 25. I like being one of the smartest people in my class.

_____ 26. I want to go to a prestigious college.

_____ 27. I want to go to a college where I can get an excellent education.

_____ 28. I want to try for an academic scholarship.

_____ 29. I want a diverse college.

_____ 30. I want a college where the students are serious about ideas.

Grading Yourself

Picking a college is not an exact science. People who are total opposites can be equally happy at the same college. Nevertheless, particular types tend to do better at some colleges than others. Each item in the survey is designed to test your feelings on an important issue related to college selection. "Sizing Up the Survey" (below) offers commentary on each item.

Taken together, your responses may help you construct a tentative blueprint for your college search. Statements 1–12 deal with the issue of size. Would you be happier at a large university or a small college? Here's the trick: Add the sum of your responses to questions 1–6. Then make a second tally of your responses to 7–12. If the sum of 1–6 is larger, you may want to consider a small college. If 7–12 is greater, then perhaps a big school would be more to your liking. If the totals are roughly equal, you should probably consider colleges of various sizes.

Statements 13–21 deal with location. The key in this section is the intensity of your feeling. If you replied to number 13 with a 10, does that mean you are going to look only at schools in warm climates? Think hard. If you consider only schools within a certain region or state, you'll be eliminating hundreds of possibilities. By examining your most intense responses—the 1s, 2s, 9s, and 10s—you'll be able to create a geographic profile of likely options.

Statements 22–30 deal with big-picture issues related to the character and personality of the college that may be in your future. As before, pay attention to your most intense responses. Read on for a look at the significance of each question.

SIZING UP THE SURVEY

1. **I enjoy participating in many activities.** Students at small colleges tend to have more opportunities to be involved in many activities. Fewer students means less competition for spots.

2. **I would like to have a prominent place in my community.** Student-council presidents and other would-be leaders take note: it is easier to be a big fish if you're swimming in a small pond.

3. **Individual attention from teachers is important to me.** Small colleges generally offer more one-on-one with faculty both in the classroom and the laboratory.

4. **I learn best when I can speak out in class and ask questions.** Students who learn from interaction and participation would be well-advised to consider a small college.

5. **I am undecided about what I will study.** Small colleges generally offer more guidance and support to students who are undecided. The exception: students who are considering a preprofessional or highly specialized major.

6. **I want to earn a Ph.D. in my chosen field of study.** A higher percentage of students at selective small colleges earn a Ph.D. than those who attend large institutions of similar quality.

7. **I learn best by listening and writing down what I hear.** Students who prefer lecture courses will find more of them at large institutions.

8. **I would like to be in a place where I can be anonymous if I choose.** At a large university, the supply of new faces is never-ending. Students who have the initiative can always reinvent themselves.

9. **I prefer devoting my time to one or two activities rather than many.** Students who are passionate about one activity—say, writing for the college newspaper—will often find higher quality at a bigger school.

10. **I want to attend a college that most people have heard of.** Big schools have more name recognition because they're bigger and have Division I athletic programs. Even the finest small colleges are relatively anonymous among the general public.

11. **I am interested in a career-oriented major.** More large institutions offer business, engineering, nursing, etc., though some excellent small institutions do so as well (depending on the field).

12. **I like to be on my own.** A higher percentage of students live off campus at large schools, which are more likely to be in urban areas than their smaller counterparts.

13. **I prefer a college in a warm or hot climate.** Keep in mind that the Southeast and the Southwest have far different personalities (not to mention humidity levels).

14. **I prefer a college in a cool or cold climate.** Consider the Midwest, where there are many fine schools that are notably less selective than those in the Northeast.

15. **I want to be near the mountains.** You're probably thinking Colorado or Vermont, but don't zero in too quickly. States from Maine to Georgia and Arkansas to Arizona have easy access to mountains.

16. **I want to be near a lake or ocean.** Oceans are only on the coasts, but keep in mind the Great Lakes, the Finger Lakes, etc. Think about whether you want to be on the water or, say, within a two-hour drive.

17. **I prefer to attend a college in a particular state or region.** Geographical blinders limit options. Even if you think you want a certain area of the country, consider at least one college located elsewhere just to be sure.

18. **I prefer to attend a college near my family.** Unless you're planning to live with Mom and Dad, it may not matter whether your college is a two-hour drive or a two-hour plane ride.

19. **I want city life within walking distance of my campus.** Check out the neighborhood(s) surrounding your campus. Urban campuses—even in the same city—can be wildly different.

20. **I want city life within driving distance of my campus.** Unless you're a hard-core urban dweller, a suburban perch near a city may beat living in the thick of one. Does public transportation or a campus shuttle help students get around?

21. **I want my campus to be surrounded by natural beauty.** A college viewbook will take you only so far. To really know if you'll fall in love with the campus, visiting is a must.

22. **I like to be surrounded by people who are freethinkers and nonconformists.** Plenty of schools cater specifically to students who buck the mainstream. Talk to your counselor or browse the *Fiske Guide to Colleges* to find some.

23. **I like the idea of joining a fraternity or sorority.** Greek life is strongest at mainstream and conservative-leaning schools. Find out if there is a split between Greeks and non-Greeks.

24. **I like rubbing shoulders with people who are bright and talented.** This is perhaps the best reason to aim for a highly selective institution, especially if you're the type who rises to the level of the competition.

25. **I like being one of the smartest people in my class.** If so, maybe you should skip the highly selective rat race. Star students get the best a college has to offer.

26. **I want to go to a prestigious college.** There is nothing wrong with wanting prestige. Think honestly about how badly you want a big-name school and act accordingly.

27. **I want to go to a college where I can get an excellent education.** Throw out the *U.S. News* rankings and think about which colleges will best meet your needs as a student.

28. **I want to try for an academic scholarship.** Students in this category should consider less-selective alternatives. Scholarships are more likely if you rank high in the applicant pool.

29. **I want a diverse college.** All colleges pay lip service to diversity. To get the truth, see the campus for yourself and take a hard look at the student-body statistics in the *Fiske Guide*'s write-ups.

30. **I want a college where students are serious about ideas.** Don't assume that a college necessarily attracts true intellectuals merely because it is highly selective. Some top schools are known for their intellectual climate—and others for their lack of it.

A Guide for Preprofessionals

The lists that follow include colleges and universities with unusual strength in each of nine preprofessional areas: architecture, art/design, business, communications/journalism, engineering, film/television, dance, drama, and music. We also offer lists covering two of today's hottest interdisciplinary majors: environmental studies and international studies. In compiling the lists, we drew on data from the thousands of surveys used to compile the *Fiske Guide*. We examined the strongest majors at each college as reported in student and administrative questionnaires, and then weighed these against the selectivity and overall academic quality of each institution. After compiling tentative lists in each subject, we queried our counselor advisory group, listed on page 815, for additional suggestions and feedback. To make the lists as useful as possible, we have included some schools that do not receive full-length write-ups in the *Fiske Guide*. Moreover, while the lists are suggestive, they are by no means all-inclusive, and there are other institutions in the *Fiske Guide* that offer fine programs in these areas. Nevertheless, we hope the lists will be a starting place for students interested in these fields.

If you are planning a career in one of the subjects below, your college search may focus largely on finding the best programs for you in that particular area. But we also recommend that you shop for a school that will give you an adequate dose of liberal arts. For that matter, you might consider a double major (or minor) in a liberal arts field to complement your area of technical expertise. If you allow yourself to get too specialized too soon, you may end up as tomorrow's equivalent of the typewriter repairman. In a rapidly changing job market, nothing is so practical as the ability to read, write, and think.

ARCHITECTURE
Private Universities Strong in Architecture

Carnegie Mellon University
The Catholic University of America
Columbia University
Cooper Union
Cornell University
Drexel University
Hobart and William Smith Colleges
Howard University
Lehigh University
Massachusetts Institute of Technology
University of Miami (FL)
Northeastern University
University of Notre Dame
Princeton University
Rensselaer Polytechnic Institute
Rice University
University of Southern California
Syracuse University
Temple University
Tuskegee University
Tulane University
Washington University in St. Louis

Public Universities Strong in Architecture

University of Arizona
UC–Berkeley
University of Cincinnati
Clemson University
University of Florida
Georgia Institute of Technology
University of Illinois at Urbana–Champaign
University of Kansas
Kansas State University
University of Maryland
Miami University (OH)
University of Michigan
University of Nebraska–Lincoln
New Jersey Institute of Technology
University of Oregon
Pennsylvania State University
SUNY–University at Buffalo
University of Texas at Austin
Texas A&M University
Virginia Tech
University of Washington

A Few Arts-Oriented Architecture Programs

Barnard College
Bennington College
Pratt Institute
Rhode Island School of Design
Savannah School of Art and Design
Wellesley College
Yale University

ART/DESIGN
Top Schools of Art and Design

Art Center College of Design
School of the Art Institute of Chicago
California College of the Arts
California Institute of the Arts
Cooper Union
Kansas City Art Institute
Maryland Institute, College of Art
Massachusetts College of Art
Moore College of Art and Design
School of the Museum of Fine Arts (MA)
North Carolina School of the Arts
Otis Institute of Art and Design
Parsons School of Design
Pratt Institute
Rhode Island School of Design
Ringling School of Art and Design
San Francisco Art Institute
Savannah College of Art and Design
School of Visual Arts (NY)

Major Universities Strong in Art or Design

American University
University of the Arts (PA)
Boston College
Boston University
Carnegie Mellon University
University of Cincinnati
Cornell University
Drexel University
Harvard University
University of Michigan
New York University
University of Pennsylvania
Syracuse University
University of Washington
Washington University in St. Louis
Yale University

Small Colleges and Universities Strong in Art or Design

Alfred University
Bard College
Brown University
Centre College
Cornell College
Dartmouth College
Furman University
Hollins University
Kenyon College
Lake Forest College
Lewis & Clark College
Manhattanville College
Mills College
Randolph College
Sarah Lawrence College
Scripps College
Skidmore College
Smith College
Southwestern University
SUNY–Purchase
Vassar College
Wheaton College (MA)
Willamette University
Williams College

BUSINESS
Major Private Universities Strong in Business

American University
Baylor University
Boston College
Boston University
Carnegie Mellon University
Case Western Reserve
University of Dayton
Emory University
Fordham University
Georgetown University
Howard University
Ithaca College
Lehigh University
Massachusetts Institute of Technology
New York University
University of Notre Dame
University of Pennsylvania
Pepperdine University
Rensselaer Polytechnic Institute
University of San Francisco
Santa Clara University
University of Southern California
Southern Methodist University
Syracuse University
Texas Christian University
Tulane University
Villanova University
Wake Forest University
Washington University in St. Louis

Public Universities Strong in Business

University of Arizona
UC–Berkeley
University of Cincinnati
University of Connecticut
University of Florida
University of Georgia
University of Illinois at Urbana–Champaign
Indiana University
James Madison University
University of Kansas
University of Maryland
University of Massachusetts Amherst
Miami University (OH)
University of Michigan
University of Minnesota
University of Missouri
University of North Carolina at Chapel Hill
Ohio State University
Ohio University
University of Oregon
Pennsylvania State University
University of Pittsburgh
Rutgers–The State University of New Jersey
University of South Carolina
SUNY–University at Albany
SUNY–Binghamton University
SUNY–University at Buffalo
SUNY–College at Geneseo
University of Tennessee Knoxville
Texas A&M University
University of Texas at Austin
University of Vermont
University of Virginia
University of Washington
College of William and Mary
University of Wisconsin–Madison

Small Colleges and Universities Strong in Business

Agnes Scott College
Babson College
Bentley University
Bucknell University
Calvin College
Claremont McKenna College
Clarkson University
Eckerd College
Fairfield University
Franklin and Marshall College
Furman University
Gettysburg College
Guilford College
Hendrix College
Lafayette College
Lake Forest College
Lehigh University
Lewis & Clark College
Millsaps College
Morehouse College
Muhlenberg College
Oglethorpe College
Ohio Wesleyan University
Presbyterian College
Rhodes College
University of Richmond
Ripon College
Skidmore College
Southwestern University
Stetson College
Susquehanna University
Trinity University
Washington and Jefferson College

Washington and Lee University
Whittier College
Wofford College
Worcester Polytechnic Institute
Xavier University of Louisiana

COMMUNICATIONS/ JOURNALISM
Colleges and Universities Strong in Communications/Journalism
American University
Arizona State University
Boston University
UC–Los Angeles
UC–San Diego
University of Florida
University of Georgia
University of Illinois at Urbana–Champaign
Indiana University
Ithaca College
University of Kansas
University of Maryland
University of Michigan
University of Missouri
University of Nebraska–Lincoln
University of North Carolina at Chapel Hill
Northwestern University
Ohio University
University of Oregon
Pepperdine University
St. Lawrence University
University of San Francisco
University of Southern California
Stanford University
Syracuse University
Texas Christian University
University of Utah
University of Wisconsin–Madison

ENGINEERING
Top Technical Institutes
California Institute of Technology
California Polytechnic Institute–San Luis Obispo
Colorado School of Mines
Cooper Union
Florida Institute of Technology
Georgia Institute of Technology
Harvey Mudd College

Illinois Institute of Technology
Massachusetts Institute of Technology
Michigan Technological University
New Jersey Institute of Technology
New Mexico Institute of Mining and Technology
Rensselaer Polytechnic Institute
Rochester Institute of Technology
Rose–Hulman Institute of Technology
Stevens Institute of Technology
Worcester Polytechnic Institute

Private Universities Strong in Engineering
Boston University
Bradley University
Brigham Young University
Brown University
Carnegie Mellon University
Case Western Reserve
The Catholic University of America
Columbia University
Cornell University
Drexel University
Duke University
The George Washington University
The Johns Hopkins University
Northeastern University
Northwestern University
University of Notre Dame
Olin College of Engineering
University of Pennsylvania
Princeton University
University of Rochester
Rochester Institute of Technology
Santa Clara University
University of Southern California
Southern Methodist University
Stanford University
Syracuse University
Tufts University
Tulane University
University of Tulsa
Vanderbilt University
Villanova University
Washington University in St. Louis

Public Universities Strong in Engineering
University of Arizona
UC–Berkeley
UC–Davis

UC–Los Angeles
UC–San Diego
University of Cincinnati
Clemson University
University of Connecticut
University of Delaware
University of Florida
University of Illinois at Urbana–Champaign
Iowa State University
University of Kansas
University of Maryland
University of Massachusetts Amherst
McGill University
University of Michigan
Michigan State University
University of Missouri–Rolla
University of New Hampshire
The College of New Jersey
North Carolina State University
Ohio State University
Oregon State University
Pennsylvania State University
Purdue University
Queen's University (CA)
University of Rhode Island
Rutgers–The State University of New Jersey
SUNY–Binghamton University
SUNY–University at Buffalo
Texas A&M University
Texas Tech University
University of Texas at Austin
University of Toronto
University of Virginia
Virginia Tech
University of Washington
University of Wisconsin

Small Colleges and Universities Strong in Engineering
Alfred University
Bucknell University
Butler University
Calvin College
Clarkson University
Dartmouth College
Lafayette College
Lehigh University
Loyola University (MD)
University of the Pacific
Rice University

Smith College
Spelman College
Swarthmore College
Trinity College
Trinity University
University of Tulsa
Tuskegee University
Union College

FILM/TELEVISION
Major Universities Strong in Film/Television
Arizona State University
Boston University
UC–Los Angeles
University of Cincinnati
DePaul University
Drexel University
Emerson College
University of Florida
Ithaca College
University of Kansas
Memphis State University
University of Michigan
New York University
Northwestern University
Pennsylvania State University
Quinnipiac University
University of Southern California
Syracuse University
University of Texas at Austin
Wayne State University

Small Colleges and Universities Strong in Film/Television
Bard College
Beloit College
Brown University
California Institute of the Arts
Columbia College (CA)
Columbia College (IL)
The Evergreen State College
Hampshire College
Hofstra University
Hollins University
Occidental College
Pitzer College
Pomona College
Sarah Lawrence College School of Visual Arts
SUNY–Purchase College
Wesleyan University

PERFORMING ARTS—DANCE
Major Universities Strong in Dance
Arizona State University
UC–Irvine
UC–Los Angeles
UC–Riverside
Case Western Reserve
Florida State University
The George Washington University
Howard University
Indiana University
University of Iowa
University of Minnesota
New York University
Ohio University
Southern Methodist University
Texas Christian University
University of Texas at Austin
University of Utah
Washington University in St. Louis

Small Colleges and Universities Strong in Dance
Amherst College
Barnard College
Bennington College
Butler University
Connecticut College
Goucher College
Hollins University
Juilliard School
Kenyon College
Middlebury College
Mills College
Muhlenberg College
North Carolina School of the Arts
Princeton University
Sarah Lawrence College
Smith College
SUNY–Purchase College

PERFORMING ARTS—DRAMA
Major Universities Strong in Drama
Boston College
Boston University
Butler University
UC–Los Angeles
Carnegie Mellon University
The Catholic University of America
University of Chicago

DePaul University
Emerson College
Florida State University
Fordham University
Indiana University
University of Iowa
University of Minnesota
New York University
Northwestern University
University of North Carolina at Chapel Hill
University of Southern California
Southern Methodist University
Syracuse University
Texas Christian University
University of Washington
Yale University

Small Colleges and Universities Strong in Drama
Beloit College
Bennington College
Centre College
Colorado College
Connecticut College
Drew University
Ithaca College
Juilliard School
Kenyon College
Lawrence University
Macalester College
Middlebury College
Muhlenberg College
Occidental College
Otterbein University
Princeton University
Rollins College
Sarah Lawrence College
Skidmore College
SUNY–Purchase College
Vassar College
Whitman College
Wittenberg University

PERFORMING ARTS—MUSIC
Top Music Conservatories
Berklee College of Music
Boston Conservatory
California Institute of the Arts
Cleveland Institute of Music
Curtis Institute of Music
Eastman School of Music

Juilliard School
Manhattan School of Music
New England Conservatory of Music
North Carolina School of the Arts
Peabody Conservatory of Music
San Francisco Conservatory of Music

Major Universities Strong in Music

Baylor University
Boston College
Boston University
UC–Los Angeles
Carnegie Mellon University
Case Western Reserve
University of Cincinnati
University of Colorado–Boulder
University of Denver
DePaul University
Florida State University
Harvard University
Indiana University
University of Miami (FL)
Miami University (OH)
University of Michigan
University of Nebraska–Lincoln
New York University
Northwestern University
University of Oklahoma
University of Southern California
Southern Methodist University
Vanderbilt University
Yale University

Small Colleges and Universities Strong in Music

Bard College
Bennington College
Bucknell University
Butler University
DePauw University
Furman University
Gordon College
Illinois Wesleyan University
Ithaca College
Knox College
Lawrence University*
Loyola University New Orleans
Manhattanville College
Mills College
Oberlin College*
University of the Pacific

Rice University
St. Mary's College of Maryland
St. Olaf College
Sarah Lawrence College
Skidmore College
Smith College
SUNY–College at Geneseo
SUNY–Purchase College
Stetson University
Wesleyan University
Wheaton College (IL)

*These two schools are unusual because they combine a world-class conservatory with a top-notch liberal arts college.

ENVIRONMENTAL STUDIES

Allegheny College
College of the Atlantic
Bowdoin College
UC–Davis
UC–Santa Barbara
University of Chicago
Clark University
Colby College
University of Colorado–Boulder
Dartmouth College
Deep Springs College
Eckerd College
The Evergreen State College
Hampshire College
Hiram College
Hobart and William Smith Colleges
McGill University
Middlebury College
University of New Hampshire
University of New Mexico
University of North Carolina Asheville
Oberlin College
Prescott College
St. Lawrence University
Tulane University
University of Vermont
University of Washington
Williams College
University of Wisconsin–Madison

INTERNATIONAL STUDIES

American University
Austin College

Brandeis University
University of British Columbia
Brown University
Bucknell University
University of Chicago
Claremont McKenna College
Clark University
Colby College
Connecticut College
Dartmouth College
Davidson College
Denison University
University of Denver
Dickinson College
Earlham College
Eckerd College
The George Washington University
Georgetown University
Goucher College
Hiram College
The Johns Hopkins University
Kalamazoo College
Lewis & Clark College
University of Mary Washington
University of Massachusetts Amherst
Middlebury College
Mount Holyoke College
Occidental College
University of the Pacific
University of Pittsburgh
Pomona College
Princeton University
University of Puget Sound
Randolph College
Reed College
Rhodes College
University of Richmond
St. Olaf College
Scripps College
University of South Carolina
Sweet Briar College
Tufts University
Wesleyan University
College of William and Mary

Learning Disabilities

Accommodation for students with learning disabilities is one of the fastest-growing academic areas in higher education. Colleges and universities recognize that a significant segment of the population may suffer problems that qualify as learning disabilities, and the range of support services offered to such students is increasing. Assistance ranges from counseling services to accommodations such as tapes of lectures or extended time on exams.

Following are two lists—the first of major universities, the second of smaller colleges—that offer particularly strong services for LD students. If you qualify for such support, you should be diligent in checking out the services at each college on your list. If possible, pay a visit to the LD support office or have a phone conversation with one of the administrators. Since many such programs depend on the expertise of one or two people, the quality of the services can change abruptly with changes in staff.

Keep in mind also that many colleges are becoming increasingly skeptical of requests for LD services, especially when the initial diagnosis is made on the eve of the college search.

STRONG SUPPORT FOR STUDENTS WITH LEARNING DISABILITIES

Major Universities

American University
University of Arizona
Clark University
University of Colorado–Boulder
University of Connecticut
University of Denver
DePaul University
Fairleigh Dickinson University
University of Georgia
Hofstra University
Northeastern University
Purdue University
Rochester Institute of Technology
Syracuse University
University of Vermont

Small Colleges

Bard College
Curry College
Landmark College
Lesley University
Loras College
Lynn University
Manhattanville College
Marist College
Mercyhurst College
Mitchell College
Muskingum College
New England College
University of New England
St. Thomas Aquinas College (NY)
West Virginia Wesleyan College
Westminster College (MO)

SAT and ACT Optional Schools

Two decades ago a small number of U.S. colleges and universities, including Bates and Bowdoin, decided that they would no longer require all applicants to submit SAT or ACT scores. They reasoned that there is a significant pool of bright students who can do quality academic work but who for one reason or another do not test well. A "test optional" policy would allow schools to tap into this market.

Over the years the number of "test optional" or, in some cases, "test flexible" schools has grown dramatically. The National Center for Fair and Open Testing (FairTest), a Cambridge, Massachusetts–based advocacy organization that is critical of standardized testing in general, has tracked this growth, and at press time its website (www.fairtest.org) listed nearly 850 such colleges and universities. Reasons for this growing aversion to college admissions tests are many. The early test optional schools have been happy with the way the policy has worked out. The SAT has been a focus of repeated controversy, especially around incidents of scoring error. In a parallel development, a number of schools and a national commission headed by William Fitzsimmons, the dean of admission and financial aid at Harvard University, have begun to argue that SAT Subject Tests, AP exams, and International Baccalaureate exams—tests that are closely tied to curriculum—are more useful than regular SAT and ACT scores. And perhaps most importantly, the whole field of "test prep" has spiraled out of control. Students and parents alike are tired of the anxiety surrounding prep courses—not to mention the financial cost of helping bolster the coffers of Kaplan or Princeton Review.

Until recently there was not much that students could do—especially if they hoped to be able to choose among a range of quality colleges. Over the last few years, however, a critical mass has emerged of quality liberal arts colleges and major state universities that are "test optional" or "test flexible" in the sense that they offer applicants a range of options for the tests they take. There are now 63 such institutions covered in the *Fiske Guide*. For the first time, students who wish to avoid getting involved in the admissions-test rat race can do so while still enjoying a range of colleges and universities from which to choose.

Accordingly, we now publish a list of those colleges and universities in the guide that are "test optional." We are not recommending that any particular student eschew college admissions tests and apply only to these schools. As a resource designed to help students and parents, we are simply pointing out that applicants now have that option.

In looking over the list below of "test optional" or "test flexible" colleges and universities described in the *Fiske Guide*, please keep a couple of things in mind. First, most of the schools are large state universities or small liberal arts colleges. You won't find many other types, including the Ivies or flagship publics. Second, keep in mind that there are different ways of being "test optional" or "test flexible." Some schools, for example, only exempt students who meet certain GPA or class rank criteria, while others on the list still require other types of tests. Qualifications are noted in the footnotes. Finally, the "test optional" field is changing daily, so go to www.fairtest.org for updated information and, above all, confirm current policy with any school to which you are thinking of applying.

University of Aberdeen (5)
Agnes Scott College
University of Arizona
College of the Atlantic
Bard College
Bates College
Bennington College
Bowdoin College
Clark University
Colorado College (5)
Connecticut College (5)
Denison University

DePaul University
Dickinson College
Earlham College
Eugene Lang College–The New School for Liberal Arts
University of Florida
Franklin and Marshall College
Furman University
George Mason University (5)
University of Glasgow
Goucher College
Guilford College (5)

Gustavus Adolphus College
Hampshire College
Hartwick College
Hobart and William Smith Colleges
College of the Holy Cross
Hood College (3)
Ithaca College
Knox College
Lake Forest College
Lawrence University
Lewis & Clark College (5)
Loyola University Maryland

Manhattanville College
Marlboro College
McGill University
Middlebury College (5)
Mount Holyoke College
Muhlenberg College
New York University (5)
Pitzer College
Providence College
University of Rochester

Rollins College
St. John's College, MD
St. John's College, NM
St. Lawrence University
Saint Michael's College
Sarah Lawrence College
Smith College
University of the South (Sewanee)
Stetson University
Susquehanna University

Trinity College (CT) (5)
Union College
Ursinus College (4)
Wake Forest University
Washington and Jefferson College
Wheaton College (MA)
Wittenberg University
Worcester Polytechnic Institute (MA)

KEY

1 = SAT/ACT used only for placement and/or academic advising

2 = SAT/ACT required only from out-of-state applicants

3 = SAT/ACT used only when minimum GPA and/or class rank is not met

4 = SAT/ACT required for some programs

5 = SAT/ACT not required if applicant submits SAT Subject Test, Advanced Placement, International Baccalaureate, applies for a score optional consideration, substitutes for a personal portfolio/presentation, or other exams

A Note to the Reader

It seems like only yesterday that a small band of journalists gathered each evening in the back of the newsroom of the *New York Times*—where I was the Education Editor—to create the first edition of the *Fiske Guide to Colleges*. Now we've been in publication for more than 30 years!

The higher education scene was quite different in the early 1980s. Tuition and room and board averaged only $3,200 at public universities and $7,000 at private institutions. Stanford had just emerged as a national university, and hardly anyone outside the South had heard of Duke. AP exams and the Common Application were in their infancy, and Columbia still had not gotten around to admitting women. Division I university presidents still had some control over their athletic directors, and *U.S.News & World Report* was little more than a mediocre newsweekly.

But important changes were on the way. By the early 1980s the last of the baby boomers had worked their way through college. Admissions directors were losing sleep over whether they could fill their classrooms, so they responded with aggressive marketing campaigns. The methods they used seem quaint by current standards: telephone calls, video tapes (remember them?), and lavish four-color brochures that overflowed the mailbox of any students whose ACT scores were larger than their shoe size.

The aggressive marketing of colleges produced a backlash—and an opportunity. Someone needed to wade in on the side of students and parents and cut through all the hype that was coming from the colleges. Thus was born the *Fiske Guide to Colleges*. Our vision was to use basic journalistic techniques to create a college guide that would provide reliable information on what it was like to be a student at the "best and most interesting" colleges and universities in the country. Since then we have done just that for millions of students, parents, and school counselors.

Consistent with changes in the culture of higher education over the last three decades, the content of the school profiles in the *Fiske Guide* has evolved. Given the impact of globalization, we have documented the proliferation of study abroad programs, and we have added write-ups on universities in Canada, Britain, Scotland, and Ireland. The write-ups reflect colleges' increased sensitivity to issues of campus safety and to alcohol and drug abuse. Colleges today talk more about racial, ethnic, and socioeconomic diversity than they did in the early 1980s, although the numbers do not always show much progress. Many large universities have created "living/learning" communities in order to offer more intense learning environments within the context of a large institution. Perhaps most importantly, colleges, for better or worse, have seen it to be in their competitive interest to invest huge amounts of resources in student centers, fitness facilities, and other amenities designed to make the undergraduate experience more comfortable.

But one thing that has not changed over the last three decades is the importance of institutional cultures. When we started out to create the *Fiske Guide* the big editorial risk was: Do we describe yet another small liberal arts college with "the faculty often invite students to their homes for dinner," which would make all liberal arts schools begin to sound alike—creating a pretty dull reading experience? But it turned out not to be a problem. The schools in the *Fiske Guide* are just as diverse as the students who apply to them. Even schools that look the same on paper have their own distinctive institutional cultures and personalities. The task of the *Fiske Guide* has been to capture those cultures and personalities of the "best and most interesting" colleges in the country. Students can then decide which schools are the best match for their own interests and learning styles.

In the age of the Internet, information is abundant and cheap. Endless facts and opinions about any particular college or university are just a few clicks away, but to know everything is to know nothing. The real challenge for college-bound students—the same challenge that faced them in the early 1980s—is to cut through the mass of information that is being thrown at them and figure out what is really important. That's what the *Fiske Guide to Colleges* has been doing with authority for more than three decades. That's what we pledge to continue to do in the decades to come.

University of Aberdeen: See page 359.

Adelphi University

BEST BUY

One South Avenue, Garden City, NY 11530

Situated in a comfortable Long Island suburb within shouting distance of Manhattan, Adelphi lets you taste urban life without being overwhelmed. Serves primarily the New York tristate region, and the campus clears out on the weekends. Strong on preprofessional programs with a solid grounding in the liberal arts. Compare to Fairfield and Quinnipiac.

Everyone loves a great comeback story. In the mid-1990s, this small Long Island university was strapped for both cash and students because of mismanagement by a free-spending president and a negligent board of trustees. Thanks to new leadership and a revamped mission, Adelphi University has undergone a renaissance, hiring more than 200 new faculty over the last decade, adding or renovating 500,000 square feet of facilities, expanding student financial aid, and implementing a policy of keeping tuition lower than peer institutions. As a result, students speak of a palpable sense of energy among students and faculty. "Adelphi is a small campus, and you really get to know other students and professors because the classes are small, too," says a junior.

Adelphi occupies 75 acres in an attractive residential suburb replete with Gothic cathedrals and stately homes. Adelphi's most popular majors have a decidedly preprofessional bent: biology and premed, nursing, various health sciences, business, psychology, and the fine and performing arts. The notable theater program draws creative students not inclined to stray far from home, while the honors college offers a rigorous liberal arts program for exceptional students. Honors students must complete all the requirements for their major within that department or school and supplement their learning with intensive honors courses. Recent honors seminar topics included Genetic Disease and Genetic Engineering; The Decline and Fall of Certainty, Censorship, and Morality; The Fate of the Earth; and Equality and Inequality. Joint degree programs have been established in a number of disciplines, including physics, dentistry, law, and physical therapy. The combined degree program in engineering with Columbia allows students to earn a B.S. in physics from Adelphi and a B.S. in engineering from Columbia in five years, or an undergraduate and graduate degree in six years. Additional undergraduate degrees include music education, studio art, and peace studies. Adelphi has a well-staffed program for students with learning disabilities.

> "To get As you must think ahead and be ready for anything."

General education requirements include a 24-credit distribution in several areas (arts, humanities and languages, natural sciences and mathematics, and social sciences) as well as courses in composition and English, a foreign language, statistics, computer programming, critical thinking, or public speaking. Freshmen take part in an orientation course and a three-credit freshman seminar that introduces students to life at Adelphi.

Adelphi prides itself on its high retention and graduation rates, which are among the highest in the area and may reflect its emphasis on experiential learning and student engagement. Academics are challenging: "It is a highly competitive atmosphere," says one junior. "To get As you must think ahead and be ready for

Website: www.adelphi.edu
Location: Suburban
Private
Total Enrollment: 7,859
Undergraduates: 5,103
Male/Female: 30/70
SAT Ranges: CR 500–600, M 510–620
ACT Ranges: 22–28
Financial Aid: 96%
Expense: Pr $
Student Loans: 87%
Average Debt: $ $ $
Phi Beta Kappa: Yes
Applicants: 9,184
Accepted: 66%
Enrolled: 16%
Grad in 6 Years: 66%
Returning Freshmen: 82%
Academics: ✍ ✍ ✍
Social: ☎ ☎
Q of L: ★ ★ ★
Admissions: (516) 877-3050
Email Address: admissions@adelphi.edu

Strongest Programs:
Nursing
Elementary Education
Biology
Accounting
Performing Arts
Psychology
Physical Education

anything from your teachers." Nearly half of all classes have 19 or fewer students, and professors are commended for their accessibility and knowledge. "I believe that the quality of teaching has been very high at Adelphi," a student says. "The professors, most of whom have their doctorate degree, have experience in their field and bring that to the classroom."

Adelphi students have a "sense of appreciation for the university, and the campus itself," asserts a senior. "I also feel that there is a high involvement of the community and the alumni base that takes part in a lot of the events that go on here, which is definitely a plus for the students at Adelphi." More than two-thirds of Adelphi undergrads are women, which is high even among other liberal arts colleges. Ninety percent of the university's student body hails from New York, and just over half graduated in the top quarter of their high school class. Minority

"This is a commuter college." enrollment is consistent with the university's proximity to the Big Apple. Ten percent of students are African American, 13 percent Hispanic, and 7 percent Asian American. Political issues don't dominate campus conversations, but students say recent debates include issues of homosexuality and the importance of voting. Adelphi offers merit scholarships to qualified students. More than 250 athletic scholarships are available.

Despite "comfortable and well-maintained" residence halls, Adelphi remains primarily a suitcase school. Seventy-six percent of students live off campus, "even if they live close to school," says one student. "The housing on campus is pretty plentiful, especially because Adelphi just built another new dorm building," says a business management major. Though some grumble about the price of food on campus, most admit that there is plenty to choose from. "The food is OK," says a senior. "They are making changes and improving it, which is promising." Campus security maintains a presence and the university recently installed additional cameras and emergency boxes throughout campus. "I feel the security is good on campus," says one junior.

"This is a commuter college," a nursing student explains. "The weekdays are great. The weekends are quiet." The school sponsors 70 clubs and organizations, including seven sororities and fraternities that attract 9 percent of the women and men, respectively. Adelphi is a dry campus, and students say that the policy is strictly enforced. Still, "as a resident assistant, I know that the 'no alcohol' policies don't work," says a senior. "Students will be tricksters!" One student describes Garden City as "a very safe, low-key residential neighborhood," if not a college town. The glitz of New York City is just 40 minutes away by train, and the Long Island beaches draw crowds when it's warm.

Adelphi fields several competitive teams, including men's and women's basketball, men's and women's soccer, men's golf, and women's volleyball. The men's basketball team is a perennial tournament competitor, and women's lacrosse is a powerhouse, having recently become the first Division II team to win four national championships and three consecutive national titles. Men's and women's cross-country have brought home a slew of ECC championships in the past few years. In addition, the university has won the coveted New York Collegiate Athletic Conference Commissioner's Cup, awarded to the most outstanding program, for several years running. Intramurals are offered in a dozen sports.

"Adelphi has changed tremendously," says one happy student. "It has become more lively and fun." Indeed, this newfound optimism is infectious and seems to permeate the campus. Signs of rebirth and renewal are everywhere, from the campus facilities to the burgeoning enrollment. Although the university's commuter heritage can leave some wanting for more social opportunities, many find that this small Northeastern school fits the bill.

Agnes Scott College

141 East College Avenue, Decatur, GA 30030

Combines the tree-lined seclusion of Decatur with the bustle of Atlanta. More money in the bank per student than most Ivy League schools, and enrollment is up 50 percent in the past two decades. Recent physical plant additions give ASC exceptional facilities for a college of its size. Small classes, sisterhood, and a more exciting location than the Sweet Briars of the world.

Agnes Scott College, founded in 1889, offers a small-town campus atmosphere and provides women with an intellectually challenging institution—absent the distractions of men. The college is known for its science and math programs, but it also produces skilled writers and artists and continues to be one of the South's leading women's schools. ASC's climate as a small, single-sex institution leads to close relationships with the faculty and very involved students—both academically and socially. "We believe in the power of women, of deep thinking, of honor, of social justice, of learning for the sake of learning," muses one senior. "We believe in being better than we were yesterday. We believe we can change the world."

> "We believe in the power of women."

The Agnes Scott campus sits on 100 acres in the historic district of Decatur, just outside of Atlanta. The well-maintained Gothic and Victorian buildings are surrounded by gardens filled with rare shrubs, bushes, and trees—all evidence of strong alumnae support. The $36.5 million Science Center at Agnes Scott includes an X-ray spectrometer, nuclear magnetic resonance imaging equipment, and a scanning tunneling microscope. The school's Delafield Planetarium has a computer-controlled Zeiss projector, one of only 10 in the United States.

Aside from outstanding instruction in the sciences, Agnes Scott provides students with solid grounding in the liberal arts. First-year students may choose seminars on innovative topics such as Shakespeare and Film; The Value of Life in Latin America; Reducing World Poverty; and Cloning, Transgenes, and Warfare: Biotechnology in Today's Society. To graduate, students must complete one semester of English composition and literature, plus courses in math, historical studies or classical civilization, fine arts, science, social and cultural analysis, and physical education. Students must also attain intermediate-level proficiency in a foreign language and, because ASC is affiliated with the Presbyterian Church, take one course in religion or philosophical thought.

> "The courses are rigorous and challenging."

Academically, Agnes Scott delivers solid programs in biology and math. The school also offers a top-notch German program. Notable majors include public health and a computer science dual degree with Emory; newer minors include public health, film and media studies, and environmental and sustainability studies. Those participating in research may attend or present results at an annual conference held in the spring. The new, three-week summer Bridge to Business program acquaints students with different aspects of business education and includes topics such as accounting,

Website: www.agnesscott.edu
Location: City Center
Private
Total Enrollment: 827
Undergraduates: 827
Male/Female: 0/100
SAT Ranges: CR 520–670, M 510–620
ACT Ranges: 22–29
Financial Aid: 100%
Expense: Pr $
Student Loans: 77%
Average Debt: $ $ $
Phi Beta Kappa: Yes
Applicants: 1,554
Accepted: 62%
Enrolled: 24%
Grad in 6 Years: 64%
Returning Freshmen: 82%
Academics: ✍ ✍ ✍
Social: ☎ ☎
Q of L: ★ ★ ★ ★
Admissions: (404) 471-6285
Email Address: admission@agnesscott.edu

Strongest Programs:
Astrophysics
Biology
Mathematics
German
Psychology
Economics
English

business communications, international business, and entrepreneurship. The overall academic climate at ASC is rigorous. "The courses are rigorous and challenging," says a senior. "In every course, there is a cross-curricular approach. You will, at the end of your four years, be an excellent writer, speaker, and critical thinker." The average first-year class size is 22 students, which encourages close student/faculty interactions in the classroom. "The professors I have had so far want me to learn and care about the quality of my education," says one anthropology major.

For those students wishing to leave Agnes Scott's idyllic campus behind for a time, there are study abroad options available in 49 countries, including Argentina, Australia, France, Ghana, India, Japan, and Thailand. The Hubert Scholars Program combines experiential learning with humanitarian service either at home or abroad. Past Hubert scholars have conducted HIV/AIDS research in South Africa and traveled to Mongolia and Tanzania. Engineers may complete their degrees through a 3–2 program with Georgia Tech. As a member of the Atlanta Regional Council for Higher Education*, Agnes Scott shares facilities and resources with 19 other schools in the area through a cross-registration program.

"Agnes Scott women do not rest on the laurels of their institution. We earn our accolades—every single one of them," a senior says. The ASC student body hails mainly from the Southeast; 56 percent are Georgia natives. One student describes the student body as "driven, somewhat idealistic, thoughtful, and motivated." Despite the school's small size, its campus is quite diverse, with 35 percent of the student body African American, 8 percent Hispanic, and 3 percent Asian American. Politics attract Scotties, and recent issues include the living wage campaign, human rights, and refugee services. An honor system, enforced by a student judiciary, allows for self-scheduled and unproctored exams. Agnes Scott awards merit scholarships averaging $18,000 annually, based on academic performance, leadership, or musical ability.

> "The upperclass dorms are really big and nice, but there is NO air-conditioning in two of the main buildings."

Eighty-five percent of Agnes Scott students live in the dorms, which are linked by tree-lined brick walks. "Students aren't allowed to move off campus, which creates a close campus community, but can be a barrier financially because room and board is so expensive," says a first-year student. Dorms are described as being spacious and well maintained compared to other colleges. Juniors and seniors can live in Avery Glen, the college-owned apartment complex, while first-years are assigned to one of two dorms (out of six total). "The upperclass dorms are really big and nice, but there is NO air-conditioning in two of the main buildings," says one student. "If you put fans in your room it is really not that bad, and it usually only sucks for the month of August and the first weeks of September." Agnes Scott has no sororities, but the college itself is a close-knit sisterhood. The selection of food at Agnes Scott dining facilities takes every type of diet into consideration. "The food is very good for campus food," says one student. "Guests always rave about it."

As for the ACS social scene, the programming group on campus (ProBo) always provides the students with something to do. "Your social life is up to you, plain and simple," says a creative writing major. "The great thing is that Atlanta is literally next door, and there is always something to do. I've had a blast going to concerts, eating at great restaurants, and going to the High Museum of Art." Convenient public transportation serves cultural landmarks and provides access to the social scene in nearby Atlanta. Underage students may not imbibe, in accordance with Georgia state law; enforcement falls under the honor code. One student says the restrictions work well, and 21-year-olds can enjoy alcohol in their dorms and at certain functions. Every October, students invite dates to a formal dance known as Black Cat. Other quaint traditions survive, too, such as throwing recently engaged classmates into

Academically, Agnes Scott delivers solid programs in biology and math. The school also offers a top-notch German program.

The average first-year class size is 22 students, which encourages close student/faculty interactions in the classroom.

the alumnae pond. And seniors who get into grad school or find jobs go to the top of the college bell tower, pealing out chimes to share the good news. "Agnes Scott is centered around traditions," says a student. "I cannot reveal too much insider information about it because it has a air of mystery for non-students and new students."

Decatur itself is not really a "college town," but there are some attractions for Agnes Scott students. "There are still nice little venues and coffee shops; very hip and fun," a student says. A lot of ASC students get involved with community service both on and off campus, with Habitat for Humanity, the DeKalb Rape Crisis Center, Girl Scouts, Hands Across Atlanta, and Best Buddies. When traveling, popular road trips include Stone Mountain and Six Flags, or New Orleans for Mardi Gras.

Agnes Scott is a member of the Great South Athletic Conference, and the most competitive teams include tennis, soccer, and softball. The Scottie Tennis team won the Great South Athletic Conference Championship in 2013 for a fifth consecutive year. About 10 percent of students participate in intramural activities, which include the standard roundup of sports plus a few more exotic options, such as Frisbee.

Small but mighty, ASC stands out for the little touches that make students feel they're part of a close-knit community, including pine-scented brochures sent to accepted applicants. "Agnes Scott is distinctive in that it is a bubble of academia in the middle of Atlanta," says a sophomore. The school offers challenging courses in science and math and supplements its instruction in many other fields with a variety of programs that allow students to explore new opportunities both on campus, in conjunction with other institutions, and abroad.

Agnes Scott has no sororities, but the college itself is a close-knit sisterhood.

Overlaps

Vanderbilt, Emory, University of Georgia, Georgia State, Spelman, Oglethorpe, Georgia Tech

If You Apply To ➢   **Agnes Scott:** Early action: Nov. 30. Regular admissions: Mar. 1. Application fee: $35 (paper), free (online). Campus and alumnae interviews: optional, evaluative. SATs or ACTs: optional. Subject Tests: optional. Accepts the Common Application. Essay question.

University of Alabama

Box 870132, Tuscaloosa, AL 35487-0166

"Roll, tide, roll" still says a lot about the University of Alabama—but not everything. Passion for the Crimson Tide is as strong as ever, but also look for strong honors programs, emphasis on undergraduate research, and pockets of professional excellence. Though its football team is back among the nation's elite, 'Bama still pales academically in comparison with rivals University of Georgia and University of Florida.

Although the University of Alabama earned its national reputation on the gridiron, the state's first university is committed to making an academic name for itself as well. UA has increased its emphasis on global perspectives, computer-based technologies, freshman learning communities, and undergraduate research in an effort to attract the South's best and brightest. It seems students have taken notice: "We are more academically based," observes one senior, "and we have better programs and facilities."

'Bama's thousand-acre campus combines classical, revival-style buildings (several of which survived the Civil War) with modern structures. One of the most stunning in the South, the campus wraps around a shaded quadrangle, the home of the main library and "Denny Chimes," a campanile carillon that rings the Westminster Chimes on the quarter hour. Capstone College of Nursing and Tanglewood Pavilion are among the newest additions to campus.

Website: www.ua.edu
Location: City Center
Public
Total Enrollment: 28,420
Undergraduates: 25,109
Male/Female: 47/53
SAT Ranges: CR 500–620, M 500–640
ACT Ranges: 22–30
Financial Aid: 42%
Expense: Pub $ $

(continued)

Student Loans: 43%

Average Debt: $ $ $

Phi Beta Kappa: Yes

Applicants: 26,409

Accepted: 53%

Enrolled: 45%

Grad in 6 Years: 67%

Returning Freshmen: 85%

Academics: ✍ ✍ ✍

Social: ☎ ☎ ☎

Q of L: ★ ★ ★

Admissions: (205) 348-5666

Email Address: admissions@ ua.edu

Strongest Programs:

Nursing

Biology

Elementary Education

Accounting

Psychology

Metallurgical and Materials Engineering

Food and Nutrition

Art and Art History

The only course 'Bama requires students to take during the first year on campus is a two-term English composition sequence.

The University of Alabama is organized into eight undergraduate colleges and schools, which together offer more than 80 undergraduate degree programs. The Culverhouse College of Commerce and Business offers strong programs in marketing and management information systems. The College of Communication and Information Sciences is one of the country's top

"Most of my teachers have been outstanding." communication schools, while respected programs in the College of Human Environmental Sciences include athletic training and family financial planning. The School of Music is a regional standout, attracting guest artists such as Itzhak Perlman and Wynton Marsalis. New College allows students to work with faculty to design their own interdisciplinary major. The most popular majors include nursing, biology, elementary education, accounting, and psychology.

The Honors College houses the three university-wide honors programs: computer-based honors, international honors, and university honors. More than 4,000 students belong to one or more UA honors programs, which feature smaller classes, early registration privileges, and the opportunity to write a senior thesis. The Blount Undergraduate Initiative is a living/learning program within the College of Arts and Sciences, where freshmen are housed with a faculty director and fellows. Other offerings include study abroad options (including 30 reciprocal exchange programs around the world) and the innovative May interim term, when students spend three weeks focusing on one course in depth.

About 20 percent of 'Bama freshmen take part in the Arts and Sciences Mentoring Program, which pairs them with faculty mentors who ease the adjustment to college through informal counseling and enrichment activities such as concerts, movies, or lectures. All students may also enroll in the two-credit Academic Potential Seminar, which covers self-assessment, motivation, personal responsibility, time management, memory, textbook reading, note-taking, and test preparation. The only course 'Bama requires students to take during the first year on campus is a two-term English composition sequence. Before graduation, students must also complete courses in writing, natural sciences, math, humanities, and social sciences, and either two semesters of a foreign language or one of computer science.

UA's core curriculum is no cakewalk, students say. "UA is a competitive school," says one senior. "The classes are pretty tough because the teachers require your best

"The social life ranges from Greek life to campuswide activities to departmental events." and nothing less." Professors teach lectures and many seminar courses, including some classes for freshmen. "Most of my teachers have been outstanding," a junior reports, "but I have had a teacher or two who just weren't approachable or didn't cover their material very well." The Freshman Learning Communities allow students to take two or three academic courses together, and a seminar taught by a full professor. The one-credit FLC seminar topic ties the academic courses together. Currently 40 individual FLCs are offered, and approximately 600 freshmen participate.

Fifty-nine percent of 'Bama's students are Alabama natives, and 3 percent are international students representing more than 45 countries. UA students are "smart, hardworking individuals who also have a good time when not studying," says a finance major. Twelve percent of UA students are African American, 1 percent are Asian American, 1 percent Native American, and 3 percent Hispanic. The biggest social and political issues on campus include free speech and diversity. 'Bama awards 272 athletic scholarships in 22 sports and has expanded the number of merit scholarships in the hopes of increasing enrollment. The average award exceeds $9,200.

Although UA requires freshmen to reside on campus, most Alabama students live in off-campus apartments in the Tuscaloosa area; only 27 percent remain in campus residence halls, where options range from private rooms and suites to apartment-style living. "Most of the dorms have suites that house one to four people, though there are cheaper double-occupancy dorms as well," notes one student. "Most of the dorms are co-ed." A freshman gives high marks to the living/learning communities, some of which are for first-year students and others that bring together students from a particular school or college. Twenty-three percent of men pledge fraternities and 33 percent of women join sororities, and they may live in chapter houses. Students report that campus dining options are edible, diverse, and expensive.

Much of 'Bama's social life revolves around the Greek system and athletic events. "The social life ranges from Greek life to campuswide activities to departmental events," says one student. Partying has remained a staple of the social scene in recent years, despite administrators' efforts to weaken it by prohibiting fraternities and sororities from having parties on campus. Those under 21 can't have alcohol in the dorms—or elsewhere, for that matter, per state law—but a student says, "Unless someone is walking around, noticeably drunk, underage offenders don't get caught. If someone is going to drink, they'll find a way to do it." Those who don't go Greek, or who don't wish to drink, will find everything from the Society for Creative Anachronism (medievalists) to Bible study groups. A modern trolley service connects the 'Bama campus to the city's thriving downtown. Tuscaloosa is described as "an awesome college town," that is "mostly centered around the university." Road trips to New Orleans (for Mardi Gras and Greek weekend formals), Atlanta, Nashville, Birmingham, and the Gulf Coast and Florida beaches are popular, too, but "many people never leave UA!" says a sophomore.

'Bama football remains the cornerstone of the university's competitive athletic programs and has regained its former glory under the direction of head coach Nick Saban. The team brought home the Southeastern Conference title in 2012. The annual Auburn–Alabama game—the Iron Bowl, one of the most intense rivalries in college sports—is the highlight of the school year. "Any Alabama football game is a festival," a sophomore says. Alabama competes in Division I, and most sports teams, including basketball, baseball, and softball, are competitive. The wheelchair basketball team has brought home a number of national titles, and women's gymnastics and women's golf were recent conference champs. 'Bama also sports a number of solid nonathletic teams as well, including the debate team and the Alabama Forensics Council, which competes in 16 regional and national speaking events and debate tournaments.

Although sports are still an integral part of the UA experience, the university's emphasis is now on technology, merit scholarships, global perspectives, and undergraduate research.

> 'Bama football remains the cornerstone of the university's competitive athletic programs and has regained its former glory under the direction of head coach Nick Saban.

Overlaps

Auburn, Florida State, University of Alabama at Birmingham, University of Florida, University of Georgia, University of Tennessee

If You Apply To ➤ | **Alabama:** Rolling admissions. Application fee: $40. Campus and alumni interviews: optional, informational. SATs or ACTs: required. Subject Tests: optional. Accepts the Common Application. No essay question.

Albion College

Albion, MI 49224

Next to evangelical Hope and Calvin and out-there Kalamazoo, Albion is Michigan's middle-of-the-road liberal arts college. Think Gerald Ford, the moderate Republican president who is the namesake of Albion's signature Institute for Public Service. Future doctors, lawyers, and businesspeople are well served.

Albion continues to attract an ambitious, involved group of students.

Albion is a small, private college in Michigan whose motto is "Liberal arts at work." The school's motto emphasizes the importance Albion places on combining learning with hands-on experience. Students at Albion often participate in leadership and service-learning seminars. Albion helps students achieve their goals "through classes, internships, projects, and a strong alumni network," says a senior. And when the work is through, students here enjoy a close-knit social life. "Albion is where I have built lifetime friendships," says a student.

Founded in 1835 by the Methodist Church, Albion is located near the banks of the Kalamazoo River. In addition to its newer Georgian-style architecture, the college has retained and restored several of its 19th-century buildings. The campus is spacious, with statuesque oaks and a beautiful nature center. Robinson Hall, the campus centerpiece, houses myriad departments, including the Gerald Ford Institute for Public Service, the Gerstacker Liberal Arts Program in Professional Management, and the Anna Howard Shaw Women's Center. The college is also home to the largest collegiate indoor riding arena in the United States.

> **"With very few exceptions, I have had professors who have challenged and encouraged me."**

Albion has a rich academic history and was the first private college in Michigan to have a Phi Beta Kappa chapter (1940). The school has also produced three Rhodes scholars. On their journey to such success, students are required to take core courses distributed among humanities, natural sciences, social sciences, fine arts, and math. They must also satisfy requirements in environmental science and gender and ethnicity studies. Freshmen must take first-year seminars designed to provide a "stimulating learning environment" in a small-class setting, while seniors participate in a capstone experience.

Albion's most distinguishing feature is the emphasis placed on citizenship and service. The Ford Institute takes a unique approach for future civic leaders. Students participate in a simulation of city government in which they play the roles of community leaders. Visiting speakers include senators and congressmen, governors and state legislators, and interest group representatives. The premedical and prelaw programs draw dedicated undergrads, and the English and economics departments are well respected. Another option is the Summer Research Program, which allows students to remain on campus during the summer to work with faculty members on different projects. Newer programs include majors in business and organizations, environmental science, and sustainability studies. The computer science and physical education majors have been dropped.

The academic climate at Albion is described as competitive but not cut-throat. One student says, "Albion has a challenging yet inviting academic climate." Top-notch academic and career counseling and low student/faculty ratios keep students on track and motivated. Class size varies, but 71 percent of classes have 19 or fewer students. Professors are interested in students' academic performance and their emotional well-being. "With very few exceptions, I have had professors who have challenged and encouraged me," says a junior. Teaching assistants are used for tutoring, not teaching. Albion's libraries feature computer facilities, an interlibrary loan service, a listening lab for language or music study, and a helpful staff. If you can't find what you need at Albion's libraries, weekly bus trips to the University of Michigan libraries in Ann Arbor provide access to even more resources.

Albion continues to attract an ambitious, involved group of students. "The typical Albion student doesn't spend the evening playing video games in his room," explains a junior, "but trying to prioritize between a student senate meeting, soccer practice, or marching band practice." Michigan residents make up 88 percent of the student population. Two percent are Asian American, 4 percent African American, and 3 percent Hispanic. Up to now, there has been little deviation from the white, upper-middle-class norm. In an effort to change this, a host-family program matches minority students with families from within the community. There are a number of merit scholarships available, averaging $16,627, but no athletic scholarships.

Ninety percent of Albion students call the residence halls home. "Housing is good," says a political science major, "especially options for upperclassmen." The majority of the freshman class inhabits Wesley Hall. During their sophomore year, many students move to Seaton or Whitehouse halls; seniors enjoy apartment-style housing called The Mae. Dorms are co-ed by hall or floor, and the information each student provides in their housing request form is used to assign rooms and roommates. Other housing options include apartment annexes and fraternity houses. Sororities do not have houses; they hold their meetings in lodges. Two large dining rooms feed campus residents on an "eat all day" meal plan. "The dining hall offers a wide variety of options on a daily basis," one junior reports.

Fifty-one percent of Albion men and 43 percent of women belong to one of the school's six national fraternities and seven sororities. Greek parties draw large crowds, composed of Greeks and non-Greeks, making them a primary part of many students' social lives. "Social life on campus is always active," says one student. A well-run union board organizes all sorts of activities—films, lectures, plays, comics, and concerts—to keep students occupied in their spare time. Several students report that the town movie theater shows "free movies if you show a valid student ID!" Those who insist on imbibing can do it at Gina's or Cascarelli's, popular bars in town. Road trips are a big part of weekends for many students. Ann Arbor, East Lansing, and Canada are frequent destinations.

The college's geographic namesake has been a victim of the economic downturn and rates poorly as a college town, according to students. "The city of Albion is going through a rough period," says a sophomore. Students focus some of their energy by working for groups supported by the Student Volunteer Bureau; in fact, half of the students volunteer on a regular basis. They are very involved in the community, including "city clean-up day, Habitat for Humanity, and volunteering at nursing homes and schools." Some traditional events that offer a nice break from academics are the Briton Bash, a fair that familiarizes students with clubs and organizations, and the Day of Woden, which is a picnic held in the spring on the last day of class.

"Social life on campus is always active."

The varsity football team competes in the Mid-America Intercollegiate Athletics Association and has won 34 conference championships—the most in Conference MIAA history. Other recent conference champs include women's tennis, women's cross-country, and women's soccer. Hope College is a bitter rival, as is Alma College. Recreational and intramural sports attract 38 percent of students and include soccer, flag football, basketball, and canoeing.

At Albion, professors are accessible and interested, and academics are challenging without being overwhelming. Students cite the appeal of a "small campus with friendly students, caring faculty, and kind staff members."

Albion has a rich academic history and was the first private college in Michigan to have a Phi Beta Kappa chapter.

Overlaps

Michigan State, University of Michigan, Hope, Grand Valley State, Alma, Central Michigan

If You Apply To ➤

Albion: Rolling admissions. Early action: Dec. 1. Application fee: $40 (paper), free (online). Campus interviews: optional, evaluative. Alumni interviews: optional, informational. SATs or ACTs: required. Subject Tests: optional. Accepts the Common Application with Albion supplement. Essay question.

Alfred University

Alumni Hall, Saxon Drive, Alfred, NY 14802-1205

Talk about an unusual combination: Alfred combines a nationally renowned college of ceramics, a school of art and design, an engineering program, and a business school wrapped up in a university of just over 2,000 students. The Finger Lakes is a region full of natural beauty, but it takes elbow grease to pry coastal types to the hinterlands of western New York.

Website: www.alfred.edu
Location: Rural
Private
Total Enrollment: 2,070
Undergraduates: 1,884
Male/Female: 49/51
SAT Ranges: CR 480–580,
  M 500–600
ACT Ranges: 21–27
Financial Aid: 85%
Expense: Pr $
Student Loans: 85%
Average Debt: $ $ $ $
Phi Beta Kappa: Yes
Applicants: 3,332
Accepted: 70%
Enrolled: 23%
Grad in 6 Years: 64%
Returning Freshmen: 68%
Academics: ✐ ✐ ✐
Social: ☎ ☎ ☎
Q of L: ★ ★ ★
Admissions: (800) 541-9229
Email Address: admissions@
  alfred.edu

Strongest Programs:
Engineering
Art and Design
Business Administration

With 2,000 students, Alfred University isn't a bustling academic factory; it's a quiet, cloistered, self-described "educational village" in a tiny town wholly dedicated to the "industry of learning." The university boasts highly respected programs in art and design, as well as ceramic engineering. Innovation not only shapes the curriculum, but also has a profound effect on campus life. Small classes and friendly competition support this diversity while encouraging individuals to succeed. Along with being able to handle the academic rigors of the college, students also have to weather brutal winters that dump snow by the foot on the region.

> **"The studio courses are challenging."**

Alfred's campus consists of a charming, close-knit group of modern and Georgian brick buildings, along with a stone castle. The Kanakadea Creek runs right through campus, and the town of Alfred consists of two colleges (the other is the Alfred State College) and a main street with one stoplight. There are a few shops and restaurants, but certainly no malls, parking lots, or tall buildings. The university has completed an addition to the performing arts facility, adding a 498-seat theater, costume room, dressing rooms, and a choral rehearsal studio to the existing space.

The university and its students share a no-nonsense approach to education. Although prospective students apply directly to one of four colleges and declare a tentative major, half of all requirements for a bachelor's degree are earned in the liberal arts college. Requirements are quite different in each school. However, the mix usually includes coursework in oral and written communication, foreign language and culture, social sciences, history, literature, philosophy, and religion.

Alfred, though private, is actually the "host" school for the New York State College of Ceramics, which is a unit of the state university system and comes with a public university price tag. Ceramic engineering (the development and refinement of ceramic materials) is the academic cornerstone and the program that brings Alfred international recognition. All engineering programs are found within the School of Engineering, and there is a degree in renewable energy engineering. The art department, with its programs in ceramics, glass, printmaking, sculpture, video, and teacher certification, is also highly regarded. The School of Art and Design offers a graphic design major in which students use the latest electronic and computer equipment. The business administration school also gets good reviews from students and provides undergraduates with work experience through a small business institute where students have real clients.

"The studio courses are challenging," says one sophomore. "I would say that Alfred is pretty competitive," adds a junior. The major in foreign language and culture sponsors trips abroad, and exchange programs are available in England, Germany, Italy, France, Japan, China, and the Czech Republic. The Track II program enables students to design their own interdisciplinary majors with personal guidance from top faculty members.

Whatever their major, all students enjoy small classes (average size is 18 students), and the quality of teaching is described as very high. "The teachers are very accessible and more than willing to help students with anything they need," says a freshman. Most classes are taught by full professors, with graduate students and teaching assistants helping out only in lab sessions. The university stresses its commitment to helping undergrads plan their future, and the academic advising and career planning services are strong enough for Alfred to deliver on its promise. Students say faculty members really want to see them succeed, both in class and in the real world. "Most teachers have high expectations, resulting in greater student performance," says one junior.

Alfred students are "creative and like to be challenged," says a business administration major. Seventy-five percent of the students at Alfred are from New York State, and 17 percent graduated from high school in the top 10th of their class. African Americans comprise 7 percent of the student body, Hispanics 6 percent, and Asian Americans 2 percent. Financial aid is available, and outstanding students can apply for many merit scholarships; National Merit finalists receive Alfred's Award of Merit. There are no athletic scholarships.

No one seems to mind the two-year on-campus residency requirement because the rooms are large and comfortable, and the dorms are equipped with lounges, kitchens, and laundry facilities. "The dorms are nice," says one student. Upperclassmen have a choice of dorms that are co-ed by floor with single rooms, suites, or apartments.

All engineering programs are found within the School of Engineering, and there is a degree in renewable energy engineering.

"The teachers are very accessible."

Freshmen enjoy their own housing divided into doubles. Seventy-six percent of all students choose to live on campus, but some juniors and about half of the seniors opt to live off campus. The school has two dining halls, and students say the offerings include plenty of selections for vegetarians and vegans. "The dining facilities are very nice and well equipped, and the food is both diverse and edible," says a junior. Campus security is good, according to most students. "There are blue lights all over campus, and AU security will provide rides or walking escorts if you feel unsafe walking alone," a biology major says.

Alfred's location in the Finger Lakes region, almost two hours from Buffalo and an hour and a half from Rochester, is isolated. The other chief complaint is the chilly, snowy weather. Social life is difficult due to the rural atmosphere and lack of Greek organizations, but the Student Activities Board brings many events to campus, including musicians, comedians, lecturers, and movies. Favorite road trips are to Letchworth and Stony Brook state parks, and to Ithaca, Rochester, Buffalo, and Toronto. Many students are skiing, hunting, camping, and rock-climbing enthusiasts. Friendly games of hackeysack, Frisbee, football, softball, and other sports can often be found on campus. Alfred is a dry campus. "Alfred doesn't have too many problems with drinking that I have heard of," a student says. The alcohol policy is enforced in the dorms, and students say it is largely respected.

Campus security is good, according to most students.

Because Alfred shares the town with Alfred State University, the dominant student population makes Alfred a good college town. "It is a small town, very close community, but nice," observes a biology major. The downtown scene provides students with an adequate number of movie theaters and eateries. Every spring brings the annual Hot Dog Weekend, a big carnival-like event that fills Main Street with game booths, bands, and lots of hot dog stands. Alfred's Division III Saxons are ominous opponents on the football, soccer, and lacrosse fields, and the alpine skiing, equestrian, and men's swimming teams have all won spots in the nation's top 10.

"Alfred University will prepare you to go into the real world," says a freshman. Although small and somewhat secluded, Alfred University is a good choice for those students who want to concentrate on the ABCs of arts, business, and ceramic engineering—just be sure to bundle up for the long, snowy winters.

Overlaps

RIT, Clarkson, Ithaca, SUNY–Geneseo, St. John Fisher, University of Rochester, SUNY–Buffalo, Hartwick

Allegheny College

520 North Main Street, Meadville, PA 16335

An unpretentious cousin to more well-heeled places like Dickinson and Bucknell. Draws heavily from the Buffalo-Cleveland-Pittsburgh area. The college's powerhouse athletic teams feast on Division III competition. A robust Greek system gives Allegheny a strong traditional college life. If you've ever wondered what lake-effect snow is, you'll find out here.

Website: www.allegheny.edu
Location: Small City
Private
Total Enrollment: 2,097
Undergraduates: 2,097
Male/Female: 46/54
SAT Ranges: CR 540–650,
   M 560–650
ACT Ranges: 24–29
Financial Aid: 99%
Expense: Pr $ $
Student Loans: N/A
Average Debt: N/A
Phi Beta Kappa: Yes
Applicants: 4,795
Accepted: 63%
Enrolled: 19%
Grad in 6 Years: 78%
Returning Freshmen: 89%
Academics: ✍ ✍ ✍
Social: ☎ ☎ ☎
Q of L: ★ ★ ★
Admissions: (800) 521-5293
Email Address: admissions@
   allegheny.edu

Strongest Programs:
Physical and Biological
   Sciences
Political Science
Managerial Economics
International Studies
Psychology

Allegheny College is a down-to-earth Eastern liberal arts school boasting a rich history of academic excellence in an intimate setting. Administrators here understand the importance of providing students with real-world experience to complement their classroom work. The school's innovative May term offers time for internships or other off-campus work and study, and a commitment to civic responsibility has spurred several new programs. Allegheny's small size means students don't suffer from lack of attention, and despite the heavy workload, anyone struggling academically will get help before the situation becomes dire. "The education you will receive at Allegheny is priceless," says one senior.

"The professors have high expectations and standards."

Allegheny's 79-acre campus is tucked away in Meadville, Pennsylvania, 90 miles north of Pittsburgh. Founded in 1815, nestled in the Norman Rockwell–esque rolling hills of northwestern Pennsylvania, the campus is home to traditional architecture and redbrick streets, as well as new additions such as apartment-style housing for upperclassmen. A nationally acclaimed science complex supports already-strong programs, and students who wish to break a sweat can do so at the Wise Sports and Fitness Center. The college also owns a 123-acre outdoor recreational complex, a 283-acre research reserve, and an 80-acre protected forest. North Village—a community of townhouse-style apartments—houses 330 students. The 40,000 square-foot Vukovich Center for Communication Arts is home to rehearsal and instructional areas, video production facilities, and a large performance space. A $5.7 million renovation of Carr Hall is now complete and houses the Richard J. Cook Center for Environmental Science, as well as the physics department.

Students at Allegheny typically work hard and do well. "The professors have high expectations and standards, and the coursework is demanding," says a psychology major. The school's strongest programs are in environmental science, managerial economics, the sciences, and international studies (which offers tracks in Middle Eastern and North African studies). Students give high marks to English, too. There is a major in biochemistry, a chemistry curriculum, and a track for students interested in entrepreneurial and managerial economics. Co-op programs include a 3–2, 3–3, 3–4 option leading to degrees in engineering, public policy and management, nursing, and allied health. The Allegheny College Center for Experiential Learning (ACCEL) is a clearinghouse for internship opportunities, service learning, and overseas study.

Allegheny has two 15-week semesters each year and each features an Academic Programming Day: Classes do not meet and students are able to participate in a number of college-sponsored programs, including open houses, advising and career counseling workshops and other campus events. General education requirements keep students busy. Juniors take a seminar in their major field, and seniors complete an intensive capstone project in their major, where they are required to orally defend a work of independent research. All students must take courses in each of three major divisions (humanities and the natural and social sciences) and must finish a minor in a division area outside their major. The First-Year/Sophomore Seminar sequence is a three-course, 12-credit sequence that is limited to 15 students. Seminar topics include Brain, Art, and Mind; Business Ethics; and Music to Die For. Sixty-four percent of courses have 19 or fewer students.

"The faculty are extremely dedicated."

Students praise Allegheny's faculty for their passion, knowledge, and accessibility. "The faculty are extremely dedicated to teaching their students, and all classes are taught by professors," a biology major says. Indeed, you won't find a TA at the lectern in any Allegheny classroom, and the college's honor code allows students to take unproctored exams. Off campus, Allegheny offers study in several U.S. cities and 17 countries, an on-campus independent study option, and semester internships or job shadowing experience. There's also a three- or four-week Experiential Learning term following spring semester for study abroad and internships not available during the year. Additionally, Allegheny is a member of the Great Lakes Colleges Association*. Thirty-one percent of students participate in some form of study abroad.

Fifty-five percent of Allegheny's students hail from Pennsylvania, and sizable contingents come from nearby Ohio, New York, and New England. "Students are hardworking and serious about their studies," one senior says, "but are also involved in numerous campus organizations, community service, and intramural sports." African Americans make up 5 percent of the student population, Hispanics 5 percent, and Asian Americans 4 percent. "Students are very aware politically," claims one sophomore. The college's Center for Political Participation engages students by fostering an appreciation for the vital link between an engaged, active citizenry and a healthy democracy. Merit scholarships are available, with an average award of $14,562, but there are no athletic scholarships. Twenty-six percent of the most recent freshman class was eligible for Pell Grants.

"There are weekend and evening events sponsored on campus."

Residence halls and houses (including TV and study rooms) accommodate 90 percent of the student body in relative style and comfort with a variety of living situations: all-freshmen dorms; co-ed and single-sex halls; small houses; and single, double, and triple rooms and suites. "The dorms are comfortable, clean, and friendly," a senior says. Housing is guaranteed for four years; the most popular dorm is the townhouse-style North Village Complex, which holds students in suites with four single bedrooms each. Students are happy with their on-campus food choices ("quite good"), as well as campus security ("very good and always available").

Greek organizations draw 28 percent of the men and 34 percent of the women, and provide a great deal of nightlife. Four of the six fraternities have their own houses, while the five sororities have on-campus living communities. There are also two campus theater series, two-dollar movie nights, and comedians, ventriloquists, and live bands provided by the center for student involvement. Large-scale philanthropic events like Make a Difference Day and the Month of Service, in March, are also popular. "There are weekend and evening events sponsored on campus," says one student. College policy states that students must be 21 to have or consume alcohol on campus, but one student says "the social scene doesn't revolve around alcohol." Homecoming, Greek Sing, Wingfest in the fall (featuring free wings), Springfest (a day full of bands, activities, and food), and Winter Fest break up the monotony of studying, and midnight breakfasts served by faculty help ease end-of-semester stress.

(continued)

Environmental Science
Neuroscience

Juniors take a seminar in their major field, and seniors complete an intensive capstone project in their major, where they are required to orally defend a work of independent research.

Downtown Meadville, lovingly referred to as Mudville, is a 10-minute walk from campus and worlds away from a "college town." It has several community playhouses, as well as schools, hospitals, children's homes, animal shelters, and other organizations that benefit from the more than 25,000 hours of service students contribute each year. "We've really gotten to know the local businesses and take pride in supporting our local community," says an English major. When more time in Meadville is too much to bear, students hit the road, venturing to factory outlets in nearby Grove City, Pennsylvania, or heading toward the bright lights of Pittsburgh, Buffalo, or Cleveland. "What's nice is that even though Meadville is small, larger cities are close by so you can get away if need be," a senior says. Nearby state parks, Conneaut Lake, and Lake Erie offer waterskiing and boating in warm weather and cross-country skiing in the winter.

As for Allegheny traditions, there's the somewhat suspect "13th Plank" ritual, which states that all freshman women must be kissed on the 13th plank of the campus bridge by an upperclassman to be considered "true Allegheny co-eds." Of course, a group of freshman men steal the plank every year at the beginning of the first semester to prevent that from happening.

Athletics play a big role in Allegheny life, and the sports and fitness complex gives students reason to cheer. Twenty-five percent of Allegheny students participate in varsity athletics, and the Gators field a number of competitive teams. Recent conference champs include women's soccer and softball, men's cross-country, and men's golf. Fifty percent of students participate in club, recreational, and intramural sports, with basketball, soccer, and volleyball drawing the most interest.

Allegheny College boasts a rich history of academic excellence in an intimate setting, augmented by a new emphasis on extracurricular experiences designed to produce well-rounded alumni. The campus's natural beauty and the genuine affection students feel for it and for each other remain unchanged. What's more, students appreciate the value placed on individuality and involvement. "Students are encouraged to explore their unusual combinations of interests, skills, and talents," says one junior. "The word 'no' is not often used here."

Thirty-one percent of students participate in some form of study abroad.

Overlaps

Washington and Jefferson College, University of Pittsburgh, Penn State, College of Wooster, Westminster, Denison, Duquesne, Susquehanna

If You Apply To ➤

Allegheny: Early decision: Nov. 15. Regular admissions: Feb. 15. Application fee: $35 (paper), free (online). Campus interviews: optional, evaluative. Alumni interviews: optional, informational. SATs or ACTs: required. Subject Tests: optional. Accepts the Common Application. Essay question.

Alma College

Alma, MI 48801-1599

The college that put the "Alma" back in "alma mater." As friendly a campus as you'll find, Alma savors its Scottish heritage and combines the liberal arts with distinctive offerings in health and preprofessional fields. On this campus of just over 1,400 students, diversity is an issue, and few out-of-staters enroll. If central Michigan eventually drives you stir-crazy, join the hordes who go abroad.

Alma College, a tiny gem on Michigan's lower peninsula, was founded in 1886 by Presbyterians with a fourfold mission: "To prepare graduates who think critically, serve generously, lead purposefully, and live responsibly as stewards of the world they bequeath to future generations." Alma has a wide array of choices for its undergraduates, including distinctive offerings in health and preprofessional fields, as

Website: www.alma.edu
Location: Small City
Private
Total Enrollment: 1,410

well as the opportunity to learn abroad. Alma students have taken part in everything from the U.S. mission to the United Nations to the reclamation of a Jewish cemetery in Poland. And the annual Highland Festival, with kilt-wearing bagpipers and competitions, has led some to dub the school "Scotland, USA."

Alma's campus features 25 Prairie-style buildings of redbrick and limestone surrounding a scenic central mall. Alma was founded more than a hundred years ago, but most of the buildings have been built or renovated in recent years. There are lots of trees and open places to sit, at least in the warmer months. Two major campus construction projects—the renovations and addition to the Eddy Music Center and the building of the Art Smith Arena adjacent to the Hogan Center—were completed in 2010–11.

The Alma experience begins with the seven-day Preterm Orientation, which is built around a one-credit academic seminar that includes readings, discussions, and research and introduces students to computer resources, on-campus life, and extracurricular activities. Trustee Honors Scholarship recipients are invited to attend a two-credit Freshman Honors Seminar during their first year. To graduate, students must satisfy general education requirements, including a first-year seminar and 12 credits in each of three divisions: humanities, social sciences, and natural sciences. Students must also demonstrate proficiency in a second language or international awareness. Alma recently put its student-centered philosophy front and center with the Alma Commitment, which offers a four-year graduation promise and a pledge that each interested student can participate in an experiential learning opportunity such as an internship, research fellowship, or study abroad. Participating students receive $2,500 in Alma Venture funding.

> **"I went to London for a Shakespeare course and it was incredible."**

Alma's academic environment is "much more collaborative than competitive," says a senior, "even within departments." Alma's top majors, per student enrollment, are business administration, education, and biology. Biology and psychology prepare students for work with wellness intervention programs and public health agencies, or graduate study in medicine, nursing, or physical therapy. The college's Service Learning Program gives students academic credit for work with nonprofit economic development organizations or educational, environmental, and social service agencies. Alma's Model United Nations teams received top recognition at the world's largest and most prestigious collegiate Model UN conference for a record 17 consecutive years (1997 through 2013), the longest of any college or university. Students interested in the Scottish arts find a range of opportunities to work with nationally known instructors of bagpipe and Highland dance, or join in seminars offered by award-winning Scottish authors. A peer-mentoring program places successful upper-class students in contact with new students to help them adapt to the opportunities and expectations of an engaged college community. A prenursing program is available for those interested in pursuing a career in nursing.

Despite Alma's small size and the fact that 91 percent of students are Michigan natives, the terms "provincial" and "insular" just don't apply here. In fact, one of the college's selling points is its wide variety of study abroad opportunities. During the one-month spring term, students enroll in a single intensive course that often includes off-campus study. Course offerings have included the study of lizards in Jamaica, a tour of cultural and educational sites in Argentina, the analysis of World War II topics at the British National Archives in London, the restoration of a Jewish Holocaust cemetery in Poland, and the analysis of ethnic politics in Scotland. In cooperation with colleges and universities overseas, Alma College offers a study abroad program with the

> **"There are so many different activities, I wish I had more time in the day."**

(continued)

Undergraduates: 1,410
Male/Female: 46/54
SAT Ranges: CR 450–620,
  M 470–590
ACT Ranges: 21–26
Financial Aid: 100%
Expense: Pr $
Student Loans: 77%
Average Debt: $ $ $ $
Phi Beta Kappa: Yes
Applicants: 2,232
Accepted: 72%
Enrolled: 27%
Grad in 6 Years: 66%
Returning Freshmen: 80%
Academics: ✐ ✐ ✐
Social: ☎ ☎ ☎
Q of L: ★ ★ ★
Admissions: (800) 321-2562
Email Address: admissions@
  alma.edu

Strongest Programs:
Business Administration
Education
Biology
History
Psychology
Exercise and Health Science
Music
Sociology and Anthropology

University of Aberdeen in Scotland. Other study and research opportunities are available in Australia, Austria, Ecuador, England, Germany, India, Italy, New Zealand, and Peru. "I went to London for a Shakespeare course and it was incredible," cheers one religious studies major. "We saw more than 15 plays and lived in flats in the city."

Back on campus, Alma's professors garner plenty of praise. "The professors truly care about getting to know the students," says a junior. None of the classes taken by freshmen have more than 100 students; 68 percent have 19 or fewer. Students say graduating in four years is seldom a problem, except for education majors, who may need a ninth semester to complete their student teaching.

Alma students are "very smart but do not want the Ivy League lifestyle," according to a sociology major. "They want to go to a smaller school with a personal touch." The campus is largely homogeneous, with African Americans accounting for 3 percent, Asian Americans 1 percent, and Hispanics 2 percent of the student population. While not an overly political campus, Alma does have its fair share of activists; personal rights and diversity concerns top the list of hot issues. Brainy types can vie for merit scholarships worth an average of $14,480; there are no athletic scholarships.

Ninety percent of Alma's students reside on campus. "The dorms are comfortable and always kept clean," says one first-year student. Freshmen are assigned rooms in single-sex and co-ed halls (some co-ed by room, others by floor), while upperclassmen play the lottery and usually get suites. Other options include an international house, a Model UN house, and a Women's Resource Center. There are fraternities and

"The professors truly care about getting to know the students."

sororities for the 21 percent of men and 27 percent of women who go Greek. Everyone buys 14 or 19 meals a week, and chows down at the all-you-can-eat Commons or at Joe's Place, a snack bar. Students say they feel safe on campus thanks to the presence of patrolling security guards. "Campus security is good. I have never felt threatened," confides one elementary education major.

When it comes time to socialize, says a student, the Alma College Union Board provides plenty of on-campus fun. "We offer music performances, movie nights, speakers, student panels, and tons of events in the dorms," says a senior. "There are so many different activities, I wish I had more time in the day." Officially, the campus alcohol policy follows Michigan law: No one under 21 can drink. "We are not a dry campus so there are parties on weekends for those that choose to go," explains one sophomore. Most students tend to agree that drinking is not a big problem on campus. Underage students caught imbibing are written up and fined. "There is no stigma for people who don't drink," one student assures.

Town/gown relations at Alma are strong, with students volunteering, taking part-time jobs, and otherwise getting involved in the community. "There is a movie theater and a few restaurants," one student says. "Other than that, there really isn't a whole lot to do." The annual Highland Festival features bagpipers and Scottish dancing; for members of the Alma marching band, who strut in kilts stitched from the college's own registered Alma College tartan, every performance might as well be a festival. Students with wheels will find diversions within easy reach, as Mount Pleasant, Saginaw, and the East Lansing campus of Michigan State are less than an hour away, and ski slopes are just a bit farther. In the warmer months, the beaches of two Great Lakes, Huron and Michigan, are also two hours away. The Alma softball team is a frequent winner of the Michigan Intercollegiate Athletic Association championship, and the Scots volleyball and football teams have also brought home titles in recent years. Four new sports debuted in 2011–12: women's lacrosse and bowling and men's lacrosse and wrestling. For nonvarsity types, there is an active intramural program—more than 50 percent of the student body participates.

"I think that Alma is special. Our professors genuinely care about our success, we have a great on-campus atmosphere, and we have many facilities that aid us in our

Students interested in the Scottish arts find a range of opportunities to work with nationally known instructors of bagpipe and Highland dance, or join in seminars offered by award-winning Scottish authors.

Alma recently put its student-centered philosophy front and center with the Alma Commitment.

Overlaps

Michigan State, Central Michigan, Grand Valley State, Western Michigan, University of Michigan, Albion, Hope, Ferris State

transition to adulthood and to our lives after school," says a happy senior. Helpful advisors and caring faculty members help Alma students chart a course on campus and in the broader world, allowing them to leave well prepared for today's competitive job market. Michigan natives and newcomers alike are sure to find a warm welcome and friendly faces at Alma.

<table>
<tr><td>If You Apply To ></td><td>Alma: Rolling admissions. Application fee: $25 (paper), free (online). Campus interviews: optional, evaluative. Alumni interviews: optional, informational. SATs or ACTs: required. Subject Tests: optional. Accepts the Common Application with Alma supplement. Optional essay question.</td></tr>
</table>

Alverno College

3401 South 39th Street, P.O. Box 343922, Milwaukee, WI 53234-3922

At last, a college that evaluates students on what they can do rather than how well they can memorize. Forget oval-blackening; students here show mastery in their chosen fields. Practical and hands-on, Alverno is at its best in preprofessional programs. The college will accept any qualified applicant, and many are beyond traditional college age. Only women need apply.

If you're the type of student who obsesses over your GPA, take heed: at Alverno College, you can forget about earning an A. That's because this Catholic, women's liberal arts college emphasizes ability-based learning instead of letter grades. Students are required to show "mastery" in a range of liberal arts courses, as well as demonstrated ability in eight key areas: communication, analysis, problem solving, values, social interaction, global perspectives, effective citizenship, and aesthetic engagement. Students move through interdisciplinary progressive levels toward a degree by being "validated" in these areas. For example, a course in sociology might contribute to validation in communication and social interaction, as well as in making independent value judgments. The learning environment is more collaborative than competitive, though the ability-based method can "create a lot of work requiring much thought," says a professional communications major.

Alverno is located in a quiet residential area. The parklike 46-acre campus is just 15 minutes from downtown Milwaukee and a 10-minute walk from shops and restaurants. Its three main academic buildings, of 1950s and '60s vintage, feature brick and stone exteriors and stained-glass windows. The Sister Joel Read Center houses 73,000 square feet of science labs, multimedia production space, and computer facilities.

Alverno offers a regular weekday program that attracts mostly traditional college-age women, the majority of whom are from Milwaukee, and the Alverno on the Weekend program allows women, most of them older with full-time jobs, to earn a degree in four years by attending classes every other weekend. Students in the weekday program may earn credit by spending four to eight hours a week in internships related to their field of study. The college ditched grades long ago and offers detailed feedback instead.

"We couldn't have more help."

First-year students take an orientation seminar and introductory courses in the arts and humanities, science, psychology and sociology, communications, and math. The student body is diverse—in age, ethnic background, and religion. "It would be very hard to make generalizations," one junior says. Religious studies aren't required,

Website: www.alverno.edu
Location: City Outskirts
Private
Total Enrollment: 1,656
Undergraduates: 1,398
Male/Female: 0/100
SAT Ranges: N/A
ACT Ranges: 17–21
Financial Aid: 100%
Expense: Pr $
Student Loans: 92%
Average Debt: $ $ $ $
Phi Beta Kappa: No
Applicants: 510
Accepted: 82%
Enrolled: 46%
Grad in 6 Years: 39%
Returning Freshmen: 72%
Academics: ✍ ✍ ✍
Social: ☎
Q of L: ★ ★ ★ ★
Admissions: (414) 382-6101
Email Address: admissions@ alverno.edu

Strongest Programs:
Nursing
Business and Management

Alverno also boasts a Career Education Center that provides career planning and job assistance to students and alumnae.

Religious studies aren't required, but for those who seek it, a Catholic liturgy is available.

Overlaps

University of Wisconsin–Milwaukee, Mount Mary College, Carroll University

but for those who seek it, a Catholic liturgy is available. Alverno's business and management programs are well established. "The level of professionalism that Alverno students have compared to those at other colleges or universities is amazing," one junior says. Students praise the professional communication and teacher education programs and the strong nursing program. Fifteen percent of Alverno students study abroad each year; Chile, France, China, India, and England are just a few of the places where students have traveled in recent years. Students are required to participate in off-campus, credit-bearing internships. Alverno also boasts a Career Education Center that provides career planning and job assistance to students and alumnae.

Many professors at Alverno teach all levels of classes, so "there is no distinct difference" in the quality of teaching for freshmen or seniors, one international business major says. "The faculty and staff really care whether you are successful," adds a social science major. "They want to see you achieve and are willing to go [above] and beyond to make sure you do." Academic counseling and individual attention run throughout students' academic careers to keep them on track. "We couldn't have more help," one junior says.

Ninety-five percent of Alverno students hail from Wisconsin. "Students are extraordinarily driven, and they know what it takes to succeed in the real world," says a junior. Dozens of student groups and cultural groups are active on campus. Students and faculty often engage in roundtable discussions to look at political or social issues, according to a sophomore. African Americans comprise 18 percent of the student body, Asian Americans 5 percent, and Hispanics 17 percent. "This is a very liberal campus," says a professional communication major, "with lots of open-minded people." Merit scholarships are awarded based on a personal evaluation of each incoming student. Sixty-three percent of the most recent freshman class were eligible for Pell Grants.

"The ability-based method can create a lot of work requiring much thought."

A three-day orientation program serves freshmen, transfer, resident, and commuter students. The majority of students are commuters, though a limited number of dorm rooms house 11 percent of students, who say the residence halls offer clean, spacious rooms with fully equipped lounges, laundry, and cooking facilities available on each floor. "Dorms are comfortable and well maintained every day, including weekends," says one junior. Male visitors are allowed, but they must sign in and be out by midnight on weekdays and 2:00 a.m. on weekends.

Most of the social life takes place off campus at local clubs, bars, coffee shops, and nearby colleges, but the student union, called the Pipeline, frequently offers on-campus activities. The campus also has an on-site childcare center, a fitness center, and a jogging track, and sponsors dance and theater groups. "Milwaukee is a thriving city of the arts—visual, theatrical, and performance—not to mention the festivals that go on every year," says one art education major. There are also parks and shopping centers, a Performing Arts Center, professional sports teams, ethnic festivals, and free outdoor concerts. Students look forward to the annual Rotunda Ball and homecoming festivities. When it comes to alcohol on campus, the combination of strict policies and a generally low amount of drinking means Alverno is rarely home to archetypal college debauchery.

Alverno competes in NCAA Division III athletics, including volleyball, tennis, softball, soccer, and cross-country. The Inferno basketball team has been especially competitive as of late, finishing a recent season with the most wins in school history and earning the honor of being the first team in Alverno history to qualify for the postseason. Non-sporting annual events include Community Day, which allows students and faculty to participate in an annual day of service.

Attending a school like Alverno promises an experience far afield in some ways from the traditional college world. The emphasis on real-world applications builds confidence in one's actual ability to perform, rather than the ability to score an A. Students and faculty are often on a first-name basis from the start and build relationships that help students find their "own unique style of learning," one senior says. It's a method that obviously works.

<table>
<tr><td>

If You Apply To ➤

</td><td>

Alverno: Rolling admissions. No application fee. Campus interviews: optional, evaluative. No alumnae interviews. ACTs: required. No Subject Tests. Does not accept the Common Application. Essay question.

</td></tr>
</table>

American University

4400 Massachusetts Avenue NW, Washington, D.C. 20016-8001

If the odds are against you at Georgetown and you can't see yourself on GW's ultra-urban campus, welcome to American University. The allure of AU is simple: Washington, D.C. American has a nice campus in a nice neighborhood with easy access to the Metro. American is about a third smaller than GW and a lot easier to get into. An additional plus for males: the student body is nearly two-thirds women.

Located just a few miles from where our country's leaders make decisions of national and global impact, American University is a breeding ground for the next generation of reporters, diplomats, lobbyists, and political leaders who will shape domestic and international policy. Alongside these eager buzzhounds is a host of students taking advantage of AU's strong programs in the arts and sciences and business. "American University is a diverse, pulsing, and dynamic school driven by some of the best faculty, staff, scholars, and students in the world," a senior says. Thanks to phenomenal internships, a comfortable suburban location, and a strong international focus, AU continues to attract top students from nearly 130 nations and all 50 states.

AU's 84-acre residential campus is located in the safe northwest corner of Washington, D.C., in a neighborhood called Tenleytown that's just minutes from downtown; free shuttle buses transport students to the nearby Metro (subway) station. There's a mix of classical and modern architecture and flower gardens alongside the parking lots. The quads have numerous sitting areas for reflection and study, and the campus has gone totally wireless. The 70,000-square-foot, environmentally friendly School of International Service building is designed to be LEED Gold certified and features 7,000 square feet of solar panels on the roof, low-flow faucets and fixtures to reduce water consumption, and the first LED-lit parking garage in Washington, D.C.

> **"American University is a diverse, pulsing, and dynamic school."**

All AU undergraduates must demonstrate competency in writing and English, either through two courses or an exam; for math or statistics, it's one semester of class or placing out through a test. The general education program requires 30 credit hours from five areas: the creative arts, traditions that shape the Western world, global and multicultural perspectives, social institutions and behavior, and the natural sciences. The requirements are typically completed during the first two years so that upperclassmen can study abroad or participate in an internship or co-op—of which there are more than 100 in 41 nations, thanks to the school's relationships with more than 900 private, nonprofit, or government institutions. The school also uses these connections in its Washington Semester* program, which attracts a wide range of majors.

Website: www.american.edu
Location: City Outskirts
Private
Total Enrollment: 9,727
Undergraduates: 6,557
Male/Female: 40/60
SAT Ranges: CR 590–690, M 570–670
ACT Ranges: 26–30
Financial Aid: 84%
Expense: Pr $ $
Student Loans: 67%
Average Debt: $ $
Phi Beta Kappa: Yes
Applicants: 17,039
Accepted: 44%
Enrolled: 21%
Grad in 6 Years: 77%
Returning Freshmen: 90%
Academics: ✑ ✑ ✑ ½
Social: ☎ ☎ ☎
Q of L: ★ ★ ★
Admissions: (202) 885-6000
Email Address: admissions@american.edu

Strongest Programs:
International Studies
Political Science/Government

In the classroom, AU has outstanding programs in political science and government, international studies, business, and communications. An honors program offers the top 15 percent of entering students small seminars, special sections of many courses, and designated floors in the residence halls, plus specialized work in their major and a senior capstone experience. In all, students may choose from more than 70 programs and have the option to design their own interdisciplinary major. The School of International Service offers a three-year Global Scholars bachelor's degree program.

"AU's academic program is rigorous."

"AU's academic program is rigorous, but the climate among the students is more collaborative than competitive," says one senior. "There is definitely a belief that one's own success does not have to come at the expense of our classmates' success." Nearly half of all classes taken by undergraduates have 19 or fewer students, and over 90 percent of professors hold the highest degree in their fields. "No classes are taught by TAs, and the majority of classes are relatively small," cheers one sophomore. "Professors are more than willing to help you and are open to questions and available for office hours."

AU continues to attract top students from approximately 130 nations and all 50 states.

"Students at AU are smart, compassionate, politically aware, and driven to make the world a better place," a senior observes. AU prides itself on drawing students from every state and approximately 130 foreign countries; just 2 percent hail from the District of Columbia. Six percent of the student body is African American, 10 percent is Hispanic, and 7 percent is Asian American. Unlike many college campuses where apathy reigns, AU is politically active—after all, this is Washington, D.C. "What really sets AU apart from other schools is that when AU students are unhappy they do something about it," a student says. The school offers hundreds of merit scholarships and a slew of athletic scholarships.

More than two-thirds of AU students, mostly freshmen and sophomores, live on campus. "All the dorms are air-conditioned and spacious," a junior says. "The lounges on each floor are nice and I like that they each have a full kitchen." There is off-campus housing for upperclassmen in luxury apartments, and a shuttle bus connects them to campus. "You are guaranteed housing for your first four semesters on campus. After that, you can be a part of a lottery system," says one student. "But most students decide to live in a group house or an apartment." Campus dining receives good reviews for its taste and variety. "It's really easy to eat healthy here and not be limited to a back room or shoved in a corner," reports one student. Students say they generally feel safe on campus, noting public safety officers are visible. "I often am at work or studying in the library until the wee hours of the morning," a senior says, "and I never feel unsafe walking back to my dorm late at night."

"All the dorms are air-conditioned and spacious."

Nearly half of all classes taken by undergraduates have 19 or fewer students.

A good deal of the social life at AU revolves around campus-related functions, such as room and frat parties; 20 percent of men and 18 percent of women go Greek, though the women lament that the bottom-heavy male/female ratio is "a little ridiculous." The immediate area around AU has restaurants and shops, but you need to get a bit farther away for true nightlife in Dupont Circle and Georgetown. While greater D.C. certainly has its share of clubs and bars, they're largely off-limits to students under 21. The AU campus is officially dry, and most students take that seriously. Happily, there is so much other stuff to do in D.C., and much of it is free—the art house movie theaters, gallery openings, pro soccer games, museums and monuments, and funky live music. "You just jump on the Metro to get anywhere in the city," says a communications major. Each year, Family Weekend brings games, rides, and popular bands to campus, along with a carnival on the quad. Homecoming and Founder's Week are also campus favorites. Popular road trips include Baltimore, Annapolis, Williamsburg, Richmond, the Ocean City shore, and nearby amusement parks and outlets.

American competes in Division I, but sports are an afterthought for most students. Although there's no football team, students are enthusiastic about Eagles basketball, where games against Bucknell, Holy Cross, and the Naval Academy top the schedule. Women's volleyball is solid, having brought home multiple Patriot League championships. Field hockey and wrestling are competitive, too. AU athletics also earned the distinction of the highest combined GPA in AU history, proving that brains and brawn are not mutually exclusive. There's a slew of intramural and club sports, which are divided into different levels of competitiveness.

AU is heaven on earth for C-SPAN junkies. But even if you are not addicted to following current events, AU and Washington, D.C. are still a top combo for a rich college life. The opportunities for real-world experience—in fields ranging from business to international studies to political science—are outstanding. But AU is small enough to keep students from feeling lost in the fast-paced world inside the Beltway. "We are a small campus, which gives the feeling of being out of the city, but yet the city is at our fingertips," a junior says.

A good deal of the social life at AU revolves around campus-related functions.

Overlaps

Boston College, Boston University, Columbia, George Washington, Georgetown, NYU

If You Apply To ➤   **American:** Early decision I: Nov. 15. Early decision II: Jan. 15. Regular admissions: Jan. 15. Application fee: $70. No campus or alumni interviews. SATs or ACTs: required. Subject Tests: optional. Accepts the Common Application. Essay question.

Amherst College

Amherst, MA 01002-5000

Original home to the well-rounded, superachieving, gentle-person jock. Compare to Williams, Middlebury, and Colby. Not Swarthmore, not Wesleyan. Amherst has always been the king in its category—in part because there are four other major institutions in easy reach to add diversity and depth. Among the few liberal arts colleges with as many men as women.

Amherst offers a dynamic curriculum in the traditional academic disciplines and in numerous interdisciplinary fields. There are no core curriculum or distribution requirements, so students choose their program based on their own individual interests and plans for the future. Indeed, the focus isn't on racking up high grade point averages. Instead, students focus on becoming people who base their thinking on a strong foundation in the liberal arts. Emphasizing "freedom to explore," the spotlight here is on learning. "If your education is really your first priority," says a sophomore, "then I don't think there's a better school."

Amherst's 1,000 acres overlook the picturesque town of Amherst and the Pioneer Valley and offer a panoramic view of the Holyoke Range and the Pelham Hills. On campus, a plot of open land housing a wildlife sanctuary and a forest shares space with academic and residential buildings, athletic fields, and facilities. While Amherst's predominant architectural style remains 19th-century academia—redbrick is key—everything from a "pale yellow octagonal structure to a garish, modern new dorm" can be found here. Amherst looks like a college is supposed to look, with trees and paths winding through the buildings to offer long, contemplative walks.

Website: www.amherst.edu
Location: Small Town
Private
Total Enrollment: 1,817
Undergraduates: 1,817
Male/Female: 51/49
SAT Ranges: CR 670–770, M 670–760
ACT Ranges: 30–34
Financial Aid: 62%
Expense: Pr $ $ $ $
Student Loans: 30%
Average Debt: $
Phi Beta Kappa: No
Applicants: 8,565
Accepted: 13%

(continued)

Enrolled: 42%
Grad in 6 Years: 96%
Returning Freshmen: 98%
Academics: ✐ ✐ ✐ ✐ ✐
Social: ☎ ☎ ☎
Q of L: ★ ★ ★ ★
Admissions: (413) 542-2328
Email Address: admissions@
amherst.edu

Strongest Programs:
English
Economics
Psychology
History
Law, Jurisprudence, and
  Social Thought
Political Science

The dance program is also strong, although it requires courses at each school in the Five College Consortium*.

The most popular majors include psychology, political science, economics, history, and English. Students may mix and match among these subjects to form dual-degree programs. About one-third of students pursue double majors, and a few overachievers even triple major. Students may create their own courses of study from Special Topics classes if the subject of their interest is not available.

"Amherst is very rigorous and most students work hard."

Amherst's unique Law, Jurisprudence, and Social Thought program is not a prelaw major; instead, it's an interdisciplinary study of the law, drawing on fields as diverse as psychology, history, philosophy, and literature, with a strong theoretical focus. The dance program is also strong, although it requires courses at each school in the Five College Consortium*. To house all of these programs, Amherst has spent millions of dollars in recent years renovating facilities, upgrading technological capabilities, and improving spaces for studying, exhibits, performances, and sports.

Amherst is home to a rich intellectual environment that centers on a wealth of acclaimed instructors. "The quality of teaching is phenomenal," says one junior. On such a small campus without graduate students, interaction with professors is encouraged. "Professors are not only wise and accomplished but they pursue teaching at Amherst because they are interested in teaching," explains a sophomore.

To graduate, students must take a first-year seminar, declare a major at the end of sophomore year, fulfill departmental program requirements, pass the requisite number of electives, and perform satisfactorily on comprehensive exams in their major field. First-year seminars, taught by two or more professors, help foster interdisciplinary approaches across topics and are offered in several subject areas. "Amherst is very rigorous and most students work hard," a philosophy major says, "but the atmosphere is not competitive."

In addition to being part of the Five College Consortium*, Amherst also belongs to the Maritime Studies Program* and the Twelve College Exchange*. All-female Smith and Mount Holyoke also add to the social life, and numerous cultural and artistic events at the other schools are open to Amherst students. Each year, approximately one-third of the junior class spends a semester or year abroad; recent students have chosen from more than 260 programs in dozens of countries, ranging from a math program in Budapest to analyzing architecture in Rome. Amherst also has a program in Kyoto, Japan, where one of the college's colonial-style buildings has been duplicated.

Amherst students are "smart, hardworking, and mostly athletic," says one sophomore. Eighty-six percent of Amherst students hail from outside Massachusetts. Eighty-three percent were in the top 10th of their high school class, and, as one junior explains, "Amherst College is populated by nearly every sort of person. Whether you are a geek, jock, hippie, or any other hard-to-define type of human being, you will find kindred spirits." The student body is unusually diverse; 11 percent are African American, 12 percent Asian American, and 12 percent Hispanic. The

"Whether you are a geek, jock, hippie, or any other hard-to–define type of human being, you will find kindred spirits."

school has made a concerted effort to enroll students eligible for Pell Grants. Amherst actively works to educate its community about issues that affect student life. Residential Life, through its staff of Resident Counselors, sponsors programs that both educate and encourage open discussion about many issues on campus, including race and gender relations, issues of sexual respect, and alcohol/drug abuse. There are no merit or athletic scholarships, but the college attracts a substantial number of low-income students by providing loan-free financial aid. Sixty percent of students receive financial aid, with grants averaging over $44,000.

Housing at Amherst is guaranteed for four years, and 99 percent of students live on campus. "The rooms are huge with lots of storage space," raves a student. Those who feel shafted by the room draw can participate in a lip-synch competition; the winner receives the top room pick for his or her class. Everyone who lives on campus, and anyone else who wants to, eats in Valentine Hall, which includes a central serving station and five dining rooms. The selection is diverse but the food overall gets mixed reviews. "It's certainly not terrible," notes a student, "but there are very few options for vegetarians."

Although frats are nothing more than a faint memory, social activities are conducted almost entirely on campus. They range from quiet gatherings of friends to dorm study breaks to campuswide parties. "The social life is diverse," says a student; "from parties to board games, you can find something that suits you." The biggest party of the year, thrown in February, is Casino Night, which includes gambling with real money. The weekend-long Bavaria festival in the spring offers a pig roast and Big Wheel joust. The Campus Center includes outdoor terraces, a formal living room, a game room, a snack bar, a small theater, and a student-run co-op coffeehouse, open three nights a week with live entertainment. Students also take advantage of the Five Colleges membership: "Because of the Five College Consortium*, there are always major events of any and every type going on nearby," says a student.

> **Recent students have chosen from more than 260 programs in dozens of countries, ranging from a math program in Budapest to analyzing architecture in Rome.**

> **"Because of the Five College Consortium*, there are always major events of any and every type going on nearby."**

Amherst is "small but charming, and has everything students need," says a sophomore. Students take part in community service projects, including "Big Brothers/ Big Sisters and Habitat for Humanity, just to name a few," says a freshman. For the many outdoorsy types, good skiing in Vermont is not far, and Boston (an hour and a half) and New York (a little over three hours) are close enough to be convenient road trip destinations.

> **The weekend-long Bavaria festival in the spring offers a pig roast and Big Wheel joust.**

Sports are taken seriously, both varsity and intramurals, and "impact" athletes get favored treatment from the admissions office. The "Lord Jeffs" compete in Division III, but the strong baseball team takes on Division I opponents as well. Solid programs include men's soccer, women's tennis, and men's and women's hockey. Men's basketball were national Division III champions in 2013. Any showdown with archrival Williams is inevitably the biggest game of the season, drawing fans from all corners of campus. Amherst's intramural, club, and varsity programs attract three-quarters of the student body. Intramurals are co-ed and open to all students, staff, and faculty; favorites include soccer, tennis, flag football, and volleyball.

Combine a lack of restrictive requirements with a cadre of professors who are focused on teaching, and it becomes clear why students here so love their institution. Says a proud student: "I see our community as made up of people who are comfortable with themselves and consequently are some of the kindest and most laid-back people I can imagine. Yet this does not deter from the fact that Amherst students are always doing extraordinary things: academically, athletically, artistically, and for the benefit of the world."

Overlaps
Brown, Columbia, Dartmouth, Harvard, University of Pennsylvania, Princeton, Williams, Yale

If You Apply To ➤ **Amherst:** Early decision: Nov. 15. Regular admissions: Jan. 1. Application fee: $60. No campus or alumni interviews. SATs or ACTs: required. Subject Tests: required (any two). Accepts the Common Application. Essay question.

University of Arizona

Robert L. Nugent Building, Tucson, AZ 85704

Tucson is an increasingly popular destination, and it isn't just because of the UA basketball team. A well-devoted honors program attracts top students, as do excellent programs in the sciences and engineering. Generally viewed as a cut above ASU in academic quality. Now offering tuition discounts to out-of-staters. Bring plenty of shorts and sunscreen.

Website: www.arizona.edu
Location: City Center
Public
Total Enrollment: 34,506
Undergraduates: 28,063
Male/Female: 47/53
SAT Ranges: CR 483–600,
   M 500–630
ACT Ranges: 21–27
Financial Aid: 82%
Expense: Pub $ $ $
Student Loans: 49%
Average Debt: $ $
Phi Beta Kappa: Yes
Applicants: 26,329
Accepted: 77%
Enrolled: 37%
Grad in 6 Years: 61%
Returning Freshmen: 80%
Academics: ✍ ✍ ✍ ½
Social: ☎ ☎ ☎ ☎
Q of L: ★ ★ ★ ★
Admissions: (520) 621-3237
Email Address: admissions@
   arizona.edu

Strongest Programs:
Management Information
   Systems
Nursing
Astronomy
Pharmacy
Creative Writing
Aerospace Engineering

With a campus that's encircled by mountain ranges and the beautiful Sonoran Desert, lined with palm trees and cacti, and set against a backdrop of stunning Tucson sunsets, it's no surprise that students at the University of Arizona love to hang out at the mall. Not the shopping center, mind you—but a huge grassy area in the middle of campus where the nearly 35,000 Wildcats gather between classes. Judging by numbers alone, that's enough people to fill a medium-sized town. But students are quick to point out that UA has a strong sense of community and offers a genuinely friendly campus. "Nobody else has a huge central meeting place like we do," says a senior marketing major. "I always see familiar and friendly faces around the mall area." With all the natural beauty that surrounds them, many Wildcats simply purr through four satisfying years.

> "Some courses can be difficult and it can be competitive."

Architecturally, the UA campus distinguishes itself from the city's regiment of adobe buildings with a design that seems a study in the versatility of redbrick. Old Main, the university's first building, is into its second century, but others verge on high-tech science facilities. The Student Recreation Center boasts state-of-the-art exercise equipment, a computer lab, student-tutoring center, and a healthy organic food restaurant. It is also LEED certified. An expansion to Arizona Stadium (home of the Wildcats football team) was completed in late 2013 to the tune of $72 million.

UA has 20 colleges and over 160 degree programs. Sciences are unquestionably the school's forte—the astronomy department is among the nation's best, helped by those clear night skies. Students have access not only to leading astronomers, but also to the most up-to-date equipment, including a huge 176-inch telescope operated jointly by the university and the Smithsonian. A $28 million aerospace and mechanical engineering building has a state-of-the-art subsonic wind tunnel and rocket-combustion test facility. The history and English departments are standouts, as are several of the social science programs. Eager shutterbugs can pore through photographer Ansel Adams's personal collection, and the Center for Creative Photography offers one of the leading photographic collections in the world. Students in the popular business and public administration school can pick racetrack management as their area of expertise, while interested anthropology students can delve into garbage research. For those seeking new vistas, there are study abroad programs available in more than 60 countries.

> "The quality of teaching has been mostly positive."

Under the core curriculum, students take 10 general education courses in common. They fall under the broad categories of arts, humanities, traditions and cultures, natural sciences, and individuals and societies. In addition, almost everyone gets a healthy dose of freshman composition, math, and foreign language. Academic competition, according to most students, is left up to both the individual and the specific concentration. "Some courses can be difficult and it can be competitive, but there is a definite laid-back atmosphere," says one sophomore.

The University Honors Center offers one of the nation's largest and most selective honors programs (students must maintain a grade point average of 3.5 to remain in the program). In addition to offering 200 honors courses per year, the center features smaller classes, personalized advising, special library privileges, and great research opportunities. The Undergraduate Biology Research Program also has a national reputation. Teaching is well regarded, with some freshman courses taught by graduate students. "The quality of teaching has been mostly positive," says one student. "Most of my professors are very well versed in their fields and continue to do research."

"The students at the U of A are very outgoing," says a senior. "There are the party animals, but there are more students here to learn instead of party." Despite tougher admission standards, the administration cites a sharp increase in freshman applications over the past few years, especially from out-of-staters, who constitute 27 percent of the student body. Hispanics account for 26 percent of the student body, African Americans 4 percent, and Asian Americans 6 percent. A diversity action council, a student minority advisory committee, and cultural resource centers help students deal with race-relation issues. An active and popular student government runs a free legal service and a tenants' complaint center, and the university has instituted many programs to help those with learning disabilities. In addition to various merit scholarships averaging $6,000, there are athletic scholarships available to qualified student-athletes.

A junior says dorm quality is "all over the board" but all are well maintained: "Dorms range from brand new with every amenity to a 1920s women's only dorm with sleeping porches that's a historical landmark." Only 21 percent of undergraduates live in the dorms; some freshmen and most upperclassmen flock to the abundant and inexpensive apartments near the school. And what about the campus food? "The dining facilities have great variety, but I think the prices are really high," says a senior. The best way to enjoy the excellent food service at the student union's seven restaurants is to use the university-issued CatCard, which helps students take advantage of the various gustatory options and frees them from carrying cash. Students report feeling safe on campus. "I think campus security is incredible! I once even had a nice campus policeman drive me home from the library when I was leaving late at night," says a student.

Despite the high percentage of off-campus residents, students stream back onto campus on weekends for parties, sports, and cultural events. "There is a thriving social life at the University of Arizona," says a student. "Day or night, you will always find students entertaining themselves with plenty available to them on campus and off." Ten percent of the men belong to fraternities, and 11 percent of the women belong to sororities. The campus is technically alcohol-free, though some question whether the frats have realized that yet. Still, most social life takes place off campus. There are a lot of different dance clubs around town, and some do have after-hours for underage people. Those who feel they must go elsewhere need only head to the Mexican town of Nogales (one hour away), where there is no drinking age. Many students are content remaining in Tucson because it offers "the most incredible sunrises and sunsets, and delightful temperatures year-round." One of the UA's most time-honored traditions is Spring Fling, said to be the largest student-run carnival in the country. On Dead Day, the day before final exams begin, seniors jump into the Old Main fountain after midnight and splash around—a ritual that may or may not be related to preceding hours of drinking.

Athletics is also somewhat of a tradition here. Over the years, UA athletes have won nearly dozens of national team championships and Pac-12 conference titles.

The University Honors Center offers one of the nation's largest and most selective honors programs.

"Day or night, you will always find students entertaining themselves."

Division I football and baseball enjoy national prominence, generate lots of money for other men's and women's sports teams, and provide great weekend entertainment.

The Wildcats basketball teams have been among the nation's leaders in recent years. Division I football and baseball enjoy national prominence, generate lots of money for other men's and women's sports teams, and provide great weekend entertainment, especially when the opposing team is big-time rival Arizona State. UA's battle cry, "Bear Down!"—frequently heard at sporting events—dates back to the 1930s, when a campus football hero, fatally injured in a car crash, whispered his last message to his teammates: "Tell them, tell them to bear down." More than 70 years later, the enigmatic slogan still appears on T-shirts and in a gym on the central campus.

The University of Arizona offers a wide variety of academic opportunities along with spectacular weather. Prospective students are warned to honestly evaluate how that will affect their ability to concentrate. UA is the place to go in pursuit of truth, knowledge, and a good tan.

Overlaps

Arizona State, University of Oregon, University of Washington, University of Colorado–Boulder, San Diego State, Colorado State, Oregon State, Northern Arizona

If You Apply To ➤

Arizona: Rolling admissions: May 1. Financial aid and housing: May 1. Application fee: $50. No campus or alumni interviews. SATs or ACTs: optional. Subject Tests: optional. Essay question: personal statement.

Arizona State University

Box 870112, Tempe, AZ 85287-0112

Want to get lost in a crowd? ASU is the largest university in the nation—with ambitions to get even bigger. Big push underway to enhance interdisciplinary research and increase socioeconomic diversity in student body. Location in the Valley of the Sun attracts plenty of Northerners fleeing the cold. No matter how appealing the thought of 59,000 new faces, you'd better find the right program to get a good education. Try the professional schools and Barrett Honors College.

Website: www.asu.edu
Location: Suburban
Public
Total Enrollment: 58,884
Undergraduates: 49,870
Male/Female: 50/50
SAT Ranges: CR 480–610, M 500–630
ACT Ranges: 21–27
Financial Aid: 85%
Expense: Pub $ $
Student Loans: 55%
Average Debt: $
Phi Beta Kappa: Yes
Applicants: 30,696
Accepted: 88%
Enrolled: 34%
Grad in 6 Years: 57%
Returning Freshmen: 80%

Arizona State University has transformed itself over the last decade into the nation's biggest public university, but playing host to 59,000 students is just the beginning of the story. With no pretense of modesty, this mega-university, situated in a desert oasis that is one of the nation's fastest-growing metro areas, describes itself as the model for a New American University—one where "massive innovation" is the norm and where an interdisciplinary culture is seen as the best means of developing "world-changing ideas." Research spending is up, as are student retention and graduation rates. Not surprisingly, ASU can seem overcrowded and overwhelming at times, but it provides motivated students who can find a manageable niche with countless opportunities for work and play.

ASU's Tempe campus offers a beautiful blend of palm-lined walkways, desert landscapes, and public art displays. The campus is officially listed as an arboretum, and ASU groundskeepers tend to more than 115 species of trees that thrive in Arizona's arid climate. Architectural styles range from turn-of-the-century historic to more modern, and campus construction is booming. The nine-acre Barrett Honors College residential community at the Tempe campus was designed by students, faculty, and staff working with nationally renowned architects. As the first four-year residential honors college within a top-tier public university in the nation, it houses more than 1,700 students and includes a sustainable living/learning community, features multiuse classroom and meeting spaces, dining hall, a fitness center, many unique outdoor courtyards, and a central amphitheater. The 3,430-square-foot Pat Tillman Veterans Center is located on the ground floor of the Memorial Union and brings together a number of academic and student support services that serve the university's continually growing enrollment of veterans and their dependents—currently more than 2,300 undergraduate and graduate students.

ASU's undergraduate schools include business, liberal arts and sciences, engineering, design and the arts, education, health solutions, journalism, nursing and health, public programs, sustainability, technology and innovation, though students apply to the institution as a whole. The School of Sustainability emphasizes the study of land use and planning models that minimize environmental harm, while the college of business ranks second in placing graduates with the Big Four accounting firms. The fine arts college features an innovative child drama program and nationally recognized majors in art, music, and dance. Engineering programs, especially microelectronics, robotics, and computer-assisted manufacturing, are sure bets; the facility for high-resolution microscopy allows students to get a uniquely close-up view of atomic structures. The most popular majors are business, biological sciences, education, engineering, and visual and performing arts.

"The courses are difficult, but the group aspect of most project work makes the hard work much less overwhelming."

The sciences (including biochemistry, chemistry, geology, and biology) and social sciences boast first-class facilities, notably the largest university-owned meteorite collection in the world. Earth and space exploration is out of this world; ASU is also a founding member of the NASA Astrobiology Institute, which focuses on studying the origin of life on Earth and elsewhere. Anthropology benefits from its association with the Institute of Human Origins' Donald C. Johannson, who discovered the 3.2-million-year-old fossil skeleton named Lucy. ASU also offers the largest teacher preparation program of any university in the nation. The B.S.E. in construction engineering focuses on a combination of design and management topics for students interested in engineering with an emphasis on the construction industry; other degrees include a B.S.E. in engineering management and a B.A. in digital culture. ASU is large enough to operate two engineering schools: The College of Technology & Innovation, located on the campus of ASU–Polytechnic, bases every course on a project in which students solve problems for a local community or company. Courses are held not in classrooms but in "studios" filled with machines and tools. The larger and more traditional Ira A. Fulton School of Engineering, located in Tempe, has built four new "eSpace" classrooms using the studio model.

"The best academic program would have to be the honors college," offers one student. "It's amazing! It offers the intellectual stimulation and individual attention of a small liberal arts college at a large research university with innumerable opportunities." Regardless of major, students must fulfill requirements in literacy and critical inquiry (including composition), mathematical studies (including college-level algebra or higher), humanities and fine arts, social and behavioral sciences, and natural sciences. Students must also complete courses in three awareness areas: global, historical, and U.S. cultural diversity. Freshman courses in fields such as mathematics and engineering are being retooled to employ adaptive-learning technologies and to provide more hand-on experiences.

"As a female student, I have always felt very safe on campus."

"The courses are difficult, but the group aspect of most project work makes the hard work much less overwhelming," says one junior. Teachers get high marks for their knowledge and accessibility. "Despite the challenging nature of the classes, professors are always willing to go above and beyond to ensure that the student is successful," says a kinesiology major. Those wishing to study abroad have access to more

(continued)

Academics: ✐ ✐ ✐

Social: 🏮 🏮 🏮 🏮 🏮

Q of L: ★ ★ ★ ★ ★

Admissions: (480) 965-7788

Email Address: admissions@ asu.edu

Strongest Programs:
Psychology
Geography
Electrical Engineering
Civil and Environmental
    Engineering
Materials Science and
    Engineering
Chemistry
History
Economics

The fine arts college features an innovative child drama program and nationally recognized majors in art, music, and dance.

than 300 programs in over 60 countries. The Fulton Undergraduate research Initiative (FURI) is designed to enhance and enrich a student's engineering education by providing hands-on lab experience, independent and thesis-based research, and travel to national conferences. Students select, design, and complete research projects under the guidance of faculty mentors and present their findings at an annual public symposium. An "e-advisor" system keeps students on track to meet degree requirements.

Twenty-three percent of the students at Arizona State come from elsewhere. "It is truly a rarity to come across someone who is not involved in several student organizations, research, or an internship—students here are go-getters, and they take advantage of the opportunities that ASU has to offer," says a student. Because ASU draws so heavily from within Arizona, 19 percent of the student body is Hispanic; African Americans contribute 5 percent, Asian Americans 6 percent, and Native Americans 2 percent. The biggest campus concern of late is the seemingly endless tuition hikes: "Students hate them," says one particularly blunt finance major. ASU offers merit scholarships averaging $7,683 to qualified students and awards 366 athletic scholarships annually to male and female athletes. ASU is one of 14 campuses serving as Tillman Military Scholar University Partner, which honors Pat Tillman, the former football star who died in combat in Iraq.

Only 20 percent of ASU students live in the co-ed dorms. "It is mostly freshmen who choose to live on campus, but our dorms are so nice! I've visited several other schools, and ASU has some of the largest rooms. The furniture in them is also replaced every five years, so nothing is old or broken," says one junior.

"ASU has an incredible amount of school spirit."

No matter where they live, students don't have to buy a meal plan and one student says "the food is edible and diverse." Students say campus security is sufficient: "As a female student, I have always felt very safe on campus," a junior says. "ASU has its own police service, which means students are the top priority and that officers are always on campus and nearby if needed."

"Sometimes I feel there is too much stuff going on that I have to pick between two or three things on a day or night or weekend," says one junior, "but, hey, that's a good problem to have!" ASU's Greek system attracts only 6 percent of the men and 7 percent of the women and "small kick-backs in dorms are just as common as huge house parties," says a sophomore. The campus is officially dry and those under the legal drinking age are also warned against drinking in student housing. Perhaps that's why students head off campus on weekends—often far off campus. Many have cars, giving them access to the mountains of Colorado, the beaches of San Diego, the natural beauty of the Grand Canyon, or the bright lights of Las Vegas. Tempe gets generally positive reviews from students. "It has great restaurants nearby, different shopping centers, and a street called Mill Ave that has stores, food and bars/nightclubs for the 21 and over set," says a communications major.

"ASU has an incredible amount of school spirit," says a junior. Arizona State's Division I athletics department is consistently ranked among the nation's best. ASU softball made its 11th consecutive NCAA appearance in 2011, while women's golf holds the record for consecutive trips to the Women's Golf NCAA Championships with 23 straight appearances. For the 11th consecutive year, students in the Walter Cronkite School of Journalism and Mass Communication took first place in the regional Society of Professional Journalists Mark of Excellence awards.

Arizona State may seem like an overwhelmingly big school with a reputation for rowdiness, but that's not the full story. "It's important for students to know that ASU is not defined by the small proportion of students who choose to drink or party," says a junior, "but that it has so much more to offer and it a fantastic place to go to school." For those not frightened away by its sheer enormity, ASU may be a good place to enjoy the weather and earn a degree.

Overlaps

University of Arizona, Northern Arizona, San Diego State, University of Oregon, University of Southern California, UCLA, University of Colorado

University of Arkansas

200 Hunt Hall, Fayetteville, AR 72701

University of Arkansas rates in the second tier of Southern public universities alongside Alabama, LSU, and Ole Miss. Though conservative by national standards, Fayetteville is progressive by those of Arkansas. With traditional strength in agriculture, U of A has also developed programs in business, engineering, and other professional fields. U of A's highest-ranked program takes the field on Saturday afternoons in the fall.

The state of Arkansas is transforming its flagship public university into a nationally competitive, student-centered research institution in an effort to help stop the flight of the state's young and talented. In the last decade, U of A undergrads have won a plethora of prestigious awards, including Goldwater scholarships, Fulbright scholarships, British Marshall scholarships, National Science Foundation Graduate Fellowships, and Rhodes scholarships. And Arkansas's riches aren't limited to academic spoils. A $300 million cash gift from the family of Walmart founder Sam Walton, the largest ever made to an American public university, put his name on the U of A's business college, and also helped endow the undergraduate Honors College, which enrolls the brightest young scholars on campus. The Walton grant also strengthens and improves the U of A's graduate school. "Come to a Razorback game in the fall when the leaves are changing in the Ozarks," says one student, "and you will be totally won over."

The Arkansas campus is nestled among the mountains, lakes, and streams of the Ozarks, in the extreme northwest corner of the state. The community is friendly and safe, and the moderate climate means recreational opportunities abound. Architectural styles range from modern concrete to buildings that date from the Depression. The center of campus is the stately brick Old Main, which once housed the entire university. There are two greenhouses for plant science majors and an Innovation Center for engineers. The $46 million Northwest Quad project includes housing for 600 students, as well as dining areas, classrooms, computer labs, and other amenities.

Established as a land grant institution in 1871, with agricultural and mechanical roots, the U of A includes six colleges and professional schools. U of A's core requirements include six credits each in English and fine arts, three credits each in U.S. history and math, eight in science, and nine in social sciences. Students in the Fulbright College of Arts and Sciences must also

> **"Come to a Razorback game in the fall and you'll be won over."**

achieve foreign language proficiency. The Walton College of Business offers two of the most popular majors on campus: marketing and finance. Other popular programs are psychology and journalism; architecture and engineering are likewise strong. The Dale Bumpers College of Agricultural, Food, and Life Sciences includes the Poultry Health Center, a national leader in research on poultry epidemics.

Students are quick to point out that although the academic climate is generally stress-free, it is competitive at times. Although introductory courses can be

Website: www.uark.edu
Location: Small City
Public
Total Enrollment: 19,391
Undergraduates: 17,687
Male/Female: 50/50
SAT Ranges: CR 500–610,
  M 520–630
ACT Ranges: 23–28
Financial Aid: 82%
Expense: Pub $
Student Loans: 45%
Average Debt: $ $
Phi Beta Kappa: Yes
Applicants: 16,749
Accepted: 63%
Enrolled: 43%
Grad in 6 Years: 60%
Returning Freshmen: 81%
Academics: ✍ ✍ ✍
Social: ☎ ☎ ☎ ☎
Q of L: ★ ★ ★
Admissions: (800) 377-8632
Email Address: uofa@uark
  .edu

Strongest Programs:
Marketing
Management
Finance
Elementary Education

challenging, the "upper-level classes are harder and require a lot more reading and study time," explains a junior. Professors are lauded for their teaching skills, but students are also likely to have graduate students leading classes. When professors take the lectern, they generally "stimulate and challenge" the students, says a psychology major.

Fifty-three percent of U of A students are homegrown, and minorities comprise 15 percent of the student body. African Americans make up 6 percent, Asian Americans 3 percent, and Hispanics 6 percent. Still, there are commonalities. Students are "laid-back" and focused on earning a degree, says a junior. The university continues to emphasize race relations, and the chancellor has personally chaired a campus task force to help boost success rates of students from underrepresented minority groups. Arkansas hands out thousands of merit scholarships each year, and there are also hundreds of athletic scholarships, representing all U of A sports teams. Additionally, the Good Neighbor program lets students from nearby states with GPAs of 3.0 or higher and ACT scores of at least 24 enroll at in-state rates.

Roughly one-quarter of all undergrads at Arkansas live in the dorms and "most freshmen and sophomores live on campus," a student says. All halls are single-sex, except for one that's co-ed by floor. Students recommend Gregson and Holcombe for freshmen, and note that as part of the First-Year Experience, Arkansas strives to put freshmen in residence halls where peers surround them. A junior recommends "Rock Camp," an optional orientation weekend in Oklahoma. "It is a great way to meet new students, get on email lists, and start making connections." When it comes to food, you can get everything from salad and burgers to sushi. "We have three cafeterias," a dietetics major says.

> **"Upper-level classes are harder and require a lot more reading and study time."**

Arkansas's Greek chapters attract 36 percent of the women and 23 percent of the men. Aside from the revelry that accompanies Razorback football and basketball, students say Greek parties are pretty much the only game in town on weekends. "There are always things going on on campus," says a senior. Dixon Street, the main drag in the town of Fayetteville (population 55,000), is full of bars and restaurants; the town also offers drive-in movies, live music at local clubs, and touring Broadway shows at the Walton Arts Center. Those with cars will find Dallas, Tulsa, Oklahoma City, Memphis, and St. Louis all within six hours' drive.

Varsity teams are the Razorbacks (wild hogs) and the Hog Call "Woooooo! Pig sooie!" rings out during football and basketball weekends, and red Razorback logos are all over town—on T-shirts, napkins, book covers, license plates, and on game day, the cheeks of ecstatic fans. "The student section is always packed, and you must arrive one to two hours early to get a seat," says a junior. Powerhouse teams include men's baseball, basketball, and track, and women's gymnastics, golf, basketball, and volleyball. Eighty-two percent of Arkansas students participate in intramurals, where sports include everything from flag football and soccer to dominoes, miniature golf, and trivia. (Who knew using your brain was a competitive sport?)

The University of Arkansas boasts "fun-loving and free-spirited" students who are "genuinely friendly," says a senior. "If they encounter someone who needs help, they help." This kind of Southern hospitality means poultry science students aren't the only ones flocking to Arkansas for a solid education at a bargain price. Northerners may feel out of their element, and those who dislike football should keep their feelings to themselves. Others may look forward to graduation day, when their names will join forever those of 120,000 other alumni, etched into the five-mile network of sidewalks on campus.

Overlaps

Missouri State, Oklahoma State, University of Oklahoma, University of Texas, University of Tulsa

Atlanta University Center

Atlanta is viewed as the preeminent city in the country for bright, talented, and successful African Americans. It became the capital of the Civil Rights movement in the 1960s—a town described by its leaders as "too busy to hate."

At the heart of this extraordinary culture is the Atlanta University Center, the largest African American educational complex in the world, replete with its own central library and computing center. The seven component institutions have educated generations of African American leaders. The Reverend Martin Luther King Jr. went to Morehouse College; his grandmother, mother, sister, and daughter went to Spelman College. Graduates spread across the country in a pattern that developed when these were among the best of the few colleges to which talented African Americans could aspire. Even now, when the options are almost limitless, alumni continue to send their children back for more.

The center consists of three undergraduate colleges (Morris Brown, Morehouse, and Spelman) and three graduate institutions (Clark Atlanta University, the Interdenominational Theological Seminary, and the Morehouse College of Medicine) on adjoining campuses in the center of Atlanta, three miles from downtown. Students at these affiliated schools can enjoy the quiet pace of their beautiful magnolia-studded campuses or plunge into all the culture and excitement of this most dynamic of Deep South cities. The six original schools—all but the medical school—became affiliated in 1929 using the model of California's Claremont Colleges, but they remain fiercely independent. Each has its own administration, board of trustees, and academic specialties, and each maintains its own dorms, cafeterias, and other facilities. There is cross-registration among the institutions (Morehouse students, for example, go to Spelman for drama and art courses) and with Georgia State and Emory University as well. The governing body of the consortium, the Atlanta University Center, Inc., administers a centerwide dual-degree program in engineering in conjunction with Georgia Tech—and it runs campus security, a student crisis center, and a joint institute of science research. There is also a centerwide service of career planning and placement, where recruiters may come and interview students from all six institutions.

Dating and social life at the coeducational institutions tend to take place within the individual schools, though Morehouse, a men's college, and Spelman, a women's college, maintain a close academic and social relationship. The Morehouse–Spelman Glee Club takes its abundance of talent around the nation, and its annual Christmas concert on the Spelman campus is a standing-room-only event.

Morehouse and Spelman (see full write-ups) constitute the Ivy League of historically African American colleges. The following are sketches of the other two institutions offering undergraduate degrees.

CLARK ATLANTA UNIVERSITY (WWW.CAU.EDU)

Formed by the consolidation of Clark College, a four-year liberal arts institution, and Atlanta University, which offered only graduate degrees, CAU is a comprehensive coeducational institution that offers undergraduate, graduate, and professional degrees. The university draws on the former strengths of both schools, offering quality programs in the health professions, public policy, and mass communications (including print journalism, radio and television production, and filmmaking). Graduate and professional programs include education, business, library information studies, social work, and arts and sciences. Undergraduate enrollment: 3,200.

MORRIS BROWN COLLEGE (WWW.MORRISBROWN.EDU)

An open-admission, four-year undergraduate institution that is related to the African Methodist Episcopal Church, MBC lost most of its students in the spring of 2003 after the college lost its accreditation. A new president and a restructured board of trustees are working hard to restore its financial and academic viability. Its most popular programs are education and business administration. Morris Brown also offers evening courses for employed adults, as well as a program of co-op work-study education.

Morehouse College

830 Westview Drive, Atlanta, GA 30314

Along with sister school Spelman, Morehouse is the most selective of the historically black schools. Alumni list reads like a *Who's Who* of African American leaders. Best known for business and popular 3–2 engineering program with Georgia Tech. Built on a Civil War battlefield, Morehouse is a symbol of the new South.

Website: www.morehouse.edu
Location: Urban
Private
Total Enrollment: 2,438
Undergraduates: 2,438
Male/Female: 100/0
SAT Ranges: CR 450–570,
   M 460–570
ACT Ranges: 19–24
Financial Aid: 97%
Expense: Pr $
Student Loans: 74%
Average Debt: $
Phi Beta Kappa: Yes
Applicants: 2,575
Accepted: 66%
Enrolled: 33%
Grad in 6 Years: 55%
Returning Freshmen: 82%
Academics: ✏ ✏ ✏
Social: ☎ ☎ ☎ ☎
Q of L: ★ ★ ★ ★
Admissions: (404) 215-2632
Email Address: admissions@
   morehouse.edu

Strongest Programs:
Economics
Business
Biology
Political Science
Psychology

Founded in 1867, Morehouse College has the distinction of being the nation's only historically African American, four-year liberal arts college for men. Top students come to Morehouse because they want an institution with a strong academic program and a supportive atmosphere in which to cultivate their success orientation and leadership skills without facing the additional barriers they might encounter at a predominantly white institution. "Morehouse is a college of young, assertive, ambitious black men," says a psychology major. Notable alumni include the Rev. Martin Luther King Jr., Samuel L. Jackson, Spike Lee, and Dr. Louis Sullivan, president emeritus of the Morehouse School of Medicine and former U.S. Secretary of Health and Human Services.

Located near downtown Atlanta, the 61-acre Morehouse campus is home to 35 buildings, including the Martin Luther King Jr. International Chapel. Over the last decade, the college has enriched its academic program, conducted a successful multimillion-dollar national fund-raising campaign, increased student scholarships and faculty salaries, doubled its endowment, improved its physical plant, and acquired additional acres of land.

The general education program includes not only 53 semester hours in four major disciplines (humanities, natural sciences, math, and social sciences), but also the study of "the unique African and African American heritage on which so much of our modern American culture is built." "Many students are here to get a greater understanding of their heritage and to promote it," attests one student. As part of their general education requirements, students also need to pass freshman, sophomore, and junior year assemblies which "celebrate Morehouse heritage and traditions." The academic climate at the House can get intense, with students learning and challenging themselves for the sake of learning and not just to bust a curve. "Morehouse offers an academic structure that is both competitive and rigorous," states a freshman. Counseling, including career counseling, is considered quite strong, although students caution applicants to expect bureaucratic red tape as they navigate Morehouse student life.

> **"Morehouse is a college of young, assertive, ambitious black men."**

As a rule of thumb, the more preprofessional your plan, the better Morehouse fits. Undergraduate programs include the traditional liberal arts majors in the humanities and social and natural sciences. While the sciences have been traditionally strong at Morehouse, business courses have risen in prominence. The college has obtained accreditation of the undergraduate business department by the American Assembly of Collegiate Schools of Business, and current students are linked to graduates who serve as mentors in the ways of the business world. The most popular major is business administration. Engineering, which trails shortly behind in popularity, is actually a 3–2 program in conjunction with Georgia Tech and other larger universities. The school also runs a program with NASA that allows students to engage in independent research. Programs that receive less favorable reviews from students are English, art, and drama, and the administration admits that physical education and some of the humanities offerings could use some strengthening. Study abroad options include programs offered through the Associated Colleges of the South* consortium. The school also offers courses and additional resources as a member of the Atlanta Regional Council for Higher Education*.

Sixty-seven percent of Morehouse students come from outside the state, with a sizable number from the Southeast and the Mid-Atlantic. Sixty-seven percent graduated in the top quarter of their high school class. Ninety-six percent are African American and 4 percent hail from other nations. More than 600 merit scholarships are available, many providing full tuition. There are roughly 120 scholarships for athletes in football, basketball, track, soccer, and tennis.

There's limited housing, leaving half of the student body to find their own off-campus accommodations. For freshmen, students recommend Graves Hall, the college's oldest building, built in 1889. Those who do get campus housing sometimes wish they hadn't. Complaints range from "too small" to "not well maintained." Most upperclassmen live off campus. The meal plan at Morehouse is mandatory for students living on campus and draws its share of complaints.

> "Morehouse offers an academic structure that is both competitive and rigorous."

Morehouse's homecoming is a joint effort between Morehouse and Spelman. The queen elected by Morehouse men has traditionally been a Spelman woman, as are the cheerleaders and majorettes, who have been known to quip, "You can always tell a Morehouse man, but you can't tell him much." The four fraternities, which sign up a very small percentage of the students, hold popular parties; "drinking is not a big deal here," most students concur. Going out on the town in Atlanta is a popular evening activity, and on-campus football games, concerts, movies, and religious programs all draw crowds.

In its early years, Morehouse left much to be desired in the area of varsity sports, but it now competes well in Division II. Track, cross-country, tennis, basketball, football, and soccer are all strong, but it is the strong intramural program that allows students a chance to become the superstars they know are lurking within them. During football season, Morehouse men road-trip to follow the games at Howard, Hampton, and Tuskegee universities.

Morehouse is well equipped to serve the modern heirs of a distinguished tradition. Morehouse students don't just attend Morehouse. They become part of what amounts to a network of "Morehouse Men" who share the bonds of having had the Morehouse experience, and graduates find that alumni stand ready and willing to help them with jobs and other needs.

As a rule of thumb, the more preprofessional your plan, the better Morehouse fits.

In its early years, Morehouse left much to be desired in the area of varsity sports, but it now competes well in Division II.

Overlaps

Atlanta, Clark, Georgia Tech, Hampton, Howard

If You Apply To ➤

Morehouse: Early action: Nov. 1. Regular admissions: Mar. 1. Application fee: $50. Campus and alumni interviews: recommended, informational. SATs or ACTs: required. Subject Tests: optional. Essay question.

350 Spelman Lane, Atlanta, GA 30314

The Wellesley of the black college world, Spelman's reputation draws students from all corners of the country. Unusually strong in the sciences with particular emphasis on undergraduate research. Wooded 42-acre Atlanta campus offers easy access to urban attractions. Significantly more selective than brother school Morehouse. Has scrapped varsity sports to emphasize lifelong physical fitness.

Website: www.spelman.edu
Location: Urban
Private
Total Enrollment: 2,145
Undergraduates: 2,145
Male/Female: 0/100
SAT Ranges: CR 480–570, M 465–560
ACT Ranges: 20–24
Financial Aid: 55%
Expense: Pr $
Student Loans: 80%
Average Debt: $
Phi Beta Kappa: Yes
Applicants: 5,864
Accepted: 38%
Enrolled: 24%
Grad in 6 Years: 73%
Returning Freshmen: 90%
Academics: ✐ ✐ ✐
Social: ☎ ☎ ☎ ☎
Q of L: ★ ★ ★ ★ ★
Admissions: (800) 982-2411
Email Address: admiss@ spelman.edu

Strongest Programs:
Biology
Engineering
Natural Sciences
Premed
Prelaw

As one of only two surviving African American women's colleges in the United States (the other is Bennett), Spelman College holds a special appeal for African American women seeking to become leaders in fields ranging from science to the arts. Students flock here for that something special that the predominantly Caucasian schools lack: an environment with first-rate academics where African American women can develop self-confidence and leadership skills before venturing into a world where they will once again be in the minority.

Founded in 1881 by two white women from New England (it was named after John D. Rockefeller's in-laws, Mr. and Mrs. Harvey Buel Spelman), the school was traditionally the starting point for teachers, nurses, and other African American female leaders. Today's emphasis is on getting Spelman grads into the courtrooms, boardrooms, and engineering labs. Honing women for leadership is the main mission, and that nurturing takes place on a classic collegiate-green campus with a $141 million endowment.

These are heady times for Spelman. Although the college finds itself competing head-on with the Seven Sisters and other prestigious and predominantly Caucasian institutions that are eager to recruit talented African American women, the college is holding its own. The college offers a well-rounded liberal arts curriculum that emphasizes the importance of critical and analytical thinking and problem solving. Usually by the end of sophomore year, students are expected to complete 34 credit hours of core requirements, including English composition, foreign language, health and physical education, mathematics, African diaspora and the world, African American women's studies, and computer literacy. In addition, freshmen are required to take First Year Orientation, and sophomores must take Sophomore Assembly. Spelman's liberal arts program introduces students to the principal branches of learning, specifically languages, literature, English, the natural sciences, humanities, social sciences, and fine arts.

> **"The school is made up of the top students from around the country."**

Spelman's established strengths lie in the natural sciences (especially biology) and the humanities, both of which have outstanding faculties. Over the last decade, the college has greatly strengthened its offerings in math and the natural sciences; extensive undergraduate research programs provide students with publishing opportunities, and many end up attending grad school to become researchers. Students have moved beyond the popular majors of the early '70s—education and the fine arts—in favor of premed and prelaw programs, and these programs remain strong. The dual-degree program in engineering (in cooperation with Georgia Tech) is also a standout. The Women's Research and Resource Center specializes in women's studies and community outreach to women.

"The academic climate is very competitive," says an English major. "The school is made up of the top students from around the country and the courses are designed to be a challenge for the best of the best." Individual attention is the hallmark of a Spelman education. About 70 percent of the faculty have doctorates, and many are African American and/or female—and thus, excellent role models, ones the students find very accessible. Except for some of the required courses, classes are small; most have fewer than 25 students. Students who want to spread their wings can venture abroad through a variety of programs, or try one of the domestic exchange arrangements with Wellesley, Mount Holyoke, Vassar, or Mills. The school also offers courses and additional resources as a member of the Atlanta Regional Council for Higher Education*.

Spelman's reputation continues to attract African American women from all over the country, including a high proportion of alumnae children. Roughly three-quarters of the students come from outside Georgia. Students represented here include high achievers looking for a supportive environment and those women with high potential who performed relatively poorly in high school. Eighty-two percent of the student body is African American, 1 percent are international. Spelman does not guarantee to meet the financial need of all those admitted, but it does offer merit scholarships. There are no athletic scholarships.

Forty-three percent of students live on campus, and housing is "dated," reports a biology major. "We have little to no air-conditioning." Still, the older dorms certainly can add to the school's historical charm, and students report having little trouble in getting a room. There are 11 dorms, and students recommend that freshmen check out the Howard Harreld dorm. The meal plan is mandatory for campus-dwellers and food is described as "edible," if not diverse.

> **"No alcohol on campus—period."**

Largely because of the Atlanta University Center, students also have plenty of chances for social interaction with other nearby colleges. "Students mingle in the student centers of all four schools all the time, especially on Fridays," a veteran explains. "Atlanta is a great college town!" gushes one junior. "If there is any place that a student can be academically enriched, it is here." Spelmanites do take advantage of the big-city nightlife; they attend plays, symphonies, and the hot Atlanta nightclubs such as Ethiopian Vibrations and Lenox Mall. Sororities are present but only in small numbers—3 percent of the students go Greek. The attitude on drinking leans toward the conservative. Says one student, "No alcohol on campus—period." The most anticipated annual events include sisterhood initiation ceremonies and the Founders Day celebration. Varsity sports, never all that important, have now been scrapped for a general fitness and nutrition program, with an extensive list of physical activities such as running and yoga.

Spelman College has spent more than 125 years furthering the education and opportunities of African American women. It has adapted its curriculum to meet the career aspirations of today's youth, built up its bankroll, and successfully met the challenge posed by affirmative action in other universities. Still an elite institution in African American society, Spelman is staking its future on its ability to provide a unique kind of education that allows its graduates to compete with anyone.

> *The college offers a well-rounded liberal arts curriculum that emphasizes the importance of critical and analytical thinking and problem solving.*

> *Eighty-two percent of the student body is African American, 1 percent are international.*

Overlaps

Atlanta, Clark, Florida A&M, Georgia State, Hampton, Howard

If You Apply To ➤

Spelman: Early action: Nov. 8. Early decision: Nov. 22. Application fee: $35. Campus interviews: optional, informational. No alumnae interviews. SATs or ACTs: required. Subject Tests: optional. Accepts the Common Application. Essay question. Seeks women who are active in school, church, or community.

105 Eden Street, Bar Harbor, ME 04609

In today's practical world, COA is as out-there as it gets—a haven for communal, earthy, vegetarian types who would rather save the world than make a buck. Lacks many of the usual trappings of college life, such as varsity teams and Greek life. With fewer than 350 students, it makes smallness an academic and social virtue.

Website: www.coa.edu

Location: Rural

Private

Total Enrollment: 316

Undergraduates: 306

Male/Female: 29/71

SAT Ranges: CR 610–690,
    M 540–680

ACT Ranges: 25–33

Financial Aid: 94%

Expense: Pr $ $

Student Loans: 56%

Average Debt: $ $

Phi Beta Kappa: No

Applicants: 378

Accepted: 71%

Enrolled: 27%

Grad in 6 Years: 64%

Returning Freshmen: 83%

Academics: ✍ ✍ ✍

Social: ☎ ☎

Q of L: ★ ★ ★

Admissions: (800) 528-0025

Email Address: inquiry@coa
    .edu

Strongest Programs:
Public Policy
International Development
Marine Science
Education
Environmental Studies
Art

The College of the Atlantic attracts rugged individualists troubled by the world's most pressing issues, notably pollution, environmental damage, and troubled inner cities around the globe. The college's curriculum is focused on human ecology—the study of the relationship between humans and their natural and social environments—which is the only major offered. "The small population and emphasis on community make COA a great place to live and discuss the world with your peers and professors," says a student. What's more, COA bucks the national obsession with growth—seeing smallness as they key to education that cuts across disciplines, eschews academic conventions, and takes a personalized approach to teaching and learning.

The 35-acre campus, covered in lush flowers, vegetable gardens, and lawns, sits on the island of Mount Desert, along the shoreline of Frenchman Bay and adjacent to the magnificent Acadia National Park. In addition, the college has acquired two offshore island research centers and a 73-acre organic farm, and has opened wood-pellet heated "green" dorms and an oceanside campus center. COA is serious about its mission, and this is reflected in the facilities: sustainability is prized, and the college uses environmentally responsible materials as much as possible. "We believe the most sustainable building is that which isn't built," says an administrator.

Most courses focus on a single aspect of humans' relationships with the world. Instead of traditional academic departments, the school has three broad resource areas: environmental science, arts and design, and applied human studies. Many students choose to concentrate on more narrowly defined topics within human ecology, such as marine studies, biological and environmental sciences, public policy, visual and performing arts, environmental design, or education. With advisors and resource specialists, each student designs an individual course of study. "Students are creative and passionate about what they study," a student says, "so the courses reflect that." The natural sciences are stellar, with excellent instruction in ecology, zoology, and marine biology. The arts are catching up, with a more formal video and performance art program run by a Guggenheim recipient created in recent years. Allied Whale, the school's marine study arm, offers hands-on research opportunities and specializes in training and research in marine mammalogy. Founded in 1972, the nonprofit program conducts research into effective methods. COA also offers exchange programs with the Olin College of Engineering, the University of Maine–Orono, and several other learning institutions around the globe. What's more, the college has launched a new International Environmental Diplomacy program. Students in this program focus on learning how to understand, critique, and even negotiate international environmental treaties. In response to some entrepreneurially minded graduates who wished that they had learned some business skills, COL has established the Hatchery, a program that encourages students to come up with ideas and gives them 10 weeks to build a prototype. The emphasis is on interdisciplinary exploration, and the most compelling ideas get a $5,000 grant from the college.

> **"Students are creative and passionate about what they study."**

Student life at COA is intense and semicommunal, beginning with an optional, rugged five-day wilderness orientation preceding the first trimester. Before graduating, students must also complete a 10-week off-campus internship and 10-week final project. Other requirements are few: Freshmen must take a human ecology core course, and two courses are required in environmental sciences, human studies, and arts and design. Sophomores must submit a writing portfolio for evaluation. All students incorporate research into their studies, whether it is a development impact study for the local government or a study on the aggression of fire ants for Acadia National Park. "I think the workload is fairly intense, and even though you take only three classes per term it can feel like a lot more," says one junior.

With advisors and resource specialists, each student designs an individual course of study.

Some areas only have a professor or two, and 96 percent of all classes have 19 or fewer students. Since the student body is small, scholars can become close to faculty members. "I've had space-cadet hippie professors that never taught me with any depth, and I've had brilliant, insightful professors who have forever changed my

"I think the workload is fairly intense."

view of academics," says one student. In lieu of grades, students receive in-depth written evaluations of their work, although they may request grades as well. They must reciprocate with an evaluation of their performance.

Students attracted to this quirky academic gem and its unique curriculum tend to be bright and idealistic; many traveled the world before beginning school and move on to the Peace Corps or Americorps. "Students are self-motivated and predominantly leftist in their attitudes," explains one student. The student body is 2 percent African American, 1 percent Asian American, and 3 percent Hispanic. Twenty percent are international students. "Most students get along very well and there is a huge diversity of cultures, religions, countries, beliefs, financial statuses, and thoughts," says a freshman. The college's governance system gives students and administrators almost equal voices in how it's run; anyone may voice concerns or vote on policy-change proposals or the hiring of new faculty at the All College Meeting. Students aren't shy about also speaking out on more worldly issues, "from 'students for a free Tibet,' to antiwar protests, to environmental justice, to the global AIDS campaign," says a sophomore.

Student life at COA is intense and semicommunal.

Thanks to the college's green waterfront housing village, 44 percent of students—freshmen, international students, upper-class students, and resident advisors—live on campus, while the balance find cozy, inexpensive apartments or houses in the nearby town of Bar Harbor. "The dorms are super-comfortable, from the new, spacious Blair/Tyson, to the eccentric, ocean-view, bay-windowed Sea Fox. Peach

"There is a huge diversity of cultures, religions, countries, beliefs, financial statuses, and thoughts."

House houses only eight people—it's a little cabin in the woods," a junior says. The dining options draw praise, too. "The food is fantastic," says a senior. "Most of the produce we buy is organic and locally grown."

Bar Harbor is a tourist community that "nearly shuts down in the winter," according to one student. A sophomore adds, "Bar Harbor is nice, but the whole island is one of the best places to go to school in the world." Students get to know the townspeople through the required 30 hours of community service. "People do lots of stuff for local organizations, including work on farms, parks, the Downeast AIDS Network, and the YMCA," says a student. On weekends, few students leave campus, since Portland, the nearest urban center, is three hours away. "On campus there are lots of social groups and events, like concerts, open mics, poetry slams, and dance parties," a human ecology major says. There are no fraternities or sororities, and students kick back at off-campus house parties, which are generally alcohol-free. There's no drinking on campus, and it's tough for underage students to get served in town. There are no varsity sports, but about half of the students

There are no varsity sports, but about half of the students sign up for the intramural program.

Overlaps

Colby, Green Mountain, Hampshire, University of Maine, University of Vermont, Warren Wilson

"When I visited COA I found myself one minute in an intense discussion about the philosophy of language and the next in the middle of a snowball fight," says one student. Indeed, College of the Atlantic is a place where Earth Day really is cause for celebration, where students have been known to ride nude through the cafeteria and on nearby streets during Bike Week, and where everyone from students to trustees jumps into frigid Frenchman Bay on the first Friday of the fall term to try to swim from the school's docks to Bar Island and back. "I think you have to be extremely self-confident in directing your own education to make the most of COA," says a senior. "You have to be independent in every way."

If You Apply To ➤

COA: Early decision: Dec. 1. Regular admissions, financial aid, and housing: Apr. 1. Application fee: $50. Campus and alumni interviews: optional, evaluative. SATs or ACTs: optional. Subject Tests: optional. Accepts the Common Application. Essay question.

Auburn University

202 Mary Martin Hall, Auburn, AL 36849-5111

Sweet Home Alabama, where the skies are so blue and the spirit of football lasts year-round. Auburn was once called Alabama Polytechnic, and today AU's programs in engineering, agriculture, and the health fields are still among its best. AU's down-home, small-town atmosphere may feel claustrophobic to those from outside the Deep South.

Website: www.auburn.edu
Location: Small City
Public
Total Enrollment: 21,060
Undergraduates: 18,419
Male/Female: 50/50
SAT Ranges: CR 530–630, M 550–650
ACT Ranges: 24–30
Financial Aid: 60%
Expense: Pub $ $
Student Loans: 45%
Average Debt: $ $
Phi Beta Kappa: No
Applicants: 17,463
Accepted: 77%
Enrolled: 29%
Grad in 6 Years: 68%
Returning Freshmen: 90%
Academics: ✍ ✍
Social: ☎ ☎ ☎
Q of L: ★ ★ ★

Founded in 1856, Auburn University is a public land grant university that excels in professional and technical fields such as architecture, engineering, and agriculture. But the school also welcomes students with frenzied athletics, warm and cozy hospitality, and Southern charm. "It truly is a family atmosphere. We are here to learn and help each other," says one happy Tiger. "That is what makes us such a great university."

The town of Auburn, which grew up amid miles of forest and farmland largely to serve the university, is depicted in an Oliver Goldsmith poem as the "loveliest village of the plain." The campus stretches for nearly 2,000 acres, graced by mossy trees, lush lawns, and majestic colonnades. Most buildings are redbrick and Georgian in style with some more modern facilities grouped in a compact central location. The Auburn Arena includes over 29,000 square feet of student-athlete space, a two-court practice facility, offices, the Auburn University Athletic Ticket Office, an AU Team Store, the Lovelace Museum, two food courts, and other amenities.

"[Students are] willing to help their classmates through tutoring or group study sessions."

Auburn's core curriculum (revamped in 2011) now includes many new courses in the humanities, social sciences, and fine arts. Some previous requirements have been made more flexible, interdisciplinary honors sequences have been added, and all core curriculum courses have been aligned with one or more of the 11 general education student learning outcomes that all Auburn graduates are expected to attain by the time they graduate. To ease the transition into college life, freshmen undergo the three-day "Camp War Eagle" session, and transfer students spend a day in orientation. The academic climate varies by department, and students say classroom competition is rare. "I have found that rather than students competing with each other for higher grades they are more willing to help their classmates through tutoring or group study sessions," says a senior. "In that respect, Auburn's academic climate isn't cut-throat." Regardless of the rigor, students say professors are always willing to go the extra mile for students. "Although I have not liked every teacher I've had, every teacher has taught me something new and useful," a junior says.

The engineering, architecture, agriculture, and pharmacy programs are stellar. Many Auburn students are eager to get started on their careers, so the co-op program, which provides pay and credit in several professional fields, is increasingly popular. Auburn has also established a first-of-its-kind program in wireless engineering for students who want to design network hardware or software for cell phones and other mobile devices. The Samuel Ginn College of Engineering has an aerospace engineering department and has graduated six NASA astronauts. Seven areas formerly designated as Peaks of Excellence compete for millions of dollars in special funding; these include cell and molecular biosciences, food safety, fisheries and allied aquacultures, and forest sustainability. Through the Auburn Abroad Experience, hundreds of students study abroad in programs lasting weeks, months, or multiple semesters.

"There is always trouble getting a room if you procrastinate and wait like I did."

The Accelerated Bachelor's/Master's Plan allows eligible students to count up to nine approved graduate hours (in a 30-hour master's program) or 12 approved graduate hours (in a 36-hour master's program) toward both a bachelor's and a master's degree. In this manner, students may be able to complete both degrees in the time it normally takes to complete just the bachelor's.

Auburn students are "mostly Southern people who are from Alabama and who have family that went to Auburn," says a junior. Indeed, 62 percent of Auburn students are Alabama natives, and many are legacies—the second or third generation in their families to attend the school. African Americans account for 7 percent of the student body, Hispanics add 3 percent, and 2 percent are Asian American. The conservative tone of this Bible Belt campus makes it hospitable for many Christian groups, and Auburn is home to one of the largest chapters in the United States of the Campus Crusade for Christ. "Half of Auburn students love politics and enjoy the political process, while the other half wouldn't know where their polling place was if you gave them a map," quips one senior. Each year, the university awards merit scholarships; the average award is $2,885. Gifted athletes vie for 407 athletic scholarships in 19 sports.

The majority of Auburn's residence halls are coed by floor, but there are several single-sex halls. On campus housing features 31 residence halls and 22 percent of undergrads live on campus. "Get on a waiting list ASAP," advises a junior. Another adds, "The dorms are always filled up. There is always trouble getting a room if you procrastinate and wait like I did." First-year students compete on a first-come, first-served basis with returning students. Twenty-one percent of Auburn men join fraternities, and 31 percent of the women join sororities, perhaps because chapters get space in the best dorms. Students grumble about the mandatory—and pricey—meal plan but say the dining has improved considerably in recent years. "It seems like they open a new dining facility each academic year and the food continues to diversify and get healthier," a student says.

Aside from sporting events and fraternity parties, Auburn sponsors concerts, free movies, and plenty of intramural sports. "Social life is great whether you are Greek or not," says a freshman. "The university holds several events throughout the year that are fun," adds a senior, "but most of the social scene is off campus at apartments or fraternity houses." The campus is officially dry, except on game days, and

(continued)

Admissions: (334) 844-6425
Email Address: admissions@ auburn.edu

Strongest Programs:
Engineering
Accounting
Interior Architecture
Human Development and
    Family Studies
Actuarial Studies

The Samuel Ginn College of Engineering has an aerospace engineering department and has graduated six NASA astronauts.

Aside from sporting events and fraternity parties, Auburn sponsors concerts, free movies, and plenty of intramural sports.

students say the alcohol policy is enforced. Long-standing traditions include the Burn the (Georgia) Bulldogs Parade and Hey Day, when everyone wears a nametag and walks around saying, "Hey!"

The overall sports program has suffered from the need to pay $11 million to a fired football coach and his staff. Auburn is a football powerhouse, and on fall Saturdays, 86,000 screaming fans turn the place into Alabama's fourth-largest city. The rallying cry "Warrrrr Eagle!" rocks the place each time an Auburn back runs to daylight; the football team brought home the NCAA national title in 2010–11. Other solid teams include men's swimming and diving (conference champs in 2011–12), equestrian (2013 national title champs), and women's golf and track and field. The McWhorter Center for Women's Athletics is one of the finest gymnastics training facilities in the country, and intramural programs are numerous and popular.

Auburn is working hard to increase the caliber of its students and academic programs, and especially to achieve a top 20 national ranking for its college of engineering. "Auburn has become more focused on the future," one senior says. But students say certain key characteristics have stayed the same—and that's a good thing. Says one student, "We just keep getting cooler."

Overlaps

University of Georgia, University of Alabama, Georgia Tech, University of Florida, University of Tennessee, Clemson

If You Apply To ➤

Auburn: Early action: Oct. 1. Regular admissions: Nov. 1. Financial aid: Mar. 1. Application fee: $50. Campus and alumni interviews: optional, informational. SATs or ACTs: required. Subject Tests: optional. Out-of-state enrollment is capped on a year-to-year basis; there are no set limits. Essay question.

Austin College

900 N. Grand Avenue, Sherman, TX 75090

The second-most-famous institution in Texas with Austin in its name. Half the size of Trinity (TX), runs neck and neck with Southwestern to be the leading Texas college with fewer than 1,500 students. Combines the liberal arts with strong programs in business, education, and the health fields. Don't look for the Roos on a map of the city of Austin. The college is actually near Dallas.

Website: www.austincollege.edu
Location: Small City
Private
Total Enrollment: 1,253
Undergraduates: 1,235
Male/Female: 48/52
SAT Ranges: CR 560–660, M 570–670
ACT Ranges: 23–29
Financial Aid: 97%
Expense: Pr $
Student Loans: 75%
Average Debt: N/A
Phi Beta Kappa: Yes
Applicants: 3,003

For historical reasons over which reasonable persons can disagree, the Kangaroo has become the symbol of all things Austin. All freshmen receive Roo Crew T-shirts at orientation, students hold a trick-or-treat alternative known as "Roo Boo" for local children, and the online career management system is known as Roo Connect. AC's preprofessional programs, most notably premed, are among the strongest in the state. Professors here even serve students breakfast at 10 p.m. the night before finals. It's just another example of the personal style that is typical of this charming Southern institution. "You feel comfortable and safe at Austin College," says a sophomore. "It becomes your second home."

Austin's 65-acre campus is in a residential area in the city of Sherman. The campus is designed in the traditional quadrangle style and comprises beige sandstone buildings, tree-lined plazas, decorative fountains, and an impressive 70-ton sculptured solstice calendar. Dorms are conveniently located approximately 200 yards from most classrooms, which eases the pain of first-period classes.

The core curriculum begins with a freshman seminar called Communication/Inquiry. Each professor who teaches the course becomes the mentor for the 20 freshmen in his or her class. Next is a three-course sequence on the Heritage of Western

Culture. Then students select from courses in three categories in humanities, social sciences, and natural sciences. Seventy-eight percent of all classes have 25 students or fewer, and no class has more than 50. "The academic climate is competitive with a close student/teacher relationship," says a freshman. "Every course does push the student to improve."

When it comes time to apply to grad school, premed and predental students at this little college have one of the highest acceptance rates of any Texas school, and aspiring lawyers also do well. AC's five-year teaching program grants students both a bachelor's and a master's degree. Science and education receive high marks from students, as do international studies, political science, and foreign languages, but psychology is the most popular major. The Jordan Language House boards 48 students studying French, German, Japanese, and Spanish, along with a native speaker of each language, and students have to speak the language in all common areas. Students can combine three of the school's majors into an interdisciplinary degree, and must complete one major and a minor or a double major to graduate. A cooperative engineering program links the college with other schools.

> **"Professors are easy to talk to and seem to have a passion for making students understand course material."**

The college also offers its students independent study, directed research, junior year abroad, and departmental honors programs. The Leadership Institute is open to approximately 15 students of each entering class, and five more can get in after their first year. Participating students enjoy a suite of privileges. Austin also provides three research areas in Grayson County. Students can focus on just one course during the January term, and many use that time to study abroad or undertake off-campus internships. Back on campus, students heap praise on the professors. "The professors are ready to help," says one student. Another adds, "Professors are easy to talk to and seem to have a passion for making students understand course material."

Ninety-one percent of Austin students hail from the Lone Star State. Hispanics and African Americans comprise 13 and 4 percent of the student body, respectively, and Asian Americans make up 13 percent. "Students are calm, confident, intelligent, aware of their interests, and easygoing," according to an art major. Students also say there is a wide range of political views on campus. Austin was founded by a Presbyterian missionary in 1849, and its continuous ties to the Presbyterian Church (USA) can be seen in the emphasis on values in the core courses, participation in service activities, and limited residence-hall visitation hours—a chief complaint of students. AC offers merit scholarships worth an average of roughly $15,000.

As for dorm life, 77 percent of undergraduates live in traditional dorm housing. "Dorms are comfortable and sufficient," a sophomore says. One dorm is co-ed, one houses language studies students, one is men-only, and two are women-only. Dean (the only co-ed residence hall) seems to be a popular choice for freshmen, despite (or perhaps because of) its reputation as being loud and social. Others say Clyce is the best bet for freshman women. The Roo Suites house juniors and seniors, with priority given to juniors. Residence hall access is computerized, and students say safety is not an issue. Nearly all students take advantage of the three-meal-a-day plan, though not all take advantage of the all-you-can-eat

> **"AC is awesome because it's small and comfortable."**

option. "Fresh fruits and vegetables are always available," a sophomore says. "The food has flavor and there's a variety to choose from." The Pouch Club, an on-campus joint, serves pizza and burgers, as well as beer and wine for those students 21 and over.

Most of the social life is either on or near campus, with the Greeks taking the lion's share of credit. Twenty-seven percent of the men and women belong to fraternities and sororities, respectively, but the Greeks are not school-funded and are

(continued)

Accepted: 59%
Enrolled: 17%
Grad in 6 Years: 77%
Returning Freshmen: 77%
Academics: ✐ ✐ ✐
Social: ☎ ☎ ☎
Q of L: ★ ★ ★
Admissions: (903) 813-3000
Email Address: admission@
  austincollege.edu

Strongest Programs:
Biology
Chemistry/Biochemistry
Political Science/International
  Studies
Psychology
Business Administration
English
History

The core curriculum begins with a freshman seminar called Communication/ Inquiry.

not allowed to advertise off-campus parties without the college's permission. Not everyone depends on the Greek system for a good time. "We also have a lot of social events," says one student, including musical performances and an on-campus carnival. Students get an eyeful during the Baker Bun Run, in which the men of Baker Hall strip to their boxers and cavort around the campus on the Monday night before finals. There are spring and fall festivals, and the Final Blowout party before finals. Students can have alcohol in dorm rooms only if they are 21 or older, and school policy prohibits booze at campus events. Popular weekend excursions are a drive to Dallas or to the college's 28-acre recreational spot on Lake Texoma (a half hour north). Sherman is "quaint" and "historic," and is becoming a better college town, students say. "There are lots of restaurants," a junior says, "but for the most part there is nothing to do late at night."

Even without athletic scholarships, varsity sports are generating increasing support. The Kangaroos compete in Division III, and the women's volleyball team won two recent division championships. The Robert T. Mason Athletic/Recreation Complex provides facilities for student-athletes and the fitness-conscious. There's also an intramural program, with basketball, softball, flag football, and lacrosse proving popular; 31 percent of undergrads participate.

"AC is awesome because it's small and comfortable," a senior says. "The professors are incredibly approachable and helpful." The preprofessional programs are among the academic strengths at this college with roots in the Presbyterian Church. And while Sherman may be a sleepy little place, Austin College is hoppin'. Says one happy student: "At the end of four years, students leave with an amazing education, lifelong friends, and happy memories."

Overlaps

Baylor, University of North Texas, Southwestern, Texas A&M, Texas Christian, Texas Tech

If You Apply To >

Austin: Early action I: Dec. 1. Early action II: Jan. 15. Regular admissions: Mar. 1. No application fee. Campus interviews: optional, evaluative. Alumni interviews: optional, informative. SATs or ACTs: required. Subject Tests: optional. Accepts the Common Application. Essay question.

Babson College

Babson Park, MA 02457-0310

The only college in the *Fiske Guide* devoted entirely to business. Babson is the birthplace of entrepreneurial studies—which continue to define the campus ethos. Only 11 miles from College Student Mecca, a.k.a. Boston, and tougher to get into than ever. Has about half as many undergraduates as Bentley, its closest competitor. The one college in Massachusetts where it is possible to be a Republican with head held high.

Babson is a preeminent training ground for budding entrepreneurs and corporate bigwigs. The college is a pioneer in the study of entrepreneurship, dating to the 1970s—a time when people thought it couldn't be taught. Here, hands-on experience is the norm; students get school funding to start businesses during their first years, and may hone their stock-picking skills by managing part of the college's endowment. Always the foremost business college in the Boston area, Babson attracts budding tycoons and entrepreneurs from around the globe.

Founded in 1919, the college sits on 370 acres near the sedate Boston suburb of Wellesley. The tract features open green spaces, gently rolling hills, and heavily wooded areas. Buildings are gently shaded and parking lots (filled with expensive

Website: www.babson.edu
Location: Suburban
Private
Total Enrollment: 3,250
Undergraduates: 2,015
Male/Female: 56/44
SAT Ranges: CR 550–640, M 610–700
ACT Ranges: 26–29

foreign cars) are relatively hidden. Architecturally, the campus is mainly neo-Georgian and modern. Several dorms and the admissions office have been renovated, and two dining facilities—Jazzman's Café and Pandini's Italian bistro—provide students with tasty meals.

Although Babson is a business school, about half of students' classes are in the liberal arts. General education requirements emphasize rhetoric (public speaking); ethics and social responsibility; international and multicultural perspectives; and leadership, teamwork, and creativity. In the Foundation Management Experience, students are split into groups of 30 to develop business plans; each group gets up to $3,000 in seed money from the college to get their concept up and running. At the end of the year, the business is liquidated and profits go to charity. Former FME groups have developed Babsonopoly (a Babson-themed version of Monopoly), opened a Krispy Kreme Doughnuts franchise, and sold customized fleece blankets. "There are 14 businesses all around campus, all trying to sell to the same 1,700 students," says a sophomore. "That's competitive, but it gives us real-world experience."

"Not only textbook: teamwork."

All Babson students major in business and then select a concentration, such as management, finance, or marketing—or even gender studies or literary and visual arts. (The Sorenson Visual Arts Center has painting, ceramics, and sculpture studios, labs for photography and digital art, a student art gallery, and workspace for artists-in-residence.) The entrepreneurship program is one of Babson's strongest, bringing in venture capitalists and executives (from companies such as Dunkin' Donuts and Jiffy Lube) for how-to lectures. Courses are rigorous, and most are small. "Not only textbook: teamwork," says a junior. For projects, students can use more than 250 workstations dotting five computer labs or their brand-new PC laptops, which are included with tuition. Since the computers are leased, upgrades are guaranteed after two years.

In the classroom, Babson relies on the case-study approach more typically employed by M.B.A. programs. (At 56/44, the school's lopsided male/female ratio is also more similar to those of M.B.A. programs than those at undergraduate business schools.) In the case-study method, students break into groups or act as officers of pseudo-corporations to address specific business situations and solve marketplace problems. Professors teach all courses, and a junior says most have 10 to 20 years of experience in their fields. Accounting students may take graduate classes at Babson in the summer and fall after finishing their bachelor's degrees, letting them sit for the CPA exam about one year earlier than most other programs. Babson offers more than 100 study abroad programs in 40 countries, as well as the Semester at Sea*. Students can go away for an entire semester or the two-week winter session, and not all programs are business-focused; the London Theatre Program, for example, focuses on arts appreciation.

"Creativity is in no shortage here. Everyone has a new idea or initiative that they're willing to test," says one freshman. Babson has partnered with the Posse Foundation to help increase diversity on campus, welcoming 10 Posse scholars from urban public high schools. Still, the campus remains largely white and wealthy, with African Americans making up 4 percent of the student body, Hispanics 10 percent, and Asian Americans 12 percent. Foreign students comprise 27 percent. Twenty-three percent of Babson students are Massachusetts natives. "One could say that Babson is very prep," admits a student. "No one blinks an eye when a student is walking around campus in a suit and many consider it a faux pas to be wearing anything less than dark jeans to class." No one seems to care about politics, but students do want to end the self-segregation of various ethnic and racial groups on campus. Merit scholarships averaging $24,000 are available, but there are no athletic scholarships.

"Creativity is in no shortage here."

(continued)

Financial Aid: 51%
Expense: Pr $ $ $
Student Loans: N/A
Average Debt: N/A
Phi Beta Kappa: No
Applicants: 5,512
Accepted: 30%
Enrolled: 29%
Grad in 6 Years: 90%
Returning Freshmen: 94%
Academics: ✍ ✍ ✍
Social: ☎ ☎
Q of L: ★ ★ ★
Admissions: (781) 239-5522
Email Address:
    ugradadmission@babson
    .edu

Strongest Programs:
Business
Chemistry
Economics
English
Finance
Political Science
Physics
History

Professors teach all courses, and a junior says most have 10 to 20 years of experience in their fields.

Babson guarantees housing for four years, and 85 percent of undergraduates live on campus, resulting in high demand for singles and suites. "The suite-style living is awesome," says a freshman. "It allows you to live with a bunch of your best friends but still have separate singles to sleep in." Dorms are air-conditioned and carpeted, and most upper-class rooms have their own bathrooms. Most halls are co-ed, but one dorm is reserved for men, and floors and wings of other buildings are reserved for women. After the first year, the large rooms are assigned by lottery, and standing is based on credits earned. At the main dining hall, you'll find sushi and make-your-own stir fry stations; every Wednesday is gourmet night, and the menu may include fresh lobster, Italian specialties, or turkey with all the trimmings. "One of my favorite places to eat is from the vegan station in the dining hall," a senior says.

Students say social life at Babson is on campus during the first two years; after that, most students are 21 and have cars, so they head to the clubs and bars of Boston proper, about 20 minutes away. (It helps that many upperclassmen do not have class on Fridays.) For those who aren't of age, or who lack wheels, the Campus Activities Board brings in comedians and organizes parties, as do Greek organizations, which attract 15 percent of the women and 25 percent of the men. The school also sponsors trips to Celtics and Red Sox games. "We have a very vibrant social life here," says a student. If

"No one blinks an eye when a student is walking around campus in a suit."

you're caught with booze while underage, or sent to the hospital because of overindulgence, you get one strike; rack up two more, and you're out of the dorms. Popular road trips include the beaches of Cape Cod and Martha's Vineyard, the ski slopes of Vermont and New Hampshire, and the bright lights of New York City and Montreal.

The "very affluent" town of Wellesley has shops and restaurants, and there is a subway stop. Students can take the T's Green Line into the city to explore Quincy Market or the campuses of Harvard, Northeastern, Emerson, and Boston Universities. Wellesley is also home to Wellesley College, and it's not uncommon for Babson students to socialize with Wellesley women; Babson also offers cross-registration at Wellesley, Brandeis, and the Olin College of Engineering. Favorite campus festivals include homecoming (great networking opportunities), Oktoberfest, and Winter and Spring Weekends, when bands come to play and parties are thrown. April 8 is Founders Day, and classes are canceled so everyone can celebrate entrepreneurship.

While making money may be the most popular "sport" at Babson, students recognize the importance of keeping their bodies in competitive condition, too. Popular intramural sports include volleyball, rugby, and ice hockey, and on the varsity level, the Beavers play in NCAA Division III. Any match against archrival Bentley and soccer games against Brandeis and Colby draw crowds. The women's basketball squad has reached the Division III Elite 8, and women's lacrosse has made it to the Division III Sweet 16.

Babson students embrace entrepreneurship as an ethos and are willing to work hard for what they want. After all, learning how to balance work with everything else that's important in life is a prerequisite to climbing the corporate ladder. And thanks to small classes, a laser-like focus on all things financial, and plenty of hands-on experience, students leave Babson well equipped to begin scampering up those rungs—without once being subjected to The Donald's hair.

If You Apply To ➤

Babson: Early decision and early action: Nov. 1. Regular admissions: Jan. 3. Financial aid: Feb. 1. Housing: May 1. Application fee: $75. Campus and alumni interviews: optional, evaluative. SATs or ACTs: required. No Subject Tests. Accepts the Common Application. Essay question.

Bard College

Annandale-on-Hudson, NY 12504

Welcome to Nonconformity-Central-on-Hudson. Like Reed on the West Coast, Bard combines unabashed individuality with rigorous traditional academics. More selective than Hampshire and with a better male/female ratio than Sarah Lawrence, Bard is a dominant presence in the world of nontraditional liberal arts colleges. Famous president Leon Botstein is an iconic figure.

Bard College has come a long way since its 1860 founding by 12 men studying to enter the seminaries of the Episcopal Church. Those pioneers would no doubt be surprised at the eclectic mix of students now running around Annandale-on-Hudson. Bard students marched to their own drummer in high school. "Many struggle their first year, when they realize everyone is just as unique as they are, and no one cares what kind of radical statement they are trying to make, because it's not revolutionary when everyone is trying to be different," says a senior. The idea that Bard is strictly a school for artists and social studies majors is slowly disappearing, and the result is a school with lots of intellectual depth—and a higher national profile.

Bard's campus occupies 600 well-landscaped acres in upstate New York's Washington Irving country. There's no prevailing architectural theme, so each ivy-covered brick building stands out—especially the dorms, which range from cottages in the woods to Russian colonial in style. Renowned architect Frank Gehry designed the $62 million Fisher Center for the Performing Arts. The 11,000-square-foot facility includes two theaters and rehearsal and teaching space for Bard's theater and dance programs. The dramatic Center for Science and Computation, designed by well-known architect Rafael Vinoly, lets students pursue the hands-on science that Bard promotes. A new conservatory building opened in 2013 and features state-of-the-art performance facilities.

Despite Bard's reputation for nonconformism, the list of requirements is extensive. Freshmen show up three weeks before classes start for the Workshop in Language and Thinking, where they read extensively in several genres, and meet in small groups to discuss reading and writing. (A literature major calls L&T "the best three weeks of my life.") Students then take the two-semester First-Year Seminar, which introduces the intellectual, artistic, and cultural ideas at the core of a liberal arts education. At the end of the second year, students write their educational autobiography and declare a major; the autobiography is more like a proposal, presented for discussion to a board of professors in the relevant area. During their junior year, students take a tutorial to prepare for their senior project—while some students run

> "Bard is great for motivated students who take their education into their own hands."

and report on a scientific experiment, or complete a 100- to 300-page critical review of literary works, others write a play or novel or compose a piece of music, and still others organize a show of their own art or choreograph a dance performance. Citizen Science is a three-week program for first-year students that examines topics not normally covered in the traditional science curriculum. Students focus on a particular issue—for example, infectious disease—for the entire length of the program, looking at the topic from different methodological and conceptual approaches.

Bard's academic climate is "intellectual and consistently challenging," says a senior. "Bard is great for motivated students who take their education into their own hands." Seventy-seven percent of classes have 19 or fewer students, and if students want more individual attention, they can devise a syllabus for their own course and

Website: www.bard.edu
Location: Rural
Private
Total Enrollment: 2,156
Undergraduates: 1,923
Male/Female: 44/56
SAT Ranges: CR 650–710, M 600–670
ACT Ranges: N/A
Financial Aid: 70%
Expense: Pr $ $ $ $
Student Loans: 49%
Average Debt: $ $
Phi Beta Kappa: No
Applicants: 5,410
Accepted: 35%
Enrolled: 28%
Grad in 6 Years: 79%
Returning Freshmen: 86%
Academics: ✑ ✑ ✑ ✑
Social: ☎ ☎ ☎
Q of L: ★ ★ ★ ★
Admissions: (845) 758-7472
Email Address: admission@bard.edu

Strongest Programs:
Political Science
Economics
Human Rights
Fine Arts
Social Sciences
Literature and Languages

find a professor to sponsor it. Bard also considers visual and performing arts as equal to other academic disciplines; as a result, photography is one of the toughest majors to get into. There are no teaching assistants here, and "students tend to know who the good professors are and rush to take classes with them." With authors such as

> "If you're a Republican or conservative, please come and add some dimension to our conversation."

John Ashbery, Ann Lauterbach, Mark Danner, and Elizabeth Frank teaching creative writing at Bard, literature is among the school's best programs. Film and political science also draw praise. Each fall, science majors may take a class

on human disease at New York City's Rockefeller University, which also reserves spots for Bard students as Summer Undergraduate Research Fellows. The distinguished scientist scholars program offers full tuition to top applicants who plan to major in science or math.

Bard established what administrators believe is the first collegiate program in human rights. There is also a five-year, dual-degree conservatory program for music students, and although Bard is far from preprofessional, it does offer combined programs with other schools in engineering, architecture, city planning, social work, public health, business and public administration, forestry, and environmental science. Study abroad is available in far-flung locales around the globe; nearly 50 percent of students take part during their time at Bard. Those interested in globalization and international affairs may participate in a residential Bard program in New York City, headquartered near Lincoln Center. The Trustee Leader Scholar program provides grants and support for student-run community service projects.

Bardians take pride in diversity, whether racial, geographical (30 percent are New Yorkers), or ideological, though they admit the latter can be lacking. "Bard students are highly motivated, creative, independent, and intellectual," says a senior. Another student adds, "If you're a Republican or conservative, please come and add some dimension to our conversation. I'm sick of agreeing with everyone."

> "You don't need perfect grades. You just need an adventurous spirit."

African Americans make up 5 percent of the student body, Asian Americans 4 percent, and Hispanics account for 3 percent. Bard offers academic scholarships but no athletic awards. Under the Excellence

and Equal Cost program, qualified high school students may apply to attend Bard for the price of a public-school education in their home state. About 200 students vie for the program's 25 available slots.

Seventy-three percent of Bard students live on campus, and freshmen are required to do so. Residence halls "vary from small, quiet dorms to large, community-oriented buildings," says a theater major. A classmate adds, "Some are old Victorian mansions, some are new modern buildings that are eco-friendly, one looks like a castle, and others are big cement monsters from the 1950s." Bard still has dorms where smoking is allowed, and the cafeteria, Kline, caters to vegetarians and vegans. Room draw can be chaotic, and since juniors and seniors are not guaranteed beds on campus, many upperclassmen move off campus. To help ease their commute, Bard runs a shuttle to the nearby towns of Red Hook and Tivoli. "Tivoli is home to a variety of restaurants (sushi, Mexican, and Cajun), a few bars (the most popular is the Black Swan), a bookstore, and a laundromat," says one student. "Red Hook is home to the Golden Wok (take-out Chinese, a student favorite), the Curry House, grocery stores, Mexican food, and more."

Social life at Bard is almost an afterthought, since New York City is just two to three hours by train. The school does offer concerts and movies, with indie films and alternative rock and hip-hop particularly popular. The Student Activities Board plans Urban Cowboy Night, the Valentine's Day Swing Dance, and Spring Fling, though there are no fraternities or sororities. When it comes to alcohol, policies are

Citizen Science is a three-week program for first-year students that examines topics not normally covered in the traditional science curriculum.

Bard also considers visual and performing arts as equal to other academic disciplines.

focused on safety and respect. "Bard is very liberal," says a student, "but I believe that the administration is trying to stop underage drinking." Bard's hometown of Annandale-on-Hudson is 20 miles from the crafts and antiques meccas of Woodstock and Rhinebeck, and not much farther from the ski slopes of the Catskills and the Berkshires. Having a car helps to prevent occasional attacks of claustrophobia.

The Raptors compete in NCAA Division III sports and are members of a number of conferences, including the Skyline Conference, Eastern Collegiate Athletic Conference, Liberty League, North East Collegiate Volleyball Association, and the College Squash Association. Bard is virtually devoid of dedicated jocks, but one student notes, "There are plenty of pseudo jocks and intellectuals in good shape." A third of the students get involved in intramurals, such as floor hockey, bowling, and table tennis, which emphasize participation and fun. Close to campus, five miles of trails stretch through the woods along the Hudson, perfect for everything from raspberry picking to jogging and hiking. "If you like the woods, it's amazing," sighs an anthropology major. "If you like the city, you'll go stir-crazy."

Bard College isn't for everyone, but thanks to the iconoclastic vision of President Leon Botstein, also erstwhile conductor of the American and Jerusalem symphonies and known by everyone simply as "Leon," it now offers strong programs in more than just the arts. "If you show that you have interests, and that you pursue them actively and can explain in an articulate manner what is important to you, Bard will accept you," one student explains. "You don't need perfect grades. You just need an adventurous spirit, an ambitious attitude toward self-improvement, and an ability to evaluate your experiences and capabilities."

Those interested in globalization and international affairs may participate in a residential Bard program in New York City, headquartered near Lincoln Center.

Overlaps
NYU, Oberlin, Reed, Vassar, Wesleyan, Skidmore

If You Apply To ➤ **Bard:** Early action: Nov. 1. Regular admissions: Jan. 1. Financial aid: Feb. 1. Housing: June 1. Application fee: $50. Campus interviews: optional, informational. No alumni interviews. SATs and ACTs: optional. Subject Tests: optional. Accepts the Common Application. Essay question.

Barnard College

New York, NY 10027

With applications running double what they were 10 years ago, Barnard rivals Wellesley as the nation's most popular women's college. Step outside and you're on Broadway; across the street lies Columbia University. Barnard women are a little more artsy and a bit more city-ish than their female counterparts at Columbia College.

Barnard students get the best of both worlds—the small, close-knit atmosphere of a liberal arts school along with the limitless opportunities of Columbia College, the Ivy League research institution just across the street. Whether they are passionate about art and music or urban studies and politics, women seeking a high-energy environment with top-notch academics are likely to find a niche here. "Barnard is a rigorous yet nurturing environment," says a senior. "Barnard students are firm believers in women's education."

Barnard's campus is on the Upper West Side of Manhattan, in the Morningside Heights neighborhood. It's just blocks from Riverside Drive, which has a lovely path parallel to the Hudson River for running, biking, or rollerblading. Trees and other greenery shade grand prewar apartment buildings, and grassy medians break up the wide expanse of Broadway itself. Barnard's architecturally diverse buildings are more

Website: www.barnard.edu
Location: City Center
Private
Total Enrollment: 2,466
Undergraduates: 2,466
Male/Female: 0/100
SAT Ranges: CR 630–730, M 620–710
ACT Ranges: 28–31
Financial Aid: 40%
Expense: Pr $ $ $

Dual-degree and joint-degree programs are available with Columbia and the Jewish Theological Seminary, and music students may also take classes at Juilliard and the Manhattan School of Music.

modern than Columbia's, and in recent years, the college has invested to upgrade labs, classrooms, animal research facilities, and the residence halls with new bathrooms, heat and air-conditioning systems, elevators, and windows. A new student center was added in 2010 and includes a black box theater, café, student dining center, art gallery, and study spaces.

Barnard's requirements are designed to reflect the changing nature of our technological society, and the fact that graduates are increasingly pursuing law, business, and other professions rather than academic careers. To that end, students take two first-year foundation courses and fulfill the "Nine Ways of Knowing," which include reason and value, social analysis, historical studies, cultures in comparison, laboratory science, quantitative and deductive reasoning, language, literature, and the visual and performing arts. Students must also take a physical education course, though most get plenty of exercise running for the bus or dashing up and down subway stairs.

> "Many students double major or take additional courses in departments other than their own."

While curricular requirements guarantee Barnard graduates have intellectual breadth, the senior thesis project, artistic performance, or research presentation ensures academic depth. Barnard students may cross-register at Columbia if they find more courses of interest there, or enroll in graduate courses in a number of Columbia's schools. Dual-degree and joint-degree programs are available with Columbia and the Jewish Theological Seminary, and music students may also take classes at Juilliard and the Manhattan School of Music. Another program offers women the chance to concentrate on dance, music, theater, visual arts, or writing—while also completing a degree in liberal arts. The school offers study abroad opportunities at Oxford, Cambridge, the University of London, and other institutions in England, France, Germany, Italy, Japan, and elsewhere around the world.

Barnard's most popular majors are English, economics, psychology, and political science, all of which happen to be among the school's best departments. Also wellsubscribed are biology (there's a healthy contingent of premeds) and history. "Many students double major or take additional courses in departments other than their own," offers one student. Barnard boasts strong support for budding writers and is a hotbed of new talent. Women's studies and education draw praise, though students in these programs must also choose another major. Human rights is a relatively new program and the administration cites foreign area studies as among the weaker programs. The Athena Center for Leadership Studies offers workshops, mentoring programs, internships, guest speakers, and other special features.

> "The quality of teaching here is unparalleled."

"Courses at Barnard are intellectually stimulating and challenging," says one junior. Many students come to Barnard because of its low student/faculty ratio. Seventy percent of classes taken by first-years have no more than 19 students. Another plus: Barnard has no graduate teaching assistants. In fact, Barnard professors enjoy Columbia's proximity almost as much as undergraduates, and each year one-third of the full-time faculty teaches in graduate departments throughout the university. Still, faculty members focus on their teaching responsibilities to undergraduates first. "The quality of teaching here is unparalleled," says one student. "One of my professors arguably founded the field I'm studying." Undergraduate research is also a priority at Barnard. The innovative Matching Alumnae to Partner with Students (MAPS) program matches students with alumnae who have agreed to help with internships and career advisement.

"Barnard students are the most intellectually curious, passionate, motivated, and diverse group of girls I have ever met," an economics and political science major says. Thirty-one percent of Barnard students are New York natives, including a sizable contingent from the East Side of Manhattan. Asian Americans make up 17 percent of the student body, while African Americans add 5 percent and Hispanics make up another 10 percent. Barnard competes head-to-head with Columbia in admissions, an interesting dilemma because Barnard is an affiliate college of Columbia University, similar to the engineering school, the medical school, the business school and, of course, Columbia College. In general, women looking for a more traditional "rah-rah" experience may prefer Columbia. Those seeking flexibility might do better at Barnard, a hotbed of liberalism where students don't shy away from rallies and protests. "We are a diverse group of smart, ambitious, and talented women," says a junior. Women's rights and race relations are among the issues that have gotten students stirred up recently. Barnard students do share a first-year orientation program with Columbia, where they mix together in small groups and take tours of the campus and city. Students can also take part in a preorientation urban volunteer program.

The innovative Matching Alumnae to Partner with Students (MAPS) program matches students with alumnae who have agreed to help with internships and career advisement.

Ninety-one percent of Barnard students live in the dorms, which have come a long way since the college's beginning as a commuter school: there's an 18-story Barnard dormitory tower, plus one dorm complex and five off-campus apartment buildings; nonresidents must be signed in by a resident, and entries are always guarded, so students say they feel safe. In addition, Barnard shares two co-ed dorms with Columbia. "The dorms and housing at Barnard are amazing," says one senior. "They are clean, comfortable, spacious (mostly!), and very well maintained." With New York's notoriously high rents and broker fees, demand for dorm beds remains high. Seniors get the best rooms through a lottery system, though one student says, "The range of housing options makes the housing process stressful." Another adds, "Barnard guarantees four years of housing, which is a relief considering how difficult and expensive it can be to find an apartment in New York City." Dorm-dwellers must buy a meal plan, which may also be used at Columbia's John Jay cafeteria, though students say Barnard's food is better.

When it comes to social life, students tend to divide their time between on campus and off. "Most of the social life takes place around campus," a junior says, "but you obviously have all of New York City to explore." Traditions on campus include Midnight Breakfast the night before finals begin, when deans and administrators serve up eggs and waffles in the gym. Women in the arts are celebrated in the annual Winterfest. Less academic pursuits are available, too. "If you still don't like what you see, you can head out to one of the bars in Morningside Heights," a student says. Fake IDs are easy to come by in Manhattan, and while they often work, Barnard students aren't likely to be drinking themselves into oblivion. "Because there is so much else to do in NYC, alcohol is not a primary amusement," explains an English and creative writing double major. Many of the city's offerings are free to students with their school ID. Road trips are infrequent—as not many students have cars—but when they happen, destinations range from Washington, D.C., to Boston, easily reached by train and plane, to skiing and snowboarding in Vermont, or spring break on the beaches of South Carolina.

"Barnard students are intellectually curious, passionate, motivated, and diverse."

Barnard athletes compete alongside their peers enrolled at Columbia, and the field hockey, soccer, lacrosse, archery, and crew teams have the largest number of participants. The fencing team is also strong. Columbia's marvelous gym and co-ed intramurals are also available to Barnard women, but many of them prefer to exercise their minds.

Students see Barnard as an "all women's college, located in a prime city, affiliated with a large research institution, with distinguished faculty, alums, and intelligent and driven students," according to one proud Barnard woman. For some, the

Overlaps

Columbia, Wellesley, University of Chicago, Georgetown, Brown, Cornell, University of Pennsylvania, NYU

supportive community created by those students and faculty is what makes this a special place. "Barnard is different because although the students here are really intelligent, they are also really down to earth, and are supported by each other and the academic community," another student says.

If You Apply To ➢ **Barnard:** Early decision: Nov. 1. Regular admissions: Jan. 1. Financial aid: Feb. 15. Housing: Jun. 1. Application fee: $65. Campus and alumni interviews: optional, evaluative. SATs or ACTs: required. Subject Tests: writing and two others required with the SAT, optional with the ACT. Accepts the Common Application. Essay question.

Bates College

23 Campus Avenue, Lewiston, ME 04240

Bowdoin got rid of its frats; Bates never had them, and therein hangs a tale. With its long-held tradition of egalitarianism, Bates is a kindred spirit to Quaker institutions such as Haverford and Swarthmore. A month-long spring term helps make Bates a leader in studying abroad. Blue-collar Lewiston is not a draw, but the New England countryside is within arm's reach.

Website: www.bates.edu
Location: Small City
Private
Total Enrollment: 1,753
Undergraduates: 1,753
Male/Female: 47/53
SAT Ranges: CR 630–718, M 630–710
ACT Ranges: 30–32
Financial Aid: 45%
Expense: Pr $ $ $ $
Student Loans: 40%
Average Debt: $ $
Phi Beta Kappa: Yes
Applicants: 4,906
Accepted: 27%
Enrolled: 39%
Grad in 6 Years: 88%
Returning Freshmen: 95%
Academics: ✐ ✐ ✐ ✐ ½
Social: ☎ ☎ ☎
Q of L: ★ ★ ★
Admissions: (855) 228-3755
Email Address: admission@ bates.edu

Strongest Programs:
Economics
Biology

Founded by abolitionists in 1855, Bates College takes pride in its heritage as a haven for seekers of guidance, freedom, and justice. Its 4–4–1 calendar offers ample opportunity for study abroad, even for just one month at year's end. The school's small size also means student/faculty interaction is plentiful, and close friendships are easily formed.

The Bates campus features a mix of Georgian and Federal buildings and Victorian homes spread out over the grassy lawns of Lewiston. Begun in March 2010, the Hedge/Roger Williams project is the fourth and final undertaking of phase I of the Campus Facilities Master Plan, which also produced the 280 College Street residence, Alumni Walk and New Commons. Together, these projects have given Bates a new campus core in terms of facilities: Bates has transformed two former student residence halls into key new academic buildings, converted a historic Victorian home into a new student residence, and dramatically renovated one of the country's earliest college football fields into a multisport turf field.

"One unique part of Bates is that just about all seniors write a thesis."

Bates emphasizes a broad-based education in the liberal arts that encompasses the humanities, sciences and mathematics, social sciences, and the arts. Although there are no core course requirements, students are expected to select a major and two thematic concentrations, each consisting of four interrelated courses structured on the basis of a central organizing principle. These concentrations may fall within one department or program, or may focus on a particular topic or area of inquiry designed by faculty from different disciplines. "One unique part of Bates is that just about all seniors write a thesis," says a chemistry major. "Some are semester-long, while others are year-long, depending on the department and what you want to do." The Ladd Library is often crowded with the 85 percent of students who write a thesis or produce an equivalent research, service, performance, or studio project. Ladd has almost 589,000 printed volumes, plus an all-night study room, computer labs, and an audiovisual room with everything from Bach to Bruce Springsteen.

While Bates was a pioneer in not requiring standardized tests for admission, don't expect to coast through. "The academic climate at Bates is extremely rigorous," says one junior. "The academic standard for an institution such as Bates is high, and students are held to that standard in all aspects across all major and minor disciplines." The most popular majors include economics, psychology, politics, history, and English, and these are also among Bates's best. The music and art departments benefit from the Olin Arts Center, which houses a performance hall, gallery, recording studio, art studios, and practice rooms. Interdisciplinary programs at Bates include American cultural studies, neuroscience, and women and gender studies. Professors teach all courses, including lab and discussion sections. "The professors are always so accessible and make a real effort to get to know their students on a personal basis," one senior states.

For those whose horizons extend beyond the charms of Lewiston, Bates offers study abroad opportunities in more than 80 foreign locations such as China, Russia, Japan, Croatia, Chile, and Austria, and more than two-thirds of students take advantage of them. The school also participates in the Washington Semester of American University* and the American Maritime Studies Program* at Mystic Seaport—all attractive options for students seeking real-world experience. Bates's 4–4–1 calendar allows for a five-week short term at the end of the academic year, and students may use this term to focus on a single subject of interest, frequently off campus. Recent examples include marine biological studies at stations on the coast of Maine; art, theater, and music studies in New York City and Europe; and field projects in economics, sociology, and psychology.

Eighty-nine percent of Bates students come from outside Maine, many from Massachusetts, Connecticut, and New York. "Students at Bates are intelligent, quirky, and eager to try new things," a student says. While the administration is trying to make Bates more diverse, minorities remain a fragment of the student population, with African Americans accounting for 4 percent, Hispanics 5 percent, and Asian Americans 4 percent. "Diversity is the biggest social issue on campus," reports a French major. Students are drawn to social and political causes, and Bates is also home of the famed undergraduate debate organization The Brooks Quimby Debate Council. Founded in the 1800s when completing a public debate was a graduation requirement at Bates, the team was one of the first in the nation to go co-ed and to include African American students. Bates, too, was the first American institution to debate with foreign universities. There are no merit or athletic scholarships available, although the college does guarantee to meet the demonstrated need of all students.

Virtually all Bates students live on campus. "Housing is great here," a student raves. Housing is guaranteed for four years, but awarded by lottery after the first year, and there are quads, singles, doubles, triples, and suites available. Students report that the campus dining hall offers tasty fare. "We have a vegan bar, a pasta bar, brick-oven pizza station, a grill station, a Euro station, soup, salad, and sandwich stations, as well as a toaster station for bagels and toast," reports one politics major. "We also have over sixty cereals in circulation in the dining hall." Students say campus security is visible and more than adequate. "Given the nature of a small campus, students know a majority of the officers' names and do not feel intimidated to approach them about a problem," explains a history major.

Since there's not much to do in Lewiston, parties, concerts, and other weekend diversions mostly occur on campus. "Whether it is parties, comedians, movies, or bands, there is always something to do for everyone on campus," a freshman says. Without a Greek system, college alcohol policies are fairly loose, a student says, and

(continued)
Psychology
History
Political Science

While Bates was a pioneer in not requiring standardized tests for admission, don't expect to coast through.

"The academic climate at Bates is extremely rigorous."

Bates's varsity teams compete in Division III, except for the ski team, which is Division I.

"There is always something to do for everyone on campus."

a ban on hard liquor is often ignored. Barbecues and clambakes are big when the weather is nice, and the annual Winter Carnival includes ice skating, snow sculpting, and a semiformal dance. During the St. Patrick's Day Puddle Jump, students of Irish descent—and all those who want to be Irish for the day—cut a hole in the ice on Lake Andrews and plunge in. Students with cars can easily road-trip to the outlet stores in Freeport and Kittery, Maine. Other popular destinations include Bar Harbor in Acadia National Park, or "Portland, for great food," says a senior. Montreal and Boston are not far, and neither are the ski slopes of Vermont and New Hampshire.

Bates's varsity teams compete in Division III, except for the ski team, which is Division I. Everyone gets excited for matches against Bowdoin and Colby, especially when they involve ice hockey. Basketball, football, and lacrosse are also popular among spectators. The intramural program, organized by the students and supervised by faculty members, is "strong and spirited" and attracts a large number of students. Intramural softball is popular, along with ultimate Frisbee, soccer, and basketball.

If you can stand the cold and the silent, starry nights, Bates may be a good choice. With caring professors, a small student body, and a focus on the liberal arts, students quickly become big fans. "I came to Bates for the people," says a sophomore. "The friends you make here will remain your friends well beyond your final days at Bates."

Overlaps

Bowdoin, Colby, Dartmouth, Middlebury, Wesleyan

If You Apply To ➤

Bates: Early decision: Nov. 15. Regular admissions: Jan. 1. Application fee: $60. Campus and alumni interviews: optional, evaluative. SATs and ACTs: optional. Subject Tests: optional. Accepts the Common Application. Essay question.

Baylor University

Waco, TX 76798

Come to Baylor and Mom can rest easy. The largest Baptist university anywhere, Baylor is avowedly Christian, which means less debauchery than is found elsewhere. It's also one of the least expensive private universities in the country. Prayers come in handy on the football field, where the team often takes a pounding by the likes of the University of Texas and the rest of the Big 12.

Website: www.baylor.edu
Location: City Center
Private
Total Enrollment: 14,700
Undergraduates: 12,589
Male/Female: 41/59
SAT Ranges: CR 550–660, M 570–670
ACT Ranges: 24–29
Financial Aid: 91%
Expense: Pr $
Student Loans: N/A
Average Debt: N/A

Baylor University offers students a solid Christian-influenced education at a bargain price. The university's Baptist tradition fosters a strong sense of community among students and faculty, and the school's 2012 vision plan promises a slew of strategic changes such as lowering the student/teacher ratio and building new residence halls.

"Everyone is trying to keep their GPA up." Under the watch of president Ken Starr (famous for his role in the impeachment of President Clinton), the university aspires to become a top-tier research university while enhancing its Christian identity. "Baylor's commitment to academic excellence and an incredible alumni network ensures a great education and a chance to get a job," says a junior.

The 432-acre Baylor campus, nicknamed Jerusalem on the Brazos, abuts the historic Brazos River near downtown Waco, Texas (population 110,000). The architectural style emphasizes the gracious tradition of the Old South, and the central part of campus, the quadrangle, was built when Baylor moved from Independence, Texas, in 1886. The campus has been witness to a number of renovations and new construction, including the 70,000 square-foot Jay and Jenny Allison Indoor Football Building and a state-of-the-art tennis facility.

Students pursue their major in arts and sciences or one of Baylor's five other schools: business, education, engineering and computer sciences, music, and nursing. "The family and consumer sciences department and the forensics department offer great programs," asserts one senior. Core requirements include four English courses and four semesters of human performance. All students also take two religion courses and two semesters of Chapel Forum, a series of lectures and meetings on various issues or Christian testimonies. The Honors College oversees the honors program (which offers opportunities for course integration and independent research) and the University Scholars Program (which waives most distribution requirements). Students may major or minor in Great Texts, an interdisciplinary program exploring "the richness and diversity of the Western intellectual heritage."

> **"Baylor's students have a heightened sense of purpose."**

Prebusiness courses are popular; popular majors include biology, psychology, mechanical engineering, and prenursing. More unusual options include church-state studies, museum studies, and institutes focusing on environmental studies and childhood learning disorders. The archaeology and geology departments benefit from fossil- and mineral-rich Texas prairies. An increasing number of Baylor students are traveling on study abroad programs, which send them to more than a dozen countries, including China, Spain, and South America.

One of Baylor's greatest strengths is the sense of campus community, fostered by the emphasis on Christianity and by the administration's efforts to focus faculty members on teaching, rather than on research and other activities, students say. Baylor also strives to keep classes small—the average class size is fewer than 30. The university's endowment is hefty and the largest among the nation's Baptist-affiliated schools. "As a nursing major, my classes are very difficult and extremely competitive," says one junior. "Everyone is trying to keep their GPA up in order to be able to get the best job after college or get into the best graduate school." Full professors often teach freshman courses, although "grad students are present to grade papers and hold study sessions," says a junior. Another adds, "My teachers have been well qualified, highly experienced, and good at communicating and teaching the students in the classroom."

"Overall, Baylor's students have a heightened sense of purpose," states a freshman. "For just about every student one meets at Baylor, they find that each person's goals are directed towards helping society. Many students are very serious, and informed, about their religious experience." Seventy-six percent are Texans. African Americans account for 7 percent of the student body, Hispanics 14 percent, and Asian Americans 6 percent. "Baylor is a conservative campus," says a student. Students vie for numerous merit scholarships and 377 athletic scholarships in 15 sports.

As might be expected on a conservative and religious campus like Baylor's, dorms are single sex and have restrictive visitation privileges, which is a big complaint among the 39 percent of students who call them home. "Some dorms are aging, but even these are well maintained," says one freshman. "Ironically, the oldest dorms are some of the most popular." Upperclassmen look off campus for cheaper housing with private rooms and fewer rules, but there is a push for more students to stay on campus with the construction of a newer residence hall with apartment-style rooms, notes one co-ed. Students report feeling safe provided they stay on campus. "There are lights everywhere on campus, and police cars constantly patrolling the grounds," one student reports. Moreover, "there are people on watch at all times, especially at night. I feel extremely safe."

(continued)

Phi Beta Kappa: Yes
Applicants: 27,828
Accepted: 61%
Enrolled: 19%
Grad in 6 Years: 75%
Returning Freshmen: 87%
Academics: ✐ ✐ ✐
Social: ☎ ☎ ☎
Q of L: ★ ★ ★
Admissions: (254) 710-3435
Email Address: admissions@ baylor.edu

Strongest Programs:
Premed
Communications Sciences and Disorders
Theater Arts

Full professors often teach freshman courses.

Thirteen percent of Baylor's men and 21 percent of the women belong to a fraternity or sorority, providing a party scene for those who want it, as well as community service outlets. With so many students residing off campus, the social life is decent but not a party atmosphere. "Common Grounds, an on campus coffee shop, hosts concerts most weekends," reports one student. "The movies are popular (a ticket only costs $5 with a student ID)." Easy road trips include Dallas, Austin, San Antonio, Bryan/College Station, and beaches at Galveston, South Padre Island, and Corpus Christi. Most destinations are within a two-and-a-half-hour drive, students say, making a set of wheels a big help, if not a necessity.

"Alcohol is much less prevalent at Baylor than at most schools," says a senior. It isn't served on campus or at campus-sponsored events. Highlights of Baylor's social calendar include the weekly Dr. Pepper Hour with free soda floats and the Dia del Oso (Day of the Bear), when classes are canceled for a day in April in favor of a campuswide carnival. Christmas on 5th Street, organized by Student Life, gives students an opportunity to enjoy the annual Christmas tree lighting, concert, and other holiday festivities. The school also has the largest collegiate homecoming parade in the nation.

When it comes to football, remember: You're in Texas. Freshmen wear team jerseys to games and take the field before the players, then sit together as a pack. "It's a very awesome part of the freshman experience," one student says. The team has been on a hot streak lately, as has the women's basketball team, which was nationally ranked for the past several years. The Baylor Bears compete in Division I and recent Big 12 champs include men's and women's tennis, and men's baseball. Women's track and field also draws fans. For weekend warriors, the McLane Student Life Center offers the tallest rock-climbing wall in Texas. The university maintains a small marina for swimming and paddle boating, and several lakes with good beaches are nearby. Forty-six percent of the student body participates in intramural sports, including flag football, indoor volleyball, and the largest collegiate dodgeball tournament in the nation.

While keeping true to its traditional Christian roots, Baylor recognizes it must remain open to new ways of thinking to achieve its stated goal of becoming a top-tier university. Baylor students may party less than their counterparts at other Texas schools. Instead, they focus on academics, spiritual nourishment, community involvement, and finding their vocational calling. One content junior says, "I will always proudly say that my decision to come to Baylor is one of the best life decisions I have ever made."

When it comes to football, remember: You're in Texas.

Overlaps

Texas A&M, University of Texas, Texas Christian, Texas Tech, Texas State, Rice, University of North Texas, University of Texas at San Antonio

If You Apply To ➤

Baylor: Early action: Nov. 1. Regular admissions: Feb. 1. Application fee: $50. Campus and alumni interviews: optional, informational. SATs or ACTs: required. No Subject Tests. Essay question: optional (with résumé and letters of recommendation).

Beloit College

700 College Street, Beloit, WI 53511

A tiny Midwestern college known for freethinking students and international focus, Beloit has steered back toward the mainstream after its heyday as an alternative school in the '60s and '70s. Wisconsin location makes Beloit easier to get into than comparable schools in sexier places. Well-known anthropology program is among the best in the nation.

Beloit College urges students to "Invent Yourself," encouraging intellectual curiosity and personal initiative by giving students freedom to explore. Known for attracting liberal freethinkers in the 1960s and '70s, the school is now steering back toward the mainstream. "The joke around campus is you can be anything here but a Republican," says a senior. What hasn't changed is its emphasis on tolerance, understanding, and the world beyond the United States. In short, "Beloit will rock your world and change your life," says one happy student.

Beloit's 40-acre campus is a Northeastern-style oasis an hour's drive from Madison and Milwaukee and 90 minutes from Chicago. Academic and administrative buildings sit on one side, with residence halls on the other. Two architectural themes dominate, says one student: "1850s colonial and obtuse 1930s." The college's Turtle Creek Bookstore is located three blocks away in downtown Beloit. A cozy coffee bar, selection of general books and magazines, and a patio for relaxing, reading, or studying augment the typical stacks of textbooks. The public library in downtown Beloit was gifted to the college and is now a state-of-the-art center for the arts.

Beloit does not have core requirements. Instead, students complete a capstone experience, a required "beyond the classroom" Liberal Arts in Practice experience, three writing-intensive courses, a quantitative reasoning class, and one intercultural literacy course. In addition to an Initiatives orientation

"Beloit will rock your world and change your life."

and discovery course in their first semester, students also tackle classes on Big Questions and Transformational Works while earning five credits across five domains that focus on systems, arts, behavior, the universe, and texts.

The academic milieu is described as challenging yet collaborative. "Whether it's an 'easy' class or a hard one, you always know that you'll be challenged and empowered to think critically and engage with real issues," says one student. Teaching is the faculty's first priority, and 76 percent of classes have 19 or fewer students. "All of the professors I have had have been very willing to meet with me one-on-one when I feel like I'm struggling in their classes or have questions about class assignments," says a senior.

Anthropology is the most popular major, followed by psychology, creative writing, health and society, and economics. "The economics, sociology, philosophy, religious studies, and biology programs are quite highly received. They have high quality professors who go out of their way to engage students," a religious studies major reports. Among the more unusual options are a museum studies minor, with hands-on restoration experience, and the rhetoric and discourse major, which asks students to reflect on current nonfiction writing while producing their own prose. The health and society major encourages students to take an interdisciplinary look at health and medical care in the United States and around the world. The communications major has been re-dubbed "media studies."

To satisfy Beloit's experiential learning and global diversity requirements, Venture Grants offer $500 to $1,500 for "entrepreneurial, self-testing activities" that benefit the community; recent awardees traveled to Santa Fe, New Mexico, to photograph and record man-made and natural earthworks or made their way to the tea plantations of Sri Lanka to study women's health issues. An internship program provides up to $2,000 for projects that address a community need, and students may conduct biological and biomedical research at Northwestern and Rush Universities in Chicago. Nearly half of Beloit's students study or do research abroad through the International Education Program, which sends students to 35 countries. The Center for Language Studies complements Beloit's own foreign language programs with intensive summer study in Chinese, Japanese, Russian, Arabic, and English as a second language. Beloit is also a member of the Associated Colleges of the Midwest* consortium, increasing students' choices.

Website: www.beloit.edu
Location: Small Town
Private
Total Enrollment: 1,266
Undergraduates: 1,266
Male/Female: 41/59
SAT Ranges: CR 550–710, M 560–690
ACT Ranges: 24–32
Financial Aid: 96%
Expense: Pr $ $
Student Loans: 57%
Average Debt: $ $ $
Phi Beta Kappa: Yes
Applicants: 2,205
Accepted: 67%
Enrolled: 21%
Grad in 6 Years: 78%
Returning Freshmen: 91%
Academics: ✐ ✐ ✐
Social: ☎ ☎ ☎
Q of L: ★ ★ ★
Admissions: (608) 363-2500
Email Address: admiss@beloit.edu

Strongest Programs:
Anthropology
Economics
English
Geology
Modern Languages and Literatures
Natural and Social Sciences
Theater Arts

Beloit does not have core requirements.

There is no archetypal Beloit student: "Talk to five Beloiters about what they're doing over the summer and you'll get five different answers: an internship in public health, a job shadow at a chemical production plant, art classes in Florence, working at an orphanage in Ghana, or a camping/running trip through the Appalachian mountains," says a student. "It's hard to describe the typical Beloit student because the whole point is that we're atypical." Eighteen percent of Beloit's student body is homegrown; 80 percent hail from out of state, including 10 percent from abroad. Hispanics comprise 8 percent of the total, African Americans 4 percent, and Asian Americans represent 2 percent. Hot-button issues include "racial and socioeconomic diversity among students," says a political science major. Merit scholarships are available, although there are no athletic scholarships.

> **"The economics, sociology, philosophy, religious studies, and biology programs are quite highly received."**

Ninety-four percent of Beloit students live on campus, where they're required to remain for three years. Many residence halls boast new carpeting, furniture, and central air-conditioning and heat; one student says good choices include Chapin and Aldrich. "The dorms are moderately well maintained and comfortable. Nothing extravagant but nothing terrible either," reports one student. Four fraternities attract 8 percent of the men, and two sororities draw 6 percent of the women; members may live in their chapter houses. Special-interest houses cater to those interested in foreign languages, music, anthropology, and other disciplines. An international business major sums up campus vittles this way: "The food is restaurant quality, everything is made from scratch, and there are provisions for vegetarians, vegans, and gluten free."

"Most of the social life is on campus," reports a student. "Clubs host events, there are sporting events, concerts, plays, dance performances, projects, the occasional beer tasting, and parties accessible only with a college ID." Two all-campus festivals liven up the calendar: the Folk and Blues Fall Music Festival brings jazz, reggae, folk, and blues bands to campus, while on Spring Day, classes give way to concerts and everyone kicks back to enjoy the (finally!) warmer weather. The Beloit Science Fiction/Fantasy Association offers movie marathons, dramatic readings, role-playing games, board and video games, and other activities for members and nonmembers alike. The school's alcohol policy is lax, students say. "We have an alcohol philosophy," says a sociology major. "Beloit would never go so far as to say 'policy.'"

The health and society major encourages students to take an interdisciplinary look at health and medical care in the United States and around the world.

"The town of Beloit is in the midst of a change. It was previously in fairly poor economic shape, however the downtown is making a comeback," a student says. Having wheels here will definitely raise your social standing, as they make it easier to take off from Beloit for Chicago or the college town of Madison, also easily reached through a cheap local bus service. For the outdoors-minded, the nearby Dells offer camping and water parks. Beloit has basic necessities, such as a few bars (check out the excellent burgers at Hanson's Pub, says a senior), a bowling alley, a movie theater, and a Walmart. "Groups such as Habitat for Humanity, Beloit Interaction Committee, and the Outreach Center work hard to integrate students into the community," says a sophomore.

Sports at Beloit are played more for fun than glory. Among the school's Division III Bucs squads, standouts include baseball, men's and women's basketball, men's and women's cross-country, and football, especially against rival Ripon College. Men's and women's lacrosse played their inaugural season last year. Intramural ultimate Frisbee typically draws hundreds of players and spectators, and more than one-third of students participate in the intramural program, with basketball, volleyball, and soccer also popular.

Beloit is a bundle of contradictions: a small liberal arts college in the heart of Big Ten state university country, where the academic program has an East Coast rigor but

Overlaps

Lawrence, Knox, Grinnell, Macalester, Oberlin, Earlham, College of Wooster, University of Wisconsin–Madison

the laid-back classroom vibe reflects the free-and-easy spirit of the Midwest. Although the school continues to evolve, "the essential core of Beloit has stayed the same," says a senior. "It is still a campus full of artistic creators, unabashed activists, and people who love making dorm room forts. We're still weird, and we like it that way."

If You Apply To ➤

Beloit: Early decision: Nov. 1. Early action: Dec. 1. Regular admissions: Jan. 15. Financial aid: Mar. 1. No application fee. Campus interviews: optional, evaluative. Alumni interviews: optional, informational. SATs or ACTs: required. Subject Tests: optional. Accepts the Common Application. Essay question.

Bennington College

Bennington, VT 05201-6003

Known for top-notch performing arts and lavish attention on every student. Arts programs rely heavily on faculty who are practitioners in their field. Less competitive than Bard and Sarah Lawrence, comparable to Hampshire. With a total enrollment of just over 800, Bennington is one-third the size of most liberal arts colleges.

Bennington College is a school where architects are teachers, biologists sculpt, and a sociologist might work on Wall Street or in graphic design. It's no wonder they strive to abandon the theory of regimented knowledge. Bennington's focus is on learning by doing. The emphasis on self-direction, field work, and personal relationships with professors sets it apart even from other liberal arts colleges of similar (small) size. Says one junior, "If you want an education you can shape yourself and you want that education to transcend your homework and the classroom, this is a great place to go to school."

Bennington sits on 470 acres at the foot of Vermont's Green Mountains. The campus was once an active dairy farm, and a converted barn houses the main classroom and administrative spaces. But don't let the quaint New England setting fool you. The Dickinson Science Building offers high-tech equipment for aspiring chemists, biologists, environmental scientists, and geneticists. The building is also home to a media lab dedicated to the study of languages, including Chinese, French, Italian, Japanese, and Spanish. A 14,000-square-foot student center offers students a snack bar, grill, convenience store, and multipurpose spaces. The Center for the Advancement of Public Action opened in 2011 and includes space for students and faculty centering their work in public action to collaborate with each other and to engage with people whose lives and work are dedicated to solving pressing world problems.

> "Teaching here is universally outstanding."

Thanks to its focus on John Dewey–style experiential learning, Bennington's academic structure differs from that of a typical college or university. Each student designs a major, although there are some academic requirements, including a seven-week internship each January and February in a field of interest and a location of the student's choice. Students receive narrative evaluations in lieu of grades (although they do have the option to request grades in addition to the evaluations). "I would describe the academic climate as collaborative," says one junior. "Students are engaged in a lot of interdisciplinary work, often in other students' projects." Professors are roundly praised for their knowledge and dedication. "Freshmen are always taught by full professors here, and teaching here is universally outstanding," says a biology major.

Website: www.bennington.edu
Location: Small Town
Private
Total Enrollment: 809
Undergraduates: 684
Male/Female: 36/64
SAT Ranges: CR 620–720, M 560–660
ACT Ranges: 26–30
Financial Aid: 90%
Expense: Pr $ $ $ $
Student Loans: 68%
Average Debt: $ $ $
Phi Beta Kappa: No
Applicants: 1,236
Accepted: 63%
Enrolled: 25%
Grad in 6 Years: 67%
Returning Freshmen: 83%
Academics: ✍ ✍ ✍
Social: ☎ ☎ ☎
Q of L: ★ ★ ★ ★
Admissions: (800) 833-6845
Email Address: admissions@bennington.edu

Strongest Programs:
Visual and Performing Arts
Social Sciences

Without academic departments, the faculty works to provide students with a well-rounded academic foundation. The most popular area of study is visual and performing arts, followed by social sciences, English, foreign languages, and liberal arts. Computing and mathematics are strong, too, although they attract a smaller number of students than many of the college's programs. "Half of the students here do work in the arts, whether it's theater or dance or studio art. Those are obviously well regarded," says a sophomore. Consistent with Bennington's judgment that traditional academics have become "insular and self-perpetuating," the Center for the

"Students are engaged in a lot of interdisciplinary work."

Advancement of Public Action invites students to put the world's most pressing problems at the center of their education via hands-on, change-the-world workshops—known as Design Labs—and three-week modules aimed at developing capacities that may be applied in a broad array of disciplines.

"Because of the plan process, we are all genuinely interested in the things we are studying, and this makes for a vibrant and fascinating environment to be in," says one senior. Four percent are from Vermont and 8 percent are foreign nationals. Curiosity and excitement about exploration and experimentation will take you far here, and if you lean liberal in the voting booth, so much the better. African Americans account for 2 percent of the student body, Hispanics 5 percent, and Asian Americans 2 percent. Students are politically motivated, and "green issues are probably the area that students are most concerned about," says a junior. Merit scholarships worth an average of $17,121 are awarded annually; there are no athletic scholarships available.

As Bennington lacks traditional departments, requirements, and even faculty tenure, it's probably not surprising that the school also lacks dorms. Ninety-five percent of students live in one of the college's co-ed houses; 12 are white New England clapboard, and six are more modern. Each house holds 25 to 30 people with an appointed chair to govern house affairs. "All of the houses are well maintained and gorgeous," cheers one social psychology and design major. "Most of the student houses on campus house fewer than 40 students, every house has large ornate common rooms and kitchens, each house has a fireplace and a piano, and most of the houses on campus sport hardwood floors, crown molding, and double hung windows." The college food service provides plenty of options, from vegetarian and vegan choices to a salad bar, wok station, and pizza machine. "As far as college food goes," says one student, "we're lucky." Security is good, and "the campus is extremely secure and virtually free of all crime," confides a literature major.

Bennington was once an all-female college, and women still outnumber men 2 to 1 here. A biology major says, "Nearly all the social life takes place on campus, with a little bit of that extending to the town of Bennington itself and onto weekend

"Green issues are probably the area that students are most concerned about."

road trips to places like New York and Boston." The annual theme parties always draw raves—themes have included Gatsby's Funeral and Mods vs. Rockers. The alcohol policies on campus are fairly standard: no one under 21 is allowed to imbibe. "I think the high level of academic expectations here make us self-regulate our drinking and partying habits," says a student.

Although the vibe on Bennington's campus is liberal, sophisticated, and cosmopolitan, the neighboring town of the same name—four miles away—is far more conservative, typical of rural New England. "The town is split up into Bennington and North Bennington," a junior explains. "North Bennington borders campus, and is a nice little village with good restaurants and a lake with a public beach. Bennington proper has the typical Walmart/fast food kind of area, but there is also the center of town, which has really nice coffee shops, galleries, and used bookstores." Students

Curiosity and excitement about exploration and experimentation will take you far here.

often find their way into the community through volunteer work in local schools and homeless shelters, though such programs can be tough because of the mandatory midyear internship term, which takes many students away from campus.

Given Bennington's rugged location, hiking, rock climbing, caving, camping, and canoeing keep students moving. Ski slopes beckon in the colder months. Twice each year, the college turns part of its huge Visual and Performing Arts complex into an indoor roller rink for a Rollerama party. For 12 hours one day each May, the campus celebrates spring with Sunfest, which includes bands, games, and other events. "Every term we also have an event called Rollerama," says a student. "We lower a disco ball in our auditorium, and the nearby roller skating rink comes and gives out all of their skates. Students dress up in wacky '70s garb and skate around to music until late into the night." And during finals week each term, the blaring of fire truck sirens tells weary students to head to the dining hall, where professors, staff, and the college president serve up French toast and other breakfast favorites. Sports aren't a big focus, but Bennington does compete in a co-ed soccer league that also includes other Northeastern colleges. The way one student sees it, "Bennington kids prefer going to a dance performance or poetry reading over playing sports."

As the first school in the nation to grant the arts equal status with other disciplines, Bennington offers a novel, participatory, and hands-on approach. Whether they're painters or writers, musicians or scientists, sculptors, dancers, or some combination thereof, what Bennington students have in common is self-motivation and a real thirst for knowledge. Bennington is likely a good fit for "students who are interested in an education that bridges academia and the 'real world' (or encourages students to not distinguish between the two)," says a senior. Crossing disciplines is encouraged, and forget about taking the road less traveled; each student here charts his or her own course. And besides, there's a tree house—and milk and cookies served at every meal. Who says going to college means growing up?

Bennington was once an all-female college, and women still outnumber men 2 to 1 here.

Overlaps

Hampshire, Bard, Sarah Lawrence, University of Vermont, Lewis & Clark, Marlboro, Eugene Lang, Skidmore

If You Apply To ➤

Bennington: Early decision: Nov. 15. Early action: Dec. 1. Regular admissions: Jan. 3. Financial aid: Feb. 15. Application fee: $60. Campus and alumni interviews: optional, evaluative. SATs or ACTs: optional. Subject Tests: optional. Accepts the Common Application. Essay question.

Bentley University

175 Forest Street, Waltham, MA 02452

Bentley means business—studying it, that is. Now competes on a nearly even footing with archrival Babson. Bentley provides career-oriented internships to more than 90 percent of its students. Bentley's scenic colonial-style campus is at arm's length from Boston with shuttles to Harvard Square.

The name may have changed, but Bentley still means business. Formerly known as Bentley College, this small New England university excels at turning out men and women who are committed to taking their place among the ranks of future business leaders. "Bentley prepares its students for the workplace by giving them comparable experiences socially, academically, and—most importantly—professionally," says a sophomore. With the university's solid

"Most of Bentley's social life takes place right on campus."

Website: www.bentley.edu
Location: Small City
Private
Total Enrollment: 4,728
Undergraduates: 4,057
Male/Female: 59/41

(continued)

SAT Ranges: CR 530–620,
    M 593–670

ACT Ranges: 25–29

Financial Aid: 73%

Expense: Pr $ $

Student Loans: 59%

Average Debt: $ $ $ $

Phi Beta Kappa: Yes

Applicants: 7,040

Accepted: 45%

Enrolled: 31%

Grad in 6 Years: 87%

Returning Freshmen: 95%

Academics: ✐ ✐ ✐

Social: ☎ ☎ ☎

Q of L: ★ ★ ★

Admissions: (800) 523-2354

Email Address:
    ugadmission@bentley.edu

Strongest Programs:
Finance
Global Studies
Management
Marketing
Mathematical Sciences
Media and Culture

Students who choose to pursue a bachelor of arts degree must also fulfill business core requirements.

courses in business, state-of-the-art facilities, and a dedication to the liberal arts, students find much to admire. "I chose Bentley because I felt like they really cared about me as a person," a student says, "and not just a name on an application."

Bentley is situated on 163 acres in Waltham, Massachusetts, just minutes west of the hustle and bustle of Boston. The dominant architectural style is Georgian, and the majority of campus buildings are classically built in redbrick. The Bentley campus was designed on a three-tier plan. The upper campus revolves around academics and features a state-of-the-art library, more than 70 "smart" classrooms and high-tech labs and centers. Mid-campus centers on student life and is anchored by the 70,000-square-foot student center. Finally, the lower campus focuses on recreation and includes the Charles A. Dana Athletic Center. Residential housing is spread throughout each tier of the campus.

"The students at Bentley are definitely unique."

Bentley has long been committed to producing "liberally educated business students," and this is reflected in the curriculum, which offers both B.A. and B.S. tracks. Every student must complete 47 credit hours of general education coursework, including courses in information technology, literature, mathematics, natural and behavioral sciences, economics, government, history, and philosophy. In addition, freshmen take a mandatory first-year seminar that is designed to help them with their overall adjustment and decision-making abilities regarding their academic and social development. The First-Year Seminar instructor also serves as the student's academic advisor for his or her first three semesters. Students who choose to pursue a bachelor of arts degree must also fulfill business core requirements, which consist of a sequence of five courses from the first two years of the general business core.

"It is definitely not a 'dog-eat-dog' campus," a management major explains, "but there are some majors that tend to be more competitive." A freshman adds, "Courses at Bentley are challenging and encourage an exploration of the subject beyond what is taught in the classroom." Not surprisingly, the most popular majors are accountancy, marketing, finance, and management. Students seeking a bachelor of science degree may choose from nearly a dozen disciplines, while those pursuing bachelor of arts degrees have a more limited selection: history, global studies, public policy, liberal arts, Spanish studies, sustainability science, media and culture, and philosophy. Motivated students may pursue the liberal studies major (LSM), a highly integrated (and optional) second major that must be paired with a business or business-related major. Current LSM concentrations include American studies; earth, environment, and global sustainability; ethics and social responsibility; global perspectives; health and industry; media arts and society; and quantitative perspectives. Students are treated to a plethora of state-of-the-art facilities and labs, including the Trading Room, which is one of the largest and most advanced financial learning labs in the nation.

"It is definitely not a 'dog-eat-dog' campus."

Twenty-six percent of classes have 19 or fewer students, and adjunct professors and senior lecturers with professional expertise teach many of the courses. "The vast majority of professors have worked in their field, so they are able to give insight as to which concepts will be important when working in the real world," a student says. As befitting the university's focus on the corporate world, approximately 90 percent of undergraduates participate in experiential learning via internships. In keeping with the university's mission to educate students to be active leaders in a global economy, the Cronin Office of International Education at Bentley offers eligible students the opportunity to participate in semester, summer or week-long faculty-led programs abroad. Each year more than 400 Bentley students participate. The top 10 percent of students in each entering class (about 90 students) are invited to participate in the honors program, which follows an intimate, highly interactive seminar format. Instructors in the honors courses are among the most distinguished teacher-scholars on the Bentley faculty.

"The students at Bentley are definitely unique. I'd classify them as a strong mix of being academically focused but definitely not having lost sight of the other facets of college life," says one student. Forty percent of Bentley students are from Massachusetts, and nearly three-quarters attended public high school. African Americans comprise 3 percent of the student body, Asian Americans 8 percent, and Hispanics 7 percent. Social and political issues generally take a backseat to studies, but diversity and equality are common concerns, according to students. Merit scholarships averaging $16,365 are doled out annually, and talented athletes vie for 53 athletic scholarships.

The university's student residences include apartments, suites, and traditional dormitories and house 78 percent of the student body. All rooms include wireless Internet access, cable TV, local telephone service, and air-conditioning. "The freshman dorms are a bit small but once you get to your sophomore year, the rooms get better because you get to live in suites or apartments," says one student. The various dining facilities offer traditional college fare, and those on the meal plan are given unlimited meals at the main dining hall. "It's important to

"Bentley prepares its students for the workplace."

The top 10 percent of students in each entering class (about 90 students) are invited to participate in the honors program.

remember with all college food that it isn't your mom's home cooking," says a student. "Bentley is no exception." Students also report feeling safe on campus, thanks to an active police patrol, 24/7 safety escorts, and various prevention programs.

"Most of Bentley's social life takes place right on campus," says a student. "There is so much involvement in Bentley's 90-plus organizations. A group is bound to have an event on any given day." Sponsored events include an annual Halloween Party, Hawaiian luaus, fashion shows, Latin dance night, a Boston scavenger hunt, "drive-in" movies on the quad, comedy nights, and Spring Day. "There is never a dull moment on campus," cheers a freshman. Although Greeks attract 11 percent of the men and women, they don't dominate the social scene. Students of legal age may have alcohol, but "peer pressure is not an issue" for those who choose not to imbibe, according to one accounting major.

Waltham may not have the cachet of nearby Boston, but students say it has the basic amenities every college student craves: restaurants, bars, shops, and salons. "A lot of students get involved with the community," says a freshman. "There is 'service learning,' where students are able to volunteer in the community and earn credits." For those seeking a bit more action, the university provides a free shuttle into Harvard Square, where students can mix and mingle with peers from other local colleges and universities. Popular road trips include jaunts to the beaches of New Hampshire, the ski resorts of Vermont, and weekend trips to the Cape.

Although Greeks attract 11 percent of the men and women, they don't dominate the social scene.

Competition at Bentley is not confined to the classroom; the university also fields 23 men's and women's varsity teams at the NCAA Division II level and a competitive Division I ice hockey team. Solid Falcon teams include men's and women's basketball, men's golf, women's volleyball, and men's and women's tennis. The men's basketball team reached the Division II Elite 8 three times since 2007, and women's basketball has competed in a record 30 NCAA tournaments. Men's field hockey has been in the NCAA Division II national championship game six times in the last 14 years. Students get fired up anytime rivals Babson and Bryant take the field, and there is the predictable T-shirt reading, "Friends don't let friends go to Babson." Intramurals draw nearly 60 percent of all students; popular activities include flag football, soccer, volleyball and street hockey.

Like the university itself, Bentley students have a keen sense of who they are and where they're headed. A marketing major says the university offers a "premium education, unlimited opportunities, and the ultimate college experience." What's more, "The combination of liberal arts, business, and technology sets Bentley apart

Overlaps
Northeastern, Babson, Boston College, Bryant, University of Massachusetts, Boston University, University of Connecticut, Villanova

from other business schools," according to a senior. For those students charting a course into the upper echelons of corporate America, Bentley may be the first step to a long and fruitful career.

If You Apply To ➤

Bentley: Early decision and early action: Nov. 1. Regular admissions: Jan. 7. Financial aid: Feb. 1. Application fee: $50. Campus interviews: optional, informational. No alumni interviews. SATs or ACTs: required. Subject Tests: optional. Accepts the Common Application. Essay question: personal statement.

Birmingham–Southern College

Box 549008, 900 Arka, Birmingham, AL 35254

One of the Deep South's better liberal arts colleges, now fighting its way back from a management and financial crisis under leadership of a retired four-star general. With just over 1,200 students, BSC is roughly the same size as Rhodes (Tennessee) and Millsaps (Mississippi). Its strong fraternity system is a throwback to the way college used to be. Relatively low tuition and plenty of scholarships.

Website: www.bsc.edu
Location: City Outskirts
Private
Total Enrollment: 1,207
Undergraduates: 1,207
Male/Female: 53/47
SAT Ranges: CR 500–610, M 510–610
ACT Ranges: 23–29
Financial Aid: 90%
Expense: Pr $
Student Loans: 50%
Average Debt: $ $ $
Phi Beta Kappa: Yes
Applicants: 1,846
Accepted: 65%
Enrolled: 18%
Grad in 6 Years: 62%
Returning Freshmen: 81%
Academics: ✍ ✍ ✍
Social: ☎ ☎ ☎
Q of L: ★ ★ ★
Admissions: (205) 226-4696
Email Address: admission@bsc.edu

Strongest Programs:
Biology
English
Business

Once an old-school conservative Southern institution, BSC is now striving to prepare students for all aspects of the modern world, with high-tech facilities and a more global curriculum. More than half the student body participates in community service through the Bunting Center for Engaged Study and Community Action, and attentive faculty add to a sense of commitment to both personal and community growth. A junior says BSC is a good choice for those students who "want to spend four years preparing, maturing, and challenging their minds so that they can make a difference in the world."

Known as the Hilltop for obvious geological reasons, BSC is the result of the 1918 merger of two smaller colleges: Birmingham College and Southern University. The campus, a green and shady oasis in an urban neighborhood, contains a pleasing hodgepodge of traditional and modern architecture, all surrounded by a security fence for added safety. Two new, LEED-certified residence halls have been completed and provide suite-style living for 167 students. When the school went through a major financial crisis several years ago, the trustees turned to General Charles Krulak, a former commandant of the U.S. Marine Corps, to become president and shape things up. Officials report that the budget is now balanced, debt is under control, and both contributions and student enrollment are on the increase.

> **"The professors are great teachers."**

The courses at BSC are "somewhat competitive" and "challenging but not impossible," according to one senior. Each student is assigned a faculty member who serves as his or her academic advisor from freshman convocation to graduation, an arrangement that students praise for its effectiveness. Equal praise goes out to faculty in the classrooms, where 65 percent of classes have 19 or fewer students. "The professors are great teachers," reports one psychology major.

Business, a division that includes programs ranging from accounting to international issues, is the most popular major, enrolling about a quarter of the students. Visual and performing arts and psychology majors are also popular, and the many premed students cite biology as a major drawing card. The Stephens Science Center gives this program, as well as the chemistry and physics departments, a further boost. English is also one of the school's strongest programs. The art, drama, dance, and music programs are all among the best in the South. Students stage several major productions each year, often including American and world premieres. An interdisciplinary major in English/theater arts is also available. Other notable majors include urban and environmental studies and media and film studies.

(continued)

Humanities
Psychology

The Explorations general education curriculum is designed to "guide students in learning how to communicate effectively, solve complex problems in creative ways, connect their coursework to the wider world, engage with their social and political world, and engage in self-directed teaching and learning." It comprises 32 units across several disciplines, including fine and performing arts, social sciences, natural sciences, and humanities, as well as three global and local citizenship courses. BSC, a member of the Associated Colleges of the South* consortium, also offers a wide variety of special programs. The Explorations term allows students to explore new areas of study, from cooking lessons to travel in China. The international studies program offers students the chance to study abroad in several different countries, and the honors program allows 25 exceptional first-year students to take small seminars with one or more professors.

Other notable majors include urban and environmental studies and media and film studies.

Fifty-five percent of the students are homegrown Alabamians, and practically all the rest hail from Deep South states, many with family ties to Southern. Though moderate by Alabama standards, the student body is quite conservative. Thirty-eight percent of the students belong to the Methodist Church. "Students at BSC possess a desire to learn from each other and professors," says a sophomore. "We enjoy discussing current national and international issues as well as our classes." Eight percent of BSC students are African American, 3 percent are Hispanic, and 4 percent are Asian American. "We have an expanding international student base and multicultural affairs and the beginning of some African American sororities. The college is taking steps to diversify," a student says. BSC offers various merit scholarships, with an average grant of $17,000. National Merit Scholars who list Birmingham–Southern as their first choice receive an automatic scholarship of $500 to $2,000, and up to 10 get full-tuition awards.

"It's not a huge party school."

Eighty-five percent of the students live on campus, including many of those whose families reside in Birmingham. Dorms are described as comfortable and convenient. "You can wake up 10 minutes before class, get ready, walk to class, and still have two or three minutes to spare," says a business administration major. More importantly, "The water pressure is great in the hall showers," cheers one picky student. Dining facilities get mixed reviews. The quality is decent and special tastes are accommodated, but the food can get repetitive. Campus security is quite visible, and students praise its effectiveness in keeping the campus safe.

The biggest social event of the year is Soco, a two-day festival.

Thirty-five percent of the men and 53 percent of the women are members of Greek organizations, which means that much of the social activity at BSC revolves around the Greek system, though plenty of opportunities are available for independents as well. "It's not a huge party school," says one student, "but there is a fair amount that goes on on campus." As for alcohol, it's not allowed on the quad, and elsewhere it must be in an opaque container, a policy most students find reasonable, described by one senior as a "'don't see it, ignore it' policy."

The biggest social event of the year is Soco, a two-day festival. Freshmen take part in a square dance during orientation. Other popular events include E-Fest and Halloween on the Hilltop, where students "dress up in costumes and the neighborhood kids go trick-or-treating." When social opportunities on campus dry up, many students take the shuttle to Birmingham for the city's nightlife. Road trips to Auburn, Nashville, and Atlanta are popular, and beaches and mountains are less than five hours away.

BSC currently fields 21 varsity teams for men and women, including men's and women's basketball, cross-country, golf, lacrosse, indoor track and field, outdoor track and field, soccer, and tennis. The Panthers compete in the Division III Southern Collegiate Athletic Conference (SCAC), where the baseball team has been

Overlaps

University of Alabama, Auburn, Rhodes, University of the South, Millsaps, Samford, Furman, University of Alabama at Birmingham

champion for the past four years. Seventy percent of students take part in the intramural program. Basketball, flag football, and soccer are popular, but less traditional sports, such as dodgeball and table tennis, are also offered.

Students at BSC continue to focus on academics while balancing community service and an active social scene. Small classes, a caring faculty, and an expanding menu of academic offerings continue to draw attention to this close-knit liberal arts school.

If You Apply To ➤

Birmingham–Southern: Early action: Nov. 15. Regular admissions: Feb. 1. Housing: May 1. Application fee: $50. Campus and alumni interviews: optional, informational. SATs or ACTs: required. Subject Tests: optional. Accepts the Common Application. Essay question.

Boston College

140 Commonwealth Avenue, Devlin Hall, Room 208, Chestnut Hill, MA 02467

Many students clamoring for a spot at Boston College are surprised to learn that it is affiliated with the Roman Catholic Church. Set on a quiet hilltop at the end of a T (subway) line, BC's location is solid gold. A close second to Notre Dame in the pecking order among true-blue Catholics. About 70 percent of the students are Catholic, compared to Georgetown's 50 percent and Notre Dame's 80 percent.

Website: www.bc.edu
Location: Suburban
Private
Total Enrollment: 13,783
Undergraduates: 9,110
Male/Female: 47/53
SAT Ranges: CR 620–710, M 640–740
ACT Ranges: 29–32
Financial Aid: 70%
Expense: Pr $ $ $ $
Student Loans: 49%
Average Debt: $
Phi Beta Kappa: Yes
Applicants: 34,061
Accepted: 29%
Enrolled: 25%
Grad in 6 Years: 92%
Returning Freshmen: 95%
Academics: ✐ ✐ ✐ ✐
Social: ☎ ☎ ☎ ☎
Q of L: ★ ★ ★
Admissions: (617) 552-3100
Email Address: N/A

Strongest Programs:
Chemistry

Boston College is a study in contrasts. The academics and the athletic teams are both well respected. The environment is safely suburban, yet barely 20 minutes from Boston, the hub of the Eastern seaboard's college scene. The Jesuit influence on the college, one of the largest Roman Catholic schools in the country, provides a guiding spirit for campus life, but the social opportunities still seem endless. Despite the paradoxes (or perhaps because of them), students at BC enjoy a college experience with much to offer.

Don't let the name fool you. Boston College is actually a university with nine schools and colleges. It has two campuses: the main campus at Chestnut Hill and the Newton campus a mile and a half away. The dominant architecture of the main campus (known as "the Heights") is Gothic Revival, with modern additions over the past few years, including a new science building. There's lots of grass and trees, not to mention a large, peaceful reservoir (perfect to jog around) right in the front yard.

Boston College was originally founded by the Jesuits to teach the sons of Irish immigrants. These days, the college's mission is to "educate skilled, knowledgeable, and responsible leaders within each new generation." To accomplish this goal, the Core Curriculum requires courses not only in literature, science, history, philosophy, social science, and theology, but also writing, mathematics, the arts, and cultural diversity, in addition to specific requirements set by each undergraduate school. "Core Curriculum forces you to take classes you might not want to take but end up enjoying," says a senior. Students in arts and sciences must also show proficiency in a modern foreign language or classical language before graduation. Freshmen are required to take a writing workshop in which each student develops a portfolio of personal and academic writing and reads a wide range of texts. Seniors participate in the University Capstone program, a series of seminars aiming to give a "big picture" perspective to the college experience.

> **"Core Curriculum forces you to take classes you might not want to take but end up enjoying."**

The academic climate is challenging and collaborative. "If you are better at science than your roommate, you will help her out," states one senior, "and perhaps when it comes time to fulfill your philosophy core requirement her love of Plato will get you through the class." Professors are praised for their passion and knowledge, as well as their accessibility. "I have certainly been challenged by my professors but also supported since they consistently make themselves available outside of the classroom through office hours or other appointments," says one history major. The Jesuits on BC's faculty (about 60 out of 900) exert an influence out of proportion to their numbers. "The philosophy, theology, and ethics departments are the most important in setting the tone of the campus because they encourage the students to be open minded," says a freshman.

The schools of arts and sciences, management, nursing, and education award bachelor's degrees. Communications, economics, biology, finance, and English are the most popular majors. Outside the traditional classroom at the McMullen Museum of Art in Devlin Hall, students find exhibitions, lectures, and gallery tours. The Music Guild sponsors professional concerts throughout the year, and music students emphasizing performance can take advantage of facilities equipped with Steinways and Yamahas. Theater majors find a home in the 600-seat E. Paul Robsham Theater Arts Center, which produces eight student-directed productions each year.

"I have certainly been challenged by my professors."

Students searching for out-of-the-ordinary offerings will be happy at BC. The PULSE program provides participants with the opportunity to fulfill their philosophy and theology requirements while engaging in social-service fieldwork at any of about 35 Boston organizations, and sometimes leads students to major in those areas. Perspectives, a four-year interdisciplinary course of study, is grounded in the great texts of Western culture and seeks to integrate the humanities and natural sciences. "It's another opportunity for freshmen to learn from some of the university's best professors in a small discussion group setting," a biology major says. There's also a Freshman-Year Experience program, which offers seminars and services to help students adjust to college life and take advantage of the school and the city. An honors program allows students to work at a more intensive pace and requires a senior thesis. Forty-one percent of Boston College undergraduates engage in an international volunteer or academic experience by the time they graduate. BC offers over 60 academic programs in 30 countries around the world, as well as three-week summer study abroad programs. Finally, the Undergraduate Faculty Research Fellows Program requires participating students to spend an average of 100 hours per semester assisting faculty with serious research, for which they receive financial aid.

"There is a pervasive spirit of compassion."

Twenty-two percent of BC students come from Massachusetts, and Catholics comprise about 70 percent of the student body. African Americans constitute 4 percent of the student body, while Asian Americans make up 10 percent and Hispanics 11 percent. "The student body is a socially conscious, environmentally responsible, academically oriented group on the whole," offers one student. "There is a pervasive spirit of compassion that runs through the student body here." Indeed, the Jesuit appeal for tolerance means that students can find support and interaction even when approaching hot-button issues that orthodox Catholicism will not condone, such as homosexuality. Nearly 300 athletic awards are doled out annually in 14 men's and women's sports; merit scholarships are worth an average of $16,661.

Eighty-five percent of BC students live on campus. When students are admitted, they are notified whether they will get on-campus housing for three or four years, and most juniors with three-year guarantees live off campus or study abroad in the fourth year. The city of Boston has a fairly reliable bus and subway system to bring

(continued)

Economics
English
Finance
Political Science
Physics
History

Boston College is actually a university with nine schools and colleges.

Seniors participate in the University Capstone program, a series of seminars aiming to give a "big picture" perspective to the college experience.

There's also a
Freshman-Year
Experience program,
which offers seminars
and services to help
students adjust to
college life and take
advantage of the
school and the city.

distant residents to campus; the few students that drive to school are required to show they need to park on campus. Another lottery system determines where on-campus residents hang their hats. "The dorms are comfortable and spacious," says an international studies major, "with the exception of forced triples for freshmen." Students pay in advance for a certain number of dining hall meals, served a la carte. "The food is expensive," a student says, "but it is great quality." BC students are serious about their work but not excessively so. "There are always events going on on campus," reports one senior, "such as concerts and performances."

BC's reputation as a hard-core party school is diminishing, now that no kegs or cases of beer are allowed on campus grounds. Those of legal age can carry in only enough beer for personal consumption. Bars and clubs in Boston ("the college town of all college towns," cheers a junior) are a big draw, along with Fenway Park. On weekends, especially in the winter, the mountains of Vermont and New Hampshire beckon outdoorsy types. The campus is replete with sporting events, movies, festivals, concerts, and plays, and "volunteer work is huge," says one student. As at other Jesuit institutions, there is no Greek system at BC, and "the social life is much more inclusive" as a result, according to a senior.

"The dorms are comfortable and spacious."

Athletic events become social events too, with tailgate and victory parties common. Football games are a big draw—the contest with Notre Dame is jokingly referred to as the "Holy War" and makes for a popular road trip. The Eagles football program has been recognized for achieving the highest graduation rate in the NCAA, and the men's ice hockey team brought home national titles in 2008, 2010, and 2012. Other solid teams include women's soccer, fencing, cross-country, golf, and basketball, and men's soccer, sailing, and fencing. The Silvio O. Conte Forum Sports Arena is well attended, and BC meets fierce competition from Atlantic Coast Conference rivals Duke, Miami, Florida State, Virginia Tech, and others. Students even get the day off from classes to line the edge of campus and cheer Boston Marathon runners up "Heartbreak Hill." Intramural sports are huge here. About 4,300 undergrads play on 42 teams—from basketball and volleyball to skiing and golf. Students rave about Boston College's recreational complex and the Yawkey Athletics Center.

BC students spend four years fine-tuning the art of the delicate balance, finding ways to make old-fashioned morals relevant to life in the 21st century and finding time for fun while still tending to their academic performance.

Overlaps

Georgetown, Harvard, Duke, Notre Dame, Brown, University of Pennsylvania, Cornell, Villanova

If You Apply To ➤

BC: Early action: Nov. 1. Regular admissions: Jan. 1. Financial aid: Feb. 1. Housing: May 1. Application fee: $70. No campus or alumni interviews. SATs or ACTs: required. Subject Tests: required (two or more). Accepts the Common Application. Apply to particular schools or programs. Essay question: personal statement.

Boston University

121 Bay State Road, Boston, MA 02215

One of the nation's biggest private universities, but easy to miss amid the bustle of the city. Boston's adjacent Back Bay neighborhood is the promised land for hordes of students nationwide seeking a funky, artsy, youth-oriented urban setting that is less in-your-face than New York City. More selective than it once was, but still more accessible than either NYU or George Washington.

Like The George Washington University and NYU, Boston University is an integral part of the city it calls home. The school's mammoth collection of nondescript high-rises straddles bustling, six-lane Commonwealth Avenue—and so do thousands upon thousands of students. Whether they're aspiring actors, musicians, journalists, or filmmakers, or wannabe doctors, dentists, or hotel managers, BU seems to offer something for all of them. "BU has endless opportunities in academics, research, study abroad, and internship experiences," raves one senior. A junior adds, "You definitely walk away from BU with a sense of accomplishment and individuality."

The BU campus is practically indistinguishable from the city that surrounds it. A measure of relief is available on the tree-lined side streets, which feature quaint Victorian brownstones. Facilities include the 35,000-square-foot Hillel House, a multilevel fitness center, a hockey arena that doubles as a concert hall, and a life science and engineering building that allows the biology, chemistry, bioinformatics, and biomedical engineering faculty to operate under one roof. The John Hancock Student Village includes a track and tennis center, as well as an apartment-style dorm. A $50 million student center opened in late 2012.

"I do not feel overwhelmed by the workload."

BU's nine undergraduate schools and colleges include the College of Arts and Sciences, which caters to the premeds and prelaw students. The College of Communication combines theory and hands-on training—some of it by adjunct professors with day jobs at major newspapers and TV networks. It also houses the nation's only center for the study of political disinformation. The School of Music benefits from its own concert hall and from faculty who also belong to the Boston Symphony Orchestra. The physical therapy program at the Sargent College of Health and Rehabilitation Sciences takes six years, culminating in B.S. and D.P.T. degrees. Students in the School of Education can test their ideas for curricular reform in the public schools of nearby Chelsea, while those in the School of Visual Arts may show their work in one of three campus galleries.

The School of Management, one of BU's top programs, offers an honors program for sophomores and minors in law and hospitality administration; the College of Engineering boasts a robotics and biomedical engineering lab. Future employers of students in the School of Hospitality Administration offer paid internships in exotic locales such as Brussels and Britain. (Students in other fields who wish to work abroad may vie for jobs from Australia to Moscow.) BU also offers highly competitive seven- and eight-year programs admitting qualified students simultaneously to the undergraduate program and the university's medical or dental school. "All of the academic programs I've encountered have an accomplished faculty that bring 'real-world' experiences into the classroom," a political science major says.

Each of BU's schools and colleges sets its own general education requirements. Students rave about FYSOP, the First-Year Student Outreach Project, which brings freshmen to campus a week early to do community service. For a break from brutal Boston winters, BU offers more than 90 study abroad programs, including internships, field work, research, language study, and liberal arts programs. There's also a marine science program at the Woods Hole Institute and the Semester at Sea*, a program welcoming students from many schools to spend a term living and studying on a cruise ship as it travels the world.

"Since we are on a lottery system it is possible to get a not-so-great room."

Back on campus, the University Honors College attracts the highest achieving students. Perhaps a further indicator of the university's elite status, BU was recently invited to join the exclusive and prestigious Association of American Universities.

The academic climate at BU encourages both cooperation and competition. "While I am consistently challenged, I do not feel overwhelmed by the workload," says one senior. Fifty-eight percent of classes have 19 or fewer students. "From the

Website: www.bu.edu
Location: City Center
Private
Total Enrollment: 25,374
Undergraduates: 16,029
Male/Female: 39/61
SAT Ranges: CR 570–670, M 610–720
ACT Ranges: 26–30
Financial Aid: 61%
Expense: Pr $ $ $
Student Loans: 59%
Average Debt: $ $ $ $
Phi Beta Kappa: Yes
Applicants: 44,006
Accepted: 46%
Enrolled: 19%
Grad in 6 Years: 84%
Returning Freshmen: 92%
Academics: ✍ ✍ ✍ ✍
Social: 🕿 🕿 🕿 🕿
Q of L: ★ ★ ★
Admissions: (617) 353-2300
Email Address: admissions@bu.edu

Strongest Programs:
Management
Communications
Biomedical Engineering
Natural Sciences
Psychology
Deaf Studies
Archeology

introduction to writing seminars of freshman year to the advanced colloquiums I've taken, all my teachers have been engaging, knowledgeable, and passionate," says a student.

"The students here are diverse," says a junior. "I feel like that is an overused word, especially when looking at colleges, but it's true. On my freshmen floor of 40 girls, seven were from outside the country and 25 were from outside of Massachusetts." Indeed, 63 percent of BU undergrads are from outside Massachusetts and 20 percent come from outside the United States. Asian Americans are the largest minority group on campus, at 14 percent of the total; African Americans add 3 percent, and Hispanics comprise 9 percent. "I would consider BU to be a very active and socially aware campus," a student reports. In all, the university offers more than one thousand merit scholarships each year; there are also more than 300 athletic scholarships in 17 sports.

Seventy-seven percent of BU students live in campus housing, which is guaranteed for four years. "Some dorms are older than others, but each residence has its perks," says a health science major. "Since we are on a lottery system it is possible to get a not-so-great room," explains a psychology major. "Freshmen/sophomore dorms are fairly typical, but housing gets better as you get to be a senior." The luxury apartments, known as the Residences at 10 Buick Street, house 814 students on 18 floors, in apartments with four single bedrooms each. Each bedroom is wired for phone and fast Internet service, and each air-conditioned apartment also includes a kitchen, living and dining area, and two full bathrooms. Meal plans are flexible, and one of the six dining halls on campus is kosher. "BU has great food!" cheers a senior. There's also a food court with chains such as Burger King, Starbucks, and D'Angelo's, a local sub shop. Students say campus security is up to the task of keeping students safe: "For being in an urban area, I feel extremely safe on campus," reports one senior.

"You have to be proactive about finding out what's going on around campus."

"The social scene at BU has a lot to offer," a student says. "We always have on-campus events every day of the week, including the weekends. If we don't feel like staying on campus, we can just hop on our Boston trains and be anywhere in the city of Boston within minutes." Eight percent of the men and 14 percent of the women go Greek, and parties at neighboring schools are an option as well. Owing to Boston's heavily Irish heritage, St. Patrick's Day is also an occasion for revelry. Drinking is fairly common, though not in the dorms, because state laws are strictly enforced and violators may find themselves without university housing. The Splash party in September, homecoming in October, and Culture Fest in March round out the social calendar. Possible road trips include Cape Cod, Cape Ann, and Providence, Rhode Island. Even better, "Fenway Park, downtown, Landsdowne Street, and Boston Common are all within walking distance," says a marine biology major.

BU doesn't field a football team, so hockey season is the athletic high point of the school year. All Terrier teams compete in NCAA Division I, and solid teams include women's tennis, men's cross-country, men's and women's swimming and diving, and men's and women's hockey. The Head of the Charles regatta, which starts at BU's crew house each fall, draws college crew teams from across the country. By far the most popular intramural sport is broomball, which is like ice hockey on sneakers, with a ball instead of a puck and a broom instead of a stick. BU has won 29 of 60 titles in the annual Beanpot men's ice hockey tournament, which pits BU against Harvard, Northeastern, and archrival Boston College.

Boston University offers more than 250 majors and minors in its nine undergraduate schools and colleges, along with dual degree and interdisciplinary opportunities. The university urges students to just "Be You" (ahem) and most are happy to do so, but they warn that coming here is not for the faint of heart. The school is "a great

BU was recently invited to join the exclusive and prestigious Association of American Universities.

BU doesn't field a football team, so hockey season is the athletic high point of the school year.

Overlaps

Northeastern, NYU, Boston College, University of Southern California, George Washington, University of Massachusetts, Syracuse

place, with lots of academic and social opportunities, but it's not for the timid student," agrees a geophysics and planetary sciences major. "You have to be proactive about finding out what's going on around campus, so that you can find your niche."

If You Apply To ➤ **BU:** Early decision: Nov. 1. Regular admissions: Jan. 1. Financial aid: Feb. 15. Housing: May 1. Application fee: $80. Campus interviews: optional, informational. No alumni interviews. SATs or ACTs (with writing): required. Subject Tests: optional (required for some programs). Apply to particular school or program. Accepts the Common Application. Essay question.

Bowdoin College

Brunswick, ME 04011

Rates with Amherst, Williams, and Wesleyan for liberal arts excellence and does not require the SAT. Bowdoin has strong science programs, and outdoor enthusiasts benefit from proximity to the Atlantic coast. Smaller than some of its competitors, with less overt competition among students.

For more than two centuries, Bowdoin College has sought to make nature, art, and friendship as integral to the student experience as the world of books. This is, after all, the alma mater of the great American poets Longfellow and Hawthorne. In fact, when they matriculate, new students sign their names in a book on Hawthorne's very desk. Though the New England weather can be brutal ("Be prepared for long, cold winters," warns a junior), students are quick to point out that good food and friendships that "transcend labels" help make campus a warm and friendly place. "Bowdoin has so many resources," says one happy freshman. "If you're passionate about anything, Bowdoin provides you with the resources to explore those passions."

Bowdoin's 205-acre campus sits in Brunswick, Maine, the state's largest town. Hidden amid the pine groves and athletic fields are 117 buildings, in styles from German Romanesque, colonial, medieval, and neoclassical to neo-Georgian, modern, and postmodern. Former fraternity houses now house academic and administrative offices, since Greek groups were phased out. In 2013, the college opened the Robert H. Edwards and Blythe Bickel Edwards Center for Art and Dance.

To graduate, Bowdoin students must complete 32 courses, including one each in natural sciences and math, social and behavioral sciences, and fine arts and humanities, in addition to a required course in the visual and performing arts. Distribution requirements emphasize issues vital to a liberal education in the 21st century and include courses within distributions such as Exploring Social Differences; Mathematical, Computational, or Statistical Reasoning; and International Perspectives. Freshmen also have their choice of seminars, capped at 16 students each, which emphasize reading and writing; recent topics included Cultural Difference and the Crime Film, The Cuban Revolution, and The Economics of Art. Academic strengths include the sciences, specifically biology, neuroscience, chemistry, and environmental studies. Making a virtue out of climatic necessity, Bowdoin also offers coursework in Arctic Studies (its mascot is the polar bear), as well as opportunities for Arctic archeological research in Labrador or ecological research at the Kent Island Scientific Station in Canada. Premeds of all persuasions will find top-of-the-line lab equipment and outstanding faculty; the field of microscale organic chemistry was developed and advanced here.

"The academic climate is very laid-back."

Website: www.bowdoin.edu
Location: Suburban
Private
Total Enrollment: 1,830
Undergraduates: 1,830
Male/Female: 50/50
SAT Ranges: CR 670–760, M 670–760
ACT Ranges: 31–33
Financial Aid: 47%
Expense: Pr $ $ $ $
Student Loans: 35%
Average Debt: $ $
Phi Beta Kappa: Yes
Applicants: 6,716
Accepted: 16%
Enrolled: 46%
Grad in 6 Years: 95%
Returning Freshmen: 97%
Academics: ✑ ✑ ✑ ✑ ✑
Social: ☎ ☎ ☎
Q of L: ★ ★ ★
Admissions: (207) 725-3100
Email Address: admissions@bowdoin.edu

Strongest Programs:
Government
Economics
Biology
History

*Freshmen also have
their choice of
seminars, capped at
16 students each,
which emphasize
reading and writing.*

*Bowdoin's robotics
lab is the home
of cutting-edge
research conducted
by computer science
faculty and students
and a robotics course
in computer science.*

"The courses at Bowdoin are definitely challenging. They force you to think in new ways and include significant amounts of reading and analysis," says one senior. "However, the academic climate is very laid-back." Students praise the art history and English departments and say the popularity of government and economics—the majors with the highest enrollment—is well deserved. Bowdoin's robotics lab is the home of cutting-edge research conducted by computer science faculty and students and a robotics course in computer science. There's also an increasing emphasis on service learning; more than half of all Bowdoin students apply their classroom work to real-world problems faced by local community groups. Undergraduate research is a priority, and it's common for juniors and seniors to conduct independent studies with faculty members, then publish their results in professional journals.

"Teachers are always willing and ready to help students."

Those same professors teach all Bowdoin classes—there are no graduate students here, and thus no TAs—and their skills in the classroom draw raves. "Teachers are always willing and ready to help students," a freshman says. "The professors are all very talented and incredible at what they do," adds a sophomore.

Before school begins, the entire entering class takes preorientation hiking, canoeing, kayaking, or community service trips that teach them about the people and landscape of Maine. There's a community service experience in Brunswick for students less interested in the outdoors. The entering class also reads the same book before arriving to start the year with a common academic experience.

Eighty-two percent of students hail from outside Maine; most are generally hardworking, fun-loving, athletic types. "Bowdoin students are also very involved in campus life. But rather than being involved just in one area, there is a lot of crossover," reports a sociology major, "so there are athletes who do community service; outdoor club leaders who do a capella; and people on student government who also do theater." African Americans make up 5 percent of the student body, Hispanics comprise 13 percent, and Asian Americans add 7 percent. Bowdoin was the first U.S. institution to make SAT I scores an optional part of the admissions process, shifting the emphasis to a student's whole body of work. Merit scholarships are available to qualified undergraduates; there are no athletic scholarships. Additionally, Bowdoin has eliminated loans from its financial aid packages and replaced them with grants.

Ninety-two percent of Bowdoin students live on campus, where "freshmen start off in a two-room triple (or if you're lucky, a two-room double), so you'll never be kept up

"Bowdoin students are also very involved in campus life."

by your roommate typing a paper at 3 a.m.," says a chemistry major. After that, students try their luck with the lottery, although members of the social houses, which have replaced sororities and fraternities, can escape by living with these groups. Upperclassmen may choose four-bedroom quads. Students give rave reviews to dining service workers and the food they serve. Students also love the lobster bake that kicks off each school year, and vegans and vegetarians are happy with the options available to them. "Dining services are very accommodating, and vegetarian, vegan, and gluten-free options are always available," confirms an anthropology major. "Bowdoin dining does a great job of providing varied, delicious, and healthy options."

With the Greeks long gone, social life at Bowdoin centers around two groups: sports teams and social houses. "Bowdoin's social life is very much centered around campus, as the town of Brunswick does not have much to offer in way of night life," says one senior. "College houses make up the main social sphere of first-year and sophomore social life, and smaller apartment parties become more popular as students become older." All parties and kegs must be registered and most students report that while underage drinking does occur, it doesn't dominate the social scene. Students look forward to homecoming, the BearAIDS benefit concert, and

Ivies Weekend, one last blast of fun before spring finals. The latter celebrates the fact that Bowdoin didn't join the Ivy League, with bands and games in the quad.

One student says Brunswick (population 21,000) is "a great, quiet college town." A car comes in handy for the 15-minute drive to the outlets of Freeport (including L.L. Bean's flagship 24/7 factory store) or a quick trip to Portland for a "real" night out. A school shuttle takes students to Boston, less than three hours away, and ski bums will find several resorts even closer. Habitat for Humanity and various mentoring programs help build bridges between local residents and students. For those who get really stir-crazy, study abroad programs are available in more than 100 countries, including warm ones like Ecuador (a welcome treat when you consider the normally brutal New England winters). Fifty percent of students take advantage of such programs.

While "the long winters are certainly not a favorite," according to a senior, they do bring out school spirit, and rooting for the ice hockey team is an important strategy for winter survival. Any sporting event against Colby—especially hockey—is exciting. "That rivalry is almost out of control," says a biology major. "The chanting is brutal, and dead fish have been known to fly onto the ice." Bowdoin's Bears compete in the Division III New England Small College Athletic Conference, and students "get blacked out" to demonstrate support, wearing all black when they attend games. The most competitive teams are field hockey, women's basketball, men's soccer, men's tennis, men's ice hockey, and women's lacrosse. Students have a big say in the start-up of intramural programs, and about 70 percent participate in recreational activities run by student organizations or the Bowdoin Outing Club.

Outdoorsy types and those who can brave the cold will find warm and inviting academics at Bowdoin, where close friendships with peers and professors are easily forged. "Being able to make friends with my professors is something I'll treasure forever," says an art history major. For those considering Bowdoin, a senior offers this assessment: "The education and opportunities will be beyond anything you'd imagine."

> *With the Greeks long gone, social life at Bowdoin centers around two groups: sports teams and social houses.*

Overlaps

Brown, Dartmouth, Middlebury, Williams, Yale, Amherst, Harvard, Princeton

If You Apply To ➤

Bowdoin: Early decision: Nov. 15. Regular admissions: Jan. 1. Financial aid: Feb. 15. Application fee: $60. Campus and alumni interviews: optional, evaluative. SATs or ACTs: optional. Subject Tests: optional. Accepts the Common Application. Essay question.

Brandeis University

Waltham, MA 02454-9110

Founded in 1948 by Jews who wanted an elite institution to call their own. Now down to 55 percent Jewish and seeking top students of all faiths. Academic specialties include the natural sciences, the Middle East, and Jewish studies. Has one of the top programs in neuroscience at a small university. Competes with Tufts in the Boston area.

Brandeis University, founded to provide educational opportunities to those facing discrimination, has always had a reputation for intense progressive thought. Now it's being recognized as a rising star among research institutions. The only nonsectarian Jewish-sponsored college in the nation, Brandeis continues its struggle to maintain its Jewish identity while attracting a well-rounded, eclectic group of students.

Set on a hilltop in a pleasant residential neighborhood nine miles west of Boston, Brandeis's attractively landscaped 235-acre campus boasts many distinctive

Website: www.brandeis.edu
Location: Suburban
Private
Total Enrollment: 5,808
Undergraduates: 3,588
Male/Female: 44/56

(continued)

SAT Ranges: CR 610–710,
  M 620–740
ACT Ranges: 28–32
Financial Aid: 64%
Expense: Pr $ $ $ $
Student Loans: 56%
Average Debt: $ $ $
Phi Beta Kappa: Yes
Applicants: 8,380
Accepted: 39%
Enrolled: 25%
Grad in 6 Years: 91%
Returning Freshmen: 95%
Academics: ✎ ✎ ✎ ✎
Social: ☎ ☎ ☎
Q of L: ★ ★ ★
Admissions: (781) 736-3500
Email Address: admissions@
  brandeis.edu

Strongest Programs:
Neuroscience
Biology
Near Eastern and Judaic
  Studies
English and American
  Literature
Theater Arts
Economics
Psychology

East Asian studies gives students a broad yet intimate knowledge of the history, politics, economics, art, and language of the major areas of East Asia.

buildings. The music building, for example, is shaped like a grand piano; the theater looks like a top hat. The 24-hour Carl and Ruth Shapiro Campus Center includes a student theater, electronic library, and bookstore. The Abraham Shapiro Academic Building houses a state-of-the-art distance-learning classroom, conference rooms, the International Center for Ethics, Justice, and Public Life, the Center for Middle Eastern Studies, the Mandel Center for Jewish Education, and faculty offices.

Biochemistry, chemistry, neuroscience, and physics are top-notch programs, while economics, biology, psychology, international global studies, and health enroll the most students. Dedicated premeds are catered to hand and foot, with special advisors, internships, and their own premedical center, with specialized laboratories designed to provide would-be M.D.s with research opportunities. With the largest faculty in the field outside of Israel, the university is virtually unrivaled in Near Eastern and Judaic studies; Hebrew is a Brandeis specialty. East Asian studies gives students a broad yet intimate knowledge of the history, politics, economics, art, and language of the major areas of East Asia. A growing number of popular interdisciplinary programs including business; journalism; and legal, environmental, Latin American, peace, and women's and gender studies add spice to the academic menu. Brandeis also maintains a commitment to the creative arts, with strong theater offerings and a theory-based music program founded by the late Leonard Bernstein. Sixty-four percent of the classes have 19 or fewer students.

> **"Professors are engaging, incredibly smart, and, most of all, care about their students."**

Undergraduates enter the College of Arts and Sciences, which offers more than 40 different majors and nearly 50 minors through its departments and interdepartmental programs. The Brandeis core curriculum is rooted in a commitment to developing strong writing, foreign language, and quantitative-reasoning skills and an interdisciplinary and cross-cultural perspective. Students complete courses in composition, foreign language, physical education, quantitative reasoning, and non-Western and comparative studies. Rising sophomores and juniors have the opportunity to earn credit through summer internships related to their studies. More than 400 off-campus programs are offered in 70 countries; 40 percent of each junior class takes advantage of these opportunities. The Schiff Undergraduate Fellows Program enables 10 Fellows each year to work with faculty mentors on research and teaching projects. The TYP program is a one-year academic program for inner city and economically disadvantaged students who typically come from under-resourced high schools and/or home communities. The program guarantees small classes, rigorous academics, and strong academic support.

> **"There is always something to do on campus."**

Twenty-five percent of the Brandeis student population is from Massachusetts, and the population is heavily bicoastal otherwise, with sizable numbers of New York, New Jersey, and California residents. The group is also very bright; 93 percent graduated in the top quarter of their high school class, and professors want them to continue working hard. Students say the academic climate here is intense. "Brandeis takes its academic integrity seriously," says a creative writing and English major. There is an out for those in need of respite; the Flex 3 option allows students to take three classes one semester if an especially rough course is required, and five the next, to stay on track for four-year graduation. The Justice Brandeis Semester allows groups of 12 to 15 students to earn credits while focusing on topics such as ethnographic fieldwork, environmental justice and legal rights, or Web programming for social networks. The linked courses feature fieldwork, internships, or research under faculty supervision. Professors are "engaging, incredibly smart, and, most of all, care about their students," according to one English major.

Though more than half the student body is Jewish, there are three chapels on campus—Catholic, Jewish, and Protestant—built so that the shadow of one never crosses the shadow of another. It's an architectural symbol that students say reflects the realities of the campus community. Muslim students, with an enrollment of more than 200, have their own dedicated prayer space. African Americans make up 4 percent of the student body, Hispanics 6 percent, and Asian Americans 13 percent. "Students who attend Brandeis are passionate, involved in student life, outgoing, friendly, think out of the box and are intellectual," says a senior. Gays and lesbians have an established presence and throw some of the liveliest parties. The unofficial fraternities and sororities that

> **"Brandeis is not only an awesome place to get an education, it's also an open, accepting place where anyone can feel at home."**

have colonized at Brandeis are clamoring for recognition from the school. Other hot-button issues include political correctness, rape awareness, and environmental causes. Even with one of the highest tuition rates in the country, Brandeis does not guarantee to meet each student's full demonstrated need, but help is generally available to those who apply on time. The level of support remains fairly constant over four years, students report. The university also offers merit scholarships to qualified students.

As befits its mold-breaking heritage, Brandeis is the only school in the nation where you can live in a replica of a Scottish castle with stairways leading to nowhere. More pedestrian housing options include traditional quadrangle dormitories, where freshmen and sophomores live in doubles, and juniors live in singles. The Foster Living Center, or the "Mods," are co-ed; university-owned townhouses are reserved for seniors. Another option is The Village, which offers singles and doubles clustered around family-style kitchens, semiprivate bathrooms, and lounges. Freshmen and sophomores are guaranteed housing, while upperclassmen play the lottery each spring. Seventy-four percent of students live on campus, and the rest find affordable off-campus housing nearby. "Housing on campus improves as you get older," one student observes. Brandeis boasts the best college food in the Boston area, as well as the most appetizing set-ups, students say, thanks to a decision to outsource dining services. Campus meal tickets buy lunch or dinner in a fast-food joint, the pub, a country store, a kosher dining hall with vegetarian selections, or the Boulevard, a cafeteria where "the salad bars are huge."

"There is always something to do on campus," cheers one student, including "dances, movie showings, gatherings on the Great Lawn." Brandeis also hosts more than 250 clubs, spanning from service and activism, to sports and religion. Some of the largest organizations include Student Events (the campus

> **"Housing on campus improves as you get older."**

programming board), WBRS 100.1FM, Waltham Group, Triskelion, BEMCo, and Student Sexuality Information Services. Weekends begin on Thursday, with live entertainment at the on-campus Stein pub. Students can party at will in the dorms providing they don't get too rambunctious, but suites are officially "dry" unless a majority of the residents are over 21. Major events on the campus calendar include a Tropics Night dance (where beachwear is required in February), the massive Bronstein Weekend festival just before spring finals, and the "Screw Your Roommate" dance, where dormies set up their roommates on blind dates. Also well attended are the homecoming soccer match and the annual lacrosse tilt against crosstown rival Bentley College.

The possibilities for off-campus diversion are nearly infinite, thanks to the proximity of Boston and Cambridge, which are accessible by the free Brandeis shuttle bus or a nearby commuter train. (A car is more trouble than it's worth.) And what about Waltham, Brandeis's host town? Waltham receives lukewarm reviews from the students, but one global studies major asks, "Who needs Waltham for excitement when Boston is a short shuttle ride away?"

Though the school does not field a football team, Brandeis has developed strong men's baseball and swimming and women's swimming, fencing, and cross-country

Sixty-four percent of the classes have 19 or fewer students.

The Schiff Undergraduate Fellows Program enables 10 Fellows each year to work with faculty mentors on research and teaching projects.

squads, all of which have taken regional championships in recent years. The Judges athletic program gets a boost from its membership in the Division III University Athletic Association, a neo-Ivy League for high-powered academic institutions such as the University of Chicago, Emory, NYU, and Carnegie Mellon. Brandeis teams compete in the 70,000-square-foot Gosman Athletic Center, which is also used by an extensive intramural program. IM contests run nearly every day of the year thanks to the artificial turf and lights on the newly renovated Gordon Field, also home to the Brandeis soccer teams.

Few private universities have come as far as Brandeis so quickly, evolving from a bare 270-acre site with the leftovers of a failed veterinary school to a modern research university of more than 100 buildings, a $700 million endowment, and ever-evolving academic opportunities. Landscaping, dining services, health services, and the campus computer network have all been dramatically improved in the past few years, students say, adding to their feelings of pride in the school. One student sums it up this way: "Brandeis is not only an awesome place to get an education, it's also an open, accepting place where anyone can feel at home."

Overlaps

Brown, Emory, University of Pennsylvania, Washington University in St. Louis, Yale, Harvard, NYU, Columbia

If You Apply To ➤

Brandeis: Early decision: Nov. 15. Regular admissions: Jan. 15. Financial aid: Feb. 1. Application fee: $75. Campus and alumni interviews: optional, evaluative. SATs or ACTs: required. Subject Tests: optional (two different subject areas). Accepts the Common Application. Essay question.

Brigham Young University

Provo, UT 84602

From the time they are knee high, Mormons in all corners of the country dream about coming to BYU. Most men and some women do a two-year stint as a missionary. Strongest academic programs are all preprofessional. The atmosphere is generally mild-mannered and conservative, but BYU goes bonkers for its sports teams.

Website: www.byu.edu
Location: City Center
Private
Total Enrollment: 30,364
Undergraduates: 28,338
Male/Female: 51/49
SAT Ranges: CR 580–690, M 590–690
ACT Ranges: 26–31
Financial Aid: 68%
Expense: Pr $
Student Loans: 31%
Average Debt: $
Phi Beta Kappa: No
Applicants: 12,557
Accepted: 55%
Enrolled: 79%
Grad in 6 Years: 77%

Brigham Young University's strong ties with the Church of Jesus Christ of Latter-Day Saints means that "BYU has high morals and a wholesome environment, which makes students feel safe and comfortable," a senior says. A sense of spirituality pervades most everything at BYU, where faith and academia are intertwined and life is governed by a strict code of ethics—covering everything from dating to academic dishonesty—that has even led to the suspension of star athletes in mid-season. Indeed, the school's commitment to church values is the reason most students choose it. "The students who attend BYU are unique," says a communications major. "Everyone is clean-cut, shaven, modestly dressed, and proper in their etiquette."

"Everyone is clean-cut, shaven, modestly dressed, and proper in their etiquette."

The church's values of prosperity, chastity, and obedience are strongly evident on BYU's 557-acre campus, where the utilitarian buildings, like everything else, are "clean, modern, and orderly." The campus sits 4,600 feet above sea level, between the shores of Utah Lake and Mount Timpanogos, with breathtaking sunsets and easy access to magnificent skiing, camping, and hiking areas. Days begin early; church bells rouse students at 8 a.m. with the first four bars of the church hymn "Come, Come Ye Saints." (The same bells also peal every hour throughout the day.) The church's influence continues when students set their schedules; students must take one religion course per term to graduate, and offerings include, of course, the Book of Mormon. BYU requires students to demonstrate proficiency in math, writing (first-year and advanced), and advanced languages, a catch-all category that can be satisfied with coursework in a foreign language or in statistics, advanced math, or advanced music. Students must also complete an extensive liberal arts core, which includes work in civilization, American heritage, biology, physical sciences, and electives in the natural sciences, social and behavioral sciences, and arts and letters. Students agree that the academic climate is demanding and students can be competitive. "It is competitive," a senior reports, and "some courses are known for being extremely difficult to pass, such as American Heritage or Econ 110."

BYU's academic offerings run the gamut, from liberal arts and sciences to professional programs in engineering, nursing, business, and law. Students say the strongest offerings include the J. Reuben Clark Law School and most departments in the Marriott School of Management, especially accounting. "One of the most popular programs has been exercise science," says a sophomore. There are also degrees in public health education, school health education, and Ancient Near Eastern Studies. Brigham Young has campuses in Idaho and Hawaii, a center in Jerusalem, and boasts the 15th largest study abroad program in the nation—166 programs in 54 nations.

Freshmen are often taught by full-time professors, who generally get good marks. "I have been very satisfied by the quality of teaching," says a student. "Most professors have a passion for their subject and for teaching." General education courses can be quite large, but the honors program, open to highly motivated students, offers small seminars with more faculty interaction and is "an excellent way to get more out of your college experience," one participant says. The strength of the faculty is one reason BYU has more full-time students than any other church-sponsored university in the United States, almost all of them undergraduates. Still, with thousands of students to accommodate, registration can be a chore. Approximately 90 percent of the men and 20 percent of the women interrupt their studies—typically after the freshman year—to serve two years as a missionary.

"The dorms are small but comfortable and very clean."

Not surprisingly, the typical BYU student is conservative. "The students are very academically and spiritually minded," confides a junior, who further describes students as "intelligent, friendly, and honest." Thirty-seven percent of BYU students are from Utah. Many others hail from California and Idaho, and 3 percent come from more than 100 other countries. Hispanic students contribute 5 percent to the student body, Asian Americans 2 percent, and African Americans less than 1 percent. The Honor Code requires students to eschew drinking, smoking, and drugs. Tuition for church members is lower than for nonmembers, because Latter-Day Saint families contribute to BYU through their tithes. Academic scholarships are available, as are roughly 250 athletic scholarships in 21 sports.

Nineteen percent of BYU undergrads—primarily freshmen—live in the single-sex residence halls, where the "very valuable" Freshman Academy program allows them to take courses and eat meals with fellow dorm-dwellers and professors. "The dorms are small but comfortable and very clean," says a student. Upperclassmen typically opt for cheaper off-campus apartments, which are also single-sex (remember the Honor Code?). When it comes to food, the student dining outlets on campus are described as adequate. "The school provides decent, affordable on-campus meal plans," says a senior.

Whether it's work with the homeless or disabled, dances, concerts, plays, or sporting events, most of BYU's social life is organized through or linked to the church. Community service is big, with students visiting patients at hospitals and care centers, performing at local festivals, and building and refurbishing houses. Social life is carried out within the church's bounds of propriety and is given a

(continued)

Returning Freshmen: 89%
Academics: ✍ ✍ ✍
Social: ☎ ☎ ☎
Q of L: ★ ★ ★ ★
Admissions: (801) 422-2507
Email Address: admissions@ byu.edu

Strongest Programs:
Business
Law
Engineering
Languages
Nursing

BYU's academic offerings run the gamut, from liberal arts and sciences to professional programs in engineering, nursing, business, and law.

Physical fitness is big here, and the intramural facilities are some of the country's best.

lighthearted feeling with groups that encourage "creative dating and lots of dating, period," says a senior. There are no fraternities and sororities to provide housing or parties, which is just fine with most students, since alcoholic drinks are banned. Don't be deterred by this, as you will still find plenty to do in the social scene. The college does what it can to keep the students busy, with activities like dances, fire-sides, and special activities within the campus religious wards (small groups of about 100 students). Road trips include Vegas or southern Utah and, with the mountains being so close, you'll find plenty of skiing and camping.

Provo itself has plenty of places to eat, shop, and play for those needing a quick getaway from the strict administration enforcing the even stricter Honor Code. "Provo wouldn't really exist without BYU," says a student, and "it's a good college town for people who don't like bustling metropolises."

Physical fitness is big here, and the intramural facilities are some of the country's best, with indoor and outdoor jogging tracks; courts for tennis, racquetball, and handball; and a pool. Also important are varsity sports; the church philosophy of discipline and obedience has worked wonders for Cougar teams, and the football rivalry against the University of Utah provides some serious end-of-season intensity. The ESPN television network has dubbed the BYU–Utah rivalry the "Holy War." One of the most popular courses offered at BYU is ballroom dancing, partly because many participants aspire to join BYU's award-winning dance team.

To most Americans, BYU probably seems old-fashioned or like a step back in time. But for young members of the Church of Jesus Christ of Latter-Day Saints, that may be just what the elder ordered. "BYU's dedicated faculty, devout atmosphere, and beautiful, clean campus set it apart from all other universities," a satisfied senior says.

Overlaps

BYU–Hawaii, BYU–Idaho, University of Utah, Utah State, Utah Valley State

If You Apply To ➤

BYU: Rolling admissions: Feb. 1. Housing: First come, first served; students are encouraged to apply a year in advance, with housing contingent on acceptance at the university. Application fee: $35. Campus and alumni interviews: optional, informational. SATs or ACTs: required. No Subject Tests. Essay question.

University of British Columbia: See page 348.

Brown University

45 Prospect Street, Providence, RI 02912

To today's stressed-out students, the thought of taking every course pass/fail seems like a dream come true. Nobody at Brown actually does this, but the pass/fail option, combined with the school's notable lack of distribution requirements, gives it the freewheeling image that students love. In reality, doing well at Brown is just as tough as at other Ivies. Bashed by conservatives as a hotbed of political correctness.

Website: www.brown.edu
Location: Small City
Private
Total Enrollment: 8,403
Undergraduates: 6,103

Brown University is a perennial "hot college," with an overwhelming number of happy students and many more clamoring to join their ranks. Once here, students not only receive a prestigious and quality education, but also a chance to explore their creative sides at a liberal arts college that does not emphasize grades and pre-professionalism and shuns required courses. Brown's environment and policies have drawn both praise and criticism over the years, but its students thrive on this discussion and lively debate. "Brown's open curriculum, though not for everyone, is incredibly liberating," says one student.

Founded in 1764 as the College in the English Colony of Rhode Island and Providence Plantations, Brown was renamed in 1804 after Nicholas Brown Jr., a major benefactor whose father—one of the school's founders—was a businessman with controversial ties to the slave trade. The university sits atop College Hill on the east side of Providence and its 140-acre campus affords an excellent view of downtown Providence. Campus architecture is a composite of old and new—plenty of grassy lawns surrounded by historic buildings that offer students refuge from the city streets beyond. One student describes it as a "melting pot of architecture's finest. We have a building that resembles a Greek temple [and] buildings in the Richardsonian tradition." The neighborhoods that surround the campus lie within a national historic district and boast beautiful tree-lined streets full of ethnic charm.

Brown's faculty has successfully resisted the notion that somewhere in their collective wisdom and experience lies a core of knowledge that every educated person should possess. As a result, aside from completing courses in a major, the only university-wide requirements for graduation are to demonstrate writing competency and complete the 30-course minimum satisfactorily. (The assumption is that students will take four courses a term for a total of 32 in four years.) Freshmen have no requirements. Those with interests in interdisciplinary fields will enjoy Brown's wide range of concentrations that cross departmental lines and cover everything from cognitive science to public policy. Indeed, there are bona fide departments in cognitive and linguistic sciences and media and modern culture. Students can also create their own concentration from the array of goodies offered. Brown also offers group independent-study projects, a popular alternative for students with the gumption to take a course they have to construct primarily by themselves, and a dual-degree program with the Rhode Island School of Design. Particularly adventurous students can choose to spend time in one of Brown's more than 50 study abroad programs in 14 countries. Closer to home, students can cross-register with Rhode Island School of Design, also on College Hill.

> "Brown's open curriculum, though not for everyone, is incredibly liberating."

Students can take their classes one of two ways: for traditional marks of A, B, C, or No Credit; or for Satisfactory/No Credit. The NC is not recorded on the transcript, while the letter grade or Satisfactory can be supplemented by a written evaluation from the professor. A habit of NCs, however, lands students in academic hot water. Any fewer than seven courses passed in two consecutive semesters makes for an academic "warning" that does find its way onto the transcript and means potential dismissal from the university. "Brown students work incredibly hard and are very passionate about academics," says a student. "Our courses are usually engaging and challenging."

The most popular majors are biological sciences, history, international relations, English, and political science. History and geology are some of the university's best, and students also praise computer science, religious studies, and applied math. Other top-notch programs include comparative literature, classics, modern languages, and the writing program in the English department. Among the sciences, engineering and the premed curriculum are standouts. Future doctors can try for a competitive eight-year liberal medical education program where students can earn an M.D.

> "We have a building that resembles a Greek temple [and] buildings in the Richardsonian tradition."

without having to sacrifice their humanity. Fields related to scientific technology have very good facilities, including an instructional technology center, while minority issues are studied at the Center for Race and Ethnicity. The Starr Fellow program awards $4,000 for a summer project to 10–15 students, and there is the potential for an additional $2,000 award in the subsequent academic year.

(continued)

Male/Female: 48/52
SAT Ranges: CR 660–760, M 670–780
ACT Ranges: 29–34
Financial Aid: 58%
Expense: Pr $ $ $ $
Student Loans: 37%
Average Debt: $ $
Phi Beta Kappa: Yes
Applicants: 28,742
Accepted: 10%
Enrolled: 56%
Grad in 6 Years: 95%
Returning Freshmen: 98%
Academics: ✍ ✍ ✍ ✍ ✍
Social: ☎ ☎ ☎ ☎
Q of L: ★ ★ ★ ★ ★
Admissions: (401) 863-2378
Email Address: admission@brown.edu

Strongest Programs:
Biological Studies
History
International Relations
English
Political Science

Freshmen have no course requirements.

Brown prides itself on undergraduate teaching and considers skill in the classroom as much as the usual scholarly credentials when making tenure decisions. Younger professors can receive fellowships for outstanding teaching, and the administration's interest in interdisciplinary instruction and imaginative course design helps cultivate high-quality instruction. The size of the faculty ranks has increased and investment in university libraries has also risen. "The professors are phenomenal," a sophomore says. Another adds, "Professors come to Brown because they want to teach undergrads, and it shows." The advising system reflects the administration's commitment to treating students as adults. The lack of predetermined requirements is supposed to challenge students, so "no one is going to tell you what to take." The advising system pairs each freshman with a professor and a peer advisor, and resident counselors in the dorms are also available to lend an ear. Sophomores utilize special advising resources, upperclassmen are assigned an advisor in their concentration, and a pool of interdisciplinary faculty counselors is on hand for general academic advising problems.

> **"Professors come to Brown because they want to teach undergrads."**

Brown offers more than 100 freshman courses via the Curricular Advising Program (CAP), and the professors in these courses officially serve as academic advisors for their students' first year. Upper-level classes are usually in the teens, CAP courses are limited to 20, and only 19 percent of introductory lectures have more than 50 students. Especially popular courses are usually jammed with students, and often there aren't enough teaching assistants to staff them effectively. Some popular smaller courses, especially writing courses in the English department and studio art courses, can be nearly impossible to get into, although the administration claims that perseverance makes perfect—in other words, show up the first day and beg shamelessly. Compared with the other Ivies, Brown's academic climate is relatively casual and students don't fret about competition. "A great deal of peer-to-peer learning occurs here at Brown," says one student. Another adds, "The only competition I've felt has been with myself to do well."

"There are some major geeks," says one student, "but most students are very well balanced and sociable." With a mere 5 percent of students hailing from Rhode Island, geographical diversity is one of Brown's hallmarks. Consistent with its Rhode Island location and with the spirit of openness that persists to this day, Brown was the first Ivy League school to accept students from all religious affiliations. Today, Brown is one of the few remaining hot spots of student activism in the nation; nary has a semester passed without at least one demonstration about the issue of the day. African Americans comprise 11 percent of the student body, Hispanics 13 percent, and Asian Americans 18 percent; 11 percent are international students. Minorities rarely miss an opportunity to speak out on issues of concern, and the gay and lesbian community is also prominent. "They throw the best dances on campus," says one science major. Ninety-eight percent of students were in the top quarter of their high school class, and 40 percent hail from private or parochial schools.

Brown admits most students regardless of their financial need (transfer and international students excepted), and although it doesn't offer athletic or academic merit scholarships, it does guarantee to meet the full demonstrated need of everyone admitted. The university has also eliminated loans for families with incomes below $100,000 a year and eliminated tuition for those with incomes up to $60,000 a year. Fifteen Starr National Service scholarships, ranging from $1,000 to $2,000, are awarded each year to students who devote a year or more to volunteer public service jobs.

Freshmen arrive on campus a few days before everyone else for orientation, which includes a trip to Newport, and there is also a Third World Transition Program. About half the freshmen are assigned to one of eight co-ed Keeney Quad dorms, in

Particularly adventurous students can choose to spend time in one of Brown's more than 50 study abroad programs in 14 countries.

"loud and rambunctious" units of 30 to 40 with several sophomore or junior dorm counselors. The other half live in the quieter Pembroke campus dorms or in a few other scattered locations. After their freshman year, students seeking on-campus housing enter a lottery. The lottery is based on seniority, and sometimes the leftovers for sophomores can be a little skimpy, though there are some special program houses set aside to give them a chance to focus their interests in residential halls.

The dorms themselves are fairly nondescript. "Dorms are good and our housing lottery lets students pick exactly which room they want, which is great," says one student. Nevertheless, there are many options from which to choose, including apartment-like suites with kitchens, three sororities, two social dorms, and three co-ed fraternities. Brown guarantees housing all four years, and a dorm with suites of singles ensures that there is room for all. A significant number of upperclassmen get "off-campus permission." Apartments nearby are becoming more plentiful and more expensive as the area gentrifies. Brown's food service, which gets high marks from students for tastiness and variety, offers meal plans ranging from seven to twenty meals a week. Everyone on a meal plan gets a credit card that allows the student to do what students at every other school only wish they could: use the meal ticket for nocturnal visits to snack bars should they miss a regular meal in one of Brown's two dining halls. Campus security is described as "very good."

Providence is an old industrial city that has undergone a renaissance of sorts. Providence is Rhode Island's capital, so many internship opportunities in state government are available, as are a few good music joints, lively bars, and a number of fine, inexpensive restaurants. The city is also home to a number of colleges and universities, which helps to liven up the social scene. For the couch potato set, there are plenty of good things right in the neighborhood. "Downtown is a 10-minute walk, but why bother when you can buy anything from Cap'n Crunch to cowboy boots on Thayer Street, which runs through the east side of campus?" asks a philosophy major. For a change of scenery, many students head to Boston or the beaches of Newport, each an hour away.

The few residential Greek organizations are generally considered much too unmellow for Brown's taste (only 15 percent of the men and 5 percent of the women sign up), hence freshmen and sophomores are their chief clientele. The nonresidential black fraternities and sororities serve a more comprehensive student-life function. Tighter drinking rules have curtailed campus drinking somewhat. The university sponsors frequent campuswide parties and plays, concerts, and special events. Funk Nite every Thursday night at the Underground, a campus pub, draws a mixed bag of dancing fools. The biggest annual bash of the year is Spring Weekend, which includes plenty of parties and a big-name band. Strong theater and dance programs, daily and weekly newspapers, a skydiving club, political organizations, and "even a Scrabble club and a successful croquet team" represent just a few of the ways Brown students manage to keep themselves entertained. "There are hundreds of different social groups on campus," says one senior. Another place for entertainment is the campus student center, which has been thoroughly renovated. For those interested in community outreach—and there are many at Brown who are—the university's nationally recognized public service center helps place students in a variety of volunteer positions. The Brown Community Outreach, in fact, is the largest student organization on campus.

Brown isn't an especially sports-minded school, but a number of teams nevertheless manage to excel. Of the 37 varsity teams, recent Ivy League champions include the baseball, women's crew, men's tennis, and men's soccer teams. Athletic facilities include an Olympic-sized swimming pool and an indoor athletic complex with everything from tennis courts to weight rooms. There's also a basketball arena

> **Brown isn't an especially sports-minded school, but a number of teams nevertheless manage to excel.**

> **"Our housing lottery lets students pick exactly which room they want."**

for those trying to perfect their slam dunks. The intramural program is solid, mixing fun with competitiveness.

Ever since the days of Roger Williams, Rhode Island has been known as a land of tolerance, and Brown certainly is a 21st-century embodiment of this tradition. The education offered at this university is decidedly different from that provided by the rest of the Ivy League, or for that matter, by most of the country's top universities. Brown is content to gather a talented bunch of students, offer a diverse and imaginative array of courses, and then let the undergraduates, with a little help, make sense of it all. It takes an enormous amount of initiative, maturity, and self-confidence to thrive at Brown, but most students feel they are up to the challenge. "You get four years of choice," says one student. "Deal with it."

Overlaps

Columbia, Dartmouth, Harvard, University of Pennsylvania, Stanford, Yale

If You Apply To ➤

Brown: Early decision: Nov. 1. Regular admissions: Jan. 1. Application fee: $75. No campus interviews. Alumni interviews: optional, informational. SATs or ACTs: required. Subject Tests: required (any two). Accepts the Common Application. Essay question: academic interests; personal statement.

Bryn Mawr College

101 North Merton Avenue, Bryn Mawr, PA 19010-2899

BMC has the most brainpower per capita of the elite women's colleges. Politics range from liberal to radical. Honor code shapes the campus culture. Bryn Mawrtyrs may take themselves a bit too seriously. The college still benefits from ties to nearby Haverford, though the relationship is not as close as in the days when Haverford was all male. A train station just off campus offers easy access to Philadelphia.

Website: www.brynmawr.edu
Location: City Outskirts
Private
Total Enrollment: 1,652
Undergraduates: 1,305
Male/Female: 0/100
SAT Ranges: CR 600–710, M 590–720
ACT Ranges: 26–30
Financial Aid: 76%
Expense: Pr $ $ $
Student Loans: 52%
Average Debt: $ $
Phi Beta Kappa: No
Applicants: 2,626
Accepted: 41%
Enrolled: 34%
Grad in 6 Years: 82%
Returning Freshmen: 90%
Academics: ✐ ✐ ✐ ✐ ✐
Social: ☎ ☎ ☎
Q of L: ★ ★ ★

Leafy suburban enclaves are a dime a dozen around Philadelphia, but only one is home to Bryn Mawr College, a top-notch liberal arts school that happens to be all-female. On this campus, students find a range of academic pursuits from archeology to film studies to physics, and a diverse yet community-oriented student body. Founded in 1885, Bryn Mawr has evolved into a hotbed of intellectualism that prepares students for life and work in a global environment. Although students here abide by a strict academic honor code and participate in a host of long-standing campus traditions, they remain doggedly individualistic. "Bryn Mawr is a place where you will figure out who you are and what you want to do with your life," says a sophomore.

> "Bryn Mawr is a place where you will figure out who you are and what you want to do."

Bryn Mawr's lovely campus is a path-laced oasis set among trees (many carefully labeled with Latin and English names) and lush green hills, perfect for an afternoon walk, bike ride, or jog. Just a 20-minute train ride from downtown Philadelphia, Bryn Mawr provides a country setting with a vital and exciting city nearby. The predominant architecture is collegiate Gothic, a combination of the Gothic architecture of Oxford and Cambridge Universities and the local landscape, a style that Bryn Mawr introduced to the United States. Ten of Bryn Mawr's buildings are listed in the National Register of Historic Places. The M. Carey Thomas Library, which was named after the school's first dean and second president, a pioneer in women's education, is also a National Historic Landmark. Variations on the collegiate Gothic theme include a sprinkling of modern buildings, such as Louis Kahn's slate-and-concrete residence hall and the redbrick foreign language dormitory.

Out of respect for their academic honor code, students refrain from discussing their grades, but they freely admit that they work hard. "Bryn Mawr is far from competitive," says a sophomore, "but it is certainly challenging." Most departments are strong, especially the sciences, classics, archeology, art history, and the foreign languages, including Russian and Chinese. Doing serious work in music, art, photography, or astronomy requires a hike over to Haverford, Bryn Mawr's nearby partner in the bicollege system. Five hundred Bryn Mawr students a year take courses at Haverford. The unique relationship between Bryn Mawr and Haverford dates to more than 25 years ago. This unique consortium allows students at each institution to take courses, use the facilities, eat, and even live in the dormitories of the other. Bryn Mawr and Haverford students cooperate on a weekly newspaper, radio station, orchestra, and other clubs and sports, and a free shuttle bus connects the campuses. Students may also cross-register with Swarthmore and Penn or participate in a 3–2 engineering program through Caltech. Approximately one-third of students study overseas during their junior year; students choose from more than 70 programs in nearly 30 countries. Projects range from fieldwork in the Aleutian Islands with the anthropology department to studying Viennese architecture with the growth and structure of cities department.

> "Bryn Mawr is far from competitive."

(continued)

Admissions: (610) 526-5152
Email Address: admissions@ brynmawr.edu

Strongest Programs:
Archeology
Growth and Structure of Cities
Physics
Mathematics
Art History
Classics
Foreign Languages

The general education requirements include two classes in each of the three divisions (social sciences, natural sciences, and the humanities), one semester of "quantitative" work, an intermediate level of competency in a foreign language, and the requirements of a major. Students are also required to take eight half-semesters of physical education and must also pass a swimming test. In addition, all freshmen are required to take two college seminars to develop their critical thinking, writing, and discussion skills. The 360-Degree program is an interdisciplinary experience that engages several aspects of a topic or theme, giving students an opportunity to thoroughly investigate a multitude of perspectives. Students take a cluster of courses focusing on the history, economic concerns, cultural intersections, and political impact of an era, decision, event, policy, or important innovation.

> "Students here are engaged, passionate, intellectual, and most carry an intensity with them that drives them to succeed."

The quality of teaching at Bryn Mawr is unquestionably high. "Professors really want to get to know you and to expand your horizons," a sophomore says. Freshmen and transfer students are initiated to the Bryn Mawr experience during Customs Week, which includes a variety of seminars and workshops as well as a tour of the campus and town. For those looking ahead to see what the steep tuition will buy in the long term, the campus has a career resource center that offers information on interviewing and building a résumé.

"Students here are engaged, passionate, intellectual, and most carry an intensity with them that drives them to succeed but can also feel overpowering to outsiders," a history major says. African Americans make up 6 percent of the student body, Hispanics 10 percent, and Asian Americans 13 percent. To encourage diversity and harmony on campus, freshmen can take an intensive four-hour session during orientation on pluralism, which teaches students to examine assumptions about class, race, and sexual orientation. "Mawrtyrs are intellectually curious and stimulating," says a biology major, who adds, "We are willing to roll up our sleeves, whether it is to solve a complex math proof or fight poverty. Many of us are idealists, and we are not afraid to admit it or fight for what we believe in." There are no merit or athletic scholarships, but the school does guarantee to meet the demonstrated financial need of everyone admitted.

Another guarantee is quality on-campus housing for all four years; 93 percent of the student body reside on campus. "I think all of our dorms are beautiful, charming,

Doing serious work in music, art, photography, or astronomy requires a hike over to Haverford, Bryn Mawr's nearby partner in the bicollege system.

Freshmen and transfer students are initiated to the Bryn Mawr experience during Customs Week.

and comfortable," says one sophomore. Dorm features include hardwood floors, window seats, and fireplaces, says another senior. For good reason, the food service has received a national award from *Restaurants and Institutions* magazine. Choices are plentiful and tasty, according to students. "Our dining halls are constantly working to provide vegetarian and vegan options," says one French major. "We also have a nutritionist available for students to consult should they have dietary restrictions as well."

Bryn Mawr is located on suburban Philly's wealthy Main Line (named after a railroad), and the campus is two blocks from the train station. "We have everything you need within walking distance," a student says. A 20-minute train ride provides students with easy access to cultural attractions, as well as social and academic events at the nearby University of Pennsylvania. "Social life comes in many forms," says a student. "If you want big frat parties, that would mostly be off campus at Haverford or UPenn. However, Bryn Mawr has parties as well, in addition to concerts, plays, readings, comedians, dances, and more."

Tradition is a very important part of the campus social scene. The Elizabethan-style May Day festivities are held the Sunday after classes end in May. Everyone wears white, eats strawberries, and watches Greek plays. Students are known to skinny-dip in the fountains and drink champagne on the lawn. The presentation of lanterns and class colors to incoming freshmen on Lantern Night, and regal pageants, such as Parade Night, Hell Week, and Step-Sings, fill life with a Gothic sense of wonder and school spirit. Says a student, "They play a big role in uniting all four classes and give students a role in the greater history of the college."

As for athletics, the Bryn Mawr Owls compete in the Division III Centennial Conference. Students are active in 12 intramural sports, including rugby, cross-country, volleyball, and field hockey. And, of course, there's always the champion badminton team. Club sports range from all-female teams, such as rugby, squash, and figure skating, to co-ed teams shared with Haverford College, such as ultimate Frisbee and fencing.

Bryn Mawr is a study in contrasts: the campus is in suburbia, but steps from a major city. Humanities programs are very strong, but science majors are also enormously popular. The students are independent but revel in college traditions. The result is overwhelmingly positive. Says a junior, "When you are surrounded by strong, talented, driven women who respect you, it inspires you to be like them."

The presentation of lanterns and class colors to incoming freshmen on Lantern Night, and regal pageants, such as Parade Night, Hell Week, and Step-Sings, fill life with a Gothic sense of wonder and school spirit.

Overlaps

Barnard, Brown, Haverford, Mount Holyoke, Smith, Swarthmore, Wellesley, Yale

If You Apply To ➤ **Bryn Mawr:** Early decision: Nov. 15. Early action and regular admissions: Jan. 15. Application fee: $50 (paper), free (online). Campus and alumnae interviews: recommended, evaluative. SATs or ACTs: required. Subject Tests: required (any two). Accepts the Common Application. Essay question.

Bucknell University

Lewisburg, PA 17837

Bucknell, Colgate, Hamilton, Lafayette—all a little more conservative than the Ivy schools, and all just a little less selective. Bucknell is the biggest of this bunch and, like Lehigh, offers engineering. Bucknell's Greek system is strong, but students don't join until they are sophomores. The central Pennsylvania campus is isolated but one of the most beautiful anywhere.

The students at Bucknell University strike a healthy balance between hitting the books and hitting the bars or the frat houses of their pastoral central Pennsylvania campus. Yes, they tend to be preppy and outdoorsy: "Bucknell students are mostly upper-middle class, relatively conservative, and materially conscious. However, they are also highly motivated and eager to succeed," says one junior. With small classes, engaging faculty, and not a subpar dorm to be found, it's no wonder students complain that "four years at Bucknell go by way too fast," says a junior.

"Bucknell is always doing structural improvements."

In addition to being comfortable and friendly, Bucknell is physically beautiful. Located on a hill just south of quaint Lewisburg, the campus overlooks the scenic Susquehanna River valley. Playing fields, shaded by leafy trees, are sprinkled among the Greek Revival buildings. While some structures date from the 19th century, lending a fairy-tale quality, others are far more modern, including an $8 million engineering building. "Bucknell is always doing structural improvements," confirms one student. Three major projects in the area south of the library include Academic East, a 60,000-square-foot facility facing Academic West; residence halls; a student commons and an arts building.

Students in Bucknell's College of Arts and Sciences must complete general education courses in three areas: Intellectual Skills (including a writing-intensive seminar), Tools for Critical Engagement, and Disciplinary Perspectives. Students must also take a foreign language, and are encouraged to take a course that addresses quantitative literacy, and an Integrated Perspectives course. In the College of Engineering, students have a common first semester, including a special course that introduces them to all five engineering disciplines. Along with major-related requirements, each student completes a capstone project during senior year, and must demonstrate competence in writing in order to graduate.

After fulfilling Bucknell's many requirements, students select from a variety of courses, including the popular Management 101, where students create and sell a product and donate their profits to charity. Approximately 45 percent of each graduating class studies abroad, and programs staffed by Bucknell professors take them to England, France, and Spain. Relationships with other colleges and universities enable students—including engineers—to travel to nearly 50 other nations, from Japan and Sweden to China,

"The coursework and overall academic climate is extremely rigorous."

Argentina, and Australia. The College of Engineering has one of the highest participation rates for study abroad for students in an engineering program. It also offers a specialized course taught by Bucknell engineering faculty and spans three weeks at the end of each spring semester in locations that have included Argentina, Western Europe, Scandinavia, and Brazil. The two-summer Institute of Leadership in Technology and Management allows engineering and management students to learn new ways to solve problems, while building their teamwork and communication skills. On-campus study the first summer is followed by an off-campus internship during the second. Honors programs attract scholars and the Presidential Scholars Program offers talented undergrads an opportunity to fulfill the work-study portion of their financial aid packages at higher wages than those for regular student employees.

Back on campus, 58 percent of courses have 19 or fewer students, and the emphasis is on discussion and group work. "The coursework and overall academic climate is extremely rigorous," says a senior. It also helps that professors come to Bucknell because they want to teach: "The quality of instruction is generally fabulous," says one vocal performance major, "with few exceptions." While Bucknell is known for engineering, management, and the natural sciences, students say academics

Website: www.bucknell.edu
Location: Small Town
Private
Total Enrollment: 3,545
Undergraduates: 3,498
Male/Female: 48/52
SAT Ranges: CR 580–680, M 620–710
ACT Ranges: 27–31
Financial Aid: 61%
Expense: Pr $ $ $ $
Student Loans: 55%
Average Debt: $
Phi Beta Kappa: Yes
Applicants: 8,291
Accepted: 27%
Enrolled: 41%
Grad in 6 Years: 90%
Returning Freshmen: 95%
Academics: ✍ ✍ ✍ ✍
Social: ☎ ☎ ☎ ☎
Q of L: ★ ★ ★
Admissions: (570) 577-1101
Email Address: admissions@ bucknell.edu

Strongest Programs:
Economics
Management
Biology
Psychology
Political Science
Chemistry
Geography
Linguistics

The College of Engineering has one of the highest participation rates for study abroad for students in an engineering program.

are strong across the curriculum and weaker programs are hard to find. "Even the smaller departments have dedicated professors and loyal students," says a junior. Administrators highlight programs in animal behavior, which benefit from an outdoor naturalistic primate facility for teaching and research, and in environmental studies, which includes not only science courses but also courses in the humanities, social policy, and civil engineering, too.

"Bucknell students are very competitive and very concerned with social life," says one junior. Twenty-two percent are Pennsylvanians, and 61 percent went to public high school. Diversity has been slow in coming; Asian Americans account for 3 percent of the student body, while African Americans comprise 3 percent and Hispanics add another 5 percent. "Students are fairly apathetic, but political groups are very active," reports one student. Hot issues include the environment and free speech, according to one senior, and the student body "is on the whole liberal." Each year, Bucknell awards a small number of merit scholarships as well as 81 athletic scholarships in 10 sports.

Eighty-six percent of Bucknellians live on campus; all first-years are required to do so, and since upperclassmen must obtain permission to leave, more than 300 live in five college-owned apartment buildings. "The dorms are wonderful for freshmen," says a senior, "but for upperclassmen not in a residential college, on-campus housing can be tough." Some singles have been converted to doubles, and doubles have become triples. About 25 percent of each entering class affiliates with one of the eight intellectually focused "colleges": Discovery, Arts, Humanities, Environmental, Global, Languages and Cultures, Social Justice, and Society and Technology; a seminar on the theme of their college replaces the required Foundation Seminar that their classmates take. Students report that Bucknell dining is better than your average institutional fare and includes "provisions for vegans and vegetarians."

"Even the smaller departments have dedicated professors and loyal students."

"Most of the social life at Bucknell takes place on campus or in the immediate vicinity," a mechanical engineering major reports. Bucknell's robust Greek system draws 39 percent of the men and 43 percent of the women, though rush is delayed until the start of sophomore year. And while the Greeks are a driving force in campus social life, there are alternatives. "Parties on campus are a lot of fun and the majority of students are active members of the social scene," one student explains. Two student organizations arrange everything from carnivals to hypnotists to religious retreats, while the nonalcoholic, school-run Uptown nightclub offers dancing 'til dawn. When it comes to drinking, a point system hasn't stopped those younger than 21 from drinking, but it does provide for clarity and proportionality when offenses occur. "The policy is well enforced and keeps everyone responsible," offers one sophomore.

Lewisburg is "small, rural, and can be a bit of a shock to students coming from larger cities," says one sophomore. Market Street has boutiques, restaurants, and an old-style movie theater that serves up first-run flicks. The nearby town of Bloomsburg offers a more ethnic feel, with Indian and Thai cuisine. Through the "I Serve 2" campaign, Bucknell is trying to get all students to complete at least two hours of community service each semester. Projects are coordinated through the Bucknellians in Service to Our Neighbors program (BISON). When students get claustrophobic, New York, Philadelphia, and Washington/Baltimore are less than three hours away; the main campus of Penn State, in State College, Pennsylvania, is even closer. Bucknell also sponsors road trips to these communities for students who lack wheels.

Favorite traditions include Midnight Mania (the official start of the basketball season), the formal Chrysalis Ball in the spring, and First Night, "a ceremony congratulating first-year students on the completion of their first semester," says a junior. "They learn the alma mater and serenade the president and his wife."

"A great tradition occurs during orientation when the entire first-year class walks through the Christy Mathewson Gates. Four years later, at graduation, you walk through the gates in the opposite direction," says a sophomore.

The Bucknell Bison have captured the Patriot League Presidents' Cup, for the league's all-sports champion, 18 times in 23 years—including seven of the last eight. Men's and women's cross-country and track and field are perennially strong and have combined for dozens of Patriot League championships since 1990. Men's and women's swimming and diving are also notable, while the women's crew team won a gold medal at Philadelphia's Dad Vail Regatta in recent years. Bucknell's biggest rivalries are with Lafayette and Lehigh, though these aren't a tremendous focus. "Bucknell is a basketball school," says one student. Notably, Bucknell's athletic program ranks among the top 10 Division I institutions in graduation rates and is fifth nationally in total number of Academic All-Americans. Intramural and club sports draw about a third of the students.

> **"Bucknell students are very competitive and very concerned with social life."**

Bucknell students get the best of several worlds: excellence in engineering and the liberal arts, abundant research opportunities, and a healthy social life. "Bucknell is the ideal college environment," says a sophomore. "The strong sense of community really instills pride in everyone." The school's central Pennsylvania location is lovely but isolated, and the preponderance of preppies may seem stifling, but this campus is slowly becoming both more liberal and more diverse. If you're seeking small classes and professors who really care, in a supportive environment with plenty of school spirit, Bucknell may be a good fit.

Overlaps

Lehigh, Villanova, Colgate, Boston College, Penn State, Lafayette, Cornell, University of Virginia

If You Apply To ➤   **Bucknell:** Early decision: Nov. 15. Regular admissions: Jan. 15. Application fee: $60. No campus or alumni interviews. SATs or ACTs: required. No Subject Tests. Accepts the Common Application. Essay question: personal statement.

Butler University

Indianapolis, IN 46208

Small, private university with an attractive campus near Indianapolis and a relaxed Midwestern feel. Butler combines a strong liberal arts emphasis with practical learning. Strong in dance and international business. Classes are small with no TAs. Students are a homogeneous lot who share Indiana's trademark passion for basketball. Larger than DePauw, smaller than Northwestern.

College hoops fans may recognize Butler University as the unheralded outsider who fought its way to the final game of the NCAA Division I Basketball Championships not once but twice in recent years. But those who attend this small Midwestern university know that Bulldogs basketball is representative of the Butler way of life, which emphasizes teamwork, tenacity, and solid fundamentals. "Butler University offers quality education, friendly and approachable professors, plenty of opportunities for involvement, and an overall friendly atmosphere," says one public and corporate communications major. Despite the sometimes claustrophobic atmosphere of the "Butler Bubble," most students find the school's cozy campus and solid academics to be a slam dunk.

Website: www.butler.edu
Location: City Center
Private
Total Enrollment: 4,272
Undergraduates: 3,923
Male/Female: 40/60
SAT Ranges: CR 530–630, M 540–650
ACT Ranges: 25–30

(continued)

Financial Aid: 92%

Expense: Pr $

Student Loans: 64%

Average Debt: $ $ $ $

Phi Beta Kappa: No

Applicants: 9,682

Accepted: 66%

Enrolled: 17%

Grad in 6 Years: 73%

Returning Freshmen: 91%

Academics: ✍ ✍ ✍

Social: ☎ ☎ ☎

Q of L: ★ ★ ★ ★

Admissions: (317) 940-8100

Email Address: admission@
   butler.edu

Strongest Programs:

Natural and Health Sciences

Dance

Business Marketing

Accounting

Education

Journalism

Communication Disorders

English and Creative Writing

International Business

*The university's most
popular programs
are also among its
best and include
pharmacy, biology,
marketing, chemistry,
and early and middle
childhood education.*

Located five miles from downtown Indianapolis in the city's historic Butler-Tarkington neighborhood, Butler University's 290-acre campus is hailed as one of the most attractive in the Midwest for its parklike setting, which includes centuries-old trees, open landscaped malls, curving sidewalks and fountains, a nature

> "Butler University offers quality education, friendly and approachable professors."

preserve, prairie, historical canal, formal botanical garden, an observatory, and jogging paths. The first building, Jordan Hall, features Gothic architecture and has set the tone for subsequent buildings. Butler's Hinkle Fieldhouse, which opened in 1928, has reigned as one of the nation's great sports arenas for more than six decades. A 42,000-square-foot pharmacy building features large, tiered lecture rooms, a pharmacy lab, patient examination rooms, offices, and study spaces. Newer facilities include a performing arts venue and Efroymson Center, home of the Butler MFA Creative Writing Program.

Courses at Butler are "challenging but manageable," says a senior. "Because the student-to-professor ratio is much smaller than at other universities, students have to be fully prepared for each class and have to be willing to participate." The university's most popular programs are also among its best and include pharmacy, biology, marketing, chemistry, and early and middle childhood education. "I believe the best academic departments are the College of Business and the College of Pharmacy and Health Sciences because they have unique curriculum and are proven to prepare students for life after graduation," says one marketing major. Other solid offerings include English and creative writing, psychology, and political science. The Risk Management and Insurance (RMI) program focuses on teaching students how to mitigate and manage risks through a combination of insurance and non-insurance techniques; graduates of the program can work in the insurance and financial services industries.

Regardless of major, students must complete Butler's core curriculum. Students enroll in two common elements: First Year Seminar, a two-semester sequence in their first year, and Global and Historical Studies, a sophomore-year sequence of courses. They must also complete courses in six general areas of inquiry: Analytic Reasoning, The Natural World, Perspectives in the Creative Arts, Physical Well-Being, The Social World, and Texts and Ideas. Butler students also complete Writing

> "Students have to be fully prepared for each class and have to be willing to participate."

Across the Curriculum and Speaking Across the Curriculum requirements, as well as two experiences designed to connect them to the campus community: the Indianapolis Community Requirement and the Butler Cultural Requirement. Fifty-one percent of classes have 19 or fewer students, and the majority of classes taken by freshmen are taught by full professors. "Every so often you get a professor that isn't that great, but never are they terrible," says a junior.

The Butler Honors program is designed to foster a diverse and challenging intellectual climate and features courses, events, independent study, and research opportunities. The competitive Undergraduate Student Research program invites up to four students annually to conduct research under the guidance of a faculty mentor; participants also receive a stipend. For those who wish to travel to far-flung locales around the globe, Butler offers more than 110 study abroad programs in over 40 countries, including Australia, Ireland, Spain, Germany, China (Hong Kong), Ghana, India, and Peru. Nearly one-third of Butler students participate. "Study abroad programs are very important to students on campus," a chemistry major confirms.

Forty-nine percent of Butler students come from Indiana, and "most come from middle- to upper-class families and are very well put together," according to one student. "They are all very bright and very welcoming. The school isn't really cliquey," adds a freshman. Seventy-seven percent ranked in the top quarter of their high school class and eight out of 10 attended public high school. African Americans account for 4 percent of the student body, Hispanics 3 percent, and Asian Americans 3 percent. Social and political issues elicit quiet shrugs from most: "I wouldn't say that there are any major social issues on campus," says one student. Still, Butler does receive its share of complaints, including the lack of parking and cost to attend. Merit and athletic scholarships are available to qualified students.

Sixty-nine percent of students live in university-sponsored housing, and all but seniors are required to do so. "Students are given the opportunity to share very comfortable places with other roommates, either in the dormitories, houses, fraternity houses, or apartments—all with Wi-Fi access," says a senior. The university offers a number of housing options, including an all-female hall, co-ed halls, a suite-style facility and apartment building for continuing students and eligible transfer students, and the Apartment Village, which houses juniors and seniors. "With so many housing options for our student body, there is no trouble getting a room," a sophomore says. Students may dine in the student union or one of two campus dining halls, where food is said to be edible and diverse. "The dining facilities are so-so. The food isn't really that great, but they make up for that by giving a wide variety of options," says a pharmacy major. And while Butler is "not in the best part of town," students report feeling safe on campus: "Butler is a very tight-knit community and we all look out for each other," says a junior, "but it also feels good to know that our campus security, BUPD, is always there."

"During the first two years, most of the social life occurs on campus," a pharmacy student reports. "A lot of students venture out to the fraternities on the weekends. Once they turn 21, a lot of students spend the weekends at local bars in Broad Ripple or downtown." Greek life attracts 27 percent of the men and 31 percent of the women, and although the university is a wet campus, students say the social scene doesn't revolve around booze. Students seeking new vibes head off campus and into Indianapolis, where bars, restaurants, and cultural events are plentiful. "Students can attend performances by the Indianapolis Symphony Orchestra, a game by the Indiana Pacers, go to Circle Center Mall, or even visit the Indianapolis Children's Museum," says one adventurous sophomore. Volunteering is a favorite pastime and traditions include homecoming week, "where students decorate the lawns of the Greek houses, participate in Yell Like Hell, and make a midnight snack run," according to a marketing and finance major.

"During the first two years, most of the social life occurs on campus."

Butler fields nearly 20 NCAA Division I teams (the Bulldogs), and all but one compete in the Horizon League—the football team is a member of the Pioneer Football League. Men's basketball, men's soccer, men's and women's cross-country, women's golf, and football are solid. Nearly half of the student body participate in intramurals; the most popular include volleyball, five-on-five basketball, flag football, outdoor soccer, and ultimate Frisbee.

Butler University desires to provide students with a strong undergraduate liberal arts experience and access to professional programs of "local impact and global reach." "Butler cares about its students as individuals," says one freshman, and students have taken note of the school's revamped programs, improved facilities, and focus on personal attention. Although the school's size can feel limiting ("It can sometimes feel like 'Butler High School,'" quips a student), most seem to value the small classes and close-knit campus vibe. "Butler truly becomes a community for our students," says a sophomore. "The students and faculty all work to make Butler life an enjoyable experience for all."

Butler offers more than 110 study abroad programs in over 40 countries, including Australia, Ireland, Spain, Germany, China (Hong Kong), Ghana, India, and Peru.

Butler fields nearly 20 NCAA Division I teams (the Bulldogs), and all but one compete in the Horizon League.

Overlaps
Indiana University, Purdue, Ball State, Miami (OH), Marquette, Drake, Xavier, DePauw

California Colleges and Universities

Once a bargain, the University of California system is now one of the priciest of any in the country. This is especially true for out-of-state students, for whom the total cost rivals expensive private institutions. California's three-tiered system of colleges and universities has long been viewed as a model of excellence by other public higher education institutions nationwide and even around the world. The system offers a wealth of educational riches, including world-class research universities, enough Nobel Prize winners to fill a classroom, and colleges on the cutting edge of everything from film to viticulture. Underlying the creation of this remarkable system was a commitment to the notion that all qualified Californians, whatever their economic status, were entitled to the benefits of a college education.

Unfortunately, the well-publicized financial turmoil that has racked the State of California is playing havoc with the ability of its public colleges and universities to fulfill their traditional mission. The state's higher education budget was slashed by $650 million in 2011 and other cuts have followed. For students, the practical impact is taking the form of larger classes, reduced course offerings, and—surprise, surprise—a big increase in student fees that pushes the cost at a UC university up over the $31,000 mark (including tuition, fees, room and board, and a supplies allowance). There is talk of eliminating the research mission of some UC universities entirely, while access to the state universities and community colleges faces restrictions.

The system is composed of the 10 combined research and teaching units of the University of California (UC) and 23 state universities (CSU), including the newest CSU campus at Channel Islands, that focus primarily on undergraduate teaching. It also includes 106 two-year community colleges that offer both terminal degrees and the possibility of transferring into four-year institutions.

Admissions requirements for the three tiers and the institutions within them vary widely. Community colleges are open to virtually everyone with or without a high school diploma. The top third of California high school graduates (as measured statewide by a combination of SAT scores and grade point average) may attend one of the CSU campuses; all applicants must have taken a course in the fine or performing arts to be considered for admission. In the past, students in the top 9 percent of their class have been eligible to attend the University of California, though admission to their top-choice campus is not guaranteed. In-state students graduating in the top 4 percent of their high school class who meet regular admissions standards will be guaranteed admission to the UC system, although not to a particular campus. The 4 percent proposal is part of a plan to broaden the representation of California applicants and to give more weight to GPA. Out-of-state students continue to face ferocious competition for a limited number of spots while still paying more. Revised admissions guidelines took effect in 2012, increasing the number of California high school graduates who are considered for undergraduate admission by an estimated 40 percent and reducing the number of students in the state who are guaranteed admission based primarily on grades and test scores.

The University of California (UC) system boasts 220,000 students, 170,000 faculty and staff, and 1.4 million living alumni. Although one university system, the nine undergraduate UC campuses (San Francisco is for upper division and graduate students) each offer a full range of academic programs, and each has its own distinctive character. The most recent addition, Merced, opened in 2005 as the first American research university to be founded in the 21st century. In recent years, UC has moved from relying primarily on statistical academic information to a "comprehensive review" that takes into consideration not only coursework and test scores, but also leadership, special talent, and the educational opportunities available to each student. Subject Tests are no longer required; however, when applying to colleges or majors that are impacted, it can be to the student's benefit to submit Subject Test scores. For example, for engineering, it is highly recommended that students submit scores in Math 2,

Chemistry, and/or Physics. Despite state laws that prohibit the university from considering race in admission, the system remains dedicated to achieving a diverse student body. The university offers a number of outreach programs designed to assist low-income or educationally disadvantaged students who have promising academic potential with admissions and support services.

The California State University System is totally separate from the University of California; in fact, the two institutions have historically competed for funds as well as students. The largest system of senior higher education in the nation, CSU focuses on undergraduate education; while its members can offer master's degrees, they can award doctorates only in collaboration with a UC institution. Research in the state university system is severely restricted, a blow to CSU's national prestige but a big plus for students. Unlike UC, where the mandate to publish or perish is alive and well, teachers in the state system are there to teach. CSU's biggest problem is the success of UC, and its frequent lament—"Anywhere else we'd be number one"—is not without justification.

The 23-campus system caters to more than 417,000 students a year. And while most of the campuses serve mainly commuters, Chico, Humboldt, Monterey Bay, San Luis Obispo, and Sonoma stand out as residential campuses. While a solid liberal arts education is offered, the stress is usually on career-oriented professional training. Size varies dramatically, from more than 37,000 students at San Diego State and Long Beach to fewer than 4,000 at several other branches, like Channel Islands. Each campus has its own specific strengths, although in most cases a student's choice of school is dictated by location rather than by academic specialties. For those with a wider choice, some of the more distinctive campuses are profiled below.

Chico (enrollment 16,000), situated in the beautiful Sacramento Valley, draws a large majority of its students from outside a 100-mile radius and continues to become more selective in its admissions. The on-campus undergraduate life is strong and the social life is great. Bakersfield (7,900) and San Bernardino (17,700) boast residential villages along with more conventional dorms. The former is in a living/learning center with affiliated faculty members; the latter has its own swimming pool. California Polytechnic at San Luis Obispo (19,500) is the toughest state university to get into. It provides excellent training in the applied branches of such fields as agriculture, architecture, business, and engineering. Fresno (22,300), located in the Verdant Central Valley, has the only viticulture school in the state outside of UC–Davis, and undergraduates can work in the school winery. Yosemite, Kings Canyon, and Sequoia national parks are nearby.

San Diego State (36,500) is the balmiest of the campuses, and since it has a more residential, outdoorsy, and campus-oriented social scene, it appeals more to traditional-age undergraduates. "You could go for the weather alone—some do," says one former student. Contrasted with most other state schools, athletics are very important, and the academic offerings are almost as oriented to the liberal arts as at its UC neighbor at San Diego.

Humboldt State (7,700) is perched at the top of the state near the Oregon border in the heart of the redwoods. Humboldt's forestry and wildlife departments have national reputations, and the natural sciences are, in general, strong. Nursing majors have been dropped. Students have the run of excellent laboratory facilities and Redwood National Park. Most in-staters come here to get away from Los Angeles and enjoy the rugged coastline north of San Francisco. California Maritime Academy, located 30 miles northeast of San Francisco with 865 students, specializes in marine transportation, engineering, and maritime technology, and requires summer cruises on the T.S. *Golden Bear*. Monterey Bay, one mile from the beach with 4,000 students, 65 percent of whom live on campus, offers an interdisciplinary focus with a global perspective, opportunities for internships, and a unique Capstone Festival featuring the culminating projects of graduating seniors, credential candidates, and master's students.

To apply to a California State University campus, complete the electronic application available at www.CSUMentor.edu. You choose one campus to complete the first application. Once this application is completed, the data will automatically transfer to each additional campus. The only screen that must be completed per campus is the Enrollment Information screen (the first screen of the application). Students who apply to Cal Poly San Luis Obispo, however, must choose a major and complete additional screens. There is a $55 application fee for each campus.

To apply for admission to the University of California, students complete the electronic application available at www.universityofcalifornia.edu/admissions. Prospective students may apply to as many as nine UC undergraduate campuses on the application, and students are encouraged to apply to a minimum of four to augment their chances of gaining admission to at least one campus. It should be understood that each campus to which a student applies reviews the application using its own methodology and criteria. Decisions are thus campus-unique. (One campus does not know what another campus is planning to do with any given applicant.) There is a $60 fee for each campus. For each campus selected, students must choose a major and (in some cases) an alternate major.

110 Sproul Hall #5800, Berkeley, CA 94720-5800

Like everything else at Berkeley, the academic offerings can be overwhelming. With more than 25,000 undergraduate overachievers crammed into such a small space, it is no wonder that the academic climate is about as intense as you can get at a public university. Don't expect to be on a first-name basis with your professor in Intro Bio.

Website: www.berkeley.edu
Location: City Center
Public
Total Enrollment: 34,399
Undergraduates: 25,018
Male/Female: 48/52
SAT Ranges: CR 590–720,
    M 630–770
ACT Ranges: 27–33
Financial Aid: N/A
Expense: Pub $ $ $
Student Loans: 40%
Average Debt: $
Phi Beta Kappa: Yes
Applicants: 61,731
Accepted: 18%
Enrolled: 37%
Grad in 6 Years: 91%
Returning Freshmen: 96%
Academics: ✑ ✑ ✑ ✑ ✑
Social: ☎ ☎ ☎ ☎
Q of L: ★ ★ ★
Admissions: (510) 642-3175
Email Address: N/A

Strongest Programs:
Engineering
Architecture
Business
Theoretical Physics
Molecular and Cell Biology
Political Science
English

Berkeley. Mention the name, and even down-to-earth students get stars in their eyes. Students who come here want the biggest and best of everything, though sometimes that ideal runs headlong into budget cuts, tuition increases, and housing shortages. Never mind. Berkeley is where the action is. If you want a quick indicator of Berkeley's academic prowess, look no farther than the parking lot. The campus is dotted with spots marked "NL"—spots reserved for resident Nobel laureates. The last time anyone counted, Berkeley boasted 22 Nobel laureates, over 400 Guggenheim fellows, and a bevy of Pulitzer Prize recipients, MacArthur fellows, and Fulbright scholars. Is it any wonder that this radical institution of the '60s still maintains the kind of reputation that makes the top private universities take note? The social climate at this mother of UC schools is not as explosive as it once seemed to be, but don't expect anything tame on today's campus. Flower children and granola chompers still abound, as do fledgling Marxists, young Republicans, and body-pierced activists.

> **"Everyone was the top student in his or her high school class."**

Spread across 1,200 scenic acres on a hill overlooking San Francisco Bay, the Berkeley campus is a parklike oasis in a small city. The startlingly wide variety of architectural styles ranges from the stunning classical amphitheater to the modern University Art Museum draped in neon sculpture. Large expanses of grass dot the campus and are just "perfect for playing Frisbee or lying in the sun." The oaks along Strawberry Creek and the eucalyptus grove date back to Berkeley's beginnings nearly 140 years ago. Sproul Plaza, in the heart of the campus, is one of the great people-watching sites of the world. Stanley Hall serves as the Berkeley headquarters for the California Institute for Quantitative Biomedical Research (QB3). An office and lab complex supports interdisciplinary teaching and research as part of the campus's Health Science Initiative.

Of course, Berkeley is not only gorgeous; it's also academically intense. "Everyone was the top student in his or her high school class, so they can't settle for anything less than number one," says one student. A classmate concedes that "it can be a stressful environment, especially during the first years." Another says tersely, "Expect very little sleep." Some introductory courses, particularly in the sciences, have as many as 800 students, and professors, who must publish or perish from the university's highly competitive teaching ranks, devote a great deal of time to research. After all, Berkeley has made a large part of its reputation on its research and graduate programs, many of which rank among the best in the nation.

And while the undergraduate education is excellent, students take a gamble with the trickle-down theory, which holds out the promise that the intellectual might of those in the ivory towers will drip down to them eventually. As a political science major explains, "This system has allowed me to hear outstanding lectures from amazing professors who write the books we read, while allowing far more personal attention by the graduate-student instructors." Another student opines, "It's better to stand 50 feet from brilliance than five feet from mediocrity." Evidence of such gravitation is seen in the promising curricula designed specifically for freshmen and sophomores that include interdisciplinary courses in writing, public speaking, and the history of civilization and an offering of small student seminars (enrollment is limited to 15) taught by regular faculty. Despite these attempts at catering to undergraduates, the sheer number of students at Berkeley makes it difficult to treat each student as an individual. As a result, such things as academic counseling suffer. "Advising? You mean to tell me they have advising here?" asks one student.

Each of Berkeley's six undergraduate colleges or schools has its own set of general education requirements, which are generally not extensive, and many can be fulfilled through Advanced Placement exams in high school. All students, however, must take English composition and literature and one term each of American history and American institutions. Also, undergrads have an American cultures requirement for graduation—an original approach (via courses offered in several departments) to comparative study of ethnic groups in the United States.

Most of the departments at Berkeley are noteworthy, and some are about the best anywhere (like engineering and architecture). Business, sociology, mathematics, physics, chemistry, history, economics, and English are just a handful of the truly dazzling departments. Berkeley offers seven departments and seven interdisciplinary programs in engineering, and the biological sciences department integrates several undergraduate majors in biochemistry, biophysics, botany, zoology, and others into more interdisciplinary programs such as integrative biology and molecular and cell biology. The College of Natural Resources has five departments and participates in five interdisciplinary research centers.

Berkeley has made a large part of its reputation on its research and graduate programs, many of which rank among the best in the nation.

"Expect very little sleep."

Special programs abound at Berkeley, though it's up to the student to find out about them. "Our class enrollment system is much like playing a low-risk lottery," opines one undergrad. "Maybe you'll win, or maybe you won't. If anything, adding courses will definitely toughen up any person." Students may study abroad on fellowships at one of 50 centers around the world, or spend time in various internships around the country. If all you want to do is study, the library system, with more than eight million volumes, is one of the largest in the nation and maintains open stacks. The system consists of the main library (Doe-Moffitt) and more than 20 branch libraries, including the Hargrove Music Library.

Special programs abound at Berkeley, though it's up to the student to find out about them.

Thirty-seven percent of the student population is Asian American, 3 percent African American, and 13 percent Hispanic. The Coalition for Excellence and Diversity in Mathematics, Science, and Engineering, which provides women and minorities with undergraduate mentors in these fields, is highly regarded. The university also provides a variety of other programs to promote diversity, including Project DARE (Diversity Awareness through Resources and Education), the Center for Racial Education, and a Sexual Harassment Peer Education Program. Despite Berkeley's liberal reputation, the recent trend is away from the legacy of the free speech movement. Business majors and fraternity members outnumber young Communists and peaceniks, though the school does produce a large number of Peace Corps volunteers. In the past few

"It's better to stand 50 feet from brilliance than five feet from mediocrity."

years, outrageous fee hikes and severe budget cuts had some students wondering if a first-rate, affordable education had gone the way of the dinosaurs. The university has taken some measures to address these concerns: It is now capping the parental contributions of families making $80,000 to $140,000 a year.

Though the dorms have room for only 26 percent of the students, freshmen are guaranteed housing for their first and second years. After that, the Cal Rentals is a good resource for finding an apartment in town. Many students live a couple of miles off campus, where "apartments are cheaper," says one student. About two-thirds of the university's highly prized dorm rooms are reserved for freshmen, and the few singles go to resident assistants. A number of student-housing projects have opened in recent years, offering a variety of rooms in low-rise and high-rise settings. In the absence of a mandatory meal plan, everybody eats "wherever and whenever they wish," including in the dorms.

If the housing shortage gets you down, the beautiful California weather will probably take your mind off it in time. The BART subway system provides easy access to San Francisco, by far one of the most pleasant cities in the world and a cultural and countercultural mecca. The Bay Area boasts myriad professional sports teams, including the Oakland A's, the San Francisco 49ers, and the 2010 World Series winning San Francisco Giants. From opera to camping, San Francisco has a wide variety of activities to offer. Get access to a car, and you can hike in Yosemite National Park, ski and gamble in Nevada, taste wine in the Napa Valley, or visit the aquarium at Monterey. But be advised that a car is only an asset when you want to go out of town—students warn that parking in Berkeley is difficult, to say the least.

"Social life at UC–Berkeley is killer!"

"Social life at UC–Berkeley is killer!" exclaims one geography major. Weekends are generally spent in Berkeley, hanging out at the many bookstores, coffeehouses, and sidewalk cafés, heading to a fraternity or sorority party, or taking advantage of the many events right on campus. Berkeley is a quintessential college town ("kind of a crazy little town," opines one anthropology major), and of course, there's always the people-watching; where else can an individual meet people trying to convert pedestrians to strange New Age religions or revolutionary political causes on every street corner? Nearby Telegraph Avenue is famous (notorious?) for such antics every weekend. More than 1,200 student clubs and groups are registered on campus, which ensures that there is an outlet for just about any interest and that no one group will ever dominate campus life.

Despite all this activity, many students use the weekend to catch up on studying.

Despite all this activity, many students use the weekend to catch up on studying. Greeks have become more popular, with 10 percent of the men and women in a fraternity or sorority. Varsity athletics have always been important, with strengths in the men's gymnastics and crew teams. A surge in popularity for the Golden Bears basketball team probably has to do with its great performance in the Pac-12. And just about everyone turns out for the "Big Game" (football), where the favorite activity on the home side of the bleachers is bad-mouthing the rival school to the south: Stanford. Intramurals are popular, and the personal fitness craze is fed by an extensive recreational facility and gorgeous weather year-round. Students are also reviving an old tradition whereby they hike up Charter Hill and paint the giant "C" their class color.

The common denominator in the Berkeley community is academic motivation, along with the self-reliance that emerges from trying to make your mark among upward of 25,000 peers. Beyond that, the diversity of town and campus makes an extraordinarily free and exciting college environment for almost anyone. "It makes one feel free to dress, say, think, or do anything and not be chastised for being unorthodox," explains a student. "At Berkeley, it is worse to be dull than odd."

Overlaps

UC–Davis, UCLA, UC–San Diego, Harvard, Stanford

If You Apply To ➤

Berkeley: Regular admissions: Nov. 30. Financial aid: Mar. 2. Application fee: $70. No campus or alumni interviews. No letters of recommendation. SATs or ACTs (with writing): required. Subject Tests: recommended. Two pieces of writing limited to 1,000 words. Apply to a particular college, school, or program.

175 MRAK Hall, Davis, CA 95616

The closest thing to a cow college in the UC system, but with a cultured, upscale feel. Premed, prevet, food science—you name it. If the subject is living things, you can study it here. A small-town alternative to the bright lights of UC–Berkeley and UCLA. As is often true at science-oriented schools, the work is hard.

At the University of California–Davis, environmental studies and most everything that has to do with agriculture or biological science is noteworthy. The Aggies' cup truly runneth over. Originally known as the University of California Farm, the campus maintains its sprawling, verdant beauty, replete with native and imported forestry, charming bike paths, and mooing cows. But lest you assume this environmentally oriented university is full of quaint country folk, think again. Davis has become an international leader in the agricultural, biological, biotechnical, and environmental sciences.

Located 15 miles west of Sacramento and 72 miles north of San Francisco, the 6,000-acre campus is in the middle of a stretch of flat farmland that even Dorothy and Toto could mistake for Kansas. It features nearly 1,000 buildings with a blend of architectural styles, from traditional dairy barn to modern concrete. The hub of the university is a central area known as the Quad, one of many grassy open spaces on campus. Additional facilities include the Center for Comparative Medicine and a variety of seismic renovations. The 34,000-square-foot teaching and research center at the UC–Davis and Robert Mondavi Institute for Wine and Food Science is home to the world's first wireless wine fermentation system. A student community center opened in January 2012.

Though it has added programs in many disciplines over the past few years—including Chinese, Japanese, food engineering, and biological systems engineering—its biological and agricultural science departments are still the ones that shine. Animal science and engineering are strong departments, and the botany program is one of the best in the country. The school is "the no. 1 choice for any prevet," and it's great for premeds, too. The food sciences major is also stellar and not for the faint of heart or those afraid of chemistry. It was Davis food scientists who gave us the square tomato (better for packing into boxes), as well as more useful things such as the method for creating orange juice concentrate. Studio art, boasting several internationally known artists, is also among the top in the nation. Noteworthy special programs include the Interdisciplinary Electronics Arts (IDEA) Lab,

> **"The university has a challenging curriculum."**

which allows students to create electronically based productions by integrating photography, video, digital editing, and the Internet. Internships and co-op programs are well established, which is why many students remain for more than four years.

Faculty members here are expected to do top-level research as well as teach, so Davis is charged with both education and research. These two are uniquely blended when undergraduate students contribute to first-class research groups as paid technicians or volunteer interns. Davis also offers the innovative Washington Program, which gives undergraduates academic credits for internships in Congress, at federal agencies, and the like. Study abroad options include more than 150 host institutions in 35 countries. Many introductory courses are quite large, but Davis also offers 40 freshman seminars taught by the best instructors. The academic advising system generally gets high marks, but you must seek out their assistance. "They helped me plan a four-year college schedule and always kept me on track," says one student.

Website: admissions.ucdavis.edu
Location: Small City
Public
Total Enrollment: 32,354
Undergraduates: 25,276
Male/Female: 45/55
SAT Ranges: CR 520–640, M 570–690
ACT Ranges: 24–30
Financial Aid: 74%
Expense: Pub $ $ $ $
Student Loans: 55%
Average Debt: $
Phi Beta Kappa: Yes
Applicants: 49,333
Accepted: 46%
Enrolled: 23%
Grad in 6 Years: 81%
Returning Freshmen: 92%
Academics: ✍ ✍ ✍ ✍
Social: ☎ ☎ ☎
Q of L: ★ ★ ★ ★
Admissions: (530) 752-2971
Email Address: admissions.ucdavis.edu

Strongest Programs:
Environmental Studies
Botany
Animal Science
Viticulture
Agricultural Sciences
Studio Art
Biological Sciences
Engineering

The general education requirements stipulate that all students take courses in three broad areas: topical breadth, social-cultural diversity, and writing experience. These areas include courses in the arts and humanities, science and engineering, and the social sciences. Students may elect to take a general education theme option (sets of general education courses that share a common intellectual theme) and may now take courses as pass/no pass to fulfill their general education requirements.

The academic demands are high, and many students describe the atmosphere as competitive if not cut-throat (especially in the biological sciences). For students who still want more, the Davis Honors Challenge is designed for highly motivated, academically talented first- and second-year students who want to enhance their education through special courses. "The university has a challenging curriculum," says a senior, "but students see the value of supporting one another versus sabotaging other students to get ahead." The quality of teaching is generally high, according to students, and professors make themselves available outside of class. "Most of the teachers I have had were very high quality. Many would come in on weekends to offer study sessions and review sessions despite the fact that they were married

"Most of the teachers I have had were very high quality."

and had children," says one junior. "Like any large research university, though I have had a few that were clearly more interested in their research than their teaching."

A famous campus saying claims that "Davis students take notes at graduation." An environmental science major says, "Everyone at Davis is extremely friendly and down to earth for the most part. Most students are driven and focused but also value their time with friends and engaging in social activities." African Americans account for 2 percent of the students, Asian Americans 37 percent, and Hispanics 16 percent. Campus hot topics include fair labor practices and political correctness. In its pledge to foster awareness of diversity issues, the university has established an Office of Campus Diversity and a Cross-Cultural Center. UC–Davis boasts a graduation rate of 81 percent. Davis awards merit scholarships averaging $5,675 and there are 240 athletic awards in 23 sports.

Virtually all freshmen inhabit campus housing, which is well maintained and includes a number of theme houses. "Dorms are really nice and new and air conditioned. Housing is guaranteed the first two years," a student says. Six different meal plans for the dining halls are available, and one student says, "Healthy eating is also very important and they have a simple system to tell you if something is a good or bad choice.

"Everyone at Davis is extremely friendly and down to earth for the most part."

Each item's description is followed by anywhere between zero and four happy apple faces to tell you how good it is for you." A variety of nearby eating establishments serve the student clientele (no word on whether or not they also employ the "happy apple face" system) as well. Campus security is said to be sufficient. "Everyone I know feels very safe on campus," says one senior. "Our biggest crime is bike theft."

A car can come in handy if you are looking for a good meal in Sacramento (15 minutes) or a great one in San Francisco (a little more than an hour). Beaches are a two-hour drive from the campus, and the ski slopes and hiking trails of Lake Tahoe and the Sierra Nevada are a little closer. But if you feel, as most Davis students do, that studies are too important to be abandoned on weekends, the town has restaurants, activities, and entertainment enough to keep the stay-at-homes happy.

In between quizzes and cram sessions, the outlying countryside offers a welcome change of pace. The town of Davis itself is small, about 50,000, and students make up half the population. If some call it a cowtown, others call it peaceful, with its tree-lined streets and quiet nights. The relationship between college and town is one of rare cooperation (partly because the students are a significant voting bloc in local elections). Health and energy consciousness runs high in town and on the vast, architecturally diverse campus, where bicycles are the main form of transportation on the incredible 46 miles of bike paths that crisscross the campus and environs. "Bicycles are the norm at Davis. Don't come without one," advises one psych major. The university has encouraged environmental awareness by sponsoring solar energy projects and promoting such novelties as contests between dorms for the lowest heating and electric bills.

UC–Davis boasts a graduation rate of 81 percent.

"Social life is booming here at UC–Davis!" cheers one student. "There are over 400 clubs to get involved in! Also, Greek life can enhance social life." On-campus activities are varied, and many university-sponsored events fill the calendar. Active drama and music departments provide frequent entertainment, and there is plenty of room for homegrown talent in the coffeehouses, which offer mellow live entertainment and poetry readings on a regular basis. The 1,800-seat Mondavi Center for the Arts features international and local groups. Fraternities and sororities attract 6 percent of the men and 7 percent of the women, respectively. Alcohol is allowed in the dorms for those over 21 years old; those too young to imbibe have trouble finding booze, unless it's supplied by peers. Major annual social events include Picnic Day, in which alumni join current students in a massive outdoor shindig; African American Week; and the Whole Earth Festival, "an earthy, tie-dyed sort of event" in celebration of the '60s.

"Dorms are really nice and new and air conditioned."

Several years ago the university's varsity athletic teams, the Aggies, made the jump to Division I, where they compete in the Big West Conference along with fellow UC campuses Irvine, Riverside, and Santa Barbara. The Davis cycling team has won multiple national collegiate cycling championships and the annual Causeway Classic against rival Sacramento State stirs passions. Other solid teams include men's and women's golf, women's gymnastics, women's track and field, and women's lacrosse. But Davis students tend to prefer being participants rather than spectators: Each year more than 19,000 of them participate in over 60 club sports and intramurals. Given the Mediterranean climate, outdoor activities are the most popular. On this outdoor campus, almost everyone does something athletic—jogging, softball, tennis, swimming, or Frisbee—if only to break up the monotony of their studies with a different kind of competition.

Proud of its small-town atmosphere, Davis is not for the lazy or faint of heart. As one student says, "There's no free ride. You are going to have to work for everything you get." And most students get a lot out of their four or more years at Davis. It's the ideal spot to combine high-powered work in science and agriculture with that famous easygoing California lifestyle.

Overlaps
UC–Santa Barbara, UCLA, UC–Irvine, Caltech, UC–San Diego, UC–Berkeley, UC–Riverside

If You Apply To ➤

Davis: Regular admissions: Nov. 30. Financial aid: Mar. 2. Housing: May 1. Application fee: $70. No campus or alumni interviews. No letters of recommendation. SATs or ACTs (with writing): required. Subject Tests: optional. Two pieces of writing limited to 1,000 words. Apply to a particular college, school, or program.

UC–Irvine

260 ADM, Irvine, CA 92697

Irvine sits in the midst of one of the nation's biggest suburbs, combining funky, modern architecture with perhaps the most conservative student body in the UC system. Premed is the featured attraction, along with various other health-related offerings. Not quite as close to the beach as Santa Barbara—but close enough for students to go there often.

Website: www.uci.edu

Location: Suburban

Public

Total Enrollment: 26,432

Undergraduates: 21,878

Male/Female: 46/54

SAT Ranges: CR 470–610,
   M 540–670

ACT Ranges: 21–27

Financial Aid: 76%

Expense: Pub $ $ $ $

Student Loans: 50%

Average Debt: $

Phi Beta Kappa: Yes

Applicants: 56,508

Accepted: 42%

Enrolled: 21%

Grad in 6 Years: 86%

Returning Freshmen: 93%

Academics: ✍ ✍ ✍ ✍

Social: ☎ ☎

Q of L: ★ ★ ★

Admissions: (949) 824-6703

Email Address: admissions@
   uci.edu

Strongest Programs:

Biological Sciences

Economics

Information and Computer
   Science

Chemistry

Premed

There is no football team, but intramurals are extremely popular, as is the 5,000-seat multipurpose gym.

On the surface, UC–Irvine's clean, contemporary campus appears to be home to students who study diligently in the busy library, wear sensible shoes to biology lab, and resist that double shot of espresso at the local coffeehouse. But that image starts to dissipate as soon as you hear that bizarre noise: "Zot! Zot! Zot!" Then a UCI student explains that "it's the sound that an anteater supposedly makes when it swipes an ant with its tongue." Hey, any school that has a marauding anteater as a mascot can't be completely straitlaced. The university is, however, serious about its reputation as a school with stellar programs in biology and creative writing. The current academic climate can be quite serious and challenging, but as one UCI student swears, the Anteaters are "also surprisingly cooperative."

Located in the heart of Orange County and founded in 1965, UCI is among the newest of the UC campuses. Although enrollment is up and the administration has dreams of further expansion, "it is the perfect size," says one English major. UCI is liberally supplied with trees and shrubs from all over the world. Futuristic buildings are arranged in a circle around a large park, "giving it the appearance of a relaxed art school," says one observer. Undergraduates have long quipped that UCI stood for "Under Construction Indefinitely."

A "premed mentality" reigns at Irvine, since the School of Biological Sciences is the best and most competitive academic division. The School of Arts offers nationally ranked programs in dance, drama, music, studio art, and musical theater, as well as a minor in digital arts. The Beall Center for Art and Technology in the Claire Trevor School of the Arts enables students to explore the relationship between digital technology and the arts and sciences. The popular interdisciplinary School of Social Ecology offers courses combining criminology, environmental and legal studies, and psychology and social behavior, and strongly emphasizes teacher/student relationships. Like most of the other UC campuses, UCI is on a 10-week quarter system, so the pace is fast and furious. Students should face registration with the same determination, too; it's a tough fight to get into the science classes of choice as a sophomore.

"UCI is fairly competitive and the courses are moderately rigorous."

Languages are strong at UCI, as are the biggest nonbiology majors: economics; information and computer science; psychology; social behavior; criminology, law, and society; and a fiction-writing program that is gaining national recognition. Other programs of note include majors in computer game science and pharmaceutical studies. "UCI is fairly competitive and the courses are moderately rigorous," says a junior. Students may be overwhelmed by the size of most classes. Even seniors find their classes packed with 100 undergrads. "Graduate students teach lower-division writing courses," says one student, adding that "most classes are overcrowded, leaving little room for personal attention." The Center for Health Sciences focuses on five areas of research: neuroscience, genetics, cancer, infectious diseases, and aging. The university also houses the Reeve-Irvine Research Center, which supports the study of spinal cord trauma and disease with emphasis on finding a cure. The "breadth requirement" means that students must take three courses each in writing, natural sciences, social and behavioral sciences, and humanities in order to graduate. There is also a foreign language requirement, and one in math, statistics, or computer science, as well as requirements in multicultural and international/global issues. Honors programs are available in humanities, economics, psychology, political science, physics, cognitive sciences, anthropology, and mathematics.

Eighty-six percent of the student body are in-staters, the majority from Southern California and many of those from wealthy Orange County. The students are in general "much more conservative than at the other UC campuses," says one applied math major. Minorities account for well over half the student body, with Asian

Americans comprising 48 percent, African Americans 2 percent, and Hispanics 20 percent. "Cultural groups seem to segregate from each other more than I really like," says a senior. Merit scholarships are awarded annually and nearly 250 athletic awards are doled out in 18 sports.

Condominium-style dorms, both single sex and co-ed, are "exceptional compared to the high-rise dormitories of other institutions," says one senior. Others agree that the homey campus dwellings provide a good experience for freshmen, though finding a room can be a challenge. "If you really want on-campus housing," warns a student, "you need to make sure you meet the deadlines." Additional housing includes those with academic themes and ones especially for fraternities and sororities; most opt to move off campus after their first year. Currently, 21 percent of freshmen live off campus—many on the beach—giving the campus a commuter-school atmosphere. One student laments, "You have to find the social life on this campus. It won't find you."

> "You have to find the social life on this campus. It won't find you."

Still, the Greek scene is vigorous, attracting 9 percent of UCI men and 10 percent of the women. There are 18 sororities and 18 fraternities, and each has something going on every weekend. As for booze, UCI is a dry campus and students say finding a drink on campus without proper ID is difficult. Irvine touts many festivals that seem to attest to a celebration of diversity: the Rainbow Festival (cultural heritage), Asian Heritage week, Black History month, Cinco de Mayo, and rush week. The one event that brings everybody out is the daylong Wayzgoose, when the campus is transformed into a medieval fair complete with mimes, jugglers, and performers dressed up in medieval costumes.

> *There are 18 sororities and 18 fraternities, and each has something going on every weekend.*

But if life on campus is slow, beyond it is not. That's because the campus is located just 50 miles from L.A., five miles from the beach, and a little more than an hour from the ski slopes. Catalina Island, with beaches and hiking trails, is a quick boat trip off Newport Harbor; Mexico is two hours away. While some students treasure the quiet setting of Irvine, others lament its "lackluster, homogeneous communities." Notes one student, "UCI and the city of Irvine seem like completely different entities; the former is slightly liberal while the latter is ultraconservative."

Irvine fields 20 athletic teams and the Anteaters compete in Division I of the NCAA. Tennis and cross-country are perennial Big West powerhouses, and men's water polo has been ranked in the top five nationally for more than 20 of the last 32 years. There is no football team, but intramurals are extremely popular, as is the 5,000-seat multipurpose gym.

What lures students to UCI is its top-name professors, innovative academic programs, and the chance to be a part of its cutting-edge research. For the students who come here prepared to keep their heads buried in a book for a few years, the reward will be an exceptional education.

Overlaps

UC–Berkeley, UC–Davis, UC–Merced, UCLA, UC–Riverside, UC–San Diego, UC–Santa Barbara, UC–Santa Cruz

If You Apply To ➤

Irvine: Regular admissions: Nov. 30. Application fee: $70. No campus or alumni interviews. No letters of recommendation. SATs or ACTs (with writing): required. Subject Tests: recommended. Two pieces of writing limited to 1,000 words. Apply to a particular college, school, or program.

UC–Los Angeles

1147 Murphy Hall, 405 Hillgard A, Los Angeles, CA 90095

Tucked into exclusive Beverly Hills with the beach, the mountains, and chic Hollywood hangouts all within easy reach. The adjacent town of Westwood is an ideal student hangout. Practically everything is offered here, but the programs in arts and media are some of the best in the world. More conservative than Berkeley and nearly as difficult to get into.

Website: www.ucla.edu
Location: City Center
Public
Total Enrollment: 39,000
Undergraduates: 27,358
Male/Female: 45/55
SAT Ranges: CR 560–680,
   M 600–760
ACT Ranges: 25–31
Financial Aid: 58%
Expense: Pub $ $ $
Student Loans: 46%
Average Debt: $
Phi Beta Kappa: No
Applicants: 72,697
Accepted: 22%
Enrolled: 35%
Grad in 6 Years: 92%
Returning Freshmen: 96%
Academics: ✑ ✑ ✑ ✑ ✑
Social: ☎ ☎ ☎
Q of L: ★ ★ ★
Admissions: (310) 825-3101
Email Address: ugadm@
   saonet.ucla.edu

Strongest Programs:
Political Science
Psychology
History
Sociology
Economics

With stellar programs in music, film and television, journalism and communication, dance, and drama, you'd think UCLA was some kind of incubator for truly talented and gifted people. Or with a long list of well-known and highly accomplished alumni, maybe UCLA's some sort of farm that grows superstar athletes. Well, UCLA is all that and more. A superb faculty, a reputation for outstanding academics, and a powerful athletics program make this university the ultimate place to study.

UCLA's prime location—sandwiched between two glamorous neighborhoods (Beverly Hills and Bel Air) and a short drive away from Hollywood, the Sunset Strip, and downtown Los Angeles—makes it appealing for students who want more from their college experience than what classes offer. The beautifully landscaped 419-acre campus features a range of architectural styles, with Romanesque/Italian Renaissance as the dominant motif, providing only one of a number of reasons students enjoy staying on campus. A wealth of gardens—botanical, Japanese, and sculpture—add a touch of quiet elegance to the campus. Additional facilities include the California Nanosystems Institute, an array of studios and theaters, and the Orthopaedic Hospital/Luck Research Center.

> **"Teachers are very devoted and always make themselves available to students."**

Strong programs abound at UCLA, and many are considered among the best in the nation. The School of Engineering and Applied Science is highly regarded and sets the tone on campus. The School of Film, Theater, and Television is first-rate, and its students have the opportunity to study in Verona, Italy, with the Theater Overseas program. The popular music department offers a course in jazz studies, and the biological sciences are also highly regarded. Research opportunities abound at UCLA, and the university ranks seventh in the nation in federal funding for research. "I think the best department here is psychology," says a student, "since it is so highly ranked and is the most popular among students." Newer programs include B.A. and B.S. degrees in human biology and society and a master's degree in ecology and evolutionary biology.

Freshmen are encouraged to participate in a three-day summer orientation, which provides workshops, counseling, and a general introduction to the campus and community. Freshmen can also take a yearlong cluster of courses on topics such as the History of Modern Thought, or seminars with titles such as Asian American Youth: Culture, Identity and Ethnicity. During their first two years, most students take required core classes that are sometimes jammed with 300 to 400 people. But administrators are quick to point out that 80 percent of all undergraduate classes have fewer than 50 students. Savvy students come to UCLA with advanced courses in their high school backgrounds and test out of the intro courses. First-year students are required to take a course involving quantitative reasoning unless they hit 600 or higher on their math SAT, and English composition requirements should also be met during freshman year. Lab science and a language requirement are also necessary for a liberal arts degree. Simply getting into classes

> **"UCLA students are smart and active and passionate."**

here can be a big challenge, and common student complaints include the rising tuition and stifling bureaucracy.

UCLA's academic environment is extremely intense. The climate can be competitive due to the sheer number of students fighting to get in—UCLA gets more applications than any other college in the country. "The academics are rigorous and challenging, but there are many on-campus student resources like peer tutoring and study groups to help," says a junior. The faculty is also impressive. "Teachers are very devoted and always make themselves available to students," a senior says. On the other hand, there is a widespread sense here that undergraduate teaching is often sacrificed on behalf of scholarly research. "It isn't until upper divisions that you really get to know professors," confides a biology major. Concerned that too many majors have been requiring too little from students, the university is now encouraging departments to require "capstone" projects in which students must use the methodological training of their discipline and integrate what they have learned across topics and fields.

"At UCLA, students participate in numerous community service projects, social organizations, and get training for their futures through internships and research," says a junior. "UCLA students are smart and active and passionate." Asian Americans account for 36 percent of UCLA's student population, Hispanics make up 17 percent, African Americans 4 percent, and Native Americans less than 1 percent. UCLA has several student-run newsmagazines, including the feminist *Together* and the Asian American newsmagazine *Pacific Ties*. UCLA is one of the few universities in the nation with a gay fraternity and a lesbian sorority. Among major research universities, UCLA has the highest number of students receiving federal financial aid. Merit scholarships are also available, averaging more than $8,000 each.

> **"Whether you're a fan of the big party scene or more of a Friday-night-movie kind of person, there are opportunities both on and off campus."**

Ninety-two percent of the students live in university housing; freshmen and sophomores are guaranteed housing, but for everyone else it's strictly a waiting list. Overcrowding is a concern, though recent housing construction should provide enough space for all students to live on campus all four years. "The dorms are very comfortable and it feels as though the campus has an army of facilities workers that respond to any student need," a student says. The campus is philosophically divided into North and South. North attracts more liberal arts aficionados, while those in math and science tend to favor South. Fifteen dining halls, restaurants, and snack bars serve meals that students rave about. "There is an abundance of healthy and fresh choices, including vegetarian and vegan dishes," a senior says. Security gets a thumbs-up, too: "Campus security is excellent. We have our very own UCLA police department that caters primarily to the students here," a student reports.

Owing to the gargantuan size of UCLA, there is no shortage of social options on campus. "Whether you're a fan of the big party scene or more of a Friday-night-movie kind of person, there are opportunities both on and off campus," a sophomore says. The hopping Westwood suburb, which borders the university, has at least 15 movie theaters and scores of restaurants, but the shops cater to the upper class. "There's nowhere to dance and only two bars, but a lot of coffee and cheap food," a junior says. UCLA's Ocean Discovery Center on the Santa Monica Pier is an innovative, hands-on ocean classroom for students and the public. The beach is five miles away, and the mountains are only a short drive. Although public transportation is cheap, it's also inconvenient, making a car almost a necessity for going outside of Westwood. Unfortunately, parking is expensive and difficult to obtain. The easiest solution is to live close to campus and ride a bike.

With all the attractions of the City of Angels at its doorstep, the campus tends to empty out on the weekends (except when the football Bruins have a home game).

The School of Engineering and Applied Science is highly regarded and sets the tone on campus.

First-year students are required to take a course involving quantitative reasoning unless they hit 600 or higher on their math SAT, and English composition requirements should also be met during freshman year.

Fiske Guide to Colleges 2015　　　　　　　　　　　　　　　　　　UC–LOS ANGELES 99

"Students involve themselves with student organizations and attend different programs hosted by students groups. Some are also involved with Greek life," says a junior. Eleven percent of the men and women join one of UCLA's 50 fraternities and sororities, respectively. The university's alcohol policy is similar to that of other UC schools—open consumption is a no-no. But according to one student, "It is extremely easy for undergrads to be served, especially at fraternities." Top-name entertainers, political figures, and speakers of all kinds come to the campus; film and theater presentations are frequent, and the air is thick with live music.

UCLA has won a staggering number of collegiate championships, including more than 1,200 NCAA titles, and has produced more than 250 Olympians. The most recent championships include women's gymnastics, women's softball, and women's golf. The men's football, basketball, baseball, and tennis teams are the undeniable superstars. Beating crosstown rival USC is the name of the game in any sport; UCLA fans regard their intracity rivals with passionate feelings. Beat SC Week, the week leading up to the football game between the two, is an event in itself, featuring a bonfire, concert, and blood drive.

A leading research center, 190 fields of study, distinguished faculty members, and outstanding athletics make UCLA one of the most prestigious universities in the nation. And despite the large size, students still feel they are part of a tight-knit community. "There is a lot of school spirit, and everyone is very friendly," a junior says.

Overlaps

UC–Berkeley, UC–Irvine, UC–San Diego, UC–Santa Barbara, USC

If You Apply To ➤

UCLA: Regular admissions: Nov. 30. Application fee: $70. No campus or alumni interviews. No letters of recommendation. SATs or ACTs (with writing): required. No Subject Tests. Two pieces of writing limited to 1,000 words. Apply to a particular college, school, or program.

UC–Riverside

Riverside, CA 92521

Most diverse UC school and the easiest to get into. Social life is relatively tame, since so many of the students commute. While some complain of a lack of nightlife in Riverside, they readily agree that activities on campus make up for it. Returning students are welcomed back every year with a campuswide block party, and Spring Splash and HEAT concerts bring in hot bands.

Lacking the big-name reputation and booming athletic programs of the other UC schools, UC–Riverside has chosen to place its emphasis on something that not all institutions consider to be an important priority in higher education: the student. Riverside offers one of the lowest student/faculty ratios in the UC system, strong programs with personalized attention, and a diverse academic community that seems to have been forgotten at other UC schools. "Students are well taken care of and get personal attention," says one satisfied senior. Though part of the UC system, UC–Riverside is a breed apart.

"Students are well taken care of and get personal attention."

Located 60 miles east of Los Angeles, UCR is surrounded by mountains on the outskirts of the city of Riverside. The beautifully landscaped, 1,200-acre campus consists of mainly modern architecture, with a 160-foot bell tower (with a 48-bell carillon) marking its center. Wide lawns and clusters of oaks create "a veritable botanical garden," where students and faculty enjoy relaxing between classes. Acres

Website: www.ucr.edu
Location: City Center
Public
Total Enrollment: 20,390
Undergraduates: 18,052
Male/Female: 48/52
SAT Ranges: CR 470–580, M 500–630
ACT Ranges: 20–25
Financial Aid: 35%
Expense: Pub $ $ $
Student Loans: 73%
Average Debt: $ $

of citrus groves form a half-circle on the outer edges of campus and perfume the air. Additional facilities include a 77,000-square-foot materials science and engineering building and the School of Medicine Research Building.

Decades ago, researchers at the Citrus Experiment Station in Riverside perfected the growing methods for the imported navel orange, making discoveries to protect the fruit from disease and pests and saving California's citrus industry. Riverside continues to excel in plant sciences and entomology. But the campus has grown since its founding in 1954 to include excellent programs in engineering, natural sciences, social sciences, humanities, the arts, business, and education. The biomedical sciences program is UCR's most prestigious and demanding course of study, and its most successful students can earn a B.S./M.D. in partnership with the medical school at UCLA. The engineering program is also quite selective, more so than the campus as a whole, which generally accepts students who are ranked in the top 12 percent of the state's high school graduates. One of the few undergraduate environmental engineering programs is at UCR, as is an undergraduate program in creative writing.

"I see more students working together to get the job done."

Graduate programs in the arts are strong, with an M.F.A. in writing for the performing arts and the nation's first doctoral program in dance history and theory. The School of Medicine is California's first new public medical school in four decades. It expands and diversifies the region's physician workforce and develops research and health care delivery programs to improve the health of medically underserved populations. The University Honors Program offers exceptional students further academic challenges in addition to extracurricular activities and special seminars for freshmen. Talented student singers, dancers, and actors can earn stipends for performing in the community through an arts outreach program funded by the Maxwell H. Gluck Foundation.

All students are required to meet extensive "breadth requirements" that include courses in English composition, natural sciences and math, humanities, and social sciences. Some majors include a foreign language requirement. State budget cuts mean that class sizes have risen over the years. The campus libraries have an impressive two million volumes, an interlibrary loan system within the UC system, and vast electronic databases. A specialized research collection in science fiction is world-class. UCR's California Museum of Photography, located in downtown Riverside and available on the Web, has grown in stature.

Students say the academic climate is cooperative rather than competitive. "Instead of being super competitive," says a student, "I see more students working together to get the job done." Research is an institutional priority for faculty, so the quality of instruction can vary dramatically from "awful to fantastic," according to one sophomore. Still, UCR has a tradition of undergraduate and faculty interaction with a wide range of undergraduate research grants available during the academic year. This may be why one in six graduates goes on to get a Ph.D. State funding woes have not gone unnoticed on campus. "We've lost a lot of core classes and financial aid does not offer as much," grumbles one student.

Ninety-seven percent of the UCR student body is from California, mainly L.A., Riverside, San Bernardino, and Orange County. Asian Americans account for 40 percent of the students, and Hispanics and African Americans 38 percent and 5 percent, respectively. As part of the UC commitment to diversity, Riverside upholds policies prohibiting sexual harassment, hazing, and physical and verbal abuses. It supports centers for various ethnicities, for women, and for gay and lesbian students. "UCR is one of the most diverse universities in the nation," a political science major says. "Because of this, there is a wide range of students at UCR that make a blended environment of different cultures, nationalities, and social statuses." Numerous merit scholarships are doled out every year, as well as Division I athletic scholarships. Scholarships are also available in specific academic departments.

(continued)

Phi Beta Kappa: Yes
Applicants: 30,395
Accepted: 63%
Enrolled: 21%
Grad in 6 Years: 70%
Returning Freshmen: 88%
Academics: ✍ ✍ ✍ ½
Social: ☎ ☎
Q of L: ★ ★ ★
Admissions: (951) 827-3411
Email Address: discover@ucr.edu

Strongest Programs:
Plant Sciences and
   Entomology
Engineering
Natural Sciences
Social Sciences
Biomedical Sciences
Humanities and Arts
Business
Education

One of the few undergraduate environmental engineering programs is at UCR, as is an undergraduate program in creative writing.

The School of Medicine is California's first new public medical school in four decades.

Housing is relatively easy to obtain, but the quality varies greatly. "While West Lothian looks like a prison, Pentland Hills is like a resort," says one student. "UCR has a ton of housing options which are all comfortable and well maintained," a sociology major reports. Thirty-one percent of the students live in the dorms, where freshmen are guaranteed a spot. Campus dining is described as adequate. "I could eat their tater tots forever," gushes one student. Students feel safe on campus; security measures include an escort service and patrolling security officers.

Fraternities and sororities attract 6 percent of men and 7 percent of the women on campus. The groups usually hold campuswide parties once a quarter. "There is always something going on, whether it be a concert, lecture, or sorority/fraternity

> **"There is always something going on, whether it be a concert, lecture, or sorority/fraternity party."**

party," one sophomore says. Campus hangouts, including The Barn, have live bands and comedy nights. Every Wednesday the campus can enjoy a "nooner," where live bands play during lunch. University Village is a commercial center offering a movie theater, restaurants, and an arcade right on the edge of campus. The campus runs a cultural arts program that brings professional shows to campus, such as Laurie Anderson and Margaret Cho.

Riverside weather is temperate except during the summer months, when the heat and haze combine to make a trip to the coast look really inviting. The coast is only about 45 minutes by freeway and the desert is an hour east. Big Bear and numerous ski resorts are also within an hour's drive.

Riverside competes in the NCAA Division I and men's and women's cross-country teams are competitive. Other successful Highlander teams include women's volleyball, men's and women's golf, and men's basketball. A recreational program in men's and women's karate has turned out national champions. A student recreation center offers a health-club atmosphere with sand volleyball, weight and workout machines, and intramural leagues.

All in all, Riverside is growing and improving, albeit not without some growing pains. "It is nice to see the campus grow, but many students suffer because of rising tuition and living costs," says one student. Although smaller than some sister UC campuses, it offers more personal attention to its students. UCR is fast becoming a nationally recognized research institution, from which students surely will benefit. "UCR has grown immensely over the past few years," one sophomore says. "The emphasis for the future is to establish a name for UCR, to let the nation know what a wonderful university this is."

Overlaps

UC–Berkeley, UC–Davis, UC–Irvine, UCLA, UC–San Diego, UC–Santa Barbara, UC–Santa Cruz

If You Apply To ➤

Riverside: Admissions deadline: Nov. 30. Financial aid: Mar. 1. Housing: May 9. Application fee: $70. No campus or alumni interviews. No letters of recommendation. SATs or ACTs (with writing): required. No Subject Tests. Two pieces of writing limited to 1,000 words. Apply to a particular college, school, or program.

UC–San Diego

9500 Gilman Drive, Department 0021, La Jolla, CA 92093-0021

Applications have doubled in the past 10 years at this seaside paradise. UCSD now rivals better-known Berkeley and UCLA as the Cal campus of choice for top students. Six undergraduate colleges break down UCSD to a more manageable size. Best known for science, engineering, and the famed Scripps Institute of Oceanography.

Some say that looking good is better than feeling good, but at UC–San Diego, they're doing a lot of both. Set against the serene beauty of La Jolla's beaches, students catch as much relaxation time as they do study time. But it's not all fun and games around this campus. The research star of the UC system, UCSD's faculty rates high nationally among public institutions in science productivity. And within each of the five undergraduate colleges, a system that offers undergraduates more intimate settings, students are honing their minds with the classics and the cutting edge in academics. Sure, San Diegans tend to be more mellow than the average Southern Californian, and UCSD students follow suit. But beneath the tanned foreheads and bright smiles, UCSD's bubbling with intellectual energy and the healthy desire to be at the top of the UC system.

"Courses are competitive."

San Diego's tree-lined campus sits high on a bluff overlooking the Pacific in the seaside resort of La Jolla. The predominant architectural theme is contemporary, with a few out-of-the-ordinary structures, including a library that looks like an inverted pyramid. Another tinge of the postmodern is the nation's largest neon sculpture, which wraps around one of the high-rise academic buildings and consists of seven-foot-tall letters that spell out the seven virtues superimposed over the seven vices.

UCSD's programs in science, engineering, and computer science have global reputations and are "not for the faint of heart," says one student. Engineering requires a B average in entry-level courses for acceptance into the major. The Scripps Institute of Oceanography is also excellent, due to the university's advantageous location. Chemistry also gets a strong recommendation, but you really can't go wrong in any of the hard sciences. Although the humanities and social sciences are not as solid in comparison, political science and psychology get strong backing from students. Imaginative interdisciplinary offerings include computer music, urban planning, ethnic studies, and a psychology/computer science program in artificial intelligence, as well as majors devised by students themselves.

San Diego operates on the quarter system, which makes for a semester's worth of work crammed into 10 weeks. Science students find the load intense. "Courses are competitive, especially in biology courses since it's the most popular major," says one senior. Students have a choice of six libraries, some good for research, others better for socializing. Despite the quality of research done by the faculty, half a dozen of whom are Nobel laureates, students find that the typical scenario of research over teaching seen at most large research universities is not as common at UC–San Diego, although "you end up teaching a lot of the material to yourself," according to an anthropology major.

"You end up teaching a lot of the material to yourself."

UC–San Diego's six undergraduate colleges have their own sets of general education requirements, their own personalities, and differing ideals on which they are based. Prospective freshmen apply to UC–San Diego—the admissions requirements are identical for each college—but students must indicate their college preference. Revelle College, the oldest, is the most rigorous and mandates that students become equally acquainted with a certain level of coursework in the humanities, sciences, and social sciences, as well as fulfill a language requirement. Muir allows more flexibility in the distribution of requirements. Thurgood Marshall College was founded to emphasize and encourage social awareness; like Revelle, it places equal weight on sciences, social sciences, and humanities. However, it stresses a liberal arts education based on "an examination of the human condition in a multicultural society." Warren has developed a highly organized internship program that gives its undergraduates more practical experience than the others do. Eleanor Roosevelt College ("Fifth") devotes its curriculum to international and cross-cultural studies. Sixth

Website: www.ucsd.edu
Location: Suburban
Public
Total Enrollment: 27,761
Undergraduates: 22,242
Male/Female: 51/49
SAT Ranges: CR 550–650, M 620–730
ACT Ranges: 26–31
Financial Aid: 75%
Expense: Pub $ $ $ $
Student Loans: 56%
Average Debt: $
Phi Beta Kappa: Yes
Applicants: 60,807
Accepted: 38%
Enrolled: 20%
Grad in 6 Years: 86%
Returning Freshmen: 94%
Academics: 🖉 🖉 🖉 🖉 🖉
Social: ☎ ☎ ☎
Q of L: ★ ★ ★ ★
Admissions: (858) 534-4831
Email Address: admissionsinfo@ucsd.edu

Strongest Programs:
Biology
Engineering and Bioengineering
Cognitive Science
Economics
Political Science
Oceanography
Communication

Although the humanities and social sciences are not as solid in comparison, political science and psychology get strong backing from students.

College focuses on art, culture, and technology. Its goal is to graduate multicultural students who can work collaboratively and enjoy working in their communities.

A theater major notes that UCSD's academic intensity "does not mean that all the students here are nerdy. We enjoy athletics and extracurricular activities, but academic excellence is our priority." A short walk to the beach, however, reveals the

"The residence halls are very nice, with all the amenities."

student body's wild and crazy half-surfers and their fans, who celebrate the "kick back." Students jumping curbs on skateboards are common on this campus. Yet these beach babies are no scholastic slouches. Most of them placed in the top 10 percent of their high school class. The average student pulls a 3.0 GPA while at UCSD. Many students here choose to take five years to graduate in order to gain a higher GPA, and many of the scientists continue their studies after graduation. UCSD also ranks highly among public colleges and universities in the percentage of graduates who go on to earn a Ph.D. and in the percentage of students accepted to medical school. Only 4 percent of students are from out of state, and another 13 percent are foreign students. Minority representation is high, with 40 percent of the student body Asian American, 15 percent Hispanic, and 2 percent African American. Diversity education includes a Cross-Cultural Center for students, faculty, and staff that provides activities, brown-bag luncheons, and programs on race relations. Merit scholarships are doled out to eligible undergraduates, and the average award exceeds $9,000. Budding athletic superstars must look elsewhere for financial awards, as there are no athletic scholarships.

Students find that the typical scenario of research over teaching seen at most large research universities is not as common at UC–San Diego.

Each of the university's colleges has its own housing complex, with either dorms or apartments. Most freshmen live on campus and are guaranteed housing for their first three years. "The residence halls are very nice, with all the amenities," says an animal physiology major. By junior year, students usually decide to take up residence in La Jolla proper or nearby Del Mar, often in beachside apartments; only 43 percent of all the students live on campus. But that can be costly: The price ends up being inversely proportional to proximity to the beach. If you are willing to relinquish the luxury of a five-minute walk to the beach, a short commute will bring you relatively affordable housing.

The immediate surroundings of UCSD, however, are definitely not affordable. "La Jolla is a rich, conservative, retired, white, snobbish community," one sophomore says. "Not a college town!" Cars are, of course, an inescapable part of Southern

"No car equals no fun."

California life, and owning one—many people do—makes off-campus living even more pleasant. "No car equals no fun," one international studies major says. Unfortunately, trying to park on campus can be difficult, though at least one student says that "parking is not nearly as bad here as it is at other schools." Dorm residents are required to buy a meal card, which gets them into any of the four campus cafeterias as well as the campus deli and burger joints.

Many students here choose to take five years to graduate in order to gain a higher GPA.

The university is dry and most of the real socializing seems to take place off campus. "Most students hang out at the dance clubs, jazz bars, and great restaurants in the Gaslamp Quarter," says a senior. Annual festivals include the Open House, Renaissance Faire, UnOlympics, and the Reggae Festival. Another annual festival pays tribute to a hideously loud and colorful statue of the Sun God, which is the unofficial mascot for this sun-streaked student body. Ten percent of the men and women try to beat the blahs by joining a fraternity or sorority. Alcoholic parties are banned in the residence halls, though students say lax RAs and good fake IDs make for easy underage drinking. Although campus life is relatively tame, students rely heavily on the surrounding area—but not La Jolla—for their entertainment. Students go to nearby Pacific Beach and downtown San Diego with the zoo, Sea World, and Balboa Park all only 12 miles away. Torrey Pines Natural Reserves are great for outdoor enthusiasts. Mexico—and the five-dollar lobster—is a half-hour drive (even nearer than the desert, where many students go hiking), and the two-hour trip to Los Angeles makes for a nice weekend jaunt.

Although San Diego will never be mistaken for a sports-crazed school (à la USC), it is rapidly becoming a Division II powerhouse, most notably in women's sports. The women's volleyball and tennis teams have won numerous national championships, and the men's water polo and volleyball teams have also done well. In all, Triton teams have captured more than two dozen national titles. For weekend competitors, classes are available in windsurfing, sailing, scuba diving, and kayaking at the nearby Mission Bay Aquatic Center. Everyone participates in one intramural league or another, and if you're not on a team, "you're not a true UCSD student." The RIMAC, an impressive sports facility for students, gets even the couch potatoes off their Barcaloungers.

The students at UCSD are exceptionally serious and out for an excellent education. But the pace (study, party, relax, study more) and the props (sun, sand, Frisbees, and flip-flops) give the rigorous curriculum offered by UCSD's six colleges an inimitable flavor that undergraduates would not change. Indeed, many believe they have the best setup in higher education: "a beautiful beachfront environment that eases a life of academic rigor."

If You Apply To ➤ **San Diego:** Regular admissions: Nov. 30. Application fee: $60. No campus or alumni interviews. No letters of recommendation. SATs or ACTs (with writing): required. Subject Tests: recommended for engineering and science students. Two pieces of writing limited to 1,000 words. Apply to a particular college, school, or program.

UC–Santa Barbara

Santa Barbara, CA 93106

Willpower is the word at UC–Santa Barbara. On a beautiful day with the sound of waves crashing in the distance, it takes willpower to hang in there with pen, paper, laptop, or book. Fairly or not, Santa Barbara is known as the party animal of the UC system. In the classroom, science is the best bet. Free spirits should check out the unusual College for Creative Studies.

For students at UC–Santa Barbara, California's famed beaches serve as both classroom and playground. On weekends, sun-worshipping students grab surfboards and don bikinis and head to the water for some serious fun. During the week, those same students can likely be found studying technology rather than tan lines. UCSB provides a comfortable mixture of work and play that is unique to the UC system and draws praise from its students. "On a nice sunny day, the beaches and grassy areas will be flooded with students," says a freshman, "but most of them are there with a book."

Located just a stone's throw from the beach, UC–Santa Barbara's 989-acre campus is bordered on two sides by the Pacific Ocean, with a clear view of the Channel Islands. On the landward side are a nature preserve and the predominantly student community of Isla Vista, and five miles to the north lie the Santa Ynez Mountains. The campus itself features mainly 1950s Southern California architecture with a Southern California atmosphere to match.

"Students here are hardworking and fun loving."

Website: www.ucsb.edu
Location: City Outskirts
Public
Total Enrollment: 21,653
Undergraduates: 18,712
Male/Female: 47/53
SAT Ranges: CR 540–660, M 570–690
ACT Ranges: 24–29
Financial Aid: 70%
Expense: Pub $ $ $ $
Student Loans: 53%
Average Debt: $
Phi Beta Kappa: Yes

(continued)

Applicants: 54,762
Accepted: 44%
Enrolled: 20%
Grad in 6 Years: 80%
Returning Freshmen: 91%
Academics: ✍ ✍ ✍ ✍
Social: 🍺 🍺 🍺 🍺
Q of L: ★ ★ ★ ★
Admissions: (805) 893-2881
Email Address: admissions@
 sa.ucsb.edu

Strongest Programs:
Marine Biology
Physics
Engineering
Chemistry
Geology
Religious Studies
Accounting
Environmental Studies

The accounting program is strong, and the courses are geared toward taking and passing the CPA exam.

The Bren School of Environmental Science and Management is open for business, and the faculty is world-renowned.

Not surprisingly, the marine biology department capitalizes on the school's aquatic resources and stands out among the university's best. Other favorites include economics, biological sciences, psychology, communications, and sociology. The accounting program is strong, and the courses are geared toward taking and passing the CPA exam, so graduation is usually followed by a mass recruitment by California's big accounting firms. "We have a good reputation for many of our programs," says one student, "from physics to economics to history. There are no departments that students tend to avoid." The College of Creative Studies offers an unstructured curriculum to about 400 self-starters ready for advanced and independent work in the arts, math, or the sciences. An interdisciplinary program called the Global Peace and Security Program combines aspects of physics, anthropology, and military science. The National Science Foundation provides funding for the $5.5 million National Center for Geographic Information and Analysis program. The Bren School of Environmental Science and Management is open for business, and the faculty is world-renowned—the college boasts five Nobel Prize winners in economics, chemistry, and physics. Still, teaching is a hit-or-miss affair, according to one junior: "Many of the professors are more interested in their research than teaching a class."

> **"Many of the professors are more interested in their research than teaching a class."**

UCSB's general education program requires all students to fulfill four subject areas: writing, non-Western cultures, quantitative relationships, and ethnicity. Other required courses include English reading and composition, foreign languages, social sciences, and art. For those who crave time away, Santa Barbara is the headquarters of the UC system's Education Abroad Program (EAP), which sends students to any of 100 host universities worldwide. In order to graduate, all students must take courses in English composition and American history and institutions, must fulfill a unit requirement, and must also meet the requirements of their individual majors. In addition, students must be registered at UCSB for a minimum of three regular quarters.

UCSB students are traditionally public-spirited; the fraternities and sororities, which attract 8 percent of men and 12 percent of women, are known for their philanthropy. The students, 94 percent of whom are California residents, are laid-back. "Students here are hardworking and fun loving," says one senior. Asian Americans comprise 23 percent of the student body; African Americans make up 4 percent, and Hispanics account for 24 percent. The campus's beach locale inspires many students to be environmentally friendly, and the campus vibe is decidedly liberal. Merit scholarships and athletic scholarships in 11 sports are available for those who qualify.

University housing, which includes both dorms and privately run residence halls, is comfortable, well maintained, and much sought after. "Our on-campus housing is amazing, right in front of the beach," a junior says. "They come fully furnished, with high-speed Internet, cable, telephone lines, and a great atmosphere." Unfortunately, there is a waiting list to get into the dorms—even with the addition of the new Manzanita Village Student Housing. Only 37 percent of students, most of whom are freshmen, snag on-campus housing. The rest find a home in neighboring Isla Vista, which has welcomed its student population—after all, most of its population is UCSB students. As a result, students are very active in the community. Meals in the dorms are available to residents and nonresidents alike, and are, according to most students, more than simply edible. "Great food and tons of it!" raves one student. While all students say they feel extremely safe on campus, one frequently used motto is "four years, four bikes," because of the frequency of bicycle thefts.

Because Isla Vista is predominantly made up of students, it's become what some students consider Party Central. "This is a real party school," says a political science major, "and most of the social life takes place on weekends." Alcohol isn't allowed on campus, but many students say the rule is easy to skirt. The local bars are off-limits to those under 21, but when the long-awaited birthday arrives, students celebrate with a quaint little ritual known as the State Street Crawl, imbibing at all the numerous establishments on the "main drag" of Santa Barbara. Movies and concerts are also available, and the mountains, Los Padres National Forest, and L.A. are all an easy drive away. The annual Extravaganza is an all-day, free concert, and students are known to go wild on Halloween and dress up for the entire weekend. "Halloween is our claim to fame," boasts one student.

Although the Greeks are strong and growing, there's an ample selection of other organizations from which to choose. A never-ending rotation of intramurals is available on and off the beach. All of UCSB's varsity teams compete in the NCAA's Division I. The most successful Gaucho teams include soccer, water polo, baseball, volleyball, swimming, and basketball. Ultimate Frisbee is also quite popular, as well as nationally competitive.

UCSB students love to work and play. They rave about their professors and the academic challenges they face. But they also know a good thing when they see it: not everyone gets to spend four years on the beach and come away with a degree. "UCSB is an environment where you will be challenged to expand your mind, push past boundaries, and take chances to experience things you have never tried before," says a senior. A junior adds, "Being a UCSB Gaucho is something I'm proud of, and I wouldn't trade it for anything in the world."

> *Although the Greeks are strong and growing, there's an ample selection of other organizations from which to choose.*

Overlaps

UCLA, UC–San Diego, UC–Irvine, UC–Berkeley, UC–Davis, UC–Santa Cruz

If You Apply To > | **Santa Barbara:** Regular admissions: Nov. 30. Financial aid: Mar. 3. Housing: Jun. 1. Application fee: $70. No campus or alumni interviews. No letters of recommendation. SATs or ACTs (with writing): required. Subject Tests: recommended. Two pieces of writing limited to 1,000 words. Apply to a particular college, school, or program.

UC–Santa Cruz

1156 High Street, Santa Cruz, CA 95064

From its flower-child beginnings, UC–Santa Cruz has wandered back toward the mainstream. The yoga mats and surfboards still abound, but the students are a lot more conventional than in its earlier incarnation, and UCSC is not quite the intellectual powerhouse of yore. Santa Cruz's relatively small size and residential college system give it a homey feel.

UC–Santa Cruz, still a baby in the UC system, was born during the radical '60s when it reigned as the ultimate alternative school. The founding vision of an integrated learning environment remains to this day, and every undergraduate affiliates with one of the residential colleges. Progressive thought continues to flourish, as does a strong academic program that strives to focus on undergraduate education. Students still come to UCSC to do their own thing.

The campus, among the most beautiful in the nation, is set on a 2,000-acre expanse of meadowland and redwood forest overlooking Monterey Bay. Bike paths and hiking trails wind throughout the redwood-tree-filled campus, and the beach is a quick drive away—or a spectacular bike ride or scenic hike. The buildings range from 1860 Cowell Ranch farm structures to the multi-award-winning modern colleges, whose styles range from Mediterranean to Japanese to sleek concrete block.

Website: www.ucsc.edu
Location: Small Town
Public
Total Enrollment: 17,085
Undergraduates: 15,721
Male/Female: 47/53
SAT Ranges: CR 470–610, M 490–630
ACT Ranges: 20–27
Financial Aid: 63%
Expense: Pub $ $ $ $

(continued)

Student Loans: 56%
Average Debt: $
Phi Beta Kappa: Yes
Applicants: 33,142
Accepted: 61%
Enrolled: 19%
Grad in 6 Years: 74%
Returning Freshmen: 91%
Academics: ✑ ✑ ✑ ✑
Social: ☎ ☎ ☎
Q of L: ★ ★ ★ ★ ★
Admissions: (831) 459-4008
Email Address: admissions@ucsc.edu

Strongest Programs:
Marine Sciences
Biology
Psychology
Linguistics

UCSC also includes the Jack Baskin School of Engineering, which was developed to accommodate the growing needs of engineering students.

Thanks to a unique building code, nothing may be built taller than two-thirds the height of the nearest redwood tree. Designed by Bohlin Cywinski Jackson—the same architectural firm that created Pixar Studios—the 26,000-square-foot Digital Arts Research Center serves as a social and intellectual hub for UCSC's Arts Division.

The bucolic surroundings are deceptive. "Courses are very rigorous, in my experience," warns one undergrad. Santa Cruz's academic offerings range as widely as its architecture and feature both traditional and innovative programs. In an effort to become what one official calls a "near-perfect hybrid" between the large university and the small college, campus life revolves around the residential colleges. Whatever one's specialty, the curriculum can be demanding. Led by marine sciences and biology, the sciences are Santa Cruz's strongest suit and frequently give students the opportunity to coauthor published research with their professors. Science facilities include state-of-the-art laboratories; the Institute of Marine Sciences, which boasts one of the largest groups of experts on marine mammals in the nation; and the nearby Lick Observatory for budding stargazers. UCSC also includes the Jack Baskin School of Engineering, which was developed to accommodate the growing needs of engineering students. UCSC also offers undergraduate majors in bioengineering and computer game design, as well as graduate degrees in education, music, and statistics/stochastic modeling.

"Courses are very rigorous, in my experience."

While the majority of students pursue traditional majors, the possibility is still there for eclectically minded students to pursue "history of consciousness" or just about anything else they can get a faculty member to OK. One of UCSC's most unusual features is that professors provide written evaluations for each student in their class and also provide letter grades. UCSC boasts more than the average number of interdisciplinary programs, including environmental, community, and feminist studies; bioinformatics; and creative writing. Field study and internships are encouraged. Overall, the emphasis is on the liberal arts, and students will find few programs with a vocational emphasis. Additional programs include robotics engineering, computer science/computer game design, Jewish studies, and cognitive science.

To meet the general education requirements, students must complete courses in cross-cultural analysis, ethnicity and race, interpreting arts and media, mathematical and formal reasoning, scientific inquiry, statistical reasoning, and textual analysis and interpretation. In addition, students must choose one of three "perspectives" courses focused on environmental awareness, human behavior, or technology and society. Finally, they must select a course on creative process, collaborative endeavor, or service learning. The main library, McHenry, houses more than 1.5 million books and 25,000 periodicals, and students have access to books at other UC campuses through an online catalog system and interlibrary loans. The science library houses an additional 300,000 volumes.

Though the curriculum is demanding and the quarter system keeps the academic pace fast, the atmosphere is emphatically noncompetitive. Such competition as there is tends to be internalized. A majority of the students eventually go on to graduate study. All UC campuses insist on faculty research, but most Santa Cruz professors are there to teach. "I've been very impressed with how accessible professors are," says a sophomore. "Whether it's via email or regular office hours, I feel very comfortable approaching and talking to all of my professors."

"I've been very impressed with how accessible professors are."

Santa Cruz remains the most liberal of the UC campuses, and, according to one student, is "still a school with a social conscience." "Before I came here I was told that UCSC was a 'hippie-dippie' college," says one student, "but it's not true at all."

Seventy-nine percent of the students are Californians, though Santa Cruz always manages to lure a few Easterners. One-third of the students are members of minority groups, with Asian Americans accounting for 21 percent of the students, Hispanics 28 percent, and African Americans 2 percent. "Racial, ethnic, and cultural diversity is celebrated and strongly encouraged by the majority of the students here," reports a politics major. Santa Cruz offers hundreds of merit scholarships, but there are no athletic scholarships.

Forty-eight percent of the undergraduate student population lives in university-sponsored housing. Some dorms have their own dining halls with reasonably good food; students may also opt to join a food co-op. Freshmen and transfer students are guaranteed on-campus housing for two years. Upperclassmen can take their chances in the lottery or move off campus.

There are a dozen fraternities and sororities (attracting but 2 percent of the student population), as well as countless established student groups, to provide an active social life. The beach and resort town of Santa Cruz, with its boardwalk and amusement park, are only 10 minutes away from campus by bike, but pedaling back up the hill takes much longer. Those looking for city lights can take the windy, mountainous highway to San Jose (35 miles away) or the slow, scenic coastal highway to San Francisco (75 miles), or ride a bus to either city. If you have a car, destinations such as Monterey, Big Sur, the Napa Valley, and the Sierras are easily accessible.

Santa Cruz remains the most liberal of the UC campuses.

Although Santa Cruz fields only a few varsity teams, students love their school mascot, Sammy the banana slug. Men's tennis is strong and won its third indoor national title and its seventh NCAA title recently; the women's rugby squad is a national champ, too. Participation in intramurals ("Friendship through Competition" is the motto) is widespread, with rugby in particular growing in popularity. Sailing and scuba diving are among the many physical education classes offered, and the student recreation department sponsors everything from whitewater rafting to cooking classes.

Santa Cruz is a progressive school with a gorgeous campus and innovative academic programs, where the main priority is the education of undergraduates. Many students are concerned that UCSC is growing too fast, and an ambitious proposal for future expansion has threatened its heretofore cozy relationship with local citizens. Still, as long as UCSC retains its belief in "to each his or her own," it will remain uniquely Santa Cruz.

Overlaps

UC–Berkeley, UC–Davis, UC–Irvine, UCLA, UC–San Diego, UC–Santa Barbara

If You Apply To >

Santa Cruz: Regular admissions: Nov. 30. Application fee: $70. No campus or alumni interviews. No letters of recommendation. SATs or ACTs (with writing): required. No Subject Tests. Two pieces of writing limited to 1,000 words. Apply to a particular college, school, or program.

California Institute of Technology

Mail Code 328-87, 1200 East California Boulevard, Pasadena, CA 91125

If you're armed with a perfect SAT score; a burning desire to study math, science, or engineering; and some independent research or published papers already under your belt, maybe you'll have a fighting chance of getting into and out of the California Institute of Technology. Caltech is best experienced with grit, a propensity for pranks, and wide-ranging intellectual curiosity.

The pass/fail grading system in the freshman year goes a long way toward easing the acclimation period for new arrivals.

The California Institute of Technology counts more than 30 Nobel Prize winners among its faculty and alumni, and with administrators' permission—which is easy to obtain—students may tap into that brilliance by taking as many classes as they can cram in each semester. Expectations are high; "Techers" are fond of saying that "the admissions office doesn't make mistakes," and it's fairly common to take time off to deal with stress and avoid burnout. "The atmosphere promotes a love of science, learning, and discovery that is truly exhilarating," says a biology major. No doubt about it—if you prefer particle physics to partying, Caltech is the place to be.

"The atmosphere promotes a love of science, learning, and discovery."

Caltech's 124-acre campus is located in Pasadena, "a wealthy suburban town about 15 miles outside Los Angeles," says a senior. "It's not a college town at all." The distance from downtown means the school is relatively isolated from the glitz, glamour, and good times that many people associate with "La La Land." Outside the classroom, at least, tranquility prevails, with olive trees, lily ponds, and plenty of flowers breaking up clusters of older Spanish-mission style buildings. Leafy courtyards and arcades link these with the more modern, "block institutional" structures. The Broad Center for the Biological Sciences offers 120,000 square feet of lab, classroom, and office space at the northwest corner of campus. It was designed by Pei Cobb Freed & Associates, the firm behind the U.S. Holocaust Memorial Museum in Washington, D.C.

Caltech's mission, one official says, is "to train the creative type of scientist or engineer urgently needed in our educational, governmental, and industrial development." After all, it was here that Albert Einstein abandoned his concept of a static cosmos and endorsed the expanding-universe model. This is also where physicist Carl Anderson discovered the positron. With these luminaries as their models, students plunge right into the demanding general requirements, which include five terms each of math and physics, three terms of chemistry with lab, one term of biology, two terms of science communication, and courses in the humanities and social sciences to round things out. Students complain about these, "and usually take no more than absolutely required," says a biology major. Still, they can be tough to get into come registration time, says a computer science major, since enrollment is limited "to allow for discussion among a small group." The pass/fail grading system in the freshman year goes a long way toward easing the acclimation period for new arrivals. And the honor system, which mandates that "no one shall take unfair advantage of any other member of the Caltech community," helps discourage competition for grades. Professors give take-home exams, and if violations of the honor code are suspected, "students decide if a violation was indeed made," one student explains.

"The quality of teaching improves as you get into your major."

Caltech made its name in physics, and students say that program remains strong. A junior says, "I love mechanical engineering. The profs are great, the subject is fun, and you get to do fun contests." Regardless of major, Caltech students benefit from state-of-the-art facilities, including the Beckman Institute, a center for fundamental research in biology and chemistry, and the Keck telescope, the largest optical telescope in the world. The Moore Laboratory has 90,000 square feet of the latest equipment for engineering and communications majors studying fiber optics and the like, and the university's endowment is the largest of the nation's engineering schools. Summer Undergraduate Research Fellowships give 300 undergraduates the chance to get a head start on their own discoveries, with help from a faculty sponsor. Some 20 percent of these students publish results from their endeavors in scientific journals.

Despite Caltech's reputation for brilliance, students say the quality of teaching is hit or miss. "At times, you get lucky and get amazing professors," says a computer science major. "Other times, you get professors who either don't care about the class they teach, or are so advanced in their field that they are unable to convey 'simple' concepts." A senior adds, "The quality of teaching improves as you get into your major." Here, the student says, professors in the humanities and social sciences really shine, since they actually want to teach, rather than hole up in a lab with mass spectrometers and computer simulations of atomic fission. Another student describes the academic climate as "collaborative, intense, and busy." While teaching assistants do lead some recitation sections affiliated with large lectures, it's not uncommon for professors to lead them, too—even for freshmen, says a sophomore. "If you don't like your TA, switching sections is a breeze," the student says.

Sixty-three percent of Techers come from California, and 40 percent are Asian American. Other minorities are less well represented, with Hispanics making up 10 percent of the student body and African Americans 2 percent. Men outnumber women, which has inspired the bittersweet observation among distaff Techers that "the odds are good, but the goods are odd." **"People live in a Tech bubble."** Social and political issues are not a big deal on campus, says a junior. "People live in a Tech bubble, where they care about nothing more than 50 meters from campus," a sophomore agrees. The school awards merit scholarships but no athletic awards.

Caltech guarantees on-campus or school-affiliated housing for all four years, and 85 percent of students live in the "comfortable and convenient" dorms. "The housing system is great," cheers one student, who describes residence life as "social support in an academically intense environment." While there are no fraternities or sororities, the seven co-ed on-campus houses inspire a loyalty worthy of the Greeks. The four older houses, which have been renovated, offer mostly single rooms, while the three newer dorms have doubles. Freshmen select their house during Rotation Week, after spending an evening of partying at each one, and indicating at week's end the four they like the most. Resident upperclassmen take it from there in a professional-sports-type draft, which places each new student in one of his or her top choices. Business-minded types, for example, may choose Avery House, which focuses on entrepreneurship. Each dorm has a dining hall, and those who live on campus must buy a meal plan, which a junior calls "quite expensive for the quality of food." A vegetarian calls the food "awful," and says that "by the end of the week, I am often wondering if we're being served the same spinach for five days in a row."

The houses are the emotional center of Caltech life, and the scene of innumerable practical jokes. On Ditch Day, seniors barricade their dorm rooms using everything from steel bars to electronic codes, leave clues as to how to overcome the obstacles, and disappear from campus. Underclassmen spend the day figuring out how to break in, using "cleverness, brute force, and finesse," to claim a reward inside, which can range from the edible to, well, anything is possible. Perhaps the best student prank occurred during the 1984 Rose Bowl game, when crosstown rival UCLA played Illinois. A group of Caltech whiz kids spent months devising a radio- **"Ask any local bartender for a Caltech Cocktail and you will get three ounces of straight water."** control device that would allow them to take control of the scoreboard in the second half, to gain national exposure for Caltech by flashing pictures of their school's mascot, the beaver, and a new version of the score that had Caltech trouncing MIT.

While drinking might seem a reasonable escape from the pressure of all that work, Caltech requires any organization hosting a party to hire a professional bartender—"and they card," says a senior. "Ask any local bartender for a Caltech Cocktail and you will get three ounces of straight water," quips a sophomore. Social life at Caltech "is horrible," agrees a junior. "There are occasional parties, but the administration does not allow students from other colleges to attend, unless accompanied by a Caltech student." So students head off campus—to Old Pasadena, nearby schools like USC, Occidental, and the Claremont colleges, or to downtown L.A., now easily reachable on the Metro's gold line. Disneyland and Hollywood are always options, and road trips to the beach, mountains, or desert—or south of the border, to Tijuana—are options for those with cars. "From yoga studios to death metal concerts, L.A. has it all," one student says. But some Caltech students still prefer to make their own fun. The annual Pumpkin Drop (on Halloween, of course) involves immersing a gourd in liquid nitrogen, and then dropping it from the library roof, so that it shatters into a zillion frozen shards. During finals week, stereos blast "The Ride of the Valkyries" at seven o'clock each morning, just the thing to get you going after that all-nighter.

Caltech fields 18 Division III teams, and the most popular include men's soccer, men's and women's track and field, and men's cross-country. The Beavers' men's basketball team became campus heroes in March 2011 when they ended a conference losing streak that dated back to 1985. The school also offers more unusual sports such as water polo and fencing. Perhaps more popular than varsity competition, though, are the intramural matches between the houses, in nine sports every year. Also popular is the annual design competition that's the culmination of Mechanical Engineering 72; it helped inspire the TV shows *Battle Bots* and *Robot Wars*. The city of Pasadena is home to the granddaddy of postseason college football competition—the storied Rose Bowl.

Caltech students must learn to thrive under intense pressure, thanks to the school's tremendous workload and lackluster social life. But students say they appreciate the freedom to think and explore—and the trust administrators place in them because of the honor code. "The unique student body, how available professors are (I call almost all of them by their first names), and how much we learn make Caltech a special place," says a sophomore.

Overlaps

MIT, Princeton, Stanford, Harvard, UC–Berkeley, Harvey Mudd, University of Chicago, Yale

---

If You Apply To ➤

Caltech: Early action: Nov. 1. Regular admissions: Jan. 3. Application fee: $75. No campus or alumni interviews. SATs or ACTs (with writing): required. Subject Tests: required (math and either physics, biology, or chemistry). Accepts the Common Application. Looks for math/science aptitude as well as research orientation or unusual academic potential. Essay question: areas of interest; personal statement.

Calvin College

3201 Burton, Grand Rapids, MI 49546

An evangelical Christian institution that ranks high on the private-college bargain list. Nearly half the students are members of the Christian Reformed Church. Archrival of Michigan neighbor Hope and Illinois cousin Wheaton. Best known in the humanities and as one of the few Christian colleges with engineering.

Website: www.calvin.edu
Location: City Outskirts
Private
Total Enrollment: 3,773
Undergraduates: 3,748
Male/Female: 46/54
SAT Ranges: CR 520–670, M 540–690

Michigan's Calvin College prides itself on being "distinctively academic, strikingly Christian." Along with Wheaton College in Illinois, it is regarded as one of the country's top evangelical colleges. Though no one is required to attend the school's daily chapel services, classes stop when worship starts, and most students view Christian values as central to the academic experience. "Calvin is a place where your individual beliefs will be challenged but not dismissed," says a student. "You will learn and grow here."

Calvin was founded in 1876, as the educational wing of the Christian Reformed Church in North America. After outgrowing one of its first homes, the college bought a tract of land on the edge of Grand Rapids, and built its present campus. Calvin spreads out over 400 beautifully landscaped acres, including playing fields and three ponds. The campus also includes a 90-acre woodland and wetland ecosystem preserve used for classes, research, and recreation. Most facilities are less than 35 years old, and were designed by a student of famed architect Frank Lloyd Wright. The east campus includes the Prince Conference Center, DeVos Communication Center, Gainey Athletic Facility, and the award-winning Bunker Interpretive Center, powered primarily by student-designed solar energy technology. The Covenant Fine Arts Center includes space for offices, classrooms, a 1,100-seat auditorium, a 3,800-square-foot art gallery, and a student lounge.

> **"Calvin is a place where your individual beliefs will be challenged but not dismissed."**

Calvin's core curriculum has four components: core gateway, studies, competencies, and capstone courses. All first-year students must take the two linked gateway courses, Prelude and Developing a Christian Mind. Students then tackle the liberal arts core, An Engagement with God's World, which challenges them to develop knowledge, skills, and Christian character. Studies courses include The Physical World, Societal Structures in North America, and Biblical Foundations. Competencies courses cover foreign languages and Rhetoric in Culture.

Preprofessional programs, such as business, engineering, education, and nursing tend to be Calvin's best bets, students say—perhaps that's why those programs, along with psychology, are the college's most popular majors. Biology, chemistry, philosophy, and religion are also regarded as strong, though faculty members in those departments are said to be tough. Students who receive bachelor's degrees in accounting from Calvin pass the CPA exam at rates well above the national average. Calvin is the only evangelical Christian college to offer an Asian studies program, and the Creation Care living/learning community gives motivated students the chance to learn about and promote environmental responsibility and Christian stewardship at the local, national, and global level.

Academically, Calvin's atmosphere is tough but collaborative. "The courses at Calvin are both rigorous and challenging, but always focused on preparing students for life after Calvin," says a senior. The school is founded on the belief that every subject—even the sciences, or mass media and popular culture—can be approached from a Christian perspective, and faculty members work hard to integrate faith and learning. A sophomore says, "The dedication of the professors is contagious and encourages me to want to learn more."

Forty percent of classes at Calvin have 49 or fewer students. Faculty members must be committed to Christian teachings, and teaching assistants won't be found behind the lecterns, so professors are expected to reserve about 10 hours per week for advising and assisting students outside of class. "The personal attention that I've received at Calvin has been absolutely outstanding," cheers one student. "I honestly can't say enough about the academic environment." Calvin offers faculty-led, semester-long off-campus programs in Britain, China, France, Ghana, Honduras, Hungary, New Mexico, Spain, Thailand, the Netherlands, and Washington, D.C. Students also participate in study abroad programs offered through Calvin or in conjunction with other colleges and universities. "Study abroad programs are an essential part of the Calvin experience," says a psychology major. Seventy percent of students participate in study abroad and the college is among the top in the nation for the number of students who study abroad.

> **"The courses at Calvin are both rigorous and challenging."**

Though Calvin still has a strongly Dutch heritage, students who are members of the Christian Reformed Church now account for less than half of the student

(continued)

ACT Ranges: 24–30
Financial Aid: 97%
Expense: Pr $
Student Loans: 63%
Average Debt: $ $ $ $
Phi Beta Kappa: No
Applicants: 3,284
Accepted: 76%
Enrolled: 39%
Grad in 6 Years: 77%
Returning Freshmen: 86%
Academics: ✍ ✍ ✍
Social: ☎ ☎ ☎
Q of L: ★ ★ ★ ★
Admissions: (616) 526-6106
Email Address: admissions@ calvin.edu

Strongest Programs:
Business
Nursing
Psychology
Biology
Engineering
Computer Science
Geology
Philosophy

"Calvin students are people who care about the condition of the world and the people who live in it," says a junior. Forty percent of Calvin students are legacies and 52 percent are Michigan natives—African Americans constitute 3 percent of the total, Hispanics comprise 3 percent, and Asian Americans add 5 percent. And how about raging social and political issues? "Two big issues would be evolution and homosexuality," says one junior. Eligible Calvin students receive scholarships based on academic merit, averaging $7,500 each. There are no athletic awards.

Sixty-one percent of Calvin students live on campus in the single-sex dorms. Freshmen and sophomores bunk in suites with two bedrooms, connected by a bathroom, while juniors and seniors move off campus or into the on-campus apartments. "The dorms at Calvin foster community and friendships while also providing a comfortable place to call home," an organizational communications major says. Each residence hall and two of the apartment buildings have computer rooms in the basement, along with free washers and dryers. Calvin offers three intentional living/learning floors—Creation Care (recreational pursuits/environmental stewardship and sustainability), Grassroots (exploring race and identity in North America), and Honors. The food gets mostly positive reviews, too—with options such as pizza, cereal, fresh fruit, made-to-order sandwiches, and ice cream and waffles available at every meal. "More menu options throughout the week would be a huge plus. But the food is edible, and pretty good," says a philosophy major.

> **"Study abroad programs are an essential part of the Calvin experience."**

Calvin has no Greek system, and—owing to its emphasis on Christianity and character—the campus is officially dry. That's no great loss, students say, because there is so much to do on campus, including movies, speakers, concerts, and dances. "With over 100 different student clubs, varsity and intramural sports, and music groups, it's not too difficult to get socially connected on campus," says one senior. A junior adds, "The college usually organizes events known as 'Buck Fridays' where students can pay just a dollar and do something fun such as ice skating downtown during the winter." Downtown Grand Rapids has plenty of amenities and "there is never a shortage of things to do," according to one student. A popular annual event is Chaos Day, which brings the dorms together for a day of athletic contests. The Airband lip-synch competition each February is also a favorite, as are athletic contests versus Hope College. Road trips include the beaches of Lake Michigan (a one-hour drive) or Chicago (three hours distant), and even Florida or California for spring break.

Calvin fields a robust athletic program that competes in the Michigan Intercollegiate Athletic Association (MIAA). During the 2012–13 season, Calvin teams claimed 12 MIAA titles and earned the MIAA Commissioner's Cup, which is awarded to the school with the best overall performance across the league's 20 athletic offerings. Men's and women's cross-country and soccer, men's golf, men's basketball, and women's volleyball are especially competitive. "Any game against Hope always turns into a big deal," says a speech pathology major. The college's intramural program offers classes, leagues, and tournaments in sports from dodgeball to ultimate Frisbee and fantasy football. Half of all undergraduates participate.

The students who come to Calvin College aren't seeking the traditional beer-soaked four years away from home. Instead, they're looking to build community with friends and faculty members who share their already-strong Christian faith. "Calvin has a distinctively Christian character and atmosphere," says a sophomore. "This college, its people, place, and mission, all revolve around a commitment to Christ and the furthering of His kingdom. Faith plays an integral part in the classrooms, offices, and dorm rooms."

Calvin has no Greek system, and—owing to its emphasis on Christianity and character—the campus is officially dry.

Calvin is the only evangelical Christian college to offer an Asian studies program.

Overlaps

Hope, Grand Valley State, Michigan State, University of Michigan, Wheaton (IL), Trinity, Taylor, Western Michigan

Carleton College

Northfield, MN 55057

Less selective than Amherst, Williams, and Swarthmore, mainly because of its out-of-the-way Minnesota location. Yet Carleton retains its position as the premier liberal arts college in the upper Midwest. Predominantly liberal, but not to the extremes of its more antiestablishment cousins, students at Carleton excel at making their own fun.

Minnesota is many things: the land of 10,000 lakes, home to the massive Mall of America, birthplace of lore from Hiawatha to Paul Bunyan, and proud parent of the Mississippi River. Beyond all that history-book stuff, tucked into a small town in the southeastern corner of the state is Carleton College, arguably the best liberal arts school in the expansive Midwest. Add to this a midwinter carnival complete with human bowling, badminton competitions that raise money to fight cancer, and an expulsion of Coca-Cola from campus for human rights violations, and you have one all-around unique institution.

Surrounded by rolling farmland, Carleton's 955-acre campus is in the small town of Northfield, whose one-time status as the center of the Holstein cattle industry brought it the motto "The City of Cows, Colleges, and Contentment." Lakes, woods, and streams abound, and you can traverse them on 12 miles of hiking and cross-country skiing trails. The city boasts of fragrant lilacs in spring, rich summer greens, red maples in the fall, and a glistening blanket of white in winter. There's even an 800-acre arboretum, put to good use by everyone from jogging jocks to bird-watching nature lovers. Carleton's architectural style is somewhat eclectic—everything from Victorian to contemporary, but mostly redbrick.

Carleton's top-notch academic programs are no less varied: the sciences—biology, physics, astronomy, chemistry, geology, and computer science—are among the best anywhere, and scores of Carleton graduates go on to earn Ph.D.s in these areas. Of all the liberal arts schools in the country, Carleton's undergrads were recently awarded the highest number of National Science Foundation fellowships for graduate studies. Engineers can opt for a 3–2 program with Columbia University or Washington University in St. Louis, and for geologists seeking fieldwork—and maybe wanting to thaw out after a long Minnesota winter—

> **"Our language departments are very strong."**

Carleton sponsors a program in Death Valley. Closer to home at the "arb," as the arboretum is affectionately known, environmental studies majors have their own wilderness field station, which includes a prairie-restoration site. At the opposite end of the academic spectrum, the arts also flourish. Music and studio art majors routinely get into top graduate programs, and may take advantage of expanded offerings in dance and theater.

Distribution requirements ensure that a Carleton education exposes students not only to rigor and depth in their chosen field, but also to "a wide range of subjects and methods of studying them," administrators say. All students must show proficiency in English composition and a foreign language while fulfilling requirements

Website: www.carleton.edu
Location: Small Town
Private
Total Enrollment: 2,035
Undergraduates: 2,035
Male/Female: 47/53
SAT Ranges: CR 670–760, M 670–760
ACT Ranges: 29–33
Financial Aid: 56%
Expense: Pr $ $ $ $
Student Loans: 40%
Average Debt: $
Phi Beta Kappa: Yes
Applicants: 5,856
Accepted: 26%
Enrolled: 35%
Grad in 6 Years: 94%
Returning Freshmen: 98%
Academics: 🖉 🖉 🖉 🖉 🖉
Social: ☎ ☎ ☎
Q of L: ★ ★ ★
Admissions: (800) 995-2275
Email Address: admissions@carleton.edu

Strongest Programs:
Mathematics
Computer Science
Chemistry
Physics
English
History
Economics
Psychology

in four broad areas: arts and literature; history, philosophy, and religion; social sciences; and math and natural sciences. There's also a Global Citizenship requirement, under which students must take at least one course dealing with a non-Western culture, and a first-year Argument and Inquiry Seminar. Carleton offers interdisciplinary programs in Asian, Jewish, urban, African and African American, and women's studies. "Obviously I'm biased," says one Latin American studies major, "but I believe that our language departments are very strong. Particularly the Spanish department, due to its breadth of available classes and engaging professors." A concentration in cross-cultural studies brings in foreign students to discuss global issues and dynamics with their American counterparts. Approximately 74 percent of students spend at least one term abroad, and many take advantage of programs available through numerous organizations, including Carleton and the Associated Colleges of the Midwest*.

With highly motivated students and a heavy workload, Carleton isn't your typical mellow Midwestern liberal arts college. The trimester calendar means finals may be just three months apart and almost every-

"Our profs are incredible." may be just three months apart and almost every-one feels the pressure. The six-week Christmas vacation is Carleton's way of dealing with the cold winters. "While Carleton certainly isn't competitive, I wouldn't call it laid-back, either. Courses here will make you work, whether that's in reading, researching, thinking, some combination thereof, or something completely different," a linguistics major says. Sixty-four percent of classes have 19 or fewer students, so Carls are expected to participate actively. Carleton's faculty members are very committed to teaching. A senior raves, "Our profs are incredible. The instruction we receive is available not just in the classroom but during office hours, phone calls, Skype sessions, and many other modes of communication."

"Carleton is definitely nerd-friendly," quips one senior, "even if people here aren't passionate about 'traditionally' nerdy things." Seventy percent hail from outside Minnesota, half are from outside the Midwest, and most attended public schools. Both coasts are heavily represented, and international students account for 10 percent of the student body. African Americans and Hispanics account for 10 percent of the total student body, and Asian Americans for another 8 percent. But most Carls have a few things in common, such as being intellectually curious, yet laid-back; individualistic, but concerned about building a community feeling on campus. Their earthy dress and attitude are a sharp contrast from that of their more traditional crosstown cousins at rival St. Olaf College. The Carleton campus is rather left of center, concerned with issues including the environment, multiculturalism, affirmative action, gay rights, and sexism. "Students are ambitious, aware, and ready to 'save the world,'" says a sophomore. Qualified students receive merit awards averaging more than $2,600, but there are no athletic scholarships.

Campus accommodations range from comfortable old townhouses to modern hotel-like residence halls. Ninety-four percent of Carleton students live on campus. "I've had very positive experiences with housing. There's a wide variety of dorm and room styles, so it's possible every year to get a different living experience. Rooms are spacious (yes, even freshmen doubles), and dorms are very clean," reports a student. Best of all are the 10 college-owned off-campus "theme" houses,

"Carleton is definitely nerd-friendly." which focus on special interests such as foreign languages, the outdoors, or nuclear power issues. With the exception of the Farm House, an environmental studies house sitting on the edge of the arb, all the theme houses are situated in an attractive residential section of town close to campus. Students who wish to live off campus must apply for a slot. Dorms are co-ed by room, but there are two halls with single-sex floors. Davis is the recommended dorm, although Burton enjoys a "fun" reputation. Everyone who stays on campus must submit to a meal plan. "The food is fairly edible," reports a student, "as long as one enjoys the exclusive use of salt as a seasoning." Students report feeling safe: "Carleton is an extremely safe place," says a political science major. "Northfield is generally a low-crime city and the campus is even safer."

Absent a Greek system, Carleton's social life tends to be relaxed and informal. "Most students stay on campus over the weekends because there is always so much happening. We have movie screenings, theater productions, dances, student bands, guest performers, and many other events," says an English major. "Students are never bored." There are activities for those who pass on imbibing; a group called Co-op sponsors dances and Wednesday socials every two weeks, free movies, and special events like Comedy Night. Students agree that Carleton makes little more than token efforts to enforce the drinking age. "I would credit good judgment by students rather than the alcohol policy, but Carleton does not suffer from too many problems surrounding alcohol," says a senior.

Absent a Greek system, Carleton's social life tends to be relaxed and informal.

Northfield itself is a history-filled town with a population of about 17,000. There are old-style shops and a beautiful old hotel. "Northfield is quaint, but there's not much to do," a sophomore says. Students often frequent the St. Olaf College campus and a nightspot known as the Reub'n'Stein. Minneapolis-St. Paul, 35 miles to the north, is a popular road-trip destination. Since students aren't allowed to have cars on campus, Carleton charters buses on weekends.

The Knights compete in NCAA Division III athletics; about a third of the students play on varsity teams. The track, swimming, tennis, basketball, and baseball teams are competitive, as are the championship cross-country ski teams. In soccer, men have won four conference titles in the last five years, while the women's team has made the NCAA tournament three times in the last four years. Popular events include the Winter Carnival, the Spring Concert, and Mai-F'te, a gala celebrated on an island in one of the two lakes on campus. Traditions include the weeklong freshman orientation program, where—during opening convocation—students bombard professors with bubbles as the faculty members process. There's also the annual spring softball game that begins at 5:30 a.m. and runs as many innings as there are years in Carleton's existence. The all-campus 10:00 p.m. scream on the eve of final exams keeps fatigued studiers awake. Another distinctive Carleton tradition is the regular liberation and dramatic reappearance—such as dangling from a helicopter over homecoming football games—of a plaster bust of Friedrich Schiller, the Romantic philosopher and buddy of Goethe.

"Rooms are spacious (yes, even freshmen doubles)."

It can be cold in Minnesota, in a face-stinging, bone-chilling kind of way. And the classes are far from easy. But Carleton is a warm campus, and the academics are challenging without being impossible. Carls toe the line between individuality and community, which makes for personal growth and lifelong friendships. Says one happy student, "At Carleton, everyone is a bit nerdy and everyone is free to be whomever they want."

Overlaps

Macalester, Middlebury, Brown, Amherst, Yale, Bowdoin, Pomona, Williams

If You Apply To ➤ **Carleton:** Early decision: Nov. 15. Regular admissions: Jan. 15. Application fee: $30 (paper), free (online). Campus and alumni interviews: optional, informational. SATs or ACTs: required. Subject Tests: recommended. Accepts the Common Application. Essay question.

Carnegie Mellon University

5000 Forbes Avenue, Pittsburgh, PA 15213-3890

Carnegie Mellon is the only premier technical university that happens to be equally strong in the arts. Applications have nearly doubled in the past 10 years, so it must be doing something right. One of the few institutions that openly matches better financial aid awards from competitor schools. Shares its suburban neighborhood with a variety of cultural institutions, including the University of Pittsburgh.

Website: www.cmu.edu

Location: City Center

Private

Total Enrollment: 10,922

Undergraduates: 6,072

Male/Female: 58/42

SAT Ranges: CR 630–730, M 680–780

ACT Ranges: 29–33

Financial Aid: 48%

Expense: Pr $ $ $ $

Student Loans: 45%

Average Debt: $ $ $ $

Phi Beta Kappa: Yes

Applicants: 17,313

Accepted: 30%

Enrolled: 29%

Grad in 6 Years: 87%

Returning Freshmen: 96%

Academics: ✑ ✑ ✑ ✑

Social: ☎ ☎ ☎

Q of L: ★ ★ ★

Admissions: (412) 268-2082

Email Address: undergraduate-admissions@ andrew.cmu.edu

Strongest Programs:
Computer Science
Engineering
Drama
Music
Industrial Management
Business
Architecture

Students at Carnegie Mellon don't have to choose between soaking up the high drama of Shakespeare and plunging into the fast-paced dot-com world. The university is known for both its science offerings and strong drama and music programs. But scholars can't be focused on just their own course of study—Carnegie Mellon continues to strive to offer both its technical and liberal arts students a well-rounded education that requires a lot of hard work, but promises great results.

"Carnegie Mellon is very intense."

Carnegie Mellon was formed by the merger of Carnegie Institute of Technology and the Mellon Institute of Research in 1967, resulting in a self-contained 144-acre campus attractively situated in Pittsburgh's affluent Oakland section. Next door is the city's largest park and its major museum, named after—you guessed it—Andrew Carnegie. Henry Hornbostel won a competition in 1904 to design the Carnegie Technical Schools, now Carnegie Mellon University. Hornbostel, who attended the École des Beaux-Arts in the 1890s, created a campus plan that is a modification of the Jefferson plan for the University of Virginia with the Beaux-Arts device of creating primary and secondary axes and grouping buildings around significant open spaces. Buildings are designed in a Renaissance style, with buff-colored brick arches and piers, tile roofs, and terra cotta and granite details.

Carnegie Mellon is divided into seven colleges, six that offer undergraduate courses: the College of Fine Arts, the College of Humanities and Social Sciences, the Carnegie Institute of Technology, the Mellon College of Science, the School of Computer Science, and the Tepper School of Business. Each college has its own distinct character and admission requirements, which applicants may want to contact the admissions office to find out about. All the colleges, however, share the university's commitment to what it calls a "liberal-professional" education, which shows the relevance of the liberal arts while stressing courses that develop technical skills and good job prospects. Humanities and social science types can major in applied history, professional writing, or information systems, for example, instead of traditional disciplinary concentrations. The Science and Humanities Scholars program allows talented undergrads to develop a course of study based on their interests in the humanities, natural sciences, math, or social sciences. In addition, the Fifth-Year Scholars program provides full tuition for outstanding students who want to remain at Carnegie Mellon for an additional year to pursue more studies that interest them.

"Sometimes there just isn't very much social life."

Most departments at Carnegie Mellon are strong, but exceptional ones include chemical engineering and electrical and computer engineering. While some humanities courses are praised, most students agree Carnegie Mellon is definitely more of a science-oriented school. Each college requires core work from freshmen; in the College of Humanities and Social Science, for example, students are introduced to computers in a required first-year philosophy course, using the machines to work on problems of logic. Two majors—logic and computation in the philosophy department and cognitive science through the psychology department—combine computer science technology with such fields as artificial intelligence and linguistics.

As one student bluntly puts it, the courses at Carnegie Mellon are "extremely rigorous with many hours expected outside of the classroom. Expect to work hard if you come here." Students at Carnegie Mellon work hard, no doubt about it. "Carnegie Mellon is very intense, so lots of time is dedicated to class assignments and group projects," a student says. However, nearly all the classes are small, with fewer than 30 students. Most students agree that the Carnegie Institute of Technology is by far the most difficult college. Professors rate high with most students, who praise their availability and willingness to help. "Most professors are very eager to help and make sure that material is understood," says a sophomore psychology major.

Carnegie Mellon's professional focus shows in its internship program. A number of five-year, dual-degree options exist, including a joint B.S./M.S. or an industrial internship co-op program in materials science and engineering, which places students in the industrial environment. Beyond traditional student exchanges with major universities around the globe, Carnegie Mellon has established a campus in the Arabian Gulf nation of Qatar. The campus offers business and undergraduate computer science degrees, and is led by renowned roboticist Charles Thorpe. The university also has a campus in California and a rapidly expanding presence in Europe and Asia, with programs and educational partnerships in locations such as Portugal, Singapore, Japan, and Greece; more than a quarter of the university's undergrads study abroad.

Carnegie Mellon remains one of the most fragmented campuses in the nation. Students divide themselves between actors, dancers, and other artsy types and engineers, scientists and architects. In any case, students are united in their quest for a good job after graduation. Still, many complain about the fact that students will give up sleep to study, and that this kind of academic orientation can often hinder social life. "Sometimes there just isn't very much social life, but many students prefer it that way," says one student. Every day includes a designated "meeting-free" time for students, allowing them time to study or participate in student activities.

> "We are very diverse and therefore very culturally aware."

Once a largely regional institution, drawing mostly Pennsylvania residents, Carnegie Mellon now counts two-thirds of its students from out of state. More than one-third are from minority groups, including 22 percent Asian American, 5 percent African American, and 7 percent Hispanic. "We are very diverse and therefore very culturally aware," a biology major says. Some students say a big issue is the nearly 2-to-1 male/female ratio. The university says it remains committed to need-blind admissions, but it provides larger proportions of outright grants in financial aid packages to "academic superstars." Carnegie Mellon has stopped guaranteeing to meet the financial need of all accepted students, but offers an early evaluation of financial aid eligibility for interested prospective students. The financial aid office actually encourages students who have received more generous packages from competing schools to let Carnegie Mellon know so they have an opportunity to match or better them.

Housing, guaranteed for all four years, offers old and newer buildings, the most popular being university-owned apartments. Upperclassmen get first pick, with freshman assignments coming from a lottery of the remainder. "The dorms are generally very comfortable and well maintained, with ample living space," says one student. The best dorms for freshmen are New House, Donner, Resnik, and Morewood Gardens. Most halls are co-ed, but a few are men-only. Students can remain in campus housing as long as they wish, and about 99 percent do so each year. The

Humanities and social science types can major in applied history, professional writing, or information systems, for example, instead of traditional disciplinary concentrations.

Two majors—logic and computation in the philosophy department and cognitive science through the psychology department—combine computer science technology with such fields as artificial intelligence and linguistics.

Carnegie Mellon Café was the first cafeteria in the nation to earn LEED certification and offers students a state-of-the-art dining space.

With all the academic pressure at Carnegie Mellon, it's a good thing there are so many opportunities to unwind, especially with the entire city of Pittsburgh close at hand. The Greek system provides the most visible form of on-campus social life, and 12 percent of the men and 13 percent of the women join fraternities and sororities, respectively. For those who choose not to fraternize, coffeehouses, inexpensive films, dances, and concerts in nearby Oakland, plus downtown Pittsburgh itself (opera, ballet, symphony, concerts, and sporting events just 20 minutes away by bus) provide plenty of alternatives. The administration is desperately trying to curtail underage drinking. Some students say the penalties for being caught are harsh, but others maintain that the rules are only "vaguely known."

One event that brings everyone together is the Spring Carnival, when the school shuts down for a day. Students set up booths with electronic games, and student groups race in buggies made of lightweight alloys designed by engineering majors. Students put on original "Scotch and Soda" presentations, two of which—*Pippin* and *Godspell*—went on to become Broadway hits. The Jill Watson Festival Across the Arts—named for an alumna and former faculty member who died on TWA Flight 800—specifically targets artists who cross boundaries in their work. The Carnegie Mellon Tartans compete in Division III. Both the women's soccer and volleyball teams recently won tournament championships, and the swim team has earned many AAU honors as well.

Carnegie Mellon appeals to those yearning for the bright lights of Broadway or the glowing computer screens of the scientific and business worlds. And with a broad range of liberal arts and technical courses not only available, but required, there's no doubt students leave Carnegie Mellon with a well-rounded education—and an impressive diploma. "It's driven, but there's no better place to be interacting with people of so many disciplines who are so focused," one satisfied senior says.

> *Carnegie Mellon remains one of the most fragmented campuses in the nation.*

Overlaps

MIT, Cornell, Princeton, Stanford, University of Pennsylvania, Columbia, UC–Berkeley, Washington University in St. Louis

If You Apply To ➤

Carnegie Mellon: Early decision: Nov. 1. Regular admissions: Jan. 1. Housing: May 1. Application fee: $70. Campus and alumni interviews: optional, evaluative. SATs or ACTs: required. Subject Tests: required (math). Accepts the Common Application. Essay question: personal statement.

Case Western Reserve

103 Tomlinson Hall, 10900 Euclid Ave, Cleveland, OH 44106-7055

Case has most of the offerings available at Carnegie Mellon or Washington U, but it has never found a niche in the national consciousness. Students sing its praises, especially since Case is less difficult in admission than other institutions of comparable quality, and students can get an outstanding technical education with solid offerings in other areas.

Website: www.case.edu
Location: City Outskirts
Private
Total Enrollment: 8,817
Undergraduates: 4,228

Cleveland's Case Western Reserve has long been in the shadow of Pittsburgh's Carnegie Mellon, but the schools also have much in common. Both are the product of mergers between a technical college, known for excellence in engineering, and a more traditional university, focused on the arts and sciences. Both are located in aging rust-belt cities, which have struggled to reinvent themselves. And both tend to attract brainy students more concerned with studying than socializing. Case has increased its investment in the arts, humanities, and social sciences, with an aim toward helping students connect these disciplines with their technical studies. "Case is challenging but friendly," says one student, "and I couldn't imagine a better combination."

Case is located on the eastern edge of Cleveland, at University Circle. This 550-acre area of parks and gardens is home to more than 40 cultural, educational, medical, and research institutions, including the city's museums of art and natural history, its botanical gardens, and Severance Hall, home of the Cleveland Orchestra.

"Case is challenging but friendly."

Campus buildings are an eclectic mix of architectural styles, and several are listed on the National Register of Historic Places. The Peter B. Lewis Building, designed by Frank Gehry, is home for the Weatherhead School of Management. It features undulating walls similar to those of Gehry's Guggenheim Museum in Bilbao, Spain, along with offices, classrooms, and meeting rooms on every floor, to encourage informal student/faculty interaction.

The product of the 1967 marriage between Case Institute of Technology and Western Reserve University, Case has four undergraduate schools: the College of Arts and Sciences, the Case School of Engineering, the Frances Payne Bolton School of Nursing, and the aforementioned Weatherhead School; all also offer graduate programs. All Case students participate in a general education program known as SAGES. The acronym stands for the Seminar Approach to General Education and Scholarship, and the program emphasizes small seminars, critical thinking, and writing. The program requires four seminars, a writing portfolio, and a senior capstone experience that can be an individual or group effort.

Case's strongest programs include engineering, especially biomedical engineering, and the school's polymer science major is one of the few such undergraduate programs in the country. "Case is well known for science and engineering programs," says one student, "and they are very rigorous programs that will prepare you for future work and studies." Strengths in the College of Arts and Sciences include music (a joint program with the nearby Cleveland Institute of Music), anthropology (especially medical anthropology), and psychology. Management and accounting are also strong. Twenty-two percent of students take part in study abroad; locales include El Salvador, Israel, Ecuador, and the Netherlands.

Courses tend to be rigorous but collaboration among students is the norm, says one junior. "It's ridiculously easy to find a study partner or group—just stick your head out of your room and shout, 'Who's doing the Math 223 problem set?' and you'll have a half-dozen people working together around a table in moments." A biochemistry major says, "While you may run across some professors who are difficult to learn from, there are far more professors who care a great deal about the students." Combined bachelor's and master's programs are popular, as is the Preprofessional Scholars program, which gives top freshmen conditional acceptance to Case's law, social work, medical, or dental schools, assuming satisfactory progress through prerequisite courses.

"Students are extremely motivated," says a senior, and "each one is clearly driven to succeed." Thirty-seven percent of Case's students are Ohio natives, and 70 percent come from public high schools. African Americans make up 5 percent of the student body, Asian Americans 18 percent, and Hispanics 5 percent. In addition to need-based financial aid, eligible students at Case receive scholarships based on academic merit. Students say conservatives

"Case is well known for science and engineering programs."

and liberals are well represented on campus. The College Now Greater Cleveland program provides additional financial aid for high school graduates from urban Cleveland and the inner-ring suburbs.

(continued)

Male/Female: 56/44
SAT Ranges: CR 600–720, M 660–760
ACT Ranges: 29–33
Financial Aid: 86%
Expense: Pr $ $
Student Loans: 52%
Average Debt: $ $ $ $
Phi Beta Kappa: Yes
Applicants: 14,778
Accepted: 54%
Enrolled: 17%
Grad in 6 Years: 78%
Returning Freshmen: 92%
Academics: ✍ ✍ ✍ ✍
Social: ☎ ☎
Q of L: ★ ★ ★
Admissions: (216) 368-4450
Email Address: admission@case.edu

Strongest Programs:
Biology
Psychology
Biomedical Engineering
Mechanical Engineering
Nursing
Management
Anthropology
Polymer Science

All Case students participate in a general education program known as SAGES.

Ninety-seven percent of students live on campus; freshmen and sophomores are required to do so. While students give the older dorms mixed reviews, they are awed by the apartment-based accommodations for upperclassmen. The complex houses about 700 upperclassmen in apartment-style suites with two to nine students each. Students enjoy full kitchens, living rooms, single rooms, and double beds. "The dorms are comfortable and clean," says a biology major. In addition to dishwashers and extra-large windows, the apartments include study rooms, laundry rooms, music practice rooms, a fitness center, and a cyber café. Another choice for upperclassmen is off-campus housing, where there are many desirable apartments within walking distance of campus. Among campus meal plan options, students say the two dining halls are OK but best on weekdays. There are also plenty of quick-service options on campus, such as Starbucks, Subway, and Einstein Bros Bagels. As for safety, "campus security is passable," says one student. "As long as students stay smart, issues don't arise too often."

Twenty-two percent of students take part in study abroad; locales include El Salvador, Israel, Ecuador, and the Netherlands.

Case is located in a quasisuburban area five miles from downtown. "It's very budget-friendly," notes one senior. Another says, "Cleveland is more than just Case and I wouldn't have it any other way." There's also the Rock & Roll Hall of Fame, and—in the warmer months—Cleveland Indians games at Progressive Field.

On campus, there are dances and fraternity parties (Greek groups draw 39 percent of the men and 33 percent of the women, respectively). "Social life on campus is basically centered on student groups," one student says. Community service projects are also big in the Greek community. Having a car is helpful, especially for road trips to nearby cities in Ohio, or for longer jaunts to Chicago or Windsor, Ontario, where students under 21 are free to drink and gamble. In Cleveland, students get unlimited bus service for around $25 a semester.

When a man at Case pledges his undying love and devotion, it can as easily be to his laptop as to a woman. Rationalizes one student: "You may have trouble finding a date on most weekends, but if your computer crashes on a Friday night, it will be up and running by Saturday morning." Popular campus traditions are Greek Week, which includes nearly everyone on campus; the Spring Fest to celebrate the end of classes; and "Study Overs," where students gather during finals week for free food, massages, study groups, and more. The annual sci-fi movie marathon is a rite of passage, while Engineering Week features a fuel-cell powered car competition.

"Students are extremely motivated."

Although sports are not a major focus on campus, the Tartans versus Spartans football game against Carnegie Mellon is big. The baseball team recently won its first UAA championship and finished as runners-up at the NCAA Midwest Regional. Men's tennis is solid and the cross-country team won an All-Ohio championship and qualified for its first NCAA championship appearance since 2008. Women's tennis and volleyball are competitive, too. Intramural competition draws 55 percent of undergrads and "ultimate Frisbee is huge," says a junior. Also popular are intramural soccer, basketball, softball, volleyball, flag football, inner-tube water polo, floor hockey, and other sports. The 26-mile Hudson Relay, held the last week of the spring semester to commemorate Case's relocation from Hudson to Cleveland, pits teams of runners from the four classes against one another, with each person running a half mile. There's also a racquetball and squash complex, and a field house with an Olympic-size pool.

Overlaps

Ohio State, University of Michigan, University of Pittsburgh, Boston University, University of Illinois

If you come to Case, students say, prepare to work hard. Studying takes priority, and one student says his favorite tradition is the Midnight Scream: "The night before you have a final, you go out on the balcony of your dorm, or lean out the window, and scream at midnight. It's great to hear other people screaming, to remind you that you aren't alone."

The Catholic University of America

Washington, D.C. 20064

There are other Roman Catholic–affiliated universities, but this is The Catholic University. Catholics make up 80 percent of the student body here (versus roughly half at nearby Georgetown). If you can't be in Rome, there is no better place than D.C. to work and play. CUA even has a Metro stop right on campus. Academic freedom is the norm except in theology.

Founded in 1887 under a charter from Pope Leo XIII, The Catholic University of America was the brainchild of United States bishops who wanted to provide an American institution where the curriculum was guided by the tenets of Christian thought. Over time, the university has garnered a reputation as a research-oriented school that also provides a strong undergraduate, preprofessional education, and an appreciation for the arts. However, the university's new strategic plan calls for an emphasis on the humanities, less large-scale research, and a return to single-sex residence halls. The changes have ruffled a few feathers; the school recently pulled out of the Association of American Universities, a group composed of 62 elite research institutions, citing differences in mission.

> "The courses are challenging and require a commitment to studying."

Catholic's campus comprises 193 tree-lined acres, an impressive layout for an urban university. Buildings range from ivy-covered brownstone and brick to ultra-modern, giving the place a true collegiate feel. Catholic is one of the few colleges in the country that began as a graduate institution (others are Clark University and The Johns Hopkins University), and grad students still account for a respectable portion of the student population. Six of its 10 schools (arts and sciences, engineering, architecture, nursing, music, and philosophy) now admit undergrads, while two others (social service and religious studies) provide undergraduate programs through arts and sciences.

Students have excellent options in almost any department at CUA. Apart from politics (which all agree sets the tone on campus), the history, English, drama, psychology, and physics departments are very strong. Philosophy and religious studies are highly regarded and have outstanding faculty members. The School of Nursing is one of the best in the nation, and engineering and architecture are also highly regarded. Architecture and physics have outstanding facilities, the latter enjoying a modern vitreous-state lab, a boon for both research and hands-on undergraduate instruction. For students interested in the arts, CUA's School of Music offers excellent vocal and instrumental training, and there's also a program in musical theater. "The courses are challenging and require a commitment to studying and learning the material in order to be successful," a senior says.

> "One of the things I really love about Catholic are the professors."

Students at CUA need at least 40 courses in order to graduate. In the School of Arts and Sciences, approximately 25 of these must be from a core curriculum spread

Website: www.cua.edu
Location: City Center
Private
Total Enrollment: 4,733
Undergraduates: 3,409
Male/Female: 45/55
SAT Ranges: CR 510–610, M 500–610
ACT Ranges: 22–27
Financial Aid: 91%
Expense: Pr $ $
Student Loans: N/A
Average Debt: N/A
Phi Beta Kappa: Yes
Applicants: 6,361
Accepted: 63%
Enrolled: 22%
Grad in 6 Years: 67%
Returning Freshmen: 84%
Academics: ✎ ✎ ✎
Social: ☎ ☎ ☎
Q of L: ★ ★ ★
Admissions: (202) 319-5305
Email Address: cua-admissions@cua.edu

Strongest Programs:
Architecture
Psychology
History
Biology
Musical Theater
Nursing

(continued)

Education
Social Work

across the humanities, social and behavioral sciences, philosophy, environmental studies, religion, math and natural sciences, and languages and literature. English composition is also required. The brightest students can enroll in a 12-course interdisciplinary honors program that offers sequences in the humanities, philosophy, and social sciences. The university offers a wide variety of semester, academic year, summer and short-term education abroad programs, as well as international internships through its CUAbroad office. Currently, there are more than 40 semester and 16 summer options available, including popular Western European destinations and programs in Africa, South America, Asia, and Australia/Oceania. The flagship Rome study abroad program for design students incorporates design studio, field study, history, theory, and the Italian language. Finally, two students are chosen each year to spend a fall semester at the Fondazione Architetto Augusto Rancilio (FAAR) in Milan to study themes including architecture, urban studies, and technology. CUA also offers accelerated degree programs in which students can earn bachelor's and master's degrees in five years, or six years for a joint B.A./J.D. CUA is part of the 11-university Consortium of Universities of the Washington Metropolitan Area* and the Oak Ridge Associated Universities Consortium*. The latter comprises 87 U.S. colleges and a contractor for the federal Energy Department. The program gives students access to federal research facilities.

The School of Nursing is one of the best in the nation, and engineering and architecture are also highly regarded.

Most classes have fewer than 25 students, which means special attention from faculty members. It also means that there's no place to hide. "One of the things I really love about Catholic are the professors," says one sophomore. "They all teach with passion and it is apparent that they love what they do." Clergy are at the helm of certain graduate schools, but the School of Arts and Sciences has a primarily lay faculty, with priests occupying less than 16 percent of the teaching posts. Its chancellor is the archbishop of Washington, and Catholic churches across the country donate a fraction of their annual collections to the university. One downside of being the only Catholic school with a papal charter is that officials in Rome, who do not always warm up to American traditions of academic freedom, keep a sharp eye on who teaches in the theology department and what they write and say.

"For most students, CUA is a large financial sacrifice."

Catholicism is clearly the tie that binds the student body. Sunday Masses are so well attended that extra services must be offered in the dorms. Most students are from the Northeast, and are primarily white. African Americans account for 4 percent of the student body, while Hispanics comprise 10 percent. Another 3 percent are Asian American, and foreign students account for 4 percent. Ninety-eight percent are from out of state, and most students are fairly conservative. Big issues on campus include abortion and gay/lesbian rights. "For most students, CUA is a large financial sacrifice," says one student. "I think in a lot of ways it drives them to do well and to succeed at whatever they're pursuing." The university maintains a need-blind admissions policy. It does not guarantee to meet the full demonstrated need of all admitted. Thirty-one lucky students—one from each archdiocese in the nation—receive a full-tuition merit scholarship. There are several hundred additional merit scholarships available worth an average of $6,736, along with various types of financial aid. There are no athletic scholarships.

The brightest students can enroll in a 12-course interdisciplinary honors program that offers sequences in the humanities, philosophy, and social sciences.

Eighty-seven percent of the students live in the dorms. "The newer dorms are more comfortable than the older dorms, but Catholic is very good about revamping and reconstructing older dorms," one student says, but many grumble that the influx of applicants has made rooms hard to come by. The spacious and ultramodern Centennial Village (eight dorms and 600 beds laid out in suites) is available to all students, many of whom flee CUA's strict visitation (no guests past 2:00 a.m.) and alcohol policies and move into apartments of their own. The best dorms for freshmen are Spellman, Flather, and Conaty. Campus fare is hit or miss: "The dining is unlimited, which is awesome for big appetites," says one student. "The problem is that it's extremely overpriced and very bland." Emergency phones, shuttle buses, and escort services are provided as part of campus security, and students agree that they always feel safe on campus as long as they are careful.

CUA students do indulge in some serious partying. Some of their favorite locales include the Irish Times, Colonel Brook Tavern, the Tune Inn, and Kitty's. It's no wonder most students agree that the social scene is "off campus at various bars, clubs, and coffeehouses in D.C." When students want to explore the city, they need only walk to the campus Metro stop and then enjoy the ride. Capitol Hill is 15 minutes away; the stylish Georgetown area, with its chic restaurants and nightspots, is only a half hour away. No one under 21 can drink on campus, and most students agree that this policy is effective in curbing underage drinking. Also, alcohol "abuse" has been added as an offense in addition to use, possession, and distribution. For those eager to repent the weekend's excesses, there are student ministry retreats. Annual festivals on the campus calendar include a weeklong homecoming celebration, Beaux Arts Ball, Christmas Holly Hop (held in New York City), and Spring Fling. A time-honored winter tradition is sledding down Flather Hill on cafeteria trays.

CUA students do indulge in some serious partying.

"The dining is unlimited, which is awesome for big appetites."

Sports on campus include varsity and intramural competition. CUA's athletic teams compete in Division III. In recent years, women's lacrosse has won four consecutive conference championships (the most recent in 2011) and advanced to the regional finals of the NCAA tournament twice; men's and women's soccer have both won conference championships, as has baseball. Men's lacrosse, softball, and field hockey are solid, too. Many students use their strength for community service, including the Christian-based Habitat for Humanity, in which they build houses for needy families.

When discussions first raised the idea of a Catholic university, the man who would become the university's first rector, Bishop John Joseph Keane, argued for an institution that would "exercise a dominant influence in the world's future" with a superior intellectual foundation. Now, more than 100 years later, CUA offers students a wealth of preprofessional courses spanning the arts and sciences. The founders' quest for "a higher synthesis of knowledge" is constantly being realized at CUA, a unique university and a capital destination.

Overlaps

Boston College, University of Maryland, Georgetown, Loyola (MD), American, George Washington

If You Apply To ➤

Catholic: Early action: Nov. 15. Regular admissions: Feb. 15. Application fee: $55. Campus interviews: optional, evaluative. No alumni interviews. SATs or ACTs: required. Subject Tests: recommended (writing and foreign language). Accepts the Common Application. Essay question.

Centre College

600 West Walnut, Danville, KY 40422

Centre may not be the most famous institution of higher learning in Kentucky, but it is certainly the best. Centre offers college the way it used to be—gentleman scholars, football games, and fraternity pranks (preferably done in the nude). There is also the unparalleled closeness between students and faculty that comes with a student body of just over 1,000. Compare to Sewanee, DePauw, and Millsaps.

Eighty-five percent of any given class takes advantage of those study abroad programs.

Centre College, the only independent school in Kentucky with a Phi Beta Kappa chapter, has produced two-thirds of the state's Rhodes scholars over the last 40 years. But the school is not all work and no play. It's also a throwback to the way college used to be, with Friday night parties on fraternity row and Saturday afternoon football games. Centre's small size offers "the ability to get involved and have a direct hand in making improvements," says a biology major. And its liberal arts focus means that despite Centre's southern location, students are progressive, intellectual, and perhaps more well-rounded than their peers at neighboring schools. "We have an amazing balance of 'Northern academics' paired with 'Southern hospitalities,'" says a sophomore.

> **"We have an amazing balance of 'Northern academics' paired with 'Southern hospitalities.'"**

Located in the heart of Kentucky Bluegrass country, Centre's campus is a mix of old Greek Revival and attractive modern buildings. More than 14 of them are listed on the National Registry of Historic Places, a fact that's less surprising when you know that Centre is the 48th oldest college in the United States. The college is home to four LEED-certified buildings, including two at the Gold level.

General education requirements include basic skills in expository writing, math, and foreign language and two courses in four contexts—aesthetic, social, scientific, and fundamental questions. Students are also required to take a computer seminar. The freshman seminar is offered during the three-week January "CentreTerm." These courses are required and are capped at 15 students each, and they offer a chance to explore topics such as cloning, baseball in American politics, and coffee and culture.

Centre's most popular majors are history, economics, English, biology, and government; not coincidentally, these are among the school's best departments. Art is also strong, and glassblowing enthusiasts will find one of the few fully equipped undergraduate facilities for their pursuit in the nation. "The academic climate is challenging, but incredibly supportive. Professors expect the best out of every student, but are also always there to provide any possible assistance," reports one senior. No course taken by a Centre freshman has more than 50 students, and 60 percent have 19 or fewer. Professors are "experts in their fields and are also excellent at transmitting their knowledge to students," says a psychology and Spanish double major. Another student adds, "With the focus on undergraduate students, Centre students have the opportunity to do research with professors as early as the summer after their freshman year."

Eighty-five percent of any given class takes advantage of those study abroad programs, which offer travel to London, France, Mexico, Japan, and Ireland during the semester, and to New Zealand, Russia, Turkey, Vietnam, and India during the January term. Centre also belongs to the Associated Colleges of the South*, through which students may select programs in Central America. A 3–2 program sends aspiring engineers on to one of four major universities, including Columbia and Vanderbilt. About one-fifth of students perform collaborative research with faculty, and the John C. Young Scholars program allows select seniors to participate in a year of guided research.

"Centre students are versatile; we are athletic, intelligent, ambitious, and skeptical of the status quo," says one freshman. "At the risk of sounding brash, Centre students are simply higher achievers than the students at our rival college." Fifty-four percent of Centre students hail from Kentucky, and three-quarters graduated from public high school. African American, Asian American, and Hispanic students together make up 10 percent of the student body. "Although Centre students have a reputation for being apathetic, there is a large number who are socially and politically engaged," a senior says. "Thanks in part to the college's robust study abroad program, students are politically engaged and aware of international concerns," says a junior. Centre offers merit scholarships and the "Centre commitment" guarantees students an internship or research experience, study abroad, and a degree in four years.

Ninety-nine percent of students live in Centre's dorms, which are "comfortable and clean," according to a senior. There are three main clusters of halls on campus—North Side, Old Centre, and the Old Quad—and each has all of the necessities of college life. Freshmen live in single-sex halls, while upperclassmen may choose buildings that are co-ed by floor. Room draw is described as "confusing," and it can be difficult to get into the most highly desired housing. Centre has also purchased and remodeled an apartment building to provide additional housing for upperclassmen, though the 41 percent of men and 38 percent of the women who go Greek may bunk in fraternity or sorority houses, respectively. Campus dining receives a hearty thumbs-up from students. "The dining hall has soup, sandwiches, pizza, pasta, a salad bar, bagels, fresh fruit, cereal, and desserts every day. Most students like the food and enjoy the atmosphere of the dining hall," notes one sated student.

"People stay on campus for the weekends," says a mathematics major. "Greek life is huge, but very inclusive." When it comes to alcohol, Centre follows federal and state law—no one under 21 can drink. "The policies generally work pretty well," a senior says. "However, alcohol is a large part of the weekend social life here for many students." The town of Danville is located in a dry county, and local restaurants only recently won permission to serve alcohol. That said, Lexington and Louisville are within an hour's drive, and it's easy to get to the countryside for camping, fishing, and other outdoor pursuits. Students also get free admission to Centre's separately endowed Norton Center for the Arts, which brings touring musicals, plays, and other performances to campus. Eighty percent of the student body does community service through the Greek system, Habitat for Humanity, and the Humane Society.

Eighty percent of the student body does community service through the Greek system, Habitat for Humanity, and the Humane Society.

Centre's football team has been around for more than a century, and while it now competes against regional opponents in Division III, that wasn't always the case. In 1921 the Colonels beat then-powerhouse Harvard, six to zero, a triumph that has been called the greatest sports upset in the first half of the 20th century. Men's basketball, women's

"We are athletic, intelligent, ambitious, and skeptical of the status quo."

soccer, men's and women's golf, and men's cross-country have all competed in the NCAA championships recently. Seventy percent of the student body regularly takes advantage of the intramural program, with flag football, softball, and soccer drawing a lot of players. Centre's archrival is nearby Transylvania University, but it's other traditions that really get students going. Those include faculty Christmas caroling for the freshmen and the "Running the Flame," which has students dashing from the fraternity houses, around a sculpture, and back—"naked, of course." Another student says, "Recently, people have started putting pennies on the new statue of Lincoln for good luck on exams."

What Centre College lacks in size, it more than makes up for in quality. With a safe, bucolic campus, an emphasis on academic excellence, and faculty and students who care about forming lasting friendships with each other, this undiscovered gem may be worth a look. "The people and just the feel of the campus were what really won me over," one satisfied junior says.

Overlaps

Transylvania, Rhodes, University of the South, Furman, Denison, Vanderbilt, Wofford, DePauw

If You Apply To ➢

Centre: Early action: Dec. 1. Regular admissions: Jan. 15. Application fee: $40 (paper), free (online). Campus and alumni interviews: optional, informational. SATs or ACTs: required. No Subject Tests. Accepts the Common Application. Essay question: Common Application questions.

Chapman University

One University Drive, Orange, CA 92866

Chapman sits at the hub of Orange County and a stone's throw away from L.A. Has parlayed its O.C. location into burgeoning popularity in film, television, and the performing arts. Those without showbiz aspirations can opt for biology, journalism, and business. Disneyland is in the neighborhood, but you need a car to get there.

Website: www.chapman.edu
Location: Suburban
Private
Total Enrollment: 6,798
Undergraduates: 5,433
Male/Female: 42/58
SAT Ranges: CR 550–650,
    M 560–660
ACT Ranges: 25–29
Financial Aid: 89%
Expense: Pr $ $ $
Student Loans: 73%
Average Debt: $
Phi Beta Kappa: Yes
Applicants: 10,489
Accepted: 44%
Enrolled: 28%
Grad in 6 Years: 72%
Returning Freshmen: 91%
Academics: ✍ ✍ ✍
Social: ☎ ☎ ☎
Q of L: ★ ★ ★
Admissions: (888) CU-APPLY
Email Address: admit@
    chapman.edu

Strongest Programs:
Film and Television Production
Business and Economics
Theater
Dance
Music
Education

Although Southern California has more than its share of budding starlets and Brad Pitt wannabes, it's also home to Chapman University, where future filmmakers and other burgeoning artists flock to hone their crafts under the watchful eye of seasoned faculty. The university offers solid programs in film, television, theater, and music, and sends students out into the world via countless internships. Even those who steer clear of show business find reason to cheer: Chapman has stellar programs in biology and journalism as well. A junior says, "A Chapman student is a leader, someone who wants to be actively involved in their community and consciously making a difference."

> "A Chapman student is a leader."

Founded in 1861, Chapman University is one of the oldest private universities in California. Originally called Hesperian College, the school later merged with California Christian College in Los Angeles. In 1934, the institution was renamed in honor of C. C. Chapman, an Orange County entrepreneur and benefactor of the school. In 1991 the college again changed its name to Chapman University, reflecting its evolution into a comprehensive institution of higher learning. The beautiful residential campus, situated on 75 tree-lined acres, features a mixture of landmark historic buildings and state-of-the-art facilities. It is located in the historic Old Towne district of Orange, near outstanding beaches, Disneyland, and the world-class cultural offerings of Orange County and Los Angeles. For what it's worth, Chapman is also home to the largest freestanding marble staircase west of the Mississippi River, as well as the largest piece of the Berlin Wall owned by an American university. Additional facilities include Oliphant Hall—featuring 14 teaching studios, a 60-seat lecture hall, and an orchestra hall—and Marion Knott Studios, which features a 500-seat theater, digital arts center, and two full-sized sound stages.

The most popular majors are business administration, film production, communication studies, public relations and advertising, and psychology. Budding filmmakers may enter the Dodge College of Film and Media Studies, a comprehensive, production-based program that includes majors in film production, television and broadcast journalism, screenwriting, public relations and advertising, and film studies, as well as internships and other active learning opportunities. Future entrepreneurs and business tycoons can take advantage of a well-stocked portfolio of business programs through the Argyos School of Business and Economics. The Economic Science Institute allows for the study of experimental economics under the direction of Nobel laureate Dr. Vernon Smith and spans the fields of accounting, economics, finance, information systems, engineering, psychology, neuroscience, computer science, and philosophy. For more artsy types, Chapman offers solid programs in theater and dance, each with frequent national and international performance components. The university's peace studies and legal studies programs are tied to internships and study abroad experiences. Additional majors include computational science, law, justice, and social change.

> "The teaching I have received has been outstanding."

Regardless of major, all students must complete a series of distribution requirements that includes credits in fine and performing arts, humanities, history, social sciences, and natural sciences. In addition, students are expected to fulfill requirements in quantitative reasoning, world cultures, human diversity, and foreign language, as well as pass a junior writing proficiency exam. Freshmen are eased into college life by Chapman's comprehensive first-year program, which provides extensive contact with peers, student mentors, faculty, and advisors, as well as an orientation. Freshmen are also assigned a life coach with whom they meet weekly to discuss goals, plan and organize, and develop skills that are critical to success as a first-year college student. Finally, new students may take part in the First-Year Experience (FYE), where they "have their own floor in one of the residence halls and participate in special programs aimed at helping them adjust to their first year of college," explains a sophomore.

Forty-two percent of classes have 19 or fewer students. Freshmen are taught by professors; there are no TAs. "The teaching I have received has been outstanding," says one student. "Many of the professors are working professionals who still work in the field so they are teaching the most up-to-date information, providing first-hand experience, and continually offer internships and research opportunities." The 144,000-square-foot Leatherby Libraries feature state-of-the-art amenities, including nine discipline-specific libraries, a 24-hour study commons, and Internet-based learning environments.

Chapman attracts a friendly, largely affluent student body. "The students at Chapman are true leaders that are committed to personal and professional development during their time in college. Most Chapman students hold multiple internships, are involved in multiple organizations, and hold many leadership positions," says a junior. Nearly two-thirds hail from California and 4 percent are international students. African Americans comprise 2 percent of the population, Asian Americans 9 percent, and Hispanics 13 percent. A junior describes fellow students as "involved, intelligent, and hardworking." Neither liberals nor conservatives dominate the political scene, and the campus is decidedly lukewarm when it comes to social and political issues. "Chapman is an extremely liberal school," a psychology major says. Eligible undergraduates receive merit scholarships worth an average of $20,818. There are no athletic scholarships.

> **"The social life is great here as there is never a shortage of things to do."**

Thirty-four percent of Chapman students call the residence halls home, and "the dorms are large and comfortable," says a freshman. A sophomore adds, "They feel like you are in your own little apartment." Braden Hall has 70 rooms that are paired into suites, while Henley Hall features a substance-free community as well as a First-Year Experience floor for incoming students. Other university-owned options include off-campus houses (for families) and nearby apartments. Campus dining is described as edible and diverse: "The dining hall serves high-quality, delicious food that looks and tastes nothing like typical college food," reports one junior. As for safety, students say that campus security is a constant presence. "I've never felt unsafe on campus," says a student.

Twenty-six percent of the men join fraternities, and sororities attract 30 percent of the women, but the Greeks don't dominate the social scene. Students are apt to hang out with friends on campus or take part in a school-sponsored event. "The social life is great here as there is never a shortage of things to do," says one senior. "Most of it takes place off campus, but our administration has been holding more weekend events on campus as of late." Although alcohol is readily available, "the RAs and Public Safety do a good job of controlling alcohol consumption" by students, according to a theater major. When students grow weary of campus life, they hit the local shops and bars or take trips to "Mexico, Disneyland, Knott's Berry Farm, the mall, and L.A.," according to a film major. Back on campus, students flock to the homecoming celebration and the annual Greek Week festival.

Future entrepreneurs and business tycoons can take advantage of a well-stocked portfolio of business programs through the Argyos School of Business and Economics.

Freshmen are eased into college life by Chapman's comprehensive first-year program.

Twenty-six percent of the men join fraternities, and sororities attract 30 percent of the women, but the Greeks don't dominate the social scene.

The city of Orange (population 135,000) is a college town only in the technical sense of the term. "It's actually a very quiet city," says a junior. It's also home to the usual litany of restaurants and shops, as well as a district known as "Old Towne Orange, the Antique Capital of California." Most of the town closes by midnight, and students looking for fun generally head into Los Angeles (40 minutes away).

The Chapman Panthers compete in Division III and the most competitive sports include baseball, football, women's tennis, and women's lacrosse (2011 Women's Collegiate Lacrosse Association champs). Intramurals are popular and students can usually be spotted playing ultimate Frisbee, volleyball, or soccer in the pristine Southern California weather.

At Chapman, the spotlight is definitely on those looking to build careers in film and television, whether it's on a movie set, behind the camera, or on a stage. Students are not only expected to hit the books, but also to actively express their creativity through hands-on learning and forays into the real world. All the while, they're encouraged to build relationships with peers and faculty and enjoy themselves, too. "We have a lot of pride," a film major says. "We are a fun school with excellent academic possibilities and opportunities."

Overlaps

Loyola Marymount, Santa Clara, University of San Diego, UC–Irvine, University of Southern California, UCLA, Cal State

If You Apply To ➤

Chapman: Early action: Nov. 1. Regular admissions: Jan. 15. Financial aid: Mar. 2. Housing: May 1. Application fee: $65. Campus and alumni interviews: optional, informational. SATs or ACTs: required. Subject Tests: optional. Requires the Common Application and Chapman supplements. Essay question.

College of Charleston

Charleston, SC 29424

A public school about half the size of the University of South Carolina that offers business, education, and the liberal arts. College of Charleston compares to William and Mary in both scale and historic surroundings but is far less rigorous academically. Addressing its housing crunch to help it reach the next level.

Website: www.cofc.edu
Location: Small City
Public
Total Enrollment: 9,967
Undergraduates: 9,674
Male/Female: 38/62
SAT Ranges: CR 550–650, M 560–650
ACT Ranges: 23–27
Financial Aid: 46%
Expense: Pub $ $ $
Student Loans: 47%
Average Debt: $ $
Phi Beta Kappa: No
Applicants: 11,962
Accepted: 68%
Enrolled: 26%

Whether sampling the traditional Low Country cuisine or delving into the wide range of courses offered at this strong liberal arts institution, students at the College of Charleston know they are getting a solid education based on creative expression and intellectual freedom. Founded in 1770 as Colonial South Carolina's first college, CofC's original commitment to the liberal arts and to the citizens of the region has helped it become a well-respected institution throughout the Southeast. And the location only adds to the experience, providing opportunities for volunteering and interning, and a robust social scene. "The school is filled with amazing, talented, intelligent, and respectful people," a senior says.

"We're all just trying to focus on ourselves and pass our classes."

Located in Charleston's famous Historic District, the campus features many of the city's most historic and venerable buildings. More than 80 of its buildings are former private residences, ranging from the typical Charleston "single" house to the Victorian, and the clap-clap of horse-drawn carriages bearing tourists is a routine sight. The wooded area in front of Randolph Hall, known as the Cistern Yard, is a student gathering point and the site of graduation ceremonies. The campus has received countless awards for its design, and has been designated a national arboretum and a National Historic Landmark. The Cato Center, a 74,000-square-foot addition to the Albert

Simons Center for the Arts, includes teaching studios, performance classrooms, and a choral and ensemble practice room, as well as a gallery space for the Halsey Institute of Contemporary Art, complete with a media room and space for special collections.

CofC has a core curriculum rooted strongly in the liberal arts and professional programs and focused on the development of writing, computing, language acquisition, and thinking skills. Each student is required to complete six hours in English, history, mathematics or logic, and social science; eight hours in natural sciences; and 12 hours in humanities. Students must also show proficiency in a foreign language. Biology and chemistry are two of the strongest programs; many of the graduates end up at the Medical University of South Carolina a few blocks down the street. Several programs have been awarded with Commendations of Excellence, including all those in the School of Sciences and Mathematics.

> "Everyone has their own style and quite frankly aren't judged for it."

Most agree that the courses at Charleston can be rigorous, but collaboration is more common than competition. "The courses are somewhat tough, but the students are not competitive with each other because we're all just trying to focus on ourselves and pass our classes," a sophomore says. Those in the honors college are given a more demanding workload. The most popular majors are biology, communication, psychology, business administration, and political science. Majors in astronomy and astrophysics are available, while data science (formerly discovery informatics)—an interdisciplinary program that integrates statistics, social sciences, math, computer science, learning theory, logic, information theory, and artificial intelligence—is one of only a handful of degrees of its type in the country. Many performing arts majors take advantage of internship opportunities with Spoleto Festival USA, Charleston's annual arts festival. Among the 40 or so study abroad options are the International Student Exchange Program and Semester at Sea*. Additional programs include Jewish studies, international studies, women's and gender studies, and computing in the arts.

Professors get high marks in and out of the classroom. "I can say I've had some of the most amazing and intelligent professors," says one freshman. A senior adds, "It isn't uncommon for a full professor to teach an introductory level course to freshmen." All new students attend Convocation, where they are introduced to the college's academic traditions, and freshman minority students participate in several support programs designed to ensure their successful transition to college. Freshmen take part in the First-Year Experience and choose between seminar and learning community options; sample seminars include Molecular Biology in the News, World History through Food, and Visual Culture in Theater Practice. Cougar Excursion is offered through the Higdon Student Leadership Center and is a three-day summer leadership retreat in which about 100 participants meet other incoming freshmen, student leaders, and administrators.

"Everyone has their own style and quite frankly aren't judged for it," says a junior. Thirty-six percent of the students hail from out of state, and 31 percent graduated in the top 10th of their high school class. Asian Americans and Hispanics make up 6 percent of the student body, African Americans account for 6 percent, and 1 percent are foreign. "While no one issue has been primary on campus, we have clubs that push their own issues," says a student. "College Democrats, College Republicans, and the Political Science Club all raised awareness during the recent presidential election." The college offers hundreds of merit scholarships and 120 athletic scholarships in 21 sports.

"On-campus housing at CofC is very nice, with the choices between dormitories, apartments, or historic houses," says one student. "Living on campus after freshman year is considered a little uncool," admits one junior, "which is kind of a nuisance because to find somewhere that's comparable in price and services, you need to go a little further from campus and find roommates." The percentage of students living on campus has slowly increased, and is now 31 percent. Parking is limited but food

(continued)

Grad in 6 Years: 69%
Returning Freshmen: 82%
Academics: ✍ ✍ ✍
Social: ☎ ☎ ☎ ☎
Q of L: ★ ★ ★ ★
Admissions: (843) 953-5670
Email Address: admissions@ cofc.edu

Strongest Programs:
Biology
Communication
Psychology
Business Administration
Political Science
Astronomy
Computer Information Systems
Jewish Studies

Among the 40 or so study abroad options are the International Student Exchange Program and Semester at Sea.*

is plentiful; there are options for all types of eaters, including "homestyle, grill, deli, salad bar, Greek, dessert, and cereal bar" selections. Vegetarian fare is available as well. Students report feeling safe on campus, thanks to an active security program. "Campus security is very tight," says one student simply.

Students party off campus in local clubs and apartments as well as on campus, where 15 percent of the men and 22 percent of the women belong to frats and sororities, respectively. "Campus clubs ensure there is always an event for on-campus fun," explains a junior. Due to a well-enforced policy on drinking, students report that it is difficult to be served on campus if you are not 21, but off campus it is not a problem. "I think the policies keep drinking to a minimum in dorms," a senior says. Women far outnumber men, but females looking to beat the odds can always go to the Medical University of South Carolina or the Citadel Military College, both in Charleston.

"I could not imagine going to college anywhere else."

Students enjoy Charleston, with its festivals, plays, and scenic plantations and gardens. "I could not imagine going to college anywhere else," a senior says. "Charleston is such an unbelievable place to spend the most important four years of your life." On weekends, students can head to beaches such as Folly Beach, Sullivan's Island, and Isle of Palms, which are merely minutes away. For those who don't mind a drive, there's "the Grand Strand," Myrtle Beach, 90 miles north, Savannah and Hilton Head to the south, and Atlanta and Clemson University to the west.

The absence of a football team is a common gripe among students, but other athletics are relatively popular. The College of Charleston is a Division I school and several teams have claimed recent conference championships, including women's soccer, women's volleyball, men's swimming and diving, and men's tennis. Sailing captured its first ever ICSA/APS Team Race National Championship title in 2012. There is a lengthy roster of intramural and club sports to choose from, including indoor soccer, tennis, and racquetball. CofC's SIFE (Students in Free Enterprise) team is solid, too, and competed in the 2011 SIFE USA Regional Competition before advancing to the national competition.

The College of Charleston has become the finest public liberal arts and sciences institution in South Carolina, propelled by an honors college, opportunities to do research and study abroad, and new living and learning facilities. "Our small-college feel with large-college advantages brings a great atmosphere to CofC," a senior says.

Overlaps

Clemson, University of South Carolina, Coastal Carolina, Winthrop, University of Georgia, UNC at Chapel Hill, Elon, James Madison

If You Apply To ➤

Charleston: Regular admissions: Apr. 1. Financial aid: Mar. 15. Housing: May 1. Application Fee: $50. No campus or alumni interviews. SATs or ACTs: required. No Subject Tests. Essay question.

University of Chicago

1116 East 59th Street, Chicago, IL 60637

Periodically, the news media reports that students at the University of Chicago are finally loosening up and having some fun. OK. Maybe so. But UChicago is still a place for true intellectuals who enjoy nothing more than the chance to debate a fresh idea. Recent investments in dorms, the arts, and athletics have helped to nearly double the undergraduate population. Now as selective as the top Ivies and just as strong. Social climbers should look elsewhere.

The University of Chicago attracts students eager to move beyond the cliquishness of high school and the superficial trappings of Ivy League prestige—the kids more concerned about learning for learning's sake than about getting a job after graduation, though they're certainly capable of the latter. "We're all nerds at heart," says a senior. Still, administrators have realized that in the 21st century, even the best schools cannot survive on intellectual might alone. To make UChicago more attractive, they've made the core curriculum less restrictive, expanded study abroad programs and career advising, and completed a bevy of new facilities. The result? A surge in applications. Says a freshman, "The fact that college here is a good time just makes us that much happier."

"**The courses are extremely rigorous because that's the way we like them.**"

The university's 215-acre tree-lined campus is in Hyde Park, an eclectic community on Chicago's South Side, surrounded by low-income neighborhoods on three sides and Lake Michigan on the other. One of 77 city neighborhoods, Hyde Park "is pretty intellectual," says one student, noting that "two-thirds of our faculty live here." Streets are lined with brownstones, row houses, and townhouses, giving way to luxury high-rises with beautiful views as you get closer to the lake; the city's Museum of Science and Industry is within spitting distance. The campus itself is self-contained and architecturally magnificent. The main quads are steel-gray Gothic—gargoyles and all—and buildings were designed by the likes of Frank Lloyd Wright, Eero Saarinen, Mies van der Rohe, and Edward Durrell Stone. The Regenstein Library ("the Reg"), symbolically located in the heart of the campus, is a national treasure. Next to the Reg is the recently opened Mansueto Library, a geodesic dome featuring millions of books stored underground and retrieved by a 50-foot underground robotic arm.

Historically, UChicago has drawn praise for its graduate programs, but in recent years administrators have realized that they must pay attention to undergraduates as well if UChicago is to compete successfully with the likes of Stanford, Harvard, and Princeton. To that end, the university remains unequivocally committed to the view that a solid foundation in the liberal arts is the best preparation for future study or work and, moreover, that theory is better than practice. Thus, music students study musicology, but also learn calculus, along with everyone else. Regardless of major, 15 to 18 of a student's 42 courses fall under general education requirements called the Common Core, which is one of the most comprehensive sets of distribution requirements anywhere. (The precise number of courses in the core depends on how much foreign language instruction a student needs to reach proficiency.)

Other core requirements include courses in the sciences and math, humanities, social sciences, and a sequence of study in a specific civilization. There is a required writing tutorial as well. Sound intense? Well, yes, students say it is, especially because UChicago pioneered the quarter system whereby class material is presented over 10-week periods, with the first term starting in late September and ending by Christmas. In practice, this means virtually uninterrupted work through the year, punctuated by a long summer vacation and three exam weeks. "The courses are extremely rigorous because that's the way we like them," says a junior. A freshman adds, "People here have bookshelves overflowing with books they have actually read. Passionate discussion and intellectual curios-

"**I don't know how professors here could get better.**"

ity are everywhere." Despite the academic rigor, collaboration is the norm. Seniors are also encouraged to do final-year projects. Helping students learn those skills are brilliant and distinguished faculty members who've won Nobel Prizes, Guggenheims, and other prestigious awards. "I don't know how professors here could get better," says a senior. "They make themselves available to students and seem genuinely interested in our ideas."

Website: www.uchicago.edu
Location: City Center
Private
Total Enrollment: 9,858
Undergraduates: 5,529
Male/Female: 53/47
SAT Ranges: CR 710–780, M 710–790
ACT Ranges: 31–34
Financial Aid: 58%
Expense: Pr $ $ $ $
Student Loans: 43%
Average Debt: $ $
Phi Beta Kappa: Yes
Applicants: 25,273
Accepted: 13%
Enrolled: 46%
Grad in 6 Years: 92%
Returning Freshmen: 99%
Academics: ✍ ✍ ✍ ✍ ✍
Social: ☎ ☎ ☎
Q of L: ★ ★ ★ ★
Admissions: (773) 702-8650
Email Address: collegeadmissions@uchicago.edu

Strongest Programs:
Economics
Biological Sciences
Political Science
Mathematics
English

The university remains unequivocally committed to the view that a solid foundation in the liberal arts is the best preparation for future study or work.

The economics department, a bastion of neoliberal or New Right thinkers, is UChicago's main academic claim to fame. Popular majors include economics, biological and biomedical sciences, political science, math, and English. The university also prides itself on interdisciplinary and area studies programs, such as those focusing on East Asia, South Asia, the Middle East, and the Slavic countries. Undergrads may take courses in any of the university's graduate and professional schools—law, divinity, social service, public policy, humanities, social sciences, biological and physical sciences, and business. In the spirit of alumni such as Mike Nichols and Elaine May, a major in theater and performance studies is available, as is the Accelerated Medical Scholars Program. While you may have to fight through a thicket of Ph.D. students to get your professor's attention, you'll be rewarded by an abundance of research assistantships—and opportunities for publication, even before you graduate. "University of Chicago students are intellectual and proud of it," says an anthropology major. "I've even discussed Max Weber at a frat party." When Chicago gets too cold and snowy, students may take advantage of study abroad programs, which reach most corners of the globe and include study at the university's center in Paris and one in Beijing.

Seventy-one percent of UChicago's students come from out of state, including many East Coasters with academic parents; another 9 percent are foreigners. Asian Americans represent 18 percent of the total, Hispanics account for 8 percent, and African Americans add 5 percent. Politically, "the conservative voice is allowed a presence on campus—the effect is to enliven debate and save us liberals from easy self-assurance," says a freshman. Students have fond memories of freshman orientation, known as O Week, an event administrators claim was invented at the university in 1924. The school hands out merit scholarships each year and has eliminated loans from the financial aid packages for families with annual incomes below $60,000. Loans have been cut in half for families with incomes below $100,000.

"Dorms are divided into units of 30 to 100 people called houses."

UChicago guarantees campus housing for four years, and more than half of all undergrads live in the dorms. "Dorms are divided into units of 30 to 100 people called houses," says a junior. "These houses become the center of social life, at least for first-years." Each dorm is different—some house less than 100 people in traditional, shared double rooms without kitchens, while another has 700 beds organized into colorful suites. The South Campus Residence Hall offers a mix of singles, doubles, and apartments in a modern building. All halls are co-ed by room or by floor. "Hyde Park has tons of really cute, cheap apartments," reports one student, so the more "independent-minded" students usually move off campus.

UChicago the school, and Chicago the city, offer what a freshman calls "infinite options: bars downtown, a film festival, a White Sox game at U.S. Cellular Field, a spoken-word performance at a Belmont coffeehouse, open-mic night at the student center." Lest you get bored, the city also offers museums galore, world-class symphony, opera, dance, and the Second City comedy troupe (invented by University of Chicago undergrads). Though everything is accessible by public transportation, cars are a nice luxury (if you can find a parking place). When it comes to drinking, campus policies are "very, um, accommodating," says one student. "The university treats us as responsible adults with common sense." Off campus, it's much harder for the underage to imbibe. Road trips are infrequent, but one popular destination is Ann Arbor, about five hours away, for concerts and more traditional collegiate fun at the University of Michigan.

Tradition is a hallmark at UChicago, and each spring, students look forward to Scavenger Hunt ("Scav"), "a pumped-up version of a regular scavenger hunt, with a list of 300 bizarre items," says a sociology major. "If you walked onto campus

The economics department, a bastion of neoliberal or New Right thinkers, is UChicago's main academic claim to fame.

during those few days, you'd think most people had lost their minds." In the winter, students head for the outdoor skating rink on the Midway, site of the 1893 World's Fair, for broomball. Students also celebrate the festival of Kangeiko, which features their naked or seminaked peers dashing across campus during the Polar Bear Run. Doc Films is the country's longest continuously running student film society. The Festival of the Arts features concerts, a fashion show, special lectures, museum exhibits, and "funky installations on the quads." Come summer, students can be found "doing Jell-O wrestling and other carnival activities" as part of Summer Breeze, which also includes a concert.

UChicago's Maroons compete in Division III, and the school belongs to the University Athletic Association, where rivals include NYU and Washington U in St. Louis. Aside from hitting the gridiron or the basketball court, "even the varsity athletes are Phi Beta Kappa (that is, very smart) and involved with university theater," a junior marvels. In fact, athletes here have a higher overall GPA than the student body as a whole. The wrestling team and women's soccer squad have boasted All-Americans in recent years, and both men's and women's soccer have been to the Division III Final Four. To everyone's surprise, the football team has also had a couple of winning seasons. When it comes to intramurals, 70 percent of undergraduates participate in sports ranging from the traditional (football, soccer, and broomball) to the offbeat (inner-tube water polo, badminton, and archery).

> "The university treats us as responsible adults with common sense."

Although T-shirts lovingly mock the university's rigor ("Where Fun Comes to Die"), the University of Chicago has moved well beyond the Spartan attitudes of former president Robert Maynard Hutchins, who led UChicago from 1929 to 1951 and once said, "When I feel like exercising I just lie down until the feeling goes away." In a lighter moment, Hutchins also said, "My idea of education is to unsettle the minds of the young and inflame their intellects." For students who choose the University of Chicago, learning is often the best—though not necessarily the only—kind of fun.

Overlaps

Northwestern, Columbia, University of Pennsylvania, Harvard, Yale, Princeton, Georgetown, Duke

---

If You Apply To ➤ **UChicago:** Early action: Nov. 1. Regular admissions: Jan. 2. Financial aid: Feb. 1. Application fee: $75. Campus and alumni interviews: optional, evaluative. SATs or ACTs: required. Subject Tests: optional. Accepts the Common Application. Essay question.

University of Cincinnati

P.O. Box 210091, Cincinnati, OH 45221-0091

In most states, UC would be the big enchilada. But with Ohio State two hours up the road and Miami U even closer, Cincinnati has to hustle to get its name out there. The inventor of co-op education, it offers quality programs in everything from engineering to art—and a competitive men's basketball team to boot.

Many first-time visitors to Cincinnati are surprised to find an attractive and very livable city. As they traverse the city's hilly roads, they are in for another surprise—its university. Not only is the University of Cincinnati renowned for its extensive research programs, but its cooperative education program is also the largest of any public college or university in the country.

Website: www.uc.edu
Location: City Center
Public
Total Enrollment: 25,212

(continued)

Undergraduates: 19,615

Male/Female: 52/48

SAT Ranges: CR 510–620,
  M 520–640

ACT Ranges: 22–27

Financial Aid: 81%

Expense: Pub $ $ $

Student Loans: 69%

Average Debt: $ $ $

Phi Beta Kappa: Yes

Applicants: 17,104

Accepted: 67%

Enrolled: 37%

Grad in 6 Years: 62%

Returning Freshmen: 86%

Academics: ✍ ✍

Social: ☎ ☎ ☎

Q of L: ★ ★ ★

Admissions: (513) 556-6000

Email Address: admissions@
  uc.edu

Strongest Programs:

Marketing

Psychology

Criminal Justice

Communication

Nursing

Architecture

Musical Theatre

Across the Cincinnati curriculum, an abundance of co-op opportunities are available, and more than 3,000 students take advantage of them.

The compact campus is a mile uphill from Cincinnati's downtown area. Ultramodern buildings rise up next to traditional ivy-covered Georgian halls. A $233 million construction project to create a "Main Street" in the center of campus and consolidate all student activities is complete. Students may also take advantage of the $113 million campus recreation center and the $100 million Richard E. Lindner Varsity Village, consisting of athletic facilities.

Research has been a UC specialty. Campus scientists have given the world anti-knock gasoline, the electronic organ, antihistamines, and the U.S. Weather Bureau. UC is also the place where, in 1906, cooperative education was born, allowing students to earn while they learn. Across the Cincinnati curriculum, an abundance of co-op opportunities are available, and more than 3,000 students take advantage of them. In all, more than 40 programs offer the popular five-year professional-practice option.

The colleges of engineering; business administration; and design, architecture, art, and planning (the schools with the most co-op students) are the best bets at UC. The university's music conservatory, one of the best programs in the field, also offers both electronic media and broadcasting training. The schools of nursing and pharmacy are well known and benefit from UC's health center and graduate medical school. The most popular major is psychology, followed by communication, marketing, criminal justice, and biology. Education students earn two bachelor's degrees: one in education and one in a liberal arts subject. Additional initiatives include a culinary arts and science degree program offered jointly with Cincinnati State, and the state's first baccalaureate program in facilities and hospitality management. UC is also one of only a handful of universities across the country with a language-immersion house, a freestanding residence where students are required to live, work, study, and play "24/7" in another language.

> "I would say that the most rigorous courses are those that are nontraditional."

The academic rigor is determined largely by the major. Fields such as engineering, business, and nursing require a substantially larger academic commitment. "I would say that the most rigorous courses are those that are nontraditional," offers one student, citing "study abroad, capstones, projects with corporate partners, and advanced topics classes." Some courses end up being quite large (in popular design courses, two people to a desk is not unusual); 90 percent of classes have 49 or fewer students. One fine asset is the school's 11 libraries, which hold four million volumes and are completely computerized.

UC has taken steps to improve the quality of the undergraduate education by strengthening its general education requirements to focus on critical thinking and expression and expanding its honors program. Freshmen must take English and math as well as a contemporary issues class; other requirements vary by college. All students are now required to complete a capstone experience as well. Additionally, UC has adopted a strategic plan known as the Academic Master Plan to place students at the center of campus life. A third of the faculty members hold outside jobs, bringing fresh, practical experience to the classroom.

"Because a large amount of UC students co-op, and most move off campus after their freshman year, I feel UC students have a firmer grasp on what's expected of them in the real world," says a student. Ten percent of the student body comes from out of state, which makes the student body fairly heterogeneous. African Americans, Asian Americans, and Hispanics comprise a mere 8, 3, and 3 percent of the student body, respectively. Diversity, feminist issues, campus construction, and rising tuition are the hot topics on campus. The school offers merit scholarships and athletic scholarships for men and women.

Nineteen percent of UC students live on campus. Many upperclassmen, especially the older and married students, consider off-campus living far better than dorm life, and inexpensive apartments can usually be found. A student says, "The Clifton area is also in the process of developing and building several new complexes that offer apartments for students." Dining facilities offer a wide variety of "edible and diverse" fare, according to a junior. Campus security gets a thumbs-up, too: "I've never felt unsafe on campus," a student says. "It's well lit and you see UCPD very often."

Merchants have turned the area surrounding UC, called Clifton, into a mini college town with plenty to do. Nine nearby bus lines take undergraduates into the heart of the "Queen City" of Cincinnati in minutes. There the students find museums, ballet, professional sports teams, parks, rivers, hills, and as many large and small shops as anyone could want. On-campus activities include 450 student clubs, with everything from mountaineering to clubs in various majors. Fraternities and sororities attract less than 10 percent of the men and women, but are still the most active places to party on campus, usually opening their functions to everyone. "I always struggle finding a good weekend to visit home," says a senior, "because there always is something fun I'll miss." The university sponsors some events, such as WorldFest and Greek Week. The most popular road trips are to the city of Cleveland and white-water rafting in West Virginia.

In sports, men's and women's basketball are solid and 19 Bearcat teams compete in the Division I Big East Conference. The men's basketball team does not turn out many graduates, but it has been to postseason play in 19 of the past 22 seasons. The women's basketball team has made postseason tournament appearances in nine of the last 12 years. Track, soccer, baseball, and women's crew are also popular. Everyone mentions the football rivalry with Miami (of Ohio) as a game you won't want to miss, and the same holds true when the men's basketball squad takes on Xavier University. Weekend athletes also take advantage of UC's first-rate sports center.

Cooperative education is the name of the game at this Ohio school. Students get to take their degrees out for a test drive before graduation thanks to the work-study co-op programs. UC also offers students a lively social scene, both on campus and minutes away in downtown Cincinnati.

> *Everyone mentions the football rivalry with Miami (of Ohio) as a game you won't want to miss, and the same holds true when the men's basketball squad takes on Xavier University.*

> **"I always struggle finding a good weekend to visit home because there always is something fun I'll miss."**

Overlaps

Ohio State, Miami (OH), Ohio University, Bowling Green State, Wright State, Xavier

If You Apply To ➤ **UC:** Rolling admissions. Application fee: $50. Campus interviews: optional, informational. No alumni interviews. SATs or ACTs: required. No Subject Tests. Essay question: personal statement. Apply to particular program.

Claremont Colleges

In 1925, James A. Blaisdell had the vision to create a group of colleges patterned after Oxford and Cambridge in England. More than a century later, the five schools that comprise the Claremont Colleges thrive as a consortium of separate and distinct undergraduate colleges with two adjoining graduate institutions, a theological seminary, and botanical gardens. Like families, the colleges coexist, interact, and experience their share of both cooperation and tension. Ultimately, however, the Claremont College Consortium* forms a mutually beneficial partnership that offers its students the vast resources and facilities one might only expect to find at a large university.

The colleges are located 35 miles east of Los Angeles on 317 acres in the suburb of Claremont, a peaceful neighborhood replete with palm trees, Spanish architecture, and the nearby San Gabriel Mountains. The picture-perfect

California weather is marred by smog, courtesy of the neighbors in nearby L.A., but the administration claims the smog level has declined dramatically in the past few years.

None of the five undergraduate colleges that make up the Claremont Colleges Consortium*—Claremont McKenna, Harvey Mudd, Pitzer, Pomona, and Scripps—is larger than a medium-size dorm at a state school. Each school retains its own institutional identity, with its own faculty, administration, admissions, and curriculum, although the boundaries of both academic work and extracurricular activities are somewhat flexible. Each of the schools also tends to specialize in a particular area that complements the offerings of all the others. Claremont McKenna, which caters mainly to students planning careers in economics, business, law, or government, has eight research institutes located on its campus, while Harvey Mudd is the choice for future scientists. Pitzer, the most liberal of the five, excels mainly in the behavioral sciences, and at the all-women Scripps, the best offerings are in art and foreign languages. The oldest of the five colleges, Pomona ranks as one of the top liberal arts colleges anywhere, and is the one Claremont school that is strong across the board, and especially superb in the humanities.

Collectively, the colleges share many services and facilities, including art studios, a student newspaper, laboratories, an extensive biological field station, a health center, auditoriums, a 2,500-seat concert hall, a 350-seat theater, bookstores, a maintenance department, and a business office. The Claremont library system makes more than 1.9 million volumes available to all students, though each campus also has a library of its own. Faculties and administrations are free to arrange joint programs or classes between all or just some of the schools. Courses at any college are open to students from the others (approximately 1,200 courses in all), but each college sets limits on the number of classes that can be taken elsewhere. Perhaps the best example of academic cooperation is the team-taught interdisciplinary courses, which are organized by instructors from the different schools and appeal to a mix of different academic interests.

The Claremont Colleges draw large numbers of students from within California, although their national reputation is growing. These days, about half the students hail from other Western and non-Western states, with a sizable contingent from the East Coast. The tone at Claremont is decidedly intellectual—more so than at Stanford or any other place in the West—and graduate programs in the arts and sciences are more common goals than business or law school. Anyone who is bright and hardworking can find a niche at one of the five schools. Unfortunately, despite their excellence, the Claremonts are also among the most underrated colleges in the nation.

The local community of Claremont is geared more to senior citizens than college seniors. "Quiet town of rich white people—boring," yawns an English major. A sophomore says, "Most of the stores have strange granny knick-knacks or cosmic aura trinkets." Still, "the Village," a quaint cluster of specialty shops (including truly remarkable candy stores), is an easy bike ride from any campus, though the shades come down and the sidewalks roll up well before sunset. Students report that the endless list of social activities offered at the colleges make up for the ho-hum town of Claremont. For hot times, Hollywood's glamour and UCLA-dominated Westwood are within sniffing distance, and a convenient shuttle bus makes them even closer for Claremont students without cars. Nearby mountains and the fabled surfing beaches make this collegiate paradise's backyard complete. Mount Baldy ski lifts, for instance, are only 15 miles away, and you'll reach Laguna Beach before the end of your favorite CD. For spring break, Mexico is cheap and a great change of pace.

On campus, extracurricular life maintains a balance between cooperation and independence. Claremont McKenna, Harvey Mudd, and Scripps field joint athletic teams, and the men's teams especially are Division III powers, due to the exploits of CMC athletes. Pomona and Pitzer also compete together. Each of the five colleges has its own dorms, and since off-campus housing is limited in Claremont proper, the social life of students revolves around their dorms. "Scripps itself is quiet, but parties at Harvey Mudd and Claremont McKenna can get pretty wild," admits a Scripps student. There are no fraternities, except at Pomona, where joining one is far from de rigueur. All cafeterias are open to all students, and most big events—films, concerts, etc.—are advertised throughout the campus. Large five-school parties are regular Thursday, Friday, and Saturday night fare. Social interaction among students at different schools, be it for meals or dates, is not what it might be. Pomona is seen as elitist, and its admissions office has been known to try to distance itself from the other colleges. Occasional political squabbles break out between liberal faculty and students at Pitzer and their conservative counterparts at Claremont McKenna. For the most part, students benefit not only from the nurturing and support within their own schools, each of which has its own academic or extracurricular emphasis, but also from the abundant resources the Claremont College Consortium* offers as a whole.

Following are profiles of each undergraduate Claremont College.

890 Columbia Avenue, Claremont, CA 91711

Make way, Pomona—this up-and-comer is no longer content with being a social sciences specialty school. CMC is half the size of a typical liberal arts college and 30 percent smaller than Pomona. CMC continues to develop its national reputation, and Californians now make up less than half the student body.

Claremont McKenna College's special niche in the Claremont College pantheon is top programs in government, economics, business, and international relations. In addition, CMC has 10 research institutes located on campus, which offer its undergraduates ample opportunities to study everything from political demographics to the environment. The arts and humanities are also available, but Claremont McKenna is better suited to those with high ambitions in business leadership and public affairs. "CMC provides students with a pragmatic liberal arts education that will prepare them for grad school and a career," a senior says. "It is a great place to spend four years."

"It is a great place to spend four years."

The 69-acre campus is mostly "California modern" architecture with lots of Spanish tile roofs and picture windows that look out on the San Gabriel Mountains. Described by one student as "more functional than aesthetic," the physical layout fits right in with the school's practical attitude. Kravis Center is a state-of-the-art academic center that houses classrooms, seminar rooms, a computer laboratory, and faculty offices. The Robert E. Tranquada Student Services Center houses health services, counseling, and psychological services for students.

Claremont McKenna offers top programs in economics and government, but the international relations, psychology, and history programs are also considered strong. The biology, chemistry, and physics departments are greatly enhanced through the use of Keck Science Center, an outstanding facility providing students with hands-on access to a variety of equipment. In addition, the 85-acre Bernard Biological Field Station is located just north of the CMC campus and is available to students for field work.

CMC's extensive general education requirements include two semesters in the humanities; three in the social sciences; one in the natural sciences; a semester each in mathematics, English composition and literary analysis, and the Freshman Humanities Seminar Program; and a senior thesis. The college offers popular 3–2 programs in management engineering and economics and engineering, a four-year B.A./M.A. program, and a 4–1 M.B.A. program in conjunction with the Claremont Graduate University. More than 40 percent of Claremont McKenna students take advantage of study abroad programs in 56 countries, including Australia, Brazil, Costa Rica, and Japan. CMC also offers active campus exchange programs with Haverford, Colby, Spelman, and Morehouse. Another popular program is the Washington Semester program, in which students can intern with E-Span, the State Department, the White House, and lobbying groups.

The academic climate is fairly strenuous at Claremont McKenna, but not overwhelming. "There are very difficult courses that will push you to the brink of your comfort zone in every major," a junior says. Professors are described as "outstanding" and praised for their accessibility. "I have met some of the most incredible teachers at CMC who are both brilliant and devoted to their students," a economics major says. Eighty-three percent of classes have 19 or fewer students ("one of the perks of a small college," says a neuroscience major). Majors in biophysics, Middle East studies, and environmental analysis have been added within the past couple of years.

Website: www.claremontmckenna.edu
Location: Suburban
Private
Total Enrollment: 1,281
Undergraduates: 1,250
Male/Female: 53/47
SAT Ranges: CR 650–750, M 660–760
ACT Ranges: 29–32
Financial Aid: 47%
Expense: Pr $ $ $ $
Student Loans: 31%
Average Debt: $ $
Phi Beta Kappa: Yes
Applicants: 5,058
Accepted: 14%
Enrolled: 42%
Grad in 6 Years: 92%
Returning Freshmen: 95%
Academics: ✍ ✍ ✍ ✍ ½
Social: ☎ ☎ ☎
Q of L: ★ ★ ★
Admissions: (909) 621-8088
Email Address: admission@claremontmckenna.edu

Strongest Programs:
Economics
Government
Psychology
International Relations
History
Sciences

A senior describes CMC students as "career-oriented, ambitious, and serious about their classes." The CMC student body is 39 percent Californian, with many from the East Coast. Many attended public high school and 63 percent graduated in the top 10th of their class. Asian Americans comprise the largest minority at 11 percent. Hispanics comprise 9 percent, while African Americans make up 3 percent. A student says, "There is a good mix of liberals, conservatives, and libertarians." All freshmen take part in a five-day orientation program that includes a Wilderness Orientation Adventure (WOA!) trip and a reception with the president and department chairs. The school guarantees to meet the demonstrated need of accepted applicants and offers merit scholarships to eligible students. CMC has partnered with the POSSE Foundation to provide full-tuition scholarships to needy students.

Majors in biophysics, Middle East studies, and environmental analysis have been added within the past couple of years.

Ninety-four percent of CMC students live on campus "because of the social life." The maid service probably doesn't hurt. "They dust and vacuum our rooms and clean our bathrooms! We do nothing (except study, of course)!" declares a happy resident. All the residence halls are co-ed; freshmen are guaranteed a room. Stark Hall, a substance-free dorm, gives students more living options. A cluster of on-campus apartments equipped with kitchen facilities is a popular option for upperclassmen. "The dorms can be like palaces," asserts a junior. "Hot palaces in August and May. Dirty palaces on weekends." Dorm food is said to be quite good, and students can eat in dining halls at any of the other four colleges, though the best bet may be CMC's Collins Dining Hall. "They have a large spread with lots of different options," says one student, including vegetarian, vegan, and organic fare.

"There are very difficult courses that will push you to the brink of your comfort zone in every major."

Most students agree that the social life at CMC is more than adequate, thanks to the five-college system. "CMC's campus is often the center of the social life for all of the Claremont Colleges," says a junior. "There are always parties, club events, barbecues, movie screenings, and other events." In addition to the usual forms of revelry, a calendar full of annual bashes includes Monte Carlo Night, Disco Inferno, Oktoberfest, and Chez Hub. Ponding, another unusual CMC tradition, involves being thrown into one of the two campus fountains on one's birthday. The college sponsors an outstanding lecture series at the Marian Miner Cook Athenaeum on Monday through Thursday nights each week. Before each lecture, students and faculty can enjoy a formal gourmet dinner together and engage in intellectual debates. Road trips to Joshua Tree, San Francisco, Las Vegas, and Mount Baldy are highly recommended by the students.

Top rivalries include Pomona, both in athletics and academics, one student claims.

Athletics are an important part of life at Claremont McKenna and the school has an overstuffed trophy case to prove it. Competitive Stag (men's) teams include cross-country, track and field, and tennis; solid women's teams (the "Athenas") include cross-country, track and field, basketball, and tennis. A third of the students play varsity sports, and CMC students tend to dominate the teams jointly fielded with Harvey Mudd and Scripps. Top rivalries include Pomona-Pitzer, both in athletics and academics, one student claims. "Basketball games rock this campus," another student says. The Claremont Colleges Debate Union has brought home three national debate championships, as well as more than 150 team and individual debate awards, in each of the past five years.

Overlaps

UC–Berkeley, UCLA, Pomona, University of Southern California, Stanford

CMC has embraced its mission to produce great leaders by providing students with ample opportunities for research and study abroad, as well as top-notch programs such as government and economics. "Leadership pervades almost everything that goes on here," says a junior. "Claremont McKenna builds character, fosters a sense of ambition among its students, and drives them to set their sights high."

Harvey Mudd College

301 Platt Blvd, Claremont, CA 91711

The finest institution that few people outside of the science and engineering world have ever heard of. Future Ph.D.s graduate from here in greater percentages than at any other school in the nation. HMC rivals Caltech for sheer brainpower and tops it in access to outstanding faculty. Offers more exposure to the liberal arts than most science- and technology-oriented schools.

A top-ranked technical school, Harvey Mudd College strives to give its students a sense of academic balance. Although it's a leading provider of high-quality programs in science and engineering, it also emphasizes a well-rounded education with knowledge in the humanities. "We're characterized as the nerd school of the five Claremonts because the classes are hardest and, yes, we talk about science and math over dinner sometimes. Mudders definitely know how to balance working and having fun, though," says a junior.

HMC's mid-'50s vintage campus of cinder-block buildings even "looks like an engineering college; it's very symmetrical and there's no romance." In addition, the buildings have little splotches all over their surfaces that students have dubbed "warts"—not a very attractive picture. The newest campus addition is a teaching and learning building that features a 300-person auditorium, recital hall, digital and electronic music studios, and an art gallery.

While most technology schools tend to have a narrow focus, HMC has come up with the novel idea that even scientists and engineers "need to know and appreciate poetry, philosophy, and non-Western thought," says an administrator. The "Common Core" includes four semesters of mathematics, three semesters of physics and associated laboratories, two semesters of chemistry and associated laboratories, two semesters of humanities and social sciences, and one course each in biology, computer science, and engineering. Students report that classes are formidable and the heavy workload is a common complaint. "Mudd is hard. It's academically challenging and can be very difficult mentally and emotionally because of the rigor," says a junior.

Of the nine on-campus majors, engineering is considered the strongest and ranks as the most popular by students, followed by computer science, mathematics, physics, and chemistry. HMC has one of the nation's top computer science programs and an award-winning math department. Students rave about the engineering clinic program, which plops real-life engineering tasks (sponsored by major corporations and government agencies to the tune of more than $30,000 per project) into the laps of students. There's also a Freshman Project that allows neophytes to tackle "some real-world engineering problems." And where else can you take a freshman seminar in integrated-circuit chip design? The absence of graduate programs means that undergraduates get uncommon amounts of attention, even from top faculty. "The professors truly care about the students' well-being," says an engineering major. "They put in countless hours to help us get the most out of our experience."

"Mudd is hard."

Website: www.hmc.edu
Location: Suburban
Private
Total Enrollment: 782
Undergraduates: 782
Male/Female: 56/44
SAT Ranges: CR 680–770, M 740–800
ACT Ranges: 33–35
Financial Aid: 82%
Expense: Pr $ $ $ $
Student Loans: 48%
Average Debt: $ $
Phi Beta Kappa: No
Applicants: 3,336
Accepted: 19%
Enrolled: 31%
Grad in 6 Years: 88%
Returning Freshmen: 98%
Academics: ✏ ✏ ✏ ✏ ½
Social: ☎ ☎ ☎
Q of L: ★ ★ ★
Admissions: (909) 621-8011
Email Address: admission@hmc.edu

Strongest Programs:
Engineering
Computer Science
Math
Physics
Chemistry

These budding technology leaders are also top achievers: 96 percent graduated in the top 10 percent of their high school class. "Each student at Mudd brings something different to the table," says one Mudder. "One student might be extremely talented at unicycling, and another might know every word to every Beatles song ever created, yet they both are in love with science." Thirty-eight percent of the students are homegrown Californians. African Americans represent 1 percent of the student body, Hispanics account for 7 percent, and Asian Americans comprise 22 percent. Political issues don't attract much attention on campus, although students report that environmental sustainability is a common concern. A handful of merit scholarships averaging $10,305 help with the hefty tuition bill, but as an NCAA Division III college, Mudd offers no athletic scholarships.

Ninety-eight percent of undergrads live on campus, and "the dorms are great and have the biggest rooms I've ever heard of," says a junior. They are all co-ed and mix the classes. "The dorms are well known by their personalities and the cultures that revolve around them; Mudd has no Greek life, so the different dorm personalities are a chance to live with similar people," one student explains. Another adds, "There are quiet dorms, loud dorms, quirky dorms, old dorms, and new dorms." The dorms are also ideal for computer whizzes: All are wired for online access to the HMC mainframe. The housing lottery can be grueling. Dining options include seven facilities scattered across the five Claremont campuses. Overall, food is described as "edible."

Despite their heavy workload, most HMC students find abundant social outlets, even if it's just joining the parade of unicycles that has overrun the campus. The college has no Greek life, and most social life takes place in and around the dorms, where there are parties every weekend. "All Mudders are a bit weird, but most have more social skills that you might expect at a technical school," says a computer science major. A student describes the town of Claremont as "a wonderful place if you're married or about to die." However, most students say there is always fun to be had on one of the five Claremont College campuses. Down-and-dirty types often frequent the Mudd Hole, a pizza/pinball/Ping-Pong hangout. Underage drinking is "compliments of a peer over 21," as one student puts it.

> "Mudd has no Greek life, so the different dorm personalities are a chance to live with similar people."

Mudd is rife with tradition. In the annual "pumpkin caroling" trip on Halloween, students serenade professors' homes with doctored-up Christmas carols. Another night of screwball fun is the Women's Pizza Party, in which men don dresses and crash a meeting of the Society of Women Engineers. There is also an annual Five Class competition among the four classes and the handful of fifth-year students, complete with amoebae soccer and relay races that include unicycles (backward), peanut butter and jelly, and slide-rule problem solving. Engineering pranks are popular but must be reversible within 24 hours.

Mudd fields varsity sports teams together with Claremont McKenna and Scripps, and mainly because of all the CMC jocks, the teams do extremely well. Men's tennis, women's soccer, men's cross-country, men's swimming, men's basketball, and women's lacrosse all won league titles in recent years. Not long ago, some enterprising Mudders stole archrival Caltech's cannon, elevating the Mudd-Caltech rivalry to include a soccer game dubbed the Cannon Bowl. Intramurals, also in conjunction with Scripps and CMC, are even more popular. Traditional sporting events include the Black and Blue Bowl, an interdorm game of tackle football, and the Freshman-Sophomore Games, which climax in a massive tug-of-war across a pit of vile stuff.

A common student refrain is "too much work," and students might welcome more time to reflect on what they are learning, but the work tends to pay off in grad

Of the nine on-campus majors, engineering is considered the strongest and ranks as the most popular by students.

Ninety-eight percent of undergrads live on campus.

Overlaps

MIT, Caltech, UC–Berkeley, Stanford, Princeton, Cornell, UCLA, Olin College of Engineering

school and in the job world. HMC is right on the heels of Caltech as the best technical school in the West. Mudd doesn't promise you'll end up with a hot job in Silicon Valley, but some students certainly do, and the college offers a gem of a technical education perfectly blended with a dash of humanities and social sciences. HMC's intimate setting also offers something bigger schools can't: a sense of family. "HMC is one of the most rigorous science schools around," says a senior, "but the thing that makes it special is that it develops you as an entire person."

If You Apply To ➤ **Harvey Mudd:** Early decision: Nov. 15. Regular admissions: Jan. 1. Financial aid: Feb. 1. Application fee: $70. Campus and alumni interviews: optional, evaluative. SATs or ACTs: required. Subject Tests: required (math II and one other). Accepts the Common Application. Essay question.

Pitzer College

1050 North Mills Avenue, Claremont, CA 91711

Offers a haven for the otherwise-minded without the hard edge of nonconformity at places like Bard and Evergreen. Traditional strengths lie in the social and behavioral sciences. Far more selective than it was 10 years ago.

As the most laid-back of the Claremont Colleges, Pitzer College offers students a creative milieu, abundant opportunities for intellectual exploration, and a sense of fierce individualism. Founded in the '60s, this small school has changed with the times but continues its emphasis on progressive thought, social responsibility, and open social attitude. In the last 15 years, Pitzer students and alums have won more than 80 Fulbright fellowships and the school continues to attract top talent from around the world.

Even the campus is, well, different. The classroom buildings are modernistic octagons, and the grass-covered "mounds" that distinguish the grounds "are perfect for sunbathing and Frisbee," says one student. Drought-tolerant landscaping pervades the campus, and there is an organic garden. Additional facilities include LEED-certified, environmentally friendly dorms and an expanded Benson Auditorium. West and East Halls opened in late 2012 and are the newest residential living areas on Pitzer's campus.

In keeping with Pitzer's philosophy of student autonomy, each student has the maximum freedom to choose which classes he or she would like to take. A lively freshman seminar program sharpens students' learning skills, especially writing. Students select from more than 40 majors in sciences, humanities, arts, and social sciences. Almost anything in the social and behavioral sciences is a sure bet, especially psychology (the most popular major), sociology, political science, media studies, and English and world literature. Pitzer is the first college in the country to offer a major in secular studies with courses such as God, Darwin,

> "The coursework is intensive but manageable."

and Design in America. Most courses in Pitzer's weaker areas can be picked up at one of the other Claremont schools. The Firestone Center for Restoration Ecology in Costa Rica is home to programs in science, language, and international studies and provides opportunities for research. There are also 33 international exchange programs and study abroad opportunities in diverse locations such as Ecuador, Italy, and China. In all, 73 percent of Pitzer students participate in study abroad programs.

Website: www.pitzer.edu
Location: Small City
Private
Total Enrollment: 1,041
Undergraduates: 1,041
Male/Female: 39/61
SAT Ranges: CR 580–710, M 590–680
ACT Ranges: 24–30
Financial Aid: 39%
Expense: Pr $ $ $ $
Student Loans: 47%
Average Debt: $
Phi Beta Kappa: No
Applicants: 4,227
Accepted: 16%
Enrolled: 38%
Grad in 6 Years: 81%
Returning Freshmen: 90%
Academics: ✐ ✐ ✐
Social: 🕿 🕿 🕿
Q of L: ★ ★ ★
Admissions: (909) 621-8129
Email Address: admission@pitzer.edu

Strongest Programs:
Psychology

Most courses in Pitzer's weaker areas can be picked up at one of the other Claremont schools.

The academic climate is demanding but cooperative. "The coursework is intensive but manageable," says a sophomore. Interdisciplinary inquiry is encouraged and original research is common. Class size is generally small, promoting close interaction between students and faculty. "Professors love being here and it shows," says a senior. "Professors are passionate and seem to enjoy what they do," adds another student.

"Professors love being here and it shows."

Individualism is a prized characteristic among Pitzer students, but one junior says the oft-bandied "hippie" label is unfair: "Pitzer people are genuinely socially conscious and academically adventurous, but do go on to good jobs." Forty-eight percent are from California and the college has a substantial minority community: African Americans comprise 7 percent of the student body, Hispanics 14 percent, and Asian Americans 9 percent. Political and social issues include the genocide in Darfur, the environment, and corporate responsibility. Pitzer offers merit scholarships, but athletic scholarships are not available.

Seventy-four percent of students live on campus and many find themselves in the new, environmentally friendly dorms; the remainder hang their hats in "old but spacious" rooms. Boarders can choose from a variety of meal plans in the dining hall (which never fails to have a vegetarian plate). Campus security is ever-present; a student says, "Pitzer seems to be [safer] than other campuses because campus security is so effective." One interesting campus curiosity is Grove House, a California craftsman-style house students saved from the wrecking ball nearly two decades ago and moved to campus. It houses a dining room, study areas, and art exhibits.

"Most students stay on campus to attend events or go to parties."

The women's water polo team has won several national championships recently.

As for the social scene, "Most students stay on campus to attend events or go to parties," says a senior. Pitzer has no Greek organizations, nor does it want any, and social life tends to be fairly low-key. Kohoutek is the big party; activities include bands, food, and a "whole week of hoopla." All parties that serve alcohol must be registered. Dances, cocktail parties, and cultural events do much to occupy students' leisure time, but without a car things can get claustrophobic.

The Pomona-Pitzer football team—"The Sagehens"—has had winning seasons and the school fields a variety of competitive teams within the Southern California Intercollegiate Athletic Conference, including women's soccer and swimming. The women's water polo team has won several national championships recently. Other strong men's teams include basketball and cross-country. Students play a large role in Pitzer's community government and sit on all policy committees, including those on curriculum and faculty promotion.

Pitzer attracts open-minded students looking for the freedom to go their own ways. Notes one student: "Pitzer is the only Claremont school that can claim to be genuinely different, in terms of race, religion, sexual orientation, and political belief. Pitzer is an amalgamation of every color of the spectrum."

Overlaps

UCLA, UC–Santa Barbara, UC–Santa Cruz, Lewis & Clark, Occidental, Pomona

If You Apply To ➤

Pitzer: Early decision: Nov. 15. Regular admissions: Jan. 1. Financial aid: Feb. 1. Application fee: $60. Campus interviews: optional, evaluative. No alumni interviews. SATs or ACTs: optional. Subject Tests: optional (English and two others). Accepts the Common Application. Essay question: Common Application.

Pomona College

333 North College Way, Claremont, CA 91711

The great Eastern-style liberal arts college of the West, and one of the few that Easterners will travel west to attend. Offers twice the resources of stand-alone competitors with access to the other Claremonts. A haven for the otherwise-minded, though not to the same extent as nonconformist neighbor Pitzer. Strong across the academic spectrum.

Pomona College, located just 35 miles east of the glitz and glamour of Hollywood, is the undisputed star of the Claremont College Consortium* and one of the top small liberal arts colleges anywhere. This small, elite institution is the best liberal arts college in the West. But the school's prestigious reputation doesn't go to the heads of Pomona's friendly students. "Students here are very open about different types of people—[Pomona] prides itself on its diverse community," chirps one Sagehen (the school's mascot).

The architecture is variously described as Spanish Mediterranean, pseudo-Italian, or, as a sophomore puts it, "a perfect mix of Northeastern Ivy and Southern California modern." The administration building, Alexander Hall, is described as "postmodern with Mediterranean influences," and one notices more than one stucco building topped with a red tile roof

> **"Students here are very open about different types of people."**

on campus, as well as eucalyptus trees, canyon live oaks, and an occasional "secretive courtyard lined with flowers." By virtue of its location and beauty, Pomona's campus has served as the quintessential collegiate milieu in various Hollywood movies.

Economics, mathematics, neuroscience, politics, and psychology are the most popular majors at Pomona. Although no specific course or department is prescribed for graduation, students must take at least one course in each of five areas: creative expression; social institutions and human behavior; history, values, ethics, and cultural studies; physical and biological sciences; and mathematical reasoning. The Critical Inquiry seminar emphasizes thoughtful reading, logical reasoning, and graceful writing through subjects such as Living with Our Genes and Penguins, Polar Bears, People, and Politics. Students must also complete foreign language and physical education requirements.

Educational opportunities abound at Pomona. Students can spend a semester at Colby or Swarthmore, pursue a 3–2 engineering plan with the California Institute of Technology, or spend a semester in Washington, D.C., working for a congressperson. More than half of the students take advantage of 51 study abroad programs offered in 32 foreign countries, and many others participate in programs focusing on six cultures and languages at the Oldenborg Center. In addition, the Summer Undergraduate Research Program (SURP) provides more than 200 students each summer with funds to conduct research mentored by a faculty member.

Classes at Pomona are challenging. "Although classes can be difficult, students help each other out and the classroom environment is an enjoyable one," offers one economics major. Students often form study groups in an effort to help one another through the demanding curriculum. One undergrad estimates the average student spends 20 to 30 hours a week studying outside the classroom.

Classes are small at Pomona—73 percent have 19 or fewer students—and the faculty makes a point of being accessible. It's not uncommon for professors to hold study sessions at their houses. "Pomona professors are bright, enthusiastic, and highly respected leaders in their respective fields," a student says. An ever-popular

Website: www.pomona.edu
Location: Suburban
Private
Total Enrollment: 1,579
Undergraduates: 1,579
Male/Female: 48/52
SAT Ranges: CR 680–770, M 680–760
ACT Ranges: 29–34
Financial Aid: 54%
Expense: Pr $ $ $
Student Loans: 32%
Average Debt: $
Phi Beta Kappa: Yes
Applicants: 7,456
Accepted: 13%
Enrolled: 41%
Grad in 6 Years: 96%
Returning Freshmen: 97%
Academics: ✍ ✍ ✍ ✍ ✍
Social: ☎ ☎ ☎
Q of L: ★ ★ ★ ★
Admissions: (909) 621-8134
Email Address: admissions@pomona.edu

Strongest Programs:
International Relations
Economics
Neuroscience
Foreign Languages
Media Studies
Chemistry
Politics

take-a-professor-to-lunch program gives students free meals when they arrive with a faculty member in tow. Better still, "We do not have graduate students or TAs teaching class," says a senior. "Thus, students do not have to wait until they are upperclassmen to enjoy the benefits of working with and learning from brilliant professors."

Pomona students "tend to be high-achieving, confident, verbal students with a fairly liberal political ideology," says a senior. "Students are laid-back in a very Southern California kind of way," adds a senior. Thirty-one percent of the students are Californians, and a growing percentage venture from the East Coast. Pomona is proud of its diverse student body: 6 percent are African American, 14 percent are Hispanic, and 11 percent are Asian American. There is a healthy mix of liberals and conservatives on campus, though the leftists, especially the feminist wing, are much more vocal. One interesting way students voice their issues is by painting the Walker Wall. Anyone is allowed to paint any message they want on the wall, and the school will even provide groups with the paint. The student government is active, and the administration is credited with respecting students' opinions. There are no merit or athletic awards.

> "Students help each other out and the classroom environment is an enjoyable one."

Pomona is need-blind in admissions and meets the full demonstrated need of all those who attend, and has replaced loans with grants in an effort to reduce the loan burden for families. The college also participates in the QuestBridge and POSSE programs. A five-day freshman orientation program divides the new arrivals into groups of six to 12 students headed by a sophomore. "We provide a great deal of support in acclimating students to a college environment," says a senior.

Virtually all Pomona students (98 percent) live on campus all four years. The dorms are co-ed, student-governed, and divided into two distinct groups. Those on South campus are family-like, fairly quiet, and offer spacious rooms, and those on the North end have smaller rooms with a livelier social scene. "Pomona's dorms are like palaces," says a student. The open courtyards and gardens are popular study spots. The new Pomona and Sontag Residence Halls, opened in 2011, are LEED platinum, feature suite-style apartments, and have common areas with full kitchens on each floor. Pomona Hall features the Outdoor Education Center. A handful of students isolate themselves in Claremont proper, where apartments are scarce and expensive. Boarders must buy at least partial meal plans. The food is good, with seafood certified by the Marine Stewardship Council, humanely raised beef and cage-free eggs, and ice cream for dessert every day. Pomona has a well-established language dorm with wings for speakers of Chinese, French, German, Japanese, Spanish, and Russian, as well as language tables at lunch for those six languages and 15 additional languages offered once or more per week. Students generally feel safe on campus. "The worst that usually happens are bike thefts," says a junior. "We're in a pretty nice suburb, so there really aren't many problems with crime."

Students at Pomona often spend Friday afternoons relaxing with friends over a brew at the Greek Theater. Social life begins in the dorms, where barbecues, parties, and study breaks are organized. There are movies several nights a week, and students also enjoy just tossing a Frisbee on the lawn. One student wanted to be sure that incoming freshmen and transfers knew of the Coop's (student union) "best milkshakes west of the Mississippi," pool tables, and large-screen TV and gaming system. "I appreciate the diversity and depth that the five-college community brings to the social life," says a student. "You are guaranteed to meet new and interesting people whenever you step off campus." Five-college parties happen nearly every weekend. During midterms and finals, however, the campus is a "social ghost town." It helps to have

> "We're in a pretty nice suburb, so there really aren't many problems with crime."

a set of wheels because "it's virtually impossible to get around in Southern California without a car," according to one student.

Pomona is unique among the Claremont Colleges in that it has three non-national fraternities (two co-ed; there are no sororities). There is "no peer pressure to join frats," and no fraternity rivalry. As for booze, "I haven't noticed any pressure to drink here," reports one student, but "alcohol is definitely present in the social scene." Harwood dorm throws the five-college costume party every Halloween. Freshman orientation gets interesting, too. "First-years have to run through the gates of Pomona with blue and white carnations while upperclassmen throw water balloons and shoot water at them," says a student. Every February or March, hundreds of students spend the morning at a nearby ski resort, then head to a local beach to swim and end the day with an oceanside cookout.

There once was a time when the Pomona Sagehens were an athletic powerhouse; the football team even knocked off mighty USC on Thanksgiving Day back in 1899. Currently, women's soccer, swimming, tennis, and water polo, and men's baseball, basketball, soccer, and water polo are strong programs. Recent conference champs include women's tennis and water polo, and men's baseball. Intense rivalry exists between the colleges in the Claremont Consortium*; basketball games between Pomona–Pitzer and CMS (Claremont–Mudd–Scripps) are "particularly heated." Intramurals, including hotly contested inner-tube water polo matches, attract many participants, and Pomona's $14 million athletic complex makes its facilities the best of the Claremonts.

"Pomona offers a unique and desirable juxtaposition of rigorous academics and comfortable social atmosphere," says a student. Another student says, "Once you take advantage of the five-college system, you realize how cool it is." The strongest link in an extremely attractive chain, Pomona continues to symbolize the rising status of the Claremont Colleges—and the West in general—in the world of higher education. There are few regrets about coming to Pomona. Says a senior, "We're in California. The sun is always shining. What's the problem?"

> *Pomona is unique among the Claremont Colleges in that it has three non-national fraternities (two co-ed; there are no sororities), each with its own party rooms on campus.*

Overlaps

UC–Berkeley, Brown, UCLA, Harvard, Stanford, Yale

If You Apply To ➤

Pomona: Early decision I: Nov. 1. Early decision II and regular admissions: Jan. 1. Application fee: $70. Campus and alumni interviews: optional, evaluative. SAT and two SAT Subject Tests or ACT (with writing recommended): required. Accepts the Common Application. Essay question.

Scripps College

1030 Columbia Avenue, Claremont, CA 91711

Scripps is easily the premier women's college on the West Coast, offering a commitment to women's education while interacting with co-ed institutions that are literally next door. Attracts more well-rounded women than either Pomona or Pitzer. Innovative Core Curriculum takes an interdisciplinary approach to learning.

Scripps College offers the best of both worlds—a close-knit women's college, where traditions include weekly tea and fresh-baked cookies, and the size and scope of a major research institution, thanks to its membership in the Claremont Colleges. Founded in 1926 by newspaper publisher Ellen Browning Scripps, the college continues to pursue her mission: "To educate women by developing their intellects and talents through active participation in a community of scholars." Students tend to

Website: www.scrippscollege
.edu
Location: Small Town
Private
Total Enrollment: 950

(continued)

Undergraduates: 934

Male/Female: 0/100

SAT Ranges: CR 640–730,
    M 620–700

ACT Ranges: 28–32

Financial Aid: 72%

Expense: Pr $ $ $ $

Student Loans: 44%

Average Debt: $

Phi Beta Kappa: Yes

Applicants: 2,373

Accepted: 32%

Enrolled: 31%

Grad in 6 Years: 88%

Returning Freshmen: 92%

Academics: ✐ ✐ ✐ ½

Social: ☏ ☏ ☏

Q of L: ★ ★ ★ ★

Admissions: (800) 770-1333

Email Address: admission@
    scrippscollege.edu

Strongest Programs:

Politics/International Relations

English

Studio Art

Biology

Psychology

Foreign Languages

Music

Everyone takes the
Core Curriculum.

More than 60 percent
of Scripps students
study abroad, typically
in the junior year.

be outgoing, articulate, and serious about their studies, though they still know how to have fun. "The atmosphere is helpful, not competitive and scary," says one student. "It is impossible to be depressed in this beautiful place."

Indeed, Scripps's scenic 30-acre campus, listed on the National Register of Historic Places, offers a tranquil, safe, and comfortable environment. The architecture is Spanish and Mediterranean, with tiled roofs and elegant landscaping. A performing arts center provides permanent space for the Claremont Concert Orchestra and Concert Choir. In addition to a 700-seat theater, the center offers a music library, recital hall, practice rooms, faculty offices, and classrooms. The Joan and David Lincoln Ceramic Art Building offers more than 5,000 square feet of work area and kiln yards.

The academic experience at Scripps emphasizes cooperation. "Scripps is a very supportive community," a junior says. "It is a place where professors encourage you to

> **"The atmosphere is helpful, not competitive and scary."**

work in groups because more brains [are] always better." Everyone takes the Core Curriculum in interdisciplinary humanities, focusing on ideas about the world and the methods used to generate them. Other requirements include courses in fine arts, letters, natural and social sciences, women's studies, race and ethnic studies, foreign language, and math. "I feel like my professors are my mentors and teachers, as well as my friends," says one student. "They are always up for a discussion, always willing to answer questions (even difficult ones), and always up to chat about how their day is going."

Popular and well-regarded majors at Scripps include psychology, English, studio art, politics, and biology. The Millard Sheets Art Center offers a state-of-the-art studio and freestanding museum-quality gallery for aspiring painters and sculptors. Premeds benefit from the Keck Science Center, a joint facility for students at Scripps, Claremont McKenna (CMC), and Pitzer. The Scripps Humanities Institute offers seminars and lectures open to the general public, along with fellowships for juniors; recently, the institute explored how and why empathy is a shared focal point in disciplines as broad as neuroscience, literary criticism, and legal studies. While Scripps doesn't offer business, students can take economics courses at the college and accounting across the street at Claremont McKenna. More than 60 percent of Scripps students study abroad, typically in the junior year. The students choose from over 100 study program options in 40 different countries.

Forty-eight percent of Scripps women are from California. African Americans account for 4 percent of the student body, Hispanics 9 percent, and Asian Americans 18 percent. "The students here are diligent, thoughtful, and really down to earth," observes one politics major. "They are usually privileged and have had the opportunity to have really impressive experiences." SCORE, the Scripps Communities of Resources and Empowerment, provides support and funding to organizations that

> **"The dorms are gorgeous."**

further promote social and political awareness, with respect to issues of class, ethnicity, gender, race, religion, sexuality, and sexual orientation. There are no athletic scholarships, but more grant money has been made available for students with financial need.

Ninety-five percent of Scripps students live in one of the eight "spectacular" dorms, where options range "from singles to seven-person suites, apartment-style living arrangements to charming Spanish Mediterranean residence halls built in the 1920s." A student says, "The dorms are gorgeous. They are well maintained and have lots of charm with French doors, balconies, or the occasional fireplace." Juniors are guaranteed single rooms. The cafeteria garners rave reviews as well: "This is not traditional college food," says a bioethics major. "The salad bar is gourmet, the bread comes from a local bakery, and the pizza is made in a wood-fired brick oven. Don't get me started about the hot cookies!"

Social life at Scripps centers on the residence halls, which take turns throwing parties. "Our social life is very much based on campus," says a chemistry major. "With five undergraduate universities literally across the street from each other, it is challenging not to have something to do—from movie screenings, art exhibits, concerts, special events like a carnival or the International Festival, and parties." The school's alcohol policy complies with state law but also specifies that if an underage student is drunk at a party, she will be helped and kept safe, rather than written up and punished. The town of Claremont also offers a farmer's market on Sundays, with fresh fruit, flowers, and gifts. For students with cars, popular road trips include Pasadena, Mount Baldy, San Diego, and even Las Vegas and Mexico; students without wheels can hop on the MetroLink commuter train and get to and from Los Angeles for less than five dollars.

Athletic rivalries aren't the focus here, but Scripps does field joint teams with CMC and Harvey Mudd.

Athletic rivalries aren't the focus here, but Scripps does field joint teams with CMC and Harvey Mudd, and when those teams face off against Pomona and Pitzer, students pay attention. All of the Athena teams compete in Division III, and the Scripps water polo, lacrosse, tennis, cross-country, track and field, and swimming and diving teams are all recent conference champs. In addition, the Claremont Colleges Ballroom Dance Company are seven-time national collegiate champions. Intramural sports are also played jointly, and popular options include inner-tube water polo, soccer, flag football, volleyball, rugby, and lacrosse. Traditions are also important at Scripps, including the Matriculation ceremony at the start of each year, and the signing of the "graffiti wall" by each class before graduation.

"Our social life is very much based on campus."

Scripps offers a winning combination of outstanding academics and personal attention, with a cooperative, nonthreatening feel. And should the women-only environment of Scripps begin to feel claustrophobic, the other Claremont Colleges beckon, with parties, intramural sports, and cross-registration privileges. Scripps students want to achieve great things, but not if that requires stepping on their classmates' toes.

Overlaps

Wellesley, Pomona, UC–Berkeley, UCLA, University of Southern California

If You Apply To ➤

Scripps: Early decision: Nov. 15. Regular admissions: Jan. 2. Application fee: $60. Campus and alumnae interviews: optional, informational. SATs or ACTs: required. Subject Tests: optional. Accepts the Common Application. Essay question. Applicants must also submit a graded analytical paper from junior or senior year of high school.

Clark University

950 Main Street, Worcester, MA 01610-1477

If Clark were located an hour to the east, it would have become the hottest thing since Harvard. Worcester is not Boston, but Clarkies bring a sense of mission to their relationship with this old industrial town. Clark is liberal, tolerant, and world-renowned in psychology and geography. Has a less national student body than some institutions of comparable quality.

A classic Clark University poster distills the school's philosophy into a single photograph: a normal green peapod, filled with multicolored peas. "Categorizing people," the poster says, "isn't something you can do here." And indeed, it's not. "At Clark you have to be prepared to be open minded and accepting since there are so many different types of people and ideas," says a junior. Clark started in 1887 as an all-graduate school on a German model, excelling in disciplines including

Website: www.clarku.edu
Location: Small City
Private
Total Enrollment: 3,096
Undergraduates: 2,233

(continued)

Male/Female: 42/58

SAT Ranges: CR 530–640,
  M 530–640

ACT Ranges: 24–29

Financial Aid: 86%

Expense: Pr $ $

Student Loans: 91%

Average Debt: $ $

Phi Beta Kappa: Yes

Applicants: 4,297

Accepted: 70%

Enrolled: 20%

Grad in 6 Years: 80%

Returning Freshmen: 92%

Academics: ✍ ✍ ✍ ✍

Social: ☎ ☎ ☎

Q of L: ★ ★ ★

Admissions: (508) 793-7431

Email Address: admissions@
  clarku.edu

Strongest Programs:
Psychology
Political Science
Biology
International Development and
  Social Change
Business Management
Geography
Screen Studies

Clark's historically strong psychology and geography departments continue to burnish their national reputations.

psychology and geography, and now welcomes undergraduates of all backgrounds and interests with small classes and no shortage of faculty attention.

Clark's compact, 50-acre campus has "enough ivy, tall maples, and collegiate brick buildings to make a traditionalist happy," even though it's located in the gritty Main South section of Worcester. Buildings range from remodeled Victorian-era residences—former homes of prosperous merchants—to the award-winning Robert Hutchings Goddard Library. Clark is always renovating something, and careful restoration has brought a renewed sense of history to the area. Clark is the only American university where famed psychoanalyst Sigmund Freud lectured, and his statue adorns the spot in the center of campus where he spoke. Blackstone Hall is home to 208 students. Each apartment houses four to six students and features modern amenities such as central air-conditioning and full kitchens. The John and Kay Bassett Admissions Center is a contemporary, 7,200-square-foot annex connected by an entrance to the current Admissions Office.

> **"Categorizing people isn't something you can do here."**

While Clark now serves primarily undergraduates, its history of graduate education is evident in its classrooms. Most courses are seminars, and two-thirds have 19 or fewer students. First-year intensives are even smaller, limited to 16 students each. They permit students to explore issues in depth in their first or second semesters, and the faculty member teaching the course acts as an academic adviser until students declare a major. "It is a nice way to immediately meet people and continue having contact with them throughout the semester, and your adviser gets to know you better," a junior communication and culture major says.

The foundation of a Clark education is the Program of Liberal Studies, which promotes the habits, skills, and perspectives essential to lifelong learning. Each student must complete eight courses: one in verbal expression, one in formal analysis, and six in perspectives—aesthetic, comparative, historical, language, scientific, and values. International Studies students take courses in those areas with an international focus. Interdisciplinary programs are popular, and students may design their own majors. Those who finish with a grade point average of 3.4 or better may take a fifth year tuition-free to obtain a master's degree.

Clark's historically strong psychology and geography departments continue to burnish their national reputations, the latter having churned out more Ph.D.s in the field than any other school in the nation, plus four members of the National Academy of Sciences (the most of any geography program). Clark is the birthplace of the American Psychological Association and the concept of adolescence as being distinct from childhood. Also strong are the sciences and programs in management, political science, international development, and communication and culture.

Regardless of major, Clark encourages students to take advantage of internship opportunities through the university itself or the 12-school Colleges of Worcester Consortium*. More than one-third of all Clark students spend at least one semester studying abroad at one of 40 programs. Even those who don't go abroad can get a taste of foreign culture by taking courses or attending international research conferences at the Clark University Center in Luxembourg. Back on campus, the academic climate is challenging, but students don't compete with one another. "The academic climate is more laid-back than competitive," says one psychology major. "You can leave your computer unattended at the library and not worry that another student will delete your essay or something crazy like that." First-years are taught by full professors who are "qualified and very enthusiastic about teaching," according to one student. About 40 percent of students participate in undergraduate research, and first-year students have access to a variety of programs aimed at helping them transition into college life.

> **"The academic climate is more laid-back than competitive."**

"Clark students are, well, *Clarkies*," says one senior. "They are weird, intelligent, talented in a quiet way, and probably the best people you will ever meet." Fifty-three percent of Clark students hail from Massachusetts, and international students from about 90 countries make up another 11 percent. African Americans account for 4 percent of the student body; Hispanics and Asian Americans combine for another 11 percent. Many Clark students do community service, and the Community Engagement and Volunteering Center is a hub for the many social activism groups. Clark offers merit scholarships ranging between $3,000 and $21,000. Nearly 86 percent of students receive some form of need- or merit-based scholarships.

First-year students and sophomores at Clark are required to live in the dorms, and all except one are co-ed by floor or wing. In all, 71 percent of the student body bunks on campus. "Housing lottery can be stressful," notes one student, "but I have never had a problem finding a place to live on campus and I have lived on campus all four years." Some students find apartments and group houses nearby. Campus dwellers must buy the meal plan, which always offers student favorites along with vegan, vegetarian, and kosher options. "The food is pretty diverse," a student says, "which is definitely a plus." Students report feeling safe on campus, despite being "in kind of a rough neighborhood," according to a senior, and "University Police are a very active presence on campus."

Clark has no Greek life, but more than 120 student-run organizations offer "a ton of concerts, bands, comedians" and other programs, says a student. "Clark is not a huge party school. Most students choose to hang out in their dorms or apartments with close friends," one senior says. First-year dorms are dry, and mixed-class halls "are dry if you are under 21," says a Spanish major. Underage drinkers, be forewarned: "They bust a lot of kids," says a senior.

Worcester and the vicinity host 12 colleges and Worcester itself is described as "a city of hidden gems," according to one student. The city has movie theaters, restaurants with every conceivable type of cuisine, and small clubs where bands can play, as well as the DCU Center, a 13,000-seat arena. "Main South Worcester is not the prettiest, quietest locale for a college, but it's got flavor and spice, and you'll either love it or hate it," a junior biology major says. Students mix with the townspeople through volunteer programs such as Clark University Brothers and Sisters. "If you like volunteering someplace that needs it, or fighting for human rights, this is your school," a junior says. To get away, Clarkies head to the larger cities of Boston and Providence, or the rural wilds of Vermont, New Hampshire, and Maine—all easily reachable by car or public transit.

Coping with the frigid New England winters includes quaffing cups of hot chocolate and dreaming about Spree Day: "Every spring classes are canceled and the administration essentially makes a carnival for students to blow off steam before finals," explains one senior. "Face paint, bouncy castles, rock climbing walls, carnival food; it's an awesome day."

The Clark Cougars compete in Division III and the university fields 17 intercollegiate teams. In recent years, men's basketball won the New England Women's and Men's Athletic Conference (NEWMAC) Championship and advanced to the second round of the NCAA tournament, and men's soccer was selected to play in the NCAA tournament. About half of the students participate in intramural sports, which range from soccer and flag football to ultimate Frisbee and volleyball. The Dolan Field House provides facilities and locker rooms for spring and fall teams, plus lighted outdoor fields. The crew team has a boathouse on Lake Quinsigamond, and the cross-country teams recently broke in a new course.

Along with Johns Hopkins, Clark started out differently, serving only graduate

About 40 percent of students participate in undergraduate research, and first-year students have access to a variety of programs aimed at helping them transition into college life.

"[Clarkies] are weird, intelligent, talented in a quiet way, and probably the best people you will ever meet."

Overlaps

Northeastern, University of Massachusetts, Boston University, Wheaton (MA), University of Vermont, Brandeis, Boston College, American University

students. Though it now caters mainly to undergraduates, the school continues to challenge convention, pioneering new teaching methods, pursuing new fields of knowledge, and finding new ways to connect thinking and doing. "Its urban location gives it a distinct identity," a senior says. "It is also fairly progressive, making room for students to satisfy a wide variety of interests."

If You Apply To ➤

Clark: Early action: Nov. 15. Regular admissions: Jan. 15. Financial aid: Feb. 1. Housing: May 1. Application fee: $50. Campus and alumni interviews: optional, informational. SATs or ACTs: optional. Subject Tests: optional. Accepts the Common Application. Essay question: Common Application questions.

Clarkson University

Holcroft House, Box 5605, Potsdam, NY 13699

You know you're in the North Country when the nearest major city is Montreal. Clarkson lies over the river and through the woods. With an informal and close-knit atmosphere, Clarkson is one of the few small, undergraduate-oriented technical universities in the nation. Compare to Lehigh, Bucknell, and Union. Out-of-the-way location makes Clarkson easier to get into, but doing well is no easy task.

Website: www.clarkson.edu
Location: Small Town
Private
Total Enrollment: 3,504
Undergraduates: 3,003
Male/Female: 72/28
SAT Ranges: CR 500–610,
   M 560–660
ACT Ranges: 23–28
Financial Aid: 99%
Expense: Pr $ $
Student Loans: 80%
Average Debt: $ $ $
Phi Beta Kappa: No
Applicants: 4,199
Accepted: 76%
Enrolled: 24%
Grad in 6 Years: 72%
Returning Freshmen: 86%
Academics: ✑ ✑ ✑
Social: ☎ ☎
Q of L: ★ ★ ★
Admissions: (315) 268-6480
Email Address: admission@
   clarkson.edu

Strongest Programs:
Engineering

At Clarkson University, engineering and ice hockey reign supreme. About half of the student body is enrolled in the engineering program, and the hockey team is a perennial contender for top honors. Students here get a quality technical education in a small-town environment that offers plenty to do, especially during the sled-dog days of winter. Clarkson "is an academically excellent school," says a sophomore, "and it will push your learning and skills to new heights."

The village of Potsdam, New York, is cloistered away between the Adirondacks and the St. Lawrence River. The campus relies mainly on modern architecture and lots of woods and wildlife. Established in 2010, the Clarkson Institute for a Sustainable Environment (ISE) is now home to Clarkson's environmental activities associated with research, interdisciplinary graduate and undergraduate degree programs, and outreach programs. The Institute was established to support Clarkson's long-standing expertise in this field, to increase collaboration among faculty in areas related to environmental sustainability, and to support educational initiatives and environmental-related research opportunities for students. A new softball field was recently completed and three new theme houses have opened to serve Greek organizations and other shared-interest groups.

> "It's competitive enough to encourage each individual's best work."

Engineering isn't the only academic offering at Clarkson, but it certainly gets top billing; nearly 50 percent of the students are in the program, and it includes three of the top five most popular majors. The combined programs in electrical/computer engineering and mechanical/aeronautical engineering earn the highest marks from students. Clarkson's School of Business has several majors to choose from, and all first-year business students actually start and run a business. The school also reorganized its undergraduate degree programs to offer courses of study in global supply chain management and innovation and entrepreneurship. Arete allows students to earn a double major in business and a liberal arts discipline. Physics and chemistry are the strongest offerings in the sciences, and would-be doctors have the benefit of a joint program combining biology and—you guessed it—engineering. There is a double major at the B.S. level titled "Social Documentation" and a new minor in war studies.

(continued)

Digital Arts and Sciences
Physical and Life Sciences
Software Engineering

As part of the university's general education requirements (Clarkson Common Experience), all students are required to complete a set of courses and a professional experience. The program emphasizes four components that serve as common threads through multiple courses: learning to communicate effectively; developing an appreciation for diversity in both living and working environments; recognizing the importance of personal, societal, and professional ethics; and understanding how technology can be used to serve humanity. Study abroad opportunities are available at 40 different schools in 24 countries, including Sweden, England, Australia, Korea, France, and Germany. The honors program includes 120 students who participate in an intensive four-year curriculum.

> **"The majority of students here study engineering and many fit the antisocial, awkward stereotype."**

Clarkson prides itself on intimacy and personalized instruction; 46 percent of classes taken by freshmen have 19 or fewer students. Eighty percent of the Foundation courses are taught by full-fledged faculty members, and nearly 200 students conduct research with a faculty mentor each year. "Professors challenge students to excel in the classroom," says one political science major, and are "easily accessible and always willing to provide assistance to students." Some students say Clarkson isn't the academic pressure cooker that many technical institutes are, but others disagree. "It's competitive enough to encourage each individual's best work," a sophomore says, "yet laid-back enough to let everyone work in a way that best fits them." The bottom line of a Clarkson education is getting a job after graduation, and students uniformly praise the career counseling office and proudly note Clarkson's high placement rate.

Study abroad opportunities are available at 40 different schools in 24 countries, including Sweden, England, Australia, Korea, France, and Germany.

At Clarkson, the students are friendly, serious-minded, and down to earth; radicals are notably absent. "We are able to balance heavy courseload and still be active members of multiple organizations. Clarkson students tend to be more social than other engineering students at rival colleges," says one student. Another adds, "The majority of students here study engineering and many fit the antisocial, awkward stereotype." Seventy-four percent of the students graduated in the top quarter of their class. Seventy-two percent are New Yorkers, and 2 percent hail from abroad. Clarkson has trouble luring minorities to its remote locale; African Americans, Hispanics, and Asian Americans combine for 11 percent of the student population. Although students are aware of local and national issues, "nothing really riles people up here in North Country," a junior says. Clarkson awards a handful of merit scholarships each year. Forty-one athletic scholarships are offered, but only ice hockey players need apply (it's Clarkson's only Division I sport).

> **"Clarkson does a great job of providing activities for those who do not party."**

Eighty-three percent of students live in campus housing. Students are required to reside on campus all four years, unless exempted to live in a Greek house. All freshmen are housed with students in their major areas of study and in some instances in their department, giving them the chance to study and learn together. Many underclassmen are housed in conventional dorms, but university-owned townhouse apartments offer more gracious living. Overall, housing is described as adequate, if less than stellar. The dining facilities get average marks for variety and taste. "The food is very edible," says a student. "Even professors eat it."

In keeping with Clarkson's "come as you are" atmosphere, the social scene is low-key. "Clarkson does a great job of providing activities for those who do not party," says one student, "such as movie nights, comedians, hypnotists, and sporting events." Twelve percent of the men and 14 percent of the women join the

Women's volleyball was Liberty League Tournament Champion for the second time in the past four seasons, winning the conference title in 2012.

Greek system. Fraternity beer blasts are the staple of weekend life, and those not into the Greek scene (and over 21) can head to the handful of bars in downtown Potsdam. "Potsdam is definitely a college town," says a student. "St. Lawrence and SUNY–Potsdam are very close by, so during the school year, downtown can be filled with college students." Drinking is permitted on campus for those of age, and even underage students can obtain alcohol easily. For those who crave the bustle of city nightlife, Ottawa and Montreal are each about an hour and a half away by car.

When it comes to sports, hockey is first and foremost in the hearts of Clarkson students. The team has been ECAC champ in recent years, and contends for the national championship with other blue-chip teams like archrivals Cornell and St. Lawrence. Women's volleyball was Liberty League Tournament Champion for the second time in the past four seasons, winning the conference title in 2012. In addition, Clarkson offers 14 Division III sports. Football has been revived as a club sport, as has women's softball. About three-quarters of students take advantage of the intramural program, with soccer, broomball, and volleyball proving popular. For weekend athletes, an abundance of skiing and other outdoor and winter sports are within easy driving distance and nearby lakes and waterways make for terrific canoeing and kayaking during the summer.

While other majors are offered, Clarkson's bread and butter are its technical programs, particularly its slew of engineering majors. Students here gain exposure to the ever-growing variety of specialties in the field. And the extended snowy winters in Potsdam are great for ice hockey fans or ski bunnies looking for fresh powder.

Overlaps

Rochester Institute of Technology, Rensselaer Polytechnic, Syracuse, Worcester Polytechnic, St. Lawrence, Northeastern, University of Rochester, Cornell

If You Apply To >

Clarkson: Early decision: Dec. 1. Regular admissions: Jan. 15. Financial aid: Mar. 1. Application fee: $50. Campus and alumni interviews: optional, informational. SATs or ACTs: required. Subject Tests: recommended. Accepts the Common Application. Essay question: optional.

Clemson University

Clemson, SC 29634

Clemson is a technically oriented public university in the mold of Georgia Tech, North Carolina State, and Virginia Tech. Smaller than the latter two and more focused on undergraduates than Georgia Tech, Clemson serves up its education with ample helpings of school spirit. Small-town location makes for a tight-knit campus, though also a hayseed image next to more sophisticated locales such as Columbia and Chapel Hill.

Website: www.clemson.edu
Location: Small Town
Public
Total Enrollment: 18,340
Undergraduates: 15,570
Male/Female: 54/46
SAT Ranges: CR 560–660, M 590–680
ACT Ranges: 26–31
Financial Aid: 38%

Nestled in the foothills of the Blue Ridge Mountains, Clemson University is a place where traditional Southern spirit continues to flourish alongside modern academics, big-time athletics, and state-of-the-art facilities. This public university has the ring of a private institution and features quality academics in technical areas such as engineering and biology. Tiger spirit is as strong as ever, as evidenced by the ubiquitous orange tiger paws that decorate the campus, and students here are happy to make tracks of their own.

CU's 1,400-acre campus is situated on what was once Fort Hill Plantation, the homestead of Thomas Green Clemson. The campus is surrounded by 17,000 acres of university farms and woodlands and offers a spectacular view of the nearby lake and mountains. Architectural styles are an eclectic mix of modern and 19th-century collegiate. Clemson Bottoms, half a mile down the road from the 80,000-seat football stadium, is home to the Calhoun Field Laboratory, a pastoral site dedicated to agricultural research that features a large, student-run organic garden.

Electrical engineering is Clemson's largest department, and computer engineering is among the nation's best in research on large-scale integrated computer circuitry and robotics. The College of Architecture, one of the school's most selective programs, offers intensive semesters at the Overseas Center for Building **"People are serious about their academics."**
Research and Urban Study in Genoa, Italy. A fantastic resource for science enthusiasts and history buffs is the library's collection of first editions of the scientific works of Galileo and Newton. Because of the prevailing technical emphasis, most students interested in the liberal arts head "down country" to the University of South Carolina. Undergraduate teaching has always been one of Clemson's strong points, and for students interested in pursuing a liberal arts curriculum, the school has degrees in fine arts, philosophy, and languages and enjoys a strong regional reputation for its history program. Although most students agree that engineering and architecture are the school's strongest programs, they also give high marks to business and agriculture. Highly motivated students should consider Calhoun College, Clemson's honors program—the oldest in South Carolina—open to freshmen who scored 1320 or above on their SATs and ranked in the top 10 percent of their high school graduating class. Clemson also offers exchange programs in Mexico, Scotland, Ecuador, Spain, England, Australia, and Italy.

General education requirements include courses in advanced writing; oral communications; mathematical, scientific, and technological literacy; social sciences; arts and humanities; cross-cultural awareness; and science and technology in society. An electronic portfolio pilot allows freshmen to build their portfolio, demonstrating changes in competencies throughout their experiences at Clemson. Academically, the level of difficulty varies. "People are serious about their academics," one senior says, "but few people are cut-throat." Professors run the gamut from average to stellar. "The quality of teaching varies," says a junior. "The best advice is to choose classes based on the professor's reputation, which is easy to find out." Students report some problems finishing a degree in four years, and class registration can be a hassle.

Clemson's student body has a decidedly Southern air, as 69 percent of the undergrads hail from South Carolina, with most of the rest from neighboring states. The average Clemson student is friendly and conservative, and though, as a public **"The quality of teaching varies."**
institution, the school isn't affiliated with any church, there is a strong Southern Baptist presence on campus. Fifty-four percent of students were in the top 10th of their high school graduating class. African Americans make up 6 percent of the student body, Hispanics account for 3 percent, and Asian Americans 2 percent. The university offers thousands of merit scholarships and hundreds of athletic scholarships. Lack of parking is the overriding complaint among students.

Housing gets positive reviews, and 41 percent of the students live on campus, usually during their first two years. Most of the dorms are single sex, though co-ed, university-owned apartment complexes are also an option. "Apartment housing is competitive, but rooms on campus are usually available," says a student. Clemson House and Calhoun Courts, the co-ed halls, are considered the best places to be. "The west campus high-rise dorms are awesome," raves a junior. The dining facilities have been improving, according to students. "They have specials and even ask students to contribute recipes," according to one student. Upperclassmen can cook for themselves, and each dorm has kitchen facilities.

After class, many students hop on their bikes and head to nearby Lake Hartwell. The beautiful Blue Ridge mountain range is also close by for hiking and camping, and

(continued)

Expense: Pub $ $ $ $
Student Loans: N/A
Average Debt: N/A
Phi Beta Kappa: Yes
Applicants: 18,500
Accepted: 58%
Enrolled: 32%
Grad in 6 Years: 82%
Returning Freshmen: 91%
Academics: ✐ ✐ ✐
Social: 🕿 🕿 🕿 🕿
Q of L: ★ ★ ★ ★
Admissions: (864) 656-2287
Email Address:
    cuadmissions@clemson.edu

Strongest Programs:
Engineering
Architecture
Landscape Architecture
Economics
Genetics
Business

Students report some problems finishing a degree in four years, and class registration can be a hassle.

Clemson has a high-powered sports scene.

beaches and ski slopes are both within driving distance. Atlanta and Charlotte are only two hours away by car, and Charleston is four hours away on the coast. Aside from the sports teams, fraternities and sororities provide most of the social life. Twenty percent of Clemson men and 33 percent of women go Greek. The town itself is pretty small, with a few bars and movie theaters, but some students love it. "Downtown is across the street from campus and has many bars," a student affairs major says.

Clemson has a high-powered sports scene and fields a number of competitive teams in the Atlantic Coast Conference (ACC). On weekends when the Tiger teams are playing, there are pep rallies, cookouts, dances, and parties for the mobs of excited fans. The roads leading to campus are painted with large orange pawprints, an insignia that symbolizes great enthusiasm for Clemson sports. So, too, are half the fans at an athletic event, making the stands look like an orange grove. Football fever starts with the annual First Friday Parade, held before the first home game, and on every game day the campus dissolves into a sea of Tiger orange. Hordes of Tiger fans cram "Death Valley" for every game and are especially rowdy when the reviled University of South Carolina Gamecocks are in town. Other very competitive athletic teams include basketball, baseball, and men's track.

Clemson is best at serving those whose interests lie in technical fields. School spirit is contagious, fueled by a love of big-time college sports, and becomes lifelong for many Clemson students. Everyone can become part of the Clemson family, from Southern belle to Northern Yankee, as long as they're friendly, easygoing, and enthusiastic about life in general and the Tigers in particular.

Overlaps

University of South Carolina, College of Charleston, Winthrop, Citadel, UNC at Chapel Hill, University of Georgia, Duke

If You Apply To ➢

Clemson: Rolling admissions: May 1. Application fee: $70. Campus interviews: optional, informational. No alumni interviews. SATs or ACTs: required. No Subject Tests. No essay question.

Colby College

Waterville, ME 04901

The northernmost outpost of private higher education in New England. Colby's picturesque small-town setting is a short hop from the sea coast or the Maine wilderness. No frats since the college abolished them nearly 30 years ago. A well-toned, outdoorsy student body in the mold of Middlebury, Williams, and Dartmouth. Invented the month-long January term.

Website: www.colby.edu
Location: Rural
Private
Total Enrollment: 1,863
Undergraduates: 1,863
Male/Female: 45/55
SAT Ranges: CR 610–710, M 630–720
ACT Ranges: 29–32
Financial Aid: 43%
Expense: Pr $ $ $ $

Colby College draws students who like to work hard and play harder, whether in the classroom or on the ski slopes. The nearby town of Waterville, Maine (population 20,000) offers few distractions, and close friendships with peers and professors help ward off the winter chill. Colby's top study abroad program offers students an opportunity to explore the world, and even those who don't spend a semester or year away can get a taste during the month of January, when Jan-Plan trips send Colby students far and wide. "Colby allows me to explore educational possibilities and experiences of all kinds, from taking a class with a top U.S. economist, to sea kayaking, to mentoring needy children in local schools," says a sophomore. "The setting is picturesque, and the faculty and students are friendly and warm."

Colby sits high on a hill, with beautiful views of the surrounding city and countryside. Its 714 acres include a wildlife preserve, miles of cross-country trails, and a pond used in winter as an ice-skating rink. Georgian architecture predominates, and the oldest buildings are redbrick with white trim, ivy, and brass nameplates above their hunter green doors. The more contemporary buildings lend a touch of modernity. One of the most iconic Colby buildings is the library tower, which is topped with a blue light. The student center features a 7,000-square-foot pavilion with a snack bar, coffee shop, and lounge areas.

As a small college with a history of innovation and educational excellence, Colby encourages students to learn for learning's sake rather than for a good grade. "Colby isn't competitive, but you're expected to do well in your courses," says a senior. Students must complete distribution requirements in English composition, foreign language, "Areas"

> **"Colby allows me to explore educational possibilities and experiences."**

(one course each in arts, historical studies, literature, quantitative reasoning, and social sciences, and two courses in natural sciences), "Diversity" (two courses focusing on how diversity has contributed to the human experience), and "Wellness" (five supper seminars over the first two semesters). Freshmen eager to fulfill that language requirement can ship off to Salamanca or Dijon to take care of it, delaying on-campus enrollment until the second semester. Popular and well-regarded programs include economics and biology, followed closely by English, government, and history. In all, Colby offers more than 50 majors. Colby's faculty is unusually devoted to undergraduate teaching. "The quality of teaching could not be better," says a sophomore. "Professors' doors are always open and they are always willing to chat." Sixty-eight percent of all classes have 19 or fewer students, allowing those highly lauded profs to spend more time with each student.

Colby was the first men's college in New England to admit women, and also the first to establish a special January term. Students must take three such terms for credit to graduate. Motivated students might use the month off to serve an internship, study abroad, or prepare an in-depth report. Less serious types head for the ski slopes or Southern beaches, and write a quick paper at the end of the month. The school also sponsors Jan-Plan trips to everywhere from Nicaragua to Vietnam, including Bermuda (for biology). Other programs include Connecticut's Mystic Seaport (for marine biology); Kyoto, Japan; and the great cities of Europe. For would-be engineers, there is a joint 3–2 program

> **"The three dining halls do a wonderful job of providing delicious food."**

with Dartmouth, and others may take exchange programs with Clark Atlanta and Howard. Given all these options, it's no surprise that half of the school's majors have an international component and more than two-thirds of Colby students spend some time abroad, taking advantage of more than 140 approved international programs. A high proportion of graduates enter the Peace Corps and the Foreign Service.

Colby students are "so different yet all united through a love of learning," offers one student. "They work as hard as they play," adds another. Only 12 percent of Colby students are Mainers; the rest learn to act like natives during the COOT program (Colby Outdoor Orientation Trips). These four-day excursions by bicycle, canoe, or foot introduce them to the beauty of the Maine wilderness or to service or theater experiences. African Americans account for 3 percent of the student body, Hispanics 5 percent, and Asian Americans 6 percent. Merit scholarships averaging $3,582 are available, and the college has eliminated student loans from all financial aid packages and replaced them with grants. There are no athletic scholarships.

Ninety-four percent of Colby students live on campus, where residence halls have live-in faculty members. "Dorms range from palatial apartments to closet-like doubles," says a junior. About 100 seniors live off campus each year in apartment-style buildings. Dining halls cater to the various tastes, lifestyles, religions, and even holidays throughout the year. "The three dining halls do a wonderful job of

(continued)

Student Loans: 34%
Average Debt: $ $
Phi Beta Kappa: Yes
Applicants: 5,241
Accepted: 29%
Enrolled: 33%
Grad in 6 Years: 90%
Returning Freshmen: 95%
Academics: ✐ ✐ ✐ ✐ ½
Social: ☎ ☎ ☎
Q of L: ★ ★ ★ ★
Admissions: (800) 723-3032
Email Address: admissions@ colby.edu

Strongest Programs:
Art
Economics
Government
English
International Studies
Environmental Studies
Natural Sciences
Music

Popular and well-regarded programs include economics and biology, followed closely by English, government, and history.

providing delicious food and unique atmospheres. Students are free to eat at whichever one they want," states a senior.

When the weekend comes, you'll find most Colby students staying close to campus. "As a college town, it isn't much," confides a senior, "but the restaurants are OK and the new Starbucks helps." Although fraternities are a thing of the past, students maintain an active party life. In response to student requests, administration has instituted a program allowing a glass of wine or beer at dinner on Friday nights in Dana dining hall for students of legal age. Still, there are options for those who choose not to imbibe, including "parties, shows, plays, talks, and concerts," according to a junior. Popular road trips include Augusta, Portland, and Freeport, Maine (home to the L.L. Bean factory and store). Also easy to reach are the bright lights of Boston and Montreal and the slopes of Sugarloaf, Maine.

The Colby administration likes to share two "big secrets" about Maine winters: they're beautiful, and they're a lot harsher in the telling than in the living. Still, an enthusiasm for chilly weather and outdoor sports are the major nonacademic credentials needed to find contentment here. Everyone looks forward to football, basketball, lacrosse, and hockey games, as well as the annual winter carnival and snow-sculpture contest. The Colby Mules have come a long way since the first intercollegiate croquet game, played at Colby in 1860. Nonvarsity athletes are eager participants in 10 club teams and six intramural sports.

Colby's traditional New England liberal arts college vibe extends far beyond its small-town setting and historic, ivy-covered buildings. It permeates the air, punctuated by the long-standing traditions, abundant school spirit, and caring faculty members who focus on developing their students' minds.

Overlaps

Bowdoin, Middlebury, Bates, Hamilton, Dartmouth, Colgate, Brown, Amherst

If You Apply To ➤ | **Colby:** Early decision: Nov. 15. Regular admissions: Jan. 1. Financial aid: Feb. 1. No application fee. Campus and alumni interviews: optional, informational. SATs or ACTs: required. Subject Tests: optional. Accepts the Common Application. Essay question.

Colgate University

13 Oak Drive, Hamilton, NY 13346

With fewer than 3,000 students, Colgate is smaller than Bucknell and Dartmouth but bigger than Hamilton and Williams. Like the other four, it offers small-town living and close interaction between students and faculty. Greek organizations and a jock mentality are still well entrenched despite administrative efforts to neutralize them.

Website: www.colgate.edu
Location: Rural
Private
Total Enrollment: 2,886
Undergraduates: 2,871
Male/Female: 46/54
SAT Ranges: CR 620–720, M 650–740
ACT Ranges: 30–32
Financial Aid: 42%

Colgate University offers small-town living, an active social scene, strong athletics, and close student/faculty interaction. While you may see the same North Face or Patagonia fleece coming and going (and coming and going) as you stroll across campus, students here aren't all spun from the same cloth. "There are the athletes, the bookworms, the partiers, the all-around kids, the preppy kids, the neat freaks, the drama kings and queens, the activists—the list goes on and on," says one denizen. From the herbarium to the Devonian fossils to the 16-inch reflecting telescope, it's clear that Colgate has more to offer than just its picture-postcard setting.

Colgate's 13 founders started the school with 13 prayers and 13 dollars. Their prayers were answered in 1880, when toothpaste mogul William Colgate gave $50,000 to the fledgling university, enough to get the name changed from Madison to his own (and less than the current annual cost to attend!). Today, the 515-acre campus sits on a hillside in rural New York, overlooking the village of Hamilton. Ivy-covered limestone buildings peek out from tree-lined drives; lush green spaces are perfect for rugby, Frisbee, or other outdoor diversions, at least in the warmer months. Rolling hills and farmland surround the campus, making for stunning vistas during the snowy season, which stretches from mid-October to mid-March.

Aside from blazing a trail to rural New York, Colgate has led its peers in emphasizing interdisciplinary study. The faculty first established an interdisciplinary core program in 1928, and it's been a foundation of the curriculum ever since. Even now, all freshmen take a first-year seminar that introduces liberal arts topics, skills, and ways of learning. The seminars are capped at 18 students each, and there are more than 40 topics, ranging from the history of rock and roll to the advent of the atomic bomb. The seminars focus on individual needs and strengths, learning from classmates, and learning from resources beyond the classroom; academic advising also comes from the seminar instructor, since students don't declare majors until the sophomore year. Students also complete two courses from each of Colgate's three academic divisions: natural sciences and math, social sciences, and humanities. Five courses in the liberal arts core—on Western traditions, the challenge of modernity, cultures, scientific perspectives, and global perspectives—round out the requirements and equip students to contemplate the issues they will face throughout their lives. Aside from a major (or two), Colgate also mandates foreign language proficiency and two physical education classes.

> **"Colgate students are committed to academic excellence."**

Students give high marks to the natural and social sciences, including economics, political science, and history, all of which are among the most popular majors. English department offerings include not only literature but a strong program in creative writing, as well as theater courses. Befitting Colgate's rugged location, there are five majors within the environmental studies program: environmental studies, environmental biology, environmental geography, environmental geology, and environmental economics. Classrooms and labs devoted to foreign language study help students gain comfort with another tongue—a good thing, since Colgate offers more than 20 semester-long off-campus study programs and a variety of extended study opportunities around the globe. Aside from programs led by faculty members in foreign locales, from England, Japan, and Nigeria to Russia and Central America, there are three domestic programs, such as one at the National Institutes of Health in Bethesda, Maryland. Colgate also participates in the Maritime Studies Program* and the Semester at Sea*.

Classes at Colgate are small, and 65 percent of those taken by freshmen have 19 or fewer students. "Students are more than willing to help each other succeed and this leads to good collaboration and group work," says a senior. A sophomore adds, "The professors are very well respected in their fields, and that shows in their teaching styles. They are confident, yet never talk down to you." Undergraduate research also wins raves, and each summer approximately 150 students work under faculty members as paid research assistants. The students who go straight into the workforce credit Colgate's strong and loyal alumni network with helping them land their first job.

> **"I would describe Hamilton as the quintessential college town."**

"Colgate students are committed to academic excellence but do not let it overshadow their overall college experience," says one junior. "Sports, extracurricular activities, and social life are all important aspects to student life, and those who fail to balance an extensive résumé of activities are an isolated minority." The students are also overwhelmingly white graduates of public high schools, and 25 percent are New Yorkers. African Americans account for 6 percent of the minority

(continued)

Expense: Pr $ $ $ $
Student Loans: 34%
Average Debt: $
Phi Beta Kappa: Yes
Applicants: 7,798
Accepted: 29%
Enrolled: 33%
Grad in 6 Years: 90%
Returning Freshmen: 95%
Academics: ✍ ✍ ✍ ✍ ½
Social: ☎ ☎ ☎
Q of L: ★ ★ ★
Admissions: (315) 228-7401
Email Address: admission@ colgate.edu

Strongest Programs:
Economics
English
Political Science
International Relations
Environmental Studies
Peace and Conflict Studies

The faculty first established an interdisciplinary core program in 1928, and it's been a foundation of the curriculum ever since.

population, Hispanics 8 percent, and Asian Americans 10 percent—better than in the past, but still insufficient, students say. Issues that draw attention include elections, human rights, and the university's increased involvement in Greek life. "The campus is pretty evenly divided between liberals and conservatives," a student says. Financial aid awards typically consist of grants, a student loan, and a campus job opportunity. Colgate Grant funds usually represent the largest portion of a regular financial aid award; for the Class of 2017 the average award for students receiving financial aid was $42,575. Athletic scholarships are available in 13 sports.

Ninety-one percent of Colgate students live in the dorms, which range from traditional buildings with fireplaces to newer facilities that seem more like hotels. "Housing has been one of my least rewarding experiences at Colgate," grumbles one student. "My freshman dorm room was far too small to accommodate two residents and my sophomore housing felt like it was a prison." About 250 upperclassmen are allowed to live off campus each year. Three dining halls provide students with a wide choice of victuals, including salad and sandwich bars, soup, cereal, and bagels. Take-out food is provided at the campus center, known as the Coop. One student reports, "The food is incredibly hit or miss, especially Frank, our main dining hall. The Coop and the Edge Bistro are a lot higher quality, though."

"Students are more than willing to help each other succeed."

"I would describe Hamilton as the quintessential college town," says one student, "with restaurants, bars, and, of course, late-night pizza." The town is within walking distance of campus, but there's also a free bus that cycles through every half hour, especially nice in the dead of winter. Students enjoy free "Take Two" movies on Friday and Saturday nights, a cappella concerts featuring their friends, and open-mic nights at Donovan's Pub or the Barge Canal Coffee Company, which Colgate opened in a downtown storefront. The coffeehouse is open to all, including townspeople, and has become very popular. The Palace draws crowds with music, dancing, a bar, and a Mexican restaurant; it's also located downtown.

Back on campus, the social scene keeps most students close to home. "If you leave campus, you miss out," one student explains. Thirty percent of the men and 32 percent of the women join the Greek system, while debates continue over the proper balance between academics and social life. In an effort to cut down on alcohol consumption, hazing, and other problems that regularly get out of hand at Colgate, the administration forced fraternities and sororities to sell their off-campus houses to the university. In addition to the required four-day orientation program, freshmen may also participate in Wilderness Adventure, where groups of six to eight canoe and hike in the Adirondacks, or in Outreach, which involves three days of community service in the surrounding area. "Community service is quite popular," confirms a senior. Colgate students remain involved in the community through work as tutors, mentors, and student teachers, on Habitat for Humanity projects,

"Colgate has a huge ice hockey rivalry with Cornell."

and with the elderly. For those with wheels, skiing is 45 minutes away in Toggenburg, and the malls and city lights of Syracuse and Utica are roughly the same distance. Everyone looks forward to Spring Party Weekend, a last blast before finals, which celebrates the thaw with a carnival, barbecues, fireworks, and multiple bands. On the eve of graduation, seniors light torches and form a circle around Lake Taylor, where they sing their alma mater and throw their torches into a bonfire.

While Colgate students participate in intramurals ranging from bowling to ultimate Frisbee, their most fervent cheers are reserved for Division I-AA football against Bucknell and Division I men's lacrosse against Cornell. Recent league champions include football, men's soccer, men's ice hockey, women's soccer, volleyball, and women's swimming and diving. "Colgate has a huge ice hockey rivalry with Cornell and each time the two teams meet, the ice rink is filled to capacity," says a senior. Even weekend warriors may take advantage of the Sanford Field House, the Lineberry natatorium, and the Seven Oaks golf course, which is ranked among the top five collegiate courses nationally. There's also a trap-shooting range, a quarry for rock-climbing, miles of trails for running and cycling, and sailing and rowing facilities at Lake Moraine, five minutes away. Forty sport clubs and 19 intramural competitions attract a healthy number of participants.

Colgate led the way in interdisciplinary work and continues to do so now. What else has remained constant? A senior offers this assessment: "I think Colgate has embraced its identity as different from other liberal arts colleges in that we are not a crunchy granola hippy school and we are not a socially progressive bastion of forward thinking. Colgate is what it is: a hidden gem in the Chenango Valley."

If You Apply To ➢

Colgate: Early decision: Nov. 15. Regular admissions and financial aid: Jan. 15. Application fee: $60. Campus and alumni interviews: optional, informational. SATs or ACTs: required. No Subject Tests. Accepts the Common Application. Essay question.

University of Colorado–Boulder

Office of Admissions, 552 UCB, Boulder, CO 80309-0552

Boulder is a legendary place that draws everyone from East Coast ski bums to California refugees. The scenery is breathtaking and the science programs are first-rate. The University of Arizona is the only public university of similar stature in the Mountain West. That said, the university's party-school reputation is a headache for administrators. Check out the residential academic programs.

Wild buffalo may be all but extinct on America's Great Plains, but they're in boisterous residence, proudly wearing gold and black, at the University of Colorado at Boulder. A bevy of scholars' programs, learning communities, and academic neighborhoods give the campus a community feel, and students choose from a solid menu of academic programs, including research experience, study abroad, and recreational pursuits. With more than 300 days of sunshine a year, is it any wonder students here are a contented lot?

Tree-shaded walkways, winding bike paths, open spaces, and an incredible view of the dramatic Flatirons rock formation make CU's 600-acre Boulder campus a haven for students from both coasts and for Colorado residents eager to pursue knowledge in a snowy paradise. The campus includes about 200 classic rural Italian-style buildings and complexes built of Colorado sandstone with red tile roofs. The 45,000-square-foot Discovery Learning Center houses 12 labs in which engineering students tackle society's challenges using video-conferencing and other high-tech capabilities. The Sierra Club has named CU–Boulder as the top public university in the nation for its efforts to protect the environment. Among other things, it was the first U.S. university to buy renewable energy credits. What's more, city bus passes are included in the cost of tuition and fees. A new biotechnology building opened in early 2012.

> **"My courses are challenging but not overwhelming."**

Website: www.colorado.edu
Location: Small City
Public
Total Enrollment: 25,873
Undergraduates: 23,474
Male/Female: 54/46
SAT Ranges: CR 530–630, M 540–650
ACT Ranges: 24–29
Financial Aid: 56%
Expense: Pub $ $ $
Student Loans: 45%
Average Debt: $ $
Phi Beta Kappa: Yes
Applicants: 21,767
Accepted: 84%
Enrolled: 30%
Grad in 6 Years: 68%
Returning Freshmen: 84%

Outstanding departments include astrophysics and planetary sciences, biochemistry, biology, business entrepreneurship, engineering, English, geography, music, and psychology.

Entering freshmen and transfer students at CU–Boulder choose from three colleges, two programs, and one school: the College of Arts and Sciences (with 70 percent of students), the College of Music, the College of Engineering and Applied Science (the hardest to enter, students say), the Program in Environmental Design, the Program in Journalism and Mass Communication, and the Leeds School of Business. Each has different entrance standards and requirements; music, for example, requires an audition. General education requirements for those who enroll in arts and sciences are designed to provide a broad background in the liberal arts to complement their major specialization. The requirements cover four skills acquisition areas—writing, quantitative reasoning and math, critical thinking, and foreign language—and seven content areas: historical context, culture and gender diversity, U.S. context, natural sciences, contemporary societies, literature and the arts, and ideals and values.

"My courses are challenging but not overwhelming," says a sophomore. "I've actually seen a lot of students banding together to get through the rigorous course load," adds a junior. CU–Boulder offers more than 3,600 courses each year in approximately 150 areas of study. Outstanding departments include astrophysics and planetary sciences, biochemistry, biology, business entrepreneurship, engineering, English, geography, music, and psychology. CU–Boulder is consistently among the top universities in the country to receive NASA funding, leading to unparalleled opportunities for the design, construction, and flight of model spacecraft—and to 18 CU–Boulder alumni having worked as astronauts. "In my experience, professors and graduate student instructors alike have taken a keen interest in students' progress, success, and learning," says one freshman, "making themselves available to students as a valuable resource for extra assistance with class concepts and assignments."

CU–Boulder has tried to make its large campus seem smaller through "academic neighborhoods" (specialized living and learning environments) focusing on topics such as leadership, diversity, natural or social sciences, international studies, engineering, music, and history, culture, and society. In these programs, students take one or two courses, each limited to 25 students, in their residence halls. "The Residential Academic Program for freshmen is essential for gaining a well-rounded experience at CU," advises a senior. The Presidents Leadership Class is a four-year scholarship program that exposes the most promising students to political, business, and community leaders through seminars, work and study trips, and site visits. Special Undergraduate Enrichment Programs offer special activities and advising for CU–Boulder's most "intellectually committed" students, chosen for their excitement about learning and academic success. CU–Boulder also offers over 300 study abroad programs in more than 65 countries.

Sixty-four percent of CU–Boulder's student body comes from Colorado, and by state regulation that percentage can be no lower than 55 percent, on average, over a three-year period. Hispanics comprise 9 percent of the undergraduate population, Asian Americans 5 percent, and African Americans make up 2 percent. "My experience at CU has led me to be around students more like myself: academically focused and socially aware," offers one freshman. "It is such a large, broad campus that just about any sort of student can be found." Qualified undergrads receive merit scholarships worth an average of $7,736, and 237 athletes receive scholarships as well. Additional programs provide debt-free financial incentives for qualified students whose family income is at or below the federal poverty line.

> **"Professors and graduate student instructors alike have taken a keen interest in students' progress."**

First-year students are required to live on campus, where rooms get mixed reviews. "The dorms on main campus are currently pretty run-down, but very close to classes," says a biochemistry major. "Most of the dorms that have been recently renovated are on the outskirts of campus." Most sophomores, juniors, and seniors find off-campus digs in Boulder, and those who want to stay on campus are advised to make early reservations for Farrand, Sewall, or Kittredge halls. An alternative to the four dining halls and nine cafés is the student-run Alferd Packer Memorial Grill, which provides fast food under innocent auspices. CU–Boulder students and trivia buffs know, however, that Packer was a controversial 19th-century folk figure known as the "Colorado Cannibal." *Bon appétit.* Generally, students say campus is safe, helped by emergency telephones along walkways and paths, near bus stops and campus buildings, and in the parking structures. CU–Boulder also offers walking and riding escorts at night via a service called CU NightRide.

Physical exercise is a popular extracurricular activity at CU–Boulder.

"Although there is plenty of socialization on campus (numerous coffee shops, performances at the university theater, and various on-campus events), I would say most students go off campus for social interaction," says one integrative psychology major. For the culturally minded, the university and the city of Boulder offer films and plays, the renowned Colorado Shakespeare Festival, art galleries and museums, and concerts by top rock bands. Denver is only 30 miles southeast, reachable by a free bus service. Eleven percent of CU–Boulder men and 16 percent of women go Greek, though fraternity and sorority parties have changed dramatically since CU–Boulder's sorority chapters became the first in the nation to voluntarily make their houses dry. On campus, the ban on alcohol is taken seriously, and dorms are officially "substance-free." Get caught with booze two times while underage, and you'll be subject to suspension. Even if you don't drink, though, you'll surely find something to do. Day trips to ski resorts like Breckenridge, Vail, and Aspen largely replace weekend getaways here, but

"Most students go off campus for social interaction."

for those who've got to get out of the cold, Las Vegas isn't so far, says one student. For a quick drive to the slopes, the Eldora ski area—with runs up to three miles long and a vertical drop of as much as 1,400 feet—is just a half hour from campus.

Physical exercise is a popular extracurricular activity at CU–Boulder. The CU–Boulder club sports program is ranked among the top three in the nation for both the athletic and academic performance of its teams. Just $177 a year (part of the mandatory student fee) gives students access to the Student Recreation Center, with swimming pools, basketball and tennis courts, an indoor running track, three weight rooms, cardiovascular training facilities, an indoor rock-climbing wall, and an ice arena. Varsity teams now compete in the Pac-12 Conference, and the Buffaloes have won more than two dozen team conference championships, including the 2013 NCAA national title for skiing. Each year, football fans flock to Denver for the game against Colorado State, and any showdown with Nebraska is sure to get students riled up. Ralphie, the live buffalo who acts as CU–Boulder's mascot, doesn't miss a game—and neither do many students.

"CU–Boulder is energy. Every student, teacher, and department always has something new and exciting going on. It would be very hard to get bored here," claims one senior. If you want to flex your muscle as well as your mind, forget the ivy-covered bricks and gray city skies endemic to so many Eastern institutions, and consider going West instead. "There are few places where quality learning and a fun college atmosphere meet with such success," says a senior.

Overlaps

Colorado State, University of Denver, University of Oregon, University of Arizona, Caltech, University of Washington, Colorado School of Mines, UC–Santa Barbara

If You Apply To ➤ **CU–Boulder:** Early action: Dec. 1. Regular admissions: Jan. 15. Financial aid: Apr. 1. Application fee: $50. Campus interviews: optional, informational. No alumni interviews. SATs or ACTs: required. No Subject Tests. Two essay questions required. Apply to individual schools or programs.

Colorado College

14 East Cache La Poudre Street, Colorado Springs, CO 80903

The Block Plan is CC's calling card. It is great for in-depth study and field trips but less suited to projects that take an extended period of time. The Rockies draw outdoor enthusiasts and East Coasters who want to ski. CC is the only top liberal arts college between Iowa and the Pacific. Colorado Springs is an ideal location at the base of the Rockies.

Website: www.colorado
   college.edu
Location: City Center
Private
Total Enrollment: 2,001
Undergraduates: 1,983
Male/Female: 46/54
SAT Ranges: CR 630–720,
   M 610–710
ACT Ranges: 28–32
Financial Aid: 52%
Expense: Pr $ $ $
Student Loans: 31%
Average Debt: $
Phi Beta Kappa: Yes
Applicants: 5,606
Accepted: 23%
Enrolled: 40%
Grad in 6 Years: 90%
Returning Freshmen: 95%
Academics: ✍ ✍ ✍ ✍
Social: ☎ ☎ ☎ ☎
Q of L: ★ ★ ★ ★
Admissions: (800) 542-7214
Email Address: admission@
   coloradocollege.edu

Strongest Programs:
Economics
Biology
Sociology
Political Science
International Political Economy

Colorado is one of the few U.S. schools offering block scheduling, also known as the "One-Course-at-a-Time" method. For more than a century, CC's focus on creative approaches to academics and its breathtaking location at the edge of the Rocky Mountains have drawn liberal-leaning liberal arts enthusiasts who also like to go out and play.

Founded in 1874, the college campus lies at the foot of Pike's Peak, in the town of Colorado Springs. The surrounding neighborhood is on the National Register of Historic Places, as are many CC buildings, including its first, Cutler Hall (1879), and Palmer Hall, named after town founder William J. Palmer, a major force behind the establishment of the college. The prevailing architectural styles are Romanesque and English Gothic, with some more modern structures thrown in. The Western Ridge dorm complex offers apartment-style living for 290 students. The Cornerstone Arts Center is a 73,300-square-foot building that includes a 433-seat auditorium, a black box performance venue, a sound stage, a 108-seat film screening room, the Interdisciplinary Experimental Arts (IDEA) Space, and a multipurpose Flex Room, which can be used as a teaching or performing space.

> **"You decide how rigorous the course is by how much effort you give."**

CC requires students to take 32 courses, at least 18 outside their major department. Within those 32 courses, two must focus on the Western tradition; three on the non-Western tradition, minority culture, or gender studies; and two on the natural sciences, including lab or field study. Foreign language proficiency is also required, and students must complete either a six-course thematic minor, which examines an issue or theme, cultural group, geographic area or historical era, or six social science courses outside their major. What really defines the academic climate, though, is the block schedule (see also Cornell College in Iowa). Students take eight courses between early September and mid-May, but focus on each one, in turn, for three and a half weeks. Some courses, such as neuroscience, are two blocks long. Four-and-a-half-day breaks separate the terms. The plan helps students stay focused, eliminating the temptation to let one course slide so that they can catch up in another. But there are trade-offs. Students say it can be hard to integrate material from courses taken one at a time. There's also the danger of burnout, because so much material is crammed into such a short span. Still, the prevailing vibe is low-key. "You decide how rigorous the course is by how much effort you give," explains a freshman. "The only person you are ever really competing with is yourself." The First Year Experience program, with a student mentor and two advisors, helps students adjust.

Students at Colorado tend to be bright and independent; they say the school's best programs include the sciences and English. "The sciences are great," says a physics major, "especially geology." The block schedule permits some classes at unique times and in unique places—for instance, astronomy at midnight, or coral biology work in the Caribbean. The college's popular program in Southwest studies includes time at its Baca campus, 175 miles away in the historic San Luis Valley. Other interesting interdisciplinary programs include Asian studies, studies in war and peace, and American-ethnic studies. In addition to giving students the option to pick semester and year-long abroad programs in over 60 countries, Colorado College faculty also teach about 25 blocks abroad during the school year and summer session. Still more options are available through the Associated Colleges of the Midwest*. And for students who want to see more of the United States, there are arts and urban studies programs in Chicago, a Washington semester for budding politicos, and a science semester at Tennessee's Oak Ridge National Laboratory.

Back on campus, the majority of classes have 19 or fewer students. Required courses aren't hard to get into, since spots are secured with an auction system. At the beginning of each year, students get 80 points to "bid" on the classes they want. Those who bid the most for a particular class get a seat. And if you're going to take only one class at a time, it helps to like the teacher. Students say that's no problem here. "The professors are very accessible, and it is easy to have a good working relationship," says a history and political science major.

> **"The students are laid-back, nature-loving hippies."**

Just 19 percent of Colorado College students are in-staters, 6 percent are international, and the rest are from elsewhere in the United States. "The students are laid-back, nature-loving hippies," says a student. Minorities account for 13 percent of the student body—2 percent are African American, 7 percent Hispanic, and 4 percent Asian American—and the school is trying to attract more diversity. The Queer Straight Alliance, the Feminist Collective, the College Republicans, the Jewish Chaverim, and the Black Student Union also provide support to students of varied backgrounds and viewpoints. "Environmental issues are especially big on campus," says a sophomore. The admissions office places great weight on students' high school records, class ranks, and essays.

Only seniors are permitted to live off campus at Colorado College, so the other 78 percent of the student body bunks in the dorms. And while seniors don't have to move, a junior says it's easy to see why they do: "There's housing for about 80 percent of our student body, but a lot of it sucks." Architecturally, dorms range from large brick halls to small houses; some are for freshmen only, others are same sex, and still others offer a language or cultural theme. Campus residents give the dining hall food a universal thumbs-down: "The food is not a highlight," quips a student. "It is very bland and there are not many options." The dining options include an organic café, coffee bar, traditional dining hall, and a coffeehouse.

> **"The food is not a highlight."**

When the weekend comes, students stay on campus for parties in friends' rooms or events sponsored by the "low-key" Greek system, which attracts 7 percent of the men and 11 percent of the women. Officially, no one under 21 is permitted to have alcohol in the dorms or elsewhere, but students say enforcement is lax. "It's fairly easy to get alcohol from an upperclassman," says a biology major. For those who don't, won't, or can't imbibe, Herb 'n' Farm offers great smoothies. Each spring, the outdoor Llamapalooza festival features bands from on and off campus. For those seeking a bit of urban culture, Denver and Boulder are a short drive away. Most CC students love heading off campus to ski or hike, either at nearby resorts or in Utah, New Mexico, or the Grand Canyon area. (Freshman outdoor orientation trips help out-of-staters sort out the options, from backpacking and hiking to rafting, bicycling, and windsurfing. Students may even reserve a college-owned mountainside cabin.) Service trips are sponsored during block breaks, and 84 percent of students do some type of community service.

Colorado College sponsors two NCAA Division I sports (the "Tigers")—men's ice hockey and women's soccer—as well as 15 Division III sports. Men's ice hockey

Some courses, such as neuroscience, are two blocks long. Four-and-a-half-day breaks separate the terms.

Only seniors are permitted to live off campus at Colorado College, so the other 78 percent of the student body bunks in the dorms.

Overlaps

University of Colorado–Boulder, University of Denver, Middlebury, Brown, Stanford, Pomona, Dartmouth, Bowdoin

is solid, and women's lacrosse and volleyball, men's soccer, and men's and women's track and field all have made national tournament appearances in recent years. There's a huge rivalry with the University of Denver. Popular intramurals include dodgeball, flag football, indoor volleyball, outdoor soccer, indoor soccer, ice hockey, basketball, kickball, racquetball, inner-tube water polo, softball, and ice broomball.

The block plan made Colorado College what it is today, and the school continues to build on this reputation. While CC is intense, and the schedule is not for everyone, "I really enjoy the people and the unique learning environment," a freshman says. "It's small and conducive to the way I learn."

If You Apply To ➤

Colorado College: Early decision and early action: Nov. 15. Regular admissions: Jan. 15. Financial aid: Feb. 15. Housing: Jun. 20. Application fee: $60. Campus interviews: optional, evaluative. Alumni interviews: optional, informational. SATs or ACTs or three exams from a list of approved category options that includes Subject Tests: required. Accepts the Common Application. Essay question.

Colorado School of Mines

1811 Elm Street, Golden, CO 80401-1842

Mines is the preeminent technical institute in the Mountain West. Getting in is not hard; graduating is another story. Twice as big as New Mexico Tech, but one-tenth the size of Texas Tech. Best known for mining-related fields but strong in many areas of engineering. Men outnumber women 3 to 1, and Golden provides little other than a nice view of the mountains.

Website: www.mines.edu
Location: Small Town
Public
Total Enrollment: 5,041
Undergraduates: 3,897
Male/Female: 73/27
SAT Ranges: CR 570–670, M 630–720
ACT Ranges: 27–31
Financial Aid: 30%
Expense: Pub $ $ $ $
Student Loans: 51%
Average Debt: $ $ $ $
Phi Beta Kappa: Yes
Applicants: 11,682
Accepted: 37%
Enrolled: 22%
Grad in 6 Years: 67%
Returning Freshmen: 89%
Academics: ✍ ✍ ✍ ½
Social: ☎ ☎ ☎
Q of L: ★ ★
Admissions: (303) 273-3220

If you're a bit of a geek whose only dilemma is what type of engineer to become, and you want to spend your scarce free time hiking, biking, and skiing with friends, then Colorado School of Mines may be the place for you. This public school's small size and rugged location endear it to the mostly male students who shoulder heavy workloads to earn their degrees. "There are often fun and entertaining conversations that could only be possible with the types of students here," says a sophomore mechanical engineering major. Just down the road from Coors Brewing Co., which taps the Rockies for its legendary brews, students at Mines learn to tap the same mountains for coal, oil, and other natural resources.

"Good time management and friends help ease the angst."

CSM's 373-acre campus sits in the shadow of the spectacular Rocky Mountains in tiny Golden, Colorado. Architectural styles range from turn-of-the-century gold dome to present-day modern, and native trees and greenery punctuate lush lawns. The $25 million Recreation Center features a swimming pool, climbing wall, recreational gym, and other facilities.

CSM academics are rigorous. All freshmen take the same first-year program, which includes chemistry, calculus, physical education, physics, design, earth and environmental systems, quantitative chemical measurement, nature and human values, and the Freshman Success Seminar, an advising and mentoring course designed to increase retention. Because of CSM's narrow focus, the undergraduate majors—or "options," as they're called—are quite good. There's plenty of variety, as long as you like engineering; programs range from geophysical, geological, and petroleum to civil, electrical, and mechanical.

Courses in a student's option start in the second semester of sophomore year, after yet more calculus, physics, and differential equations. Mines offers the only B.S. degree in economics in Colorado. Physics has grown, now enrolling nearly 10 percent of undergraduates, and the school has been investing more in humanities and social sciences.

Pass/fail grading is unheard of at Mines, but failing grades are not. "The courses are hard," says a junior, "but good time management and friends" help ease the angst. Professors are qualified and helpful, and adjunct professors, who work in the fields they teach, draw raves for bringing real-world application into the classroom. "Most of the teachers have industry experience and bring that into the classroom," a chemistry major says. Forty percent of freshman classes have 25 or fewer students, but 5 percent are packed with more than 100 students. The required two-semester EPICS program—the acronym stands for Engineering Practices Introductory Course Sequence—helps develop communications, teamwork, and problem-solving skills with weekly presentations and written reports. Students say teamwork helps soften the load a bit. "We are all working together," one student says.

CSM supplements coursework with a required six-week summer field session, enabling students to gain hands-on experience. About 100 undergraduates participate in the McBride Honors Program in Public Affairs, which includes seminars and off-campus activities that encourage them to think differently about the implications of technology. CSM also offers the opportunity to live and study at more than 50 universities in Europe, Australia, Latin America, Asia, and the Middle East, but only 7 to 10 percent of students take part. Each year, 100 to 120 undergraduates participate in research with faculty members or on their own.

Mines is a state school, making it a good deal for homegrown students, who comprise 60 percent of the student body. "Most of the students would be considered nerds or geeks at other schools," a civil engineering major explains, "but almost everyone fits in here." Hispanics comprise 8 percent of the student body, Asian Americans 5 percent, and African Americans account for 1 percent. Students are generally too wrapped up in academics to pay attention to political issues, according to a physics major. Merit scholarships are available to qualified students, and student-athletes may vie for roughly 250 athletic scholarships.

"We are all working together."

Forty-three percent of CSM students—mostly freshmen—live in the residence halls. Most buildings are co-ed, though the preponderance of men results in a few single-sex dorms. "All the residence halls have been refurbished and are looking better than ever," a sophomore says. Most upperclassmen move to fraternity or sorority housing, college-owned apartments, or off-campus condos and houses. There's only one cafeteria, and a junior says, "The vegetarian options are not very good unless you really like cereal and salad" (presumably not during the same meal).

There is life outside of the computer labs here. "There is a lot that goes on on campus," a junior says. "There is always a club putting together an event or just students throwing parties." CU–Boulder offers more partying 20 minutes away. Mines also has an active Greek system, with fraternities and sororities attracting 12 percent of the men and 16 percent of the women. Still, rush is dry, and, owing to Mines' small size, those serving the alcohol almost always know the age of those trying to obtain it, making it tough for the underaged to imbibe. Social life also includes comedy shows, homecoming, and Engineering Days—a three-day party with fireworks, a pig roast, tricycle races, taco-eating contests, and 25-cent beers. New student orientation includes the M-climb, in which freshmen hike up Mount Zion lugging a 10-pound rock, "and whitewash it, and each other," says one participant. The rock is added to an M formation atop the mountain, then "seniors return to take down a rock, completing the cycle."

(continued)

Email Address: admit@mines
.edu

Strongest Programs:
Geology/Geophysics
Mining Engineering
Petroleum Engineering
Metallurgy and Materials
  Engineering
Chemical Engineering
Engineering Physics

Courses in a student's option start in the second semester of sophomore year.

Pass/fail grading is unheard of at Mines, but failing grades are not.

CSM's location at the base of the Rockies means gorgeous Colorado weather (make sure to bring sunscreen) and easy access to skiing, hiking, mountain climbing, and biking. Denver is also nearby, and aside from its museums, concerts, and sports teams, the city is home to many government agencies and businesses involved in natural resources, computers, and technology, including the regional offices of the U.S. Geological Survey and Bureau of Mines. Golden hosts the National Earthquake Center, the National Renewable Energy Laboratory, and, of course, the Coors Brewery. (The 3,000-foot pipeline that runs from the Coors plant to campus is there to convert excess steam from the brewery into heat for the school—not to supply the frats with the foamy stuff.) The biggest complaints are too much homework and (among guys) not enough women. Road trips to Las Vegas or Texas provide some respite.

> **"There is a lot that goes on on campus."**

CSM fields 16 Division II varsity teams, which is more varsity teams than any other college or university in the state. Especially competitive Oredigger teams include men's and women's cross-country, as well as women's track and basketball. The intramural program has grown dramatically, with 70 percent of students now participating.

While time spent in the classroom at Mines may not be fun, for those who are focused on engineering, educational options don't get much better than those offered here. "Lots of companies recruit our students," says one senior, thanks to a stellar reputation in the fields of mining and engineering. "It is a great school," says a junior. "When you leave here, you're prepared for anything." Especially if you are an engineer.

Overlaps

University of Colorado, Colorado State, University of Denver, MIT, Texas A&M, University of Texas

If You Apply To ➤

CSM: Rolling admissions. Application fee: $45 (paper), free (online). Campus and alumni interviews: optional, informational. SATs or ACTs: required. Subject Tests: optional. No essay question.

Colorado State University

Fort Collins, CO 80523

It lacks Boulder's glitz and glamour, but Colorado State offers a more authentic slice of the Rocky Mountain West. Known throughout the region for its prevet program, CSU turns out more STEM (science, technology, engineering, math) graduates than any other Colorado campus. Has a traditional college feel with a first-rate student center and strong ties to the local community.

Website: www.colostate.edu
Location: Small City
Public
Total Enrollment: 23,533
Undergraduates: 20,884
Male/Female: 48/52
SAT Ranges: CR 500–620, M 520–640
ACT Ranges: 22–27

Founded in 1870 as the Colorado Agricultural College, Colorado State University began with five students, two faculty members, and a mission "to serve society through teaching, research, and outreach." Today, the university boasts approximately 1,400 faculty across eight colleges and 52 academic departments, as well as more than 116,000 living alumni, including state governors, heads of corporations, Olympic gold medalists, teachers, researchers, and artists. Students here enjoy ample research opportunities, a slew of solid academic programs, and an unbeatable location, so it's little wonder they take pride in calling CSU home. "CSU has a great community and a wonderful friendliness about it," says one happy Ram. "It really is a fun and comfortable place to be."

Situated at the foot of the spectacular Rocky Mountains, CSU gives students easy access to abundant natural resources. The open space on the main campus reflects the university's heritage as a land grant institution. The Oval, a wide expanse of lawn encircled by towering elm trees, anchors the northwest corner of campus. Architectural styles range from Beaux-Arts to Renaissance Revival, and the campus features a spacious outdoor plaza, 32 acres of recreation fields, and stunning views of Long's Peak. The South Campus is the site of the Veterinary Teaching Hospital and Natural Resource Research Center, the Foothills Campus is home to facilities specializing in everything from equine science to disease control, and the Pingree Park Campus is an ideal location for field research in the heart of the Rockies. Groundwork has begun for a new stadium and sports complex.

> "CSU has a great community and a wonderful friendliness about it."

CSU offers more than 60 undergraduate majors, the most popular of which include health and exercise science, psychology, biological science, construction management, and human development/family studies. "Our science programs are really strong," a sophomore says. The prevet program is also distinguished, and graphic design and business draw praise from students. The performing arts have received a boost thanks to improved facilities, but the humanities are not as solid as other departments. Other notable undergraduate majors are available in applied computing technology and biomedical sciences, as are concentrations in horticulture therapy, viticulture and enology, and conservation biology. Biomedical engineering and international studies degrees are also available.

All CSU students complete a university-wide core curriculum that includes 31 credit hours of coursework in written communication, mathematics, oral communication, biological and physical sciences, arts and humanities, social and behavioral sciences, historical perspectives, and global and cultural awareness. The academic climate is competitive—especially in the preprofessional programs—and students say classes can be difficult. "The courses are hard, but manageable," a junior says. Eighty-one percent of classes have 49 or fewer students, and "professors are very knowledgeable," according to one student. Another says, "If you express an interest in their area of study, they may invite you to do research in their lab, write a paper and be published in a major journal, or help you with graduate school applications—who knows!" Freshmen may also participate in a midsummer orientation and a variety of first-year seminars designed to ease the transition from high school to college. Qualified students can opt for the honors program or take part in the Hughes Undergraduate Research Scholars program, which allows students to conduct long-term research alongside a faculty mentor. Additional hands-on learning opportunities include a four-week geology field camp, a watershed management field camp, and an undergraduate research symposium. "The number one program that students should know about is the Key Communities," says one sophomore.

> "The courses are hard, but manageable."

"As a key student you take three classes with a cluster of 19 people who you meet before classes start. This is so nice because you immediately have friends and people you know who also live in Braiden Hall and can help you study."

"The students at CSU are friendly and accepting," says a junior. "Students who attend this university are passionate about what they study and want to change the world." Seventy-eight percent of CSU students are from Colorado. African Americans account for 2 percent of the student body, Asian Americans 2 percent, and Hispanics 10 percent. Two percent hail from abroad. CSU is a politically active campus, and liberal and conservative viewpoints are both well represented. "The biggest issues on campus are probably environmental issues," says a student, "due mainly to our proximity to the Rocky Mountains." Merit scholarships averaging

(continued)

Financial Aid: 77%
Expense: Pub $ $
Student Loans: 63%
Average Debt: $ $
Phi Beta Kappa: Yes
Applicants: 17,929
Accepted: 75%
Enrolled: 34%
Grad in 6 Years: 64%
Returning Freshmen: 84%
Academics: ✍ ✍ ✍
Social: ☎ ☎ ☎ ☎
Q of L: ★ ★ ★ ★
Admissions: (970) 491-6909
Email Address: admissions@ colostate.edu

Strongest Programs:
Life Sciences
Graphic Design
Engineering
Veterinary Medicine
Construction Management
Business

The performing arts have received a boost thanks to improved facilities, but the humanities are not as solid as other departments.

$7,822 are handed out each year, and athletes vie for 208 scholarships in 16 men's and women's sports.

Twenty-five percent of CSU students live on campus in residence halls and campus apartments. "All freshmen are required to live in the dorms," a sophomore reports, "but most move off campus after their first year." Another student adds, "Of the residence halls, 75 percent have been renovated or built within the past five years, so they are in great condition and more like a resort than the dorms we all picture from movies." Campus residents may choose from among six meal plans, and the residence hall dining center provides an all-you-can-eat option. "The food is awesome," a student says. "I think it is as good as any restaurant in town." Students also report feeling safe on campus; security measures include a "safe walk" escort program, emergency phones, and an active security staff.

Although the Greek scene attracts 6 percent of the men and 10 percent of the women, students say social life is divided between on-campus activities (including art exhibits, picnics, and comedians) and off-campus fun. "Campus activities, such as free movies or concerts, draw a large crowd,"

"There is no tolerance for alcohol in the residence halls."

says one student, "while parties and other gatherings off campus do the same." The Lory Student Center hosts events on a regular basis, and "there are over 300 clubs," says a junior, "which many students use as a social outlet." The CSU campus is dry and "there is no tolerance for alcohol in the residence halls," one biochemistry major says. "The policies are enforced."

Fort Collins is "a fun city that revolves around the school," says one junior. "There is a definite sense of community and support for CSU in the town," a senior adds. Students not only frequent the downtown bars, shops, and eateries, but also can often be found performing volunteer work or community service alongside the locals. Popular road trips include quick getaways to nearby ski resorts and hiking trails, and longer treks to Utah and Nevada. Back on campus, students enjoy a number of traditions: "We have a huge homecoming," says one student, "with a bonfire, lighting of the 'A,' parade, and football game."

The CSU Rams compete in Division I-A as members of the Mountain West Conference, and the most competitive teams include volleyball, men's golf, women's cross-country, and women's swimming. Women's volleyball has made 18 consecutive trips to the NCAA championship tournament. The University of Colorado is the hated rival—especially in football—and "the Rocky Mountain Showdown is probably the biggest event of the year," says a family and consumer sciences major. Intramurals attract nearly one-third of the student body and "some of the most popular are soccer, flag football, and basketball," a senior says. The Student Recreation Center features an indoor track, basketball and volleyball courts, cardio machines and free weights, and a host of other facilities for students who want to stay in shape.

Despite ubiquitous complaints about limited parking, rising tuition, and the need for more bike racks, students at Colorado State are quick to say why they appreciate their alma mater: "Because CSU rocks! It is an awesome school to go to and has lots to offer students of all ages and backgrounds," cheers one senior. What's more, it's a "fun and beautiful place to be," says a junior, "and you know that your degree will mean something."

Overlaps

University of Arizona, University of Colorado, Colorado School of Mines, University of Denver, University of Northern Colorado

If You Apply To ➤ | **CSU:** Early action: Dec. 1. Regular admissions and financial aid: Feb. 1. Application fee: $50. No campus or alumni interviews. SATs or ACTs: required. No Subject Tests. Accepts the Common Application and prefers electronic applications. Essay question: personal statement.

Columbia University

212 Hamilton Hall, New York, NY 10027

Once an Ivy League also-ran, Columbia now rivals the Ivy League's "big three" in selectivity. Applications have doubled in the past 10 years for one simple reason: Manhattan trumps New Haven, Providence, Ithaca, and every other Ivy League city, with the possible exception of Boston. The often overlooked engineering program is among the best in the nation for undergraduates. The heart of Columbia is still its core curriculum.

Though students entering Columbia will, of course, expect the rigorous academic program they'll encounter at this Ivy League school, they must also be streetwise, urbane, and together enough to handle one of the most cosmopolitan cities in the world. Columbia lets its students experience life in the Big Apple, but serves as a refuge when it becomes necessary to escape from New York; ideally, Columbians can easily be part of the "real world" while simultaneously immersing themselves in the best academia has to offer. "Columbia students all share at least two reasons for coming to this university," says a freshman: "The Core Curriculum and New York City. This means the students here want a classical liberal arts education and that they do not want to live in a college bubble." Famous alums can be found in the highest echelons of their chosen professions, whether it be politics, literature, sports, or entertainment.

With a total university-wide enrollment of more than 25,000 students, says one, "it's easy to feel lost." Columbia's undergraduates are divided into two divisions: the flagship Columbia College and the School of Engineering and Applied Science. (Sister school Barnard College, affiliated with Columbia but governed by its own board of trustees, has an additional 2,200 students.) Columbia's campus has a large central quadrangle in front of Butler Library and at the foot of the steps leading past the statue of Alma Mater to Low Library, which is now the administration building. The redbrick, copper-roofed neoclassical buildings are "stunning," and the layout, says an undergrad, "is well thought out and manages to provide a beautiful setting with an economy of space." The Campbell Sports Center opened in late 2012 and features a theater-style meeting room, conference rooms, a strength and conditioning center, and a student-athlete lounge.

Columbia is an intellectual school, not a preprofessional one, and even though 60 percent of the students aspire to law or medical school (they enjoy a 90 percent acceptance rate), "we are mostly content to be liberal artists for as long as possible," says an English major. Even students in the School of Engineering and Applied Sciences pursue "technical education" with a liberal arts base. Almost all departments that offer undergraduate majors are strong, notably English, history, political science, and psychology. Chemistry and biology are

> **"Students here want a classical liberal arts education and that they do not want to live in a college bubble."**

among the best of Columbia's high-quality science offerings. The earth and environmental science department owns 200 acres in Rockland County, home to many rocks and much seismographic equipment. There are over 40 offerings in foreign languages, ranging from Serbo-Croatian to Uzbek to Hausa. The fine arts are not fabulous, but are improving, thanks to departmental reorganization, new facilities, and joint offerings with schools such as the Juilliard School of Music. Columbia offers many challenging combined majors such as philosophy/economics and biology/psychology. The East Asian languages and cultures department is one of the

Website: www.columbia.edu
Location: City Center
Private
Total Enrollment: 25,208
Undergraduates: 6,068
Male/Female: 53/47
SAT Ranges: CR 690–780,
   M 700–790
ACT Ranges: 31–34
Financial Aid: 52%
Expense: Pr $ $ $ $
Student Loans: N/A
Average Debt: N/A
Phi Beta Kappa: Yes
Applicants: 31,851
Accepted: 7%
Enrolled: 60%
Grad in 6 Years: 97%
Returning Freshmen: 99%
Academics: ✍ ✍ ✍ ✍ ✍
Social: ☎ ☎ ☎
Q of L: ★ ★ ★ ★
Admissions: (212) 854-2522
Email Address: ugrad-ask@
   columbia.edu

Strongest Programs:
English
History
Political Science
Economics
Biology
Music
Drama
Mechanical Engineering

best anywhere. There is also an African American studies major, and a women's studies major that delves into topics from the Asian woman's perspective to the lesbian experience in literature.

The kernel of the undergraduate experience is Columbia's renowned core curriculum. While these courses occupy most of the first two years and can become laborious, students generally praise them as worthwhile and enriching: "It truly unifies the school in a way that transcends most social limitations and gives us all a great basis for further pursuits of knowledge," says a freshman. As it has since World War I, the college remains committed to the core while at the same time expanding the diversity of the canon and requiring core classes on non-Western cultures. "Students who come to Columbia dive into the Core Curriculum and are able to explore different cultures and non-western civilizations and perhaps spark some interest in a subject they had never thought of before!" says a junior.

> "The nice thing about Columbia is that it has an internal rating system that lets students review their professors anonymously."

There are over 40 offerings in foreign languages, ranging from Serbo-Croatian to Uzbek to Hausa.

Two of the most demanding introductory courses in the Ivy League—Contemporary Civilization (CC) and Literature Humanities—form the basis of the core. Both are yearlong and taught in small sections, generally by full profs. LitHum (as it is affectionately called) covers about 26 masterpieces of literature from Homer to Dostoyevsky, usually with some Sappho, Jane Austen, and Virginia Woolf thrown in for alternative perspectives. CC examines political and moral philosophy from Plato to Camus, though professors have some leeway in choosing 20th-century selections. "Many of the concepts can be hard to grasp, but in the end, it's rewarding to make it through something like Homer's *Iliad* or Plato's *Republic* and feel like you understand the basic concept," a sophomore says. One semester each of art and humanities is required and, while they are not given the same reverence as their literary counterparts, they are eye-opening all the same. Foreign language proficiency is required, as are two semesters of science; two semesters of "global core," classes dealing in cultures not covered in the other core requirements; two semesters of phys ed; and logic and rhetoric, a one-semester, argumentative writing class that first-year students reportedly "either love or hate." Students at the School of Engineering complete approximately half of the core curriculum. "Columbia has amazing professors who will change your life and awful professors who make you hate everything about a subject that once mesmerized you," says a philosophy major. "The nice thing about Columbia is that it has an internal rating system that lets students review their professors anonymously."

Columbia is tough, and students always have something to read or write. Student/faculty interaction is largely dependent on student initiative. Additional interaction stems from professorial involvement in campus politics and forums and from the faculty-in-residence program, which houses professors and their families in spruced-up apartments in several of the residence halls. First-year students are assigned an advisor and receive a faculty advisor when they declare a major at the end of sophomore year. Columbia students can take classes at Barnard and graduate-level courses in several departments, notably political science, gaining access to the resources of the School of International and Public Affairs and its multitude of regional institutes. For students wishing to spend time away from New York, Columbia offers credit through more than 200 programs in dozens of spots around the world, including Paris, Mumbai, Beijing, Nairobi, and Istanbul.

> "The thing that really sets us apart is our hunger for interdisciplinary knowledge."

"The thing that really sets us apart is our hunger for interdisciplinary knowledge," a student says. "As a student in Columbia College, I'm required to do a third of my coursework in areas not related to my major—in great books, in non-Western cultures, in a language, in art humanities, in music history, in the cutting edge of science, in the foundations of writing." Columbia has the largest percentage of students of color in the Ivy League; 12 percent are African American, 15 percent are Hispanic, and 20 percent are Asian American. Twenty-seven percent of the students come from New York. Socially, the campus is also diverse. The university has eliminated loans for all students receiving financial aid and replaced them with additional grants. Students coming from families with annual incomes below $60,000 are not expected to contribute to the cost of tuition, fees, room, or board.

Columbia remains one of the nation's most liberal campuses, but a computer science major cautions against generalizing: "The stereotypical characterization of Columbia students has some flaws. We are not all raging liberals that protest on campus daily." Although 10 percent of the students go Greek, Columbia is hardly a Hellenocentric campus, namely because, as a junior argues, "the frats are chock-full of athletic recruits, the organizations—even the co-ed ones—are deemed elitist and politically incorrect, and there are too many better things to do in NYC on a Friday night than getting trashed in the basement of some random house." The advent of co-ed houses has raised interest in Greek life, as has the arrival of sororities open to both Columbia and Barnard women.

With the New York housing market out of control, 94 percent of Columbia students live in university housing, which is guaranteed for four years. "The spaces are kind of small, but that's university housing for you," says one student. "It's much cheaper than living in apartments around the city." Security at the dorms is rated as excellent by students. "I think the best feature of campus safety is the security guards that swipe students into dorms 24/7," says a senior. One exciting aspect of Columbia housing is that many rooms are singles, and it is possible to go all four years without a roommate. Carman Hall is the exclusively first-year dorm, and "the fact that you get to meet your classmates compensates for the noise and hideous cinderblock walls," says a music major. First-year students can also live in buildings with students of all years. First-year students are automatically placed on a 19-meal-a-week plan and take most of those meals at John Jay, an all-you-can-eat "binge-a-rama with salad bar, deli, grill, and huge dessert bar." Many soon-bloated students scale down their meal plans or convert to points, a buy-what-you-want arrangement with account information stored electronically on their ID cards. "The food is pretty awful," gripes one student. "I would not suggest getting the meal plan." Several dorms have kitchens, allowing students to do their own cooking. Kosher dining is also available.

"Columbia has an excellent relationship with its Morningside Heights neighborhood," explains a freshman. The social scene starts on the Columbia campus and spills over into the bustling streets of New York City. "We are in Morningside Heights, which is a very particular kind of neighborhood—a kind of eclectic mix of native New Yorkers, academics, and students. I think it's a fantastic college town," says one student. Rarely are there big all-inclusive bashes, the exceptions being fall's '60s throwback, Realityfest, and spring's Columbia-fest. "I love that no one activity dominates the social scene," says a freshman. "You do not have to attend the basketball and football games to be 'in,' nor do you have to pledge fraternities and sororities."

Columbia athletics don't inspire the rabid loyalty of, say, a Notre Dame, because "Columbia students are individualists," according to one sophomore. "This is not a school that rallies together at football games." Still, the Lions field 31 Division I Ivy League sports and have won more than a dozen Ivy championships in the last

The kernel of the undergraduate experience is Columbia's renowned core curriculum.

"Columbia has an excellent relationship with its Morningside Heights neighborhood."

Columbia is tough, and students always have something to read or write.

four years. As an urban school, Columbia lacks team field facilities on campus; however, 100 blocks to the north is the modern Baker Field, home of the football stadium, the soccer fields, an Olympic track, and the crew boathouse. On campus, the Dodge Gymnasium, an underground facility, houses four levels of basketball courts, swimming pools, weight rooms, and exercise equipment. The gym is often crowded and not all the facilities are wonderful. "It does the job, as well as providing for the best pickup basketball this side of Riverside Park," notes a sophomore. Intramural and club sports are popular, with men's and women's ultimate Frisbee both national competitors.

Columbians are proud that they are going to college in New York City, and most would have it no other way. Explains a freshman: "Columbia's five biggest selling points are the Core Curriculum, the location, the strength of its academic programs, the availability of research opportunities, and the vibe on campus. The fifth one I tend to think is the most important. Come to Columbia if you feel like you'd absolutely love living here for the next four years."

Overlaps

Harvard, MIT, University of Pennsylvania, Princeton, Stanford, Yale

If You Apply To ➤

Columbia: Early decision: Nov. 1. Regular admissions: Jan. 1. Financial aid: Mar. 3. Application fee: $85. Campus interviews: not available. Alumni interviews: optional, evaluative. SATs or ACTs: required. Subject Tests: required (any two; math and chemistry or physics for engineering applicants). Accepts the Common Application. Essay: personal statement.

University of Connecticut

Tasker Building, 2131 Hillside, Storrs, CT 06269-3088

Squeezed in among the likes of Brown, UMass, Trinity, Wesleyan, and Yale—all within a two-hour drive—UConn could be forgiven for having an inferiority complex. But championship basketball teams, both men's and women's, have ignited Husky pride and boosted selectivity. Storrs is nobody's idea of an exciting destination, but it does offer easy access to beautiful countryside.

Website: www.uconn.edu
Location: Rural
Public
Total Enrollment: 21,687
Undergraduates: 16,587
Male/Female: 51/49
SAT Ranges: CR 550–650, M 580–680
ACT Ranges: 26–30
Financial Aid: 53%
Expense: Pub $ $ $
Student Loans: 62%
Average Debt: $ $
Phi Beta Kappa: Yes
Applicants: 29,966
Accepted: 45%
Enrolled: 23%
Grad in 6 Years: 82%

The top public university in New England, the University of Connecticut has seen billions of dollars poured into improving and expanding its facilities in recent years. Couple the new buildings with the glow of two championship basketball teams, a wealth of research opportunities, and more than 250 clubs and organizations, and it's clear why students who in the past might have dismissed it as a "cow college" are choosing UConn, even when they have other options. "I'm incredibly proud to be a UConn student," says a senior, "and the four years I've spent here have been the best of my life." UConn is also the only public university in New England with its own law school, medical school, dental school, and school of social work. What's more, it's one of the few major public universities that continues to significantly expand their faculty ranks, including a commitment to create nearly 300 tenure-track positions over the next four years.

"I'm incredibly proud to be a UConn student."

UConn's 4,000-acre campus is about 23 miles northeast of Hartford. Building styles range from collegiate Gothic and neoclassical to half-century-old redbrick. Dense woods surround the campus, which also boasts two lakes, Swan and Mirror. Ongoing renovations are the norm, sparking jokes about the "University of Construction," but the results are impressive: an expanded and renovated student union, the expanded Neag School of Education, a school of pharmacy, a state-of-the-art biophysics building, a five-story Information Technologies Engineering Building, a 40,000-seat football stadium, new student housing, and other ongoing projects. In fact, since 1995, more than 100 capital projects have been completed.

Students say UConn's strongest offerings are preprofessional, including business, engineering, education, pharmacy, and allied health, including nursing and physical therapy. Also notable are basic sciences, history, linguistics, psychology, and, of course, agriculture. (UConn was founded more than a century ago as a farm school; it's where America learned to get more eggs per chicken by leaving the lights on in the coops.) In addition to new buildings, UConn continues to add new curricula, including electrical engineering, materials science and engineering, and mechanical engineering. There are also notable programs in biomolecular engineering, neurosciences, cognitive science, American studies, aquaculture, survey research, coastal studies, urban and community studies, and human rights. Engineering is demanding, and, as at many schools, it has a relatively high attrition rate, with many students switching to the less rigorous major in management information systems. A special program in medicine and dentistry allows students to earn bachelor's degrees in any of UConn's more than 100 disciplines, and guarantees admission to the School of Medicine or Dental Medicine if they meet all criteria.

> "The academic climate here is quite rigorous."

UConn's academic atmosphere is described as moderately competitive and challenging, depending on a student's course of study. "The academic climate here is quite rigorous," says a molecular cell biology major. UConn's core requirements include courses in four basic areas: arts and humanities, social sciences, diversity/multiculturalism, and science and technology. Also required are two foreign language courses, waived if a student has studied three years of a single language in high school, and competency in computer technology and information literacy. Seminar-style writing classes are available to all freshmen, and 75 percent also take one or more First Year Experience courses focusing on time management, how to use the library, and other useful skills. The Academic Center for Exploratory Students helps freshmen and sophomores who still need to decide on a major. Students generally applaud the enthusiasm of their professors—and the graduate teaching assistants who administer tests, collect assignments, and run labs and discussion groups—but note that some seem more interested in research than teaching. "Some lack the ability to connect with students and the skills to teach students effectively," grumbles one senior.

UConn's engineering, business, pharmacy, and honors students are required to undertake research projects, and each year two teams of finance majors run the $1 million student-managed investment fund. Students who aspire to graduate school in academic fields, rather than professional certification, may win grants to work independently under faculty members through the undergraduate summer research program. The 9 percent of students who qualify for the honors program gain access to special floors and dorms; several programs for disadvantaged students are also available. In addition, 15 percent of students participate in the study abroad program, which offers 200 programs in more than 65 countries. UConn's five campuses around Connecticut offer the first two years of the undergraduate program and some four-year degree programs. Students who satisfactorily complete work at these schools are automatically accepted at the Storrs campus for their last two years.

> "UConn students are hardworking, responsible, intelligent, passionate, and inspirational."

UConn students are "hardworking, responsible, intelligent, passionate, and inspirational," according to one psychology major. Seventy-six percent of UConn students are from Connecticut, and 22 percent are minorities—6 percent African American, 7 percent Hispanic, and 9 percent Asian American. There are cultural

(continued)

Returning Freshmen: 93%
Academics: ✎ ✎ ✎ ✎
Social: ☎ ☎ ☎
Q of L: ★ ★ ★
Admissions: (860) 486-3137
Email Address: beahusky@ uconn.edu

Strongest Programs:
Biosciences
Communication Sciences
Business
Education
Engineering
Pharmacy
Psychology
Physical Therapy

Intramurals are offered at three levels, from recreational to competitive.

centers for African American, Asian American, Latin American, and Puerto Rican students, as well as the Rainbow Center, a resource for gay, lesbian, bisexual, and transgender students. "Students are very much concerned with what is going on today in our world," a student says. Eligible UConn students receive merit scholarships averaging $6,500, and 466 athletic scholarships are available in 18 sports.

The 9 percent of students who qualify for the honors program gain access to special floors and dorms.

Seventy-two percent of the students live in university housing, which is available to all undergraduates. "All the dorms are very well maintained," says a senior. Though a few dorms are single sex, most are co-ed by floor. Nearly all campus housing has high-speed Internet, cable, and data networking service in the rooms, not just in student lounges. Eight dining halls offer plenty of choices, even for vegetarians and vegans, though many students would just as soon visit the snack bar for some ice cream, freshly made with help from the cows grazing nearby. "The food at UConn each night is diverse and a student can always find something he or she wants," one student says. Students report feeling safe on campus. "There are blue lights everywhere, crime is so low we think it doesn't exist, the police don't bother anyone unless they have to, and we have a great system of security alerts," says a junior.

"Social life is the best part of college life and includes clubs, frats, sports, and so much more," says one student. "As you get involved, you will be wicked busy!" The freshman dorms are officially dry, and students in other dorms are allowed to possess no more than a six-pack of beer, one bottle of wine, or a small bottle of liquor. Students under 21 who are caught with booze may be evicted from campus housing. Late-night activities at the student union and other campus events provide a lot of alternatives to alcohol use. Fraternities attract 10 percent of the men, and sororities claim 13 percent of the women; members can live in chapter housing at the Husky Village. On weekends, there are buses to Hartford (only 30 minutes away), Boston, New Haven, New York, and Providence. Cape Cod and the Vermont ski slopes are within weekend driving distance.

"Social life is the best part of college life."

The town of Storrs "is basically UConn," says one student. New community developments are on the way and will include shops, restaurants, and a town green, says one student. The university provides transportation for students who volunteer in area schools and hospitals. Legend holds that UConn also offers one diversion most other colleges can't: cow tipping—that is, sneaking up on unsuspecting cows, which sleep standing up, and tipping them over. The administration contends that this is a myth, though students always claim to "know someone who did it."

UConn's teams are known as the Huskies (UConn. Yukon. Get it?).

UConn's teams are known as the Huskies (UConn. Yukon. Get it?), and in a state without major league professional sports teams, the UConn women's basketball team routinely sells out the Hartford Civic Center. Both men's and women's basketball won the national Division I titles in 2014. Other championships have been racked up in men's soccer and field hockey, and UConn boasts four National Intercollegiate Women's Polo championships. Intramurals are offered at three levels, from recreational to competitive. Popular offerings range from underwater hockey to inner-tube water polo to basketball, volleyball, and flag football. Favorite annual campus events include the mud volleyball tournament, carnival-style "UConn Late Nights," midnight breakfasts during finals, homecoming, Winter Weekend, and Midnight Madness—the first official day of basketball practice. In addition to cheering for the Huskies, "it is good luck to rub the nose of the bronze statue of our mascot, Jonathan," says a sophomore.

Despite the school's agricultural roots, UConn students aren't "cowed" by the plethora of offerings. Those seeking greener pastures will be hard-pressed to find a more dynamic public institution. "We are a well-rounded campus with students from every background," a junior pharmacy student says. And with the campus undergoing a complete face-lift, a student says it's an exciting time to be at UConn.

Overlaps

Boston University, Northeastern, University of Delaware, University of Massachusetts, University of Rhode Island

Connecticut College

270 Mohegan Avenue, New London, CT 06320-4196

Like Skidmore and Vassar, Connecticut College made a successful transition from women's college to co-ed. That means a slightly more progressive campus tenor than at, say, Hamilton or Trinity. The college is strong in the humanities and renowned for its study abroad programs. It is also an SAT- or ACT-optional school. New London does not offer much, but at least it is on the ocean.

Students at Connecticut College follow the example of their mascot, the camel—they take pride in drinking up and storing knowledge. The student-run honor code means finals are not proctored; they're even self-scheduled, whenever students prefer, during a 10-day window. Thanks to the code, students also feel comfortable leaving doors and bikes unlocked. Utopian? Perhaps. "What makes CC stand out among its peer institutions is the honor code and commitment to interdisciplinary studies," says one junior.

Placed majestically atop a hill, the Conn College campus sits within a 750-acre arboretum with a pond, wetlands, wooded areas, and hiking trails. It offers beautiful views of the Thames River (pronounced the way it looks, not like the "Temz" that Wordsworth so dearly loved) on one side and Long Island Sound on the other. The granite campus buildings are a mixture of modern and collegiate Gothic in style, with some neo-Gothic and neoclassical architecture thrown in for good measure.

Conn was founded in 1911 as a women's college, and since then has been dedicated to the liberal arts, broadly defined. The general education requirements are aimed at fostering intellectual breadth, critical thinking, and acquisition of the fundamental skills and habits of minds conducive to lifelong inquiry, engaged citizenship, and personal growth. To that end, students are required to complete a series of at least seven courses that introduce them to the natural and social sciences, humanities, and arts. Academics are definitely the focus here. "Upper-level courses are challenging, require frequent participation by all students, and the professors hold us to high standards," says one senior. Professors "have a passion for teaching students" and "are genuinely excited about teacher/student interactions," says a student.

> **"Upper-level courses are challenging."**

Conn's dance and drama departments are superb, and it's not uncommon for dancers to take time off to study with professional companies. Aspiring actors, directors, and stagehands may work with the Eugene O'Neill Theater Institute, named for New London's best-known literary son. Chemistry majors may use high-tech gas chromatograms and mass spectrometers from their very first day, and students say Conn also offers excellent programs in biology and physics. The Ammerman Center for Arts and Technology allows students to examine the connections between artistic pursuits and the worlds of math and computer science. The most popular majors are economics, biology, environmental studies, English, and international relations. The teacher certification program also wins raves.

Website: www.conncoll.edu
Location: Suburban
Private
Total Enrollment: 1,816
Undergraduates: 1,812
Male/Female: 41/59
SAT Ranges: CR 620–710, M 615–700
ACT Ranges: 28–31
Financial Aid: 48%
Expense: Pr $ $ $ $
Student Loans: 50%
Average Debt: $ $
Phi Beta Kappa: Yes
Applicants: 4,837
Accepted: 36%
Enrolled: 29%
Grad in 6 Years: 85%
Returning Freshmen: 92%
Academics: ✍ ✍ ✍ ✍
Social: ☎ ☎ ☎
Q of L: ★ ★ ★ ★
Admissions: (860) 439-2200
Email Address: admissions@conncoll.edu

Strongest Programs:
Fine and Performing Arts
Environmental Studies
Economics
Psychology
Anthropology
International Studies
Government

To escape Conn's small size and occasionally claustrophobic feel, the Study Away/Teach Away initiative allows groups of 15 to 30 Conn students and two faculty members to spend a semester living and working together at an overseas university, in locations as far-flung as Egypt, Ghana, Tanzania, and Vietnam. Over half of students study abroad, and virtually any major can be "internationalized" through language study or paid overseas internships. Conn also participates in the Twelve College Exchange Program*, bringing the total number of foreign study programs to more than 40. A gift from Conn helps students secure extraordinary summer internships; everyone who participates in a set of workshops is guaranteed one $3,000 grant during his or her four years to help cover housing or other costs incurred while gaining real-world work experience.

"Almost all students live on campus."

Conn's dance and drama departments are superb.

Conn is a "perfect mix of preppy New Englanders, hard-core athletes, passionate artists, and inspired intellectuals," says a student. Only 17 percent of Conn College students come from Connecticut, and 49 percent graduated from public high schools. African Americans comprise 4 percent and Asian Americans make up 3 percent of the student body, respectively; Hispanic students add 8 percent. Freshmen must attend a session on issues of race, class, and gender, run by a panel of peers representing different cultures, socioeconomic backgrounds, sexual orientations, and physical disabilities. Efforts to improve diversity have been helped by the school's decision to emphasize high school transcripts rather than the SAT as a measure of achievement and potential in the admissions process. There are no merit or athletic scholarships. Loan reduction is available for students of highest need.

"Almost all students live on campus," says a history major. "I met seniors who lived on my floor as a freshman. It made me feel included and like I was actually integrated into the community." Dorms house students of all ages, and are run by seniors who apply to be "house fellows." Roommates tend to be well matched because incoming students complete a three-page questionnaire about personal habits before coming to campus, says a sophomore. Among the seven specialty houses are Earth House (environmental awareness), the Abbey House co-op (where students cook their own meals), and houses dedicated to substance-free living, quiet lifestyles, and international languages. "There is a great sense of house pride on campus," says one student. "There is even an entire weekend devoted to honoring your house." The campus dining hall offers traditional main courses, as well as "fast food, stir-fry, pizza, pasta, vegetarian options, deli sandwiches, salad bars, and an ice cream bar," says a psychology major.

"Most of the partying takes place on campus."

Because Conn lacks a Greek system, most activities revolve around the dorms, which sponsor weekly keg and theme parties.

Because Conn lacks a Greek system, most activities—including co-ed intramural sports—revolve around the dorms, which sponsor weekly theme parties. "There is a strong sense of community that goes with a residential college," confirms a sophomore. Also keeping students busy are movie nights, comedy shows, student productions, and dances—sometimes with out-of-town bands and DJs. The alcohol policy falls under the honor code, so those under 21 can't imbibe at the campus bar, and students take that prohibition seriously. "Most of the partying takes place on campus," reports a student, but "campus safety has cracked down significantly since I started as a freshman." Conn is helping to revitalize New London, where defense contractor General Dynamics has operations. Students volunteer at the local schools, aquarium, youth community center, and women's center; a college van makes it easy to get to and from work sites. When students get the urge to roam, the beaches of Mystic and other shore towns are 20 minutes from campus, and the Mohegan Sun casino is also very close. Trains go to Providence, Rhode Island, New York City, or Boston, while Vermont and upstate New York offer camping, hiking, and skiing. Conn's traditions include October's Camelympics, which pit dorms against each other in a 24-hour marathon of games from Scrabble to Capture the Flag; the winter Festivus ("the festival for the rest of us"); and Floralia, an all-day music festival the weekend before spring finals, recently headlined by the Dave Matthews Band.

The Conn Camels compete in Division III, and men's ice hockey games against NESCAC rival Wesleyan draw crowds, though students say Conn doesn't really have any true athletic rivalries. A T-shirt brags that Conn football has been undefeated since 1911; of course, Conn—as a former women's college—has never had a team. In 2010 the men's lacrosse team was nationally ranked in the top 10 in Division III and competed in the NCAA tournament. More than 700 students participate in intramural and club sports, the most popular of which are ultimate Frisbee and broomball. Between classes or at the end of the day, all students may use the natatorium's pool and fitness center and the rowing tanks and climbing walls at the field house.

On its friendly campus, Conn College fosters strong student/faculty bonds and takes pride in its ability to challenge—and trust—students, both in and out of the classroom. But getting the most out of the Conn experience depends on being receptive—and on taking initiative, students say. "If you want to be a number, Conn is not the place for you."

The Conn Camels compete in Division III.

Overlaps

Bates, Brown, Colby, Skidmore, Vassar, Wesleyan

If You Apply To ➤ **Conn College:** Early decision: Nov. 15. Regular admissions: Jan. 1. Application fee: $60. Campus interviews: recommended, evaluative. Alumni interviews: optional, evaluative. SAT or two SAT Subject Tests or ACT: optional. Accepts the Common Application. Essay question.

Cooper Union

BEST BUY

30 Cooper Square, New York, NY 10003

As college costs skyrocket, so does the popularity of Cooper Union's low-cost education in art, architecture, and engineering. Expect Ivy-level competition for a place in the class here. Instead of a conventional campus, Cooper Union has the East Village—which is quite a deal. But be prepared to spend your nights hitting the books rather than the bars.

Tuition is no longer free at Cooper Union for the Advancement of Science and Art. But if you manage to get accepted into this technical institute, you get a half-tuition scholarship and some of the nation's finest academic offerings in architecture, engineering, and art. With cool and funky Greenwich Village in the background and rigorous studying in the forefront, college life at Cooper Union may seem to be faster than a New York minute. Whatever the pace, though, no one can deny that a CU education is one of the best bargains around—probably the best anywhere. The only complication is that the number of applicants is booming and its acceptance rate is comparable to the Ivies.

The school was founded in 1859 by entrepreneur Peter Cooper, who believed that education should be "as free as water and air." With hefty contributions from J. P. Morgan, Frederick Vanderbilt, Andrew Carnegie, and various other assorted robber barons, the school was able to stay afloat in order to recruit poor students of "strong moral character."

In place of a traditional collegiate setting are three academic buildings and one dorm plunked down in one of New York's most eclectic and exciting neighborhoods. The stately brick art and architecture building is a beautiful historic landmark. Built

Website: www.cooper.edu
Location: City Center
Private
Total Enrollment: 897
Undergraduates: 848
Male/Female: 64/36
SAT Ranges: CR 620–710, M 610–770
ACT Ranges: 29–33
Financial Aid: 100%
Expense: Pr $ $
Student Loans: 23%
Average Debt: $
Phi Beta Kappa: No
Applicants: 3,573

(continued)

Accepted: 7%

Enrolled: 76%

Grad in 6 Years: 82%

Returning Freshmen: 90%

Academics: ✍ ✍ ✍ ½

Social: ☎

Q of L: ★ ★ ★

Admissions: (212) 353-4120

Email Address: admissions@
cooper.edu

Strongest Programs:
Fine Arts
Architecture
Engineering

*Tuition is no longer
free at Cooper Union
for the Advancement
of Science and Art.*

of brick and topped by a classic water tower, the dorm blends right in with the neighborhood. The Great Hall was the site of Lincoln's "Right Makes Might" speech and the birthplace of the NAACP, the American Red Cross, and the national women's suffrage movement. Wedged between two busy avenues in the East Village, Cooper Union offers an environment for survivors. A LEED-certified academic building opened in late 2009—the first academic building in New York City to achieve LEED Platinum status, the highest and most rigorous level of certification. A new residence hall is expected to open in late 2014.

The academic climate is intense. "Although the courses are difficult and the coursework is challenging, the students are more than willing to cooperate with one another and collaborate when studying," says one freshman. The curriculum is highly structured, and all students must take a sequence of required courses in the humanities and social sciences. The first year is devoted to language and literature and the second to the making of the modern world. In some special circumstances, students are allowed to take courses at nearby New York University and the New School for Social Research. The nationally renowned engineering school, the first in the nation to have a female dean, offers both bachelor's and master's degrees in chemical, electrical, mechanical, and civil engineering as well as a bachelor of science in general engineering studies. "Architecture and engineering are the most acclaimed, but then, these occupations are more mainstream, and graduates get big money and success," reflects an art major. "It's harder to measure success in the art school." The art school offers a broad-based generalist curriculum that includes graphic design, drawing, painting, sculpture, photography, printmaking, film, and video. The architecture school, in the words of one pleased participant, is "phenomenal—even unparalleled." Requirements for getting into each of these schools vary widely—each looks for different strengths and talents—hence the differences in test-score ranges.

> **"Students are more than willing to cooperate with one another and collaborate when studying."**

Classes are small and, with a little persistence, not too difficult to get into. While teaching quality is hit or miss, students report that professors are generally engaging. "I've received excellent teaching," a chemical engineering major says. A professional counseling and referral service is available, as is academic counseling, but the school's small size and its rigorously structured academic programs set the classes the students take and eliminate a lot of confusion or decision making. Students "tend to talk to other students, recommending or insulting various classes and profs around registration time," notes a senior.

Strong moral character is no longer a prerequisite for admission, but an outstanding high school academic average most certainly is. Prospective applicants should note, however, that art and architecture students are picked primarily on the basis of a faculty evaluation of their creative works. For engineering students, admission is primarily based on a review of the high school record, SAT scores, and the SAT IIs in mathematics and physics or chemistry. The admissions office also carefully reads student writing and considers extracurricular involvement before finalizing admissions decisions.

> **"Architecture and engineering are the most acclaimed."**

CU students "range from being complete geeks who love math, science, and gaming to artsy and out of this world," one student says. Fifty-five percent of the students are from New York State, and about half grew up in the city. Most are from public schools, and many are the first in their family to attend college. Forty percent of the students are from minority groups, most of them Asian Americans (25 percent); 6 percent are African American, and 9 percent are Hispanic. One student attests that diversity is not an issue at CU: "We are a racially mixed student body that stays mixed. There's no overt hostility and rare self-segregation." The campus is home to ethnically based student clubs, but, according to one student, membership is not exclusive: "In other words, you can be white and be a member of Onyx—a student group promoting black awareness." According to one senior, CU is a very liberal place: "If you can't accept different kinds of people, you shouldn't come here." Students must pay for room and board; those who demonstrate financial need receive help with living expenses.

Students love the dorm, a 15-story residence hall that saves many students from commuting into the Village or cramming themselves into expensive apartments. It is noteworthy that housing here is guaranteed only to freshmen, thus only 20 percent of the student body resides on campus. The facility is composed of furnished apartments with kitchenettes and bathrooms complete with showers or tubs and is "in great condition and well maintained," states one resident. A less enraptured dweller notes, "Rooms are barely big enough to fit a bed, a table, and a clothes cabinet." Still, each apartment does have enough space for a stove, microwave, and refrigerator. So you can cook for yourself or eat at the unexciting but affordable school cafeteria or at one of the myriad nearby delis and coffee bars.

The combination of intense workload and CU's location means that campus social life is limited, though the administration contends the dorm promotes more on-campus social activities. "The social life here is centered around the many clubs and activities offered on campus," says one student. "This is where most people find their crowd." Five percent of the men belong to professional societies. Drinking on campus is allowed during school-sponsored parties for students over 21—otherwise, no alcohol on campus. But as one student puts it, "This is New York; one can be served anywhere." McSorley's bar is right around the corner, the Grassroots Tavern is just down the block, and nearby Chinatown and Little Italy are also popular destinations. The heart of the Village, with its abundance of theaters, art galleries, and cafés, is just a few blocks to the west. The Bowery and SoHo's galleries and restaurants are due south; all of midtown Manhattan spreads to the northern horizon.

Cooper teams compete in the Division III Hudson Valley Athletic Conference, and the most competitive teams include men's and women's tennis and women's cross-country. The intramural sports program is held in several different facilities in the city, and the games are popular. Students organize clubs and outings around interests such as soccer, basketball, skiing, fencing, Ping-Pong, classical music, religion, and drama. "Professional societies are very active at Cooper (American Society of Civil Engineers)," notes a senior.

Getting into Cooper Union is tough, and once admitted, students find that dealing with the onslaught of city and school is plenty tough as well. But most students like the challenge. "The workload, living alone in New York, and the administrative policies force you to act like an adult and take care of yourself," explains a senior. Surviving the school's academic rigors requires talent, self-sufficiency, and a clear sense of one's career objectives. Students who don't have it all can be sure that there are six or seven people in line ready to take their places. That's quite an incentive to succeed.

> *The combination of intense workload and CU's location means that campus social life is limited, though the administration contends the dorm promotes more on-campus social activities.*

> **"If you can't accept different kinds of people, you shouldn't come here."**

Overlaps

Cornell, Columbia, Carnegie Mellon, Pratt, Massachusetts Institute of Technology, Rensselaer, NYU, Rhode Island School of Design

If You Apply To ➢

Cooper Union: Early decision: Dec. 1. Regular admissions: Jan. 1. Financial aid and housing: May 1. All students receive half-tuition scholarships. Application fee: $70. Campus interviews: optional, evaluative. No alumni interviews. (Portfolio Day strongly recommended for art applicants.) SATs or ACTs: required. Subject Tests: required for engineering (math and physics or chemistry). Apply to particular program. Essay question.

Cornell College

600 First Street West, Mount Vernon, IA 42314-1098

The one-course-at-a-time model is Cornell's calling card. Cornell's main challenge: trying to lure top students to rural Iowa. Three-and-a-half-week terms allow students to do off-campus study in distant corners of the world. With a student body of about 1,000, Cornell showers its students with personal attention. Though primarily a liberal arts institution, Cornell has small programs in business and education.

Website: www.cornellcollege
.edu

Location: Small Town

Private

Total Enrollment: 1,174

Undergraduates: 1,174

Male/Female: 46/54

SAT Ranges: CR 535–685,
M 540–690

ACT Ranges: 24–30

Financial Aid: 75%

Expense: Pr $

Student Loans: 81%

Average Debt: $ $ $

Phi Beta Kappa: Yes

Applicants: 2,718

Accepted: 53%

Enrolled: 21%

Grad in 6 Years: 70%

Returning Freshmen: 84%

Academics: ✍ ✍ ✍

Social: ☎ ☎ ☎

Q of L: ★ ★ ★

Admissions: (800) 747-1112

Email Address: admission@
cornellcollege.edu

Strongest Programs:

Psychology

Economics and Business

Biochemistry and Molecular
Biology

Kinesiology

English

Theater

Classics

Cornell College attracts the type of student who seeks an intense yet flexible, self-designed program and a liberal, progressive atmosphere in which to solidify strict habits and routines. If you're not satisfied with easy answers, don't mind heading to the rural Midwest, and do want loads of personal attention while you focus on one class, Cornell College may be worth a look. "One-Course-at-a-Time is an incredible way to learn," says a sophomore.

Aside from its distinctive schedule (shared by only one other school, Colorado College), Cornell has one of only two U.S. college or university campuses listed in its entirety on the National Register of Historic Places. The majestic bell tower of King Chapel offers an unparalleled view of the Cedar River valley. A pedestrian mall runs through campus, and other campus facilities include suite-style residence halls for 96 upper-class students. Cornell's Thomas Commons has undergone a complete renovation and expansion that brings sweeping changes to the college's student center.

> **"At Cornell, a semester's worth of work is completed in a month."**

Cornell awards the bachelor of arts (B.A.) in nearly 40 academic majors, as well as an extensive group of preprofessional programs. The college also offers the bachelor of special studies, pursued by 5 percent of students, which administrators describe as "an opportunity which permits students to combine courses in an individualized fashion and to broaden or deepen their studies beyond the traditional framework of the bachelor of arts." The One-Course-at-a-Time method can be intense here because "it is difficult to learn a language in three and a half weeks," a junior says. A sophomore adds, "At Cornell, a semester's worth of work is completed in a month. This makes for a fast-paced class that is normally composed of a couple papers, maybe some annotations, a midterm, a final, and a final project."

Current general education requirements include two humanities courses, one math, one science, one social science, and one fine arts; eight 300-level courses, and 124 semester hours to graduate. Block scheduling makes it easier for some students to graduate early; others use the flexibility to finish with a double major. If that sounds intimidating, it can be. But administrators say it also improves the quality of Cornell's liberal arts education by helping students acclimate to the business world, where "what needs to be done needs to be done quickly and done well." The One-Course method also helps in academic advising—with grades every four weeks, signs of trouble are quickly apparent. Block scheduling does have drawbacks, though. "Courses are completed in 18 days, so each class is pretty intense," says a junior biology and Spanish major.

> **"Most of the courses at Cornell are extremely challenging."**

"Most of the courses at Cornell are extremely challenging and require a lot of focus and studying to be successful," admits one sophomore. Among the most popular programs are psychology, history, economics, English, and kinesiology; other strong options include philosophy, politics, and theater. Smaller areas include German, Latin American studies, and Russian. Professors are described as dedicated and knowledgeable: "Our professors are the best. They really care about their students on an individual basis and return timely, thoughtful comments and encourage lively discussion."

More than 40 percent of Cornell students study off campus during their time at Cornell. Each year, approximately 20 courses travel internationally or domestically, including Ocean Ecology in the Bahamas, Religions of China and Japan in Mongolia, Greek Archaeology in Greece, Advanced Spanish in Argentina, Macroeconomics Seminar: Wealth and Poverty in Uruguay, Chinese Gender and Culture in China, and Geology in New Zealand. Students can also spend a semester at sea or in one of nearly 40 countries through the Associated Colleges of the Midwest* consortium. During the short breaks between courses, students can take advantage of symposia, Music Mondays, carnivals, and athletic events. The school's Cole Library is also the town of Mount Vernon's public library, one of only two such libraries in the country. The Berry Center for Economics, Business, and Public Policy provides academic enrichment programs for undergraduates in applied economics and public policy.

Cornell students are, in a word, quirky: "We have swing dancers who knit and basketball players who love Latin and mandolin players who are passionate about education," says one student. "I think that the students here are well organized, motivated, and focused," adds a kinesiology major. One of Cornell's biggest challenges is drawing students to its rural Iowa campus, but administrators are doing well on that score: only 16 percent of students are homegrown. African Americans represent 6 percent of the student population, Hispanics 11 percent, and Asian Americans 4 percent. Six percent hail from other nations. Politically, Cornell leans liberal. "The biggest social issue on campus would probably be veganism, which has gotten really popular with the rise of the animal rights group on campus," a student explains. Merit scholarships are offered to qualified students, although there are no athletic awards.

Ninety-two percent of students live on campus. "It's no five-star hotel and small maintenance matters are a constant concern, but rooms are pretty big as dorm rooms go and the buildings are cleaned every weekday and on any additional need basis," a freshman says. Another student adds, "Even freshman rooms are really big and comfortable!" Nearly 10 percent of students participate in living/learning communities. Everyone eats together in the Commons. Bon Appétit runs the kitchen, and the food is "usually good," a junior says. Vegetarian options are always available. Campus security receives a thumbs-up: "The campus security at Cornell is very good, and they do a good job of patrolling campus throughout the day and night," a student says.

"Even freshman rooms are really big and comfortable!"

On campus, the fraternities draw 24 percent of the men and 17 percent of the women, though they are not associated with national Greek systems. "Performing Arts and Activities Council (PAAC) is also in charge of bringing entertainment to campus including bands, comedians, speakers, musicians, hypnotists, and many other programs which are great to attend with friends," notes one student. Some dorms and floors are substance free; in the others, only students over 21 may have alcohol. Policies to control underage drinking tend to be effective, according to students. Mount Vernon itself is "small, but very welcoming," says a physical education major. "Mount Vernon has one main street that is great for a nice day's stroll. There is an organic market, a few places to get a haircut, a grocery store, a couple coffee shops, and a farmer's market every week," a sophomore says. Students either love the town's idyllic pace—a few local bars; an acclaimed restaurant; some funky shops; and a lot of peace, quiet, and safety—or long for more excitement. The latter is available in Cedar Rapids (home of archrival Coe College) or Iowa City (home to the University of Iowa), each less than half an hour away. Chicago is less than four hours away.

The One-Course method also helps in academic advising—with grades every four weeks, signs of trouble are quickly apparent.

On campus, the fraternities draw 24 percent of the men and 17 percent of the women, though they are not associated with national Greek systems.

On the field or on the court, Cornell's competition with Coe "is intense, and the entire student body is involved," says one student, especially when it comes to football or basketball. "Every time a rival plays us at home in men's basketball, it's a tradition that we throw rolls of toilet paper out on the floor after we score our first basket," adds another—perhaps to show how Cornell plans to "clean up" its opponent. Cornell teams compete in the Midwest Conference and competitive teams include volleyball, basketball, and softball. The women's volleyball team qualified for the NCAA Championships for the second year in a row by going undefeated in conference play, while the women's basketball team engineered the best season in Cornell's history with a 24–1 regular season record and a conference title. Twenty percent of students, and some faculty and staff, participate in intramural sports.

Cornell offers a top-notch education and a supportive community—if you can take the bitter winters and relative isolation of rural Iowa. And while the curriculum requires students to focus on just one course at a time, "it is the most practical and interesting way to learn," declares a senior. A junior adds, "We are very much a nurturing happy microcosm that is turning out great things and wonderful, socially conscious people." Indeed, life here allows them to explore just about anything.

Overlaps

Knox, Coe, Grinnell, Beloit, DePaul, Augustana, St. Olaf, Colorado College

If You Apply To ➢

Cornell College: Early decision: Nov. 1. Early action: Dec. 1. Regular admissions: Feb. 1. Financial aid: Mar. 1. Application fee: $30 (paper), free (online). Campus interviews: optional, evaluative. No alumni interviews. SATs or ACTs: required. Subject Tests: optional. Accepts the Common Application. Essay question.

Cornell University

Ithaca, NY 14850

Cornell University's reputation as a pressure cooker comes from its preprofessional attitude and "we try harder" mentality. Spans seven colleges—four private and three public—and tuition varies accordingly. Strong in engineering and architecture, world-famous in hotel administration. Easiest Ivy to get into, and also the farthest from an urban center. Ithaca is a great college town.

Cornell University has a long tradition for being the lone wolf among the Ivy League universities. So it should come as no surprise that Cornell has taken another huge step away from its Ivy League counterparts by announcing its intention to become the finest research university for undergraduate education in the nation. Cornell has launched a $400 million, 10-year plan to improve undergraduate education by combining education and research and having all freshmen live in the same residential area. And the mixture of state and private, preprofessional, and liberal arts at one institution provides a diversity of students rare among America's colleges. "Cornell offers a diversity of opportunities in and outside of the classroom," says one student.

Aside from the great strides in undergraduate education, Cornell also has its stunning campus to lure students to upstate New York. Perched atop a hill that commands a view of both Ithaca and Cayuga lakes, the campus is breathtakingly scenic; or, as the saying goes, "Ithaca is gorges." Ravines, waterfalls, and parks border all sides of the school's campus. The Cornell Plantation, more than 3,000 acres of woodlands, natural trails, streams, and gorges, provides space for walking, picnicking, or contemplation. The Human Ecology Building provides state-of-the-art teaching and research facilities. The Physical Sciences Building joins the Department

Website: www.cornell.edu
Location: Rural
Private
Total Enrollment: 21,211
Undergraduates: 14,186
Male/Female: 49/51
SAT Ranges: CR 640–740, M 670–780
ACT Ranges: 30–33
Financial Aid: 64%
Expense: Pr $ $ $ $
Student Loans: 45%
Average Debt: $
Phi Beta Kappa: Yes
Applicants: 37,808
Accepted: 17%

of Physics, the School of Applied and Engineering Physics, and the Department of Chemistry and Chemical Biology under one roof. Milstein Hall opened in 2011 and offers 47,000 square feet of amenities, including studio space, a 275-seat auditorium, a small exhibition space, and approximately 6,000 square feet of critique space.

At the undergraduate level, the university has four privately endowed colleges: architecture, art, and planning; arts and sciences; engineering; and hotel administration. Cornell is also New York State's land grant university. Therefore, Cornell operates three other colleges under contract with New York State: agriculture and life sciences, human ecology, and the school of industrial and labor relations (ILR). Thirty-three percent of the students in these state-assisted colleges are New York State residents who pick up their Ivy League degrees at an almost-public price (as tuition at these schools is slightly steeper than SUNY rates).

Cornell's College of Arts and Sciences boasts considerable strength in history, government, and just about all the natural and physical sciences. The English program has turned out a number of renowned writers, including Toni Morrison, Thomas Pynchon, and Kurt Vonnegut. Foreign languages, required for all arts and sciences students, are also strong, and the performing arts, mathematics, and most social science departments are considered good. The agriculture college is solid and a good bet for anyone hoping to make it into a veterinary school (there's one at Cornell with state support). The School of Industrial and Labor Relations is the preeminent school of its kind, and the Department of Applied Economics and Management offers an undergraduate business major. The Johnson Museum of Art, designed by I. M. Pei, has been rated as one of the 10 best university museums in America. Students enjoy the $22 million theater arts center, designed specifically for undergraduates.

Student/faculty relations are a mixed bag, but for the most part students do have a lot of respect for their professors. "The quality of teaching is top-notch because the majority of professors are regarded as experts in their respective fields," says one student. "Some of the educators struggle to communicate their knowledge, but the professors have great command of their subject matters." First-year courses in the sciences and social sciences are generally large lectures, though many are taught by "charismatic profs" who try to remain accessible. "Freshman year it was difficult to build personal relationships with faculty because the classes are so large," a senior observes, "but as the years pass, classes become smaller and more intimate, which is a big advantage from a student perspective."

The Fund for Educational Initiatives gives professors money to implement innovative approaches to undergraduate education, which have included a visual learning laboratory and a course on electronic music. Cornell was early among universities to add women's studies to the curriculum and continues to be an innovator, with programs in China and Asia Pacific studies (which requires a semester's study in China and a semester's study in Washington, D.C.) and by offering its students programs like Sea Semester*.

Cornell academics are demanding and foster an intensity found on few campuses. "Cornell, without a doubt, fosters a competitive academic climate. Everyone here really wants to succeed and works as hard as possible to meet their end goal," says one senior. Ninety-one percent of Cornell students ranked in the top 10th of their high school class, so those who were

> **"Freshman year it was difficult to build personal relationships with faculty because the classes are so large."**

the class genius in high school should be prepared for a struggle to rise to the top. A number of well-publicized suicide incidents in recent years has led to the development of a strong mental health support program. To cope with the anxieties that the high-powered atmosphere creates, the university has one of the best psychological counseling networks in the nation, including an alcohol-awareness program, peer

(continued)

Enrolled: 51%
Grad in 6 Years: 93%
Returning Freshmen: 96%
Academics: ✍ ✍ ✍ ✍ ✍
Social: ☎ ☎ ☎ ☎
Q of L: ★ ★ ★
Admissions: (607) 255-5241
Email Address: admissions@ cornell.edu

Strongest Programs:
Biology
Physical Science/Math
English
Architecture
Hotel Administration
Industrial and Labor Relations
Agriculture
Economics/Business

sex counselors, personal-growth workshops, and EARS (Empathy, Assistance, and Referral Service).

The library system is superb. Cornell students have access to more than seven million volumes, 63,000 journals, and 1,000 networked resources in the 20 libraries comprising Cornell's library system. The resources are available to a wide range of students, faculty, staff, and, in some cases, the community. Also, the digital initiative has made many resources and collections available online. Within the beautiful underground Carl A. Kroch Library, students study in sky-lit atriums and reading rooms and move about the renowned Fiske Icelandic Collection and the Echols Collections, the finest Cambodian collection on display.

Cornell operates three other colleges under contract with New York State: agriculture and life sciences, human ecology, and the school of industrial and labor relations (ILR).

Cornell offers more than 4,000 courses in a wide range of pursuits, including programs in viticulture and enology, statistical science, and environmental engineering. A co-op program is available to engineering students, and Cornell-in-Washington, with its own dorm, is popular among students from all seven undergraduate colleges. Students looking to study abroad can choose from more than 200 programs and universities throughout the world, including those in Indonesia, Belgium, Ireland, and Nepal. "Studying abroad is a celebrated opportunity at Cornell," says a sophomore. "The number of quality programs seems inexhaustible." The College of Human Ecology offers exchange programs with Hong Kong Polytechnic University and the University of New South Wales. Nearly 50 percent of undergraduates participate in a mentored research experience with Cornell faculty at some point during their four years; popular options include the Human Ecology Urban Semester Program and the Student Project Teams found in the College of Engineering.

Prospective students apply to one of the seven colleges or schools through the central admissions office, and admissions standards vary by school. "We are cooler than the nerdy kids, and nerdier than the cool kids," quips one senior. "Cornellians often feel the need to vindicate themselves because we don't quite fit in anywhere else. We by and large didn't get into other Ivies, so compared to those students we feel a need to validate and distinguish ourselves through hard work and a more robust social life." Twenty-six percent of Cornell's students hail from New York; another 19 percent are international. African Americans constitute 6 percent of the student body, Hispanics account for 11 percent, and Asian Americans comprise 16 percent. Cornell offers many workshops and discussion groups aimed at increasing tolerance. The state-assisted schools draw a large number of in-staters, as well as students from New Jersey, Pennsylvania, and New England, while arts and sciences and engineering draw from the tristate metropolitan New York City area, Pennsylvania, Massachusetts, and California. Whatever their origin, students seem self-motivated and studious. Upon graduation, nearly one-third of Cornell students attend graduate and professional schools.

"The quality of teaching is top-notch."

Cornell is need-blind in admissions and guarantees to meet the demonstrated need of all accepted applicants, but the proportion of outright grants—as opposed to loans that must be repaid—in the financial aid package varies depending on how eager the university is to get you to enroll. The Cornell Installment Plan (CIP) allows students or their parents to pay a year's or semester's tuition in monthly interest-free installments. Cornell has expanded its financial aid initiatives by eliminating the parental contribution for students from families with incomes below $60,000 and assets below $100,000, capping need-based student loans at $7,500 annually for students who have financial need and whose families have annual incomes above $120,000, and reducing the parental contribution for selected students who have financial need and whose families have annual incomes above $60,000.

Cornell academics are demanding and foster an intensity found on few campuses.

"Housing was one of the main reasons I chose Cornell," says one junior. "I was able to essentially guarantee myself a single room even freshman year. My room was huge, and my dorm was quiet." North Campus residence halls are the home of all freshmen. A few students are housed in two dorms on the edge of Collegetown, the blocks of apartments and houses within walking distance of the campus. There are dorms devoted to everything from ecology to music, and cultural houses include the International Living Center, Latino Living Center, Ujamaa Residential College, and Akwe:kon, a program house focusing on American Indian culture (the only facility of its kind in the nation). Also available are a small number of highly coveted suites—six large double rooms with kitchens and a common living area. Just under half of Cornell's students live in university housing, though many try their luck in Collegetown, where demand keeps the housing market tight and rents high. Cornell's food service is reputedly among the best in the nation. There are eight residential meal plan dining halls that function independently, so, one student enthuses, "the food is very diverse and super tasty!" Another adds, "With the hotel school and agriculture school, Cornell has access to some of the best chefs and freshest vegetables and fruit in the area."

Despite the intense academic atmosphere—or maybe because of it—Cornell social life beats most of the other Ivies hands down. Once the weekend arrives, local parties and ski slopes are filled with Cornell students who have managed to strike a balance between study and play. With 28 percent of men and 24 percent of women pledging, fraternities and sororities also play

> "We are cooler than the nerdy kids, and nerdier than the cool kids."

a significant role in the social scene. "Social life at Cornell is really built around Greek life, especially for those under 21. Students who go Greek tend to have busy social schedules, and those who don't really need to find an organization they are passionate about," advises one student. Alcohol is part of the social scene, but underage drinkers beware: "The university is cracking down on high-risk drinking," says one student. "Freshmen are not allowed to attend fraternity parties during the fall semester and after freshmen receive a bid to a house in the spring there is an eight-week dry period." Big events include Fun in the Sun (a day of friendly athletic competition), Dragon Day (architecture students build a dragon and parade it through campus), and Springfest (a concert on Libe Slope). Students celebrate the last day of classes—Slope Day—by hanging out at Libe Slope. There are also innumerable concerts and sporting events. In addition, there are nearly 900 student organizations.

Cornell has won dozens of Ivy League team titles over the last decade with individual NCAA champions and a slew of high-profile national championship appearances. Wrestling has finished among the top six in the NCAA in five straight seasons, while women's ice hockey has three Frozen Four appearances in the last four years. Men's lacrosse has advanced to the NCAA Final Four four times in the last seven years and has won 10 of the last 11 Ivy League titles. Men's basketball reached the Sweet 16 in 2010 and earned its third consecutive trip to the NCAA tournament. Still, hockey is unquestionably the dominant sport on campus (the chief goal being to defeat Harvard), and camping out for season tickets is an annual ritual. Lightweight rowing has brought home three consecutive Intercollegiate Rowing Association titles. Cornell boasts the largest intramural program in the Ivy League; it includes more than a dozen sports, including 100 hockey teams organized around dorms, fraternities, and other organizations. The aforementioned "four seasons of Ithaca" can make walking to class across the vast and hilly campus challenging, but with the first snow of the winter, "traying" down Libe Slope becomes the sport of choice for hordes of fun-loving Cornellians. Ithaca boasts "wonderful outdoor enthusiast stores," says one student. It also hosts Greek Peak Mountain for nearby skiing, Cayuga Lake for boating and swimming, and lots of space for hiking and watching the clouds roll by.

One junior sums up the Cornell experience like this: "The people are passionate, the academics are rigorous, and the extracurricular activities are empowering." Like

Despite the intense academic atmosphere—or maybe because of it—Cornell social life beats most of the other Ivies hands down.

Overlaps

Harvard, University of Pennsylvania, Princeton, Stanford, Yale

most other Ivy League universities, Cornell is a premier research institution with a distinguished faculty and outstanding academics. What sets it apart is the university's willingness to stray from the traditional Ivy League path. Cornell University is a pioneer in the world of education, and students unafraid to blaze their own trails will feel at home here.

If You Apply To ➢

Cornell University: Early decision: Nov. 1. Regular admissions: Jan. 2. Financial aid: Feb. 15. Application fee: $75. No campus interviews. Alumni interviews: optional, informational (varies by program). SATs or ACTs (with writing): required. Subject Tests: required (varies by program). Accepts the Common Application. Essay question: Common Application. Apply to individual programs or schools.

University of Dallas

Irving, TX 75062

Bulwark of academic traditionalism in Big D. Despite being a "university," UD has fewer than 1,400 undergraduates. The curriculum is exclusively liberal arts. The only outpost of Roman Catholic education between Loyola of New Orleans and University of San Diego. A big drawing card is the university's program in Rome, pursued by most sophomores.

Website: www.udallas.edu
Location: Small City
Private
Total Enrollment: 1,611
Undergraduates: 1,329
Male/Female: 48/52
SAT Ranges: CR 550–670, M 530–640
ACT Ranges: 23–29
Financial Aid: 62%
Expense: Pr $
Student Loans: 58%
Average Debt: $ $ $ $
Phi Beta Kappa: Yes
Applicants: 1,178
Accepted: 88%
Enrolled: 34%
Grad in 6 Years: 69%
Returning Freshmen: 80%
Academics: ✑ ✑ ✑
Social: ☎ ☎
Q of L: ★ ★ ★
Admissions: (972) 721-5266
Email Address: ugadmis@udallas.edu

Strongest Programs:
English

While many universities around the nation have reexamined their Eurocentric core curriculums, the University of Dallas—the best Roman Catholic college south of Washington, D.C.—remains proudly dedicated to fostering students in the study of great deeds and works of Western civilization. "We have a very strong academic program," says a senior. "You will get a very good education here and also have a lot of fun."

UD's 744-acre campus occupies a pastoral home in a Dallas suburb on top of "the closest thing this region has to a hill." A major portion of the campus is situated around the Braniff Mall, a landscaped and lighted gathering place near the Braniff Memorial Tower, the school's landmark. The primary tone of the buildings is brown, and the architecture, as described by one student, is "post-1950s, done in brick, typical Catholic—institutional." While it may not be a picture-perfect school, it does have a beautiful chapel and a state-of-the-art science building. The Art Village has five buildings, and each art major has private studio space.

At UD, students choose from 29 majors and 32 concentrations. The social sciences are popular, as is business, English, biology, and psychology. The business program draws on the learning opportunities in the Dallas Metroplex to develop responsible and competent managers through classroom and industry experiences. Political philosophy is also a popular major, although students claim that most courses tend to be slanted toward the conservative side. Premed students are well served by the biology and chemistry programs, and 80 percent of UD graduates plan to go on to grad school.

> "You will get a very good education here and also have a lot of fun."

Appropriately for a Roman Catholic school, much of the focus is on Rome, where 80 percent of the sophomore class treks every year. The unique and intense program focuses on the art and architecture of Rome, the philosophy of man, classical literature, Italian, and the development of Western civilization. The Rome semester is part of UD's four-semester Western civilization core curriculum. "The study abroad program is an integral part of the University of Dallas," confirms a psychology major. Included in the core are philosophy, English, math, fine arts, science, American civilization, Western civilization, politics, and economics, as well as a serious foreign language requirement. Two theology courses (including Scripture and Western Theological Tradition) are also required of all students. Those inclined toward the sciences may take advantage of the John B. O'Hara Chemical Science Institute, which offers a hands-on eight-week summer program to prepare new students for independent research and earns them eight credits in chemistry.

(continued)

Biology
History
Politics
Philosophy
Premed

"The University of Dallas is very much like a coffeehouse," says one junior. "It is laid-back, but intellectual, it is fun, and all your friends are there with you." The university uses no teaching assistants, and professors are easy to get to know. "The professors are brilliant and have chosen to teach at UD because they understand the education the core entails," says a theology major. Fifty-five percent of classes taken by freshmen have 19 or fewer students.

"The students are fun, friendly, caring, dedicated, smart, and spiritual," one student says. "They study hard but know when to stop and have fun." Eighty-one percent of UD students are Roman Catholic, and many of them choose this school because of its religious affiliation. Eighteen percent of the student body is Hispanic; Asian Americans account for 4 percent; and 1 percent are African American. UDers tend to lean to the right politically, with topics such as abortion and homosexuality leading the discussions. "We are a Catholic institution and most students are conservative," a senior explains. UD offers various merit scholarships.

With no fraternities or sororities at UD, the student government sponsors most on-campus entertainment.

Sixty-five percent of students live on campus, where tradition and religion govern conduct. Students under 21 who don't reside at home with their parents must live on campus in single-sex dorms, "where visitation regulations are relatively strict," one student reports. "The dorms are like living at a summer camp," a junior says. "You do have to make a few sacrifices, but honestly it is a blast!" The most popular dorms are Jerome (all-female) and Madonna (all-male). At Gregory, the dorm reserved for those who like to party, the goings-on are less than saintly. In addition to a spacious and comfortable dining hall with a wonderful view of north Dallas, there is the Rathskeller, which serves snacks and fast food (and great conversation). "We have a personal chef who always makes sure everything is fresh and keeps the menu changing at all times," a junior explains.

"The dorms are like living at a summer camp."

With no fraternities or sororities at UD, the student government sponsors most on-campus entertainment. Three free movies a week, dances, and visiting speakers are usually on the agenda. Church-related and religious activities provide fulfilling social outlets for a good number of students. "There are plenty of things to do," says a junior, "and almost every weekend there is some big event happening." Annual events include Mallapalooza, a spring music festival, and Groundhog, a party on Groundhog Day weekend. Then there's Charity Week in the fall, when the junior class plans a week's worth of fund-raising events. Each year, students dread Sadie Hawkins Day and the annual Revenge of the Roommate dance—dark nights of the soul, each. The university can be vigorous in enforcing restrictive drinking rules and, as a result, it is difficult for a minor to drink at campus events. "The Office of Student Life runs a tight ship regarding alcohol," a student warns.

Intramural sports are well organized and very popular, with volleyball attracting the most players.

Students describe Irving (population 216,000) as "a suburb just like any other," but the Metroplex offers almost unlimited possibilities, including a full agenda for bar-hopping on Lower Greenville Avenue, about 15 minutes away. The West End and Deep Ellum offer a taste of shopping and Dallas's alternative music scene. And for the more adventurous, Austin and San Antonio aren't too far away.

The University of Dallas is unusual for a Texas school in that its entire population does not salivate at the sight of a football or basketball. But baseball and men's basketball are competitive, as is women's soccer, which has reached the NCAA Division III tournament multiple times. Intramural sports are well organized and very popular, with volleyball attracting the most players. Chess is also a favored activity.

UD appeals to those students who pride themselves on being the "philosopher kings of the 21st century," but whose roots go back to the Roman thinkers of an earlier era. The mix of religion and liberal arts can serve a certain breed of students well. In the words of one senior, "Come here to have fun, build sincere friendships, work hard, and graduate with a deep sense of your place in the Western cultural tradition."

If You Apply To ➤

Dallas: Early action I: Nov. 1. Early action II: Dec. 1. Regular admissions: Mar. 1. Application fee: $50. Campus interviews: optional, informational. No alumni interviews. SATs or ACTs: required. Subject Tests: optional. Accepts the Common Application. Essay question: personal statement.

Dartmouth College

6016 McNutt Hall, Hanover, NH 03755

The smallest Ivy and the one with the strongest emphasis on undergraduates. Traditionally the most conservative member of the Ivy League, it has steered toward more student diversity, more serious scholars, and fewer party animals in recent years. Ivy ties notwithstanding, Dartmouth has more in common with places like Colgate, Middlebury, and Williams. Great for those who like the outdoors.

Website: www.dartmouth.edu
Location: Small Town
Private
Total Enrollment: 6,030
Undergraduates: 4,098
Male/Female: 50/50
SAT Ranges: CR 670–780, M 680–780
ACT Ranges: 30–34
Financial Aid: 54%
Expense: Pr $ $ $ $
Student Loans: 46%
Average Debt: $
Phi Beta Kappa: Yes
Applicants: 23,110
Accepted: 10%
Enrolled: 49%
Grad in 6 Years: 95%
Returning Freshmen: 98%
Academics: ✍ ✍ ✍ ✍ ✍
Social: ☎ ☎ ☎ ☎ ☎
Q of L: ★ ★ ★
Admissions: (603) 646-2875

Unlike the other seven members of the Ivy League, which trace their roots to Puritan New Englanders or progressive Quaker colonists, Dartmouth College was founded in 1769 to educate Native Americans. The student body has always been the smallest in the Ancient Eight, and the school's focus on undergraduate education differentiates Dartmouth from its peers, though the college does offer graduate programs in engineering, business, and medicine. Dartmouth's campus is probably the most remote of the Ivies, and its winters may be the coldest, with the possible exception of those at Cornell. The Big Green compensates with the warmth of community, keeping sophomores on campus for the summer to build closeness, and using intensive language training and study abroad to emphasize the importance of global ties.

While tradition is revered at Dartmouth, the school also continues to grow, change, and evolve. Former president Jim Yong Kim was the first physician to serve in that role, and he came to Dartmouth after founding Partners in Health and leading the HIV/AIDS Department at the World Health Organization. Dr. Kim honored Dartmouth's long-standing tradition of taking on the "world's troubles" by establishing new innovations like the Center for Health Care Delivery sciences (a collaboration of Dartmouth's schools of engineering, business, and medicine). Today's Dartmouth hardly resembles the college of yesteryear, whose rowdy Greek scene inspired the movie *Animal House*. The school still attracts plenty of hiking and skiing enthusiasts, and the most popular extracurricular organization is the Dartmouth Outing Club, the oldest collegiate outdoors club in the nation. But these days, students are just as likely to join a hip-hop dance group called Sheba, or to spend a vacation doing Dartmouth-sponsored community service in South America.

"The whole campus is one giant, interactive, constant learning community."

Set in the "small, Norman Rockwell town" of Hanover, New Hampshire, which is bisected by the Appalachian Trail, Dartmouth's picturesque campus is arranged around a traditional New England green. It's bounded by the impressive library at one end, and by the college-owned Hanover Inn at the other. Architectural styles range from Romanesque to postmodern, but the dominant theme is copper-topped colonial frame. The nearest big city, Boston, is two hours away, but major artists like Itzhak Perlman routinely visit Dartmouth's Hopkins Center for the Creative and Performing Arts, adding a touch of culture. The Black Family Visual Arts Center opened recently and includes the Hopkins Center for the Arts and the Hood Museum of Art.

Dartmouth's status as a member of the Ivy League means academic excellence is a given. But that doesn't mean students have complete freedom when it comes to choosing courses. First-years must take a seminar that involves both independent research and small-group discussion; about 75 are offered each year. The seminars "ensure that every student's writing is up to par," while supplementing the usual introductory survey courses available in most disciplines and offering a glimpse of the self-directed scholarship expected at the college level. Students must also demonstrate proficiency in at least one foreign language. And they must take three world culture courses (one non-Western, one Western, and one Culture and Identity), and 10 courses from various distribution areas: the arts; literature; systems and traditions of thought, meaning, and value; international or comparative studies; social analysis; quantitative and deductive science; natural or physical science and technology; or applied science. In addition, Dartmouth has a senior culminating activity—a thesis, public report, exhibition, seminar, production, or demonstration—that allows students to pull together work done in their major with a creative and intellectual twist of their own. "The whole campus is one giant, interactive, constant learning community," says a senior.

> "The academic climate at Dartmouth is challenging but supportive."

Though Dartmouth students work hard, the climate is far from cut-throat. "The academic climate at Dartmouth is challenging but supportive. The courses increase in difficulty as you advance in the department," says one junior. The most popular majors are social sciences, biological/life science, business/marketing, psychology, and English. The languages are also well regarded, and students benefit from the Intensive Language Model developed by Professor John Rassias. Computer science offerings are among the best in the nation, thanks in no small part to the late John Kemeny, the former Dartmouth president who coinvented time-sharing and the BASIC language. Indeed, computing is a way of life here; well before the Internet, all of Dartmouth's dorm rooms were networked, and students would "Blitzmail" each other to set up meetings, discussions, or meals. Now, a Voice-over-Internet Protocol phone system also lets students use their laptops as telephones, which means long-distance calls home are free.

Professors get high marks at Dartmouth, perhaps because of the school's focus on undergraduates. The isolated location also helps; faculty make a conscious choice to teach here, leaving behind some of the distractions afflicting their peers at more urban schools. "Dartmouth is a rare school that is an undergraduate institution first," says a religion major. "Teaching is clearly a big part of that commitment to excellence." Sixty-five percent of classes taken by freshmen have 19 or fewer students. The Presidential Scholars Program offers one-on-one research assistantships with faculty, and the Senior Fellowship Program enables 10 to 12 students a year to pursue interdisciplinary research projects and to pay no tuition for their final term. The Policy Research Shop helps undergraduate public policy students write policy briefs for state legislators and government agencies in New Hampshire and Vermont. The Women in Science Project encourages female students to pursue courses and

(continued)

Email Address: admissions
.reply@dartmouth.edu

Strongest Programs:
Biological Sciences
Computer Science
Engineering
Economics
Languages
Psychological and Brain
 Sciences

Though Dartmouth students work hard, the climate is far from cut-throat.

careers in science, math, and engineering with mentors, speakers, and even research positions for first-years. The Montgomery Fellowships bring well-known politicians, writers, and others to campus for periods ranging from a few days to several months, while the Visionary in Residence program invites notable thinkers to campus to share their talents and insights.

The school's most notable eccentricity is the Dartmouth Plan, or "D Plan"—four 10-week terms a year, including one during the summer. Students must be on campus for three terms during the freshman and senior years, and also during the summer after the sophomore year, but otherwise, as long as they're on track to graduate, they can take off whenever they wish. More than half of the students use terms away for one of Dartmouth's 44 study abroad programs, where they may focus on the classics in Greece or the environment in Zimbabwe; other students pursue part-time jobs, internships, or independent travel. The college also participates in the Twelve College Exchange Program* and the Maritime Studies Program*.

"Dartmouth is a rare school that is an undergraduate institution first."

Dartmouth went co-ed in 1972, and women now make up half of the student body. Minorities also comprise a substantial portion, with African Americans making up 6 percent, Asian Americans 13 percent, and Hispanics 6 percent. Students here have a "true, true love for this school and a passion for learning not simply for the grade but for the experience," says a senior. Students retain that passion after graduation, as Dartmouth has the most elaborate network of alumni organizations of any college in the country. Admissions are need-blind, even for students who get in off the waitlist, and the school offers free tuition and no loans to students from families with incomes below $100,000 a year. No merit or athletic scholarships are awarded; the Ivy League prohibits the latter.

Eighty-six percent of Dartmouth students live on campus in one of more than 30 dorms, which have been grouped into 11 clusters to help create a sense of community. "The dorms are spacious and comfortable and very well maintained," says an environmental studies major. "You can live in a single, double, triple, or quad, with anywhere from one to three rooms of different shapes and sizes." First-year students may choose freshman-only housing, or dorms where all classes live together. Sophomores may get squeezed during the housing lottery, but because of the D Plan, people are always coming and going; it may be easier to find a new room or roommate than at schools on the semester system. Dining facilities are open until 2:30 a.m. for those needing sustenance during late-night study sessions. Seniors may move off campus, into group houses, and many choose to do so. Safety is not a big concern here. "Safety and Security [S&S] is a constant presence around the clock," a student says.

"Social life at Dartmouth takes place through many of the organizations and groups that exist on campus," says a geography major. "Almost all of it takes place on campus at fraternities or sororities." Dartmouth's Greek system attracts 48 percent of the men and 47 percent of the women; it's "big, but not exclusive—all parties are open to everyone," says a junior. The Greeks have become less of a force in campus social life because of the Student Life Initiative, a steering committee that developed more rigorous behavior standards. Parties and kegs must also be registered, and the houses where they're being held are subject to walk-throughs by college safety and security personnel. Alcohol policies are aimed at keeping booze away from those under 21. Indeed, recognizing that the nickname of its hometown has long been "Hangover," Dartmouth was one of the first schools to develop a counseling and educational program to combat alcohol abuse. And students say a campus bar called the Lone Pine Tavern is more likely to be the scene of Scrabble and chess tournaments than hardcore drinking games. Popular road trips include Montreal or Boston, for a dose of bright lights and the big city, or the White Mountains for camping. (Dartmouth has a

Now, a Voice-over-Internet Protocol phone system also lets students use their laptops as telephones, which means long-distance calls home are free.

27,000-acre land grant in the northeast corner of New Hampshire where cabins may be rented for five dollars a night.) Still, "the social life revolves almost 100 percent around the college itself," a senior says. "Very little occurs off campus."

"I was sold on Dartmouth because it is steeped in tradition," says one senior. Weekends include traditions such as a 75-foot-tall bonfire at homecoming and Winter Carnival, which includes ski racing at the college's bowl, 20 minutes away, as well as snow-sculpture contests and partiers from all over the Eastern seaboard. Spring brings mud as the snow slowly melts, and also Green Key weekend, which one student calls "an excuse to drink under the guise of community service." (The school is striving for 100 percent participation in community service by graduation, "and we're close," says one student. "I've traveled twice to rural Nicaragua on a Dartmouth-sponsored, student-organized cross-cultural education and service program; we provide medical assistance to villagers and construct clinics, compostable latrines, and organic farms.")

> More than half of the students use terms away for one of Dartmouth's 44 study abroad programs.

Love of the outdoors at Dartmouth extends to varsity athletics. The women's ice hockey team is a perennial powerhouse, and other competitive Big Green teams include men's soccer, ice hockey, and baseball, and women's lacrosse, basketball, and skiing. Hanover residents support the basketball teams, and few Dartmouth students miss a trip to Cambridge for the biennial Dartmouth–Harvard football game. The school's sports facility boasts a 2,100-seat arena, a 4,000-square-foot fitness center, and the only permanent three-glass-wall squash court in North America. Three-quarters of the student body participate in nearly 50 intramural sports. Nonathletes beware: Dartmouth does have a nontimed swimming test

"The dorms are spacious and comfortable."

and a physical education requirement for graduation; you can fulfill the latter with classes such as fencing or ballet, or participation in a club or intramural sport.

"Dartmouth is really a place for a go-getter," advises one student. The college attracts outdoorsy, down-to-earth students who develop extremely strong ties to the school—and each other—during four years together in the hinterlands. It seems as if every other grad has a title like deputy assistant class secretary, and many return to Hanover when they retire, further cementing their bonds with the college, and driving local real estate prices beyond the reach of most faculty members. You'll have to be made of hardy stock to survive the harsh New Hampshire winters. But once you defrost, you'll be rewarded with lifelong friends and a solid grounding in the liberal arts, sciences, and technology.

Overlaps

Brown, Cornell, Duke, Harvard, University of Pennsylvania, Princeton, Stanford, Yale

If You Apply To > **Dartmouth:** Early decision: Nov. 1. Regular admissions: Jan. 1. Financial aid: Feb. 1. Application fee: $80. No campus interviews. Alumni interviews: optional, evaluative. SATs or ACTs (with writing): required. Subject Tests: required (any two). Accepts the Common Application. Essay question.

Davidson College

P.O. Box 7156, Davidson, NC 28035

Has always been styled as the "Dartmouth of the South." Goes head-to-head with Washington and Lee (VA) as the top liberal arts college below the Mason–Dixon Line. An early leader in the trend to replace loans with grants, it boasts a strong honor system that sets the campus tone. Small-town location is a stone's throw from Charlotte and near prime vacation spots.

Website: www.davidson.edu

Location: Suburban

Private

Total Enrollment: 1,790

Undergraduates: 1,790

Male/Female: 50/50

SAT Ranges: CR 625–720,
   M 635–720

ACT Ranges: 29–32

Financial Aid: 47%

Expense: Pr $ $ $

Student Loans: 22%

Average Debt: $ $

Phi Beta Kappa: Yes

Applicants: 4,770

Accepted: 25%

Enrolled: 42%

Grad in 6 Years: 93%

Returning Freshmen: 97%

Academics: ✍ ✍ ✍ ✍ ½

Social: ☎ ☎ ☎

Q of L: ★ ★ ★ ★ ★

Admissions: (800) 768-0380

Email Address: admission@
   davidson.edu

Strongest Programs:

Biology

Psychology

English

Political Science

Theater

Chemistry

International Studies

History

Davidson's academic climate is rigorous but not grueling.

Davidson College boasts the Southern tradition and gentility of neighbors like Rhodes and Sewanee, with the academic prowess more common to Northern liberal arts powerhouses such as Dartmouth and Middlebury. Often overlooked because of its small size and Carolinas location, Davidson offers students strong interdisciplinary, international, and preprofessional programs, as well as a thriving social scene. "Davidson offers one of the best undergraduate experiences and is the liberal arts school of the South," says a senior economics major.

> **"Because of an Honor Code that works, Davidson students are able to walk around campus feeling safe."**

Located in a beautiful stretch of the North Carolina Piedmont, Davidson's wooded campus features Georgian and Greek Revival architecture. The central campus is designated as a national arboretum, and college staff lovingly maintain a collection of the woody plants that thrive in the area. Davidson retains its original quadrangle, which dates from 1837, plus literary society halls built in the 1850s. A new residence hall for 251 students was completed in 2012.

Davidson's Honor Code allows students to take exams independently and to feel comfortable leaving doors unlocked. "Because of an Honor Code that works, Davidson students are able to walk around campus feeling safe and can leave their belongings anywhere without worrying that they will be stolen," says a senior. Every entering freshman agrees to abide by the code, and all work submitted to professors is signed with the word "pledged." Core requirements include one course each in historical thought; literary studies; creative writing and rhetoric; mathematical and quantitative thought; natural science; philosophical and religious perspectives; social-scientific thought; visual and performing arts; and liberal studies. Students must also take a class in a foreign language, diversity, and first year writing. Four physical education classes are required, including Davidson 101, two lifetime activities, and a team sport. Many requirements, including in-depth or comparative studies of another culture, may be met through the two-year interdisciplinary humanities program.

Davidson's academic climate is rigorous but not grueling. "Davidson has to be one of the toughest places," says a sophomore. "There are times when I find myself staying up several nights during the week to finish up papers, projects, and tests." Professors are highly lauded for being friendly and accessible, and with no graduate students around, opportunities to work with faculty members on research projects abound. "Every professor is extremely intelligent and most are great teachers," one student reports. The most popular majors are political science, psychology, English, biology, and history.

> **"Every professor is extremely intelligent and most are great teachers."**

For those whose academic interests lie outside the mainstream, Davidson's Center for Interdisciplinary Studies allows students to develop and design their own majors with faculty or on their own. Environmental studies majors may apply to the School for Field Studies to spend a month or a semester studying environmental issues in other countries or to work and conduct research at Biosphere 2. The Dean Rusk International Studies Program, named for the Davidson alumnus who served as secretary of state to presidents Kennedy and Johnson, brings speakers to campus and provides more than $100,000 annually to students to help them study and travel abroad. The South Asia studies program focuses on India, Pakistan, Bangladesh, Sri Lanka, Nepal, and Bhutan; study abroad is also available in countries from France, Germany, and England to Cyprus and Zambia, and 71 percent of the students graduate with some foreign experience. "If you want to study abroad, you can do it through Davidson," says a student. "It's a very internationally focused campus." A 3–2 engineering program is available with five larger universities. On campus, class size is restricted; the only room with more than 35 students is the cafeteria.

Twenty-two percent of Davidson students come from North Carolina and 6 percent from abroad. While the school embraces its Presbyterian heritage, Davidson "is alive with an ecumenical spirit, so all students of all religious backgrounds feel comfortable while here," a political science major explains. Seven percent of the student body is African American, with 6 percent Hispanic and 5 percent Asian American. A student says, "The Honor Code is a cornerstone not just for academics, but for all aspects of life at Davidson," which means that student attitudes and behaviors are shaped by their respect for the code. Davidson lures top students with generous merit scholarships, and under its highly touted Davidson Trust, the college has replaced all loans with grants. Nearly 200 athletic scholarships are available.

Ninety-two percent of Davidson's students live on campus in co-ed or single-sex dorms. "The dorms are generally nice and centrally located," a sophomore says. Freshmen are housed together and eat in Vail Commons, where the "food is great— all you can eat, and lots of options, though it's hard to be a vegan at Davidson." Upperclassmen may live in the dorms or off campus with permission of the residence life office. Laundry service is offered to students as part of the mandatory fees they pay—a reminder of Davidson's days as an all-male school when such services were the only way to keep undergrads socially presentable. Seniors get apartment-style housing with private bedrooms. Most upperclassmen take meals at one of the fraternities or eating houses. These groups have their own cooks and serve meals family style.

"Because we are such a small school it's not uncommon that you meet someone in a class, on a team, or at a service project and end up hanging out with them and being great friends," says a student. The eating clubs are the center of social life on campus, as is the Alvarez College Union. All but one are in Patterson Court, which freshmen are not allowed to enter for the first three weeks of school. The dues charged by these clubs cover meals, as well as parties and other campuswide events. The fraternities, which claim 10 percent of Davidson's men, are not much different from the eating clubs, and freshmen simply sign up for the group they want to join on Self-Selection Night, with no "rushing" allowed. There is one sorority on campus that draws 1 percent of Davidson women. And even if you don't join up, don't despair; Davidson requires that most parties—"at least two per weekend" at the eating clubs—be open to the entire community. Alcohol policies comply with North Carolina law; officially, no one under 21 can be served. "Policies are tied into the Honor Code, so they are enforced," a student says.

Davidson's five-day freshman orientation includes the Cake Race, which provides runners with about 200 cakes they select based on order of finish. Orientation also introduces students to the cozy town of Davidson, which has coffee shops and cafés and to the college's 100-acre Lake Norman campus which provides for sailing, swimming, and waterskiing. "Davidson is a great college town," a chemistry major says. The equally quaint town of Cornelius is adjacent to Davidson, so it's a common destination for dinner and a movie or a relaxed night out. When those diversions grow old, North Carolina's largest city, Charlotte, is just 20 miles away with clubs and other attractions. A car definitely helps here, as Myrtle Beach and skiing are several hours from Davidson, in different directions. Students without wheels of their own can rent a car through the college's We Car program.

Davidson fields 21 teams (the "Wildcats") that compete in Division I, as well as non-scholarship football. About 20 percent of students are varsity athletes. Basketball, soccer, swimming, lacrosse, golf, volleyball, and wrestling are the strongest programs. Intramural and club sports are also varied and popular.

Despite its North Carolina location, Davidson has the look and feel of a New England liberal arts college and continues to attract top students to its charming

A 3–2 engineering program is available with five larger universities.

"The dorms are generally nice and centrally located."

Basketball, soccer, swimming, lacrosse, golf, volleyball, and wrestling are the strongest programs.

Overlaps

UNC at Chapel Hill, Duke, Wake Forest, Washington and Lee, University of Virginia, Vanderbilt, Furman, College of William and Mary

neck of the woods. "So many factors contribute to Davidson being such a great place," says a junior. "If it's the right college for you, you can probably tell from the moment you step on campus." From study abroad and independent research to a strawberries-and-champagne reception with the college president for graduating seniors, students here combine tradition with forward thinking to make great memories, friends, and intellectual strides.

University of Dayton

Dayton, OH 45469-1323

Among a cohort of second-tier Midwest Roman Catholic institutions that includes DePaul, Duquesne, Loyola of Chicago, Saint Louis University, and Xavier (OH). Drawing cards include business, education, and the social sciences. The city of Dayton is not particularly enticing, and UD's appeal is largely regional.

Website: www.udayton.edu
Location: City Outskirts
Private
Total Enrollment: 9,357
Undergraduates: 7,441
Male/Female: 51/49
SAT Ranges: CR 510–620, M 503–640
ACT Ranges: 24–29
Financial Aid: 97%
Expense: Pr $
Student Loans: 62%
Average Debt: $ $ $ $
Phi Beta Kappa: No
Applicants: 15,101
Accepted: 55%
Enrolled: 25%
Grad in 6 Years: 78%
Returning Freshmen: 88%
Academics: ✏ ✏ ✏
Social: ☎ ☎ ☎ ☎ ☎
Q of L: ★ ★ ★
Admissions: (937) 229-4411
Email Address: admission@udayton.edu

Strongest Programs:
Education

Anyone who thinks college students of today subscribe to postmodern cynicism ought to take a peek at Dayton, where optimism and Christian charity are alive and well. "If you used one word to describe UD students, it would be 'friendly,'" a senior says. "Everyone on campus is very welcoming. We smile and say 'hi' to people we don't know and hold the doors open for each other." There's good reason for the cheery disposition: Applications are at an all-time high and selectivity continues to increase.

> "The classes are certainly academically challenging."

Although its name suggests that it is a public university, Dayton was founded by the Society of Mary (Marianists) and continues to emphasize that order's devotion to service. The majority of UD students volunteer their time in 30 different public service areas. Christmas on campus, when UD students "adopt" local elementary students for a night of crafts, games, and a visit with Santa, is one of the most student-involved activities. "We bring in about 1,000 inner-city Dayton school kids and walk them around campus, which has been transformed into a winter wonderland," says one student.

The parklike campus is on the southern boundary of the city, secluded from the traffic and bustle of downtown. The more historic buildings make up the central core of the campus and blend architectural charm with modern technological conveniences. A $25 million fitness and recreation complex, dubbed the "RecPlex," houses classrooms, a climbing wall, basketball and volleyball courts, a juice bar, and many other sports-related facilities. A 400-bed residence hall with amenities such as a post office and credit union is in the heart of campus. ArtStreet, a $9 million arts-centered living/learning complex, includes six two-story townhouses and five loft apartments above performance spaces, art studios, the campus radio station, and a recording studio.

"The classes are certainly academically challenging," says one junior. UD students take full advantage of the strong offerings found in communication, mechanical engineering, psychology, accounting, and management—the most popular majors. Weaker offerings include theater and physical education. Entrepreneurship is the fastest-growing major in the School of Business Administration and participating sophomores are given $3,000 loans to start their own businesses, with any profits going to charity. The program includes mentoring by local entrepreneurs and courses taught by entrepreneurs and Ph.D. faculty.

Dayton's Common Academic Program (CAP) will begin to replace the current general education requirements; over the next three years the two programs will exist on parallel tracks. The prestigious Berry Scholars program includes seminars, study abroad opportunities, service and leadership projects, and a major independent research project. Consistent with its religious mission, Dayton offers a major in human rights. Students with at least a 1300 combined SAT score or a 30 ACT score and who place in the top 10 percent of their graduating class or have a 3.7 GPA may join the University Honors Program, which provides guest speakers in small classes and requires an honors thesis project.

> **"Professors are more than willing to set aside time to meet with students."**

The Interdepartmental Summer Study Abroad Program is a popular ticket to the world's most exciting cities, while the Immersion Program in Third World countries is much praised by participants. The University of Dayton Research Institute (UDRI) is one of the nation's leading university-based research organizations. All students purchase a notebook computer upon entering UD. Students speak enthusiastically about the quality of teaching, stating that professors are enthusiastic about their courses. "Professors are more than willing to set aside time to meet with students," a sophomore says, "going above and beyond regular office hours." New students unsure of their majors can take advantage of First Year Experience, a structured program where students are required to meet with their advisors once a week.

"Students at UD love one word above all," says a sophomore: "community." Fifty-one percent of Dayton's students are from Ohio, and minorities make up just 6 percent of the student population: 3 percent are African American, 2 percent are Hispanic, and 1 percent are Asian American. The Task Force on Women's Issues, the Office of Diverse Student Populations, and an updated sexual-harassment policy demonstrate UD's growing sensitivity to campus issues. Twenty-six percent of incoming students rank in the top 10th of their high school class, and the school is becoming more selective. Dayton's 200 athletic scholarships go to athletes in 12 men's and women's sports. There are also many merit awards, averaging nearly $9,313.

Seventy-four percent of students are campus residents; those who live off campus generally live adjacent to it. "All first-year students live in one of four traditional residence halls," a senior explains. "Sophomores opt to live in suites or apartments, while upper-class students live in university-owned houses, apartments, or townhouses." Students say the dorms are well

> **"There is a 'three strikes, you're out' policy regarding drinking."**

maintained yet somewhat outdated. Sophomores have an opportunity to live in Virginia Kettering, a residence hall whose amenities evoke luxurious apartments. The food in the dining halls that dot the campus is generally well received; one dining hall is located in one of the first-year dorms, another in the sophomore complex, the third is centrally located in the student union, and a fourth is in Marianist Hall.

The student neighborhood (a.k.a. "the Ghetto") serves as a sort of continuous social center. A lit porchlight beckons party-seeking students to join the weekend festivities. Because the university owns most of the properties, a 24-hour campus security patrol keeps watch over the area. "You never really need to leave campus to have a memorable time," says a junior. The more adventurous weekend excursions are trips to Ohio State University, Ohio University, Indianapolis, and the restaurants, shops, and sports arenas in Cincinnati. But the best road trip is the

(continued)
Communication
Marketing
Finance
Psychology

Dayton's Common Academic Program (CAP) will begin to replace the current general education requirements.

Twenty-six percent of incoming students rank in the top 10th of their high school class.

Dayton-to-Daytona trip after spring finals, a 17-hour trek that draws loads of students each year. Partying on campus is commonplace and controlled, but parties have sized down due to the university's enforcement of the 21-year-old drinking age. "There is a 'no keg' policy that most students ignore," admits one student. Still, "There is a 'three strikes, you're out' policy regarding drinking," which students say makes them cautious. Greek organizations draw 9 percent of UD men and 15 percent of the women, with all chapters playing an active role in community service and social life.

More important, though, are sports, particularly basketball. "The Xavier game is our biggest rivalry and attracts the attention of most students," says a student. The football team, which is Division I-AA, plays in the Pioneer Football League and is a perennial powerhouse; UD is in the Atlantic 10 for Division I athletics in all other sports. Women's volleyball, women's basketball, women's soccer, and men's baseball are the most competitive teams. When students aren't cheering, they can participate in an intramural program that offers 45 sports. Other activities in the city include a minor-league baseball team, an art institute, an aviation museum, and a symphony and ballet in the Schuster Performing Arts Center. Two large shopping malls are also easily accessible.

The success of Dayton's attempts to provide its students with a high quality of life and a sense of cohesiveness is reflected in many of the students' comments about the terrific social life and familylike atmosphere among both students and faculty. As a midsize university where the undergraduates come first, Dayton has managed to maintain an exciting balance of personal attention, academic challenge, and all-American fun. Students do have one complaint, according to a sophomore: "We have to leave after four years."

Women's volleyball, women's basketball, women's soccer, and men's baseball are the most competitive teams.

Overlaps

Miami (OH), Ohio State, University of Cincinnati, Xavier, Ohio University, Marquette, Indiana University, Saint Louis University

If You Apply To ➢

Dayton: Early action: Dec. 15. Regular admissions: Mar. 1. Housing: May 1. Application fee: $50 (paper), free (online). Campus and alumni interviews: optional, informational. SATs or ACTs: required. Subject Tests: optional. Essay question.

Deep Springs College

Deep Springs, CA; Mailing Address: Dyer, NV 89010-9803

BEST BUY

Picture 25 Ivy League-caliber men living and learning in a remote desert outpost—that's Deep Springs. DS is the most elite two-year institution in the nation, and also the most unusual—and not just because of its free tuition. Occupies a handful of ranch-style buildings set on 50,000 acres on the arid border of Nevada and California. Students transfer to highly selective colleges after two years. The college hopes to go co-ed.

If the thought of spending countless hours under the fluorescent lights of the classroom makes you grimace, you may consider getting your hands dirty at Deep Springs College. This two-year institution doubles as a working ranch. Bonding is easy here, and students enjoy a demanding and individualized education supplemented by the challenges and lessons of ranch life. Both, it seems, demand the same things: hard work, commitment, and pride in a job well done. Deep Springs College students are also rewarded for their efforts in other ways: tuition is free and so is room and board. Students pay only for books, travel, and personal items; the average cost of

Website: www.deepsprings.edu
Location: Rural
Private
Total Enrollment: 28
Undergraduates: 28
Male/Female: 100/0

one year at Deep Springs is $2,000. Still, students do have a few complaints: loneliness, saddle-chafing, and no girls. Many of the men who work, study, and live at this college have shunned acceptance at Ivy League schools to embrace the rigors of a truly unique approach to learning. Deep Springs students tend to be of the academic Renaissance-man variety with wide-ranging interests in many fields. Almost all transfer to the Ivies or other prestigious universities after their two-year program, and 70 percent eventually earn a Ph.D. or law degree. Efforts to go co-ed have thus far been blocked by the courts.

California's White Mountains provide a stunning backdrop for the Deep Springs campus, set on a barren plain 5,200 feet above sea level, near the only water supply for miles around. The campus is an oasislike cluster of trees and a lawn with eight ranch-style buildings that were built from scratch by the class of 1917. Deep Springs is 28 miles from the nearest town, a thriving metropolis known as Big Pine, population 950. The focal point of campus is the Main Building, a venerable ranch-style building with wide eaves that includes a computer room and offices. Dorm rooms are housed in the spacious Student Residence. Faculty houses and the dining facilities are grouped around the circular lawn a few yards away, and the trappings of farm life surround the tiny settlement. The college has 170 acres under cultivation, mostly with alfalfa, and an assortment of barnyard animals. A solar array produces twice as much energy as the college requires and is the most efficient array in North America.

"Deep Springers tend to think of academics as part of our community life."

Founded in 1917 by an industrialist who made a fortune in the electric-power industry, Deep Springs today remains true to its charter "to combine taxing practical work, rigorous academics, and genuine self-government." Ideals of self-government, reflectiveness, frugality, and community activity have weathered more than 85 years of a grueling academic climate. "Deep Springers tend to think of academics as part of our community life," says one student. "The courses are challenging," says another. "All students have an intense devotion to the material," adds a second-year student. Students are also required to perform 20 hours per week of labor, which can include everything from harvesting alfalfa to cooking dinner.

Students' input carries a lot of weight at this school. The student body committees are an essential part of the self-governance pillar at DS. There are four committees: the student-run Applications Committee, which is made up of eight students, a faculty member, and a staff member; the Curriculum Committee; the Review and Reinvitations Committee; and the Communications Committee. They help choose the college's faculty and even elect two of their own to be full-voting members on the board of trustees. They play a determining role in admissions and curricular decisions. And they abide by a Spartan community code that bans all drugs, including alcohol, and forbids anyone to leave Deep Springs Valley (the 50 square miles of desert surrounding the campus) while classes are in session, except for medical visits and college business. Lest these rules sound unnecessarily strict, keep in mind that these are all decided on and enforced by the student body, not the administration.

Like almost everything else about it, Deep Springs has an unorthodox academic schedule: two summer terms of seven weeks each, and a fall and spring semester of 14 weeks each. Between 7 and 10 classes are offered every term. The faculty consists of three "permanent" professors (they sign on for two years, but can stay for up to six), plus an average of three others who are hired on a temporary basis to teach for a term or two. The quality of particular academic areas varies as professors come and go. "The teachers range from superb to mediocre," observes one student. Although the curriculum is altered yearly, students predict that the humanities will always remain superior. The students control the academic program and

"The teachers range from superb to mediocre."

(continued)

SAT Ranges: CR 750–800, M 710–760
ACT Ranges: 31–36
Financial Aid: 100%
Expense: Pr $
Student Loans: N/A
Average Debt: N/A
Phi Beta Kappa: No
Applicants: 200
Accepted: 7%
Enrolled: 87%
Grad in 6 Years: 100%
Returning Freshmen: 92%
Academics: ✎ ✎ ✎ ✎ ½
Social: ☎
Q of L: ★ ★ ★
Admissions: (760) 872-2000
Email Address: apcom@ deepsprings.edu

Strongest Programs:
Humanities
Liberal Arts
Environmental Studies
Philosophy

A solar array produces twice as much energy as the college requires and is the most efficient array in North America.

quickly replace courses—and faculty—that do not work out. Currently, the only required courses are public speaking and composition.

Deep Springers aren't much for the latest conveniences, but almost every student room has a computer, plus there are several in a common area. Deep Springs used to have one telephone line for the whole school; now it has six. With class sizes ranging from two to 14, there is ample opportunity for close student/faculty interaction. Close living arrangements have fostered a kind of kinship between faculty and students. Students routinely visit their mentors in their homes, sometimes to confer on academic matters and sometimes to play soccer with their children.

Deep Springers can truly boast of being handpicked to attend; of the approximately 200 applications received each year, only a few students are accepted. Most DS students are from upper-middle-class families and typically rank in the top 3 percent of their high school class. "The students are extremely motivated, hardworking, and intelligent," a student says. Many Deep Springers are transplanted urbanites; the rest hail from points scattered across the nation or across the seas. Political leanings run the gamut, and there is diversity even among this small population, although that may only translate to one or two students of color here.

> "The students are extremely motivated, hardworking, and intelligent."

Dorm selection and maintenance is entirely the responsibility of the students. "Compared to other college dorms," says a student, "the Deep Springs dorm is a palace." Students all pitch in preparing the meals, from butchering the meat to milking the cows to washing the dishes. "The food is usually five stars," boasts a student. "Vegetarians are usually provided for, but we are a cattle ranch." And what about security? "Unless a tractor runs over you, you're fine," says a freshman. A classmate adds, "Sometimes the bulls get loose."

Social life can be a challenge. "Most students socialize over meals or midnight snacks," reports one student. And loneliness can be an issue. Still, "we're too busy with the three pillars—academics, labor, and self-governance—to have much of a social life." When the moon is full, students go out en masse in the middle of the night to frolic in the 700-foot-high Eureka Sand Dunes with Frisbees and skis. "We slide down the Eureka Valley sand dunes au naturel," says one student. Perhaps the most popular social activity on campus is conversation over a cup of coffee in the Boarding House (Deep Springs's dining hall), where the chatter is usually lively until the wee hours of the morning. Other common activities are road trips to nearby national parks, hikes in the nearby mountains, and horseback riding. The Turkey Bowl; the potato harvest; the two-on-two basketball tournament; and Sludgefest, an annual event involving cleaning out the reservoir, are only some of the time-honored Deep Springs traditions.

Critics of Deep Springs charge that DS cultivates arrogance and social backwardness among students who were too intellectual to be in the social mainstream during high school. They argue that students who come here are doomed to be misfits for life. While that charge is debatable, even supporters of Deep Springs confess to a love-hate relationship with the college. Although the interpretations may vary, one common thread winds through the DS mission from application to graduation: training for a life of service to humanity.

> "The food is usually five stars."

Perhaps more than any other school in the nation, Deep Springs is a community where students and faculty interact day-to-day on an intensely personal level. Though the financial commitment is small, the school demands an intense level of personal commitment. All must quickly learn how to get along in a community where the actions of each person affect everyone. "We are oriented toward serving humanity," says a freshman, "and we try to understand what service means in a nuanced and

Deep Springs has an unorthodox academic schedule: two summer terms of seven weeks each, and a fall and spring semester of 14 weeks each.

Critics of Deep Springs charge that DS cultivates arrogance and social backwardness among students who were too intellectual to be in the social mainstream during high school.

Overlaps

Brown, Cornell, Yale, University of Chicago, Harvard, Columbia, Stanford, Princeton

original way." Urban cowboys who dream of riding into the sunset are in for a rude awakening. For a select few, however, the camaraderie and soul-searching fostered in this tight-knit community can be mighty tempting—just stay clear of those bulls.

If You Apply To ➢

Deep Springs: Regular admissions: Nov. 7. No application fee. Campus interviews: recommended, evaluative. No alumni interviews. SATs: required. Subject Tests: optional. Essay questions: describe yourself, critical analysis of book or other work of art, and why Deep Springs.

University of Delaware

116 Hullihen Hall, Newark, DE 19716

Plenty of students dream of someday becoming Nittany Lions or Cavaliers—even Terrapins—but not many aspire to be Blue Hens. The challenge for UD is how to win its share of students without the name recognition that comes from big-time sports. The state of Delaware is tiny, and less than half the students are in-staters. Check out the variety of residential learning options.

The University of Delaware is a public gem that boasts more than 145 solid academic programs, from engineering to education. Though lacking a big-time sports program, UD attracts its share of students who are looking for solid academics and a friendly atmosphere. It all adds up to "the small-school feel with the opportunities of a larger university," as one junior says.

Delaware's 1,000-acre campus has an attractive mix of colonial and modern geometric buildings, set among one of the nation's oldest Dutch elm groves. The hub of the campus is a grassy green mall, flanked by classic Georgian buildings. Mechanical Hall is a climate-controlled art gallery and home to the Paul R. Jones collection. Hotel and restaurant management students benefit from a Courtyard by Marriott right on campus, which doubles as a learning and research facility.

Delaware's academic menu includes more than 145 majors, ranging from the liberal arts and sciences to more professional programs such as apparel design and fashion merchandising. To graduate, students must pass freshman English (critical reading and writing) and earn at least three credits of discovery-based or experiential learning, such as an internship, research, or study abroad; other requirements vary by college. Biological sciences and nursing are the most popular majors, followed by finance, exercise science, and psychology. Other majors include agriculture, human services, marketing, natural resource management, sport management, and landscape design. "The academic climate of the University of Delaware is very competitive," a student reports. "The courses and professors challenge you to do your best, and your peers give you the support and competitive drive to work hard." A senior adds, "I love having the chance to learn from individuals who have worked in their respective fields and can translate their experience into classroom learning."

Engineering, especially chemical engineering, is one of UD's specialties, and the school benefits from the close proximity of DuPont, the chemical giant that has been a major benefactor of the university. "Our engineering department is amazing," says one student, "but those kids hardly ever sleep because it's so demanding."

> "Everyone on campus is so friendly, and that makes going to school here comfortable and makes it feel like home."

Website: www.udel.edu
Location: Small City
Public
Total Enrollment: 18,709
Undergraduates: 15,896
Male/Female: 42/58
SAT Ranges: CR 540–650, M 560–660
ACT Ranges: 24–29
Financial Aid: 82%
Expense: Pub $ $ $
Student Loans: 56%
Average Debt: $ $ $ $
Phi Beta Kappa: Yes
Applicants: 26,225
Accepted: 57%
Enrolled: 26%
Grad in 6 Years: 80%
Returning Freshmen: 92%
Academics: ✍ ✍ ✍
Social: ☎ ☎ ☎ ☎ ☎
Q of L: ★ ★ ★
Admissions: (302) 831-8123
Email Address: admissions@udel.edu

Strongest Programs:
Biological Sciences
Nursing
Finance

The music department is another attraction, with a 350-member marching band and several faculty members holding impressive professional performance credits. UD created the nation's first study abroad program in 1923, and more than 70 study abroad programs are available on all seven continents. Journalism students can take a winter-term trip to Antarctica aboard a Russian icebreaker. Each year, about 600 UD students hold research apprenticeships with faculty members; in fact, the Carnegie Endowment Reinvention Center at SUNY–Stony Brook has called Delaware a "national model" for undergraduate research.

As UD has grown in popularity, academic standards have become more rigorous. Delaware routinely gets the highest number of nonresident applications for state-affiliated U.S. institutions. "In the last few years, Delaware has become more competitive and more expensive," says a senior. "Particularly, the out-of-state tuition has become a topic of dissent." About 500 new students enter the University Honors Program each year, which offers interdisciplinary colloquia, priority seating in "honors" sections of regular courses, along with talented faculty, personal attention, and extracurricular and residence hall programming.

Engineering, especially chemical engineering, is one of UD's specialties, and the school benefits from the close proximity of DuPont.

More than one-third of students at Delaware hail from the First State; many of the rest are from the Northeast. Minority enrollment continues to increase; 5 percent of the student body are African American, 6 percent are Hispanic, and 4 percent are Asian American. International students provide a strong presence on campus, and the majority hail from China. "The students are relatively preppy, very inclusive, and enjoy social events," one sophomore says. Merit scholarships and athletic scholarships are offered. The university also maintains a search program to ensure that deserving Delaware students are aware of the scholarships for which they are eligible. The Commitment to Delawareans initiative began in 2009 and is designed to meet the full need of state residents. Need is calculated based on the annual cost of tuition and fees, on-campus housing, meals, and books.

"The students are relatively preppy, very inclusive, and enjoy social events."

Forty-four percent of students live on campus, including all freshmen—except those commuting from home. After that, dorm housing is guaranteed and awarded by lottery, though many juniors and seniors move into off-campus apartments. "The new residence halls are amazing. The rooms are huge," an international relations major says. Those who stay on campus find a range of accommodations: co-ed and single-sex halls with single and double rooms, as well as suites and apartment-style buildings. Honors students also live together in designated residence halls and special interest housing is also available. Campus dwellers must buy the meal plan: "The food is certainly not mom's home-cooked meal," says a student, "but it is still good." Campus security is comprehensive, according to students. "I definitely feel safe on campus," says a junior.

"Social life is bustling at University of Delaware," says one junior. "There are parties on and off campus for those interested, and also clubs for those interested in those events." Delaware students know how to let loose, though a ban on alcohol at campus parties has really taken things down a notch. "The three-strike policy works fairly well, especially in the freshman dorms," says a student. (First two strikes: fines and meetings. Third strike: suspension.) Fraternities attract 15 percent of the men and sororities 17 percent of the women. Greek groups often throw parties, but there are plenty of other options, from concerts and plays on campus to casual gatherings in friends' rooms or apartments.

Greek groups often throw parties, but there are plenty of other options.

Main Street, the heart of downtown Newark, "practically runs right through campus," one student says. "It's easy walking distance from anywhere, and there are tons of coffee shops, pizza places, restaurants, a movie theater, a bowling alley, bookstores, and shops—anything you could possibly want." For those seeking further excitement, New York, the Washington/Baltimore area, and Philadelphia are all within a two-hour drive. When the weather is warm, the beaches of Rehoboth and Dewey beckon, and in chilly months, the Pennsylvania ski slopes aren't too far. Mallstock is the annual spring bacchanal, bringing music and a carnival to the central campus green.

Delaware's Blue Hens compete in Division I, and on Saturdays in the fall, watch out. "Football is big," says one student. "Now that our football team won the NCAA I-AA championship, it is getting more popular. The cheerleaders are also very good." Tailgate picnics are popular before and after the game. In 2012–13, the women's basketball team won the Colonial Athletic Association title and was undefeated in league play and the volleyball team won its fifth consecutive league title in 2011–12. Delaware's sports center has space for 6,000 to cheer; intramural sports are popular.

"Everyone on campus is so friendly, and that makes going to school here comfortable and makes it feel like home," muses one student. Aspiring engineers and educators, and practically everyone in between, can find something to delve into at the University of Delaware. With a challenging and stimulating academic environment, comfortable size, an increasingly smart student body, a healthy social scene, and up-and-coming athletic teams, UD offers a blend of strengths that would make many schools envious—and leads to many happy Blue Hens.

Overlaps

Boston University, University of Connecticut, James Madison, University of Maryland, Penn State, Rutgers

If You Apply To ➤ **Delaware:** Regular admissions: Jan. 15. Application fee: $75. Campus and alumni interviews: optional, evaluative. SATs or ACTs: required. Subject Tests: recommended. Accepts the Common Application. Essay question.

Denison University

Granville, OH 43023

Not quite as selective as Kenyon, Denison draws more Easterners than competitors such as Wittenberg and Ohio Wesleyan, and it fashions itself as a sort of Midwestern Haverford. Denison has a middle-of-the-road to conservative student body, lots of preppies, and one of the most beautiful campuses anywhere. Increasing selectivity has helped create a more serious student body.

Denison University, tucked into the "quaint, small, and beautiful" hamlet of Granville, draws "driven, competitive, and highly involved" students from diverse backgrounds, says a senior. Thanks to Denison's small size, there's ample opportunity to interact (and do research with) professors and to form close relationships with peers as everyone focuses on the liberal arts. One student advises, "If you are willing to sacrifice some of your time and effort to get involved on campus and take advantage of the opportunities presented you, then Denison will be everything you dreamed it would be."

Denison's campus is set atop rolling hills in central Ohio. Huge maples shade the sloping walkways, which offer a panoramic view of the surrounding valley. And don't be surprised if you're reminded of New York's Central Park—Denison retained park architect Frederick Law Olmsted for its first master plan back in the early 1900s. The Georgian style of many buildings—redbrick with white columns—also evokes shades of New England and its private liberal arts colleges. A

Website: www.denison.edu
Location: Suburban
Private
Total Enrollment: 2,305
Undergraduates: 2,305
Male/Female: 42/58
SAT Ranges: CR 600–720, M 600–680
ACT Ranges: 27–31
Financial Aid: 96%
Expense: Pr $ $ $
Student Loans: 45%
Average Debt: $

$38.5 million construction project has resulted in the renovation and expansion of Mitchell Center, a centerpiece of the college's athletics and recreation facilities. The space includes new classrooms, gathering areas, the Trumbull Aquatics Center, and the Crown Fitness Center.

Denison's general education requirements are comprehensive. Students take two first-year seminars, and then during their four years, two courses each in the fine arts, the sciences (one with lab), the social sciences, the humanities, and a foreign language. Some courses may be double-counted to fulfill oral communication

"If you fall behind in the reading it becomes difficult."

and quantitative reasoning requirements. Students must also complete an "interdivisional requirement" by selecting a course from one of seven interdisciplinary programs, including black studies, East Asian studies, environmental studies, international studies, Latin American and Caribbean studies, queer studies, and women's studies. The Power and Justice requirement seeks to give students the ability to "question their own place in the structures of power and privilege that constitute human societies." Students say the environment is more collaborative than competitive and the key to success is effective time management. "If you fall behind in the reading it becomes difficult, but as long as you do your homework and prepare for class, the coursework is definitely manageable," a senior says.

Students say that some of the best majors are distinctive to Denison. The PPE major is effectively a triple major in philosophy, political science, and economics. "The modern languages department is excellent and offers great opportunities outside the classroom," advises one student. Another says, "Physics is an extremely strong (but underappreciated) department. That department has some of the best

"The modern languages department is excellent."

faculty members on campus, the courses are excellent, and the other students are great." Denison's 350-acre biological reserve is a boon for environmental studies majors. Denison's signature Summer Scholar Program provides scholarships for more than 150 students to stay on campus during the summer and complete 10 weeks of full-time research in collaboration with faculty members. Typically, more than 50 percent of the summer scholars are science students.

Classes are small, and individual attention is the norm. "Professors are highly qualified and always place the emphasis on teaching as opposed to their own research," one English major says. Twenty-seven percent of freshman classes are taught by senior faculty and 66 percent of classes have 19 or fewer students. Students with wanderlust can sign up for internships and off-campus studies through the Great Lakes Colleges Association* and the Associated Colleges of the Midwest*. Those considering a run for office may be interested in the Richard G. Lugar Program in American Politics and Public Service, which includes political science courses on campus and culminates in a House or Senate internship in Washington. (The former senator happens to be a Denison grad.) As a participant in the Denison Internship Program, formerly known as May Term, students select from more than 250 internships around the country.

Thirty percent of Denison's population is homegrown, and 7 percent come from abroad. The Denison stereotype used to be a "preppy, East Coaster with pearls and Ugg boots," says a senior. "But today, Denison is much more diverse." To that end, the Posse Program funds 20 full-tuition scholarships per class for multicultural student leaders from Chicago and Boston public high schools. African Americans now constitute 8 percent of the student body, while Hispanics and Asian Americans combine for another 11 percent. "The environment, social justice, and fair trade are the largest issues on campus. The percentage of liberal students on campus is relatively high despite the somewhat conservative and wealthy backgrounds of many

Students say the environment is more collaborative than competitive and the key to success is effective time management.

students," explains a student. The average non-need-based award is more than $20,000, and there are no athletic scholarships.

Ninety-nine percent of Denison students live on campus; the only ones allowed to live elsewhere are those commuting from home. (One exception is the dozen Homesteaders, who live in three student-built solar-paneled cabins on a farm a mile away, and grow much of their own food.) Options range from singles to apartments with kitchens. "Some dorms are newer and in better condition than others, but Denison does a fairly good job of regularly renovating and maintaining all of the buildings," one student says. Housing is guaranteed for four years, but "the lottery can be painful," says a senior. Entrées in the two dining halls change daily. "They generally don't measure up to a home-cooked meal or restaurant-quality offerings," a student says, but the staff does "make an effort to offer a variety of options and to offer different menu items each day." Safety is considered a given here: "Granville is a *very* safe town," says a senior. "Parents can feel comfortable sending their kids to this school."

"Professors are highly qualified."

"The social life is mainly on campus, with bars in town for students who are 21," says a communication major. "There are often concerts or other activities going on during the weekend, so students who aren't interested in the party scene have plenty to get involved with." The school also runs trips to the local mall and to Meijer, a Midwestern superstore similar to Walmart, and the student government has even been known to hold fireworks shows. Alcohol policies are less punitive and more focused on ensuring safety. "Alcohol consumption is common and frequently high. Thankfully, everything at Denison is within walking distance," says one student. Though the Greek system is nonresidential, 35 percent of the men and 41 percent of the women still join up. Students also look forward to three blowout parties each year—November's D-Day, Culture Jam, and Aestavalia. There's also "Naked Week" in February, which affords the more "freewheeling" students a chance to frolic naked around campus.

Granville (population 3,500) "is a quaint, almost surreal town scattered with colorful flowers, beautiful parks, forested hills, and the friendliest families," says one student. Another adds, "If you held up each month of a Norman Rockwell calendar while looking at the village for the respective months, you might think you were looking at the same thing!" There are four churches on the corners of the town's main intersection, along with "two bars, a coffee shop, a bank, a greasy spoon restaurant, a library, and gift shops," says another student. Most stores and restaurants close by 8 p.m., though students appreciate the feeling of safety and security that results. The Denison

"The environment, social justice, and fair trade are the largest issues on campus."

Campus Association frequently sends students into Granville and nearby Newark to provide tutoring, mentoring, and environmental cleanup. Popular road trips include Ohio University, Ohio State (in the state capital, Columbus), and Miami University in Oxford, Ohio. Pittsburgh, Cleveland, Cincinnati, and Dayton are also close by.

Denison students are enthusiastic supporters of the Big Red, and men's lacrosse games against Ohio Wesleyan always draw large crowds. The university finished in first place in the North Coast Athletic Conference (NCAC) Dennis M. Collins All-Sports Award in 2010–11; the award is based on each institution's conference finish in the NCAC's 23 championship sports. Denison captured championships in women's basketball, men's lacrosse, women's lacrosse, softball, men's swimming and diving, women's swimming and diving, and women's tennis. Enthusiasm reaches a fever pitch during homecoming weekend, when the all-campus gala always includes a chocolate volcano. Intramurals and club sports remain popular too, drawing upwards of 80 percent of students to a variety of pursuits, including dodgeball, floor hockey, flag football, basketball, golf, volleyball, indoor soccer, tennis, sand volleyball, and softball.

Denison University aims to graduate independent thinkers who become active citizens of a democratic society. "Denison is a fun and interactive place to get an education," says one senior. The school continues to value tradition—woe to the student who steps on the school seal in front of the chapel, for doing so will cause him to fail all his finals—while growing and evolving to emphasize academics and the life of the mind. Throw in a vibrant social scene and you've found a recipe for a dynamic college experience. A recent graduate says, "Denison is distinctive for its commitment to preparing its students to be lifelong learners. The liberal arts tradition at Denison teaches students how to become analytical and critical thinkers— something valued in nearly any field of work."

If You Apply To ➤

Denison: Early decision: Nov. 15. Regular admissions: Jan. 15. Financial aid: Feb. 15. Application fee: $40 (paper), free (online). Campus and alumni interviews: recommended, evaluative. SATs or ACTs: optional. No Subject Tests. Accepts the Common Application. Essay question.

University of Denver

2199 South University Boulevard, Mary Reed Building, Denver, CO 80208

The only major midsized private university between Tulsa and the West Coast, DU's campus in residential Denver is pleasant but uninspiring. Brochures instead tout Rocky Mountain landscapes. DU remains a haven for ski bums and business majors. Has gotten more selective in recent years.

The oldest private university in the Rocky Mountain region, the University of Denver is where former secretary of state Condoleezza Rice earned her B.A. in political science at age 19 and later returned for a Ph.D. in international studies. Her mentor was Soviet specialist Joseph Korbel, father of former secretary of state Madeline Albright. Thus, it's not surprising that DU boasts strong programs in political science, international studies, and public affairs. However, many students opt for DU's business program, and the campus location offers ample opportunities for networking, skiing, and taking in the beautiful Colorado landscape. "Academics are high, social life is awesome, friendships are easily formed, and it's four years of unforgettable memories," a junior says.

DU's 125-acre main campus is located in a comfortable residential neighborhood only eight miles from downtown Denver and an hour east of major ski areas. The north campus is home to several programs, including the Women's College, and approximately $500 million has been invested in 11 new buildings and more than a dozen renovation projects in recent years. Architectural styles vary, and include collegiate Gothic, brick, limestone, Colorado sandstone, and copper. Nearby Mount Evans (14,264 feet) is home to the world's loftiest observatory, a DU facility available to both professors and students. Ruffatto Hall was made possible by a $10 million gift and is home to the Morgridge College of Education (MCE), the Learning Effectiveness Program, and the Disability Services Program at the University of Denver. Recent campus projects include a $32 million library renovation.

> **"Academics are high, social life is awesome, friendships are easily formed."**

Website: www.du.edu
Location: City Outskirts
Private
Total Enrollment: 8,289
Undergraduates: 4,957
Male/Female: 44/56
SAT Ranges: CR 550–640, M 569–660
ACT Ranges: 25–30
Financial Aid: 85%
Expense: Pr $ $
Student Loans: 43%
Average Debt: $ $ $ $
Phi Beta Kappa: Yes
Applicants: 11,448
Accepted: 68%
Enrolled: 16%
Grad in 6 Years: 76%
Returning Freshmen: 86%
Academics: ✍ ✍ ✍
Social: 🐘 🐘 🐘 🐘
Q of L: ★ ★ ★ ★

DU is known for its business school—especially the hotel, restaurant, and tourism management offerings. Preprofessional programs are feeders for graduate schools in business, international studies, engineering, and the arts. Chemistry, atmospheric physics, music, psychology, and computer science have solid reputations. Undergrads can opt for a five-year program toward a master's degree in business, international studies, or law. Students report that the academic climate can be demanding but is mostly relaxed. "While many of the courses are challenging, professors and students are willing to work collaboratively to ensure that everyone succeeds," says a senior. Professors receive high marks for their intelligence and passion. "Most of the professors at DU have had practical experience in their field so they understand how to bridge the gap between theory and practice and makes for a much more interesting and fulfilling class," a student says.

> "Most of the professors at DU have had practical experience in their field."

(continued)

Admissions: (303) 871-2036
Email Address: admission@ du.edu

Strongest Programs:
Biological Sciences
Business
Psychology
History
English
Political Science
Public Affairs
International Studies

Under the general education requirements, undergraduate students choose from a series of courses from the Common Curriculum that emphasize writing and rhetoric, language, analytical inquiry, and scientific inquiry. These courses are supplemented by a first-year seminar and an advanced seminar, which serve as capstones to the curriculum model. A freshman orientation program brings new students onto campus a week early, during which they spend 10 hours with a small group of students and a professor discussing a collection of essays by prominent writers. Freshmen also take a four-credit, first-year seminar limited to 15 students. "I really appreciated the orientation program and the first-year program," says a junior. The honors program draws more than 400 students; in the past six years, the university has produced Rhodes, Marshall, Goldwater, Truman, and Fulbright scholars.

University rules stipulate that all core courses must be taught by senior faculty. "At first I thought, 'Who wants to take these science, art, and English classes?'" explains a business major. "But now that I've completed the core, I feel better about myself and my world knowledge. Now I can speak of Goya, Berlioz, and define my favorite artists with a knowledge of the period, styles, and works." All juniors and seniors have the chance to study abroad at no extra cost and students say the programs are an integral part of the DU experience. "As a junior, the question isn't 'Are you going abroad?'" says one student. "It's '*Where* are you going abroad?'" Dual-degree programs are available for students who want to accelerate their graduate studies by up to one year.

DU is known for its business school—especially the hotel, restaurant, and tourism management offerings.

"The students at DU are passionate, adventurous, intelligent, driven, motivated leaders. Although there are a few students who are a bit pretentious and privileged, the majority are down to earth," says one sophomore. Forty-one percent of the students are from Colorado, and 78 percent graduated in the top quarter of their high school class. African Americans account for 5 percent of the student body, Asian Americans contribute 4 percent, and Hispanics comprise 8 percent. Because it is one of the few private colleges in the West, DU is also among the most expensive in the region. In a nod to the diminishing importance of standardized test scores and GPAs, the university now conducts personal interviews of every candidate for undergraduate admissions, either in person or by phone. There are hundreds of merit scholarships averaging more than $13,700 and nearly 200 athletic scholarships.

Dual-degree programs are available for students who want to accelerate their graduate studies by up to one year.

Students are required to spend their first two years on campus in the residence halls. "No matter what dorm you live in you will love your experience and the people surrounding you," insists a sophomore. The Johnson-McFarlane hall ("J-Mac") is supposed to be the best place for freshmen, though another student says that the Towers are a much quieter on-campus option. "The only issue is that the housing selection system for sophomore students can be an absolute drag," grumbles one student. "It used to be a lottery-based system, but now it's a first-come, first-served system for which people spend hours in line." Greeks can live and dine together in their houses. Most juniors and seniors opt for the decent quarters found within walking distance of campus. The campus dining options receive mixed reviews: "The food is fine, but after eating it every day for two years it gets pretty old," says one student. Students also report feeling safe on campus thanks to a highly visible security patrol.

With consistently beautiful, sunny weather and great skiing, hiking, and camping less than an hour away in the Rockies, many DU students head for the hills on weekends. "During the winter weekends, the campus is empty because everyone is skiing," a senior says. Besides various ski areas, one can explore Estes Park, Mount Evans, and Echo Lake. Additionally, DU is not far from Moab, Albuquerque, and Las Vegas. Since Denver is not primarily a college town, many students with cars head for Boulder (home of the University of Colorado), about 30 miles away. For those staying home, the transit system makes it easy to get to downtown Denver. "The city of Denver is fantastic!" cheers one sophomore. "It is safe, fun, and accessible." The options there are tremendous and include great local restaurants, bars, and stores, many of which cater to students. Twenty-five percent of the men and women belong to a fraternity or sorority, and Greeks tend to dominate the social life. Drinking policies abound, and the university "tries to make sure that students are making responsible decisions about drinking," says a senior.

> "Students are passionate, adventurous, intelligent, driven, motivated leaders."

The students unite when the DU hockey team, a national powerhouse, skates out onto the ice, especially against archrival Colorado College. The Pioneers ski team brought home national titles in recent years, while women's golf brought home Sun Belt Conference titles. Other competitive programs include men's and women's lacrosse, women's soccer, and men's golf. Intramural and club sports are varied and popular; approximately 85 percent of students take part. Each January, academics are put aside for the three-day Winter Carnival. Top administrators, professors, and students all pack off to Steamboat Springs, Crested Butte, or another ski area to catch some fresh powder and see who can ski the fastest, skate the best, or build the most artistic ice sculptures. "The biggest DU traditions are Winter Carnival, the hockey season ticket campout, and the hockey games against our rivals, Colorado College," says one student.

Students like the University of Denver for its modest size and friendly atmosphere. And while there remain some moneyed students with attitude problems, plenty of others are more down to earth. As the school pushes for a more ethnically diverse student body and improves its curriculum and facilities, the University of Denver is striving to become better known for its intellectual rigor than for its gorgeous setting in the Rocky Mountains. That's a tough challenge!

> *Twenty-five percent of the men and women belong to a fraternity or sorority, and Greeks tend to dominate the social life.*

Overlaps

University of Colorado, Colorado State, Santa Clara University, Colorado College, Stanford, University of Oregon, University of San Diego, University of Vermont

---

If You Apply To ➤ | **DU:** Early action: Nov. 1. Regular admissions: Jan. 15. Housing: May 1. Application fee: $60. No campus or alumni interviews. SATs or ACTs: required. Subject Tests: optional. Accepts the Common Application. Essay question: Common Application.

DePaul University

Chicago, IL 60604

Few universities have come so far, so fast. DePaul gets the nod over Loyola as the best Roman Catholic university in Chicago. DePaul's Lincoln Park setting is like a Midwestern version of New York's Greenwich Village or Upper West Side. About half of the student body is Catholic. Especially strong in business, film, and the performing arts.

There is no refuting that DePaul is the largest Roman Catholic university in the nation, and students claim its diversity and liberal leanings set it apart from rival institutions. Based in the heart of the city, DePaul is a feeder to Chicago's business community. A spate of campus construction has transformed it from the "little school under the tracks" to Chicago's version of NYU.

DePaul has two residential campuses. The Lincoln Park campus, with its state-of-the-art library and new student center, is home to the College of Liberal Arts and Sciences, the College of Education, the Theatre School, and the School of Music, as well as residence halls and academic and recreational facilities. Lincoln Park itself is a fashionable Chicago neighborhood with century-old brownstone homes, theaters, cafés, parks, and shops. The Loop, or "vertical" campus, 20 minutes away by elevated train in downtown Chicago, houses the College of Law, the School for New Learning, the Driehaus College of Business, the College of Communication, and the College of Computing and Digital Media. The DePaul Center, a $70 million teaching, learning, and research complex, is the cornerstone of this campus. The Arts & Letters Hall opened recently and houses 47 classrooms and the departments of English and History of Art & Architecture.

DePaul's name is closely associated with Midwestern business and law, and undergraduates can find internships with local legal and commercial institutions. The School of Accountancy and MIS draws many majors and is reported to be the most challenging department in the College of Commerce. The College of Communication offers majors in journalism, public relations and advertising, communication and media, and others. The College of Science and Health encompasses programs in biology, chemistry, physics, nursing, psychology, environmental science, math, and statistics. The college also includes the health sciences program, which prepares students for a variety of health care professions by "combining biomedical instruction and preparation for medical practice with an understanding of how societal factors impact health." DePaul's academic climate is demanding but not overwhelming. "The courseload is rigorous at times, but if a student is dedicated to their studies, it is nothing that can't be handled," says a senior.

"The courseload is rigorous at times."

Classes are small and professors teach at all levels. The administration appoints student representatives from each school and college to faculty promotion and tenure committees. "DePaul professors are respectful, intelligent, and don't put up with nonsense," says one senior. All freshmen take a course called Discover Chicago or its alternative, Explore Chicago. "This class is one of the best things about DePaul. It's really fun and valuable," says a senior. Other common core courses include composition and rhetoric as well as quantitative reasoning for freshmen, a sophomore seminar on multiculturalism in the United States, and a junior-year program in experiential learning. Students also complete a series of "learning domains," consisting of arts and literature, philosophical inquiry, religious dimensions, scientific inquiry, social science, and history. To earn a B.A., students must take three foreign language courses. The highly selective honors program includes interdisciplinary courses, a modern language requirement, and a senior thesis. Fifteen percent of students participate in study abroad programs that take them to more than 40 locations around the world, including Paris, Nairobi, Istanbul, and Buenos Aires.

DePaul's president is a priest, and clerics teach some courses and celebrate (voluntary) mass every day. In addition, the University Ministry hosts other religious services and leads programs to teach students about other faiths. Eighty-two percent of DePaul students hail from Illinois. Hispanics represent 17 percent of the student body, African Americans 8 percent, and Asian Americans 8 percent. DePaul hopes to boost those figures by reaching out to disadvantaged inner-city students with high academic potential. "The students at DePaul are very diverse," says a sophomore.

Website: www.depaul.edu
Location: City Center
Private
Total Enrollment: 18,895
Undergraduates: 13,627
Male/Female: 46/54
SAT Ranges: CR 530–640,
    M 510–630
ACT Ranges: 23–28
Financial Aid: 70%
Expense: Pr $
Student Loans: 63%
Average Debt: $ $ $
Phi Beta Kappa: Yes
Applicants: 18,160
Accepted: 62%
Enrolled: 23%
Grad in 6 Years: 68%
Returning Freshmen: 85%
Academics: ✏️ ✏️ ✏️
Social: ☎ ☎
Q of L: ★ ★ ★
Admissions: (312) 362-8300
Email Address: admission@
    depaul.edu

Strongest Programs:
Psychology
Accounting
Finance
Public Relations and
    Advertising
Marketing
Hospitality and Leadership

The administration appoints student representatives from each school and college to faculty promotion and tenure committees.

"There are student organizations to represent all different faiths, ethnicities, and backgrounds." DePaul has a reputation for being liberal, and "it has become more liberal in recent years," says a junior. In addition to merit scholarships, DePaul also awards scholarships to students who have artistic talent or strong leadership skills or those who participate in community service.

One student complains, "Weekends can be boring because many students go home." Traditionally, DePaul has been a commuter school, but 17 percent of students live in university housing. Students find the dorms comfortable and well maintained, but they advise applying early to secure a bed, especially after sophomore year. "Housing is in high demand around here,"

> "There are student organizations to represent all different faiths, ethnicities, and backgrounds."

says a junior. The Lincoln Park campus includes eight modern co-ed dorms, several townhouses, and apartments. At the Loop campus, a 1,700-student residence hall includes a rooftop garden, fitness center, and music, art, and study rooms. Although students like campus housing, some find the food overpriced and limited. "I'm a vegan, and there is not a large or good variety," says a junior. While Chicago may have a high-crime reputation, students say campus security is visible, with officers patrolling in cars and on foot, emergency blue lights on campus, and dorms requiring students to swipe ID cards at two or three places before allowing entrance.

DePaul's president is a priest, and clerics teach some courses and celebrate (voluntary) mass every day.

Fraternities and sororities draw just 3 percent of DePaul men and 9 percent of women, respectively. Not surprisingly, with the school's proximity to Chicago's clubs (especially on Rush Street), sporting events, and bars, most social life occurs off campus. In the warmer months, the beaches of Lake Michigan beckon downtown students, while the huge annual outdoor Fest concert attracts large crowds from both campuses. "Chicago is the ultimate college town," says a music major. "There is everything to do here." On campus, the alcohol policy forbids beer for underage students, but students say that enforcement doesn't always work.

DePaul is a member of the Big East Conference, and the Blue Demons compete in NCAA Division I in 13 sports. Men's basketball is the headline story, beginning with the Midnight Madness of each fall's first practice in October. The game against Notre Dame always draws a capacity crowd, though Loyola is DePaul's oldest rival. The men's and women's soccer teams, men's and

> "Weekends can be boring because many students go home."

women's track and field teams, and women's tennis and basketball are competitive, too. Intramurals and club sports are big draws and the Campus Recreation department offers a 123,000-square-foot fitness and recreation facility, which includes a four-court gymnasium, 25-yard pool, three racquetball courts, 200-meter track, five exercise studios, and more than 100 pieces of cardio and selectorized equipment.

DePaul's student body has become more diverse while increasing in size, an admirable achievement. The administration credits the school's "increased academic reputation" for growth, but students say DePaul's popularity is due as much to the special bonds they feel with fellow Blue Demons. "DePaul University provides students a unique atmosphere in which to learn and grow," says a sophomore. "The campus and its students are friendly, open, and always inviting."

Overlaps

University of Illinois, Loyola University, Columbia College, Illinois State, Northwestern, Northern Illinois, Marquette

If You Apply To ➤   **DePaul:** Early action: Nov. 15. Regular admissions: Feb. 1. Financial aid: Mar. 1. Application fee: $40 (paper), $25 (online). Campus interviews: optional, informational. No alumni interviews. SATs or ACTs: optional. Subject Tests: optional. Essay question.

DePauw University

315 South Locust Street, P.O. Box 37, Greencastle, IN 46135

DePauw is a solid Midwestern liberal arts institution in the mold of Denison, Dickinson, Illinois Wesleyan, and Ohio Wesleyan. Its Greek system is among the strongest in the nation and full of students destined for Indiana's business and governmental elite. DePauw's center for management and entrepreneurship is a major draw for career-oriented students.

DePauw University offers a liberal arts education with an orientation toward experiential learning. Art history, creative writing, and music are solid, as are (more surprisingly) computer science and economics. Indeed, students here are career-oriented and happy to take advantage of the rigorous classwork and ample real world experiences. And with an undergraduate population of nearly 2,300 students, close ties to classmates and faculty are a given.

Founded in 1837 and named after the first American bishop of the Methodist Church, DePauw is set amid the gently rolling hills of west-central Indiana. The lush green campus has a mix of older buildings and more modern redbrick structures, centered on a well-kept park with fountains and a reflecting pool. Notable facilities include the William Weston Clarke Emison Museum of Art, the Janet Prindle Institute for Ethics, and a $29 million center for performing arts.

> "The classroom environment is highly collaborative."

DePauw's first-year program helps students transition into college by combining academically challenging coursework with cocurricular activities and programs. When they arrive, students are assigned to mentor-groups with 10 to 12 peers, plus an upperclassman advisor and a faculty member who will teach their first-year seminar and serve as their academic advisor. By graduation, students must demonstrate competence in writing, quantitative reasoning, and oral communication. And they must fulfill distribution requirements in natural science and math, social and behavioral sciences, literature and the arts, historical and philosophical understanding, foreign language, and self-expression through performance and participation.

Academically, the DePauw student body is as career-oriented as they come. Aspiring business leaders benefit from courses, speakers, and internships offered through the McDermond Center for Management and Entrepreneurship. Future reporters, editors, anchors, and producers will find a home in the Pulliam Center for Contemporary Media, which supplements DePauw's strong student-run newspaper, TV station, and radio stations. And DePauw's School of Music is also worth a mention, offering all students the chance to take lessons, join ensembles, and perform, in genres from orchestra to jazz to opera. For exceptionally motivated students, five programs of distinction offer the chance to focus on an area of interest, such as media, management, scientific research, or information technology. The latter program includes real-world work experience, both in IT departments at DePauw and with off-campus employers. The curriculum also includes majors in theater and film studies, and a five-year dual-degree program in music performance/liberal arts.

The DePauw curriculum includes a January term, during which first-year students remain on campus for a focused, interdisciplinary course, while upperclassmen pursue independent study or off-campus study or service in the United States or abroad. Approximately 60 percent of DePauw students spend a semester off campus, and when the January term is included, that fraction rises to more than 80

Website: www.depauw.edu
Location: Small Town
Private
Total Enrollment: 2,292
Undergraduates: 2,292
Male/Female: 45/55
SAT Ranges: CR 530–650, M 550–680
ACT Ranges: 24–30
Financial Aid: 53%
Expense: Pr $ $
Student Loans: 54%
Average Debt: $ $ $
Phi Beta Kappa: Yes
Applicants: 4,835
Accepted: 63%
Enrolled: 19%
Grad in 6 Years: 78%
Returning Freshmen: 89%
Academics: ✐ ✐ ✐ ½
Social: ☎ ☎ ☎
Q of L: ★ ★
Admissions: (765) 658-4006
Email Address: admission@depauw.edu

Strongest Programs:
Chemistry and Biochemistry
Biology
Political Science
Computer Science
Economics
Theater
English and Creative Writing
Communication

percent. The school offers its own programs as well as those arranged by the Great Lakes Colleges Association*. Students say that the classes are rigorous but well supported. "The classroom environment is highly collaborative and encouraging," says one sophomore, "and in many courses the students and professors engage in class discussions that more closely model academic conversations than traditional lectures." Another student adds, "I have been lucky to have professors that care about my education."

One student describes her peers at DePauw as "intellectually curious, philanthropically minded, and socially active." The minority presence has grown, thanks in part to recruitment of Posse Foundation students from New York and Chicago. African Americans now account for 6 percent of the student body, with Hispanics adding 4 percent, and Asian Americans 3 percent. Merit scholarships are available, although there are no athletic scholarships. Three-quarters of DePauw students volunteer with area churches and social service agencies, which can also help them qualify for scholarships.

Virtually all DePauw students live in university housing, which is guaranteed for four years. Overcrowding is a thing of the past, since the school has opened more than a dozen new duplexes and renovated another 46 apartments in recent years. The homey buildings have computer labs, common areas, and TV lounges; students recommend Humbert Hall for freshmen because of its hotel-like atmosphere. A whopping 76 percent of DePauw's men and 65 percent of the women go Greek. That's not surprising: The first modern-day sorority, Kappa Alpha Theta, began here in 1870, and the university is home to the longest continually running fraternity anywhere.

> **"Students love being at DePauw on the weekends."**

"Students love being at DePauw on the weekends," says a student. Perhaps because of the prevalence of Greeks on campus, and spurred by the disciplining of a sorority accused of purging its overweight members, these groups have worked hard to change the stereotypes of fraternities and sororities. They've devised a risk-management policy and instituted a community council to review conduct violations. In addition, rush is delayed until second semester so freshmen can first get their feet on the ground academically. Fraternities still maintain the old custom of having "house moms." Still, students say it's easy for underage drinkers to imbibe, especially at fraternity parties. Off campus, however, fake IDs "get confiscated quicker than you can take them out," one student warns.

The town of Greencastle has a movie theater, a bowling alley, and several pizza places, but it "lacks an atmosphere," says a recent grad. "It is fine for sustaining day-to-day living, but doesn't offer many alternatives to the university." In good weather, several state parks offer hiking trails and a lake for the sailing club; Indianapolis is only a 45-minute drive, and St. Louis, Chicago, and Cincinnati make for good road trips. Another cherished tradition is a takeoff on Indiana University's famed Little 500 bike race, itself a takeoff on the Indianapolis 500 auto race—teams of cyclists compete on a course that circles the heart of the DePauw campus.

Aside from Greek parties, social life at DePauw revolves around varsity athletics, especially the annual football game against Wabash College, derisively dubbed the "Wallies." The Wabash–DePauw rivalry is the oldest west of the Alleghenies, and the winner of each year's contest gets the much-cherished Monon Bell, hence the popular T-shirt: "Beat the bell out of Wabash." Several Tigers teams have played in Division III championship games, including women's soccer and golf, men's and women's cross-country and tennis, and men's golf. Women's basketball brought home the Division III national championship—the university's first—several years ago. Intramural sports attract some 75 percent of students, and club sports are popular as well.

DePauw's School of Music is also worth a mention, offering all students the chance to take lessons, join ensembles, and perform, in genres from orchestra to jazz to opera.

Aside from Greek parties, social life at DePauw revolves around varsity athletics.

Overlaps
Indiana, Miami (OH), Notre Dame, Vanderbilt, Washington University in St. Louis

For a small school, DePauw offers a multitude of opportunities, balancing strong academics with a healthy dose of school spirit and a wealth of opportunities to lead—whether in one of the abundant extracurricular activities or by blazing a trail through study abroad.

If You Apply To ➤

DePauw: Early decision: Nov. 15. Early action: Dec. 1. Regular admissions: Feb. 1. Application fee: $40 (paper), free (online). Campus interviews: recommended, evaluative. No alumni interviews. SATs or ACTs: required. Subject Tests: optional. Accepts the Common Application. Essay question: Common Application questions.

Dickinson College

P.O. Box 1773, Carlisle, PA 17013

With traditions dating to the time of the American Revolution, Dickinson occupies a historic setting in the foothills of central Pennsylvania. "Engage the World" model signals its emphasis on international studies, foreign languages, and study abroad. Student-run organic farm is core of push for sustainable development. With underrepresented minorities, international students, and hippies more numerous, Dickinson has shed its image as a preppy haven. Competes head to head with nearby Gettysburg.

Dickinson College won its charter just six days after the Treaty of Paris recognized the United States as a sovereign nation in 1783, and this small liberal arts school has been blazing trails ever since. The moving force behind it was Dr. Benjamin Rush, the famous physician and signer of the Declaration of Independence. Rush convinced John Dickinson, the then governor of Pennsylvania, to lend his name to the new school. Today, the college asks students to challenge what is safe and comfortable and to meet the future with a voice that reflects America and engages the world. To that end, its more than 40 study abroad programs in 24 countries draw well over half of the student body. Now, administrators are focused on diversity, global education, and attracting the best and brightest academic talent. Says one senior, "If you're looking for a college with a focus on the world and all it has to offer, Dickinson may be perfect."

Almost all of Dickinson's Georgian buildings are carved from gray limestone from the college's own quarry, which lends a certain architectural consistency. The campus is part of the historic district of Carlisle, an economically prosperous central Pennsylvania county seat nestled in a fertile valley. The third phase of the $62 million Rector Science Complex was completed in late 2013. Phases I and II are complete and provide space for undergraduate science studies and research. The school has made a big push for reliance on solar and wind power, and set a target of 2020 for zero new emissions.

"It's not uncommon to see students staying up studying in the library until closing."

Dickinson is best known for its workshop approach to science education, for its outstanding and comprehensive international education program, and for the depth of its foreign language program with more than a dozen languages offered, including Arabic, Chinese, Japanese, Hebrew, Portuguese, and Italian. A 3–3 program with Penn State's Dickinson School of Law allows students to obtain undergraduate and J.D. degrees in six years. The popular international business and management major includes coursework in economics, history, and financial analysis, as well

Website: www.dickinson.edu
Location: Small Town
Private
Total Enrollment: 2,328
Undergraduates: 2,328
Male/Female: 45/55
SAT Ranges: CR 590–690,
M 600–690
ACT Ranges: 27–30
Financial Aid: 73%
Expense: Pr $ $ $ $
Student Loans: 53%
Average Debt: $ $ $
Phi Beta Kappa: Yes
Applicants: 5,818
Accepted: 40%
Enrolled: 26%
Grad in 6 Years: 85%
Returning Freshmen: 91%
Academics: ✑ ✑ ✑ ✑
Social: ☎ ☎ ☎
Q of L: ★ ★ ★
Admissions: (717) 245-1231
Email Address: admit@
dickinson.edu

Strongest Programs:
English

*Dickinson is best
known for its
workshop approach
to science education.*

as internships and overseas education. Dickinson offers innovative interdisciplinary academic programs; science programs range from biochemistry and molecular biology to neuroscience to workshop physics, and majors participate in firsthand research and work in state-of-the-art labs alongside renowned professors. Certificate programs in security studies and health studies bring together insights and perspectives from a wide range of disciplines and are centered on emerging issues of immediate contemporary significance. Students can affect global change in social justice and cultural understanding through women's and gender studies, and they gain a hands-on understanding of human culture and behavior by studying archaeology in an on-campus simulation lab and through off-campus fieldwork in locations such as Mycenae, Greece. They bring their work to life by staging plays and productions at Dickinson's own Mathers Theatre or curating an art exhibition at The Trout Gallery.

Regardless of major, about half of all students complete internships, where they may learn about stock trading at a brokerage firm, assist a judge in a common pleas court, or work with the editorial staff of a magazine. The required First Year Seminar Program introduces new students to college-level study and reflection, with interdisciplinary courses such as The Idea of Freedom, and Knowing America through Baseball. To help students understand how the liberal arts fit into the broader world, Dickinson requires distribution courses in the arts and humanities, social sciences, and laboratory sciences; writing; and quantitative reasoning; and physical education. Required cross-cultural studies courses include comparative civilizations, United States diversity, and a foreign language.

"It's a special type of person who comes to Dickinson."

Academics are demanding, but not cut-throat. "It's not uncommon to see students staying up studying in the library until closing, though this is mostly because students are very involved in campus life and activities during the afternoon and evenings and use the late night to catch up on work," says one sociology major. Seventy-three percent of classes have 19 or fewer students, allowing freshmen easy access to their professors. A junior says, "I am taught by incredibly talented teachers who lead interesting lives, publish highly respected scholarship, and are willing advise and work with me on questions I have about course material or aid me in pursuing my own interests outside of a course." For those students wishing to get away, Dickinson sponsors more than 40 study abroad programs in 24 countries; 56 percent of students participate. A student says, "Dickinson took us to Sydney and Byron Bay, and even paid for field trips for one class. I spent a week on the Great Barrier Reef snorkeling and conducting real research—pretty cool for a non-science major!"

"It's a special type of person who comes to Dickinson," says one junior: "It's someone who really wants to learn and better themselves so they can better the world." Twenty percent of the student body hails from the Keystone State, and 75 percent come from the Virginia-Maine corridor. African Americans account for 3 percent of the student population, Asian Americans and Hispanics combine for another 8 percent, and international students comprise 7 percent. Dickinson has been enrolling a growing number of minority and international students, especially through partnerships with New York's Posse Foundation and the Philadelphia Futures Foundation, and with schools and foundations abroad. Perennial hot topics include sustainability, foreign affairs, and social justice. Dickinson awards three types of merit scholarships worth an average of $16,885; the school does not offer athletic scholarships.

"Students tend to socialize on campus."

Given that only seniors are allowed to live off campus and Dickinson guarantees four years of housing, 95 percent of students remain in the dorms. The residences are "normal college housing," says a freshman. "Freshman dorms have small rooms but they can be made quite comfortable." The college offers a wide variety of housing, ranging from traditional residence halls to small houses and apartments, all of which are coeducational. The college transformed an abandoned factory into a combination of art studios and loft-style apartments, with 118 beds for juniors and seniors, and also recently renovated Morgan Hall, the largest dorm on campus. All Greek houses are owned and maintained by the college, and special interest housing includes communal living opportunities based on French and Spanish language immersion, volunteerism, cultural diversity, and the environment. The 50-acre Dickinson College Farm, mostly student run, supplies vittles to the dining halls and a local food bank and serves as a classroom and work-study opportunity for students interested in sustainable development. Campus dining options are diverse, students report, and most of the fare is tasty and healthy. "They make an effort to give a lot of options," says one student.

Most social life at Dickinson occurs on campus and "there is something for every taste," says a senior. Another student adds, "Students tend to socialize on campus. There are dances and late-night events sponsored by the college every weekend, and between improv shows, open-mic nights, and settling down for a 2 a.m. pizza run at the Quarry, there is a lot to do!" Fraternities and sororities attract 11 percent of the men and 29 percent of the women, respectively, and they throw open parties. At the aforementioned Quarry, a former frat house, you can grab a cup of coffee, play some video games, or show your moves on the dance floor. When it comes to booze, Dickinson follows Pennsylvania state law, so you must be 21 to drink; monitors check IDs at parties. Kegs aren't permitted in any college housing, and four underage drinking incidents will get you suspended. "The policy works relatively well," a student says, "but sometimes students feel like campus security is a bit overbearing." There's a big concert each semester and Hub-All-Night includes "music, food, and lots of free stuff," says a political science and economics major. Each fall brings an arts festival, and a spring carnival gives students one last blast before finals.

"Today, Dickinson is a great school."

Carlisle is 20 miles from the Pennsylvania state capital of Harrisburg, and has plenty of "cool little shops that you wouldn't find in big cities," says a student. "It's a fun place to be," adds a senior. For those seeking more of a college town vibe, Amy's Thai and Pomfret Street Books are good bets. Big Brothers Big Sisters programs, the Alpha Phi Omega community service fraternity, and programs like Adopt-a-Grandparent help bring the school and community together. In the spring and early fall, Maryland and Delaware beaches beckon; they're just a two- to three-hour drive. Come winter, good skiing is a half hour away. Nature lovers will enjoy hiking the nearby Appalachian Trail. For those craving urban stimulation, the best road trips are to Philadelphia, New York, and Washington, D.C. All are accessible by bus or train—a good thing, since first-years can't have cars.

Dickinson students get riled up for any match against top rival Franklin and Marshall; the schools battle it out each year for the Conestoga Wagon trophy. The Red Devils also square off with Gettysburg College each year for the Little Brown Bucket. Football, women's basketball, cross-country, soccer, and indoor and outdoor track and field squads have won Centennial Conference championships in the past few years. About three-quarters of the men and half the women take part in intramurals, where dodgeball, basketball, floor hockey, and soccer are most popular. The soccer, softball, baseball, and varsity football fields sit within a 30-acre park, and they're lighted for night games. There is an outdoor track, jogging trails, and an indoor rock-climbing wall. Students may also organize club teams to compete with other schools in sports like ice hockey or ultimate Frisbee, where Dickinson doesn't field varsity squads.

Although Dickinson was founded more than two centuries ago, some things remain the same. Seniors still share a champagne toast before graduation. And the steps of Old West, the first college building, are still used only twice a year—in the fall,

Overlaps

Gettysburg, Franklin and Marshall, University of Richmond, Middlebury, College of William & Mary, American, Lafayette, Colgate

at the convocation ceremony that welcomes new students, and in the spring, for commencement. Dickinson continues to honor Rush's global vision, with its wealth of study abroad options and its demand that students cross the traditional borders of academic disciplines to grasp the interrelated nature of knowledge. "Five years ago, Dickinson was a good school," says one senior. "Today, Dickinson is a great school."

<table>
<tr><td rowspan="3">If You Apply To ➤</td><td>Dickinson: Early decision: Nov. 15. Early action: Dec. 1. Regular admissions and financial aid: Feb. 1. Application fee: $65. Campus interviews: recommended, informational. Alumni interviews: optional, informational. SATs or ACTs: optional. Subject Tests: recommended. Accepts the Common Application. Essay question.</td></tr>
</table>

Drew University

Madison, NJ 07940-4063

From Drew's wooded perch in suburban Jersey, Manhattan is only a 30-minute train ride away. That means Wall Street and the UN are both frequent destinations for Drew interns. Drew is New Jersey's only prominent liberal arts college and one of the few in the greater New York City area. About 60 percent of the students are from Jersey, and Drew is still struggling to find a national identity.

Website: www.drew.edu
Location: Small Town
Private
Total Enrollment: 1,912
Undergraduates: 1,562
Male/Female: 40/60
SAT Ranges: CR 490–620, M 480–600
ACT Ranges: 21–28
Financial Aid: 94%
Expense: Pr $ $ $
Student Loans: 66%
Average Debt: $ $
Phi Beta Kappa: Yes
Applicants: 3,872
Accepted: 85%
Enrolled: 11%
Grad in 6 Years: 69%
Returning Freshmen: 75%
Academics: ✍ ✍ ✍
Social: ☎ ☎ ☎
Q of L: ★ ★ ★
Admissions: (973) 408-3739
Email Address: cadm@drew.edu

Strongest Programs:
Political Science

Founded more than a century ago as a Methodist university, Drew University has grown into a place where an emphasis on hands-on learning, research, independent studies, and internships is just as important as performance in the classroom. The university sends its students abroad for month-long educational ventures, promotes internships on Wall Street, and encourages theater and the arts to thrive. "Come to Drew if you want individual attention and want to be treated as a name rather than a number," says a senior.

"Our English and theater departments are amazing."

The school occupies 186 acres of peaceful woodland in the upscale New York City suburb of Madison and is known as "The University in the Forest." Fifty-six campus buildings peek through splendid oak trees and boast classic and contemporary styles, a physical reflection of Drew's respect for both scholarly traditions and progressive education. The Ehinger Center is the heart of student life outside of the classroom. The building features expansive windows, fireplaces, a two-story rotunda, and a dining hall with a barrel-vaulted ceiling. It is home to the 1867 Lounge, Crawford Hall, The Space, and the C'80 Pub.

Political science is Drew's strongest undergraduate department, and future politicos can take advantage of off-campus opportunities in Washington, D.C. and London and at the United Nations in New York City. Other popular majors include economics, psychology, English, and sociology. The Dana Research Institute for Scientists Emeriti offers opportunities for students to do research with distinguished retired industrial scientists and recently won the lofty Merck Innovation Award for Undergraduate Science Education for fresh thinking and imaginative use of resources. Even more impressive is a program whereby students can earn a B.A. and M.D. from Drew and the University of Medicine and Dentistry of New Jersey/New Jersey Medical School in seven years. Future financiers can follow in the footsteps of the school's founder Daniel Drew, a financier and railroad tycoon, and take advantage of the Wall Street Semester, an on-site study of the national and international finance communities.

Drew's general education requirements include coursework in six areas: depth of study (courses within the student's chosen major); breadth of knowledge; proficiencies (writing, quantitative literacy, foreign language, and information literacy); local and global citizenship; an off-campus experience; and a first-year experience (College Seminar, first-year writing, and Common Hour courses). The university's commitment to liberal arts education includes the lofty goal of universal computer literacy. The Baldwin Honors program includes master classes with elite speakers, special trips, and exclusive activities. Drew's Center for Civic Engagement supports teaching, research, scholarship, art, and other university-based activities that benefit communities.

(continued)

Psychology
Economics
English
Biology
Sociology

The theater arts department works closely with the Playwrights Theater of New Jersey to produce plays that are written, directed, and designed by students. "Our English and theater departments are amazing," a senior raves. "There are tons of resources and the professors are great." Drew has long been a proponent of study abroad programs, including the Drew International Seminar program, where students study another culture in-depth on campus, then spend three to four weeks in that country. "These seminars are a great way of learning firsthand about a country and experiencing a once-in-a-lifetime chance to put your education into practice," says one student.

"Drew's academic climate is not overtly competitive."

"Drew's academic climate is not overtly competitive, but it doesn't have a completely carefree feeling either," says a sophomore. "Creativity is what's prized; being outspoken, worldly, artistic, or 'coffee' intellectualism are the more desired traits." Maintaining a rigorous study schedule is key, according to many upperclassmen. A cast of highly praised, interactive faculty who generate enthusiasm and ambition fuels the industrious grind of hard work. "They are accessible, friendly, and extraordinarily knowledgeable," a student observes.

A cast of highly praised, interactive faculty who generate enthusiasm and ambition fuels the industrious grind of hard work.

"People at Drew are friendly, funny, and down to earth," says one senior. Sixty-four percent of students are from New Jersey and most attended public high schools. The school continues to work on increasing its racial diversity—5 percent are Asian American, 10 percent are African American, and Hispanics comprise 14 percent. And the differences extend past heritage: "My favorite thing about Drew is that although people are politically and socially active, they are more interested in listening to what others have to say than in projecting their own opinions," says a senior. Merit awards average $11,778, although there are no athletic scholarships available.

Seventy-eight percent of the students live in university housing, which includes both single-sex and co-ed dorms, and theme houses. "The dorms are reasonably equipped; they are not luxury homes, but they are certainly updated and provide sufficient space," says a sophomore. Several housing options are available to upperclassmen, from dorm rooms of all sizes to suites and townhouses. A lottery gives housing preference to seniors and juniors, and most freshmen reside in dorms situated at the back of campus. "Room picks can be a grueling affair, but you only have to go through it once a year," says a senior. Drew's dining options receive modest reviews and are described by a junior as "generally edible" and "fairly diverse."

"Parties are a popular option."

There is no Greek system, and social life mostly takes place on campus. "Parties are a popular option, but for those who aren't interested, there's a healthy array of cultural and intellectual things to do," advises one student. "You just need to actively seek out the fun—sitting around in your dorm room won't do you any good!" Officially, nobody under 21 is allowed to drink, but alcohol is said to be easy to come by. There is a 21-and-over pub on campus as well as two coffeehouses. New York City's Pennsylvania Station is less than an hour away by commuter train, and

Philadelphia, the Jersey shore, and the Delaware River are close by. The First Annual Picnic, held on the last day of classes and numbered like Super Bowls (FAP XVII), provides an opportunity to enjoy live music and food. On Multicultural Awareness Day, students are excused from one day of classes to celebrate cultural diversity by attending lectures, workshops, and social events.

The commuter town of Madison (population 15,700) doesn't have the amenities of larger metropolitan areas, of course, but "there are little shops, restaurants, and a pharmacy," says one student. "It is a quiet and safe town." Approximately 50 percent of students volunteer in activities such as Mentors at Drew and The Honduras Project, in which a group of Drew students travel to Honduras to help at an orphanage. Madison does provide several unique shops and restaurants within walking distance of campus, though the town "is a nice college town according to my parents, but not to students. Everything closes up pretty early." Nearby Morristown is more of a college place. The Shakespeare Theatre of New Jersey is in residence part of every year and offers both performances and internships.

Students used to seem more interested in intramural sports than in the school's Division III varsity teams, but interest has grown as the Rangers have become more successful. The most competitive teams are men's tennis, men's soccer, men's lacrosse, women's tennis, women's lacrosse, and women's soccer. Championships include men's tennis (winners of 13 consecutive conference titles), women's soccer (2010 ECAC Metro/South champions), and baseball (2012 conference champs). The $15 million athletic center is a 126,000-square-foot state-of-the-art facility that seats 4,000 and is used by varsity sports teams and intramural programs.

"Don't overlook Drew if you are looking for a small, tight-knit community that takes academic creativity seriously," cautions a sophomore. Indeed, Drew offers its small body of students a wide range of opportunities in a classic liberal arts structure. "It's easy to get involved, make friends, and feel like you make a difference," says a senior. Not too bad for a school in the forest.

There is no Greek system, and social life mostly takes place on campus.

Overlaps

Rutgers, College of New Jersey, Muhlenberg, NYU, Boston University

If You Apply To ➤

Drew: Early decision: Nov. 1. Early action: Jan. 15. Regular admissions and financial aid: Feb. 15. Application fee: $60. Campus and alumni interviews: optional, evaluative. SATs: required. No Subject Tests. Accepts the Common Application. Essay question.

Drexel University

3141 Chestnut Street, Philadelphia, PA 19104

Drexel is a streetwise, no-nonsense technical university in the heart of Philadelphia. Go to school, work an internship, go to school again, work again—that's the Drexel way. Like Lehigh, Drexel also offers programs in business and arts and sciences, and its most distinctive offering is a College of Media Arts and Design. The university is a financial bargain compared with other leading technical schools.

Website: www.drexel.edu
Location: City Center
Private
Total Enrollment: 25,500
Undergraduates: 15,876

For career-minded students who want to bypass the soul-searching of their liberal arts counterparts, Drexel University offers both solid academics and an innovative co-op education that combines high-tech academics with paying job opportunities—a mix that's particularly appealing in today's economic reality. "If you want a good job, you go to Drexel and you do co-op." Drexel is out to increase its visibility, and it is on track to increase the number of undergraduates by nearly a third. To do so, it has adopted aggressive recruiting and a fast-track early application process that emphasizes early decisions.

"Drexel's campus is impressive for its downtown Philadelphia location, with gardens and greenery on every block," says a student, "but the campus is woven tightly into the fabric of the city." The buildings are simple and made of brick; most are modern and in good condition. Sitting just west of the city center and right across the street from the University of Pennsylvania, the campus is condensed into about a four-block radius. Additional facilities include the Edmond Bossone Research Center and Ross Commons.

Cooperative education is the hallmark of Drexel's curriculum, which alternates periods of full-time study and full-time employment for four or five years, providing students with six to 18 months of money-making job experience before they gradu- **"The courses are very rigorous."** ate. And the co-op possibilities are unlimited: students can co-op virtually anywhere in this country, or in 11 foreign countries, and 98 percent of undergraduates choose this route. Freshman and senior years of the five-year programs are spent on campus, and the three intervening years (sophomore, prejunior, and junior) usually consist of six months of work and six months of school. A precooperative education course covers such topics as skills assessment, ethics in the workplace, résumé writing, interviewing skills, and stress management. Each co-op student has the opportunity to earn from $7,000 to $30,000 while attending Drexel. And although some students complain that jobs can turn out to be six months of make-work, most enjoy making important contacts in their potential fields and learning while earning. "The courses are very rigorous," explains a junior. "The profs tend to move very fast to fit everything into the 10-week terms."

To accommodate the co-op students, Drexel operates year-round. Flexibility in requirements varies by college, but in the first year everyone must take freshman seminar, English composition, mathematics, and Cooperative Education 101; engineering majors must also complete the Drexel Engineering Curriculum, which integrates math, physics, chemistry, and engineering to make sure that even techies enter the workforce well rounded and able to write as well as they can compute and design. Students enjoy the 700,000-volume library, which offers good hours and lots of room for studying. What's more, each entering freshmen is assigned a "personal librarian" charged with helping them make the best use of library facilities. Professors receive high praise from most, and are noted for their accessibility and warmth. Says one student, "I have had exceptional teachers who go out of their way to ensure the success of their students."

Drexel's greatest strength is its engineering college, which churns out more than 1 percent of all the nation's engineering graduates, B.S. through Ph.D. The electrical and architectural engineering programs are particular standouts. The College of Arts and Sciences is well recognized for theoretical and atmospheric physics; chemistry is also recommended. The futuristic Center for Automated Technology complements the strong computer science program. Students mention that the biology and chemistry departments are weak, primarily due to lack of organization and foreign teachers, who are hard **"Students are professional, experienced, bright, and ambitious."** to comprehend. Newer programs include urban environmental studies, entertainment and arts management, and the Drexel College of Law, which accepted its first class in 2012.

Drexel students are "professional, experienced, bright, and ambitious," according to one junior. The student body is 38 percent Pennsylvanian, with another large chunk of students from adjacent New Jersey. The international student population is 14 percent, Asian Americans and African Americans account for 19 percent of

(continued)

Male/Female: 54/46
SAT Ranges: CR 540–640, M 580–680
ACT Ranges: 24–29
Financial Aid: 98%
Expense: Pr $ $
Student Loans: 60%
Average Debt: N/A
Phi Beta Kappa: Yes
Applicants: 40,586
Accepted: 75%
Enrolled: 10%
Grad in 6 Years: 65%
Returning Freshmen: 85%
Academics: ✐ ✐ ✐
Social: ☎ ☎
Q of L: ★ ★
Admissions: (800) 2-DREXEL
Email Address: enroll@ drexel.edu

Strongest Programs:
Engineering
Graphic Design
Architecture
Film and Video

To accommodate the co-op students, Drexel operates year-round.

the student body, and Hispanics comprise 7 percent. Nearly one-third of Drexel undergrads graduated in the top 10th of their high school class, and the student body tends to lean right politically. "This is a science and technology school full of conservative students who don't really have the time to worry about liberal issues," says a student. In addition to need-based financial aid, a wide range of athletic and merit scholarships are offered.

Freshmen live in one of six co-ed residence halls, including a luxurious high-rise, but many upperclassmen reside in nearby apartments or the fraternities, which are frequently cheaper and more private than university housing. Overall, 34 percent of the students live in the dorms; another third commute to campus from home. The cafeteria offers adequate food and plenty of hamburgers and hot dogs, but it's far away from the dorms. While on-campus freshmen are forced to sign up for a meal plan, most upperclassmen make their own meals; the dorms have cooking facilities on each floor. If all else fails, nomadic food trucks park around campus, providing quick lunches. Students are encouraged to use a shuttle bus between the library and dorm at night, and access to dorms, the library, and the physical education center is restricted to students with ID, so most feel safe on campus.

With so many students living off campus and the city of Philadelphia at their disposal, Drexel tends to be a bit deserted on weekends. A student notes, "In a single weekend, I may play paintball in the Poconos, swim at the Jersey shore, see an opera in Philadelphia, and go mountain biking in nearby Wissahickon Park." Friday-night flicks are cheap and popular with those who stay around, and dorms sponsor floor parties. The dozen or so fraternities also contribute to the party scene, especially freshman year, but a handful of smaller sororities has little impact. Still, Greek Week is well attended by members of both sexes, as is the spring Block Party, which attracts four or five bands. The Greeks recruit 9 percent of the men and 8 percent of the women. Drinking is "not a big deal to everyone," and campus policies are strict; dorms require those of age to sign in alcohol and limit the quantities they may bring in. "This policy encourages many students to explore non-alcohol related activities," says an education major.

Drexel's co-op program often undermines any sense of class unity, and can strain personal relationships. Activities that depend on some continuity of enrollment for success—music, drama, student government, athletics—suffer most. "It's hard to get people involved because of the amount of schoolwork and co-ops," says one student. There is no football team, but men's basketball and soccer are strong. "Our biggest rivalry is our feud with Delaware," admits one frenzied student. "We delight in sacrificing blue plastic chickens [Delaware's mascot]!" Men's and women's swimming and women's volleyball also generate interest. An extensive intramural program serves all students, and joggers can head for the steps of the Philadelphia Art Museum, just as Rocky did in the movies. Students take full advantage of their urban location by frequenting clubs, restaurants, cultural attractions, and shopping malls in Philadelphia, easily accessible by public transportation.

Aspiring poets, musicians, and historians may find Drexel a bit confusing. But for future computer scientists, engineers, and other technically oriented minds, the university's unique approach to learning inside and outside the classroom could give your career a fantastic jump-start. As one satisfied student explains, "The terms are intense, the activities unlimited, but Drexel graduates are surely among the most capable and motivated individuals I have ever met. When I graduate, I will be prepared and proud of it."

The futuristic Center for Automated Technology complements the strong computer science program.

"Drinking is not a big deal to everyone."

Greek Week is well attended by members of both sexes, as is the spring Block Party, which attracts four or five bands.

Overlaps

University of Delaware, Northeastern, Penn State, University of Pittsburgh, Rutgers, Temple

If You Apply To ➤

Drexel: Early action: Nov. 2. Regular admissions: Jan. 15. Application fee: $75. Campus interviews: recommended, informational and evaluative. No alumni interviews. SATs or ACTs: required. Subject Tests: optional. Accepts the Common Application. Apply to particular schools or programs.

Duke University

2138 Campus Drive, Durham, NC 27708

What fun to be at Duke—face painted blue, rocking Cameron Indoor Stadium as the Blue Devils win again. Duke is the most prestigious private university in the South—more selective than Rice and Vanderbilt, and academically competitive with the Ivies and Stanford. Strong in engineering as well as the humanities, it offers public policy and economics rather than business. Big emphasis on study across disciplines.

Duke University is one of the few elite U.S. colleges where strong academics and championship-caliber sports teams manage to coexist. It might be south of the Mason-Dixon Line, and may seem a bit wet behind the ears compared to those ancient and prestigious Northeastern schools known for the erstwhile foliage on their walls, but Duke is competing with them and winning its fair share of intellectually serious superachievers as well as lots of top athletes.

Founded in 1838 as the Union Institute (later Trinity College), Duke University is young for a school of its stature. It sprouted up in 1924, thanks to a stack of tobacco-stained dollars called the Duke Endowment. Duke's campus in the lush forest of North Carolina Piedmont is divided into two main sections, West and East. With 8,300 acres of adjacent forest, it offers enough open space to satisfy even the most diehard outdoors enthusiast. West Campus, the hub of the university, is laid out in spacious quadrangles and dominated by the impressive Gothic chapel, a symbol of the university's Methodist tradition. Constructed in the 1930s, West includes collegiate Gothic residential and classroom quads, the administration building, Perkins Library (with almost six million volumes, nearly 18 million manuscripts, and two million public documents), and the student union. East Campus, built in the 1920s, consists primarily of Georgian redbrick buildings. East and West are connected by shuttle buses, though many students enjoy the mile-or-so walk or bike ride between them along wooded Campus Drive. Recent construction includes the Keohane Quad Hall, a five-story residence hall with 148 beds. The 7,000-acre Duke Forest is a rich laboratory for environmental research.

> **"Students at Duke are ambitious and diligent."**

Students opt for one of two undergraduate schools: the Pratt School of Engineering and Trinity College of Arts & Sciences (the latter resulted from a merger in the 1970s of the previously separate men's and women's liberal arts colleges). The school's engineering programs—particularly electrical and biomedical—are national standouts. Natural sciences, most notably ecology, biology, and neuroscience, are also first-rate. The proximity of the Medical Center enhances study in biochemistry and pharmacology. Public policy attracts the most majors, followed by psychology, economics, political science, and biology.

Duke's Sanford School of Public Policy offers an interdisciplinary major—unusual at the undergraduate level—that trains aspiring public servants in the machinations of the media, nonprofit organizations, government agencies, and other bodies that govern public life. Internships and apprenticeships are a big part of the program.

Website: www.duke.edu
Location: Small City
Private
Total Enrollment: 14,591
Undergraduates: 6,484
Male/Female: 50/50
SAT Ranges: CR 660–750, M 690–780
ACT Ranges: 30–34
Financial Aid: 61%
Expense: Pr $ $ $ $
Student Loans: 39%
Average Debt: $
Phi Beta Kappa: Yes
Applicants: 30,374
Accepted: 13%
Enrolled: 42%
Grad in 6 Years: 94%
Returning Freshmen: 97%
Academics: ✍ ✍ ✍ ✍ ✍
Social: ☎ ☎ ☎ ☎
Q of L: ★ ★ ★ ★
Admissions: (919) 684-3214
Email Address: undergrad-admissions@duke.edu

Strongest Programs:
Biology
Ecology
Neuroscience
Public Policy
Economics
Literary/Cultural Studies

"From personal experience, the public policy department is difficult but top-notch," says one student. There is a major available in statistical science, as well as a performance concentration in the existing music major. In addition, a dance major is now available to undergraduates. More than 25 interdisciplinary certificates are available in specialties such as ethics, documentary studies, and markets and management. Duke has more than 60 interdisciplinary centers, including the Duke Global Health Institute, the Nicholas Institute for Environmental Policy Solutions, and the John Hope Franklin Humanities Institute. Students say the language offerings can be weak.

Fifty percent of Duke's students study abroad, and there are ample opportunities for those who want a break from campus life without leaving the country. DukeEngage, an ambitious and innovative program backed by a $30 million endowment, makes civic engagement an integral part of the undergraduate experience. It supports students willing to spend summers working on projects ranging from building schools in Kenya to working with Gulf Coast flood victims. Nearly 400 students are admitted into the program each year; the program has become a centerpiece of President Richard Brodhead's commitment to "knowledge in service to society."

Trinity College's curriculum, part of the traditional undergraduate coursework known as Program I, requires courses in five general areas of knowledge: arts, literature, and performance; civilizations; social sciences; natural sciences; and quantitative studies. Students must also fulfill requirements in six modes of inquiry, including foreign language, writing, research, and ethical inquiry. All students must also complete three Small Group Learning Experiences: one seminar course during the freshman year—offered in topics such as Imagining Dinosaurs and The Psychology of Social Influence—and two more as upperclassmen. Students must finish 34 courses to graduate; those who wish to explore subjects outside and between usual majors and minors may choose Program II, to which they are admitted after proposing a topic, question, or theme for which they plan an individualized curriculum with faculty advisors and deans. "Students are given considerable freedom, and with it, responsibility," says a student.

When college counselors say Duke is hot, they're not referring to the boiling temperatures in the South. Duke competes with the Ivies and a select few other colleges for top-notch students. Courses here are rigorous and the academic atmosphere has become more intense, particularly in the sciences and engineering. "Students at Duke are ambitious and diligent, and the collective work ethic definitely has the potential to create competition," a freshman says. In recent years, the university has focused resources on undergraduate education and having senior professors teach more classes. Its president, lured from Yale, has made the expansion of interdisciplinary work—already part of the Duke culture—a priority for faculty and students alike. "I have met some really incredible professors in my time at Duke. If I had to give a net rating, it would definitely be positive. At any school there are some professors who aren't as engaging as others, but the great ones I have had have definitely made up for the others," says a junior. The nationally recognized FOCUS program offers groups of seminars with 15 or fewer students clustered around a single broad theme such as biotechnology and social change or humanitarian challenges at home and abroad. It is "an incredible opportunity to engage with the university's top professors," a senior says.

"There is constant pressure to succeed, both inside and outside of the classroom."

"The students at Duke are very ambitious," observes one history major. "There is constant pressure to succeed, both inside and outside of the classroom." Only 10 percent of Duke students are from North Carolina; the Northeastern corridor sends a fair-sized contingent, as does California. About 9 percent of undergraduates now hail from overseas. Despite the unmistakable air of wealth on campus, two-thirds come from public high schools. Ten percent of students are African American, 6 percent are Hispanic, and the growing Asian American contingent has reached 21 percent. Students of different ethnicities and races tend to "self-segregate," students say, producing little tension but also little interaction. Overcoming these self-imposed barriers has been an ongoing quest for administrators and students who created a Center for Race Relations, which seeks to evaluate and improve the way Duke educates its students about diversity and conflict resolution.

Duke's Southern gentility is reflected in campus attire, which is generally neatly pressed on guys and maybe a bit outfit-y on women, in contrast to the thrown-together antistatus uniform of jeans and sweats that dominates on some other campuses. Undergraduate women sometimes complain that they feel pressured to be "perfect" in all respects, from appearance to achievement. Duke is also a culturally active campus; theater groups thrive, and the relatively new Nasher Museum of Art, with its world-class exhibits by Picasso, Calder, and El Greco, among others, has become a popular social hub as well. During the summer, Duke plays host to the splendid American Dance Festival.

> **"Duke students are the type who will start a club if they are interested in something that nobody else is doing."**

Duke admits students without regard to financial need and has eliminated loans and the expected family contribution for families with incomes below $40,000 a year. The university has also eliminated the family contribution and/or capped loans for many families with incomes up to $60,000 a year. More than 40 percent of students receive need-based financial aid, and Duke offers a small number of merit scholarships, including some earmarked for outstanding African Americans. Like other NCAA Division I universities, Duke hands out lots of athletic scholarships.

Duke undergrads are required to live on campus for three years. Students live in residence halls or quads that house both unaffiliated students and members of selective living groups such as fraternities. Freshmen all reside in dorms on the East Campus led by a faculty member and his or her family. "The dorms look like castles on the outside and feel like *Harry Potter*," says a junior, who adds that the new dorms "are like five-star hotels." Seniors can move off campus, but "the apartments vary in quality." The decision to have all freshmen live on the East Campus was aimed at making it easier to adjust to academic life and insulating them from the wilder aspects of Duke's vigorous social scene. "The freshman year experience is marked by either bonding about having no air conditioner or bonding about living in Bell Tower, the nicest dorm on East Campus," says one freshman. Sophomores move to West Campus, where there are also special-interest dorms focused on themes such as women's studies, the arts, languages, and community service. Students say the dining choices range from edible to excellent. "There are over 20 eateries to choose from," says a junior, who notes that off-campus restaurants—many of which will deliver—are linked to the Duke meal plan. A percentage of unused "money" from prepaid meal cards is refunded at the end of the semester, an unusual and much-appreciated policy.

When college counselors say Duke is hot, they're not referring to the boiling temperatures in the South.

Duke undergrads take both their studies and their play seriously. "Duke students are the type who will start a club if they are interested in something that nobody else is doing, work hard on a paper late into the night, and then go out Thursday, Friday, and Saturday," says a public policy major. Students agree that most social life takes place on campus or in surrounding houses and apartments. Although it has been pushed away from the center of campus, "the Greek scene dominates," says a history major. Fraternities and sororities attract 29 percent of men and 42 percent of women, respectively. Fraternity parties are open to everyone, and the free shuttle bus service that connects the school's various dorm and apartment complexes runs until 4 a.m., making it easy to socialize in rooms or suites. There are three tightly regulated bars on campus, including the Washington Duke Inn, for students who are of age to drink. "Alcohol, it seems, is quite easy to find," says a freshman, at least on West Campus. "The university struggles with the drinking culture," explains a student, "and continues to tinker with the policies."

During the basketball season, men's games sell out, and the town is proud of its Durham Bulls, the local minor-league baseball team, which coined the term "bull-

"There is something magical about Duke basketball."

pen." Popular road trips include Franklin Street in nearby Chapel Hill, home of archrival UNC, and Raleigh, the state capital and home of North Carolina State University. In warm weather, the broad beaches on North Carolina's outer banks are two to three hours away, while winter ski slopes are three to four hours distant. The popular Springternational festival brings in live bands and vendors peddling local crafts and exotic foods each spring, and the traditional Joe College Day has been revived as a fall day affair filled with food, arts and crafts, and music.

Durham is a small, working class city that has had its share of racial tensions but also boasts a vibrant African American middle class and good political leadership. The contrast between Duke's wealth and the economic depression afflicting some of Durham's residents is obvious. But Duke as an institution has been active in the community, especially in public schools, and hundreds of undergrads are involved in service learning, tutoring, and related activities. "Everyone is involved in volunteer work," says one student. Downtown Durham is undergoing a revival, with old tobacco warehouses being converted into restaurants, stores, offices, and apartments. The *New York Times* frequently writes up Durham as a foodie destination. Students have access to discounted tickets to traveling Broadway shows at the state's largest performing arts center. No one misses the irony of the fact that Durham, once known as the "City of Tobacco," now bills itself as the "City of Medicine." Durham includes most of the Research Triangle Park, the largest research center of its kind in the world. Duke, North Carolina State, and the University of North Carolina at Chapel Hill created the park for nonprofit, scientific, and sociological research. Many Silicon Valley technology companies have East Coast outposts in the park, which has helped make the Raleigh-Durham area one of the most productive regions in the nation, with the highest percentage of Ph.D.s per capita in the United States.

Duke's official motto is *Eruditio et Religio* only to a few straitlaced administrators; everyone else knows it as Eruditio et Basketballio, which translates more or less as "Go to hell, Carolina"—meaning UNC at Chapel Hill, Duke's archrival in the rough and tough Atlantic Coast Conference. At games, students transform into the legendary Cameron Crazies and get the best courtside seats, where they make life miserable for the visiting team. Their efforts paid off in 2010 when the Blue Devils won the national Division I men's basketball championship for the fourth time in a decade. "By far, basketball season brings out the best of student support," a senior says. Sports-crazed Blue Devils erect a temporary tent city—dubbed "Krzyzewskiville" after the surname of fabled coach Mike—to vie for the best seats. This is far from "roughing it"—students form groups to hold their places so that some fraction can go to class and keep their peers on track academically while those who hold down the fort check their email through wireless connections. "There is something magical about Duke basketball, and the feeling of being in the student section with the Cameron Crazies during the Duke–UNC game is something that can't be captured in words. Revered by fans and hated by our rivals, the devotion of the Duke students is impressive and incredible," says one fan. The women's basketball team has become a dynasty in its own right and sometimes makes it to the Final Four. The lacrosse

Undergraduate women sometimes complain that they feel pressured to be "perfect" in all respects.

team, a national powerhouse that is trying to forget the scandal of a few years ago resulting from off-the-field behavior by some its members, bounced back to win the national championship in 2013. Football has undergone a renaissance under coach David Cutcliffe—a process that led to the university's first trip to the ACC title game in 2013. The Duke debate team is stellar, too, and brought home the national title recently. Intramurals are big and operate on two levels, one for competitive types and one for strictly weekend athletes. These draw heavy participation from the Greeks and guys.

Meandering around Duke's up-to-date campus, you can see the latest technology, but you can also hear the whisper of the Old South through those big old trees. "If you come here, there isn't a chance in the world that you won't fall in love with it, with its possibilities and opportunities and people and beauty," one student says. In addition to blending old and new, Duke also does an amazing job combining sports and academia, producing students who almost define the term "well-rounded." But this may be changing. Says a junior, "It's attracting better students, shifting the focus away from basketball and fraternities, and trying to create a more intellectual environment on campus."

> ## Overlaps
> **Brown, Dartmouth, Harvard, Penn, Princeton, Stanford, Yale**

If You Apply To ➤

Duke: Early decision: Nov. 1. Regular admissions: Jan. 2. Application fee: $85. Campus interviews: optional, informational. Alumni interviews: optional, evaluative. SAT and two SAT subject tests or ACT (with writing): required. Accepts the Common Application. Essay question.

Earlham College

Richmond, IN 47374

Earlham is a member of the proud circle of liberal colleges in the Midwest that includes Beloit, Grinnell, Kenyon, and Oberlin, to name just a few. Less than half the size of Oberlin and comparable to the other three, Earlham is distinctive for its Quaker orientation and international perspective. Its struggle is to lure progressive-minded students to a nondescript city in southern Indiana.

Earlham is a study in contradictions—a top-notch liberal arts college in a conservative city that few could place on a map, and an institution that even in the 21st century remains true to the traditions of community, peace, and justice that are hallmarks of its Quaker heritage. Earlham's curriculum and programs engage students with the world by exposing them to classmates from approximately 70 nations and offering more than 200 academic courses that incorporate an international perspective. A variety of study abroad programs offers close faculty involvement and a thoughtful focus on cross-cultural perspectives.

"Fine arts majors definitely get the short end of the stick when it comes to space, resources, and professors."

Earlham's 800-acre campus sits in the small, quintessentially Midwestern city of Richmond, just a short distance from Cincinnati and Indianapolis. Georgian-style buildings dominate, surrounded by mature trees and plantings, while the Japanese gardens symbolize the college's long friendship and closeness with Japan. With upwards of 95 percent of students living on campus, the college has committed to improving its residence halls, including the recent modernization of Earlham Hall. A renovated science building and admissions welcome center opened in late 2013.

Website: www.earlham.edu
Location: City Center
Private
Total Enrollment: 1,080
Undergraduates: 1,011
Male/Female: 44/56
SAT Ranges: CR 550–700, M 530–660
ACT Ranges: 23–30
Financial Aid: 88%
Expense: Pr $ $
Student Loans: 59%
Average Debt: $ $ $
Phi Beta Kappa: Yes
Applicants: 1,408
Accepted: 75%

(continued)

Enrolled: 27%
Grad in 6 Years: 73%
Returning Freshmen: 83%
Academics: ✐ ✐ ✐ ✐
Social: ☎ ☎ ☎
Q of L: ★ ★ ★ ★ ★
Admissions: (765) 983-1600
Email Address: admissions@
earlham.edu

Strongest Programs:
Biology
Interdisciplinary Studies
Social Science
Psychology
Visual and Performing Arts
Neuroscience
Peace and Global Studies

During their undergrad years, more than 70 percent of Earlham students participate in at least one off-campus study experience.

To graduate, students must complete general education requirements in the arts, analytical reasoning, wellness, scientific inquiry, foreign language, and, not surprisingly, diversity. Biology is the most popular major, followed by psychology, fine arts, interdisciplinary studies, and sociology. A wide range of interdisciplinary offerings includes such programs as peace and global studies, legal studies, Quaker studies, Latin American studies, and Japanese studies, a field in which Earlham is a national leader. Students are hard pressed to identify weaker programs, but say that some departments could use more resources. "Fine arts majors definitely get the short end of the stick when it comes to space, resources, and professors," says one senior, adding, "Our best departments are probably Japanese studies, biology, sociology/anthropology, and peace and global studies."

"If you're a health nut or just really picky about quality of food...then the dining hall isn't great."

Challenged to think and meet high academic expectations, students see themselves as capable and eager to learn. "The courses are not only intellectually stimulating," says one student, "but they encourage students to think critically." Class discussion, rather than lecture, is the predominant learning style here. Earlham faculty members are selected for their excellence in teaching and their ability to cross disciplinary lines. "Faculty are always willing to meet with students to chat about pretty much anything," says a history major. While profs are available, class outlines demand that individuals "figure things out" by taking the initiative to take their work seriously.

About three-quarters of students eventually pursue postgraduate study, often after taking some time off for a job or to participate in volunteer or service programs. During their undergrad years, more than 70 percent of Earlham students participate in at least one off-campus study experience. Earlham offers study abroad programs in more than two dozen countries, including Mexico, India, England, Spain, Martinique, Northern Ireland, France, New Zealand, East Africa, and Japan. In a Border Studies program, students live with families in Tucson or Ciudad Juarez and take courses focusing on United States-Mexico border issues. Most programs are managed by the college; students first receive preparation for a multicultural experience, and most programs have an on-site director. The popular May Term courses send students off campus with faculty for one-month intensive courses in various locations around the world.

Earlham may be small, but its student body is exceptionally diverse. "We have all kinds of people from social activists and artsy hippies to gamers and people obsessed with anime to old school jocks," says a religion major, "and most of us aren't just one of these archetypes, we're a strange mishmash of them, and other things too." Only 19 percent of the students are Hoosiers; 18 percent hail from abroad, representing approximately 70 countries. Another 10 percent are African American, with Hispanics adding 6 percent and Asian American students contributing 2 percent. With a strong emphasis on conversation, the campus is full of well-intentioned activists blazing their own trails through life, albeit on "Earlham Time" (a tardy-favorable clock widely accepted in this laid-back climate). Merit scholarships are available for qualified students; there are no athletic scholarships.

Ninety-six percent of Earlham students live on campus in nine residence halls. "The dorms are comfortable and well maintained," says a sophomore. Single, double, and triple rooms are available in the two older dorms, which connect with the newer Mills Hall. Along with wireless Internet connectivity, the hall features two- to four-bedroom suites sharing private baths and, on each floor, a kitchen, study room, laundry, and, yes, TV lounges. Dorm space is reserved for first-years, and upperclassmen enter a lottery for the remaining rooms or petition to live together in small houses. Most students eat in the college dining hall, which offers a diverse selection for special diets. "There are options for vegetarians," reports one student, "but if you're a health nut or just really picky about quality of food and how your food is cooked, then the dining hall isn't great." Students say campus security is adequate and safety officers are helpful in all situations: "Once, I had a conversation with a campus security officer about the best places to hide on campus in case of a zombie attack," quips a senior.

Quaker beliefs and Indiana's liquor laws prohibit alcohol on campus, making Earlham a dry campus, at least technically. While any college has its dissenters on alcohol policy—making it more realistically a "damp campus"—Earlham seems to embrace its policy well enough. "Our alcohol policy is in transition, but currently we are a dry campus. We prefer the term 'pleasantly moist,'" says a history major. The atmosphere this creates is very respectful of nondrinkers' decisions and avoids pressure.

With no fraternities or sororities at Earlham, gatherings and parties on weekends may be hard to find and quiet when they do happen, but on-campus activities abound. "Most social life happens on campus," a theater major confirms. Students enjoy improv comedy, a cappella music, equestrian programs, a lip-synch competition, fall and spring festivals, concerts, and sports. Student organizations include numerous cultural, ethnic, and religious groups as well as left-of-center organizations such as Amnesty International and the Earlham Progressive Union. Apart from day trips to Cincinnati, Indianapolis, or Columbus, students stick with a laid-back social atmosphere of visiting with others or checking out one of the musicians, speakers, or other groups that Earlham brings to campus.

With no fraternities or sororities at Earlham, gatherings and parties on weekends may be hard to find.

Richmond and the surrounding county offer standard American as well as Mexican restaurants, a popular French bistro, movie theaters, bowling alleys, rollerskating, and golf. Students fan out into the city, racking up more than 40,000 hours of volunteer service a year. Guaranteed to impress, outreach programs are truly getting students involved in their community and building a close relationship with the city. "Volunteerism is an important value of many Earlham students, and despite class work and other commitments, many students still make time to volunteer," says a first-year.

"Volunteerism is an important value of many Earlham students."

Basketball, flag football, racquetball, and soccer are especially popular recreational sports. The school's varsity teams attract nearly a third of the student body and compete in Division III sports, including basketball, track, cross-country, baseball, volleyball, and tennis. Men's and women's tennis and soccer are among the school's strongest squads.

Although Earlham students are based in the Midwest, they graduate ready to take on the world, thanks to the school's cooperative, can-do spirit, international perspective, and caring student/faculty community. Earlham has much to offer, says one student. "It allows an individual to pursue many areas of interest, and the people you meet will be friends for a lifetime."

Overlaps
Oberlin, Beloit, College of Wooster, Grinnell, Knox

If You Apply To ➤

Earlham: Early decision: Nov. 1. Early action: Dec. 1. Regular admissions: Feb. 1. No application fee. Campus and alumni interviews: optional, evaluative. SATs or ACTs: optional. Subject Tests: optional. Accepts the Common Application. Essay question.

Eckerd College

4200 54th Avenue South, St. Petersburg, FL 33711

There are worse places to attend than a college with its own stretch of beach on the shores of Tampa Bay. Eckerd's only direct competitor in Florida is Rollins, which has a business school but is otherwise similar. Marine science, environmental studies, and international studies are among Eckerd's biggest draws. The student body is mainly from out of state, with plenty of Yankee accents.

Website: www.eckerd.edu
Location: Suburban
Private
Total Enrollment: 1,825
Undergraduates: 1,825
Male/Female: 41/59
SAT Ranges: CR 510–620,
   M 500–610
ACT Ranges: 23–28
Financial Aid: 90%
Expense: Pr $ $
Student Loans: 58%
Average Debt: $ $ $ $
Phi Beta Kappa: Yes
Applicants: 3,910
Accepted: 71%
Enrolled: 19%
Grad in 6 Years: 60%
Returning Freshmen: 81%
Academics: ✍ ✍ ✍
Social: ☎ ☎ ☎
Q of L: ★ ★ ★ ★ ★
Admissions: (727) 864-8331
Email Address: admissions@
   eckerd.edu

Strongest Programs:
Marine Science
Biology
Psychology
International Relations
Creative Writing and Literature
Management and International
   Business
Environmental Studies

Attending Eckerd College demands a special sort of willpower. Why? In the words of an international business major: "We are right on the water, and it is like going to college in a resort." With free canoes, kayaks, boats, coolers, and tents always available for student use, it's a wonder anyone finds time to study. But study they do, as administrators continue to lure capable students to Eckerd with small classes, skilled professors, and a thriving social scene. "Few schools are located right on the beach," says a sophomore. "It's Eckerd's paradise-like setting that seals the deal for most prospective students."

Founded in 1958 as Florida Presbyterian College and renamed 12 years later after a generous benefactor (of drugstore fame), Eckerd considers itself nonsectarian. Still, the school maintains a formal "covenant" with the major Presbyterian denomination, from which it receives some funds. The lush, grassy campus is on the tip of a peninsula bounded by the Gulf of Mexico and Tampa Bay, with plenty of flowering bushes, trees, and small ponds—it's not unusual to spot dolphins frolicking in the adjacent waters. Campus buildings are modern, and none are taller than three stories. The GO Pavilion takes advantage of Florida's year-round outdoor living climate and offers nearly 10,000 square feet of open-air space for sports, concerts, and other events. The Center for Molecular and Life Sciences houses the biology, chemistry, and biochemistry programs.

> **"It is like going to college in a resort."**

Freshmen arrive three weeks early for orientation and take a one-credit seminar on the skills required for college-level work. First-years also take a yearlong course called Western Heritage in a Global Context, which focuses on influential books, and students must meet composition, foreign language, information technology, oral communication, and quantitative skills requirements. Also required are one course in each of the four academic areas—arts, humanities, natural sciences, and social sciences—plus one course each in environmental and global perspectives. The capstone senior seminar, organized around the theme "Quest for Meaning," asks students to draw on what they've learned during college to find solutions to important issues. Popular majors include marine science, environmental studies, international business, psychology, and communication.

"Although the classes are intellectually stimulating, engaging, and challenging, there is not too much competition among the students," one junior observes. Wet subjects are especially strong. "Eckerd College is renowned for its marine science program," says a student. "The close proximity to the ocean gives [students in] this major a great amount of hands-on, close-up experience." The college was granted a Phi Beta Kappa chapter in 2003, making it the youngest private college ever to receive the honor. Eckerd was a pioneer of the 4–1–4 term schedule, in which students work on a single project for credit each January. Every student has a faculty mentor, and there are no graduate assistants. "The faculty here are amazing," says a psychology major. "They are here for us and they want us to do well." A Freeman Foundation grant funds significant coursework in the Chinese and Japanese languages.

While St. Petersburg isn't exactly a college town (a freshman says it is "more a vacationing spot"), a side benefit to the school's location is the Academy of Senior Professionals, a group of senior citizens who mentor undergrads. Academy members, who come from all walks of life, take classes with students, work with professors on curriculum development, help students with career choices, and lead workshops in their areas of expertise. Sixty percent of Eckerd's students study abroad, in countries ranging from Austria and France to Bermuda. The school also maintains study centers in London, Latin America, and China. Marine science programs include a Sea Semester* and the Eckerd College Search and Rescue, which performs more than 500 marine rescues annually and inspires a popular campus T-shirt that tells students to "GET LOST! Support Eckerd Search and Rescue."

Eckerd's president once referred to students as "intellectuals in sandals," says a junior. "I like the quote and it really works." Another student says Eckerd attracts "friendly, liberal, free-spirited, and intelligent" students who enjoy the great outdoors. Seventy-eight percent of the student body hail from out of state, with a large contingent coming from the Northeast; 3 percent are foreign. Hispanics account for 8 percent of the student body, African Americans comprise 3 percent, and Asian Americans constitute 1 percent. Eleven athletic scholarships are awarded annually in baseball and basketball, and merit scholarships are available to qualified "barefoot and brainy" types.

> *Popular majors include marine science, environmental studies, international business, psychology, and communication.*

> **"There is not too much competition among the students."**

"The dorms at Eckerd vary greatly," reports one student. "The traditional dorms are basic and unsightly, while the newer dorms are fantastic and aesthetically pleasing." Eighty-one percent of students live in the housing quads, separated from the rest of campus by the imaginatively named Dorm Drive. Rooms are fairly large and air-conditioned, and waterfront views and beach access are a given—and free. Two trendy townhouse- and apartment-style residence halls provide suite living, and other dorms have been renovated to add computer labs and kitchens in lounges. "There is usually no problem getting a room and most students do not live off campus," says a senior. And how about the food? "Dining is superior," says one student, "with a variety of food choices ranging from traditional hamburgers and pizza, to a lively and diverse vegetarian and global selection."

> *The college was granted a Phi Beta Kappa chapter in 2003, making it the youngest private college ever to receive the honor.*

There are no Greek organizations at Eckerd, and a strict alcohol policy—no kegs on campus, no alcohol at university events—means wristbands at campus parties, even for those over 21. The policy has been relaxed a bit to allow students of drinking age to imbibe at the campus bar, the Triton Pub, and to drink in public areas of the dorms. Students say those who are underage still manage to get booze and consume it in their rooms, away from prying eyes. "Most students learn how to stay out of trouble and play by the rules," says a sophomore. Off campus, it's next to impossible for underage students to be served at bars and restaurants, students say—though they do enjoy the Baywalk shopping complex, about 15 minutes from campus, with a stadium-seating movie theater, bars, and restaurants.

> **"The traditional dorms are basic and unsightly, while the newer dorms are fantastic."**

On campus, students can partake in concerts, lectures, shows, and games arranged by the student activity board. At the Festival of Hope, seniors present their Quest for Meaning social work. "Social life is primarily on campus and it really is what you make it," a junior states. The Kappa Karnival offers rides and games galore. Off campus, students can take in the nightclubs and bars of Latin-flavored Ybor City about 30 minutes away. Tampa and St. Pete also offer a Salvador Dali museum—which Eckerd students get into for free—and professional baseball, football, hockey, and soccer teams. Tempting road trips include Orlando's Walt Disney World and Islands of Adventure theme parks, Miami's South Beach, and that hub of debauchery on the delta, New Orleans.

> *There are no Greek organizations at Eckerd.*

Varsity teams (the "Tritons") compete in NCAA Division II, and the men's basketball and baseball teams are especially competitive. "Men's basketball is the only sport that attracts lots of fans and spectators," a senior says, and a night of Midnight Madness helps kick off the season. The co-ed sailing team has claimed several recent divisional and regional championships. Eckerd doesn't have a football team, but popular intramurals include flag football, soccer, baseball, softball, and the assassin game, in which students try to shoot their peers with dart guns.

"Eckerd is the place where your dreams can become realities and where new dreams can take flight," says one enraptured junior. Eckerd is striving to add "experiential, service, and international learning" to the traditional classroom experience and attract a higher caliber of students. That mission, combined with new facilities and the fun to be had in the Florida sun, gives Eckerd its distinctive flavor.

Overlaps

College of Charleston, Elon, Florida Southern, University of Miami (FL), New College of Florida, Rollins, Roger Williams, University of Tampa

If You Apply To ➢

Eckerd: Rolling admissions. Early action: Nov. 15. Application fee: $40. Campus and alumni interviews: recommended, evaluative. SATs or ACTs: required. Subject Tests: optional. Accepts the Common Application. Essay question.

University of Edinburgh: See page 362.

Elon University

Elon, NC 27244

A rapidly rising star among liberal arts colleges in the Southeast and an emerging name nationwide. With a welcoming environment and a supportive faculty, Elon is good at taking average students and turning them on to the life of the mind. Strong emphasis on global perspectives and hands-on learning in the classroom. Classic-looking campus adds to the appeal.

Website: www.elon.edu
Location: Suburban
Private
Total Enrollment: 5,732
Undergraduates: 5,194
Male/Female: 41/59
SAT Ranges: CR 570–660, M 560–660
ACT Ranges: 25–29
Financial Aid: 68%
Expense: Pr $
Student Loans: 44%
Average Debt: $ $ $
Phi Beta Kappa: Yes
Applicants: 10,241
Accepted: 52%

Elon University derives its name from the Hebrew word for "oak," which is fitting when you consider the many ways in which the school is growing. At each year's opening convocation, entering students are given an acorn. Four years later, they are presented with an oak sapling at commencement. It's a charming tradition and a reminder of how things grow and change. Indeed, it seems everything is changing here—from the name to the buildings, academic majors, and programs. With an emphasis on undergraduate research, group work, service learning, and study abroad, the university also provides its students with plenty of opportunities to grow—intellectually and socially. A junior says, "Students will have the chance to hone their passions, discover new ones, study abroad, deepen their academic focus with the help of professors and mentors, and make lifelong friends in the process."

"Students tend to gravitate toward communications because the department is so good."

Elon was founded in 1889 and occupies a 620-acre campus in North Carolina's Piedmont region. With apologies to Miami (OH), it is arguably the most architecturally consistent campus in the nation. Buildings are Georgian-style brick with white trim, and newer buildings have been adapted to modern architectural lines while maintaining this classic collegiate feel. At the center of campus is Lake Mary Nell, home to an abundance of geese and ducks. Academic buildings are organized in three clusters: an arts and sciences quad near a fountain in the older section of the campus; an Academic Village, complete with a colonnade and amphitheater; and business and science centers in close proximity to the student center. The Academic Village serves as an informal gathering spot where students and faculty come together weekly for bagels and coffee, a tradition since 1984. The Gerald L. Francis Center houses the recently established School of Health Sciences.

All of the newer facilities have been designed to support Elon's highly interactive academic programs. The university offers more than 60 undergraduate degrees, with strong programs in biology, communications, psychology, education, and business. The School of Communications is nationally recognized and benefits from two ultramodern digital television studios. "Students tend to gravitate toward communications because the department is so good," a junior explains. Students agree the academic climate is rigorous but varies greatly depending on your major. "The academic climate at Elon is highly competitive," says a marketing major. "Students

> **"It is easy to take for granted how personable and accessible our professors are at Elon."**

have to put in a lot of work to get good grades." Elon has established a new international business dual-degree program and new majors in early childhood education, marketing, management, applied mathematics, entrepreneurship, finance, biophysics/biomedical engineering, and environmental and ecological science.

Elon has an elaborate support system designed to ensure that first-year students don't fall through the cracks. Students begin general studies with a first-year course called The Global Experience, a seminar-style interdisciplinary class that investigates challenges facing the world. First-year orientations include Move-In Day, in which faculty and staff members literally help students lug their belongings from their cars to their new rooms, and an optional experiential learning program that partners 90 freshmen with returning students for activities ranging from white-water rafting to volunteer work. Elon 101 is taken by all first-years; students meet weekly in groups of no more than 17 during the first semester and discuss academic, social, and personal concerns with a faculty member and an upper-level student.

Students must complete a core that includes English, mathematics, wellness, eight courses in liberal arts and sciences, three courses at the advanced level, an experiential learning component, a foreign language component, and a general studies interdisciplinary seminar. The university places a big emphasis on service learning and undergraduate research. Nearly 20 percent of undergrads are engaged in research work with faculty. Seventy-three percent study abroad, thanks to the 4–1–4 academic calendar and more than 100 study abroad programs. The Honors Program offers a series of demanding courses that focus on writing and critical thinking skills, and the university offers a variety of prestigious Fellows programs. Fifty-two percent of all classes have 49 or fewer students, and professors are highly praised. A senior says, "It is easy to take for granted how personable and accessible our professors are at Elon because it is the norm, but it is something that is very special and has made for an incomparable learning experience."

Elon has traditionally prided itself on attracting students who may not have been academic stars in high school (but who have leadership potential) and turning them on to the life of the mind. "As part of an Elon education there are five Elon Experiences, and each student is required to complete one before they graduate," a senior explains. "The five experiences are internship, leadership, service, study abroad, and undergraduate research. While each student is required to complete one of these experiences, many will go above and beyond the requirement and complete multiple experiences in their four years at Elon." Seventy-three percent come from

(continued)

Enrolled: 27%
Grad in 6 Years: 83%
Returning Freshmen: 90%
Academics: ✍ ✍ ✍
Social: ☎ ☎ ☎ ☎
Q of L: ★ ★ ★ ★
Admissions: (800) 334-8448
Email Address: admissions@elon.edu

Strongest Programs:
Business
Communications
Psychology
Biology
Education
International Studies

All of the newer facilities have been designed to support Elon's highly interactive academic programs.

outside North Carolina. Eighty-two percent of Elon's student body are Caucasian, 6 percent African American, 4 percent Hispanic, 2 percent Asian American, and 2 percent international. Students are also keen to discuss political and social issues. "Being a fairly rich, white, and preppy campus, Elon hits the topic of diversity fairly often along with discussions of homosexuality, ethical conduct, sustainability, and social justice," says one student. The well-known Elon University Poll, which the school runs as a public service, tracks political and public policy issues. The top 25 percent of admitted applicants are automatically considered for the Presidential Scholarship. Students can also vie for merit scholarships averaging $5,563, and there are 267 athletic scholarships available in 16 sports.

Sixty percent of students reside on campus and are required to for their first two years. "Many students choose to live off campus junior/senior year because it costs a little less and they have more freedom with the meal plan," says one junior. Another student adds, "All halls are air-conditioned, large, and there isn't a problem finding adequate housing on campus." Options include traditional residence halls, an academic village complex where students and faculty live and study together, and university-owned apartments. Campus dining gets good reviews: "For such a small school our dining facilities are extensive and well maintained," says one student.

> **"Being a fairly rich, white, and preppy campus, Elon hits the topic of diversity fairly often."**

When it's time to let off steam, students generally turn to the active Greek scene—which attracts 22 percent of the men and 38 percent of the women—or countless activities on campus. "Parties are definitely a student favorite and while some do take place on campus (usually in apartments), most take place off campus," a student says. "Elon offers many cultural and social events, so there is always something to do on campus and most students stay in Elon for the weekend," adds an international studies major. Students say that while alcohol is ever present, there is little pressure to drink. Says a student, "The campus is cracking down on underage drinking. There are severe consequences for breaking the law." Road trips to the beach (three hours), the mountains (one hour), and Washington, D.C. (five hours) are popular diversions.

The tiny town of Elon (population 7,300) is virtually indistinguishable from the university, which even owns the two main restaurants. Students take an active role in the community through volunteer projects. "Service is one of the bigger components of life as an Elon student. It's one of our five 'Elon Experiences' along with internships, research, study abroad, and leadership—things that nearly everyone on campus has taken part in." Popular campus events include homecoming and a weekly College Coffee, where students and faculty mingle over free breakfast and coffee.

Elon recently made the move from the Southern Conference to the Colonial Athletic Association and continues to offer nine women's sports and seven for men; the most competitive include men's soccer (2011 conference champs), men's baseball (2013 SoCon tournament champs), women's volleyball, and women's softball. There's also an intramural program covering more than 20 sports, in which 30 percent of students take part, and a successful club sports program that lets students compete with those at other schools. Elon's mock trial team is consistently competitive on the national level. For the second time in three years the team has reached the opening round of the American Mock Trial Association's National Championship Tournament.

Without a doubt, Elon University has come a long way in recent years. "Elon is truly an up-and-coming school," a student says. "Our programs of study are getting better and better and the campus is growing by leaps and bounds," a communications major reports. By steadily ramping up its educational offerings, growing and improving its facilities, and upping its admissions standards, this quality liberal arts university is quickly outgrowing its local reputation and making a name for itself across the country.

The top 25 percent of admitted applicants are automatically considered for the Presidential Scholarship.

Overlaps

UNC at Chapel Hill, Wake Forest, University of Virginia, American University, Clemson, North Carolina State, Boston College, University of Richmond

Emerson College

120 Boylston Street, Boston, MA 02116-4624

Emerson is strategically located on Boston Common in the heart of Boston's theater district and within walking distance of the city's major attractions. Specializes in theater, film, creative writing, and communications. With roughly 3,000 undergraduates, Emerson is a smaller alternative to neighboring giants Boston U and Northeastern. Like most Beantown institutions, it is way more selective than it once was.

Those who aspire to a career in Hollywood or Manhattan may want to start with a four-year stint in Boston. There they will find Emerson College, a small liberal arts school that offers strong programs in communications and the performing arts. At Emerson, students take notes from professors who also happen to be working directors, producers, actors, and writers. It's an approach that helps talented, city-savvy students find their voices and prepare for the spotlight. Emerson allows students to "do whatever they dream up," says a junior. But prospective students take note: getting into Emerson requires more than dreams. You'll need solid test scores and plenty of talent, too.

Founded in 1880, Emerson is located by Boston Common in the middle of the city's theater district and features a mix of traditional and modern high-rise buildings. Nearly half of the campus facilities have been refurbished or newly built since 2002, and much of the surrounding city is accessible by foot, including the historic Freedom Trail and the Boston Public Garden. The historic 1,200-seat Cutler Majestic Theatre is the anchor of Emerson's campus. The college completed restoration of this landmark to its original 1903 appearance and constructed an 11-story performance and production center for rehearsal space, a theater design/technology center, costume shop, makeup lab, and television studio. The restored Paramount Center includes a scene shop, black box theater, sound stage, film screening room, and student residence hall.

Emerson was founded with an emphasis on communications and performance, and the school still offers a plethora of strong programs in this vein. Undergraduates may choose from more than a dozen majors, including acting, broadcast journalism, print and multimedia journalism, film, communication sciences, television/radio, political communication, and theater design/technology. General education requirements consist of a combination of interdisciplinary seminars and traditional courses. All students must take courses in three areas: foundations, which includes courses in writing, oral communications, and quantitative reasoning; perspectives, which includes courses in aesthetics, ethics and values, history, literature, and scientific, social, and psychological perspectives; and multicultural diversity, which includes classes in global and U.S. diversity. Interdisciplinary seminars of no more than 20 students stress the interrelationships between different communication fields; recent seminars include Minds and Machines; The City; Ways of Knowing: Philosophy and Literature; and Words, Imagination, Expression.

The most popular major is creative writing; film/video production, performing arts, journalism, and marketing communication are also popular. In visual and media

> "Classes are thought provoking."

Website: www.emerson.edu
Location: City Center
Private
Total Enrollment: 4,321
Undergraduates: 3,586
Male/Female: 38/62
SAT Ranges: CR 590–680, M 560–650
ACT Ranges: 26–29
Financial Aid: 58%
Expense: Pr $ $
Student Loans: 60%
Average Debt: $ $
Phi Beta Kappa: Yes
Applicants: 7,465
Accepted: 48%
Enrolled: 24%
Grad in 6 Years: 82%
Returning Freshmen: 88%
Academics: ✐ ✐ ✐
Social: ☎ ☎
Q of L: ★ ★ ★
Admissions: (617) 824-8600
Email Address: admission@emerson.edu

Strongest Programs:
Film/Video Production
Writing
Literature and Publishing
Performing Arts
Journalism
Marketing Communication

arts, production courses focus on animation, screenwriting, and digital media. The college also provides students with access to state-of-the-art equipment and facilities—including digital labs, audio postproduction suites, sound mix studios, radio stations, an all-digital newsroom, and television studios—and the campus is home to the oldest noncommercial radio station in Boston. The entrepreneurship minor features a business plan competition known as the Entrepreneurship Exposition; students vie for $12,000 in startup funds. "Above all, extracurriculars are the backbone of an Emerson education," a film production major says. "Classes are thought provoking but nothing prepares you for the real world better than actually getting out into the field to practice as much as possible."

The most popular major is creative writing; film/ video production, performing arts, journalism, and marketing communication are also popular.

For those seeking a spotlight and stage in a different setting, Emerson offers a semester-abroad program at Kasteel Well (the Netherlands), where students are housed in a restored 12th-century castle complete with moats, gardens, a gate house, and peacocks. Film students may attend a production program in the Czech Republic, and communications/journalism majors have the option to travel to Taiwan. Each year about 200 students spend a semester at Emerson's Los Angeles Center. There, they can participate in internships with companies such as Interscope Records, CNN, Warner Bros., Dreamworks, and NBC. A semester-long program sends participants to Washington, D.C., for classes and internships. Back on campus, students may cross-register with nearby Suffolk University and the six-member Boston ProArts Consortium (which includes the Berklee College of Music). Sixty-two percent of all classes have 19 or fewer students, and professors receive high marks for their real-world experience. "The majority of my professors have been awesome," a senior says. "I've learned from each and every one of them and I think I've become a better writer, communicator, and thinker because of them."

"The majority of my professors have been awesome."

"Emerson students are usually motivated, competitive people, intent on succeeding," says a junior. Seventy-seven percent hail from outside of Massachusetts, and most come from public high schools. African Americans account for 3 percent of the student body, Hispanics 10 percent, and Asian Americans another 4 percent. Hot campus issues include politics and government. "We're a very liberal campus," says a sophomore, "so most students advocate for world peace, social justice, and the environment." Emerson offers merit scholarships to qualified applicants, averaging more than $14,000, as well as scholarships to support underrepresented students. There are no athletic scholarships.

Each year about 200 students spend a semester at Emerson's Los Angeles Center. There, they can participate in internships with companies such as Interscope Records, CNN, Warner Bros., Dreamworks, and NBC.

Fifty-seven percent of students live on campus, some in dorms with special theme floors, including the Writers' Block (ahem), and the Digital Culture floor. Freshmen are guaranteed on-campus housing, and the 14-story residence hall overlooking Boston Common helps to create a residential feel to the campus. "There is a limited amount of dorm space at Emerson College. It can be hard for juniors, and nearly impossible for seniors, to live on campus," says one student. Campus dining is not only about eating but also, according to one sophomore, "the social mecca for kids on campus." The food rates well with lots of options for vegans, vegetarians, and those with special diets. "The food is good, although by the end of the semester you might get sick of it," says one student, "and choose to take advantage of the full kitchens in the colonial building to do some cooking." Students feel safe on campus. Each building requires an ID to enter, and public safety officers regularly patrol the streets outside the buildings. "We're in the heart of the city," a student says, "but I have never felt unsafe."

"Emerson students are usually motivated, competitive people, intent on succeeding."

"Students spend time bonding and socializing with each other through learning communities, student organizations, panel discussions, and Greek life," says one theater studies major. "Students also hang out off campus." Fun also includes plays and film shoots that take place on a regular basis. More than 60 student clubs, organizations, and performance groups offer students ample opportunity for involvement, including two radio stations, six humor and literary journals, 10 performance troupes, and six production organizations. "People make tons of friends in organizations," a senior says. A few party animals can be found among performing arts majors who "use substances to thrive," according to one student, and among members of the Greek scene, which attracts 2 percent of Emerson men and 3 percent of the women. Though the campus is considered "dry," parties at off-campus apartments make it possible for students to drink. That said, "alcohol is not a huge problem," says a sophomore.

When students tire of on-campus events, they can step off campus into Boston.

When students tire of on-campus events, they can step off campus into Boston. One student says, "Boston is definitely the best college town in the U.S. There's always something to do, whether culturally enriching or just to have fun." Another gushes, "Emerson students live, study, work, and volunteer in almost every major

"Students also hang out off campus."

neighborhood and area of the city." There are plenty of diversions, including museums, the Franklin Park Zoo, Freedom Trail, the Boston Symphony Orchestra, and major league baseball at Fenway Park. Back on campus, students enjoy poetry slams and comedy sketches. Popular festivities include EVVY Awards, the largest student production/organization in the country. There is also Hand-Me-Down Night (during which outgoing club officers "hand down" their positions to incoming officers), Greek Week, and the New Student Revue.

Emerson fields 13 Division III athletic teams, and the Lions compete as a member of the Eastern College Athletic Conference and the Great Northeast Athletic Conference. Men's basketball, women's soccer, men's tennis, women's softball, and the cross-country team are perennial GNAC conference finalists. The college has built a new athletic field and gym to support a growing intercollegiate presence. Emersonians also enjoy an active intramural program and take advantage of the 10,000-square-foot fitness center featuring state-of-the-art equipment, classes, and wellness workshops.

While you are not guaranteed to become the next Meryl Streep, Will Smith, or Michael Bay, the possibility for stardom exists at Emerson. "Emerson nurtures students without treating them like children," says one happy freshman. And even if a lifestyle of fame is not for you, the excellent education, small classes, and attentive professors may teach you how to be the "star" of your own life.

Overlaps

NYU, Boston University, Northeastern, Ithaca, Syracuse, University of Massachusetts, University of Southern California, Fordham

If You Apply To ➤ | **Emerson:** Early action: Nov. 1. Regular admissions: Jan. 5. Financial aid: Mar. 1. Application fee: $65. No campus or alumni interviews. SATs or ACTs: required. Subject Tests: optional. Accepts the Common Application. Essay question: personal statement.

Emory University

200 Boisfeuillet Jones Center, Atlanta, GA 30322-1950

Often compared to Duke and Vanderbilt, Emory may be most similar to Washington University in St. Louis. Both are in major cities and both tout business and premed as major draws. Emory's suburban Atlanta location is unbeatable. Also consider Oxford College, Emory's two-year small-town liberal arts campus. Still attracts a larger contingent from the Northeast than more Southern competitors such as Vanderbilt.

Emory belongs to the Atlanta Regional Council for Higher Education, which lets students take courses at other area schools.

Emory University may lack the liberal arts prowess of the Northeastern schools with which it competes, but it's a favorite of preprofessional students from both U.S. coasts. They come for its size (big, but not too big), location, and national reputation. Though most students are clean-cut and career-oriented, a freshman says the population ranges "from preppy, to Northeast and very designer-oriented, to hippie, and everything in between." Regardless of how they're dressed, students are challenged, not coddled, in the classroom; they form study groups and work together to succeed. An atmosphere of friendliness and Southern hospitality enhances the vibrant campus life.

"Many courses are challenging, but they are also exciting."

Set on 631 acres of woods and rolling hills in the Druid Hills suburb of Atlanta, Emory's campus spreads out from an academic quad of marble-covered, red-roofed buildings. Contemporary structures dot the periphery of the lush, green grounds. In recent years, Emory has expanded science and math research facilities, constructed an apartment-style living complex for upper-class students, added a performing arts center and a psychology building, and opened freshman residence halls, which make up a freshman quad. "I enjoy our location because it offers a homey, 'neighborhood' feel, while providing the optimal location just 15 minutes from downtown Atlanta," says one senior.

Emory's distribution requirements aim to develop competence in writing, quantitative methods, a second language, and physical education, and include exposure to the humanities, social sciences, and the natural sciences. Other required coursework helps broaden students' perspectives on national, regional, and global history and culture. Finally, students take two seminars—one as freshmen (50 to 60 are available each term, limited to 15 students each) and one at an upper level. Entering freshmen seeking a smaller environment may want to consider Emory's two-year Oxford College, located in a "small-town" atmosphere 30 miles away. There, 725 students earn associate's degrees and then continue to the main campus to finish up. (Interested students should apply directly to Oxford.) Additionally, all freshmen participate in PACE (Pre-Major Advising Connections at Emory).

"You'll see talent sprinkled everywhere."

The program brings together faculty, staff, and student leaders to mentor first-year students on the aspects of college life. Emory belongs to the Atlanta Regional Council for Higher Education, which lets students take courses at other area schools. The Center for International Programs Abroad (CIPA) offers more than 100 study programs on six continents. Participants earn Emory credit and Emory grades, and they can receive Emory financial aid, scholarships, and grants.

Emory can be challenging, even for those accustomed to hard work. "My friends and I jokingly call ourselves 'the students formerly known as gifted,'" quips a sophomore. A senior adds, "Many courses are challenging, but they are also exciting." Just as Emory has invested in its physical plant, the school has spent lavishly in the past to add star faculty members to key departments, such as Archbishop Desmond Tutu in the school of theology, the Dalai Lama, and Salman Rushdie. "They're passionate about the subject matter and concerned with making sure their students get the most out of their education," says one student, and personal attention is nearly a given. Chemistry and biology benefit from physical proximity to the federal Centers for Disease Control, while many political science professors have ties to the Carter Center (named for the former president, who holds a town hall meeting on campus each year), and serve as regular guests on nearby CNN.

The most popular majors are business, economics, biology, psychology, and nursing. Dual degree programs allow students to earn a bachelor's degree at Emory and a bachelor's degree in engineering at Georgia Tech, or a bachelor's degree at Emory and a master's in engineering at Georgia Tech. Emory has received a significant portion of Nobel laureate Seamus Heaney's archive, and its Irish studies program is said to rival those of Notre Dame and Boston College. There are minors in predictive health, sustainability, and bioethics.

"Every Emory student angles to be a part of Dooley's entourage (our unofficial skeleton mascot)," says a senior. "You'll see talent sprinkled everywhere from breathtaking Theater Emory shows to First Fridays (a cappella concerts that draw crowds on the first Friday of every month)." Only 24 percent of Emory students are Georgians, and one-third are from the Southeast. New York, New Jersey, California, and Florida are also well represented. African Americans make up 10 percent of the student body, Asian Americans 23 percent, and Hispanics 6 percent. Politically, the campus is less conservative than many Southern institutions. "Most people are very aware of what's going on in the world and bring humanitarian and political activism onto campus," a sociology major says. Merit scholarships worth an average of $21,047 are awarded annually; there are no athletic scholarships. Under the "Loan Cap Program," the university has capped loans at $15,000 for families with incomes between $50,000 and $100,000.

Chemistry and biology benefit from physical proximity to the federal Centers for Disease Control.

Sixty-seven percent of Emory students live on campus; freshmen and sophomores are required to do so. Lucky juniors and seniors may hang their hats in the one- to four-bedroom Clairmont Campus apartments, which boast private bedrooms with full-size beds, kitchens, and baths, and

"There is a very active social scene both on and off campus."

a washer-dryer in each unit. Clairmont residents also get an activity center with basketball, volleyball, and tennis courts; a heated, outdoor, Olympic-sized pool; and weight-training facilities. Housing is guaranteed for two years, and students can request to live in a building that is co-ed by floor, co-ed by room, or single sex. "I lived in the oldest, smallest freshman hall (Dobbs) during my first year at Emory, but I loved it," a student says. "The sense of community was stronger than in any other dorm." They can also request a specific roommate. In addition to the dining halls, there are small cafés, grills, and a food court on campus, each providing tasty fare. "The food is pretty good," says a freshman.

"Emory has an amazing social life that combines on-campus fun with the best Atlanta has to offer," says a junior. "There is a very active social scene both on and off campus," adds another student. Fraternities and sororities attract 30 percent of Emory's men and 31 percent of the women so, of course, Greek parties are prevalent. Upperclassmen enjoy the Atlanta bar scene. Other options include college nights at local dance clubs and concerts organized by the Student Programming Committee. Alcohol isn't allowed in the freshman dorms, and "anyone caught will definitely suffer consequences," a freshman says. A very popular highlight of the social calendar is Dooley's Week, a spring festival in honor of Emory's enigmatic mascot, James W. Dooley, a skeleton who reportedly escaped from the biology lab almost 100 years ago. If Dooley walks into your class, the class is dismissed, and the week culminates with a costume ball in his honor. Freshman halls also have Songfest, a competition where residents make up spirit-filled song-and-dance routines. Popular road trips include Stone Mountain, Athens, Savannah, and the beaches of Florida and the Carolinas.

Merit scholarships worth an average of $21,047 are awarded annually; there are no athletic scholarships.

Atlanta also offers a multitude of diversions, from Braves baseball and Hawks basketball to plays at the Fox Theatre, exhibits at the High Museum of Art, marine wildlife at the Georgia Aquarium, and shopping at Underground Atlanta or the Lenox Mall, to which Emory provides a free shuttle every Saturday.

Emory doesn't field a varsity football team, but the Eagles have produced a number of national champs, including women's swimming and diving and men's tennis. Men's swimming and diving, baseball, women's volleyball, and men's golf are competitive as well. Men's basketball competes against such academic powerhouses as the University of Chicago, Johns Hopkins, and Carnegie Mellon. Most students join

Overlaps

Duke, Georgetown, University of Pennsylvania, Vanderbilt, Washington University in St. Louis

at least one intramural sports team at either a competitive or a recreational level. Popular intramurals include flag football, volleyball, soccer, basketball, water polo, and ultimate Frisbee.

While many Southern schools suffer from a regional provincialism, that isn't true at Emory, which blends a focus on teaching and research to nurture creativity and graduate leaders who are highly sought after in the working world—and by postgraduate law, medical, and business programs. "Emory provides a rich community that students truly love to be part of," says a senior.

<table>
<tr><td>If You Apply To ➤</td><td>Emory: Early decision: Nov. 1. Regular admissions: Jan. 15. Financial aid: Mar. 1. Housing: May 1. Application fee: $50. No campus or alumni interviews. SATs or ACTs: required. Subject Tests: recommended. Accepts the Common Application. Essay question. Recommend that serious applicants visit the campus.</td></tr>
</table>

Eugene Lang College–The New School for Liberal Arts

65 West 11th Street, New York, NY 10011

Eugene Lang College–The New School for Liberal Arts is home to 1,355 street-savvy, freethinking students and has finally caught on as a desirable alternative to NYU in New York's chic Greenwich Village. The city is its campus, and Lang per se offers little sense of community. In keeping with the New School's history, an internationalist perspective is predominant. Strong in the arts and humanities; its student body is nearly 70 percent female.

Website: www.newschool.edu
Location: City Center
Private
Total Enrollment: 1,355
Undergraduates: 1,355
Male/Female: 31/69
SAT Ranges: CR 550–655, M 500–610
ACT Ranges: 24–27
Financial Aid: N/A
Expense: Pr $ $
Student Loans: 44%
Average Debt: $ $ $ $
Phi Beta Kappa: No
Applicants: 1,543
Accepted: 73%
Enrolled: 25%
Grad in 6 Years: 52%
Returning Freshmen: 80%
Academics: ✍ ✍ ✍
Social: ☎
Q of L: ★ ★ ★

Students seeking a typical college experience—large lectures, rowdy football games, and rigid academic requirements—would do well to steer clear of Eugene Lang College. That's because Lang has seminars instead of traditional lectures, minimal required coursework, and not a single varsity sport. Instead, this small, urban liberal arts college offers individualized academic programs, small classes, and a campus that reflects the quirky and kinetic atmosphere of Greenwich Village. "We don't want to become business leaders, but instead teachers, community organizers, thinkers, professors, and writers," a junior says. "Students here want to change the world."

"Students here want to change the world."

Lang fits right in amid the brownstones and trendy boutiques of one of New York's most vibrant neighborhoods. The majority of Lang's classrooms and facilities are in a single five-story building between Fifth and Sixth avenues on West 11th Street, although The New School occupies 16 buildings along Fifth Avenue. NYU and the excitement of Greenwich Village and Washington Square Park are just a few blocks away. The new University Center offers state-of-the-art facilities, including fully wired "smart" classrooms, design studios, a residence hall, and an auditorium.

The New School was founded in 1919 by a band of progressive scholars that included John Dewey, Charles Beard, and Thorstein Veblen. A decade and a half later, it became a haven for European intellectuals fleeing Nazi persecution, and over the years it has been the teaching home of many notable thinkers, including Buckminster Fuller and Hannah Arendt. Created in 1978, the undergraduate college was renamed in the late '80s for Eugene Lang, a philanthropist who made a significant donation to the school.

In addition to Eugene Lang College, today's New School includes a graduate program in social research, a school of management, and various arts programs, most notably the former Parsons School of Design, now known as Parsons-The New School for Design. At night, the New School for Public Engagement is host to a huge assortment of lectures and continuing education courses.

The two most distinctive features of Lang College are the small classes—85 percent have fewer than 19 students—and undergraduates pursuing their own path of study with minimal general education requirements. As freshmen, students choose from a broad-based menu of seminars, and as sophomores,

"The coursework and expectations are demanding."

they select from 16 paths of study: the arts (dance, theater, music, visual studies); culture and media; economics; education studies; environmental studies; global studies; interdisciplinary studies; history; literary studies; philosophy; politics; psychology; religious studies; social inquiry; urban studies; and self-designed liberal arts. In their final year, students take on advanced "senior work" through a seminar or independent project that synthesizes their educational experience. The standard courseload is at least four seminars a semester, with topics such as From Standup to Shakespeare and The History of Jazz. All first-year students must take one year of writing and workshops focusing on nonacademic concerns and library research skills. Cooperation, not competition, is the norm. "The coursework and expectations are demanding," a senior says, but the focus is on "communal and collaborative learning."

Lang's top offerings include political and social theory, writing, history, literature, and literary theory. Its city location lends strength to the urban studies and education programs. Writing is highly praised, especially fiction and journalism, and the arts programs are generally strong. While introductory language courses are plentiful, upper-level language offerings are limited. And the college has beefed up its offerings on the history and literature of Third World and minority peoples, which were already better than those at most colleges. The professors at Lang are well versed and engaging, according to many students. "I appreciate the way that class discussions are so well planned and thought out," says one student.

The main academic complaint is the limited range of seminars, but outside programs offer more variety. After their first year, students may enroll in a limited number of approved classes in other divisions of The New School. More than a dozen joint B.A./M.A. and B.A./M.S. programs are available, including media studies, international affairs, nonprofit management, psychology, philosophy, and economics. Exchange programs with Sarah Lawrence College, American University of Paris, and John Cabot University (among others) provide motivated students with additional academic opportunities. The New School's library is small, but students have access to the massive Bobst Library at nearby New York University.

Lang College attracts a disparate group of undergraduates, but most of them can be described as idealistic and independent. "We are nontraditional college students who relish in this difference and exciting uniqueness that sets us apart from conforming NYU students," a junior says. Some are slightly older than conventional college age and are used to looking

"We do have dances and club activities within the school facilities."

after themselves. Twenty percent are African American or Hispanic, and another 5 percent are Asian American. Less than 20 percent of Lang's students are from New York and many cite the school's location as one of its best features. "Whatever is desired can be found somewhere in New York City," says a junior. "It's a nice place to be if you want to party or be a stone-cold intellectual." Lang College admits students regardless of their finances and strives to meet the demonstrated need of those enrolled. However, the school does not guarantee to meet the demonstrated financial need of all admits. A deferred-payment plan allows students to pay tuition in 10

(continued)

Admissions: (212) 229-5665
Email Address: lang@ newschool.edu

Strongest Programs:
Film
Writing
Fine Arts
Education Studies
Culture and Media
Philosophy

The standard courseload is at least four seminars a semester, with topics such as From Standup to Shakespeare and The History of Jazz.

installments, and there are various loan programs available. There are a handful of merit scholarships, but no varsity teams means no athletic awards.

Dorm life at Lang attracts roughly one-quarter of the student body, and the rooms are reported to be in good shape. Stuyvesant Park and University Center are the newest dorms; Stuy Park caters predominantly to first-year students. Off-campus dwellers live in apartments in the Village, if they can afford it, or in Brooklyn or elsewhere in the New York City area. A meal plan is available, but most students opt for the hundreds of delis, coffee shops, and restaurants that line Sixth Avenue.

The social network at Lang is quite small and, like many things, is left up to the student. "Our lack of campus kind of makes all activity 'off campus,' though we do have dances and club activities within the school facilities themselves," a junior says. The social activities found on campus generally involve intellectual pursuits such as poetry readings and open-mic nights, as well as typical college activities like the student newspaper and the literary magazine. Occasionally, students organize dances and parties. Students generally avoid drinking on campus, and when they do imbibe, alcohol is "far from the central focus of activity," says a junior. Athletics barely register here, although the school does field three teams: men's basketball, and men's and women's cross-country.

Despite the seeming lack of tradition and sense of community, Eugene Lang College's stock continues to rise. Students relish the freedom and independence they have at Eugene Lang College. For a student who yearns for four years of "traditional" college experiences, Lang would likely be a disappointment. But for those desiring an intimate education in America's cultural capital, Lang offers all the stimulation of the city it calls home.

The New School's library is small, but students have access to the massive Bobst Library at nearby New York University.

If You Apply To ➢ **Eugene Lang:** Early decision: Nov. 1. Regular admissions: Jan. 6. Housing: Jul. 1. Application fee: $50. No campus or alumni interviews. SATs or ACTs: optional. Subject Tests: optional. Accepts the Common Application. Essay question.

The Evergreen State College

Olympia, WA 98505

There's no mistaking Evergreen for a typical public college. Never mind the way-out garb favored by its students; Evergreen's interdisciplinary, team-taught curriculum is unique. To find anything remotely like Evergreen, you'll need to go private and travel East to places like Hampshire or Sarah Lawrence. Evergreen is no longer as selective as it once was, and its graduation rate has suffered accordingly.

In "La Vie Bohème," the anthem of Jonathan Larson's rock opera *Rent*, one of the characters asks, "Anyone out of the mainstream / Is anyone in the mainstream?" At The Evergreen State College, the answer has always been a vehement "No!" The school's unofficial motto is *Omnia Extares*, Latin for "Let it all hang out." Founded in 1967 as Washington State's experimental college, Evergreen lacks grades, majors, and even departments. This system may sound strange, but it works for those seeking the freedom to chart their own course. "The character of the school is openly artistic, earth-friendly, musically open, and a place to truly be an individual," says a freshman. "Students are free to explore and be whoever they want to be," agrees a sophomore.

Website: www.evergreen.edu
Location: Small City
Public
Total Enrollment: 4,062
Undergraduates: 3,863
Male/Female: 47/53
SAT Ranges: CR 510–640, M 460–590
ACT Ranges: 21–27

Evergreen lies in a fir forest at the edge of the 90-mile-long Puget Sound. The peaceful, 1,000-acre campus includes an organic plant and animal farm, as well as 3,300 feet of undeveloped beach. Most of Evergreen's buildings are boxy concrete-and-steel creations, though the Longhouse Education and Cultural Center is designed in the Native American style typical of the Pacific Northwest. In keeping with Evergreen's progressive nature, all new building projects strive to comply with LEED standards, and intercity bus passes are included in the cost of tuition. Recent additions include a new sustainable agriculture laboratory.

At first glance, Evergreen's wide-open curriculum looks like Easy Street: it's based on nine "planning units"—native programs; critical and creative practices; culture, text, and language; environmental studies; expressive arts; sustainability and justice; scientific inquiry; consciousness studies; and society, politics, behavior, and change—which

> "The academic climate at Evergreen is robust, collaborative, and engaging."

means no required classes and few traditional exams to slog through at the end of each 10-week quarter. And instead of signing up for unrelated courses to fulfill distribution requirements, students enroll in a coordinated "program," often team-taught by multiple professors. Recent offerings include Food, Health, and Sustainability; Living in the Sacred Garden; Music, Math, and Motion; and Positive Restlessness. Still, there is some structure at the college. Many freshmen select an interdisciplinary core program tailored for first-year students, while upperclassmen concentrate in more specialized areas, often writing a thesis or fulfilling an Individual Learning Contract developed in partnership with a faculty sponsor. "Freshman Core programs, which are entirely for freshmen, are really good introductions to Evergreen, and do a lot to introduce students to support services available on campus," says one student.

Students praise Evergreen's environmental science offerings, which span ornithology, marine biology, and wetlands studies. To supplement their coursework, environmental scientists may also study marine animals while sailing in Puget Sound, spend seven weeks at a bird sanctuary in Oregon, or trek to the Grand Canyon or the tropical rainforests of Costa Rica. Various arts programs—dance, writing, visual arts, and media arts—also get high marks. And regardless of what they study, students warn that—while the integrated approach to learning may improve comprehension and deepen understanding—it likewise means a lot of work. "The academic climate at Evergreen is robust, collaborative, and engaging," says a junior. "It gives space for both self-directed learning and small learning communi-

> "The apartments have been remodeled so they are clean and everything is in good condition."

ties." Capstone programs include internships, contracts, and opportunities within specific programs. There are also formal opportunities to complete a capstone project, such as the Expressive Arts Senior Thesis.

Because Evergreen attracts many nontraditional students and students who are older than the typical college freshman, administrators take advising and career counseling seriously. They've also asked faculty members to do more to help students adjust to life on campus. "The teachers have such a personal connection with the students," one senior says. Another bonus: because Evergreen doesn't award tenure, there's less pressure for professors to conduct research and publish their findings—and less to distract them from teaching undergraduates. "The quality of teaching is incredible. Professors actually get to know each individual student and are very knowledgeable," says a student.

Students not only think outside of the box, says a freshman, but "burn the box and create our own way of thinking." Seventy-five percent of Evergreen's students are Washington natives; African Americans and Hispanics account for 12 percent of the student body, while Asian Americans add another 6 percent. "For the most part people are very liberal and tend to be very involved in organizing around an

(continued)

Financial Aid: 63%
Expense: Pub $ $
Student Loans: 48%
Average Debt: $
Phi Beta Kappa: No
Applicants: 1,650
Accepted: 98%
Enrolled: 32%
Grad in 6 Years: 54%
Returning Freshmen: 72%
Academics: ✍ ✍ ✍
Social: ☎ ☎ ☎
Q of L: ★ ★ ★ ★
Admissions: (360) 687-6170
Email Address: admissions@ evergreen.edu

Strongest Programs:
Social Sciences
Humanities
Interdisciplinary Studies
Environmental Sciences
Liberal Arts

issue they feel is important," a senior says. Another adds, "Greeners want to be open minded, intelligent, and actually meaningful to the world in which they live."

Twenty percent of Evergreen students, mostly freshmen and sophomores, live on campus. The school's apartment complexes have single bedrooms, shared bathrooms—with bathtubs, not just shower stalls—and full kitchens, according to one student. "The apartments have been remodeled so they are clean and everything is in good condition. They are very spacious and most students have their own bedroom," says one student. Still, because campus housing can be expensive, most upperclassmen live off campus. There's an efficient bus system to get nonresidents to class on time, though it helps to have a car. Evergreen's food service offers a wide variety of dishes. "We have the amazing student-run cafe: The Flaming Eggplant. They serve delicious, locally sourced food that caters to special diets," cheers one student. Campus security is "adequate, reliable, and friendly," according to one American studies major, and students report feeling safe on campus.

Given the pervasive individualism that flavors Evergreen, it's little surprise that the college lacks a Greek system. Still, students say the housing office organizes plenty of weekend events—including open-mic nights, soccer, and other field games, performances, and parties. "Social life happens both on and off campus," a creative writing major says. "There are on campus lectures, plays, concerts, festivals…On the weekend there will be a lot happening downtown Olympia or at house parties." Nearby Olympia (the state capital) doesn't really qualify as a college town, but it is progressive and open minded, with art walks through local galleries, coffee shops, clothing stores, co-ops, and lots of live music. Even better, "Evergreen is 10 minutes from theaters, parks, and recreation, an hour or so from skiing, hiking, or the beach, and about an hour from Seattle," says a student concentrating in sociology. The college offers all types of outdoor equipment for rent, from backpacks and skis to kayaks and sailboats. Its large College Activities Building houses a radio station and the student newspaper, along with space for student gatherings. Portland and the rugged Oregon coast (three to four hours away) provide other changes of scenery for students with wheels; everything is kept green and lush by the (interminable) rain, which stops in time for summer break and resumes by October.

> **"On the weekend there will be a lot happening downtown Olympia or at house parties."**

You may chuckle at Evergreen's mascot, an eight-foot clam named "Speedy" (a nod to the large geoduck clams found in Puget Sound), but the school is serious about organized sports. Its basketball, cross-country, soccer, and women's volleyball teams compete in the Division II Cascade Conference. While those squads haven't brought home any titles yet, Evergreen has produced All-American players. Students may choose to participate in recreational or intramural sports, which include Frisbee, volleyball, skiing, tennis, basketball, and sailing.

Evergreen isn't for everyone; indeed, this remains one of the best choices for students who think they were born several decades too late. Freed from requirements and grades, Greeners delight in exploring the connections between disparate disciplines at their own pace. Succeeding in that endeavor, however, requires an incredible ability to focus; while some students would find the task burdensome, students here welcome the challenge. "It's up to us to learn what to believe in, not some instructor telling us what it's going to be," says a satisfied math and computer science student.

Overlaps

University of Washington, Western Washington, Hampshire, Seattle University, UC–Santa Cruz, Central Washington, Lewis & Clark

If You Apply To ➤

Evergreen: Regular admissions: Feb. 1. Financial aid: Mar. 1. Housing: Jul. 14. Application fee: $50. Campus interviews: optional, informational. No alumni interviews. SATs or ACTs: required. Subject Tests: optional. Essay question.

Fairfield, CT 06824

Fairfield is one of the up-and-coming schools in the Roman Catholic higher education scene. Undergraduate enrollment has grown in recent years. Strategic location near New York City is a major attraction. Lack of big-time sports keeps Fairfield from enjoying the visibility of Boston College or Holy Cross. Business is the biggest academic draw. Check out the beach house on Long Island Sound.

No doubt about it, Fairfield University is moving into the same class as older, more revered East Coast Jesuit institutions. The school provides a dynamic living and learning environment, combining solid academics, real-world opportunities in and outside of the classroom, and an abundance of community service projects. Although the number of Jesuit faculty members is declining, a new on-campus residence, boldly contemporary and centrally located, is intended to enhance their visibility on campus and to enlist the help of lay faculty in pursuing the ideals of Jesuit education. "There is an outstanding sense of community on campus," says one senior, "and being a smaller school, the needs of students are addressed rapidly and efficiently."

The physical beauty of the university's scenic, tree-lined campus just 90 minutes from Manhattan is a source of pride. The administration takes pains to preserve a lush atmosphere of sprawling lawns, ponds, and natural woodlands. Buildings are a blend of collegiate Gothic, Norman chateau, English manor, and modern. Students enjoy a 24-hour computer lab, Geographic Information Systems lab, wireless 125-person computer lab in the School of Nursing, and wireless area in the Barone Campus Center. Two new residential facilities were recently completed and two others were substantially renovated.

Students may have difficulty finding time to savor the beautiful facilities. A demanding class schedule requires everyone to complete the liberal arts core curriculum over four years, with two to five courses from each of five areas: math and natural sciences; history and social and behavioral sciences; philosophy, religious studies, and applied ethics; English and visual and performing arts; and modern and classical languages. The core constitutes almost half of a student's total courseload. Fairfield's main academic strengths are business (marketing, finance, and management), nursing, communications, and psychology. "The core is extensive but extremely rewarding," says an English major. Upperclassmen with the necessary academic standing can design their own majors.

> **"There is an outstanding sense of community on campus."**

Fairfield's academic climate is demanding. "Our courses are challenging but stimulating at the same time," says a biology major. "The way I look at it is that if it's something you really enjoy, you're willing to work at it." Irish studies has strong ties to the University of Galway and Italian studies features links to the Florence University of the Arts. Engineering students may enroll in joint five-year programs with the Rensselaer Polytechnic Institute, Columbia University, the University of Connecticut, or Stevens Institute of Technology. M.B.A. candidates can choose a concentration in ebusiness or minor in information systems or operations management. Since 1993, more than three dozen Fairfield students have been awarded Fulbright scholarships for studies abroad. About 5 percent are part of the four-year honors program.

Students looking to travel abroad without committing a full semester can take a trip with one of several professors who lead educational summer tours for credit.

Website: www.fairfield.edu
Location: Suburban
Private
Total Enrollment: 3,813
Undergraduates: 3,456
Male/Female: 41/59
SAT Ranges: CR 530–620, M 550–630
ACT Ranges: 24–27
Financial Aid: 78%
Expense: Pr $ $ $
Student Loans: 67%
Average Debt: $ $ $
Phi Beta Kappa: Yes
Applicants: 9,254
Accepted: 71%
Enrolled: 15%
Grad in 6 Years: 81%
Returning Freshmen: 87%
Academics: ✐ ✐ ✐
Social: 🐀 🐀 🐀 🐀
Q of L: ★ ★ ★ ★
Admissions: (203) 254-4100
Email Address: admis@ fairfield.edu

Strongest Programs:
Nursing
Accounting
Communication
Biology
Religious Studies
Business

Approximately 45 percent of students study abroad each year, through their choice of approximately 100 programs in 50 nations. Sophomores can join the Ignatian Residential College; afterward, they can continue on to the Companions program, which includes cultural activities and mentoring. Students enrolled in the Dolan School of Business have access to a state-of-the-art, multipurpose financial markets classroom known as the Business Experiential, Simulation, and Trading Floor (BEST) classroom. Approximately 21 percent of students carry out undergraduate research projects during their time at Fairfield.

Freshmen are introduced to Fairfield with a thorough orientation program. A formal academic convocation in the first week of classes includes a speaker chosen to reflect the school's Jesuit values. There are no teaching assistants at Fairfield; 40 percent of classes have 19 or fewer students. "Every professor I ever contacted was willing to meet me during his or her office hours to clarify questions regarding various projects, papers, and assignments," a junior says.

The vast majority of Fairfield's students come from Roman Catholic families, and 35 percent are from Connecticut. Minority enrollment is small, with African Americans constituting 3 percent of the student body, Hispanics 8 percent, and Asian Americans 2 percent. "Students are incredibly hardworking, motivated, and passionate. Nurses are willing to wake up at four in the morning to go to clinical, while liberal arts and business students intern for two or three companies on average throughout their four years here," a communication major says. Hot-button issues include environmental, gender, and sexuality issues, according to an accounting major. To help students with Fairfield's steep price, the school offers merit scholarships annually, averaging $16,105, as well as 255 athletic scholarships in 20 sports.

Fairfield's residence halls house 82 percent of the student body. Overcrowding is a real concern, and some students are squeezed into triples or fail to get a room at all. "The newer dorms are definitely nicer and provide more space and luxury for students. There is never trouble getting a room, as on campus housing is guaranteed all four years should you need it, but the nicer dorms get chosen (in the lottery) first," a senior reports. Seniors are given the opportunity to experience living off campus, and among the most popular options are the privately owned beach houses and apartments on Long Island Sound made available to students off-season. Several living/learning communities are available, too, for first-year students; options include women in math and sciences, healthy living, and community service floors. Meal plan options are available to all students, and many say the menu is middling at best. "They have salads available all the time but otherwise don't have special dishes for vegetarians, vegans, or those that eat kosher," grumbles one freshman. Campus security receives higher praise: "Campus security is fantastic!" raves one student. "I have never felt unsafe walking around at campus at night. All of the gates close at 11:00 p.m. with the exception of the main entrance where a Public Safety officer is stationed to check our student ID cards."

Fairfield's proximity to the beaches of the Long Island Sound, a quick five-minute drive from campus, provides students with a scenic social space for everything from romantic retreats to lively parties. "On a Friday night, there are students hopping in taxis going to Fairfield Beach for a party, walking up to the townhouse, or watching a movie in the auditorium," says one student. "There is something for everyone at Fairfield, should they be someone who parties or does not." On campus, sponsored events range from dances to hanging out at the coffeehouse and on-campus pub to concerts. "While it isn't a huge campus, there is usually a lot to do," says a sophomore. Harvest Weekend at the end of October and Dogwoods Weekend at the end of April provide relief from the stress of studying. Road trips

Irish studies has strong ties to the University of Galway and Italian studies features links to the Florence University of the Arts.

"Our courses are challenging but stimulating."

To help students with Fairfield's steep price, the school offers merit scholarships annually, averaging $16,105, as well as 255 athletic scholarships in 20 sports.

to New York (an hour by train) and Boston (two hours away) are popular. Students report alcohol policies to be effective in curbing underage drinking, although "if you want a drink, you can find it," says one freshman. The Campus Ministry draws a large following, with daily masses, retreats about three times a semester, and regular community service work, including two weeks of programs in the Caribbean and Latin America. But one student complains, "Our Jesuit identity needs to be expressed more clearly and something more must be done to excite students about the spiritual life."

As for the surrounding area, some students say the quaint, wealthy Fairfield area can feel a bit "snobby," though there are plenty of shopping outlets and restaurants that fit college student budgets. Beach residents don't always approve of beach-apartment students and their activities. "Community members are not often comfortable participating in university events and vice versa," a student says. Volunteerism abounds, much of it in the nearby city of Bridgeport. "The influence of Bridgeport on my Fairfield experience has been profound," says a student.

Athletics have come of age at Fairfield. The university's Division I athletic program was awarded the Metro Atlantic Athletic Conference (MAAC) 2012 Commissioner's Cup, the league's highest honor. Competitive Stags teams include men's and women's soccer, men's and women's lacrosse, and men's and women's tennis, volleyball, and softball. Men's and women's basketball both draw crowds, and the boisterous home-court fans, who come to games in full Fairfield regalia, have been dubbed the "Red Sea." Living up to the Jesuit motto of sound mind and body, about half of the students play on one of 25 intramural teams, whose exploits are copiously chronicled in the campus newspaper. "Many students sign up and create teams with their friends, and have a great time playing during the weekends," one student says. The school also takes pride in its high graduation rate for athletes, regularly one of the highest rates in the country.

Fairfield University has combined several traditions to create a rich undergraduate experience, including close bonds with faculty, an emphasis on community involvement, challenging academics, and an emphasis on the holistic development of each student. "Fairfield seeks to help people realize that there is more to life than your marketing degree," a satisfied student says. "Students are taught to open their eyes and see the real world."

> *The university's Division I athletic program was awarded the Metro Atlantic Athletic Conference (MAAC) 2012 Commissioner's Cup, the league's highest honor.*

> **"Students are incredibly hardworking, motivated, and passionate."**

Overlaps

Providence, Quinnipiac, Loyola (MD), Fordham, University of Connecticut, Sacred Heart, Boston College, Stonehill College

If You Apply To ➤ | **Fairfield:** Early action: Nov. 1. Regular admissions: Jan. 15. Financial aid: Feb. 15. Housing: May 1. Application fee: $60. Campus and alumni interviews: optional, evaluative. SATs or ACTs: required. Subject Tests: optional. Accepts the Common Application. Essay question: Common Application; personal statement.

University of Florida

Gainesville, FL 32611

It should come as no surprise that UF is a world leader in citrus science. Add communications, engineering, and Latin American studies to the list of renowned programs. Among Deep South public universities, only the University of Georgia rivals UF in overall quality. None rivals it in alcohol consumption. Top-shelf varsity sports teams are a year-round draw.

Website: www.ufl.edu

Location: Suburban

Public

Total Enrollment: 42,608

Undergraduates: 29,984

Male/Female: 45/55

SAT Ranges: CR 580–670,
  M 590–690

ACT Ranges: 26–31

Financial Aid: 96%

Expense: Pub $

Student Loans: 41%

Average Debt: $

Phi Beta Kappa: Yes

Applicants: 27,419

Accepted: 44%

Enrolled: 52%

Grad in 6 Years: 85%

Returning Freshmen: 96%

Academics: ✍ ✍ ✍ ✍

Social: 🍷 🍷 🍷 🍷 🍷

Q of L: ★ ★ ★ ★

Admissions: (352) 392-1365

Email Address:
  webrequests@admissions
  .ufl.edu

Strongest Programs:
Journalism
Chemistry
Pharmacy
Anthropology
Material Sciences
English
Citrus Science

Set on 2,000 acres of rolling, heavily forested terrain in north-central Florida, the University of Florida is an athletic powerhouse, and administrators are working hard to gain the same level of national recognition for their academic offerings as well. The school is massive and continues to grow, and in this case, bigger does seem to be better. While some students certainly get lost in the shuffle, those who can navigate the bureaucratic red tape will find ample resources at their fingertips, including the world's largest collection of butterflies and moths and an $85 million Cancer and Genetics Research Complex. The state's flagship university has become more selective in its admissions and continues to wage an aggressive campaign against its long-standing tradition of free-flowing alcohol.

> **"UF is fairly competitive–it's hard to get in to, so students who attend are eager to get ahead."**

UF's central campus has more than 20 buildings on the National Register of Historic Places. Most are collegiate Gothic in style—redbrick with white trim. They're augmented by more modern facilities, including a 173,000-square-foot complex for nursing, pharmacy, and the health professions; and an honors dorm complex, which offers suite-style living, a computer lab, classrooms, and a full-time honors staff in residence. UF's research capabilities and equipment are likewise impressive, and a boon to aspiring physicians. The school has one of the nation's few self-contained intensive care hyperbaric chambers for treatment of near-drowning victims, and a world-class, federally funded brain institute. Media types flock to the school's public TV and radio stations, and to its two commercial radio stations. Pugh Hall houses the Bob Graham Center for Public Service and trains students in languages, culture, and other skills vital to careers in public service.

Academically, UF's strongest programs are those with a preprofessional bent, including engineering, tax law, and pharmacy. Popular majors include psychology, biology, political science, mechanical engineering, and finance. Students also give high marks to the College of Journalism and Communications, the first in the nation to offer students an electronic newsroom. Students with weighted high school GPAs of 4.0 or higher and SAT scores of at least 1400 are invited into the Honors Program, where most classes are limited to 25 students. The program offers honors sections in standard academic subjects, and interdisciplinary courses such as Masterworks of Music, Writing, and Love, and the History of Rock and Roll. Additionally, honors students are invited to live in the Honors Residential College. The University Scholars Program offers $2,500 stipends to 205 students each year for one-on-one research with a faculty member. Results must be published in the online *Journal for Undergraduate Research* or another peer-reviewed journal. Even if you don't qualify for those options, you should find something of interest, since only Ohio State and the University of Minnesota offer more degree programs on one campus than UF, among the five largest universities in the nation.

> **"Students love living on campus and feel comfortable in their dorms."**

The University Scholars Program offers $2,500 stipends to 205 students each year for one-on-one research with a faculty member.

To balance students' preprofessional coursework, UF's general education program requires credits in composition, math, humanities, social and behavioral sciences, and physical and biological sciences. Students must also take six credits in the humanities or social or physical sciences that focus on themes of internationalism or diversity. Approximately 4 percent of the student body study abroad each year through more than 80 university-sponsored programs, over 100 exchange programs, and thousands of non-university sponsored options.

"UF is fairly competitive—it's hard to get in to, so students who attend are eager to get ahead. In large classes, students are looking to prove themselves and stand out to their professors," says one political science major. While UF offers programs in every conceivable discipline, like many supersized schools, it also forces students to climb a mountain of bureaucracy to get the courses and credits they need. Occasionally, for example, lectures in the College of Business Administration have to be videotaped and rebroadcast on the campus cable network so that everyone can see them. Still, administrators are working to fix these problems. Professors often have deep professional experience and bring enthusiasm to their work, though students often find TAs behind the lectern. "Many of the lower division courses are taught by graduate students," says a student, "and while some are good instructors, others may be too engrossed in their own work to provide adequate teaching."

Florida Gators "accept no limits, work hard in all aspects of their lives as students, and are the ultimate well-rounded individuals," according to one senior. UF is Florida's flagship university, and 95 percent of students here hail from the Sunshine State. Despite the geographical homogeneity, they're an ethnically diverse bunch, with African Americans adding 8 percent of the student body, Asian Americans 8 percent, and Hispanics 18 percent. UF offers 425 athletic scholarships and thousands of merit scholarships averaging $3,868. National Merit Scholars automatically qualify if they list UF as their first choice by the required date.

Twenty-four percent of Florida's undergrads live on campus, and students say rooms are tough to come by if you're not a first-year student. Doubles, triples, and suites in the co-ed dorms are awarded by lottery, based on social security numbers, and there just isn't enough room for everyone. Dorm-dwellers buy the campus meal plan or use kitchens in their residence halls. "Students love living on campus and feel comfortable in their dorms," says a junior. Nineteen percent of UF's men and women go Greek; rush is held before classes start in the fall and again in the spring. The traditional fraternities and Panhellenic Council sororities have privately owned houses in Gainesville, which also offer meal service. Nine historically African American Greek groups and seven culturally based Greek organizations also recruit at various times during the year; they don't offer housing.

"Fraternity row is generally hopping every Friday and Saturday night."

UF students know how to party and the campus continues to be a haven for those who love alcohol. Still, the binge drinking rate has fallen sharply as a result of tougher enforcement, a ban on drinking games, and other means. "Later Gator" buses pick up students who stagger out of bars in the early hours and deliver them home safely. Freshmen must pass a 90-minute online alcohol education course in order to register for their spring semester. "Fraternity row is generally hopping every Friday and Saturday night, but off-campus parties are certainly a fixture as well. Midtown, located right across from the stadium, is the typical place for students to find night life," a senior reports. Students say Gainesville, a city of about 125,000 between the Atlantic Ocean and the Gulf of Mexico, is a great college town. "Gainesville revolves around UF," a student says. There are plenty of stores, restaurants, and bars, as well as a sports arena and the Center for Performing Arts, which brings in world-class symphony orchestras, Broadway plays, opera, and large-scale ballet productions. The university owns a nearby lake, which is "great for lazy Sundays" and more vigorous water sports, and there's a plethora of parks, forests, rivers, and streams for backpacking, camping, and canoeing. Beaches are also a popular destination.

Sports are a year-round obsession here, and the students go wild anytime the Gators take to the court or the gridiron, especially when they're squaring off against rivals Florida State or the University of Georgia. The annual homecoming extravaganza, known as "Gator Growl," is billed as the biggest student-run pep rally in the country. Other sports are not forgotten, though; the university has one of the top intercollegiate programs in the nation, with varsity competition (in the brutal Southeastern Conference) for men and women in 16 sports, including

Overlaps

Florida State, University of Central Florida, University of South Florida, University of Miami, Florida Atlantic, Florida International, University of North Florida, UNC at Chapel Hill

nationally ranked teams in baseball, track, golf, tennis, gymnastics, volleyball, swimming, and diving. Intramural sports are popular (44 percent of students participate), and for those who don't want to join a team, the 60,000-square-foot fitness park offers aerobics classes, martial arts, strength training equipment, and squash and racquetball courts.

For some students, Florida's sheer size is overwhelming. For others, it's a drawing card. "UF is a school with an impressive history," says a senior, "and its students and alumni remain proud of that." Combine great weather with nationally recognized programs in engineering and business, and nationally ranked athletic teams, and it's easy to see why Sunshine State natives clamor to study here.

If You Apply To ➢	**Florida:** Regular admissions: Nov. 1 (for fall semester). Application fee: $30. No campus or alumni interviews. SATs or ACTs: not used. Subject Tests: optional. Students apply to a particular school within UF. Essay question.

Florida Institute of Technology

Melbourne, FL 32901-6975

FIT is practically a branch of the nearby Kennedy Space Center, so aeronautics and aviation are popular specialties. The Atlantic Ocean is close at hand, making the school an ideal spot for marine biology. Only drawback to otherwise ideal location is the occasional early-fall hurricane evacuation. With a total enrollment of about 3,700, FIT is the smallest of the major technical institutions in the Southeast.

Website: www.fit.edu
Location: Small City
Private
Total Enrollment: 3,786
Undergraduates: 2,779
Male/Female: 72/28
SAT Ranges: CR 500–540, M 610–640
ACT Ranges: 22–28
Financial Aid: 85%
Expense: Pr $
Student Loans: 61%
Average Debt: $ $ $ $
Phi Beta Kappa: No
Applicants: 7,428
Accepted: 59%
Enrolled: 17%
Grad in 6 Years: 55%
Returning Freshmen: 79%
Academics: ✐ ✐ ✐
Social: ☎ ☎ ☎
Q of L: ★ ★ ★
Admissions: (800) 888-4248

Students at the Florida Institute of Technology can explore the endless depths of the ocean or shoot for the stars. Located just 40 minutes from one of NASA's primary launch pads, Florida Tech is a child of the nation's space program. The school's subtropical setting is perfect for scientific research and study in oceanography, meteorology, marine biology, and environmental science. It comes as no surprise that some of the most cutting-edge work in space and water-related sciences happens here. The combination of academic excellence and a convenient central Florida location—just an hour from the dizzying bustle of Walt Disney World—draws students to this high-flying and innovative school.

Founded in 1958 to meet the academic needs of engineers and scientists working at what is now the Kennedy Space Center, Florida Tech's contemporary 130-acre

"Florida Tech is very competitive."

campus features more than 200 species of palm trees and botanical gardens in a tropical setting. Campus architecture ranges from modern to Georgian Gothic. The university has opened a number of new facilities in recent years, including the Florida Tech Commons, a 63,000-square-foot building that offers a "one-stop shop" for students needing admission, registration, housing, or financial aid service.

If you're considering Florida Tech, the only independent technological university in the Southeast, make sure you have a strong background in math and science, especially chemistry and physics. Few students major in the less practical sciences. Though many students grouse that Florida Tech is too expensive for their tastes, those who plan their education well are able to get high-paying technical jobs as soon as they graduate. Prospective aviation students can major in aviation management, aviation meteorology, or aviation computer science, as well as aeronautics with or without a flight option. The flight school has a modern fleet of 30 airplanes and three flight-training devices, and the precision-flying team regularly wins titles. The most popular majors are aerospace engineering, mechanical engineering, electrical engineering, civil engineering, and marine biology. Incoming freshmen are welcomed with a weeklong orientation program highlighted by trips to Disney World and the beach, just three miles away. On campus, freshmen may take part in the University Experience Program, which helps first-years adapt to college life; nearly 99 percent participate.

The academic climate at FIT is challenging. "Florida Tech is very competitive because of the nature of the majors," says one junior. More than half of classes have 19 or fewer students and the majority are taught by full professors. All majors offer co-op programs and senior independent research at the Indian River Lagoon or on the *RV Delphinus*, a 60-foot research boat the school owns. Marine research has included manatee preservation, beach erosion, and sea turtle studies. Everyone must take courses in communication, physical or life science, mathematics, humanities, and social sciences, and be proficient in using computers. The ProTrack cooperative education program allows students in the College of Engineering to complete three semester-long paid work experiences. Students graduate with their employers' names on their final transcripts. Study abroad options are available in France and other European countries.

"If you don't have a car of your own, it may be hard because public transportation is limited."

Thirty-four percent of Florida Tech students are out-of-staters, while 28 percent hail from outside the country. "It is a microcosm of intelligent people representing 97 countries," says a sophomore. "It's like traveling the world in four years." African Americans comprise 5 percent of the student body, Asian Americans 2 percent, and Hispanics 6 percent. "There is no 'typical' Florida Tech student," explains one junior. Florida Tech offers merit scholarships averaging $12,306 and 233 athletic scholarships in 17 sports.

There is a growing selection of dorms at Florida Tech, and they are modern and well maintained. Forty-seven percent of students make their home on campus, though some complain about the cost. Still, the rooms are well received. "Residence Life takes a holistic approach to making every resident feel right at home," says a junior. Freshmen are required to live on campus in large double rooms. Four-student apartments are available to a small percentage of qualifying upperclassmen by lottery. Students who live off campus are drawn by cheap rent and not much else, because Melbourne is "quiet and is not a typical college town," reports an aerospace engineering major. The meal plan is an open, unlimited arrangement, and students report the food is fair to middling.

Watching space shots from campus with a trained eye and a cold brew is a treasured pastime. The campus bar, the Rat, is a popular hangout, and there are more than 100 active clubs and organizations on campus. Among the most popular are performance-oriented groups such as Pep Band, The College Players, and Florida Tech cheerleading. Fraternities and sororities are becoming more popular at Florida Tech, claiming 14 percent of the men and 11 percent of the women, respectively. While the campus is officially dry, every frat party has beer that the underage eagerly guzzle, students say. Besides partying, students spend their downtime surfing, fishing, hanging out at the beach, shopping, or going for a "Sunday drive" (in the sky) with a flight school student. Most Florida Tech students who don't have cars choose bikes as their favorite mode of transportation. "If you don't have a car of your own, it may be hard because public transportation is limited," cautions one student. Diversions can be found in Orlando (with Epcot, Disney Hollywood Studios, and Animal Kingdom abutting Disney World) or at the Kennedy Space Center. Students

(continued)

Email Address: admission@ fit.edu

Strongest Programs:
Computer Science
Marine Science
Electrical Engineering
Aerospace Engineering
Computer Engineering
Mechanical Engineering
Aviation Management

The most popular majors are aerospace engineering, mechanical engineering, electrical engineering, civil engineering, and marine biology.

Watching space shots from campus with a trained eye and a cold brew is a treasured pastime.

also hit the road for other Sunshine State cities, including Tampa, Key West, Miami, Daytona, and St. Augustine. Every April, students brace for the invasion of other collegians on spring break.

Techies also look forward to Greek Week and intramural sports competitions. The Florida Tech Panthers compete in Division II and the baseball team is competitive, as are women's cross-country, rowing, golf, and tennis and men's golf and rowing (gold medal winners in 2013 at Dad Vail Regatta). The university's Precision Flight Team, the Falcons, recently earned first place for top pilot and safety at the National Intercollegiate Flying Association's Regional Safety and Flight Evaluation Conference. In 2011–12, Tech was awarded the Sunshine State Conference Mayor's Cup for the men's division.

Whether it's surveying marine coral 50 feet below the sea or the sky 30,000 feet above, students at Florida Tech get hands-on experience that serves to sharpen the school's already specialized, high-quality academics. The administration continues to focus on capital improvements, sponsor cutting-edge research, and embrace diversity. And with beaches and amusements close at hand, students can have some real fun in the sun while they prepare for high-flying or low-lying careers.

Overlaps

University of Central Florida, Embry–Riddle Aeronautical, University of South Florida, University of Florida, Purdue, Florida State, Rochester Institute of Technology, Florida International

If You Apply To ➢

Florida Tech: Rolling admissions. No application fee. Campus and alumni interviews: optional, informational. SATs or ACTs: required. Subject Tests: optional. No essay question.

Florida Southern College

111 Lake Hollingsworth Drive, Lakeland, FL 33801

FSC combines top-ranked Division II athletics, strong career-oriented programs, a strong Greek system, and a picturesque campus that doubles as a Frank Lloyd Wright museum. Located between Tampa and Orlando. Competes with Rollins and Eckerd, but its reputation is more regional and its student body more conservative.

Founded in 1883, Florida Southern College remains committed to providing students with a solid liberal arts foundation and exceptional signature programs. Students enjoy a bevy of academic choices, including outstanding preprofessional programs, comprehensive undergraduate research opportunities, and a vigorous study abroad program. They also appreciate the college's United Methodist affiliation and its mission to develop well-rounded graduates.

> **"The best departments are also some of the most challenging."**

Situated on 100 sloping acres overlooking pristine Lake Hollingsworth, Florida Southern features the world's largest concentration of buildings designed by famed architect Frank Lloyd Wright. The architecture is uniquely Floridian and makes use of many native materials, including cypress wood, sand, and coquina shell. Twelve of Wright's initial designs were ultimately built—10 buildings, a 45-foot-high water dome, and a one-and-a-half-mile network of covered walkways connecting the buildings. Wright's Annie Pfeiffer Chapel is a popular meeting and performance venue for student organizations as well as religious services. The campus also features two buildings designed by renowned architect Robert A. M. Stern, dean of the Yale School of Architecture: a humanities building and the 80,000-square-foot Residential Life Center boasting a state-of-the-art living and learning environment with meeting

Website: www.flsouthern.edu
Location: City Center
Private
Total Enrollment: 2,455
Undergraduates: 2,257
Male/Female: 40/60
SAT Ranges: CR 500–590, M 480–600
ACT Ranges: 22–26
Financial Aid: 84%
Expense: Pr $
Student Loans: 54%
Average Debt: N/A
Phi Beta Kappa: No
Applicants: 4,453
Accepted: 56%
Enrolled: 22%

rooms, lounges, study rooms, kitchens, and bedrooms. The 22,500-square-foot Dr. Marcene H. and Robert E. Christoverson Humanities Building opened in late 2010 and includes high-tech classrooms, a film studies theater, a state-of-the-art modern language learning lab, and an art gallery.

Florida Southern's core curriculum is based on student learning outcomes in the following eight areas: critical and creative thinking, quantitative reasoning, effective oral and written communication, personal and social responsibility, meaning and value, knowledge of the social world, knowledge of the natural world, and artistic interpretation and expression. The college formerly followed a traditional, three-credit-hour model that included lecture courses. Most classes now meet for four hours a week, with at least one of those hours fully devoted to engaged learning techniques such as debate, small group discussions, case studies, and research. Service learning also is a central feature of the new curriculum, and most students will graduate having completed at least one service learning course. In keeping with the college's United Methodist affiliation, all students are required to attend the monthly Convocation Series. The curriculum features a plethora of active learning techniques, in which students are guided by faculty mentors through hands-on learning experiences.

> "The environment is laid-back but the courses are challenging."

In all, FSC students may choose from 50 undergraduate majors and more than 40 minors. The most popular majors include business administration, biology, nursing, psychology, and communications, and these are among the college's strongest programs. "The best departments are also some of the most challenging," says a sophomore. The premed program boasts a nearly 100 percent placement rate in medical, dental, or pharmacy programs nationwide and FSC honors students receive priority admittance to the University of South Florida medical school. Speaking of the honors program, qualified students may enroll in the highly selective honors core, which offers specialized courses in cultural, environmental, artistic, and social heritage. Additionally, Florida Southern College has become the first private college in the state of Florida to affiliate with the prestigious Washington Center, a D.C.-based internship provider that allows students to study and work in the nation's capital as well as other major cities around the world. In fact, all students are guaranteed an internship in their fields of study. Students have interned with OPEC, ESPN, Fox News, Lockheed Martin, Merrill Lynch, The Disney Company, and NASA (among others).

Academics are a priority at FSC, and "the environment is laid-back but the courses are challenging," says one biology major. "At FSC, you have teachers that are willing to help you even though the courses are quite hard." Freshmen are assigned a faculty mentor who meets with them on a regular basis to help them set goals and successfully adjust to college life. First-year students also take part in the Examined Life seminar, which encourages students to form close relationships with peers and professors in a small class setting. Professors are lauded for their enthusiasm and skill behind the lectern. "From the time I was a freshman I have had extraordinary professors who do their best to cover their material in depth and who genuinely want to see their students succeed," a psychology major says. When students tire of the Florida heat and humidity, they can take advantage of the robust study abroad program, which sends kids packing to exotic locales around the globe, including the United Kingdom, France, Italy, Spain, China, The Bahamas, Peru, Greece, and Turkey. The college also offers year-long study through Regent's College in London and a popular modern language school in Spain. Approximately 20 percent of students carry out undergraduate research projects during their time at FSC.

> "People are not really concerned with political issues."

Approximately 20 percent of students carry out undergraduate research projects during their time at FSC.

(continued)

Grad in 6 Years: 55%
Returning Freshmen: 76%
Academics: ✍ ✍ ✍
Social: ☎ ☎ ☎
Q of L: ★ ★ ★
Admissions: (800) 274-4131
Email Address: fscadm@ flsouthern.edu

Strongest Programs:
English
Music
Natural Sciences
Psychology
Education

Florida Southern students are "very down to earth and easy to get along with," says one student. Just under two-thirds of the student body hail from Florida and roughly 80 percent attended public high schools. "The majority of students here are white, Christian, and probably middle- to upper-class," says a junior. African Americans account for 6 percent of the population, Asian Americans 2 percent, and Hispanics 9 percent. "People are not really concerned with political issues," reports one student. "They tend to mind their own businesses and have fun with their friends." The college awards merit scholarships, as well as more than 250 athletic awards in 21 sports. Students from low-income families vie for the Florida Southern Grant and also receive a greater portion of gift aid than students who are not in need.

Seventy-four percent of FSC students reside in student housing. First-year students hang their hats in one of three residence halls, Joseph Reynolds, Allan Spivey, or Hollis, while sophomores, juniors, and seniors choose from among six residence halls, including Jenkins (all-male, traditional, and suite-style doubles), Dell (co-ed doubles), and the new, state-of-the-art Barnett Residential Life Center with its stunning lake views. "If you live on campus, you get some great experiences," says a sophomore. The cafeteria serves up a variety of "OK" fare, including special options for vegetarians. "Since my freshman year, the food has improved dramatically because of student feedback and suggestions," says a senior. "There are many tasty and healthy options for students to choose as well as the much less healthy comfort foods." Students report feeling safe on campus, thanks to an active security program.

The social scene is active on campus. "The college sponsors a myriad of social programs on campus such as cookouts, concerts, and sporting events that allow students to stay entertained on campus if they lack transportation," says one student. "In addition, the school also sponsors various bimonthly wellness trips that vary from paintball to snorkeling with manatees." Thirty-two percent of the men and 27 percent of the women go Greek, but Greek life doesn't dominate the social scene. Neither does alcohol, according to students. "FSC is an alcohol-prohibited campus," notes one psychology major. "Our 'no alcohol' policy is strictly enforced and violators are punished accordingly," a junior adds. In addition to the nearly 90 student clubs and organizations, FSC offers a number of traditions, including the annual Christmas tree lighting, the Fair-Well Carnival, and Founders Week.

A junior describes Lakeland as "a quaint town with a thriving indie art and music scene." A senior adds, "Lakeland is very much a college town. It offers a lot of local dining and activities including several malls, movie theaters, and an old downtown district with many unique shops and attractions." Many students venture out into the local community to volunteer or take part in off-campus church services. "Greek life is huge here, which allows you to get involved with the community," says one sophomore. For those with access to wheels, popular road trips include excursions to Tampa's sandy beaches, Orlando's famed theme parks, or the Florida Keys.

The dominant Florida Southern Moccasins ("Mocs") compete in Division II as members of the Sunshine State Conference. Overall, the college's 20 varsity teams have won more than two dozen national titles and nearly 150 conference championships, and have produced approximately 430 All-Americans. The most competitive teams include men's baseball and basketball, women's softball and volleyball, and men's and women's golf, tennis, and cross-country. "Our athletes dominate Division II sports every year," boasts one student, and the University of Tampa is the Mocs' chief rival. Twenty-one intramural sports and activities attract 41 percent of undergraduates; the most popular activities include flag football, basketball, and soccer. Students also take advantage of a variety of fitness and recreational programs, as well as a 12,000-square-foot wellness center.

The social scene is active on campus.

"If you live on campus, you get some great experiences."

The dominant Florida Southern Moccasins ("Mocs") compete in Division II as members of the Sunshine State Conference.

Overlaps

University of Central Florida, University of Florida, Rollins College, University of South Florida, Stetson University, University of Tampa

Florida Southern College has a lot going for it. Despite the ubiquitous college student laments of limited parking, so-so food, and constant construction, most are quick to point out that they have access to strong academic programs, championship athletics, and all the sun and fun a person could want. "Florida Southern College is a great community where students can grow academically, socially, and emotionally," says one senior. "It truly becomes your home away from home."

<table>
<tr><td>If You Apply To ➤</td><td>Florida Southern: Rolling admissions. Application fee: $30. Campus interviews: recommended, evaluative. Alumni interviews: optional, informational. SATs or ACTs: required. Subject Tests: optional. Accepts the Common Application. Essay question: personal statement.</td></tr>
</table>

Florida State University

A2500 University Center, Tallahassee, FL 32306-2400

Located in Florida's down-home panhandle, FSU is far from the glitz of South Beach or Daytona. The motion picture school is among the best around, and business and the arts are also strong. Notable programs include several living/learning options for freshmen.

At Florida State University, you could have a Nobel laureate for a professor, study in one of the finest science facilities in the Southeast, or network at the state capitol. The choices are plentiful here and the pace of life makes it possible to taste a little of everything: a wide array of solid academic choices, blistering Florida sunshine, and plenty to do, from football to Tallahassee hangouts.

FSU is located in the "Other Florida": the one with rolling hills, flowering azaleas and dogwoods, and a canopy of moss-draped oaks. Glistening Gulf of Mexico waters are only half an hour away. The main campus features collegiate Jacobean structures surrounded by plenty of shade trees, with some modern facilities sprinkled in. Situated on 450 compact acres, the campus is the smallest in the state university system—it's just a 10-minute walk from the main gate on the east side to the science complex on the west side. Bicycling and skating are popular forms of transportation, and a free shuttle bus circles campus for those without wheels.

FSU has outstanding programs in music, drama, art, and dance. The sciences are strong, too, especially chemistry, ecology and evolutionary biology, and physics. Communications, statistics, and business (especially accounting) have strong reputations in the Southeast. The English department and the School of Motion Picture, Television, and Recording Arts have consistently won an impressive array of national and international awards. Most of the more than 80 honors courses offered each academic year have fewer than 25 students, giving gifted students the opportunity to rub shoulders with top faculty. Certain students can even earn their degrees in three years. Directed individual study courses offer undergraduates the chance to participate in independent research projects with faculty direction. Internships and political jobs abound for tomorrow's politicians, since the state capitol and Supreme Court are nearby.

Students report the academic climate is somewhat laid-back but that "the courses are rigorous." Freshmen can take advantage of the First-Year Experience (FYE), Living/Learning Communities, and Freshmen Interest Groups (FIGs). FYE is

> "The quality of teaching is excellent."

Website: www.fsu.edu
Location: Small City
Public
Total Enrollment: 34,469
Undergraduates: 28,530
Male/Female: 44/56
SAT Ranges: CR 560–640, M 560–640
ACT Ranges: 25–29
Financial Aid: 85%
Expense: Pub $
Student Loans: 51%
Average Debt: $ $
Phi Beta Kappa: Yes
Applicants: 30,040
Accepted: 54%
Enrolled: 36%
Grad in 6 Years: 74%
Returning Freshmen: 91%
Academics: ✍ ✍ ✍
Social: ☎ ☎ ☎
Q of L: ★ ★ ★ ★ ★
Admissions: (850) 644-6200
Email Address: admissions@ admin.fsu.edu

Strongest Programs:
Accounting

FYE is an extended orientation that introduces students to campus organizations, events, and activities.

an extended orientation that introduces students to campus organizations, events, and activities; students who enroll in FIGs attend classes with the same group of peers who have similar academic interests.

Within FSU's liberal studies program, students must also complete six hours of multicultural understanding coursework focusing on diversity within the Western experience and cross-cultural studies. Freshmen must take math and English, and may find a TA at the helm in these courses. But overall, faculty members do teach. "The quality of teaching is excellent," a senior says. For those with wanderlust, FSU offers extensive study abroad options. They include a branch campus in Panama, year-round programs in Italy, England, and Spain, and summer programs in Greece, Vietnam, Switzerland, France, Costa Rica, Russia, the Czech Republic, Ireland, Japan, Belize, Brazil, and China. The university is making strides in the world of distance learning, allowing some students with an associate's degree to earn their bachelor's degree online.

Perhaps not surprisingly, FSU's student body has a distinctly Floridian flavor: in-staters comprise 90 percent of the group. Nine percent are African American, 3 percent are Asian American, and 16 percent are Hispanic. There's little evidence of racial tension on the diverse campus. Seminoles are a mixture of friendly small-towners and city dwellers, and political tastes tend toward the conservative. Hot topics include voter registration, the environment, and student government concerns. Merit scholarships averaging $2,295 are available to qualified scholars, and student-athletes vie for 245 scholarships in 20 sports.

Twenty percent of FSU's undergrads live in the university dorms, all of which are air-conditioned (a must in Florida). Students may opt for typically spacious older halls or newer ones that tend to be more cramped. The dorms get mixed reviews from students, and the number who can live in them is limited, so rooms are assigned on a first-come, first-served basis. Upperclassmen generally forsake the housing rat race and move into nearby apartments, houses, or trailers, where they take advantage of the city and campus bus systems to get to school. The dorms are equipped with kitchens; meal plans that offer "good but expensive" food are also available.

"The social life is fine."

When they're not studying, FSU students keep busy with plays, films, concerts, and dorm parties. "The social life is fine," a freshman says. Those with a valid ID can head for one of Tallahassee's bars or restaurants, which fall somewhere between "college hangout" and "real world." Generally, though, students give the area a thumbs-up. As for Greek life, 16 percent of the men and 19 percent of the women join fraternities and sororities, respectively, which constitute another important segment of the social scene.

In sports, the Seminole football team won two national titles in the '90s and has dominated the Atlantic Coast Conference. FSU's baseball team also draws an enthusiastic following, as do women's basketball, volleyball, soccer, and softball teams. Recent conference champs include men's basketball, men's indoor track and field, and women's volleyball. Nearly 70 percent of students participate in recreational activities, including over 40 intramural sports and nearly 50 sports clubs.

Florida State remains a solid choice for those seeking knowledge under the blazing Florida sun. FSU students take pride in their school and what it has to offer. "It is a place I can consider almost like my home," says a business major.

Overlaps

University of Florida, University of Central Florida, University of South Florida, Florida International, University of Miami, Florida Atlantic, University of North Florida, University of West Florida

If You Apply To ➤

Florida State: Regular admissions: Jan. 15. Financial aid: Feb. 1. Housing: May 1. Application fee: $30. No campus or alumni interviews. SATs or ACTs: required. Subject Tests: optional. Essay question.

Fordham University

Rose Hill Campus: 441 East Fordham Road, Bronx, NY 10458
Lincoln Center Campus: 113 West 60th Street, New York, NY 10023

New York City's Fordham is riding the wave of euphoria for colleges in New York. Though still an underdog to places like NYU and Boston College, Fordham now accepts less than half its applicants. There is no better location than Lincoln Center in Manhattan, where the performing arts programs are housed. The Bronx location is less appealing but adjacent to the New York Botanical Garden and Bronx Zoo.

At Fordham University, the Jesuit tradition pervades all aspects of life, from the quality of teaching, to the emphasis on personal relationships, to the pursuit of both "wisdom and learning," which also happens to be the school's motto. Students benefit from two campuses: the gated Bronx community of Rose Hill and the Lincoln Center facility, just a short subway ride away from the heart of midtown Manhattan. Small classes offer individual attention, and though half of the student population is from New York, there's plenty of variation in ethnic background and in students' political and social views. Fordham is "more diverse than Boston College, less funky than NYU," says a German and English double major. "We have an even mix of preppy, athletic types, and independent, Manhattan types, the latter more so at the Lincoln Center campus."

> **"Core courses tend to be easier than major courses."**

The 85-acre Rose Hill campus is an oasis of trees, grass, and Gothic architecture; it's close to the New York Botanical Garden and Yankee Stadium and had cameo appearances in films such as *A Beautiful Mind*. Rose Hill is home to Fordham College, the largest liberal arts school at the university, as well as the Gabelli School of Business. The Lincoln Center campus benefits from its proximity to the Juilliard School, to the CBS and ABC television studios between Tenth and Eleventh Avenues, and to Lincoln Center itself, Manhattan's performing arts hub. This campus has its own undergraduate college, and also houses Fordham's law school and other graduate programs. Started as an alternative-style urban institution with no grades, the Lincoln Center campus has become more traditional over the years, and now uses the same 18-course core curriculum as Rose Hill. Shuttles run between the two campuses. Recently renovated Hughes Hall now houses the Gabelli School of Business and features "smart" classrooms with state-of-the-art technology, multiple conference rooms, an information and technology center, and a 144-seat auditorium.

No matter where at Fordham you study, humanities are a good choice. Strengths at Rose Hill include history, philosophy, psychology, and economics, while at Lincoln Center theater, English, and communications shine. The B.F.A. in dance is offered along with the Alvin Ailey American Dance Theater; students must be accepted both by Fordham and by the Ailey audition panel. Fordham's public radio station, WFUV, offers hands-on experience for aspiring deejays and radio journalists, and there are TV production studios in both Manhattan and Rose Hill, but so far, no university-sponsored station.

> **"Dining is probably the one major drawback at Fordham."**

Both colleges offer interdisciplinary majors, such as African American and Latin American studies, as well as 3–2 engineering programs with Columbia and Case Western Reserve, a 3–3 program with Fordham Law School, and a teacher-certification program. The latter may include a fifth year, culminating in a master's degree in education.

Website: www.fordham.edu
Location: City Center
Private
Total Enrollment: 11,911
Undergraduates: 7,691
Male/Female: 47/53
SAT Ranges: CR 570–670, M 580–670
ACT Ranges: 26–30
Financial Aid: 62%
Expense: Pr $ $ $
Student Loans: N/A
Average Debt: N/A
Phi Beta Kappa: Yes
Applicants: 34,069
Accepted: 43%
Enrolled: 13%
Grad in 6 Years: 81%
Returning Freshmen: 88%
Academics: ✍ ✍ ✍
Social: ☎ ☎ ☎
Q of L: ★ ★ ★
Admissions: (718) 817-4000
Email Address: enroll@ fordham.edu

Strongest Programs:
Business Administration
Communication and Media Studies
Psychology
English
History
Mathematics
Social Work

"Core courses tend to be easier than major courses," says a junior. "Everyone here is interested in their academic passions." Popular and well-regarded majors include business, history, communications, psychology, and English language and literature. Helped by alumni connections, business students often obtain internships on Wall Street or elsewhere in the Manhattan financial community; some of these positions lead to jobs after graduation. The GLOBE Program in international business includes an international internship or study abroad assignment, two courses with an international focus, and proficiency in a foreign language. Core requirements include English, social and natural sciences, philosophy, theology, history, math/computer science, fine arts, and foreign languages. Students also complete four *Eloquentia Perfecta* seminars, including a capstone senior seminar on values.

Forty-eight percent of classes have 19 or fewer students, and professors are lauded for their abilities behind the lectern. "Most of the professors here really know their stuff and are engaging and helpful," a philosophy major says. "Many of the lower-level core courses are taught by adjunct professors, but I have never had a bad experience with a professor," adds a sophomore.

"Fordham students constantly want to do 'magis,' the Jesuit term for 'more,'" says a student, "whether in class or in the community." Fifty-two percent of the students at Fordham are from New York State, and many of the rest are Roman Catholics from elsewhere on the East Coast, even though the school is independent of the church. The atmosphere is less intellectual than at nearby Columbia and NYU, but "students are driven to do well academically and to get good jobs after graduation," says a senior. "Our Democrat and Republican groups go at it!" says a marketing major. African Americans comprise 5 percent of the student body, Asian Americans make up 9 percent, and Hispanics 14 percent. In the Jesuit tradition of "men and women for others," students travel as far away as Romania and Belize during vacations for intensive study and service projects. There are hundreds of merit scholarships available to eligible students, and the university now awards football scholarships to those students who demonstrate a gift on the gridiron.

> "Here I feel like an individual, an adult, and part of a community."

Fifty-six percent of Fordham students live in the dorms, and they are guaranteed university housing for four years. Those lucky enough to snag rooms in the 20-story, 850-bed residence hall near Lincoln Center are saved from the borough's unscrupulous brokers and unconscionable rents. At Rose Hill, "dorms are spacious, and community bathrooms are cleaned daily," says a senior. Students must sign in to gain admission to dorms other than their own, and Rose Hill has its own security personnel, but the Bronx "is very much an eye-opener for all the suburban white kids," one student quips. "It's a good experience if you have the common sense to keep a low profile among the locals." Those who venture off campus often choose to live in the Bronx's answer to Little Italy, says a senior. Campus food is described as "passable," though on the upswing. Still, "Dining is probably the one major drawback at Fordham," admits one junior.

Fordham's social life is an embarrassment of riches. "We go to school in New York City," says a student. "If you're bored here, it's your own fault." Fordham sponsors an intramurals program, as well as movies and concerts on both campuses. There's a "huge bar scene, both in the Bronx and in Manhattan," one student says—presumably aimed at students over 21, but this being New York, fake IDs are easy to come by, and sometimes they work. Off-campus parties also provide another opportunity to imbibe, if students are interested. The Rose Hill campus backs up against the Bronx Zoo and it's around the corner from Arthur Avenue, another Little Italy. Both provide welcome weekend diversions. Students look forward to homecoming, Fall Fest, Fordham Week, Spring Weekend, and Senior Week, as well as to

Strengths at Rose Hill include history, philosophy, psychology, and economics, while at Lincoln Center theater, English, and communications shine.

Those lucky enough to snag rooms in the 20-story, 850-bed residence hall near Lincoln Center are saved from the borough's unscrupulous brokers and unconscionable rents.

the Columbia–Fordham football game and the Irish vs. Italian rugby match. "The 10 o'clock scream," a Thursday night ritual in which everyone leans out their window and screams for one minute, is a favored stress reliever.

Fordham competes in Division I and the Atlantic 10 Conference, and its location near the Hudson River has also helped to produce the women's rowing Metropolitan champs. The football team is competitive and promises to improve now that scholarships are awarded. Women's softball brought home conference titles in 2011 and 2013. The marvelous Lombardi Memorial Athletic Center (named for Vince, an alumnus) supports 11 club sports and 24 intramurals, including ultimate Frisbee and tae kwon do, as well as "grandstand athletes," who root for the varsity basketball team. With a new head coach and strong recruiting classes, basketball is poised for increasing competitiveness.

Consistent with its Jesuit tradition, Fordham fancies itself a family. Indeed, students are often so happy with what they find that they preach the gospel to younger siblings, who obligingly follow them to one of the school's three campuses. Some things are changing at Fordham—including its admission and academic standards, which are inching up, and its national profile, which is also far higher than in years past. What hasn't changed is the idea that diversity and community can coexist, instilling confidence and pride in Fordham students and loyalty in the expanding alumni base. "Here I feel like an individual, an adult, and part of a community," says one student. "When it comes to student life and satisfaction, you want to be here."

If You Apply To ➤

Fordham: Early action: Nov. 1. Regular admissions: Jan. 1. Financial aid: Feb. 1. Application fee: $70. No campus or alumni interviews. SATs or ACTs: required. Subject Tests: optional. Apply to particular school or program. Accepts the Common Application. Essay question.

Franklin and Marshall College

637 College Avenue, Lancaster, PA 17604-3003

F&M is known for churning out hardworking preprofessional students. Faces tough competition from the likes of Bucknell, Dickinson, Gettysburg, and Lafayette for Pennsylvania-bound students. Known for natural sciences, business, and internships on Capitol Hill. Uses merit scholarships to lure top students from Bucknell and Lafayette.

At Franklin and Marshall College, set in the serene hills of Pennsylvania's Amish country, you might come nose-to-nose with a horse and buggy, but you can still enjoy the perks of being in one of the country's 50 largest metro areas. While the city has modernized beautifully, parts of this historic town look much the same as they did when two acclaimed but struggling colleges decided to pool their resources. Marshall College (named for Chief Justice John Marshall) merged with Franklin College (started with a donation of 200 English pounds from Ben himself) in Lancaster. These days, F&M is trying to modernize too, particularly by bringing a more international bent to the curriculum. "At F&M you have the chance to really explore and find yourself," says a junior.

F&M's 125-acre campus is surrounded by a quiet residential neighborhood shaded by majestic maple and oak trees. A major urban renewal project is underway

Website: www.fandm.edu
Location: Small City
Private
Total Enrollment: 2,302
Undergraduates: 2,302
Male/Female: 48/52
SAT Ranges: CR 600–690, M 613–710
ACT Ranges: 28–31
Financial Aid: 54%
Expense: Pr $ $ $ $

that will eventually expand its geographical reach. The campus itself is an arboretum and boasts 47 buildings of Gothic and colonial architecture. The College Square complex appeals to students seeking a study respite. Other notable facilities include the Life Sciences and Philosophy Building, the Brooks Tennis Center, and a 400-bed residential facility.

Although there are no required courses freshman year, nine out of 10 students enroll in First-Year Residential Seminars. Participating students live together in groups of 16 on co-ed freshman floors and study a major theme or concept within a discipline. General education requirements include writing and language requirements, two "Foundation" courses, and distribution requirements in the arts, humanities, social sciences, sciences, and non-Western cultures. Collaborations are optional opportunities to get course credit for an experience that includes working with others. F&M has long been known for being strong in the natural sciences, and the school is now placing more emphasis on courses with a service-learning component. All majors can be combined with the international studies concentration that requires students to study abroad and become proficient in a foreign language. Nearly 50 percent of F&M students engage in directed research under the guidance of faculty, including students in the Hackman Summer Research Scholars program. A preprofessional college in line with Lafayette and Bucknell, F&M has an excellent reputation for preparing undergrads for medical school, law school, and other careers.

> "At F&M you have the chance to really explore and find yourself."

Students uniformly describe the coursework as strenuous and demanding, but say the environment remains more cooperative than competitive. "The courses are challenging, as professors aim to push students to new levels," a senior says. Still, "people are happy for each other if they do well," says a junior. Students say teaching is outstanding, and the relatively small student body and intimate class sizes help create a strong sense of community between students and professors. "Professors care about their students both inside and outside of the classroom," says a business major, "and make Franklin and Marshall an exciting and comfortable place to learn." F&M offers cross-registration with two other small Pennsylvania colleges— Dickinson and Gettysburg—and several domestic-exchange and cooperative-degree programs. In the summer, the college sends students to countries such as Japan and Russia, and approximately half study in locations around the world during their time at F&M. Others participate in the Sea Semester*.

> "Professors aim to push students to new levels."

"Students here are open minded and very free spirited," says a sophomore. Eighty-six percent of students rank in the top quarter of their graduating high school class, and 63 percent hail from Pennsylvania. Asian American students comprise 4 percent of the student body, African Americans 4 percent, and Hispanics 6 percent. An occasional political debate may waft through the murmurs of light social exchanges during dinner, but "intense political debate is uncommon," according to a senior. Fummers do, however, take an interest when it comes to extracurricular activities and social opportunities. The 100-plus clubs on campus attest to that, as does an unusually high level of participation in community service activities.

Collaborations are optional opportunities to get course credit for an experience that includes working with others.

Approximately 50 Marshall and 75 Presidential scholars are named each year. Marshalls receive a $12,500 tuition grant, a Mac, and the chance to apply for up to $3,000 in research travel funds. Presidential scholars receive a $7,500 tuition grant. F&M also offers two Rouse scholarships worth full tuition, books, and fees, and about 40 Buchanan community service grants of $5,000 each. The school has eliminated merit scholarships and redirected the funds toward need-based financial aid. There are no athletic scholarships.

The college requires students to live in college-operated housing all four years and housing options include dorms, special interest housing, suites, and apartments. A faculty-led College House system is designed to increase the quality of the residential experience. "The dorms are very cozy and clean," says a junior, "and there is never any trouble getting a room." Boarders eat most of their meals in the campus cafeteria under a flexible meal plan, but students are issued debit cards that they may use at a number of different food stops on campus. Campus security is described as "efficient and friendly," and students report feeling safe on campus.

The seven fraternities attract 28 percent of men, and two sororities attract 34 percent of women. They are integral to much of the nightlife, although the residence halls and special-interest groups offer a range of alternatives, including concerts and comedians. Ben's Underground, a popular student-run nightclub, and Hildy's, a tiny local bar, are favorite meeting places. "Off-campus parties dominate the lives of students on the weekends," one student says. "Aside from the mall and the movies, frat houses are the only places to go for fun." In recent years, the student-run and college-funded College Entertainment Committee has brought a number of popular musicians and bands to the campus.

Lancaster is a historical and well-to-do city of 60,000 people located in a larger metro area of more than 400,000. Lancaster offers a 16-screen cinema, scores of shops, a farmer's market, brick-and-cobblestone streets, and a plethora of quaint restaurants and cafés. Students have a measured, realistic appreciation of its urban amenities and rural ambiance. "Lancaster is a lot of fun," muses one student. "There are great restaurants and bars." The Amish culture draws the interest of some students, although "the city is not full of Amish like many people expect," says a senior. Those with a hankering for contemporary action take road trips to Philly, Baltimore, Washington, D.C., and New York City. The biggest annual event is Spring Arts, held the weekend before finals, which includes student air-band contests, live concerts, art exhibits, games, booths, and barbecues. Other highlights include the freshman Pajama Parade, the Sophomore Sensation, the Senior Surprise, International Day, Black Cultural Arts Weekend, Flapjack Fest (when professors serve pancakes to students), and Fum Follies, a faculty-produced play.

"Students here are open minded and very free spirited."

The college has a good selection of intramural sports, which include popular co-ed competitions. With the exception of wrestling (Division I), Diplomat teams compete in Division III. F&M boasts Centennial Conference championships in men's swimming, football, and baseball, and women's swimming. The women's lacrosse team has brought home national championships in recent years. Varsity squads are called the Diplomats, a moniker that gained currency in 1935 when the football team nearly upset national powerhouse Fordham. The annual football game against Dickinson for the Conestoga Wagon trophy is always a crowd pleaser.

The school's illustrious namesakes would no doubt be proud of the institution which bears their names. "We have a stellar reputation and the best faculty," says one happy senior. "An F&M education will prep you for any job, and alumni jump at the chance to help."

F&M offers cross-registration with two other small Pennsylvania colleges—Dickinson and Gettysburg.

Approximately 50 Marshall and 75 Presidential scholars are named each year.

Overlaps
Bucknell, Colgate, University of Delaware, Dickinson, Gettysburg, Lafayette, Lehigh, Penn State

If You Apply To ➤   **F&M:** Early decision: Nov. 15. Regular admissions: Jan. 15. Financial aid: Feb. 15. Application fee: $60. Campus and alumni interviews: optional, evaluative. SATs or ACTs: optional (required for international students). Subject Tests: optional. Accepts the Common Application. Essay question: Common Application and F&M supplement.

Furman University

3300 Poinsett Highway, Greenville, SC 29613-5245

Furman's campus is one of the most beautiful in the nation, and the swans are definitely a nice touch. At just under 2,700 total enrollment, Furman is nearly twice the size of Davidson and half the size of Wake Forest. Academic programs include a strong emphasis on student research. As befits its Baptist heritage, Furman is a conservative place and still a largely regional institution.

Furman University has been called the "Country Club of the South." And if you're Southern, white, Christian, and conservative, you're likely to feel like a member. As a political science major says, "Students here tend to be sheltered and ignorant of real-world issues. They are very image-conscious and our gym stays busier than most others." Beyond the country club vibe, though, students find small classes led by caring faculty and plenty of opportunities for independent research. Prominent alums include Nobel Prize-winning physicist Charles Townes and Keith Lockhart, director of the Boston Pops Orchestra.

Furman's 750-acre campus is one of the country's most beautiful, with tree-lined malls, fountains, a formal rose garden and Japanese garden, and a 30-acre lake filled with swans and ducks. Flowering shrubs dot the well-kept lawns, which surround buildings in the classical revival, Colonial Williamsburg, and modern architectural styles. Many have porches, pediments, and other Southern touches, such as hand-made Virginia brick. The Townes Science Complex was recently completed, and the Physical Activities Center was renovated.

Furman operates under the "semester-plus" system. The school year begins in late August, and the first semester ends prior to the December holiday break. Students begin the second semester in January and then have the option of attending a three-week "Maymester" in (you guessed it) May. General education requirements include two first-year seminars (one must be a writing seminar) and a series of core requirements that fulfill the following "ways of knowing": empirical studies; human cultures; mathematical and formal reasoning; foreign language; ultimate questions; and body and mind. Finally, students must fulfill global awareness requirements.

Furman's academic climate is challenging. "Furman students all understand that the courses are difficult and seem to commiserate with one another," says one junior.

> **"Bowties and button-downs are expected for guys on game day at tailgates."**

Forty-nine percent of classes taken by freshmen have 19 or fewer students, helping students get to know faculty members well. "They are absolutely brilliant and love to both learn and teach," says a political science major. "Furman professors are also some of the most accessible people. Whether it is sitting in their office for a chat or going down to the dining hall with them, they are always willing to talk." The Furman Advantage program helps fund research fellowships and teaching assistantships for more than 120 students a year. Furman also typically sends one of the largest student delegations to the annual National Conference of Undergraduate Research. More than 250 students study abroad each year, through one of more than a dozen Furman-sponsored programs on five continents, including a special exchange with Japan's Kansai-Gaidai University. Furman also belongs to the Associated Colleges of the South*. Entering freshmen have the opportunity to travel in small groups to an island off the coast of Charleston, the mountains of North Carolina, or even China during the summer before they enroll.

Furman broke with the South Carolina Baptist Convention in 1992, but it remains in South Carolina, where religion ranks second only to football. Students are

---

Website: www.furman.edu
Location: Suburban
Private
Total Enrollment: 2,672
Undergraduates: 2,618
Male/Female: 43/57
SAT Ranges: CR 550–650, M 560–660
ACT Ranges: 25–29
Financial Aid: 85%
Expense: Pr $ $ $
Student Loans: 43%
Average Debt: $ $ $
Phi Beta Kappa: Yes
Applicants: 6,035
Accepted: 77%
Enrolled: 15%
Grad in 6 Years: 83%
Returning Freshmen: 90%
Academics: ✍ ✍ ✍ ½
Social: ☎ ☎ ☎
Q of L: ★ ★ ★
Admissions: (864) 294-2034
Email Address: admissions@furman.edu

Strongest Programs:
Political Science
Health Sciences
Business Administration
Biology
Communication Studies
Chemistry
Psychology
Music

mostly white, upper-middle-class Southerners. "Everyone dresses in the stereotypical Southern preppy style of Brooks Brothers, Lilly Pulitzer, and Southern Proper," says a senior. "Bowties and button-downs are expected for guys on game day at tailgates, and girls wouldn't be caught dead without their Longchamp totes and Tory Burch flats." Furman is trying to diversify, but those efforts have been slow to bear fruit. African Americans make up 5 percent of the student body, Hispanics comprise 3 percent, and Asian Americans add 2 percent. Every year, Furman awards a number of merit scholarships (averaging $16,000), plus 260 athletic scholarships in 18 sports.

Ninety-six percent of students live on campus, as Furman has a four-year residency requirement. "The dorms are quite large, comfortable, and well maintained," says a global commerce major. Furman is no longer a completely dry campus, although the policy is strictly enforced in freshman and sophomore dorms, where underage students shouldn't be imbibing anyway. The atmosphere is more relaxed for students of legal drinking age who may consume alcohol in North Village, a newer, university-owned apartment complex of 10 buildings for juniors and seniors. All dorms are equipped with telephone,

> **"If you are looking for a party school, Furman definitely is not it."**

cable TV, and Internet access, and students enjoy the camaraderie that results from a residential campus. Meal plan credits can be used in the dining hall or food court, which always offers student favorites like hamburgers and hot dogs. Overall, students say campus fare is tasty and diverse. Campus security helps provide a relatively safe environment. "Furman has its own police force," notes a senior.

"If you are looking for a party school, Furman definitely is not it. Greeks are the ones that have the most active social lives with their formals and functions and parties," says a student. When the weekend comes, Furman's Student Activities Board sponsors "free movies, weekend trips, restaurant deals, huge concerts, and basically always something to do," adds a communication major. Fraternities claim 38 percent of the men and sororities 51 percent of the women, and off-campus Greek parties draw crowds. "Greenville is a great city that is seeing a large amount of growth," says a senior. "The downtown is booming and is a really fun place to visit." The Peace Center for the Performing Arts, located downtown, brings in touring casts of Broadway shows and other top-rated acts. More than 60 percent of Furman's students devote spare time to the Heller Service Corps, which provides volunteers to more than 85 community agencies and organizes the annual May Day-Play Day carnival, converting the campus into a playground for underprivileged kids. However, one freshman remarks, "A good amount of students volunteer, yes, but most are content to simply live out their privileged lives in the peace of the Furman bubble." The best road trips are to the mountains of Asheville (only 45 minutes away), Atlanta (for the big city and shopping, about two hours), and Charleston or Myrtle Beach (four hours).

Furman's athletic teams are the Paladins (after the toughest warrior in Charlemagne's court) and they compete in the Division I Southern Conference. The men's tennis and soccer and women's volleyball, soccer, tennis, and golf teams have brought home conference titles within the past few years. Students happily yell out the school's tongue-in-cheek cheer ("F.U. one time, F.U. two times, F.U. three times, F.U. all the time!") during football games against archrivals Wofford and Georgia Southern. More than 70 percent of the student body competes for the coveted All Sports Trophy by participating in intramurals, which range from flag football to horseshoes. Furman's Mock Trial program is nationally recognized and competes in intercollegiate tournaments with schools ranging from those in the Ivy League to major research universities.

Furman may call itself a university, but its educational approach is closer to that of a liberal arts college, emphasizing problem solving, projects, and experience-based

The Furman Advantage program helps fund research fellowships and teaching assistantships for more than 120 students a year.

Furman's athletic teams are the Paladins (after the toughest warrior in Charlemagne's court).

Overlaps

Clemson, University of South Carolina, University of Georgia, University of North Carolina, Elon, College of Charleston, Wofford, Wake Forest

learning. Two decades after severing its religious ties, the school continues to evolve, drawing more academically capable students from increasingly diverse backgrounds.

If You Apply To >

Furman: Early decision: Nov. 1. Early action: Nov. 15. Regular admissions, financial aid, and housing: Jan. 15. Application fee: $50. Campus interviews: optional, evaluative. Alumni interviews: optional, informational. SATs or ACTs: optional. Subject Tests: optional. Accepts the Common Application. Essay question: Common Application questions.

George Mason University

4400 University Drive, Fairfax, VA 22030-4444

Capitalizes, so to speak, on its location next to Washington, D.C., in the northern Virginia suburbs. Leading center of conservative, political, and economic thought. Now challenging UVA and Virginia Tech in many fields. A university shuttle bus goes to the D.C. Metro. Dorm construction continues as GMU works on becoming more than a commuter school.

Website: www.gmu.edu
Location: Suburban
Public
Total Enrollment: 20,234
Undergraduates: 16,238
Male/Female: 48/52
SAT Ranges: CR 520–620, M 530–630
ACT Ranges: 23–28
Financial Aid: 52%
Expense: Pub $ $
Student Loans: 57%
Average Debt: $ $ $
Phi Beta Kappa: No
Applicants: 14,703
Accepted: 66%
Enrolled: 28%
Grad in 6 Years: 66%
Returning Freshmen: 86%
Academics: ✐ ✐ ✐
Social: ☎ ☎
Q of L: ★ ★
Admissions: (703) 993-2400
Email Address: admissions@gmu.edu

Strongest Programs:
Economics
Engineering
Public Policy
Nursing

Located in the middle of greater Washington, D.C.'s budding high-tech corridor, George Mason University features an urban campus and symbiotic relationship with the surrounding region that contrasts starkly with Virginia's two other major universities, which have held classes for a hundred years in the relative isolation of Charlottesville and Blacksburg. Mason has grown by leaps and bounds for most of the past two decades and now boasts nearly 21,000 students pursuing majors in nearly 150 degree programs. "The university's biggest drives are for diversity and innovation, and this is reflected in the programs offered to the student body," says a sophomore.

> "The university's biggest drives are for diversity and innovation."

Founded as a sleepy outpost of the University of Virginia, GMU sits on a 583-acre wooded campus thirty miles from Washington, D.C., in suburban Fairfax, Virginia. Campus architecture is modern and nondescript; most structures were erected after the mid-1970s. GMU's 10,000-seat arena, the Patriot Center, hosts both sporting and entertainment events. And although GMU's campus doesn't have the colonial ambiance or tradition of William and Mary or UVA, its namesake does have the same Old Virginia credentials. George Mason drafted Virginia's influential Declaration of Rights in 1776, and he later opposed ratification of the federal Constitution because there was no Bill of Rights attached.

Mason's general education requirements stipulate that all students take the equivalent of two courses in English composition, humanities, social sciences, and math and sciences. Students who prefer to find their own way can design a major under the Bachelor of Individualized Study program. The academic climate is intense but manageable. "Depending on the faculty member and academic program, classes can range anywhere from 'relaxingly manageable' to 'kill me now,'" says a sophomore. Professors are praised for their knowledge, and Mason has the distinction of being the only university in Virginia to have two Nobel Prize winners on its faculty. "I have never had a professor who was not entirely dedicated to the class," says one student.

> "Classes can range anywhere from 'relaxingly manageable' to 'kill me now.'"

Notable degrees include degree programs in conflict analysis and resolution, computer game design, and applied computer science. Another option is the New

Century College degree program, which teams small groups of faculty and under-graduates on projects that can be easily connected to the world outside GMU. Though it is growing up fast, Mason's youth shows in a number of ways. First, programs taken for granted at more established universities are just hitting their stride here. Next, GMU's relatively small endowment means almost constant tuition increases. Last, some of the school's facilities are just plain inadequate for its more than 20,000 students. The library, for example, has fewer than 700,000 volumes, though it now subscribes to more than 300 online databases and allows students to borrow books from all eight members of the Washington Research Library Consortium.

The lack of resources in the library may present less of a problem for GMU's career-focused students, who seem to like learning on the job: 70 percent enter the working world after graduation, and just 20 percent proceed to graduate and profes-sional schools. Psychology tops the list of popular majors, and economics—which boasts its own Nobel laureate—is probably the strongest department. Other well-regarded majors include computer science, nursing, engineering, and English; not surprisingly, given the school's location, the public policy department also receives accolades. The drama department, once a weak sister, is now part of the Institute of the Arts, created to make the arts an intrinsic part of every student's GMU experi-ence. The institute includes a professional theater company, which hosts actors and playwrights in residence. The university recently partnered with the Smithsonian Institution to create the "Smithsonian Semester," which allows students to live on-site at the Conservation and Research Center of the Smithsonian's National Zoo and study global conservation issues and civic concerns.

Notable degrees include degree programs in conflict analysis and resolution, computer game design, and applied computer science.

"The students at GMU are hard workers and intelligent scholars," says a junior. "They know how to relax and have a good time, and these activities are generally community focused." Eighty-four percent of GMU stu-dents are from Virginia, and the remainder hail from all 50 states and 134 nations. Minorities make up a third of the student population—9 percent African American, 11 percent Hispanic, and 17 percent Asian American. Students are politi-cally aware and tend to lean rightward. That said, racial tensions haven't been a problem, perhaps thanks to the four-year-old Stop, Look, and Learn program. The program attempts to increase campus discussion on prejudice, discrimination, and harassment. Athletic and merit scholarships are available to those who qualify.

"The students at GMU are hard workers and intelligent scholars."

George Mason has traditionally been a commuter school; 28 percent of students live on campus or around campus in university-sponsored housing. The administra-tion admits that room and board costs are inflated because the university's entire housing stock dates from 1978 or later, which means the buildings are modern and air-conditioned—but still being paid for. One student explains, "Housing is constantly growing and changing at Mason. The dorms are all well maintained and quite nice compared to almost every other university I've been to, likely because they are quite new." Freshmen live together in Presidents Park, while other students get rooms on a first-come, first-served basis based on class status. Those looking for an active social life should definitely consider a stint in the dorms, particularly in Presidents Park or the Freshman Center, but freshman dorms are dry, and you can get the boot if you're caught having a party with alcohol. Three percent of the men and women go Greek.

The drama department, once a weak sister, is now part of the Institute of the Arts.

GMU's University Center, with its food court, movie theater, classrooms, com-puter labs, and study areas, has become the center of on-campus social life. The cen-ter is a convenience and a lure for students who commute to school and have gaps between classes. On the weekends, students find a predictable assortment of malls and shopping centers in Fairfax, just southwest of D.C., but off-campus parties and the sights and sounds of downtown Washington, Georgetown, and Old Town Alexandria beckon when the sun goes down. Best of all, these are only a short commute away via

Three percent of the men and women go Greek.

a free shuttle bus to the subway. Those searching for a more lively collegiate scene take road trips to other local schools, including James Madison and UVA.

With barely a generation of history under its belt, Mason is notably lacking in traditions and annual events: "Come here and invent one!" a student urges. Patriots Day and Mason Day are the two major bashes, in addition to homecoming and International Week. GMU competes in Division I, and the basketball team is the marquee program—any game against James Madison University draws a big crowd. Other successful Patriots teams include women's soccer, men's and women's track, and women's volleyball. Intramurals are catching on now that many games are held in the Patriot Center.

"Nearly every aspect of Mason is developing at breakneck speed. We haven't hit our best yet," says one student. It has already established itself as a bastion of conservative thinking on social issues. The name of George Mason may not have the cachet of George Washington, James Madison, or the other luminaries of Virginia history who have had universities named for them, but with improving academics, an ever-expanding physical campus, and the rich cultural and economic resources of Washington, D.C., Mason's namesake may be set to follow in those other schools' footsteps.

If You Apply To ➤

Mason: Early action: Nov. 1. Regular admissions: Jan. 15. Financial aid: Mar. 1. Housing: May 1. Application fee: $60. Campus interviews: optional, informational. No alumni interviews. SATs or ACTs: required (unless student applies for "score optional" consideration). No Subject Tests. Essay question.

The George Washington University

Washington, D.C., 20052

Not so long ago, GW was a backup school with an almost 80 percent acceptance rate and maligned for its lack of identity. But the allure of Washington, D.C., coupled with an intellectually stimulating educational environment, has made it increasingly selective. Located steps away from the White House. One of the most expensive private schools in the country, it is also the nation's leader in internships per capita.

Like Washington, D.C., itself, The George Washington University draws students from all over America—and around the world. Upon arrival, they find a bustling campus in the heart of D.C., enriched with cultural and intellectual opportunities. Students have easy access to the Smithsonian Institution museums, the Folger Shakespeare Library, the Library of Congress, and other national treasures. GW also offers top political officials as guest speakers and visiting professors. "The location of the school is awesome, and there are lots of opportunities for jobs and internships and study abroad," cheers one junior.

"Students push themselves on a personal level."

George Washington was established in 1821 by an act of Congress as a testament to George Washington's dream of a national institution of higher learning. Today, The George Washington University is composed of three campuses—the main, older campus in the Foggy Bottom neighborhood on Pennsylvania Avenue near the White House, the Mount Vernon campus, site of the former Mount Vernon College for Women, three miles away, and a science and technology campus located in Ashburn, Virginia. The Foggy Bottom campus has a mix of renovated federal row

Website: www.gwu.edu
Location: City Center
Private
Total Enrollment: 17,391
Undergraduates: 9,758
Male/Female: 45/55
SAT Ranges: CR 600–690, M 600–700
ACT Ranges: 27–31
Financial Aid: 66%
Expense: Pr $ $ $ $
Student Loans: 48%
Average Debt: $ $ $ $
Phi Beta Kappa: Yes
Applicants: 21,756

houses and modern buildings and is virtually indistinguishable from the rest of the neighborhood, while the wooded Mount Vernon campus spans 26 acres near Georgetown and includes athletic fields, tennis courts, and an outdoor pool.

Freshmen may enroll in the School of Engineering and Applied Science, the School of Business, the Elliott School of International Affairs, the School of Public Health and Health Services, and the Columbian College of Arts and Sciences, which is the largest undergraduate division. During freshman year, all undergraduates take English composition. The G-PAC (General Education Curriculum-Perspective, Analysis, Communication) requirements include three credits in mathematics or statistics; six credits in natural and/or physical laboratory sciences; six credits in social sciences; six credits in humanities and three credits in art (visual, performing, critical, and historical practices). Of the analytic courses, students must take one that includes a global or cross-cultural perspective and one that includes local/civic engagement.

"I have had fantastic professors at GW."

For highly motivated and capable undergraduates seeking a challenge, the University Honors Program offers special seminars, independent study, and a university symposium on both campuses. The School of Engineering and Applied Science also offers an honors program in which students work with professors on research projects. GW's political communications major, which combines political science, journalism, and electronic media courses, is one of the few undergraduate programs of its kind and benefits from its Washington location. "International affairs is so interdisciplinary," says a senior. "I've taken courses in economics, foreign language, anthropology, and business." More than 350 study abroad options are available in 60 countries, and the university offers a number of combined undergraduate/graduate degree programs.

"My classes have been challenging, but I have learned a lot, and I have definitely retained the information," says one freshman. Competition isn't a concern, says a senior. "Students push themselves on a personal level and do not necessarily judge themselves in comparison to other students." Fifty-five percent of the classes taken by freshmen have 19 or fewer students; professors handle lectures and seminars, and TAs facilitate discussions or labs. "I have had fantastic professors at GW," a student says. Almost half of GW's faculty members divide their time between the halls of academia and the corridors of power, with many holding high-level government positions. "Its really enlightening to have a class about political communications taught by a journalist for the *Washington Post* or a class on Middle Eastern politics taught by a former ambassador," says one senior. "You really learn to understand the material in a whole new light by having classroom experiences with these types of professors."

Given GW's location and its improved academic reputation, students are "really open minded, ambitious, and self-motivated," says one student. A senior adds, "GW students tend to be very proactive and involved in the city." Seven percent of the students are African American, 7 percent are Hispanic, 10 percent are Asian American, and 8 percent hail from foreign countries. As you might expect, political issues are important here and the biggest concerns include "anything and everything," according to a criminal justice major. Merit scholarships worth an average of $20,201 are awarded annually and student-athletes vie for 148 awards in 23 sports. Though tuition is really steep, the university has adopted a fixed-rate plan that guarantees tuition will not increase for up to five years of full-time undergraduate study. Students who receive need-based grant aid for their first year are guaranteed the same amount of aid for up to five years. The administration recently conceded that, contrary to the impressions that it had been giving, GW is not need-blind in its admissions.

"The social life on campus is vibrant."

Sixty-eight percent of GW students live in campus housing, where freshmen and sophomores are guaranteed housing. "Housing can be described in one word,"

(continued)

Accepted: 33%
Enrolled: 33%
Grad in 6 Years: 81%
Returning Freshmen: 92%
Academics: ✑ ✑ ✑ ½
Social: ☎ ☎ ☎
Q of L: ★ ★ ★
Admissions: (202) 994-6040
Email Address: gwadm@ gwu.edu

Strongest Programs:
International Affairs
Political Science
Psychology
Finance
Marketing

George Washington was established in 1821 by an act of Congress.

says a student: "Fantastic!" Another counters, "The residence halls are enormous and provide many amenities, but the housing staff can be slow and inefficient." Those who move off campus typically find group houses in Foggy Bottom or go to nearby neighborhoods like Dupont Circle and Georgetown, just a short walk from campus. Some also choose the Maryland or Virginia suburbs, where housing stock is newer, a little more affordable, and just a short subway ride away. Many freshmen are assigned to suites with up to four roommates in Thurston Hall, the biggest and rowdiest dorm on campus. They may also apply for Affinity Housing, which accommodates groups of students who share similar interests. Despite the university's urban location, students say the campus is safe and security is reliable.

GW's political communications major, which combines political science, journalism, and electronic media courses, is one of the few undergraduate programs of its kind.

"The social life on campus is vibrant," an international affairs major says. "Many social fraternities and sororities exist as well as a strong club scene." Twenty-three percent of GW men and women go Greek, and "there are over 350 student organizations on campus so there is always something going on," a senior says. Although underage drinking does occur, a D.C. police crackdown has made it extremely difficult for those under 21 to be served at off-campus restaurants and pubs. Major annual events include the Fall Fest and Spring Fling carnivals, with free food and such nationally known entertainment as The Roots and Busta Rhymes. Popular road trips include the beaches of Ocean City, Maryland, and Virginia Beach, Virginia. Philadelphia and New York City are easily accessible by bus or train, a boon because most GW students don't have cars.

GW doesn't field a football team, but its 23 varsity teams (the "Colonials") are competitive in Division I Atlantic 10 Conference play. Solid teams include men's golf (2012 Atlantic 10 champs), women's rowing (2013 Atlantic 10 Varsity 8 winners), men's soccer, softball, and men's squash. The gymnastics squad is also strong. Approximately 20 percent of undergraduates participate in the intramural sports program, which offers more than 30 events throughout the year. The school's unofficial mascot is the hippopotamus.

Overlaps

Boston University, NYU, American University, Georgetown, Northeastern, Boston College, University of Pennsylvania, University of Southern California

"GW has a great location which affords its students so many opportunities for jobs and internships," says one student. Despite the bureaucratic annoyances, the university continues to build its national reputation. "GWU has become a much more well-known institution," a sophomore says. "Standards are higher and admission criteria are much more competitive." For students interested in urban living in the heart of the nation's political establishment, GW may fit the bill. But the bill will be hefty.

If You Apply To ➤ | **GW:** Early decision: Nov. 10. Regular admissions: Jan. 10. Financial aid: Feb. 1. Housing: Apr. 15. Application fee: $75. Campus and alumni interviews: optional, evaluative. SATs or ACTs: required. Subject Tests: recommended. Accepts the Common Application. Essay question.

Georgetown University

37th and O Streets NW, Washington, D.C. 20057

For anyone who wants to be a master of the political universe, this is the place. Strong international and intercultural culture. In the excitement of studying in D.C., students may pay little attention to the Jesuit affiliation, which adds a conservative tinge to the campus. Getting in is also easier if you're Roman Catholic. Occupies a tree-lined neighborhood that is home to many of the nation's most powerful people.

As the oldest and most selective of the nation's Roman Catholic schools, Georgetown University offers students unparalleled access to Washington, D.C.'s corridors of power. Aspiring politicos benefit from the university's emphasis on public policy, international business, and foreign service. The national spotlight shines brightly on this elite institution, drawing dynamic students and athletes from around the world. "Georgetown is one of the most prestigious schools in the nation," a senior observes. "It balances academics, social life, and faith in an all-encompassing college experience based on 'care of the whole person.'"

"Students take their coursework very seriously."

From its scenic location just blocks from the Potomac River, Georgetown affords its students an excellent vantage point from which to survey the world. The 104-acre campus reflects the history and growth of the nation's oldest Jesuit university. The Federal style of Old North, home of the School of Business Administration, which once housed guests such as George Washington and Lafayette, contrasts with the towers of the Flemish Romanesque-style Healy Hall, a post–Civil War landmark on the National Register of Historic Places.

Although Georgetown is a Catholic university (founded in 1789 by the Society of Jesus), the religious atmosphere is by no means oppressive. Just more than half of the undergraduates are Catholic, but all major faiths are respected and practiced on campus. That's partially due to the pronounced international influence here. International relations, diplomatic history, and international economics are among the hottest programs, as evidenced by former secretary of state Madeline Albright's return to the School of Foreign Service. Through its broad liberal arts curriculum, GU focuses on developing the intellectual prowess and moral rigor its students will need in future national and international leadership roles. The curriculum has a strong multidisciplinary and intercultural slant, and students can choose among several programs abroad to round out their classroom experiences.

Would-be Hoyas may apply to one of four undergraduate schools: Georgetown College for liberal arts, the School of Nursing and Health Studies, McDonough School of Business, and the Walsh School of Foreign Service (SFS), which gives future diplomats, journalists, and others a strong grounding in the social sciences. Prospective freshmen must declare intended majors on their applications, and their secondary school records are judged accordingly. This means, among other things, intense competition within the college for the limited number of spaces in Georgetown's popular premed program.

"TAs never teach courses. They only lead discussion sections and recitations."

"Students take their coursework very seriously," says a senior. "The courses are challenging, but it certainly isn't impossible to do well." The most popular programs include international affairs, government, international politics, finance, and nursing. Of course, the theology department is also strong. The School of Foreign Service stands out for its international economics, regional and comparative studies, and diplomatic history offerings. SFS also offers several five-year undergraduate and graduate degree programs in conjunction with the Graduate School of Arts and Sciences. The business school balances liberal arts with professional training, which translates into strong offerings in international and intercultural business as well as an emphasis on ethical and public policy issues. Curiously, given its location in D.C., Georgetown does not offer an undergraduate public policy major. The School of Nursing and Health Studies runs an integrated program combining the liberal arts and humanities with professional nursing theory and practice, and offers majors in nursing and health studies. The Faculty of Languages and Linguistics, the only undergraduate program of its kind nationwide, grants degrees in nine languages, as well as degrees in linguistics and comparative literature.

Website: www.georgetown.edu

Location: City Center

Private

Total Enrollment: 13,831

Undergraduates: 7,006

Male/Female: 44/56

SAT Ranges: CR 650–750, M 660–750

ACT Ranges: 29–33

Financial Aid: 56%

Expense: Pr $ $ $ $

Student Loans: 39%

Average Debt: $ $ $

Phi Beta Kappa: Yes

Applicants: 20,115

Accepted: 17%

Enrolled: 46%

Grad in 6 Years: 93%

Returning Freshmen: 96%

Academics: ✍ ✍ ✍ ✍ ½

Social: ☎ ☎ ☎ ☎

Q of L: ★ ★ ★ ★

Admissions: (202) 687-3600

Email Address: guadmiss@georgetown.edu

Strongest Programs:
Government
Chemistry
Philosophy
Business
International Relations
Diplomatic History
International Economics

Prospective freshmen must declare intended majors on their applications, and their secondary school records are judged accordingly.

All students must complete requirements in humanities and writing, philosophy, and theology; other requirements are specific to each school. That GU views most subjects through an international lens is evidenced by the number of students who study abroad. The Office of International Programs offers more than 120 programs in 39 countries. First-years read the same novel during the summer and the author visits campus during the first few weeks for a day-long seminar. There are no special academic requirements for the freshman year, but about 30 Georgetown College freshmen are accepted annually into the liberal arts colloquium. Georgetown likes to boast about its faculty, and well it should. "The professors are outstanding and the teaching is first-rate," says an American studies major. A culture and politics major adds, "TAs never teach courses. They only lead discussion sections and recitations." The school's hefty endowment is the largest among the nation's Jesuit colleges and universities.

There are no special academic requirements for the freshman year, but about 30 Georgetown College freshmen are accepted annually into the liberal arts colloquium.

A senior says GU students are not the stereotypical "pastel polo and pearl-clad preppies from Long Island." The GU community includes students from all over the United States. African Americans make up 7 percent of undergrads, Hispanics 8 percent, and Asian Americans comprise 9 percent. Almost half the students come from private or parochial schools. A student committee works with the vice president for student affairs to improve race relations and develop strategies for improving inclusiveness and sensitivity to issues of multiculturalism. Georgetown offers no academic merit scholarships, but it does guarantee to meet the full demonstrated need of every admit, and more than 120 athletic scholarships draw male and female athletes of all stripes. The Georgetown Scholarship Program offers additional financial incentives to eligible students.

"Social life is a major part of campus."

University-owned dorms, townhouses, and apartments accommodate some 67 percent of undergrads, and "housing is extremely nice," says a senior. All dorms are co-ed, and some have more activities and community than others. "All have great amenities like Ethernet and landscaping," adds one student. Two dining halls serve "steadily improving" but expensive fare. GU students feel relatively safe on campus, thanks to the school's ever-present Department of Public Safety and its walking and riding after-dark escort services.

Jesuits, who know a thing or two about secret societies, frown upon fraternities and sororities at their colleges, and so there are none at Georgetown. The university's strict enforcement of the 21-year-old drinking age has led to a somewhat decentralized social life, which is not necessarily a bad thing. Alcohol is forbidden in undergrad dorms, and all parties must be registered. The dozens of bars, nightclubs, and restaurants in Georgetown—Martin's Tavern and the Tombs are always popular—are a big draw for students who are legal, but they can get pricey. The Hoyas, a campus pub in the spectacular student activity center, is a more affordable alternative. Popular annual formals such as the Diplomatic and the Blue/Gray Ball force students to dress up and pair off. "Social life is a major part of campus," says a student. "Kids can easily find their niche." Georgetown has a reputation as a gay-friendly campus, and regular events include Gay Pride Month and a popular drag ball called Genderfunk.

Jesuits, who know a thing or two about secret societies, frown upon fraternities and sororities at their colleges, and so there are none at Georgetown.

Washington offers unsurpassed cultural resources, ranging from the museums of the Smithsonian to the Kennedy Center. "Washington is an ideal place to spend your college years," says a student. "The city has everything students could want, including culture, shopping, museums, monuments, social life, and the clean and convenient Metro for transportation." Given the absence of on-campus parking, a car is probably more trouble than it's worth. Road trips are said to be not popular.

Should you notice the hills begin to tremble with a deep, resounding, primitive chant—"Hoya Saxa Hoya Saxa"—don't worry; it's probably just another Georgetown basketball game. Hoya is derived from the Greek and Latin phrase *hoya saxa*, which means, "What rocks!" Some say it originated in a cheer referring to the stones that formed the school's outer walls. The Hoya men's basketball team has a long history of prominence. The Hoyas are also competitive in men's and women's lacrosse and sailing; the women's lacrosse team has won numerous Big East Championships. The thrill of victory in intramural competition at the superb underground Yates Memorial Field House is not to be missed, either.

For anyone interested in discovering the world, Georgetown offers an outstanding menu of choices in one of the nation's most dynamic cities. Professors truly pay attention to their undergrads and the diverse students, who are "hardworking, diligent, caring individuals," says one sophomore. "Georgetown is a place where students of all backgrounds, all traditions, and all faiths come together for a common purpose of educating each other and making an impact on the world."

If You Apply To >

Georgetown: Early action: Nov. 1. Regular admissions: Jan. 10. Application fee: $75. Campus interviews: optional, evaluative. Alumni interviews: required, evaluative. SATs or ACTs: required. Subject Tests: recommended. Apply to particular schools or programs. Essay question: personal statement plus one additional question for each school.

University of Georgia

212 Terrell Hall, Athens, GA 30602-1633

What a difference (nearly) free tuition makes. Top Georgia students now choose UGA over highly selective private institutions. Business and social and natural sciences head the list of strong and sought-after programs. The college town of Athens boasts a great nightlife and is within easy reach of Atlanta. The university's Center for Undergraduate Research offers unique opportunities.

College-aged Georgians hit the jackpot when the state began using lottery receipts to fund the Hope Scholarship program. The program covers 90 percent of tuition at the University of Georgia for all four years for students who finish high school in the state with a B average and maintain that average in college. In fact, the scholarship has made it much tougher to get into UGA, which not long ago was known mostly for its dynamite football team and raucous parties. In the last decade, UGA students have received nearly 60 major scholarships including Rhodes, Goldwater, Truman, Marshall, Udall, and Merage awards. "Georgia offers the most complete 'Southern college experience' in the South," says a senior.

Founded in 1785, Georgia was the nation's first state-chartered university (UNC was chartered later but was the first public university to open its doors). Its attractive 706-acre campus is dotted with greenery and wooded walks. The older north campus houses the administrative offices and law school, and features 19th-century architecture and landscaping. The southern end of campus has more modern buildings and residence halls. The most recent campus addition is the Richard B. Russell Special Collections Libraries, a 115,000-square-foot facility featuring climate- and humidity-controlled vault storage for rare manuscripts and historical documents.

"Entry-level (weedout) courses are highly competitive."

UGA's core curriculum includes one course in life sciences and one in physical sciences, as well as courses in world languages and culture, humanities, and the arts.

Website: www.uga.edu
Location: Small City
Public
Total Enrollment: 30,940
Undergraduates: 24,416
Male/Female: 42/58
SAT Ranges: CR 560–660, M 580–670
ACT Ranges: 26–30
Financial Aid: 39%
Expense: Pub $ $ $
Student Loans: 44%
Average Debt: $
Phi Beta Kappa: Yes
Applicants: 18,458
Accepted: 56%
Enrolled: 48%
Grad in 6 Years: 83%
Returning Freshmen: 94%
Academics: ✐ ✐ ✐

(continued)

Social: 🐶 🐶 🐶 🐶 🐶
Q of L: ★ ★ ★
Admissions: (706) 542-8776
Email Address: adm-info@
   uga.edu

Strongest Programs:
Life Sciences
Ecology and Environmental
   Studies
Agriculture
International and Public Affairs
Business
Education
Journalism/Mass
   Communication

Computing, calculus, engineering, and statistics courses are also emphasized. Before the semester starts, freshmen may spend a month on campus to learn their way around, meet new friends, and even earn six hours of credit. Don't want to stay for an entire month? Choose the Dawg Camp weekend retreat, which promotes networking and leadership skills and includes programs on time and stress management, diversity, and "What It Means to Be a Georgia Bulldog." During the year, freshman seminars allow first-year students to study under a senior faculty member in a small, personalized setting while earning an hour of academic credit. "UGA offers tremendous opportunities for freshmen to get plugged in on campus, both before classes start and after," confirms a senior. Students give high marks to UGA's Terry College of Business, Grady College of Journalism, the School of Public and International Affairs, and the colleges of education and of agriculture and environmental sciences.

"The teachers at UGA are wonderful."

"I would say the competitiveness of the classes varies," says a junior. "Many of the upper-level courses in certain business majors are quite relaxed, but the entry-level (weed-out) courses are highly competitive." As you might expect, large lecture classes are common. A computerized registration system helps students sign up for courses; first pick usually goes to the 2,500 honors students and to UGA's varsity athletes, with everyone else prioritized by class standing. The Center for Undergraduate Research Opportunities allows students to conduct a research or service project, write a thesis, develop a creative work with close faculty supervision. "The teachers at UGA are wonderful," a finance major says. "The professors have a strong desire to help students out who are actively trying to learn the material." About 26 percent of undergrads have an international education experience, through more than 100 study abroad programs and 50 student exchange programs. UGA operates year-round residential study abroad programs of its own in Oxford, England; Avignon, France; and Cortona, Italy; and the school has an ecological research center in Costa Rica.

Eighty-seven percent of UGA students are Georgian.

Eighty-seven percent of UGA students are Georgian, and 90 percent graduated in the top quarter of their high school class. African Americans account for 7 percent and Asian Americans 8 percent of the student body, and Hispanics add another 5 percent. Politically, the school tends to lean right and "since most of the student body are from the South, the silent majority on campus are white-collar conservatives," says a senior. Merit scholarships are available and UGA also doles out 412 athletic scholarships in 12 sports. As many as 100 top undergraduates are named Foundation Fellows, netting a full scholarship plus stipends for international travel and research.

"The party scene is alive and well."

Thirty-six percent of Bulldogs live in the dorms, and freshmen are required to do so. Dorm life is "a great way to get plugged into the UGA community," says one senior. "The dorms aren't the Ritz, but freshman year is so much fun you never notice," adds a political science/speech communication major. Most keep their meal cards even after moving off campus. "The dining facilities are incredible!" says a student. "We even have a dining hall with 24-hour service during the school week." There are four campus dining halls—each with its own specialty cuisine—and a snack bar, and the excellence of UGA's food service program has been recognized with the Ivy Award.

When the weekend comes, students know how to have a good time.

When the weekend comes, students know how to have a good time. "The party scene is alive and well with house parties, frat parties, and downtown Athens," says a senior. There are also more than 500 student organizations; fraternities and sororities attract 21 percent of the men and 28 percent of the women, respectively. More significant than Greek life is the funky mix of shops, restaurants and clubs, and various cultural events found in downtown Athens, a 10-minute walk from most residence halls.

"Most people are very excited about the counterculture of Athens," says one student. "Everyone loves going downtown to shows, art events, and to eclectic restaurants." Many clubs in Athens cater to UGA students and admit those under 21, as long as they get a stamp saying they can't drink. Alcohol is prohibited in the dorms, but as at most schools, the determined manage to imbibe anyway. Athens is also "far enough away from Atlanta to maintain the college community, yet close enough to provide an escape," a senior says. Other popular road trips include the Florida and Carolina beaches, and anywhere the Bulldogs are playing on a fall Saturday.

Indeed, Athens residents worship UGA's perennially fierce football team. The Georgia–Florida rivalry—billed as the "World's Largest Cocktail Party"—is particularly notable: "The game takes place on neutral ground in Jacksonville, and since it coincides with fall break, 90 percent of the students go," says an accounting major. The women's gymnastics team (the Gym Dogs) won its fifth consecutive national championship in 2009. The women's equestrian team brought home three straight titles from 2005 to 2009. Men's tennis has won national titles as well. Women's and men's golf are also competitive. For the weekend warrior, there are intramural teams in 15 sports and the Oconee River Greenway, a 13-mile paved trail.

UGA's sheer size means you could coast through four years here as nothing more than a number. But with a little effort, that doesn't have to happen. Freshman seminars, research projects, study abroad, and honors courses offer the opportunity to graduate with a solid background in any number of areas and fond memories of Saturdays spent cheering on the Bulldogs—along with 92,000 of your closest friends. "Coming into UGA is like coming into a family," a junior says. "UGA cares about its people and the people care about UGA."

Athens residents worship UGA's perennially fierce football team.

Overlaps

Georgia Tech, UNC at Chapel Hill, University of Texas, University of South Carolina, Emory, University of Virginia, Clemson, University of Florida

If You Apply To ➤

Georgia: Early action: Oct. 15. Regular admissions: Jan. 15. Financial aid: Jul. 15. Housing: May 15. Application fee: $60. No campus or alumni interviews. SATs or ACTs: required. Subject Tests: optional. Essay question.

Georgia Institute of Technology

Atlanta, GA 30332-0320

As the South's premier technically oriented university, Ma Tech does not coddle her young. Students must survive the sometimes mean streets of downtown Atlanta and fight through a wall of graduate students to talk with their professors. Architecture and big-time sports supplement the engineering focus. Tech's 67/33 male/female ratio is offset by women from all-female Agnes Scott.

If you're looking for lazy days on the college green and hard-partying weekends, look elsewhere. You won't find those at Georgia Institute of Technology, the South's premier tech university, and, since 2009, a member of the elite Association of American Universities. What you will find are challenging courses that prepare you for a high-paying job as an engineer, architect, or computer scientist. "Tech is tough," reasons a graduate student. "You have to want to be here." Still, even those who want to be here are happy to finally arrive at graduation day. What makes Tech a special place? "The fact that I survived it and got out with a degree," says a computer science major, only partially joking.

Website: www.gatech.edu
Location: City Center
Public
Total Enrollment: 18,741
Undergraduates: 13,190
Male/Female: 67/33
SAT Ranges: CR 600–700, M 660–760

(continued)

ACT Ranges: 28–32
Financial Aid: 43%
Expense: Pub $ $ $
Student Loans: 44%
Average Debt: $ $ $
Phi Beta Kappa: No
Applicants: 14,645
Accepted: 55%
Enrolled: 38%
Grad in 6 Years: 79%
Returning Freshmen: 95%
Academics: ✏️ ✏️ ✏️ ✏️ ✏️
Social: ☎ ☎
Q of L: ★ ★
Admissions: (404) 894-4154
Email Address: admission@
gatech.edu

Strongest Programs:
Engineering
Computer Science
Management

Located just off the interstate in Georgia's capital city, Tech's 450-acre campus includes 42 residence halls, an aquatic center, a sports performance complex, and an amphitheater. Reflective of the history of Georgia Tech, the building styles include the Georgian Revival and collegiate Gothic of the historic Hill District (listed on the National Register of Historic Places) and surrounding area, the International style buildings constructed from the 1940s into the 1960s, the modernist structures of the 1970s and '80s, the postmodern facilities of the '90s, and the newly built high-tech facilities. All these styles coexist comfortably on a tree-filled and landscaped campus seen as a green oasis in the midst of a dense urban environment.

Courses at Tech are "extremely rigorous," says a senior, at least in the sciences and engineering. "Grading on a curve creates hypercompetitive situations because your absolute grade is largely irrelevant—you just have to do better than most of the others." Strong programs include math and computer science ("It's hard to have a life and be a CS student," one major sighs) as well as most types of engineering, especially industrial, biomedical, and aerospace. Tech also offers civil, electrical, environmental, mechanical, computer, materials, and nuclear engineering. Tech has plenty of liberal arts courses, but a grad student says history, philosophy, and English aren't the reasons why most students enroll.

"Tech is tough."

Aside from the technical fare, Tech's management college is increasingly popular, and its school of architecture has done pioneering work in historic preservation and energy conservation. Among the architecture program's alumni is Michael Arad, whose winning design for the September 11 memorial in lower Manhattan was selected from a field of more than 5,200. The prelaw certificate is a boon to aspiring patent attorneys, as is the minor in law, science, and technology. As most courses need computers, the school requires students to bring their own laptops.

Regardless of major, students must complete nine semester hours of social sciences, eight hours of science, six hours each of English and humanities, four hours of math, three hours of U.S. or Georgia history, U.S. Perspectives Overlay, a global perspectives course, and two hours of wellness. As students move from those core and required courses to upper-level options within their majors, the quality of teaching improves. "It's absolutely horrible for things like freshman math classes," says a computer science major. "You're typically taught by TAs, maybe half of whom have only the slightest grasp of English. Things get better as you progress and get to know professors." That's because those professors are indeed exceptional; some have worked on projects such as the Star Wars missile-defense system and the space shuttle. Still, classes are big—23 percent of those taken by undergraduates have more than 49 students. "Students are generally stressed and tired," says a grad student. "Not working hard is not an option here."

Tech's management college is increasingly popular, and its school of architecture has done pioneering work in historic preservation and energy conservation.

In fact, Tech's demanding workload means it's common to spend five years getting your degree. There's also the frustrating course selection process: "Sleep through your registration time ticket, and you may blow your semester because you won't get into anything," warns a senior. Also contributing to delayed graduation dates is the popular co-op program, through which almost 2,700 students earn money for their education while gaining on-the-job experience. Those eager to experience another culture or environment can tap into more than 80 exchange programs and 30 group-led faculty programs; over 25 percent of Tech students have an international experience by the time they graduate.

"Grading on a curve creates hypercompetitive situations."

Two-thirds of Georgia Tech's students come from Georgia, and most are too focused on school or their co-op jobs to care about politics, causes, or any of the issues that get their peers riled up on nearby campuses. "There are a lot of left-brain types here—high on the introspection and thinking, low on the social skills," says a senior. And though they may be united in their pursuit of technical expertise, the campus is hardly homogenous: African Americans account for 7 percent of the student body, Hispanics 7 percent, and Asian Americans 19 percent. To limit burgeoning enrollment, out-of-state applicants must meet slightly higher criteria than their Georgia counterparts. The university awards merit scholarships to nearly half of the undergraduate population. There are also more than 300 athletic scholarships available to student-athletes. In addition, Tech has eliminated loans for Georgia residents with family incomes below $33,300 a year.

Fifty-six percent of students live in the dorms, where freshmen are guaranteed a room. A senior says that the quality of residence halls varies widely. "Some dorms are new, apartment-style, and nice," the student says. "Others are foul dungeons." Many dorms have full kitchen facilities, though, and while most halls are single-sex, visitation rules are lenient. Off-campus housing is generally comfortable, but parts of the surrounding neighborhood are unsavory. "Far too many cars are broken into or stolen," says one student. "There's usually a couple of armed robberies (at least) a semester." The campus dining halls offer "little variety and less quality," according to another student.

Fortunately, even if mystery meat is on the day's menu at Tech, the school is smack-dab in the middle of "Hot-Lanta," with its endless supply of clubs, bars, movie theaters, restaurants, shopping, and museums, both in midtown Atlanta and the Buckhead district. "Atlanta is not a college town," reasons a computer science

Tech's demanding workload means it's common to spend five years getting your degree.

"You're typically taught by TAs, maybe half of whom have only the slightest grasp of English."

major. "However, it is the best thing going in Georgia," with friendly, young residents, good cultural activities, beautiful green spaces, and a booming economy. The city also offers plenty of community service opportunities. Fraternities draw 23 percent of Tech's men and sororities draw 29 percent of the women, and members may live in their chapter houses. Alcohol flows freely at frat parties, but otherwise, students say, Tech's policies against open containers and underage drinking are strictly enforced. "There's not much in the way of social life here outside of the frats," says a senior. "You have your group of friends and you do your own thing." The best road trips include Florida's beaches, which are a half-day's drive, and Athens, Georgia, for basketball or football games against the University of Georgia.

Tech's varsity sports teams (the "Yellowjackets") have become as big-time as any in the South.

Tech's varsity sports teams (the "Yellowjackets") have become as big-time as any in the South, and when the weekend comes, students throw off their lab coats and become wild members of the "Rambling Wreck from Georgia Tech." Solid Division I teams include women's basketball, softball, football, golf, and men's cross-country. Among Tech's many other traditions is "stealing the T," in which students try to remove the huge yellow letter T from the tower on the administration building and return it to the school by presenting it to a member of the faculty or administration. The addition of alarms, motion sensors, and heat sensors on the T has made the task more difficult, but "certainly not impossible for a Georgia Tech engineer," says an electrical engineering major. And then there's the Mini 500, a 15-lap tricycle race around a parking garage with three pit stops, a tire change, and a driver rotation.

Forget fitting the mold; the engineers of Georgia Tech are proud to say they make it. Self-direction, ambition, and motivation will take you far here, as will dexterity with a graphing calculator and a fondness for highly complex software algorithms. And despite their complaints about the workload, the social life (or lack thereof), the safety of their surrounding neighborhood, and the impact of budget cuts, Tech students do have a soft spot for their school. Says one student, "I love a good challenge, and Tech is perfect for that."

Overlaps

University of Florida, University of Georgia, University of Virginia, MIT, Carnegie Mellon, Cornell, Emory, UC–Berkeley

Gettysburg College

300 North Washington Street, Gettysburg, PA 17325-1484

The college by the battlefield is strong in U.S. history—that's a given. The natural sciences and business are also popular, and political science majors enjoy good connections in D.C. and New York City. Students can also take courses down the road at Dickinson and Franklin and Marshall—as long as they don't mind being on rival turf.

Website: www.gettysburg.edu
Location: Suburban
Private
Total Enrollment: 2,573
Undergraduates: 2,573
Male/Female: 47/53
SAT Ranges: CR 600–690, M 610–670
ACT Ranges: N/A
Financial Aid: 55%
Expense: Pr $ $ $
Student Loans: 58%
Average Debt: $ $ $
Phi Beta Kappa: Yes
Applicants: 5,620
Accepted: 40%
Enrolled: 34%
Grad in 6 Years: 84%
Returning Freshmen: 91%
Academics: ✐ ✐ ✐ ½
Social: ☎ ☎ ☎
Q of L: ★ ★ ★
Admissions: (717) 337-6100
Email Address: admiss@gettysburg.edu

Strongest Programs:
English
History
Psychology
Natural Sciences
Business
Political Science

Whether the reference is to the Pennsylvania town steeped in Civil War history or the small, high-caliber college located in the famed battlefield's backyard, a certain pride and reverence are immediately evident when the name "Gettysburg" is uttered. This feeling is not lost on students at Gettysburg College, who come to southeastern Pennsylvania to acquaint themselves with American history while gearing up for the future. "We add a personal touch to everything," says a student.

Situated in the midst of gently rolling hills, Gettysburg's 200-acre campus is "a historical treasure," an eclectic assemblage of Georgian, Greek, Romanesque, Gothic Revival, and modern architecture, plus several styles not easily categorized. One campus building—Penn Hall—was actually used as a hospital during the Battle of Gettysburg. Rumor has it that ghostly soldiers can still be seen walking the grounds.

Indoors, the English department, home of the *Gettysburg Review*, is among the strongest at Gettysburg, as are the natural sciences, which are well endowed with state-of-the-art equipment. The fine psychology department offers opportunities for students to participate in faculty research. The management major is the most popular. Also popular, of course, is the excellent history department, which is bolstered by the school's nationally recognized and prestigious Civil War Institute. The library system boasts nearly 400,000 volumes, a library/learning resource center, and an online computer catalog search. "The college is engaging," says a student, and "courses require students to play an active role."

"All of the students maintain a rigorous academic schedule and have a heavy course load," says one sophomore. "However, everyone is supported and encouraged to do their best." The small class sizes make for close student/faculty relationships, and the academic honor code contributes to the atmosphere of community and mutual trust. "Classes are engaging and fun, as long as students are willing to meet the professor halfway," says one junior. "The quality of teaching is superb,"

"Classes are engaging and fun." adds another student. The popular first-year seminars explore topics such as Why Do People Dance?; participants live in the same residence hall and are in the same first-year residential college program. "First-Year orientation, seminars, the honor code, and the RISE program are important because they are all learning experiences," says one student. Another popular program is the Area Studies Symposium, which focuses each year on a different region of the world and offers lectures and films for the whole campus, in addition to academic credit for participating students. There are disciplinary programs such as environmental studies, Latin American studies, and biochemistry and molecular biology. Students may pursue a Music in Performance degree within the Sunderman Conservatory of Music; there are also degrees in globalization studies, Arabic language, and prebusiness advising.

Gettysburg sponsors a Washington semester with American University, a United Nations semester through Drew University in New Jersey, and cooperative dual-degree programs in engineering and forestry. Most departments offer structured internships, and the chemistry department offers a summer cooperative research program between students and professors in which most majors participate and work on a joint publication. Through the Central Pennsylvania Consortium, students may take courses at two nearby colleges—Dickinson and Franklin and Marshall. Outstanding seniors may participate in the Senior Scholars' Seminar, with independent study on a major contemporary issue, but all students have a chance to do independent work and/or design their own majors. Study abroad programs are global and popular, with 57 percent of the students taking part during their college career. A political science and public policy major says, "All students are encouraged to study abroad. The faculty really wants the students to have that global experience because the perspectives they bring back to the classroom are so insightful."

> Social life at the 'Burg involves the Greek system and other activities.

The Gettysburg student body is mostly middle- to upper-middle-class and 73 percent hail from outside Pennsylvania. Students who attend Gettysburg tend to be "happy and passionate," according to one senior. "Students are barely in their residence halls because there is so much to do, and students have such a love for this college and everything it offers." African American, Asian American, and Hispanic enrollment accounts for 10 percent of the student body. Seventy-two percent of the students were in the top 10th of their high school class. Students are so interested in public service that the school set up a Center for Public Service to direct their community activities. Big issues include Darfur and homelessness, although "we aren't a very politically charged school," says a junior. No athletic scholarships are available, but academic scholarships average $13,444.

> "Students are barely in their residence halls because there is so much to do."

Campus housing is guaranteed all four years, and students can choose from apartment-style residence halls, special interest halls, and the Quarry Suites. A student says, "Every living option has pros and cons, but students can choose what will work best for them. First-year dorms are pretty standard: white cinderblocks, linoleum floors, and shared bathrooms. The living spaces are definitely big enough for two people, and we never do forced triples." The top scholars in each class get first crack at the best rooms. Student rooms have been added in renovated historical properties (some reputed to be haunted) on campus, and there are more options for interesting housing and suite living. Off-campus apartments lure 8 percent of the student body away, while freshmen are required to remain in the residence halls. There are a variety of dining options, including the ever popular Café 101, the campus snack bar, and grill room where many students take their regular meals. Kitchens are also available in the residences for upperclassmen. "There are always lots of options for vegetarians, vegans, and students with special dietary needs," states a senior. "I have a few friends with gluten allergies, and they are so satisfied with the options they are given."

> There are disciplinary programs such as environmental studies, Latin American studies, and biochemistry and molecular biology.

Social life at the 'Burg involves the Greek system and other activities. Thirty-six percent of the men belong to the dozen fraternities; the seven sororities draw 32 percent of the women. Greek parties are open and attract crowds eager to dance the night away, although students insist they're not the only source of fun on campus. A Student Activities Committee provides alternative social events, including concerts, comedians, bus trips to Georgetown, movies, and campus coffeehouses. "There are always things going on," says one student. "Everyone can stay busy without leaving campus." Officially the campus is dry, but as on many such campuses, drinking can be done, albeit carefully, students report. The orchards and rolling countryside surrounding the campus are peaceful and scenic, and there is a

"The school attracts individuals who will push themselves and have a great time doing it."

small ski slope nearby. Students also get free passes to the historic attractions in town. Many participate in the November 19 Fortenbaugh Lecture by noted historians commemorating the Gettysburg Address and in the yearly wreath-laying ceremony in front of the Eisenhower Admissions Office to commemorate the general's birthday. Tourist season is a common complaint among students. But those who want to escape can do so—the campus is within an hour and a half of Washington, D.C., and considerably closer to Baltimore, where students enjoy the scenic Inner Harbor area.

The management major is the most popular.

Gettysburg sponsors 24 varsity sports—12 for men and 12 for women—that compete at the NCAA Division III intercollegiate level. The annual football game against Dickinson draws a good turnout, and the Little Brown Bucket, mahogany with silver handles, is passed to the team that wins. Both track and swimming frequently produce All-Americans. The college is a frequent winner of the President's Cup, awarded to the top overall athletic program in the Centennial Conference. Competitive teams include men's and women's lacrosse, men's and women's swimming (both 2012 conference champs), and women's volleyball. Ninety-two percent of students participate in intramural and club sports and recreational fitness programs.

At Gettysburg, students stay true to their slogan: "Work Hard, Play Smart." A senior says, "The school attracts individuals who will push themselves and have a great time doing it." Students wanting personal attention from professors, solid academics, and an area rich with history might consider getting their education with a Gettysburg address.

Overlaps

Dickinson, Bucknell, University of Richmond, Franklin and Marshall, Lafayette, George Washington

If You Apply To ➤ **Gettysburg:** Early decision: Nov. 15. Regular admissions: Feb. 1. Financial aid: Feb. 15. Application fee: $60. Campus interviews: optional, informational. No alumni interviews. SATs or ACTs: required. Subject Tests: optional. Accepts the Common Application. Essay question: describe how you have made a difference to your school or community; why Gettysburg?

University of Glasgow: See page 365.

Gonzaga University

502 East Boone Avenue, Spokane, WA 99258-0102

Best known outside the Northwest for its unlikely successes on the basketball court, Gonzaga is a medium-sized private university with a picturesque residential campus in an urban setting. Offers classic Jesuit education with rigorous core and emphasis on service, though only half of undergrads are Roman Catholic. Spokane is not as cosmopolitan as Seattle or San Francisco. Gonzaga is less selective than Santa Clara or USD, comparable to USF. Good bet for those who relish school spirit.

Gonzaga University burst into the nation's frontal lobes in 1999 when its men's basketball team fought their way to the quarterfinals of the NCAA Division I tournament. Consistent success in the tournament since then has softened the Zag's image as a mid-sized David doing battle with Goliaths like UConn. What has lingered, though, is the image of a solid

"To be a Zag is something that transcends a four-year time frame."

regional liberal arts university committed to the Jesuit ideal of educating the whole person: mind, body, and spirit. In the case of Gonzaga, "spirit" takes on multiple meanings. "To be a Zag is something that transcends a four-year time frame," says one student. "It's for life."

Founded in 1887 as a Jesuit mission, the school takes its name from St. Aloysius Gonzaga, a 16th century Italian aristocrat who joined the Society of Jesus and was martyred while serving victims of an epidemic. The campus occupies 131 picturesque acres along the Spokane River, only a 15-minute walk from downtown. A 37-mile paved bike trail borders the campus and river. Architectural styles range from the Romanesque College Hall to the sleek PACCAR Center for Applied Science. The library's Crosby Collection contains recordings, photographs and other memorabilia pertaining to Gonzaga's most famous alumnus, crooner Bing. The Boone Retail Center opened in 2013 and serves as the dining hall for residential students while the University Center is under construction. An indoor tennis and golf facility opens in 2014.

With just over 200,000 residents, Spokane is the second largest city in Washington but has the feel of a much smaller city. Students describe it as "a great college town" with a relaxed atmosphere and "a ton of cool little shops and music venues." Local businesses offer student discounts. "They love the school almost as much as students do—especially during basketball season," observes a public relations major. The administration points out that, with an average annual rainfall of 16 inches, Spokane has about 260 days of sunshine a year and four distinct seasons. Maybe so, but students grouse about the weather on the other 105 days. "I am used to it being warm and sunny for almost nine months out of the year," says an Arizonian. "I feel homesick on gray, cold days."

Consistent with its Jesuit liberal arts traditions, Gonzaga requires undergraduates to complete an extensive core curriculum, including a seven-credit "Thought and Expression" block of courses in English composition, speech communication, and critical reasoning. There are also heavy doses of philosophy and religious studies, literature, and mathematics. Writing and analytic skills are emphasized throughout the core curriculum. "The holistic Jesuit philosophy of educating the whole person means that classes from our core curriculum tie into courses from our majors and

"I feel homesick on gray, cold days."

minors, which is really fun," reports a business administration major. "Students graduate from Gonzaga knowing about so much more than just their majors because of our core."

Students describe the academic climate as rigorous but not particularly competitive. "I think classes are fair," says one student. "Sure, there's a lot of studying and reading going on, but our professors are truly brilliant and that it makes it fun." As elsewhere, science courses are said to "require massive amounts of time." Although Gonzaga is a Jesuit school and offers 24 spiritual retreats annually, only 50 percent of students are Roman Catholic. There are no requirements to attend mass or chapel.

Gonzaga offers 75 academic majors and programs in five undergraduate divisions: the College of Arts and Sciences and the schools of Business, Education, Engineering and Applied Science, and Professional Studies. All courses at Gonzaga are taught by regular professors, and 37 percent of all classes have 19 or fewer students. Students say the strongest programs are engineering and business, with accounting a particular strength. Psychology is also popular because, as one such major puts it,

Website: www.gonzaga.edu
Location: Small City
Private
Total Enrollment: 5,564
Undergraduates: 4,762
Male/Female: 46/54
SAT Ranges: CR 540–640, M 550–650
ACT Ranges: 24–29
Financial Aid: 95%
Expense: Pr $
Student Loans: 66%
Average Debt: $ $ $
Phi Beta Kappa: Yes
Applicants: 6,991
Accepted: 67%
Enrolled: 24%
Grad in 6 Years: 81%
Returning Freshmen: 94%
Academics: ✍ ✍ ✍
Social: ☎ ☎ ☎ ☎
Q of L: ★ ★ ★
Admissions: (800) 322-2584
Email Address: admissions@gonzaga.edu

Strongest Programs:
Business
Engineering
Psychology/Social Sciences
Communication/Journalism/
    Broadcasting
Biological/Health Sciences

"the professors have lived such colorful lives that inspire their students." Psych students may focus on specialized areas of interest such as child psychology and clinical research. Arts and Sciences recently established an Environmental Studies major and offers interdisciplinary concentrations in Women's and Gender Studies and Native American Studies. A major in human physiology draws students interested in sports medicine and physical therapy. Biology majors have the option of adding a "research" concentration to their degree, while English majors have the choice between literature and writing tracks. Depending on academic major, students may participate in a variety of Capstone programs, including a "Senior Design" option for engineers. Many students participate in "Undergraduate Research Week" when they have a chance to show off their research projects. Gonzaga offers good support for students with learning disabilities.

Consistent with its Jesuit liberal arts traditions, Gonzaga requires undergraduates to complete an extensive core curriculum.

The Freshman Retreat offers incoming students the chance to escape for a weekend and bond with classmates through games and other activities ("the best thing I did my freshman year"), while Pathways, a single-credit course in the fall, introduces newcomers to the university and its host city. Other special offerings include the three-year Hogan Entrepreneurial Leadership Program, open to high-achieving freshmen seeking an Entrepreneurial Leadership concentration in addition to their regular majors. Another three-year option for freshmen is the Comprehensive Leadership Program, which leads to a concentration in, you guessed it, leadership studies. Gonzaga's Army ROTC program ("Bulldog Battalion") ranks as one of the best anywhere.

"Our professors are easy to approach outside of classes."

All classes are taught by full-time professors, 10 percent of whom are Jesuits. "Our professors are easy to approach outside of classes, and they actually get to know us on a personal level," says a junior. The centerpiece program for study abroad is Gonzaga-in-Florence, which offers students of any major, including engineering, the opportunity to study at Gonzaga's campus in Florence, Italy, without interrupting their four-year path to graduation. The university runs programs in Zambia for students involved in service leadership, education, or psychology, as well as environmentally focused field studies programs in Latin America, the Caribbean, and Australia. Other sponsored program sites range from China to Scotland. "I studied in Paris the fall semester of my junior year and took classes at a French university with 10 other Gonzaga students," says a business administration major. "I received my Gonzaga scholarship while abroad, and all the credits that I took transferred easily."

Three out of four Zags are Caucasian, with 8 percent Hispanic, 4 percent Asian American, and only 1 percent African American. One percent of students are from other countries, with the rest fairly equally divided between Washingtonians and out-of-staters. Hardly anyone pays the sticker price. Ninety-five percent receive some sort of financial aid, with an average award of $10,488, and the school offers 100 athletic scholarships in 18 sports. Gonzaga's Family Discount policy guarantees discounts to siblings attending GU at the same time.

There are no requirements to attend mass or chapel.

Freshmen and sophomore students are required to live on campus and purchase a campus meal plan, while juniors and seniors usually head elsewhere. All in all, 57 percent of students live in university housing. The 24 on-campus residence halls offer a variety of living styles, including both co-ed and single-sex corridors and floors and several living/learning communities. The so-called Hotel Coughlin, the newest residence hall, offers living communities around themes such as cultural diversity, health and wellness, and leadership. One junior describes the dorms as "pretty nice (well, nice for dorm rooms)." A sophomore adds, "Put it this way: if you can walk around the dorm barefoot without being worried about contracting something nasty, you've got it made." GU operates 25 "themed" off-campus houses for juniors and seniors, but a junior notes that "students complain about the limited amount of on-campus housing for upperclassmen." GU has one main dining facility, known as the COG (a Latin acronym meaning "gathering of all the Gonzagans"), where the food is variously described by students as "convenient," "edible," and "neither horrible nor four-star restaurant." A student says, "Sometimes it's amazing and my taste buds celebrate whatever culinary concoction is being served for dinner. Other nights, I have to settle for cereal." Students report feeling safe on campus. "Campus Police, lovingly referred to as CAMPO, is the bomb dot com," cheers one junior. "They have a super quick response rate and are constantly driving around patrolling campus and the surrounding neighborhood."

Consistent with what Jesuits have learned about secret societies over the centuries, there are no fraternities or sororities at Gonzaga, but students say that their absence has hardly put a damper on social life either on or off campus. "We are a very social and active campus," reports a junior. The Crosby Student Center (remember Bing?) sponsors campus events such as trivia nights and coffee houses, and a classmate reports that "there is a noticeable party scene off campus in the houses of upperclassmen." Underage students found in possession of alcohol may be fined or required to take an alcohol awareness and safety program. A public relations major notes that "GU has a deal with the Spokane Police so if any Gonzaga student is caught off campus with alcohol, they get referred back to the school instead of having to deal with the state." A sophomore adds, "If people drink here, they don't become belligerent and act like idiots."

Gonzaga's Army ROTC program ("Bulldog Battalion") ranks as one of the best anywhere.

Gonzaga's debate program has a long history of excellence and competes successfully in national debate competitions, and the culture of Gonzaga places strong emphasis on issues of social justice and service. "We're required to take a service-learning course which combines a core class with a volunteer requirement. Being involved in the community is a specific Jesuit trait that we all try to live out," says one student. Each spring, nearly 200 students travel to sites across the nation to participate in community service projects through "Mission Possible," and the university ranks third in alumni Peace Corps volunteers nationwide. Social activism on campus revolves around issues

"Campus Police, lovingly referred to as CAMPO, is the bomb dot com."

such as human trafficking and the environment, and a junior comments, "In the last five years, Gonzaga has begun to address social issues in ways that would not typically be supported by the Catholic Church." Many Gonzaga students actively supported the successful effort in 2012 to permit single-sex marriage in Washington.

GU's 14 intercollegiate teams, known as the Zags or Bulldogs, compete in the NCAA Division I West Coast Conference. In the absence of football (shut down in 1941 and never resurrected), basketball is both king and queen. Other teams that consistently win conference championships are men's baseball and women's crew. GU has a strong intramural program, mostly run by students themselves, that attracts two-thirds of undergraduates each year. "There are three divisions—recreational, intermediate, and competitive—so anyone can participate," explains an environmental studies major. The most popular intramural sports are basketball, flag football, ultimate Frisbee, soccer, and an annual triathlon competition. There are four ski areas within a 90-mile radius, and GU Outdoors sponsors rafting, hiking, and skiing excursions, including trips in Montana and Canada.

School spirit is a big deal at Gonzaga—mainly when it comes to sports and especially when the opponent is California-based St. Mary's. "There are a few things that all of Gonzaga truly despise: required philosophy classes, when the snow turns to slush, and St. Mary's," asserts a junior. Since Gonzaga's mascot is the Bulldog, the student cheering section is naturally known as the Kennel. Students go through an elaborate process for tickets to big home basketball games that involves strategic Tweeting and living in a Tent City days before the opening tap. "It's insanity,"

Overlaps

University of Portland, University of Washington, Santa Clara, Seattle University, Washington State, University of San Diego, Whitworth, Western Washington

confesses one sophomore, "but it's so much fun." A junior adds, "Every Zag should experience this at least once."

Basketball may inspire the most vocal outpourings of school spirit at Gonzaga, but students say that the religious and humanistic values to which the university has long been committed run deep. "Community is a word tossed around quite frequently at all college campuses," says a psych major, "but at GU community is almost a belief. People come from all walks of life, be it socioeconomic, religious, ethnic, etc. We accept our differences, embrace the things that make us different, and learn from each other. I think this sense of community is what sets GU apart."

If You Apply To >

Gonzaga: Early action: Nov. 15. Regular admissions: Feb. 1. Financial aid: Feb. 1. Housing: May 1. Application fee: $50. Campus interviews: optional, evaluative. No alumni interviews. SATs or ACTs: required. No Subject Tests.

Gordon College

255 Grapevine Road, Wenham, MA 01984

Gordon is the most prominent Christian college in New England and competes nationally with Messiah, Wheaton (IL), and Calvin. Not quite in Boston, but close enough to be within easy reach. Extensive core curriculum shapes the undergraduate experience. Emphasis on integrating faith and learning.

Website: www.gordon.edu
Location: Small Town
Private
Total Enrollment: 1,652
Undergraduates: 1,548
Male/Female: 38/62
SAT Ranges: CR 510–646, M 506–642
ACT Ranges: 23–29
Financial Aid: 97%
Expense: Pr $
Student Loans: 81%
Average Debt: $ $ $ $
Phi Beta Kappa: No
Applicants: 4,008
Accepted: 40%
Enrolled: 29%
Grad in 6 Years: 74%
Returning Freshmen: 80%
Academics: ✐ ✐ ✐
Social: ☎ ☎
Q of L: ★ ★ ★ ★
Admissions: (866) 464-6736
Email Address: admissions@gordon.edu

Evangelical Christian values are at the heart of almost all aspects of life at this New England college, where faith and religious values set the tone for campus life inside and outside the classroom. The college, founded as a missionary training school "to prepare the people of God to do the work of God," is always evolving, sharpening its offerings across the board, from neuroscience to music education, and looking to increase its diversity. The students revel in the atmosphere. "We offer a deeper education in regard to biblical context," says a sophomore. "Gordon is a challenging school."

Gordon is located on Massachusetts's scenic North Shore, three miles from the Atlantic Coast and 30 miles from Boston. The campus sits on more than 300 forested acres with five lakes. Most campus structures are Georgian-influenced traditional redbrick, except for the old stone mansion that houses administration and faculty offices. The Ken Olsen Science Center, an 80,000-square-foot science and technology center at the heart of the campus, is home to new physics, mathematics, and psychology labs. Wenham offers "cute shops and restaurants along with other oddities—like used bookstores, jewelry shops, and fresh markets."

"Gordon is a challenging school."

Religious commitment at Gordon is seen as the foundation of serious academic learning rather than a threat to free inquiry. Gordon's core curriculum includes 52 hours of instruction distributed among religion, the fine arts, humanities, social and behavioral sciences, natural sciences, math, and computer science. Required courses include theology and Old and New Testament. Freshmen also take a first-year seminar to help them learn how to integrate faith into their academic experience. The Clarendon Program provides urban students with mentoring and support both on campus and at home. The most popular majors are psychology, business administration, English, communication arts, and biology. Finance is available as a major—a rarity at small Christian colleges—and a 3–2 engineering program is also available.

"The best academic programs are definitely the sciences, specifically biology, kinesiology, and chemistry," contends one history major. "They are taught by incredibly bright people and are challenging to the point where students know that they can't slack off if they truly want to succeed."

The academic climate is serious and somewhat competitive, according to students. "Classes are difficult and include a significant amount of reading, but give students an opportunity to take responsibility for their education," a sophomore says. "I'm always learning something new each class, and come out with a feeling of accomplishment because of that. If I ever don't understand something, I know that I can meet with my professor during office hours or even during lunch," adds another student. Off-campus opportunities include stints in Washington, D.C., for aspiring politicos, in Michigan for environmentalists, and in Los Angeles for filmmakers, as well as trips abroad through the Christian College Consortium*. The college also has its own programs in Orvieto, Italy, focused on the country's history, art, and language; Aix-en-Provence in France; and at Oxford University in England; and partners with programs elsewhere around the world, from Africa to Israel. Business majors can take advantage of a China seminar.

> "Classes are difficult and include a significant amount of reading."

(continued)

Strongest Programs:
Education
Psychology
English
Biblical/Theological Studies
Music

Business majors can take advantage of a China seminar.

Applicants to Gordon are asked to describe how their faith impacts their lives and to recognize the Bible as "the Word of God and hence fully authoritative in matters of faith and conduct." While observation of the Sabbath is expected, Gordon gives students a bit more latitude than some Christian colleges in determining how they will "separate themselves from worldliness." "Students at Gordon College are very kind and compassionate. Many of the kids here really exemplify what it is like to be a young Christian," a kinesiology major says. Up to 4 percent of students are Roman Catholics. African Americans constitute 3 percent of the campus, while Asian Americans add 3 percent, and Hispanics comprise 7 percent. Merit scholarships worth an average of $11,629 are offered.

"Even the oldest residence halls are nice and spacious," says a freshman. Ninety percent of Gordon students live in the co-ed dorms, where men and women live in separate wings of the same buildings—separated by a lobby, a lounge, and a laundry room. Persons of the opposite sex may traverse these barriers only at specified times. That policy draws some complaints from students, and the Student Council has been trying to extend the hours. Permission to move off campus may be granted by petition. "Most students choose to live on campus because the community and living experience at Gordon is so valuable," says a sophomore. Campus dining options receive good—if not great—reviews, and campus security is said to be up to the task. "Campus security is excellent and they respond very fast. Whenever there is an emergency, they are very efficient," says a sophomore.

> "On weekends Gordon is a ghost town."

Social life at Gordon is hit or miss. "Although leaps and bounds have been made to host more on-campus activities for the student body, on weekends Gordon is a ghost town," laments one freshman. Since drinking and smoking are forbidden on campus (and may result in suspension or expulsion), students focus on other activities. "On campus, there are always a variety of events, movies, and coffeehouse happenings," says a biology major. Those who are 21 or older may drink off campus, but are expected to do so responsibly. Other options include weekend excursions to Boston (25 miles away by a five-minute walk to the T, the city's public transit system), the beach, church-related functions, movies, and an occasional square dance.

Everyone looks forward to homecoming, the Winter Ball formal, and the Last Blast spring party. Each year, the most popular guys in each class face off in the "hilarious" Golden Goose talent show, where the winner is crowned "Mr. Gordon." Gordon has no Greek system—so drunken toga parties are out. For outdoorsy types,

Applicants to Gordon are asked to describe how their faith impacts their lives.

Gordon's setting on rugged Cape Ann is ideal, and it attracts its share of tourists. The campus has cross-country ski trails and ponds for swimming, canoeing, and skating. The ocean is a quick bike ride away, nice beaches are available on Cape Cod and in Maine, and students frequently ski New Hampshire's nearby White Mountains. Having a car is essential. Volunteering through a prison ministry and in soup kitchens and local churches is popular, and missionary road trips take students to Tennessee, Florida, and Washington, D.C., and around the world. "Gordon takes volunteerism very, very seriously," a sophomore reports. A psych major says that discussions of hot-button social issues such as gay marriage and human trafficking are vigorous but adds, "because it's a Christian school, even the liberals aren't too liberal. Everything is pretty good natured."

Gordon's Fighting Scots compete in NCAA Division III athletics, and "a good portion of the student body comes out to the games" when the opponent is rival Endicott College, says a history major. Another adds: "The basketball games are standing-room-only when we play them." The men's and women's lacrosse teams are competitive; other popular sports are men's and women's soccer. Approximately 50 percent of the student body participates in intramural sports.

For many students, Gordon's combination of Christian values, strong academics, and a relaxed setting is a winning one. "It's not unusual for students to have really deep, honest conversations with each other about their faith, their lives and what they're struggling with," says a sophomore. Gordon wants to graduate men and women of academic excellence and high Christian character. And as the school tries to attract students of different backgrounds, those here already find it welcoming. Says one freshman, "You'll be challenged, supported, and you will learn a lot about who you are and what you'd like to do."

> **Volunteering through a prison ministry and in soup kitchens and local churches is popular.**

Overlaps

Messiah, Wheaton (IL), Houghton, Liberty, Eastern, Calvin

If You Apply To ➤

Gordon: Rolling admissions: Feb. 1. Early decision and early action: Nov. 15. Application fee: $50. Campus interviews: required, evaluative. No alumni interviews. SATs or ACTs: required. Subject Tests: optional. Does not accept the Common Application. Essay question.

Goucher College

Baltimore, MD 21204

This is not your grandmother's Goucher. Once a staid women's college, Goucher added men and a more progressive ambiance, making it similar to places like Sarah Lawrence and Skidmore. Strategically located near Baltimore and not far from D.C., Goucher offers an excellent internship program and is among the few colleges that requires all students to spend time studying or working abroad.

Goucher is the kind of place where a student starts off with a dance class, then dashes to a lab to use a nuclear magnetic resonance spectrometer, and finally wraps up the afternoon chatting with a professor about studying abroad in Ghana. The school's mission is to prepare students for a life of inquiry, creativity, and critical and analytical thinking. According to students, the atmosphere is academically challenging and competitive but not uptight. A sophomore says it succinctly: "We're a family."

A former women's college that went co-ed in 1987, Goucher has a long-standing history of excellence. Phi Beta Kappa established a chapter on campus only 20 years after the college was founded, and the college ranks among the nation's top 50

Website: www.goucher.edu
Location: Suburban
Private
Total Enrollment: 1,625
Undergraduates: 1,441
Male/Female: 33/67
SAT Ranges: CR 510–640, M 480–620

liberal arts colleges in turning out students destined for Ph.D.s in the sciences. Set on 287 landscaped acres in the suburbs of Baltimore, Goucher's wooded campus features lush lawns, stately fieldstone buildings (the fieldstone is mined from local quarries), and rare trees and shrubs from all corners of the globe. The Athenaeum houses the library, an open forum for performances, an art gallery, exercise spaces, a café, and other vital college facilities.

A rigorous Liberal Education Requirements (LERs) program forms the foundation of every Goucher student's education and includes courses in academic writing/writing proficiency; foreign language; perspectives; social sciences; natural sciences; mathematical reasoning; artistic/creative expression; textual analysis and critical perspectives; diversity; study abroad; and environmental sustainability.

Of Goucher's offerings, the science departments (especially biology and chemistry) are arguably the strongest, with the nuclear magnetic resonance spectrometer and scientific visualization lab available for student use. Other facilities include dedicated research space, a greenhouse, and an observatory with a six-inch refractor telescope. The dance department is especially strong, while anthropology is reported to be weak. There's also a German minor offered through Loyola College (MD), and future engineers can take advantage of the 3–2 program offered in conjunction with the Whiting School of Engineering at The Johns Hopkins University. Goucher students may take courses at nearby Johns Hopkins and seven smaller area colleges. Two new programs have been added recently: art history and biochemistry and molecular biology.

> "The two words that best describe the student body at Goucher are 'Quirky Community.'"

"Goucher provides students with demanding yet manageable academic environment in which they can develop both an understanding of the material and how it applies to their own experiences in the outside world," says a first-year student. Faculty members here devote most of their time and energy to undergraduate teaching and have a good rapport with students. "Goucher has taught me to stop looking at professors as superior beings with infinite knowledge, but instead to see them as fellow intellectuals that can facilitate classroom conversation," says a psychology major. Each freshman has a faculty advisor to assist with the academic and overall adjustment to college life, which is made easier by Goucher's trademark small classes and individual instruction. "Goucher has small classes, and the professors always keep their office doors open if you need help," says one sophomore.

In addition to their academic work, all Goucher students are required to do a three-credit internship or off-campus experience related to their major. Popular choices include congressional offices, museums, law firms, and newspapers. Another option is the three-week-long Public Policy

> "The party scene is not particularly strong on campus."

Seminar in Washington, D.C., where students meet informally with political luminaries. Goucher also hosts College Summit, a nonprofit organization that works with economically challenged high school students. It offers summer mentoring workshops where members of the campus community serve as writing coaches. Goucher was the first college in the nation to require all of its undergraduates to study abroad at least once before graduation; the college provides every student with a $1,200 voucher to offset the cost.

"The two words that best describe the student body at Goucher are 'Quirky Community.' We are a group of individuals who aren't afraid to be ourselves and to be ourselves loudly," says a student. Twenty-seven percent of Goucher's students are homegrown, and most of the rest hail from Pennsylvania, Virginia, New York, and New Jersey. African Americans make up 9 percent of the student body, Hispanics 8 percent, Asian Americans 3 percent, and international students 3 percent. The

(continued)

ACT Ranges: 27–29
Financial Aid: 84%
Expense: Pr $ $
Student Loans: 43%
Average Debt: $ $ $
Phi Beta Kappa: Yes
Applicants: 3,615
Accepted: 72%
Enrolled: 16%
Grad in 6 Years: 70%
Returning Freshmen: 84%
Academics: ✍ ✍ ✍
Social: ☎ ☎ ☎
Q of L: ★ ★ ★
Admissions: (410) 337-6100
Email Address: admissions@ goucher.edu

Strongest Programs:
Dance
Creative Writing
Biology
Political Science
International Relations

Goucher students may take courses at nearby Johns Hopkins and seven smaller area colleges.

administration hosts "campus conversations" with students, faculty, and the college president to discuss various issues. Newer, more intensive programs such as the Study Circle on Diversity and the peace studies dialogue sessions have also been implemented to address diversity issues. Goucher offers merit scholarships for those who are qualified, some providing full tuition and room and board each year.

Eighty-six percent of students live on campus and freshmen double up in spacious rooms, while upperclassmen select housing through lotteries. The available singles usually go to juniors and seniors, though a lucky sophomore may occasionally get one. "Housekeeping is friendly and most students get the rooms that they want. It's a very familylike atmosphere," says a sophomore. Campus dining options include vegan and vegetarian fare. "No matter what your taste is you can find at least five items in each dining hall to satisfy your need," asserts one student.

"The party scene is not particularly strong on campus, but there are plenty of students who get together in each other's rooms to kick back and relax on the weekends," an environmental studies major says. "If nothing else, there are plenty of ways to get off campus and explore all that Towson and Baltimore have to offer." Another student says, "Most students go off campus at least one night a weekend," so access to a car is a virtual necessity because many students travel to nearby universities (Loyola and Towson State) or Baltimore's Inner Harbor for entertainment. The CollTown Network, however, provides transportation to nearly 20 colleges in the area. Students who are of age frequent restaurants and bars in Towson, the small but bustling college town a five-minute walk away. Goucher has no sororities or fraternities, but the close-knit housing units hold periodic events, and the college hosts weekend movies, concerts, and lectures. Alcohol is ever-present but not the hub of the social scene, according to one junior: "Sometimes I feel alone in my decision not to drink, but other students never pressure me to drink, either." Major annual social events include Rocktoberfest, Spring Fling, and the Blind Date Ball. "In the fall, we have Opening Celebrations, which is my favorite Goucher tradition," muses one communication and media studies major. "Every class has a specific class color, and we all gather in the residential quad and march toward the lawn next to the library with the rest of our classes. The faculty and staff are there to cheer on the students as we enter into the new semester."

> "You will form a family at Goucher."

The Cardinals field a number of competitive teams in the Division III Landmark Conference. As Goucher was a women's college for so long, women's athletics are more highly developed than those at many co-ed schools. The women's lacrosse team is popular, along with men's basketball and lacrosse. Men's lacrosse won the 2011–12 conference title. The equestrian team is competitive and the genteel sport of horseback riding is popular, thanks to the indoor equestrian ring, stables, and beautiful wooded campus trails. Goucher also has several tennis courts, a driving range, practice fields, a swimming pool, and saunas.

Goucher is far from a stagnant place. Indeed, it is constantly rethinking its mission and redirecting its resources to broaden student experiences. With self-designed interdisciplinary majors, an emphasis on experiential learning, and several partnerships with other top schools, Goucher students find themselves sampling from a buffet of options. "Goucher is unique and the students are creative and fun," says a sophomore. "You will form a family at Goucher."

> *Goucher was the first college in the nation to require all of its undergraduates to study abroad at least once before graduation.*

Overlaps

Towson, American, University of Maryland–College Park, McDaniel, Skidmore, Clark, University of Maryland Baltimore County, University of Vermont

If You Apply To ➢ **Goucher:** Early decision: Nov. 15. Early action: Dec. 1. Regular admissions and financial aid: Feb. 1. Housing: May 1. Application fee: $55. Campus and alumni interviews: optional, informational. SATs or ACTs: optional. No Subject Tests. Accepts the Common Application. Essay question.

Grinnell College

Grinnell, IA 50112

Iowa cornfields provide a surreal backdrop for Grinnell's funky, progressive, and talented student body. With about 1,600 students, Grinnell's population is 1,000 less than Oberlin's. That translates into tiny classes and tutorials of 19 students or fewer. Second only to Carleton as the best liberal arts college in the Midwest. Grinnell's biggest challenge is simply getting prospective students to the campus. College in the cornfields makes for a tight-knit campus community.

"Go West, young man, go West," Horace Greeley said to Josiah B. Grinnell in 1846. The result of Grinnell's wanderings into the rural cornfields, about an hour from Des Moines and Iowa City, is the remarkable college that bears his name. Despite its physical isolation, Grinnell is a powerhouse on the national scene. Ever progressive, it was the first college west of the Mississippi to admit African Americans and women, and the first in the country to establish an undergraduate political science department. It was once a stop on the Underground Railroad, and its graduates include Harry Hopkins, architect of the New Deal, and Robert Noyce, inventor of the integrated circuit, two people who did as much as anyone to change the face of American society in the 20th century.

> **"Due to the college's enormous endowment, the sciences are top-notch."**

The school's 120-acre campus is an attractive blend of collegiate Gothic and modern Bauhaus academic buildings and Prairie-style houses. (Architecture buffs should take note of the dazzling Louis Sullivan bank facade just off campus.) True to its liberal arts focus, Grinnell mandates a first-semester writing tutorial, modeled after Oxford University's program, but doesn't require anything else. The more than 30 tutorials, limited to about 12 students each, help enhance critical thinking, research, writing, and discussion skills, and allow first-year students to work individually with professors. When it comes to declaring a major, students determine their own course of study with help from faculty. Strong departments include the natural sciences and foreign languages, including German and Russian, bolstered by an influx of research grants, including one from the National Science Foundation. "Due to the college's enormous endowment, the sciences are top-notch," offers one student. "With the best equipment and graduate-level research at the undergraduate level, Grinnell's science division is a popular choice." The chemistry department draws majors with independent research projects, and English, psychology, and foreign languages and literature are popular, too.

Grinnell's admissions standards are high—92 percent of students were in the top quarter of their high school class—and nearly one-third of graduates move on directly to graduate and professional schools. Students who don't mind studying, even on weekends, will be happiest here. "The academic climate is fairly intense," says one junior, "but not competitive." During finals, perhaps to help ease the stress, costumed superheroes run around the library giving out candy, says a sociology major. Teaching is the top priority for Grinnell faculty members, and because the college awards no graduate degrees, there are no teaching assistants. "In general, profs are here to teach and have generous office hours," a sophomore says.

> **"The academic climate is fairly intense."**

Academic advising is also highly regarded, as students are assisted by the professor who leads their first-year tutorial, and then choose another faculty member in their major discipline. "Tutorials are fun, interesting, and a great introduction

Website: www.grinnell.edu
Location: Small Town
Private
Total Enrollment: 1,609
Undergraduates: 1,609
Male/Female: 45/55
SAT Ranges: CR 630–750, M 630–750
ACT Ranges: 29–33
Financial Aid: 86%
Expense: Pr $ $ $
Student Loans: 55%
Average Debt: $
Phi Beta Kappa: Yes
Applicants: 4,021
Accepted: 36%
Enrolled: 30%
Grad in 6 Years: 88%
Returning Freshmen: 95%
Academics: ✍ ✍ ✍ ✍ ½
Social: ☎ ☎
Q of L: ★ ★ ★
Admissions: (641) 269-3600
Email Address: askgrin@grinnell.edu

Strongest Programs:
Foreign Languages
Biology
Chemistry
History

to the academic possibilities that Grinnell has to offer," one student says. Sixty-five percent of classes taken by freshmen have 19 or fewer students; none have more than 49. When the urge to travel arises, students may study abroad in more than 100 locations, through the Associated Colleges of the Midwest* consortium and Grinnell-in-London. Nearly 60 percent of students spend some time away from campus, and financial aid extends to study abroad, administrators say, and there are opportunities for research across disciplines. Recent excursions have included trips to Asia, Australia, Latin America, Europe, the Middle East, and Africa. Co-ops in architecture, business, law, and medicine, and 3–2 engineering programs are also available.

Grinnell is a bit of Greenwich Village in corn country. Despite the rural environment, the college attracts an urban clientele, especially from the Chicago area. Only 10 percent of Grinnell students are from Iowa, and 12 percent are international. "We're quirky, often hippie and liberal, though increasingly diverse," a student observes. The student body is 7 percent Hispanic, 7 percent Asian American, and 6 percent African American. Women's rights, gay rights, labor rights, human rights, globalization, the environment, and groups such as PAFA (the Politically Active Feminist Alliance), GEAR (Grinnell Escalating AIDS Response), and Fearless (formed to combat gender-based violence) set the tone. All told, Grinnell's hefty endowment funds 50 percent of the college's operating budget. Merit awards averaging $13,626 are handed out annually, but there are no athletic awards. In an effort to limit student debt, the college is gradually capping the amount of loans in its financial aid packages.

> "Grinnell is not a dry campus, but there are no bars on campus and there is no peer pressure to drink."

The college guarantees four years of campus housing, and 88 percent of students take advantage of the dorms, each of which has kitchen facilities, cable television, and a computer room. All but two dorms are co-ed, and after freshman year, students participate in a room draw, which can be stressful but usually works out. "The dorms are good," a student says, "with no ridiculously small rooms." Students who move off campus, mostly seniors, live just across the street. Despite being located in the middle of Iowa, students say they are glad to have campus security available. "Campus security is pretty good," says a student.

With no fraternities or sororities, intramurals and all-campus parties revolve mainly around the dorms. "I liken the experience to that of a cruise ship," says one student, "in that the students all stay in one place and entertainment is brought to campus." Each dorm periodically sponsors a party using wordplay from its name in the title. For instance, Mary B. James Hall puts on the Mary-Be-James party, for which everyone comes in drag. As for alcohol, a senior reports, "Grinnell is not a dry campus, but there are no bars on campus and there is no peer pressure to drink or culture of problematic drinking. There are liberal limits on how much alcohol can be served at parties and these events always have trained servers who check ID." Nondrinkers need not sit home, however. Grinnell's social groups and activities range from the Society for Creative Anachronism and the Black Cultural Center to improvisational workshops, poetry readings, symposia, concerts, and movies.

Highlights of the campus calendar include semiformal Winter and Spring Waltzes, where "most people wear formals and look very nice, not a common occurrence at a school where comfort is the usual standard and women rarely wear makeup," notes one student. At Disco, "everyone dresses up in clothes from the '70s and dances all night." Other noteworthy events include a band/tie-dyeing fest called Alice in Wonderland, Titular Head (a festival of five-minute student films), and Pipe Cleaner Day (May 5 generally brings upwards of 20,000 of the sculptable wires to campus).

Grinnell (population 9,100), is "a small farming community with a nice downtown." Community service helps bridge the town-gown gap, with some students serving as tutors and student teachers at the local high school and others participating in mentoring programs and community meals, among other projects. Outdoor recreation is popular, and nearby Rock Creek State Park lends itself to biking, running, camping, kayaking, and cross-country skiing, as well as other pursuits sponsored by the Grinnell Outdoor Recreation Program, or GORP. There are a few bars and pizza joints downtown, but for those craving bright lights, Iowa City and Des Moines are within an hour's drive, and the college runs a shuttle service to them. Chicago and Minneapolis are each about four hours distant.

The Grinnell Pioneers compete in Division III athletics, and the men's basketball team has won national attention for an unusual run-and-gun offense that uses waves of five players like hockey shifts in an effort to wear down opponents. Recent conference champions include men's and women's cross-country, swimming, track, and tennis. One psychology major explains, "Because almost 40 percent of the student body participates in intercollegiate athletics, the intramural program isn't as extensive as it would be in a larger school."

Grinnell wouldn't put a grin on every prospective college student's face. "Most of us don't apologize for what at first turns people off about Grinnell," explains a senior. "We like being in the middle of Iowa, we like that you've probably never heard of us, we love that you won't come here because you want a big name." But there's no denying that Grinnell—a first-rate liberal arts college in the cornfields—is a real gem of a school.

> ## Overlaps
> **Carleton, Brown, Amherst, Northwestern, Pomona, Bowdoin, Macalester, Swarthmore**

If You Apply To ➢ | **Grinnell:** Early decision: Nov. 15. Regular admissions: Jan. 15. Application fee: $30 (paper), free (online). Campus and alumni interviews: optional, evaluative. SATs or ACTs: required. No Subject Tests. Accepts the Common Application. Essay question: Common Application.

Guilford College

5800 West Friendly Avenue, Greensboro, NC 27410

Guilford is one of the few schools of Quaker heritage in the South. Emphasizes a collaborative approach and is among the most liberal institutions below the Mason-Dixon line. Has a notably high African American population. A kindred spirit to Earlham in Indiana. Guilford's signature program is justice and policy studies. Campus in suburban Greensboro has plenty of open space but is not particularly picturesque.

If your idea of a rousing road trip is protesting in Washington, D.C., you'll likely find plenty of kindred spirits at Guilford College. This generally left-leaning campus loves to debate just about any issue and get involved in the world around it. There's none of that college "bubble" that envelops many other colleges. Instead, enrollment numbers are going up and the student body is becoming more diverse. "The students are extremely open to different ideas," says a senior. Founded in 1837 by the Religious Society of Friends (Quakers), Guilford is sticking to its original principles of inclusiveness as it constantly encourages its students to broaden their minds. Inclusiveness is enhanced by an ambitious adult education program. Nearly half of full-time undergraduates are 23 or older,

> "The students here are all very free spirited and extremely accepting."

Website: www.guilford.edu
Location: Small City
Private
Total Enrollment: 1,945
Undergraduates: 1,945
Male/Female: 43/57
SAT Ranges: CR 480–620, M 490–660
ACT Ranges: 21–26
Financial Aid: 99%

During the senior year, students take an interdisciplinary studies course to meet the Capstone requirement.

who benefit from a large selection of evening classes and their own orientation and counseling services.

Located on 340 wooded acres in northwest Greensboro, Guilford's redbrick buildings are mainly in the Georgian style. The school is the only liberal arts college in the Southeast with Quaker roots, as well as the oldest coeducational institution in the South and the third oldest in the nation. During the Civil War, Guilford was one of a few Southern colleges that remained open—perhaps because it was also an embarkation point on the Underground Railroad. Since 2002, the college has invested $30 million in campus improvements.

The central theme of the Guilford education is "principled problem solving," according to administrators, and students fulfill general education requirements in three areas: Foundations, Explorations, and Capstone. All students must also demonstrate quantitative literacy. Foundations consists of four skills and perspectives courses. The college has five areas of study—arts, business and policy, humanities, natural sciences and math, and social science—and the first set of Explorations courses provides academic breadth outside the area covered by a student's major and concentration. The second set of Explorations courses consists of three critical perspectives classes, one each from the categories of intercultural, social justice and environmental responsibility, and U.S. diversity. During the senior year, students take an interdisciplinary studies course to meet the Capstone requirement.

> "Guilford students are known to unify and protest."

A senior says, "As a student coming to Guilford one should be prepared to learn as well as to work hard in order to achieve excellence. The college is centered on the Quaker religious values of community, diversity, equality, excellence, integrity, justice, and stewardship." Students say Guilford's best programs include physics, religious studies, peace and conflict studies (owing to the Quaker influence), and political science. "The English and art departments are really good," offers one freshman. Guilford believes that experiential learning adds immeasurably to classroom work, so the college offers study abroad from China and Japan to Mexico, Germany, and France; 20 percent of the student body participate. In the summer, students may participate in a five-week seminar that includes hiking, camping, and geological and biological research in the Grand Canyon, or in a seminar on the East African rift, which includes a three-week trip to Africa.

Despite its small size, Guilford gives students the tools needed for groundbreaking work. Physics majors get professional-grade optics and robotics equipment, and students working on complex geology and chemistry projects have access to the Scientific Computation and Visualization Facility, with more than 20 Unix workstations for information-based modeling. Significantly, Guilford publishes both the *Journal of Undergraduate Mathematics* and the *Journal of Undergraduate Research in Physics*. Wireless Internet connections are available in the Hege Library, where students may check out laptop computers from the circulation desk. Students call professors by their first names and "the quality of teaching is high," says one student. Another adds, "The professors at Guilford are 100 percent dedicated to the success of their students. This is one aspect of Guilford College that has made me realize I ended up where I needed to be." Adult students are most likely to take evening classes, have their own student government, and benefit from their own orientation and counseling services.

Guilford students come from across the globe and a range of socioeconomic backgrounds; most are liberal. Students "tend to be sympathetic to the little man," says a sophomore. A junior adds, "The students here are all very free spirited and extremely accepting." African Americans comprise 32 percent of the student body, Hispanics 6 percent, and Asian Americans 2 percent. While traditional students are evenly split along gender lines, nearly three-quarters of the adult students are female. "There are two major groups of students at Guilford," says a freshman, "those that came here because it's small, liberal, and Quaker and those who were recruited for sports teams." Students aren't shy about tackling social and political causes, says a sophomore. "Guilford students are known to unify and protest or advocate aspects of local, national, or international importance." Qualified Guilford students receive merit scholarships, although there are no athletic scholarships.

Seventy-seven percent of Guilford students live in the dorms, which feature big-screen TVs, remodeled kitchens, and upgraded heating and air-conditioning systems. "Housing is very comfortable," says one student. "The cleaning staff is so helpful." On-campus apartments for juniors and seniors are comparable in price to off-campus digs—a good thing, since getting permission to move off campus is tough. Bryan is the party dorm, and English (for men) and Shore (for women) are the single-sex quiet dorms. The female residents of Mary Hobbs, a co-op dorm built in 1907, do their own housekeeping in exchange for cheaper rent. The college is also piloting a "Community Agreements" project to strengthen community life in a first- and second-year residence hall. Food options include vegan and ethnic dishes, although "the food isn't always like mother used to make," says a particularly snarky student.

Guilford students come from across the globe and a range of socioeconomic backgrounds.

Guilford's social life revolves around various clubs and organizations, ranging from the Entrepreneur's Network and Strategic Games Society to Hillel and the African American Cultural Society. "There is a good balance between on- and off-campus social activities," says one student. "It is not unusual for people to hang out in their dorm rooms or apart-

"There is a good balance between on- and off-campus social activities."

ments, however, it is common to hear of people going off campus in Greensboro or traveling to the mountains of Asheville or the coast of Wilmington." No alcohol is allowed at college functions, but it remains fairly easy for underage students to drink—despite efforts to impose fines on those who are caught. Serendipity, a celebration of spring with games, mud wrestling, streakers, famed musicians such as the Violent Femmes, and "a sense of mass disorientation," is a cherished tradition. "If you love to drink and be loud, and throw chairs and trash cans off of balconies and buildings, then you will have a great time," says one student.

Beyond the campus gates, students find all of the essentials—Walmart, some clubs in downtown Greensboro (only 10 minutes away), the ethnic restaurants of Tate Street, the college's Quaker Village, a pool hall, and a Starbucks. Popular road trips include UNC at Chapel Hill (one hour), Asheville and the mountains (three and a half hours), and the famous Outer Banks beaches (four and a half hours).

Guilford's athletic teams compete as the Fighting Quakers.

Guilford's athletic teams compete as the Fighting Quakers, and students love the oxymoron, as in their cheer: "Fight, fight, inner light! Kill, Quakers, kill!" Students root for the football team in the annual Soup Bowl against Greensboro College, while the men's golf team has brought home a slew of conference titles in recent years (and as recently as 2013). The women's basketball team and the women's lacrosse team are strong, too. Because of Guilford's emphasis on developing the whole person, physically, mentally, and spiritually, students are encouraged to participate in school-sponsored outdoor adventures, such as a ropes course, sailing, and white-water rafting.

A popular Guilford mantra is "how are you going to change the world?" And with students who'd rather get involved than sit back and watch, you can expect some pretty passionate answers to that question. It all goes back to Guilford's traditional Quaker goal of "educating individuals not only to live, but to live well." As one student explains it, the college "supports me while allowing me to grow as a person." She then adds, in typical Guilford-speak: "It gives me the tools I need to make a change in the world when I leave."

Overlaps
UNC Greensboro, Appalachian State, North Carolina State, UNC Charlotte, Elon, UNC at Chapel Hill, UNC Asheville, High Point

Gustavus Adolphus College

800 West College Avenue, St. Peter, MN 56082

A touch of Scandinavia in southern Minnesota, GA is a guardian of the tried and true in Lutheran education. With Minnesotans comprising three-quarters of the students, GA is less national than cross-state rival St. Olaf. Extensive distribution requirements include exploring values and moral reasoning. Tiny minority enrollment makes for a homogeneous student body.

Website: www.gustavus.edu
Location: Small Town
Private
Total Enrollment: 2,482
Undergraduates: 2,482
Male/Female: 44/56
SAT Ranges: CR 570–700, M 570–670
ACT Ranges: 25–30
Financial Aid: 97%
Expense: Pr $ $
Student Loans: 75%
Average Debt: $ $
Phi Beta Kappa: Yes
Applicants: 4,881
Accepted: 63%
Enrolled: 22%
Grad in 6 Years: 83%
Returning Freshmen: 90%
Academics: ✍ ✍ ✍
Social: ☎ ☎ ☎
Q of L: ★ ★ ★
Admissions: (507) 933-7676
Email Address: admission@gustavus.edu

Strongest Programs:
Biology
Biochemistry
Education
Music
Physics
Psychology
Political Science

Gustavus Adolphus College is named for Sweden's King Gustav II Adolph (1594–1632), who is credited with making Sweden a major European power and defending Lutheranism against the Roman Catholics. While the king's battle victories earned him the title Lion of the North, he was also an advocate of education and culture. Save for the women now attending classes, King Gustav would probably feel at home at the college that bears his name, where a not-so-subtle Swedish influence pervades everything from the buildings to the curriculum. Gustavus is the "epitome of Minnesota nice," says one sophomore.

The 340-acre GA campus is about 65 miles southwest of the Twin Cities. Not surprisingly, the prevailing architectural theme is Scandinavian, with mostly modern and semimodern brown brick buildings. Highlights include the 134-year-old Old Main and the centrally located Christ Chapel, with spires and shafts resembling a crown. Thirty bronze works by sculptor-in-residence Paul Granlund are strategically placed, and the 135-acre Linnaeus Arboretum and Interpretive Center offers plant study and retreats. The sidewalk running through the middle of campus is nicknamed the Hello Walk, because it's a tradition for students to greet one another as they pass—whether they know each other or not.

> **"Gustavus is the epitome of Minnesota nice."**

In the classroom, students find an academic smorgasbord, as GA aims to offer an education both "interdisciplinary and international in perspective." There are interdisciplinary programs in Scandinavian studies, environmental studies, women's studies, and materials science, and if neither those nor traditional departments suffice, students may design their own courses of study. While the social sciences—psychology, economics, communication studies—are among the most popular majors, students give the highest marks to GA's science and premed programs and its offerings in music and education. Students also say weak departments are hard to find, although some programs do enroll only a small number of students. Outside the classroom, learning opportunities come from several internationally renowned meetings, such as the Nobel Conference, which brings Nobel laureates and other experts to campus for two days each October.

To fulfill core requirements, Gustavus students have two options. Curriculum I includes 12 courses from seven areas of knowledge, plus a first-term seminar covering critical thinking, writing, speaking, and recognizing and exploring values. Curriculum II is an integrated 12-course sequence focused on related classic works from various disciplines. Sixty students may select this option on a first-come, first-served basis. In addition to the core courses, students must satisfy a "writing across the curriculum" requirement, with three courses that have a substantial amount of writing, and the first-term Values in Writing seminar, which explores questions of value while emphasizing critical thinking, writing, and speaking.

Overall, academics at Gustavus are rigorous, but study groups are common, and students don't compete for grades. "The courses require a lot of work both inside and outside the classroom," says one junior. "Professors expect you to give your best every day and in return they give you their best." Undergraduate research is a hallmark and Gustavus Adolphus consistently ranks in the top 10 of papers presented at the National Conference on Undergraduate Research. The President's Scholarship Program offers qualified students awards of $15,000 to $17,000; the only renewability requirement is a 3.25 GPA. For the professionally minded, Gustavus offers 3–2 engineering programs with the University of Minnesota and Minnesota State in Mankato.

"Professors expect you to give your best every day."

During the January term, when winter winds force almost everyone indoors, Gustavus students (known as Gusties) may take concentrated courses on campus or pursue travel and co-op opportunities. The school sponsors study abroad programs at five colleges and universities in—surprise, surprise—Sweden, as well as in non-Scandinavian haunts such as Japan, India, Malaysia, Australia, Russia, the Netherlands, and Scotland, and about half of the students participate. Back on campus, students find faculty members knowledgeable and friendly. "The quality of teaching has been excellent," says one student. "Professors go the extra step to make sure students are learning in a positive environment." Profs even serve up a free meal for students during Midnight Express, which precedes final exams. "In no way have I ever been an anonymous face in a sea of faces," a student says.

Overall, academics at Gustavus are rigorous, but study groups are common.

"Students are very involved," says one biology major, and they "shuffle about campus from classes, music ensembles, sports practices, interest groups, and community service." For all its good points, though, this liberal arts college is hardly a model of diversity. In fact, the population is more reminiscent of Garrison Keillor's Lake Wobegon: 84 percent of students are Caucasian, 81 percent are Minnesotan, and more than half are Lutheran. The school is trying to boost diversity, though African Americans and Hispanics together account for only 6 percent of the student body, and Asian Americans add 4 percent. Politically, the campus has its fair share of both conservatives and liberals, and students debate everything from campus issues to topics of global concern. Merit scholarships averaging just over $15,500 are awarded annually, but there are no athletic scholarships.

"There is never a shortage of things to do on the weekends."

Eighty-six percent of Gusties live in the dorms, and why not? Housing is guaranteed for four years, and all residences are smoke-free; even the halls without suites or apartments have kitchenettes, 24-hour computer labs, and foosball tables. "The dorms are wonderful," says a student. "They stay full on the weekends and are well maintained." Substance-free floors are available, as is the Crossroads International House, for students interested in languages and contemporary global issues. Norelius is exclusively for freshmen and sophomores, which helps students form friendships by encouraging group activities. Two dorms with single rooms and apartment-style suites, and some college-owned houses, are exclusively for upperclassmen, who get priority at room draw. Juniors and seniors (and all students over 21) may also request permission to live off campus. Students rave about the a la carte meal plan, and especially about the Marketplace dining hall, which is open from 7 a.m. until 11 p.m. daily. "Dining facilities are outstanding!" cheers a sophomore.

Politically, the campus has its fair share of both conservatives and liberals.

Only 11 percent of the men and 12 percent of the women go Greek, so GA's social life does not revolve around fraternities and sororities. In fact, service projects are far more important, with about two-thirds of students participating, and giving 15,000 hours of service each semester. Projects include working with children, the elderly, and the local animal shelter, as well as with Habitat for Humanity. "From concerts, to sporting events, to movies and dances, there is never a shortage of things to do on the weekends," says one senior. While the town of St. Peter has coffee shops and bowling, the college offers periodic trips to Mankato, 10 miles away, and to the Twin Cities, for "real" shopping at the Mall of America or for a professional baseball, basketball, or hockey game. Because students 21 and older may drink in their rooms—with the door closed—underage students can get alcohol if they want it, but students say drinking isn't a popular pastime here. GA's many musical ensembles all perform together at the Christmas in Christ Chapel concert. The chapel holds 1,500 people and there are a total of five performances, all of which usually sell out.

When it comes to athletics, "any time, any sport—if St. Olaf is in town, the event is packed," says a lusty Gustie fan. GA competes in Division III, and men's golf and men's and women's tennis, swimming, and Nordic skiing are competitive, as are men's basketball and women's cross-country. Both the men's and women's hockey teams won Minnesota Intercollegiate Athletic Conference championships recently. The college's forensics team is solid, too, having earned a Top 20 national ranking for four consecutive years. The fitness center features treadmills, stairclimbers, Nautilus equipment, and a pristine weight room. Approximately 70 percent of Gusties participate in intramurals.

The Gustavus Adolphus campus may be gorgeous in the spring and fall and too cold in the winter, but it's warmhearted all year long. Small classes, one-on-one academic attention, a plethora of research opportunities, and an active campus social life go a long way toward making St. Peter, Minnesota, seem a lot less isolated. Says one senior, "Our core values of community, service, faith, justice, and excellence prevail both in and out of the classroom, and students commit themselves and their time here to such values."

> Only 11 percent of the men and 12 percent of the women go Greek, so GA's social life does not revolve around fraternities and sororities.

Overlaps

University of Minnesota, St. Olaf, St. Thomas, St. John's University, Luther, Carleton, University of Wisconsin

If You Apply To ➤ **Gustavus Adolphus:** Rolling admissions. Early action: Nov. 1. Financial aid: May 1. Housing: Jun. 1. No application fee. Campus and alumni interviews: optional, informational. SATs or ACTs: optional. Subject Tests: optional. Accepts the Common Application. Essay question.

Hamilton College

198 College Hill Road, Clinton, NY 13323

Hamilton is part of the network of elite, rural, Northeastern liberal arts colleges that extends from Colby in Maine through Middlebury and Williams to Colgate, about half an hour's drive to Hamilton's south. Hamilton is on the small side of this group and emphasizes close contact with faculty and a senior project requirement. Strong Greek system makes for traditional campus social life.

Website: www.hamilton.edu
Location: Small Town
Private
Total Enrollment: 1,868
Undergraduates: 1,868

Back in 1978, Hamilton College seemed to have everything: money, prestige, and academic excellence. Everything, that is, except women. So, after 166 years of bachelorhood, Hamilton walked down the aisle with nearby Kirkland College, the artsy women's college founded under its auspices a decade before. The arrangement took some getting used to, but ultimately, it's been a success. Hamilton's student body is now evenly split between men and women, and students of both sexes benefit from the mix of old-boy tradition and right-brain flair. "Come to Hamilton because you will learn much more than simple facts and data," says an economics major. "You will learn how to think critically, communicate clearly, and lead effectively."

Set on a picturesque hilltop overlooking the small town of Clinton, the old Hamilton campus features collegiate Victorian architecture rendered in rich, warm brownstone. In fact, the only facility interrupting the rhythmic beauty of campus is the eyesore housing the library. By contrast, the adjacent Kirkland campus consists mostly of boxy concrete structures of a 1960s "brutalist" vintage, otherwise described as "faux I. M. Pei." Straddling the ravine that divides the campuses and joining them literally and figuratively is a student activities building with a diner, lounges, and areas for student and faculty relaxation. Surrounding the campuses are more than 1,200 college-owned acres of woodlands, open fields, and glens, with trails for hiking or cross-country skiing. The college has invested $200 million over the past decade in new and renovated facilities, including a Student Activities Center and a museum of art. A new theater and studio arts building is slated to open in 2014.

> **"Come to Hamilton because you will learn much more than simple facts and data."**

In the classroom, Hamilton is pure liberal arts. Economics, government, math, psychology, and international relations are the most popular majors. "The economics and Chinese departments have strong professors with work experience and a passion to teach," says a student. Weak departments are hard to find, students say. Hamilton's Arthur Levitt Public Affairs Center, named for the former New York State comptroller, is a working think tank where students can pursue research for local, regional, and state social service groups and government agencies. The natural sciences are strong, bolstered by a $56 million science center. A grant from the National Science Foundation helps send geoscience students to Antarctica for research each year, while Hamilton's rocky terrain provides fertile ground for those who remain.

The general education curriculum has no distribution requirements and features a series of proseminars—classes of no more than 16 that require intensive interaction—that emphasize writing, speaking, and discussion. The optional sophomore program stresses interdisciplinary learning and culminates in an integrative project with public presentation. In fact, Hamilton is among a minority of schools requiring all students to undertake a senior program in their area of concentration. Another interesting development is the administration's decision to let students choose which standardized tests to submit with their application for admission, including SAT I, the ACT, three SAT IIs, or three Advanced Placement (AP) or International Baccalaureate (IB) exams. Students may also select more than one type of test, so long as their portfolio includes an English test and a quantitative test, plus one other exam.

> **"The economics and Chinese departments have strong professors with work experience and a passion to teach."**

Academically, students say that the emphasis is on performance, allowing students to remain laid-back rather than competitive. "Courses are difficult and challenge students to manage their time well," says one senior. "That said, there is no sense of competition between students and everyone is supportive of others' academic pursuits and achievements." You'll always find a professor, not a teaching assistant, at the lectern. Says one government major: "Professors are top-notch academics with relevant experience, but also are sensitive to the needs of individual students." Even with the intimate size of most classes, students report few problems getting needed courses, once they declare a major. A chemistry major says, "If you're in chemistry and you want to do research, you are almost guaranteed to find a faculty member willing to take you on." When the town of Clinton gets

(continued)

Male/Female: 49/51
SAT Ranges: CR 650–740, M 650–740
ACT Ranges: 29–33
Financial Aid: 55%
Expense: Pr $ $ $ $
Student Loans: 39%
Average Debt: $
Phi Beta Kappa: Yes
Applicants: 5,107
Accepted: 27%
Enrolled: 34%
Grad in 6 Years: 91%
Returning Freshmen: 96%
Academics: ✍ ✍ ✍ ✍ ½
Social: 🍺 🍺 🍺 🍺
Q of L: ★ ★ ★
Admissions: (315) 859-4421
Email Address: admission@ hamilton.edu

Strongest Programs:
Economics
Mathematics
Government
Biology
Psychology

In the classroom, Hamilton is pure liberal arts. Economics, government, math, psychology, and international relations are the most popular majors.

claustrophobic, students can spend a semester or a year in France, China, Spain, or India, or take a term in Washington, D.C. or New York; 52 percent of undergraduates have studied abroad.

"It's cool to be passionate about things here," says a psychology major. "Students are so involved in a range of different activities; it's kind of lame if you only go to class and don't have a whole bunch of extracurriculars." Thirty-one percent of Hamilton students are New York residents, and 79 percent were in the top 10th of their high school class. African Americans constitute 4 percent of the student body, while Hispanics comprise 7 percent, and Asian Americans 8 percent. Although the campus is no political hotbed, students report that current issues (both global and local) receive ample attention from student activists. There are no merit or athletic scholarships, but the college has a need-blind admissions policy for domestic students.

Ninety-eight percent of the students reside on campus. Options range from old fraternity houses renovated and turned into dorms to stately mansions with posh amenities, and newer apartments that accommodate three to four students each. "Hamilton provides great housing and it's possible to get decent housing even as a rising sophomore," says a student. Smart students become resident assistants, which guarantees them a single and lets them bypass the hated lottery. The Hamilton side of campus is the place for party animals; Dunham gets cheers for being social, but some students liken it to a "dungeon." The Kirkland dorms have a more mellow reputation. Students may also choose to live in a co-ed cooperative house, or in residences that are substance-free or quiet. And how about the food? "The food is surprisingly good for college food," one senior admits.

"Hamilton provides
excellent social, academic,
and cultural opportunities."

Social life at Hamilton ranges from the campus pub, which occupies an old barn, to programming arranged by the campus activities board, such as comedy shows, a casino night, an award-winning acoustic coffeehouse series, and concerts by Macklemore & Ryan Lewis, Ellis Paul, The Shins, Guster, Ben Folds, Joshua Redman, Jason Mraz, Talib Kweli, Keller Williams, SouLive, and Rahzel. "Campus parties tend to be dominated by underclassmen. The upperclassmen attend them occasionally, but they generally make their own parties in the suites or the quads or they go downtown to the two bars," one student says. There's also the Greek system, which draws 26 percent of the men and 17 percent of the women. Clinton itself is "a picturesque village good for pizza and coffee," says a sophomore. Because there's relatively little to do, much of the social life does revolve around alcohol, one student says, although stiff punishments are meted out to underage imbibers. The nearest small city, Utica, is only 10 minutes away by car. The college maintains a jitney service and sponsors two Zipcars for student transportation. Other popular road trips include Syracuse and New York City, while Boston, Toronto, and Montreal are each less than five hours away.

In athletics, Hamilton (the "Continentals") offers 29 intercollegiate varsity sports and is a member of the highbrow New England Small College Athletic Conference. The women's lacrosse team has brought home a national title and several conference titles; men's basketball, men's and women's soccer, men's golf, and men's and women's swimming and diving programs have also competed in the NCAA championships in recent years. Even some school traditions are athletically minded. Class and Charter Day marks the last day of classes in the spring with ceremonies, a picnic, a concert, and even a triathlon the week before. "Many students believe this day is better than Christmas," says an economics major.

"Hamilton provides excellent social, academic, and cultural opportunities," says one senior. Hamilton students are, by necessity, hearty. They're used to the cold and the snow—and perhaps that's what leads to the strong sense of community evident on campus. "Make sure you enjoy the snow; the winters are long, and if you need sunny days to be happy, this is not the place for you," a student warns. For those who can tough it out, Hamilton may be a solid choice.

<table>
<tr><td>

If You Apply To ➤

</td><td>

Hamilton: Early decision: Nov. 15. Regular admissions: Jan. 1. Financial aid: Feb. 15. Application fee: $60. Campus interviews: optional, evaluative. Alumni interviews: required, evaluative. SATs or ACTs: required. Subject Tests: required. (Students may also substitute three AP or IB exams, including one English, one quantitative, and one other.) Accepts the Common Application. Essay question. Students must also submit a graded expository writing sample.

</td></tr>
</table>

Hampden–Sydney College

P.O. Box 667, Hampden Sydney, VA 23943

The last bastion of the Southern gentleman and one of two all-male colleges in the nation. Feeder school to the economic establishment in Richmond. Picturesque rural setting evokes the old South, though some would argue that H–SC is out of step with the realities of today's world. Accepts roughly half of its applicants, while neighboring (and co-ed) Washington and Lee accepts less than one-third.

Perhaps a bit of an anachronism in a society increasingly focused on diversity, the all-male Hampden–Sydney College still aims to expose its small student body to a broad liberal arts education, which is entirely focused on undergraduate success. H–SC is one of only two all-male colleges without a coordinate women's college in the nation (see Wabash). "We are an all-male college," says one student, "which provides for a special sense of brotherhood and community." Tradition reigns here and students like to call themselves "Southern gentlemen." Of course, there's plenty of not-always-gentlemanly fun to be had when you have nearly 1,100 guys together.

Hampden–Sydney's 1,340-acre campus, surrounded by farmland and woods, features mainly redbrick buildings in the Federal style. The nearby town of Farmville, population 6,600 and home to Longwood College, offers restaurants, stores, and a movie theater; it's just five miles from H–SC, but one student describes the town as "a black hole inside a time warp." The Kirk Athletic Center includes a heated and air-conditioned auditorium with seating for 500.

Hampden–Sydney's most popular major is economics, which may help explain why more than half of the school's alumni have pursued business careers. The department offers several concentrations, including managerial and mathematical concepts; instruction is "intensive," a junior says. History, economics, biology, and psychology are also popular. The Wilson Center for Leadership in the Public Interest puts a public service focus on the study of political science, preparing students for government work and garnering high marks in return. The school's small size offers many opportunities to work closely with professors, but has some academic drawbacks, including few computer courses and fewer than 30 majors. The fine arts program, with concentrations in music, theater, and visual arts, has begun emphasizing performance rather than the study of these disciplines.

"Easy As are few and far between."

Students at Hampden–Sydney say there are no free passes when it comes to classwork. "Easy As are few and far between," says a freshman. To graduate, students must demonstrate proficiency in rhetoric and a foreign language, along with

Website: www.hsc.edu
Location: Rural
Private
Total Enrollment: 1,080
Undergraduates: 1,080
Male/Female: 100/0
SAT Ranges: CR 490–620, M 510–615
ACT Ranges: 21–26
Financial Aid: 99%
Expense: Pr $ $
Student Loans: 55%
Average Debt: $ $ $
Phi Beta Kappa: Yes
Applicants: 2,630
Accepted: 56%
Enrolled: 23%
Grad in 6 Years: 67%
Returning Freshmen: 78%
Academics: ✏ ✏ ✏
Social: ☎ ☎ ☎ ☎
Q of L: ★ ★ ★ ★
Admissions: (434) 223-6120
Email Address: hsapp@hsc .edu

Strongest Programs:
Economics
History

completing seven humanities courses, three in the social sciences, and four in the natural sciences and mathematics. All freshmen have a special advising program, and 60 percent take freshman seminars. Classes are small; all have fewer than 50 students. "Professors are always available and eager to help students out with any problems that arise," says one junior. Most H–SC professors live on campus and encourage students to drop by their offices often. Some even make house calls to find out why a student missed class. "I have been invited to numerous dinners at professors' homes, and professors encourage us to contact them whenever we have a question, even if that means at nine o'clock on a Wednesday night," says a junior. The Tigerfund allows students to manage an equity fund, and more than 100 study abroad options are available in 25 countries.

One thing you won't see a lot of at H–SC are students with long hair, body piercing, or much else that would not fit into a clean-cut profile. "Students are wealthy and Southern and very proud of it," says a senior. Sixty-nine percent of students are state residents, and 83 percent are Caucasian. African Americans make up 8 percent of the student body, Hispanics constitute 2 percent, and Asian Americans comprise 1 percent. The college has added a director of intercultural affairs to help increase tolerance for diversity, and students say diversity is among the hot-button political issues found on campus. As a Division III school, Hampden–Sydney offers no athletic scholarships. There are, however, merit awards worth an average of $18,949.

> **One thing you won't see a lot of at H–SC are students with long hair, body piercing, or much else that would not fit into a clean-cut profile.**

Ninety-six percent of students live on campus, as housing is guaranteed for four years, and H–SC is renovating older residence halls with mostly single rooms to offer more apartment-style living. "Freshmen are usually grouped in the larger housing areas in order for them to get the college roommate experience," says one student. All rooms have Internet connections and cable. Cushing Hall, built in 1824, is the dorm of choice for first-year students, with "big rooms, excellent parties, and at least three ghosts." The dining facilities are only a few years old and supply hungry students with "decent" fare. Campus security includes seven full-time police officers who provide 24/7 coverage.

> **"Professors encourage us to contact them whenever we have a question."**

Students praise the close-knit atmosphere fostered by Hampden–Sydney's all-male status. "The social life is something magical," says a sophomore. "Most social events take place in the heart of the campus." One student reports that showering during the week is really optional: "We clean up on Fridays before the girls come." Men seeking members of the opposite sex can find them at three all-female schools nearby—Sweet Briar, Hollins, and Mary Baldwin. Those who make a love connection will be glad to know that H–SC's dorms have 24-hour visitation.

> **Perhaps because of all that testosterone on campus, Hampden–Sydney men are competitive, and that spells excellence in athletics.**

Hampden–Sydney's social nexus is the Circle, the site of 11 of the school's 12 fraternities, which claim 30 percent of the students. "On the weekends, everyone goes to 'frat circle' where all the fraternities have houses on campus," says a student. Students under 21 can't drink, but where there's a will, there's a way. Campus security will crack down if students get wild, but "handle yourself properly and you won't get into too much trouble," says an English major. The annual spring Greek Week brings out the *Animal House* aspect of Hampden–Sydney's budding gentlemen. Homecoming and various music festivals are also eagerly anticipated.

Despite its lack of bright lights ("Farmville sucks. You come here for the school, not the town," grumbles one student), nearby Farmville does provide numerous community service and outreach opportunities. A campus volunteer group called Good Men, Good Citizens spearheads projects such as tutoring, highway cleanup, and Habitat for Humanity home-building. When rural Virginia gets too insular, H–SC students can be found on road trips to the University of Virginia and James Madison University, Virginia's beaches, or Washington, D.C. The ski slopes of Wintergreen are within three hours' drive.

Perhaps because of all that testosterone on campus, Hampden–Sydney men are competitive, and that spells excellence in athletics. Tigers football is big; students attend games in coat and tie, and H–SC's football rivalry with Randolph-Macon (not the former women's college!) is the oldest in the South. At the annual pregame bonfire, the college rallies to sing songs and hear student and faculty leaders vilify the enemy and extol "the garnet and gray." Basketball, baseball, soccer, and lacrosse are also competitive. For weekend warriors, intramurals are available in several sports, including football, baseball, soccer, and lacrosse.

"Most social events take place in the heart of the campus."

So it's largely conservative and a bit homogeneous, but Hampden–Sydney offers more than just a flat demographic profile. Two centuries of tradition and a tight-knit student body make for a rich undergraduate experience. One confident junior sums up the rewards of the Hampden–Sydney experience like this: "If you're looking to improve your speaking and writing skills and mold yourself into a true gentleman that women love and employers desire to hire, this is the school for you."

If You Apply To ➢

Hampden–Sydney: Early decision: Nov. 15. Early action: Jan. 15. Regular admissions: Mar. 1. Application fee: $30. Campus interviews: optional, evaluative. Alumni interviews: optional, informational. SATs or ACTs: required. Subject Tests: optional. Accepts the Common Application. Essay question.

Hampshire College

P.O. Box 5001, Amherst, MA 01002-5001

Part of a posse of nonconformist colleges that includes Bard, Bennington, Eugene Lang, and Sarah Lawrence. Instead of conventional majors, students complete self-designed interdisciplinary concentrations and independent projects. Gains breadth and resources from the Five College Consortium*. Campus architecture is postmodern rather than traditional.

Passion reigns at Hampshire College. It's found in just about everything students do—from devising their own courses to starting new clubs to debating the most current social issues. There's no one way to do things at Hampshire, and the students revel in the freedom they have to direct the path of their education. "We love what we are studying because we get to choose what we are studying," says a junior studying sustainable agricultural methods. Without the yoke of traditional majors and the nail-biting stress of regular grades, Hampshire offers a virtually boundary-free exercise in intellectual nirvana.

Located in the Pioneer Valley of western Massachusetts, Hampshire's 800-acre campus sits amid former orchards, farmland, and forest. Buildings are eclectic and contemporary, and the school is most proud of its bio-shelter, arts village, and multisports and multimedia centers. Two nationally known museums—the National Yiddish Book Center and the Eric Carle Museum of Picturebook Art—are located right on campus.

Instead of grades, Hampshire professors hand out "narrative evaluations," which consist of written evaluations and critiques. Degrees are obtained by passing a series of examinations—not tests, but portfolios of academic work, evaluations, and students' self-reflections on their academic development. The first hurdle, known as

Website: www.hampshire.edu
Location: Small City
Private
Total Enrollment: 1,438
Undergraduates: 1,438
Male/Female: 42/58
SAT Ranges: CR 600–700, M 540–650
ACT Ranges: 25–29
Financial Aid: 70%
Expense: Pr $ $ $ $
Student Loans: 55%
Average Debt: $ $
Phi Beta Kappa: No
Applicants: 2,856
Accepted: 64%
Enrolled: 20%

(continued)

Grad in 6 Years: 64%
Returning Freshmen: 82%
Academics: ✍ ✍ ✍ ✍
Social: ☎ ☎ ☎
Q of L: ★ ★ ★
Admissions: (413) 559-5471
Email Address: admissions@ hampshire.edu

Strongest Programs:
Film and Television
Environmental Studies
Cognitive Science
Creative Writing
Natural Science
History
Human Health
Agriculture

Instead of grades, Hampshire professors hand out "narrative evaluations."

Division I, begins with a course in each of five multidisciplinary schools: natural science; social science; cognitive science; interdisciplinary arts; humanities, arts, and cultural studies; and other coursework.

The second hurdle, Division II, is each student's "concentration"—the rough equivalent of a major elsewhere. Unlike a major, the requirements of a concentration are unique to each student, emerging from regular discussions with two faculty members, and include courses, independent study, and fieldwork or internships. Division III, or "advanced study," begins in the fourth year. Students are asked to complete a sizable independent study project centered on a specific topic, question, or idea, much like a master's thesis. In recent years, students have created smartphone software to monitor blood sugar, studied monologues on mountaintop removal in Appalachia, explored how Aztec ants protect coffee, and suggested alternative microcredit models. The Campus Engaged Learning (CEL) program requires all students to commit to 40 hours of service or a semester-long equivalent. Because of the division system, there are as many curricula at Hampshire as there are students; each individual must devise a viable, coherent program specific to himself or herself. The common denominator is a heavy workload, an emphasis on self-initiated study, close contact with faculty advisors, and the assumption that students will eventually function as do graduate students at other institutions. "Our environment encourages self-motivated learning," says one student.

"Our environment encourages self-motivated learning."

Given the emphasis on close working relationships with faculty and those "narrative evaluations," the importance of qualified, attentive faculty is not to be underestimated. Students at Hampshire heap praise on their professors. "This is my first year," raves a freshman, "and I'm already assisting two professors with research projects and heading a research team of my own." The Hampshire academic year has fall and spring semesters, each four months long; an optional January term; and internships and other real-world experience are encouraged during all three. Befitting Hampshire's entrepreneurial nature, a large percentage of grads do go on to graduate school, and many Hampshire students begin their own businesses.

Hampshire's flexibility is ideal for artists, and the departments of film and photography are dazzling, which is also the reason they are overcrowded. Communications, creative writing, and environmental studies are also good bets, and Hampshire was the first college in the nation to offer an undergraduate program in cognitive science. A popular program called Invention, Innovation, and Creativity exposes students to the independent reasoning and thinking essential to the process of inventing. "Culture, Brain, and Development" emerged several years ago with funding from the Foundation for Psychosocial Research, and the college is actively transforming itself into a "language learning community" thanks to a gift from the Andrew W.

"We are not cookie-cutter students."

Mellon Foundation. The study of languages is integrated into topics and questions of interest to individual students. Students also have access to selected courses at sister schools in the Five College Consortium*.

Although the school's library is a quiet and pleasant place to study, and if you count the library resources at all five institutions, students have ready access to more than eight million volumes. There is no extra cost to use the other schools' facilities or the buses that link them. And use them they do—Hampshire students take 1,200 classes per year at the other schools. Hampshire offers its own study abroad programs in China, Cuba, and Germany, and students may also participate in programs through more than 130 institutions in 38 countries.

Hampshire draws students from across the country who tend to be "driven and passionate about their studies," says one sophomore. "We are not cookie-cutter students. We are students who passionately teach ourselves in a school that is deliberately unique and experimental." For a school that's so focused on social issues, the minority community is relatively small—3 percent of students are African American, 9 percent Hispanic, and 2 percent Asian American—and most students would like to see these numbers rise. Another 5 percent are international. The school is "100 percent politicized in every way," says a philosophy major. "Political correctness doesn't even begin to describe it." Merit scholarships are available to qualified students.

Eighty-two percent of undergraduates live on campus. First-year students live in co-ed dorms, about 25 percent in double rooms. Many single rooms are available for older students who may move to one of more than 100 "mods"—apartments in which groups of four to 10 students share the responsibility for cleaning, cooking, and maintaining their space. "The dorms and apartments were quickly and cheaply built, and have problems," warns a senior. Special quarters are available for nonsmokers, vegetarians, and others with special preferences. The dining options are diverse and include "many great vegan and vegetarian options," says one nanotechnology major.

On weekends, some students head for Boston, New York, Hartford, or, in season, the ski trails of Vermont and New Hampshire. But there are plenty of cultural resources within the Five College area, and the free buses to Amherst (the ultimate college town), Northampton, and South Hadley (all within 10 miles) are always crowded. From edgy record stores to ethnic restaurants

"Political correctness doesn't even begin to describe Hampshire."

and boutiques, the area abounds with diversions. The annual Spring Jam brings live bands to campus, and throughout the year there's almost always a party going on, including the drag ball and the much-anticipated Halloween bash—an intense, all-campus blowout complete with fireworks. A tradition called "Div Free Bell" celebrates the completion of Division III requirements—and graduation—with soon-to-be alumni ringing a bell outside the library, surrounded by friends.

Hampshire is no place for competitive jocks, since many sports are co-ed and primarily for entertainment (there never was a football team here). Hampshire is affiliated with the United States Collegiate Athletic Association (USCAA) and also is a member of the Yankee Small College Conference (YSCC). The school offers paid instructors in a handful of sports, but most students organize their own clubs (men's and women's soccer, basketball, and fencing are the biggies, and there's also the competitive Red Scare Ultimate Frisbee Team) and intramural teams. The outdoors program offers mountain biking, cross-country skiing, and kayaking; equipment may be borrowed free. The school also has its own climbing wall and cave, a gym with solar-heated pool, and a co-ed sauna.

"If you're an independent student and like to think outside the box, then Hampshire is for you," says an animal behavior major. There's a niche for every type of student, and even those pigeonholes are blown apart quite regularly. When you can make up your own education, and do it with great faculty and the option of studying at several other top-notch schools, there's little Hampshire students can't accomplish. "You set limits with yourself, and then push those limits and strive even higher," says one student, who adds, "This is the only place where I could see myself being happy."

Overlaps

Bard, Bennington, Mount Holyoke, NYU, Oberlin, Reed, Sarah Lawrence, Smith

If You Apply To ➤ **Hampshire:** Early decision I: Nov. 15. Early decision II: Jan. 1. Early action: Dec. 1. Regular admissions: Jan. 1. Application fee: $60 (paper), free (online). Campus and alumni interviews: optional, evaluative. SATs or ACTs: optional. Subject Tests: optional. Accepts the Common Application. Essay question.

Oneonta, NY 13820

Hartwick is known for its cozy atmosphere and ability to take good care of students. Combines arts and sciences with a nursing program. The campus is beautiful, but small-town upstate New York has proven to be a hard sell in recent years. New general education program emphasizes hands-on learning, and three-year bachelor's degree is an option. Most strong students can get at least a small merit award.

Website: www.hartwick.edu
Location: Small City
Private
Total Enrollment: 1,503
Undergraduates: 1,503
Male/Female: 41/59
SAT Ranges: CR 520–610,
   M 500–610
ACT Ranges: 24–27
Financial Aid: 80%
Expense: Pr $ $
Student Loans: 69%
Average Debt: $ $ $
Phi Beta Kappa: No
Applicants: 5,795
Accepted: 85%
Enrolled: 9%
Grad in 6 Years: 57%
Returning Freshmen: 73%
Academics: ✑ ✑ ✑ ✑
Social: 🐿 🐿 🐿 🐿
Q of L: ★ ★ ★
Admissions: (607) 431-4150
Email Address: admissions@
   hartwick.edu

Strongest Programs:
Nursing
Biology
Business Administration
Psychology
Sociology

In recent years, Hartwick College has transformed itself by choosing to better focus on its ever-improving liberal arts profile. Hartwick emphasizes study abroad—especially for freshmen—crystallizing the school's philosophy that learning isn't about rote memorization, it's about creating experiential knowledge and developing skills. The students here take full advantage of what's offered and feel at home on this close-knit campus. "Hartwick College is characterized by its strong liberal arts curriculum and its close community ties," says one student. "When coming here, you will feel like you instantly become an active and important member of the community."

> **"Hartwick College is characterized by its strong liberal arts curriculum."**

Hartwick's campus has a New England feel with its ivy-covered, redbrick buildings and white cupolas, gables, and trim. The campus setting on the Oyaron Hill, overlooking the city and the Susquehanna Valley, provides a breathtaking view, though the steepness of the campus may have some wishing for the legs of a mountain goat. Campus facilities include a tissue culture lab, electron microscopes, a greenhouse, a herbarium, a cold room, a biotechnology "clean lab," and a graphics imaging lab. The college continues to expand and improve the campus thanks to a robust and highly successful capital campaign.

The most popular major is business administration, followed by nursing, biology, psychology, and English. The music and art programs receive high marks, too. Student/faculty collaborations are the norm, as is the emphasis on learning through real-world experiences, from working in a Jamaican hospital to interning with the New York Mets. Another example of Hartwick's academic enrichment is the honors program, which provides students with the opportunity to design and carry out a coherent program of study characterized by challenges exceeding those offered in typical coursework required for graduation.

Hartwick's general education program (The Liberal Arts in Practice) is divided into seven areas and places emphasis on experiential and integrative learning. Among the voluminous requirements are courses in humanities, physical and life sciences, social and behavioral sciences, foreign language, writing competency, and quantitative/formal reasoning.

> **"The professors and students make [Hartwick] fun and exciting."**

In addition, students must complete a first-year seminar and a senior capstone project. The course offerings are necessarily limited by Hartwick's small size, but the Individual Student Program (ISP) enables students to create their own major dealing with a particular interest. Students may take courses at the nearby State University College at Oneonta (SUCO). The Three-Year Degree Program allows students to take on a larger courseload and pursue January term courses on and off campus in order to earn a B.A. or B.S. within three years. The program is designed to save enrolled students more than $40,000 off the cost of earning a degree. Students may choose from 24 major areas of study including biology, business administration, computer science, economics, information science, and religious studies.

Hartwick's academic environment is challenging but doesn't foster intense competition among students. "The courses are challenging yet the professors and students make it fun and exciting," says a sophomore. Hartwick offers other unconventional learning options, many of them in off-campus locations. Students have traveled to all parts of the world while pursuing their Hartwick education—first-year students are especially encouraged to leave the "Bubble on the Hill," as some call Hartwick. The optional Awakening Program, completed by 12 percent of freshmen as part of orientation, is also an option for management majors who want to test their leadership skills. The four-week January term is also a favorite time to explore the world beyond Oneonta. The faculty wins nearly universal praise from the students. "I have only encountered two professors in my time here who I thought to be average," says one senior. "Otherwise, they have all been supportive, incredibly knowledgeable, are able to challenge their students, and foster learning." Private tutoring and help sessions are offered, along with an innovative freshman early-warning program that identifies struggling students early and offers counseling. "Many students do research alongside professors," says a biology major.

The four-week January term is also a favorite time to explore the world beyond Oneonta.

Hartwick has traditionally attracted a somewhat less academically oriented student body than most of the colleges with which it competes, but it has improved its academic position in recent years, thanks to a focused recruitment program. "We have the granola kids, the hipsters, the preps, the frat boys, the jocks, and everything in between," says a junior. Twenty percent of students come from the top 10th of their class. Seventy percent are from New York State, especially upstate, and most of the rest come from New England or the mid-Atlantic States. Hartwick has worked hard to improve the diversity of its student body: African Americans, Hispanics, and Asian Americans combine for 12 percent. Political and social issues receive a fair amount of attention from students: "Our students are always involved and trying to change things," says a sophomore. Hartwick College awards merit scholarships averaging more than $18,000, as well as 18 athletic scholarships for Division I men's soccer and women's water polo.

"I have never felt unsafe on campus."

Seventy-eight percent of the student body resides on campus. "We have a variety of different housing options including regular dorms, suites, townhouses, and honors housing," explains one sophomore. "The dorms are all a comfortable size and are maintained properly." Upperclassmen covet a place in one of the four townhouses described by one as "the yuppie version of on-campus living." Freshmen, sophomores, and juniors are required to live on campus, though the latter may move into one of the fraternity or special-interest houses. Each dorm has designated quiet hours, though they may not always be observed. Hartwick's 920-acre environmental campus, Pine Lake, has cabins that are heated by pellet stoves and a lodge where environmentally inclined students can live in rustic style. On-campus dining receives high marks; a psychology major says the school offers a "huge variety of foods for any culture or diet." Campus security is praised, too. "I have never felt unsafe on campus," says an English major.

Hartwick's social scene is found both on and off campus, according to students, and tends to be as mellow or rowdy as one chooses. From campus it's only a short walk, bike ride, or bus ride downhill into the small city of Oneonta, with its tantalizing profusion of bars. But the underage Hartwick students usually don't get past the front doors of these taverns, and the administration is tough about enforcement on campus. "There is not a lot of drinking on campus, but many people drink off campus," says a sophomore. Tamer entertainment includes Sunday night movies as well as occasional lecturers and comedians, and just hanging out at the student union. The Greek system attracts 3 percent of the men and 5 percent of the women. Popular campuswide bashes include a Last Day of Classes party, the Holiday Ball,

Hartwick is nationally ranked at the Division I level in men's soccer.

and Winter and Spring Weekends, the latter of which features the notorious "Wick Wars," a schoolwide sports competition. There's also the Breakfast of Champions before final exams, when professors and administrators serve students breakfast between 11 p.m. and 2 a.m. Walking to class each day provides great hill workouts for your ski legs, and skiing is popular throughout the region. Oneonta is a "quaint, peaceful town," according to one student. "There aren't very many things to do but my friends and I haven't gotten bored yet."

Oneonta is big on sports, and Hartwick delivers. The Mayor's Cup Soccer Tournament weekend is a big event. Hartwick is nationally ranked at the Division I level in men's soccer. The women's water polo team has brought home the CPA Northern Division title six of the last eight years, and the remainder of the teams compete in Division III. Intramurals are popular as well—20 percent of the student body takes part.

Change is good, the sages say, and the folks at Hartwick would definitely agree. By focusing its efforts on recruiting higher-caliber students and emphasizing top-notch experiential learning, Hartwick is bolstering its image as a solid liberal arts college. Even some of the T-shirts sold on campus broadcast the students' attitudes about their education: one simply says "Smartwick."

If You Apply To ➤

Hartwick: Rolling admissions. Early decision: Nov. 1. No application fee. Campus and alumni interviews: optional, informational. SATs or ACTs: optional. Subject Tests: optional. Accepts the Common Application. Essay question.

Harvard University

86 Brattle Street, Cambridge, MA 02138

An acceptance here is the gold standard of American education. Gets periodic slings and arrows for not paying enough attention to undergraduates, some of which is carping from people who didn't get in. It takes moxie to keep your self-image in the midst of all those geniuses, but most Harvard students can do it. ("I go to school in Boston.") The recent recession put a crimp in Harvard's budget because much of its spending relies on income from investments.

Over the past 375 years, the name Harvard has become synonymous with excellence, prestige, and achievement. At this point, Harvard University, the nation's first institution of higher learning, is the benchmark against which all other colleges are compared. It attracts the best students, the most academically accomplished faculty, and the most lavish donors of any institution of higher education nationwide. Sure, some academic departments at Hah-vahd are smaller than others, but all have faculty members who have made a name for themselves, many of whom have written the standard texts in their fields. Olympic athletes, concert pianists, and Rhodes scholars blend in easily here, ready to embrace the challenges and rewards only Harvard's quintessential Ivy League milieu can offer.

Spiritually as well as geographically, the campus centers on the famed Harvard Yard, a classic quadrangle of Georgian brick buildings whose walls seem to echo with the voices of William James, Henry Adams, and other intellectual greats who trod its shaded paths in centuries past. Beyond the yard's wrought-iron gates, the campus is an architectural mix, ranging from the modern ziggurat of the science center to the white towers of college-owned houses along the Charles River. Loker Commons, a student center beneath the new Annenberg freshman dining hall, provides a place for students to meet and philosophize over gourmet coffee or burritos of epic proportions. The Barker Center for humanities has emerged from the shell of the Union and the old freshman dining hall. Harvard is embarking on creating a huge new science complex across the river in Allston.

Harvard's state-of-the-art physical facilities are surpassed only by the unparalleled brilliance of its faculty. Under its "star" system, Harvard grants tenure only to scholars who have already made it—usually someplace else—and then gives them free rein for research. It seems like every time you turn around, a Harvard professor is winning a Nobel

> **"You can have unlimited contact with professors, but it must be on your initiative."**

Prize or being interviewed on CNN; every four years, half the government and econ departments move to Washington to hash out national policy. But one of Harvard's finest qualities is also one of its biggest problems. "You can have unlimited contact with professors, but it must be on your initiative," notes a biology major. "This is not a small liberal arts college where people will reach out to you." That's not to say profs are completely uncaring. Most teach at least one undergraduate course per semester, and even the luminaries occasionally conduct small undergraduate seminars (including those reserved for freshmen, which can be taken pass/fail). Harvard also sponsors a faculty dining program, encouraging professors to eat at the various residential houses and chew over ideas as well as lamb chops.

Harvard's best-known departments tend to be its largest; economics, government, biology, English, and biochemistry account for a large chunk of majors. But many smaller departments are gems as well: East Asian studies is easily tops in the nation. And under the leadership of Henry Louis Gates, the African American studies department has assembled the most high-powered group of black intellectuals in American higher education. Smaller, interdisciplinary honors majors, to which students apply for admission, boast solid instruction and happy undergraduates too. These programs—social studies, history and science, history and literature, and folklore and mythology—are the only majors that require a senior thesis, although many students elect to do one in other departments.

Harvard's visual and environmental studies major serves filmmakers, studio artists, and urban planners, and concentrations in women's studies and environmental sciences have been well received. Students can also petition for individualized majors, typically during the sophomore year. All students must choose some sort of major at the end of their freshman year, a year earlier than most schools. The field of concentration can be changed later, but Harvard expects its students to hit the ground running. Regardless of the department, students uniformly complain about the overuse of teaching fellows (graduate

> **"The courses are difficult, particularly in the beginning as students make the transition from high school to college."**

students) for introductory courses in mathematics and the languages. TFs aren't all bad, though, says a junior: "They can give good advice, having just been in our position." Besides, it's easier to ask "dumb questions" of mere mortals than of the demigod professors.

Back in the mid-1970s, Harvard helped launch the current curriculum reform movement. The core curriculum that emerged ranks as perhaps the most exciting collection of academic offerings in all of American higher education. The best and brightest freshmen can apply for advanced standing if they have enough Advanced Placement credits. And should you not find a class you are looking for, admittedly highly unlikely, Harvard offers cross-registration with several of its graduate schools and the Massachusetts Institute of Technology.

(continued)

Applicants: 34,216
Accepted: 6%
Enrolled: 84%
Grad in 6 Years: 97%
Returning Freshmen: 97%
Academics: ✍ ✍ ✍ ✍ ✍
Social: ☎ ☎ ☎
Q of L: ★ ★ ★ ★
Admissions: (617) 495-1551
Email Address: college@fas.harvard.edu

Strongest Programs:
Economics
Biology
Social Studies
Government
English
African American Studies
East Asian Studies
Anthropology
Music
History of Science

In formal terms, the core requires students to complete one letter-graded course in each of eight categories: Aesthetic and Interpretive Understanding, Culture and Belief, Empirical and Mathematical Reasoning, Ethical Reasoning, Science of Living Systems, Science of the Physical Universe, Societies of the World, and United States in the World. One of these eight courses must also engage substantially with the Study of the Past.

For many students, the most rewarding form of instruction is the sophomore and junior tutorial, a small-group directed study in a student's field of concentration that is required in most departments within the humanities and social sciences. Teaching of the tutorials is split between professors and graduate students, and the weight of each party's responsibility varies with the subject and the professor. Juniors and seniors seek out professors with whom they want to work.

The oft-made claim that "the hardest thing about Harvard is getting in" is right on target. Flunking out takes serious and sustained effort. Once on campus, the possibilities are endless for those who are motivated. Then again, Harvard can feel uncaring and antisocial. While it offers unparalleled resources—including fellow students—brilliant overachievers who desire the occasional ego stroke might be better off at a small liberal arts college. Although most students feel little competition, the academic climate is still intense. "The courses are difficult, particularly in the beginning as students make the transition from high school to college," says one student. "But it's definitely doable." Sooner or later, all roads lead to Widener Library, where incredible facilities lie in wait (and where snow-covered steps make prime sledding runs in the winter).

Harvard does have one thing its $31 billion endowment can't buy: a diverse, high-powered, ambitious, and exciting student body. You will meet smooth-talking government majors who appear to have begun their senatorial campaigns in kindergarten. You will meet flamboyant fine arts majors who have cultivated an affected accent all their own. You will sample the intensity of Harvard's extracurricular scene, where more than 6,600 of the world's sharpest undergrads compete for leadership positions in a luminous galaxy of extracurricular opportunities. "Most of the social life takes place on campus through extracurricular activities or just in people's dorm rooms," says a psychology major. Stressed-out students can count on help from a variety of quarters, including the various deans' offices, the Bureau of Study Counsel, the Office of Career Services ("dedicated to working with Harvard students and alums for the rest of their lives," claims a senior), and counselors associated with each residential house. All students participate in weeklong orientation, and the First-Year Urban and Outdoor Programs help students acquaint themselves with one another and the Boston area.

"The dorms are incredible."

No one can tell you exactly what it takes to gain admission to Harvard (and if anyone tries, apply a large grain of salt), but here's a hint: More than three-quarters of the current student body ranked in the top 10th of their high school class and two-thirds went to public high school. Though there are a few old-money types who probably spit up their baby food on a Harvard sweatshirt, their numbers are smaller than one might imagine on this liberal campus. (Many enter as sophomores when no one is looking.) Undergrads come from all 50 states and scores of foreign countries, although the student body is weighted toward the Northeast. African Americans account for 6 percent of the student body, Hispanics 9 percent, and Asian Americans 15 percent. There are no merit or athletic scholarships to ease the pain of Harvard's hefty tuition, but Harvard has eliminated the expected family contribution for students from families with incomes up to $60,000 a year and limited the family contribution for families with incomes up to $180,000 to fixed percentages of their incomes, ranging from 1 to 10 percent. No-loan financial aid packages are

Smaller, interdisciplinary honors majors, to which students apply for admission, boast solid instruction and happy undergraduates.

optional. Under former president Larry Summers, the university overextended itself financially; resulting budget cuts have forced faculty and students to give up some of their most prized perks, including hot breakfasts in most dorms and cookies at faculty meetings.

In the past, female students benefited from "dual citizenship" in both Harvard and Radcliffe colleges, receiving degrees ratified by the presidents of both colleges. However, Radcliffe has long since been phased out as a separate institution; everyone is now considered a Harvard student, though students can still take advantage of Radcliffe's network of professional women, researchers, and alumnae.

Every first-year class lives and eats as a single unit in Harvard Yard, a privilege made more enticing by recent renovation of all the freshman dorms. Freshmen now eat in Annenberg Hall, the new name for beautifully renovated Memorial Hall. For their last three years, students live in one of 12 residential houses, built around their own courtyards with their own dining halls and libraries. All the houses are co-ed, and each holds between 300 and 500 students. Designed as learning communities, the upper-class houses come equipped with a complement of resident tutors, affiliated faculty members, and special facilities—from art studios to squash courts. Each house has a student council, which plans programs and parties and arranges the fielding of intramural teams. Students are now randomly assigned (with up to 15 friends) to one of the houses, but some houses still retain a personality from the days of old when each stood for a particular ideology, interest, or economic class. "The housing is one of the best parts of Harvard!" raves one student. "The dorms are incredible."

The nine houses along the Charles River feature suites of rooms, while the three houses at the Radcliffe Quad, a half mile away, offer a mixture of suites and single rooms. Some students value the greater privacy of the Quad houses' singles; others consider it equivalent to a Siberian exile, especially during harsh Cambridge winters. The older dorms provide spacious wood-paneled rooms, working fireplaces, and the gentle reminders of Harvard's rich traditions. Most rooms are also wired for direct Internet access. With all these features and amenities, it's no wonder few students move off campus.

Socializing at Harvard tends to occur on campus and in small groups. "It's certainly normal to spend Friday and Saturday nights studying," says a philosophy major. With the exception of the annual all-school Freshman Mixer and the annual theme festivals each house throws, parties tend to be private affairs in individual dorm rooms. A student-run website provides information and commentary on parties for those in the dark. Though Harvard does enforce the drinking age at university events, in individual houses it's up to the resident tutors. For some, the key to happiness in Harvard's high-powered environment is finding a niche, a comfortable academic or extracurricular circle around which to build your life. Outside activities include about 80 plays performed annually, two newspapers and several journals, and plenty of community service projects.

The possibilities of Harvard's social life are increased tenfold by Cambridge and Boston, where there are many places to have fun. Harvard Square itself is a legendary gathering place for tourists, shoppers, bearded intellectuals, and coffeehouse denizens. The American Repertory Theater, transplanted from Yale in the mid-1980s, offers a season of professional productions and nearly as many professional student shows. Cambridge also enjoys an exceptional selection of new and used bookstores, including the Starr Bookshop (behind the Lampoon building), McIntyre & Moore, Grolier Books, and, of course, the Harvard Bookstore and the mammoth Harvard Co-op, known universally as "the Coop." Boston itself features Faneuil Hall, the Red Sox, the Celtics, and 52 other colleges. "Cambridge's Harvard Square is the perfect college town," a student boasts. "There are tons of shops, restaurants, and bars."

All students must choose some sort of major at the end of their freshman year, a year earlier than most schools.

Harvard does have one thing its $31 billion endowment can't buy: a diverse, high-powered, ambitious, and exciting student body.

Harvard has 41 varsity sports (21 men, 20 women), which is the most of any Division I school and the most women's sports. The athletic facilities are across the river from the campus, and their incredible offerings often go unnoticed by students buried in the books. Both the men's and women's squash and crew teams are perennial national powers, and the men's ice hockey team draws a crowd of a few dedicated fans. The women's lacrosse team is strong, as are tennis, swimming, and sailing. As for football, the team has been doing better in recent years, but the season always boils down to the Yale game, memorable as much for the antics of the spectators and marching band as for the fumbles of the players. Intramural sports teams are divided up by house, and each fall, league champs play teams from Yale the weekend of the game. Another fall highlight is the annual Head of the Charles crew race, the largest event of its kind in the world, where as many as 200,000 people gather to watch the racing shells glide by.

> "I have quickly gained exposure to major theories in literature, psychology, anthropology, social sciences, and evolutionary biology."

Nowhere but Harvard does the identity of a school—its history, its presence, its pretense—intrude so much into the details of undergraduate life. Admission here opens the door to a world of intellectual wonder, academic challenges, and faculty minds unmatched in the United States—but then drops students on the threshold. "I have quickly gained exposure to major theories in literature, psychology, anthropology, social sciences, and evolutionary biology," says a junior. "I gauge myself by how many allusions in the *New Yorker* I understand." That's the way Harvard is; what other kind of place could produce statesmen John Quincy Adams and John F. Kennedy, pioneers W. E. B. DuBois and Helen Keller, and artists T. S. Eliot and Leonard Bernstein? Even its dropouts are movers and shakers (witness Bill Gates). But beware: it is only the most motivated and dedicated student who can take full advantage of the Harvard experience. Others who attempt to drink from the school's perennially overflowing cup of knowledge may find themselves drowning in its depths.

Overlaps

MIT, Princeton, Stanford, Yale

If You Apply To ➤ **Harvard:** Early action: Nov. 1. Regular admissions: Jan 1. Application fee: $75. Campus interviews: optional, evaluative. Alumni interviews: recommended, evaluative. SATs or ACTs: required. Subject Tests: required (two). Accepts the Common Application. Essay question: Common Application questions.

Harvey Mudd College: See page 141.

Harvey Mudd College: See page 141.

Haverford College

Haverford, PA 19041-1392

Quietly prestigious college of Quaker heritage. With an enrollment of about 1,200, Haverford is half the size of some competitors but benefits from its relationship with nearby Bryn Mawr. Close cousin to nearby Swarthmore but not as far left politically. Exceptionally strong sense of community. Parklike campus amid the bustle of suburban Philadelphia. Your only option if you want to play cricket.

An overarching honor code covering everything from the classroom to the dorm room defines student life at Haverford College. Students schedule their own final exams, take unproctored tests, and police underage drinking on their own. "The honor code, in some respects, is a self-selecting system which draws many students to Haverford. For this reason, nearly all students who come here share common values of trust, concern, and respect for others as well as academic integrity," says a junior econ major. Haverford may be smaller and less well-known than some of its peers, but it holds its own against the finest liberal arts colleges in the country, especially for students who are willing to work hard. "Haverford offers an opportunity to work hard, be trusted, and learn about issues, while still feeling comfortable," says a senior.

Founded under Quaker auspices in 1833, Haverford functions much like a family. The campus consists of 204 acres just off Philadelphia's Main Line railroad, and resembles a peaceful, well-ordered summer camp. The densely wooded campus has an arboretum, duck pond, nature trails, and more than 400 species of shrubs and trees. Architectural styles range from 19th- and early-20th-century stone buildings to a sprinkling of modern structures here and there. The combination enhances the sense of a balanced community, bringing together two traditional Quaker philosophies: development of the intellect and appreciation of nature. The 188,000-square-foot, $50 million Koshland Center for Integrated Natural Sciences (for the departments of astronomy, biology, chemistry, physics, math, and more) provides a place for interdisciplinary teaching, learning, and research.

"The professors are only here for us."

Haverford's curriculum reflects commitment to the liberal arts. English, biology, economics, psychology, and political science are among the most popular majors. There are more than a dozen areas of concentration—which are different from minors—that are attached to certain majors, including peace and conflict studies, neural and behavioral sciences, and mathematical economics. Unusual offerings include a philosophy seminar called From Zen Buddhism to Contemporary Public Black Intellectuals and a course called Happiness, Virtue, and the Good Life. Comparative literature, East Asian studies, and computer science are newer, growing majors. Haverford's general education requirements call for taking three courses in each of the three divisions: social sciences, natural sciences, and humanities. One of these nine courses must fulfill a quantitative reasoning requirement, and every student must also study a foreign language for a year and complete a freshman writing seminar.

The bicollege system with Bryn Mawr College, a nearby women's school, allows Haverford students to major in subjects such as art history, growth and structure of cities, and environmental studies. The unique relationship between Bryn Mawr and Haverford dates to the days when Haverford was all-male, more than 25 years ago. This unique consortium allows students at each institution to take courses, use the facilities, eat, and even live in the dormitories of the other. Haverford and Bryn Mawr students cooperate on a weekly newspaper, radio station, orchestra, and other clubs and sports, and a free shuttle bus connects the campuses. About half of Haverford graduates have taken a course at Bryn Mawr. Cross-registration is also available at Swarthmore and the University of Pennsylvania. Study abroad programs in 38 countries attract 40 percent of students. Additional programs include a 3–2 engineering program with Caltech and a major in Middle Eastern and Islamic studies.

Since there are no graduate students at Haverford, undergraduates often help professors with research, and several publish papers each year. In fact, Haverford's biggest strength may be its faculty members, 50 percent of whom live on campus and are said to be very accessible. A junior political science student notes that one

Website: www.haverford.edu
Location: Suburban
Private
Total Enrollment: 1,205
Undergraduates: 1,205
Male/Female: 47/53
SAT Ranges: CR 650–760,
    M 660–760
ACT Ranges: 29–33
Financial Aid: 56%
Expense: Pr $ $ $ $
Student Loans: 33%
Average Debt: $
Phi Beta Kappa: Yes
Applicants: 3,626
Accepted: 23%
Enrolled: 39%
Grad in 6 Years: 94%
Returning Freshmen: 96%
Academics: ✍ ✍ ✍ ✍ ✍
Social: ☎ ☎ ☎
Q of L: ★ ★ ★ ★ ★
Admissions: (610) 896-1350
Email Address: admission@ haverford.edu

Strongest Programs:
Biological and Physical
    Sciences
English
History
Political Science
Economics

Unusual offerings include a philosophy seminar called From Zen Buddhism to Contemporary Public Black Intellectuals and a course called Happiness, Virtue, and the Good Life.

professor personalized a 90-student class by dividing it up into groups of 10 and having each group over for a pre-exam dessert. "The professors are only here for us. They really enjoy teaching as well as involving us in research."

Perhaps because of the intense classroom interaction, the workload is sizable, although students say they don't worry about each other's grades and try to squeeze in nonscholarly pursuits, too. "Haverford is very challenging," says one geology major. "As a student, you expect to put in a lot of work." Advising is ever-present: freshmen are matched with professors who work with them from their arrival until they declare majors two years later, while upper-class "Customs people" are resources and mentors for living groups of eight to 16 first-year students.

One of Haverford's most distinctive features is the honor code that governs all aspects of campus life. "I can take my final exam at 3 a.m. on Founder's Green," says a junior, who says the honor code "means we look out for ourselves." The code, administered by students and debated and reratified each year at a meeting called Plenary, helps instill the values of "integrity, honesty, and concern for others." While the social honor code encourages students to "voice virtually any opinion so long as it is expressed rationally," this can also mean self-censorship, says a philosophy major. "Sometimes you feel like you are walking on eggshells to avoid offending anyone," the student says. In good Quaker tradition, decisions are made by consensus rather than formal voting, and students play a large role in college policy.

Only 12 percent of Haverford's students hail from Pennsylvania, but a large percentage are East Coasters nonetheless. "Students are very academically motivated, but we have a good mix of partiers and shut-ins," a student explains. Seven percent of students are Asian American, 9 percent Hispanic, and 6 percent African American. Though the college is nonsectarian, the Quaker influence lives on in the form of an optional meeting each week. "Although students tend to be very well informed on political issues and have great concern about these issues, few are very involved in political activism," says a philosophy major. Haverford has eliminated loans from its financial aid packages and replaced them with grants.

Haverford's residence halls are spacious and well maintained, and most rooms are singles—even for freshmen—so it's not surprising that 99 percent of all students live on campus. All dorms are co-ed, but students may request single-sex floors. Freshmen are guaranteed housing, and even sophomores, who draw last in the lottery, can usually get decent rooms. The extremely popular, school-owned Haverford College Apartments sit on the edge of campus. These include one- and two-bedroom units, each with a living room, kitchen, and bathroom. Upperclassmen in the apartments may cook for themselves, but all others living on campus (and all freshmen regardless of where they live) must buy the meal plan, which includes weekend board. "Some of the dorms are incredible. The apartments are the best freshman housing anywhere," says an economics student. Crime is virtually nonexistent, owing to the school's location in the ritzy Philadelphia suburbs. "There is little to worry about coming from the surrounding area," explains a philosophy major: "There is a very safe and trusting relationship between students and security."

While the community spirit at Haverford works well for academics and personal development, it doesn't always carry over to the social scene. Without fraternities and sororities, Haverford and Bryn Mawr hold joint campus parties. These affairs can get tiresome after freshman and sophomore years, which is why students tend to spend at least part of their junior year abroad. The alcohol policy is connected to the honor code. "Haverford is very unusual in that the drug and alcohol policy is set and administered by the student body," explains a junior. For nondrinkers, there are frequently free movies, concerts, and other activities on campus. Other traditional

About half of Haverford graduates have taken a course at Bryn Mawr.

"As a student, you expect to put in a lot of work."

In good Quaker tradition, decisions are made by consensus rather than formal voting, and students play a large role in college policy.

events include the weekend-long pre-exams Haverfest—Haverford's approximation of Woodstock—as well as the winter Snowball dance and Taste the Rainbow drag ball. Life in the close-knit, introspective environment that is Haverford can get stifling, but there are easy escapes: downtown Philadelphia is 20 minutes away by train. New York City, Washington, D.C., the New Jersey beaches, Pocono ski areas, and Atlantic City are only a couple hours away by car or train. Many students participate in the Eighth Dimension, which coordinates volunteer opportunities.

The "Ford's" rich athletic history dates back more than 100 years, when the soccer team played in its first intercollegiate game. The men's cross-country team is a perennial national contender and men's and women's soccer, men's outdoor track and field, and women's squash each brought home conference titles in

> **"We have a good mix of partiers and shut-ins."**

2012–13. "The Haverford–Swarthmore men's basketball and lacrosse games are the two biggest athletic events of the year," says one student. Haverford also boasts the number-one varsity college cricket team in the country because, well, it's the only school that has one! Intramural sports are popular, especially because participation counts toward the six quarters of athletic credit Haverford requires during the freshman and sophomore years. In spite of all the rivalries, these Quakers have struggled to justify their peace-loving heritage with the desire to bash opponents' brains out on the court or the field. For now, students root for the Black Squirrels and chant, "Fight, fight, inner light—kill, Quakers, kill!"

Haverford's student body may be beyond the norm in regards to personal values, but the downside of the honor code is that "students are challenged to meet an ideal set before them of creating the best community possible. For this reason, students are constantly criticizing themselves and the community as a whole to find ways of solving the problems facing them." See? Mom was right. With freedom comes responsibility.

Overlaps

Swarthmore, Brown, Wesleyan, University of Pennsylvania, Princeton, Amherst, Yale, Williams

University of Hawaii–Manoa

2530 Dole Street, Room C200, Honolulu, HI 96822

Who wouldn't be tempted to go to Hawaii for college? To make it work, aim for one of UH's specialties, such as Asian studies, marine science, or travel industry management. Bear in mind the measly 56 percent graduation rate after six years. (There's a reason Barack Obama did not stay for college.) Too many luaus and not enough studying can be a bad combination.

One of the goals of the University of Hawaii at Manoa is to "serve as a bridge between East and West." This multiculturalism is evident in everything from course offerings to the student body. And while you may be thinking about surfing as much as studying, don't be fooled: it will take more than a great tan and the ability to catch a wave to earn your degree here. Unfortunately, not everything at UH is so sunny: the state's budget crisis has put strains on the university, resulting in bulging classrooms and talk of merging programs and laying off faculty members.

Website: www.manoa.hawaii.edu
Location: City Center
Public
Total Enrollment: 14,784
Undergraduates: 11,721

(continued)

Male/Female: 46/54
SAT Ranges: CR 480–580,
    M 500–610
ACT Ranges: 21–27
Financial Aid: 78%
Expense: Pub $ $
Student Loans: 42%
Average Debt: $ $
Phi Beta Kappa: No
Applicants: 6,810
Accepted: 81%
Enrolled: 36%
Grad in 6 Years: 56%
Returning Freshmen: 79%
Academics: ✐ ✐
Social: ☎ ☎ ☎
Q of L: ★ ★ ★
Admissions: (808) 956-8975
Email Address: uhmanoa
    .admissions@hawaii.edu

Strongest Programs:
Astronomy
Asian and Pacific Area Studies
Languages
Travel Industry Management

It should come as no surprise that marine and ocean-related programs are also first-rate.

If you're thinking about off-campus housing, take note: housing in Honolulu is scarce and expensive.

The UH campus occupies 300 acres in the Manoa Valley, a residential Honolulu neighborhood. The architecture is regionally eclectic, mirroring historical and modern Asian Pacific motifs, and is enhanced by extensive subtropical landscaping. Frear Hall provides housing for 810 students in two interconnected 12-story towers.

UH offers bachelor's degrees in nearly 90 fields. Among the best are astronomy, Asian and Pacific area studies, languages and the arts, ethnomusicology, and tropical agriculture. It should come as no surprise that marine and ocean-related programs are also first-rate. The university takes pride in its programs in engineering, geology and geophysics, international business, political science, and travel industry management. UH also offers a B.A. degree in information and computer science. Beyond these few specialties, programs are adequate but hardly worth four years of trans-Pacific flights for students from the mainland.

"The courses can be challenging."

Core requirements are extensive: all students must take a semester in expository writing and math, two courses in world civilization, two years of a foreign language or Hawaiian, and three courses each in the humanities, social sciences, and natural sciences. Freshman seminar classes offer small-group learning in a variety of subjects. Desirable classes and times are said to be difficult to get into for freshmen and sophomores. "The courses can be challenging based on what you take and the major you declare," says a senior. The Honors Program provides qualified freshmen and sophomores the opportunity for general education courses in small, intensive classes. Professors received generally favorable reviews and "teachers range from seasoned lecturers to tenured professors," says a senior. Students who tire of Hawaii's endless beaches and beatific sunsets can study abroad in locations around the world, including Asia, Europe, Latin America, and Russia.

Hawaii stands out among major American universities in that 41 percent of the students are of Asian descent. Caucasians account for 21 percent, African Americans 2 percent, and Hispanics 2 percent. "Every ethnicity from around the planet can be found here," says a junior. A senior adds, "We all care about one another." Political and social issues often take a backseat to academics and play, but among the more prominent concerns are the environment and native Hawaiian rights. Especially promising students can compete for merit scholarships. The university also offers approximately 200 athletic scholarships in 15 sports.

Less than a quarter of students live in campus housing, which is parceled out by a priority system that gives preference to those who are from across the sea. "Most students live off campus because housing is so limited," says one senior. Fortunately, once you are accepted into housing, continuous residency is not that difficult to obtain. Students recommend the four towers, Ilima, Lehua, Lokelani, and Mokihana;

"Social life at the college is nonexistent, especially after 4 p.m."

the rooms are small and the hallways are happening. If you're thinking about off-campus housing, take note: housing in Honolulu is scarce and expensive. Cafeterias are located throughout the campus and serve diverse and adequate fare. Students complain that security is less than effective. "I think we need more lighting around the campus," says one senior. "Campus security means well," adds a classmate, "but their funds are used poorly."

Because of all the commuters, UH is pretty sedate after dark. "Social life at the college is nonexistent, especially after 4 p.m.," says a psychology major. A senior counters, "There are a lot of activities and concerts at the campus center and a lot of clubs to join." Only 1 percent of the men and women join the tiny Greek system. Drinking is not allowed in the dorms. A couple of local hangouts provide an escape, and the campus pub, Manoa Garden, is also an option. Lest anyone forget, some of the world's most beautiful resorts—Diamond Head and all the rest—are less than a 20-minute drive away. Waikiki Beach? Within two miles' reach. And round-trip airfare to the neighboring islands—including Maui, Kauai, and the Big Island—is not unreasonable.

The athletic teams, the Rainbow Warriors, generate the most excitement on campus with basketball, baseball, and swimming among the top draws. The Rainbow women's teams are also well supported, especially the championship volleyball team and the cheerleading squad, which brought home first- and fifth-place trophies in 2009. The homecoming dance is one of the most popular events of the year. But what students really look forward to is Kanikapila, a festival of Hawaiian music, dance, and culture. Don Ho, eat your heart out.

> **"You're only young once— might as well be 20 in Hawaii."**

Students seeking warm weather and great surfing won't be disappointed, but mainlanders should think twice about making the leap to UH unless they are set on one of the university's specialized programs. It's up to you, one student says, to get the best out of Hawaii. "The location allows mainland students to get a different cultural experience," adds another. "You're only young once—might as well be 20 in Hawaii."

Overlaps
UCLA, Hawaii Pacific, UH–Hilo, University of Southern California, University of Washington

If You Apply To >

UH: Regular admissions: Jan. 4. Application fee: $70. No campus or alumni interviews. SATs or ACTs: required. Subject Tests: optional. No essay question.

Hendrix College

1600 Washington Avenue, Conway, AR 72032

Hendrix is in the same class of mid-South liberal arts colleges as Millsaps and Rhodes. The smallest and most progressive of the three, Hendrix has a strong emphasis on international awareness. Small-town Arkansas is a tough sell, and the college accepts the vast majority of students who apply. About half of Hendrix students are from Arkansas, and most of the rest are Southerners.

For a school in the heart of the Bible Belt, Hendrix College is surprisingly liberal. In fact, it's among the South's most progressive liberal arts colleges. Academics are demanding but students are laid-back—even radical—in their political and social views. Ironically, healthy dialogue about tough issues such as gay rights, the environment, and capital punishment draws students together. "People here are passionate, intelligent, and fun," says a freshman. "They really want to change the world."

Hendrix's compact and comfortable campus stretches for 180 acres between the Ouachita and the Ozark mountains. College land boasts more than 80 varieties of trees and shrubs, and more than 10,000 budding flowers each spring. The main campus—with its own lily pool, fountain, and gazebo—occupies about one-fourth of the total acreage. The redbrick buildings are a mix of old and new, and a pedestrian overpass connects the main campus to the college's athletic facilities and a wooded fitness trail. The campus is undergoing a building boom. An 80,000-square-foot student life and technology center houses state-of-the-art educational technology space, as well as a coffee shop and dining facility. Most recently, a multisport stadium, athletic center, and tennis center were completed.

Hendrix is strong in many areas, but natural and social sciences are definitely the school's forte. Twenty percent of students major in biology or psychology, the

Website: www.hendrix.edu
Location: Suburban
Private
Total Enrollment: 1,369
Undergraduates: 1,356
Male/Female: 43/57
SAT Ranges: CR 550–680, M 540–670
ACT Ranges: 26–32
Financial Aid: 100%
Expense: Pr $ $
Student Loans: 52%
Average Debt: $ $
Phi Beta Kappa: Yes
Applicants: 1,656
Accepted: 83%
Enrolled: 27%

(continued)

Grad in 6 Years: 72%
Returning Freshmen: 86%
Academics: ✍ ✍ ✍
Social: ☎ ☎ ☎ ☎
Q of L: ★ ★ ★ ★
Admissions: (501) 450-1362
Email Address: adm@
  hendrix.edu

Strongest Programs:
Biology
Chemistry
History
Religion
Psychology

Participants in the Accademia dell'Arte program travel to Arezzo, Italy, to experience Italian culture while studying European theater, vocal arts, and dance.

All but one of Hendrix's dorms are single-sex, and freshmen are required to live on campus.

school's two most popular majors. Students also give high marks to English, history, religion, philosophy, and politics. Doing well at Hendrix means keeping up with the workload. "I would describe the academic climate as 'hard-core,'" says one junior. "The premed track will suck your soul away." A freshman agrees, "Academics are definitely the priority here." Thankfully, engaging professors are available to help students navigate the coursework. "There are very few bad faculty, and those are usually in temporary positions and are soon weeded out," a senior says. Sixty-five percent of classes have 19 or fewer students, so personal attention is the norm.

At Hendrix, undergraduate research takes priority, especially within the sciences, and students get the chance to present original papers at regional and national symposia. Hendrix offers exchange programs in Austria and England, sends aspiring

"People here are passionate, intelligent, and fun."

ecologists to Costa Rica for two weeks and budding artists to Italy, and allows other students to get course credit for internships at U.S. embassies and organizations such as the National Institutes of Health and Agency for International Development. The Hendrix-in-Brussels program allows students to study issues of European identity, integration, and public policy in the capital of the European Union. Participants in the Accademia dell'Arte program travel to Arezzo, Italy, to experience Italian culture while studying European theater, vocal arts, and dance. Thirty-six percent of all Hendrix students have a significant international experience through programs that provide opportunities for students to work, study, research, and serve abroad. The school is also a member of the Associated Colleges of the South* consortium, and offers five-year programs with Columbia, Vanderbilt, and Washington University in St. Louis for aspiring engineers.

Hendrix freshmen participate in a weeklong orientation program, which includes a two-day, off-campus trip emphasizing outdoor experiences, urban exposure, or volunteer service. Professors from many departments teach the course, which considers the lasting importance and global influence of Western and non-Western traditions. General education requirements have been recently realigned and retitled as "Collegiate Center"; coursework includes the freshman commons course, the freshman seminar, the learning domains, the capacities, and the Odyssey Program. The former Journeys program is now called "The Engaged Citizen" and pairs faculty with common themes. Hendrix has also reintroduced minors in kinesiology, public health, medical humanities, and neuroscience.

"Our students live up to our motto of 'unto the whole person.' We challenge each other to explore new subjects, new perspectives, new hobbies, new lifestyles,"

"We challenge each other to explore new subjects, new perspectives, new hobbies, new lifestyles."

says one junior. Forty-five percent of Hendrix students are from Arkansas. African Americans and Hispanics combine for 8 percent of the student body; Asian Americans make up 3 percent. Social and political issues garner attention, according to one senior, and hot topics include environmental issues such as "pushing to make the campus more green friendly through recycling, Earth Day programs, and other initiatives." The college offers a variety of merit scholarships averaging more than $21,000 to academically qualified students, but there are no athletic scholarships.

All but one of Hendrix's dorms are single-sex, and freshmen are required to live on campus, which students say adds to the sense of community. Eighty-eight percent of students live on campus, which has led to some overcrowding as of late. Still, most report the dorms to be comfortable. "The housing facilities are good," says a senior: "Easy access to laundry, cooking utensils and such in the kitchen, and comfy common rooms." Students generally praise the dining options and report that plenty of choices are available for those with special dietary needs. "Our dining hall is extremely fun," cheers one economics major. "The staff knows students by name, and they make the dining experience very personal. On birthdays, students get bombarded with a cake and with an enthusiastic dining staff who leads the entire cafeteria in singing their special birthday song." Students also report feeling safe on campus, due in part to a visible security program and the close-knit nature of the Hendrix community.

Greek life—a staple of most Southern schools—is conspicuously absent at Hendrix. Students are proud of their independence; the annual Hendrix Olympics allows them to celebrate the absence of Alphas, Betas, and Gammas from campus. Other major affairs include the Toga Party, Oktoberfest, and Beach Bash, as well as the annual Toad Suck Daze, a rollicking carnival that features bluegrass music. Last but not least is the Shirttail Serenade, in which first-year men and women from each dorm croon out a song-and-dance routine in their shirts, ties, shoes, and socks for classmates. Judges rate each performance on the basis of singing, creativity, legs, and so on.

Despite being home to three colleges, Conway is essentially a "ghost town" for those seeking typical college-town activities. There are a number of shops and restaurants, but the 30-minute ride to Little Rock is the preferred destination. "Basically, all social life takes place on campus," a sophomore explains. Faulkner County, where the school is located, is officially dry, so students must travel to buy booze—or find older peers to help out. School policies prohibit underage drinking, but "the alcohol policies could use some work," says one student. Other popular road trips are Memphis (two hours by car) and Dallas and Oklahoma City (each a five-hour drive) for concerts and the like. For those who stay in town, the Volunteer Activities Center coordinates participation in projects on Service Saturdays.

Hendrix fields a number of competitive varsity teams, including men's baseball and women's softball and field hockey. Football—that other staple of Southern schools—is back at Hendrix for the first time since 1961. Rhodes College is the chief rival. For outdoor buffs, the college sponsors trips around Arkansas for canoeing, biking, rock climbing, and spelunking. Intramurals attract about 60 percent of the student body.

Musician Jimi Hendrix—whose mug inevitably adorns a new campus T-shirt each year—once asked listeners, "Are you experienced?" After four years at Hendrix College, with small classes, an emphasis on research, and a laid-back atmosphere in which to test their beliefs and boundaries, students here can likely answer, "Yes!"

Hendrix fields a number of competitive varsity teams, including men's baseball and women's softball and field hockey.

"Basically, all social life takes place on campus."

Overlaps

University of Arkansas, University of Central Arkansas, Rhodes, University of Texas, Arkansas State, University of Tulsa, University of the South, Southwestern

If You Apply To ➤ **Hendrix:** Rolling admissions. Early action: Nov. 15. Financial aid: Mar. 1. Housing: May 1. Application fee: $40. Campus and alumni interviews: optional, evaluative. SATs or ACTs: required. Subject Tests: optional. Accepts the Common Application. Essay question.

Hiram College

P.O. Box 96, Hiram, OH 44234

The smallest of the prominent Ohio liberal arts colleges. Less nationally known than Denison or Wooster, Hiram draws the vast majority of its students from in state. Lots of classes are taught in seminar format, and an extensive core curriculum ensures a broad education and undergraduate research opportunities.

Website: www.hiram.edu

Location: Rural

Private

Total Enrollment: 1,324

Undergraduates: 1,293

Male/Female: 44/56

SAT Ranges: CR 440–560,
  M 440–570

ACT Ranges: 20–25

Financial Aid: 100%

Expense: Pr $

Student Loans: 82%

Average Debt: $ $ $

Phi Beta Kappa: Yes

Applicants: 2,378

Accepted: 62%

Enrolled: 21%

Grad in 6 Years: 63%

Returning Freshmen: 75%

Academics: ✏ ✏ ✏

Social: ☎ ☎ ☎

Q of L: ★ ★ ★

Admissions: (330) 569-5169

Email Address: admission@
  hiram.edu

Strongest Programs:

Biology

Chemistry

History

English

Psychobiology

Environmental Studies

Communications

Creative Writing

The sciences, especially chemistry, are strong, and the music program has been bolstered by the addition of a student-created marching band.

Hiram College offers students a solid liberal arts education and plenty of opportunities to travel the globe. In fact, more than half study abroad in exotic locales ranging from Europe to Australia to Costa Rica. But no matter where they hang their hats, students here take advantage of ample research opportunities and a close-knit environment that ensures every Hiram Dawg has his or her day. "Hiram has a unique character," extols one junior. "Because of its small size, students get noticed, not lost in the shuffle."

Set on a charming hilltop campus that occupies the second-highest spot in Ohio, Hiram is blessed with an abundance of flowers and trees as well as a nice view of the valley below. The prevailing architectural motif is New England brick, and many Hiram buildings are restored 19th-century homes. The Les & Kathy Coleman Sports, Recreation, and Fitness Center houses a competition gymnasium; two multipurpose field houses that feature tennis, volleyball, and basketball courts; a pool; an indoor track; and facilities for fitness training. Hiram's bio majors work at a 260-acre, college-owned ecology field study station a mile away, with a specialized lab, a 70-acre beech and maple forest, artificial river, and numerous plant and animal species.

> **"Students get noticed, not lost in the shuffle."**

The Hiram Plan allows students to cover a breadth of material in three courses during each semester's longer 12-week session and to focus on a seminar-style class during the additional three-week term. Even nonseminars are small, though; 95 percent of Hiram's courses have 25 or fewer students, allowing for an impressive degree of faculty accessibility. "They are involved and are fun to talk with," says a freshman. Hiram's core curriculum is extensive. Students are required to select courses from at least six different academic disciplines that fall under two categories, "Ways of Knowing" and "Ways of Developing Responsible Citizenship." Through their studies, students learn various methods for acquiring knowledge and understanding about human beings and the world while exploring what it means to be socially responsible citizens. In addition, Hiram has the Freshman Colloquium, a writing and speaking skills seminar, and an upper-division interdisciplinary requirement. First-year students are also enrolled in a seminar with a focus on Western intellectual traditions and an emphasis on writing. Though the academic climate can be challenging, "there are a lot of resources to help students on campus," says a freshman, including tutors, the writing center, and help from peers or profs. The sciences, especially chemistry, are strong, and the music program has been bolstered by the addition of a student-created marching band.

Hiram offers several unusual summer opportunities, most notably the Northwoods Station up in the wilds of northern Michigan, where students choose courses ranging from photography to botany and geology to writing. And Hiram is the only affiliate college of the Shoals Marine Lab, run by Cornell University and the University of New Hampshire, which offers summer study in marine science, ecology, coastal and oceanic law, and underwater archeology.

Hiram goes to great lengths to offer outstanding travel abroad programs. Trips led by professors make it to all corners of the globe, and all participating students get academic credit. Students can also study at Hiram's Rome affiliate, John Cabot International University, and transfer their credits. Hiram's unique academic calendar allows ample opportunity for off-campus endeavors of all types, including the Washington Semester* at American University, which Hiram helped found.

Seventy-five percent of Hiram students are in-staters, and many of the rest hail from New York and Pennsylvania, though the administration is working aggressively to recruit more minority and international students. Minority students are present, too, with African Americans constituting 12 percent and Asian Americans and Hispanics together comprising another 4 percent. Hiram offers a dorm program called Dialogue in Black and White that encourages open discussion on multicultural issues. There's also a one-credit course that has as its final project the creation of a plan of action on campus race relations. In addition to need-based financial aid, Hiram awards merit scholarships. Hiram lures good students with irresistible financial aid. "My financial aid package at Hiram is unbelievable," says a junior. "After applying to larger, cheaper public universities, I came to realize it would actually cost me less to attend Hiram."

Almost all Hiram students—90 percent—live on campus, and everyone who wants a room gets one. "Ours are much better than some I have seen at other schools," says a junior. Community lounges in each hall boast big-screen TVs and computer labs. Most halls are co-ed, and upperclassmen who like their location can stay in the same room year after year. Most students live in two-person suites; the popular (and larger) triples and quads are scarcer and thus harder to get.

When the weekend rolls around, don't expect to find all Hiram students gathered around a keg. There are dorms designated as totally dry, and the college has cracked down on underage drinking. Still, students admit that it's easy for underage students to get alcohol if they really want to drink. Hiram is a bit isolated, and there are few distractions in town, so students must make their own fun. Typically, that means hanging out in each other's rooms, or if they're 21, at the on-campus pub that serves pizza (and features karaoke on Tuesdays). The Student Programming Board plans concerts, comedians, speakers, movies, and both formal and informal dances. "We always have tons of things happening on campus," says one student, noting the college also sponsors trips to events.

> **"There are a lot of resources to help students on campus."**

Cleveland's Progressive Field is a short road trip away. Cleveland's Rock and Roll Hall of Fame can get students rockin' all year-round. Sometimes the college offers free tickets to concerts, plays, and ballets in town. Every semester also brings a surprise Campus Day, when classes are canceled and a slew of activities are planned. Other diversions include an excellent golf course three miles away, a college-owned cross-country ski trail, and good downhill slopes about an hour distant.

Hiram is hardly a mecca for budding athletic superstars, but it does have a decent Division III sports program, including a volleyball team that has gone to the NCAA Tournament in recent years. Football, baseball, and soccer are among the most popular men's Terriers teams, while soccer and softball attract women. Intramurals, including soccer, floor hockey, basketball, and dodgeball are popular.

Those looking for a school where anonymity will be ensured need not apply. People here are so close that they share an equivalent of the secret handshake. "Everyone smiles at you as you pass—faculty, staff, a senior football player, a freshman chemistry major, the lady that vacuums in the morning, the gardener," says a junior. Indeed, those seeking a friendly, all-American institution with a touch of internationalism might want to give Hiram a look.

Hiram goes to great lengths to offer outstanding travel abroad programs.

Overlaps

John Carroll, Miami University (OH), Mount Union, Wittenberg, College of Wooster

If You Apply To ➢ | **Hiram:** Rolling admissions. No application fee. Campus interviews: recommended (required for scholarship consideration), evaluative. Alumni interviews: optional, informational. SATs or ACTs: required. Subject Tests: optional. Accepts the Common Application. Essay question.

Coordinate single-sex colleges overlooking one of New York's picturesque Finger Lakes. Two-college system makes for somewhat more traditional relations between the sexes, though most dorms are co-ed. Most social life takes place on campus, especially in the fraternities, but skiing and other outdoor activities beckon. HWS takes pride in personal attention from full professors and a culture of community service.

Website: www.hws.edu
Location: Small City
Private
Total Enrollment: 2,275
Undergraduates: 2,267
Male/Female: 45/55
SAT Ranges: CR 570–650, M 565–660
ACT Ranges: 26–29
Financial Aid: 87%
Expense: Pr $ $ $ $
Student Loans: 53%
Average Debt: $ $ $ $
Phi Beta Kappa: Yes
Applicants: 4,473
Accepted: 53%
Enrolled: 26%
Grad in 6 Years: 76%
Returning Freshmen: 88%
Academics: ✑ ✑ ✑
Social: ☎ ☎ ☎
Q of L: ★ ★ ★
Admissions: (315) 781-3622
Email Address: admissions@ hws.edu

Strongest Programs:
Creative Writing
Environmental Studies
Architectural Studies
Biology
Political Science
History
Economics
Elementary, Secondary, and
   Special Education

If you're unsure about a single-sex institution, the Hobart and William Smith "coordinate system" may offer the best of both worlds. Students eat together, study together, and even live together in co-ed residence halls, but also take advantage of unique traditions and programs generally reserved for single-sex establishments. If you can tolerate the frigid winters of upstate New York, you'll be rewarded with small classes, caring faculty, and a place where tradition still matters. "Life here is vibrant and busy," says one senior, "and this makes it quite easy to get involved and find your niche amongst a group of friends."

"You certainly have to work hard to succeed."

Hobart College was founded in 1822 by Episcopal Bishop John Henry Hobart, who conceived it to be an outpost for civilized and learned behavior. In 1908 William Smith College opened. The college bears the name of a wealthy businessman who wanted to introduce women to opportunities that were largely unrecognized at the time. The HWS campus stretches for 200 tree-lined acres and includes a forest, farmland, and a wildlife preserve. Architectural styles range from colonial to postmodern, with stately Greek Revival mansions and ivy-clad brick residences and classrooms. Stern Hall houses the departments of economics, political science, anthropology, sociology, and Asian languages and cultures. There's a boathouse on the shores of Seneca Lake for the nationally ranked sailing team.

The innovative HWS curriculum has no distribution requirements. Instead, students take an interdisciplinary seminar in the first year, constructed around a different interest, such as flight, consumerism, or rock and roll music. Students must also complete a major and minor or a double major, one from a traditional department and one from an interdisciplinary program. Popular majors include economics, English, political science, psychology, and environmental science, and the long list of minors includes Sacred in Cross-Cultural Perspective, men's studies, The Good Society, and aesthetics. Other solid programs include architectural studies, which is staffed by three professionally trained designers, and environmental studies, which requires students to select courses from the natural sciences, social sciences, and humanities.

"You certainly have to work hard to succeed, however there are always people lining up to help you out," says a sophomore. Small classes are the norm here: 65 percent have 19 or fewer. "At HWS the quality of teaching is fantastic across the board," gushes one senior. "We have great professors who are eager to teach and learn from students. They take our education personally and want to see us succeed." The Finger Lakes Institute at the college gives students wide opportunities to work in various fields of scientific inquiry, as well as public policy. HWS students may take a term away from campus and, in recent years, HWS has offered off-campus programs on six continents, including such locations as Auckland, New Zealand; Dakar, Senegal; Galway, Ireland; London, England; Hanoi, Vietnam; Madrid, Spain; Queensland, Australia; Quito, Ecuador; Rome, Italy; and Washington, D.C. Each

"Students at HWS are motivated, determined, and constantly engaged in stimulating conversation."

year, about 30 seniors elect to "do Honors," producing a research or critical paper or an equivalent creative work and then taking written and oral exams on their projects. The Senior Symposium offers seniors an opportunity to share their intellectual passions. They present research findings, discuss theory, display and discuss creative works, or present other significant scholarly activities. All seniors in all majors are invited to participate in this showcase of HWS's best student work.

"For the most part, students are preppy, friendly, and outgoing," says one junior. New Yorkers make up 41 percent of the HWS student body. African Americans and Hispanics combine for 5 percent of the total, while Asian Americans account for 1 percent. The departments of women's, African American, and Third World cultural studies are small but flourishing. Politically, the colleges lean liberal, but "everyone is respectful of each other's opinions." "Students at HWS are motivated, determined, and constantly engaged in stimulating conversation. They continue their interests in academics beyond the classroom," says a senior. Merit scholarships averaging more than $15,000 are awarded to qualified students; there are no athletic scholarships.

Ninety percent of HWS students live on campus, where first-years may opt for single-sex or co-ed dorms, and "a quarter of the people on your floor will be in your first-year seminar," says a sophomore. Caird and de Cordova halls are student favorites and each houses 88 residents in 20 singles, 24 doubles, and five quads. Durfee, Bartlett, and Hale halls are also popular among Hobart men. Sophomores, who may lose out in the "unlucky" housing lottery, typically live in a large co-ed complex known as J-P-R (for Jackson, Potter, and Rees halls). Juniors and seniors may choose Victorian houses with high ceilings and wood floors, or the more modern "Village at Odell's Pond," where townhouses have four to five bedrooms and two bathrooms each. Housing is guaranteed for four years, and only seniors are allowed to live off campus, though few choose to do so. When it comes to campus dining, reviews are mixed. "Because HWS is a small school, the food isn't the greatest," laments one student. "We don't have a ton of options."

"Students rarely leave campus on the weekends and if they do, it is to go skiing with friends or to go into New York City or Boston," says one art history major. Six Hobart fraternities claim 20 percent of the men, who aren't permitted to pledge until **"Life here is vibrant and busy."** sophomore year, but there are no sororities at William Smith. William Smith has also retained a number of traditions typical of women's colleges, such as Moving Up Day, in which seniors symbolically hand over their leadership role to juniors. (Hobart, not to be left out, has a similar event called Charter Day.) Social life includes Greek parties and bashes at off-campus houses, while the Campus Activity Board plans movies, concerts, dances, plays, and other events each weekend. There's a "zero tolerance" policy for underage drinking, and students caught with booze must attend alcohol awareness classes and may face social probation.

The old industrial city of Geneva "is not the best college town, but it's getting better," says a senior. But features that get rave reviews are Seneca Lake and the Smith Opera House, which "offers unique events, free or discounted to students, that you might not expect in a small, rural area," praises one junior. Other notable perks include movie theaters, restaurants and bars, a state park, an outlet mall, and a bowling alley—if not right in town, then not far, as long as you've got a car. Popular road trips include Rochester, Ithaca, and Syracuse, all about 45 minutes away; more intrepid (or bored) souls trek as far as New York City; Washington, D.C.; and Toronto, Canada. Most of the campus takes part in Days of Service, which brings students, faculty, and staff together for several days of community service. "Community service is a huge component to everyday life," confirms one senior, "ranging from mandatory community service during orientation to a variety of service-learning classes and three days of service for the entire campus."

HWS students may take a term away from campus and, in recent years, HWS has offered off-campus programs on six continents.

All seniors in all majors are invited to participate in this showcase of HWS's best student work.

Sports are the most popular diversion from studying here, whether you're a spectator or participant.

Sports are the most popular diversion from studying here, whether you're a spectator or participant. HWS teams compete in Division III, except for men's lacrosse, which won 16 straight NCAA Division III championships before joining Division I. Hobart football, ice hockey, sailing, soccer, and squash, and William Smith field hockey, rowing, sailing, soccer, and squash are all perennially competitive. Recent conference champs include William Smith cross-country, Hobart football, Hobart hockey, Hobart rowing, and William Smith soccer. The HWS Debate Team, only in its fifth year, has had much success as well.

The HWS coordinate system may not be for everyone, but the benefits are many for those who decide to stay, including intimate classes, robust community service opportunities, and a bevy of traditions. Says a psychology major, "HWS really cares about their students."

If You Apply To ➤

HWS: Early decision: Nov. 1. Regular admissions: Feb. 1. Financial aid: Feb. 15. Application fee: $45 (paper), free (online). Campus and alumni interviews: optional, evaluative. SATs or ACTs: optional. Subject Tests: optional. Accepts the Common Application. Essay question: Common Application questions.

Hofstra University

Hempstead, NY 11549

Offers a combination of suburban setting with ready access to the Big Apple. Hofstra has outgrown its commuter-school origins and offers a broad range of pre-professional and other academic programs. Greek system is an option but does not dominate the social scene. Well-known as a lacrosse powerhouse. Has become more selective in recent years, but for many it is still a backup to urban schools like BU and Northeastern.

Website: www.hofstra.edu
Location: Suburban
Private
Total Enrollment: 9,253
Undergraduates: 6,347
Male/Female: 47/53
SAT Ranges: CR 530–630, M 540–630
ACT Ranges: 23–28
Financial Aid: 66%
Expense: Pr $ $
Student Loans: 67%
Average Debt: N/A
Phi Beta Kappa: Yes
Applicants: 22,733
Accepted: 59%
Enrolled: 11%
Grad in 6 Years: 61%
Returning Freshmen: 78%
Academics: ✍ ✍ ✍

Although it sits within easy striking distance of Manhattan, Hofstra University occupies one of the prettiest campuses you'll find anywhere. Its bucolic setting is not only an accredited museum and arboretum but is also home to the school's blossoming professional offerings. Whatever their field, Hofstra students enjoy study abroad options, research opportunities, and first-year programs that help harried freshmen get off to a good start. One film major says the best parts of the Hofstra experience include "the diversity, the educational quality, the great campus life, and awesome friends."

Founded in 1935 with one building—the Dutch colonial mansion left in trust by Kate and William Hofstra on their 15-acre estate—the campus is now home to 115 buildings on 240 acres. The suburban campus offers a parklike environment with a variety of architecture, from ivy-covered stone buildings to modern facilities with sleek angles and electronic signage, which surround open green quads, where students gather, play sports, or enjoy outdoor classes when weather permits. The campus is especially beautiful in the spring, when its 100,000 tulips, a tribute to the Dutch heritage of Hofstra's founders, are in bloom. Recent construction includes an expansion and refurbishment to the fitness center and new, state-of-the-art bioengineering labs.

With more than 140 academic programs for undergraduates, Hofstra offers students plenty of options. With the establishment of a School of Engineering and Applied Science and with joint undergraduate programs with its medical school,

Hofstra seeks to model itself on much larger and better-known Northeastern universities like NYU and Syracuse. Signature programs include communications and engineering. Accounting, biology, drama, and international business are especially strong, with business and psychology among the most popular. The Zarb School of Business offers separate majors in marketing and finance. First Year Connections offers new students a combined social and academic experience centered on small seminars (limited to 18 students) taught by senior faculty; recent seminars include Art Is Really Dangerous, Baseball in America, and Reading Karl Marx in the Capitalist Meltdown. Freshmen may also enroll in clusters of thematically related courses. The Honors College offers approximately 200 qualified entering students a multidisciplinary program that allows them to graduate with both a bachelor's degree and Honors College designation. They may also take advantage of faculty mentors and special housing.

"Students at Hofstra are very goal oriented."

(continued)

Social: ☎ ☎ ☎
Q of L: ★ ★ ★
Admissions: (516) 463-6700
Email Address: admission@ hofstra.edu

Strongest Programs:
Business
Communication
Biology
Psychology
Education

Support for students with learning disabilities is strong, and students with wanderlust can take advantage of study abroad options around the world, including programs in England, Italy, Mali, Japan, France, Peru, and South Korea. Hofstra is home to one of the largest simulated trading rooms in the New York area, boasting 34 dual-panel Bloomberg terminals. The Department of Dance and Drama has turned out such luminaries as Francis Ford Coppola, the late Madeline Kahn, and *Everybody Loves Raymond* creator Phil Rosenthal.

Regardless of what major they choose, all undergrad students must complete distribution requirements, including coursework in humanities, natural sciences and mathematics/computer science, social sciences, cross-cultural studies, and interdisciplinary studies. Students must also pass the English Proficiency Exam. "I'd say the school is fairly competitive," says one junior. "My classes are challenging but I budget my time so as not to be overwhelmed," adds a freshman. Fifty percent of classes have 19 or fewer students, giving them plenty of access to professors. "At Hofstra, we pride ourselves on the fact that most professors have the highest degree in their field of study and/or are currently working in their field," boasts one senior. "No students are taught by TAs."

The Honors College offers approximately 200 qualified entering students a multidisciplinary program that allows them to graduate with both a bachelor's degree and Honors College designation.

Sixty-three percent of freshmen hail from New York, and 61 percent ranked in the top quarter of their high school class. "Students at Hofstra are very goal oriented," a broadcast journalism major says. African Americans account for 9 percent of the student body, Hispanics 11 percent, and Asian Americans 8 percent. "Kids are very opinionated here," says a student, and hot topics include gay rights, women's rights, and abortion. The university offers merit scholarships worth an average of $11,003 and 249 athletic scholarships in 17 men's and women's sports.

Seventy-one percent of students live in university housing. "Dorm rooms are pretty big, definitely big enough to live in without any trouble," a student says. Although the housing restrictions leave many students grumbling, the dining options receive high marks. "The dining facilities are good," says a sophomore. "Hofstra offers 20 different eateries around campus and that's including Au Bon Pain, Nathan's, Subway, and even Red Mango. There are also two Starbucks locations on campus and all these accept the Hofstra dining plan." Students report feeling safe on campus. "Campus security is very good," says a marketing major.

"You're bound to find a club or organization that interests you."

"Every day there seems to be something going on and you're bound to find a club or organization that interests you," says one student. "Being involved is absolutely crucial to having a social life on campus," adds a sophomore. "This is where Hofstra excels, though, offering an incredible number of clubs, in-dorm activities, and departmental organizations." Eleven percent of the men and 9 percent of the women go Greek, but they don't dominate the social landscape. Alcohol policies include severe consequences for underage drinkers, "but most students assume the risk and consume anyway," says a junior. Festivals include Greek Week, and "the Irish, Italian, and Dutch festivals are really fun events," a student says. When students tire of on-campus activities, they trek into New York City (40 minutes away) for more urban activities.

"Hempstead is not really a college town. Hofstra just happens to be in the middle of it. That's why most things that go on, happen on campus," says a sophomore. Long Island has "absolutely everything" and many students get involved in the community through service clubs or organizations on campus.

Hofstra teams compete in Division I and play an important role in shaping campus culture. In the past two years, men's lacrosse, softball, women's soccer, and wrestling have participated in their respective NCAA tournaments, and women's basketball has participated in the WNIT. Men's basketball has averaged 20 wins per season over the past few years. Intramurals and recreational sports attract approximately 38 percent of undergrads, and students take advantage of the Fitness Center, which features daily fitness classes, a multipurpose gym, and a fully equipped weight room.

Hofstra succeeds at making the transition from high school to college less overwhelming. A Spanish and secondary education major says, "There are plenty of things to do on campus, and even with such a large student body, you get to know so many people." By offering solid academics and a bevy of programs aimed at first-year students, the university seeks to put its students in a New York state of mind.

Overlaps
Fordham, NYU, Drexel, SUNY–Stony Brook, Syracuse, Boston University, Penn State, Northeastern

If You Apply To ➢ **Hofstra:** Rolling admissions. Early action: Nov. 15. Financial aid: Feb. 15. Housing: May 1. Application fee: $70. Campus interviews: optional, informational. No alumni interviews. SATs or ACTs: required (optional for some programs). Subject Tests: recommended. Accepts the Common Application. Essay question: personal statement.

Hollins University

(formerly Hollins College) P.O. Box 9707, Roanoke, VA 24020

Hollins competes with Sweet Briar for the mantle of leading Virginia women's college. Sweet Briar is rural and Hollins is on the edge of Roanoke, the biggest city in southwest Virginia. Hollins has long been noted for creative writing and its equestrian program. Social life often depends on road trips to Virginia Tech and Washington and Lee, both about an hour's drive.

Website: www.hollins.edu
Location: City Outskirts
Private
Total Enrollment: 647
Undergraduates: 591
Male/Female: 0/100
SAT Ranges: CR 500–650, M 460–590
ACT Ranges: 21–27
Financial Aid: 98%
Expense: Pr $

Traditions rule at Hollins University, a private, single-sex college on a lush 475-acre campus in the Virginia mountains. Each fall, students and staff hike up Tinker Mountain for skits, a picnic lunch, and a bird's-eye view of the changing foliage. There's a secret society known as Fraeya, since the school doesn't have sororities. And there are males on campus, too, since Hollins offers co-ed graduate programs in children's literature, creative writing, dance, screenwriting and film studies, liberal studies, and teaching. "A student should only attend Hollins if they want to be a part of a close-knit community that fosters creative minds and ambitious spirits," says a senior.

Described by the *New York Times* as "achingly picturesque," the neoclassical redbrick buildings at Hollins date back to the mid-19th century. There are some modern structures, too, such as the Wetherill Visual Arts Center, which opened in 2004. Several buildings have been renovated in recent years, including Turner

Hall, Presser Hall, and Bradley Hall, which is now home to the university's Batten Leadership Institute.

General education requirements (known as Education through Skills and Perspective) stress breadth and depth across the curriculum. The skills component teaches students to write successfully, reason quantitatively, express themselves effectively, research astutely, and be adept technologically. The perspectives component includes seven areas of knowledge that help to explain how people view and understand the world: Aesthetic Analysis, Creative Expression, Premodern Worlds, Modern and Contemporary Worlds, Scientific Inquiry, Social and Cultural Diversities, and Global Systems and Languages. Two terms of physical education are also mandatory, as is Orientation Week, which includes academic programming, a day of community service, and plenty of time to form friendships with new classmates. Freshmen also participate in a mandatory first-year seminar.

> "This is an environment that encourages you to give your all."

Motivated students are encouraged to design their majors. Additionally, because Hollins belongs to the Seven-College Exchange*, its students may cross-register at any of the other six institutions. In addition to Hollins Abroad programs in Paris and London—to which students from all colleges and universities are invited to apply—Hollins offers its own students the opportunity to study on affiliated programs in countries around the world, including Argentina, Spain, Japan, Mexico, Ghana, Italy, Ireland, Greece, Germany, and South Africa. The annual Science Seminar features undergrad research in biology, chemistry, psychology, physics, and math, while the Batten Leadership Institute is the only college program in the nation that promotes personal and professional growth with videotaped performance reviews, senior mentoring, intensive communication skills groups, and board governance experience. The shorter January term offers a break for on-campus projects, travel, or internships, and alumnae help arrange housing in Washington and other cities. Students may earn a certificate in leadership studies through the Hollins Batten Leadership Institute. Students participate in classes, skill-building groups, seminars, and hands-on projects.

Academics are a top priority at Hollins, though competition is rare. "This is an environment that encourages you to give your all," explains one senior. "Faculty and students support one another throughout the more challenging courses." English, psychology, business, studio art, and communication studies are the most popular majors. Artists benefit from extensive internship opportunities at Christie's, Sotheby's, and various parts of the Smithsonian Institution, while the Hollins Repertory Dance Company, closely affiliated with the American Dance Festival, has been selected to perform at the Kennedy Center and at Aaron Davis Hall, Harlem's premier performing arts center. Classes are small and professors are well regarded. "The overall quality of teaching at Hollins is excellent. I have never been in doubt of my professors' intelligence, and their collective passion for and ability to pass on that knowledge is excellent," says one student.

"A common characteristic is that we're all go-getters. Hollins women are known for always working (for classes, clubs, jobs, and internships). We've also been described as quirky, and we are! We embrace our silly traditions and show off all the unique personalities here," says an English major. Fifty-two percent are Virginians; African Americans make up 12 percent of the total, while Asian Americans and Hispanics add 2 and 5 percent, respectively. "We have a very

> "A common characteristic is that we're all go-getters."

active gay and lesbian club called Outloud, and also an active women's studies department, that put together a lot of rallies and events," says a freshman. "Our campus has a definite liberal leaning, although there is a small, committed Republican group." Hollins hands out merit scholarships averaging more than $18,600 but no athletic scholarships.

(continued)

Student Loans: 77%
Average Debt: $ $ $ $
Phi Beta Kappa: Yes
Applicants: 814
Accepted: 66%
Enrolled: 24%
Grad in 6 Years: 56%
Returning Freshmen: 70%
Academics: ✏ ✏ ✏
Social: ☎ ☎ ☎
Q of L: ★ ★ ★ ★
Admissions: (540) 362-6401
Email Address: huadm@ hollins.edu

Strongest Programs:
English/Creative Writing
Visual and Performing Arts
Psychology
Communication Studies
Biology
Political Science

The annual Science Seminar features undergrad research in biology, chemistry, psychology, physics, and math.

Seventy-seven percent of Hollins students live in the dorms; they have to, unless they're married, older than 23, or living at home in Roanoke with their parents. "Most of the dorms are beautiful historic buildings full of character and comfort," says a student. Freshmen live in Randolph and Tinker; upperclassmen in Main, West, and East, which have 10-foot ceilings and hardwood floors. Singles are only available to upperclassmen, and there is a fee. Some rooms in Main, West, and East also boast brass doorknobs, walk-in closets, and even fireplaces. Students chow down in Moody or at the campus coffee shop, which is open late. "In general, this is the part of campus that people have the most problems with. The meal plan is mandatory (and overpriced)and provides sub par food," grumbles one student.

"Most of Hollins' social life occurs on campus," says a student. "There are lots of events and programs to attend each week, with occasional off-campus offerings that are also very popular." Hollins shuns sororities, but sporadic student efforts to bring them to campus draw lively debate. To fill the gap, the school organizes mixers, concerts, dances, and second-run movies each weekend. There's also a free shuttle to help students get around Roanoke, a city with "malls, shopping centers, and movie and live theaters," says a freshman. "It has a nice historic downtown with an organic farmer's market, but it is not densely urban like New York or Washington, D.C." As a result, road-tripping remains the preferred social option—to Hampden–Sydney College, Virginia Tech, the University of Virginia, or Washington and Lee.

The Hollins Outdoor Program offers hiking, spelunking, and other activities in the beautiful Shenandoah Valley and Blue Ridge Mountains. The on-campus stable complements the school's top-notch equestrian program, which has brought home the Old Dominion Athletic Conference championship multiple times in recent years. Women's tennis is also a recent conference champion, and the swim team has won national Division III championships. In addition to the varsity lacrosse, golf, soccer, basketball, volleyball, swimming, and tennis teams, fencing and field hockey are available as club sports.

"Hollins has continually pushed me to be better, to achieve more, to experience more," says a senior. As the number of women's colleges continues to dwindle, Hollins remains committed to offering single-sex education and a close-knit community. Students leave with confidence, critical thinking skills, and intellectual depth, thanks to a solid grounding in the liberal arts. And the school's Southern heritage doesn't hurt, either. "Hollins is a great school that empowers women," says one senior. "It has made me independent."

If You Apply To ➤ **Hollins:** Rolling admissions. Early decision: Nov. 1. Early action: Dec. 1. Financial aid: Feb. 15. Application fee: $40 (paper), free (online). Campus and alumnae interviews: optional, informational. SATs or ACTs: required. Subject Tests: optional. Accepts the Common Application. Essay question.

College of the Holy Cross

Worcester, MA 01610

A tight-knit Roman Catholic community steeped in church and tradition, much more so than relatively secularized Boston College. Many students are the second or third generation to attend. Set high on a hill above gritty Worcester, an hour from Boston. Sports teams compete with (and occasionally beat) schools 10 times HC's size.

Students at Holy Cross, a Roman Catholic college in the heart of New England, are devoted to the Jesuit tradition of becoming "men and women for others." Students on "the hill" are driven to do something for their college or community, whether it's a football player becoming a Big Brother or an off-campus senior becoming a student government senator. Peers and professors alike offer support and spiritual guidance, and bonds forged in the lab or on the field are strengthened through activities like SPUD (Student Programs for Urban Development), which provides community service opportunities. The classroom focus is critical thinking and writing, but the school's proximity to nine other colleges in the Boston area means Crusaders focus on their social lives as well.

> **"All students are taught by full professors."**

Located on one of the seven hills overlooking the industrial city of Worcester, the 174-acre Holy Cross campus is a registered arboretum. The school's landscaping has won national awards, including two first-place prizes as the best-designed and best-planted campus in the nation. Architectural styles range from classical to modern.

Holy Cross offers small classes—65 percent of those taken by freshmen have 19 or fewer students—which help faculty members keep in touch with undergraduates. HC's premed program boasts that it has twice the number of students accepted to medical school as the national average. Students also give high marks to the English, history, and economics and accounting programs. As might be expected, philosophy and religious studies are strong, and concentrations in Latin American studies and peace and conflict studies are popular, as these are the disciplines central to Jesuit missionary work. Community-based learning courses include two to two and a half hours of weekly service with local volunteer, education, or health organizations, in addition to time in the classroom.

All first-year students participate in Montserrat, a comprehensive program designed to enhance each student's academic and campus experience by integrating living and learning. The program features small, full-year seminars that facilitate collaboration among students and professors. The seminars are organized into five clusters, each devoted to a specific theme: the divine, the self, the natural world, global society, and core human questions. Students also live in the same residence hall and participate in cluster activities. "The ability to see familiar faces and interact both in the dorm and in the classroom is a great way for students to meet each other when they first arrive at Holy Cross," says a history major.

Holy Cross's general education requirements comprise 12 courses in 10 areas: modern or classical languages, social sciences, arts, literature, religion, philosophy, history, cross-cultural studies, science, and mathematics. Ideas and thinking are the focus rather than preparation for a specific vocation. Students say the climate is demanding and the classes intense, though most agree that the competition is healthy. "I would not say that the academic climate is overly competitive or cutthroat. Students want to see each other succeed and many participate in peer tutoring programs," says one junior. Professors earn high marks for their knowledge and compassion. "Professors are very accessible, personable, and willing to help," says one junior. Another student adds, "One of the great things about Holy Cross is that since it is solely undergraduate, all students are taught by full professors."

> **"HC students are outspoken and focused."**

Holy Cross is part of the Worcester Consortium*, which offers registration privileges at the region's most prestigious colleges and universities. Aspiring teachers will find education courses and student-teaching opportunities at local primary and secondary schools and a teacher certification program accredited by the Massachusetts Department of Education. Would-be engineers can choose Holy

---

Website: www.holycross.edu
Location: City Outskirts
Private
Total Enrollment: 2,891
Undergraduates: 2,891
Male/Female: 49/51
SAT Ranges: CR 600–700, M 620–680
ACT Ranges: 27–30
Financial Aid: 58%
Expense: Pr $ $ $
Student Loans: 55%
Average Debt: $ $ $
Phi Beta Kappa: Yes
Applicants: 7,228
Accepted: 34%
Enrolled: 32%
Grad in 6 Years: 93%
Returning Freshmen: 95%
Academics: ✍ ✍ ✍ ✍
Social: ☎ ☎ ☎ ☎
Q of L: ★ ★ ★ ★
Admissions: (508) 793-2443
Email Address: admissions@holycross.edu

Strongest Programs:
Biology/Premed
History
Economics
English

As might be expected, philosophy and religious studies are strong.

Cross's 3–2 dual-degree programs with Columbia or Dartmouth; a partnership with nearby Clark offers a B.A. and M.B.A., or a B.A. and M.A. in finance, in five years. Off-campus opportunities include academic internships in the community, 25 study abroad programs in 15 nations, and the Washington Semester*. "Students who participate in study abroad and the First Year Program usually speak highly of the programs," a senior says. HC's honors program enables a small number of juniors and seniors to enroll in exclusive courses and thesis-writing seminars, while the Fenwick Scholars program helps students design and carry out independent projects. Each April, approximately 300 Holy Cross students participate in a four-day conference that provides them with an opportunity to present the results of their independent work.

Would-be engineers can choose Holy Cross's 3–2 dual-degree programs with Columbia or Dartmouth.

HC students are "outspoken and focused," according to one senior. The religious influence at Holy Cross is somewhat greater than at other Jesuit schools—most students are Roman Catholic, 36 percent are in-staters, and just under half attended public high school—but daily mass is not required. The chaplain's office does offer an optional five-day silent retreat four times a year, in which student volunteers follow the spiritual exercises of Jesuit founder St. Ignatius Loyola. African Americans make up 5 percent of the student body, Asian Americans comprise 5 percent, and Hispanics account for 10 percent. Hot political issues include social justice, campus diversity, and homosexuality. Merit scholarships are awarded annually, with an average payout of $28,000, and student-athletes may vie for 58 athletic scholarships in seven sports.

Ninety-one percent of Holy Cross students live in the residence halls, where freshmen and sophomores have double rooms, and juniors and seniors may opt for two- and three-bedroom suites—with living rooms and bathrooms, but no kitchens. Floors are single sex; buildings are co-ed. Most first-years live on "Easy Street," the row of five dorms (Healy, Leahy, Hanselman, Clark, and Mulledy) on the college's central hill next to the Hogan Campus Center. Wheeler, Loyola, Alumni, and Carlin house mostly upperclassmen. "Holy Cross has a cleaning service and they clean the bathrooms and take the trash out on a regular basis, which helps keep the residence halls well maintained," a psychology major reports. Because there are no Greek organizations, dorm life takes center stage. Each dorm has its own T-shirt, and they compete against each other for prizes in athletic and other contests, says a philosophy major. Doors have combination locks, which means no worries about forgetting your keys when you walk to the shower. Dining options include several campus eateries and the main dining hall; students report the food to be tasty and plentiful. Students say they feel safe on campus. "Campus security is great," a student observes. "The officers are friendly and helpful."

"Volunteering is one way students live out the Holy Cross mission."

An hour from Beantown, Cape Cod's beaches, and the ski slopes of the White Mountains, Worcester is "a great college town," says a student. Another adds, "Currently, there are over twelve colleges in Worcester, making it a city that accepts college students and has a lot of things for students to explore." A school shuttle service takes students to the orchestra, the Worcester Centrum for athletic events and rock concerts, and the town's museum. HC abides by Massachusetts liquor law: Students under 21 can't drink at the campus pub. If they're caught with alcohol, they're put on probation and parents are notified. Still, as with most schools, students who seek to imbibe can find booze, regardless of their age. Since students are discouraged from having cars, most take advantage of events organized by the Campus Activities Board. "Most of the social life at the College does take place on campus because most people live in the dorms. The Campus Activities Board and other organizations do offer events in the campus center and elsewhere especially

Tradition is big at Holy Cross.

for those under the age of 21," a student says. The college also organizes trips to New York City and Providence, Rhode Island, and there are countless service opportunities. "Volunteering is one way students live out the Holy Cross mission," a student says.

Tradition is big at Holy Cross, from Alumni Weekend to HC by the Sea (a week in Cape Cod at the end of the year). Midnight breakfasts provide sustenance as students cram for finals, while the 100 Days weekend begins the senior class countdown to graduation. Spring Weekend brings well-known performers. Would-be matchmakers can set up their roommates on dates at the Opportunity Knocks dance. And of course, given the high percentage of Irish Catholic students, St. Patrick's Day is an occasion for celebration. Recent Patriot League champs include women's ice hockey and men's football. Seventy percent of HC students participate in intramural sports.

Holy Cross is keeping the faith—its emphasis on Catholicism and the Jesuit tradition, that is—even as administrators place a renewed emphasis on academics and small classes. "There is an unrivaled sense of community here," says a senior. "Holy Cross has so much to offer." Indeed, the close-knit atmosphere offers students a multitude of opportunities to serve others, challenge themselves, and create lasting friendships.

If You Apply To ➤

Holy Cross: Early decision: Dec. 15. Regular admissions: Jan. 15. Financial aid: Feb. 1. Housing: May 1. Application fee: $60. Campus and alumni interviews: optional, evaluative. SATs or ACTs: optional. Subject Tests: optional. Accepts the Common Application. Essay question: Common Application.

Hood College

401 Rosemont Avenue, Frederick, MD 21701

With a decade of coeducation under its belt, Hood faces the challenge of building a fully co-ed environment. Male enrollment is now over 30 percent. A major asset: Hood's strategic location, one hour from D.C. and Baltimore. Hood's distinctive core curriculum stresses thematic study.

Founded as a women's college in 1893, Hood College undertook a bold reinvention of itself in 2003. That's the year it began admitting men as regular residential students (males had been commuting students since 1971). Now members of both sexes have the opportunity to partake of Hood's traditional mix of professional and liberal arts offerings on a campus strategically located in a historic Civil War setting.

Hood's strikingly beautiful 50-acre campus features redbrick buildings and lush, tree-shaded lawns. Situated in the Civil War town of Frederick, Hood is within an hour and a half of nearly 30 colleges and within minutes of a major National Cancer Institute research complex, high-tech firms, small and large businesses, and both Washington, D.C., and Baltimore. On campus, technology programs, which are already important, get a further boost thanks to the Hodson Science and Technology Center.

"Hood is not extraordinarily competitive."

Students see their school's biggest strength in its people: students, staff, and faculty. "There are so many cultures and ethnicities and traditions to be shared," says one junior. "I love living here. I'm having the time of my life." First-year students

Website: www.hood.edu
Location: Small City
Private
Total Enrollment: 1,383
Undergraduates: 1,270
Male/Female: 34/66
SAT Ranges: CR 470–610, M 470–590
ACT Ranges: 20–25
Financial Aid: 98%
Expense: Pr $
Student Loans: 75%
Average Debt: $ $ $
Phi Beta Kappa: No
Applicants: 1,788

(continued)

Accepted: 77%

Enrolled: 20%

Grad in 6 Years: 68%

Returning Freshmen: 77%

Academics: ✍ ✍ ✍

Social: ☎ ☎ ☎

Q of L: ★ ★ ★

Admissions: (800) 922-1599

Email Address: admissions@
hood.edu

Strongest Programs:
Psychology
Management
Biology
Education
Art
Social Work

Education, especially
early childhood, is
a program of note,
as are psychology,
communications,
English, and
management.

participate in Hood's First-Year Read program, and can opt to enroll in writing-intensive First-Year Seminars and Living Learning Communities, all designed to provide the kinds of informal learning opportunities and structured classroom environments that help build academic skills, confidence, and a sense of belonging.

"Hood is not extraordinarily competitive," says a sophomore, "although hard work is required to do well." Hood's required core curriculum is divided into three parts. Foundation courses include English, foreign language, computation, physical education, and fitness. Methods of Inquiry offers courses that acquaint students with scientific thought, historical and social/behavioral analysis, and philosophy. The Civilization section requires coursework in modern technology and Western and non-Western civilization at the junior/senior level. Even with these comprehensive requirements, there is still a great deal of flexibility; creative interdepartmental majors are often approved.

Hood's major strength lies in the sciences, especially the biology department, with its special emphases on molecular biology, marine biology, and environmental science and policy. A semester-long coastal studies program takes students along the East Coast on a biological educational mission. Education, especially early childhood, is a program of note, as are psychology, communications, English, and management. The graduate school of mostly commuting students is as large as the undergraduate program. Middle Eastern studies and a B.S. in nursing completion program are available as well.

Students say the learning environment is more rigorous than competitive. "The professors here are extremely intelligent with excellent credentials," raves one student. In general, Hood students are "interested in their education and are serious and hardworking," says a sophomore. Hood students praise the competence and accessibility of the faculty. "The teachers want their students to succeed and are very accessible when students need help," says a math major. Only labs are taught by graduate assistants, and 67 percent of freshman classes have 19 or fewer students.

"The traditions are amazing."

If you really want to stimulate the brain cells, the four-year honors program features team-taught courses and a sophomore-year seminar on the ethics of social and individual responsibility with student involvement in a community service project. Ten percent of students complete internships that include overseas jobs for language and business majors and legislative and cultural positions in Washington, D.C. With the outstanding resources of the Catherine Filene Shouse Career Center (including a national electronic listing for résumés), students have a leg up on their next step in life, whether it be their career or graduate school. Other study abroad destinations include the Dominican Republic, Korea, Japan, South America, Spain, France, Australia, Egypt, and South Africa.

One student says that characterizing her classmates is difficult because "we all come from such different financial, cultural, ethnic, and personal backgrounds. The only thing I can say for sure is that we come here to learn." Twelve percent of the student body are African American, while Hispanics and Asian Americans combine for another 10 percent. Students say the campus leans slightly left, politically speaking, and key issues include the environment and fiscal concerns. Hood provides merit scholarships worth an average of $14,658.

Hood's residence halls are well liked, with good-sized, air-conditioned rooms. One of the dorms, Shriner Hall, has been recently renovated. The lottery system is based on seniority, and 56 percent of students live on campus. Freshmen can expect to be assigned to doubles (seniors and juniors can compete for singles), and language majors may choose to live in French-, Spanish-, or German-language houses. First-year students can also elect to live in themed living/learning communities within the residence halls.

Social life among the students is centered on the dorms, as each has its own personality as well as its own house council, rules, and social activities. Students report that there are parties every weekend, along with movies, dances, or other forms of entertainment. The Whitaker Campus Center, with its pool tables, snack bar, bookstore, and meeting rooms, offers a great gathering place for residents and commuters 24 hours a day. "If you don't like to stay on campus, there are restaurants, bars, clubs, malls, and coffeehouses within 10 minutes of the college by car," explains an English major. A one-hour car ride delivers students to the multiple diversions in Baltimore and Washington, D.C. Campus alcohol policies have been tightened and follow state law, but drinking is generally not a big deal at Hood. "At parties and events, you have to show ID to get alcohol," one senior says. "However, in the dorms at other times, it is possible for underage students to get alcohol from those 'of age.'" Students also frequent scenic Frederick, which is described as small, safe, and beautiful.

With over a century of history, Hood is rife with traditions. Some of the most important ones include Class Ring dinner and formal, a performance of Handel's *Messiah*, and Spring Parties, a weekend of carnival activities and dances. The Blazers compete in Division III and competitive teams include men's and women's track and men's basketball. Recreational and intramural sports attract 20 percent of undergraduates; popular activities include soccer, touch football, kickball, basketball, and volleyball.

While Hood has undergone the major change from a women's college to a co-ed institution, its mission remains the same: to prepare students to face the challenges of a fast-changing society and professional environment. "The traditions are amazing," boasts a sophomore, "topped only by professors who care and friends you'll have forever."

> *The lottery system is based on seniority, and 56 percent of students live on campus.*

Overlaps

Towson, Salisbury, Stevenson, Montgomery College, University of Maryland, McDaniel

If You Apply To ➤ **Hood:** Early decision: Nov. 15. Early action: Dec. 1. Regular admissions: Feb. 15. Financial aid: Feb. 15. Housing: May 1. Application fee: $35 (paper), free (online). Campus interviews: optional, informational. No alumni interviews. SATs or ACTs: required (optional for those with qualifying GPA). Subject Tests: optional. Accepts the Common Application. No essay question.

Hope College

P.O. Box 9000, Holland, MI 49422

Hope has an in-between size—bigger than most small colleges but smaller than a university. It is evangelical in orientation, but less than a quarter of the students are members of the Reformed Church in America. In addition to the liberal arts, Hope offers education, engineering, and nursing, and makes undergraduate research a priority.

Each fall since 1897, Hope College freshmen have spent three grueling hours engaged in "the Pull," an epic tug-of-war against the sophomores, who stand assembled on the opposite end of a 650-pound rope across the 250-foot-wide Black River. This well-known annual tradition evokes the daily struggle Hope students face: maintaining their faith in a world eager to challenge it at every turn. The heritage of Hope's Dutch founders remains strong and visible on campus, but you don't have to be a member of the Reformed Church in America to appreciate this conservative Christian college. "The academic programs, particularly the research and collaboration opportunities, far surpass those of Hope's rivals," says a sophomore.

Website: www.hope.edu
Location: Small City
Private
Total Enrollment: 3,191
Undergraduates: 3,191
Male/Female: 40/60
SAT Ranges: CR 510–660, M 520–670

(continued)

ACT Ranges: 23–29
Financial Aid: 89%
Expense: Pr $
Student Loans: 65%
Average Debt: $ $ $ $
Phi Beta Kappa: Yes
Applicants: 3,491
Accepted: 85%
Enrolled: 30%
Grad in 6 Years: 77%
Returning Freshmen: 90%
Academics: ✑ ✑ ✑
Social: ☎ ☎ ☎
Q of L: ★ ★ ★
Admissions: (616) 395-7850
Email Address: admissions@
   hope.edu

Strongest Programs:
Biology
Chemistry
Dance
Education
English
Political Science
Psychology
Religion

*Professors are
generally lauded for
their knowledge and
their skill behind
the lectern.*

The college, founded in 1866, is situated on six blocks near downtown Holland, the tulip capital of the nation (population 60,000), and a short bike ride from the shores of Lake Michigan. There's a lush pine grove in the center of campus, which features an eclectic array of buildings in architectural styles ranging from 19th-century Flemish to modern. The college has undergone a bit of a building boom, opening $70 million in new facilities in the last few years.

Among Hope's academic offerings, the sciences (especially biology and chemistry) stand out, with excellent laboratory facilities and faculty who are eager to involve students in their funded research. During the school year, undergraduates often conduct advanced experiments and even publish papers; come summer, close to 180 geology, chemistry, mathematics, computer science, and physics and engineering majors participate in research full-time. Not surprisingly, many science majors go on to medical and engineering schools and Ph.D. programs. For those otherwise inclined, Hope's offerings in political science, psychology, dance, English, and business administration are solid, too. Hope's Department of Communication is one of the Speech Communication Association's two nationwide Programs of Excellence.

> **"There is a focus on teamwork and community."**

The academic climate is demanding and collaborative. "While there is a competitive edge to classes, there is also a focus on teamwork and community," says a senior. Most Hope students select a major from one of the college's fields, although the truly adventurous may design their own composite major. Hope's general education program, designed around the themes "knowing how" and "knowing about," includes a first-year seminar, which provides "an intellectual transition into Hope." Courses in expository writing, health dynamics, math and natural science, foreign language, religious studies, social sciences, the arts, and cultural heritage are also required; some must have a focus on cultural diversity. Students also complete a senior seminar, and a two-credit freshman seminar linked with academic advising. Professors are generally lauded for their knowledge and their skill behind the lectern. "The professors are definitely above average," says a senior. "Each class is taught by a full professor, including freshman classes."

Hope offers off-campus programs through the Great Lakes Colleges Association*, including semesters at other U.S. colleges and options combining classes and internships. Students may study abroad in more than 60 countries; approximately one-third do so. The modern and classical language departments offer students proficient in a second language the chance to use their skills in volunteer work and research with faculty members, while the Visiting Writers Series gives students an opportunity to interact with noteworthy authors.

Less than a fourth of Hope's students belong to the Reformed Church in America, and the students "tend to be very involved in academics, extracurriculars, athletics, and social events," says a junior. Within the college's prevailing Christian atmosphere, most students say there is room for other voices and viewpoints. With some effort, they can find a diversity of opinions and backgrounds amongst the friendly, fairly homogeneous student body. "Hope students are unique in their desire to incorporate faith into learning," says a junior. "Hope students are not required to attend chapel, but the chapel is full to a standing-room-only capacity on a regular basis." Sixty-eight percent of students hail from Michigan; African Americans account for 3 percent of the student body, while Hispanics and Asian Americans combine for 8 percent. "Currently, the biggest social issue on campus is the college's position on homosexuality," reports one student. Merit scholarships averaging $7,919 are available to qualified students, but there are no athletic scholarships.

> **"The professors are definitely above average."**

Eighty-one percent of Hope students live in university-sponsored housing. Hope's housing options include on-campus apartments, small houses called cottages, and traditional dorms, arranged in freshman clusters by gender or co-ed by suite. "Dorm rooms tend to be a bit small, but the dorms themselves are comfortable and well maintained," says a student. First-year students are assigned dorms and roommates; upperclassmen get first pick in the annual lottery. Only seniors and married students may live off campus. Students complain about the lack of parking, but there are few negative comments about campus security. On-campus students eat in one of two large dining halls where the fare—especially homemade bread and desserts—is tasty. "The staff is friendly and the food is relatively edible," says a philosophy major.

For those who stay around on weekends, "most social life takes place on campus," says one student. "Some students party, but there is no pressure to do so." The Social Activities Committee brings in comedians, bands, and hypnotists, shows movies in campus auditoriums, and plans the Spring Festival carnival and Winter Fantasia dance. "'Good clean fun' is their motto," says a student, "and that's exactly what it is." Seven fraternities and eight sororities, all local organizations, claim 10 percent of the men and 12 percent of the women, respectively. Students caught drinking must perform community service, although plenty of students do that anyway. Among the 80 student organizations are a

The Visiting Writers Series gives students an opportunity to interact with noteworthy authors.

"Some students party, but there is no pressure to do so."

variety of active religious life organizations, including the Fellowship of Christian Athletes, Hope for the Nations (ministry), and InterVarsity Christian Fellowship. There are a slew of unique student clubs, including Silent Praise, which seeks to praise God through American Sign Language (ASL) and worship music.

Holland is also the site of spring's Tulip Time, one of the largest U.S. flower festivals. When Hope's cozy campus and the quaint town of Holland get too close for comfort, students find relief at the beaches of Lake Michigan or drive 30 minutes to Grand Rapids, which offers some large-city amenities and good weekend rental deals at the ski slopes. Chicago and Detroit are other typical destinations for those trying to hit the road.

On the field and on the court, Hope's Flying Dutchmen are fearless and talented Division III competitors. Hope teams are frequent conference champions; solid programs include football, men's golf, men's and women's basketball, and men's swimming and diving. The college has also won the Commissioner's Cup of the Michigan Intercollegiate Athletic Association multiple times; the trophy recognizes the conference's best cumulative sports program for men and women. Especially important are any competitions against Calvin (a century-old rivalry) and football versus Albion and Kalamazoo. Nearly two-thirds of students take part in 17 intramural sports, which range from soccer and softball to inner-tube water polo.

Hope's academic and athletic programs continue to grow and prosper, helped out by an array of new facilities. For those seeking an institution with traditional Christian roots and an emphasis on undergraduates, Hope may be worth a look. "Hope is a place where students are challenged to become better students," says one senior, "but, more important, better people."

Overlaps

Grand Valley State, Michigan State, University of Michigan, Calvin, Albion, Western Michigan, Alma, Central Michigan

If You Apply To ➤

Hope: Rolling admissions. Financial aid: Mar. 1. Housing: May 1. Application fee: $50 (paper), $35 (online). Campus interviews: evaluative. No alumni interviews. SATs or ACTs: required. No Subject Tests. Essay question.

The mid-Atlantic's premier evangelical Christian college. Women outnumber men nearly 2 to 1. All students are required to take Biblical literature and Introduction to Christianity, and most go to chapel three times a week. Perks include a 386-acre horseback-riding facility. When rural New York gets claustrophobic, the college offers a variety of possibilities for a semester away.

Website: www.houghton.edu
Location: Rural
Private
Total Enrollment: 1,094
Undergraduates: 1,084
Male/Female: 34/66
SAT Ranges: CR 530–640, M 510–620
ACT Ranges: 22–27
Financial Aid: 97%
Expense: Pr $
Student Loans: 79%
Average Debt: $ $
Phi Beta Kappa: No
Applicants: 830
Accepted: 73%
Enrolled: 38%
Grad in 6 Years: 67%
Returning Freshmen: 88%
Academics: ✍ ✍ ✍
Social: ☎ ☎ ☎
Q of L: ★ ★ ★ ★
Admissions: (800) 777-2556
Email Address: admission@houghton.edu

Strongest Programs:
Music
Biology
Bible
English
Education
Psychology

Located in the bucolic New York town that shares its name, Houghton College offers a solid, growing academic program and strong athletic teams, while remaining committed to its core mission as a Christian liberal arts school. Sponsored by The Wesleyan Church, Houghton celebrates its Christian heritage and tries to ensure that students do the same. Applicants must explain in their essays why they desire to be a part of a Christian academic community, and current students are expected to attend a set amount of chapel services throughout the semester. These expectations help create true community on campus. One junior says, "Houghton combines academic rigor, athletic excellence, and intentional spiritual formation in a fun-loving and Christ-centered community."

Houghton's scenic hilltop campus covers 1,300 acres of rural beauty, surrounded by vast expanses of western New York countryside. The academic buildings are a mix of area fieldstone and brick with ivy-covered walls. Current construction includes new athletic facilities slated to open in 2014.

Houghton students must complete general education requirements known as Integrative Studies, designed to provide a context and framework for the entire educational program. Freshmen must take Biblical Literature, Writing in the Liberal Arts, and a course titled Transitions, aimed at easing the transition to college. The Houghton Honors Program allows qualified students an intensive, hands-on experience in the sciences or in the humanities along with study abroad experiences in Eastern Europe, Central Europe, or the United Kingdom. The Science Honors Program allows select students to engage a significant scientific question in a research-oriented program. According to the administration, all physics students are involved in ongoing research with their professors, providing a model that will be utilized in chemistry and biology as well.

The school's most popular programs include business administration, biology, inclusive childhood education, psychology, and communication. "Communications is the fastest growing department, with fantastic faculty and classes," cheers one sophomore. Unusual minors such as equestrian studies—which takes advantage of Houghton's 386-acre riding facility—are available. Students say Houghton's academic climate is rigorous, but not overwhelmingly so. "The academic climate is fairly serious. It's competitive in the sense that the tests, assignments, and work load are challenging, but the teachers are very willing to help students achieve their goals," says a junior. Across departments, the faculty is lauded. "All the professors are open to sharing their career journey and use real world examples often to cement important theories or concepts in our minds," says a student.

"The social life mostly revolves around campus."

Forty-six percent of Houghton students have taken advantage of off-campus study, with programs in Australia, New Zealand, Tanzania, Thailand, Honduras, Sierra Leone, Costa Rica, and other far-flung locales around the globe. Students who want to get away within the U.S. can spend a semester at any Christian College Consortium* member school or participate in the American Studies program in Washington, D.C., sponsored by the Council for Christian Colleges and Universities*. A 3–2 engineering program with Clarkson University (NY) is also available. New degrees in international development and fine arts have been added recently.

More than half of those who enroll at Houghton are from New York. "Students that attend Houghton tend to have a global vision," says one communication major. "They are often missions-minded and like to serve others," adds a classmate. African Americans account for 3 percent of the student body; Hispanics 2 percent; and Asian Americans 1 percent. "The issues that get the most attention on campus are homosexuality, abortion, and social justice," a senior reports. "Houghton students tend to be politically conservative and big on being the hands and feet of Christ to a hurting world." Qualified undergrads receive merit scholarships—97 percent of all undergraduates receive some form of financial aid.

All physics students are involved in ongoing research with their professors.

Houghton's single-sex dorms, townhouses, and apartments house 87 percent of students. "Dorm life was great and the people on my floor became like a family to me," cheers one sophomore. Students are required to live in the residence halls as freshmen and sophomores. After their first two years, some students move off campus, but many opt for college-approved townhouses where regulations are self-imposed. Students say the dining options are edible if not diverse and security is not cause for great concern. "Campus security is quite good, and students feel completely safe and at ease," says a sophomore.

"Homecoming weekend is a huge event in the fall."

Houghton's boondocks village is truly small, lacking even a traffic light, says a student. "Besides the college, there is a post office, a Chinese restaurant, a church, a Subway, and a dance studio," says one student. "That's about it." Students are involved in service projects such as Big Brothers Big Sisters and nursing home visitation, because the area surrounding the college is one of the poorest in New York State. "The social life mostly revolves around campus. There is always lots of student programming available from the Campus Activities Board and other student programs," says an art major. The college even has its own ski trails. The town of Houghton is dry and college policy forbids alcohol. "The policy is pretty clear that students are not to drink on campus, and you sign a community covenant that states you will not use any inebriating substances during your time as a student of Houghton," says a senior. Students eagerly anticipate annual celebrations for homecoming, Christian Life Emphasis Week, and the annual Christmas Prism. "Homecoming weekend is a huge event in the fall," says a freshman.

More than half of those who enroll at Houghton are from New York.

Soccer is the spectator sport of choice at Houghton, especially since there is no football team. The women's squad brought home eight consecutive American Mideast Conference titles between 2002 and 2010. The college has recently been approved for NCAA Division III provisional membership and a $24 million field house and is under construction to accommodate for the college's expanding athletic teams including baseball, lacrosse, tennis, and golf. Sixty-five percent of students participate in intramural sports.

Students don't come to Houghton for the surrounding town, which is 30 minutes by car from the nearest mall, or for the weather, which can be tough once winter sets in. But they do come, and for good reason, says a sophomore: there's little to distract them from their studies, their campus's natural beauty, and their connection to God. "Houghton has a great atmosphere," observes one student. "Not only is it a reputable academic institution, but it is an institution with a global vision that strives to equip students to make an impact."

Overlaps

Gordon, Roberts Wesleyan, Messiah, Grove City, Cedarville, Liberty, Wheaton (IL), Geneva

If You Apply To ➤

Houghton: Rolling admissions. Application fee: $40. Campus interviews: optional, evaluative. No alumni interviews. SATs or ACTs: required. Subject Tests: optional. Music majors apply directly to music program. Essay question.

2400 Sixth Street NW, Washington, D.C., 20059

The flagship university of black America and the first to integrate the black experience into all areas of study. Strategically located in D.C., Howard depends on Congress for much of its funding. Preprofessional programs such as nursing, business, and architecture are among the most popular. Only 7 percent of the students are an ethnicity other than African American.

Website: www.howard.edu

Location: City Center

Private

Total Enrollment: 10,002

Undergraduates: 6,688

Male/Female: 33/67

SAT Ranges: CR 490–580, M 480–580

ACT Ranges: 21–26

Financial Aid: 93%

Expense: Pr $

Student Loans: 69%

Average Debt: N/A

Phi Beta Kappa: Yes

Applicants: 9,015

Accepted: 54%

Enrolled: 32%

Grad in 6 Years: 63%

Returning Freshmen: 81%

Academics: ✍ ✍

Social: ☎ ☎ ☎

Q of L: ★ ★ ★

Admissions: (202) 806-2763

Email Address: admissions@howard.edu

Strongest Programs:
Biology
Psychology
Business
History
Communications

Contrary to the advice of early black leaders such as Booker T. Washington, who argued in favor of technical training, Howard has promoted the liberal arts since its inception. This focus has served the school well; Howard's law school counts the late Supreme Court Justice Thurgood Marshall among its alumni, and Nobel Prize–winning author Toni Morrison went here, too. In recent years, Howard has strengthened its financial position and has begun implementing a strategic plan structured around "Leadership for America and the Global Community." The four-part plan focuses on strengthening academic programs and services, promoting excellence in teaching and research, increasing private support, and enhancing national and community service.

> **"Come to Howard ready to study."**

Founded in 1866 by General Oliver Howard primarily to educate freed slaves, the university now operates five campuses and serves roughly 10,000 students. The 89-acre main campus houses most classrooms, dorms, and administrative offices, as well as the university center, the Founders, and undergraduate and medical and dental libraries. The Howard Law Center, with a new library, is on the west campus near Rock Creek Park; the Divinity School is on a 22-acre site in northeast Washington; and there's also a 108-acre campus in suburban Beltsville, Maryland, and a campus in Silver Spring. Architecturally, the main campus is a blend of old and new, with numerous sculptures and murals created by Jacob Lawrence, Richard Hunt, Elizabeth Catlett, and the late Romare Bearden. The campus is an easy bus ride from the attractions of the nation's capital.

The school has excellent programs in business, computer sciences, and psychology, and it has intensified offerings in the STEM fields—science, technology, engineering, and math—and Africana and diaspora studies. Other intriguing academic options are accelerated programs for a B.S. on the way to a medical or dental degree, coursework in the institute of jazz studies, programs in zoology and engineering (especially electrical engineering), and programs in communication science and disorders. The most popular major is biology, followed by political science, psychology, information sciences, and radio and television. The programs in ancient Mediterranean and international studies have become robust.

All students must complete general education requirements, which vary by school or college but uniformly encompass 18 credits in science, social sciences, humanities, computer literacy, math, languages, and one Afro-American studies course. Freshman seminars and various other special programs for first-year students are available in the undergraduate schools, such as communication, engineering, and arts and sciences. Seniors in arts and sciences must weather a comprehensive exam to graduate.

In general, students say that the workload at Howard is demanding. "Some courses are more rigorous than others. But overall this school is tough," says a junior. Another student adds, "Come to Howard ready to study." Most students agree that professors are ready and willing to help when asked, though academic advising is not Howard's strength. "Sometimes you may get professors who do not know how to break down anything," explains a psychology major. "Then it is your job to talk up and ask questions. You must ask questions because a closed mouth does not get fed!" Students who need a break from the academic scene seek out internships in town or across the country. Many also study abroad at one of the more than 200 institutions in 36 countries where Howard grants credit. Howard students can cross-register for courses at 13 other area schools including (among others) American University, Catholic University, Georgetown, George Washington, and Corcoran College of Art & Design.

Ninety-three percent of Howard students are African American, and 96 percent hail from outside of the District of Columbia. Most come from decidedly middle-class backgrounds. Although Howard seems to be a very cohesive community, career-minded and highly motivated men and women fit in best, students say, and most are politically liberal. "It's a very competitive school, from grades to fashion," says a junior. Hot issues include women's empowerment, student government, and fraternities and sororities. Fraternities and sororities do not have their own housing or dining facilities, and only 2 percent of men and 3 percent of women go Greek. Howard awards more than 100 athletic scholarships in a variety of sports. A range of renewable merit scholarships are available on a first-come, first-served basis to freshman applicants based on their standardized test scores and GPA. Transfer students are also eligible for a separate pool of merit scholarships. A deferred-payment plan also allows families to pay each semester's tuition in three installments.

The school has excellent programs in business, computer sciences, and psychology.

Interestingly, Howard is one of a handful of universities in the nation supported partly by federal subsidies; these days, the school gets about 55 percent of its budget from Congress. Bethune Hall, a $14 million housing complex, has helped ease the space crunch, but less than half of Howard's students are accommodated on campus, and facilities receive less-than-stellar reviews. "It is quite difficult to get a room at times," says a sophomore economics major. "Housing at Howard is average in regards to availability, maintenance, and comfort," says one student. Freshmen get room assignments, while upperclassmen take their chances in a lottery. Many students live off campus purely to avoid the mandatory meal plan. Still, the administration is doing its best to bring students back, and Drew, Meridian Hill, Baldwin, Carver, Truth, and Crandall halls have recently gotten face-lifts.

"It's a very competitive school, from grades to fashion."

Weekends bring an assortment of social happenings to campus, many of which take place in the student center. On-campus parties and sports events are always big draws, but the bars of Georgetown and Adams Morgan, the restaurants and clubs in the "New U" Street corridor, and the MCI Center arena (home to the NBA's Wizards and the NHL's Capitals)—most accessible by public transit—also beckon. Though small in numbers, the Greeks are "an integral part of the university."

The programs in ancient Mediterranean and international studies have become robust.

Athletics are also an important presence on campus, particularly Bison basketball, soccer, football, women's cross-country, and volleyball, and the highlight of the season is always the grudge match with Hampton University to decide which school is the "true HU." Students list Howard's homecoming as one of the best annual events, along with various Greekfests, concerts, and talent shows that alumni, current students, and members of the community enjoy together.

Among America's historically black colleges and universities, Howard stands out as the standard-bearer, a longtime center of excellence and leadership. Its scholarship and collections of artworks, rare books, manuscripts, and photographs are a repository of the African American experience and offer students unique educational opportunities.

Overlaps
Atlanta, Clark, Florida A&M, Hampton, Morgan State, Spelman

The College of Idaho

(formerly Albertson College) Caldwell, ID 83605

Got a map? You'll need a sharp eye to spot C of I, the *Fiske Guide*'s only liberal arts school between the Rocky Mountains and the West Coast. Innovative programs include leadership studies and environmental studies. Over two-thirds of the students are from Idaho.

Website: www.collegeofidaho .edu

Location: Small Town

Private

Total Enrollment: 1,016

Undergraduates: 1,002

Male/Female: 42/58

SAT Ranges: CR 470–630, M 480–600

ACT Ranges: 22–27

Financial Aid: 98%

Expense: Pr $

Student Loans: 55%

Average Debt: $ $ $

Phi Beta Kappa: No

Applicants: 1,388

Accepted: 65%

Enrolled: 32%

Grad in 6 Years: 64%

Returning Freshmen: 83%

Academics: ✐ ✐ ✐

Social: ☎ ☎ ☎

Q of L: ★ ★ ★

Admissions: (208) 459-5305

Email Address: admission@ collegeofidaho.edu

Strongest Programs:
Biology
Business
Psychology
English
Political Science

With an emphasis on education and experiential learning, The College of Idaho (formerly Albertson College), the state's oldest four-year university, offers students an opportunity to earn a solid liberal arts education through small classes in a small town. Outside class, the school's scenic environment allows sports and nature enthusiasts to explore freely before heading back into the classrooms. At C of I, you'll be exposed to "hard work, great opportunities, and a healthy amount of fun," says a freshman.

The college is in the small town of Caldwell, where the atmosphere is calm and serene. For those looking for a little excitement, the state capital of Boise is a short drive from campus. Also nearby are some of Idaho's most scenic locations such as beautiful mountains, deserts, and white-water rivers. The school, originally a Presbyterian college, first planted roots in downtown Caldwell in 1891 and then moved to its present site in 1910, where its 21 buildings now inhabit 43 acres.

The school's academic schedule is composed of 12-week semesters, spring and fall, separated by a four-week winter session, during which students can assist professors with research, take an internship, volunteer, or travel abroad. The PEAK program offers a distinctive undergraduate curriculum that allows students to graduate with an academic major and three minors in a total of four academic areas—the humanities, social sciences, natural sciences, and a professional field. Freshmen go through a first-year program that includes reading a common book, a junior or senior mentor, a team of advisors, and a weeklong orientation that includes an off-campus overnight stay. First-year students demonstrating leadership potential are invited to a series of seminars to draw them into the leadership studies program, a business minor. The two libraries have nearly 200,000 volumes and are accessible online 24 hours a day.

> **"Almost everything, from the traditions to the pub, is initiated by students."**

The College of Idaho offers more than 25 majors; biology, business, psychology, health, and history are among the majors recommended by students, and preprofessional majors, such as premed, prenursing, and prelaw are also popular and strong. "Our history department is absolutely wonderful," raves one student. "I came from high school hating history and, after taking a few courses, I've come to love it." Undergraduate research opportunities are available in all fields, including biology, chemistry, and psychology, and students present their findings at state and regional conferences. The college cooperates with the University of Idaho to offer a five-year course of study in engineering. The Center for Experiential Learning coordinates out-of-classroom experiences, such as international education and service learning. For those who want to venture abroad (physically or mentally), the college offers several options, including attending a foreign university, traveling overseas during the summer and winter breaks, and taking international studies on campus. Travel has really taken off, with study abroad opportunities in nearly 60 countries around the world.

The academic climate demands plenty of attention. "The classes are fairly tough," says one student, but "people aren't really competing to be at the top of their class." Sixty percent of all classes at C of I have 19 or fewer students and faculty are praised for their knowledge and accessibility. "The teachers at The College of Idaho are truly phenomenal. Freshmen are always taught by full professors," a senior says. The school's small size also allows students to skip the registration hassles that plague larger institutions.

"Our student body is very laid-back," says one senior. "We're also very liberal in our views and opinions." Seventy-five percent of the students are from Idaho. Fourteen percent are Hispanic, 2 percent are African American, and Asian Americans add another 3 percent. Political issues receive plenty of attention on campus, and debates about the school's honor code are not uncommon among students. The college offers merit scholarships, as well as 203 athletic scholarships in 18 sports. Not surprisingly, some of those dollars are set aside for skiers.

Sixty-two percent of students live on campus. Each room in the five residence halls has individual heating and cooling and hookups for Internet access, and each hall has a computer lab. "Dorm life is great," says a senior. "The dorms have been remodeled lately, which has made a big difference," adds an accounting major. For those looking to get their food on, C of I provides "a grill, deli, salad bar, pizza, and vegetarian options" that are "to die for," according to one student. Students feel safe on campus; the college recently implemented a round-the-clock escort system, and there are many emergency stations around campus.

Fifteen percent of men and 22 percent of women participate in the Greek system, which dominates campus social life. Annual social highlights include Winterfest, Spring Fling, and homecoming week. Games against rival Northwest Nazarene also attract attention. "Everyone hangs out on or around campus," says one student. Another adds, "There are plenty of events on campus." Caldwell, with 46,000 people, is not a great spot for college students, but students get involved by helping out the local school district. "Finals breakfasts" offer something for bleary-eyed students to look forward to during finals week. At midnight on Tuesday, faculty and staff cook breakfast for students. Nearby Boise is a popular destination for shopping, dining, cultural events, and volunteering. Many students take advantage of hiking, kayaking, and skiing in the surrounding area, and many hit the road during a week-long break taken every six weeks.

Men's basketball is a crowd-pleaser, and the team has made C of I students proud, chalking up victories in the NAIA Division II competition. The women's Coyotes team is solid, too, and is ranked in the NAIA Top 25. Women's cross-country finished second at nationals in 2012 and women's volleyball has won seven consecutive conference titles. For those who enjoy the game but might not make the team, there is an active intramurals program, an outdoors program that offers instruction in areas such as rock climbing and fly-fishing, and the large J. A. Albertson Activities Center. "Intramurals are huge at our school," says a sophomore.

C of I has much to offer its "Yotes" (translation: "We are the coyotes"). They enjoy a solid liberal arts education and personal academic attention on a campus striving to keep its offerings on the cutting edge. What's more, students here are encouraged to take an active role in the school's future. "Almost everything, from the traditions to the pub, is initiated by students," says a sophomore. "We are involved in all aspects of campus life."

Travel has really taken off, with study abroad opportunities in nearly 60 countries around the world.

"The classes are fairly tough."

Women's cross-country finished second at nationals in 2012 and women's volleyball has won seven consecutive conference titles.

Overlaps
Boise State, University of Idaho, Idaho State, College of Western Idaho, Westminster, Earlham, Northwest Nazarene

University of Illinois at Urbana–Champaign

901 West Illinois, Urbana, IL 61801

Half a step behind Michigan and neck and neck with Wisconsin among top Midwestern public universities. U of I's strengths include business, communications, engineering, architecture, and the natural sciences. Nearly 80 percent of the student body hails from in state. Has reformed admissions in the wake of a scandal over favoritism for applicants favored by political bigwigs.

Website: www.illinois.edu

Location: City Center

Public

Total Enrollment: 44,520

Undergraduates: 32,281

Male/Female: 55/45

SAT Ranges: CR 550–680, M 680–790

ACT Ranges: 26–31

Financial Aid: 45%

Expense: Pub $ $ $ $

Student Loans: 52%

Average Debt: $ $

Phi Beta Kappa: Yes

Applicants: 31,454

Accepted: 63%

Enrolled: 22%

Grad in 6 Years: 84%

Returning Freshmen: 94%

Academics: ✑ ✑ ✑ ✑ ✑

Social: ☎ ☎ ☎

Q of L: ★ ★ ★

Admissions: (217) 333-0302

Email Address: admissions@illinois.edu

Strongest Programs:
Accounting
Engineering
Agricultural Economics
Architecture
Business Administration/
  Business Management
Psychology

Like many of its Midwestern neighbors, the University of Illinois has its roots in agriculture. The Morrow Plots, the oldest experimental fields in the nation, still rest in the middle of campus—and when the wind blows the wrong way, students are not-so-subtly reminded of their heritage as a farm school. Like most big, public universities, U of I has a barn full of choices, and with a strong Greek system and 1,200 clubs, social activities are more than plentiful. Homecoming weekend was invented at the University of Illinois, and whether cheering for the Illini, pledging one of nearly 100 Greek houses, or celebrating Moms', Dads', or Siblings' Weekends, students here stir up a vibrant mix of school spirit and good times. This may look and feel like a laid-back Midwestern campus, but make no mistake: Illinois is a budget Ivy with stellar academics and learning communities that are among the best found anywhere.

Befitting the oldest land grant institution, the Illinois campus was built in farm country between the twin cities of Champaign and Urbana. The parklike campus was designed along a mile-long axis where trees and walkways separate stately white-columned Georgian structures made of brick. Physically challenged students tend to appreciate the campus because it is flat and well equipped with ramps and widened doorways. A 250,000-square-foot computer science center and physical education center are notable, as is the Technology Commercialization Laboratory, which provides faculty and students the opportunity to benefit from the commercialization of their research.

Illinois has eight undergraduate colleges and more than 150 undergraduate programs; if nothing strikes your fancy, you may design your own. Requirements include composition, quantitative reasoning, proficiency in a foreign language, and six hours each of cultural studies, natural sciences and technology, humanities and arts, and social and behavioral sciences. Engineering, business, education, and the sciences—especially agriculture and veterinary medicine—get high marks from students and lots of resources from administrators. "Overall, classes are demanding," says a senior. "The academic climate is engaging," a junior adds.

> **"The academic climate is engaging."**

Partially because of its size, Illinois can afford to support excellent programs across the university, including the expansion of undergraduate minors campuswide. For a huge university, registration can be relatively painless, thanks to an online system allowing course selection from one's own computer. Nevertheless, freshmen and sophomores, who register last, may have trouble getting into certain general education classes, such as foreign languages. Professors and academic advisors can usually help if classes you need are full, and students appreciate their dedication. "The quality of teaching is high with few exceptions," explains a psychology major. "They are truly invested in our success," adds one senior.

The impressive Illinois library system, the largest public university collection of its kind worldwide, makes it easier to keep up with classwork. Aside from engineering and business, another notable program at Illinois includes the Beckman Institute for Advanced Science and Technology, an interdisciplinary center designed to bring biological and physical sciences together to pursue new insights in human and artificial intelligence. Illinois was a pioneer in developing academic computing, and the National Center for Supercomputing Applications at Illinois developed Mosaic, the predecessor to Netscape's Navigator World Wide Web browser. The undergraduate honors program includes faculty mentoring, intensive seminars, advanced sections of regular courses, and access to special resources. More than a quarter of undergraduates travel and study abroad each year, roaming 50 countries around the globe, while the Ronald E. McNair Scholars Program helps fund independent, original research by minority, low-income, and first-generation college students who are completing bachelor's degrees.

> "The quality of teaching is high with few exceptions."

Illinois was a pioneer in developing academic computing.

Illinois has its share of stellar faculty, including Nobel laureates, National Medal of Science winners, and dozens of members of the National Academy of Sciences. Even freshmen stuck in large lectures (750 seats) will find some personal attention in the associated discussion sections, led by graduate teaching assistants. (Although many students note that due to budget cutbacks, even these classes are getting larger.) Freshman Discovery Courses, seminars limited to 19 students, enable first-year students to interact closely with full professors. First-semester freshmen can ease into the rigors of college-level work in one of the Learning Communities.

Seventy-nine percent of Illinois undergrads are homegrown and "the school is continuously getting more diverse," a sophomore says. Since Illinois stretches from the wealthy north suburbs of sophisticated Chicago to the unspoiled rural hills bordering Kentucky and encompasses classic farm towns as well as factory towns, students do come from multiple backgrounds and fit less into the stereotypical "Midwest" mold than one might think. Minorities make up 14 percent of the student body, while international students account for 14 percent. Merit scholarships averaging $4,747, and more than 200 athletic awards are doled out annually. The Illinois Promise Program provides financial aid for qualified freshmen and sophomores whose family income is at or below the federal poverty level.

> "We have a great reputation and it only grows stronger and stronger."

Fifty percent of students live in the U of I's co-ed and single-sex residence halls, which range in size from 51 to 660 beds and are arranged in quadrangle-like groups. Some dorms are quite a hike from classrooms, veterans warn. Daniels Residence has been renovated. All bedrooms have high-speed Internet connections, and many residence halls house living/learning programs, such as WIMSE (Women in Math, Science, and Engineering) and Unit One (academic support and educationally focused programming). Each residence hall is a mini-neighborhood, with dining halls, darkrooms, libraries, music practice rooms, computers, and lounges creating a sense of community. Chefs keep the food interesting, and campus security maintains a visible presence.

Even freshmen stuck in large lectures (750 seats) will find some personal attention in the associated discussion sections.

Many sophomores live in fraternity or sorority houses; Illinois claims to have the largest Greek system anywhere, with nearly 100 chapters drawing 21 percent of men and women. Illinois attracts many socially oriented students who love parties and intramural sports, which may be why the Greek influence is particularly strong. Independents don't have to suffer boredom, though, as there are also more than

1,200 registered student clubs and organizations ranging from the rugby team to ethnic advocacy groups. "It is a big campus that likes to have a lot of fun," a student says. On most weekends, the Illini Union showcases bands, comedians, and hypnotists in its central café. The impressive Krannert Center for the Performing Arts, with four theaters and more than 350 annual performances, serves as the area's cultural center, while Assembly Hall hosts national touring acts, including popular musicians and musicals. Students get a discount at both facilities. Chicago and the shores of Lake Michigan beckon when the weather warms up, and Mardi Gras makes for a good road trip in the dead of winter. Though drinking is prohibited in the dorms, the campus policies regarding alcohol are a "token gesture," a business major says. "You only need to be 19 to get into bars, but 21 to drink. In Champaign, the ticket for underage drinking is around $300, so don't risk it!" For those who itch for the stimulation of a big city, the campus is just about equidistant from Chicago, Indianapolis, and St. Louis.

Many sophomores live in fraternity or sorority houses; Illinois claims to have the largest Greek system anywhere.

The Illini compete in the Big Ten, and men's basketball and baseball have winning traditions. Other solid programs include women's cross-country and track and field; men's soccer; men's wrestling; and men's gymnastics. The intramural program is extensive with available facilities that include 16 full-length basketball courts, five pools, 19 handball/racquetball courts, a skating rink, a baseball stadium, and the $5.1 million Atkins Tennis Center, with six indoor and eight outdoor courts. Ninety percent of the student body participate in intramurals. Illinois has a strong athletic program for students with disabilities, including wheelchair basketball, which Illinois invented.

While the University of Illinois may seem mammoth to some students, don't be scared off by this giant institution. Academic and social opportunities are incredibly diverse, and classroom sizes, while growing, are supplemented by smaller group discussions. The breadth of the programs offered, combined with an active campus life makes for a well-rounded college experience, students say. "We have a great reputation and it only grows stronger and stronger."

Overlaps

University of Iowa, University of Michigan, Northwestern, Purdue, University of Wisconsin, Washington University in St. Louis

If You Apply To ➤

Illinois: Regular admissions: Jan. 2. Financial aid: Mar. 15. Housing: May 15. Application fee: $50. Campus interviews: optional, informational. Alumni interviews: not available. SATs or ACTs: required. Subject Tests: optional. Apply to particular schools or programs; music, dance, and theater applicants must audition. Essay question: personal statement.

Illinois Institute of Technology

10 West 33rd Street, Chicago, IL 60616

Forget about cheerleaders, homecoming games, and other traditional trappings of college life. IIT is about learning about technology, getting a degree, and landing a job. IIT is all engineering with a little bit of architecture thrown in for good measure. If your goal is a technical job in the Chicago area, this is your place. Though private, IIT is relatively inexpensive.

Website: www.iit.edu
Location: City Center
Private
Total Enrollment: 6,268

Engineers unite at the Illinois Institute of Technology, where classwork and real-world experience promise to propel students to the top of their fields. After all, when you're taught by Nobel laureates, engaged in comprehensive undergraduate research, and able to take advantage of state-of-the-art labs, you're nearly guaranteed a high-paying job after graduation. IIT programs may be hard, says a junior, but the work "will pay off in the end" as students enter the workforce. Indeed, kids here tend to burn the midnight oil, but frequently escape to downtown Chicago for much-deserved fun and culture.

IIT's home is an urban, 120-acre campus designed by Ludwig Mies van der Rohe, the influential 20th-century architect who directed the architecture school for 20 years. Founded in 1890, the school is just three miles south of Chicago's Loop, one mile west of Lake Michigan. Miesian-style buildings are adorned by trees and grassy open parks. U.S. Cellular Field, home of the White Sox, is located directly across from the campus. The S.R. Crown Hall, home of IIT's College of Architecture, is considered a landmark.

"The courses are very difficult."

Engineering sets the tone at IIT, and every engineering department is outstanding. Architecture is the most popular major, followed by mechanical engineering, electrical engineering, aerospace engineering, and civil engineering. "Architecture has a strong faculty," says one student, "and biomedical engineering is very new and well funded." The sciences, physics in particular, are first-rate; high-energy physicist and Nobel laureate Leon Lederman teaches freshman—yes, freshman—physics. Computer literacy is demanded of all students. In addition, all freshmen take an introduction to the professions seminar, which includes discussion of innovation, ethics, teamwork, communication, and leadership. Incoming "first-years" also receive Apple iPads; students work with professors to create new applications in order to "enhance their educational experience."

Multidisciplinary, group-based learning is big at IIT. Every student must complete two semester-long interprofession projects that sharpen real-world skills. The architecture curriculum emphasizes a team approach that mixes third- through fifth-year students under the supervision of a master professor. Guided by an academic reorganization, the physical sciences have been bolstered, grouped together with career-oriented fields such as psychology, political science, and computer information systems. Other academic options include majors in business administration, applied science, and dual admissions programs in pharmacy, optometry, and osteopathic medicine.

Along with humanities and social science courses, students must fulfill general education requirements that include mathematics, computer science, natural science, and engineering; writing is emphasized across the curriculum. IIT's academic climate is pretty unforgiving, students say.

"Professors take an active role in their students' education."

Both the workload and the competition are fierce. "The courses are very difficult," says a junior. Professors always teach their own classes at IIT, while TAs are available for labs and extra help. Most students praise the faculty for their knowledge and tendency to offer as much help as is needed. "Professors take an active role in their students' education," states a biochemistry major. Fifty-seven percent of the classes have 19 or fewer students.

In addition to meeting outside of class to go over problem sets or for career direction, IIT students and professors often work side by side on research projects. The College of Science and Letters awards several $5,000 scholarships to undergrads to perform research work under the supervision of faculty during the summer. Engineering students have the use of sophisticated labs, and independent research labs in Chicago are also available. The five-year co-op program—another possibility for hands-on experience—helps lead IIT grads into high-paying jobs after graduation. There are study abroad programs that send students to more than 100 locales around the globe, including France, Spain, Scotland, and Germany.

"Students at IIT are nerds," reports a communications major, but "in a good way." Eighty-two percent of IIT students graduated in the top quarter of their high

(continued)

Undergraduates: 2,609
Male/Female: 69/31
SAT Ranges: CR 513–630, M 610–710
ACT Ranges: 24–30
Financial Aid: 96%
Expense: Pr $ $
Student Loans: 65%
Average Debt: $ $ $ $
Phi Beta Kappa: No
Applicants: 2,597
Accepted: 55%
Enrolled: 29%
Grad in 6 Years: 68%
Returning Freshmen: 92%
Academics: ✐ ✐ ✐ ½
Social: ☎ ☎
Q of L: ★ ★
Admissions: (312) 567-3025
Email Address: admission@iit.edu

Strongest Programs:
Electrical Engineering
Chemical Engineering
Mechanical Engineering
Aerospace Engineering
Architecture

All freshmen take an introduction to the professions seminar, which includes discussion of innovation, ethics, teamwork, communication, and leadership.

school class. Out-of-state students account for nearly one quarter of the undergraduate population, and 16 percent hail from foreign countries, one of the highest rates of any U.S. college or university. African Americans and Hispanics together constitute 21 percent of the student body, and Asian American students comprise another 11 percent. Students say International Fest is one of the year's most popular events, and IIT offers a multitude of cultural awareness workshops and sponsors "awareness" weeks and months on different topics to help avert potential problems. A three-day workshop on topics including race relations, international diversity, homophobia, and sexism is required of all new students. IIT offers merit scholarships averaging approximately $19,440 each and athletic scholarships in five sports. IIT's ROTC program has grown and matured into one of the finest in the nation and even hosts a popular annual formal ball.

As befits the school's urban location, a large chunk of students commute. The 59 percent of students who live in residence halls report that rooms are nice, but can be difficult to get. Six of the seven dorms are co-ed, with one hall for women only. The McCormick Student Village is popular, and South and North are said to be the nicest dorms. Fowler has the biggest rooms, but no air-conditioning; the rest of the dorms have AC. Some students live in apartments in the area or on Chicago's North Side; others inhabit one of the eight fraternities, which claim 14 percent of the men. Sororities attract 15 percent of the women, and many students say the social aspect of Greek life is a welcome addition to campus. The dining hall has several meal plans and a special vegetarian menu. Breakfast and lunch can also be eaten in the cafeteria at the student union, while the campus pub serves lunch and dinner. Engineers and architects—notorious late-night studiers—have to hit the library early, since it closes at 10 p.m.

IIT's six-block campus is contiguous to Chicago's "Gap" community, where historic but rundown homes are being rehabilitated to form one of the city's hottest new urban residential areas. Most students love exploring Chicago; the city skyline is beautiful and a veritable museum, with buildings designed by the likes of Frank Lloyd Wright, Louis Sullivan, and, of course, Mies van der Rohe. "Chicago provides educational opportunities, internship opportunities, and countless things to do," says one biomedical engineering major. Thus, the university provides free shuttle bus service to downtown on weekends. Lake Michigan is within jogging distance, and Chinatown is a walk away for lunch or dinner.

"The social life at IIT has improved."

Although students who stick around campus on weekends must work hard to find social events, "The social life at IIT has improved over my four years," says a senior. The Union Board offers movies, concerts, and comedians, and the Bog brings in bands on Thursdays and Saturdays. Students can also plan events like a formal on the *Odyssey*, a sightseeing boat, or an outing to the Chicago Symphony. The eight-day Winter Festival and the Spring Formal are other popular annual events. Returning sophomores are invited to a weekend retreat in Lake Geneva, Wisconsin, for some bonding time and to celebrate making it through their first year. As for alcohol, the school follows the national drinking age and students say it generally works.

In sports-crazy Chicago, IIT athletic teams (the "Scarlet Hawks") are not much of a draw. Students praise the men's baseball, cross-country, and basketball teams along with women's volleyball, which compete in the NAIA Division I. Men's and women's soccer is competitive, as is men's swimming and diving, which has produced more than 20 All-Americans in the last few years. The intramural program is strong, but students lament the fact that the facilities close at 5 p.m. on weekends. The Olympics occur every year at IIT when Greek Week and Sports Fest kick off, featuring Olympic-type competition for all students.

Shipping off to Chi-town to take on the mammoth workload at IIT means hitting the books for hours upon hours and a fair share of all-nighters. But the payoff is undeniable. One student says bluntly, "This school is for people who want to make a lot of money after college." Indeed, students who take advantage of this small school's ever-improving engineering departments are likely to have their pick of careers after graduation. And with the innumerable diversions offered in the Windy City, students at IIT revel in the best of two worlds: a challenging academic climate and a great city in which to let off all that steam.

If You Apply To ➤

IIT: Rolling admissions: Aug. 1. Early action: Dec. 1. No application fee. Campus and alumni interviews: optional, informational. SATs or ACTs: required. Subject Tests: optional. Accepts the Common Application. Essay question: share your goals; optional personal statement.

Illinois Wesleyan University

Bloomington, IL 61702-2900

IWU is a small Midwestern college with an emphasis on creativity and the spirit of inquiry. The curriculum is basic liberal arts with additional divisions devoted to fine arts and nursing. An optional three-week term in May allows students to travel or explore an interest. IWU's reputation is limited outside Illinois and surrounding states.

Illinois Wesleyan University has its sights set on a special breed of student—the kind who isn't afraid to be many things at once. Its mission statement highlights the school's goal of becoming the ideal liberal arts institution by providing unique opportunities, fostering creativity, and preparing students for a life in a global society. Students here are very much encouraged to pursue multiple passions, and IWU is a mecca for students who have preprofessional interests, especially those with unusual pairings like management and music. "What makes Wesleyan really stand out is its care and attention for each student as an individual," says a junior. "You will feel at home here."

Founded in 1850, IWU occupies an 80-acre campus site in a north-side residential district of Bloomington. The heart of campus is the central quadrangle, and tree-lined walkways connect buildings that range in style from gray stone Gothic to ultramodern steel and glass. The College of Fine Arts houses the three separate schools of music, art, and drama; music is the standout, having turned out such talents as opera star Dawn Upshaw.

Among the top-notch programs in the College of Liberal Arts are biology, English, chemistry, and math. In addition to the usual fall and spring semesters, IWU has an optional three-week May term. The courses during this term must have one of five features: curricular experimentation, nontraditional approaches to traditional subject matter, student/faculty collaboration, crossing of disciplinary boundaries, or experiential learning through travel, service, or internships. Over half the students take a May term class, and about one-fourth take off-campus travel courses. The university's study abroad program offers students the opportunity to travel to more than 70 countries, including England, Denmark, and Japan. The business administration department offers a Portfolio Management

> "The teachers really care about their students."

Website: www.iwu.edu
Location: Small City
Private
Total Enrollment: 2,002
Undergraduates: 2,002
Male/Female: 42/58
SAT Ranges: CR 540–650, M 570–700
ACT Ranges: 25–30
Financial Aid: 99%
Expense: Pr $ $
Student Loans: 70%
Average Debt: $ $ $ $
Phi Beta Kappa: Yes
Applicants: 3,297
Accepted: 60%
Enrolled: 25%
Grad in 6 Years: 82%
Returning Freshmen: 89%
Academics: ✍ ✍ ✍ ½
Social: ☎ ☎ ☎
Q of L: ★ ★ ★ ★
Admissions: (800) 332-2498
Email Address: iwuadmit@iwu.edu

(continued)

Strongest Programs:

Accounting

Biology

Computer Science

International Studies

Political Science

Philosophy

Economics

Psychology

course, in which students buy and sell orders overseen by a client board composed of university trustees. IWU hosts an annual student research conference that attracts people from all disciplines.

Illinois Wesleyan's general education requirements emphasize critical thinking, imagination, intellectual independence, social awareness, and sensitivity to others. All first-year students must take a Gateway Colloquium, a topic-based, seminar-style class of 15 that stresses critical reading, writing, discussion, and analytical skills, and introduces students to the intellectual life of the university. Some of the topics include Jesus at the Movies, Are We What We Eat?, The Mommy Wars, and Jewish Humor. Students have differing views regarding which programs are weaker, but most agree that specific professors are avoided rather than departments. Additional programs include a major in Greek and Roman studies. Students do jockey for high grades, especially since the introduction of a plus/minus grading system. "IWU is a competitive school," says one student. Professors are lauded for their knowledge and accessibility. "The teachers really care about their students," says a sophomore.

> "The students are generally smart and friendly, but not stuck up."

Students at IWU are mostly the homegrown variety, with 84 percent hailing from Illinois. "The students are generally smart and friendly, but not stuck up," a sophomore says. Although IWU began admitting African American students in 1867, the campus is still predominantly white. African Americans and Asian Americans each account for 5 percent of the student body; Hispanics account for 5 percent. A multicultural task force has been formed to address the issue of diversity. The university has placed great emphasis on educating students about sexual harassment. Part of freshman orientation is spent role-playing harassment situations. Active participation in groups like Circle K, the Alpha Phi Omega service fraternity, and Habitat for Humanity provides evidence for the social consciousness of the IWU campus. Merit scholarships are available to qualified students; there are no athletic scholarships.

IWU hosts an annual student research conference that attracts people from all disciplines.

Housing is guaranteed for four years, and 71 percent of the students live in the dorms, which receive stellar marks from residents. "Everything is well maintained and getting housing is easy," according to one junior. Students must be 21 to live off campus. The food gets high marks as well. "The food at the Commons is very good," says a psychology major. Most students say campus security is good, though common sense must be exercised.

Thirty-one percent of the men and 33 percent of the women go Greek because fraternities and sororities are the focus of IWU's social life. Non-Greeks also use the system for social life, but if partying isn't your thing, there are plenty of other options. "Our student center always has free stuff going on like comedians, hypnotists, movies, and bands every Friday and Saturday night," says one senior. The alcohol policy allows drinking on campus for those over the age of 21, and students admit that the policies don't always stop underage drinkers. "Lots of students drink," one junior says. Each fall during homecoming, the fraternities and residence halls compete in the Titan Games to get appropriately psyched. Other annual festivities include the Far Left Carnival, the Gospel Festival, and Earthapalooza (on Earth Day). The Student Senate also sponsors guest speakers; Spike Lee, Bonnie Blair, and Maya Angelou have addressed audiences in recent years.

Thirty-one percent of the men and 33 percent of the women go Greek because fraternities and sororities are the focus of IWU's social life.

Thanks to the proximity of Illinois State University in nearby Normal, IWU offers more than the typical small college town atmosphere. The total area school population of about 25,000 helps to offer students at tiny IWU "the best of both worlds," says a senior. An accounting major says, "Bloomington has the highest restaurant-per-capita ratio of any community. The students love this." The best road trips are to Peoria or Urbana–Champaign (home of the University of Illinois) or to Chicago or St. Louis, each two and a half hours away.

In the IWU arena, baseball and football are well and good, but Titans basketball really gets students going. The Fort Natatorium houses a whopping 14-lane swimming pool, and the swim team has had its share of stars along with the track team. Intramural sports include volleyball, badminton, and co-ed inner-tube water polo. Forty percent of IWU men and 10 percent of women participate.

One of the Midwest's better-kept secrets, Illinois Wesleyan is at once cozy and diverse, loaded with opportunities for ambitious students with traditional or offbeat interests. As one junior advises, "The school provides a multitude of paths down which one can travel, and it is up to the student to decide which path to take. IWU allows you to become who you want to be, but only if you let it."

If You Apply To ➤ | **Illinois Wesleyan:** Rolling admissions. Early action: Nov. 15. No application fee. Campus interviews: recommended, informational. No alumni interviews. SATs or ACTs: required. No Subject Tests. Accepts the Common Application. Essay question.

Indiana University

300 North Jordan Avenue, Bloomington, IN 47405

Though men's basketball is IU's most famous program, it may not be its best. That distinction could easily go to the world-renowned music school or to the distinguished foreign language program. IU enrolls three times as many out-of-staters as the University of Illinois. Bloomington is a great college town, and most students live off campus after freshman year.

With more than 37,000 students on its enormous campus, Indiana University is the prototype of the large Midwestern school. With strong academics, a thriving social scene, and some of the best sports teams around, this top-notch public institution is a testament to Hoosier determination.

Located in southern Indiana's gently rolling hills, the 1,900-acre campus boasts architecture from Italianate brick to collegiate Gothic limestone to the distinctive style of world-famous architect I. M. Pei. Other unique campus features include fountains, gargoyles, an arboretum of more than 450 trees and shrubs surrounding two reflecting pools, a limestone gazebo, and the Jordan River, a pretty creek that runs alongside a shaded path.

IU's schools and colleges offer many majors and minors, cross-disciplinary study, an individually designed curriculum, intense honors and research programs, and overseas study in 52 countries. The highly touted business school, with its respected international studies component, is among the most popular majors, as are biology and journalism. The internationally known Kinsey Institute for the Study of Human Sexual Behavior is housed on IU's campus, and the music school is tops in its field, setting the, ahem, tone for much of the campus. Students don't complain about many departmental weaknesses but note that large introductory lectures, especially in the sciences, are a hazard of IU's size. Indiana prides itself on its liberal arts education—freshmen are admitted not to preprofessional schools but to the "university division." Majors are declared after one or two years, and the university discourages premature specialization. IU's communications and culture department advances

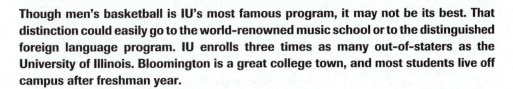

"With 4,000 different courses per semester, a variety of intensity levels exist."

Website: www.iub.edu
Location: Small City
Public
Total Enrollment: 37,090
Undergraduates: 30,845
Male/Female: 49/51
SAT Ranges: CR 510–620, M 540–660
ACT Ranges: 24–29
Financial Aid: 71%
Expense: Pub $ $
Student Loans: 52%
Average Debt: $ $ $
Phi Beta Kappa: Yes
Applicants: 35,247
Accepted: 74%
Enrolled: 29%
Grad in 6 Years: 75%
Returning Freshmen: 88%
Academics: ✍ ✍ ✍ ✍
Social: ☎ ☎ ☎ ☎
Q of L: ★ ★ ★ ★
Admissions: (812) 855-0661

Majors are declared after one or two years, and the university discourages premature specialization.

the study of communication as a cultural practice, while the Environmental Science Joint Program is an undergraduate degree program that specifically considers the environment as a scientific entity.

General education requirements vary from school to school but usually include math, science, arts and humanities, social and behavioral sciences, English and writing, culture, and a foreign language. Students describe the academic climate as rigorous but not cut-throat. "With 4,000 different courses per semester, a variety of intensity levels exist," says a marketing major. "There is a balance with room for both competitive overachievers and laid-back, carefree individuals." Students say they regularly share ideas with each other, and group projects are commonplace. Faculty members bring their research results directly to students, and some profs bring undergrads into their labs to assist with ongoing projects. Students say the quality of teaching is excellent. "The professors here are remarkable," says an art history/telecommunications major. As for advising, many students seem surprised by the personal attention they receive at such a large university, and they soon learn that many available resources are helpful to those students who seek them out. Some students, though, complain of confusing bureaucracies and parking problems.

Sixty-four percent of IU students are from in state, while the remainder hail from out of state and more than 100 foreign countries. Out-of-staters face much more rigorous minimum admissions standards, including rank in the top quarter of their high school class and SAT scores in the 1050 to 1100 range. African Americans comprise 4 percent of the student body, Hispanics 4 percent, and Asian Americans 4 percent. By and large, students do not seem to dwell on political or social issues. The school's rolling admissions system enables students to know their fate a month after their application is filed. And while IU does not guarantee to meet the full demonstrated need of every student, it admits on a need-blind basis and offers the Early

"The professors here are remarkable."

Approximate Student Eligibility (EASE) program to help prospective freshmen gauge how much financial aid they will get. Merit scholarships (averaging $7,719) are awarded to qualified students; applicants must be in the top 10 percent of their graduating class and have a combined SAT score of 1200. More than 500 athletic scholarships are available for qualified jocks.

Housing ranges from Gothic quads (co-ed by building) to 13-floor high-rises (co-ed by floor or unit, except for one all-women dorm), and halls are considered "clean and comfortable." One student explains the housing situation this way: "All dorms have laundry facilities, cafeterias, computer clusters, and undergraduate advisors, and some even have special amenities like language-speaking floors." A junior adds, "There is no trouble getting a room, but preference of dorm may be harder." Academic floors (requiring a GPA of 3.1 or better) are popular with more serious students who are not interested in intense nightlife. Housing is guaranteed to all incoming freshmen, and those who stay in the university housing system won't ever face rent increases. Based on results from a student survey, some dining halls have been modernized to resemble mall food courts with outlets offering international and healthful menus sprinkled among the fast-food options. Alcohol is prohibited in the dorms, which may help explain why 62 percent of the student body lives off campus. Most off-campus residents choose apartments or small houses with big front porches within walking distance of the campus or of the IU bus system.

As for advising, many students seem surprised by the personal attention they receive at such a large university.

Although campus organizations host numerous events, the most active on-campus groups, in terms of social life, seem to be the Greeks. Some complain of a polarized atmosphere. "There is a large separation between the Greek community and the rest of the student body," says a senior. Every fall there is a 36-hour Dance Marathon to raise money for Riley's Children's Hospital in Indianapolis. The Little 500 bike race, which was modeled after the Indianapolis 500, is one of the most highly attended events of the year in the Indiana campus. With concerts, ballets, recitals, and festivals right on campus, students are not lacking for things to keep them busy. The IU student union is the largest in the nation, and the range of extracurricular organizations is also impressive. The Office of Diversity Programs, Committee on Multicultural Understanding, and Students Organized Against Racism are a few more ways students can make a difference on campus.

With concerts, ballets, recitals, and festivals right on campus, students are not lacking for things to keep them busy.

"Bloomington is a great small-college town," says one senior. There are many excellent bars, shops, and restaurants, including one of the few Tibetan restaurants in the country. Locally, the area offers some impressive rock quarries (often used as illegal but refreshing swimming pools), miles of public forests, and three nearby lakes. Spelunkers will find heaven down below in the many nearby caves. Chicago, Cincinnati, Indianapolis, St. Louis, and even New Orleans are popular road trips.

Intramurals pale in comparison with varsity athletics here; basketball is an established religion in the state of Indiana. Although students and faculty are all eligible for tickets, they've got to get requests in early—and even those lucky enough to get tickets don't count on going to more than a quarter of home games. In recent years, women's swimming and diving, men's soccer, and men's indoor track and field have claimed Big Ten championships, and even the football team draws red and white crowds. Purdue is IU's traditional athletic rival, and teams play for the Old Oaken Bucket, found on a farm in southern Indiana in 1925 and alleged to have been used during the Civil War.

"Bloomington is a great small-college town."

Despite IU's reputation as a basketball powerhouse, it also provides committed students with stellar programs ranging from foreign languages to music, and a social scene that's hard to beat. For those not frightened away by throngs of classmates, Indiana University may be a great fit.

Overlaps

Purdue, Ball State, University of Illinois, University of Iowa, Miami (OH)

If You Apply To ➤ **Indiana:** Rolling admissions. Financial aid: Mar. 10. Application fee: $55. Campus interviews: optional, informational. No alumni interviews. SATs or ACTs: required. Subject Tests: recommended. No essay question.

International Colleges and Universities

Do you thrive on new experiences? Like to meet new people? Want to learn about different cultures? You can do all that at a college or university in the United States, but if you really want to jump in with both feet, think about attending a school in a foreign country. This section highlights the opportunities available in Canada and Great Britain, by far the most common destinations outside the United States for degree-seeking undergraduates.

The absence of a language barrier is the most obvious reason why Canada, Britain, and Ireland are the preferred destinations for study abroad. Plenty of students do a junior year abroad where the language is Spanish or Swahili, but only a handful can realistically expect to earn an entire degree in a foreign tongue. A growing number of European universities are offering instruction in English, not only to Americans but to students from throughout the world. A smattering of American universities do exist in places ranging from Paris to Cairo, but most are small and the majority of their enrollment is students from other countries seeking an American-style education. If you're willing to venture halfway around the world, Australia is an English-speaking destination that might be worth a look for its combination of beautiful scenery and bargain-basement tuition.

Look for coverage of Australian institutions in a future edition of the *Fiske Guide*. The following sections examine Canada and Britain in more detail, followed by full-length articles on selected institutions.

Canadian Colleges and Universities

Horace Greeley told ambitious young men of his generation to "go West." Today his admonition to young men and women seeking a quality college education at a fraction of the usual cost would probably be to "go North"—to Canada. A growing number of American students are discovering the educational riches that lie just above their northern border in this huge land of 30 million people that is known for its rugged mountains, bicultural politics, spirited ice hockey, and cold ale. What's drawing them is easy to discern.

The top Canadian universities are the academic equals of most flagship public universities and many leading privates in the United States, but the expense of a bachelor's degree is far lower, even taking travel into account. Canadian campuses and the cities in which they are located are safe places and, unless one opts for a French course of study, there are no language and few cultural barriers. Canadian schools are strong on international exchange programs, and their degrees carry weight with U.S. graduate schools.

Canada has 90 institutions of higher learning, ranging from internationally recognized research universities to the small undergraduate teaching institutions in the country's more rural areas; Canada ranks second after the United States in the percentage of citizens attending university. Most of the larger universities are located in highly urban centers, but some are situated in smaller towns where they dominate the life of the community. Most are almost literally next door to the United States, within 100 miles of the Canada–U.S. border. In this guide, we feature four of Canada's strongest universities: the University of British Columbia, McGill University, Queen's University, and the University of Toronto.

Institutions of higher learning in Canada were established from the earliest days of French settlement in the mid-17th century, making them some of the oldest in North America. The precursors to the public universities in Canada were the small, elite, denominational colleges that sprang up in Quebec, in the Maritimes, and later in Ontario. A few private denominational colleges and universities still exist in Canada, but most have been subsumed into affiliations or associations with the larger universities. Education in Canada, including university education, became the exclusive jurisdiction of provincial governments. As the Canadian West was developed, the large Western provinces of British Columbia, Alberta, Manitoba, and Saskatchewan set up provincially chartered universities similar to land grant colleges in the United States.

One of the key differences between Canadian and U.S. universities is that Canadian universities (and this is what they are, not "colleges") are primarily funded from public monies. Despite steady tuition increases in the past five years, the average Canadian student still only pays on average about $2,500 in Canadian dollars, which are about the same as a U.S. dollar. Although non-Canadians may be charged up to six times the domestic rate, most costs are still lower than out-of-state tuition in the United States. Tuition at the four universities described on the following pages ranges from U.S. $5,500 to $9,200.

Canadians have come to expect easy and affordable access to a uniformly high quality of education whether they live in Halifax or Vancouver. After diminishing government funding in the past several years, a now booming economy, a large government surplus, new federal initiatives, grants for innovations and scholarships, and the universities' own aggressive fund-raising campaigns bode well for the continued growth and quality of Canadian higher education in the immediate future.

Federal and provincial loans and grants that are readily available to Canadian students are generally not available to students from the United States and other countries. However, the majority of universities with competitive admissions, particularly those featured in the *Fiske Guide*, offer merit-based awards and scholarships to students of all nationalities. American students who attend leading Canadian schools can apply their U.S. student assistance funds, including Stafford Loans and Pell Grants, as well as the recently implemented HOPE Scholarship and Lifetime Learning tax credits.

The requirements for obtaining a degree are set by each institution, as are the admission requirements and prerequisites. Unlike the United States, Canada does not offer nor require its own students to take a Canadian college entrance test. Some Canadian universities admitting students from the United States will require SAT or ACT scores along with high school marks from academic subjects in the last two or three years of high school. In general, top universities are about as selective as their American counterparts.

Application fees vary by institution, as do deadlines. Canadian universities are aware of the May 1 deadline operative in the United States, and they try to accommodate. Applications to the University of Toronto and Queen's University in Ontario are handled centrally through the Ontario Universities' Application Service. McGill handles applications directly and accepts both Web-based and paper applications. British Columbia has its own application; it can be mailed, but students are encouraged to apply online. Canadian universities differ widely in the amount of credit and/or advanced standing they offer for Advanced Placement examinations or International Baccalaureate Higher Level examinations.

The following admission requirements apply to applicants from an American school system. The University of British Columbia bases admission decisions on the average of eight full-year academic courses over the last two years of high school, and there are also specific program requirements for students entering the science-based faculties. SAT test results are not required, but if students submit them, the results can be helpful in the evaluation process. McGill bases its assessment of American high school graduates on the overall record of marks in academic subjects during the final three years of high school, class standing, and results obtained in SAT I and SAT II and/or ACT tests. Queen's wants applicants with a minimum score of 1200 on SAT I (with at least 580 in Critical Reading and 520 in Mathematics) and looks at class rank. There are also program-specific requirements for programs where mathematics and/or biology, chemistry, and physics are a requirement. Toronto's Arts and Science faculties want a high grade point average and good scores on the SAT I and on three SAT II subject tests. ACT and CEEB Advanced Placement Examination scores are also considered.

It is hard to beat Canadian universities for the quality of student life. Although many students commute, most of the universities in Canada offer on-campus housing; some even guarantee campus housing for first-year students. Universities offer active intramural and intercollegiate sports programs for both men and women, and the usual student clubs, newspapers, and radio stations provide students with opportunities to get involved and develop friendships. As in the United States, student-run organizations are active participants in university life, with leaders serving on university committees and lobbying on issues ranging from creating more bicycle paths to keeping tuition low. Few Canadian campuses are troubled by issues of student safety or rowdiness. In the larger urban centers, Canadian campuses reflect the rich diversity of Canada's cultural mosaic, and most encourage their students to gain international experience by spending a term or a full year abroad.

Americans wondering about the currency of a Canadian degree in the United States should be reassured that top American and multinational countries—the likes of Archer Daniels Midland, Chase Manhattan, IBM, Microsoft, Nortel Networks, and Solomon Smith Barney—actively recruit on Canadian campuses, as do American graduate schools. According to the Institute of International Education in New York, more than 7,000 Canadians are currently enrolled in graduate schools in the United States.

The one thing that is different for U.S. and other international students intending to study in Canada is that they will have to obtain a Student Authorization, equivalent to a visa, from Canadian immigration authorities. Getting a Student Authorization is fairly straightforward for American citizens, but this slight bureaucratic hurdle is a reminder that Canada, for all of its similarities in language and culture with the United States, is still another country. For many American students who have chosen to study in Canada, this is part of the draw—they get to enjoy all the excitement of studying abroad in a foreign country with few of the cultural and none of the linguistic barriers to overcome.

The Association of Universities and Colleges of Canada has a website at www.aucc.ca. Another source of information is the website of the Canadian Embassy in Washington, D.C., at www.canadainternational.gc.ca/ci-ci /study-etudie/index.aspx.

Canadian universities are currently playing host to about 10,000 American undergraduate and graduate students on their campuses and, as a result of funding cutbacks and internationalization policies in the early 1990s, they have become increasingly active in recruiting students from south of the border. This is but one more reason why it makes sense for more young Americans to check out the "Canadian option." Canada, eh?

University of British Columbia

Vancouver, British Columbia V67 1Z1 CAN

Natural beauty is the first thing that draws Americans to Vancouver—and Canada's premier western university. A similar scale to places like University of Washington but with two major differences—no big-time sports to unite the campus and limited dorm life. The university is active in recruiting overseas, which creates an international ambience.

Website: www.connections
forlife.ubc.ca
Location: City Outskirts
Public
Total Enrollment: 34,965
Undergraduates: 22,955
Male/Female: 47/53
SAT Ranges: 1700 or above
(combined)
ACT Ranges: 26 or above
Financial Aid: N/A
Expense: Pub $ $ $ $
Student Loans: N/A
Average Debt: N/A
Phi Beta Kappa: No
Applicants: 29,086
Accepted: 46%
Enrolled: 49%
Grad in 6 Years: 77%
Returning Freshmen: 92%
Academics: ✐ ✐ ✐ ✐ ½
Social: ☎ ☎
Q of L: ★ ★ ★ ★
Admissions: (877) 272-1422
Email Address: www.askme.
ubc.ca

Strongest Programs:
Economics
Microbiology
Computer Science
Asian Studies
International Relations

What do two prime ministers of Canada, three provincial premiers, an astronaut, a world-renowned opera singer, and a Nobel Prize winner have in common? They are all graduates of the University of British Columbia. Founded in 1908, UBC offers students hundreds of solid programs such as business, science, engineering, the social sciences, and fine arts, as well as ready access to beaches and mountains and a diploma with instant name recognition. Though the massive campus can sometimes feel isolating, students are nevertheless happy to be here in such illustrious company.

Located just 25 minutes from downtown Vancouver, UBC's striking Point Grey campus covers a peninsula that borders the Pacific Ocean and is bounded by an old-growth forest. Mountains—perfect for skiing—loom in the distance. Architectural styles are a mix of Gothic and modern, and students can enjoy a leisurely stroll through the university's botanical gardens. Other notable campus facilities include the Kaiser Building (the central hub of engineering), the Barber Learning Centre, and the Mitchell Thunderbird Sports Arena. The university also has a smaller campus—UBC Okanagan—located in Kelowna, in the Okanagan Valley. New facilities include the Faculty of Pharmaceutical Sciences building and a student commons.

Strong programs include microbiology, international relations, economics, and business administration. Asian studies is highly regarded, and music majors benefit from the Chan Centre for the Performing Arts. Other popular majors include psychology, English, and computer science. The administration concedes that some home economics and agricultural science courses could be strengthened, and one student grumbles about his 8 a.m. philosophy lecture: "Who can focus on the big questions at that time of the morning?" A slew of new undergraduate programs includes majors in applied animal biology, applied plant and soil sciences, geographical biogeosciences, and zoology.

Freshmen benefit from a wide array of first-year programs, including Imagine UBC and Create UBC Okanagan, a first-day orientation. Arts One and the Coordinated Arts programs offer enriched, integrated approaches to broad interdisciplinary themes in arts and humanities. Qualified students can take advantage of Science One, featuring team-taught courses in biology, chemistry, math, and physics. Student exchange programs are available through 174 partner universities in 45 different countries, and co-op programs in engineering, science, arts, commerce, and forestry give students an opportunity to earn while they learn. In addition, honors and double-honors programs are available to superbrains and budding geniuses. Students in the School of Human Kinetics choose from one of three majors at the end of their second year; choices include kinesiology and health science, physical and health education, and interdisciplinary studies in human kinetics. Additionally, applicants to undergrad programs following the U.S. curriculum are required to submit test scores for the SAT (minimum 1700) or ACT (minimum 26).

"Courses can be hard."

The academic climate is exactly what you would expect from a university of UBC's international stature. "Courses can be hard," says one student, "but success is based on your interest and willingness to learn." Most classes have fewer than 50 students, while larger lectures are supplemented with smaller labs and discussion groups. Overall, the faculty receives good marks. "The professors are extremely intelligent people who are truly dedicated to their discipline," says a junior. Academic advising is a mixed bag, with some students complaining that finding a knowledgeable advisor can be time-consuming.

With 35,000 students attending the Vancouver campus, it's no surprise that UBC's student population is a melting pot. "There is a huge diversity here that many smaller schools may lack," says a sophomore. The typical UBC student is bright, hardworking, and gregarious. A history major divides his classmates into two categories: commuters and "those who live on campus and enjoy the community spirit." Minorities are well represented on campus (Asians make up the largest contingency), and the university encourages diversity through a series of special programs and active recruiting. Hot political issues include gay and lesbian rights, abortion, and global genocide. UBC offers merit scholarships to qualified students and athletic scholarships in many varsity sports.

A mere 25 percent of students live on campus. A space is guaranteed to new first-year students who come from beyond local areas; the rest must fend for themselves against Vancouver's pricey rental market or commute from home. On-campus options include co-ed complexes (primarily for freshmen), university apartments, and family units for upperclassmen. Theme houses are another alternative, and offer like-minded students the opportunity to mingle, including three international houses—Korea University/UBC House, Tec de Monterrey/UBC House, and Ritsumeiken House. "Housing is awesome," chirps one senior. Hungry students will find a wide variety of meal options, including "Japanese, Lebanese, Italian, and vegetarian" plates, according to one student.

> "There is a huge diversity here that many smaller schools may lack."

On such a large campus, isolation is a real threat. "You need to get in touch with other students quickly when you get here or you could feel lost on such a big campus," says a freshman. A history major offers another point of view, "One of the biggest complaints is that UBC is too big. I totally disagree with this. I think that the school's biggest strength is its size; there are so many opportunities here." Social life happens mostly on campus but largely "depends on the crowd you hang with," according to one student. For partying types, there are the requisite bashes, courtesy of UBC's small but active Greek scene—one of the few places where underage drinkers may sneak a sip of booze. Alternatives include university-sponsored events, such as movies and guest speakers. Popular campus events include Storm the Wall, longboat racing, and the Arts County Fair.

Vancouver offers students countless opportunities, though one health science major says, "It isn't a college town. It is a well-developed semicosmopolitan city." Another adds, "Vancouver is one of the most livable cities in the world and UBC is located in the nicest, most beautiful part—it's not too hard to imagine what a pleasure it is to go to school with that surrounding you." Beautiful weather draws students outdoors and to nearby beaches and mountains for in-line skating, snowboarding, and swimming. Varsity and intramural competition are favorite pastimes; popular sports include soccer, basketball, hockey, volleyball, and skiing. UBC has 37 varsity teams in 14 sports and those teams have brought home nearly 100 championships—the most of any institution in Canada.

"If you don't get involved in the nonacademics, you'll graduate with only half an education. Academics aren't everything," counsels a junior. Indeed, spending four years at this mammoth university can be isolating for the shy student. But for those willing to take control of their social lives, UBC offers an impressive academic milieu.

Freshmen benefit from a wide array of first-year programs, including Imagine UBC and Create UBC Okanagan, a first-day orientation.

On such a large campus, isolation is a real threat.

Overlaps

University of Toronto, McGill, Simon Fraser, University of Victoria, University of Washington, Queen's University, UC–Berkeley, McMaster

McGill University

Montreal, Quebec H3A 2T5 CAN

The Canadian university best known south of the border. Though instruction is in English, McGill is located in French–speaking Montreal. Individualism is encouraged, and there's a strong international flavor. Only about 10 percent of students live in university housing, and anyone coming here will be on their own for housing after freshman year.

Website: www.mcgill.ca
Location: City Center
Public
Total Enrollment: 37,835
Undergraduates: 25,938
Male/Female: 41/59
SAT Ranges: CR 640–740, M 650–720
ACT Ranges: 29–32
Financial Aid: 18%
Expense: Pub $ $ $ $
Student Loans: N/A
Average Debt: N/A
Phi Beta Kappa: No
Applicants: 21,242
Accepted: 54%
Enrolled: 44%
Grad in 6 Years: 86%
Returning Freshmen: 93%
Academics: ✐ ✐ ✐ ✐ ½
Social: ☎ ☎ ☎ ☎
Q of L: ★ ★ ★ ★
Admissions: (514) 398-3910
Email Address: admissions@mcgill.ca

Strongest Programs:
Medicine
Law
Engineering
Management
Environmental Studies
Music

With such strong preprofessional programs and a diverse student body, it's easy to see why enterprising men and women from around the world flock to McGill University. But beware: This is not a cookie-cutter school, and fitting in actually seems to be discouraged. "McGill is a university where people are allowed to become individuals," a senior says. "Difference and creativity are celebrated here."

Montreal's climate alternates between hot summers and freezing winters. A junior describes McGill's 88-acre main campus as "an oasis in the heart of the city." Located in downtown Montreal amidst the hustle and bustle, the campus provides students with ample green space and a welcome respite from the decidedly urban atmosphere of the city. Campus buildings range from "Gothic-like" structures with vines growing up the sides to more modern structures. Trees and greenery dot the campus landscape, and the sprawling recreation trails of Mount Royal rise to its immediate north. Newer construction includes a $71 million life sciences complex that serves as the centerpiece of the largest research complex of its kind in Eastern Canada and the Montreal Neurological Institute. The Schulich School of Music offers an ultramodern symphony and multimedia hall that functions as a recording studio, performance venue, and research studio. A short drive west of downtown, the Macdonald Campus occupies 1,600 acres of woods and fields on the shores of Lac St-Louis, providing unique opportunities for fieldwork and research.

> **"It is important to consider the university on the basis of which faculty you would be interested in."**

Though the most popular majors are psychology, political science, commerce, and education, there is no denying that the university's strengths lie in preprofessional programs such as medicine, law, and engineering. The sciences receive uniform praise, as does the School of Environment, where environment-related courses are offered. For those who want to escape Montreal's brutal winters, there are internships; field studies in Barbados, Africa, and the Smithsonian Tropical Research Institute in Panama; exchange programs with more than 500 partner universities around the world; and study abroad options via the Canadian University Study Abroad Program (CUSAP).

To fulfill the university's general education requirements, students must first choose which discipline (or faculty) to enter. A senior says, "It is important to consider the university on the basis of which faculty you would be interested in, because they vary greatly and operate almost as independent units." On average, students must earn 120 credits to graduate with a four-year degree. Freshmen must accumulate six to 12 credits in three of four disciplines, including languages, math and science, social sciences, and humanities, and declare a major before their sophomore year. Upon entering their major, students have a menu of course options that includes honors programs and double majors. A double-degree interdisciplinary program allows students to combine a bachelor of arts program with one in the sciences. Several programs help freshmen with the transition to college, and some are tailored to international students, which includes those from the United States.

Regardless of the major, students can expect classes to be demanding. "McGill has a very stressful and competitive atmosphere," a finance major says. Classes tend to be large—especially for freshmen, who have more than 100 students in two-thirds of their classes—and students must be willing to seek out professors and advisors. "The quality of teaching is generally above average," a student says. "Many of the professors are kind, intelligent, and devoted to their students." Academic advising is a bureaucratic tangle, and students grumble that red tape is part of the McGill experience. "There is way too much red tape and dealing with the administration can be horrible," says one senior.

McGill students are a diverse lot—more than 140 countries are represented here—and the only common thread among students seems to be their fierce independence. A geography major says McGill students are "hardworking, driven, very intellectual, and research-oriented." Environmental issues are a big concern, and students report that political and social concerns receive ample attention on campus. Qualified students are eligible for merit scholarships, but there are no awards for athletes. There is also a work-study program for those in need of financial assistance.

The university's six traditional and 14 alternative residence halls house 12 percent of undergrads in dorms, apartments, and shared facilities houses. Dorms run the gamut but one recent acquisition is, according to a senior, a "four-star hotel, turned into a six-star dorm." Party animals will feel free to crank up the stereo in Molson or McConnell, while bookworms might be better suited for Gardener. Douglas denizens enjoy their hall's quaint charm, and women who want to skip the co-ed scene can find a room in Royal Victoria College, an all-female dorm. "The dining facilities are good," says a sophomore. Off-campus apartments are a popular alternative for upperclassmen, who take advantage of Montreal's clean, affordable housing. Despite its urban location, the McGill campus is safe and security is considered more than adequate. "There are student organizations like 'Walksafe' and 'Drivesafe' that will walk or drive students to their residences at night regardless of where they are or where they are going," reports one student.

"McGill students are very sociable and love to party!" says one student. Though there are "considerable on-campus social activities, with many clubs and associations," many students venture off campus into Montreal for fun and adventure. "A cultural epicenter, Montreal is home to some of the world's best museums, galleries, restaurants, shops, and music," a senior says. "There are always free concerts and festivals all over the city throughout the year." Drinking is a popular pastime, but underage drinkers are few and far between since the legal age in Quebec is 18. "McGill treats its students as mature, educated adults and offers them the decision to choose whether or not to drink. Their decision is respected," reports a senior English major. Well-attended campus events include homecoming, Winter Carnival, and Frosh Week activities. Popular road trips include New York City, Ottawa, and Toronto. Ski slopes are less than an hour away.

Rugby, ice hockey, and women's soccer are among the most popular varsity sports, and all have captured recent championships. According to one student, "The McGill-Harvard rugby match is a must-watch." Women's synchronized swimming has won four consecutive national championships and women's hockey also brought home a national title in 2008. Intramurals offer would-be jocks an opportunity to

Upon entering their major, students have a menu of course options that includes honors programs and double majors.

"McGill has a very stressful and competitive atmosphere."

Well-attended campus events include homecoming, Winter Carnival, and Frosh Week activities.

Overlaps

University of British Columbia, Concordia, University of Montreal, NYU, Queen's University, University of Toronto

blow off steam after classes and on weekends, with soccer and ice hockey attracting the most interest.

In recent years the government of Quebec has been less than enthusiastic about funding its English-speaking academic gem, and large classes and mountains of red tape are undeniably part of the McGill experience. Nevertheless, most denizens seem happy. "The students who go to McGill are very invested in their academic life and are proud of their school," a student says.

If You Apply To >

McGill: Regular admissions: Jan 15. Application fee: $100 ($161.56 for music applicants). No campus or alumni interviews. SATs or ACTs: optional. Subject Tests: optional (varies by program). No essay question.

Queen's University

Kingston, Ontario K7L 3N6 CAN

With "only" 15,952 undergraduates, Queen's is the smallest of the major Canadian universities. It is also the only one set in a metropolitan area of modest size. Engineering is perhaps its strongest area, with business a close second. Toronto and Montreal are both about three hours away. With 90 percent of its students in the dorms, Queen's has more active residential life than other Canadian universities.

Website: www.queensu.ca
Location: City Center
Public
Total Enrollment: 22,168
Undergraduates: 15,952
Male/Female: 41/59
SAT Ranges: 1200 or above (combined)
ACT Ranges: 26 or above
Financial Aid: 52%
Expense: Pub $ $ $
Student Loans: 30%
Average Debt: N/A
Phi Beta Kappa: No
Applicants: 29,000
Accepted: 47%
Enrolled: 31%
Grad in 6 Years: 91%
Returning Freshmen: 94%
Academics: ✍ ✍ ✍ ✍ ½
Social: 🍺 🍺 🍺 🍺
Q of L: ★ ★ ★ ★
Admissions: (613) 533-2218
Email Address: admission@ queensu.ca

Students at Queen's University approach work and play with equal zeal and enjoy a potent mix of school spirit and intellectual drive. Success requires energy and a willingness to get into the thick of things. "People who aren't interested in being a part of the school community are better off at a school that isn't such a big family," warns a sophomore. Solid academics, a pervasive school spirit, and long-standing traditions make life at this storied university unique—and demanding. "Getting into Queen's is just the first challenge," says a senior. "Succeeding at Queen's is another battle."

The 161-acre Queen's campus is located on the north shore of Lake Ontario, just minutes from the heart of Kingston, Ontario ("the limestone city") and directly between Montreal and Toronto. "Almost all buildings are constructed using limestone," explains a senior. Historically significant buildings have been maintained, and "there are some modern buildings with a lot of glass to provide a bright and welcoming atmosphere." Ample greenery and open spaces provide students a place to stretch out under the sky and hit the books. Additional features include the $230 million Queen's Centre, which features facilities for the School of Kinesiology and Health Studies, and a recent expansion to Goodes Hall.

> **"Getting into Queen's is just the first challenge."**

Established in 1841 by Royal Charter of Queen Victoria, Queen's University offers undergraduate degrees in a variety of faculties, including arts, science, engineering, commerce, education, music, nursing science, and fine art. Academics are unilaterally solid, but the most demanding are engineering and commerce. The bachelor of commerce program was the first of its kind in Canada and provides students with an internationally focused liberal business education, enhanced by leadership modules and the integration of technology. The School of Computing offers bachelor of computer degrees in biomedical computing, cognitive science, and software design, as well as B.A. and B.S. degrees. Computing and the Creative Arts is a multidisciplinary program that allows students to use cutting-edge software programs for music, drama, art, and film production. General education requirements vary by program, but all students can expect to complete a rigorous series of core and elective courses. Students participating in the Queen's International Study Centre are whisked away to the university's England campus, where they enjoy small classes and integrated field studies while residing in a 15th-century castle. In addition, there are exchange programs with universities around the world.

(continued)

Strongest Programs:
Engineering
Fine Art
Commerce
Film
Drama
Music

"The academic climate is quite competitive and the courses are often theory-driven and require a substantial amount of work to prepare for class and complete assignments," says one senior. The general consensus among struggling students is that As are hard to come by. "After working your butt off and reading stacks of textbooks, your grades pale in comparison to the marks of students at other universities," gripes a biology major. Classes tend to be large for freshmen and sophomores, but dwindle in size as

"The courses are often theory-driven and require a substantial amount of work."

one approaches graduation. The majority of classes are taught by full professors, who receive praise for their accessibility and intelligence. "The teachers I have had have been thorough, challenging, and concerned about my success," says a junior. Office hours and special "wine and cheese" functions give students ample opportunity to mingle with faculty. Students report that there is little trouble getting into desired classes, and "there is lots of counseling available for students who need it."

Queen's students are an industrious, intelligent group, and most are used to academic success. "Students take pride and honor in their work and are deeply involved in the Queen's community," asserts one student. School spirit runs high and campus issues include rising tuition fees—and determining just who is responsible for the cost. Students come from every Canadian province and 80 countries, and a sociology major says that "Queen's is very PC and inclusive, regardless of gender, race, religion, or sexual orientation." A large percentage of the student body is active in extracurriculars, and school spirit is a must. Though there are no athletic scholarships, hundreds of merit awards averaging $2,000 are handed out annually. "I have had great help through scholarships and financial aid," relates a senior. "There is quite a lot of money for you. You just have to go after it." International students need not apply for scholarships separately; they are automatically considered for available merit awards.

The School of Computing offers bachelor of computer degrees in biomedical computing, cognitive science, and software design.

Ninety percent of students live in one of 11 residence halls, and all freshmen are guaranteed a place to hang their hats. The residence halls are "comfortable, extremely well maintained, and offer a number of services for students," says a senior. Co-ed and single-sex dorms are available. A mandatory meal plan gives freshmen a wide variety of foods to choose from, including pasta, salad, pizza, and a soup-and-salad bar. The surrounding city also offers a plethora of dining options. "Kingston is known in our house as the 'city of restaurants,'" says a student. "They are everywhere." After freshman year, most students pack their bags and head off campus to the

"Social life is huge at Queen's."

"student village," where comfortable apartments are available. In fact, 80 percent of Queen's students live within a 15-minute walk of campus. Though always a concern, safety is practically a nonissue on campus. Students report that they feel quite safe and that security is more than adequate.

Make no mistake about it, Queen's students know how to have a good time. "Social life is huge at Queen's," says a student. Adds another, "Campus pubs and city pubs have both found their niche." On Thursday nights, students flock to campus bars such as Afie's for a drink or two (or three), while Saturday nights are reserved for city bars and nightclubs. The legal drinking age is 19, and kiddies will have a tough time skirting the law. "The bouncers in Kingston actually have a couple of brain cells and can spot a fake ID from 90 kilometers away," says a senior. Nonalcoholic alternatives include school-sponsored movies and extracurricular clubs (there are more than

A large percentage of the student body is active in extracurriculars, and school spirit is a must.

220!). "Extracurricular activities are a must, not an option!" says one student. Frosh Week is a favorite event, with "cheers that even the most blasé of students will be shouting out with pride by the end of the week." The school is steeped in Scottish tradition, and it's normal to see kilt-wearing bandsmen at important campus events.

The school is steeped in Scottish tradition, and it's normal to see kilt-wearing bandsmen at important campus events.

Once the capital of Canada, Kingston is described as "very much a university town." There are several universities in the area (including the Royal Military College), and downtown provides students with places to shop. "Kingston itself has several clubs, three malls, a number of museums, numerous gyms, and three or four movie theaters," says a student. The city's relative isolation makes it the favored stomping ground for students without wheels. Town/gown relations are good, and students are very active in the community. Toronto and Montreal (less than three hours away) are popular road trips.

With more than 40 varsity teams, Queen's athletic program is not only the largest in Canada, but also ranks with Harvard University and MIT for the largest programs in North America. Competitive sports include men's and women's rugby; women's squash; men's soccer, rowing, golf; and women's lacrosse. The annual "kill McGill" football game against rival McGill University draws pigskin-crazed students from every corner of campus; homecoming is reputed to be a raucous affair featuring "alumni from the 1920s parading around the football field during halftime." Intramural competition is fierce, too, and nearly every student is involved on some level. A student says, "There is so much school spirit, sometimes it makes you sick."

Life at Queen's University is one of extremes. "Our spirit is second to none," says a senior. Though the academic climate can be tough and the winters long, students here find much to praise. "One of the great things about Queen's is that it's constantly growing and expanding to meet the needs of its students," says one senior, "but at the same time, it never loses sight of where it came from or what it stands for."

Overlaps

University of British Columbia, McGill, University of Toronto, University of Waterloo, University of Western Ontario, York

If You Apply To > **Queen's:** Rolling admissions: Feb. 1. Application fee: $105 (Canadian funds). No campus or alumni interviews. SATs: required. Subject Tests: optional (required for engineering candidates only). No essay question; students must complete online personal statement of experience.

University of Toronto

BEST BUY

Toronto, Ontario M5S 1A3 CAN

U of T is one of the largest institutions in the *Fiske Guide* and one of the biggest in the world. It is also, for most readers, in a foreign country. If ever there were a place where go-getterism is a necessity, this is it. In the absence of American-style school spirit, U of T students cut loose to find their fun in the city. Toronto is one of the most diverse and cosmopolitan cities in the world, with nearly half of its citizens born outside of Canada.

Website: www.utoronto.ca
Location: City Center
Public
Total Enrollment: 67,339
Undergraduates: 57,507
Male/Female: 43/57

Students at the University of Toronto avoid getting lost in the shuffle by taking part in a unique residential college system that allows them to model their educational experience after their own personalities. Each college has a distinct character and appeal, yet blends seamlessly into the university's overall academic milieu. And when it comes to academics, the U of T delivers, says a senior: "The students were likely at the top of their class in high school and are very competitive—more so than at Queen's or York universities."

Indeed, the University of Toronto is so large that it spans three campuses. The St. George campus in downtown Toronto features Gothic architecture and historic buildings. The suburban campuses in Mississauga and Scarborough feature more modern structures. Other facilities include the Centre for Biological Timing and Cognition, where researchers will study how sleep cycles affect learning and physical and mental health. The Varsity Centre for Physical Activity and Health includes regulation football and soccer fields and a score of additional amenities.

Students apply directly to one of Toronto's nine colleges, seven of which are on the St. George campus. U.S. citizens who are admitted typically have a high school diploma, SAT or ACT (including the writing test) results, plus three SAT II or AP/IB scores in appropriate subjects. Students are expected to present composite scores of at least 1700 for the SAT or 26 for the ACT; most programs require higher scores. Scores below 500 on any component of the SAT or SAT II are not acceptable. Prerequisite courses should be taken at a twelfth-grade level. The most popular majors include arts, science, commerce, engineering, and physical health and education. The concurrent education program allows undergraduates to complete the requirements for a bachelor of education, professional teacher certification, and a second undergraduate degree simultaneously.

"The University of Toronto is known for its rigorous academic environment."

First-Year Seminars, capped at 24 students each, are "a good transition from high school to university," says a senior, and give incoming freshmen the chance to learn from leading faculty members in a less intimidating environment. In addition, the Trinity One and Vic One programs each offer 25 to 50 highly capable students the opportunity to develop their critical thinking, speaking, and writing skills, while fostering close relationships with fellow students, instructors, guest lecturers, and visiting scholars. The U of T Music Faculty is the oldest in Canada and offers bachelor's, master's, and doctoral degrees in all of their programs. As befitting such a gargantuan institution, the university's endowment is the largest of any Canadian college or university.

Courses require a great deal of reading outside the classroom and are typically demanding. "The University of Toronto is known for its rigorous academic environment and I can certainly attest to this," says one linguistics major. Large lecture classes are accompanied by smaller tutorials, facilitating personal attention, and professors get high marks for their teaching skills and their smarts. "The quality of teaching is very good," one student says. Another adds, "Almost all classes are taught by full professors." Students complain that administrators continue to shift the focus from undergraduates in favor of "grad programs and the departments that bring in the big money."

U of T students are "very academic and goal-oriented, motivated, studious, and serious workers," says a student. Only 9 percent of those enrolled are "foreign"—from outside Canada, that is—and the most significant issue on campus is rising tuition and fees, blamed on the provincial and national governments. The Ontario Public Interest Research Group and Amnesty International attract sizable followings, and students turn out in droves to celebrate PRIDE, the largest gay pride event in North America, along with Frosh Week, which includes wacky fun such as bed races between the colleges. (Presumably, these involve carrying new friends from place to place on a bed, not racing to see who can be first to hop under the covers with the guy or gal from down the hall.) There are no athletic scholarships.

"Almost all classes are taught by full professors."

Twenty-five percent of first-year students live in campus housing and are guaranteed rooms. "There are new buildings, and historic old buildings that are beautiful," says an anthropology major. "They are cozy and comfortable and pretty well maintained." All of the dorms are affiliated with one of the nine undergraduate colleges,

(continued)

SAT Ranges: N/A
ACT Ranges: N/A
Financial Aid: 49%
Expense: Pub $
Student Loans: N/A
Average Debt: N/A
Phi Beta Kappa: Yes
Applicants: 67,703
Accepted: 69%
Enrolled: 30%
Grad in 6 Years: 82%
Returning Freshmen: 91%
Academics: ✍ ✍ ✍ ✍ ½
Social: ☎ ☎ ☎
Q of L: ★ ★ ★
Admissions: (416) 978-2190
Email Address: admissions
   .help@utoronto.ca

Strongest Programs:
Arts
Science
Engineering
Medicine
Education
Music

The most popular majors include arts, science, commerce, engineering, and physical health and education.

which act as "local neighborhoods" and center on specialties, including Buddhism, Celtic studies, and criminology. The dining options receive generally good marks, although the food is "nothing spectacular," according to a student. Campus security is good, thanks in part to a walking-escort service that operates after dark.

Social life here revolves around the very energetic city in which the school is located, says a sociology and English major. "The social life on campus is pretty tame," says one senior. Toronto boasts great culture, super shopping, a clean and safe nightlife district—and the picturesque shores of Lake Ontario, lovely in warmer weather. "Toronto has a huge club scene, and U of T pub nights happen in the city," the student explains. The legal drinking age here is 19; students who are of age may have alcohol in their rooms, but not in common spaces, and anyone caught violating local laws or the open container policy is reported to the dean of the residence.

"The social life on campus is pretty tame."

Those wishing to party alcohol-free will find plenty of school-sponsored events, such as movies, guest speakers, and countless clubs. There are no fraternities or sororities, but there is a club for nearly every interest, including curling, Magic: The Gathering, an engineering Lego group, a female fast-pitch softball team, and broomball intramurals.

Sports are not a focus of campus life at Toronto, though hockey, volleyball, and basketball are among the varsity teams that draw something of a following, especially when the opponent is Queen's University or the University of Western Ontario. The intramural program, however, is another story. It's the largest in Canada, involving over 8,500 students in 26 sports and 57 leagues each year. Residence halls and groups of friends compete in everything from badminton to indoor cricket, innertube water polo, squash, triathlon, and ultimate Frisbee. Students can also be found cheering the city's many professional teams, including the Blue Jays (baseball), the Raptors (basketball), and the Maple Leafs (hockey).

Toronto's biggest liability, its sheer and sometimes overwhelming size, may also be its biggest asset, students say—as long as they learn to speak up, and proactively take advantage of all of the school's resources. "I have met many people here from countries I'd only read about, and have learned a lot about different cultural beliefs and practices," says a junior. "There are lots of people from all over the globe," adds a senior. "You learn about what is happening not only in your country, but in others as well."

Overlaps

University of British Columbia, Guelph, MacMaster, McGill, Queen's, Ryerson, University of Western Ontario

If You Apply To ➤

University of Toronto: Regular admissions. Application fee: $95. No campus or alumni interviews. SATs or ACTs: required. Subject Tests: required. No essay question.

British and Irish Colleges and Universities

If going to college in Canada sounds adventuresome, you'll need even more moxie to venture overseas. But give it some thought. As the most popular overseas destination, Great Britain currently has about 2,300 Americans enrolled in undergraduate degree programs, and another 30,000 per year are pursuing shorter study abroad stints. Hundreds more have found their way to the Republic of Ireland. Studying in Britain or Ireland is not as cheap as in Canada—count on a total bill of $35,000 to $40,000 or so depending on the university—but the top British and Irish universities offer a richer international experience, infused with historical and cultural perspectives, than you will find on this side of the Atlantic.

Before we go further, here's a word to moms and dads: You may get queasy at the thought of sending your little cherub across a 3,000-mile ocean, but a flight to Dublin or London is quicker than driving 10 hours to get to First Choice U. Once you're there, the cities are at least as safe as those in the U.S., and the small towns have a crime rate roughly equivalent to that of the town of Mayberry on *The Andy Griffith Show*. The best part for parents: You'll need to visit at least once—and preferably more.

For those who are hazy on their geography, England, Scotland, and Wales make up Great Britain; throw in Northern Ireland and the moniker changes to the United Kingdom. The Republic of Ireland, occupying the southern part of the Emerald Isle across the Irish Sea, used to be part of Great Britain, but won its independence in 1921. Ireland is the closest European nation to the East Coast of the U.S., and the only English-speaking country in the eurozone. Britain and Ireland make the most sense for American students interested in studying English literature, history, foreign languages, and anything related to international studies. If medieval history is your passion, why not go to school where the remains of that long-ago world still dot the landscape? If you're looking for a career in international business, perhaps consider a country where the global village has been a way of life, and you will be making lifelong friends from around the world. Though Britain is an English-speaking country, it offers far better instruction in European and other languages than you can get in the U.S., and Ireland's favorable corporate tax rates have led U.S. companies such as Google, Microsoft, and GlaxoSmithKline to make it their European headquarters (think internships). No matter what your academic interests, your classmates will include a cross section of nationalities that would be the envy of any North American institution. Most importantly, study in Britain and Ireland has the potential to be a life-changing experience that will broaden your horizons and deepen your understanding of our increasingly globalized world. With cheap flights and trains readily available, travel to Continental Europe and beyond becomes a way of life.

With all of these benefits come some challenges. American students in Britain need to adjust to a different tenor of academic life than is found at U.S. colleges and universities. There are no campus "bubbles" to protect you from the real world. Students are treated as adults and expected to behave accordingly. The legal drinking age is 18, which obviates the need for fake IDs but puts the onus on students to behave responsibly. Dorms are generally the domain of first-year students; expect to find a "flat" (apartment) for subsequent years. "Sport" means playing, not watching. The student body will not come out on a Saturday afternoon for the big game for a simple reason: There are no big games. Most faculty members (a.k.a. tutors) are ready to help you if you are struggling with your studies, but only if you take the initiative. There is no Dean of Student Hand-Holding in British universities (nor do they offer landing pads for Helicopter Parents).

Americans thinking about studying in Britain and Ireland should also be aware of differences in the academic system "across the Pond." Most important: Whereas American universities generally require students to sample a variety of fields for two years before choosing a major, British and Irish institutions expect students to identify their field of concentration before they set foot on campus. That's because students take their general education courses in high school. Thus students in Britain and Ireland take only two or three courses at a time, mostly related to their major. American-style distribution requirements are all but unheard of—good news for students who want to get out of those nasty math or foreign language requirements. But keep in mind that since British and Irish students tend to take courses only in subjects that seriously interest them, all classes are taught at a high level, even introductory ones. Moreover, although students get fewer hours in class, they are expected to put in more hours of study per course outside of class. Anyone who wants to change majors after a year or two may encounter difficulty.

Another important academic difference is that British and Irish universities evaluate applicants almost entirely on the basis of academic credentials, with emphasis on demonstrated ability in their field of study. No essays about page 236 of your autobiography or need to present yourself as a well-rounded overachiever who will enrich the campus environment. As one administrator put it, "We don't do social engineering." Along with Trinity College Dublin, the top British universities, especially the four "ancient" Scottish universities, are thus a good bet for U.S. students who may have the smarts to do Ivy League work, but whose résumés do not include an Olympic medal or building a school in Belize during spring vacation. Standards are high; St. Andrews, for example, looks for minimum score of 1950 on the SAT I, and 28 on the ACT. Aberdeen is a bit less choosy: 1800 and 27 respectively. Trinity College Dublin wants 1300 on any two SATs, a GPA of 3.3 from an academically strong school, and at least 29 on the ACT. Institutions tend to prefer the SAT over the ACT, though many will accept either. Scores from SAT II or AP tests may also be required. For the application essay, the British usually ask about commitment to your intended major and why you want to study it. They view American-style personal essays as fluff.

While the price tag for all this cross-cultural enrichment is about one-third less than that of a selective private institution in the U.S., the downside is that academic scholarships are scarce and institutional financial aid all but nonexistent. British and Irish students, along with those from the European Union, generally receive government funding. Federal aid such as Stafford loans and Pell Grants can be transported, but many, if not most, families will find themselves paying the full freight. And because exchange rates fluctuate, the bill can vary significantly depending on whether the dollar is weak or strong. For a searchable database of the few scholarships available for study in Great Britain, visit the British Council at www.britishcouncil.org/usa. One reason that financially strapped British universities have recently begun showing a greater interest in recruiting U.S. students is that they are a source of much-needed revenue. By and large, the academic bars for U.S. students are slightly lower than for native Brits.

If you are considering a British university, you may be picturing yourself in England, the most populous region of Great Britain that includes London as well as fabled universities such as Oxford and Cambridge. But here's the rub: the English have a system of higher education that makes degree study impractical in many cases. In England, undergraduate degrees are completed in three years, not four, and students are generally assumed to have completed 13 years of schooling rather than 12. As a result, the most selective English universities are reluctant to admit American high school graduates—some refuse to admit any—and the students who do get in will find themselves navigating a world more appropriate for juniors and seniors in college. One note on terminology: in Britain and Ireland, a program of study is called a "course." The British word for what we call a course is "module."

The University of Cambridge (www.cam.ac.uk) is particularly blunt about "the possible mismatch between the broad liberal arts curriculum of the North American high school and the specialist emphasis of British degree courses." The University of Oxford (www.ox.ac.uk) does offer a glimmer of hope for a select few superachievers, and has recently ramped up its recruiting efforts in the former Colonies. Oxford will consider American students who graduate in the top 2 percent of their class, and it has recently stepped up its recruiting efforts in U.S. high schools. In a recent year it enrolled about 30 U.S. students. Even so, the odds of admission to Oxford are lower than at any college in the U.S., including Harvard. The vast majority of American undergraduates at both Oxford and Cambridge are there for a second bachelor's degree after earning one from an American institution. Students with their hearts set on the Oxbridge institutions should consider them for graduate school, where both welcome Americans (and their dollars) in significant amounts.

Students will hear a similar story at the third-most recognized name in English higher education, the London School of Economics (www2.lse.ac.uk), which enrolls about 3,600 undergraduates. The LSE says it will not normally consider U.S. students until they have a year of higher education under their belts. Less selective English institutions are more receptive to Americans, but, once again, only those who feel certain of what they would like to study should apply. If you are in this category, there is one potential benefit to an English degree: the three-year degree program will save you a year of tuition bills.

So what to do? One answer is to cast your gaze on Scotland, England's less populous neighbor, where universities offer four-year degrees that are much better suited to the needs of American high school graduates. Scotland, which lies north of England, was an independent nation until 1706, and has its own parliament that exercises considerable power when it comes to domestic policy. It has an illustrious intellectual history and has produced the likes of David Hume, Adam Smith, Rudyard Kipling, Robert Louis Stevenson, J. K. Rowling, and the world's most famous ogre, Shrek. Scotland is more egalitarian in feel than England—less hung up on social class.

The Scots take great pride in their universities, which are central to their national identity and have deep historical ties with American higher education. The American-style liberal arts institution was imported directly from Scotland in the person of John Witherspoon, a graduate of the University of Edinburgh who was lured to the U.S. in 1768 to head Princeton University. With the model of his alma mater in mind, Witherspoon transformed Princeton from a small-time school for ministers into a broad-based institution that taught philosophy, history, geography, science, mathematics, and theology. Like their U.S. counterparts, Scottish universities offer four-year programs; thus, they represent something of a middle ground between the American system and that of Oxford and Cambridge with their three-year, entirely specialized programs. Scottish universities expect early specialization, but there is some room to explore fields outside your major during the first two years. One downside of studying in Scotland is its northern location, which makes for long winter nights. Scotland has also been historically regarded as a "dreich" corner of Britain—a Highland term referring to weather variously described as dull, overcast, drizzly, cold, misty, and miserable, or a combination thereof. Scottish higher education is noted for its four "ancient" universities—Aberdeen, Edinburgh, Glasgow, and St. Andrews—each of which is profiled in the pages that follow.

There are seven universities in Ireland, but Trinity College Dublin is by far the most distinguished, and it is the only one that operates on a four-year system for undergraduates. TCD was founded in 1592 by Queen Elizabeth as an Irish counterpart to Oxford and Cambridge to train Anglican clergymen. While TCD follows the Scottish system, its cultural ties remain distinctly English, and graduates who subsequently enroll in Oxford or Cambridge are automatically entitled to an "ad eundem" courtesy degree from the English university. TCD was founded as the University of Dublin with the expectation that it would serve as "the mother of a university" and other colleges would grow up around it à la Oxbridge. This never happened, though, so for all practical purposes Trinity College Dublin is the University of Dublin. Roman Catholics make up the overwhelming majority of students despite the fact that until as late as 1972 they needed special permission from church authorities to attend this bastion of Anglican scholarship.

Students applying to UK institutions should generally use the Universities and Colleges Admissions Service (UCAS, www.ucas.ac.uk), which functions like the Common Application group in the U.S. The UCAS form asks you to list all your courses and the grades you received in them, as well as your SAT and/or ACT scores. It also requires an essay and a letter of recommendation. Most institutions will accept applications through the spring, though we recommend that you apply by the deadline for British students, January 15. The deadline for applying to Oxford and Cambridge, or to apply to any program in medicine, is October 15 for entrance the following fall. Many institutions have rolling admissions, another reason to apply early. Applicants to Trinity College Dublin apply directly to the university. It has rolling admissions with an early-decision deadline of November 1.

A high proportion of U.S. students currently enrolled in British universities come from families with international connections, such as close relatives living in other countries or diplomat parents, but prior international experience is by no means required. College in Britain is not for the faint of heart, but it can be richly rewarding for those with the initiative to take the plunge. After college in Britain, students will have the skills and savvy to succeed almost anywhere in the world.

University of Aberdeen

Aberdeen, Scotland AB24 3FX GB

Located in Scotland's third largest city, Aberdeen is the most accessible of the four "ancient" universities. Notable for the flexibility of its curriculum and emphasis on independent learning. Major attractions include engineering, life sciences, and anything related to Europe. City of Aberdeen combines charm with the bustle of a small city. Outdoor enthusiasts will find the Scottish Highlands at arm's length.

The University of Aberdeen was founded in 1495, three years after a certain well-known explorer sailed from Spain to the New World. Students seeking the flavor of old Europe will not be disappointed. With plenty of cobblestone streets and buildings made of ancient stone (it's the Granite City), the university has a distinctly medieval aura. It offers top-notch academics, a curriculum that is unusually flexible by UK standards, and a slice of life far richer than any U.S. institution can muster. "It's great fun and has a lot of opportunities," says a senior, "both academically and socially."

With a population of 240,000, the port city of Aberdeen is Scotland's third largest city. Once a center for fishing, shipbuilding, and textiles, it is now a center for the thriving oil extraction business in the North Sea. With two universities—the other is Robert Gordon—it is the educational capital of Northeastern Scotland. Aberdeen is perched at a latitude roughly the same as Juneau, Alaska, but because of the Gulf Stream, winter temperatures are generally milder than those on the East Coast of the United States. December days are short in winter, but sky-gazers are often treated to glimpses of the fabled Northern Lights.

"The students aren't hypercompetitive."

Website: www.abdn.ac.uk/sras
Location: Small City
Public
Total Enrollment: 16,500
Undergraduates: 11,000
Male/Female: 49/51
SAT Ranges: 1800 (combined)
ACT Ranges: 27 or above
Financial Aid: N/A
Expense: Pub $ $ $ $
Student Loans: N/A
Average Debt: N/A
Phi Beta Kappa: No
Applicants: 13,000

(continued)

Accepted: 27%
Enrolled: N/A
Grad in 6 Years: N/A
Returning Freshmen: N/A
Academics: ✐ ✐ ✐ ✐ ½
Social: 🍷 🍷 🍷 🍷
Q of L: ★ ★ ★ ★
Admissions: (+44) (0) 1224
   27209
Email Address: sras@abdn.
   ac.uk

Strongest Programs:
Divinity
Biological Studies
Engineering
English
French
Geography
History
Law
Medicine
Politics and International
   Relations

*Aberdeen is divided
into three colleges:
the College of Arts
and Social Sciences,
the College of Life
Sciences and Medicine,
and the College of
Physical Sciences.*

Most university buildings are concentrated in a quiet enclave known as "Old Aberdeen." The campus is crowned, literally, by a 16th-century tower in the shape of an imperial crown. Lightly traveled streets pass through the campus, and the multitude of green lawns and picturesque courtyards are ideal for lounging on sunny days. As part of its "Sixth Century Campaign," the university has begun investing $450 million in infrastructure and facilities over the next decade, starting with a new library.

Aberdeen is divided into three colleges: the College of Arts and Social Sciences, the College of Life Sciences and Medicine, and the College of Physical Sciences. The

"I have found my professors very approachable."

university is in the midst of a curriculum overhaul designed to add flexibility and bring it more into line with the academic systems of Harvard, Melbourne, Hong Kong, and top universities around the world. Thus it has introduced a series of interdisciplinary Sixth Century Courses such as Science and the Media or Oceans and Society that students are expected to sample during their first two years. Other curriculum innovations are designed to encourage students to pursue interests outside their core disciplines—what might be called "electives" in an American context. Popular majors include English literature, biology, religious studies, environmental science, and a joint international relations/politics concentration. Engineering is also strong, especially for programs related to the oil industry. The Centre for Learning and Teaching helps faculty members find ways to enhance the learning experience, while the Student Learning Service helps students develop their academic skills.

With approximately 16,000 students, Aberdeen is a medium-sized university by U.S. standards. The academic climate is described as relaxed. "The students aren't hypercompetitive," reports a biology major, "but if you are motivated to push yourself, there are always people to help you." Courses in the first two years generally consist of lectures supplemented by smaller weekly discussion sections. "One of the finest points about Aberdeen is that you are always lectured to by full professors starting in the first year," declares an English major. "I have found my professors very approachable, friendly, and helpful," chirps a history

"The university has a relaxed climate."

major. Professors typically team-teach introductory "modules," with each covering the topics that are his or her specialty. As in other Scottish universities, students generally take only three subjects at a time in the first two years, with extensive reading and research outside of class generally taken for granted. "Often we are expected to come to class prepared to discuss certain topics, but given no minimum reading assignment. The professor gives out a list of selected readings from which we can choose," says a history major. Grades are typically determined by end-of-the-term evaluations with few intermediate assignments. At the end of their second year, students must typically pass exams in order to advance to "honors level," the equivalent of the junior and senior years of college in the States. Upper-level science students typically spend long hours in the lab. One nice feature: There is generally no limit to the number of students who can enroll in a particular course, thereby giving students the freedom to sign up for anything that strikes their fancy. "The university has a relaxed climate," says a junior, who adds the "emphasis is on self-study with strong background support."

Overall, 57 percent of undergraduates hail from Scotland, 17 percent from the rest of the UK, and 20 percent arrive from 120 different countries, including 65 U.S. undergrads and another hundred or so Yankees doing study abroad. "Wandering around campus, you are bound to hear at least three different languages being spoken in a day," reports a first-year student, adding, "The people here are extremely friendly and outgoing." The political climate on campus is described as conservative and relatively subdued. Upon their arrival at the university, students partake of Freshers Week, when student organizations sponsor informational meetings.

Aberdeen is a selective institution for U.S. students, though less so than the other three "ancient" universities.

On-campus housing at Aberdeen is varied and guaranteed to all first-year students. "Accommodations themselves are basic," notes one student, "but you get what you pay for." A majority of the international students live in Hillhead Halls of Residence, a complex of houses and flats that is about a 15-minute walk from the campus. Students may elect catered rooms (two meals per day) or self-catering, wherein they cook their own food with kitchen facilities generally located down the hall from the rooms. Many students choose to move off campus after their first year, and a variety of housing options are available near the campus. Only a few students own cars, as the university is within easy walking distance of the city center and the North Sea and is on a regular bus route. Parking permits are made available to those students who require them.

As in other Scottish universities, students generally take only three subjects at a time in the first two years.

The drinking age in Britain is 18, so social life at Aberdeen revolves around legal consumption rather than drinking on the sly. "Most people go out on most nights if only for a pint at the pub," reports an exchange student. Aberdeen offers a varied nightlife with clubs and bars to suit all tastes. You may find yourself doing what Britons call "the pub crawl," which means sampling the refreshment of several pubs before heading home in the wee hours. For those who overdo it, the university has a standing deal with a local cab company to take home any student who needs a ride with the fare put on the student's university bill.

"There's always something going on."

"Social life is great," raves one student. "There's always something going on." The campus claims over 150 clubs and societies. Popular campus social events include periodic formal balls, to which the men wear kilts and the women wear evening gowns. Perhaps the biggest campus event of the year is the Torcher's Parade, which is held every spring and features floats made by various student organizations. The city center offers a variety of pubs and clubs as well as inexpensive cinemas, music, and theater. Sports are mainly for playing rather than watching, with 50 sports clubs at students' disposal. Individual sports rather than team intramurals are the staple of weekend warriors, and students can purchase passes for various athletic facilities depending on their interests.

On-campus housing at Aberdeen is varied and guaranteed to all first-year students.

Aberdeen is described by one student as "a fantastic college town!" The city has plenty of old-world charm, and outdoorsy types will love the dramatic scenery that is everywhere in northeast Scotland. Picturesque cliffs overlooking the North Sea are within an easy bus or train ride. Fifteen miles south of Aberdeen is breathtaking Dunnottar Castle, a 14th-century ruin set high on a rocky outcrop that was the set for Mel Gibson's film rendition of *Hamlet*. Within a half-hour ride inland is the edge of the legendary Scottish Highlands. Famous castles are in all directions, including the royal family's summer hideaway, Balmoral. For the Scottish version of the big city, Glasgow and Edinburgh are close by and two hours on a plane will get you to most places in Western Europe.

Though Aberdeen may lack some of the conveniences of home, most Americans are happy they came. "Between classes on a sunny day, students will buy something from the bakery and sit on the grass in the midst of 500-year-old buildings and cobblestone streets. It is such a carefree atmosphere with that special touch of Scottish tradition," says a satisfied history major. If you're the kind of person who likes to meet new people and learn about different cultures, you might thrive on the Aberdeen air.

Overlaps
Dundee, Edinburgh, Glasgow, St. Andrews, Stirling

If You Apply To >

Aberdeen: Regular admissions: Jan.15. Application fee: $36. Campus Interviews: informational. SATs, ACTs, APs, IB (any one): required. UCAS essay only.

University of Edinburgh

Old College, South Bridge, Edinburgh, Scotland EH8 9YL UK

With close ties to the city that founded it in the 16th century, Edinburgh is the most prestigious of Scotland's major research universities. Combines deep roots in Scottish culture and history with the cosmopolitan flavor and cultural riches of a sophisticated capital city. Competitive admissions for top British students, but better odds for Americans with Ivy-level academic credentials. More diverse student body than St. Andrews.

Website: www.ed.ac.uk
Location: City Center
Public
Total Enrollment: 30,000
Undergraduates: 20,000
Male/Female: 44/56
SAT Ranges: N/A
ACT Ranges: N/A
Financial Aid: N/A
Expense: Pub $ $ $ $
Student Loans: N/A
Average Debt: N/A
Phi Beta Kappa: No
Applicants: 41,000
Accepted: 36%
Enrolled: 33%
Grad in 6 Years: 94%
Returning Freshmen: 95%
Academics: ✏ ✏ ✏
Social: ☎ ☎ ☎
Q of L: ★ ★ ★
Admissions: (+44) (0) 1 3165 042
Email Address: usaenquiries@ed.ac.uk

Strongest Programs:
English Literature
History
International Relations
Natural Sciences
Business

The largest and best-known of the ancient Scottish universities, the University of Edinburgh is part and parcel of Scotland's most vibrant urban center. The city of Edinburgh is home to the Scottish Parliament, reconstituted in 1999 after nearly three centuries under the political thumb of London, as well as to the national museum, abundant historical sites, winding streets, and countless restaurants and pubs. The university, like the city, has an unmistakable international feel, including long-standing connections across the pond. In addition to the likes of Charles Darwin and J. K. Rowling, eminent graduates include two signatories of the U.S. Declaration of Independence, Benjamin Rush and John Witherspoon. "Students know that by coming to Edinburgh they are attending not only a prestigious university but the city that goes along with it," says a modern language student.

Edinburgh is unique among the major Scottish universities in that it was founded (in 1583) by a municipality rather than under religious auspices. There is no central campus per se. Its buildings are spread throughout the city, which, with 454,000 residents, is really an overgrown town. Public transport is good, but just about everything is within walking distance. The older university buildings are Georgian and tend to bear names from the Scottish Enlightenment (David Hume and Dugald Stewart), while more modern ones date to the '60s and '70s. The George Square complex is home to the recently renovated School of Business, and there is a new building for philosophy, psychology, and IT.

The university is organized around three colleges: Humanities and Social Science, Science and Engineering, and Medicine and Veterinary. Edinburgh has traditionally been strong in the sciences, and historical ties to economists like Adam Smith and philosophers like John Locke have contributed to strong programs in those fields. English literature attracts a lot of U.S. students, and history is strong, Scottish and otherwise. Unlike in the U.S., the programs in medicine and veterinary science are five-year programs for undergraduates. Veterinary graduates can go on to practice immediately in the U.S. A new program in sustainable development is attracting a diverse group of students. A merger with the Edinburgh College of Art has made possible a concentration in studio-based art. Some 200 study abroad programs are offered at leading universities around the world.

"The faculty is very international."

Applicants apply to study a particular subject, such as physics or English literature, but, unlike the situation in the leading English universities, it is possible to make changes once enrolled. There is no core curriculum, and no one has to endure a science or any other subject in which they have little interest. Students normally take three courses for each of their first two years in a variety of fields and then concentrate on one or two subjects the last two years. Each course involves a combination of lectures, which are taught by full professors, and weekly tutorials, or groups of 10 to 20 students led by tutors. "Although not full professors, my tutors have been fantastic," reports an international relations student. Another student adds, "The faculty is very international, so you don't have to worry about having a professor with too thick of a Scottish accent."

Coursework throughout the year mostly involves essays, with final exams in late April or May accounting for most of the final grade. The academic system is built around self-study. "Students are expected to find their own way," reports an American student. "We are not hand held or told what to do—which breeds a very different kind of learner and academic." The academic pressure at Edinburgh is said to be intense, with little grade inflation. "As befits one of the elite universities in the UK, the students are highly intelligent, and this intelligence is reflected inside the classroom," reports a sophomore. "Students know how to study and get their work in on time, but they also know how to go out and have fun." Faculty members do not see their role as seeking out students who may need help. "That being said, professors and tutors are more than happy to help out when you ask," says one American denizen.

"Students are expected to find their own way."

Edinburgh is the leading destination for top-performing Scottish students, who face tighter admissions standards than North Americans. Half of undergraduates hail from Scotland, with 30 percent from the United Kingdom and Europe, and 20 percent international. There are nearly 600 regular American undergrads as well as another 740 doing study abroad. Edinburgh students tend to be more middle class than their counterparts at St. Andrews, which is more upper class. With total costs of about US$36,000, Edinburgh is slightly more expensive than the other ancient Scottish universities but a bargain compared to the Ivies in the U.S. The university makes scholarships available to international students, and American students can use their U.S. student loans to attend. Like all the prestigious Scottish universities, admissions and financial aid decisions are based entirely on academic grounds, with SAT scores playing a big role. The fact that you spent a spring vacation helping build housing in the slums of Honduras won't bolster your chances of admissions. Given the nature of the student body, there is plenty of discussion of global issues. "Scotland is inherently left-leaning as a country," reports a language student, "but the international students want to share their views while also listening to the opinions of others." Not surprisingly, the most pressing issue is possible increases in tuition fees for British and Scottish students.

Edinburgh guarantees housing to all international first-year students. Catered accommodations are available in the Pollock Halls and come with 14 meals per week in the university dining hall—breakfast and dinner during the week and brunch on the weekends. Pollock accommodates 2,000 students with various styles of rooms (and prices), including some with private bathrooms. Nine out of 10 are singles. "There are common rooms and communal pantries with basic amenities such as a refrigerator and a microwave," explains one resident. Students can also choose self-catered options in which they make their own cooking arrangements. Self-catered flats (apartments) generally consist of three to five students, each with an individual room, sharing a large common living and kitchen area. All accommodations are described as clean and well maintained. Most students move off campus after their first year. "Edinburgh is a student-oriented city with many cheap flats which are directed especially at students," says a third-year student. The Student Union Advice Place will help you find a place. Cafeteria food is described as "fine but not that diverse," and one student adds that "there are many cheap cafés near the university to grab sandwiches or baked potatoes."

There is no core curriculum, and no one has to endure a science or any other subject in which they have little interest.

Since the university is so closely tied to the city, it's no surprise that social life takes place both on and off campus. "First-years tend to explore club life in the city center," explains an American student, "and as they get into their second and third years, the partying transfers homeward into flat parties." But the two student unions offer their own entertainment options. "Teviot has several bars inside, most notably the Library Bar, which is a popular student hangout for a pint as well as for lunch or dinner during the week," explains a language student. "Potterow during the day has a café for coffee but on weekend nights becomes a nightclub that plays cheesy '90s music." All in all, he adds, the social options include "pub crawls, comedy nights, amazing music, top-notch student theater, cinema, dance, and book fairs." Since the drinking age is 18, the university has no school policy on the serving of alcohol. The city of Edinburgh offers its own menu of ancient and contemporary traditions. The Beltane Fire Festival, with roots in pagan times, celebrates the arrival of spring, and every August the city is host to the huge Fringe Festival, which draws artists and spectators from all over the world. Thanks to affordable trains and low-cost airlines like Ryanair and easyJet, trips throughout Britain and all over Europe are easy to arrange. "You get good at traveling," says one American undergrad.

The Edinburgh University Student Association and the Edinburgh University Sports Union combine to offer what one American describes as "just about every sport, charity, or special interest society/club conceivable." A fair is held during Freshers' Week to give first-year students a sense of the options. Does the Chocolate Lovers Society sound tasty? Edinburgh's varsity athletic teams, which compete against other Scottish and European universities in sports like rugby, soccer, and field hockey, do well, "but the competition is laid-back." Most attention goes to the "very strong and popular intramural sports program,

"First-years tend to explore club life in the city center."

which, depending on the sport, has quite a high caliber of play." Many of the teams are co-ed, and there are eight levels of rugby. One student adds that "ancient Scottish sports like shinty that aren't well known globally make us unique." The Centre for Sport and Exercise has "top-notch, newly renovated sports equipment, studios, weight rooms, archery ranges, and stretching stations," adds a third-year student.

Much of the fun of going to college in Scotland comes from taking part in centuries-old traditions, of which Edinburgh has an abundance. Various societies and degree programs sponsor weekly or monthly ceilidhs, or traditional Scottish Dance Nights. Robert Burns Night is a big deal, as is Guy Fawkes Night on November 5, when students set off fireworks throughout the city. Whereas American commencements feature students moving the tassel of their mortarboards from one side to the other, Edinburgh places a common cap on the head of each student in turn that contains a piece of the trousers of John Knox and a NASA emblem that accompanied an Edinburgh graduate on a space mission.

American students tend to do well at Edinburgh. "They are smart and well traveled and tend to be independent thinkers," observed a faculty member. "This university has allowed me to become an adult and challenge myself because of the independent style of the education," reports an international studies major. Another American transplant hailed the fact that Edinburgh is "incredibly international but still Scottish," adding that "the bagpipes playing in the city streets, the ethereal castle, and the wee pubs constantly remind where I am."

Overlaps

University of Aberdeen, University of Glasgow, King's College, University College London, University of Oxford, University of St. Andrews

If You Apply To ➤ **Edinburgh:** Rolling admissions: Jun. 30. Housing: Aug. 1. SATs or ACTs: required. Subject Tests: required. Campus interviews: optional, informational. No alumni interviews.

University Gardens, Glasgow, Lanarkshire, Scotland G12 8QQ UK

A major urban research university located in the bohemian section of a working-class city. Glasgow is slightly smaller than Edinburgh and the atmosphere somewhat more laid-back. The West End is student-friendly, with lots of cafés and shops. Glasgow is a financial and shopping center also known for its nightlife. Locals claim "you can have more fun at a Glasgow funeral than at an Edinburgh wedding." Glasgow students get the point.

The second oldest of Scotland's major universities, the University of Glasgow shares the history and culture of Scotland's largest city. Glasgow (population 599,000) was a major center of the 18th-century Scottish Enlightenment and the 19th-century Industrial Revolution, and it now ranks as Britain's largest financial center after London. The University of Glasgow was founded in 1461 with quarters in Glasgow Cathedral before moving to its own main campus in Gilmorehill in the city's West End in 1870. In contrast to the elitist traditions of other ancient British universities, Glasgow pioneered in serving the educational needs of the growing urban and commercial classes and in 1894 became the first Scottish university to grant degrees to women. Along with Edinburgh, it belongs to the two major groups of research universities: the Russell Group (British) and Universitas 21 (global).

Not surprisingly for a place with more than five centuries of history, the dominant architectural style on campus is neo-Gothic, with a healthy mix of Victorian thrown in. While other sections of Glasgow retain the hardscrabble feel of a depressed industrial area, the West End is a bohemian residential area with an abundance of restaurants, cafés, and shops catering to the college crowd. "The area is very student-oriented, with plenty of venues offering student discounts," reports one student. A literature major describes the university as "a huge school with a small-town feel." The city center, a 15-minute walk from the university, offers an abundance of historical sites and museums as well as the best shopping in Britain outside London. Kelvingrove Park and the Botanical Gardens are down the street from the main gate of the university. A new sporting facility is planned for late 2014.

Students describe the academic climate as pressured but balanced. "The academic climate at the University of Glasgow is quite competitive. Professors know their field and are excellent at providing students with an enormous amount of insight into the courses and subjects," says a European politics major. But another warns, "Specific assignments aren't given. You're told which books go with the course, and you'd better read them on your own!" The

> **"Professors know their field and are excellent at providing students with an enormous amount of insight."**

workload is said to increase noticeably in later years, but because students apply to study in a particular field, they "rarely find themselves in courses they would prefer to avoid because of distribution requirements." First-year students go through a Fresher's Week, with tours of the university, concerts, and other events, and special orientation is also provided for international students.

Slightly smaller than Edinburgh, Glasgow is the only Scottish university with the full range of both professional and academic offerings. The university is divided into four colleges: Arts, Social Sciences, Science and Engineering, and Veterinary and Life Sciences. Befitting the alma mater of physicist Lord Kelvin, the sciences are strong. The economics department is proud that it turned out Adam Smith. Glasgow maintains the only department of Scottish Literature anywhere, and eastern European

Website: www.glasgow.ac.uk
Location: City Center
Public
Total Enrollment: 23,162
Undergraduates: 16,916
Male/Female: 44/56
SAT Ranges: N/A
ACT Ranges: N/A
Financial Aid: N/A
Expense: Pub $ $ $ $
Student Loans: N/A
Average Debt: N/A
Phi Beta Kappa: No
Applicants: N/A
Accepted: N/A
Enrolled: N/A
Grad in 6 Years: N/A
Returning Freshmen: N/A
Academics: ✍ ✍ ✍
Social: ☎ ☎ ☎
Q of L: ★ ★ ★
Admissions: (+011) (141) 330 606
Email Address: student.recruitment@glasgow.ac.uk

Strongest Programs:
Economics
Scottish Literature
European Languages
History of Art
Archeology

languages like Czech and Polish are specialties. One major suggests that "visiting students would do well to take a literature course in this department to gain an understanding of the country which they are visiting." The university gained a faculty of education in 1999 when it merged with the St. Andrews College of Education, and it offers joint studies with the Glasgow School of Art and in naval architecture with the nearby University of Stratheclyde.

Students describe faculty members as respected and well published in their fields. "In my freshman year, I was taught by psychology experts who included their own recent research into lectures," says a psychology major. Lectures are offered by full professors, and tutorials of about 15 students are handled by graduate students, whose teaching is described as "hit-or-miss." Semester-long or year-long study abroad programs are popular, especially through the Erasmus program that allows students to take courses at European universities, and a year of foreign study during their third year is mandatory for foreign language students. "The university seems to believe that a world culture is very important and values it," says a Scottish literature major.

> **"In my freshman year, I was taught by psychology experts who included their own recent research into lectures."**

Consistent with the university's cosmopolitan setting and traditions, the student body is a diverse lot with regard to nationality, race, religion, and socioeconomic backgrounds. Students hail from 120 countries, with 40 percent from Scotland and a similar proportion from the rest of the UK. Expats include 571 Americans. "You don't have an exclusive student body," reports a sophomore. "Dealing and working with people from different backgrounds is the norm."

Freshmen usually live in university housing, which is not on campus but spread throughout the northwest sections of the city, and then move into readily available independent housing in later years. The dorms are generally comfortable, and international students are guaranteed housing. One student recalls, "My first year I was in a student apartment in an old Victorian tenement flat. It was very beautiful. I had friends who stayed in the more modern student flats, and those were nice as well." Students describe campus security as good. "I always felt safe on campus," says an archeology major. As for dining, only one of the seven residence halls offers catered food, and it is located away from the main campus. The others are self-catered, which means that students cook for themselves or savor the offerings of dining facilities sprinkled throughout the campus. "The on-campus dining is very good, and they have a range of foods from Indian to Scottish on various days," reports one denizen. "There is also typically a vegan dish available upon request." A psych major reports living in a noncatered hall with an ample and well-equipped kitchen. "I enjoyed the independence of making all my own meals and found that I was able to save a lot of money by doing so," she says.

Social life is equally divided between on- and off-campus activities. Glasgow offers an abundance of quality restaurants, clubs, and pubs. There are plenty of ceilidhs, or Gaelic social gatherings, and the city sponsors an International Comedy Festival each March. Glasgow has a vigorous music scene. "In my time here, Rise Against, Dropkick Murphys, The Dwarfs, and Blink-182 have or will have played in Glasgow," enthuses

> **"Dealing and working with people from different backgrounds is the norm."**

one student. Much of the on-campus social life revolves around the two student-run university unions, the Glasgow University Union and the Queen Margaret Union, which host student organizations, provide dining and social activities and, of course, have their own bars. Since most students are above the drinking age of 18, underage imbibing is a nonissue. GUU favors sports and debates, while QMU is big on music. One popular event is GUU's Daft Friday, a black-tie affair at the end of the first term

Students describe the academic climate as pressured but balanced.

First-year students go through a Fresher's Week, with tours of the university, concerts, and other events, and special orientation is also provided for international students.

where the entire building is elaborately decorated around a secret theme. The Student Representative Council sponsors an annual Raising and Giving week to aid volunteer organizations and raise awareness of volunteer opportunities. Social activism tends to be most vigorous when the issue involves tuition cuts to the university budget and increases in tuition levels, but there are plenty of student groups organized around issues such as the environment, gender equality, and LGBT rights. Road trips are a major attraction of studying in Scotland, both to in-country destinations like Edinburgh and beyond. "It's easy to get to visit Europe while studying in Glasgow with cheap flights and accommodation," reports one student. "I recently visited Paris with an 18-pound return flight!"

"The on-campus dining is very good, and they have a range of foods from Indian to Scottish on various days."

Intercollegiate debating is taken seriously, and the university has won the world championship five times. The university offers 47 varieties of sports clubs, from aikido to windsurfing, but the only athletic rivalry of any consequence in town is the off-campus competition between the two Glasgow soccer clubs, Celtic (Roman Catholic) and the Rangers (Protestant). A student warns, "It's better not to get involved, as the games are just staging grounds for sectarian hatred. Much of the city's police funding goes to monitoring these violent affairs."

The city of Glasgow has a rough reputation, but undergrads describe their experience living and studying in the West End as rewarding. One American sums up her experience as follows: "Glasgow offers a good mix of academics and fun. It's a highly rated school with many good departments, not too competitive, and has all types of students. And other than the weather, Glasgow is a great city to live in."

The economics department is proud that it turned out Adam Smith.

Overlaps
University of Edinburgh, University of St. Andrews

If You Apply To ➤ | **Glasgow:** Rolling admissions: Jun. 30. Financial aid: Apr. 26. No application fee. SATs or ACTs: optional. Subject Tests: optional. No campus or alumni interviews.

University of St. Andrews

St. Andrews, Scotland KY16 9AJ GB

The most international of Scotland's four "ancient" universities and the most popular destination for Americans studying in the UK. Small by British standards and comparable in feel and stature to Brown. Major drawing cards include English literature, international relations, medieval history, and modern languages. St. Andrews is inseparable from the town, which boasts the famed "Old Course" where the British Open is played every five years. With 600 years to gestate, traditions reign supreme.

Harvard likes to brag about the fact that it was founded back in 1636. Think that's old? Try 1413, the date Pope Benedict XIII issued a Papal Bull recognizing the University of St. Andrews as Scotland's first university and the third in the English-speaking world. Set in an ancient town on the North Sea opposite Norway, St. Andrews is an ideal spot for adventuresome Americans who want a world-class education and an introduction to life outside North America. It now numbers more than 900 Yankees among its 6,000 undergrads, with the number on the rise. Success here requires a go-getter mentality. Support services are available, but students on this side of the

Website: www.st-andrews.ac.uk
Location: Small Town
Public
Total Enrollment: 7,775
Undergraduates: 6,169
Male/Female: 44/56

(continued)

SAT Ranges: CR 680–740,
  M 650–700

ACT Ranges: 28 or above

Financial Aid: N/A

Expense: Pub $ $ $ $

Student Loans: N/A

Average Debt: N/A

Phi Beta Kappa: No

Applicants: 13,000

Accepted: 38%

Enrolled: 16%

Grad in 6 Years: 98%

Returning Freshmen: 98%

Academics: ✍ ✍ ✍ ✍ ½

Social: ☎ ☎ ☎

Q of L: ★ ★ ★

Admissions: (+44) (0) 1334
  46215

Email Address:
  international@st-andrews
  .ac.uk

Strongest Programs:
English Literature
Medieval History
International Relations
Psychology
Philosophy
Marine Biology
Physics
Modern Languages

Atlantic are accustomed to being treated like adults. "They don't hold your hand," says one U.S. student. "You're going to be dropped in, and it's sink or swim."

St. Andrews is the only institution in the *Fiske Guide* whose most prominent landmark is the spot where a student was burned at the stake. In 1528, a Protestant reformer named Patrick Hamilton fell victim to a prolonged burning imposed by the local archbishop. Tradition deems that if you step on the stones that mark the spot where he was martyred, you will fail your final exams, unless you submerge yourself in the North Sea just before dawn the first day of May as part of a tradition called the May Dip. Academic buildings are interspersed through the town's narrow medieval

"They don't hold your hand." streets, and for all practical purposes, says one student, "St. Andrews University *is* the town."

Buildings are constructed of ancient stone and include the ruins of a 13th-century castle and a cathedral. Narrow alleys, called "wynds" by the Scots, lead to secluded gardens and courtyards that add to the old-world charm. A number of academic buildings are perched on cliffs overlooking the North Sea, and white beaches are a two-minute walk from some of the dorms. The newest of these is the School of Medical and Biological Sciences, which opened in 2010 on a new campus nearby that boasts the only contemporary architecture. The library, known as the Palace of Mustard because of unfortunate color choices by an apparently color-blind interior decorator, is set for a much-needed renovation.

Though more flexible than most British universities, St. Andrews offer less latitude to explore a variety of subjects than U.S. institutions. "It's the best of both worlds—an academic focus, but you can still take some courses outside your major," says a junior. Students typically take three yearlong classes, or "modules," in each of their first two years, continue with two of them in the second year, and then opt for a single or double honors program the final two years. "Pick your courses carefully," counsels one U.S. student. "You can't major in something you haven't taken the first year." Modules generally consist of three lectures per week with 100 or more students and a tutorial with 10 to 20, while honors-level courses are generally taught in seminar format. Fewer courses means less time in class and more emphasis on outside reading—"much more than in the States," says a UCLA study abroad student. Modules typically end with papers or exams that account for most of the grade, and there is a full week without classes prior to exams. More so than in the United States, the onus is on the students to keep current with their work and seek

"It's the best of both worlds—an academic focus, but you can still take some courses outside your major." help only when necessary. "St. Andrews is a very rigorous environment, where you are encouraged to take on independent research," says a junior. "If you make it through, you'll be strong." Nevertheless, the faculty gets high marks, and students like having professors who are internationally known in their fields. "Our lecturers are very good," reports a junior. "Tutorials can vary in their usefulness, however, depending on the kind of tutor you get."

Signature offerings at St. Andrews include international relations (IR), psychology (especially neuroscience), physics, marine biology, and modern languages, and the university is a world leader in the study of international terrorism. Americans at St. Andrews tend to cluster in a few departments, notably psychology and international relations. "I thought doing international relations in the U.S. would be a bit silly," says one American. Standards in foreign language are higher than in the United States, an opportunity but also a challenge. "I got close to 700 on my SAT IIs in French and I was completely lost," says a second-year student. As at many U.S. universities, natural science students tend to work the hardest. While there are few weak majors, several students report that access to information technology has been less than they expected.

St. Andrews is one of the world's most international universities, with one-third of its students from Scotland, another third from the UK and Europe, and another third from the rest of the world, including sizable contingents from Scandinavia, Eastern Europe, Asia, the Middle East, and, of course, the U.S. Having friends from around the world is both enriching and convenient because, as one American student explains, "you have lots of choices of places to go on vacation." The international melting pot seems to work, although the upper-middle-class background of the English students lends a more conservative tenor to the campus than some Americans might expect.

St. Andrews is inviting enough to attract the likes of Prince William and Kate Middleton, who met there. While it is competitive for European students, who must be in the top 10th academically, it is more accessible for U.S. students who have the brains to make it into the Ivies but can't throw a football or play a Liszt concerto. Many of the Americans at St. Andrews arrive with an international orientation, including "diplobrats" whose parents have worked in international organizations such as the World Bank or the State Department. The British and internationals typically give Americans a warm welcome. Tuition varies depending on the course, but the total bill for a year at St. Andrews is likely to be about $36,000, depending on the exchange rate. Students can spend two years at the College of William and Mary and two years at St. Andrews and earn degrees from both institutions.

Housing is guaranteed only for first-year students, and students can request a single or shared room. They also have the option of the university meal plan or "self-catering," in which they use kitchens in the dorms to prepare their food. Catered dorms, however, are the most central, ancient, and tend to be populated by

"If you make it through, you'll be strong."

Americans and internationals. Reviews of the food are generally negative. "British cuisine is not world renowned. There is good reason for this," says one student. Nor should students expect the glitzy food courts or all-you-can-eat service typical in the States. Meals are served at specified times with limited portions. On the plus side, dorm life includes once-a-week maid service. After their first year, students generally move to one of the many apartments (flats) in town. "There is a bit of a scramble for flats in February, but most students are able to find good accommodations," reports an IR and French major.

Given the symbiosis of town and gown, social life "takes place in the town's pubs, the student union, the dorms, and apartments," reports an English major. A peek inside the student union reveals something never seen on a U.S. campus: a fully equipped bar with everything from vodka to vermouth (not to mention scotch). The drinking age is 18 in Britain, and St. Andrews boasts 18 pubs. Though there may not be more alcohol than at an American institution, it is certainly more out in the open and thus less of an issue. Black-tie balls are also a staple, as are ceilidhs (pronounced "kaylees"), which feature traditional Scottish dancing akin to square dancing. Like other Scottish universities, St. Andrews offers "a society for everything you can think of," says a senior. Interested in whiskey tasting? Philosophical debate? Belly dancing? Harry Potter? Tunnocks Caramel Wafers? Then there's a society just waiting for you, probably with meetings at a pub. St. Andrews boasts the oldest debating society in the world, founded in 1793, and it continues to do well in international competitions. The annual Charities Campaign is well supported by students. Political activism is muted. "It's not the place to start protesting," reports a junior.

Soccer, a.k.a. football, is the national sport, and students congregate to watch pro teams in the pubs or on the big-screen TV at the union. University sports such as rugby draw few spectators—"you don't have 40,000 screaming fans"—but "hall sport" competitions, the equivalent of intramurals in the U.S., are alive and well in sports ranging from rugby and ultimate Frisbee to shinty, a violent Scottish mix of field hockey and lacrosse. There is a pay-per-use sports center with facilities ranging from basketball to squash. The fabled Old Course, where golf was invented in the 1500s, offers student discounts, but few students play and most bristle at the mention of the game. Golf is the only scholarship sport.

As befitting a 600-year-old institution, St. Andrews is rife with traditions. Red gowns, once the student uniform, are only worn on special occasions, but pubs are

"It's not the place to start protesting."

still forbidden to serve anyone wearing one. The aforementioned May Dip, aimed at purging oneself of academic bad luck, has roots in pagan times. One student explains that during Raisin Weekend in November, first-year students "equipped with multiple cans of shaving foam and dressed up in costume are taken by their adopted academic parents (older students who will take the first-years under their wing) to a huge shaving foam fight in one of the school squares." Students emerging from their last exam are greeted by their friends and doused with buckets of cold water.

The nearest road-trip destination is the medium-sized city of Dundee, about 20 minutes away, which offers nightclubs, a mall, movie theaters, and a McDonald's. (Subway is the only American fast-food joint to crack the St. Andrews market thus far.) Scotland's two largest cities, Edinburgh and Glasgow, are about an hour away, and for outdoorsy types, the legendary Scottish Highlands are within easy reach. The Student Association helps with overseas travel.

Although St. Andrews comes the closest of any of the Scottish universities to having the feel of a liberal arts college, this is not the United States. Those who come here must be ready to adjust to a different way of life—not to mention thick accents and winter nights that begin with sunset at 3:30 p.m.—and the tight identification of the university and the town can eventually make for a bit of claustrophobia. But these are small prices to pay for Scotland in all its ancient glory. U.S. institutions may trumpet their diversity, but nothing stateside compares to the richness of living abroad among the best and brightest from all corners of the globe. St. Andrews delivers it all against a hauntingly beautiful backdrop that will remain forever etched in the minds of all who come here. And there's always the chance that you will meet a future king or queen of England.

Meals are served at specified times with limited portions. On the plus side, dorm life includes once-a-week maid service.

Overlaps

Georgetown, Brown, NYU, Columbia, Tufts, Harvard, McGill, Yale

If You Apply To ➤ **St. Andrews:** Rolling admissions: May 1. Housing: Jun. 30. Application fee: $75. No campus or alumni interviews. SATs or ACTs: recommended. Accepts the Common Application. Essay: reasons for wishing to study at St. Andrews.

Trinity College Dublin

College Green, Dublin 2, Ireland

The only four-year university in Ireland, Trinity College Dublin is the youngest in a peer group consisting of Oxbridge and the four ancient Scottish universities—albeit with a more European feel. Combines rich academic offerings across the curriculum with life in one of the world's youngest and most vibrant capital cities. Traditions abound, academic and otherwise. Where else do honors students get the right to graze their sheep on the college green?

Founded in 1592 by Queen Elizabeth as an Irish counterpart to Oxford and Cambridge, Trinity College Dublin is the largest and most distinguished of the seven universities in Ireland and one of the strongest anywhere. Although best known for its offerings in the humanities and social sciences, TCD is strong across the curriculum, including in new specialties such as nanoscience. The university has produced enough distinguished alumni to fill an encyclopedia (Jonathan Swift, Oscar Wilde, Edmund Burke, and Ernest Walton for starters), and its students bathe in centuries-old academic traditions while enjoying life in one of Europe's most vibrant capital cities. "Dublin is an incredibly student-friendly city," says a junior. "It offers students whatever the university doesn't."

Trinity College Dublin occupies a 47-acre oasis in the heart of Dublin, within easy walking distance of the national museums, government buildings, and other major cultural attractions. "When you pass under the archway you move from the bustle of the city to a traditional liberal arts setting, complete with rugby and cricket pitches," says a sophomore. Most of the central buildings are built of light gray Georgian stone, including its iconic Campanile, whose bells ring on the hour and 10 minutes before exams. The Trinity College Library is Ireland's deposit library and home to the Book of Kells, an illuminated Latin manuscript of the Gospels that draws a steady stream of tourists onto the campus. Another library bears the name of James Ussher, the university's first student, who went on to make a name for himself by calculating that the world started at 6:00 p.m. on October 22, 4004 BC. Trinity College Dublin essentially coexists with a city that, with four large universities in its midst, has the youngest population in Europe and boasts a vibrant music and cultural scene. Where else can you go pub crawling in the footsteps of James Joyce and Bram Stoker? "Everything Dublin has to offer is within walking distance of the Front Gate," says one student. Security is strong, so TCD "has always felt safe despite being in the city center," says a sophomore. One freshman describes Dublin as "a fantastic city in all regards," but warns, "Let's not go overboard. There is also a lot of rain."

TCD is organized around three schools in each of the traditional areas: arts, humanities, and social sciences; engineering, math, and science; and health sciences. There are no "core" courses that everyone is required to take. The college has traditionally been best known for its English and literature offerings along with history, geography, political science, and international studies. Nevertheless, it is a world leader in mathematics, and the sciences are also strong, especially molecular biology and genetics, immunology, and chemistry. The Trinity Biomedical Sciences Institute is a new state-of-the-art research facility, while the Trinity Long Room Hub opened in 2010 for research in the arts and humanities. Nanoscience, Physics, and Chemistry of Advanced Materials (N-PCAM) is a four-year honors degree dealing with the physics and chemistry of small-scale matter. The BESS program (Business, Economics, and Social Studies) is particularly popular among American students, who as a rule tend to shy away from the sciences.

"The major difference between Trinity and American universities is that the onus falls much more on the students."

TCD has a strong interdisciplinary culture, and the Broad Curriculum option encourages students to exercise their curiosity in a module (course) outside their specialty, such as film studies or globalization.

Unlike other universities in Ireland, Trinity College Dublin offers a four-year undergraduate program parallel to the four "ancient" universities in Scotland. Students describe the academic climate at TCD as "challenging, but not stressful if you manage your time well." The academic year runs for 12 weeks each in the fall and spring, followed by three weeks of exams. Students accumulate 60 credits per year through modules offering various numbers of credits, with strong weight given to final exams, although the balance of continuous and final assessment varies by

Website: www.tcd.ie
Location: City Center
Public
Total Enrollment: 14,643
Undergraduates: 11,427
Male/Female: 41/59
SAT Ranges: N/A
ACT Ranges: N/A
Financial Aid: N/A
Expense: Pub $ $ $ $
Student Loans: N/A
Average Debt: N/A
Phi Beta Kappa: No
Applicants: 18,437
Accepted: 15%
Enrolled: N/A
Grad in 6 Years: 86%
Returning Freshmen: 95%
Academics: ✍ ✍ ✍ ✍ ✍
Social: ☎ ☎ ☎ ☎
Q of L: ★ ★ ★
Admissions: (+353) 1 896 4444
Email Address: admissions@ tcd.ie

Strongest Programs:
Business
Economics and Social
   Sciences
Law
Engineering
Computer Science
Sciences

course. "The major difference between Trinity and American universities is that the onus falls much more on the students," says a junior. A history major warns, "If you cram near the end then you are setting yourself up to panic come May." Lectures coupled with weekly tutorials are common the first two years but then give way to small seminars the last two years. A junior observes that TCD "invests some of its best faculty towards teaching undergraduate freshmen." Each entering student is assigned a faculty tutor, not one of his or her professors, who will be available for personal and academic advice over four years and, if necessary, become an advocate. American students can also sign up for a three-week Semester Start-Up Program to help them get the hang of the university and its setting.

Nanoscience, Physics, and Chemistry of Advanced Materials (N-PCAM) is a four-year honors degree dealing with the physics and chemistry of small-scale matter.

As the top university in Ireland, TCD is highly competitive academically. There are about 200 Americans pursuing four-year degrees, most of whom would probably qualify on strict academic grounds for admission to Ivy League schools. Since TCD is the closest European university to the East Coast of the U.S., it draws heavily from New York and New England, but it is attracting an increasing number of Texans and Californians who find access to the University of California frustrating. "As European students don't have to pay fees to attend TCD, there are students from every wealth bracket," says a senior. Ten percent of undergraduates are international students from 122 nations, with the U.S. and Canada making up the largest group. Most U.S. students have no Irish family connections, hail from elite public high schools and prep schools, and have traveled abroad. "I've never had a student who had to apply for a passport," says an administrator. Admission is based entirely on test scores and a 300-word academic statement, which makes Trinity an option for top students who are strong on academics but who neglected to edit their high school newspaper, star on the soccer team, or do community service in Bujumbura.

"The campus is as safe as a nursery school."

TCD students are encouraged to take advantage of the nearly 300 foreign study options, including with leading institutions in Australia, Canada, China, and Singapore. TCD participates in the Erasmus Program with other European universities and has special relationships in the U.S. with Brown, Chicago, and Columbia. The college recently launched a Global Relations Strategy intended to promote partnerships with other international universities, increase the number of international students, and build alumni and philanthropic relationships around the world. A political science major warns that some of the non-European universities "have still not worked out the kinks in transferring grades."

Unlike other universities in Ireland, Trinity College Dublin offers a four-year undergraduate program parallel to the four "ancient" universities in Scotland.

While TCD is less expensive than the four historic Scottish universities, it offers no institutional financial aid to U.S. students. Nevertheless, all students can try their luck in a series of competitive tests that sophomores can take just after Christmas known as the Foundation Scholarship Exams. More than 400 students typically sit for the exams, with about one in five becoming either "scholars" or "foundation scholars." Scholars become members of the university's governing board. Other benefits include five years of free or heavily discounted tuition, free accommodations and evening meals, and, best of all, the privileges of carrying a sword into an exam and grazing their sheep on the campus green.

One drawback of TCD's self-contained campus is that it can accommodate only 10 percent of undergrads. Most first-year students live in Trinity Hall, a modern residence about 20 minutes by bus that offers comfortable six-person apartments with kitchens and living areas. "It is pretty much where all freshmen live, all together, so it is lots of fun," says a political science major. Students generally move into private accommodations in town for their second and third years, and some seniors will then find on-campus rooms "in order to be closer to the college resources in their important final year." Preference for on-campus rooms goes to seniors, students with the highest grades, campus leaders, and international students. TCD offers no university-wide meal plan. "There are four restaurants on campus, but they really only do breakfast and lunch," says a history major. "Most students learn to cook for themselves or eat at places with cheap student deals near campus." Despite its urban location, "the campus is as safe as a nursery school," quips one sophomore.

Extracurricular activities may not help you to get into TCD, but they play an important role in campus culture once you get there. There are more than 110 student societies devoted to activities from yoga to traditional Irish music to entrepreneurialism. "Most students sign up for a bunch of them when they first arrive and then gradually concentrate on just a few," reports an economics major. The most famous are the Philosophical Society, which is the oldest debating club in the English-speaking world (1684), and its rival, the Historical Society. The two groups share a building, sponsor weekly public debates, and award medals to notable visiting speakers. "We had Conan O'Brien and two Nobel laureates in economics in the past three weeks," says a junior. The Metaphysical Society ("the Metafizz") also gives students a chance to show off how much they know about Plato or Bertrand Russell. As far as the political climate on campus is concerned, a political science major reports that "the student body as a whole does not tend to get that political other than to protest rises in student fees."

> "There is a big pub scene—it is Ireland, after all."

Social life takes place both on and off campus. "The social scene is fantastic," exudes an English major. "There is a big pub scene—it is Ireland, after all—and we are in the city center." Student clubs are mandated to throw events once a month, so there is plenty to choose from every day of the week. Most students attend "Pav Fridays," where the on-campus Pavilion Bar offers cheap beer and cider. With the drinking age 18, "alcohol is not stigmatized, but there are rules and limits," says a freshman. "You can't walk around campus drinking alcohol. By and large people drink responsibly." St. Patrick's Day is always a time to celebrate, but unquestionably the biggest event is the weeklong Trinity Week. It starts on Monday, when the new Scholars are announced, given black robes, and invited to take on current Scholars in a game of marbles on the steps of the chapel. Festivities culminate on Friday with the Trinity Ball, frequently described as "the largest private party in Europe." "It's a massive music festival where many popular Irish and European bands perform," says a recent graduate. "It draws 8,000 students, staff, and alumni in formal dress and takes over the city."

Sports are for playing not watching. "Our school culture does not revolve around sports," says a history major. "There is no school mascot or particular set of colors that students wear. People tend to do sport mainly as an extracurricular activity. It's not really a status symbol." Nevertheless, there are at least 60 club and intramural sports, with Gaelic

> "There is no school mascot or particular set of colors that students wear."

football, rugby, and rowing among the most popular. Other offerings range from sailing and squash to frisbee and water polo. Although the English invented rugby, students at TCD started the first club, and the boat club is also one of the oldest. The university does hire coaches for some intercollegiate sports, such as rugby and soccer, and team leaders are eligible for scholarships. TCD is ideally located for travel to European and other destinations. "There are cheap buses from Dublin to any corner of Ireland," reports a senior. "It is also possible to fly to continental Europe or the UK for well under 50 euros. Instead of a road trip, you can go on a Euro-trip!"

Trinity College Dublin combines strong academics with the benefits of a beautiful campus in the midst of a thriving capital city that is also a gateway to the rest of Europe. "You get a top-tier degree that costs less than most private colleges in the U.S. and gives you the international experience of a lifetime," comments one American denizen. "And I met the nicest, most interesting, and hilarious people—the Irish."

TCD students are encouraged to take advantage of the nearly 300 foreign study options, including with leading institutions in Australia, Canada, China, and Singapore.

Overlaps

University of Edinburgh, University College London, University of St. Andrews, University of Toronto, University of Warwick

Trinity: Rolling admissions: Jun. 30. Early decision: Nov. 1. Application fee: $40. No campus or alumni interviews. SATs or ACTs: required. Subject tests: recommended.

University of Iowa

107 Calvin Hall, Iowa City, IA 52242-1396

A bargain compared with other Big Ten schools such as Michigan and Illinois. Iowa is world-famous for its creative writing program and Writers' Workshop. Other areas of strength include health sciences, social and behavioral sciences, and space physics. Future scientists should check out the Research Scholars Program. The university is a regional draw, with 34 percent of the students from out of state.

Website: www.uiowa.edu
Location: Small City
Public
Total Enrollment: 24,382
Undergraduates: 19,449
Male/Female: 48/52
SAT Ranges: CR 470–630, M 550–690
ACT Ranges: 22–28
Financial Aid: 80%
Expense: Pub $ $
Student Loans: 55%
Average Debt: $ $ $
Phi Beta Kappa: Yes
Applicants: 19,430
Accepted: 78%
Enrolled: 29%
Grad in 6 Years: 70%
Returning Freshmen: 86%
Academics: ✍ ✍ ✍ ✍
Social: ☎ ☎ ☎
Q of L: ★ ★ ★
Admissions: (319) 335-3847
Email Address: admissions@ uiowa.edu

Strongest Programs:
Business
Engineering
Psychology
English
Communication Studies
Art

At first glance, one might dismiss Iowa as a standard-issue Midwestern State U. But look beyond the endless miles of fields and corn and you'll find one of the most dynamic schools in the country—and one of the best values to boot. Iowa is known for breeding stellar nurses, future doctors, and of course, wrestlers. "I feel like I'm at home when I'm here," says a sophomore. "Iowa has a great vibe." Iowa was the first public university in the 19th century to admit men and women on an equal basis and the first to accept theater, music, and the other arts as equal to more traditional areas of academic research. The university has long been a major player in the creative worlds, particularly writing, and its small-town atmosphere is just one of many reasons students nationwide flock to this "budget Ivy League."

> **"I feel like I'm at home when I'm here."**

The 1,880-acre campus is located in the rolling hills of the Iowa River valley. Among the 90 primary buildings is Old Capitol, the first capitol of Iowa, a national historic landmark and the symbol of the university. The primary architectural styles of the campus buildings are Greek Revival and modern. The face of the campus is changing, with a slew of new buildings recently opened and several more on the way. Notable facilities include a 216,000-square-foot, state-of-the-art recreation and wellness center and the College of Public Health Building. A new residence hall is slated to open prior to the 2015 academic year.

Iowa has a long tradition in creative arts. It was one of the first universities to award graduate degrees for creative work and is also the home of the famed Writers' Workshop, a two-year graduate program for emerging authors whose graduates have included Jane Smiley and John Irving. The school also prides itself on its International Writing Program. "The English department is stellar," raves one English major. "It's possibly the best in the country—at least for creative writing." Iowa's on-campus hospital is one of the largest teaching hospitals in the United States. Undergraduates benefit from the strong programs in health professions such as physician's assistant and medical technician. Iowa is also strong in the social and behavioral sciences, space physics, and paleontology. Combined degree programs permit students to earn degrees in liberal arts and their choice of business, engineering, nursing, or medicine. The University Honors Program provides special academic, cultural, and social opportunities to undergraduates who maintain a cumulative grade point average of 3.3 or higher. Iowa's 140 study abroad programs give students a choice of more than three dozen countries.

> **"It is competitive in fields such as nursing and the College of Medicine."**

Agriculture, veterinary medicine, forestry, architecture, and animal science are not offered at Iowa but are taught at its sister institution, Iowa State. Other notable majors include international relations and environmental policy and planning.

Students report the academic climate depends on the program. "It is competitive in fields such as nursing and the College of Medicine," says one microbiology major, "but it seems to be laid-back in programs such as communication studies and business." Each of the three undergraduate colleges has its own general education requirements. Liberal arts students must take courses in rhetoric, natural science, social sciences, foreign language, historical perspectives, humanities, and quantitative or formal reasoning. Also required are general education courses in the areas of cultural diversity, foreign civilization and culture, and physical education. Most classes have fewer than 50 students, but "freshmen do tend to spend a majority of their time in large lectures," says a senior. The University of Iowa's Four-Year Graduation Plan guarantees that students who fulfill certain requirements will not have their graduation delayed by unavailability of a needed course. On Iowa! immerses incoming freshmen in the campus culture and introduces them to traditions that will define their Iowa experience. "In short, they'll learn what it means to be a Hawkeye," says an administrator.

The University Honors Program provides special academic, cultural, and social opportunities to undergraduates who maintain a cumulative grade point average of 3.3 or higher.

"I think that the students here are more open minded than at our closest rival," says a premed student. "I think this is because of the strong artistic and performing culture present here." Fifty-seven percent of the undergraduates hail from Iowa, with most of the rest coming from contiguous states, especially Illinois. African Americans, Hispanics, Asian Americans, and Native Americans account for 11 percent of the student body, but as the administration points out, the state of Iowa has only a 4 percent minority population. Students say the campus is extremely tolerant and a community atmosphere is fostered in and out of the classroom. In addition to the 424 athletic scholarships, there are academic scholarships, averaging $4,500 for eligible students. The Roy J. Carver Scholarships—the first such awards to be named in honor of a homeless man—are awarded to 82 students who have overcome social or psychological barriers.

"The dorms have a very comfortable atmosphere and are cleaned daily."

Students say that campus residence halls are very sociable and therefore not very quiet. "The dorms have a very comfortable atmosphere and are cleaned daily," says a sophomore. All are co-ed by floor or wing. Students can choose to live in one of more than 30 "learning communities," such as women in science and engineering, or performing arts. "For the past several years, a few hundred students get put in temporary housing until rooms open up," says one student. Ninety-three percent of the students live in university housing, and more than half live in apartments or houses adjacent to the campus. Many students move off campus after their freshman year. The "very nice" dining halls are "set up like food courts, with numerous options for varying ethnic and special taste backgrounds," says a senior. The student union includes a pastry and coffee shop, two cafeterias, and the State Room Restaurant.

Most classes have fewer than 50 students.

Eleven percent of the men and 15 percent of women belong to fraternities and sororities, and these groups tend to play less of a role in the social life than they do elsewhere. "The weekends are a major part of college life," a student says. Football, basketball, and wrestling events are especially popular on campus. On weekends, students often venture to the downtown area, across the street from campus, which "is built with the college student in mind," a student says. "There are two university theaters right on campus and many affordable cultural events take place at Hancher Auditorium. The Union Bar and Grill, Mickey's, Sports Column, and George's are all popular hangouts with students." The school officially follows the state policy

Ninety-three percent of the students live in university housing, and more than half live in apartments or houses adjacent to the campus.

regarding alcohol. "Students disobey the policy," says a student, "but there are fines and academic ramifications." For a change of scene, Chicago, Kansas City, or St. Louis are all within six hours by car, a short road trip by Midwestern standards. Riverfest, held at the Iowa Memorial Union and on the banks of the Iowa River, is a weeklong, all-campus event celebrating the long-awaited spring. "It is a unique tradition that brings the campus and the community together," says a sophomore. Students also look forward to the annual Iowa City Jazz Festival, homecoming, Dance Marathon, and Big Ten football, especially the game against Iowa State.

Iowa's football team is a national power and regularly appears in New Year's Day bowl games. Iowa teams are the Hawkeyes, named after a legendary 19th-century Indian chief, Black Hawk. Hawkeye fans are serious about their team: "The whole town is basked in black and gold," a freshman says. Recent Big Ten champions include men's field hockey and women's basketball. The men's wrestling team also brought home its 23rd NCAA championship in 2010. There are more than 30 individual, dual, or team sports, and popular intramurals include flag football, volleyball, indoor soccer, and darts.

Much more than a campus among the cornfields, Iowa boasts a beautiful university that is ever evolving. "The University of Iowa is continually renovating and improving its facilities to stay modern and keep up with technology," says a sophomore. The scope of its academic programs is broad and social activities abound—especially when it comes to rooting for their Hawkeyes.

> ### Overlaps
>
> **Iowa State, University of Northern Iowa, Drake, Wartburg, Central College, Luther**

If You Apply To ➤ | **Iowa:** Regular admissions: Apr. 1. Application fee: $40. No campus or alumni interviews. SATs or ACTs: required. No Subject Tests. No essay question.

Iowa State University

100 Alumni Hall, Ames, IA 50011

Agriculture and engineering are the twin pillars of the curriculum, and the university is a magnet for prevets. Ames is a small city and ISU must still endure barbs from certain snobby people in Iowa City. In truth, ISU is relatively cosmopolitan, with students hailing from more than 100 foreign countries. While others retrench ISU continues to expand.

Website: www.iastate.edu
Location: Small City
Public
Total Enrollment: 27,296
Undergraduates: 24,016
Male/Female: 56/44
SAT Ranges: CR 460–620, M 530–680
ACT Ranges: 22–28
Financial Aid: 87%
Expense: Pub $
Student Loans: 65%

Love for Iowa State University runs as deep as its Midwestern roots. Strong programs in engineering, business, and agriculture attract students from around the globe. The close-knit, small-town atmosphere fostered at this school of more than 24,000 undergraduates keeps them here. At a time when many state universities are tightening the purse strings and retrenching, Iowa State has its eyes set on future growth. The university is planning to add more than 200 faculty members, mostly in research-oriented fields such as agricultural biotechnology and biorenewable energy.

The university has lavished attention on its parklike campus, located on a 1,984-acre tract in the middle of Ames, population 50,000. The campus, which boasts a combination of dignified old buildings and award-winning new ones, is a model of landscape design with numerous shady quadrangles with floral plantings and artwork that create a garden-like quality. History and tradition prevail, from the campanile, which serenades the campus with its carillon bells, to the huge public art collection including sculptures by Danish artist Christian Petersen. Howe Hall, home to aerospace engineering, boasts a virtual reality application center and a six-sided virtual reality cave. Along with Hoover Hall, the complex provides the teaching and researching home for the College of Engineering. Much of the campus is closed to cars, largely for the benefit of walking, bicycling, and in-line skating students, as well as the swans (named Sir Lancelot and Lady Elaine) and ducks that reside on Lake LaVerne. The CyRide fare-free bus system delivers students around campus and the city. New construction includes a state-of-the-art biorenewables research lab.

"We have some world-class profs here."

When Iowa State opened in 1869 as a land grant university, agriculture and engineering ruled the academic roost. These days, though, the liberal arts are just as popular, and the College of Liberal Arts and Sciences is the largest of ISU's seven colleges. Among the university's 100-plus majors, the College of Agriculture still fields outstanding programs in animal science, turf grass management, agribusiness, and agronomy. Other colleges include business, design, veterinary medicine, human sciences (formerly family consumer sciences and education), and the graduate college. Other programs include a B.S./M.S. in diet and exercise, a B.S. in software engineering, a B.A. in criminology and criminal justice, and a minor in engineering studies. Students find the academic climate competitive, but report that it varies by program.

All undergraduates must take two semesters of English composition their freshman year and demonstrate proficiency in English prior to graduation. Other general education requirements, which vary by college, focus on gaining breadth in the natural and social sciences, but everyone takes a half-credit course on the use of the library and must satisfy a three-credit requirement in diversity. Students can also use the AccessPlus system of electronic kiosks sprinkled around campus to check the status of their university bill or financial aid package, print an unofficial transcript, or get their current schedule. Iowa's highly touted learning communities offer transfer students and freshmen the opportunity to join a group of other newcomers who share similar academic interests in taking a common set of classes together or living together on the same residence hall floor.

"We have a lot of farmers and small-town Iowans."

An honors program enrolls 400 outstanding freshmen each year, many of whom live in honors housing. Iowa State ranks in the top 20 for sending students overseas; popular destinations include Italy, the United Kingdom, Spain, Australia, and Ireland. Despite the university's size, professors teach most classes, with the exception of some freshman English options. "We have some world-class profs here who are doing important research," one senior says. Academic and career counseling draw praise, too, and advisors are "always readily available" to help students.

Sixty-seven percent of ISU's students are Iowans, though all 50 states and more than 100 countries are represented in the student body. Foreign students comprise 8 percent of the student body. Iowa State was the first co-ed land grant institution, but attracting minorities has proven more difficult: Hispanics comprise 4 percent, Asian Americans 3 percent, and African Americans 3 percent. "We have a lot of farmers and small-town Iowans," says a senior. "This is a pretty white campus." To help remedy this situation, ISU launched a $25 million campaign aimed at increasing the number of scholarships available for minority students, student athletes, and student leaders. In addition to need-based financial aid and hundreds of athletic scholarships, many merit awards are available.

Thirty-four percent of students live in on-campus residence halls and apartments and another 2,600 live in Greek housing. Eaton Residence Hall offers suite-style

(continued)

Average Debt: $ $ $ $
Phi Beta Kappa: No
Applicants: 16,539
Accepted: 83%
Enrolled: 39%
Grad in 6 Years: 71%
Returning Freshmen: 86%
Academics: ✑ ✑ ✑
Social: ☎ ☎ ☎ ☎
Q of L: ★ ★ ★
Admissions: (515) 294-5836
Email Address: admissions@ iastate.edu

Strongest Programs:
Exercise Science
Apparel Design
Chemistry
Physics
Engineering
Business
Architecture
Animal Science

Students find the academic climate competitive, but report that it varies by program.

rooms. Single-sex and co-ed dorms are available, and rooms are said to be comfortable and well maintained. One student indicates that the janitors throw a picnic every spring. "The dorms are sterile to begin with but the traditions are very strong here and students transform them into home with their own personal touch," explains a junior. Special floors are available for international students, teetotalers, and particularly studious undergraduates; separate housing is available for married students and students with dependent children. The college boasts dining at the Union Drive Marketplace.

Iowa State is not simply located in Ames—in many respects it *is* Ames, but whether or not it qualifies as a college town depends on who you ask. Des Moines, the state capital, is about 30 minutes away, and Iowa City, Minneapolis, and Chicago are other easy and enjoyable road trips. Socializing tends to stay on campus, with big-name bands playing at Hilton Coliseum and parties always rocking. There are also 500 student organizations that cater to just about any interest.

"Advisors are always readily available."

Fourteen percent of men and 17 percent of women go Greek. The campus is officially dry but, according to one sophomore, many older students will buy alcohol for minors. The big event every spring is a weeklong campus festival called VEISHEA (an acronym for ISU's original five colleges), which features parades, exhibitions, food, and a fun-run. Another tradition is campaniling, where students must kiss under the campanile at the stroke of midnight to be considered "true" co-eds. And students have learned not to walk over the zodiac sign in the Memorial Union—it brings bad luck.

In sports, Cyclones basketball is king; the men's and women's teams are usual invitees to the NCAA tournament. The university boasts college wrestling's only four-time undefeated champion and an Olympic gold medalist as the head coach. Football, track and field, and women's volleyball are also competitive. A majority of students participate in one of the largest intramural sports programs in the nation. The Hawkeye rivalry is one of the strongest in the nation.

From that first class of 28 men and two women in 1869, Iowa State has taken to heart Abraham Lincoln's land grant ideal; to open higher education to all, to teach practical courses, and to share that knowledge beyond the borders of the school. According to one junior, it's this dynamic combination that draws "hardworking, kind students" from near and far.

Overlaps

Purdue, University of Illinois, University of Iowa, University of Minnesota, University of Wisconsin, University of Missouri, University of Nebraska, University of Northern Iowa

If You Apply To ➤

Iowa State: Rolling admissions. Application fee: $40 (paper), free (online). No campus or alumni interviews. SATs or ACTs: required. No Subject Tests. No essay question.

Ithaca College

100 Job Hall, Ithaca, NY 14850-7020

Ithaca offers an unusually wide array of programs for a smallish university. Students looking at Ithaca College also apply to Boston University, NYU, and Syracuse. The common thread? Outstanding programs in the arts and media. Students also clamor to get into physical therapy. Crosstown neighbor Cornell adds curricular and social opportunities.

Over South Hill, at the center of the upstate New York Finger Lakes region, sits Ithaca College. The school has a close-knit community, along with strong programs in music, theater, communications, and health sciences, such as physical and occupational therapy. With a "gorges" campus and a size that allows for easy friendships with peers and professors alike, Ithaca draws students from all over the U.S.—and dozens of other countries. IC may be overshadowed on the national scene by its Ivy League neighbor, Cornell University, but its focus on undergraduate education and "hands-on" learning differentiates IC from its larger rival down the road, and helps prepare students for the rigors of life outside institutional walls. "Ithaca is a diverse college," says one freshman, "with so much to offer in creating the well-rounded, successful person you will become."

Ithaca's campus, midway between Syracuse and Binghamton, in the beautiful Finger Lakes region, lies on the city's southern hill overlooking Cornell and Cayuga Lake. None of the streamlined, modern campus buildings on the 757-acre plot are more than a **"Ithaca is a diverse college."** few decades old, since the college did not move to its present location until the 1960s. The surrounding area is dotted with forests, waterfalls, rolling hills, and, of course, those ever-present gorges. In fact, author Tom Wolfe dubbed the college "the emerald eminence at the fingertip of Lake Cayuga." In 2011, the $65.5 million Athletics and Events Center opened. Featuring state-of-the-art spaces to gather, learn, train, and compete, the facility is the largest construction project undertaken by the college.

Ithaca has five schools—music, communications, business, health sciences and human performance, and humanities and sciences—and a division of interdisciplinary and international studies. Together, they offer more than 100 undergraduate majors. All students complete the Integrative Core Curriculum, the centerpiece of which is a "Themes and Perspectives" sequence that includes courses from the natural sciences, creative arts, humanities, and social sciences, all focusing on a general theme such as "Inquiry, Imagination, and Innovation" or "Quest for a Sustainable Future." Additional elements include a first-semester seminar, a learning portfolio, a senior capstone experience, and coursework in writing, diversity, and quantitative literacy. The natural sciences benefit from a $23 million facility. The documentary studies and production major features courses from the television, journalism, cinema, photography, and media arts departments, with a mixture of real-world production experience and opportunities for industry internships.

Although they praise Ithaca's programs in writing and sociology, students reserve their highest acclaim for the school's preprofessional programs—and for its conservatory of music, which dates to 1892, when the college was founded. "The music school has always been lauded and maintained an excellent academic program," a freshman says. The conservatory takes students by audition only, making it a destination for already-accomplished musicians and composers. Students in the School of Health **"The music school has always been lauded."** Sciences and Human Performance boast of a nearly 100 percent job-placement rate at graduation. The Park School of Communications has a $12 million facility, housing programs in radio and TV production, photography, and cinema. Ithaca's business school has grown rapidly; students choose one of six concentrations after their first or second year.

To ease the transition to college, all students read the same book before arriving, then discuss it the day after Convocation. Some students also come to campus early for "Community Plunge," a service-learning experience. Students enrolled in the School of Humanities and Sciences may also take a freshman seminar, which meets for four hours a week instead of the usual three. These classes have about 15 students each and include offerings such as Growing Up with Television or The Relevance of History. Professors and students together decide how to use the "extra" hour,

Website: www.ithaca.edu
Location: Suburban
Private
Total Enrollment: 6,576
Undergraduates: 6,147
Male/Female: 44/56
SAT Ranges: CR 520–630, M 530–640
ACT Ranges: N/A
Financial Aid: 92%
Expense: Pr $ $
Student Loans: N/A
Average Debt: N/A
Phi Beta Kappa: No
Applicants: 13,813
Accepted: 65%
Enrolled: 18%
Grad in 6 Years: 77%
Returning Freshmen: 84%
Academics: ✐ ✐ ✐
Social: ☎ ☎ ☎ ☎ ☎
Q of L: ★ ★ ★
Admissions: (607) 274-3124
Email Address: admission@ithaca.edu

Strongest Programs:
Music
Physical Therapy
Theater
Communications
Natural Sciences
Psychology

covering themes such as personal, social, and academic responsibility. The Honors Program in the School of Humanities and Sciences offers special, intensive seminars and an array of out-of-class activities to qualified students.

"The academic climate at Ithaca College is competitive," says one student, "especially when it comes to courses in your major." A sophomore adds, "If you do struggle, as I have, there are lifelines in the form of TAs, free tutoring (in most cases), and persistent professor interaction." Those same professors are praised for their knowledge and enthusiasm. "The teaching approach here is discussion-based and hands-on. Students don't learn from simply reading and listening, we learn from applying course material," says a junior. For students tired of Ithaca's small size, cross-registration is available at Cornell and Wells College. Those seeking respite from the harsh winters may pursue internships in Washington, D.C., or Los Angeles—or a one-semester "Walkabout" in Australia, which includes stints at three different universities Down Under. In all, Ithaca offers study abroad in more than 50 countries, from Japan to Chile and Italy to Zimbabwe. Closer to home, students have the option to enter the Ithaca College Communications Program in Los Angeles, which hosts between 30 and 80 students per semester.

> **"The academic climate at Ithaca College is competitive."**

Forty-four percent of Ithaca students hail from New York State. Many of the rest come from elsewhere in New England; 2 percent hail from other nations. African Americans and Asian Americans combine for 7 percent of the student body and Hispanics add another 6 percent; students recognize and lament the lack of ethnic diversity on campus and say administrators are working hard to address it. "Just like any other school, we have activists, athletes, music kids, theatre kids, and other typical stereotypes. However, what makes Ithaca students unique is our sense of community," says one student. While tuition continues to rise, students may vie for hundreds of merit scholarships each year worth an average of $10,666, although there are no athletic awards.

More than two-thirds of Ithaca's students live on campus, thanks partly to the College Circle Apartments, which have full kitchens and space for 630 upperclassmen in units accommodating two to six people each. "The residence halls are strategically located across campus so that walking to class is never a hassle, and the rooms themselves are above average," a student says. Since everyone is guaranteed space in the residence halls, first-years may find themselves in triples that used to be doubles or packed into a common-room lounge. The situation usually sorts itself out by Thanksgiving, students report. Dorm dwellers can eat in one of three dining halls, each with a different daily menu. "There's a big emphasis on local foods and vendors," says one student, adding, "They make it really easy for you to eat healthy, but there's still unlimited ice cream in every dining hall too." Students report feeling secure on campus. "I have never felt unsafe," says a senior. "I feel that we have an extremely safe community of students as well as good security measures."

> **"There is a very busy social life at Ithaca."**

Ithaca recognizes only academic fraternities or sororities, not social organizations, but that doesn't slow down the campus social scene. "There is a very busy social life at Ithaca; if you are bored it is only because you choose to be bored. There is always something going on on campus, from movies in one of our bigger classrooms, to open-mic nights, comedy nights, sporting events, guest speakers, floor events, or full-campus events like Spirit Week," one student says. The Student Activities Board, IC After Dark, and the Bureau of Concerts bring in comedians and guest speakers, show movies, and organize karaoke and open-mic nights. "There are over 150 organizations here on campus; there is something for everyone," a student says. Bars and clubs in Ithaca are 18 to enter, 21 to drink, and there's a mall, bowling alley, movie theaters, and go-carting in town. "Students here like to drink, but they also do other

Ithaca has five schools—music, communications, business, health sciences and human performance, and humanities and sciences.

Students reserve their highest acclaim for the school's preprofessional programs—and for its conservatory of music, which dates to 1892.

things too," says one biochemistry major. "Being straightedge here doesn't mean you're frowned upon or looked at as an unsocial person." Each fall brings Applefest, which celebrates the harvest, and in the winter, Chilifest helps students warm up. Cornell's fraternity houses make up for the scant Greek life at Ithaca, and the area's hilly terrain and proximity to the Shawangunk Mountains provide opportunities for hiking, biking, sledding, and skiing. Ithaca—described by one student as "a great little college town"—still is relatively isolated, and long, cold winters mean students often make their own fun. Popular road trips include Syracuse and Binghamton (each an hour away, with plenty of malls), and Philadelphia, Washington, D.C., New York City, or Canada, less than six hours' drive.

Ithaca competes in Division III athletics. The biggest annual tradition is the "Cortaca Jug" football game, pitting the Ithaca Bombers against rival SUNY–Cortland. (The winner gets the jug-shaped trophy, and "it's the only Division III football game you can bet on in Vegas," boasts a sophomore.) The Bombers teams have won 25 conference titles in the past two years. Women's soccer, tennis, basketball, and volleyball are solid; men's basketball is competitive, too. There are two levels of intramural competition at Ithaca, depending on just how competitive you want to be, and popular options include soccer, flag football, basketball, and floor hockey. Students may also train to referee these matches—and get paid for doing so. Ithaca also offers half-credit physical education courses in badminton, scuba diving, and cross-country skiing.

If you can endure the harsh winters ("Come mid-February or so, we hate the snow!" gripes one senior), you'll appreciate the small size and personal attention characteristic of Ithaca College. These qualities help it stand out among the many Northeastern schools with excellent communications programs, such as Boston University, Emerson College, and nearby Syracuse. Ithaca also boasts superior options in the health sciences, music, and theater. "Everybody who is part of the Ithaca College community knows that they are part of something special," observes one student. "At other schools, you're a number. At Ithaca, we know your name."

The Honors Program in the School of Humanities and Sciences offers special, intensive seminars and an array of out-of-class activities to qualified students.

Overlaps

Syracuse, University of Massachusetts, Boston University, Quinnipiac, University of Vermont, Northeastern, SUNY–Binghamton, NYU

If You Apply To ➤

Ithaca: Early decision: Nov. 15. Early action: Dec. 1. Regular admissions: Feb. 1. Application fee: $60. Campus and alumni interviews: optional, informational. SATs or ACTs: optional. Subject Tests: optional. Apply to particular school or program. Accepts the Common Application. Essay question.

James Madison University

Harrisonburg, VA 22807

JMU has carved out a comfortable niche among Virginia's superb public universities. More undergrads than UVA and nearly three times as many as William and Mary, though the city of Harrisonburg gives JMU a more down-home feel. Strong in preprofessional fields such as business, health professions, and education. Undergraduates rule the roost.

No doubt about it: Students at James Madison University get down to business. In fact, the school's business programs continue to garner national attention and attract top-notch students from coast to coast. The university has been growing at a phenomenal rate, causing some to feel growth pains. But an emphasis on undergraduate teaching, close student/faculty interaction, and a warm and welcoming climate are business as usual at JMU, so students have plenty of things to cheer about. "Every student 'bleeds purple,'" says a junior, "and if you spend a day here, you will too."

Website: www.jmu.edu
Location: Small City
Public
Total Enrollment: 18,933
Undergraduates: 17,302
Male/Female: 41/59

(continued)

SAT Ranges: CR 520–620,
   M 530–630

ACT Ranges: 23–27

Financial Aid: 17%

Expense: Pub $ $

Student Loans: 54%

Average Debt: $ $

Phi Beta Kappa: Yes

Applicants: 22,648

Accepted: 64%

Enrolled: 30%

Grad in 6 Years: 80%

Returning Freshmen: 91%

Academics: ✍ ✍ ✍

Social: ☎ ☎ ☎ ☎

Q of L: ★ ★ ★ ★

Admissions: (540) 568-5681

Email Address: admissions@
   jmu.edu

Strongest Programs:
Teacher Education
Business
Communication Sciences and
   Disorders
Integrated Science and
   Technology

*Freshmen are offered
a variety of programs
to help smooth
their transition into
the university.*

JMU is in the heart of the Shenandoah Valley, two hours from Washington, D.C., and Richmond, Virginia. Three types of architecture make up the campus. The buildings on Front campus have red-tile roofs and are constructed of a distinctive limestone block known as bluestone. Back campus has more modern, redbrick structures. The College of Integrated Science and Technology campus features modern beige buildings. The university straddles Interstate 81, an outlet to several major East Coast cities. Recent campus projects include the Forbes Center for the Performing Arts.

James Madison University is recognized nationally for its programs within the business major, while social sciences and education are also strong. The most popular majors at JMU are health sciences, biology, marketing, finance, and accounting. Undergraduates in the biology department have even employed recombinant DNA technology to help develop organisms that produce biodegradable plastics. Also worth noting is the geology and geography departments' summer geology field camp for undergraduates. A mathematical modeling laboratory is used by select undergrads to solve real-world applied math problems.

"For the most part, classes are challenging and competitive," says a sophomore. A junior adds, "JMU definitely has its difficult courses. There were some that I really struggled with and others that I was able to breeze through without a problem." The General Education Program requires each student to take courses in several clusters,

"For the most part, classes are challenging and competitive."

including Skills for the 21st Century, Arts and Humanities, the Natural World, Social and Cultural Processes, and Individuals in the Human Community. The idea is to offer students a basis for lifelong learning by challenging them to become active in their own education and to explore the foundations of knowledge. Freshmen are offered a variety of programs to help smooth their transition into the university. Outdoor Adventures, held before classes begin, gives first-year students an opportunity to meet while hiking and mountain climbing in the Shenandoah Mountains.

With undergraduates far outnumbering grad students, JMU's main mission is undergraduate teaching. "All of the teachers are professors with degrees in their field and no classes are taught by grad students or TAs," says one psychology major. Those looking for a more intense intellectual experience can check out the honors program, which offers small classes and opportunities for independent study. Many upper-level programs encourage undergraduate participation with faculty research, another plus of this school. JMU offers semester abroad programs in Antwerp, Florence, London, and Salamanca throughout the academic year (fall, spring, and summer). Another option is the Chinese Business Studies Minor, an 11-week summer semester, in Chengdu, China. In addition, there are summer programs in Argentina, Canada, the Czech Republic, Ghana, Ireland, Kenya, Malta, Nicaragua, the Philippines, Rome, and Scotland.

You won't find a lot of ethnic diversity among fellow students at JMU, but "anyone can find their niche here," assures one student. "We've got athletes, punk rockers, preps, nerds, tree huggers, and politicians!" Most attended public high school, and 73 percent are from Virginia. In fact, there's a general effort to keep out-of-state enrollment below 30 percent. African Americans account for 4 percent of JMU's student body, and Hispanics and Asian Americans combine for another 8 percent. Students are friendly and comfortable with each other. As for political involvement, students are "very justice oriented and politically active," according to one sociology major. A group calling itself Orange Band tries to get people talking about current issues, and students say all views on the political spectrum are represented on campus. JMU offers merit scholarships averaging $3,126 and hundreds of athletic scholarships.

Thirty-five percent of the students live in the dorms, which run the gamut from the old high-ceiling variety to newer, air-conditioned rooms that come complete with carpet and a fitness center in the building. "The dorms are well maintained and a close walk to everything," says a junior. A senior adds, "Half of the dorms have AC while the other half don't, but it's only really hot in Harrisonburg the first couple weeks and the last couple weeks of school so if you pile up some fans then you'll be good to go." Freshmen are guaranteed a room, but the school's enrollment growth means some students wind up in triples. Most upperclassmen opt to move off campus. Students rave about the meal plan, which has a growing number of options to choose from, including a salad bar and low-calorie meals. "There are 14 dining halls on campus, so you can get literally anything that you could ever want. They have vegetarian, vegan, and gluten-free options all over the place," cheers an international affairs major.

With undergraduates far outnumbering grad students, JMU's main mission is undergraduate teaching.

"Social life is really fun for a rural area," reports one student. "The students mostly gather at off-campus apartments via a bus that runs into the late hours. Bars and clubs are not particularly popular because there aren't that many." The Greek system attracts 10 percent of the men and 12 percent of the women. Greeks and independents alike participate in JMU's many

"We've got athletes, punk rockers, preps, nerds, tree huggers, and politicians!"

annual rites, including homecoming and Christmas on the Quad. The school cracks down on underage drinking on campus and after three strikes "students are asked to leave," says a student. As for road trips, the favorite destination seems to be the University of Virginia, almost an hour's drive to the south. Equally enticing, however, are the many natural delights of the Shenandoah Valley, including hiking, camping, and even skiing, all nearby. Most students find local Harrisonburg a friendly Southern town, though it doesn't necessarily embrace the college.

Sports fans here are known as the Electric Zoo and are enthusiastic about their teams, which are all Division I. Among the most competitive sports are football, baseball, women's basketball, and men's and women's soccer. The field hockey team has brought home conference titles, as have the softball team and the lacrosse team. More than two-thirds of students participate in the intramural program's many offerings. JMU's debate team was named the top public debate program in the nation by the Cross Examination Debate Association.

Though JMU still has a ways to go before establishing itself as a front-rank national university, it is making considerable progress. The school is growing, but not outgrowing its Southern charm. "The school spirit is really what sets us apart," says an elementary education major. "No matter where you go on campus, you are always going to find someone wearing purple and gold."

Overlaps

George Mason, Penn State, University of Delaware, University of Virginia, Virginia Commonwealth, Virginia Tech

If You Apply To ➢ | **James Madison:** Early action: Nov. 1. Regular admissions: Jan. 15. Application fee: $50. No campus or alumni interviews. SATs or ACTs: required. No Subject Tests. Essay question: one-page personal statement.

The Johns Hopkins University

3400 North Charles Street, Baltimore, MD 21218

The Hop's reputation as a premed factory can be misleading. It's apt, but Hopkins also has fine programs in international studies (with D.C. close at hand) as well as in the humanities and social sciences. For non-premeds, JHU is much easier to get into than other top-tier schools. With total enrollment just over 7,000 (and 5,000 undergraduates), Hopkins is smaller than most people think.

Website: www.jhu.edu

Location: City Outskirts

Private

Total Enrollment: 7,082

Undergraduates: 5,149

Male/Female: 52/48

SAT Ranges: CR 640–740,
   M 670–770

ACT Ranges: 30–34

Financial Aid: 55%

Expense: Pr $ $ $ $

Student Loans: 49%

Average Debt: $ $

Phi Beta Kappa: Yes

Applicants: 20,502

Accepted: 18%

Enrolled: 37%

Grad in 6 Years: 94%

Returning Freshmen: 97%

Academics: ✍ ✍ ✍ ✍ ✍

Social: ☎ ☎ ☎

Q of L: ★ ★ ★

Admissions: (410) 516-8171

Email Address: gotojhu@
   jhu.edu

Strongest Programs:

Public Health Studies

International Studies

Biomedical Engineering

Neuroscience

Biology

English/Writing

Archaeology

Physics

The typical student at The Johns Hopkins University is fueled by the pursuit of academic excellence and a need to achieve. This midsize Baltimore school, one of the few U.S. universities initially founded as a graduate school, has garnered widespread acclaim for its exceptional professors, incredible resources, and unparalleled research opportunities. Though the university has a reputation as a top-notch premed factory, the administration has been working for a number of years to make it clear that Johns Hopkins has plenty to offer those undergrads whose interests are decidedly nonmedical or nonscience based. Students who attend this elite university know they are at the top of the game, and they burn the midnight oil to stay there. "Students are very driven and motivated to succeed at Hopkins," says a senior.

> **"Many [students] are involved in some form of research."**

The arts and sciences and engineering schools are on the picturesque 140-acre Homewood campus, just three miles north of Baltimore's revitalized Inner Harbor. Tree-lined quadrangles, open lawns, and playing fields make for an idyllic setting on the edge of a major urban center. The architecture on this woody urban campus is mainly Georgian redbrick, with several recently built, more modern structures scattered throughout. Hodson Hall is home to high-tech classrooms, and a new chemistry building houses several research programs. Decker Quadrangle includes Mason Hall, a 28,000-square-foot visitor center, an interdisciplinary computational sciences building, and a 604-space underground parking garage. The Brody Learning Commons opened in 2012, connects to the library, and offers the latest learning technology, including interactive projectors and video teleconferencing.

As much as some try to deny it, premeds dominate the campus. Public health studies tops the list of most popular majors (followed by international studies, biomedical engineering, neuroscience, and molecular and cellular biology). Excellent research opportunities abound on the Homewood campus and for those who hop the crosstown shuttle to the medical campus. "Many [students] are involved in some form of research," says a junior biomedical engineering student. "That's a big part of Hopkins." The Johns Hopkins Hospital and Medical School play such a major role in the identity of Hopkins that students sometimes fear it "overshadows the vibrant undergrad life that exists at Homewood." But administrators say the school is paying more attention to the undergraduate programs and emphasizing interdisciplinary, collaborative approaches to the coursework. Engineering majors also enjoy strong departments, such as mechanical engineering, chemical and biomedical engineering, electrical and computer engineering, and computer science. Many say it's the hardest department at the school, thanks to its intense workload. But that doesn't deter a Hopkins student. "The courses are rigorous but not impossible, and there is ample opportunity to succeed," says one freshman.

Students are generally happy with the quality of teaching at Hopkins. "My professors always infuse lectures with their own research, which is usually at the forefront of his or her respective field. This makes even highly theoretical courses very engaging," says one sophomore. Although Johns Hopkins is a firm supporter of traditional scholarship, there are no university-wide requirements other than a four-course writing component. Each major has its own distribution requirements, and there are several creative seminar offerings for freshmen. Students can receive a B.A. in creative writing through the Writing Seminars program, where they study with authors and playwrights such as Alice McDermott and Stephen Dixon. The Humanities Center espouses a casual, interdisciplinary approach, and with maximum curriculum flexibility allowed them, undergraduates are free to range as broadly or focus as specifically as they want. Students can get a dual degree in music performance with the university's Peabody Conservatory. There also are broad "area

> **"The courses are rigorous but not impossible."**

majors," such as social sciences and behavioral sciences, humanistic studies, or natural sciences, and students can choose from a cluster of related disciplines to design their own program. Even the strictly structured engineering course plan stresses the importance of interdisciplinary and interdepartmental exposure. "Students at Johns Hopkins are often generalized as premed or engineering students as a result of the high reputations of these respective programs," notes one freshman. "However, the university is also home to some of the country's top humanities programs."

Students also benefit from the well-developed graduate side of Johns Hopkins. The International Studies Program, for example, is enriched by its offerings at the university's Bologna Center in Italy, Nanjing Center in China, and at its Nitze School of Advanced International Studies in nearby Washington, D.C. Undergraduate research is a hallmark of the Johns Hopkins experience, with 70 percent of students having at least one research experience. The provost awards 60 grants of up to $2,500 each for undergraduate research. There is a premajor advisor for freshmen, and arts and sciences students are encouraged to wait until at least their sophomore year to declare a major. Currently, first-semester freshmen grades are recorded as satisfactory or unsatisfactory. After this "honeymoon" period, students buckle down to a herculean workload. They get some relief from the optional January intersession, during which students can take courses or pursue independent study for one or two credits.

Hopkins students are remarkably talented and motivated, with 84 percent from the top 10th of their high school class. The image Johns Hopkins students once had as antisocial bookworms is giving way to more focus on social life. "Hopkins students are incredibly passionate and normally pretty well-rounded," a freshman says. Still, another student adds, "Schoolwork is a socially acceptable excuse or reason to choose not to attend different functions or events on campus because all students acknowledge the academic rigor of this institution." Nineteen percent of students are Asian American, 5 percent African American, and 10 percent Hispanic. Geographically, most students come from the mid-Atlantic states and New England. The campus is fairly liberal and "most students are accepting of other's beliefs," according to one chemical and biomolecular engineering major. At $2 billion, Hopkins's endowment is among the top 25 in the country, and it strives to meet the full demonstrated financial need of nearly every admit. Hopkins generously rewards the extraordinarily talented with hefty Hodson Trust scholarships worth $27,500 annually, regardless of need, and renewable annually for those who keep a 3.0 GPA. The Hodson Success Scholarship, based on need, replaces the loans in the aid packages of selected students from underrepresented minority groups. Forty-four athletic scholarships are also awarded in women's and men's lacrosse, where Hopkins is a perennial national powerhouse. Hopkins also provides loan-free financial packages for qualified students, and all accepted residents of Baltimore City who attend a Baltimore City public school for the final three years of high school receive full tuition scholarships.

Fifty-four percent of Hopkins students live in student housing; freshmen and sophomores are required to do so. "There is a variety of dorm styles from traditional co-ed hallway style to dorms that are more like apartments," says an international relations major. "All freshmen and sophomores are required to live in residence and have no trouble getting a room." Upperclassmen often choose to scope out the row houses and apartment buildings that surround Hopkins, but 25 percent are now guaranteed housing in the Charles Commons or one of six other residence halls or university-owned "luxury" apartments. The dining facilities have improved markedly in recent years, according to students. "Dining services does a good job in terms of accommodating dietary needs, such as vegetarian, vegan, and kosher," says a junior. As for campus security: "The campus security here is dense and the measures

Engineering majors also enjoy strong departments, such as mechanical engineering, chemical and biomedical engineering, electrical and computer engineering, and computer science.

"The university is also home to some of the country's top humanities programs."

The Humanities Center espouses a casual, interdisciplinary approach, and with maximum curriculum flexibility allowed them, undergraduates are free to range as broadly or focus as specifically as they want.

in place make everyone feel safe at any hour of the day," says an economics major. "The security measures also extend into the surrounding community, so even students living off campus feel safe."

"The social life is incredibly inclusive," says a mathematics and philosophy double major. "Greek life doesn't dominate the social scene at Hopkins as it might at some other schools, but it enhances and provides additional social outlets for all students at Hopkins." Indeed, rowdy dorm parties and all-campus events are few and far between, but fraternity parties can be found on the weekends; 20 percent of the men and 23 percent of the women belong to Greek life. There are also more than 350 clubs and student organizations, including several a cappella groups. "Students can get alcohol at frat parties, but sometimes it's more difficult at local bars," one senior says. In general, "alcohol problems are not pervasive on campus," a student says.

The biggest and most popular undergraduate social event of the year is the annual student-organized Spring Fair, which draws crowds from the surrounding communities as well. Downtown Baltimore and the famed Inner Harbor are not too distant, and some of the city's best attractions, such as the Baltimore Museum of Art, Wyman Park, and the funky Hampden neighborhood are right near campus. Trendy Baltimore hot spots—like Canton, Fells Point, and Little Italy—draw big crowds.

"The social life is incredibly inclusive."

Students also head downtown for plays, the symphony, films, clubs, restaurants, the zoo, and major league sports; Camden Yards, home of baseball's Orioles, is the most commodious park in the country. "Baltimore is not wild and crazy, but it grows on you," says a junior. Of course, the urban reality means parking can be hard on campus, some students say. Those with wheels can take off for Annapolis, less than an hour away. Washington, D.C., only an hour's train ride, beckons with tourist activities and "a great nightlife." In the warmer months, a trek out to the Delaware and Maryland beaches takes the mind off the books.

When the stellar men's lacrosse team takes the road against opponents, students often take advantage of the opportunity to road-trip with them. Undergrads come together—even leaving the library at times—to cheer on their nationally acclaimed Division I Blue Jays and release some study tension. The rest of the Hopkins athletic program competes in Division III. The football, men's and women's soccer, men's and women's tennis, women's field hockey, and men's basketball and baseball teams have brought home recent Centennial Conference titles. Men's and women's swimming are perennial top-10 finishers in the Division III national meet. The Woodrow Wilson Debate Council recently placed fifth in the nation in the American Parliamentary Debate Association. Eighty-three percent of undergraduates use the recreation center for intramurals, sports clubs, experiential education, and fitness activities.

With one of the world's premier medical schools, top science programs, as well as first-rate programs in areas as diverse as writing, international studies, environmental engineering, and philosophy, The Johns Hopkins University is clearly among the best schools in the country. "Hopkins is a place that attracts people who want to do well in whatever they do," says a freshman. For those seeking top-notch professors, incredible resources, and unparalleled research opportunities, Johns Hopkins is hard to beat. Students truly take pride in the fact that they belong to the cream of the academic crop.

Overlaps

Harvard, Princeton, Yale, Cornell, University of Pennsylvania, Duke, Columbia, Stanford

If You Apply To ➤

Johns Hopkins: Early decision: Nov. 1. Regular admissions: Jan. 1. Financial aid: Mar. 1. Housing: May 30. Application fee: $70. Campus and alumni interviews: optional, informational. SATs or ACTs: required. Subject Tests: recommended. Biomedical engineering students must apply to that program. Accepts the Common Application. Essay question.

1700 Moore Street, Huntingdon, PA 16652

Located in the middle of Pennsylvania's rural hinterland, Juniata boasts one of the best undergraduate science programs among liberal arts colleges. Students are encouraged to design their own majors and to think globally. Peace and conflict studies are a specialty. Lots of merit scholarships, but not much diversity among students.

Set amid the ridges and valleys of central Pennsylvania, Juniata College offers students a tantalizing mix of academic flexibility, small classes, and surprisingly solid programs in the natural sciences. Students here create their own majors, conduct research alongside faculty, and pack their bags for study abroad opportunities around the world. What's more, Juniata students share a desire to change themselves and the world. "If you value world change over personal gain, then Juniata is for you," says a senior.

> **"Juniata College is very competitive, particularly in the sciences."**

Juniata College's 110-acre campus features a central stand of structures reflecting three architectural styles. The college's landmark building, Founders Hall, is a colonial Revival structure, built of brick atop a stone foundation. Halbritter Center for the Performing Arts, Ellis Hall, and the von Liebig Center for Science are all Classical Revival buildings, the prominent pillars on each visible all over campus. The college also boasts a Beaux-Arts building, Carnegie Hall, originally built as a Carnegie library in 1907 and redesigned on the interior to house the college's art museum. Founder's Hall recently received a makeover that earned LEED Gold certification for sustainability. The grounds are dotted with hardwoods, including Chinese Elms, American Elms, and several species of oak and maple.

In order to graduate, all Juniata students must complete six credit hours of coursework in five specific liberal arts–related areas: fine arts, international studies, social sciences, humanities, and natural sciences. Students also are expected to complete at least four communications courses—two of which must be writing-based and two of which may be speech-based—and must demonstrate that they have a basic competency in statistics as well as an understanding of basic mathematical skills. To satisfy the requirement, students have three options: complete a course which deals explicitly with both statistical and mathematical skills; complete one statistical and one mathematical course; or pass proficiency exams in math and statistics. All Juniata students complete two general education courses after attaining sophomore standing. One course is chosen from the Interdisciplinary Colloquia offerings and another from the Cultural Analysis offerings. In addition, all

> **"Most of my professors have been really good."**

freshmen complete the College Writing Seminar, an interdisciplinary course that introduces students to basic writing skills and communication. The course also integrates basic computer, library, and Internet research and study skills; career planning; and other issues relevant to first-year college students.

In lieu of preset majors, Juniata students may develop their own Programs of Emphasis (POEs) and approximately one-third do so. Each student works with two advisors to combine two existing POEs into a third course of study or create an entirely new program. "Juniata College is very competitive, particularly in the sciences," says one digital media major, but that doesn't necessarily translate into vicious competition for grades. "Juniata is very community-centered," a student says. Students may also choose a course of study from more than 50 existing POEs, and the most popular include business, biological/life sciences, psychology,

Website: www.juniata.edu
Location: Small Town
Private
Total Enrollment: 1,458
Undergraduates: 1,451
Male/Female: 45/55
SAT Ranges: CR 520–640, M 530–645
ACT Ranges: N/A
Financial Aid: 100%
Expense: Pr $ $
Student Loans: 72%
Average Debt: $ $ $ $
Phi Beta Kappa: No
Applicants: 2,418
Accepted: 66%
Enrolled: 25%
Grad in 6 Years: 76%
Returning Freshmen: 90%
Academics: ✍ ✍ ✍
Social: ☎ ☎ ☎
Q of L: ★ ★ ★
Admissions: (877) 586-4282
Email Address: admissions@juniata.edu

Strongest Programs:
Biological/Life Sciences
Business/Marketing
Education
Natural Resources and Conservation
Psychology
Museum Studies
Geology
Peace and Conflict Studies

education, and social sciences. "Juniata has long been known as a school for the natural sciences," a senior explains. "True to that reputation, those departments are still considered to be the top academic areas." Peace and Conflict Studies is one of the oldest and most comprehensive programs of its kind in the United States, and includes study abroad opportunities and internships. The communication program is praised, too: "The professors are known for their extensive networks in the marketing and communication fields and have a high success rate for getting their students internships and jobs," explains a senior. There are also POEs in digital media and performing arts management.

Sixty-eight percent of classes have 19 or fewer students, which allows for plenty of interaction between professors and students. "Most of my professors have been really good," says a sophomore. "They are available during office hours." Juniata has international exchange/study abroad agreements with colleges and universities in 16 countries, and 41 percent of all Juniata students participate in study abroad. The Inbound program allows new students to spend a week on campus as part of a particular club or activity in order to "make their first few days of immersion into college life easier," according to one student.

"Juniata students are self-motivated, driven, and ready to conquer the world when given the chance," says a marketing communication major. Sixty-one percent of Juniata students hail from Pennsylvania and 74 percent graduated in the top quarter of their high school class. The student population is about as homogeneous as it gets: African Americans and Asian Americans combine for 5 percent of the student body, Hispanics 4 percent, and international students 9 percent. Although the campus tends to lean left, students report that all viewpoints are represented and respected. "We're big on sustainability," says a student. "Students will literally pick plastic bottles out of the trash to recycle them." Another adds, "Compared to schools in New England, we're Bible-thumpers, whereas compared to schools in the South, we're socialists." Hundreds of merit scholarships are available, averaging more than $16,000 each, but there are no athletic scholarships.

"Compared to schools in New England, we're Bible-thumpers."

Eighty-one percent of the students live on campus in a variety of housing options, including traditional residence halls with cable and high-speed Internet access in each room and off-campus apartments for juniors and seniors. "Some dorms are newer, some are bigger, but they're all good dorms," says a sophomore. Campus fare is available at the Baker Refectory or Muddy Run Café (among others) and is "not Grandma's home cooking but is very tasty and certainly nutritious," one senior says. Students report feeling safe on campus thanks to an active security program that includes a warning siren, patrolling officers, and locked dorms.

"Juniata social life is definitely an on-campus thing," a senior explains. "There are over 90 clubs and organizations and they come through in a big way." Activities include live bands, trivia shows, poker tournaments, dinners, and dances. Students of legal age may drink on campus, and even those under the age of 21 have little trouble finding alcohol, despite policies that prohibit underage drinking. There are no fraternities or sororities, but students enjoy a number of traditions, including Mountain Day (classes are canceled for the day and students attend outdoor activities), Madrigal Dinner, and the Pig Roast. "I love the traditions at Juniata," cheers one psychology major. Students also take part in the "storming of the arch," in which "freshmen attempt to run into an arch defended by the rugby team," according to one student.

Huntingdon (population 17,000) is "a relatively small place for a college," says one student, but does provide the basic necessities for college students, including several restaurants and a movie theater. Walmart recently moved in, offering students "an opportunity to buy socks five minutes away rather than driving 40 minutes to Altoona," says a student. Community service is popular, as are road trips

In lieu of preset majors, Juniata students may develop their own Programs of Emphasis (POEs) and approximately one-third do so.

In addition to 20 varsity sports, Juniata students have the chance to participate in a variety of club, intramural, and individual activities, including basketball, soccer, volleyball, and ultimate Frisbee.

to Penn State (40 minutes away), Baltimore, Philadelphia, and Pittsburgh. "If you choose to stay on campus on weekends," observes one student, "you can definitely have a great social life."

The Juniata Eagles compete in Division III, and competitive teams include men's and women's volleyball, men's basketball, and women's field hockey. Juniata teams have earned 47 conference championships in a variety of sports, as well as eight national titles in men's and women's volleyball. In addition to 20 varsity sports, Juniata students have the chance to participate in a variety of club, intramural, and individual activities, including basketball, soccer, volleyball, and ultimate Frisbee. "A decent amount of students participate and they are a lot of fun," one student says.

Although students sometimes complain about the limitations of attending a small college in a small town, most seem excited to be part of such an inviting academic institution. "Juniata is a really comfortable community," says one junior. "Students can develop strong and beneficial relationships with faculty and staff that will impact their future careers." Those seeking "big football games, raging frat parties, and a vibrant urban setting" should look elsewhere, a senior adds. However, "if you are more interested in an intensive and personal academic environment with an extremely tight-knit and supportive community, then Juniata is the place for you."

If You Apply To ➤

Juniata: Early decision: Nov. 15. Regular admissions: Mar. 15. Housing: May 1. Application fee: $30 (paper), free (online). Campus interviews: optional, evaluative. No alumni interviews. SATs or ACTs: required. Subject Tests: recommended. Accepts the Common Application. Essay question: personal statement.

Kalamazoo College

1200 Academy Street, Kalamazoo, MI 49006-3295

Kalamazoo is a small liberal arts school that opens up the world to its students—literally. A whopping 80 percent of Kalamazoo Hornets study abroad thanks to the ingenious K-Plan, a quarter system that allows students to study abroad one, two, or three academic terms. And if you need an extra boost to round out that résumé, there is an extensive internship program.

Kalamazoo College is a small school in a small city in America's heartland. But college subsidies enable the majority of students to go abroad during their years here, making the school a launching pad to the world. In addition to international education, the school's K-Plan emphasizes teaching, internships (80 percent of students have at least one), and independent research (as seniors, all students complete a senior individualized project, with one-on-one faculty supervision). Students are exposed to a demanding academic schedule and high expectations from faculty. "K is a very rigorous place," warns one student, "characterized by people who want to do well and are passionate about their work."

Life on Kalamazoo's wooded, 60-acre campus centers on the Quad, a green lawn where students ponder their destinies and play ultimate Frisbee with equal ease. With its rolling hills, Georgian architecture, and cobblestone streets, the campus has the quaint look more typical of historic New England than of nearby Kalamazoo, which, with surrounding communities, has 225,000 residents. The Hicks Student Center was recently renovated and awarded LEED Silver certification. The school's athletic field complex and field house were renovated in 2012.

Website: www.kzoo.edu
Location: Small City
Private
Total Enrollment: 1,338
Undergraduates: 1,338
Male/Female: 42/58
SAT Ranges: CR 540–670, M 520–660
ACT Ranges: 26–30
Financial Aid: 99%
Expense: Pr $ $
Student Loans: 53%
Average Debt: $ $ $
Phi Beta Kappa: Yes
Applicants: 2,294

(continued)

Accepted: 69%

Enrolled: 21%

Grad in 6 Years: 80%

Returning Freshmen: 94%

Academics: ✐ ✐ ✐

Social: ☎ ☎ ☎

Q of L: ★ ★ ★

Admissions: (800) 253-3602

Email Address: admission@
kzoo.edu

Strongest Programs:

Business and Economics

Biological Sciences

English

Psychology

Chemistry

Fine Arts

Humanities

Languages

Kalamazoo aims to prepare students for real life by helping them synthesize the liberal arts education they receive on campus with their experiences abroad.

Founded in 1833 and formerly associated with the American Baptist Churches, Kalamazoo is the oldest college in Michigan. The college operates on the quarter system, and students must spend their entire first year on campus. Still, many freshmen begin the year with a "land/sea adventure," three weeks of climbing, rappelling, canoeing, and backpacking in the mountains of the Adirondacks. By the end, they're convinced they can survive anything, including the rigors of a Kalamazoo education and the long Michigan winters. Once safely back on campus, they take a liberal arts curriculum that includes language proficiency, a first-year writing seminar, sophomore and senior seminars, as well as a senior individualized project—an internship, artistic work, directed research, student teaching, or a traditional thesis, basically anything that caps off each student's education in some meaningful way.

> **"A future student should expect to work hard on school nights."**

After their freshman year, most of Kalamazoo's undergrads meet life's challenges with suitcase in hand, studying wherever their heart takes them, for the regular tuition price. The college offers three-, six-, and nine-month immersive study abroad programs that are available to all students regardless of major; all credit earned during study abroad transfers back to Kalamazoo College. "I studied abroad in Clermont-Ferrand, France, for nine months. I went to a French university, lived with a French family, and was completely immersed in French culture. It was a huge learning and growing experience, and I am very thankful to have been able to do it," says one student. Eighty percent of students take part in study abroad programs, including those offered by the Great Lakes College Association*. In fact, Kalamazoo offers students the opportunity to study via 41 programs in 21 countries on six continents. Kalamazoo's Center for Experiential Education is another resource for information on careers, internships, and study abroad.

Kalamazoo aims to prepare students for real life by helping them synthesize the liberal arts education they receive on campus with their experiences abroad. The result is an academic environment that is challenging. "A future student should expect to work hard on school nights," says a sophomore. The natural sciences are exceptionally good and students heap praise on the psychology and languages departments. "Being a liberal arts school, people are doing very cool and exciting things in all of the departments," one student says. Professors give students lots of individual attention and are rewarded with some of Michigan's highest faculty salaries. "The quality of teaching at Kalamazoo is superb. Every professor I've had has been passionate about what they teach and accessible outside of class," says a senior.

"Students are quirky, motivated, and highly involved in their community," says a senior. "Everybody here has a certain amount of weirdness to them, and we love each other for it," adds another student. Thirty-eight percent of students come from out of state, and minorities account for 19 percent of the student body—4 percent African American, 9 percent Hispanic, 5 percent Asian American, and 1 percent

> **"Students are quirky, motivated, and highly involved in their community."**

Native American. Many Kalamazoo students crave more diversity on campus. The administration says it is continuing efforts to educate students on intercultural understanding, and the campus has a decidedly progressive tone. "I think LGBT rights and racial justice are the two biggest issues on campus," offers one student. Merit scholarships are available to qualified students although athletic scholarships are not available.

Seventy-five percent of students live on campus. "The dorms are comfortable and a great way to get to know people. Community bathrooms are cleaned every day, and private bathrooms are cleaned once per week," a student explains. With 200 to 300 students away each term thanks to the K-Plan, a certain instability pervades all activities, from athletics to student government to living groups in the co-ed residence halls, where suites hold one to six students. Dorms are divided by class standing, and three dorms are available for freshmen. For those who tire of campus life, "Off-campus housing is both cheap and located close to campus, so it is a popular option," says a sophomore. While there are no Greek organizations at Kalamazoo, theme houses offer a more community-oriented atmosphere, including family-style dinners. "The food is great and the cooks are very friendly," says a student. Students also say campus security is good. "On campus, I have always felt safe and sheltered from danger," an economics major says.

"Most of the social life takes place within the college community," a junior reports. "There are movies and events on campus each weekend, but many students attend parties at upperclassmen's houses off campus." Students look forward to a casino night called Monte Carlo, homecoming, Spring Fling, and the Day of Gracious Living, a spring day where, without prior warning, classes are canceled and students relax by taking day trips or helping beautify the campus. (One popular T-shirt: "The end of learning is gracious living.") The city of Kalamazoo is a "fun city with lots going on and many ways to get involved," according to one political science major. Students volunteer at a variety of local churches and schools. Kalamazoo also offers the typical collection of restaurants, theaters, and bars; Kalamazoo students also benefit from the physical proximity of colleges such as Western Michigan University, where they may use the library or attend cultural events. Students appreciate the city's proximity to Lake Michigan's beaches and Chicago's urban playground.

> **"The dorms are comfortable and a great way to get to know people."**

For those who equate college with big-time athletics, Kalamazoo has something to offer—even if it's not nationally televised games or tens of thousands of screaming fans. The Kalamazoo Hornets have a long-standing rivalry with Hope College, culminating in the football teams' annual competition for the "infamous wooden shoes," where the Hornets are cheered on by fans known as "the stingers." Kalamazoo also has an outstanding men's tennis team, which has won conference titles for 75 (!) consecutive years. The Kalamazoo men's and women's swimming squads are also top-notch. Fifty percent of the student body participate in intramural sports.

Kalamazoo is best suited for those "looking for a place where everyone is really enthusiastic about learning and thrives in that kind of environment," says one student. A classmate adds that it can be tough for students to "find a balance between the academic life and recreation." Despite the isolating nature of the program, Kalamazoo offers students a truly global education.

Kalamazoo has an outstanding men's tennis team, which has won conference titles for 75 (!) consecutive years.

Overlaps

University of Michigan, Michigan State, Hope, College of Wooster, Grand Valley State, Albion, St. Olaf

If You Apply To ➤

Kalamazoo: Early decision: Nov. 10. Early action: Nov. 20. Regular admissions: Feb. 1. Financial aid: Feb. 15. Application fee: $40. Campus interviews: optional, evaluative. Alumni interviews: optional, informational. SATs or ACTs (with writing): required. No Subject Tests. Accepts the Common Application. Essay question.

University of Kansas

1502 Iowa Street, Lawrence, KS 66045

Often overlooked because of its heartland location, KU has the sophistication of the leading Big Ten universities but is much easier to get into. Stereotypes of Kansas to the contrary, Lawrence is not flat as a pancake. Excellent honors programs and a solid slate of professional schools. The University Honors Program is among the nation's best.

Despite its conservative Midwest location, the University of Kansas is an oasis of progressive activism and tolerance. And those students who are extremely dedicated can plunge into a great honors program the school provides to court them in its efforts to raise its academic profile. With solid academics, outstanding extracurricular programs, winning athletics, and a stellar social life, the University of Kansas has a bounty of opportunities for motivated Jayhawks. "You name it, we have it," cheers one satisfied junior.

The 1,000-acre campus is set atop Mount Oread ridge—once a lookout point for pioneer wagon trains—and spread out on rolling green hills overlooking valleys. The land of Dorothy and *The Wizard of Oz* isn't the first place that comes to many people's minds when asked to think about beautiful scenery, but the wooded and hilly

> **"The journalism school is amazing because it offers students excellent opportunities to get hands-on experience."**

Lawrence campus is actually one of the loveliest in the United States. Many of the buildings are made of indigenous Kansas limestone and are famed for their red roofs. But the real beauty of the campus lies in its landscape, particularly the breathtaking foliage that appears each autumn. There are almost as many trees on campus—29,525 at last count—as there are students. The Dole Institute of Politics is home to the world's largest Congressional archives and a World Trade Center memorial.

KU applicants apply to the individual school of their choice. Freshmen may apply to the schools of Architecture, Business, Engineering, Journalism, Music, and the College of Liberal Arts and Sciences. Those not admitted to one of the professional schools will automatically be considered for admission to the College of Liberal Arts and Sciences, where nearly 60 percent of the undergraduate population is enrolled. Students in the other professional schools spend their first two years completing the liberal arts requirements. The general education curriculum is intended to expose students to the foundations of the humanities, sciences, and social sciences over 120 credit hours. Foreign language and laboratory science courses are also required for all B.A. candidates.

Of the graduate and professional schools, those most noted for undergraduate programs are architecture and urban design, allied health, music, social welfare, pharmacy, nursing, education, business, and engineering. The architecture and business programs receive rave reviews from students and the School of Journalism and Mass Communication perpetuates the legacy of famed 19th-century journalist William

> **"The quality of teaching is certainly very good, but not perfect."**

Allen White. "The journalism school is amazing because it offers students excellent opportunities to get hands-on experience," says a senior. KU is a major player in behavioral research, and the School of Business has added its seventh undergraduate program—supply chain management and logistics—in response to strong demand from regional business leaders.

Students describe the academic atmosphere as highly variable: "KU is challenging and is a big environment, which is why some characterize KU as being unforgiving," says a sophomore. Students report the quality of teaching to be generally high, although interaction with professors is limited in some of the larger courses. "The quality of teaching is certainly very good, but not perfect," a student reports. "Because it is a research university, many of the general education courses are taught by researchers first, teachers second." Forty-two percent of all undergraduate classes have 19 or fewer students, and select freshmen can apply for the University Honors Program, which provides academically motivated students with honors courses, special advising, tutorials, and opportunities for scholarships and research grants. Other options for undergraduates include independent study or study abroad programs over 70 countries, including Brazil, France, Germany, and Ghana. Kansas

Students describe the academic atmosphere as highly variable.

provides several area study programs supported by language instruction in more than 40 languages. The Office of Student Affairs, run by its own vice provost, wins praise for its academic advising and for its help with internships, disability services, and extracurriculars. It publishes a monthly newsletter to parents.

Seventy-two percent of the students are from Kansas, and most of the rest are fellow Midwesterners (many from Chicago). African Americans, Hispanics, Native Americans, and Asian Americans account for 14 percent of the student body. "I think there is a good mix of students. There are the preppy students, liberal students, conservative students, ROTC students, hipster students, and just a wide variety of majors as well," a senior says. Out-of-staters must have a 2.5 high school core-curriculum GPA, be in the top third of their graduating class, or score a 24 on the ACT to get in. KU grants four-year renewable merit scholarships ranging from $4,000 to $40,000 to eligible freshmen.

Less than a quarter of Kansas students live in university housing, and both co-ed and single-sex dorms are available. Overall, students are pretty happy with the housing, much of which is being spruced up. "Most freshmen live in very comfortable, spacious dorms; I've stayed in five of the eight residence halls on campus at one point or another, and was never disappointed," says one junior. Students with 2.5 GPAs can live in one of the scholarship halls where 50 men or women live in a cooperative-type arrangement, resulting in "a unique, close-knit, communal environment," says one participant. Groups of 20

> **"Most freshmen live in very comfortable, spacious dorms."**

students can live in thematic learning communities on their residence hall floors—past themes include aerospace engineering and the meaning of film. A vast majority of KU students live off campus in Lawrence apartments, which are considered expensive only by Kansas standards. A dining complex called Mrs. E's provides extended-hour access to food-court-style meals for 2,500 residence-hall occupants. "There are always tons of options," a student says. "You can get anything from a simple sandwich to sushi."

"Much of the social life (beyond hanging out in dorm rooms) takes place in houses and apartments off campus," says a linguistics major. The Greek system, which attracts 14 percent of men and 20 percent of women, tends to be a major force in on-campus social life, though tension does exist between Greeks and independents. Sorority rush is completely dry, but rumor has it that the frats are a little more lenient when it comes to alcohol. "Just like the students, the social life at KU is very diverse," says a communication studies major. More than 600 organized groups keep things lively; other extracurricular activities include movies, poetry readings, and concerts. Scholarship halls, dorms, and other student groups sponsor large campus parties and events, but most of the social life takes place off campus. The university's bus system is run entirely by students and is much appreciated by tenderfeet, especially because that great big hill seems to double in size during the cold, windy winters. Lawrence, with its myriad boutiques, restaurants, and bars, receives rave reviews from students. "Lawrence is the American college town," says one enthusiastic Jayhawk. "Period." City slickers can trek off to Topeka, the state capital, or to Kansas City, each less than an hour's drive. The KC airport makes for easy long-distance transportation, and the area is also served by Amtrak.

KU varsity teams—the only ones in the nation that carry the name Jayhawks—compete in the rough-and-tumble Big 12 Conference. The football team is improving and KU was one of only three schools to send both men's and women's basketball teams to the NCAA Sweet 16; the men's team won its ninth straight conference title in 2013. James Naismith, who invented basketball, was KU's first coach—and the only one with a losing record. The school year kicks off with Hawk Week, the official welcome for new students. The traditional "Rock Chalk Jayhawk" KU cheer

The Office of Student Affairs, run by its own vice provost, wins praise for its academic advising and for its help with internships, disability services, and extracurriculars.

More than 600 organized groups keep things lively; other extracurricular activities include movies, poetry readings, and concerts.

and steam whistle denoting class change is enough to bring a pang of nostalgia to the heart of even the most grizzled Kansas alum. To demonstrate their loyalty to the Jayhawks, thousands of students show up for the first basketball practice of the season. This nocturnal tradition is lovingly labeled "Late Night in the Phog"—an allusion to the late, great coach Phog Allen. The women's basketball, softball, and volleyball teams are also worth watching. "One of KU's defining characteristics is the tradition on campus. The Rock Chalk chant is widely recognizable, creating a sort of bond between all Jayhawks, past and present," says one student.

> "Much of the social life (beyond hanging out in dorm rooms) takes place in houses and apartments off campus."

KU's academic value is hard to beat. With nearly 50 nationally ranked academic programs, Kansas's reputation (the nonbasketball one) continues to grow. Comprehensive study abroad programs, extensive undergraduate research opportunities, and a thriving social scene are just some of the reasons students choose to be a Jayhawk. "No school has a better balance of academics, athletics, and social life than KU," a finance major says.

If You Apply To ➤

Kansas: Rolling admissions: Aug. 18. Application fee: $30. No campus or alumni interviews. SATs or ACTs: required. No Subject Tests. Apply to particular school or program. Essay question.

University of Kentucky

100 Funkhouser Building, Lexington, KY 40506-0032

The state of Kentucky is better known for horses and hoops than higher education, but the University of Kentucky is working to change that. The basketball team is still a championship contender, but so too are programs in business, engineering, and health fields. About one in five students come from out of state, mostly from Tennessee and Ohio.

You probably recognize the University of Kentucky Wildcats as a perennial force in the NCAA postseason basketball tournament. But the University of Kentucky's claim to excellence stretches beyond its winning athletic teams—into outstanding medical and premedical programs, scientific research involving both professors and students, and a social calendar packed so full of Southern tradition that it would make even the most composed debutante's head spin. UK is also a national leader in efforts to support first-generation college students and has established a living/learning community for such students. Nothing if not ambitious, the college has initiated a strategy that seeks to make UK a top-20 public research university by 2020, but budget cuts have stymied the effort for the time being. Stay tuned.

> "I do wish I had more assistance from my advisors."

The University of Kentucky campus contains a mixture of old and new, modern and traditional buildings that date back to the late 1890s. The campus buildings indicate a transition beginning with the original redbrick structures to designs using contemporary glass and concrete as one moves south following the path of development. Most visitors would agree that the grounds are well maintained, organized around the comfortable parklike spaces influenced by Frederick Law Olmsted's design. The campus contains a vast amount of mature trees and lawns set in a natural arrangement of open spaces, typical of the great land grant universities. Of course, UK's location in the heart of one of the finest horse-breeding areas in the world makes it a natural place for the Gluck Equine Research Center, a headquarters for research into horse diseases. The William T. Young Library is ranked 30th among public research libraries by the Association of Research Libraries.

Students sing the praises of many departments at UK, but several unique programs stand out. The Lexington campus is home to the Gaines Center of the Humanities, which is unusual in its study of public higher education. Lexington also hosts the Patterson School of International Diplomacy, one of the smallest yet most respected schools of its type in the country. The chemistry department has turned out three National Science Foundation fellowship winners. Weaker areas include lower-level "monster" science classes, which one student describes as "extremely large and not at all personalized." Undergrads complain about trouble getting into courses they need, especially entry-level offerings. According to a marketing major, students "have difficulty if they are freshmen, because most of them have to take the same classes, and sometimes they don't get the right times—or the classes at all." It's hard to complete the engineering, health, business, and architecture programs in four years, students say. Term-time internships, known as co-ops, also complicate—but enliven—the picture.

"UK students are typically self-assured, slightly competitive, and outgoing."

Students praise UK's professors. "My professors have always shown a genuine concern for my grades," says a sophomore. TAs and full professors teach about the same number of freshman classes. The Central Advising Service, or CAS, is helping to improve the quality of academic guidance, though one student notes, "I do wish I had more assistance from my advisors on which classes to take."

To graduate, all students must take mathematics and a foreign language, as well as written and oral communication classes and a statistics, calculus, or logic course. The core program, called University Studies, also requires exposure to natural and social sciences, humanities, an introduction to cross-disciplinary education, and experience with non-Western ways of thinking. Additionally, all freshmen are encouraged to take an academic orientation class called UK101, designed to help them adjust to college life. The academic climate is laid-back, but students shouldn't expect easy As. "When it comes to study time and class work, the students are always competing with themselves to earn the best grades they can," explains a junior.

For upperclassmen, UK offers a number of joint programs with other colleges and universities, including Transylvania, Centre, and Georgetown (in Kentucky). There's also a cooperative program with the Army and Air Force ROTC. Students studying prevet at UK will find coveted slots reserved for them at Auburn and Tuskegee in the advanced veterinary medicine program, at in-state tuition rates. UK is a member of the Academic Common Market, which provides students in 15 states the opportunity to pay in-state tuition at any of these states' schools if they want to enroll in a program not offered in their home state.

"UK students are typically self-assured, slightly competitive, and outgoing," says a psychology major (perhaps practicing analysis for her future career). The UK student body hails from all 50 counties in Kentucky, with 21 percent from out of state. The student body is predominantly white; African Americans account for 8 percent of students, and Hispanics and Asian Americans combine for 5 percent. Despite these small numbers, students say diversity is valued. "Respectfulness is an issue," says one student, "but Southern hospitality abounds." The university aims to be an

(continued)

Enrolled: 36%
Grad in 6 Years: 59%
Returning Freshmen: 81%
Academics: ✍ ✍ ✍
Social: ☎ ☎ ☎ ☎
Q of L: ★ ★ ★
Admissions: (866) 900-4685
Email Address: admissions@ uky.edu

Strongest Programs:
Business
Premed
Predentistry
Nursing
Engineering
Chemistry

The chemistry department has turned out three National Science Foundation fellowship winners.

Students praise UK's professors.

"inclusive learning community," achieving academic excellence by working toward "social responsibility and community building, with particular focus on equity, fairness, and safety for each person," among other initiatives. Merit scholarships are offered to qualified students.

Kentucky's dorms are clean and convenient, as well as a great way to meet people, students say, though there's quite a range of what amenities you may get. Dorms are located on three parts of the campus—north, central, and south. North campus housing is old, but the halls are small, so they afford a chance to form close relationships. They're also within a short walking distance of classrooms, the student center, and the bookstore. South campus offers newer dorms with small rooms and air-conditioning, while central campus offers the biggest rooms. Recommended for freshmen: Kirwan-Blanding Complex, since "everything seems to happen there." Getting a room is not a problem as long as you apply by the deadline. Also, since students are not required to live on campus, only 26 percent do so.

Students say that while Lexington is a great place to go to school, it's not a typical college town. "Lexington is almost 250,000 people strong," an upperclassman explains. "It's small enough to drive across town easily, but large enough not to see everyone you know when you go to Walmart." Despite the lack of diversity on campus, Lexington abounds with a multitude of ethnic eateries, as well as theaters, shopping malls, and nightspots. On campus, students enjoy movies, presentations, seminars, and athletic events, the most popular being basketball games at the legendary Rupp Arena. Other campus activities include the Little Kentucky Derby, a weeklong student-run festival that features a balloon race and concerts. Among the highlights of any student's career at UK are two one-month periods—one in the fall, one in the spring—when students spend afternoons at Keeneland Race Track enjoying the tradition of Kentucky horse racing.

"In Kentucky, basketball is like a second religion."

Sixteen percent of Kentucky men and 25 percent of women go Greek, but fraternities and sororities offer the great majority of on-campus activities, as well as opportunities for volunteer work in the community. The university has a strict no-alcohol-on-campus policy, but it doesn't tend to affect students with fake IDs. When it's time for a road trip, UK students head to Cincinnati or Louisville (one hour away), or to Atlanta or Chicago (six hours)—that is, if they're not taking leisurely Sunday drives through nearby Bluegrass country.

The best road-trip destinations are anywhere there's a steamy, noisy gym and a basketball team ready to play UK's always-strong Wildcats. Home games at Lexington's Rupp Arena—what one student calls "a magical experience"—are consistently packed. "In Kentucky, basketball is like a second religion," agrees another true-blue Wildcat fan. Although screaming yourself hoarse for five guys hitting the hardwood may not be as genteel as cheering while sipping a mint julep at the track, for many students, the mix of collegiate craziness and old-world Southern hospitality found in Lexington is just what they want.

If You Apply To ➤

Kentucky: Rolling admissions: Feb. 15. Application fee: $50. Campus and alumni interviews: optional, informational. SATs or ACTs: required. Subject Tests: optional. No essay question.

Kenyon College

Ransom Hall, Gambier, OH 43022-9623

Kenyon is a vintage liberal arts college plunked down in the middle of the Ohio countryside. More mainstream than Oberlin, more serious than Denison, and more selective than Wooster, Kenyon is best known for English and a small but distinguished drama program. Located in a tiny village where faculty and staff are the main residents. Swimming and diving teams are dominant.

Kenyon College provides students with an accessible and pure liberal arts experience that rivals those of leading East Coast institutions. Students here are proud of what sets Kenyon apart from other liberal arts colleges. "The one thing that unites us all is that we are passionate about something," explains one student. "Whether it be drama, physics, writing, activism—Kenyon students care!" The college continues to increase its selectivity and build on its reputation as a supportive academic environment.

> **"People work hard, and it is expected that you'll get your work done on time."**

The oldest private college in Ohio, Kenyon's 1,200-acre campus sits on a hillside overlooking a scenic view of river, woods, and fields in a secluded village of roughly 600 residents. The college's oldest building, Old Kenyon, dates from 1826; it is said to be the first collegiate Gothic building in America, and the campus is on the National Register of Historic Places. The Brown Family Environmental Center includes a butterfly garden and extensive perennial gardens planted with community donations. The sleek, modern Kenyon Athletic Center offers 263,000 square feet of fitness and recreational space, including a basketball/volleyball arena, 22-lane swimming pool, 200-meter track, four racquetball courts, a 120-seat theater, and a sushi bar. A spate of new facilities are planned for 2014, including an art gallery, studio art building, and new townhouse apartments for students.

Kenyon's focus on liberal arts makes for a challenging, but largely noncompetitive, learning environment. "People work hard, and it is expected that you'll get your work done on time, but there is no competitiveness," says a student. In fact, at Kenyon, it's hard to find a weak department—especially since there are so many opportunities for independent study. "It's hard to say there are bad departments, only apathetic and unimaginative students," says a religious studies major. English, a nationally renowned subject at Kenyon since the 1930s, is the most popular major, and it, along with the drama department (which turned out Paul Newman), sets the tone of campus life. Kenyon is, after all, the home of the *Kenyon Review*, a prestigious literary quarterly, and a school about which alum E. L. Doctorow

> **"Kenyon's professors are generally top-notch."**

has said, "Poetry is what we did at Kenyon, the way at Ohio State they played football." Political science is said to be solid, drawing undecided majors with its introductory class, Quest for Justice. The Integrated Program in Humane Studies, which incorporates English, history, political science, and art history, is also popular.

The hallmark of Kenyon's academic philosophy is an almost fanatical devotion to the liberal arts and sciences. "Academic life at Kenyon is rooted in three strong tenets," an administrator explains. "That students thrive when they can work closely with their professors; that they can best explore their own potential when they have enough flexibility to experiment; and that they learn most productively in an atmosphere of cooperation." A unique program is a farming independent study, which places students on nearby farms for fieldwork each week. Preprofessional content opportunities include 3–2 engineering programs with several universities, and with high

Website: www.kenyon.edu
Location: Rural
Private
Total Enrollment: 1,657
Undergraduates: 1,657
Male/Female: 47/53
SAT Ranges: CR 630–730, M 610–680
ACT Ranges: 28–32
Financial Aid: 52%
Expense: Pr $ $ $ $
Student Loans: 41%
Average Debt: $
Phi Beta Kappa: Yes
Applicants: 3,947
Accepted: 36%
Enrolled: 31%
Grad in 6 Years: 90%
Returning Freshmen: 94%
Academics: ✎ ✎ ✎ ✎
Social: ☎ ☎ ☎
Q of L: ★ ★ ★
Admissions: (740) 427-5776
Email Address: admissions@kenyon.edu

Strongest Programs:
English
Psychology
Economics
Political Science
History
Neuroscience
Microbiology

acceptance rates to graduate programs in law, business, and medicine. On-campus Summer Science research scholarships provide opportunities for collaborative research for aspiring scientists and doctors. The Career Development Center helps sort out grad schools and employment opportunities, both summer and postgraduation.

While there is no core curriculum at Kenyon, all students must have proficiency in a second language. Students must also complete requirements in quantitative reasoning. A bevy of academic counselors, including upperclassmen and professors, help ensure that freshmen stay on the right track. About 20 percent of juniors are invited by their departments to read for honors, and approximately 11 percent graduate with departmental honors. The culmination of each student's coursework at Kenyon is the senior exercise, which may take the form of a comprehensive examination, an integrative paper, a research project, a performance, or some combination of these.

Classes are small at Kenyon and even the larger introductory courses use a two-part format in which students meet for lectures one week and split up for discussion sections with the professor the next. "Kenyon's professors are generally top-notch. I have had more incredibly talented and passionate professors than I could ever list," says a senior. Many profs live close to campus, which enhances the close-knit environment. Half of the student body takes part in study abroad; they may choose from more than 150 programs in more than 50 countries.

> **The hallmark of Kenyon's academic philosophy is an almost fanatical devotion to the liberal arts and sciences.**

"Whether Kenyon students are into Greek life, athletics, art, or something else entirely, they all are nerdy in some way," says a senior. Fifteen percent of Kenyon students are Ohioans, and one-third hail from New England and Mid-Atlantic states. "Kenyon students are preppy, rich, classy, liberal, well educated, and high class," says a freshman. Students also have a global mind-set. African Americans account for 3 percent of the student body, Hispanics 5 percent, and Asian Americans 7 percent. The lack of diversity is noticed on campus. Kenyon awards merit scholarships averaging $12,094. Thanks in part to a $10 million gift from Paul Newman, the college also guarantees a loan-free education for 25 selected students with the greatest need who bring the qualities of creativity, community service, and leadership to Kenyon.

"Kenyon students are preppy, rich, classy, liberal, well educated, and high class."

Ninety-eight percent of the students live on campus, with housing guaranteed for four years. Freshmen start in five dorms at the north end of campus, and most move south to recently remodeled housing the next year. Renovations and expansions are always in the works, with 15 north campus townhouses recently opened, and five more under construction. Rooms are selected via a sometimes harrowing housing lottery, and upperclassmen typically try to get into one of the historic dorms. Housing options include a variety of spaces, from three-, four-, and six-person apartments to singles, suites, and traditional double rooms. Most dorms are co-ed. Rather than their own houses, fraternities occupy sections of the south campus dorms, making that area the center of the party scene. "Frats have parties but these are definitely not your typical frats," says one student. Everyone, including those in the apartments with kitchens, must buy college food. Campus safety is described as adequate. "I have never once felt unsafe on campus, even when walking home from the library late at night," says a freshman. "This is mostly due to the fact that Kenyon is located in a remarkably small town in the middle of rural Ohio."

> **The school's Greek system draws 14 percent of the men and 16 percent of the women, and the frats throw lively parties that are open to all.**

The school's Greek system draws 14 percent of the men and 16 percent of the women, and the frats throw lively parties that are open to all. "Most of Kenyon's parties involve beer and dancing, but students who want a different scene can usually make it happen," says one student. A senior adds, "Every student performance—sports games, public presentations, music recitals, art shows—is incredibly well attended." Gambier is a small town, with a couple of bars and no movie theaters, but there are a few more options 10 minutes away in Mount Vernon, to which the college runs a daytime shuttle bus. On-campus events and college-sponsored activities are growing more popular to help keep boredom at bay. With its deli, market, coffeehouse, inn, restaurant, bank, and post office, Gambier is at least quaint. Students enjoy buying real maple syrup, fresh bread, and cheese from Amish farmers with stands on the main street on Saturdays.

Kenyon remains defined by its traditions.

Kenyon remains defined by its traditions, the most hallowed of which is renewed each year as incoming freshmen sing college songs to the rest of the community from the steps of Rosse Hall. Departing seniors sing the same songs at graduation. On Matriculation Day each October, after a formal ceremony, freshmen sign a book that contains the signatures of virtually every Kenyon student since the early 1800s. Other major events include homecoming and the Summer Send-Off. To break February's icy cold, the school holds a formal ball called Philander's Phling, remembering founder Philander Chase; an alum donates money for the dance. There are two small ski areas near campus, but for those seeking adventure farther from home, Columbus and Ohio State University are a 45-minute drive south. The adventurous sometimes take road trips to Cleveland (home of the Rock and Roll Hall of Fame), Cincinnati, Chicago, or even Canada.

Kenyon's varsity teams are known as the Lords and the Ladies. Women's and men's tennis and men's soccer are competitive, but the flagship sport is definitely swimming. Kenyon's swimming and diving teams dominate Division III competition, with the men's team having won a record 32 times in a row. "Kenyon's rivalry with Denison is huge," says one student, "especially between the swim teams." Kenyon was instrumental in establishing the North Coast Athletic Conference, which includes a number of academically strong Midwestern schools, including longtime rival Denison. A junior cites the annual hockey game versus Denison, when "both teams have to drive to Newark and a surprising number of fans from both colleges attend." Soccer games against Ohio Wesleyan draw large crowds. Clubs sponsor everything from ultimate Frisbee to water polo.

"Kenyon's rivalry with Denison is huge."

Kenyon students are liberal, global thinkers who are as devoted to one another as their studies. While Gambier might be a bit of a culture shock for urbanites, one student says, "Kenyon's rural setting is one of its greatest advantages." Rituals and traditions of the past are still alive and well at Kenyon. The *Kenyon Review*, the legend of alumnus Paul Newman, and national-championship swimming give the college an identity that's hard to match.

Overlaps

Oberlin, Carleton, Middlebury, Brown, Vassar, Wesleyan, Denison, Grinnell

If You Apply To ➤

Kenyon: Early decision I: Nov. 15. Early decision II and regular admissions: Jan. 15. Financial aid: Feb. 15. Housing: May 1. Application fee: $50 (paper), free (online). Campus and alumni interviews: optional, evaluative. SATs or ACTs: required. Subject Tests: optional. Accepts the Common Application. Essay question.

Knox College

2 East South Street, Galesburg, IL 61401

This friendly and progressive Illinois college was among the first in the nation to admit African Americans and women. Offers a strong writing program and exceptional sciences. More mainstream than Beloit and Grinnell and just over half as big as Illinois Wesleyan. With a student body of about 1,400, Knox offers an unusual degree of personal attention, even by the standards of small colleges.

With the unconventional Prairie Fire as its mascot, Knox College has long made a name for itself by breaking away from the conventions of the day. Founded by abolitionists in 1837 as the Knox Manual Labor College, this liberal arts college has a tradition of debate that extends beyond the Lincoln-Douglas event that occurred there in 1858. And through a warm and supportive academic community, the college continues to foster a strong sense of individualism.

> **"Knox is challenging but not overwhelming."**

Located in the heart of the Midwest—almost midway between Chicago and St. Louis—the 82-acre campus has spacious, tree-lined lawns and a dynamic mixture of architecture that reflects the 145-year span of construction dates of existing buildings. Old Main, constructed in 1857, is a National Historic Landmark and the only building remaining from the 1858 Lincoln-Douglas debates. Additional facilities include a fully renovated football venue, a student lounge, and Borzello Hall, which houses faculty offices and classroom space.

Students say the academic relationships at Knox are infused with a spirit of cooperation and equality. Beyond the classroom, students, faculty, and administrators make decisions on boards together, each with identical voting power. First-year students confront the core issues of liberal education in Preceptorial, a one-term seminar examining questions of ethics and truth through multidisciplinary reading and critical writing. But while many schools have small, intense classes for first-year students, Knox takes things a bit further by mandating an advanced preceptorial for seniors. This class connects their expertise in their major to a broad topic.

The general education curriculum requires students to take one course each in the arts, the natural and social sciences, and the humanities, as well as courses in writing, speaking, mathematics, information technology, foreign language, and human diversity. Knox also boasts the Ford Foundation Research Fellowship Program, which was created in the mid-1980s to encourage students to consider careers in college teaching and research. Ford Fellows work with selected faculty mentors to design and carry out a research project in an area of interest. Through this permanently endowed foundation, Knox is able to offer stipends for summer research to a full one-fifth of the junior class. Moves like these have helped Knox earn a national reputation for its independent undergraduate research. More than 85 percent of students do some type of independent study.

Strong departments include creative writing, math, psychology, political science, and the natural sciences, with biology attracting lots of research grant money. The school's literary journal, *Catch*, has won national awards. Students can take part in the Chicago Semester in the Arts, and dramatists also benefit from several theaters, including one with a revolving stage. Study abroad options include more than 30 programs in 18 countries, and 28 percent of students participate. The college is also a member of the Associated Colleges of the Midwest Consortium*.

Knox operates on an honor system that allows students to take tests unproctored in any public area, but few students would even think of cheating. "Knox is

> **"Students who attend Knox are involved in their community."**

challenging but not overwhelming," says a senior. Where faculty is concerned, students offer uniformly glowing reviews for their performance in the classroom and availability outside of it. "The quality of teaching is very high," a student says. Sixty-five percent of classes have fewer than 19 students. Knox's trimester system packs a great deal of studying into a short period, but students are only required to take three courses per term.

Students praise Knox's student advising system. "Academic advising has been excellent for me, and advisors are always available to discuss anything ranging from future plans to personal problems," says a junior. An early identification of premed freshmen guarantees six students admission to Rush Medical College in Chicago if they maintain a four-year B average. Knox also offers 3–2 or 3–4 programs in engineering, nursing, medical technology, law, and architecture.

"Students who attend Knox are involved in their community (campus and otherwise) and are independent thinkers," says a senior. Forty-five percent of students are from Illinois, and 11 percent of students come from foreign countries. Students of color make up 23 percent of the student body (7 percent African American, 6 percent Asian American, and 10 percent Hispanic) and maintain an active profile on campus. While Knox is not a terribly politically active school, there appears to be a commitment to diversity across campus. One of the most popular forms of activism is "chalking," where students write messages in chalk on campus walkways. "The biggest social and political issues on campus involve student governance," a senior reports. Most students went to public high school, and 66 percent graduated in the top quarter of their class. Merit scholarships averaging more than $12,000 are available, but athletic scholarships are not.

Housing is not a problem on the Knox campus; 85 percent of students reside in campus digs. Renovations have improved housing for most students, though some students complain that most rooms are not air-conditioned. "The dorms are comfortable and have adequate space," one senior reasons. Co-ed living arrangements are available, although most freshmen live in single-sex suites with one or two upperclassmen as residential advisors. Students suggest freshman women would be happiest in Post Hall, while men should try to live anywhere in Old Quad. Older students may band together with friends to form a special-interest or theme suite. Twenty-one percent of men belong to fraternities, while 16 percent of women join sororities. It takes a minor miracle for students to obtain permission to move off campus, which has become a common complaint among juniors and seniors. Students say campus dining options are edible if not overly diverse.

> "The biggest social and political issues on campus involve student governance."

Weekends are filled with dances, campus activities, and fraternity parties. "Most of the social life happens on campus," a creative writing major says. The alcohol policy is strict, students say, and the administration is quick to deal with underage drinkers. Galesburg is a small Midwestern railroad town, and some students say they've had trouble adjusting to the sounds of locomotives, although the Amtrak station makes travel easy and relatively cheap. At one time this city of about 35,000 was a center of abolitionism, and the honorary degree that the college bestowed on then presidential candidate Abraham Lincoln was his first formal title. A senior says, "Galesburg is a small town with a lot of hidden treasures." Nearby Lake Storey offers boating, water slides, and nature trails, and students looking for more excitement can travel to Peoria, about 40 miles away. Slightly farther away, Chicago is about 140 miles to the northeast. One of the best all-time traditions is Flunk Day. At 5:30 on a spring morning, Old Main's bell rings, whistles blow, and classes are canceled to make way for dunk tanks and Jell-O pits.

Prairie Fire athletics generate a reasonable degree of enthusiasm. Both the men's and women's golf teams are strong, and every fall, the football team endures lots of hard Knox against archrival Monmouth to bring home the highly prized Bronze Turkey Award, a throwback to the time when the game was played on Thanksgiving Day.

Knox may not be a well-known school, but students here have little else to complain about. Academics are the priority and students are encouraged to be individuals, but the close-knit atmosphere helps them form strong connections with different types of students and down-to-earth professors. Says a student, "There is a 'freedom to flourish' at Knox. My opportunities are limitless."

Ford Fellows work with selected faculty mentors to design and carry out a research project in an area of interest.

Students can take part in the Chicago Semester in the Arts, and dramatists also benefit from several theaters.

Overlaps
Beloit, University of Chicago, Grinnell, University of Illinois, Illinois Wesleyan, Lawrence

Lafayette College

Easton, PA 18020

Geographically close to Lehigh, but closer kin to Colgate and Hamilton. Does offer engineering, as do Bucknell, Swarthmore, Trinity (CT), and Union. Attracts relatively conservative, athletic students who work hard and play hard. A recent spate of building shows Lafayette's financial health. One of the smallest institutions to play Division I sports.

Website: www.lafayette.edu
Location: Suburban
Private
Total Enrollment: 2,436
Undergraduates: 2,436
Male/Female: 53/47
SAT Ranges: CR 580–680, M 610–710
ACT Ranges: 27–30
Financial Aid: 64%
Expense: Pr $ $ $
Student Loans: 56%
Average Debt: $ $ $
Phi Beta Kappa: Yes
Applicants: 6,660
Accepted: 34%
Enrolled: 28%
Grad in 6 Years: 91%
Returning Freshmen: 95%
Academics: ◣ ◣ ◣ ◣
Social: ☎ ☎ ☎ ☎ ☎
Q of L: ★ ★ ★
Admissions: (610) 330-5100
Email Address: admissions@ lafayette.edu

Strongest Programs:
Engineering
Economics/Business
Government/Law
Psychology

Lafayette College has become one of the small elite liberal arts colleges with a huge presence abroad. Lafayette is a national leader in undergraduate faculty-mentored research and is ranked among the top colleges in study abroad participation. The liberal arts curriculum mixes nicely with engineering in a small college atmosphere. The number of applications has increased, signaling that the world beyond the Lafayette campus has taken notice.

> **"The largest class I've ever had was only 50 students."**

Lafayette is situated on a stately hill in Easton, Pennsylvania, just an hour and a half west of New York City and even closer to Philadelphia. The campus has an eclectic blend of architectural styles and more than 125 species of trees. The main library holds more than 500,000 volumes, with a 24-hour study area and online access to the card catalog from the comfort of dorm rooms. A $22 million expansion of the Skillman library has added 30,000 square feet of open learning space—a common theme in many Lafayette buildings. The 90,000-square-foot Acopian Engineering Center stays open all night and weekends, and features lots of open workspaces and glass walls to build a sense of shared purpose—and allow for extra mingling.

Lafayette's economics, psychology, government and law, mechanical engineering, and English programs are among the most popular majors. A Common Course of Study (CCS) has been implemented for the class of 2016 and requirements include a first-year seminar and courses in lab science, social sciences, mathematics, humanities, writing, global and multicultural proficiency, and a foreign language. Lafayette has one of the highest study abroad participation rates among liberal arts colleges; the school offers several faculty-led, semester-long programs for its students and also offers faculty-led, short-term study abroad programs for credit during the January and May interim terms. The Economic Empowerment and Global Learning Project allows students from all disciplines to relate classroom lessons to real-world problems in the U.S. and abroad. The EXCEL program pays students who take research positions with faculty.

> **"A large number of students attended private high schools or boarding schools, which lends a particular 'preppiness' to areas of the campus."**

Engineering students, too, may explore a foreign culture through an unusual arrangement with the Free University of Brussels, which allows them to study abroad while maintaining normal progress toward their degrees. There is also cross-registration available with other schools in the Lehigh Valley Association of Independent Colleges*. Back on campus, students report classes to be challenging.

"The academic climate is challenging," says a sophomore, "but there are lots of resources that really encourage you to explore all of your interests." The quality of teaching is uniformly high, students say, and professors are accessible and friendly. "All the classes are taught by professors, and the largest class I've ever had was only 50 students. I especially have enjoyed the seminar classes," says one student.

"Students at Lafayette largely come from Pennsylvania and New Jersey. The campus currently lacks a broad cultural and ethnic diversity, although it has been becoming more diverse with each successive class year. A large number of students attended private high schools or boarding schools, which lends a particular 'preppiness' to areas of the campus, especially Greek life," a junior says. Seventy-eight percent of Lafayette students are from out of state and most tend to shy away from politics, although there are plenty of student groups for everything from the environment to getting out the vote. African Americans account for 5 percent of the student body, and Hispanics and Asian Americans combine for another 9 percent. "Students are less political than one might imagine," a student explains, "even though the College Democrats, Republicans, and Libertarians all have a pretty loud voice on campus." Hundreds of merit scholarships worth an average of nearly $20,000 each are available to qualified students; there are 83 athletic scholarships available in 11 men's and women's sports.

The EXCEL program pays students who take research positions with faculty.

"The student-led Lafayette Activities Forum arranges events almost every week that are open to all students."

Ninety-two percent of students live on campus, and housing is guaranteed for all four years. Possibilities include Greek houses as well as independent dormitories and college-owned apartments with a variety of living and eating arrangements. Experienced students recommend Keefe, South, Kirby, or PT Farinon/Conway. A 60-person residence hall has special-interest floors organized around themes such as science and technology. "The dorms are decent and students are always guaranteed housing," a junior says. There's a lottery system that determines which dorm a student will live in, but most get into the dorm of their choice. Ruef and South College are more social, while Watson Hall and Kirby House are quieter, students say. Most upperclassmen, including women and non-Greek males, join meal plans at fraternities or the social dorms. "The food is quite edible and dining services attempts to serve a variety of foods while also trying to satisfy picky eaters," says one international affairs major. Students report feeling safe while traversing the campus. "Campus security is good and continues to improve," reports one junior.

There is also cross-registration available with other schools in the Lehigh Valley Association of Independent Colleges*.

"Most of the social life is on campus as the student-led Lafayette Activities Forum arranges events almost every week that are open to all students. There is also an on-campus nightclub called The Spot that hosts events every Friday and Saturday night," explains one student. Greek life attracts 19 percent of the men and 39 percent of the women. For students with cars, or those willing to hop a bus or train, the bright lights of Philadelphia, New York, and Atlantic City beckon on weekends; for a change of pace, there is also hiking the Appalachian Trail. A popular excursion is touring the nearby Binney & Smith factory where Crayola crayons are made. Parties are BYOB, and all sororities and some fraternities are dry. The arts program brings a range of performers to campus. Blue-collar Easton "gets a bad rap, but is really nice," says a senior. "A lot of restaurants on the hill, lots of nice shops, great health and beauty salons. I really like Easton." From College Hill and Downtown to the South Side, the city offers plenty of opportunities for volunteer work in schools, prisons, rehabilitation centers, hospitals, and environmental sites, under the auspices of Lafayette's Community Outreach Center.

There's a lottery system that determines which dorm a student will live in, but most get into the dorm of their choice.

Sports add much flavor to the Lafayette experience. Competitive teams include men's baseball, football, soccer, and lacrosse and women's basketball. Recent Patriot League champions include women's field hockey and men's soccer. The annual football game against nearby Lehigh is intense—students claim it's the oldest rivalry in the U.S. All Leopard varsity teams compete in Division I except for football, which is I-AA. For those not up to varsity level, there is an extensive intramural program, buoyed by the state-of-the-art, $35 million Kirby Sports Center. The most important nonathletic campus event of the year is All-College Day, a spring festival with beach balls, bathing suits, bands, and the like.

Students looking for tradition and close contact with professors—and who aren't afraid of some serious study—should take a look. "There's more to college life than drinking," advises one senior. "Keep an open mind, get involved, and follow your interests and dreams!"

If You Apply To ➤

Lafayette: Early decision: Nov. 15. Regular admissions: Jan. 15. Application fee: $65. Campus interviews: optional, evaluative. Alumni interviews: optional, informational. SATs or ACTs: required. SAT Subject Tests: recommended. Accepts the Common Application. Essay question.

Lake Forest College

555 Sheridan Road, Lake Forest, IL 60045

The only small, selective, private college in the Chicago area. Lake Forest generally attracts middle-of-the-road and conservative students. In the exclusive town from which the school takes its name, students can babysit for corporate CEOs at night and get internships at their corporations during the day. Large numbers of Foresters also study abroad.

Located just 30 miles north of the downtown Loop, Lake Forest College offers excellent programs in business, communications, and psychology, along with abundant opportunities for study abroad and professional internships at Chicagoland companies such as *Rolling Stone*, the Chicago Blackhawks, and the Chicago Board of Trade. Academic improvements at Lake Forest are drawing attention; applications are up significantly and the school is attracting high-caliber students from around the nation. "Students are friendly, motivated, and actively involved in campus life," says a senior. What's more, the school is shedding its image as a haven for spoiled rich kids, says a senior, in favor of "increasingly challenging academics, more student engagement, and more responsible students."

With its mixture of century-old Gothic and modern glass structures, Lake Forest's 107-acre campus is storybook beautiful. Located on Chicago's North Shore, in a wealthy, quiet city of 25,000, the campus has three contiguous parts divided by natural wooded ravines: North, Middle, and South. Each has a mix of residence halls and academic buildings. The state-of-the-art Donnelley and Lee Library offers a 24-hour computer lab, wireless access to the campus network, and state-of-the-art "smart classrooms," along with space where students can work collaboratively on projects. The Mohr Student Center offers a central gathering place for students outside of the classroom and features large-screen televisions, lounges, game rooms, and a deli. A $17 million sports and recreation addition offers three multipurpose courts, a suspended recreational track, an aerobic and dance studio, lobby café, and 11,500 square feet of strength, cardio, and fitness spaces. A new, 230-bed residence hall opened in late 2013.

> **"The academic climate at Lake Forest is generally laid-back."**

General education requirements include the First-Year Studies Program, featuring "very small classes designed to help freshmen integrate into the college," says an English major. "These courses are writing intensive and offer a variety of opportunities, including trips to Chicago for plays and museum visits." Students also complete two credits in each of three liberal arts areas (humanities, social sciences and natural sciences, and math), two cultural-diversity courses, and a senior-studies capstone course. Those seeking academic autonomy benefit from the Independent Scholar program, which allows undergrads to create their own majors outside the boundaries of traditional disciplines. Each year, about 35 students become Richter Apprentice Scholars. They participate in an interdisciplinary seminar and a 10-week paid research assistantship during the summer before their sophomore year. As upperclassmen, Richter scholars live and work together and take part in a weekly student/faculty colloquium designed to help them learn about—and pursue—careers in academics and primary research.

"Professors come trained from extremely prestigious schools and are wonderful teachers."

"The academic climate at Lake Forest is generally laid-back," says one neuroscience major. "Students are eager to help each other and work together so everyone can succeed." Students say Lake Forest's best and most popular departments include communications, business, English, economics, and psychology. In addition, "all natural and social sciences are great," according to one senior. Students who don't like what's offered at Lake Forest can create their own classes, provided they find professors to teach them. Accelerated and dual degree programs—including three-year degree programs in philosophy and communications and dual degree programs in law—are available, as is an accelerated degree in international relations. Newer majors in neuroscience and finance have been introduced, as have minors in digital media design, cinema studies, social justice, neuroscience, finance, and medieval Renaissance studies.

Indeed, while Foresters like the school's small class sizes, flexible academic guidelines, and large doses of individual attention, nothing seems to compare to the quality of the faculty. "The quality of teaching here is fantastic," a student raves. "Professors come trained from extremely prestigious schools and are wonderful teachers." The Career Advancement Center is run by the same person who oversees admissions, meaning that the person who brings you to Lake Forest is also looking out for you as you graduate and move into the workforce.

"Students actively participate to bring about change and make a difference."

The center offers symposia, workshops, and résumé clinics, and students benefit from the college's proximity to downtown Chicago, just an hour away by train. Many pursue term-time internships in the city's business district, known as the Loop, or at nonprofits and other organizations in surrounding communities.

Study abroad is also integral to the Lake Forest experience and 35 percent of students travel abroad during their time at Lake Forest. "Students are encouraged to go abroad," a freshman explains. The college's program in Greece uses archeological sites and museums to study the ancient Aegean world, while the international program in Paris allows aspiring international executives to hone their language and financial skills. The programs in Beijing and Granada also allow students the opportunity to participate in internships while abroad. If those choices aren't sufficient, Lake Forest also belongs to the Associated Colleges of the Midwest*, which offers programs in Russia, Zimbabwe, Japan, India, and central Europe, among other locales.

Forty-nine percent of Lake Forest students hail from the Land of Lincoln, and most are serious about their studies and having fun. "There are a lot of intelligent, bright students who attend, and many of them put their knowledge to good use in extracurriculars as well," says one student. Another adds, "The most successful students are self-starters and over-involved in the campus community. These students

(continued)

Email Address: admissions@ lakeforest.edu

Strongest Programs:
Communication
Economics
Politics
Business
Psychology
Latin American Studies

Students who don't like what's offered at Lake Forest can create their own classes, provided they find professors to teach them.

are a part of at least three organizations, hold at least one leadership title, and are responsible with their coursework." African Americans make up 6 percent of the student body, and Hispanics and Asian Americans combine for another 18 percent. Political issues include diversity, campus alcohol policies, and homosexuality. "Students actively participate to bring about change and make a difference," a physics major says. Competitive financial aid packages are helping to bring more students of color and those from less-advantaged backgrounds to LFC. LFC awards numerous merit scholarships but does not offer athletic scholarships.

Competitive financial aid packages are helping to bring more students of color and those from less-advantaged backgrounds to LFC.

Seventy-two percent of students live in the dorms, which vary in age and appearance. An English major says, "Different halls attract different people. I preferred living in the older buildings because they felt homier than the new buildings, which felt more like a hotel." Nollen and Deerpath have been renovated and given central air-conditioning; the latter "has themed suites for five or six people," says a senior. Freshmen are assigned rooms by the Dean of Students, while upperclassmen participate in a lottery based on seniority. Overall, students say the residence halls are well

"Most social life takes place on campus." maintained, if not a bit institutional. Everybody eats in the central dining hall, where food is prepared to order at pizza, pasta, stir-fry, and other stations, and helpings are unlimited. "Along with the cafeteria, there are also several cafés on campus, including Java City, which is in the Donnelley and Lee Library," a senior reports. "The cafés are often open longer than the cafeteria, which allows students to have a late-night snack while finishing a paper or studying for an exam."

LFC offers an active social life, with one fraternity and five sororities. They attract 7 percent of the men and 11 percent of the women, respectively, and their parties are open to all. "Most social life takes place on campus. There are always events being put on by different organizations on campus and the events tend to be well attended," a senior reports. The Campus Entertainment Committee books movies, comedians, and big-name bands, while the Garrick Players also put on several productions per year. A crackdown on underage drinking and alcohol abuse is shifting the focus of LFC social life away from booze-soaked bashes. Everyone enjoys the tradition of homecoming, as well as the semiformal Winter Ball, the annual Day of Service, the Spring Concert, and the Drag Show lip-synch contest planned by PRIDE.

Varsity athletics are a modest draw at Lake Forest; students are more likely to cheer for the ultimate Frisbee team than their Foresters.

The town of Lake Forest is "cute but not really a college town," says a student. Another adds, "The town is actually in a forest, so the whole place is beautiful, and it feels like you live tucked away in a safe haven." There's a commuter train station five minutes away and the Lake Michigan beach is just as close. LFC also offers a weekend shuttle service to local malls and movie theaters, though a car is helpful. Seven student organizations are devoted to community service, and Greek organizations sponsor blood drives, bake sales, and car washes. One program sends students to the Appalachian Mountains in Virginia and Tennessee every spring break to help local townspeople repair substandard housing.

Varsity athletics are a modest draw at Lake Forest; students are more likely to cheer for the ultimate Frisbee team than their Foresters. Still, in recent years more than a dozen varsity sports teams qualified for their respective national or conference postseason championship. Football, men's soccer, and women's soccer each won a Midwest Conference championship in 2012–13. Club and intramural sports programs attract a good number of students; lacrosse and indoor soccer are especially popular.

Although Lake Forest still has its fair share of "preppy" types, students are quick to emphasize that the college is taking steps to increase diversity, curb the excessive partying, and encourage school pride. "The administration is more attuned to student issues," says an English major. "Lake Forest takes very good care of its students by providing challenging academics, comfortable living, lots of entertainment, and a small-town feel with access to a big city," concludes a senior. "What more could anyone want?"

Overlaps

DePaul, Macalester, DePauw, University of Illinois, Marquette, Knox, Hobart & William Smith, Carleton

<table>
<tr><td>

If You Apply To ➤

</td><td>

Lake Forest: Early decision and early action: Nov. 15. Regular admissions: Feb. 15. Financial aid: Mar. 1. Housing: May 1. No application fee. Campus interviews: optional, informational. No alumni interviews. SATs or ACTs: optional (ACTs preferred). Subject Tests: optional. Accepts the Common Application. Essay question: Personal statement. Applicants must also submit a graded paper.

</td></tr>
</table>

Lawrence University

711 East Boldt Way, Appleton, WI 54911

One of three small colleges in the nation that combines the liberal arts with a first-rate music conservatory (Bard and Oberlin are the others). Lawrence is half the size of Oberlin and comparable to Beloit and Grinnell, though Lawrence's personality is more mainstream than any of the three. Occupies a scenic bluff in northeastern Wisconsin. Remote location limits national appeal.

Lawrence University is an unpretentious school that can appeal to both the left and right side of students' brains. For those with an analytical bent, there is Lawrence's uncommon physics program. More creative types can take advantage of the school's renowned Conservatory of Music. "I came to Lawrence because I found no other school where I could seriously study music and academics," says a senior. "At all the other schools, you had to pick one or the other." It's this eclectic approach to learning that attracts interested and interesting students from around the world. "I think what makes Lawrence students stand out is that they are involved with such a wide range of activities," says a physics major. "When someone explains all the things they are doing on campus, it sort of blows your mind."

Lawrence's campus is on a wooded bluff above the Fox River, perfect for long walks, jogging, or simply meditating underneath the trees. It was chosen in 1847 by one of Appleton's earliest settlers. The pristine 84-acre campus reflects several architectural styles of the past 150 years, including classical revival, 1920s Georgian-inspired, and 1950s and 1960s institutional, unified by their limestone color. The award-winning Wriston Art Center and the Conservatory's Ruth Harwood Shattuck Hall of Music (both designed by Lawrence graduates) bring contemporary architectural touches to the campus. A campus center provides more than 100,000 square feet of space for food services, student organizations, a campus store, and a movie theater.

> **"Music is the unifying theme at Lawrence."**

The second coeducational college established in the nation, Lawrence was founded to educate German immigrants and Native Americans. While coeducation was shocking, innovators at Lawrence didn't stop there. More than 50 years ago, administrators introduced the Freshman Studies program, a required two-term course focusing primarily on the great works of art, music, and literature of both Western and non-Western origin. These days, general education requirements at Lawrence include freshman studies; distribution requirements; and diversity, foreign language, and writing-intensive courses. There is also a senior capstone experience.

At the school's Conservatory of Music, the instrument collection includes an 1815 Broadwood piano identical to Beethoven's Broadwood, and a Guarneri violin. There are first-rate jazz ensembles along with classical and world music programs; the college offers a bachelor's degree in music within its liberal arts environment. "Music is the unifying theme at Lawrence," says one student. "Almost everybody plays it or studies it or likes to listen to it and talk about it." The most popular major

Website: www.lawrence.edu
Location: Small City
Private
Total Enrollment: 1,435
Undergraduates: 1,435
Male/Female: 47/53
SAT Ranges: CR 580–720, M 580–710
ACT Ranges: 25–31
Financial Aid: 97%
Expense: Pr $ $
Student Loans: 65%
Average Debt: $ $ $ $
Phi Beta Kappa: Yes
Applicants: 2,599
Accepted: 76%
Enrolled: 21%
Grad in 6 Years: 73%
Returning Freshmen: 91%
Academics: ✐ ✐ ✐ ✐
Social: ☎ ☎ ☎
Q of L: ★ ★ ★
Admissions: (920) 832-6500
Email Address: excel@lawrence.edu

Strongest Programs:
Music
History
Biology
Physics
Psychology
English

is music, followed by biology, government, English, and psychology. Students are encouraged to spend at least one term of their college career off campus and 38 percent of undergrads do so during their time at Lawrence. The university is known for its London Study Center, which allows students to take classes "across the pond" while taking advantage of the city's many cultural activities. Other off-campus programs involve the Kurgan Technical Pedagogical Institute in Russia, Waseda University in Japan, and the École des Beaux-Arts in France. Programs in marine biology research are held in the Cayman Islands. In all, 45 off-campus programs are available in more than two dozen countries.

Back on campus, Lawrence students appreciate their professors' expertise and experience. "The quality of teaching is superb. I could not imagine myself in a more stimulating academic environment," says one student. Because of the three-term calendar, the academic climate is intimate and intense. "The difficulty of courses and the academic rigor are mitigated by the constant help and support of friendly professors, accessible student tutors, and the general Lawrence community," a sophomore says. Languages offered include Chinese, Japanese, and Arabic. All seniors—in all degree programs—are required to produce a final project demonstrating proficiency in their major field of study.

Most of Lawrence's students hail from Wisconsin or elsewhere in the Midwest. Most attended public high school, and 71 percent graduated in the top quarter of their class. "Students at Lawrence are quirky, down to earth, and humble," says one history major. A biochemistry major adds, "LU students are involved in everything, sometimes to the point where we don't know how all of our activities could possibly fit in one day, but we love what we do and we're passionate about the groups we join and establish." African Americans and Asian Americans each make up 3 percent of the student body, and Hispanics comprise another 4 percent. There is a sizable international population representing more than 40 countries. The political climate on campus is somewhat liberal—there's a leftist newspaper—and students are "knowledgeable about current social and political issues," according to one student. There are no athletic scholarships, but brainy types vie for merit scholarships averaging $15,250 each.

The dorms at Lawrence are well populated; all but 2 percent of students live on campus. "Ninety-eight percent of students live on campus in seven residence halls and several theme or formal houses that provide options ranging from single rooms, to suite-style quads with private bathrooms. These are very warm, comfortable, and well maintained," reports one sophomore. Greek life attracts 18 percent of Lawrence men and 9 percent of the women. All halls are co-ed, by room or by floor, and all have laundry facilities, kitchens, televisions, Internet links, and lounges. Students praise the variety of housing choices. They report the older halls are more elegant, but the newer ones are more practical, with extra storage space and other amenities. On-campus students have a choice of meal plans and report that the food is edible and diverse. Students report feeling safe on campus, thanks in part to the surrounding area. "Campus security is fantastic," says a junior, and "if you ever feel unsafe campus security is happy to escort you so you don't go anywhere alone."

Social life at Lawrence is as varied and eclectic as the students. "The social life is mostly contained on campus, as there is always a music recital or a theater production or movie showing or party going on," a psychology major says, "sometimes all at once!" Alcohol policies aren't enforced, according to many students. Although it's almost impossible for underage students to be served at the on-campus bar, the story is different at private parties and dorm rooms. The school radio station also broadcasts a 50-hour trivia contest in January, in which each hall has its own team, and students stay up for the entire weekend answering offbeat questions. Octoberfest

There are first-rate jazz ensembles along with classical and world music programs.

"I could not imagine myself in a more stimulating academic environment."

In all, 45 off-campus programs are available in more than two dozen countries.

is also a big weekend event, held in conjunction with the city of Appleton, which draws people in from nearby cities. A Shack-A-Thon has become a popular way to raise money for Habitat for Humanity.

There are good relations between Lawrence and Appleton. "The town is safe and has lots to do," says a student, including "cafés, restaurants, shops, nightlife, performing arts, and farmers markets." The nearest grocery store is a five-minute drive away, as is the nearest theater, and many students see a car as a necessity. Volunteerism is popular, and students regularly take part in activities such as tutoring at local schools. The best road trips are to Milwaukee (two hours), Green Bay (half an hour), and Chicago (four hours). There are also weekend seminars at Bjorklunden, the college's 425-acre estate on the shores of Lake Michigan.

And what would a Midwest fall Saturday be without football? The Lawrence Vikings draw good crowds almost every weekend. Women's soccer claimed the 2011 Midwest Conference North Division championship; men's cross-country brought home a **"Campus security is fantastic."** title in 2012. Men's hockey has competed in the conference semifinals for five of the past seven seasons. The sparkling recreation center helps students fend off midwinter blues. Participating in a rousing game of intramural broomball, which is ice hockey played on shoes with brooms as sticks and kickballs as pucks, is a must for students, even if all you do is watch. Ultimate Frisbee is a popular club sport. "There are lots of fun intramural and club sports open to everyone," says a sophomore, "though not everyone participates."

With its outstanding liberal arts curriculum, knowledgeable and caring faculty, an administration that treats students like adults, and a charming country setting, Lawrence University is easily one of the best little-known schools in the country. "The people are just so nice and warm and welcoming here," raves a sophomore. And for students with a musical ear, Lawrence's symphony of offerings strikes just the right chord.

Octoberfest is also a big weekend event, held in conjunction with the city of Appleton, which draws people in from nearby cities.

Overlaps

Oberlin, St. Olaf, Beloit, University of Wisconsin, Carleton, Macalester, Northwestern, Knox

If You Apply To ➤ **Lawrence:** Early decision: Nov. 1. Early action: Nov. 15. Regular admissions: Jan. 15. Application fee: $40. Campus interviews: optional, informational. No alumni interviews. SATs or ACTs: optional. Subject Tests: optional. Music applicants must audition. Accepts the Common Application. Essay question: Common Application.

Lehigh University

27 Memorial Drive West, Bethlehem, PA 18015

Built on the powerful combination of business and engineering, Lehigh occupies a middle ground between techie havens such as Drexel and Rensselaer and the liberal arts/engineering institutions such as Bucknell and Union. By graduation, students are primed for the global job market. Hillside campus means that students get plenty of exercise. A wrestling powerhouse.

From the College of Arts and Sciences to the College of Business and Economics, Lehigh University combines the academic resources of a large research university with the collegial atmosphere of a much smaller institution. "It is so easy to make a difference during your four years here at Lehigh," says one happy student. "Your professors want to help you every step of the way and the Lehigh community is always supporting you."

Website: www.lehigh.edu
Location: Small City
Private
Total Enrollment: 5,991
Undergraduates: 4,804

Lehigh also offers more than 200 study abroad options in 60 countries.

Grand old oaks shade the buildings on Lehigh's 1,600-acre campus, which is tucked into the side of an eastern Pennsylvania mountain. Architectural styles range from ivy-covered collegiate Gothic to modern glass and steel. In an apt symbol of Lehigh's efforts to link tradition with what it takes to be part of a global workforce, the 1878 collegiate Gothic Linderman Library in the center of campus has been completely gutted and rebuilt with attention to computer access, group study areas, and a café. The Murray H. Goodman Campus provides first-class practice and playing facilities for Lehigh's sports teams, including a 16,000-seat stadium, a 5,600-seat basketball arena and two turf fields, and facilities for many of the school's 25 Division I varsity sports teams.

Because much of Lehigh's reputation rests on its consistently strong engineering program, the school has invested millions of dollars to enhance critical academic programs such as optical technologies, nanotechnology, bioscience, biotechnology, and optoelectronics. Distribution requirements are divided into four domains—the mathematical sciences, the natural sciences, the social sciences, and the arts and humanities. Additionally, some degrees include a mandatory internship. Special degree options include a B.A./M.D. seven-year program with Drexel University College of Medicine, a B.A./D.M.D. seven-year dental program with the University of Pennsylvania, a B.A./O.D. seven-year program with SUNY State College of Optometry, and a five-year arts and engineering program, leading to B.A. and B.S. degrees. Co-ops allow students to spend eight months working for a major-related company—and getting paid to do so—while still graduating in four years.

> **"Your professors want to help you every step of the way."**

Lehigh is big on connecting traditionally separate disciplines and prides itself on offering innovative, special programs such as Integrated Business and Engineering (IBE), Integrated Product Development (IPD), bioengineering, computer science and business, environmental engineering, environmental studies, design arts, applied life science, and minors in business, ethics, engineering leadership, and engineering. IPD brings engineering, business, and arts students together to design and make products for sponsoring companies. The IDEAS (Integrated Degree in Engineering, Arts, and Sciences) program is a four-year honors curriculum that allows students to blend two focus areas—engineering and the arts, humanities, or natural sciences—into a single course of study.

Lehigh also offers more than 200 study abroad options in 60 countries, with exchange programs in nine countries and winter and summer faculty-led programs in 13 countries. In recent years, Lehigh summer programs have been conducted in Belgium, England, France, the Czech Republic, Italy, and China. Recent winter-term programs have been offered in England, Italy, Costa Rica, Spain, and Ghana. Thirty-five percent of students take part in study abroad at some point during their time at Lehigh.

The workload at Lehigh is heavy; students are ambitious, and many pursue double majors. "All of our classes are manageable as long as you are willing to work hard and be an active student in class," says a junior. The burden is lightened somewhat by exceptional teachers. "The professors become invested in the students and want to see us succeed," a student says. "They are a great resource for any information you need or if you need to meet with them during office hours for extra help." Forty-eight percent of courses contain 19 or fewer students and courses aren't hard to get into. Through the President's Scholars program, top Lehigh students who meet certain requirements and graduate with a 3.75 GPA or better are eligible for a fifth year of study tuition-free.

> **"You have the studious, the nerdy, the privileged, and the jocks."**

"Lehigh students vary," says a student. "You have the studious, the nerdy, the privileged, and the jocks. But I feel that the groups intermingle pretty well."

Twenty-four percent of Lehigh's students come from Pennsylvania, and many others hail from other Northeastern states; African Americans account for 4 percent, Hispanics 8 percent, and Asian Americans 6 percent. In addition, special interest housing such as the UMOJA House (the Swahili word for "unity"), established to encourage a sense of unity and pride among students of diverse backgrounds, exists to promote positive cultural exchanges. "The biggest social issue is the divide between the campus community," laments one junior. "It is very separated into Greeks, non-Greeks, first-years, and athletes." Merit scholarships averaging $10,259 are awarded annually and student-athletes vie for 60 athletic scholarships in 23 sports.

Sixty-nine percent of Lehigh students live on campus; first- and second-year students are required to do so. "The dorms are kept very well and they keep remodeling the buildings to keep them up to date," says one student. Many upperclassmen choose to live in apartment-style dorms, Greek houses, and off-campus apartments. Other options include Campus Square, a residential and commercial complex that houses 250 upper-class students. Lehigh's dining service has been honored with the Ivy Award, given by the restaurant industry to first-class restaurants as well as to educational institutions. "The dining on campus is great! I am an extremely picky eater and can always find something delicious to eat," cheers one student. Students' biggest complaint is the plethora of stairs around campus and the walk uphill to the dorms, which makes gaining the "Freshman 15" near impossible. "The inventor of escalators graduated from Lehigh yet we have no escalators," a junior says. "Ironic."

An active Greek scene (38 percent of the men join fraternities and 44 percent of the women belong to sororities) fuels the campus social life. "Lehigh students pride ourselves on knowing how to have a great time," says a cognitive psychology major. "The proliferation of campus clubs and organizations makes for a very vibrant evening and nightlife, and a plethora of daytime activities all week long. Greek organizations are responsible for some parties, but are not the only way to experience an excellent social life." No one under 21 is allowed to drink alcohol, and "Lehigh takes underage drinking very seriously," a junior says, although underage students still find ways to skirt the rules. Historic Bethlehem is five minutes from campus, and students volunteered more than 75,000 hours last year both locally and nationally with a variety of charities, including the Boys and Girls Club of America and America Reads. In addition, about 85 percent of students participate in intramural sports and club programs at Lehigh.

> **"It is very separated into Greeks, non-Greeks, first-years, and athletes."**

The bustling campus has helped revive Bethlehem, a once-great steel town in the heart of the Lehigh Valley, where some 27,000 students are enrolled in academic institutions. "Bethlehem is an up-and-coming community," a senior explains. In early August the city hosts Musikfest, a 10-day music festival that attracts more than one million people and showcases nearly every musical style with hundreds of acts from throughout the country, international foods, arts and crafts, and free concerts. Shortly thereafter in September, Celtic Classic is underway, featuring the best of the Emerald Isle against a backdrop of autumn foliage. For those with wheels, Philadelphia is 50 miles to the south and New York City is 75 miles to the east. Skiers will appreciate the close proximity of the Poconos in the winter, while sun worshippers can enjoy the nearby Jersey shore in the early fall and late spring.

The Lehigh Mountain Hawks field a number of competitive teams. Lehigh's wrestling program is a powerhouse, having brought home numerous EIWA Championships. Other solid programs include men's cross-country, men's lacrosse, men's and women's golf, men's tennis, and women's softball. Fans flock to the annual Lehigh versus Lafayette football game, the most played rivalry in college football. Even weekend warriors will find something to cheer about in the Welch

> *An active Greek scene (38 percent of the men join fraternities and 44 percent of the women belong to sororities) fuels the campus social life.*

Overlaps

Villanova, Penn State, Boston College, Rensselaer Polytechnic, University of Virginia, University of Maryland, Rutgers, University of Delaware

Fitness Center's weight room in Taylor Gym—two pools, a climbing wall, free weights, cardio equipment, racquetball and squash courts, and more.

Lehigh students proudly juggle rigorous classes and a packed extracurricular calendar. "The type of student who will do best at Lehigh is the one who prefers to be too involved rather than sit back and observe," advises one senior. They give college life more than the old college try—and expect to succeed. Says one student, "Not only will students gain an excellent education, but they will also study something they're passionate about. I've had the best time of my life at Lehigh."

Lewis & Clark College

Portland, OR 97219

The West Coast's leader in international and study abroad programs. Politically liberal, but not as far out as crosstown neighbor Reed. Portfolio Path to admission allows students to finesse standardized tests. With Mount Hood visible in the distance (sometimes), there is a wealth of outdoor possibilities. Located in suburban Portland, at arm's length from the bustle of downtown.

Website: www.lclark.edu
Location: City Outskirts
Private
Total Enrollment: 3,175
Undergraduates: 2,021
Male/Female: 40/60
SAT Ranges: CR 600–700, M 590–670
ACT Ranges: 26–31
Financial Aid: 86%
Expense: Pr $ $
Student Loans: 50%
Average Debt: $ $
Phi Beta Kappa: Yes
Applicants: 6,488
Accepted: 64%
Enrolled: 13%
Grad in 6 Years: 76%
Returning Freshmen: 89%
Academics: ✐ ✐ ✐
Social: ☎ ☎ ☎
Q of L: ★ ★ ★
Admissions: (503) 768-7040
Email Address: admissions@lclark.edu

The 19th-century explorers Lewis and Clark struck out from Middle America to find where the trail ended, and their travels took them to Portland, a lush, green paradise by the Willamette River. The college that bears the explorers' names encourages students to explore, too. Since 1962, more than 9,000 students and 200 faculty members have traveled to 66 different countries as part of one of the oldest off-campus student programs in the United States. Lewis & Clark "is an excellent, hands-on education in a beautiful national forest," boasts one junior.

Lest students become too enchanted overseas, Lewis & Clark lures them back with a gorgeous campus perched atop fir-covered bluffs overlooking the river. The campus is an old estate, complete with elaborate gardens, fountains, and pools, where cement is almost nonexistent and the roads are paved with cobblestones. Lewis & Clark demonstrated its commitment to the environment by signing the Talloires Declaration, an agreement with other colleges to promote sustainable development. Along those lines, the 50,000-square-foot John R. Howard Hall was built with the environment in mind, and received a gold certification from the U.S. Green Building Council. Howard Hall is one of four other energy-saving, environmentally friendly buildings, including three residence halls and Wood Hall. The newest residence hall opened in 2012 and accommodates nearly 170 students. The "green" building is built according to sustainable practices and features a bicycle storage room, outdoor fireplace and patio, and energy reduction technology.

Lewis & Clark requires that all students achieve competency in a foreign language and international studies; half of the students fulfill these requirements by studying overseas for a semester or more. Students may travel to countries including Australia, China, Colombia, Ecuador, Japan, Kenya, Germany, France, and

> **"Most of the classes are small and discussion-based."**

Scotland, and may also study in a number of American cities—some study in two or three countries. In addition to the international studies requirement, students must complete courses in scientific and quantitative reasoning, creative arts, and physical education.

Not surprisingly, one of the most popular majors at Lewis & Clark is international affairs; others include psychology, art, and biology. Minors in computer science, dance, and classical studies that cover the culture and history of ancient Greece and Rome are offered, and honors programs are available in all majors; 3–2 programs in engineering are also offered. The John S. Rogers Science Research Program teams students and faculty on research projects ranging from the adhesive power of geckos to molecular science. Additional majors include studio art and computer science; there are also minors in environmental studies and ethnic studies.

> **"Students here are socially conscious, motivated, and involved."**

(continued)

Strongest Programs:
Psychology
International Affairs
Foreign Languages
Biology and Environmental
   Sciences
Sociology
Anthropology

Lewis & Clark offers a Portfolio Path to admission, where students present a package representing their talents and interests in lieu of standardized test scores. In addition to the essays and other items required of students who send in test scores, PP students supply two teacher recommendations and two graded samples of high school work: one quantitative sample and one analytical writing sample. Some students who use this approach feel standardized tests don't do them justice, while others have "incredible test scores." The key to a good portfolio is a "well-rounded approach," administrators say. "The more creative, the better, but be sure it's not solely artwork or writing samples."

Given this open attitude, it's not surprising that L&C students are given flexible deadlines yet are expected to follow through with a challenging workload. "Classes are hard but not impossible," says a freshman. Freshmen and graduating seniors get priority in the registration process, helping ensure graduation in four years for those who declare majors early and plan a way to fit in all of the requirements. Professors get high marks for being knowledgeable and passionate. "The quality of teaching is excellent," says a sophomore. "Most of the classes are small and discussion-based so there is a lot of time for personal questions."

Lewis & Clark requires that all students achieve competency in a foreign language and international studies.

"Students here are socially conscious, motivated, and involved," says an international affairs major. Lewis & Clark tends to attract West Coasters (almost half of the student body) who are seeking an emphasis on the liberal arts; it is also a haven for well-off Easterners who see L&C as a refreshing contrast to the typical prep school or fancy suburban high school scene. "Everyone from emerging activists to sports players to nature lovers to musicians converge on campus," says a biology major, "which makes for an interesting and broad mix." The campus is politically active and predominantly left-leaning. The student body is 4 percent Asian American, 2 percent African American, and 7 percent Hispanic. Students pour their energies into community service and political activism via numerous campus organizations and activities. Merit scholarships are available for qualified students, but student-athletes must go elsewhere for funding.

> **"Students here look outside their lives and experiences in order to find something greater."**

Lewis & Clark's residency requirement keeps students on campus their first two years; 62 percent of all undergraduates live on campus. Owing to the college's hilltop location, lucky dorm residents have views of Mount St. Helens, Mount Hood, or the Portland skyline—at least when it's not raining. Students involved in performing arts, foreign languages, outdoor pursuits, and other programs can live in theme wings. Dorms are unique and convenient. "The most common room is a double, but there are also quads and singles, all which have sufficient room for their respective residents," reports a student. Despite L&C's location in a residential section of Portland, safety is a priority—residence halls have card-swipe entry systems and door alarms, and campus security has officers on duty 24 hours. Dining halls cater to the different diets and "we have a great selection," says a student.

Fun seekers at Lewis & Clark rely primarily on SOFA (Students Organized for Activities) for on-campus movies, contests, dances, and talent shows. Yearly events include Casino Night in February, the Watzek Rocks Concert in the spring, and the homecoming dance in the fall. On the weekends, College Outdoors sponsors trips to Mount Hood (great skiing, about an hour distant) or the coastal beaches (an hour and a half). Seattle and Vancouver, BC, three- and six-hour drives, are favorite road trips, as are San Francisco and Las Vegas when there's more time. Despite the famous rains of the Pacific Northwest, the campus is officially dry. Per Oregon law, no one under 21 may drink alcohol. "You can get in trouble if you get caught," says a sophomore, "but the repercussions aren't that severe." The neighborhood immediately surrounding the college is pleasant, affluent suburbia, which means a few stores, restaurants, or bars. The activity of downtown Portland—mostly on Hawthorne Boulevard in the southeast section, and in the Pearl District or on 23rd Street in the northwest quadrant—is 15 minutes away on the city's public transit system or the free campus shuttle service, the Pioneer Express.

Pioneer teams compete in the NCAA Division III Northwest Conference and the most competitive teams include women's cross-country and women's basketball (both 2013 conference champs). As might be expected at a school in the outdoorsy Northwest, Lewis & Clark has a well-organized intramural program and plenty of outdoor activities. Men's basketball, women's crew, and volleyball are popular.

Students at Lewis & Clark College enjoy a rather laid-back atmosphere. Many are outdoor enthusiasts who are also unafraid to champion social causes. Like the school's namesakes, students are knowledge-seeking pioneers—ones who would have made Lewis and Clark, the explorers, proud. "Students here look outside their lives and experiences in order to find something greater," says a senior. "We constantly question, and search for the answers."

Lewis & Clark's residency requirement keeps students on campus their first two years.

Overlaps

Willamette, University of Puget Sound, UC–Berkeley, Pitzer, Whitman, University of Oregon, UC–Santa Cruz, Occidental

If You Apply To ➤ **Lewis & Clark:** Early action: Nov. 1. Regular admissions: Jan. 15. Financial aid: Feb. 15. Housing: May 1. Application fee: $50 (paper), free (online). Campus and alumni interviews: optional, informational. SATs or ACTs: required (except Portfolio Path). Subject Tests: optional. Accepts the Common Application. Essay question.

Louisiana State University

1146 Pleasant Hall, Baton Rouge, LA 70803

In the state that invented Mardi Gras, students come to LSU for a great time as well as a good education. Finding the former is a no-brainer. The latter can be had in business, engineering, and life science fields. Administrators are trying to make LSU a more serious place with higher admission standards and less underage drinking. More than a quarter of students live in the dorms, which have been upgraded.

Website: www.lsu.edu
Location: City Center
Public
Total Enrollment: 27,033

From abundant azaleas and Japanese magnolias, to the smell of Cajun cuisine, the sororities' antebellum mansions, and the "huge and legendary" rivalries with Alabama and Florida, few schools evoke the spirit of the South like Louisiana State University in Baton Rouge. The university continues to offer solid programs in business, engineering, and the life sciences, and admissions standards continue to rise.

"I feel that LSU's academic achievements have been underrated," says one senior. "There are so many ways to learn and grow, both in and out of the classroom."

LSU sits on 2,000 acres along the banks of the Mississippi River on the grounds of a former plantation. Most of the 250 buildings are Italian Renaissance in style, with tan stucco walls and red tile roofs. Lakes and huge oak trees dot the landscape, helping to diffuse the strong sun and temper Louisiana's legendary humidity. Recent campus projects include a new Business Education Complex, designed to accommodate undergraduate and graduate students.

LSU was once an open-admissions university for state residents but standards have gone up in recent years, and with them, the caliber of students. Before enrolling, freshmen must complete 19 high school core units in designated academic areas, including four units each of English, math, science, and social studies, two in a foreign language, and one in fine arts. For out-of-state applicants, grades and test scores are weighed equally. Once on campus, students must complete a broad core curriculum, with six hours of coursework in each of three disciplines (English composition, analytical reasoning, and social sciences), nine hours in the humanities, nine hours in the natural sciences, and three hours in the arts.

LSU students choose from 70 undergraduate degrees and tend to focus on practical courses of study, which will help them get into graduate school or find jobs after graduation. To that end, popular majors include biological sciences and psychology—both typical for premeds—as well as mechanical engineering, mass communication, and kinesiology.

"Some classes can have hundreds of students in an auditorium."

Students also give high marks to LSU's programs in math and engineering. Given its location and history as a sea grant college, LSU's offerings in coastal studies and coastal ecology are notable as well. Professors are lauded for their enthusiasm and skill behind the lectern. "Overall the professors here at LSU love their material and are dedicated to teaching," one student says. Classes can be large, to the chagrin of many students. "Some classes can have hundreds of students in an auditorium," says one student. "That changes the dynamic of the classroom experience." Students interested in working on projects at the interface between the biological and computational sciences are encouraged to apply to the Louisiana Biomedical Research Network Undergraduate Research Program, which hosts nine-week research opportunities. The Chancellors Future Leaders in Research program provides undergraduates the chance to work side by side with professors in a research setting, such as a laboratory or in the field, to learn what a career in a chosen field might be like.

Seventy-nine percent of LSU Tigers are Louisiana natives, but that's where the similarities end. "Many of the students here are partiers and social butterflies," says one sophomore. "They tend to hang out, go to clubs, bars, and restaurants on a regular basis." African Americans make up 11 percent of the student body, Asian Americans 3 percent, and Hispanics 5 percent. "The biggest political issue is concerning budget cuts in the state and how they affect higher education," says a student. Thousands of merit scholarships are available, averaging $8,900 each. LSU also hands out nearly 500 athletic scholarships each year in 18 sports. The Pelican Promise Scholarship provides additional financial aid to low-income students; to qualify, students must be Pell Grant eligible and come from a family whose income is no more than 150 percent of the federal poverty level.

Twenty-seven percent of the students live on campus. "The on-campus dorms are small and dated," grumbles one junior. Over the past decade, the university has invested more than $150 million in housing facilities and new programs, with more than 50 percent of undergraduate housing either newly constructed or renovated. Campus dining halls offer a variety of dishes, and students say most are tasty.

(continued)

Undergraduates: 22,567
Male/Female: 49/51
SAT Ranges: CR 500–620, M 520–630
ACT Ranges: 23–28
Financial Aid: 85%
Expense: Pub $
Student Loans: 39%
Average Debt: $
Phi Beta Kappa: Yes
Applicants: 16,169
Accepted: 76%
Enrolled: 47%
Grad in 6 Years: 67%
Returning Freshmen: 83%
Academics: ✐ ✐
Social: ☎ ☎ ☎ ☎ ☎
Q of L: ★ ★ ★
Admissions: (225) 578-1175
Email Address: admissions@lsu.edu

Strongest Programs:
Biological Sciences
Kinesiology
Mass Communication
Mechanical Engineering
Petroleum Engineering

Given its location and history as a sea grant college, LSU's offerings in coastal studies and coastal ecology are notable as well.

There are also a variety of eateries near campus that are "delicious and inexpensive," according to one student. Despite Baton Rouge's high crime rate, students report feeling safe on campus. LSU has nearly 100 full-time officers and a transit system so that students don't have to walk alone after dark.

Social life at LSU "is never ending," cheers a student. "Plenty of students enjoy off-campus fun with house parties and plenty of bars nearby in Tigerland," adds another. Fifteen percent of the men and 22 percent of the women go Greek, and while doing so "is always a good way to meet people, it can be expensive," says a finance major. When it comes to drinking, you must be 21, though all bets are off on game days. "Tailgating on game day is a big party for everyone," says a senior, and the rowdy LSU contingent at away games has earned a reputation worth of English soccer fans. Everyone looks forward to homecoming and to annual festivals such as Groovin' on the Grounds, "where big-name bands come play for the students, with lots of food and games—all free!" says a junior. Road trips to the Florida beaches are common during spring break.

Tiger football is king in Baton Rouge, having won national championships in 2003 and 2007 and a conference title in 2011. The men's and women's track teams also brought home titles in recent years. The Tiger baseball team is a dynasty, having brought home its most recent Southeastern Conference title in 2012. When the Tigers are on the road, many students follow the team (and the fun) to Oxford, Mississippi (home of Ole Miss), or Auburn, Alabama (home of the Auburn Tigers). Intramural soccer, football, and softball are popular, and even those who don't play may work out at the recreation center. It features a pool; courts for basketball, racquetball, and tennis; an indoor track; a cardio and free weights area; a circuit room; and a climbing gym.

"There is never a boring day at LSU," gushes one psychology major. The trees and traditions date back more than 100 years. Change is now the norm here, as the Chancellor's Flagship Agenda works to increase both enrollment and admission standards. "Just a few years ago, LSU was named the number-one party school," notes one student. "Today, it's not even listed in the top 10." Though it may be a while before the school's academic profile matches its athletic prowess, that's what administrators are aiming for. In the meantime, students are happy to *laissez les bons temps roulez!*

Tiger football is king in Baton Rouge, having won national championships in 2003 and 2007 and a conference title in 2011.

"There is never a boring day at LSU."

Overlaps

University of Alabama, Texas A&M, Louisiana Tech, University of Louisiana, Tulane, University of Mississippi, University of Texas, University of Georgia

If You Apply To ➤

LSU: Regular admissions: Apr. 15. Financial aid: Nov. 15. Application fee: $40. No campus or alumni interviews. SATs or ACTs: required. No Subject Tests. Essay question: only required for Honors College and scholarship candidates.

Loyola University Maryland

Baltimore, MD 21210

Vintage Jesuit school with a rigorous liberal arts curriculum, caring faculty, and a strong sense of community. Baltimore location a plus for those with "I don't want to miss anything" attitude. Same size as Providence, smaller than BC, Fordham, and other Catholic schools in urban settings. No varsity football, but top-ranked men's lacrosse team evokes plenty of school spirit.

Four U.S. universities bear the name of St. Francis Loyola, founder of the Jesuit order, but this one is the granddaddy of them all. Founded in 1851 (and the one that laid claim to www.loyola.edu), Loyola University Maryland combines the virtues of a residential campus with ready access to a major city on the Amtrak corridor. Loyola jumped up from "college" to "university" status in 2009, and, with a "big enough but not too big" feel, manages to strike a balance between real-world experience and the traditional Jesuit ideals of academic excellence, a liberal arts curriculum, and *cura personals* (a.k.a. education of the whole person).

Loyola's Evergreen campus, the home to undergraduates, sits on 80 green and wooded acres in a mixed residential area in northern Baltimore, about 15 minutes from the heart of the city. Graduate students are shunted off to their own campuses in Columbia and Timonium, MD. The academic Quad features the largest collection of Collegiate Gothic building in Baltimore, including the Alumni Memorial Chapel with its lovely stained-glass windows. Architectural variety is provided by the Tudor-style Humanities Center, built in 1895, and the Sellinger School of Business and Management, a contemporary 50,000-square-foot facility notable for its atrium and five-story glass façade. A $12 million expansion of the Donnelly Science Center was completed in 2011.

Students describe the academic program at Loyola as challenging but supportive. "Students are generally not competing against each other for the best grades, but rather tend to work together on projects or while studying," says a senior. Teaching assistants are an unknown species, and an English major reports, "Classes are never bigger than 30. Most of mine have ranged from 15 to 30 students." Students praise their professors' emphasis on teaching and getting to know students. "I cannot imagine what it would be like not to have a professor know my name," comments a senior. A political science major reports that "professors tend to shy away from boring lectures in favor of engaging discussions."

Undergraduate academics at Loyola are organized around the School of Education, the Sellinger School of Business and Management, and Loyola College, the arts and sciences college. Consistent with Jesuit academic tradition, Loyola students pursue a core curriculum that covers "basic knowledge and concepts in the humanities, math, science, and the social sciences" and "encourages students to think and to solve problems in a variety of ways and to critically examine a cross-section of ideas." Among the requirements are two theology courses, an ethics course, and the choice of a course designated "diversity"—with a focus on global or domestic diversity or justice awareness. The business program is said to be strong, as are most of the humanities, where "professors find ways to make the humanities relevant to real life," says a psych major. But a biology major warns, "Some students avoid humanities courses because, while those classes are very interesting, they require a lot of reading and writing, and not everyone is into that." Other strong areas, students say, include education, speech pathology, biology, and engineering. Fine arts "does not attract very many people," reports a global studies major. The School of Education, which is growing in popularity, offers students four years of field experience as well as a capstone course that melds theory with effective practice, while the Hauber Research Program pairs undergraduates with professors to conduct original research over the summer.

First-year students jump-start their college careers with various pre-orientation programs in which they meet a small group of fellow students and focus on some special interest. Loyola 101 is a one-credit course in the fall semester that brings in guest speakers and introduces students to the resources available throughout Baltimore. The Messina is a new first-year living/learning program—soon to be extended to all

"As a Christian, I love the fact that I can openly talk about my religion and that others accept my beliefs."

Website: www.loyola.edu
Location: City Outskirts
Private
Total Enrollment: 4,530
Undergraduates: 3,871
Male/Female: 39/61
SAT Ranges: CR 540–630, M 545–630
ACT Ranges: 24–29
Financial Aid: 66%
Expense: Pr $ $ $
Student Loans: 63%
Average Debt: $ $ $ $
Phi Beta Kappa: Yes
Applicants: 12,664
Accepted: 65%
Enrolled: 13%
Grad in 6 Years: 84%
Returning Freshmen: 88%
Academics: ✏ ✏ ✏
Social: ☎ ☎ ☎
Q of L: ★ ★ ★
Admissions: (410) 617-5012
Email Address: admissions@loyola.edu

Strongest Programs:
Business
Communication
Biology
Psychology
Speech Language/Pathology
Information Systems
Theology

freshmen—in which students enroll in a small seminar class guided by a professor and an older student who also lives with the same students. "It makes new students feel like they are a part of the Loyola community and realize how many people care about them here," says a biology major. For top students, the new Honors Program provides an interdisciplinary route through a more ambitious core curriculum.

Foreign study plays a "huge part" in Loyola academics, reports a communications major, adding that nearly 60 percent of juniors study abroad for a semester or more. The university offers at least 50 study abroad options, including some that focus on specific academic areas. Venues for business students range from Bangkok and Singapore to Melbourne and Accra, while language students set out for Spain, France, China, and elsewhere in search of native speakers. Loyola students are encouraged to do community service while abroad and to submit an Immersion Research Project upon return. "I studied in Cork, Ireland, and it was one of the highlights of my college experience!" cheers a senior.

Students at Loyola tend to be, in the words of one senior, "fairly preppy." With the exception of a contingent from California, most hail from the East Coast, particularly New York, New Jersey, and Maryland. A slight majority (54 percent) graduated from public high schools, and minorities make up 16 percent of the students body, half of whom are Hispanic. A quarter of freshmen graduated in the top 10 percent of their classes, 59 percent in the top half. At least 75 percent of undergrads describe themselves as Catholics, and there are seven Jesuits on the faculty. "Religion has a huge impact on campus," says one non-Catholic, who adds, "As a Christian, I love the fact that I can openly talk about my religion and that others accept my beliefs." Many students attend mass and take part in retreats. Two-thirds of undergraduates receive some financial aid, with an average merit award of $13,700. Loyola offers 185 athletic scholarships in 16 men's and women's sports. Sixty-three percent of students borrow to finance their education, with cumulative debt averaging $32,000. Fifteen percent of students are eligible for Pell Grants.

> "Most of Loyola's social life takes place off campus."

Loyola students (and admissions officers) gush about the Loyola's 16 residential halls, which are located west of the main campus and connected by a pedestrian bridge spanning Charles Street. Facilities are spacious and modern, with air-conditioning, laundry facilities, vending machines, and recreation areas. "We have some of the best dorms in the country," says a senior. A classmate adds, "We are spoiled here." A senior English major's experience is typical. "My first year included dorm-style living, sophomore and junior years [were] apartment living with six people, and my senior year included an on-campus townhouse," she says. Not surprisingly, most students live on campus, at least until their senior year. Campus security is not an issue. "We are in a relatively dangerous part of the city," says an accounting major, "but the Loyola police do a good job to make us all feel safe on campus." A blue-light system is readily available, as is an on-call escort service. On-campus dining has been a source of complaints in recent years, but a senior reports, "We have a new dining service this year, and the quality of food is now much better, with vegetarian, gluten-free, and other options." The main dining facility is Boulder Garden Café, but other options range from the Reading Room to Starbucks. Loyola recently replaced its a la carte menu with a "meal swipe" or "declining balance" dining plan, but not everyone approves. "I did not enjoy adding $1,000 to my tuition bill for my final year," grouses a senior.

The business program is said to be strong, as are most of the humanities.

Like most Jesuit schools, Loyola has no fraternities and sororities, but given the proximity to Baltimore, this arrangement is just fine with students. "Most of Loyola's social life takes place off campus," says a communications major. "Bars and clubs are very close to campus, and the penalties for throwing a party in your room are pretty steep." That's not to say that on-campus life is monastic. "The campus is always buzzing with things like concerts and festivals," says an English major. "Sporting events and music programs are popular." The undisputed high point of the social calendar is Loyolapalooza, the spring festival held on the last weekend before final exams to celebrate the academic year. Students gather on the Quad for a concert, games, and food. "It is definitely my favorite thing to do at Loyola," exudes a senior. A close second is Luck O'Loyola, the annual St. Patrick's Day celebration that features traditional Irish bagpipes, dancing, and music. "It's a fun time for everyone, whether Irish for a day or Irish for the year," says a communications major. Students raise funds for charity at the 12-hour Relay for Life, a series of running events that "transforms our gym into a track for hope." Popular road trip destinations are the nearby Towson Mall as well as to the Inner Harbor and Washington, D.C.

Not surprisingly, community service plays a large role in campus life. "The passion for service runs very strong through the veins of Loyola," reports a senior. The Center for Community Service and Justice helps students find opportunities ranging from one-time services to service-oriented international trips and service-learning courses. "It is extremely atypical not to participate in service while attending Loyola," one senior says. A political science major says that "social justice is a huge initiative at Loyola, with abortion, immigration reform, gay marriage, homelessness, and hunger and gender equality just some of the issues that students at Loyola are fighting for/against." A senior adds that gay and lesbian rights are a major topic. "We have a group on campus called Spectrum specifically for the LGBT community and its allies," she notes.

The city of Baltimore offers an abundance of sights, including the famed Inner Harbor, with its many restaurants and museums, as well as major league sports. A senior calls it "a city with a hometown feel." Loyola's neighbors include numerous other colleges and universities, including Johns Hopkins and Towson University. "Loyola students do not regard this as a 'college town' per se, but it has plenty of young-adult neighborhoods and pockets of entertainment," reports an accounting major. Public transportation is poor in Baltimore, but a "college town" shuttle takes students between the various schools, the mall, and downtown attractions.

Loyola eschews varsity football, but the Greyhounds compete in the Division I Patriot League in eight men's and nine women's sports. Consistent with its Maryland location, both men's and women men's lacrosse are strong, with the men taking home the national championship 2012. Men's and women's soccer and men's golf were conference champions last year. For those with more modest athletic ambitions, Loyola sponsors 23 co-ed and single-sex club sports leagues that draw about 40 percent of students. Flag football, lacrosse, volleyball, and soccer are popular. "The teams are great outlets to make friends and form connections with peers in a healthy way," says an English major. The state-of-the-art Fitness and Aquatic Center boasts a well-equipped 6,000-square-foot fitness center, while the Mangione Aquatic Center features an eight-lane pool as well as a sauna and hot tubs.

Some Loyola denizens lament the absence of football and the dearth of parties on campus, but such complaints seem a small price to pay for four years as part of a close-knit community that takes it humanistic, academic, and social values seriously. "We care for each other, and our Jesuit mission rings true in our day-to-day lives," says a senior. A classmate adds, "You will always have someone who cares about you here. The good food, residence halls, and location don't hurt either."

First-year students jump-start their college careers with various pre-orientation programs in which they meet a small group of fellow students and focus on some special interest.

Overlaps

Boston College, Villanova, Fordham, University of Maryland, University of Delaware, Providence, Fairfield, Penn State, St. Joseph's, James Madison

If You Apply To ➤

Loyola: Early action and regular admissions: Nov. 1. Financial aid: Feb. 15. Housing: May 1. Application fee: $50. Campus interviews: optional, informational. No alumni interviews. SATs or ACTs: considered if submitted. No Subject Tests. Accepts the Common Application.

I LMU Drive, Suite 100, Los Angeles, CA 90045

LMU is a Roman Catholic university known for its strategic L.A. location and strong programs in film and television, business, and communications. Compare to Chapman, Santa Clara, and University of San Diego. Strong international emphasis in film and theater. To take full advantage of L.A., access to a car is highly beneficial.

Website: www.lmu.edu
Location: Suburban
Private
Total Enrollment: 8,316
Undergraduates: 5,818
Male/Female: 42/58
SAT Ranges: CR 550–640, M 560–660
ACT Ranges: 24–29
Financial Aid: 84%
Expense: Pr $ $
Student Loans: 57%
Average Debt: $ $ $ $
Phi Beta Kappa: No
Applicants: 11,913
Accepted: 50%
Enrolled: 21%
Grad in 6 Years: 75%
Returning Freshmen: 89%
Academics: ✍ ✍ ✍
Social: ☎ ☎ ☎
Q of L: ★ ★ ★
Admissions: (800) LMU-INFO
Email Address: admissions@lmu.edu

Strongest Programs:
Communication Studies
Psychology
Marketing
Political Science
English

At Loyola Marymount University, students are treated to ideal weather year-round, a vast array of internship opportunities, and a stellar academic lineup that includes solid programs in television and film, liberal arts and sciences, and business. What's more, LMU has the distinction of being the only Roman Catholic university in Los Angeles. "LMU is more than an academic institution," says a junior. "It is a community dedicated to helping students grow and thrive."

Established in 1911, LMU occupies a 142-acre Westchester campus perched on a bluff overlooking the Pacific Ocean and Marina del Rey in a peaceful residential neighborhood of Los Angeles. As part of an ambitious 10-year construction program, the university opened two new apartment buildings and a traditional residence hall. The William H. Hannon Library is located on the bluff, between the Leavey Residence Halls and the Jesuit Community, and provides a variety of seating and work space, including 33 small-group study rooms that may be reserved in advance online. The Gersten Annex was completed in 2011 and offers 18,000 square feet of space for student-athletes, including locker rooms, conference facilities, and a 4,000-square-foot weight room. A new life sciences building is under construction slated to open in early 2015.

LMU offers 60 baccalaureate programs in six colleges and schools. The general education requirements (known as the "core curriculum") are designed to encourage intellectual breadth, tackling themes such as faith and reason, virtue and justice, culture, art and society, and science, nature, and society. "The nice thing about LMU's academics is that the core requirements encourage students to be open to various studies," says a freshman, "from science to theology to philosophy." Freshmen may take part in a number of programs designed to support first-year students, including an honors program. "The first-year program begins helping freshmen before they even arrive on campus," says one student. "The program seeks to integrate the freshmen so their first year will be successful."

The most popular programs include communication studies, psychology, political science, film and television production, and English, and these are also among the university's strongest. Other solid programs include engineering and business. Students in the School of Film and Television have access to a number of resources, including a student-run production office, a television stage, and a film soundstage with a professional "green screen" (for those cool CGI effects!). They also benefit

> **"The first-year program begins helping freshmen before they even arrive on campus."**

from the program's strong international emphasis, including opportunities to study in Germany and Moscow. Those in the College of Science and Engineering take part in national competitions to design steel bridges and race eco-friendly cars. Thanks to its hip Los Angeles locale, LMU offers a plethora of internships to experience-hungry students, including stints at Disney, MTV, and Warner Brothers. The university offers 41 exchange-semester and study abroad programs in diverse locations such as Greece, Honduras, China, and many other countries.

Like nearby Tinseltown, LMU manages to be both competitive and laid-back. "Depending on the course, a lot of work might be required or barely any homework could be given," says a freshman. A theology major adds, "Most of the intro classes seem more laid-back and the upper division classes are more rigorous." Fifty-one percent of classes have 19 or fewer students and students say teacher-student interaction is a given. "Professors truly know their students and take a personal interest in their learning," says a junior. Another student adds, "All of them encourage students to interact and to get to know them better."

LMU students hail from all 50 states and 86 foreign countries; about three-quarters come from California. "LMU is known for its sense of community and its friendliness," says a student. Another adds, "There is an optimistic atmosphere on this campus because students want to be here." African Americans comprise 6 percent of the student body, Hispanics 22 percent, and Asian Americans 10 percent. Student activism is alive and well on campus and diversity is a perpetually hot issue. Merit scholarships averaging $12,477 are available for qualified students, and student-athletes vie for 233 athletic scholarships in 11 sports.

> **"There is an optimistic atmosphere on this campus because students want to be here."**

Those in the College of Science and Engineering take part in national competitions to design steel bridges and race eco-friendly cars.

Fifty-two percent of LMU students live on campus. "Housing is pretty nice," says a student. A number of themed living communities are available, including those dedicated to social action, substance-free living, and multicultural living. The university offers a variety of meal plan options and dining facilities and "all types of food are available," according to a political science major. Students describe campus security as good, too; "I have never felt unsafe," a junior says.

The social life at LMU takes place "both on and off campus," says one student. "There is always something to do on campus," a senior explains, "whether it is a party or events hosted by different clubs." Student service organizations and clubs frequently host activities for the student body, and Greek life influences the scene, too, and attracts 16 percent of the men and 33 percent of the women. Alcohol is readily available, but students say there is little pressure to drink. "If students want to drink, they can find alcohol," says a freshman. "Those that don't want to, don't have to." The university's Jesuit heritage promotes a social atmosphere that "motivates students to improve themselves by helping others," a student says. "Whether it's Greek life, service organizations, or intramurals, students have a number of possibilities." The area of Westchester is "definitely not a college town," groans a sophomore. Fortunately, Marina del Rey and Santa Monica are a short car or bus ride away, and it's only a mile to the beach. "Since L.A. is a big city, there are plenty of places for a college student to eat, shop, and find entertainment." Popular road trips include San Diego, Santa Barbara, Las Vegas, and Mexico.

With its dynamic mix of solid academics, Jesuit tradition, and thriving social life, LMU offers students substance and style.

Back on campus, LMU's varsity teams compete in Division I and field a number of competitive teams; men's and women's water polo and men's soccer each won their respective conference titles within the last few years. The Lions' rivalry with nearby Pepperdine always draws a huge crowd and the basketball teams' annual pep rally—Madness at Midnight—"is a pretty big event," says a student. Intramurals are popular and include softball, basketball, soccer, volleyball, and ultimate Frisbee. LMU's debate team is a standout, too, having placed among finalists in national championship tournaments on more than 350 separate occasions in policy, value, and parliamentary debate.

With its dynamic mix of solid academics, Jesuit tradition, and thriving social life, LMU offers students substance and style. "We're very friendly with a gorgeous campus," says a student. Whether you're a budding scientist or a future filmmaker, Loyola Marymount University may be worth a look.

Overlaps
University of Southern California, UCLA, Santa Clara, University of San Diego, UC–San Diego, UC–Santa Barbara, Chapman, Stanford

Loyola University New Orleans

6363 St. Charles Ave., Box 89, New Orleans, LA 70118

Of the four Loyolas in the nation, this is the only one where you can go to Mardi Gras and still get up in time for class. New Orleans is an ideal setting for this Roman Catholic university with strengths in business, communications, and the arts. New Orleans is the most progressive Deep South city, and Loyola's politics are mainly liberal.

Website: www.loyno.edu
Location: Suburban
Private
Total Enrollment: 3,834
Undergraduates: 2,949
Male/Female: 41/59
SAT Ranges: CR 530–650,
   M 510–620
ACT Ranges: 22–27
Financial Aid: 95%
Expense: Pr $
Student Loans: 66%
Average Debt: $ $
Phi Beta Kappa: No
Applicants: 6,486
Accepted: 66%
Enrolled: 20%
Grad in 6 Years: 58%
Returning Freshmen: 74%
Academics: ✐ ✐ ✐
Social: 🐘 🐘 🐘
Q of L: ★ ★ ★
Admissions: (800) 4-LOYOLA
Email Address: admit@loyno
   .edu

Strongest Programs:
Music
Music Industry
Advertising/Public Relations
Journalism
Biological Sciences/Premed
International Business
English/Creative Writing
Psychology

In the aftermath of Hurricane Katrina, Loyola University's president called upon students to "be part of the resurrection." It's a clever turn of phrase, and one that sums up the faith and resilient character of this Jesuit liberal arts school. The university continues to enhance its rich tradition through extensive service-learning programs, increasing admissions standards, and a renewed commitment to diversifying the student body. As a Loyola student, "you will be challenged, motivated, and inspired to do more," says one happy senior.

The school's attractive and well-kept 20-acre main campus, in the University section of Uptown New Orleans, mixes Tudor, Gothic, and modern structures. It overlooks acres of Audubon Park and, beyond, the mighty Mississippi River. Two blocks up St. Charles Avenue, Loyola's Broadway campus has an additional four acres. The J. Edgar and Louise S. Monroe Library houses 500,000 volumes, the Lindy Boggs National Center for Community Literacy, and an art gallery. More recent additions include a multimedia classroom and computer lab, a learning commons, and a video-conferencing room in the library.

Loyola offers comprehensive undergraduate degree programs in the College of Humanities and Natural Sciences and in the College of Social Sciences. The School of Mass Communications wins points with students. Also in demand is the international business program in the College of Business and virtually any major in the College of Music and Fine Arts. "We have a vast amount of resources invested in the College of Music and the Thelonious Monk Institute of Jazz Performance has just graduated its first class," a student says. The graphic arts program continues to grow and the music therapy department is one of the oldest in the U.S. There are also programs in history prelaw, which offers a multitude of history courses focused entirely on the evolution of the law, and Latin American studies, which aims to foster an understanding and appreciation of Latin American culture, society, and history.

> **"You will be challenged, motivated, and inspired to do more."**

There are no teaching assistants, and nearly all professors hold doctorate or terminal degrees in their field. "I think the quality is sound," a biology major says, "and I am extremely happy that actual professors teach the classes—not TAs." Students take 24 credits of introductory courses and 24 more of advanced courses in English, history, math, philosophy, religious studies, and natural science. The academic climate is challenging but not cut-throat. "Classmates study together, seek each other out for help, and wish one another good luck," one freshman says.

First-year students participate in a three-day orientation followed by a comprehensive first-year experience that includes a common reading program, a series of lectures and panel discussions, educational excursions, exhibits, and service-learning projects coordinated around a common academic theme. An Executive Mentoring program lets freshman business students meet regularly with local business leaders to discuss their career and personal development. A peer mentoring program helps new students adjust to college life during their initial semester. Loyolans also benefit from the New Orleans Consortium, with cross-registration and library access at other schools in the area. Study abroad programs are available in more than 50 countries, including Belgium, Mexico, Spain, Germany, Japan, and the Netherlands; 36 percent of undergrads take part.

A peer mentoring program helps new students adjust to college life during their initial semester.

"Loyola's students are warm, approachable, and easy to talk to," a marketing major says. Forty-four percent of Loyola students are Louisiana natives and many of the remaining students are from the Southeast. Religion—specifically Roman Catholicism—has a significant influence on campus. Daily mass is voluntary, but many students attend. Hispanics constitute

"Loyola's students are warm, approachable, and easy to talk to."

16 percent of the student body, African Americans 16 percent, and Asian Americans 5 percent. Students are generally well informed and passionate about political and social issues. Loyola awards merit scholarships each year and athletic scholarships in men's and women's basketball.

Many Loyola students commute from home or off-campus apartments; 65 percent of all undergraduates reside on campus. "The residences are spacious and comfortable," a freshman says. Campus dining is good and students may choose from an array of culinary delights, including "sushi, salads, and sandwiches," says a sophomore. As for security, the campus is well lit and students feel safe thanks to the "very present" campus security.

Students volunteer their sweat equity with the Loyola University Community Action Program, a coalition of 11 organizations that provides community service opportunities. With the help of the service-learning office, about 500 students make service learning part of their studies. "Loyola gives us lots of cool things to do on campus," a philosophy major says, including musical performances and sporting events. Fraternities and sororities are rarities at Jesuit schools, but are popular at Loyola, with 3 percent of the men and 6 percent of the women choosing to belong. Major campuswide social events include the Gator Crawl, Wolves on the Prowl community service day, Loyolapalooza spring music festival, and the Fr. Carter lecture series. February brings Mardi Gras, of course—the school shuts down that week. As for underage drinking, Louisiana law requires that you be at least 21 to buy alcohol, but only 18 to consume it in a private residence. While Loyola maintains that dorms are private residences, the school has also established a Coalition to Reduce Underage Drinking. But as one student says: "We live in New Orleans. They can't be too strict."

Students are generally well informed and passionate about political and social issues.

Wolfpack teams compete in the Southern States Athletic Conference. Men's basketball is solid, having won the 2012 SSAC West Division Championship. Women's hoops is strong, too. Other competitive teams include baseball, women's soccer, and volleyball. Women's tennis is now a varsity sport, while basketball, men's flag football (no real pigskins at Loyola), and women's volleyball are popular pastimes.

Students at Loyola know how to pull together and draw strength from their faith. Whether they're working closely with caring professors or relaxing with friends amid the Big Easy's boundless energy, students are satisfied with their choice. "Overall, Loyola is an awesome small Jesuit college with a lot to offer as a community and academic institution," a sophomore says.

Overlaps

Louisiana State, Loyola University of Chicago, Saint Louis University, Tulane, University of Miami (FL)

Macalester College

1600 Grand Avenue, St. Paul, MN 55105

Former UN secretary-general Kofi Annan, '61, typifies one of Mac's hallmarks: an internationalist view of the world. Carleton has a slightly bigger national reputation, but Mac has St. Paul, a progressive capital city. The only leading Midwestern liberal arts college in an urban setting. Over three-quarters of the student body hails from outside Minnesota.

Website: www.macalester.edu

Location: City Center

Private

Total Enrollment: 2,031

Undergraduates: 2,031

Male/Female: 40/60

SAT Ranges: CR 630–740, M 640–730

ACT Ranges: 28–32

Financial Aid: 77%

Expense: Pr $ $ $

Student Loans: 60%

Average Debt: $ $

Phi Beta Kappa: Yes

Applicants: 6,030

Accepted: 37%

Enrolled: 24%

Grad in 6 Years: 90%

Returning Freshmen: 94%

Academics: ✏ ✏ ✏ ✏ ½

Social: ☎ ☎ ☎

Q of L: ★ ★ ★ ★

Admissions: (800) 231-7974

Email Address: admissions@ macalester.edu

Strongest Programs:

Biology

Chemistry

Economics

Environmental Studies

International Studies

Mathematics

Political Science

Macalester College is an international island in the heart of the Great Plains. Liberal not only describes its curriculum; it also describes its politics. Students here get riled up over all sorts of issues with local, national, or international import—from sweatshops and fair trade to gay rights. Mac students come to the school "deeply caring about a social justice issue," says one student, "and throughout their years at Mac, their passions expand and deepen." With its Scottish roots and international focus, Mac has created its own special culture.

Macalester is located in a friendly, family-oriented neighborhood in St. Paul, Minnesota, one mile from the Mississippi River, which divides St. Paul from Minneapolis. Summit Avenue, a tree-lined street with the longest, best-preserved stretch of Victorian homes in the nation, forms the campus's northern boundary. The self-contained, 53-acre campus is arranged around 115-year-old Old Main, a splendid Victorian structure listed on the National Register of Historic Places. The unifying theme is redbrick, the better to set off the octagonal Weyerhauser Chapel, constructed of black glass. A new fine arts center opened in 2012 and renovations to the art building were completed recently.

"Classrooms are collaborative."

Mac's general requirements include two courses in social sciences, a course in quantitative reasoning, a course in writing, and two in natural sciences and math, plus one to two courses in fine arts and in humanities. Two courses must address cultural diversity, in the United States and internationally. Every student also completes a capstone experience during his or her senior year, such as an independent research project, performance, artistic work, or original work. Mac's academic strengths include economics, chemistry, and biology; the school's impressive science facilities include an observatory, an animal operant chamber, and labs for electronic instrumentation and laser spectroscopy. Students may also take advantage of a critical theory concentration.

Mac emphasizes collaboration and working together to handle the challenging workload, and students say most pressure to do well comes from within. "Classrooms are collaborative, with students and professors working together to create a comfortable yet academically stimulating environment," says a junior. Teaching is paramount, with professors often having students over for dinner or taking their students for drinks at a local watering hole. "Classes are taught by professors of incredible skill, knowledge, and experience," an anthropology major says. Another student adds, "Both young professors and established faculty seem to have this desire to continue the learning process along with their students and continually engage with new ideas, theories, and works." Mac attracts the best and the brightest, which might account for the competitive appearance of some programs. More than 100 students do stipend-supported research with Mac professors each summer, and since a number of faculty members play intramurals, students may find professors dishing off passes on the basketball court. Students may choose from among 110 study abroad programs in more than 70 nations via approved independent programs or the Associated Colleges of the Midwest*. Before graduation, 60 percent of students complete an internship at a Twin Cities business, law firm, hospital, financial institution, government agency, or non-profit organization.

"Macalester's students are very opinionated and are mostly open to discussion and to learn from others," says one junior. "They are, in general, self-motivated learners who do not passively wait to be inspired but initiate in relationships with professors, other students, and to engage with the material presented to them." Fifteen percent of Macalester students hail from Minnesota, and the rest come from every state, the District of Columbia, and dozens of other countries. Despite Mac's small size, the student body is 3 percent African American, 6 percent Hispanic, and 7 percent Asian American—and 12 percent of the student body are international. Political debate is lively. "Mac students are activists," says a senior. "Whether working on political campaigns, raising awareness for AIDS victims in South Africa, or voicing discontent with college policies, Macalester students make their opinions known." Says another student: "Everyone is left of liberal, except the economics majors." Merit scholarships are available to brainy types; there are no athletic scholarships. Twenty percent of a recent freshman class were eligible for Pell Grants.

> "Both young professors and established faculty seem to have this desire to continue the learning process along with their students."

All freshmen and sophomores live in college housing; 62 percent of students remain in college-owned digs, and more say they'd stay, if only they could get rooms. They live in traditional residences, with double rooms for the first two years, when they're required to live on campus, and suites for upperclassmen. Single-sex floors are guaranteed to those who want them; many students have single rooms, and some live in language houses. "Dupre is the largest and least comfortable dorm although many students enjoy great community there," a student reports. "Turk and Doty have sinks in the rooms, which is really nice. In general, housing at Mac is good and sometimes great." Residents of the kosher house prepare their own meals, while the opening of the Campus Center has vastly improved food elsewhere on campus. "Café Mac is one of the reasons I came here," says a student. "Each day is an adventure in global cuisine." Students also praise campus security: "The neighborhood around Macalester is incredibly safe, and as a young woman who likes to take walks around the area alone, I have never once felt unsafe in this community," says a junior.

Without Greek organizations and given the proximity of a major metropolitan area, much of Mac's social life takes place off campus, although there are plenty of events in the "Macalester bubble" for those loath to leave. "In general, there is not a lot of peer pressure surrounding social life; whatever your own personal preference is, people will respect it, and you'll be able to find a great group of people to hang out with," a student reports. Minneapolis and St. Paul are close, with their bookstores, coffee shops, restaurants, bars, and movie theaters, plus dance and jazz clubs and professional sports teams. The Mall of America is also

> "Whenever the weather's nice students dot the lawns playing Frisbee, soccer, or cricket—yes, cricket!"

All freshmen and sophomores live in college housing.

Without Greek organizations and given the proximity of a major metropolitan area, much of Mac's social life takes place off campus.

nearby, though Mac students tend to tire of it quickly, and the Twin Cities' public transportation isn't the greatest. Still, with about a dozen colleges and universities in town, there's plenty to do and the Twin Cities are an excellent place to live. For those with wheels, the best road trips include Chicago, Madison, and Duluth—and Bemidji, Minnesota, "to see Babe the Blue Ox," reports a senior.

Competitive Scots teams include men's and women's soccer, football, and baseball. Popular events include Spring Fest and the annual Brain Bowl football game against in-state rival Carleton, "the only school we can't chant 'We are smarter than you!' to," says a communications major. Macalester has one of the oldest competitive debate programs in the nation and the mock trial program is ranked in the top 10 nationally. The Club Sports Program provides opportunities for students to participate in a variety of sports and recreational activities including crew, rugby, and hockey. More than half of the student body participates. "Although the student body seems to take pride in being much more focused on academia, whenever the weather's nice students dot the lawns playing Frisbee, soccer, or cricket—yes, cricket!" says one student.

Macalester provides an atmosphere of high-powered scholarship and success, pairing academic rigor with global perspective. As the school's story travels, the skill and diversity of the student body is rising. "I love its multiculturalism, diversity, small-but-lovely campus, wonderful location, and, above all, its academic excellence," raves an economics student.

Overlaps
Carleton, Brown, Grinnell, Middlebury, Wesleyan, Oberlin, Tufts, University of Chicago

If You Apply To ➤

Macalester: Early decision: Nov. 15. Regular admissions: Jan. 15. Financial aid: Feb. 8. Application fee: $40. Campus interviews: optional, evaluative. Alumni interviews: optional, informational. SATs or ACTs: required. Subject Tests: optional. Accepts the Common Application. Essay question.

University of Maine–Orono

Orono, ME 04469

A sleeper choice for out-of-staters amid better-known public universities such as UMass, UNH, and UVM. Not coincidentally, Maine is the least expensive—and easiest in admission—of the four. A popular marine sciences program flourishes here, as does engineering. Offers a solid honors program and one of the top varsity hockey programs in the nation.

Website: www.umaine.edu
Location: Small Town
Public
Total Enrollment: 8,480
Undergraduates: 7,477
Male/Female: 52/48
SAT Ranges: CR 480–590, M 490–610
ACT Ranges: 21–26
Financial Aid: 71%
Expense: Pub $ $ $
Student Loans: 78%

At the University of Maine–Orono, just under 7,500 undergraduates help themselves to a range of strong academic programs at a reasonable cost. UMaine is not only the state's only land grant university, but also the only sea grant, and attracts top students to its marine sciences program. UMaine has become more academically competitive over the past several years. "It is becoming harder to get in because the school is well known and very academic. A lot of the classes are competitive and have a large workload," explains a junior social work major.

Situated on an island between the Stillwater and Penobscot rivers, UMaine's campus is 660 acres, centered on a large, tree-shaded grass mall. Architectural themes at this flagship of the state university system range from English academic to contemporary. An 87,000-square-foot recreation center features a fitness center, recreational pools, an elevated track, volleyball and basketball courts, and additional facilities. New facilities include the Innovative Media Research and Commercialization

Center, which houses state-of-the-art studios for traditional arts, as well as a computer-driven 3D router, a video production lab, and rich-media classrooms.

UMaine's five undergraduate colleges are education and human development; business, public policy, and health; engineering; liberal arts and sciences; and natural sciences, forestry, and agriculture. The growing Honors College, which has arisen out of one of the oldest honors programs in the nation, now enrolls about 700 students. Specific general education requirements vary from college to college, though all students must demonstrate writing proficiency and take two physical or biological science courses, 18 credits in human value and social context, six credits in math (including statistics and computer science), and at least one ethics course. A capstone experience in the major is also mandatory.

> "The climate here is competitive enough that you always feel challenged to do your best."

The engineering programs are widely viewed as the most demanding on campus. Other best bets include new media, business, marine science, and the health professions. "The climate here is competitive enough that you always feel challenged to do your best," says one sophomore. The interdisciplinary Institute for Quaternary Studies collaborates with other research centers around the world in focusing on the Quaternary period, a time of glacial and interglacial cycles leading up to the present. Research is a key part of an undergraduate education at UMaine and is woven into many areas of the curriculum. Professors are generally lauded for their accessibility. "There is a lot of room for personalized instruction," says a psychology major. Ocean Classroom Foundation (OCF) and the University of Maine offer a semester at sea experience for students aboard a 19th-century-style schooner. SEAmester features a four-course, 12-credit science and humanities curriculum integrated with the journey and ports of call throughout the Eastern Seaboard, Caribbean Islands, and Central America.

The university library, the state's largest, is the regional depository for American and Canadian government documents and houses some of alumnus Stephen King's papers. Former U.S. senator William S. Cohen, a UMaine faculty member before he became defense secretary in the Clinton administration, donated his personal papers to the university as well. The papers, which chronicle Cohen's 24-year congressional career, will be used to develop a nonpartisan center on international policy and commerce focused on teaching, research, and public service, named in Cohen's honor.

UMaine's Academic and Career Exploration program lets students work with professionals in different areas before declaring their degree choices. "The students here are very active in everything from outdoor activities, such as rock climbing and hiking, to politically active (on every side of things), and generally take interest in one another," says a senior. Fifty-five percent of all classes have 19 or fewer students, which means personal attention from professors. Students also report that the quality of teaching is high. "The quality of teaching is great," says a microbiology major, "especially in the lab sciences, which usually focus heavily on hands-on learning." Outside the classroom, internships and co-ops are available in most

> "There is a lot of room for personalized instruction."

fields, and there's a Lobster Institute for nautical types. Juniors who want a reprieve from Maine's frigid winters can head for Brazil, while the heartier types choose Canada, Scandinavia, and Ireland.

UMaine students are "generally fun loving, laid-back, and down to earth," says one sophomore. Most are immune to the frigid New England temperatures, too, since 79 percent are from Maine and many of the rest hail from other parts of New England. African Americans account for 2 percent of the student body, Asian Americans 1 percent, and Hispanics 2 percent; international students comprise 1

(continued)

Average Debt: $ $ $ $
Phi Beta Kappa: Yes
Applicants: 8,306
Accepted: 81%
Enrolled: 30%
Grad in 6 Years: 59%
Returning Freshmen: 76%
Academics: ✍ ✍
Social: ☎ ☎ ☎ ☎
Q of L: ★ ★ ★
Admissions: (207) 581-1561
Email Address: um-admit@maine.edu

Strongest Programs:
Marine Science
Environmental Science
Engineering
Forestry
New Media
Biological Science
Physics
Psychology

A capstone experience in the major is also mandatory.

percent. Merit scholarships offer an average of more than $4,254 a year for qualified students, and 221 athletic scholarships are available in 16 sports.

Forty percent of UMaine students live on campus; the remainder seek shelter in Orono, nearby Bangor, or the sparsely populated area in between. Dorms are co-ed; some have gyms, computer labs, or apartment-style suites. "Dorms are a decent size and they are in great condition," a sociology major says. Some housing is set aside for specific majors. The First Year Residential Experience (FYRE) is based in the first-year residence halls and helps students make a successful transition from high school to college. Dining options have been overhauled and students say the facilities offer a wide variety of tasty fare. "The best part about UMaine dining is the ability to give constant feedback," says a mass communication major. "Like something? Hate something? If you let dining services know they will do their best to accommodate." Greeks can eat in their chapter houses. When it comes to campus safety, students say they have few concerns: "Campus security is fantastic," raves a junior.

Despite—or possibly because of—UMaine's relatively isolated location, the campus pulses with social life; nearly 240 student organizations plan plays, carnival nights, concerts, and comedy hours, with a different activity offered each night. "Whatever your lifestyle, you can find something to do," a junior says. Partiers find their niche off campus, at bars, clubs, and house parties. "The police are good at fishing out the parties and giving out citations if necessary," warns one psychology major. Come spring, students go all out for April's Bumstock Weekend, a three-day event featuring bands playing outdoors from dawn till dusk. Maine Day features a parade, cookout, and campuswide cleanup.

> "The students here are very active."

The midsized town of Orono—described by one sophomore as a "great college town"—offers a few bars, a theater, and some other hangouts. Buses to Bangor, a fair-sized city 10 minutes away, run every 15 to 20 minutes. A car is helpful, although there are gripes about parking. UMaine students tend to be outdoor enthusiasts, and popular road trips include Acadia National Park, skiing at Sugarloaf USA, L.L. Bean's 24-hour store in Freeport, and the real-life Mount Katahdin, which appears on Bean's logo. More urban types enjoy Bar Harbor, Boston, or Montreal, just four hours away (and with a lower drinking age and cheaper drinks).

Hockey reigns here, especially when played against Boston College, Boston University, or New Hampshire, and the Black Bears are perennial champions. Men's baseball, women's ice hockey, and cross-country have claimed the America East championship. The Shawn Walsh Hockey Center houses the ice hockey teams and athletic facilities, and the recreation center includes a pool and elevated jogging track. The popular intramural program covers a range of sports from swimming and wrestling to hoopball (golf with a basketball) and broomball (ice hockey with a dodgeball and a broom, played with shoes instead of skates).

UMaine is a medium-sized school with a small-school atmosphere. Combine the state's natural beauty with an increased emphasis on top-quality facilities and more intimate student/faculty interaction, and it's no surprise that this campus draws more die-hard "Maine-iaks" each year. "We are straight-up awesome!" cheers one junior.

Forty percent of UMaine students live on campus.

Overlaps

University of New Hampshire, University of Vermont, University of Massachusetts, University of Rhode Island, University of Connecticut, University of Southern Maine, Northeastern, University of New England

If You Apply To ➤

Maine: Rolling admissions. Early action: Dec. 15. Financial aid: Mar. 1. Application fee: $40. Campus interviews: optional, evaluative. No alumni interviews. SATs or ACTs: required. Accepts Common Application. Essay question.

Though co-ed for more than 40 years, Manhattanville is still two-thirds female. Strong programs include art, education, and psychology. Among the few small colleges in the NYC area, Manhattanville is a quick train ride from the city. Portfolio system emphasizes competency rather than rote learning. Despite its roots as a commuter school, nearly 80 percent of Manhattanville's students live on campus.

Manhattanville sees its mission as "educating students to become ethically and socially responsible leaders for the global community." The Portfolio System, Manhattanville's distinct approach to undergraduate education, requires students to create a body of work reflecting their entire college career. However, that's only one way Manhattanville encourages individuality and personal growth. Personal attention is another. "I like how our president is involved in everything and gets to know everyone," a junior says.

Manhattanville College, which began as a Roman Catholic academy for girls on Houston Street in New York City, pulled up stakes in the 1950s for a 125-acre estate in Purchase, New York. This estate is located in wealthy Westchester County, near the town of White Plains—home to several major corporations, but just 28 miles from the excitement of the Big Apple. The focal point of the campus, which was designed by Central Park architect Frederick Law Olmsted, is Reid Hall, a 19th-century replica of a Norman castle. Recent construction includes a renovation of the quad.

M-ville's distribution requirements include courses in five areas: humanities, social sciences, fine arts, mathematics and sciences, and languages. Under the Portfolio System, students must craft a freshman assessment essay, a study plan and program evaluation, specific examples of work in writing and research, and a résumé. Freshmen complete the Preceptorial, a two-semester introduction to college-level work, as well as a library and information studies course, and are required to participate in free weekend trips into New York City. Manhattanville's strongest offerings include art and design (enhanced by the proximity of New York City's many museums and galleries), music, and education, while management, psychology, and history are also popular. Manhattanville's School of Education, which offers two five-year master's programs,

> "Manhattanville professors are knowledgeable and passionate about their fields."

boasts a near-perfect passage rate for the New York State Teaching Exam. The languages attract the fewest majors. Students may design their own major, and those studying psychology, biology, or chemistry can conduct research with faculty. Career Services, which offers internship opportunities at more than 350 locations in the New York metro area and beyond, is "phenomenal," securing placements at places such as MTV, the Metropolitan Museum of Art, Fox News, U.S. Senate offices, MasterCard, PepsiCo, and the Westchester County Board of Legislators.

The academic climate at Manhattanville can be challenging or laid-back, depending on the major. The low student/faculty ratio and the quality of teaching get high marks. Seventy-three percent of freshmen classes have 19 or fewer students. "Overall, Manhattanville professors are knowledgeable and passionate about their fields and about sharing that knowledge with students," a senior says. The Board of Trustees scholarships offer qualified students an Honors Preceptorial. An Honors Seminar and honors programs within majors are also available. The college also offers dual-degree programs with New York Medical College (M.S. in physical

Website: www.mville.edu
Location: Suburban
Private
Total Enrollment: 1,977
Undergraduates: 1,652
Male/Female: 36/64
SAT Ranges: CR 480–570, M 480–570
ACT Ranges: 21–24
Financial Aid: 81%
Expense: Pr $
Student Loans: 69%
Average Debt: $ $ $ $
Phi Beta Kappa: No
Applicants: 4,193
Accepted: 69%
Enrolled: 18%
Grad in 6 Years: 56%
Returning Freshmen: 73%
Academics: ✍ ✍ ✍
Social: 🎭 🎭 🎭
Q of L: ★ ★ ★
Admissions: (914) 323-5464
Email Address: admissions@mville.edu

Strongest Programs:
Business Administration and Management
Visual and Performing Arts
Psychology
Communications
English

therapy or M.S. in speech language pathology) and Polytechnic University (M.S. in computer science or M.S. in information technology). The college has exchange programs with Mills College and with American University's World Capitals Program, plus study abroad options in England, France, Germany, Ireland, Italy, Japan, Mexico, and Spain.

More than 50 countries are represented in Manhattanville's student body, and females outnumber males more than 2 to 1.

More than 50 countries are represented in Manhattanville's student body, and females outnumber males more than 2 to 1. "Since the college is small, it just feels like all the students belong to one big family," says a senior. Thirty-eight percent of undergraduates come from outside of New York, including 12 percent from overseas. Hispanics comprise the largest minority group at 30 percent, followed by African Americans at 12 percent, and Asian Americans at 5 percent. The college does not guarantee to meet the need of every student admitted, but there are hundreds of merit scholarships for qualified students.

Seventy-six percent of Manhattanville's students live on campus in one of four dorms, which have lounges, communal kitchens, and laundry rooms. Freshmen are assigned rooms that are "spacious and very comfortable" according to a student, while upperclassmen enter a lottery—and complain they never get what they want. Themed cottages are also available to upperclass students. Campus dwellers can choose 15- or 19-meal-a-week plans, and can also use their meal cards at The Pub (a deli-type eatery) and vending machines. The dining hall has been renovated and offers fresh-baked goods and a well-stocked salad bar. "Many people complain but I think it's up to the individual and their willingness to try something new or something other than their mom's cooking," a mathematics major says. Security is perceived as hit or miss: "I think that campus safety could do a little better to patrol and monitor the front gate, with a more rigorous swipe system or something of that nature," says one senior.

"I think that campus safety could do a little better."

Manhattanville's hometown, Purchase, "is not a college town. It is an affluent area with mansions all over. It's gorgeous," a junior says. The city of White Plains is five minutes away, and New York City is 45 minutes away. With increasing numbers of male students enrolling, the campus social scene seems to be picking up, and with no fraternities or sororities, off-campus parties are usually open to all. The student programming board is working to improve the social life, with weekend events such as dinners, formals in the castle, parties, comedy and talent shows, plays, and concerts. The student center has a movie theater. Fifty student-run organizations help fulfill the interests of the student body, but off-campus bars still draw many students—whether of age or not. On-campus alcohol policies are said to be strict. Road trips include Rye Beach in the warmer months and upstate New York or Vermont for skiing in the winter. The college offers a free Valiant Express bus service that runs into NYC, and to nearby venues. Every spring, students look forward to Quad Jam, "an all-day, all-night concert and carnival and party." There's also a Fall Jam and midnight brunches during finals served by faculty and staff.

Manhattanville has invested heavily in athletics as a way of making the school better known and attracting more males.

Manhattanville has invested heavily in athletics as a way of making the school better known and attracting more males. Valiant teams have earned more than 40 conference regular-season championships and dozens of conference tournament titles in program history, and as a result the school has made more than two dozen appearances in the NCAA Tournament. There's an intramural program, and weekend warriors and letter-winners alike applaud the college's gym, fitness center, swimming pool, tennis courts, and athletic fields.

Manhattanville's size can be both an asset and an annoyance, say students. The familial atmosphere can get claustrophobic at times, but for those wishing to be part of a close but growing community where values matter, Manhattanville may be worth a look. "It's a nice, close-knit community," a sophomore says.

Overlaps

Fordham, Iona, Manhattan College, Pace, St. John's University, Marist

Marlboro College

Marlboro, VT 05344

Marlboro is a hilltop home to a few hundred nonconformist souls. Each develops a plan of concentration that culminates in a senior project. One of the few colleges in the country that is governed in town-meeting style, where student votes carry the same weight as those of the faculty. About two-thirds of the students graduate in six years. Where else can you cheer for the Fighting Dead Trees?

Marlboro College is only a half-century old, but it is known far and wide as an innovator in liberal arts education. It was founded on the principles of independent and in-depth study just after World War II, when returning GIs renovated an old barn as the college's first building while living in Quonset huts. And today's Marlboro students are just as trailblazing; they prepare for the future by digging into self-developed Plans of Concentration. With fewer than 250 undergrads and fewer than 50 faculty members, Marlboro is its own little world, which students enter as novices and leave as pros.

Positioned atop a small mountain, surrounded by maples and pines and with a gorgeous view of southern Vermont, Marlboro's physical beauty is striking. Buildings are adapted from barns, sheds, and houses that stood on three old farms that today make up the 350-acre campus. Among the renovated structures, many with passive solar heating, are nine dormitories, a library, a science building, art studios, music practice rooms, a 350-seat theater, and a campus center. Above the science building is the college's astronomical observatory. The school has expanded the campus center; a 4,270-square-foot addition houses the health center. While some schools see growth as a sign of success, Marlboro intends to remain one of the nation's smallest liberal arts institutions. Administrators believe the size stimulates dynamic relationships between students and faculty, making learning happen both inside and outside the classroom. This isn't a place where students can fade into the background: the institution relies on everyone to share their talents and skills. The same philosophy applies to the college's Graduate Center; its programs are as innovative as the college's heritage.

"Marlboro students are more collaborative than competitive."

The cornerstone of a Marlboro education is the Plan of Concentration, which each undergraduate student develops independently. Juniors and seniors "on plan" take most coursework in one-on-one tutorials with the faculty sponsors. Seniors present their thesis or project to their sponsors, who are backed up by outside examiners, experts in the student's field unaffiliated with the college. The administration boasts that by bringing in these outsiders for two- to three-hour oral examinations of its seniors, Marlboro has created its own accountability system, ensuring that neither students nor faculty at this isolated institution are cut off from the most current academic thinking. Faculty members often find the exams as stressful as the students, as it means outsiders are judging their teaching. The only other requirement is the Clear Writing course, usually completed by the end of the third semester,

Website: www.marlboro.edu
Location: Rural
Private
Total Enrollment: 235
Undergraduates: 235
Male/Female: 53/47
SAT Ranges: CR 560–730, M 520–650
ACT Ranges: 24–32
Financial Aid: 86%
Expense: Pr $ $
Student Loans: 71%
Average Debt: $
Phi Beta Kappa: No
Applicants: 256
Accepted: 79%
Enrolled: 24%
Grad in 6 Years: 68%
Returning Freshmen: 68%
Academics: ✑ ✑ ✑
Social: ☎ ☎ ☎
Q of L: ★ ★ ★ ★
Admissions: (800) 343-0049
Email Address: admissions@marlboro.edu

Strongest Programs:
Literature
Writing
Photography
Theater
Film
Political Science

(continued)

Asian Studies
Social Sciences

Marlboro's flexibility should not be confused with academic flabbiness.

Students can veto the faculty members on hiring and retention decisions, and it takes a two-thirds vote of the faculty to override them.

with a 21-page portfolio reviewed by faculty. Marlboro offers solid instruction in literature, writing, social sciences, and fine arts. Administrators and students alike praise the World Studies Program (WSP), which provides an eight-month professional internship and/or study abroad experience; 30 percent of students take part, and 40 percent do some type of study abroad.

Marlboro's flexibility should not be confused with academic flabbiness. Grades are an integral part of the evaluation process, professors are stingy with As, and most students work hard. "Although academics are rigorous, Marlboro students are more collaborative than competitive," says one junior. Students give most profs high marks and appreciate the low student/teacher ratio: "I love the Marlboro professors," cheers one student, "because they too want to learn and share their ideas." Another adds, "Teachers are very knowledgeable, quick to answer questions, spark discussion, and explore new territory."

In the old independent Yankee spirit, Marlboro's library operates on the honor system, where students sign out their own books 24 hours a day. It is the same for

"Teachers are very knowledgeable."

the computer center and the science and humanities buildings. The school has only one security guard. "I feel really safe here," says one freshman. "Everyone is out at night and nobody's worried about assault—except maybe by bears." Indeed, the college operates on a New England town-meeting style of government involving students, faculty, and the staff and their spouses in every aspect of policymaking. Students can veto the faculty members on hiring and retention decisions, and it takes a two-thirds vote of the faculty to override them.

"The typical Marlboro student runs on caffeine and cigarettes and enjoys talking about haughty subjects," says a senior, "but still enjoys an impromptu snowball fight and sledding down the hill on dining hall trays." Marlboro remains a liberal-leaning campus, but students are quick to point out that campus politics don't dominate the scene. All students hail from outside Vermont and minority enrollment continues to be low: Asian Americans make up 3 percent of students, and African Americans and Hispanics each make up less than 1 percent. The college offers merit scholarships but no athletic scholarships.

The dorms house 84 percent of Marlboro students and are mostly co-ed; students say they have a "rustic" appeal. "The rooms are cozy and friendly, not sterile like some dorms," says one dorm dweller. Housing is based on credits, so freshmen have triples, sophomores have doubles, and upperclassmen have singles. There is one dining hall where "the entire community eats together." Food gets mixed reviews ("not phenomenal nor phenomenally diverse") but students agree it is adequate for putting on the "freshman 15." A small percentage of students live off campus in Brattleboro, 20 minutes away, and shuttle to and from campus in a school van.

Students agree that the town of Marlboro, recognizable by a post office and general store, has little to write home about. "Marlboro isn't a town so much as a few buildings with a college a mile or so down the road," observes one literature major. Most head to Brattleboro for its restaurants, bookstores, and coffee shops.

"The typical Marlboro student runs on caffeine and cigarettes."

As might be expected, Marlboro has no Greek organizations; a staff member was hired to coordinate the planning of student activities like poetry readings, trips to Boston and New York City, vans to local movie theaters, and pumpkin-carving contests. Snowball fights by the library are a big draw in winter. On Community Work Day, students and faculty skip class and work together to improve the campus through various manual labor projects. The annual Cabaret and Halloween parties are unofficial costume contests showcasing student creativity.

The school mascot, the Fighting Dead Trees, is emblazoned on the shirts of the ever-popular co-ed soccer team. Fencing is competitive, too. Broomball, a variation of ice hockey played using shoes instead of ice skates, brooms instead of sticks, and a kickball instead of a puck, is also always popular for athletes and spectators. The intramural program, which has a 40 percent participation rate, also offers dodgeball, ultimate Frisbee, and volleyball, among other sports. The "incredibly dynamic" outing club ensures plenty of opportunities to enjoy the local wilderness, including hiking and cross-country skiing on runs that radiate from the center of campus. Excellent downhill skiing is only a few minutes' drive away.

This iconoclastic school continues to push the academic envelope and remains proud of doing—and being—the unexpected. And that suits its students just fine. Says a sophomore, "We tend to have students here who are a little left of center, very interested in the details, intelligent, engaged, interested in hands-on learning, passionate, and who will always go the extra mile to learn everything about their subject."

Overlaps

Bard, Bennington, Hampshire, Reed, Sarah Lawrence, Warren Wilson

If You Apply To ➤

Marlboro: Early decision: Nov. 15. Early action: Jan. 15. Regular admissions: Mar. 1. Application fee: $50. Campus interviews: recommended, evaluative. Alumni interviews: optional, evaluative. SATs or ACTs: optional. Subject Tests: optional. Accepts the Common Application. Essay question. Encourages "nontraditional" students.

Marquette University

Milwaukee, WI 53201-1881

Marquette is an old-line Roman Catholic university along the lines of Saint Louis University and Loyola of Chicago. Milwaukee is not a selling point, and the university's student body is mainly from the southern Wisconsin/northern Illinois corridor. About 80 percent of the students are Catholic and half live on campus. The university is relatively inexpensive, in keeping with its middle- and working-class clientele.

At Marquette University, students practice what they preach. The college experience at this Roman Catholic institution includes an emphasis on civic responsibility, community service, and personal growth. "Marquette students really are a community. Everyone supports everyone else," says a senior. Innovative programs combine classroom theory with volunteer opportunities in Milwaukee and beyond.

Marquette occupies 80 acres of "concrete with interludes of grass and trees" just a few blocks from the heart of downtown Milwaukee. While offering the advantages of an urban setting, its campus does have plenty of open spaces suitable for everything from throwing a Frisbee to throwing a barbecue. Although most of the buildings are relatively modern, the campus is the site of the St. Joan of Arc Chapel, which was built in France more than 500 years ago and later transported to Wisconsin. It is said to be the only medieval structure in the Western Hemisphere dedicated to its original purpose. The university is currently engaged in a renovation project that includes three campus buildings.

The 36-hour general education core curriculum is composed of nine "knowledge areas": diverse cultures, human nature and ethics, histories of cultures and societies, individual and social behavior, theology, literature/performing arts, mathematical reasoning, rhetoric, and science and nature. In addition to myriad study abroad programs (85 programs on six continents), the university is the proud owner of the

Website: www.marquette.edu
Location: City Center
Private
Total Enrollment: 10,032
Undergraduates: 7,938
Male/Female: 48/52
SAT Ranges: CR 520–630, M 550–650
ACT Ranges: 24–29
Financial Aid: 98%
Expense: Pr $
Student Loans: 65%
Average Debt: $ $ $ $
Phi Beta Kappa: Yes
Applicants: 22,900
Accepted: 55%
Enrolled: 15%
Grad in 6 Years: 80%

Marquette has its own art museum and an active theater program.

Les Aspin Center for Government in Washington, D.C., which allows students to take courses while participating in an internship with a federal government agency. Closer to home, students intern with local and state government agencies. The Honors Program, which offers small classes, admits 100 qualified freshmen annually. Each year, more than 1,800 students enroll in service-learning courses and participate in service opportunities in more than 100 community settings.

Through an affiliation with the Milwaukee Institute of Art and Design, two art minors (studio art and art history) are available. Marquette has its own art museum and an active theater program. The foreign languages and literature departments are currently shifting focus and consequently are not as strong as other offerings. B.S. degrees in construction management engineering, computational mathematics, and elementary education are available.

Most classes have fewer than 25 students, and students report little difficulty getting into the ones they want. The administration encourages students to "put our beliefs into practice" through volunteer activity, which serves the elderly, the sick, and the poor in the Milwaukee area and elsewhere. "Volunteer work is huge at Marquette and there are departments that work to get anyone involved who wants to be involved," a junior says. Administrators say students contributed more than 420,000 hours of community service during the 2012–13 school year. Student religious organizations are active, and weekly masses are held in the dorms by the resident priest. Roman Catholics understandably predominate in the student body, but religious practice is left to the individual. The academic climate is described as challenging and competitive, although this varies by program. A senior says, "The classes are intense, but professors are always willing to help out if you just ask." Freshmen take a mandatory rhetoric course after reading the same book over the summer (a recent title was Marjane Satrapi's *Persepolis I: The Story of a Childhood*), and a first-semester seminar attracts about a quarter of entering students. The Freshman Frontier program offers admission and intensive assistance to students "who did not reach full academic potential in high school."

Although Marquette actively recruits in 35 or so states and several U.S. territories, most of the student body is from the Midwest, 34 percent from Wisconsin itself. In general, Marquette boasts a friendly collection of traditional, middle-class students. "Students are very involved," a sophomore says, "whether in community service, sports, student government, or other activities." African Americans make up 5 percent of the student body, and Hispanics and Asian Americans combine for another 15 percent. Marquette offers a very successful Educational Opportunity Program, which enables low-income, disadvantaged students, most of whom are minorities, to have the advantage of a college education. Merit scholarships averaging $8,000 are available, as are 154 athletic scholarships in 14 sports. Seventeen percent of freshmen are eligible for Pell Grants.

"Volunteer work is huge at Marquette."

Fifty-four percent of Marquette students make their home on campus; all but two residence halls are co-ed, and there are more than 400 apartments (which come with a separate electric bill). Residency is required for freshmen and sophomores, but by junior year an overwhelming majority of students choose to move off campus, though housing is guaranteed for all undergraduate students through a lottery. "Dorms are well taken care of," one student says, and are "small but cozy." Within the dorms are five different living/learning communities, including ones for freshman honors students, engineering majors, and nursing students. Dining hall fare is described as "decent" and there are plenty of choices on the menu. The university works hard to keep the campus safe. "Although Marquette is located in an urban environment, public safety does an absolutely outstanding job ensuring that students are safe and know how to remain safe in the area," a senior says.

The Golden Eagles basketball and golf are highly competitive, as are women's basketball and soccer.

Social life is mainly on campus, and "there are always things to do," says a senior. Students don't characterize Milwaukee as a college town, but still say there are many good things about being there. For one, students say they have plenty of opportunities for community service. An old advertising slogan once claimed that "Milwaukee Means Beer," and few Marquette students would disagree. Marquette is stricter than most universities in enforcing the drinking age, but getting served off campus is not as difficult; students report that alcohol is there for the getting. There are fraternities and sororities, and they attract 11 percent of the men and 14 percent of the women, respectively. Another well-loved tradition is the Miracle on Central Mall, the annual lighting of the campus Christmas tree and accompanying mass.

As the school grows, varsity sports are gaining a higher profile. The Golden Eagles basketball and golf are highly competitive, as are women's basketball and soccer. Seventy percent of students participate in at least one of the 41 intramural or 32 club sports. Sports fans will be impressed with Milwaukee's Bradley Center, close to campus and home to Marquette basketball and the NBA's Milwaukee Bucks. Nature lovers can head to Lake Michigan, a 40-minute walk from campus, or to Kettle Moraine, a glaciated region ideal for hiking and cross-country skiing. Chicago is only 95 miles away.

> "The classes are intense, but professors are always willing to help out if you just ask."

Still, no matter how dynamic Marquette's athletic teams or how impressive the facilities, it's the familial atmosphere that makes Marquette what it is. "Students here are very friendly," a junior says. "It is always easy to meet new people and become friends quickly."

Overlaps

University of Wisconsin, University of Illinois, Loyola University of Chicago, University of Minnesota, Saint Louis University, University of Iowa, DePaul, Indiana University

---

If You Apply To ➤

Marquette: Regular admissions: Dec. 2. Financial aid: Feb. 3. Housing: May 1. Application fee: $30 (paper), free (online). Campus and alumni interviews: optional, informational. SATs or ACTs: required. Subject Tests: optional. Accepts the Common Application. Essay question.

University of Mary Washington

1301 College Avenue, Fredericksburg, VA 22401

Mary Washington could easily be mistaken for one of Virginia's elite private colleges. It offers just as much history and tradition—for a much lower price. Once a women's college, it is still about two-thirds female, and administrators failed in an effort to drop "Mary" from the name to attract more men. On the selectivity chart, UMW ranks behind only UVA and William and Mary among Virginia public universities.

Strolling among the university's elegant buildings of redbrick with white columns has led more than one pleased parent to declare, "Now this is what a college should look like." Indeed, for an aura of history and tradition, few schools stack up to this small college in Fredericksburg, a site of Civil War action and the boyhood town of George Washington. Mary Washington is a good place to spend four years "because it is a strong community of socially conscious and academically focused students," says one senior.

The University of Mary Washington campus features classical Jeffersonian buildings, sweeping lawns, brick walkways, and breathtaking foliage. If the campus architecture puts some people in mind of the University of Virginia, it's no accident:

Website: www.umw.edu
Location: Small City
Public
Total Enrollment: 4,001
Undergraduates: 3,861
Male/Female: 35/65
SAT Ranges: CR 520–630, M 510–600
ACT Ranges: 22–27

(continued)

Financial Aid: 58%

Expense: Pub $ $

Student Loans: 45%

Average Debt: $ $

Phi Beta Kappa: Yes

Applicants: 4,847

Accepted: 77%

Enrolled: 25%

Grad in 6 Years: 76%

Returning Freshmen: 83%

Academics: ✏️ ✏️ ✏️ ½

Social: ☎ ☎ ☎

Q of L: ★ ★ ★ ★

Admissions: (540) 654-2000

Email Address: admit@umw
.edu

Strongest Programs:

Historic Preservation

Psychology

English

Biology

International Affairs

History

Political Science

Business Administration

Virtually every major requires students to complete a capstone project or experience or to take a senior-level initiative seminar.

UMW (formerly Mary Washington College) was the all-female branch of that august institution before going co-ed in 1970 and cutting its ties in 1972. Construction is underway on a state-of-the-art convergence center that will feature open, flexible gathering spaces where technology, information, and teaching resources will come together. UMW has several construction projects underway, including an Information and Technology Convergence Center that will house a data center, classrooms, media labs, and a digital theater.

Mary Washington has gained a reputation as one of the premium public liberal arts colleges in the country and continues to attract bright students from around the globe. The core curriculum emphasizes a strong liberal arts focus. The general education requirements include a first-year seminar and courses in quantitative reasoning; natural science; human experience and society; global inquiry; language, arts, literature, and performance; experiential learning; and a writing intensive. Virtually every major requires students to complete a capstone project or experience or to take a senior-level initiative seminar. The program in historic preservation is solid: "It's pretty unique and has great local partners for internships," says a senior. Among the sciences, biology is the clear favorite.

> **"The courses are challenging and engaging."**

"The courses are challenging and engaging," says a senior, and they "push students out of the classroom and into experiential opportunities." Students are encouraged to take on research projects of their own design, and science students are eligible for a 10-week summer research program. Several departments offer grants for work abroad or in the United States, and many students study abroad during their junior year. The college's location, roughly an hour from both Washington, D.C., and the state capital, Richmond, is a handy asset for the approximately 350 budding politicos who seek internships every year. The close ties between students and faculty are a great source of pride at Mary Washington. Classes rarely have more than 25 students, and the hiring of additional faculty may allow for even smaller classes. "Since Mary Washington is a smaller school, most of the professors know their students on a first-name basis, which help students thrive," says one student. First-year seminars are available, and UMW 101 covers a variety of topics designed to make the transition to college life as glitch-free as possible.

"The students at Mary Washington are very inquisitive and are not afraid to stand up for what they believe in. Many students are very involved with community

> **"Most of the professors know their students on a first-name basis."**

service, whether helping the school community or within the Fredericksburg area," a senior says. Eighty-five percent of the student body is from Virginia. African Americans make up 7 percent of the student population, Hispanics 7 percent, and Asian Americans 5 percent. A large majority continue on to jobs after graduation, rather than graduate school. Students tend to be politically aware and channel that energy into social issues. "The students at UMW care a lot about other people," says an English major. "Clubs and organizations advocate for children in Africa (we have a UNICEF club on campus), sexual abuse victims, families in poverty, and so much more." Eligible undergraduates receive merit scholarships, but there are no athletic scholarships.

An unusually strong sense of community characterizes everything from academics to dorm life at UMW. The 18 residence halls offer a variety of living arrangements, including suites, singles, doubles, and even quads. "The dorms are very well maintained," says a sophomore. "The cleaning staff works hard to keep housing comfortable for the students." Two recently renovated 1950s residence halls have been transformed into high-tech living and learning communities. Although many upperclassmen move to private housing, most stay within a mile of campus. All told, 60 percent of students live in university housing. Campus dining gets a resounding thumbs-up from students. "I love UMW food!" cheers a freshman. Security is described as good and students report feeling safe on campus. "The campus police are very friendly and willing to help with anything," says a student, "whether it's giving you a ride back from the parking lot or helping you when your car battery dies."

Although there are parties both on and off campus on any given weekend, alcohol does not dominate the social scene, and there are no fraternities or sororities. "There are over 120 student clubs and organizations on campus which hold weekly events," says a senior. Another student says, "There is always something to do on campus on the weekends, whether it's a concert or comedian or a movie at Cheap Seats." Small and friendly, nearby Fredericksburg is an "interesting mix of Civil War relics, antique shops, museums, and Mary Washington," according to a history major. While it lacks some of the nightlife of a larger community, there are historic homes to visit, museums with Civil War exhibits, a mall, and restaurants that offer discounts to students.

> "There are over 120 student clubs and organizations on campus."

For dance clubs and bars, students drive to Richmond or D.C. Also an hour's drive away is the scenery of the Chesapeake Bay, due east, and the Blue Ridge Mountains, due west. On campus, student organizations offer special events each Friday, such as a student film festival or a Mardi Gras celebration.

Mary Washington students take an uncommon interest in traditions. Several annual outdoor parties, including Grill on the Hill and Weststock, never fail to attract a large crowd. All third-year students brace themselves for Junior Ring Week, during which they are the victims of practical jokes prior to receiving their rings from the school's president. Another tradition is Devil-Goat Day, an all-day competition pitting odd- and even-year classes against each other in events such as sumo wrestling, jousting, and the Velcro wall. Homecoming is observed with the usual round of sporting events (particularly soccer), dances, and dinners. The Multicultural Fair is also popular.

Mary Washington doesn't have a football team, but other Eagles sports are alive and well. Since the inception of the Capital Athletic Conference, UMW has won more conference championships than all other conference members combined. In 2013, the university captured seven conference championships and six second-place finishes to earn the CAC All-Sport Award, given to the best overall athletic programs. Nonvarsity types also use the 76-acre sports and field complex, complete with an Olympic-size pool, for a variety of intramural and club sports, including men's and women's rugby and crew. Flag football, soccer, and basketball are popular intramurals. "'Intramural Champions' is the most coveted T-shirt on campus," says a senior.

A train stop on the way from UVA to Washington, D.C., and Richmond, the University of Mary Washington offers a first-rate liberal arts education. It has the feel of a private school with a public school price tag and is an option that should be explored, says a happy junior. "I feel that [UMW] is overlooked by many due to its smaller size. But I feel if people took a closer look, they would see its real beauty and excellence."

First-year seminars are available, and UMW 101 covers a variety of topics designed to make the transition to college life as glitch-free as possible.

In 2013, the university captured seven conference championships and six second-place finishes to earn the CAC All-Sport Award.

Overlaps

University of Virginia, College of William and Mary, James Madison, Virginia Tech, Christopher Newport, George Mason, University of Richmond, Longwood

If You Apply To ➤

Mary Washington: Early action: Nov. 15. Regular admissions: Feb. 1. Financial aid: Mar. 1. Housing: May 22. Application fee: $50. No campus or alumni interviews. SATs or ACTs: required. Subject Tests: optional. Accepts the Common Application. Essay question.

College Park, MD 20742

The name says Maryland, but the location says Washington, D.C. Students in College Park can jump on the Metro just as they do at American or Georgetown. Maryland is nothing if not big, and savvy students will look to programs such as the honors program and living/learning communities for some personal attention.

Website: www.maryland.umd.edu

Location: Suburban

Public

Total Enrollment: 32,098

Undergraduates: 24,364

Male/Female: 53/47

SAT Ranges: CR 580–690, M 610–720

ACT Ranges: N/A

Financial Aid: 52%

Expense: Pub $ $

Student Loans: 46%

Average Debt: $ $

Phi Beta Kappa: Yes

Applicants: 25,239

Accepted: 47%

Enrolled: 33%

Grad in 6 Years: 80%

Returning Freshmen: 94%

Academics: ✐ ✐ ✐

Social: ☎ ☎ ☎

Q of L: ★ ★ ★

Admissions: (301) 314-8385

Email Address: um-admit@uga.umd.edu

Strongest Programs:
Business
Engineering
Journalism
Computer Science
Government and Politics
Physics

For good luck on exams, University of Maryland students rub the nose of Testudo, the school's terrapin mascot. But even without touching the revered statue, most students here feel lucky to be at a school with so many courses, such a diverse student body, and state-of-the-art research programs and institutes. Despite the school's daunting size, students find plenty to cheer about. "With hundreds of different student organizations," says a senior, "students will always be able to find their niche."

Maryland's 1,200-acre campus embraces an array of architectural styles, including the Georgian brick buildings ringing the oak-lined mall at the heart of the campus. Students now have their own athletic arena—the Comcast Center. The South Campus Commons Building 7 provides additional residential space, and two new facilities opened in 2011: Oakland Hall, a new dormitory housing 700 students, and Denton Dining Hall. Phase I of the new physical sciences complex was substantially completed in late 2013.

Students select a major from within one of the university's schools and colleges; Maryland has earned a strong reputation for its engineering, physics, and computer science departments, as well as the Robert H. Smith School of Business and Philip Merrill College of Journalism. General education requirements require students to complete 40 to 46 credits in a number of areas, including writing, oral communication, mathematics, analytic reasoning, history and social sciences, humanities, natural sciences, and diversity. Students must also take an "I-Series" course that emphasizes "broad, analytical thinking about significant issues." For students at the extremes of the academic spectrum, there are several honors programs and an intensive educational development and tutoring program. Students participating in individual studies combine established majors and create their own programs; other options include internships in nearby Washington, D.C., and Baltimore, and study abroad in locations such as Costa Rica, Israel, and Sweden.

Maryland's coursework is challenging, "but there are always resources available to make [it] easier," says one senior. Lower-level courses tend to be large and impersonal ("easy to hide in, even easier to skip"), but the corresponding weekly discussion sections led by teaching assistants offer personal attention. The situation improves by junior year, when classes of 20 to 40 students become the norm. "The quality of teaching has been incredible with very few exceptions," a bioengineering major says. Faculty members are "always there to help," but, as might be expected given Maryland's size, students must seek them out for extra help, feedback, or assistance. The university is putting more emphasis on helping students make timely progress toward their degree. A two-day orientation, seminars, and course clusters are offered for freshmen.

> **"The quality of teaching has been incredible with very few exceptions."**

Seventy-five percent of students are Maryland natives, and New York and New Jersey are also well represented. Diversity is more than just a buzzword: 12 percent of students are African American, 8 percent are Hispanic, and another 15 percent are Asian American. Big issues on campus range from gay and lesbian rights to tuition hikes. "The activism is great," a sophomore says. "Being so close to Washington, D.C., has a great impact." The Maryland Pathways program provides three avenues to help students from low-income families attend the university without assuming excessive amounts of debt. In addition, qualified undergrads receive merit awards and athletes vie for hundreds of athletic scholarships.

Forty-seven percent of students live on campus in single-sex or co-ed dorms; freshmen are guaranteed housing, and while many juniors and seniors seek off-campus accommodations, those who stay on campus all four years will find that their digs improve as they gain seniority. (Upperclassmen also have the option of on-campus apartments and suites.) "Dorms are great and an essential part of the freshman experience," one senior says. Decisions on financial aid and housing are affected by acceptance date, so the earlier you apply, the better off you'll be. Freshmen generally live in high-rises or low-rises; South Campus (more relaxing than the louder North Campus) features air-conditioning, carpeting, and new furniture. Safety features include triple locks on dorm-room doors, blue-light emergency phones, and walking and riding escort services to transport students after dark. "The area has its rough spots but it is constantly becoming safer," a sophomore says, noting the campus itself tends to be "extremely safe."

> *Students participating in individual studies combine established majors and create their own programs.*

Social life at Maryland revolves around nonalcoholic events such as concerts, movies, and speakers, as well as around the traditional fraternity parties and football and basketball games. "Social life is epic here," raves one history and education double major. The uni-

"Social life is epic here."

versity's reputation as a haven for those who prefer partying to studying is changing as students with better credentials apply, but there is still always something happening in the dorms, at local pubs, and in nearby Baltimore and Washington, D.C. On campus, only students over 21 may drink, in accordance with state law. "They say no tolerance and in recent years, there have been crackdowns. As a result, policies have increased in effectiveness," says one student. Fifteen percent of men and women go Greek, but they don't dominate the tone of campus life.

Despite College Park's highly social atmosphere, Maryland's suburban campus can feel too small. A few bucks and a few minutes on the Metro (Washington's subway system) brings Terrapins into downtown D.C. at a hare's pace. Back on campus, Art Attack is a favorite annual event in which local artists share their crafts and national touring artists perform an evening concert. Other popular events include Maryland Day and homecoming.

> *Fifteen percent of men and women go Greek, but they don't dominate the tone of campus life.*

Terrapin basketball fans are unsinkable and not always civilized, turning out en masse to cheer against opponents, especially now that have fled the Atlantic Coast Conference to become the 14th member of the storied Big Ten. "Students here have a lot of school spirit," a junior says. "Terrapin pride runs rampant around here." The basketball program is always impressive, as are the women's lacrosse, volleyball, and basketball teams. The men's soccer team was ACC tournament champion in 2010 and men's wrestling brought home conference titles in recent years. A handful of intramural sports are offered, along with an array of club-level sports.

The University of Maryland's overwhelming size is both a blessing and a curse for the increasingly capable undergraduates here. On one hand, "the diversity of the student body and the opportunities afforded are infinite," a sophomore says. On the other, largeness can translate into crowded dorms, big classes, parking problems, and hassles everywhere. Still, most students agree that the threat of anonymity is overshadowed by the countless opportunities for success. "Our campus is gorgeous, academics are competitive, and we have school spirit," says one student. "Why wouldn't you want to be a Terp?"

Overlaps

Penn State, University of Michigan, University of Maryland Baltimore County, Virginia Tech, University of Delaware

University of Maryland Baltimore County

Baltimore, MD 21250

A midsize public university with the feel of a private one. Strategically located in a suburban setting between Washington, D.C., and Baltimore, UMBC invests heavily in learning communities and other efforts to ensure that its undergraduates thrive. Nationally known for selective Meyerhoff Scholars Program and a chess team that routinely bests its Ivy League competition. Working on commuter reputation.

Website: www.umbc.edu
Location: City Outskirts
Public
Total Enrollment: 10,490
Undergraduates: 9,357
Male/Female: 55/45
SAT Ranges: CR 550–650,
    M 580–670
ACT Ranges: 24–29
Financial Aid: 61%
Expense: Pub $ $
Student Loans: 53%
Average Debt: $ $
Phi Beta Kappa: Yes
Applicants: 8,514
Accepted: 60%
Enrolled: 30%
Grad in 6 Years: 61%
Returning Freshmen: 85%
Academics: ✍ ✍ ✍
Social: ☎ ☎ ☎
Q of L: ★ ★ ★
Admissions: (800)
    UMBC-4U2
Email Address: admissions@
    umbc.edu

Strongest Programs:
Information Systems
Psychology
Biological Sciences
Computer Science
Visual Arts

At the University of Maryland Baltimore County, you can be king or queen of your academic world. Students here are given access to academic and social resources usually reserved for those attending mammoth public institutions or pricey private colleges. In addition to solid programs in the sciences and humanities, UMBC offers students a seemingly endless menu of social options. "There are so many ways to get involved academically and socially," says a student, "whether it's through clubs, research, internships, or service learning." What's more, the school fields a killer chess team that regularly mops the floor with the competition. UMBC encourages exploration and expects students to support one another and the community at large. It's your move.

UMBC's 500-acre suburban campus is located within the D.C.-Baltimore corridor, offering students access to an array of cultural attractions including restaurants, art galleries, specialty shops, and museums. In the past decade, the university has invested more than $300 million in new facilities. The Information Technology and Engineering Building offers state-of-the-art amenities and the Chemistry and Biochemistry Building has undergone extensive renovations. A new performing arts and humanities building and performance center opened in late 2012.

UMBC's most popular programs are also its strongest, including social sciences, biology, computer and information systems, psychology, and visual and performing arts. The interdisciplinary studies major gives students a chance to create individualized majors drawing on a wide range of disciplines; past majors include biomechanics, criminal justice, medical illustration, and intercultural conflict resolution. The Brown Center for Entrepreneurship sponsors programs and courses to inspire entrepreneurial thinking among students and faculty, while budding researchers may compete for undergraduate research awards through the Provost's Office and via Undergraduate Research and Creative Achievement Day (URCAD). The highly selective Meyerhoff Scholars Program addresses the shortage of African Americans in the sciences and engineering; today, it is one of the nation's top producers of African American science, engineering, and math undergrads who matriculate into Ph.D. programs. Each year, the Shriver Center places more than 1,200 UMBC students in internship and co-op experiences, and several hundred students participate in study abroad programs.

> **"It's not a cut-throat environment."**

"The classes are definitely tough," says one chemical engineering major, "but it's not a cut-throat environment." All students must complete general foundation requirements, which include three courses in the arts and humanities, three social science courses, one math course, and two biological/physical science courses. In addition, students must complete a foreign language requirement. The university offers a number of programs designed to help freshmen ease into college life. First-Year Academic Seminars allow students to partner with faculty members to explore course material in an intimate, active learning environment. Students focus on creative and critical thinking skills and written and oral communication, and take part in faculty and peer critiques. The Small Study Groups program encourages freshmen and sophomores to form study groups, and Campus Connect provides additional mentoring to undecided freshmen who appear at risk for not completing their degrees. The quality of teaching is hit or miss, students say. "Some of my professors are very engaged and focused on student success," says a junior, while "others seems to be disinterested. Most are in the middle."

Fifty-six percent of students graduated in the top quarter of their high school class and 91 percent hail from Maryland. "Students here tend to be on the nerdy end of the spectrum," says one senior, "but we embrace it." African Americans account for 19 percent of the student body, Hispanics 6 percent, and Asian Americans 23 percent. Students say political activism is largely confined to political organizations on campus. "It is an open campus and people debate freely without getting too out of control," a junior says. UMBC awards merit scholarships worth an average of $8,331.

Seventy-five percent of the student body resides in university housing. "I love residential life," says a senior. "Even the lowest quality freshmen dorms have their own private bathrooms and brand new furniture." Students say off-campus housing is plentiful and cheap, although parking on campus can be a chore. Living/Learning Communities connect students with similar interests and house them together in themed residence halls, which include the Center for Women and Information Technology, Emergency Health Services, Honors College, and Exploratory Learners. Campus dining options include a dining hall and the Commons, which offers a variety of fare, including Italian, Chinese, and Mexican cuisines. Campus security is described as "decent" and "UMBC actually has its own police force located on campus," says a junior. In addition, students must swipe their student ID to get into residence halls, and emergency call boxes are stationed throughout the campus.

Students complain that social life can be slow on campus. "A lot of students are not here on the weekends since they are commuters," says one student, "so there are fewer activities." Those who remain flock to campus clubs and service organizations in search of a good time. A student says, "Most social groups are formed through the organizations on campus—volunteer, cultural, religious, academic, and others." Only 5 percent of the men and women go Greek, and you're unlikely to find any alcohol-fueled toga parties here. "UMBC is not a place where alcohol and partying dictates who is cool or not," says a junior. "For this reason, alcohol abuse is not prevalent among the students." National acts—including comedians and rock stars—have been known to make an appearance at Quadmania, much to the students' delight. "Past performers have been the Violent Femmes, My Chemical Romance, All-American Rejects, and T-Pain," says a political science major. Block Party is "another carnival where all the residential students can win prizes and play games," gushes a student. "Last year I got to hit my Community Director in the face with a pie at one of the booths!" Homecoming always draws big crowds and popular road trips include treks into Baltimore (10 minutes away) and Washington, D.C. (40 minutes away).

The UMBC Retrievers compete in Division I and field a number of competitive teams, including men's soccer, volleyball, men's and women's track and field, men's

The Small Study Groups program encourages freshmen and sophomores to form study groups.

"Students here tend to be on the nerdy end of the spectrum."

Students complain that social life can be slow on campus.

and women's lacrosse, and men's and women's tennis. The men's basketball and lacrosse teams each brought home a conference title in recent years and men's swimming and diving have captured nine consecutive titles. UMBC is a perennial collegiate chess powerhouse (and regularly makes the Final Four of College Chess), and the university lures talented players with a bevy of scholarships. Intramurals are strong, too, and offer more than 15 sports and activities each semester. "There are intramurals and club teams all year-round," says a student. "Football is especially popular for the guys, and there are co-ed teams for the ladies, too." The Retriever Activities Center offers students 18,000 square feet of fitness and recreation space, including a gymnasium, weight room, fitness studio, indoor pool, and tennis courts.

> "UMBC is not a place where alcohol and partying dictates who is cool or not."

"I would say that UMBC is a school just coming into its own," says a junior. Unlike the gargantuan University of Maryland at College Park, UMBC capitalizes on its small size by providing students with intimate learning communities, solid academics, and ample resources on a manageable scale. It's a combination that appeals to a certain kind of student, according to one junior: "We're focused on doing big things and being influential people."

Overlaps

University of Maryland College Park, Towson, Johns Hopkins, University of Delaware, Virginia Tech

If You Apply To ➤ **UMBC:** Early action: Nov. 2. Regular admissions: Feb. 1. Financial aid: Feb. 14. Housing: May 1. Application fee: $50. Campus and alumni interviews: optional, informational. SATs: required. No Subject Tests. Essay question.

University of Massachusetts Amherst

Amherst, MA 01003

A liberal mecca in cosmopolitan and scenic western Massachusetts. UMass boasts strong study abroad programs and an international flavor. Science and engineering are also strong. Ready access to privates Amherst, Hampshire, Mount Holyoke, and Smith via the Five College Consortium*. Lack of big-time sports makes for a lower national profile than the likes of Michigan or UNC.

Website: www.umass.edu
Location: Small Town
Public
Total Enrollment: 22,429
Undergraduates: 20,177
Male/Female: 52/48
SAT Ranges: CR 530–630, M 560–660
ACT Ranges: 24–28
Financial Aid: 68%
Expense: Pub $ $ $ $
Student Loans: 71%
Average Debt: $ $ $
Phi Beta Kappa: Yes
Applicants: 34,326

A leading land grant university with more than a century of tradition, the University of Massachusetts Amherst offers students a dizzying array of majors and extracurricular options and the chance to take courses at nearby private colleges that are among the best anywhere. Students can live in one of the nation's top college towns, take advantage of an extensive research program and strong honors program, and enjoy an endless supply of social opportunities—without emptying their wallets. "We have so many resources," cheers one junior. "If we don't have what you want, we'll give you the opportunity to create it!"

> "We have nerds, jocks, theater buffs, hippies, and future CEOs."

UMass's sprawling 1,463-acre campus is centered on a pond full of ducks and swans, while architectural styles range from colonial to modern. The school is located on the outskirts of Amherst, a city that combines the energy of a bustling cosmopolitan center with the quaintness of an old New England town. Students agree that Amherst caters to college life.

UMass offers more than 100 undergraduate majors, and among them management and engineering are top-ranked. The English department is notable, and political science and creative writing also draw praise. Students report little difficulty getting into courses they want or are required to take, but some regard math, computer science, and the natural sciences as especially tough. Engineering students may face a bit of a challenge in finishing in four years; while most programs require 120 credit hours, the requirement of some engineering students may exceed that amount.

All undergraduates must complete two courses in writing; two courses in basic mathematics and analytic reasoning; two courses in the biological and physical world; four courses in the social world; two courses in social and cultural diversity; and an integrative experience. The writing requirement includes a freshman course taught in sections of 24 or fewer. Commonwealth Honors College offers qualified students special courses and sponsors interdisciplinary seminars, student gatherings, service projects, and a state-of-the-art residential complex that opened in late 2013. Students seeking to stand out from the "masses" might consider the interdisciplinary major in social thought and political economy, or the bachelor's degree in individual concentration, a design-it-yourself major. Twenty-two percent of a typical UMass class studies abroad at some point; more than 70 study abroad programs are available in over 40 countries. A growing number of service-learning courses provide opportunities for internships and community service. The Center for Student Business offers one of the most imaginative programs at UMass, allowing students to staff and manage nine campus businesses and learn how to work with others and resolve conflicts professionally.

> "There is literally always something to do on campus."

UMass's intellectual and political climate is extraordinarily fertile for a state university, perhaps in part because of its membership in the Five College Consortium*. This special alliance allows students to attend UMass and take courses at the other four consortium schools: Amherst College, Hampshire, Mount Holyoke, and Smith. The university is "definitely competitive," says a student. "The faculty have responded to the demands of serious students by challenging us to learn how to succeed." Full professors teach most courses, and some of the larger ones are broken down into smaller sections with graduate-level teaching assistants. "I have had some amazing, out-of-this-world professors," says a junior, "and some abysmal ones." Academic and career counseling receive mixed reviews, and it is usually up to students to pursue career help.

The majority of students are white public school graduates from Massachusetts. Out-of-state enrollment is capped at 25 percent of the student body, but applicants from other New England states are treated as Massachusetts residents for admission purposes if their own state schools don't offer the programs they want. "We have nerds, jocks, theater buffs, hippies, and future CEOs," says a senior. Four percent of UMass students are African American, while 8 percent are Asian American, and another 5 percent are Hispanic. The university has established cultural centers on campus, providing activities and support for students from different backgrounds, but affirmative action is still an issue, students report. "There are always rallies about better programs and aid for minorities," says a senior. Merit scholarships are handed out each year, and student athletes vie for 376 athletic scholarships in 21 sports.

UMass has the sixth-largest residence-hall system in the country. Sixty-one percent of students are housed among six residential areas. Freshmen can choose single-sex or co-ed living and also submit a list of their preferred living areas, but they're required to live on campus until sophomore year. About half of the freshmen end up in the Southwest Area, a "huge, city-like complex" with five high-rise towers and 11 low-rise residence halls. "The dorms are comfortable and safe," says a student. Approximately 4,000 first-year students participate in Epoch, a yearlong residential program, or one of the university's other living/learning communities. Upperclassmen tend to move off campus.

(continued)

Accepted: 63%
Enrolled: 21%
Grad in 6 Years: 70%
Returning Freshmen: 88%
Academics: ✍ ✍ ✍ ½
Social: 🐿 🐿 🐿 🐿
Q of L: ★ ★ ★
Admissions: (413) 545-0222
Email Address: mail@ admissions.umass.edu

Strongest Programs:
Psychology
Communication
Biology
Accounting
Hospitality and Tourism
  Management

Students seeking to stand out from the "masses" might consider the interdisciplinary major in social thought and political economy, or the bachelor's degree in individual concentration, a design-it-yourself major.

UMass has the sixth-largest residence-hall system in the country.

UMass offers "a vast social life," says a student, with noisy dorms, overflowing frat houses, and frequent off-campus parties. "There is literally always something to do on campus," a junior says. Both on campus and off, alcohol policies are strict and well enforced; underage drinking is many times confined to students' rooms, if they can get away with it. First-time underage offenders are sent to alcohol-education programs. Six percent of the men and 6 percent of the women belong to one of the nearly two dozen fraternities and sororities, respectively, but they are somewhat out of the mainstream. A free public transportation system allows maximum mobility—not only among the Five Colleges, but also to nearby towns, which are graced with a number of exceptional bookshops.

Settled in the Pioneer Valley and surrounded by the Berkshire foothills, Amherst is close to good skiing, hiking, and canoeing areas. It's also 90 miles west of Boston, 150 miles north of New York City, and 25 miles south of Vermont and New Hampshire, making a car very useful (and very expensive if you get too many tickets from overzealous campus cops, students say).

Varsity sports are popular, and UMass Minutemen have been a model for achieving gender equity in athletics. The football team recently joined the Mid-American Conference and the Football Bowl Division. The men's lacrosse and swimming and diving squads are solid, as are women's lacrosse, field hockey, and softball. Two on-campus gyms offer facilities for the recreational athlete, and two Olympic-size skating rinks mark the recent reintroduction of intercollegiate hockey to the university. Additionally, the recreation center includes a weight and fitness center, a three-court gym, lounge spaces, and multipurpose rooms.

UMass is big enough to offer a vast number of academic and extracurricular opportunities, though at times it can feel impersonal and overwhelming. But with special residential programs that group students with similar languages, cultures, and lifestyles, many students will easily find a home in Amherst.

Overlaps

Northeastern, Boston University, University of Connecticut, University of Vermont, University of New Hampshire, Boston College, Tufts, University of Rhode Island

If You Apply To ➤

UMass: Early action: Nov. 1. Regular admissions: Jan. 15. Application fee: $75. Campus and alumni interviews: optional, informational. SATs or ACTs: required. Subject Tests: optional. Accepts the Common Application. Essay question.

Massachusetts Institute of Technology

Room 3–108, 77 Massa, Cambridge, MA 02139

If you're a science genius, come to MIT to find out how little you really know. No other school makes such a massive assault on the ego (with little in the way of support to help you pick up the pieces). Technology is a given, but MIT also prides itself on leading programs in economics, political science, and management. Those who don't study 24/7 can enjoy MIT's prime location near downtown Boston.

Website: web.mit.edu
Location: City Center
Private
Total Enrollment: 10,955
Undergraduates: 4,456
Male/Female: 55/45

Founded in 1861, the Massachusetts Institute of Technology continues to attract the brightest minds from near and far. MIT teachers and students have discovered many of the technological innovations that we take for granted, from electromagnets and radar to pocket calculators and the decoding of the human genome. The school is a magnet for minds like Tim Berners-Lee, the Brit who invented the World Wide Web, to Noam Chomsky, the linguist and antiwar activist. Graduates have formed more than 25,000 companies that, among other things, employ a quarter of the workforce of Silicon Valley. While Harvard stuck to the English model of Oxbridge classical education, with its emphasis on Latin and Greek, MIT looked to the German system of learning based on research and hands-on experimentation. This emphasis is enshrined in the school motto—*Mens et Manus*, or Mind and Hand—as well as its logo, showing a gowned scholar standing beside an ironmonger bearing a hammer and anvil. Intellect and craftsmanship pervade the classrooms and students here are not so much taught as engaged and inspired.

MIT is located on 168 acres that extend more than a mile along the Cambridge side of the Charles River basin facing historic Beacon Hill and the central sections of Boston. The main campus of neoclassical architecture carved from limestone was designed by Welles Bosworth and constructed between 1913 and 1920. Since then, more modern designs in brick and glass have been added. The buildings have a utilitarian aura; most are even known by number instead of by name. Athletic playing fields, recreational buildings, dorms, and dining halls are closely arranged on the campus and provide a sense of unity. Sculptures and murals, including the works of Alexander Calder, Henry Moore, and Louise Nevelson, are found throughout the campus. The university's Brain and Cognitive Sciences Complex is the world's largest neuroscience center.

> **"The courses demand your full attention and a lot of extra work."**

Originally called Boston Tech and now frequently referred to as "the Tute," MIT stresses science and engineering studies with a "concern for human values and social goals." Every science and engineering department is superb. The biology department is a leader in medical technology and the search for designer genes. Nevertheless, pure sciences tend to play second fiddle to the engineering fields that, along with computer science, draw the bulk of the majors. Electrical engineering and computer science are almost universally credited as tops in the nation. Students in these two areas may pursue a five-year-degree option, where they can obtain a professional master's degree upon completion of their studies. Biomedical, chemical, and mechanical engineering; physics; and the aeronautics department are also highly praised programs. The most popular majors include electrical engineering and computer science, mechanical engineering, computer science and engineering, physics, and mathematics. The humanities are strong here as well, though not on par with science and technology-oriented programs.

MIT has always attracted top professors in a broad range of fields. Political science, management, urban studies, linguistics, graphics for modern art, and holography—and just about anything else that can be linked to a computer—are strong, and the minority who major in these subjects receive enough personal attention to make any college student envious. "Some professors really know how to engage the interest of the student," says a senior.

MIT is tops in technology, but also strong in the social sciences, especially economics. The administration worries that engineers of the future will need first-rate technical skills coupled with a good understanding of technology's social context and marketplace. As one dean puts it, "Too many MIT graduates end up working for too many Princeton and Harvard graduates." Hence, a minor in management is now offered "in response to employers seeking graduates who are better prepared for today's increasingly complex responsibilities." Perhaps to help ensure that they will be able to make their future discoveries known, students must take four communication-intensive subjects. Of course, there is also the intensive science requirement, which includes six math/science courses and two restricted electives in science, as well as a lab or two. There's also an eight-credit physical education requirement and a swimming test.

> **"MIT is intense and will take you for quite a ride."**

One of MIT's most successful innovations is the Undergraduate Research Opportunities Program (UROP), a year-round program that facilitates student/faculty

(continued)

SAT Ranges: CR 670–770, M 740–800
ACT Ranges: 32–35
Financial Aid: 89%
Expense: Pr $ $ $
Student Loans: 41%
Average Debt: $
Phi Beta Kappa: Yes
Applicants: 18,109
Accepted: 9%
Enrolled: 70%
Grad in 6 Years: 93%
Returning Freshmen: 97%
Academics: ✐ ✐ ✐ ✐ ✐
Social: ☎ ☎ ☎
Q of L: ★ ★ ★
Admissions: (617) 253-3400
Email Address: admissions@mit.edu

Strongest Programs:
Engineering
Computer Science
Management Science
Natural Sciences

Intellect and craftsmanship pervade the classrooms and students here are not so much taught as engaged and inspired.

research projects. Considered one of the best programs of its kind in the nation, it allows students to earn course credit or stipends for doing research. Flexible, small-group alternatives for freshmen include five learning communities and the Experimental Study Group, which allows a self-paced course of study based on tutorials instead of a traditional lecture format. Not only can these offer support, but they can also engage geniuses who excel on exams without attending the lectures. The traditionally humongous introductory physics lectures have also been replaced with smaller, hands-on classes that emphasize collaboration. Along with Harvard, the university has founded an online learning consortium called edX that allows students around the world access to many courses. On campus, students have access to world-renowned professors and the Nobel Prize winners who carry lighter teaching loads to allow them time for research and interaction with students. Faculty advising is "pretty good for freshmen," one student says, but after that, "it's as good as you make it." The vast library system contains more than two million volumes, including some one-of-a-kind manuscripts on the history of science and technology. One library is even open 24 hours a day, and "some students spend the majority of their time (awake or asleep) there," one student reports.

> "The average MIT student can be characterized as having a passion and singular drive for what they really want in life."

A pass/no record grading system helps freshmen adjust to "MIT brainstretching": In the first semester, freshmen receive grades of P, D, or F in all subjects they take. P means a C-or-better performance; Ds or Fs do not receive credit or appear on the permanent record. In the second semester, the Ps are replaced by A, B, or C; Ds and Fs do not receive credit and are only noted internally. Grades or not, most MIT students set themselves a breathtaking pace. "MIT is intense and will take you for quite a ride," a biology/premed student says. "The courses demand your full attention and a lot of extra work," another says. Additional relief from "tooling" (that is, studying) is found through the optional January Independent Activities Period, which offers noncredit seminars, workshops, and activities in fields outside the regular curriculum, as well as for-credit subjects. Participation in the engineering co-op program, junior year abroad (including a major program at Cambridge University in England), or cross-registration at all-female Wellesley College are other helpful ways to get young noses away from the grindstone. Terrascope is an integrated studies program that encourages first-year students to explore how core disciplines, as well as engineering and the humanities, can help us grasp the structure and evolution of our planet.

While MIT somewhat justly earned an image as a "conservative, rich, white boys' school" in the past, there is certainly enough racial and ethnic variety to beat that rap today. African Americans account for 6 percent of the student body, Hispanics 15 percent, and Asian Americans a hefty 24 percent. Ninety-eight percent of students come from the top 10th of their high school class, and average SAT and ACT scores are simply mind-boggling. "The average MIT student can be characterized as having a passion and singular drive for what they really want in life," offers a chemical engineering major. In an effort to help financially needy students, MIT has eliminated both loans and tuition for families with incomes below $75,000 a year. And thanks to a $24 million gift, the university will increase undergraduate enrollment by 250, to 4,500 students.

Ninety percent of undergraduates live on campus, and all freshmen are required to live in the dorms. Guaranteed housing is either single-sex or co-ed; the dorms are in the middle of campus, and most of the fraternities and living groups are a mile or less away across the Charles. Meal plans can be mandatory for dorms that don't have kitchens, or optional for equipped quarters. Frat types feast on

The university's Brain and Cognitive Sciences Complex is the world's largest neuroscience center.

spreads prepared by their full-time cooks, and the Kosher Kitchen provides some refuge for others.

MIT's social scene is varied. There are campus movies and lectures if one can escape the ubiquitous workload worming its way into the uneasy consciousness of a techie's every waking hour. And there's the student-friendly city of Boston, with its many restaurants, clubs, parks, shopping opportunities, and more than 50 other colleges. On-campus dances, parties, and dorm activities keep other students busy. Most on-campus drinking for over-21 students is relaxed and accepted, "as long as the alcohol does not result in unlawful behavior or cause any problems," a student explains. The Greek scene attracts 42 percent of the men and 31 percent of the women. For those with the urge to roam, the multifaceted greater Boston metropolis sits only a few subway stops away. MIT's alcohol-prevention program is considered a national model, and drug-prevention initiatives are also comprehensive.

When the MIT megabrains take a break, practical jokes, or "hacks" (described by one student as "practical jokes with technical merit") are sure to follow. In past years, popular hacks have included disguising the dome of the main academic building as a giant breast, dismantling a campus police car and reassembling its body at the top of the tower, unscrewing and reversing all the chairs in a 500-seat lecture hall, and, of course, welding shut Harvard's gates. Hacking can also involve Harry Potter–style late-night explorations by students in the tunnels and shafts that run through restricted parts of the campus, a practice that's definitely frowned upon by the school.

When not studying or hacking, these engineering jocks often turn into real jocks. MIT has 33 varsity sports, the most of any Division III school. The Engineers field a number of competitive teams and have earned 19 NEWMAC championships in the past two years. Solid teams include men's tennis and cross-country; men's soccer, men's water polo, men's and women's track and field, women's fencing, and women's volleyball. Hockey is popular, and even more popular is the extensive, well-organized intramural program (75 percent participate), with sports ranging from Ping-Pong, billiards, and bowling to the more traditional basketball and volleyball. Everyone has access to MIT's extensive athletic facilities. Supposedly, there are more clubs and organizations at MIT than at any other school in the country, and a sampling of the offerings explains why. The Rocket Society, the Guild of Bell Ringers, and a singing group called the Chorallaries are only a few of the diverse interests on this campus.

Though students often wonder what life at a so-called typical college would have been like, chances of survival and even satisfaction at MIT are excellent. Students are able to comprehend the incredible experience of attending one of the nation's leading academic powerhouses. A biology major puts it bluntly: "It will take you right up to what you think your limits are, and then MIT will shatter them and make you realize how great your potential is."

The most popular majors include electrical engineering and computer science, mechanical engineering, computer science and engineering, physics, and mathematics.

"MIT will shatter [your limits] and make you realize how great your potential is."

Overlaps

Harvard, Princeton, Stanford, Yale, Caltech, Columbia, Cornell, University of Pennslyvania

If You Apply To ➤

MIT: Early action: Nov. 1. Regular admissions: Jan. 1. Financial aid: Feb. 15. Application fee: $75. No campus interviews. Alumni interviews: recommended, evaluative. SATs or ACTs: required. Subject Tests: required (math, science). Short essays. Looks for aptitude in math and science.

McGill University: See page 350.

P.O. Box 248025, Coral Gables, FL 33124-4616

Football is the main reason UM is on the map, but it's hardly the only one. Renowned programs in marine science and music are big draws; business is also strong. Housing takes the form of a distinctive residential college system that offers living/learning opportunities. Attracts more Northerners than other leading Florida universities.

Website: www.miami.edu
Location: Suburban
Private
Total Enrollment: 14,744
Undergraduates: 9,759
Male/Female: 49/51
SAT Ranges: CR 600–700,
   M 630–720
ACT Ranges: 28–32
Financial Aid: 76%
Expense: Pr $ $ $
Student Loans: 45%
Average Debt: $ $ $
Phi Beta Kappa: Yes
Applicants: 27,757
Accepted: 40%
Enrolled: 18%
Grad in 6 Years: 81%
Returning Freshmen: 91%
Academics: ✍ ✍ ✍
Social: ☎ ☎ ☎ ☎
Q of L: ★ ★ ★
Admissions: (305) 284-4323
Email Address: admission@
   miami.edu

Strongest Programs:
Business
Biology
Communications
Health Professions

Year-round sunshine and the colorful Miami culture could make even the most dedicated students forget why they are at college. But at the University of Miami, students can have their fun and get a solid education at the same time. The university boasts strong programs in marine science, music, and business, and the preprofessional programs are red hot. Sound academics, a diverse and energetic student population, and sandy beaches and subtropical climate create a perfect storm that attracts talented Hurricanes from far and wide. "The University of Miami is consistently evolving," says a senior. "We have climbed in the national rankings, and our school has become more innovative and overall a more complete college experience."

> **"Our school has become more innovative and overall a more complete college experience."**

Twenty minutes from Key Biscayne and Miami's beaches, and 10 minutes from downtown Miami, the university's 239-acre campus is located in tranquil suburbia and boasts tall palms, wide lawns, flowering vines, outdoor sculptures, and even a butterfly garden. With its own lake in the middle of the campus (and on the cover of most brochures), the campus is architecturally varied, from postwar, international-style structures to modern buildings, most with open-air breezeways to let in the warm winds. Recent campus additions include the Neuroscience Annex, the Schwartz Center for Athletic Excellence, and an addition to the wellness center.

Miami has one of the nation's top programs in marine biology and was the first American university to offer a four-year undergraduate degree in music engineering. With 12 schools and colleges and more than 180 majors and programs, UM offers a broad range of preprofessional options as well as those across the liberal arts. It also boasts a unique program in jazz. The university's Dual-Degree Honors Programs in medicine, marine geology, Latin American studies, exercise physiology, law, and biochemistry and molecular biology receive high marks. Also valued is the University's signature Hands-On, Early-On approach, which encourages undergraduates to carry out research in collaboration with faculty and peers. Business/marketing is the most popular degree, followed by biological/life sciences, social sciences, communication/journalism, and health professions and related programs.

> **"There is a high level of cooperation and a high level of academic excellence at the same time."**

UM's academic environment manages to be intense yet laid-back. "There is a high level of cooperation and a high level of academic excellence at the same time," says a junior. "A school does not have to be cut-throat in order to foster a high degree of achievement, a sentiment carried by teachers and students alike." Students give professors high marks for knowledge and accessibility, with full professors teaching most courses, including those with freshmen. "Most of the professors are really knowledgeable about the topic they're teaching and want you to do well," says a junior. The new Cognates Program of General Education features three areas of knowledge: arts and humanities; people and society; and STEM (science, technology, engineering, and math). Students looking for a change of pace can take advantage of Miami's summer semester program in the Bahamas or more than 100 other options in dozens of countries such as Australia, Israel, France, Japan, the Netherlands, and Argentina.

The university invites the top 10 percent of the entering freshmen class to join the General Honors Program, where students maintain an overall academic average of 3.5 and complete at least two honors courses per academic year. The stereotypical beach bum who drops by for a couple of classes in the morning, spends the rest of the day at the beach, and almost never sees the inside of the library need not apply to UM.

Fifty-two percent of UM undergraduates come from out of state, including quite a few from the Northeast and upper Midwest, seeking respite from harsh weather. UM is unusual due to the incredible diversity of its student body; Hispanics account for a substantial 23 percent of the total, African Americans 7 percent, and Asian Americans 6 percent. International students, who account for 12 percent of undergraduates, play an integral role in the life of the university. Students say that such diversity is one of UM's best assets. "You're not going to see clones walking around our campus," says a microbiology major. Students say it sometimes seems as if Spanish is the university's mother tongue. Nearly 2,000 merit scholarships are available as well as athletic scholarships.

Miami offers a distinctive system of five co-ed residential colleges, modeled after those at Oxford or Cambridge. Each residential college is directed by a master—a senior faculty member who organizes seminars, concerts, lectures, social events, and dinners. Faculty members often host study breaks in their homes and provide guest speakers from all walks of life to discuss current issues. Generally, students give the dorms average marks; 39 percent of undergrads live on campus, and others bunk in off-campus apartments or commute. Each floor of the two freshmen residential colleges is assigned to a single gender, while the other three residential colleges are set up in a suite arrangement and assigned one gender per suite. Scrounging up food on **"We are a college in a big city."** campus is easy; the residential colleges have their own cafeterias with a variety of plans, from eight to unlimited meals, and there is a kosher alternative. "People always seem to worry about food," says one student, "but I have found it to be quite enjoyable at UM as long as you do not get stuck behind the football players in line— nothing left after!" Campus security is said to be strong. "Campus security is excellent, and students always feel safe," a biomedical engineering major reports. "The Emergency Notification Network sends out texts, calls, and emails to all students in the event of the any incident on campus or close by."

Coral Gables is not a college town. "We are a college in a big city," says a junior, which means access to events such as Art Basel, the Ultra Music Festival, and professional sports teams (Dolphins, Heat, Marlins). On the weekends, Miami students frequent nearby bars or the campus. Rathskeller, a popular student meeting place that offers food, entertainment, and a venue for postgame parties, serves alcohol to students at least 21 years old, but alcohol policies on campus are strict for underage students. Fraternities still manage to thrive, accounting for 16 percent of the men and providing a space for much of the underage drinking at UM (although not during rush, which is dry). The sororities, with no housing of their own, attract 16 percent of the women. Although the 34 fraternities and sororities claim 1,600 brothers and sisters, a junior points out that "unlike other schools, our social life does not revolve only around Greek life." The biggest non-sports-related event each year is Ghandi Day, which students spend doing community service.

UM offers a plethora of other social opportunities. "There are some schools where it's basically house parties, frat parties, bars, or nothing," muses an advertising major. "Here, this is not the case. While all of those things are still offered, we

Business/marketing is the most popular degree, followed by biological/ life sciences, social sciences, communication/ journalism, and health professions and related programs.

The stereotypical beach bum who drops by for a couple of classes in the morning, spends the rest of the day at the beach, and almost never sees the inside of the library need not apply to UM.

also have a busy on-campus social life, with multiple events being held all throughout the weekends including movies, concerts, and more." Those who shun sand between their toes head to the boutiques in Coconut Grove, Bayside, or South Beach, or attend on-campus events, such as International Week and Sportsfest, which pits dorms against each other in sports ranging from flag football to obstacle courses. Public transportation and the Hurry 'Cane Shuttle service run in front of the residential colleges, but most students recommend a car in order to get "the full Florida effect." Parking can be a problem, though, says a senior: "If you want a parking space, you need to get to school by 8:00 a.m." The best road trips are Key West, Key Largo, the everglades, and, of course, UM football games against the University of Florida and Florida State.

Several years ago the university's athletic program was embroiled in a major scandal involving allegations of improper gifts to athletes and coaches by overzealous boosters, but such challenges have barely put a damper on students' enthusiasm for big-time athletics. UM competes in the Atlantic Coast Conference. The most competitive intercollegiate teams are football, baseball, basketball, women's tennis and women's basketball, which won the ACC regular season championship in 2011. The men's basketball team won the regular season and tournament championship in 2013. In a bow to Harry Potter fans, the extensive intramural sports program includes quidditch. The university also has a state-of-the-art fitness, recreation, and wellness facility that includes an 18,000-square-foot fitness room and basketball, racquetball, squash, and tennis courts, plus an indoor pool and a juice bar.

It's hard to imagine a school in the Sunshine State without a generous allotment of fun, and UM is no exception. "Though we're not the number one party school in the nation anymore, we still really love to have a great time," observes a junior. That said, UM students these days are just as likely to search long and hard for the perfect instrumental phrase or mathematical proof as they are to scope out the perfect wave. "It is the whole college experience at U of M," says one sophomore. "It is so fulfilling and rewarding."

Overlaps

University of Florida, Florida State, University of Central Florida, University of South Florida, Boston University, Florida International, NYU, University of Southern California

If You Apply To ➤

Miami: Early decision and early action: Nov. 1. Regular admissions: Jan. 1. Financial aid: Feb. 1. Housing: May 1. Application fee: $70. Campus interviews: optional, informational. No alumni interviews. SATs or ACTs: required. Subject Tests: optional; math and science required for dual-degree Honors Program in Medicine. Apply to particular schools or programs. Accepts the Common Application. Essay question.

Miami University (OH)

301 S. Campus Avenue, Oxford, OH 45056

Rather than disappear into the black hole of Ohio State, top students in the Buckeye state come here to feel as if they are going to an elite private university. MU is the honors public university in one of the nation's largest states. Twice the size of William and Mary, it has the same classic look but is much less selective. Miami's top draw is business, and its tenor is preppy/conservative. Bring your best clothes.

Website: www.miamioh.edu
Location: Small Town
Public
Total Enrollment: 15,655

This Miami is about 1,000 miles from South Beach, but that doesn't mean it's without sizzle. The academic kind, that is. Miami University is actually tucked into a corner of Ohio and is gaining national recognition as an excellent state university that has the true look and feel of a private, with a picture-perfect campus and high-caliber student body.

The university is staked out on 2,000 wooded acres in the center of an urban triangle of approximately three million people, encompassing Cincinnati and Dayton, Ohio, and Richmond, Indiana. The campus is dressed in the modified Georgian style of the colonial American period, and it remains as impeccably groomed as its sharply attired students. A number of renovations have been completed, including upgrades to the Shriver Center Bookstore and Laws Hall. New residence halls opened in late 2013 and a huge, state-of-the-art student center opens in winter 2014.

Miami University was founded in 1809 to provide a classical liberal education and has never strayed from its central commitment to liberal arts. All undergraduates must complete the Global Miami Plan, which provides them with a background in fine arts, humanities, social sciences, natural sciences, formal reasoning, and globally oriented courses/study abroad. Popular majors include marketing, finance, accountancy, zoology, and psychology. For those with an inclination toward forestry or the paper industry, the university offers a concentration in paper science and engineering and an undergraduate degree in engineering management with a technical specialty in paper and environmental engineering.

"Miami really emphasizes study abroad."

University requirements, or foundation courses, provide for a broad education, and all undergraduates must complete foundation courses in English composition; fine arts; humanities; social sciences; biological and physical sciences; mathematics; formal reasoning or technology; and global perspectives. Additional requirements include 12 credits of an advanced liberal education focus consisting of nine credits of thematic and sequential study outside of the student's major, and three credits of the Senior Capstone Experience, which ties in liberal education with the specialized knowledge of their major. Interdisciplinary studies, economics, and music are well regarded.

The academic atmosphere at Miami is competitive but not cut-throat. "The classes are difficult but very enjoyable," says one sophomore. "The teachers are always pushing me to become a better student and person." Those professors are also lauded for their knowledge and willingness to help. "The teaching at Miami is incredible. Professors are always available to talk and if they are too busy to meet with you, there are several professors in each division who you can be referred to and who can answer your questions," one student says. Thirty percent of classes have fewer than 19 students, and most are taught by full professors, though graduate students do appear behind the lectern from time to time. Many students complain that it's increasingly difficult to get into required classes—especially foundation courses—and that this can complicate the task of graduating in four years. "I've had to force-add classes or wait to take them in the summer," gripes a speech communications major.

Forty-two percent of students head for foreign climes each year. "Miami really emphasizes study abroad," confirms one junior. The Dolibois European Center in Luxembourg offers a semester- or year-long program in the liberal arts and an opportunity to live with a foreign family. Other exchange opportunities include universities in Denmark, Japan, Mexico, Austria, and England, as well as summer programs in over 90 countries. Undergraduate research gets a lot of attention at Miami—the competitive Undergraduate Summer Scholars Program gives 100 students a stipend, free tuition, and a project allowance to complete a nine-week faculty-mentored project. The Winter Term allows students to take a class, study abroad, conduct research, or participate in an internship during the three-week term.

"Miami is made up of a lot of preps who are well dressed and have money to spend," says one student. Another adds that students are ambitious and well rounded: "Most students on campus are involved in some sort of extracurricular activity, whether it's a student organization or Greek life. And most will graduate having spent some time abroad or having worked in a professional setting thanks to

(continued)

Undergraduates: 14,605
Male/Female: 48/52
SAT Ranges: CR 530–630, M 550–660
ACT Ranges: 24–29
Financial Aid: 66%
Expense: Pub $ $ $ $
Student Loans: 55%
Average Debt: $ $ $
Phi Beta Kappa: Yes
Applicants: 20,314
Accepted: 73%
Enrolled: 25%
Grad in 6 Years: 80%
Returning Freshmen: 89%
Academics: ✍ ✍ ✍ ✍ ½
Social: ☎ ☎ ☎
Q of L: ★ ★ ★
Admissions: (513) 529-2531
Email Address: admission@miamioh.edu

Strongest Programs:
Finance
Marketing
Accountancy
Zoology
Psychology

When it comes to social issues like abortion and gay marriage, however, students remain decidedly liberal.

an internship." Four percent of the student body is African American, 3 percent Hispanic, and 2 percent Asian American. Sixty-six percent of students are from Ohio, and the campus has a reputation for conservatism. "This is a hyperengaged campus," says one sophomore. Paul Ryan, the unsuccessful Republican candidate for

> **"Students tend to live off campus after their second year."**

vice president in 2012, learned his trickle-down economics here. The *New York Times* suggested that Miami appeals to Republican families as "a place unlikely to turn their children against them." When it comes to social issues like abortion and gay marriage, however, students remain decidedly liberal. The Office of Diversity Affairs, the Vice President for Institutional Diversity, and various student groups regularly hold events designed to encourage engagement around issues of difference, diversity, and privilege. Thousands of merit scholarships and 270 athletic scholarships are awarded annually.

Forty-eight percent of the student body call the campus home. "Students tend to live off campus after their second year, but the dorms are comfortable and typically well maintained," says one junior. A few of the dorms remain single-sex and are accompanied by visitation rules, and "the furniture is fine and all are livable," according to one student. Students report that campus dining options are diverse and tasty, and campus security is said to be good, "mostly due to the fact that we are in a sleepy little town in Ohio."

"Miami is pretty much in the middle of nowhere Southwest Ohio, so the students stay on campus," says one student. Drinking is a popular pastime, but doesn't dominate the social scene. The school is "very strict about alcohol violations," explains one student. "There is no tolerance for minors drinking on campus." A lot of socializing takes place in the restaurants, bars, and clubs of Oxford. Twenty-four percent of the men and 25 percent of the women belong to fraternities or sororities, respectively. In fact, Miami is known as the "mother of fraternities" because several national ones began here. Despite the hard-partying reputation of the Greeks, Miami boasts one of the best graduation rates in the nation among public institutions.

"Oxford may be a small town, but there is plenty to do," says a strategic communications major. For students who crave brighter lights and bigger city, Cincinnati is about 35 miles away. Other annual events include Make a Difference Day in cooperation with Oxford, homecoming, and continued rivalries with Ohio University.

Traditionally, Miami's ice hockey, men's basketball, women's volleyball, synchronized skating, softball, women's swimming, and women's tennis teams are the most successful.

Traditionally, Miami's ice hockey, men's basketball, women's volleyball, synchronized skating, softball, women's swimming, and women's tennis teams are the most successful. In the past two years, a number of Redhawks teams have won championships, including field hockey, women's tennis (fifth straight MAC championship and NCAA appearance), ice hockey, women's soccer, women's swimming, softball, and synchronized skating (ninth consecutive national title in collegiate Division I). Intramurals and club sports attract more than 9,000 participants annually, and popular sports include broomball, soccer, flag football, and ultimate Frisbee.

Miami University of Ohio, with its strong emphasis on liberal arts and its opportunities for research, travel abroad, and leadership, is looked upon as one of the rising stars among state universities. The school effectively combines a wide range of academic programs with the personal attention ordinarily found only at much smaller upscale institutions.

Overlaps

Ohio State, University of Dayton, Ohio University, University of Cincinnati, Indiana University, Xavier, University of Michigan, University of Kentucky

---

If You Apply To ➤

Miami (OH): Early decision: Nov. 15. Early action: Dec. 1. Regular admissions: Feb. 1. Financial aid: Feb. 15. Application fee: $50. No campus or alumni interviews. SATs or ACTs: required. Subject Tests: recommended. Accepts the Common Application. Essay question: Common Application.

1220 Student Activities Building, Ann Arbor, MI 48109-1316

The most interesting mass of humanity east of UC–Berkeley. UM is among the nation's best in most subjects, but undergraduates must elbow their way to the front to get the full benefit. Superb honors and living/learning programs are the best bet for highly motivated students. Out-of-state families may need a second mortgage to cover pricey tuition.

One of the nation's elite public universities, Michigan offers an excellent faculty, dynamite athletics, an endless number of special programs, and the most interesting collection of students east of Berkeley. "Michigan is a special place because it has a deep history and reputation," says a senior. "It is an excellent school and no matter what degree you have, it is respected."

Situated on 3,129 acres, Michigan's campus is so extensive that newcomers may want to come equipped with maps and a GPS system to find their way to class. The university is divided into two main campuses. Central Campus, the heart of the university, houses most of Michigan's 19 schools and colleges. North Campus, which is two miles northeast of Central, is home to the College of Engineering; the School of Music, Theatre, and Dance; the School of Art and Design; and the College of Architecture and Urban Planning. Other campus areas include the Medical Center Complex, containing seven hospitals and 15 outpatient facilities, and South Campus, featuring state-of-the art athletic facilities. Architecturally, the main drag of campus features a wide range of styles, from the classical Angell Hall to the recently completed ultracontemporary Museum of Art addition.

Academically, students describe the courses as challenging and rigorous but not cut-throat competitive. "People always want to do their best, and they work very hard to do so," says a senior. The university ranks among the best in the nation in many fields of study, mainly because it attracts some of the biggest names in academia to teach and research in Ann Arbor. The College of Literature, Science, and the Arts is the largest school at Michigan. The College of Engineering and School of Business are well respected, and the university's programs in health-related fields are also top-notch.

> "Michigan is a special place because it has a deep history and reputation."

Students report that professors are "knowledgeable." One student says, "The professors here are intelligent and seem to enjoy teaching." Students claim there is excellent academic and career advising available, but only for those who seek it. The administration, however, notes that the advising office, which registers nearly 12,000 clients each year, offers individually tailored services and workshops. The campus Career Center processes about 120,000 transactions each year, provides individual and group career counseling/planning and individual job placement, and works with 950 companies annually in recruiting UM graduating students.

Michigan's special academic programs seek to offer the best of both worlds—personalized attention and a large university setting. More than 600 active degree programs, including more than 200 undergraduate majors as well as individualized concentrations, are offered, mainly through the College of Literature, Science, and the Arts. Special programs include double majors, accelerated programs, independent study, field study, and internships. The Screen Arts & Cultures major balances studies and production, with studies occupying approximately two-thirds of a student's coursework and the remaining one-third devoted to creative, hands-on projects. In addition, students can choose from several small interdisciplinary programs.

Website: www.umich.edu
Location: Small City
Public
Total Enrollment: 40,721
Undergraduates: 26,954
Male/Female: 51/49
SAT Ranges: CR 610–700, M 650–760
ACT Ranges: 28–32
Financial Aid: 55%
Expense: Pub $ $ $ $
Student Loans: 44%
Average Debt: $ $ $
Phi Beta Kappa: Yes
Applicants: 42,544
Accepted: 37%
Enrolled: 39%
Grad in 6 Years: 90%
Returning Freshmen: 97%
Academics: ✐ ✐ ✐ ✐ ✐
Social: ☎ ☎ ☎
Q of L: ★ ★ ★
Admissions: (734) 764-7433
Email Address: N/A

Strongest Programs:
Premed
Engineering
Art and Design
Architecture
Music
Business

The instructors live and teach in the residential hall, the Residential College, and the Lloyd Hall Scholars Program. The Comprehensive Studies Program allows students to become part of a community of scholars who work in programs designed to best realize an individual student's potential.

Students have the chance to visit and study abroad in more than 40 countries.

The University of Michigan's long-established honors program, considered to be one of the best in the nation, offers qualified students special honors courses and opportunities to participate in individual research or collaborative research, seminars, and special academic advisors. A preferred admissions program guarantees 150 top high school students admission to Michigan's professional programs in dentistry, biomedical engineering, social work, architecture, or pharmacy, provided they make satisfactory progress during their first years. The Undergraduate Research Opportunities Program enables students to work outside the classroom with a small group of students and a faculty member of their choice. The most popular majors at University of Michigan are psychology, economics, political science, business administration, and English. Michigan also offers a number of foreign language majors not found at many other places, including Arabic, Armenian, Persian, Turkish, and Islamic studies.

No courses are required of all freshmen at Michigan, but all students are required to complete some coursework in English (including composition), foreign languages, natural sciences, social sciences, and humanities. Students in the College of Literature, Science, and the Arts must also take courses in quantitative reasoning and race or ethnicity. In addition, the university offers a series of seminars designed specifically for freshmen and sophomores, which are taught by tenured and tenure-track faculty. Off-campus opportunities abound at UM. Students have the chance to visit and study abroad in more than 40 countries. Specific programs include a year abroad in a French or German university, a business program in Paris, summer internships in selected majors, and special trips organized by individual departments. Michigan produces more Fulbright scholars than any other U.S. university.

The University of Michigan's admissions office sifts through some of the best students in the country. Sixty-two percent hail from Michigan. The student body is remarkably diverse for a state university. In fact, Michigan's Program on Intergroup Relations, Conflict, and Community was recognized by former president Clinton's Initiative on Race as one of 14 "promising practices" that

"Ann Arbor is the quintessential college town."

successfully bridge racial divides in communities across America. Minorities now comprise more than one-fourth of UM's total enrollment: African Americans and Hispanics combined make up 8 percent of the student body, and Asian Americans make up another 12 percent. There is a large and well-organized Jewish community at Michigan, and gays and lesbians are also organized and prominent. While the student body is more conservative today than it was a decade ago, it is still "most noticeably liberal," says a history major, and political issues flare up from time to time on campus. Michigan really socks it to out-of-staters with a hefty surcharge roughly triple the in-state rate. Students can vie for thousands of merit scholarships averaging $9,756, as well as 486 athletic scholarships for men and women in 27 sports. The "M-Pact" Program replaces loans with grants for the most needy in-state applicants (those with an expected family contribution of $6,000 or less).

The Comprehensive Studies Program allows students to become part of a community of scholars who work in programs designed to best realize an individual student's potential.

Dormitories at UM traditionally have well-defined personalities. After a year-long renovation, East Quad reopened for the fall 2013 term. As the home to the Residential College, the Michigan Community Scholars Program, and the Gender-Inclusive Learning Experience, East Quad is perhaps the most "open-minded" dorm on campus. North Quad is the newest dorm on campus and the focal point for international and intercultural programming. On-campus housing is comfortable and well maintained, and 34 percent of students reside there. "Many of the juniors and seniors live off campus. The housing is nothing to write home about," says a senior.

Housing is guaranteed for all incoming freshmen, leaving many upperclassmen to play the lottery. For the student who wants to live off campus, the UM housing office provides information, listings, and advice for finding suitable accommodations. Other alternatives include fraternity and sorority houses, and a large number of college- and privately owned co-ops. As for concerns about safety on campus, a student says, "Campus security is pretty good and most people I know feel safe."

Detroit is a little less than an hour away, but most students become quite fond of the picturesque town of Ann Arbor. "Ann Arbor is the quintessential college town, with a wide range of cultural opportunities and ways for students to get involved," a sophomore says. A surprising variety of visual and performing arts are offered in town and on campus. A senior has a stern warning for any potential underage drinkers: "Your fake ID will be taken. Plan on it. Do not be surprised, no matter how good it is." An annual art fair held in Ann Arbor draws craftspeople from throughout the nation and Canada. Many lakes and swimming holes lie only a short drive away and seem to keep the large summer-term population happy. As one junior says, "We are ranked high enough to be known for our academic success, but we still have a reputation for having a good time." Michigan winters, though, are known for being cold and brutal. Sixteen percent of the men and 21 percent of the women go Greek. Many students also volunteer in the community. One senior explains, "Most students get involved, especially if it has something to do with helping kids."

> **The College of Engineering and School of Business are well respected.**

> **"The housing is nothing to write home about."**

Football overshadows nearly everything each fall as students gather to cheer, "Go Blue." Despite a few shaky seasons on the gridiron, the Wolverines are hoping to rebound. Attending football games is an integral part of the UM experience, students say, and "you shouldn't be allowed to graduate if you haven't gone to a hockey game," quips a sophomore. The Little Brown Jug competition with Minnesota is popular. Men's basketball, gymnastics, swimming, ice hockey, and cross-country are strong, as are women's cross-country, gymnastics, and softball. Intramurals, which were invented at the University of Michigan, provide students with a more casual form of athletics.

The University of Michigan strives to offer its students a delicate balance between academics, athletics, and social activities. On one hand, this is an American college as it's characterized in movies like *Animal House*—football and fraternities. But it's also a world-class university with a fine faculty and top-rated programs, intent on making America competitive in the 21st century. For assertive students who crave spirit and action as well as outstanding academics, Michigan is an excellent choice.

Overlaps

Michigan State, Northwestern, Cornell, University of Illinois, Washington University in St. Louis, University of Wisconsin, UC–Berkeley, UCLA

If You Apply To ➤ **Michigan:** Rolling admissions. Early action: Nov. 1. Application fee: $65. No campus or alumni interviews. SATs or ACTs: required. Subject Tests: required for homeschooled students (English, math, science, foreign language, and social studies). Essay question. Apply to particular school or program. Policies and deadlines vary by school.

Michigan State University

250 Administration Building, East Lansing, MI 48824-0590

Most people don't realize that Michigan State is significantly bigger than University of Michigan. Students can find a niche in strong preprofessional programs such as hotel and restaurant management, prevet, business, and engineering. MSU's self-contained campus is like a town unto itself, with shuttle buses available to go from one side to the other.

Website: www.beaspartan
.msu.edu

Location: Suburban

Public

Total Enrollment: 41,801

Undergraduates: 34,002

Male/Female: 49/51

SAT Ranges: CR 430–590,
    M 540–680

ACT Ranges: 23–28

Financial Aid: 53%

Expense: Pub $ $ $

Student Loans: 46%

Average Debt: $ $

Phi Beta Kappa: Yes

Applicants: 30,224

Accepted: 71%

Enrolled: 39%

Grad in 6 Years: 79%

Returning Freshmen: 91%

Academics: ✍ ✍ ✍

Social: 🕿 🕿 🕿 🕿

Q of L: ★ ★ ★

Admissions: (517) 355-8332

Email Address: admin@msu
    .edu

Strongest Programs:
Business/Marketing
Social Sciences
Communication/Journalism
Education
Supply Chain Management
Video Game Design

*More than 2,000
alumni have served
in the Peace Corps
during the school's
44-year partnership
with the agency, a
milestone reached
by only four other
universities.*

Michigan State's roots are agricultural—the school became the state's first land grant institution in 1862—and future farmers and veterinarians still flourish here. So do those with wanderlust, thanks to study abroad programs on each of the world's seven continents. MSU's programs in natural sciences and multidisciplinary social sciences offer students the feel of a small, liberal arts college and the resources of a large research university. "Resources here abound," says a senior, "and that alone is a very worthwhile trait, giving students nearly limitless opportunities to succeed."

"Resources here abound."

The heart of the MSU campus, north of the Red Cedar River, boasts ivy-covered brick buildings, some of which predate the Civil War and are listed on the National Register of Historic Places. This area houses five colleges plus the MSU Union and 10 residence halls. Across the river are the medical complex, newer dorms, and two 18-hole golf courses. On the southernmost part of campus is University Farms, where researchers find ways to grow fatter hogs and cows that produce more milk. The 200,000-square-foot Biomedical and Physical Sciences Building has six floors of labs and another four of offices. The building connects MSU's Chemistry and Biochemistry buildings and is near the Plant Biology Laboratories and the National Superconducting Cyloctron Lab.

Michigan State students tend to be preprofessional and clear about their interests; the premed and prevet programs are strong, and the most popular majors include business, communications and journalism, education, various fields in the social sciences, and engineering. More unusual options include museum studies, supply-chain management, and hospitality management; students in the latter program get real-world experience by staffing the university hotel. To graduate, all students must satisfy university requirements in math and writing, complete a major, and take a minimum of 26 credits in the integrative studies program, which includes arts and humanities; social, behavioral, and economic sciences; and biological and physical sciences. There is a strong international component as well, with more than 275 study abroad programs in 60 countries.

The climate at MSU gets tougher as students advance through their majors, says a junior. "Many of our courses are very competitive because they play a part in determining whether or not you are accepted into a specific program," adds a classmate. Freshmen may participate in special study-away programs or take part in residential programs that focus on international themes, political science, and the environment, among others. Students say that, for the most part, professors are accessible and dedicated. "I've learned so much from my professors," says one senior.

"The students here are friendly and diverse."

"The students here are friendly and diverse," says an elementary education major. "We also have a large international population, which is really cool because it gives you the opportunity to get to know people and cultures from all over the world." Whether they come from gritty Motor City or pretty Traverse City, or from somewhere outside the Midwest, Michigan State students care about the world around them. Indeed, more than 2,000 alumni have served in the Peace Corps during the school's 44-year partnership with the agency, a milestone reached by only four other universities. There's a balance between conservative and liberal factions on campus, says a premed student. African Americans make up 7 percent of the student body, Asian Americans add 4 percent, and Hispanics constitute 4 percent. Eighty percent hail from in-state. The fall 2012 freshmen class included more students from China—nearly 1,000—than came from Illinois, Indiana, Ohio, Pennsylvania, and Wisconsin combined. Scholarships are offered in more than 20 Division I sports, and thousands of students also receive grants and awards based on academic merit.

Forty-two percent of MSU students—but nearly all freshmen—live in Michigan State's dorms, which one sophomore describes as "very convenient and well maintained." Those seeking the "traditional" college experience can bunk in one of three huge living/learning complexes, each with about four residence halls plus libraries, faculty offices, classrooms, cafeterias, and recreation areas. There are also residential colleges housing less than 1,000 students each: Students in James Madison focus on the social sciences, while those in Lyman Briggs study the natural sciences and math. An honors college allows the brightest freshmen to live together, if they wish, and assigns them a special advisor. Other living/learning programs, known by their catchy acronyms, include RISE (focus on the environment), ROIAL (arts and letters), ROSES (science and engineering), and STAR (Support Teamwork Achievement Resources). All 25 of the school's residence halls are to be updated by 2020. MSU's dining services dish out 32,000 meals a day at 16 cafeterias, where salad, soup, and dessert bars help satisfy those who crave variety. "All the food is edible," says a senior.

Safety is not a huge issue here; green-light emergency telephones are sprinkled throughout the campus, walking escorts are available for those who stay late at the library, and Lansing's bus system offers cheaper night-owl rates for those living father away. Still, parking places are in chronically short supply, and students complain about the tickets they receive as a result. Once they've earned 28 credits, which can be as soon as the spring of the first year, students may move off campus. Many do so because the city of East Lansing, just outside Michigan's capital, offers all the positive aspects of a large urban area, along with the safety and community feel of a much smaller town. Indeed, the population of the area more than doubles when school is in session.

"The social life at MSU is very lively on the weekends," says one student. Eight percent of MSU men and 7 percent of MSU women go Greek; those under 21 may not drink alcohol, but Michigan State gives the policy teeth by permitting police to Breathalyze any student suspected of being under the influence. Other weekend alternatives include bands, dances, and comedians brought in by the Student Activities Board. Movies that have left the theaters but haven't yet hit the video store are also shown in Wells Hall—free for campus dwellers, and a couple of bucks for those who live off campus.

Weekends are dominated by Big Ten athletic competitions, with the Michigan-MSU rivalry especially fierce. "Our large campus is filled from end to end with individuals sporting green and white; alcohol-free tailgating is also available," says a junior. "Seeing 150,000 people in a space that usually has about 60,000 is quite an experience." Men's and women's golf and women's

"The social life at MSU is very lively on the weekends."

rowing are strong, as are men's and women's basketball. MSU's marching band wins national awards as well. After more than six decades of standing guard at Kalamazoo Street and Red Cedar Road, the school's mascot, affectionately known as "Sparty," has moved indoors to protect him from the elements (and sneaky Wolverines). However, a replica stands outside and is guarded by students when the University of Michigan comes to town. Students are still able to paint "the Rock," a large boulder donated in the 1960s, to advertise campus events, birthdays, anniversaries, and the like.

Although the majority of MSU students are from the state of Michigan, they're far from a homogeneous lot. Future leaders, physicians, and financiers happily coexist here, in a "diverse, friendly, and expressive" bunch. And despite the university's size, "the majority of people are incredibly nice, outgoing, and laid-back," says a food-science major. "We are more willing to enjoy life and try new things than our counterparts at the University of Michigan."

Overlaps

Grand Valley State, Indiana University, University of Michigan, Central Michigan, Western Michigan, Purdue

If You Apply To ➤

MSU: Rolling admissions. Housing: May 1. Application fee: $50. Campus and alumni interviews: optional, informational. SATs or ACTs: required. Subject Tests: optional. Essay question: personal statement.

Middlebury College

Middlebury, VT 05753

One of the small liberal arts colleges where applications have surged most significantly in recent years. Students are drawn to the beauty of Middlebury's Green Mountain location and strong programs in hot areas such as international studies and environmental science. Known worldwide for its summer foreign language programs.

Website: www.middlebury.edu
Location: Rural
Private
Total Enrollment: 2,516
Undergraduates: 2,516
Male/Female: 49/51
SAT Ranges: CR 630–740, M 640–740
ACT Ranges: 31–33
Financial Aid: 41%
Expense: Pr $ $ $ $
Student Loans: 49%
Average Debt: $
Phi Beta Kappa: Yes
Applicants: 8,847
Accepted: 17%
Enrolled: 40%
Grad in 6 Years: 94%
Returning Freshmen: 97%
Academics: ✐ ✐ ✐ ✐ ½
Social: ☎ ☎ ☎
Q of L: ★ ★ ★
Admissions: (802) 443-3000
Email Address: admissions@middlebury.edu

Strongest Programs:
Social Sciences
Environmental Studies
Biology
English/Literary Studies
International Studies
Dance and Theater
Film and Media Culture
Languages

Middlebury College's nickname—"Club Midd"—may bring to mind a resort, but this school's rigorous workload means four years here is far from a vacation. The campus, with its picturesque sunsets, excellent skiing, and rural Vermont charm is a paradise for those interested in environmental studies, second and third languages, and a tight-knit community where highly motivated and intelligent students and faculty truly care about each other.

"The quality of teaching is excellent."

The college's 350-acre main campus overlooks the village of Middlebury, Vermont, which a junior calls a "small, quaint Vermont town of 8,000 people and five stoplights." The 1,800-acre mountain campus, site of the Bread Loaf School of English, the Bread Loaf Writers' Conference, and the college's Snow Bowl, is nearby. Old Stone Row cuts across the campus, where buildings with simple lines and rectangular shapes evoke the mills of early New England. (Middlebury was founded in 1800.) Academic halls and dormitories of marble and limestone sit in quadrangles and feature views of the Adirondack and Green mountains. The Axinn Center features advanced classroom and lecture spaces, as well as state-of-the-art facilities for the school's film and media culture department.

Between June and August, Middlebury banishes English from its campus and hundreds of students live, learn, and, hopefully, think only in their chosen language, some wearing T-shirts that proclaim "No English spoken here." The language departments continue their excellent instruction during the school year; especially notable are German, Chinese, Japanese, and Hebrew. Although there is no foreign language requirement, just about everyone studies another tongue, if only to take advantage of Middlebury's campuses in France, Germany, Italy, Spain, Russia, Mexico, Egypt, Brazil, Argentina, Chile, China, and Uruguay. Foreign language students benefit from Middlebury's affiliation with the Monterey Institute of International Studies in California, which in 2010 became the graduate school of Middlebury. In fact, almost half of the departments on campus are affiliated with the international studies major. The school is also a member of the Maritime Studies

"We're gregarious and come from all over the world."

Program* and there are 90 college-approved study abroad programs in total; about 60 percent of juniors take advantage of them. Other highly touted Middlebury departments include English (one of the school's most popular majors, bolstered by its connections to the famed Bread Loaf Writers' Conference), economics, and psychology. Middlebury also excels in the sciences, due to its small classes and lab sizes, research facilities, and opportunities for students to engage in research.

"There is very little competition between students," says one senior. "To be honest, I've never heard anyone here talk about the grades they've received on tests or projects or even about their GPAs as relative to others." Midd kids must take a discussion-based, writing-intensive First-Year Seminar with only 15 students; the instructor serves as advisor to those enrolled until they declare a major. By the end of sophomore year, students must complete a second writing-intensive course. In addition to a 10- to 16-credit major, students must also satisfy distribution requirements in seven of eight academic areas: literature, the arts, philosophical and religious studies, history, physical and life sciences, deductive reasoning and analytical processes, social analysis, and foreign language. Students also take four cultures and civilizations classes and two noncredit courses in physical education. With all of these requirements, it's no wonder students and faculty become close. "The quality of teaching is excellent, and I would say it is the absolute best part of Middlebury," cheers one student. "All classes are taught by professors, most are relatively small, and discussions are generally encouraged."

"The great thing about Middlebury is that you can't really characterize the student body," says one senior, who then makes an attempt to do so: "We're gregarious and come from all over the world. We occupy every niche imaginable and with a considerable amount of swagger, I might add." Eighty-six percent of Middlebury's students graduated in the top 10th of their high school class, and students of color constitute 15 percent of the student body: 6 percent are Asian American, 7 percent are Hispanic, and 2 percent are African American. The campus leans left politically and hot-button issues include human rights and environmental causes. In fact, the Sierra Club rates Middlebury top in the nation for its environmental efforts, which include reliance on a wind turbine and systematic efforts to help students recycle. The workload, the lacking social scene, and the cold weather are familiar complaints. There are no merit or athletic scholarships.

Few Middlebury students live off campus (3 percent), since housing is guaranteed for four years. A variety of co-ed dorms offer suites, augmented by college-owned group houses, the Environmental House (where residents cook all of their own food), academic interest houses, and more

Middlebury also excels in the sciences, due to its small classes and lab sizes, research facilities, and opportunities for students to engage in research.

"There is very little competition between students."

"standard" situations. Rooms for upperclassmen are distributed by a lottery based on seniority, a system that a sophomore calls "a confusing and elaborate process." A sophomore reports, "The dorms are in great condition. Housing is one of the things that make Middlebury so comfortable." The meal plan is served at five dining halls, which get high marks for both their decor and their victuals. "The food is fantastic," a sophomore raves.

Students at Middlebury play as hard on the weekends as they work during the week. "Social life is almost completely contained on campus and it is hit or miss," says one student. "Parties are fun when you're younger, but as you get older you long for something a bit more diverse and interesting." Those who stay on campus are treated to school-sponsored dances, plays, dance performances, or parties at the Greek-like co-ed social houses, which draw 9 percent of students. Kegs are prohibited in the dorms but permitted at parties, which must be registered and also offer nonalcoholic drinks and snacks. Despite the policies, alcohol consumption is common among underage students and "the college is pretty lenient about alcohol," a Spanish and geography double-major reports.

Off campus, Middlebury is "the quintessential New England town, straight out of Norman Rockwell" that is "intrinsically linked to the school." It has necessities such as fast food, grocery stores, drug stores, hardware stores, and clothing shops, but the administration regularly brings in culture and entertainment. February can be grim because the snow here comes early and stays late, so road trips are popular. The progressive city of Burlington is 45 minutes away, while Montreal is a three-hour drive, Boston four, and New York City five. Middlebury's own Snow Bowl ($100 for the season) and proximity to most Vermont ski slopes make this a paradise for ski fanatics, a breed Middlebury attracts in predictably large numbers.

Middlebury athletics draw rabid fans, especially when cheering on the powerful Panthers ice hockey teams—men's and women's—that compete in Division III

Middlebury athletics draw rabid fans.

against archrival Norwich; the teams' members also engage in tutoring in local schools. The college has won more than 30 national titles since 1995 and offers 31 varsity sports. Students are also active in the large intramural program, with soccer, hockey, football, basketball, and softball drawing the most interest. Perhaps the biggest outdoor activity of all is the three-day Winter Carnival, an annual extravaganza including parties, cultural events, an all-school formal, sporting competitions, snow sculpture, and ice-skating at an outdoor rink. Townspeople support the school's hockey games, and students—including members of the hockey team—give back through volunteer work with children, women, the elderly, and local schools. "Community service is a big part of who we are here at Midd," says a sophomore.

Students have noticed physical changes at Middlebury over the past few years, with more in the works, and have seen the school grow more rigorous and competitive. But some things have remained the same—namely, the combination of "excellent academics with endless extracurricular opportunities," says a sophomore. "We're a small liberal arts college [that is] big on individuality and character," a sophomore says. "Whatever your character, you'll find your niche."

If You Apply To ➤ **Middlebury:** Early decision: Nov. 1. Regular admissions and housing: Jan. 1. Financial aid: Feb. 1. Application fee: $65. No campus interviews. Alumni interviews: optional, evaluative. SATs or ACTs or three Subject Tests: required. Accepts the Common Application. Essay question and copy of recent graded essay.

Mills College

5000 MacArthur Boulevard, Oakland, CA 94613

One of two major women's colleges on the West Coast. Mills has the Oakland area to fall back on, including UC–Berkeley, where students can take classes. Mills is strongest in the arts and math, though it does offer smaller programs in preprofessional areas such as communications and business economics. Still the only women's college to turn back coeducation with a massive protest, which it did in 1990.

At Mills College, women receive more than just a liberal arts education. Students are expected to graduate with a deeper understanding of social issues and a broad knowledge base to help ensure they will be technologically savvy and artistically aware of the world around them. The school's dedication to equality is obvious: Mills was the first women's college in the West to award bachelor's degrees and also the first to offer a computer science major. Today, this small bastion of higher learning continues to provide ambitious women with a stellar education and a host of opportunities.

"The quality of teaching is extraordinary."

The school's fascinating history started in 1852, when it began as a young ladies' seminary serving the children of California Gold Rush adventurers who were determined to see their daughters raised in an atmosphere of gentility. Now, the combination of student diversity and educational opportunity helps guarantee that no one will graduate without having her horizons well expanded. Mills is a place where issues are debated and analyzed in the classroom, even if some students perceive an apathetic atmosphere on campus with regard to social, political, and racial concerns. The enclosed, parklike 135-acre campus boasts both historic and modern architecture set among rolling meadows, woods, and a meandering creek.

The general education curriculum is designed to graduate students who are able to write clearly, think across disciplines, work productively with others, analyze, and reason clearly; who are technology savvy, artistically sensitive, adept in scientific and historical thinking; and who are aware of multiculturalism, the influence of social institutions, and the issues facing women in society. Course requirements cover three broad areas: writing, quantitative, and technological skills; interdisciplinary, gender, and multicultural perspectives; and knowledge of arts, history, natural science, and human behavior. Nearly all majors require a capstone experience of either a research thesis or project.

Mills's academic climate is described as tough but cooperative. "The courses at Mills are challenging, and they have given me the opportunity to think in new ways, without being judged or made to feel silly," says one junior. The professors are highly regarded, friendly, and accessible, and since most of them are women, there's no shortage of strong female role models. "The quality of teaching is extraordinary. The faculty are extremely dedicated to being good teachers and mentors," one psychology major says. Strong programs abound: "Anthropology, sociology, women's studies, and biology are some of the best departments because of the awesome and outstanding professors," says one student. In addition to a premed program, Mills offers a prenursing program. Popular among prelaw students is the interdisciplinary program in political, legal, and economic analysis. The fine arts department is Mills's traditional stronghold, and electronic and computer music specializations within the music program are worthy of note. Mills students are encouraged to explore beyond the Oakland campus, and one-quarter take advantage of programs abroad and exchanges with East Coast colleges. Mills has concurrent cross-registration agreements with UC–Berkeley and many other Bay Area colleges, as well as a five-year engineering program in conjunction with USC.

"Mills students are strong, intelligent, caring, and oriented towards social justice and change," says one sophomore. Seventy-nine percent of Mills women are from California, and 78 percent attended public school. African Americans constitute 6 percent of the student body, Hispanics make up 22 percent, and another 12 percent are Asian Americans. An influential subgroup of students consists of "resumers"—women who are returning to college after a break of several years. Merit scholarships averaging $15,326 are doled out annually to qualified students, but Mills does not award athletic scholarships.

"There are several on-campus housing options, including dormitories, apartments, and graduate housing," says one student. "The rooms are generally comfortable and spacious." The beautiful, Mediterranean-style 1920s- and 1930s-era dorms are homey and "there is not much problem getting a room," a junior reports. Fifty-eight percent of students live on campus. "Most of the rooms in the dorms on campus are singles, which is uncommon for a college. If you want a roommate, you really have to TRY to get a roommate. I love having my own little area to call my own," explains a student. Campus dining receives cheers from students. "Honestly, compared to the college food of other universities, we have it made. We have a private catering company preparing fresh meals everyday from scratch," cheers one senior. Mills is a gated campus with one entrance, and students say they feel safe on campus.

Fears linger about a stunted social life on this tiny campus. "Most of my social life takes place on campus," reports a student, "but it is easy to escape Mills for a little while by using shuttle which goes to UC–Berkeley and a BART station." What the campus may lack in social options, however, can be found in Berkeley or San Francisco, both accessible via public transportation, beginning with a bus stop

"Most of the rooms in the dorms on campus are singles, which is uncommon for a college."

(continued)

Grad in 6 Years: 63%
Returning Freshmen: 77%
Academics: ✍ ✍ ✍
Social: ☎ ☎
Q of L: ★ ★ ★
Admissions: (800) 87-MILLS
Email Address: admission@ mills.edu

Strongest Programs:
English
Studio Art
Psychology
Chemistry
Economics
Biology
Anthropology
Sociology

Nearly all majors require a capstone experience of either a research thesis or project.

The fine arts department is Mills's traditional stronghold, and electronic and computer music specializations within the music program are worthy of note.

outside the front gate. Those with the means can take ski trips to Lake Tahoe or go to the sunny Santa Cruz beaches. Back on campus, one of the most popular traditions is Latina Heritage Month, when the student group Mujeres Unidas plans an "incredible" collection of events that "honor Latinos and all human beings," as one student describes it.

The Cyclones compete in the Association of Division III Independents in six sports: cross-country, rowing, soccer, swimming, tennis, and volleyball; rowing is the most competitive. There are no intramurals, but a number of students stay busy volunteering in the local community.

Despite some complaints about campus life, Mills students enjoy small classes with excellent teaching in one of the country's most desirable locations close to San Francisco. One student concludes, "Mills is the perfect place to get an unbeatable education that not only teaches you more about the world we live in, but also more about yourself. The women who graduate from Mills are strong, independent, and know what they want." With an educational program that emphasizes skills critical for understanding today's society and succeeding in the real world, the college's women are sure to graduate as independent thinkers capable of making it on their own. Says one junior: "We are all about empowering women."

Overlaps

UC–Davis, UC–Berkeley, UC–Santa Cruz, UCLA, UC–Santa Barbara, University of San Francisco, San Francisco State, Smith

If You Apply To ➤

Mills: Early action: Nov. 15. Regular admissions: Jan. 15. Financial aid: Feb. 15. Housing: Jun. 1. Application fee: $50. Campus and alumnae interviews: optional, evaluative. SATs or ACTs: required. Subject Tests: recommended. Accepts the Common Application. Writing sample: Submit a graded analytic paper or essay.

Millsaps College

1701 North State Street, Jackson, MS 39210

Millsaps is the strongest liberal arts college in the deep, Deep South and by far the most progressive. Its largely preprofessional student body typically has sights set on business, law, or medicine. Usually compared to Hendrix, Rhodes, and Sewanee, though less selective than the last two. More than half the students come from out of state, generally from other Deep South states.

Website: www.millsaps.edu
Location: City Center
Private
Total Enrollment: 909
Undergraduates: 843
Male/Female: 51/49
SAT Ranges: CR 490–610, M 520–610
ACT Ranges: 23–29
Financial Aid: 96%
Expense: Pr $
Student Loans: 55%
Average Debt: N/A
Phi Beta Kappa: Yes
Applicants: 2,255

Millsaps College has long been recognized as a finishing school for well-bred Southern belles and gentlemen. Less well-known outside the Deep South is that this is also one of the region's top liberal arts institutions. Millsaps's motto, *ad excellentiam*, means "promoting excellence"—which is what the college still does. What differentiates the school is its focus on scholarly inquiry, spiritual growth, and community service, along with its Heritage Program, an interdisciplinary approach to world culture. "Millsaps is the perfect package," says a freshman, "strongly academic, small enough to build relationships, yet big-thinking enough to build the mind."

Millsaps's 100-acre campus sits in the center of Jackson, on the highest point in the city. A mix of modern and traditional buildings is arranged around the Bowl, a sequestered glen surrounded by old-growth trees and shrubs. Recent construction includes three new residence halls that house approximately 141 juniors and seniors in suite-style living.

Millsaps requires students to complete 128 semester hours to earn a degree, all but eight of which must be taken for a letter grade. All students must also complete

10 multidisciplinary courses designed to develop skills in reasoning, communication, quantitative thinking, valuing, and decision making—including four in the humanities and four in the sciences and math. All freshmen also take a one-hour Perspectives class, led by an academic advisor, to help adjust to college life. New students also take the Introduction to Liberal Studies seminar, which focuses on critical thinking and writing.

Millsaps offers more than 30 majors and 40 minors, including the option of a self-designed major. Among the best programs at Millsaps are English and education, where students get involved with the Jackson Public Schools from introductory-level classes. "The courses are rigorous as the professors continue to push the students' academic boundaries," says a sophomore. The Millsaps

> **"The courses are rigorous as the professors continue to push the students' academic boundaries."**

College Writing Program is top-notch and the Writing Across the Curriculum initiative ensures that every student develops writing skills. Each year, a few select upperclassmen join the Ford Teaching Fellows Program, letting them work closely with a faculty member to learn about teaching—and paying them for their time in the classroom. Also well regarded are history, philosophy, and religious studies. Premed courses, including those in biology and chemistry, are strong, and the college's medical mentoring program pairs students with practitioners in their chosen field, allowing students to earn credit for real medical experience. The Wiener Premedical Summer Research Fellowships are available to students seeking careers in medicine, while cooperative agreements allow students to opt for nursing degrees in partnership with the University of Mississippi Medical Center and Vanderbilt University. Millsaps also offers engineering opportunities in cooperation with Auburn, Columbia, Vanderbilt, and Washington universities. Lastly, a new creative writing major has been established as a supplement to the English and communications studies majors.

No course at Millsaps has more than 50 students. "The quality of the teaching surpasses all of my expectations," says a student. Students may do research for credit at the Blue Ridge Center for Environmental Stewardship in Virginia and at Yellowstone National Park, or they may intern for credit with local businesses or in state government offices in Jackson. The college also maintains a 4,000-acre biological reserve in the rainforest of the Yucatán Peninsula, which hosts courses exploring Mayan culture and the Mayan coral reef, with course topics ranging from the literature of the Spanish conquest to Mayan mathematics and astronomy. Approximately 50 percent of Millsaps students study abroad, and courses are offered in nearly 20 nations, including Albania, Israel, Tanzania, China, Greece, and Costa Rica. Students eager to see how government works may participate in the Washington Semester*. Cooperative programs are also available through the Associated Colleges of the South* consortium, of which Millsaps is a founding member.

"The students at Millsaps are very diverse," says a sophomore. "They range from athletes to scholars, from the outspoken to the quiet, from liberal to conservative, and from religious to atheist." Millsaps has broadened its recruiting efforts, and 63 percent of students now come from out of state, though the

> **"The students at Millsaps are very diverse."**

campus is still far from diverse. Millsaps was the first college in Mississippi to voluntarily open its doors to minority students, and African Americans now make up 11 percent of the student body, Asian Americans add 5 percent, and Hispanics 2 percent. "The campus is very activist and very political—well split between conservatives and liberals," says a political science major. "All views are respected; poverty and human rights are hot topics." Qualified Millsaps students get some non-need-based academic scholarships. However, there are no athletic scholarships.

(continued)

Accepted: 55%

Enrolled: 17%

Grad in 6 Years: 72%

Returning Freshmen: 77%

Academics: ✍ ✍ ✍

Social: ☎ ☎ ☎

Q of L: ★ ★ ★

Admissions: (601) 974-1050

Email Address: admissions@ millsaps.edu

Strongest Programs:
Accounting
Business Administration
Biology/Chemistry/Premed
English
History
Sociology/Anthropology
Religious Studies
Education

The Millsaps College Writing Program is top-notch and the Writing Across the Curriculum initiative ensures that every student develops writing skills.

Many Mississippians view Millsaps as a hotbed of liberalism, and the school's co-ed dorms confirm their worst fears, though freshmen must still live in single-sex halls. Eighty-six percent of students stay in campus housing—mostly, grouses a sophomore, because those who move off campus lose 30 percent of their financial aid. The robust Greek system claims 60 percent of men and 56 percent of women; sophomore, junior, and senior men may live in one of four fraternity houses, but there is no sorority housing. "Housing is average," a psychology major says. Students say campus food is decent and "there is something for everyone," according to a senior.

The social scene at Millsaps revolves around the fraternity houses, which are usually open and rocking from Wednesday through Saturday nights. "The Greek life is the center of Millsaps's social life," a student explains. Greek rush is now held after fall midterms instead of during the first hectic week of school, but that hasn't dampened the party spirit. Underage students caught drinking are fined, but students say enforcement of the policy is lax. Major Madness is a favorite annual event, offering

"Housing is average." a week of open-mic nights, hypnotists, and comedians and culminating in a weekend-long festival in the Bowl, with a crawfish boil, carnival games, and live music. The city of Jackson also offers a wealth of options, including professional symphony, opera, and ballet, and the city is a nexus for Mississippi's legendary blues and "roots rock" musical traditions. Easy road trips include New Orleans, Memphis, and the riverfront casinos in Vicksburg, Mississippi; closer to campus, 10 miles to the north, is a huge reservoir that is popular for weekend water sports. For students who enjoy the great outdoors, the Natchez Trace offers easy access to wooded trails and bicycling paths.

The Millsaps Majors compete in NCAA Division III as a member of the Southern Collegiate Athletic Conference (SCAC), so it isn't nearly as sports crazy as most Southern campuses. For the men, football, basketball, baseball, and soccer draw the largest crowds; basketball, soccer, softball, and volleyball are the most popular among women's teams. Newer varsity sports include men's and women's lacrosse and men's and women's cross-country. The college has also garnered recognition for the caliber of its student-athletes, bringing home Mississippi's Halbrook Award for the highest student-athlete graduation rate 18 of the last 24 years. There are more than 25 intramural sports, plus group exercise classes and sports clubs, so even students with recreational interests and abilities can find a game to play. Everyone benefits from the 65,000-square-foot Hall Activities Center, which has facilities for weight training, aerobics, basketball, racquetball, squash, and volleyball, along with an outdoor pool.

In a state renowned for blues, booze, barbecue, and the tradition of old magnolia trees and grand plantations, progressive Millsaps College is an anomaly. "We offer the sort of prestigious education generally only available in New England," a junior explains. "Millsaps is a magnet for accomplished students from strong backgrounds and the kind of college not usually found in the South." Small classes ensure plenty of time to get to know fellow students and faculty members. "It's a challenging atmosphere where everyone actually cares about school," agrees a business major. "The faculty knows you as a person, not a number." And that's one tradition that never gets "too old."

Overlaps

Hendrix, Loyola, University of Mississippi, Rhodes, University of the South, University of Southern Mississippi, Spring Hill, Tulane

University of Minnesota

240 Williamson, 231 Pillsbur, Minneapolis, MN 55455

Not quite as highly rated as the University of Michigan or the University of Wisconsin, but not nearly as expensive for nonresidents either. In a university the size of Minnesota, the best bet is to find a niche, such as the honors program in the liberal arts college. Strong programs include engineering, management, and health fields.

The University of Minnesota, like the nearby Mall of America, can be overwhelming, given its seemingly limitless variety of offerings and gargantuan size. With nearly 150 majors and largest study abroad program in the nation, the U of M offers an abundance of academic choices. Be warned, though—winters can be frigid and it can take a cool customer to navigate the endless choices here.

The vast Twin Cities campus actually consists of two campuses with three main sections, and within each the architecture is highly diverse. The St. Paul campus encompasses the College of Food, Agricultural, and Natural Resource Sciences; the College of Biological Sciences; the College of Veterinary Medicine; and the College of Continuing Studies. The Minneapolis campus is divided by the Mississippi River into an East Bank and a West Bank that are home to the other colleges and most of the dormitories, as well as most of the fraternities and sororities. Both campuses offer a blend of traditional and modern architecture, with columned buildings seated next to sleek geometric structures. The two campuses are five miles apart and linked by a free bus service. Academic facilities are excellent, beginning with the five-million-volume library system, which is the 14th largest in North America. Every one of the colleges has its own library, many of which are good places to study. A 695-acre arboretum is used for research and teaching. The West Bank Arts Quarter makes the U of M the only public university in the nation with all of its art disciplines in the same district.

> **"The classes are relatively difficult."**

Minnesota offers more than 140 undergraduate majors in seven separate schools. The Institute of Technology is notable for the options it offers for tutorials and internships; the electrical and mechanical engineering programs are particularly strong and well subscribed. Social sciences, engineering, biology, business, and English are among the most popular majors. Undergraduates also have access to more esoteric fields, from aging studies and biometry to therapeutic recreation and mortuary science.

While efforts to limit class size have been stepped up and the university is focusing more on undergraduates, classes can reach 300-plus, with introductory classes typically the largest. "The size can be overwhelming, but oftentimes students figure out classes and find it quite fitting," says a senior. Helpful teaching assistants are abundant, and the excellent honors program in the liberal arts college allows close contact with faculty members as well as leeway to enroll in certain graduate courses and seminars. Students say the academic climate varies by school. "The classes are relatively difficult," a junior says, but "it really depends on the subject."

> **"The instructors have been exemplary."**

While undergraduates have had a difficult time enrolling in courses, one junior reveals, "If a class is closed and somebody really needs it, they can usually get a magic number from the department to be able to register for it." The administration attributes the school's low six-year graduation rate to the fact that students are likely to center their lives in spheres outside the university—in work and off-campus homes. However, the four-year plan guarantees graduation in four years provided students follow program requirements, including frequent academic counseling and specific coursework.

Website: www.umn.edu
Location: Urban
Public
Total Enrollment: 37,657
Undergraduates: 27,866
Male/Female: 49/51
SAT Ranges: CR 550–690, M 620–740
ACT Ranges: 26–30
Financial Aid: 55%
Expense: Pub $ $ $ $
Student Loans: 61%
Average Debt: $ $ $
Phi Beta Kappa: Yes
Applicants: 43,048
Accepted: 44%
Enrolled: 29%
Grad in 6 Years: 73%
Returning Freshmen: 90%
Academics: ✑ ✑ ✑ ✑
Social: ☎ ☎ ☎
Q of L: ★ ★ ★
Admissions: (612) 625-5000
Email Address: N/A

Strongest Programs:
Chemical Engineering
Management Information Systems
Mechanical Engineering

Minnesota offers more than 140 undergraduate majors in seven separate schools.

Professors receive high marks from most students as being approachable and knowledgeable. "The instructors have been exemplary due to their passion for the subject matter and commitment to their students," an archeology major says. Students find plenty of internship opportunities at the many corporations and government agencies in the Twin Cities area, and the university pushes its more than 300 study, work, and volunteer programs in more than 60 nations. These draw 30 percent of undergrads, including engineering students. The university is on a semester system, and almost all classes have a pass/fail option (limited to no more than a quarter of a student's courses).

Most U of M students are "motivated and hardworking," says a junior. Eighty-two percent of students come from the top quarter of their high school class, and 63 percent are from Minnesota. Minorities constitute 16 percent of the student body, with 4 percent African American, 3 percent Hispanic, and 9 percent Asian American. Tuition hikes are a main gripe of students, but there is need-based financial aid, as well as merit scholarships and athletic awards in all major sports.

Dorm life at Minnesota follows the big school, wait-in-line theme. Less than one-quarter of all undergraduates live in residence halls; there are eight traditional halls and three university-run apartment facilities. Dorm rooms are hard to obtain, and parking spaces for all those commuters are almost as scarce. Students who have rooms get the chance to keep them for the next year. "Dorms are adequate," says one student, although "some can be a bit cramped."

"Most social life takes place right off campus."

Once you're there, you're required to join a meal plan. Opinions vary on the quality and variety of food. But "fresh fruit and veggies are always available," notes a junior. Lest anyone fear the dietitians are excessively health-obsessed, she adds, "They have the best chocolate chip cookies." Campus security is adequate. "We have a dedicated police force as well as a free escort program," notes a junior.

Many U of M students live in apartments and have a thriving social life away from campus. "Most social life takes place right off campus," says one student, "but there are loads of activities available on campus, such as bowling, theater, late-night activities, and movies." Underage drinking is banned, and students say the policy usually works. The downtown areas of the Twin Cities are easy to get to by bus, and there are scores of good bars, restaurants, nightspots, and movie theaters.

Here, being "under the weather" can be a good thing, as campus designers found a way to get around—or under—wet or wintry conditions by linking many of the campus buildings with tunnels. For those who love it, there is Snow Week, and happy skiers and skaters become colorful spots all over the state's white backdrop. In the spring and summer, Minnesota's famed 10,000 lakes offer swimming, boating, and fishing. "Activities are all over campus, all over the Twin Cities, and students have a variety to choose from any day of the week," says a senior. The union's bowling alley, pool tables, movie theater, and live music dance club are good places to meet people. And there are more than 500 student groups on campus. The Carnival Weekend put on by the Greeks each April to raise funds for charity is a huge event. Spring Jam is described by one student as "homecoming in spring—but better," and Campus Kickoff Days in the beginning of the fall quarter is much anticipated.

This is an athletically inclined bunch of students, as both intramural and varsity sports are popular. Wrestling, baseball, and golf have brought home championship trophies recently, as has men's track and field. Students always hope the current season will be one in which the gridiron Gophers take home the roses in a bowl victory, but short of that, a win over Michigan for custody of the Little Brown Jug is cause for celebration. The football program is enhanced by the recent completion of an on-campus stadium. Intramural competition can go on well past midnight.

Anonymity is almost a given at a university of this size, but then size does have its virtues in the countless array of campus resources. A senior says, "It offers unparalleled opportunities for students to grow academically, socially, and personally." The University of Minnesota is ideal for those who appreciate an urban setting and a good, old-fashioned, button-up-your-overcoat winter.

University of Minnesota Morris

600 East 4th Street, Morris, MN 56267-2199

The plains of western Minnesota may seem an unlikely place to find a liberal arts college—and a public one at that. Morris is cut from the same cloth as Mary Washington, UNC Asheville, and St. Mary's of Maryland. The draw: private college education at a public university price. So remote that students go to Winnipeg for city life.

The University of Minnesota Morris is far more comprehensive than the small size of its student body might suggest. Originally founded to educate Native Americans, Morris has grown into a solid public liberal arts college with strong programs in biology, psychology, music, and computer science. "There is a place for everyone here," a junior says. A classmate adds, "If you actually want to learn and if you like a challenge, Morris would fit you very well."

The 130-acre Morris campus includes 26 traditional brick-and-mortar buildings, loosely arranged around a central mall. A high-powered wind turbine generates nearly half of the power Morris requires each day. The renovated welcome center meets LEED standards and is the first building in Minnesota (and the first on the National Register of Historic Places) to use energy-efficient chilled beam technology. A new, suite-style residence hall opened in late 2013.

General education requirements at Morris span 60 credits. Everyone starts with the First-Year seminar, an introduction to the liberal arts, and the Intellectual Community (IC) seminar, which introduces students to the skills necessary to engage in discussions with one another and encourages active involvement with the material, peers, and faculty. Students then move on to as many as five courses under the umbrella of Skills for the Liberal Arts: writing, foreign languages, math and symbolic reasoning, and artistic performance. Finally, students take eight courses in Expanding Perspectives, one each in history, fine arts, social sciences, and humanities, and two each in natural sciences and in "the global village," which encompasses human diversity, international perspectives, and related disciplines. The most popular majors are biology, management, English, chemistry, and political science; students also give high marks to the music, art, and economics programs. Notable undergraduate programs include sports management and German studies.

Students describe the academic climate as challenging. "The academic climate is somewhat competitive, since everyone wants to do well, both here and after college,"

> "Students at Morris tend to be leaders who are not afraid to stand up for what they believe in."

Website: www.morris.umn.edu
Location: Rural
Public
Total Enrollment: 1,788
Undergraduates: 1,788
Male/Female: 46/54
SAT Ranges: CR 510–650, M 540–670
ACT Ranges: 23–28
Financial Aid: 91%
Expense: Pub $ $ $
Student Loans: 66%
Average Debt: $ $
Phi Beta Kappa: No
Applicants: 2,349
Accepted: 60%
Enrolled: 29%
Grad in 6 Years: 60%
Returning Freshmen: 78%
Academics: ✑ ✑ ✑ ½
Social: ☎ ☎
Q of L: ★ ★ ★
Admissions: (888) 866-3382
Email Address: admisfa@ morris.umn.edu

Strongest Programs:
Biology

The Morris Honors Program provides high achievers with various honors courses, a senior honors project, and a core course titled Traditions in Human Thought.

The Golden Gophers compete in the Division III Upper Midwest Athletic Conference.

says an economics major. Courses are "competitive and rigorous but very thorough and build upon other subject areas to provide a broad-spectrum view of the material," adds a junior. Nearly two-thirds of classes at Morris have 19 students or fewer, and virtually none have more than 100. Professors are respected for their knowledge and real-world experience. "Classes are always taught by a professor and all of them are extremely knowledgeable," says one student. "The devotion to student success and assistance outside of class time is unrivaled." Every freshman is assigned an academic advisor who must approve his or her schedule. Morris also offers service-learning projects as part of the classroom experiences. The Morris Honors Program provides high achievers with various honors courses, a senior honors project, and a core course titled Traditions in Human Thought. Morris continues to integrate study abroad opportunities into the curriculum, offering more than 300 options for students wishing to study overseas; 57 percent of undergraduates participate. It has also added more than 50 programs to enable students in nontraditional disciplines to study abroad.

"Students at Morris tend to be leaders who are not afraid to stand up for what they believe in. Being around people like this gives you confidence to stand up for what you believe in also," says a senior. Eighty-one percent of Morris students are Minnesota natives; Native Americans are the largest minority group on campus, comprising 15 percent. Asian Americans add 3 percent, and African American and Hispanic students combine for 4 percent. Political issues don't dominate campus conversation, but students tend to be engaged in issues of local and national concern. "GLBTQ, gender, and feminist issues are very important to many students on campus," notes one junior. Merit scholarships are available but there are no athletic awards. Financial incentives for low-income students include full tuition and fees for Pell-eligible students.

"On campus is where all the action is."

Forty-six percent of Morris students live on campus, in one of the five residence halls or in an apartment complex reserved for upperclassmen. It's easy to get a room, though many opt for less-expensive housing off campus. "The campus housing options are comfortable and typically easy to get into," a student says. There is no Greek system, but students say there's always something to do. "Morris's social life keeps students extremely busy through intramural sports, student organizations, and activities or campus events," says a junior. "On campus is where all the action is," another student agrees. "Road trips are usually taken by small groups of friends, who get together on the weekends to go to Perkins in Alexandria, or to the mall in St. Cloud." Winnipeg, about five hours away, is also a popular destination.

Other campus traditions include the pancake breakfast served by professors during final exams. There's also the annual tug-of-war competition between two dorms, Clayton Gay Hall and Indy Hall. "Hundreds of students show up!" says one. In all, there are more than 100 student organizations, including the Morris Campus Student Association, which does everything from lobbying for lower tuition to presenting weekend movie nights. The drinking age is 21, and it's strictly enforced on campus and in local bars. And how about the surrounding town? "Morris is a small town but is a very friendly place," says one sophomore. "We have everything that a student could need while they are here and more."

The Golden Gophers compete in the Division III Upper Midwest Athletic Conference. Strong programs include football, volleyball, and men's and women's soccer. In addition, 80 percent of Morris students participate in intramural sports—including bowling, dodgeball, broomball, and sand volleyball—or use the Regional Fitness Center or hiking and biking trails.

One of the smaller campuses in the University of Minnesota system, Morris may just epitomize the idea of "Minnesota nice." Tucked away from the state's big cities, some students might find the campus isolated. But the school's location means fewer distractions—and more time for its happy students to focus on independent reading and research, or just getting to know their peers. "Morris has a community feel to it," says a sophomore. "Everyone is friendly around here."

If You Apply To ➤

Morris: Rolling admissions: Mar. 15. Application fee: $35 (paper), free (online). Campus interviews: optional, informational. No alumni interviews. SATs or ACTs: required. Subject Tests: optional. Essay question.

University of Mississippi

Oxford, MS 38677

Located in the progressive town of Oxford, Ole Miss has put its redneck past in the rearview mirror. Strong on public policy and international studies. Honors College is special. Location near Faulkner's old hangouts is an ideal place to soak up Southern literary traditions. Colonel Reb no longer the mascot, but spirit of Ole Miss Rebels lives on, especially against LSU and Mississippi State.

The University of Mississippi (more commonly known as "Ole Miss" after the nickname of the yearbook) offers students an educational experience steeped in tradition and thick with school spirit. Students have access to a host of academic offerings, including a top-notch honors college and an innovative public policy leadership major, and to a vibrant community of like-minded Rebels always ready to have a good time. Whether they're hitting the books, cheering on their teams, or simply hanging out, Ole Miss students display a love for their school that is hard to miss.

Founded in 1848, the University of Mississippi is located on 640 acres of rolling land in the center of Oxford. The main campus consists of 188 buildings and a mix of architectural styles, including Greek Revival, Beaux-Arts Classicism, Georgian Revival, and modern. The Robert C. Khayat Law Center features 165,000 square feet of space to house the School of Law and related programs.

Students say coursework can be demanding, depending on the program, but the atmosphere is collaborative rather than competitive. "The classes are definitely challenging at times," says one freshman, "but doable with the right amount of work." The most popular majors include biology, accountancy, elementary education, psychology, and criminal justice, and these are among the strongest, too. The Lott Leadership Institute is a standout that offers public policy leadership majors an innovative curriculum that combines the systematic study of public policy with the development of leadership

> "It is not at all uncommon for full professors to teach freshmen."

qualities. "The atmosphere of the Lott Institute is conducive to learning and team building," says one broadcast journalism major. "Conversational and debate classes are a change from the regular classroom, and Lott offers both." Gifted students may enroll in the Sally McDonnell Barksdale Honors College (SMBHC), where they take part in small, discussion-based honors courses offered in a number of disciplines. Honors students also complete research and a senior thesis to graduate as an SMBHC Scholar.

Regardless of major, students must complete six hours of English composition; three hours of college algebra or quantitative reasoning or statistics (taken from a

Website: www.olemiss.edu
Location: Small Town
Public
Total Enrollment: 16,647
Undergraduates: 14,691
Male/Female: 45/55
SAT Ranges: CR 480–600, M 480–600
ACT Ranges: 21–29
Financial Aid: 80%
Expense: Pub $
Student Loans: N/A
Average Debt: N/A
Phi Beta Kappa: Yes
Applicants: 13,934
Accepted: 61%
Enrolled: 40%
Grad in 6 Years: 58%
Returning Freshmen: 81%
Academics: ✍ ✍ ✍
Social: 🕭 🕭 🕭
Q of L: ★ ★ ★
Admissions: (662) 915-7226
Email Address: admissions@olemiss.edu

Strongest Programs:
Accountancy
Creative Writing

(continued)

Modern Languages
International Programs
Pharmacy

department of mathematics) or a more advanced mathematics course; six hours of laboratory science; and 15 hours of humanities, social/behavioral sciences, and fine arts (to include at least three hours of coursework from each area). Approximately 50 percent of first-year students sign up for the Freshman Year Experience (FYE), a seminar-style course that helps new students transition from high school into a successful college career. The newly established Center for Writing and Rhetoric administers two mandatory composition courses for freshman. "The quality of teaching is superior," cheers one senior. "It is not at all uncommon for full professors to teach freshmen and even offer tutoring to freshmen during their office hours."

Ole Miss offers numerous study abroad options in diverse locations around the world.

For students itching to have their passports stamped, Ole Miss offers numerous study abroad options in diverse locations around the world, including Argentina, Botswana, China, Greece, Japan, Madagascar, Peru, and Thailand. "Our study abroad program is exceptional," gushes one senior. "Not only do they offer you the opportunity to travel basically anywhere that you want, they offer many different scholarships to make study abroad less costly." Another option is the Croft Institute for International Studies, which accepts 55 students each fall into the international studies program. Participating students study international politics, economics, and culture both in the classroom and via study abroad.

"Ole Miss students are ambitious, hospitable, and well rounded," says one public policy leadership major. They are also overwhelmingly white and homegrown. African Americans account for 18 percent of the student body, Hispanics 4 percent, and Asian Americans 2 percent. "The outside view of UM is that everyone is a sorority girl or a frat guy," a mathematics major complains, "but in fact there is a very diverse student body. We have people of all categories and cultures." Sixty percent hail from Mississippi and 47 percent graduated in the top quarter of their high school class. Merit scholarships averaging $4,939 are awarded annually, as are 318 athletic scholarships in 14 sports.

The Ole Miss social scene is dominated by the Greeks.

Thirty percent of students live in the dorms, which are a hit-or-miss affair. "Some of the older dorms have seen better days, but there is a new focus on campus to renovate and rebuild housing," a student reports. Options include apartments, traditional residence halls, and residential colleges. Traditional dorm living is "a once-in-a-lifetime experience," says one student. Another adds, "The residence halls are great. They provide a sense of community and family that makes Ole Miss unique." Campus dining options are reported to be plentiful and tasty. "We offer several different dining halls," says a student, "some of which are all you can eat and some of which are cafeteria style." Students give campus security a thumbs-up too: "Ole Miss is the kind of place where people look out for each other. Aside from that, we have a campus police department that works diligently to make sure the campus is safe."

"Our study abroad program is exceptional."

The Ole Miss social scene is dominated by the Greeks, which attract 30 percent of the men and 39 percent of the women, although non-Greeks find plenty to cheer about as well. "Ole Miss social life is one of a kind," says a senior. The Student Programming Board hosts a variety of on-campus activities each week, including movies, pageants, concerts, and multicultural events. Alcohol is forbidden on campus and students say the "two strikes and you're out" policy is effective at curbing consumption. Campus worship organizations have a strong presence on campus, and students find plenty of other ways to get involved, including student government and volunteer opportunities in Oxford. An overenthusiastic junior describes the city as "the best college town in the nation." A senior adds, "There are lots of locally owned businesses and restaurants that are unique to the area and very charming." Famed author William Faulkner grew up here and attended Ole Miss for three semesters before dropping out, and the slew of local cultural events includes

Overall, students at Ole Miss seem to be a contented lot.

the annual Faulkner and Yoknapatawpha Conference, featuring lectures and discussions by literary scholars and critics. Unfortunately, Faulkner's papers left home for the University of Virginia before the powers that be at Ole Miss figured out how important he was.

The Ole Miss Rebels compete in the gauntlet known as the Southeastern Conference, where they face the likes of Alabama's Crimson Tide, the Florida Gators, and the LSU Tigers. Solid teams include men's and women's tennis, football (2013 Compass Bowl winners), men's and women's golf, men's and women's basketball, volleyball, and men's and women's track and field. School spirit is on full display, especially when LSU is in town. On game days, frenzied fans gather to support their team. "Before every home football game, students, alums, and supporters can be seen enjoying warm fall days tailgating on our beautiful campus," says one happy Rebel. "The Grove is a place where people come together regardless of their differences to support our Ole Miss Rebs and share in a community that we all love." Intramurals are popular, too, and students may choose from 17 different activities each semester.

> **"Some of the older dorms have seen better days."**

Overall, students at Ole Miss seem to be a contented lot. Despite the lack of diversity and standard complaints over the lack of parking, it's clear that these Rebels have much to cheer about, including strong academics, game days in the Grove, and a healthy dose of school spirit. "Ole Miss has a welcoming sense of community, provides a challenging education, and is in a charming town," says one senior.

Overlaps

Mississippi State, University of Southern Mississippi, University of Alabama, Auburn, University of Tennessee, University of Memphis

---

If You Apply To ➤

Ole Miss: Rolling admissions. Financial aid: Mar. 1. Application fee: $35. No campus or alumni interviews. SATs or ACTs: required. Subject Tests: optional. Essay question.

University of Missouri

130 Jesse Hall, Columbia, MO 65211

Mizzou is renowned for one of the top journalism schools in the nation, but education, agriculture, and the health sciences are also standouts. Columbia is a quintessential college town. Often overlooked because many of the brightest Missourians head to Illinois for higher education.

In 1839, the residents of Boone County, Missouri, raised enough money to create the state university in Columbia. Today, Missouri's flagship university has evolved into a top research institution, yet continues to uphold the belief of its founders in the great value of higher education that is accessible to all. Currently in the thick of a $1 billion campaign, the university continues to expand programs and facilities in ways that benefit students, including new residential halls and renovations to the dining hall.

> **"Our academic climate supports a competitive and challenging atmosphere."**

The oldest public university west of the Mississippi, Mizzou's 1,358-acre campus is flanked by mansionlike fraternity and sorority houses. The entire campus has been designated as a botanic garden and features more than 5,400 trees and 650 varieties of plants. The Francis Quadrangle Historical District, with 19 National Historic Landmark buildings, is the core of the Red Campus (so named for the predominant

Website: www.missouri.edu
Location: Small City
Public
Total Enrollment: 30,120
Undergraduates: 25,046
Male/Female: 48/52
SAT Ranges: CR 510–640, M 530–650
ACT Ranges: 23–28
Financial Aid: 59%
Expense: Pub $ $
Student Loans: 56%

(continued)

Average Debt: $ $
Phi Beta Kappa: Yes
Applicants: 20,564
Accepted: 82%
Enrolled: 39%
Grad in 6 Years: 71%
Returning Freshmen: 84%
Academics: 🎓 🎓 🎓
Social: 🏆 🏆 🏆 🏆
Q of L: ★ ★ ★
Admissions: (573) 882-7786
Email Address: MU4U@
   missouri.edu

Strongest Programs:
Journalism
Biology
Psychology
English
Education
Physical Therapy
Food Science and Nutrition
Agriculture

The J-school has created a convergence sequence to introduce students to new digital technologies.

color of brick). Central to this area are the 60-foot granite columns of the original Academic Hall—the building was destroyed by fire in 1892. To the east of the columns is the original tombstone of Thomas Jefferson, which the Jefferson family gave to Mizzou (not UVA!) in the 19th century as a symbol of his championing of state-supported education. The White Campus consists of vine-covered limestone buildings, symbolized by the Memorial Union Tower.

With more than 270 degree programs and 19 schools and colleges, Mizzou offers a comprehensive set of choices for basic and advanced study. Aspiring journalists can get hands-on experience working on the *Columbia Missourian*, the 7,000-circulation local daily paper edited by J-school faculty members and students, or at KOMU-TV, the nation's only university-owned commercial television station. KBIA, MU's National Public Radio station, is popular among journalism students and listeners alike. The J-school has created a convergence sequence to introduce students to new digital technologies, and all journalism students are required to have their own laptops. Agriculture is also nationally ranked, especially in the areas of agricultural economics and applied research for farm communities. The College of Engineering maintains several notable undergraduate segments, including biological and civil engineering. The College of Business is highly competitive and features a five-year bachelor's/master's accounting program. The film studies curriculum offers an eight-semester program of courses focused on analyzing the social and cultural significance of film—plus a handful of screenwriting and production options.

> "The dorms are incredibly nice and spacious."

Committed preprofessionals will be glad to know that MU offers highly able and directed freshmen guaranteed admission to its graduate-level programs in medicine, law, veterinary medicine, nursing, and health professions. Mizzou is also one of the leading public research institutions in the country for the number and range of lab and scholarly opportunities it offers undergraduates, a task made easier through the new undergraduate research office. More than 250 undergrads do research each year, and about 2,500 enroll in service-learning courses. MU sends more students abroad each year—more than 900—than any other higher education institution in the state. Students may choose from more than 300 programs in more than 60 countries.

MU undergraduates must meet an array of general education requirements. They include courses in exposition and argumentation, algebra, math reasoning proficiency, and American history or political science. Students also must complete 27 hours in three content areas: social and behavioral sciences, physical and biological sciences and mathematics, and humanistic studies and fine arts. All students must take a course in computer literacy, although the content of those courses varies by degree program. Two writing-intensive courses are also required. Full professors teach the lecture courses at Mizzou, supplemented by a weekly discussion session led by a teaching assistant to go over material presented in class. Professors "make a conscious effort to convey their knowledge in a way that allows them to discover new facts and evidence on their own," a senior explains. Mizzou is one of only six public universities to have law, medicine, and veterinary medicine on one campus.

> "Our university does a great job of hosting and sponsoring events on campus."

Students say the courses at Mizzou are challenging but not impossible if you are willing to work hard. "Our academic climate supports a competitive and challenging atmosphere," says one communication major, adding that the overall vibe is "laid-back." Owing to MU's size, classes can fill up quickly, but professors do give overrides for students who must take certain credits at specific times. Missouri guarantees the availability of coursework to complete a degree in four years.

Seventy-seven percent of Mizzou students hail from the Show-Me State, though every state in the union and more than 100 foreign countries are represented. One student says, "The students at MU are change seekers, driven, ambitious, diverse, and passionate about anything related to the university." African Americans account for 8 percent of the student body, while Asian Americans and Hispanics combine for 5 percent. To boost its minority population, Mizzou has established several scholarship programs designed especially for minorities. It's also opened a Black Culture Center and an Asian Affairs Center. The Diversity Week program features workshops, speakers, and other events. Merit scholarships are available averaging $3,565, and student athletes may compete for 429 awards in 20 Division I sports.

The film studies curriculum offers an eight-semester program of courses focused on analyzing the social and cultural significance of film.

Twenty-six percent of MU students live on campus, and freshmen under age 20 are required to do so. "The dorms are incredibly nice and spacious, and are well located on campus," says a strategic communication major. "I lived in one of the oldest dorms that hadn't been renovated and it was never an issue for me," relates one sophomore. "I even promote it to incoming students because the rooms are a tad bit bigger and the location of my dorm was great." Residence halls have double rooms and are often crowded and noisy—and thus are fun places to be, though single-sex halls, a few single rooms, and round-the-clock quiet floors are also available. Dorm choice is first come, first served, and half of the halls offer co-ed living by floor or wing. Students can also choose to live in one of 25 living/learning communities, where residents share a common interest, such as engineering, arts, or nursing. About 50 percent of students choose a Freshman Interest Group—there are more than 100 to choose from—where 15 to 20 students with shared academic interests live in the same residence hall and enroll in three core classes together. Dorm dwellers are required to purchase meal plans, but credits can be used at all-you-can-eat dining halls, coffee bars, and take-out stands, among many options. "If you are vegetarian, vegan, or have any special dietary needs, our dining halls does a great job with providing a range of food and drink," says a hospitality management major. The fraternity and sorority houses are livable (the frat houses less so); 22 percent of Mizzou men and 28 percent of women go Greek.

"Columbia is a bustling college town."

Students at Mizzou, a champion of tough alcohol policies, have adopted the school's stance and agreed to ban alcohol from all fraternities and sororities, making it one of the largest Greek systems in the nation to go dry. The rule is lifted when alumni come home to visit. Students say MU's social life is packed with options, including movies, shopping, eating out, the usual Greek parties, and great parks and hiking areas on the outskirts of town. "Our university does a great job of hosting and sponsoring events on campus for incoming students and those without cars," says one student, "from bringing in special guests or celebrities, to offering Mizzou After Dark themed events held every Friday for free for students."

Students say the courses at Mizzou are challenging but not impossible.

"Columbia is a bustling college town that is high-energy most weekends," says one student. Students support the town by engaging in community service, and the community caters to them in return; their concern even goes beyond the borders of campus to the plight of the wild tiger and the preservation of its habitat. "Mizzou wouldn't be Mizzou without a million things to do," says a senior. Road trips to St. Louis, Kansas City, and Lake of the Ozarks offer a change of scenery.

As of 2012, Mizzou's Tigers compete in the rough-and-tumble Southeastern Conference, and basketball and football games draw big crowds. In fact, the entire town turns out in black and gold for any football game. The women's softball team recently won its fifth straight regional championship, and the football team earned its way to a postseason bowl game, where it handily defeated North Carolina. Facilities include a 2,000-seat indoor practice complex for football, baseball, softball,

Overlaps

University of Illinois, Indiana University, University of Iowa, Iowa State, University of Kansas, Kansas State

and soccer. MU's popular intramural program has nearly two dozen sports and two skill divisions, attracting more than a quarter of the student body.

Mizzou is a school on the rise. "It is a college that will shape your life and help guide you into the future," says a student. It continues to grow academically and physically, as evidenced by the ambitious capital campaign, while sticking with its longtime traditions. What's more, students are constantly challenged at every turn by quality teaching and ample research opportunities.

If You Apply To ➤

Mizzou: Rolling admissions. Financial aid: Mar. 1. Housing: Apr. 1. Application fee: $50. Campus interviews: optional, informational. No alumni interviews. SATs or ACTs: required. No Subject Tests. No essay question.

Morehouse College: See page 32.

Mount Holyoke College

50 College Street, South Hadley, MA 01075-1488

One of two women's colleges, along with Smith, that are members of the Five College Consortium in western Massachusetts. Less nonconformist than Bryn Mawr and Smith. MHC is strongest in the natural and social sciences, and one of few colleges to have a program devoted to leadership. One of the most selective institutions that is test-optional in admissions.

Website: www.mtholyoke.edu
Location: Small Town
Private
Total Enrollment: 2,281
Undergraduates: 2,274
Male/Female: 0/100
SAT Ranges: CR 610–720, M 610–700
ACT Ranges: 28–31
Financial Aid: 82%
Expense: Pr $ $
Student Loans: 65%
Average Debt: $ $
Phi Beta Kappa: Yes
Applicants: 3,876
Accepted: 42%
Enrolled: 31%
Grad in 6 Years: 81%
Returning Freshmen: 92%
Academics: ✍ ✍ ✍ ✍
Social: ☎ ☎ ☎
Q of L: ★ ★ ★ ★

The women who choose Mount Holyoke College value tradition, leadership, and achievement and eagerly support one another as each strives to meet her goals. Mount Holyoke pioneered women's higher education in 1837, and students rave about the quality of teaching and the small classes. While they complain about the heavy workload, most bring that challenge upon themselves as they seek intellectual fulfillment. "We have a long history of preparing excellent women to become world leaders and pursue their passions against all odds," says a senior. "We basically rock!"

Mount Holyoke is located in the heart of New England, on 800 acres of rolling hills dotted with lakes and waterfalls. Modern glass-and-stone buildings stand along-

> **"We have a long history of preparing excellent women to become world leaders."**

side more traditional ivy-covered sandstone structures. Highlights include the Japanese Meditation Garden and Teahouse, an art building with studios and a bronze-casting foundry, an 18-hole championship golf course, and an equestrian center. The music hall includes a two-story addition that has a 40-seat classroom, three studio offices, and a student lounge. The $33 million science center continues to advance the college's reputation as a leader in science education and houses classrooms, labs, and offices for eight departments.

Despite changes to the campus, curriculum at this 169-year-old institution remains decidedly traditional. Students are required to complete 128 total credits to graduate—32 in their major and 16 in their minor. Required courses include three humanities courses, two courses from science and mathematics disciplines (with at least one lab), two social science courses, one course in multicultural perspectives, and a language requirement. The college offers roughly 40 first-year seminars each fall and about 20 in the spring, covering a wide variety of topics and disciplines. The focus of these courses is developing skills in analysis and critical inquiry through speaking and writing. Some also include field trips to museums or events in Boston and New York.

(continued)

Admissions: (413) 538-2023
Email Address: admissions@ mtholyoke.edu

Strongest Programs:
English
Biology
Psychology
Economics
International Relations

The academic climate is rigorous. "The courses can be difficult but the support and relationships formed with professors and other students make the classroom experience overwhelmingly positive," says one senior. "Mount Holyoke students are ambitious but never cut-throat." Professors

"Mount Holyoke students are ambitious but never cut-throat."

are roundly praised for their teaching skills and genuine interest in students' success. "The professors are not only engaged in their research, but are fully present and teach all of the Mount Holyoke classes," says a student. The top-of-the-line chemistry labs, along with a solar greenhouse, a scanning electron microscope, several nuclear magnetic resonance spectrometers, and a linear accelerator, provide the students with state-of-the-art equipment necessary to be the best. Five-year dual-degree programs enable students to combine degrees from MHC with B.S. degrees in engineering from Caltech or Dartmouth. Students may also pursue a dual degree in engineering from the University of Massachusetts at Amherst.

Although some of Mount Holyoke's intro courses have 50 or more students, 95 percent of classes have 49 or fewer. Since the required curriculum is so diverse, there is little trouble getting into the smaller classes and finishing in four years. The school's honor code makes possible self-scheduled, self-proctored final exams. After those tests is the optional January winter term, where many students opt for a noncredit, nontraditional course, or an off-campus internship in New York or Washington, D.C. About 40 percent

"Students at Mount Holyoke are academically driven and very quirky."

of MHC students seeking a complete change of scenery spend all or part of junior year in another country. The Twelve College Exchange Program* offers opportunities in more than two dozen locales, while Mount Holyoke also sponsors its own study abroad programs, including stints in China and Costa Rica. Those interested in the sea may be interested in the semester at the Marine Biological Laboratory at Woods Hole, Massachusetts.

Mount Holyoke attracts students from all over the nation and the world, but 24 percent are Massachusetts natives. "Students at Mount Holyoke are academically driven and very quirky," says an African American studies major. "The student body is highly self-selected, so we end up with a curious, thoughtful, and academically serious bunch who do not necessarily fit any particular mold." African Americans make up 6 percent of the student body, Asian Americans 7 percent, and Hispanics 8 percent. "Social justice and human rights are big issues on campus," says one student. The Student Coalition for Action is a very large and popular campus group dedicated to social change. Merit scholarships are available, averaging $15,718, but there are no athletic scholarships. Twenty-one percent of freshmen are eligible for Pell Grants.

Ninety-five percent of Mount Holyoke students live in the residence halls, most of which have their own dining facility. "Some of the dorms are not the most aesthetically pleasing externally, but they all have a beautiful view of the surrounding campus," says a senior. Most dorms are also very homey, with living rooms, TV lounges, and baby grand pianos; all serve milk and cookies (as well as healthier fare like hummus and vegetables) most nights at 9:30 p.m. Students from all four classes live together and housing is guaranteed for all four years. Some residence halls also offer apartment-style living. Several dining halls serve tasty fare, including vegan and vegetarian options. "We get to eat food that is locally

The college offers roughly 40 first-year seminars each fall and about 20 in the spring, covering a wide variety of topics and disciplines.

grown and produced, which is more organic and healthy," an economics major says. Students also report feeling safe on campus thanks to an active security program. "I see Public Safety patrolling the campus at all hours of the night," says one African American studies major, "and think that they have a great relationship with students."

Students find the Five College Consortium* one of Mount Holyoke's greatest assets. A free bus service runs every 20 minutes between MHC and Amherst, Hampshire, UMass, and Smith, multiplying a Mount Holyoke woman's access to academic, social, and cultural opportunities. "Social life varies at Mount Holyoke. Many students stay on campus and party or hang out with friends or watch a movie or whatever, but a bunch of students also socialize off campus," confirms one student. The majority of social opportunities are on campus, such as parties, plays, concerts, speakers, and cultural events. If on-campus activities aren't appealing, road trips to Boston, Vermont, and New York City are also popular. Closer to campus, the South Hadley Center has eateries, a pub, shops, and apartments, though students say that Amherst and Northampton provide more shopping options. If you are 21, you are allowed to buy and have alcohol on campus; however, if you are underage and caught drinking, "a warning or a counseling session may be required," says a sophomore.

Perhaps more than their counterparts at Smith and Wellesley, Mount Holyoke women have made a virtue out of the school's most visible "vice": the lack of men.

"Some of the dorms are not the most aesthetically pleasing externally."

Women fill all leadership positions, thanks to a strong and supportive community spirit, and boys are just down the road at Amherst or UMass. Like most happy families, Mount Holyoke students take pride in tradition. Each class also has a color and a mascot, and class spirit is huge, especially for the annual Junior Show. Every fall on Mountain Day, students wake up to ringing bells, classes are canceled (even the library is closed), and everyone treks up Mount Holyoke to picnic and see the foliage. The *Mount Holyoke News* is the oldest continuously running college newspaper in the country, and the campus is also home to the Mount Holyoke College Victory Eights, the oldest continuing female collegiate a cappella group in the United States.

For those breaks in studying, the athletics at Mount Holyoke, such as crew, riding, field hockey, and lacrosse, are popular. For the third year in a row and the 20th time in program history, the college's equestrian team advanced to the national championships, finishing in third place overall. The squash team picked up its fifth straight Seven Sisters Championship and ended the season ranked 12th nationally. The college encourages athletic participation at all levels with a demanding 18-hole golf course, jogging trails, and two lakes. The 120-acre equestrian center includes a 69-stall barn, two riding areas, a training and show area, and seating for 300. Crew regattas and rugby take the place of football games, and students come out in force when the opponent is another of the Seven Sisters.

The traditions of academic excellence, modern upgrades, and easy access to New York and Boston provide a small college atmosphere with nearby cultural education. A history major says, "Students who are interested in a welcoming student body, challenging classes, an active schedule, and wonderful memories should really consider Mount Holyoke."

If You Apply To ➤ **MHC:** Early decision: Nov. 15. Regular admissions: Jan. 15. Financial aid: Feb. 12. Application fee: $60 (paper), free (online). Campus and alumnae interviews: optional, evaluative. SATs or ACTs: optional. Subject Tests: optional. Accepts the Common Application. Essay question.

Muhlenberg College

2400 Chew Street, Allentown, PA 18104-5586

There is a definite Muhlenberg type: ambitious, studious, and preprofessional. Takes its Lutheran affiliation and values seriously, but one-third of students are Jewish and another third are Catholic. Strong in premed, prelaw, pre-anything. Has a more humble, middle-class persona than more upscale Dickinson and Lafayette.

When a popular school pseudonym is "The Caring College" rather than some line referring to sun, booze, or babes, you know you're in for a different experience. That's the case with Muhlenberg College, a small liberal arts school that nurtures its students. Founded on solid Lutheran roots, the school continues to encourage religious diversity among students and to attract the best and brightest to its top premed school.

Set on 91 parklike acres, the 'Berg campus is a combination of older Gothic stone structures and newer buildings in a variety of architectural styles. Prominent facilities include a lovely chapel, the high-tech Trexler Library, a 40-acre biological field station and wildlife sanctuary, and a 48-acre arboretum with more than 300 species of wildflowers, broadleaf evergreens, and conifer trees. The campus also boasts a football stadium and all-weather track, and the 50,000-square-foot Trexler Pavilion for the Performing Arts that has a dramatic 45-foot glass outer shell and houses a variety of performing spaces. Renovations to the residence halls are currently underway.

> **"Teachers often conduct classes outside on nice days."**

Muhlenberg's regional reputation rests on its premedical program, which continues to attract large numbers of students. An agreement with Philadelphia's Drexel University College of Medicine guarantees seats for up to six Muhlenberg students each year. The college's theater arts program is also a national draw, and a few alumni have even gone on to star on Broadway. Science lab equipment at Muhlenberg is cutting-edge, and a comprehensive natural science major allows for a sampling of it all. The Living Writers course is offered every other year and has brought a number of noted authors to campus, including Robert Pinsky, Jay Wright, and Alice Fulton. Muhlenberg sends study groups to Washington, D.C., and students may spend semesters abroad in countries from England, France, Spain, and Germany to Argentina, the Czech Republic, Japan, Australia, and Scotland. Programs sponsored by the International Student Exchange are also available, and Muhlenberg is a member of the Lehigh Valley Association of Independent Colleges*.

The college offers three honors programs, the Muhlenberg Scholars Program, the Dana Scholars Program, and the R. J. Fellows Program, which focuses on the ramifications of change. Each is limited to 15 students per entering class. They carry an annual $4,000 stipend and culminate in an in-depth mentored senior research project. Business is Muhlenberg's most popular major, followed by psychology, theater arts, media and communication, and biology, and these are high-profile programs. Still, "I would say that whatever your interests, Muhlenberg offers them as competitive and well-taught courses," says a junior. Minors in public health and African American studies are available, and there are joint programs in physical therapy and occupational therapy available with Thomas Jefferson University. Students may also spend a semester at the Jewish Theological Seminary in New York City.

> **"There is a niche for everyone at the 'Berg."**

General Education requirements have been reorganized by faculty to include the popular First-Year Seminars, a two-course cluster in the sophomore or junior

---

Website: www.muhlenberg .edu
Location: City Outskirts
Private
Total Enrollment: 2,287
Undergraduates: 2,287
Male/Female: 41/59
SAT Ranges: CR 570–670, M 570–670
ACT Ranges: 25–31
Financial Aid: 85%
Expense: Pr $ $ $
Student Loans: 65%
Average Debt: $ $ $
Phi Beta Kappa: Yes
Applicants: 5,152
Accepted: 46%
Enrolled: 24%
Grad in 6 Years: 86%
Returning Freshmen: 91%
Academics: ✑ ✑ ✑
Social: ☎ ☎ ☎
Q of L: ★ ★ ★
Admissions: (484) 664-3200
Email Address: admissions@ muhlenberg.edu

Strongest Programs:
Premed/Biology
Prelaw
English/Writing
Theater Arts and Dance
Business
Psychology

year aimed at helping students connect different disciplines, two writing intensive courses, and a Culminating Undergraduate Experience (CUE) now required in each major program. The advising program continues to be strong.

The fun-filled, three-day freshman orientation program carries one requirement: learning the alma mater and then hightailing it to the president's house to serenade him. All freshmen also take a writing-intensive, discussion-intensive First-Year Seminar, with enrollment capped at 15. Seniors may take advantage of the Senior Year Experience program that helps students make the transition from college to "whatever comes next." The program is organized around the concepts of transition, integration, and reflection and includes workshops and seminars. Seventy-one percent of courses have 19 or fewer students, and since there are no graduate students, there are no teaching assistants. "The student/faculty relationship is truly unique on this campus," a student says. "Teachers often conduct classes outside on nice days, have classes over to their houses, and can be seen at college-sponsored events."

Muhlenberg sends study groups to Washington, D.C., and students may spend semesters abroad.

"There is a niche for everyone at the 'Berg," says a senior, "whether your interests are in knitting or theater, comedy or football, politics or hip-hop dancing." Muhlenberg draws 21 percent of its students from Pennsylvania, and many from adjacent New Jersey. "We have a diverse pool of interests, which creates a lively campus in terms of politics and social awareness," says a biology major. African Americans account for 3 percent of the student body, Hispanics 5 percent, and Asian Americans 3 percent. Cultural appreciation is emphasized as Muhlenberg continues to foster an ethnically and religiously varied campus. Students stay involved in the community by volunteering as tutors and with groups such as Habitat for Humanity and Planned Parenthood. A political science professor has started a student-run polling institute, which is raising campus awareness and activism. Merit scholarships are available but there are no athletic scholarships.

Muhlenberg's regional reputation rests on its premedical program.

Muhlenberg encourages students to live on campus and guarantees housing to all undergraduates except transfers, so 92 percent of students live in campus residences. All dorms have computer labs, study lounges, and vending machines. Prosser's co-ed wing makes a good choice for freshmen, while upperclassmen praise the Muhlenberg Independent Living Experience, or MILE, townhouses. Two dorms, Robertson and South, house 140 students in single, air-conditioned rooms overlooking Lake Muhlenberg. Other popular choices include Taylor and Benfer, where students live in eight-person suites that have their own bathrooms. "Dorms are comfortable and clean," says one senior. Freshmen choose from a seven- or five-day meal plan, and students agree that dining options continue to improve. "They try to make provisions for special tastes and the school does a good job to make different foods on different days of the week."

"Dorms are comfortable and clean."

Most social life at Muhlenberg takes place on campus. "The most fun I've had at school has been in my dorm hallway," says a student. "Just hanging out with people I meet is fun." The Muhlenberg Activities Council (MAC) provides comedians every Thursday evening—recent visitors have included Jimmy Fallon—current movies in the Red Door Café, live band concerts, and new movies on the lawn. "For those who enjoy different entertainment, it is easy to get together a group of friends, go somewhere, or make your own fun," says one student. Hillel is the largest student organization. City buses stop five minutes from campus for trips to Allentown proper and area malls. There also are daily bus runs to New York City (for clubbing and theater), Philadelphia (for nightlife and cheesesteaks), and Baltimore and Washington, D.C. Outdoorsy students can pick up the Appalachian Trail for a little hiking.

The fun-filled, three-day freshman orientation program carries one requirement: learning the alma mater and then hightailing it to the president's house to serenade him.

Eighteen percent of Muhlenberg men and 24 percent of the women pledge their undergraduate years to fraternities and sororities, respectively, but Greek life does not dominate the social scene—and it's becoming less important now that rush doesn't occur until sophomore year. Alcohol is forbidden if you're underage, per Pennsylvania law, and the school takes its policies seriously. Big social events include East Fest, homecoming, Deck Party, the Scotty Wood basketball tournament, the Mr. Muhlenberg awards—which parody the Miss America pageant—and the Henry Awards, the college's version of the Oscars. There's also a candlelight ceremony where freshmen write down their college goals, to be reexamined the day before graduation.

For the athletically inclined, the Muhlenberg Mules compete in the Centennial Conference. Football and women's basketball and softball have won conference championships in the past two years. Muhlenberg's Life Sports Center offers a pool, a basketball court, and other all-purpose courts, and a jogging track. Also popular is Frisbee golf; there's an 18-hole course on campus, where play goes on during all seasons and all hours of the day and night. Students say any contest against Johns Hopkins draws crowds.

Muhlenberg earns its moniker as "The Caring College" by offering students an intimate academic milieu and plenty of support. It's a winning formula that draws students from far and wide. Says one happy student, "The warm and friendly campus makes me feel at home."

> ### Overlaps
> **Lafayette, Ithaca, Franklin & Marshall, Skidmore, Gettysburg, Dickinson, Urisinus, University of Delaware**

If You Apply To ➤ **Muhlenberg:** Early decision and regular admissions: Feb. 15. Financial aid: Mar. 1. Application fee: $50. Campus interviews: optional, evaluative (required, along with a graded paper, if students choose not to submit SAT scores). No alumni interviews. SATs or ACTs: optional. Subject Tests: optional. Accepts the Common Application. Essay question: Common Application questions.

University of Nebraska–Lincoln

12 Administration Building, Lincoln, NE 68588-0415

Everybody knows Nebraska football, but in other areas UNL has a lower profile. Fewer out-of-staters attend Nebraska than, say, Iowa or University of Kansas. The flip side is that UNL has a corner on the market for Nebraskans without a major competitor like Iowa State or Kansas State. Agriculture is still the biggest drawing card, and the music program is also strong. Because of the state's demographic makeup, diversity is a scarce commodity.

On crisp fall weekends, when spirits are high and the Big Red football arcs through the air, Huskers cheer and paint the town of Lincoln red and white in a show of appreciation for their alma mater. In fact, on home-game Saturdays, the stadium is the third largest "city" in the state, holding 5 percent of the population. Away from the stadium, students at the University of Nebraska–Lincoln have more reasons to cheer with top programs ranging from bioengineering to agriculture to journalism.

UNL spreads across two campuses. The East Campus is home to the colleges of agricultural sciences and natural resources, human resources and family sciences, law, and dentistry. Most entering students end up on the larger City Campus, home of seven undergraduate colleges: architecture, arts and sciences, journalism and mass communications, business administration, fine and performing arts, engineering and technology, and the teachers college. On City Campus, the architectural style ranges from the modern Sheldon Art Gallery designed by Philip Johnson to the architecture building, which is on the National Register of Historic Places. There are also several malls, an arboretum, and a sculpture garden.

> **Website**: www.unl.edu
> **Location**: Small City
> **Public**
> **Total Enrollment**: 20,452
> **Undergraduates**: 17,766
> **Male/Female**: 54/46
> **SAT Ranges**: CR 510–660, M 540–680
> **ACT Ranges**: 22–29
> **Financial Aid**: 75%
> **Expense**: Pub $ $
> **Student Loans**: 60%
> **Average Debt**: $ $
> **Phi Beta Kappa**: Yes

(continued)

Applicants: 10,350
Accepted: 64%
Enrolled: 59%
Grad in 6 Years: 65%
Returning Freshmen: 84%
Academics: ✍ ✍ ✍
Social: 🐭 🐭 🐭 🐭
Q of L: ★ ★ ★
Admissions: (800) 742-8800
Email Address: admissions@
    unl.edu

Strongest Programs:
Business Administration
Psychology
Accounting
Biological Sciences
Finance
Bioengineering
Nanoscale Science

The Jeffrey S.
Raikes School of
Computer Science
and Management
provides a curriculum
in technology and
management.

UNL is big and there's
a group or activity
for everyone.

Nebraska's Comprehensive Education Program provides students with a common set of educational experiences across the majors and colleges. It has four components: Information Discovery and Retrieval (one course), Essential Studies (nine courses), Integrative Studies (10 courses), and Co-Curricular Experience. To help freshmen get oriented, a one-semester University Foundations class covers the inner and outer workings of the campus, organized around academic subjects. Big Red Welcome combines entertainment and food in a carnival setting to welcome new students, and the SIPS program (Summer Institute for Promising Scholars) is a six-week preorientation session for incoming minority students. The UNL Honors Program gives qualified students research opportunities to complement their coursework. Also, the Undergraduate Creative Activity and Research Experience (UCARE) program provides a stipend for students after freshman year who want to participate in research with a professor. Students also can study abroad in more than 140 foreign places such as Costa Rica, Germany, Mexico, and Japan. Nebraska's College of Agricultural Sciences and Natural Resources is known for its outstanding programs in food science and technology, agribusiness, and animal science. The school of music's opera program has received national attention, and the performing arts programs benefit from the Lied Center for the Performing Arts, which seats 2,300. The Jeffrey S. Raikes School of Computer Science and Management provides a curriculum in technology and management with the aim of developing leaders for this era of "expanding information technology and business globalization."

> **"I would say that the majority of my professors do a pretty good job."**

Getting into courses in the most popular areas, especially education, business, and engineering, can be a problem, students say; preregistration is a must. UNL can be academically challenging and competitive "among some circles of students," says an education major. Graduate students teach some freshman courses, but top professors can be found inside the classroom, too. "I would say that the majority of my professors do a pretty good job," says a sophomore. The UNL student body is "fairly conservative and welcoming," one student says. "They value hard work." Seventy-eight percent hail from in state and 54 percent graduated in the top quarter of their high school class. Asian Americans make up 2 percent of the student body, with African Americans and Hispanics combining for an additional 7 percent. Merit scholarships are available and the average award is $5,059. Student athletes vie for 413 athletic scholarships in 19 sports.

Forty-one percent of students live in the university's single-sex or co-ed dorms, and there's usually no trouble getting a room. Dorm lotteries favor those wanting to stay in the same room or on the same floor. "Dorms are phenomenal," enthuses one senior, who notes that rooms are "huge" and offer a "great community setting." Each room also is wired for Internet. Freshmen, who must live on campus, are welcomed to the residence halls through the FINK program, which is friendlier than it sounds (the acronym stands for Freshman Indoctrination of New Kids). In addition, there are a number of living/learning communities for interested students. Dining facilities are "new and wonderful," says one student, "and always have a wide variety of food selections."

> **"The entire state shuts down on football Saturdays."**

UNL is big and there's a group or activity for everyone; fraternity and house parties, roller skating, the movies, eating out, visiting coffee shops and bars (for those of age), and road trips to Omaha or Kansas City are just some of the activities that keep students busy. For many, the fall semester revolves around football weekends and postseason bowl games. "The entire state shuts down on football Saturdays," one junior says. Fraternities draw 17 percent of UNL men and sororities attract 21 percent of the women. They offer both social events and a chance to get involved in the Lincoln community. Homecoming, Greek Week, and Ivy Day are among the most anticipated campus events, as is The End, alcohol-free programming at the end of each semester during "dead week" and finals week. For those who want to indulge, plenty of bars are within walking distance of UNL, providing relief to students dissatisfied with the dry campus.

The Cornhuskers have a reputation as a powerhouse in a number of sports.

"Lincoln is a great college town, especially during football season!" exclaims one business administration major. Another student adds, "Thirty bars within a two-minute walk of campus." Town/gown relations are good and "the community is always eager for students to return in the fall," according to one premed student. That said, Omaha is only 45 minutes away. Pachyderm enthusiasts will be delighted by the Nebraska Museum of Natural History's outstanding collection of prehistoric elephant skeletons. Beyond the sidewalks are miles of flat roads and plains, ideal for biking, cross-country skiing, and snowmobiling.

"UNL is a good makeup of a variety of attitudes and personalities."

The Cornhuskers have a reputation as a powerhouse in a number of sports. Men's track and baseball and women's bowling, volleyball, gymnastics, track, and softball have all brought home Division I titles. And who hasn't heard of the classy Nebraska football? The biggest football rivalries are with Colorado and Oklahoma. Husker fans proclaim that if forced to choose between going to Oklahoma and going to hell in the afterlife—well, it would be a tough choice. Recreational and intramural sports are popular, with flag football, broomball, and basketball drawing the most participants.

At Nebraska, future agricultural experts mingle with techno-whizzes, while teachers-in-training brush elbows with architecture mavens. "UNL is a good makeup of a variety of attitudes and personalities. Overall, most people are down to earth and very 'Nebraskan'—lots of small-town people," says one senior. Whether studying overseas, immersing themselves in internships, or going wild on Saturday afternoon, students here know how to make the most of their time as Cornhuskers.

Overlaps

University of Nebraska at Omaha, University of Nebraska at Kearney, Iowa State, Nebraska Wesleyan, Creighton, University of Missouri, University of Kansas, Doane

If You Apply To ➤   **Nebraska:** Rolling admissions: May 1. Application fee: $45. Campus and alumni interviews: optional, informational. SATs or ACTs: required. No Subject Tests. No essay question.

New College of Florida

5700 North Tamiami Trail, Sarasota, FL 34243-2197

New College is the South's most liberal institution of higher learning—apologies to Guilford. With an enrollment of just over 800, New College is about one-third the size of a typical liberal arts college. The kicker: It's a public institution and a great bargain. Don't expect to hear many Southern accents; most students are transplants even if they went to high school in Florida.

The mere existence of New College of Florida is proof that it's possible to find success through individualism. This school has done away with grades and GPAs, so students compete with themselves rather than their classmates. The laid-back student body and rigorous academic program "proves to students that learning can be a self-directed, fun, and productive experience," a sophomore says. Indeed, college alumni include a Rhodes scholar, a Field Medal winner, two Carnegie and Mellon Fellows,

Website: www.ncf.edu
Location: Suburban
Public
Total Enrollment: 832
Undergraduates: 832

(continued)

Male/Female: 41/59

SAT Ranges: CR 620–740, M 570–670

ACT Ranges: 26–31

Financial Aid: 57%

Expense: Pub $

Student Loans: 39%

Average Debt: $

Phi Beta Kappa: Yes

Applicants: 1,348

Accepted: 60%

Enrolled: 28%

Grad in 6 Years: 69%

Returning Freshmen: 83%

Academics: ✑ ✑ ✑ ✑

Social: ☎ ☎ ☎

Q of L: ★ ★ ★

Admissions: (941) 487-5000

Email Address: admissions@ncf.edu

Strongest Programs:

Psychology

Political Science

Conservation Ecology

Biology

Literature

Anthropology

Math

Marine Biology

Students work out a "contract" with their advisor each semester and receive written evaluations instead of grades.

and a Gates Cambridge Fellow. What's more, NCF has produced 36 Fulbright scholars since 2001. Strong programs in psychology, biology, and anthropology complement the liberal arts offerings and boost the reputation of this fast-rising star. "New College does not produce cookie-cutter graduates," asserts one senior. "We are intellects, activists, and sometimes a little self-righteous."

New College began in 1960 as an alternative private college for academically talented students, but when inflation threatened its existence in the mid-1970s, it offered its campus to the University of South Florida. Today, NCF serves as Florida's honors college but is an academically independent entity. New College's campus is adjacent to Sarasota Bay and consists of historic mansions from the former estate of circus magnate Charles Ringling, abutting modern dorms designed by I. M. Pei. The central quad is filled with palm trees, and sunsets over the bay are spectacular. New College shares its campus with the Sarasota branch of USF, which offers upper-level courses in business, education, and engineering. A new academic building features 10 classrooms, 36 faculty offices, and a state-of-the-art computer lab.

"We are intellects, activists, and sometimes a little self-righteous."

The administration once had no required core curriculum, but has added requirements to provide "each student with the depth and breadth of knowledge characteristic of a good liberal arts education." All undergraduates must complete at least eight courses in the liberal arts curriculum, including courses in humanities, social sciences, and natural sciences, and show literacy in math and computers. The school calendar, however, is still unusual: The two 14-week semesters are separated by a month-long January Interterm, during which students devise and carry out their own research or conduct group projects. Students work out a "contract" with their advisor each semester and receive written evaluations instead of grades. The seven semester-long contracts and three independent study projects lead to an area of concentration, capped by a senior project thesis and an oral baccalaureate examination.

Due to the highly individualized nature of the curriculum, getting into some classes can be a challenge, especially for science majors looking to fulfill requirements for grad school admission. Courses are rigorous and challenging, but the environment is not competitive, students say. "New College is not competitive like normal universities because we do not have a GPA," says a biology major. "Instead, competitiveness can be seen in what internships people apply for, who gets to work with a professor on their research, how many students get prestigious awards like Truman scholars and Fulbrights." The shape of any student's program depends heavily on the outlook of his or her faculty sponsor, and students say advising—both academic and career—is readily available.

New College doesn't offer the specialized courses of a large university, but there's still plenty to choose from across the academic spectrum. A 1,100-gallon sea water system is available for lab experiments in animal behavior and physiology. Anthropology wins raves, and many students gravitate to biology, psychology, political science, and sociology. Academic programs are constantly changing to best suit students' needs; an example is the beefing up of offerings in environmental studies, religion, and economics. The Jane Bancroft Cook Library makes up for its small size—fewer than 300,000 volumes—with a language lab, videotape viewing area, an interlibrary loan program with the entire state university system of Florida, and a classroom equipped for teleconferences. A program in Chinese language and culture is available, as is a concentration in applied mathematics.

"For a small college with limited resources, we have an incredibly thought-provoking and challenging curriculum."

Students praise the personalized attention they receive from professors; graduate students and teaching assistants don't lead classes here and 73 percent of classes have 19 or fewer students. All disciplines provide the opportunity for original research and students also may conduct field research around the globe. "For a small college with limited resources, we have an incredibly thought-provoking and challenging curriculum," says one student. "Our biggest asset is our professors, who are not only experts in their fields but are extremely accessible to students and invested in our education."

In keeping with the revolution theme, students on this relatively cosmopolitan campus tend to be creative liberal types with '60s nuances and social habits. "New College students are brilliant, and they take their minds off of their intensive studies by partying hard," one senior explains. "They are thought of as being the people who were the 'weird kids' in high school, but I think that this stereotype is a little unfair because my peers here are very social and outgoing." Eighty percent hail from Florida, perhaps because New College has yet to make a national name for itself. Minorities account for nearly 20 percent of the student body; Hispanics account for 14 percent, 2 percent are Asian Americans, and African Americans make up 2 percent. Students are active and highly aware of social and political issues, tending to lean to the left. Issues run the gamut from women's rights to poverty and commercialism. Merit scholarships are available to qualified students although there are no athletic awards.

Seventy-five percent of students live in campus housing. "We just built five new dorms," says one student, "which some people like but others think are too stiff." The Dart dorms, two apartment-style halls, accommodate 140 students in two-bedroom, two-bath suites with a kitchen, living area, and—of course—air-conditioning. Rooms are chosen by lottery and there has been a room shortage as of late, forcing some to find off-campus housing. Dining gets a hearty thumbs-down from students. "The food at Hamilton center (our only dining hall) is notoriously awful," groans one student. As for security, the campus is considered exceptionally safe. A student quips, "I could walk across the entire campus at four a.m. completely naked and be safe" (although it's not recommended).

The abundance of students sporting T-shirts and shorts on Friday night reflects the laid-back campus social scene and the shortage of school-sponsored events. "New College has a very active social life," a senior says. "There are frequent parties on the weekends, campuswide social events such as the Gatsby Party and Woodstock. For those who do not like the partying scene, there are a great deal of substance-free events thrown by the Resident Advisors." The PCPs (Palm Court Parties) are "blow-out-of-proportion" social gatherings that occur during Halloween, Valentine's Day, and graduation. Alcohol policies are "almost frighteningly sanguine," a student says, "but this makes for a much safer and supportive environment." Sarasota offers little more than "beaches and old people," according to one sophomore. The Ringling Museum of Art and the Asolo State Theater adjoin the campus, and many New College instrumentalists perform with the Florida West Coast Symphony, Sarasota's professionally led symphony orchestra. The open road to Tampa, Gainesville, Key West, Orlando, New Orleans, Atlanta, and even Washington, D.C. ("to protest stuff"), beckons when Sarasota becomes too quiet.

New College is definitely not a haven for jocks; it fields no varsity teams, although the school is a member of the Intercollegiate Sailing Association. Many students take advantage of intramural sports, which range from basketball, soccer, and softball to swimming and sailing. The yearly faculty/student kickball game is popular, and anyone can play. Students also look forward to the Crucial Barbecue in January with music and mud wrestling; the Male Chauvinist Pig Roast; the SemiNormal, a semi-formal event on the bay; and the Bowling Ball, a formal-dress occasion at a bowling

The shape of any student's program depends heavily on the outlook of his or her faculty sponsor.

"For those who do not like the partying scene, there are a great deal of substance-free events thrown by the Resident Advisors."

Merit scholarships are available to qualified students although there are no athletic awards.

Overlaps

University of Florida, Florida State, University of Central Florida, University of South Florida, Rollins, University of Miami, Hampshire

alley. While the school has a 25-meter swimming pool, students complain that it closes at 10 p.m. The nearby ocean (which is open 24/7 barring hurricanes or red tide) is a bigger draw. "The beaches are gorgeous—white sand and blue water," says a student.

Without a Greek scene, grades, or crazy football games, NCF is definitely not your typical Southern institution. But the eccentricity doesn't impede students' academic motivation or their love of learning—whether it's belly dancing, biology, origami, or psychology. "If you want to get hands-on experience, work side by side with published professors, and leave with knowledge greater than what can get you a good score on a standardized test, then go to New College," says one happy senior.

<table>
<tr><td>If You Apply To ➤</td><td>New College: Regular admissions: Apr. 15. Application fee: $30. Campus interviews: optional, informational. No alumni interviews. SATs or ACTs: required. Subject Tests: optional. Accepts the Common Application. Essay question: views on an important issue.</td></tr>
</table>

University of New Hampshire

Grant House, 4 Garrison Avenue, Durham, NH 03824-3510

UNH is a public university that looks and feels like a private college, and its tuition hits the pocketbook with similar force. Expensive though it may be, UNH draws nearly half of its students from out of state. Strong in the life sciences, especially marine biology, and in business and engineering. With only a few graduate students, UNH's focus is squarely on undergrads.

Website: www.unh.edu
Location: Small Town
Public
Total Enrollment: 13,540
Undergraduates: 12,582
Male/Female: 46/54
SAT Ranges: CR 490–590, M 500–610
ACT Ranges: 22–27
Financial Aid: 81%
Expense: Pub $ $ $ $
Student Loans: 78%
Average Debt: $ $ $ $
Phi Beta Kappa: Yes
Applicants: 17,234
Accepted: 78%
Enrolled: 22%
Grad in 6 Years: 77%
Returning Freshmen: 86%
Academics: ✍ ✍ ✍
Social: ☺ ☺ ☺ ☺ ☺
Q of L: ★ ★ ★ ★ ★
Admissions: (603) 862-1360

Students at the University of New Hampshire know how to get their hands dirty, and this solid public institution provides them with countless opportunities to do so. UNH is one of just eight universities in the nation to receive the land-grant, sea-grant, and space-grant designations. Its research mission has grown dramatically in the last decade, yet the university remains a moderate-sized institution that emphasizes undergraduate instruction. Unlike many large research universities, the UNH faculty teach all students, including freshmen, and value teaching as much as they do their research. A love of the outdoors is a must, as well as the ability to withstand long, cold winters. "We are the bomb!" cheers one sophomore.

The university's wide-open grassy campus hosts a blend of modern facilities and ivy-covered brick buildings. The sprawling lawns are surrounded by nearly 3,000

"We are the bomb!" acres of farms, fields, and woods. During the past few years, UNH has invested in large-scale construction and renovation projects, including new residence halls, student apartments, a physics building, and an addition to Coastal Marine Lab. The latest addition is a new, 120,000-square-foot building for the Peter T. Paul College of Business and Economics.

Interdisciplinary programs enhance UNH's emphasis on traditional academic programs and the many research opportunities offered by its seven undergraduate schools. Business and engineering are among the most respected programs, and the English department has a solid creative writing program. The Peter T. Paul College of Business and Economics includes options in entrepreneurial venture creations, information systems, international business, and economics, management, marketing, and accounting; students can also design their own tracks. Marine biology is also considered stellar, due to UNH's proximity to the ocean and a freshwater bay. The

Discovery Program places a curricular emphasis on the first-year experience, a focus on the interdisciplinary learning experience, and integration of the UNH Discovery Program with the academic major and research. Qualifying students can begin an honors program featuring small classes during freshman year.

The university's general education requirements apply across the board and mandate completion of 10 courses from eight categories: writing skills; quantitative reasoning; biological, physical, and technological sciences; historical perspectives; foreign cultures; fine arts; social science; and works of philosophy, literature, and ideas. Freshman composition is mandatory as part of a four-course writing intensive requirement. Classes are relatively small, almost always 50 students or fewer, and TAs only facilitate discussion sections or labs. "We have world-class professors, many of which participate in research and include students as research assistants. Office hours are always provided, and many professors reach out to struggling students and make themselves available for whatever a student may need," says a senior.

"There is a huge party life at UNH."

UNH prides itself on producing undergraduates with research experience. The Undergraduate Research Opportunities Program provides about 100 research awards each year for undergraduates to work closely with faculty on original projects. In 2010, 30 percent of UNH students participated. Budding scientists and sociologists have opportunities to work at research centers for space science and family violence; other students can take advantage of the Institute for Policy and Social Science Research; the Center for Humanities; the Institute for the Study of Earth, Oceans, and Space; and the Center to Advance Molecular Interaction Sciences. The Interoperability Lab enables students to work with professors and businesses on cutting-edge problems of computing equipment compatibility. The Isle of Shoals Marine Laboratory, which operates several research projects with Cornell University, is just seven miles off the coast. And then there's UNH's Technology, Society, and Values Program, designed to address the ethical implications of the computer age. UNH's study abroad program offers exchange programs with 15 countries and additional opportunities are available through the Center for International Education.

While UNH is New Hampshire's major public institution, it has long been popular with out-of-staters, who make up 40 percent of its students. "Students at UNH are very involved and passionate about their education and their futures," says one student. "Most are very well rounded and take part in a lot of on-campus activities and events." African Americans account for 1 percent of the student population, Asian Americans 2 percent, and Hispanics 3 percent. A special task force at the university is working on keeping the minority students in school until graduation and helping them network. Social issues at UNH include alcohol awareness and—as might be expected in a place with such lush natural beauty—the environment. The school offers hundreds of merit scholarships, averaging $8,460, and 168 awards are available for gifted athletes.

"Students at UNH are very involved and passionate."

Fifty-seven percent of UNHers live in the school's co-ed dorms. "Some of the freshmen dorms are too far away from the main area of campus (Williamson and Christenson)," says one senior. "The rooms in these dorms are not great either. Stoke is a major party dorm full of freshies but it is also a dirty dorm." The dorms offer special-interest groupings, lounges, fireplaces, TV and study rooms, and kitchenettes. Freshmen and sophomores are guaranteed dorm rooms; most upperclassmen live off campus or in Gables and Woodside, on-campus apartment complexes. Students gripe that parking is difficult on campus but say campus dining is finger-licking good. "The food is always fresh," says an animal science major. "I would say it is restaurant quality."

"There is a huge party life at UNH," cheers one student. "Everyone here seems to be relaxed and love to have a good time." Greek groups claim 8 percent of UNH men

(continued)

Email Address: admissions@ unh.edu

Strongest Programs:
Business Administration
Psychology
English
Mechanical Engineering
Biomedical Science
Marine Science
Ocean Engineering
Sustainability

The Discovery Program places a curricular emphasis on the first-year experience, a focus on the interdisciplinary learning experience.

The Interoperability Lab enables students to work with professors and businesses on cutting-edge problems of computing equipment compatibility.

and 10 percent of UNH women. The Greeks also throw parties, which are subject to the university's no-tolerance alcohol policy that evicts from on-campus housing underage students caught with alcohol more than once. For nondrinkers, the university offers weekend social events including concerts, dances, movies, and gatherings at local coffeehouses.

Less than a five-minute walk from campus is the beautiful little town of Durham, which caters to the student clientele. Along Main Street, Durham has many restaurants and coffeehouses, a grocery store, an ice cream parlor, and a few bars, which have been divided into separate sections (for legal consumers of alcohol and everyone else). Durham is UNH, students say, and the one complaint is that the city closes down on weekends. Popular road trips include Boston and the White Mountains, or apple picking at a nearby farm. Late nights at L.L. Bean have also become commonplace, and homecoming, Greek Week, Winter Carnival, Casino Night, and Spring Fling draw crowds every year. Every four years, New Hampshire takes the spotlight when the state holds the nation's earliest presidential primaries.

UNH teams that regularly enjoy national rankings and generate strong spectator interest include men's and women's ice hockey, and students celebrate the first UNH goal of each game by inexplicably throwing a large fish onto the ice. Other solid teams include football, women's field hockey, and women's swimming and diving. When the hockey team plays its rival, the University of Maine–Orono, students wear white to "white out" the stadium. The university has a strong intramural sports program involving thousands of students. Broomball—played with brooms, balls, and sneakers on the ice—is very popular. "Intramurals are great!" cheers one senior.

When there's no game to watch or postgame revelry to indulge in, nature provides UNH students with more than enough to do—if they can find time off. (The school's nickname is the University of No Holidays, since an exceptionally generous winter break limits the number of days off during other seasons.) Skiing, camping, fishing, and hiking in nearby forests are favorite seasonal pastimes, and the Outing Club is among the most popular student activities.

New Hampshire's only major public university offers a huge variety of programs. That's one reason it attracts so many students from out of state. The laid-back atmosphere and multitude of both academic and social opportunities makes the UNH experience worth every dime.

Overlaps

University of Massachusetts, University of Vermont, University of Connecticut, University of Rhode Island, Northeastern, Keene State, University of Delaware, Syracuse

If You Apply To ➤ **New Hampshire:** Early action: Nov. 15. Regular admissions: Feb. 1. Financial aid and housing: May 1. Application fee: $50. No campus or alumni interviews. SATs or ACTs: required. No Subject Tests. Accepts the Common Application. Apply to particular school or program. Essay question.

The College of New Jersey

P.O. Box 7718, Ewing, NJ 08628-0718

A public liberal arts institution in the mold of UNC Asheville or William and Mary. Also offers business and education. With more than nine-tenths of the students homegrown Garden Staters, TCNJ has little appeal beyond Jersey. On the other hand, it is now the state's second most selective institution, next to a certain school in Princeton. A smaller, more personal alternative to Rutgers.

The College of New Jersey is an up-and-coming public institution with special focus on undergraduates, an emphasis more commonly found at a private school. TCNJ offers professors focused on teaching and a campus physically similar to one found down the road at Princeton University—without the Ivy League price tag. Formerly a teachers' college, TCNJ strives to provide students opportunities in a host of other fields. The small size makes for closeness among students and faculty.

TCNJ is set on 289 wooded and landscaped acres in suburban Ewing Township, six miles from Trenton. The picturesque Georgian colonial architecture centers on Quimby's Prairie, surrounded by the original academic buildings of the 1930s. A flock of Canada geese makes its home in one of the two campus lakes. Additional facilities include a science complex, spiritual center, and three parking garages. More recent buildings include an art and interactive multimedia building and an education building.

To graduate, students must earn 120 credits for all B.S. programs in the School of Business, B.A. programs except for teacher preparation, and the bachelor of science in nursing. In addition, the list of majors and study abroad opportunities continues to grow. The First Year Experience program is a required two-semester sequence consisting of two courses—From Athens to New York, and Society, Ethics, and Technology. It is designed to ease students into the demanding reality of college life with an approach that integrates academics, individual development, and social understanding. Ten hours of community service is part of the require-ment. Also required of incoming freshmen: Expectations, a one-day program to help students and parents under-

"Most of the dorms are really nice."

stand what they can expect from the college and what the college expects of them; the 10-week College Seminar, to smooth the transition to college; Welcome Week, which gives freshmen a chance to meet their classmates and become acquainted with the campus; and Summer Readings, which exposes students to the kind of scholar-ship and dialogue they can expect at The College of New Jersey. Other requirements include two semesters each of rhetoric and mathematics, 26 credits of Perspectives on the World, and three semesters of foreign language (arts and sciences students only).

Consistent with the school's origins as a teachers' college, elementary educa-tion is popular and the business school is strong, as are the natural sciences. Sociology, health, and physical education are less solid. Academically, TCNJ is com-petitive and getting more so. "The academic climate is somewhat intense," confides a sophomore. "Some students and professors try to downplay the competitive nature, but overall it's pretty driven." The college offers a combined four-and-a-half-year B.S./M.A. in law and justice, taught jointly by TCNJ and Rutgers; a seven-year B.S./M.D. degree program with the University of Medicine and Dentistry of New Jersey; and a seven-year B.S./O.D. degree with SUNY College of Optometry. TCNJ also offers foreign study in 11 countries and is a member of the International Student Exchange Program, giving students access to more than 130 colleges and universities across the United States, including Alaska, the Virgin Islands, Puerto Rico, and Guam. The college has no teaching assistants, and faculty members get high marks, though quality can vary by department. "My professors are very pas-sionate about their work and field of study," says a psychology major. Another student adds, "Some have had a great influence on my life, and some would be better off choosing another profession."

The typical TCNJ student is "overly book smart" with "low social skills," accord-ing to one junior. A graduate student says, "TCNJ is really big on the 'community' feel." The school has no cap on out-of-state admissions, but only 4 percent of TCNJ's students are non-Jerseyans; 58 percent of the freshmen graduated in the top 10th of their high school class, and the majority attended public high school. The college has aggressively pursued minority students, and today, African Americans account

Website: www.tcnj.edu
Location: Suburban
Public
Total Enrollment: 6,494
Undergraduates: 6,287
Male/Female: 44/56
SAT Ranges: CR 550–660, M 580–680
ACT Ranges: 24–29
Financial Aid: 70%
Expense: Pub $ $ $ $
Student Loans: 60%
Average Debt: $ $ $ $
Phi Beta Kappa: No
Applicants: 10,295
Accepted: 46%
Enrolled: 29%
Grad in 6 Years: 87%
Returning Freshmen: 94%
Academics: ✍ ✍ ✍ ✍
Social: ☎ ☎ ☎
Q of L: ★ ★ ★
Admissions: (609) 771-2131
Email Address: tcnjinfo@tcnj.edu

Strongest Programs:
Biology
Chemistry
History
Elementary Education
Music
Psychology
Business
Computer Science

The College of New Jersey's 21 varsity teams (the Lions) are kings of the NCAA Division III jungle.

for 5 percent of the student body, Hispanics 11 percent, and Asian Americans 9 percent. "If you don't leave this school very well educated in political correctness, then you were obviously unconscious," says a marketing major, who praises the school for its diversity. Merit scholarships are available to qualified students. "TCNJ brings in many of the best New Jersey students who are accepted to Ivy League schools but cannot afford them," says a senior.

Dorm housing is only guaranteed for freshmen and sophomores, though approximately half of all students live on campus. "Most of the dorms are really nice," says a student, "but a few are older and outdated." Freshmen hang their hats in either Travers-Wolfe, a two-building, 10-story hall, or Lakeside, a four-building complex. After that, students can enter the lottery for about 2,100 upperclassmen spaces in the apartment-style townhouses, Community Commons, and the recently built residence hall, or try one of several local apartment complexes.

Although suburban Ewing doesn't really cater to students, funky New Hope, Pennsylvania, and preppy Princeton, New Jersey, are just up the road; restaurants, bars, movie theaters—and, this being New Jersey, many malls—are within a short drive. State alcohol policies are strictly enforced, and the underage shouldn't hope to imbibe at the campus bar, the Rathskeller. Nine percent of men and 11 percent of women belong to fraternities and sororities, respectively, which provide many of the off-campus parties. Campus programming includes dances, concerts, and movies. Road trips to Philadelphia and New York, each about an hour away and accessible by train, are also highly recommended.

> "My professors are very passionate about their work and field of study."

The College of New Jersey's 21 varsity teams (the Lions) are kings of the NCAA Division III jungle; they've won dozens of Division III crowns and runner-up titles. Students rally around the football and basketball squads, especially when archrival Rowan comes to town, and the women's field hockey, lacrosse, and soccer teams have a faithful following. TCNJers also look forward to several annual events, including homecoming, a Family Fest Day, and—the springtime favorite—Senior Week. The college also offers 14 intramural sports and 16 club sports programs.

The College of New Jersey is one of the nation's "budget Ivies," with reasonable tuition and a location that offers media types, artists, and budding scientists a relaxed suburban haven within shouting distance of the editors, producers, directors, curators, and pharmaceutical companies of New Jersey, Pennsylvania, and New York.

Consistent with the school's origins as a teachers' college, elementary education is popular.

Overlaps

University of Delaware, Drexel, Lehigh, University of Maryland, NYU, Penn State, Rutgers, Villanova

If You Apply To ➤ **TCNJ:** Early decision: Nov. 15. Regular admissions: Jan. 15. Application fee: $75. Campus and alumni interviews: optional, informational. SATs or ACTs: required. No Subject Tests. Accepts the Common Application. Essay question.

New Jersey Institute of Technology

University Heights, Newark, NJ 07102

NJIT is one of the few public technical institutes in the Northeast. It occupies a middle ground between the behemoth Rutgers and smallish Stevens Institute. Offers engineering, architecture, and management. At nearly four to one, NJIT's gender ratio is particularly skewed. Then again, no one comes to NJIT for the social life.

The New Jersey Institute of Technology provides a no-frills technological education that prepares students for a future in an ever-changing global workplace. NJIT's challenging programs emphasize education, research, service, and (not surprisingly) economic development. It's an enticing combination for students seeking a high-tech, low-cost education.

NJIT's urban 45-acre campus is dotted with 24 buildings of diverse architectural styles, ranging from Elizabethan Gothic to contemporary design. Some of New Jersey's greatest cultural institutions are just blocks away, including the Newark Museum, Symphony Hall, and the New Jersey Center for the Performing Arts.

NJIT is composed of the Newark College of Engineering, the College of Architecture and Design (composed of the New Jersey School of Architecture and the School of Art and Design), the School of Management, the College of Science and Liberal Arts, and the Albert Dorman Honors College (which enrolls almost 500 students). Top applicants are offered a spot in Dorman as NJIT freshmen, and they can stay as long as they keep their grades up. Perks of Dorman membership include guaranteed dorm rooms, research opportunities, and acceptance into the B.S./M.S. program after completion of five courses for the under- **"We need women."** graduate major. Engineering, architecture, and computer science garner the most student praise, while mechanical and electrical engineering are especially challenging. The administration acknowledges that interdisciplinary studies is among the weaker programs.

To graduate, students must fulfill general education requirements in areas ranging from English to management. All freshmen take Calculus I and II, English composition, computer science, physical education, and Freshman Seminar, a course that introduces students to university life. NJIT has worked with Rutgers to create a number of joint-degree programs from biology to history. Other programs include business information systems, biophysics, and bioelectronics. The university has also launched a prelaw program with an emphasis on technology. Learning communities in selected majors are available for incoming freshmen.

Most NJIT courses have 50 students or fewer. While some say the atmosphere can be low-pressure in certain fields, an electrical engineering student relates his experience this way: "The academic climate is extremely competitive. It requires hours of study just to keep up." The administration assists students if they are having a difficult time, arranging for leaves of absence or extra semesters with a lighter courseload. Some have problems getting into classes with enrollment caps that are offered only once a year. But one student calculates that if a freshman has all of the prerequisite courses, he or she has a good chance of graduating on time.

Students give teaching quality average to high marks. Since most profs have worked in their industry, they can offer job information along with academic assistance. Academic advising isn't as helpful as it could be, say some students. "My advisors just look at the courses I choose and make sure that I am supposed to be taking them. I wish they knew more," says one junior. Career counseling, though, is helpful in preparing students for the job hunt. NJIT's most-favored academic option is the co-op program, which enables juniors to get paid for two six-month periods of work at technical companies.

As New Jersey's comprehensive technological public university, NJIT attracts a wide range of students with different interests. But, one sophomore laments, "We need women." African Americans comprise 10 percent of the student body, Hispanics represent 20 percent, Asian Americans account for 21 percent, and 1 percent are Native American. Tolerance is not a problem here as it is on some other campuses. One student praises the Educational Opportunity Program, saying, "If it weren't for them, I would not be here. They make it easy to be a minority." NJIT has a chapter of Tau Beta Pi, the national engineering honor society. The university does

Website: www.njit.edu
Location: City Center
Public
Total Enrollment: 6,900
Undergraduates: 5,393
Male/Female: 79/21
SAT Ranges: CR 470–580,
  M 540–650
ACT Ranges: N/A
Financial Aid: 82%
Expense: Pub $ $ $ $
Student Loans: 61%
Average Debt: $ $ $ $
Phi Beta Kappa: No
Applicants: 4,216
Accepted: 64%
Enrolled: 38%

Grad in 6 Years: 54%
Returning Freshmen: 82%
Academics: ✍ ✍ ✍
Social: ☎
Q of L: ★ ★
Admissions: (973) 596-3300
Email Address: admissions@
  njit.edu

Strongest Programs:
Architecture
Computer Science
Applied Mathematics
Engineering
Environmental Science

Most NJIT courses have 50 students or fewer.

not guarantee to meet the financial aid of all admits, but offers merit scholarships to qualified students. There are also more than 100 athletic scholarships.

NJIT's four residence halls can accommodate one-third of the students, and 26 percent live on campus. "I love housing," says a junior. "We get free cable, fast Internet connections. We have very big rooms." He does advise, however, that you should get your application in on time in order to get one of those roomy rooms. Freshmen and students living farthest away get first crack at the rooms, and those who get in are guaranteed space the next year. Consensus has it that the best freshman dorms are Redwood Hall and Cypress. Upperclassmen move into fraternity houses or nearby off-campus apartments. The dorms and frats both have kitchen facilities, which many students welcome because the food service fare at times draws a few grumbles from students left with grumbling stomachs after dinner. Because of its urban location, safety is always a consideration at NJIT. However, students praise the security efforts the school has undertaken. "Public safety officers are always around," says an electrical engineering major.

NJIT has a chapter of Tau Beta Pi, the national engineering honor society.

The 4-to-1 male/female student ratio definitely puts a crimp in the social life. There are some outlets, though. Five percent of the men and three percent of the women join the Greek system. One of the best annual campus events is Spring Week, which includes bands, novelties, and a semiformal. Diwali, the Indian festival of lights, and Chinese New Year also give undergrads pause to party. "We have a lot of barbecues that bring people together," says an architecture major. Another option is the beach, an hour away, with windsurfing and sailing equipment courtesy of NJIT. Most students agree that the administration's strict alcohol policies are effective.

NJIT students take pride in their athletic prowess, though their teams operate at the bottom of the Division I food chain. Unable to join a regional conference, the Highlanders belong to the Great West Conference that pits them against unlikely and distant rivals such as Texas-Pan American and North Dakota as far as 1,950 miles from Newark. Men's soccer and baseball and women's swimming are the most popular sports on campus, followed by basketball, men's swimming, and tennis. The outstanding athletic facilities are open to all, and include an indoor running track, fitness center, racquetball and squash courts, a six-lane pool, and areas for weight training, archery, or aerobics. Outdoor facilities include lighted tennis courts, a sand volleyball court, and a multiuse soccer stadium seating 1,000. A proud (and sweaty) tradition is the Hi-Tech Soccer Classic, which pits NJIT athletes against rivals from MIT, RPI, and Stevens Institute.

"Students here are hardworking, smart, and aggressive."

"Students here are hardworking, smart, and aggressive," says an engineering management student. NJIT people have chosen their school because they want a top-notch technical education without the topflight price tag. Academics are the priority here, and if the social life is less than electrifying, students deal with it. After all, they know highly skilled jobs will beckon after graduation. Getting through is a challenge, but there's ample compensation available for NJIT alums in the technologically dependent workplaces of today—and tomorrow.

Overlaps

Drexel, College of New Jersey, Rowan University, Rutgers, Stevens Institute

If You Apply To ➤ **NJIT:** Regular admissions: Mar. 1. Application fee: $70. Campus and alumni interviews: optional, evaluative. SATs: required. Subject Tests: optional. Essay question. Architecture applicants must submit portfolio of work.

University of New Mexico

P.O. Box 4895, Albuquerque, NM 87196-4895

UNM is shaped by the intersection of Hispanic, Native American, and white cultures. Studies related to Hispanic and Native cultures are strong, and in a land of picture-perfect sunsets, photography is a major deal. Technical programs are fueled by government labs in Albuquerque and Los Alamos, and the business school produces an outsized percentage of New Mexico's commercial elite.

The University of New Mexico's heritage goes back to 1889 when New Mexico wasn't even a state, and the university's strengths are still rooted in the rich history of the American Southwest. New Mexico excels in areas such as Latin American affairs and Southwest Hispanic studies. Lest you think it is a typical state school, consider that many students are commuters or of nontraditional age. UNM also boasts New Mexico's only law, medical, and architecture and urban planning schools, as well as its only doctor of pharmacy program.

"The academic climate is very laid-back."

Seated at the foot of the gorgeous Sandia Mountains in the lap of Albuquerque, the beautifully landscaped campus sports both Spanish and Pueblo Indian architectural influences, with lots of patios and balconies. The duck pond is a favorite spot for sunbathing, and the mountains, which rise majestically to the east, are visible from virtually any point on campus. New construction includes a spate of student residences.

UNM offers more than 4,000 courses in 11 colleges and two independent divisions, running the gamut from arts and sciences, education, and engineering to management, fine arts, and the allied health fields. Academic and general education requirements vary, but the core curriculum mandates three English courses focused on writing and speaking; two courses each in the humanities, social, and behavioral sciences, and physical and natural sciences; and one course each of fine arts, a second language, and math. Those reluctant to specialize can spend a few semesters in the broad University College, which also offers the most popular degree, a bachelor of university studies. Freshmen are encouraged to participate in the Freshman Forum and Core Legacy Courses. Engineering and fine arts freshmen can join interest groups who share suites in a dorm. The Tamarind Institute, a nationally recognized center housed at UNM's School of Fine Arts, offers training, study, and research in fine-art lithography. Anthropologists may root around one of

"Students here are pretty chill."

New Mexico's many archeological sites, and engineers may join in major solar-energy projects. Other solid programs include Native American studies, Chicano-Mexicano-Hispano studies, and Latin American studies. Students may also enroll in a Navajo language program.

The academic climate is "very laid-back and depends on what field of study you are going into," according to a senior. Students are quick to help one another study, and competition for grades is the exception rather than the rule. As for professors, "I would have to give them a B," says a student. "There have been some very good ones and some that were very knowledgeable but didn't know how to teach."

By virtue of its location, UNM enjoys a diverse mix of cultures, even though the vast majority of students are state residents. A large minority student enrollment—43 percent Hispanic, 3 percent African American, and 3 percent Asian American—reflects this cultural diversity. A cultural awareness task force and student diversity council work to keep race relations from becoming rancorous, while

Website: www.unm.edu
Location: City Center
Public
Total Enrollment: 20,364
Undergraduates: 16,788
Male/Female: 45/55
SAT Ranges: CR 470–610, M 470–600
ACT Ranges: 19–25
Financial Aid: 85%
Expense: Pub $
Student Loans: N/A
Average Debt: $ $ $ $
Phi Beta Kappa: Yes
Applicants: 11,467
Accepted: 65%
Enrolled: 46%
Grad in 6 Years: 45%
Returning Freshmen: 77%
Academics: ✍ ✍ ✍
Social: ☎ ☎ ☎
Q of L: ★ ★ ★
Admissions: (800) 255-5866
Email Address: apply@unm.edu

Strongest Programs:
Southwest Hispanic Studies
Photography
Lithography
Geology
Environmental Studies
Laser Optics
Latin American Affairs

the student orientation program includes a cultural awareness component, and a full-time human awareness coordinator develops diversity-related programs for the residence halls. UNM also hosts the Arts of the Americas, a broad cross-cultural program that involves U.S. and Latin American artists in festivals, classes, and exhibits. "Students here are pretty chill," says a journalism major. "We hang out and stuff, but for the most part we are focused on school." Many classes, and several complete degree programs, are offered in late afternoon and evening sessions, and about half of the student body takes advantage of these after-hours options. Half of the undergraduate population receive merit scholarships and the average award is more than $2,000. Over 250 athletic scholarships are available as well.

Many UNM students commute, and they say finding parking spots continues to be difficult as a result. Thanks to new residence halls, 45 percent of students now live on campus. Still, "This is a commuter campus," one senior says. An escort service, emergency phones, good lighting, and police who patrol around the clock help students feel safe. Students are happy with the variety of food available to them, and note that the remodeled student union building includes chain restaurants and a restaurant that serves food from different cultures every week.

Albuquerque—sometimes referred to as ABQ—is New Mexico's largest city, and it offers a variety of cultural attractions, including the nation's largest hot air balloon fiesta, a growing artists' colony, and concert tours to charm the ears. Santa Fe is an hour away. Those with cars or pickup trucks take advantage of the state's natural attractions: superb skiing in Taos, the Carlsbad Caverns, the Sandias, as well as excellent hiking and camping opportunities. For the historically inclined, numerous Spanish and Indian ruins are within an easy drive. And for those who yearn for more exotic locales, study abroad programs beckon from Mexico, Brazil, Venezuela, Costa Rica, and Scotland.

Alcohol, though banned on the UNM campus, is readily available, according to most students, especially at Greek parties. Speaking of the Greeks—a mere 3 percent of men and women join. Other students find their fun off campus in Albuquerque's clubs and restaurants. "Social life takes place both on and off campus," a junior says. For the more socially conscious, the college sponsors Spring Storm, an outing of roughly a thousand students who volunteer around the city on a Saturday. Annual social events include Welcome Back Days in the fall and Nizhoni Days, a celebration of Native American culture. Each spring, the whole campus turns out for a four-day fiesta with food and live music.

The UNM Lobos compete in the Mountain West Conference and the men's basketball and football squads and the women's softball, soccer, and volleyball teams usually draw crowds. Recreational and intramural sports are popular; students flock to flag football, volleyball, soccer, and basketball.

UNM offers a sun-drenched location that satisfies—precisely because its academic climate is as relaxed as the rolling desert dunes. "People here are serious and accepting," says a senior, "which makes UNM a comfortable environment."

Overlaps

Arizona State, University of Colorado, Eastern New Mexico, Highlands, New Mexico State, University of Texas–El Paso

If You Apply To ➤ **UNM:** Rolling admissions. Application fee: $20. No campus or alumni interviews. SATs or ACTs: required. Subject Tests: optional, required for homeschooled students or those at nonaccredited high schools. Essay question: your educational and career goals and any other information the admissions committee should know.

Campus Station, Socorro, NM 87801

Boutique technical education with a Southwestern flair. Smaller than Rose–Hulman and somewhat larger than Harvey Mudd, Tech offers intense programs in an ever-widening number of technical fields. Skewed gender ratio and nothing-to-do town make social life bleak. Don't count on getting through in only four years.

New Mexico Institute of Mining and Technology has evolved so much since its founding that it has outgrown its name. Founded as the New Mexico School of Mines, the college now emphasizes computer science, chemical and electrical engineering, and information technology. New Mexico Tech continues to expand and change with the times, as evidenced by its growing reputation in antiterrorism training and research. Although the social life can leave one wanting, those seeking solid academics may be right at home here. "The students that are successful at NM Tech are those who are up for a challenge," says a senior. "You don't come here to party. You come here to learn."

"You don't come here to party. You come here to learn."

Tech's tree-lined campus, located 76 miles south of Albuquerque, is dotted with picturesque white adobe, red-tiled buildings, and plenty of grassy open spaces that "capture the spirit of the Southwest." The Jones Hall Annex houses classrooms, labs, and offices. NMT owns 20,000 acres adjacent to the town of Socorro (population 9,000), including Socorro Peak, which provides a mother lode of research and testing facilities. A thunderstorm lab sits on another mountaintop 20 miles away. Not surprisingly, mountain bikers, runners, astronomers, hikers, campers, rock climbers, geologists, rock hounds, and scenery enthusiasts feel right at home here.

NMT offers many excellent programs in three main areas: science, engineering, and natural resources. The departments of earth and environmental science, petroleum, and environmental engineering are among Tech's best, as is the program in hydrology. The technical communications program is on such an upswing now that administrators have hired a stable corps of instructors. Freshmen can participate in the First Year Experience Program, in which they are grouped by major under a peer facilitator. Other notable programs include information technology and mechanical engineering, as well as a master's in electrical engineering and a doctorate in applied mathematics.

As might be expected, students are drawn to Tech's library, which holds over 200,000 books. Computer facilities are, naturally, quite good. And teaching gets high marks, though because of Tech's relatively small size, most courses in the technical fields are offered sequentially. Students who don't take a cluster all the way through may wait several semesters before the necessary course is offered again. To graduate, students must take courses in calculus, physics, chemistry, English, technical writing, humanities, social sciences, and foreign language. Students say it's tough to finish all requirements in four years. A chemical engineering major says students get frustrated because "they never have enough time to finish projects and homework."

Tech's student/faculty ratio is low for a technical school, and though professors are research-oriented, they do take teaching seriously. "The quality is very high," says one student. Class sizes vary, though 93 percent have 50 or fewer students. Jobs with mineral industries, research laboratories, and government agencies are available through the five-year cooperative work-study program. Undergraduates can also work part-time at research divisions on campus, including the New Mexico Bureau of Mines and Mineral Resources, the Petroleum Research and Recovery Center, the Energetic Materials Research and Testing Center, and the National Radio Astronomy

Website: www.nmt.edu
Location: Small Town
Public
Total Enrollment: 1,607
Undergraduates: 1,359
Male/Female: 73/27
SAT Ranges: CR 550–670, M 590–700
ACT Ranges: 23–29
Financial Aid: 35%
Expense: Pub $
Student Loans: 42%
Average Debt: $
Phi Beta Kappa: No
Applicants: 1,188
Accepted: 31%
Enrolled: 94%
Grad in 6 Years: 49%
Returning Freshmen: 74%
Academics: ✑ ✑ ✑
Social: ☎ ☎
Q of L: ★ ★
Admissions: (800) 428-TECH
Email Address: admission@admin.nmt.edu

Strongest Programs:
Earth Science
Electrical Engineering
Materials Engineering
Physics

Observatory's VLA and VLBA facilities. The antiterrorism training and research comes through NM Tech's association with the Energetic Materials Research and Testing Center. Because 99 percent of the faculty does research and most hire undergraduates, opportunities for scientific investigation and independent study are plentiful. Quality advising, on the other hand, is not: "Some advisors really care about their students and try to help, while others sign your forms and can't wait to get back to their research," gripes a biology major.

Tech students are "highly intelligent, hardworking, resourceful, and scientifically inclined," says a senior. Only 18 percent of Tech's undergraduates are from out of state, and 1 percent are foreign nationals. Hispanics account for 27 percent of the student body, African Americans 2 percent, and Asian Americans 3 percent. "The issues mostly are about how someone got a better grade than so-and-so," says a chemical engineering student. Tech's housing facilities have improved and expanded since the days when women resided in the school's trailer park. Students can now live in suites with private bedrooms, a kitchen, and a living room. Less than half of students live on campus, which one resident describes as "comfortable but a little crowded." A bit of legwork can turn up decent and "incredibly cheap" housing off campus. When it's time to rustle up some food, students can eat in the cafeteria (via a mandatory meal plan) or hit the local restaurants for tasty Mexican food.

"The issues mostly are about how someone got a better grade than so-and-so."

Otherwise, the town of Socorro is far from being a student paradise. It is a mining-turned-farming area in one of the most sparsely populated areas in the Southwest that can only be described as tiny. Boredom may be a problem here, especially if you are under 21, says a senior, though he admits that in its own way, Socorro "grows on a person." The good news is the spectacular weather, where the meterological phenomenon known as rain is in danger of becoming a distant memory, and the nearby desert and spectacular mountains provide a wealth of outdoor opportunities. According to one Techie, "This is a small Western town with a deep Hispanic and Indian culture—it's very relaxed." Still, even those who enjoy the scenery and their classmates' company see a direct correlation between sanity and access to a car, which can take them to Albuquerque and El Paso or the Taos ski slopes.

With no Greek system and little excitement in Socorro, it's no wonder students at Tech have always had to work to make their own fun. The alcohol policy—"in your room only, over 21 only"—works in residence halls with active resident advisors. But a senior says, "It is very easy for minors to find alcohol." There are no varsity sports at Tech, but the men's and women's rugby and soccer teams do travel to challenge other schools. Many students also enjoy an extensive intramural program and the school's 18-hole golf course. And in the absence of teams to cheer for, Tech's most popular annual events are 49ers Weekend, a homecoming tribute to the miners of yore with gunfighters and a bordello/casino, and Spring Fling, a mini-homecoming. Fall Fest welcomes new and old students back to campus.

NMT boasts one of the most intimate and up-to-date technical educations—and certainly some of the best weather—in the nation. NMT is an island of intensity in the otherwise calm New Mexico desert, but those who make it through four years (or five or six) leave with a solid technical education at a rock-bottom price.

NMT offers many excellent programs in three main areas: science, engineering, and natural resources.

Students say it's tough to finish all requirements in four years.

Overlaps

Colorado School of Mines, MIT, University of New Mexico, New Mexico State, Texas Tech

If You Apply To ➤

New Mexico Tech: Rolling admissions: Aug. 1. Application fee: $15. Campus interviews: optional, informational. No alumni interviews. SATs or ACTs: required (ACT preferred). No Subject Tests. No essay question.

Eugene Lang College–The New School for Liberal Arts: See page 238.

New York University

22 Washington Square, New York, NY 10012

Don't count on getting into NYU just because Big Sis did. From safety school to global brand, NYU's rise has been breathtaking. The siren song of Greenwich Village now extends to a dozen study centers from Abu Dhabi to Shanghai. Major draws include the renowned Tisch School of the Arts and the best undergraduate business school this side of Penn.

With the world at its doorstep, New York University invites its student body to jump right in. Firmly planted in the heart of Greenwich Village, arguably one of the most eclectic and energizing neighborhoods in New York City, NYU has set its sights on becoming the world's first truly global university. Its growing student body, burgeoning new facilities, and multiple opportunities for high-level internships and research projects have made it a top option for a rising number of students. One senior observes, "The prestige of the university has certainly increased." What's more, "NYU is a place to gain street smarts in addition to book smarts," says a senior. "The combination of strong academics and an amazing location give NYU a big advantage."

It doesn't get more real world than the venue that NYU calls home. NYU has campuses and centers throughout the city but is centered on Washington Square. Trendy shops, galleries, clubs, bars, and eateries crowd neighboring blocks; SoHo, Little Italy, and Chinatown are just blocks away. Academic NYU buildings—both modern and historic—blend with 19th-century brick townhouses surrounding Washington Square Park (the closest thing NYU has to a quad). Kimmel Center for University Life houses meeting space for NYU's nearly 400 student clubs, plus areas for the frequent recruitment fairs and lectures featuring national and international leaders. It houses the Skirball Center for the Performing Arts' 860-seat theater, which is the largest performing arts facility south of 42nd Street.

> **"NYU is a place to gain street smarts in addition to book smarts."**

The city scene is a core element of the NYU experience. So, too, is the wide range of academic programs. The Tisch School of the Arts trained such famed actors and directors as Marcia Gay Harden, Alec Baldwin, Martin Scorcese, and Spike Lee, and current undergrads continue to win many national student filmmaker awards. Tisch also boasts excellent drama, dance, photography, and television departments, and it's not uncommon to see students who haven't yet finished B.F.A. degrees performing in Broadway shows.

Wall Street's future bulls and bears make their home at the Stern School of Business, where they benefit from a business and political economy program. Another favorite department among students (and the New York corporations who recruit them after graduation) is accounting, known for its high job-placement rate. The arts and sciences are strong, with English, journalism, history, political science, and applied math winning highest marks. There's an increased emphasis on foreign exchange and study abroad, with a dozen sites in Paris, Berlin, Shanghai, London, Florence, Madrid, Prague, Accra, Tel Aviv, and elsewhere, as

Website: www.nyu.edu
Location: City Center
Private
Total Enrollment: 34,497
Undergraduates: 20,950
Male/Female: 40/60
SAT Ranges: CR 620–710, M 630–740
ACT Ranges: 28–32
Financial Aid: 61%
Expense: Pr $ $ $ $
Student Loans: 53%
Average Debt: $ $ $ $
Phi Beta Kappa: Yes
Applicants: 42,807
Accepted: 35%
Enrolled: 34%
Grad in 6 Years: 85%
Returning Freshmen: 92%
Academics: ✑ ✑ ✑ ✑ ½
Social: ☎ ☎ ☎
Q of L: ★ ★ ★
Admissions: (212) 998-4500
Email Address: admissions@nyu.edu

Strongest Programs:
Drama/Theater Arts
Dance
Business
Art and Design
Film and Television
Music

well as exchange agreements with universities in other locations throughout the world. The Gallatin School of Individualized Study provides flexible schedules and freedom from requirements for those wishing to engage in independent study or develop their own programs. An annual undergraduate research conference at the College of Arts and Sciences gives students the chance to present findings from their research. The Steinhardt School of Culture, Education, and Human Development, the Silver School of Social Work, the College of Nursing, and the Preston Robert Tisch Center for Hospitality and Sports Management offer a plethora of career-based programs, including art, education, nutrition, and sports and leisure studies.

The city scene is a core element of the NYU experience.

Finding a cheap New York apartment may be easier than sailing through NYU's academics. The climate "is quite diverse across the various schools and programs," says one junior. "The classes can be very challenging," adds a senior, "but students have a plethora of resources to help them succeed." Everyone is very focused on career preparation—it's never enough to just concentrate on your classes. Premed, prelaw, and prebusiness students may encounter packed schedules and competitive classes, while Gallatin and Tisch students may have lots of spare time, students say. "It's hard to avoid the pressure," says a student majoring in drama and politics, with nine hours of acting class a day and writing-intensive academic courses, too. At least the NYU library is accommodating—it's one of the largest open-stack facilities in the country, with more than 5.1 million volumes.

Under the Morse Academic Plan, freshmen and sophomores take courses including foreign language, expository writing, foundations of contemporary culture, and foundations of scientific inquiry. The language offerings, though, go beyond the typical Spanish-French-German—among the choices are Cantonese, Hindi, Modern Irish, Swahili, and Tagalog—and students are required to show medium proficiency. Despite the university's mammoth size, 63 percent of classes taken by freshmen have 19 or fewer students. Graduate students might lead

"The classes can be very challenging."

foreign language sections, writing workshops, and the recitations that accompany lectures, but students still say teaching is top-notch. "Surprisingly, most of our introductory courses are taught by really great and well-known professors," says one student. "I have found professors to be accessible and willing to help their students succeed," a history major adds. Those qualifying for freshmen honors seminars study in small classes under top faculty and eminent visiting professors.

The variety of degree options here may tempt students to hang around the Village for more than four years. There's a seven-year dental program and a five-year joint engineering program with New Jersey's Stevens Institute of Technology. Freshmen selected as University Scholars travel abroad each year. Point to a spot on a world map and you'll likely hit a country hosting NYU students. Locally, internships range from jobs on Wall Street to assignments with film industry giants. The career center is "amazingly personal and well run," says an econ major, and has thousands of listings for on-campus jobs, full-time jobs, and internships.

Finding a cheap New York apartment may be easier than sailing through NYU's academics.

An international politics major says NYU students are "high achieving individuals, cosmopolitan, independent, self-driven, confident, and able to manage academics, part-time jobs, and internships while having active social lives." Thanks in part to the university's investment in new housing, a majority of students (67 percent) now come from outside New York State. The NYU students who are from New York State come primarily from the city and nearby suburbs. African Americans make up 4 percent of the student body, Asian Americans 20 percent, and Hispanics 10 percent. On this generally liberal campus, gender issues, social justice, the Israeli-Palestinian conflict, and rights of all kinds—gay, lesbian, transgender, animal, human, and workers'—are important now, students say. "NYU is primarily a pretty liberal university," says a sophomore, "but conservative folks are welcome here, too!"

Because NYU is large and fairly decentralized, the Student Resource Center helps students navigate university resources and services. The university's Wellness Exchange provides students with a hotline that connects them with professionals who can help them address daily challenges or crises they may encounter. Students also meet with academic advisors—usually professors in their major department—at least once a semester. For concerned parents and students, the Office of Student Life, Protection, and Residence Halls hosts a series of workshops on keeping safe at NYU, and programs like the NYU Trolley and Escort Van Service provide door-to-door service for students until 3:00 a.m. "I always feel safe," says a linguistics major. "I can't walk more than one block without seeing an NYU security officer or an NYPD car just patrolling the area."

> "NYU is primarily a pretty liberal university."

While NYU students once had to fend for themselves in New York's outrageous housing market, the university guarantees four years of housing to all freshmen (and most transfers) who seek it. Twenty-one residence halls, ranging from old hotels to a converted monastery, provide a wide range of accommodations. Most rooms have private baths and are larger, cleaner, newer, and better equipped than many city apartments, enticing 50 percent of students to stay on campus. Freshmen are housed largely in freshman residence halls, many of which have theme floors, and rooms are assigned by lottery each spring. Amenities include central air-conditioning, computer centers, musical practice rooms, kitchens, and even, in some buildings, small theaters. The university provides free shuttle buses to dorms that are further uptown or downtown. The dining halls offer extensive choices—from wraps to sushi to Burger King. "The dining halls really try to accommodate everyone," says one student. Of course, downtown's array of ethnic restaurants also offers a variety of food at cheap prices.

> Students can't say enough good things about NYU's social life.

Students can't say enough good things about NYU's social life. "You're in New York City," says a student. "Why would you bother staying in your dorm at night when you're within minutes of internationally renowned art, world-class theater on Broadway, shopping in SoHo, and dining in Little Italy?" Another adds: "Greenwich Village is full of students, professors, artists, families; it's the most exciting, alive, cultural part of New York City." On campus, there are concerts, movies, fraternity and sorority events (only 8 percent of the men and 5 percent of the women go Greek), and nearly 400 clubs. The springtime Strawberry Festival includes free berries, cotton candy, outdoor concerts, and carnival amusements. Many students march in the city's Halloween Parade, which literally takes over Greenwich Village, while most spring and fall weekends find a city-sponsored street fair somewhere nearby. The Violet Ball, a dinner/dance held each fall in the atrium of Bobst Library, is an excuse to get dressed up. As for alcohol, underage students caught with it in public areas of dorms may lose their housing. The rest take their chances with the notoriously strict bouncers at bars and clubs around Manhattan. "They card like crazy," says one junior.

> "I can't walk more than one block without seeing an NYU security officer or an NYPD car just patrolling the area."

While sports have not traditionally been NYU's strength, successful Violets programs include men's cross-country, women's basketball, men's soccer, women's fencing, and men's indoor track and field, all of which compete in Division III. Nearly 40 percent of undergrads participate in intramural sports, which include touch football, bowling, and quickball. The Palladium Athletic Facility boasts a big swimming pool and a 30-foot-high indoor climbing wall.

Though it might seem hard to concentrate on schoolwork as the heartbeat of New York City thumps day and night, NYU students thrive on all that energy, and

Overlaps

UC–Berkeley, Columbia, Cornell, Harvard, Northwestern, University of Southern California

know how to spread it among their studies and social lives. "To be an NYU student is to be part college student, part New Yorker," a senior says. "Don't come here if you're not up to working hard and moving fast."

University of North Carolina Asheville

I University Heights, Asheville, NC 28804-8503

The "other" UNC happens to be one of the best educational bargains in the country. At just under 3,000 full-time, degree-seeking students, UNC Asheville is about half the size of fellow public liberal arts college William and Mary and 1,000 students smaller than Mary Washington. Picturesque mountain location in one of the most livable small cities anywhere. By Southern standards, a progressive university in a progressive city.

Website: www.unca.edu

Location: Small City

Public

Total Enrollment: 2,936

Undergraduates: 2,936

Male/Female: 43/57

SAT Ranges: CR 550–650, M 550–640

ACT Ranges: 23–27

Financial Aid: 71%

Expense: Pub $

Student Loans: 58%

Average Debt: $

Phi Beta Kappa: No

Applicants: 3,018

Accepted: 61%

Enrolled: 33%

Grad in 6 Years: 55%

Returning Freshmen: 78%

Academics: ✏ ✏ ✏ ✏

Social: ☎ ☎ ☎

Q of L: ★ ★ ★ ★

Admissions: (828) 251-6481

Email Address: admissions@ unca.edu

Strongest Programs:
Psychology
Literature

Whether it's the lush environment or the money you're saving, the University of North Carolina Asheville will have you seeing green. This public liberal arts university offers all of the perks that are generally associated with pricier private institutions: rigorous academics, small classes, and a beautiful setting. And it does it for a fraction of the cost. The university continues to integrate experiential learning into its traditional curriculum, emphasizing internships and service-learning experiences. Any way you look at it, UNC Asheville is a bargain that may have your friends turning green with envy.

Located in the heart of North Carolina's gorgeous Blue Ridge Mountains, the 360-acre campus lies in the middle of 1 million acres of federal and state forest near the tallest mountain in the East and the most heavily visited national park in the country. The campus was built in the 1960s, and much of the brick architecture reflects the style of that decade, although half of the buildings were added within the past few years. The Botanical Gardens at Asheville, adjacent to the main campus, features thousands of labeled plants and trees, and serves as a wildlife refuge and study center for biology students. Highsmith University Union features modern space for gatherings and student organizations, as well as an Intercultural Center, bookstore, game room, gallery space, and food court. A new, 400-bed residence hall features 75 double rooms and 150 singles.

"The quality of teaching at UNC Asheville is superb."

The university is dedicated to providing a liberal arts education that teaches students to fulfill their bright potential and become lifelong learners. The general education curriculum is known as Integrative Liberal Studies. The program is characterized by first-year and senior capstone liberal arts colloquia; a humanities core that addresses development and beliefs of Western and non-Western cultures; topical cluster courses in natural and social sciences; and courses in written communication, critical thinking, diversity, and information literacy. There are also requirements for foreign language study as well as health promotion and wellness.

Students report that the academic climate is largely dependent on the individual: "We have students that take their studies very seriously and some less so," says one sophomore. Political science, humanities, and literature receive near-unanimous praise, and one student says the math department "is undoubtedly the strongest on campus." The most popular majors are psychology, literature, interdisciplinary studies, art, and environmental studies. A joint B.S. degree in engineering (with a concentration in mechatronics) has been established with North Carolina State University and is the only such program in the state. The Freshman Living-Learning Intensive Program (FLLIP) helps first-year students develop relationships with peers, faculty, and staff through introductory colloquium classes, special extracurricular activities, and residential living. Other notable programs include a major in women's, gender, and sexuality studies and a minor in Asian studies.

(continued)
Interdisciplinary Studies
Art
Environmental Studies
Classics
Chemistry

Asheville also offers 2+2 programs with NC State in engineering, forestry, and textile chemistry; study abroad is an option in Europe, Asia, Africa, and South America. The UNC Asheville honors program offers special courses—as well as cultural and social opportunities—to motivated students who can make the grade, and nearly half of all students will have an undergraduate research experi-

"Compared to schools like UNC Chapel Hill, we are more liberal, less preppy, and definitely weirder."

ence by graduation. Students can take advantage of Asheville's strengths as a global source of information for weather forecasting and as a center of digital imaging, and, of course, fine arts and studio crafts. Professors are given high marks and noted for their passion and experience. "The quality of teaching at UNC Asheville is superb," says one senior. "I specifically chose this institution for the faculty, their desire to mentor students, and for the quality of teaching."

"Compared to schools like UNC Chapel Hill, we are more liberal, less preppy, and definitely weirder," says one student. "But it's that weirdness that makes the students at UNC Asheville so awesome." The head count at Asheville has risen steadily over the past decade, but only 12 percent of the student body comes from out of state. (The state limits its out-of-state admits to 18 percent.) Asheville is moving away from its early reputation as a hippie haven, but students still value this individualism—with more "geeks than beer-swillers." A substantial number of transfer students add their own brand of diversity to the campus. Students "like to be green in a number of ways," one student reports, "from recycling to being vegan to conserving water." Currently, the student body is 85 percent Caucasian, 3 percent African American, 4 percent Hispanic, and 1 percent Asian American, but Asheville is making special efforts to bring more students who are underrepresented to the campus. Asheville offers 166 athletic scholarships in 15 sports, as well as merit scholarships averaging $4,612.

Asheville is working hard to build up its on-campus housing. One-third of the students live in dorms. Students can choose from air-conditioned suites in Mills Hall, double occupancy in the Founders Residence Hall, or singles in the wooded Governors Village complex. There is no lottery, and freshmen are mixed in with

"The food is healthy, clean, and fresh."

upperclassmen. "The residence halls are not dorms where students are stuffed in and hope to survive," says one student. "They are communities." For meals, students may eat dining-hall fare or grab a bite at Café Ramsey. "The food is healthy, clean, and fresh," a senior says. "The pricing is affordable and with over 30 percent of students self-identifying as vegetarians, the vendors do a wonderful job of providing adequate options for all dining needs."

After class, there are plenty of opportunities for fun, especially for the many Asheville students with a hankering for the great outdoors. "The social life is very relaxed," says a sophomore. "A typical night out would include a hangout session with friends and then heading out to go to dinner." The college is surrounded by the Blue Ridge Mountains and the Smokies, where students can hike and rock climb;

A joint B.S. degree in engineering (with a concentration in mechatronics) has been established with North Carolina State University and is the only such program in the state.

Asheville is working hard to build up its on-campus housing.

water buffs can go rafting on the nearby French Broad River. Preorientation wilderness trips help build friendships among freshmen. For students with cars, the Blue Ridge Parkway is a short drive away, while Spartanburg and Charlotte are one and two hours away, respectively. Real big-city action takes extra effort, though, since Atlanta is a four-hour trek.

Asheville (named one of *Good Morning America*'s "10 Most Beautiful Places in America") offers a tame but inviting nightlife, with popular hangouts like Mellow Mushroom, Urban Burrito, Tupelo Honey, and Rosetta's Kitchen, and the city has been named Beer City USA several times. Asheville is also home to a bevy of street performers, outdoor music festivals, and a host of live entertainment events. Most parties take place off campus, especially since RAs stalk underage drinkers in the dorms. "There is no tolerance for unsafe, underage, or unwise drinking," says a student. Two percent of the men and 4 percent of the women belong to fraternities and sororities, respectively, but their presence is not influential. There are more than 70 campus organizations, including a student newspaper, the *Blue Banner*.

Several campuswide events bring the school together each year, including Founders Day in October, homecoming, a spring lawn party, and a mock casino night with an auction. Greenfest, a semester-based environment and beautification project, is also very popular. "There are lots of annual events, but the one I feel makes our campus unique is the annual Greenfest," says a student. "All groups on campus—faculty, staff, and students—come together for two or three days to help make a designated section of campus more beautiful."

Involvement is no problem for the athletic teams, who play in Division I. The Bulldogs boast Big South conference championship teams in men's basketball (winners of two of the last three conference titles), volleyball, women's soccer, and baseball. Other competitive teams include men's soccer and women's cross-country. Intramurals are at least as popular as the varsity sports. The Justice Center sports complex houses a pool, weight room, racquetball courts, and dance studio.

"I toured 57 universities and colleges, but came to UNC Asheville for three reasons," says one student: "The residence halls are communities, the campus is beautiful, and it's an undergraduate university." Indeed, all the ingredients for a superior college experience lie in wait at Asheville: strong academics, dedicated professors, and an administration that continues to push for excellence. It's a place to get the kind of liberal arts education usually associated with private colleges—but for a lot fewer greenbacks.

The Bulldogs boast Big South conference championship teams in men's basketball (winners of two of the last three conference titles), volleyball, women's soccer, and baseball.

Overlaps

Appalachian State, North Carolina State, UNC at Chapel Hill, UNC Greensboro, Western Carolina, UNC Wilmington, UNC Charlotte, Elon

---

If You Apply To ➤   **UNC Asheville:** Early action: Nov. 15. Regular admissions: Feb. 15. Financial aid: Mar. 1. Housing: May 1. Application fee: $50. Campus interviews: optional, evaluative. No alumni interviews. SATs or ACTs: required. Subject Tests: optional. No essay question.

University of North Carolina at Chapel Hill

CB 2200, Jackson Hall, Chapel Hill, NC 27599-2200

Close on the heels of UVA as the South's most prestigious public university. With more than 80 percent of the spots in each class reserved for in-staters, admission is next to impossible for out-of-staters who aren't 6'9" with a 43-inch vertical jump. But they keep trying by the thousands. Chapel Hill is a quintessential college town that is morphing into a medium-sized city.

Welcome to "the Southern part of heaven," a place where the sky is Carolina Blue and the academics are red-hot. As the flagship campus of the state university system, UNC at Chapel Hill has earned its place among the South's most prestigious universities. The atmosphere here is a unique brand of Southern, a rowdy mixture of hard work, sports fanaticism, progressive social values, and traditions that seems to attract bright, fun-loving students from everywhere.

Chartered in 1789, UNC pioneered public higher education in the United States and North Carolinians still take pride in Carolina's identity as "the University of the people." UNC's gorgeous and comfortable campus occupies 730 acres lush with trees and lawns and brick-paved walkways. The architecture ranges from Palladian, Federal, and Georgian to postmodern, with redbrick the prevailing motif. The original administration building is a replica of the central section of Princeton's gorgeous Nassau Hall, but sleek efficiency defines the latest architectural additions to the campus, which include buildings for medical biomolecular research and for bioinformatics.

"I am always impressed with how well-rounded students are."

Chapel Hill offers more than 75 undergraduate degree programs. Some of the strongest are sociology, philosophy, chemistry, business, political science, journalism and mass communications, classics, and biology. UNC's honors program is nationally recognized as among the best in the country, and exceptionally bright students may take part. With original funding from the Ewing Marion Kauffman Foundation, the university has developed a broad range of educational and experiential opportunities to help students in business, liberal arts, and sciences become entrepreneurial, including an entrepreneurship minor and the Carolina Challenge, a student-run competition that awards up to $50,000 in prizes each year for the best business plan. Undergraduate research opportunities are available to students in all disciplines, and students may be eligible to present their findings at professional conferences, publish results in academic journals, and win fellowships to support summer research in the United States and abroad.

The general education curriculum requires all students to complete 38 to 44 credit hours of coursework in three broad themes: Foundations, Approaches, and Connections. Coursework includes physical and life sciences, social and behavioral sciences, humanities and fine arts, composition and rhetoric, foreign language, quantitative reasoning, and lifetime fitness. The academic climate is challenging but not overwhelming. "Class discussions are very intellectual and sometimes intimidating," says one sophomore. Academic and social life are governed by a student-run honor system. In addition, the "Maymester" provides undergraduates with additional opportunities for work and study off campus. The three-week breaks occur between the fall and spring semesters and the second summer session and the fall semester.

Access to registration is based on seniority. If you get closed out of a class, "be persistent," advises a freshman. "Email the professor. You can get in!" For those tired of the classroom rush, Research Triangle Park, a nearby research and corporate community and home of the National Humanities Center, employs many students as research assistants. UNC offers more than 300 study abroad programs in 70 countries. The Carolina faculty is, for the most part, top-notch. Professors keep regular office hours and welcome those students who seek them out. "I am impressed by how passionate and inclusive professors can be here," says one student. Global studies (formerly international studies) is one of the fastest-growing majors with its emphasis on social, political, and cultural matters, while the newly formed curriculum in the environment and ecology consolidates undergraduate degree programs in environmental studies and environmental sciences within the College of Arts and Sciences.

"The pickiest of the picky could be happy with Carolina Dining Services."

Website: www.unc.edu
Location: Suburban
Public
Total Enrollment: 24,428
Undergraduates: 17,506
Male/Female: 42/58
SAT Ranges: CR 590–690, M 610–710
ACT Ranges: 28–32
Financial Aid: 64%
Expense: Pub $ $
Student Loans: 35%
Average Debt: $
Phi Beta Kappa: Yes
Applicants: 28,436
Accepted: 28%
Enrolled: 50%
Grad in 6 Years: 90%
Returning Freshmen: 97%
Academics: ✍ ✍ ✍ ✍
Social: 🎉 🎉 🎉 🎉
Q of L: ★ ★ ★ ★
Admissions: (919) 966-3621
Email Address: unchelp@ admissions.unc.edu

Strongest Programs:
Communications/Media Studies
Psychology
Biology
Political Science
Economics
Linguistics
Classics

The academic climate is challenging but not overwhelming.

"I am always impressed with how well-rounded students are," says a junior. "Academics are important, of course, but students consider other activities such as community service, art, and sports to be priorities as well." Under state guidelines, 82 percent of UNC's freshman class must be state residents, and the admissions office has no problem filling this quota with the cream of the North Carolinian crop. Thus, unless you're an athlete, out-of-state admission is extremely tough. Big social and political issues on campus include multiculturalism, gender roles, local and national elections, and religious issues. African Americans account for 9 percent of the student body, Asian Americans 8 percent, Native Americans 1 percent, and Hispanics 8 percent. This sports-minded school awards more than 500 athletic scholarships in all of the major sports. Students also can vie for thousands of merit scholarships worth an average of $8,452. The innovative Carolina Covenant program enables low-income students to graduate debt-free if they work on campus for 10 to 12 hours weekly in a federal work-study job instead of borrowing. Eligible students must come from families whose income is at or below 200 percent of the federal poverty level.

Forty-six percent of undergraduates live in university housing. "Our housing system is pretty darn good!" says a senior. Freshmen and returning students are guaranteed university housing, and returning students may reserve their rooms for the upcoming academic year. Housing on the north side of campus offers old and newly renovated dorms; the south side offers several brand-new housing options, which are a good hike from classroom buildings (not to worry—there's a free campus shuttle). Students may opt to be part of a living/learning community; house themes include foreign languages, substance-free, wellness, and women's issues. "The pickiest of the picky could be happy with Carolina Dining Services," says a freshman. "If you don't see it, you can request it. Great vegetarian options. Lots of variety." Campus security is praised for its constant presence on campus. "The university takes precautionary measures," says an education major. These include free bus and shuttle rides, emergency call boxes, and a fully accredited campus police department.

"'College town' in the dictionary should show a picture of Chapel Hill," boasts one senior. Franklin Street, the main drag in town that runs across the northern boundary of campus, offers Mexican and Chinese restaurants, ice cream parlors, coffeehouses, vegetarian eateries, bakeries, a dance club, and a generous supply of bars. Fraternities and sororities may account for only 17 percent of men and women, but they exert an influence far beyond their numbers. "Fraternities are also a social hub, and many students flock to their off campus parties," confirms one student. "But, Carolina students are very active and always searching for adventure, so one does not have to be up for the night scene to meet great people and have an incredible college experience." FallFest kicks off the school year with an emphasis on the idea that you don't have to drink to have fun. Students look forward to several annual festivals: the Carolina Jazz Festival and Halloween Celebration on Franklin Street are always, shall we say, raucous. The North Carolina Literary Festival is held biannually. Students are involved in the community, many through a unique service-learning program for which they receive academic credit.

UNC's athletic program has been wracked by a series of scandals that have tarnished the school's public image. Nevertheless, the varsity sports teams remain popular, especially football. The word "popular" doesn't do justice to the basketball games. A contest between the top NCAA rated Tar Heel Basketball Team and NC State makes any Carolina fan's heart beat faster, but Duke takes the prize as the most reviled rival of all. The slam-dunking Tar Heels play in the 21,750-seat Smith Center, named for retired coach Dean Smith, one of the winningest college basketball

Access to registration is based on seniority.

"'College town' in the dictionary should show a picture of Chapel Hill."

Fraternities and sororities may account for only 17 percent of men and women, but they exert an influence far beyond their numbers.

coaches of all time. Men's and women's basketball, lacrosse, field hockey, and men's soccer won a national championship in 2011–12, but the team with one of the best records in college sports history is women's soccer, which has won nearly two dozen national championships since 1981. Carolina has finished in the Top 10 nationally for the Directors Cup in 10 of the last 11 years. A strong intramural program draws heavy participation. Those less competitive can enjoy the $4.9 million student recreation center, which includes a weight-training facil-

"If God is not a Tar Heel, why is the sky Carolina blue?"

ity, an area for aerobic dance, and the student wellness center. Those who crave fresh air can take advantage of the Outdoor Education Center, which offers mountain bike trails, an 18-hole Frisbee golf course, rope courses, and one of the longest zip lines on the East Coast.

As a popular saying goes, "If God is not a Tar Heel, why is the sky Carolina blue?" It's a cute turn of phrase, but also points to something that is well-known in these parts: As one of the best college buys in the country, the University of North Carolina at Chapel Hill gives students everything they want, both academically and socially. Despite recent budget cuts enacted by anti-intellectual forces in the legislature and Governor's Mansion, the 200-year history of this school creates an atmosphere of extreme pride, a love of tradition, and monumental school spirit. One freshman, full of that school spirit, says, "Southern hospitality blended with a high level of thinking, an overwhelming dose of friendliness and pep, and a spectacularly gorgeous campus make Chapel Hill my favorite place in the world."

> ## Overlaps
>
> **Duke, North Carolina State, University of Virginia, Vanderbilt, Harvard, Wake Forest, Yale, Princeton**

If You Apply To ➤ **UNC at Chapel Hill:** Early action: Nov. 3. Regular admissions: Jan. 7. Financial aid: Mar. 2. Housing: May 15. Application fee: $80. No campus or alumni interviews. SATs or ACTs (with writing): required. Subject Tests: recommended. Accepts the Common Application. Essay question.

University of North Carolina Wilmington

Wilmington, NC 28403-5963

Still overshadowed by Chapel Hill and the other biggies in the strong UNC system, but making a name for itself. Strong in marine biology and other sciences. You won't see the Seahawks in the NCAA Final Four any time soon, but you will be able to get to know your professors. About 15 percent of incoming students come from out of state, most of those hailing from Mid-Atlantic, Northeast, and New England states.

At the University of North Carolina Wilmington, students enjoy extensive undergraduate research opportunities, a slate of solid sciences, and a close-knit community of like-minded individuals who like their modern academics mixed with a bit of old-fashioned Southern charm. The university's close proximity to the ocean provides motivated students with ample opportunities for fun in the sun and serves as a natural lab for the school's stellar marine biology program. Whether diving into the sea or their studies, UNCW students are filled with school spirit. "We are so proud of our university and it's easy to tell," says a student. "Every Tuesday we wear teal, but we are Seahawks every day of the week!"

Founded as Wilmington College in 1947, UNCW moved to its present location in the heart of New Hanover County in 1961. The 650-acre campus is only minutes from Wrightsville Beach and historic downtown Wilmington and features Georgian

Website: www.uncw.edu
Location: Small City
Public
Total Enrollment: 11,688
Undergraduates: 11,179
Male/Female: 41/59
SAT Ranges: CR 540–620, M 560–630
ACT Ranges: 22–26
Financial Aid: 58%
Expense: Pub $

UNCW offers 53 bachelor's degree programs and 38 graduate programs.

The Cornerstone Learning Communities are home to approximately 225 freshmen, who complete coursework together.

architecture and designated conservation areas. These conservation areas are significant zones of natural beauty with their longleaf pines, oaks, dogwoods, and native magnolias. Notable campus landmarks include the clock tower, Leutze Hall's Gates (portico), Chancellor's Walk, and the new Teaching Laboratory. The Campus Life complex serves as the hub of the university community and includes the Fisher Student Center, which houses a bookstore, game room, 360-seat movie theater, and student meeting space. The Campus Commons provides outdoor space for concerts and student gatherings. The School of Nursing moved into its new building in 2010, which boasts a state-of-the-art critical care laboratory designed to support student learning of complex and critical patient care skills.

"We are Seahawks every day of the week!"

UNCW offers 53 bachelor's degree programs and 38 graduate programs, which include a Ph.D. in marine biology and an Ed.D. in educational leadership. The most popular majors include communication, psychology, marketing, biology, and finance. The university's strengths lie in the natural sciences, especially biology, chemistry, and other disciplines that form the core of the marine sciences. Outside of the sciences, UNCW offers solid programs in film studies, creative writing, and business. The UNCW Honors College accepts approximately 125 students each year to participate in living/learning communities, advanced coursework, and experiential seminars; honors students must also complete a senior honors capstone research project. Undergraduate and independent research opportunities are available, too, including the Paul E. Hosier Undergraduate Research and Creativity Fellowship, which awards $1,000 for innovative research. "Although some classes and majors may be more challenging than others, UNCW professors are great at what they do and the workload is manageable," says one psychology major.

UNCW's University Studies requirements include courses in composition, physical education, humanities, fine arts, natural sciences and mathematical sciences, social and behavioral sciences, and interdisciplinary perspectives. Students must also demonstrate computer proficiency and complete courses pertaining to diversity and global awareness. Freshmen are taught by full professors who are lauded for their knowledge and involvement. "The great thing about UNCW professors is how much they care about their students," a business major says. Enrollments in introductory courses sometimes swell to more than 100, and 9 percent of all classes have 19 or fewer students. Freshmen benefit from a slate of special programs designed to ease the transition into college life. The Cornerstone Learning Communities are home to approximately 225 freshmen, who complete coursework together. All freshmen are required to attend a two-day orientation. Each freshman seminar has a Seahawk "link": students who help with the transition into UNCW life. For those yearning to experience new vistas, the university offers more than 500 study abroad programs in 50 countries; 26 percent of students participate.

"UNCW professors are great at what they do."

UNCW students are "friendly, outgoing, and involved," says a psychology major. "We wear flip-flops for most of the year, but we still make it to class and take pride in our school work," adds a sophomore. Fifteen percent of undergrads come from outside North Carolina, mostly from the South. African Americans account for 4 percent of the student body, Hispanics 6 percent, and Asian Americans 2 percent. The campus is moderately political, students say, and hot-button issues include sustainability, the credit crisis, and the most recent presidential election. Outstanding students can vie for hundreds of scholarships, while student athletes compete for 369 athletic scholarships in 11 sports. Under UNCW's Support Opportunity Access Responsibility (SOAR) program, students from families whose income is below 200 percent of the federal poverty line may receive a $1,000 Stafford Loan, $2,500 in federal work-study, and the balance in grants up to the cost of tuition. Students must maintain a 2.5 GPA to remain in the program.

Thirty-three percent of all undergraduates live on campus; housing options include eight residence halls, 19 apartment buildings, and seven suite-style buildings. "We have the traditional, hallway-style housing, upperclassmen apartments, sophomore suites, and specialty housing for fraternities, sororities, athletes, honors, international, and Cornerstone students," says one student. "Residence halls are always well taken care of," adds a senior. The demand for housing is high and "only about a third of students live on campus because of the lack of available dorm space," reports a junior. All students living in a residence hall, suite, or apartment purchase a meal plan; campus eateries include Wagoner Hall, the Hawks Nest food court, Dubs Café, and Einstein Brothers Bagels. "Our dining facilities are good," says one student, "and they are improving." Students also report feeling safe on campus, thanks to an active safety program that includes campus police, security guards, and ample lighting.

UNCW fields varsity teams that compete in Division I.

"Participating in organizations on campus is a great way to meet people and create a social life at UNCW," says one senior. Fraternities and sororities attract approximately 11 percent of the men and 13 percent of the women, respectively. Downtown Wilmington offers its share of restaurants, shops, and bars, and is "a very scenic and beautiful city," says a marine biology major.
Many students are active in the local com-

"The workload is manageable"

munity through school-sponsored volunteer work: "Our student body is huge on giving back and getting involved in the community," says a senior. The party scene is far from raucous, students say, and underage drinkers face stiff penalties if caught. "There will be serious consequences to deal with," warns a business major. Road trips include jaunts to Myrtle Beach, the Outer Banks, Washington, D.C., and the Appalachian Mountains.

UNCW fields varsity teams that compete in Division I, and the university is a member of the Colonial Athletic Association. Competitive Seahawk teams include men's basketball, baseball, golf, and tennis, and women's basketball, softball, volleyball, and soccer. "Seahawk basketball is huge!" raves one freshman. "Everybody looks forward to basketball season." Recreational and intramural sports are also popular and attract more than half of all undergraduates; students flock to soccer, flag football, basketball, field hockey, and ultimate Frisbee. Other popular events include homecoming, the Azalea Festival, and the annual Oozeball Tournament, "where teams of six compete in games of volleyball that take place on a court filled a foot deep with mud," according to a film studies major.

Despite complaints of limited parking, expensive food, and the lack of football, students at the University of North Carolina Wilmington seem to be a happy lot. "UNCW has the most bang for your buck," says a senior, and offers strong academics (especially the sciences), an unbeatable beach location, and tons of school spirit. A marketing major says, "We really bleed teal here! UNCW has so much to offer."

Overlaps

North Carolina State, East Carolina State, Appalachian State, UNC at Chapel Hill, UNC Charlotte, UNC Greensboro, University of South Carolina, Western Carolina

If You Apply To ➤

UNC Wilmington: Early decision and early action: Nov. 1. Regular admissions: Feb. 1. Financial aid: Mar. 1. Housing: May 1. Application fee: $75. No campus or alumni interviews. SATs or ACTs: required. No Subject Tests. Accepts the Common Application. Essay question: personal statement.

Box 7103, Raleigh, NC 27695-7103

It is hard for NC State not to have an inferiority complex next to highfalutin neighbors like Duke and UNC. But having them as neighbors is also a blessing—just ask the thousands of graduates who have gotten jobs in the Research Triangle. Engineering and business are the most popular programs. Compare to Clemson and Virginia Tech.

Website: www.ncsu.edu
Location: City Outskirts
Public
Total Enrollment: 26,894
Undergraduates: 21,665
Male/Female: 56/44
SAT Ranges: CR 550–630,
    M 580–670
ACT Ranges: 24–29
Financial Aid: 48%
Expense: Pub $ $
Student Loans: 57%
Average Debt: $ $
Phi Beta Kappa: Yes
Applicants: 20,435
Accepted: 50%
Enrolled: 42%
Grad in 6 Years: 72%
Returning Freshmen: 92%
Academics: ✍ ✍ ✍
Social: ☎ ☎ ☎
Q of L: ★ ★ ★
Admissions: (919) 515-2434
Email Address: undergrad_
    admissions@ncsu.edu

Strongest Programs:
Design
Statistics
Engineering
Pulp and Paper Science
Agriculture
Forestry
Textiles

North Carolina State is one of the bright leaves of the Tobacco Belt. Whether you're looking for a stellar education or a top-rated basketball program, NCSU offers students the benefits of a large school—highly regarded professors, a diverse student body, and plenty to do on weekends—while making sure that no one feels left out. Says one student, "No matter how weird or crazy you are, there is someone just like you on campus." Another adds, "NCSU offers wonderful opportunities for any prospective student."

> "NCSU offers wonderful opportunities for any prospective student."

The 107-year-old, 1,900-acre campus consists of redbrick buildings, brick-lined walks, and cozy courtyards dotted with pine trees. There is no dominant style, but more of an architectural stream of consciousness that reveals a campus that grew and changed with time. Holladay Hall has been designated as a historic site by the Raleigh City Council and newer campus additions include an engineering building and the Terry Companion Veterans Medical Center. NCSU's Centennial Campus is a 1,000-acre advanced technology community for university, government, and industrial partners.

NCSU excels in the professional areas of engineering, pulp and paper science, statistics, design, agriculture, and forestry, which are the largest and the most demanding divisions. Not surprisingly, given its location in the heart of textile country, the school also boasts a first-rate textile school, the largest and one of the best such programs in the country. Engineering tops the list of most popular majors, followed by business, biological sciences, agriculture, and social sciences. Even the most technical of majors requires students to take a broad range of liberal arts courses, although the humanities are far from the strongest programs on campus. Programs are also available in engineering mechatronics (with UNC Asheville), international studies, sport management, Africana studies, and turfgrass science. General education requirements include 20 hours of math and natural sciences; 21 hours of humanities and social sciences; seven hours of writing, speaking, and information literacy; three hours of science, technology, and society; two hours of physical education; and computer literacy courses.

> "NCSU is a very competitive college with challenging courses."

Students also must demonstrate proficiency in a foreign language. "NCSU is a very competitive college with challenging courses," says a junior. There are notable undergraduate degrees in genetics and soil and land development.

An important feature of NC State's approach to education is the cooperative education program, through which students in all schools can alternate semesters of on-site work with traditional classroom time. There are also domestic and international exchanges with nearly 100 countries, and a Residential Scholars program in which academic standouts live together and participate in weekly activities such as guest lectures. A First Year College program provides guidance and counseling for incoming students to introduce them to all possible majors. Students in the University Honors Program take part in a dedicated living/learning community and a plethora of honors courses, as well as a capstone project. Many classes at NC State are large, but the faculty gets high grades for being accessible, interested in teaching, and friendly. "Teaching quality is great," a senior says. "Professors are so knowledgeable and caring."

The university benefits greatly from its relationships with Duke, the University of North Carolina at Chapel Hill, and private industry through the state's high-tech Research Triangle Park. Its star continues to rise as it becomes more selective. The students at NC State are largely hardworking, bright North Carolinians. Some 81 percent are in-state students. "Our students are committed to their studies but know how to enjoy themselves," says a communications major. Eighty-seven percent graduated in the top quarter of their high school class, and nine out of 10 attended public high school. Eight percent of the student body is African American, while Hispanics and Asian Americans make up another 10 percent. Amid the public school diversity, conservatism abounds, and the largest political organization is the College Republicans. Jocks and sports fans are visible, and the university offers nearly 300 scholarships for men and women athletes. Those with outstanding academic qualifications can compete for one of thousands of merit scholarships. The Pack Promise guarantees that the university's neediest students will have 100 percent of their financial need met through a combination of scholarships, grants, work-study employment, and need-based loans.

As for housing, 27 percent choose to stay on campus. "Dorms are like home away from home," says a student, "and if anything is wrong, maintenance can fix it in a flash." All students are guaranteed rooms for all four years. Sullivan and Lee are recommended for freshmen because they provide a mixture of academic and social activities. Rooms range in size from spacious to cramped. Students report that dorm dwelling is actually more expensive than several off-campus units. Off-campus housing and social activities are plentiful. A small percentage of students are housed in fraternities and sororities, and the international house is also an option. The dining halls feed all freshmen and anyone else who cares to join the meal plan. "The food really is good," says a student. "There is such a variety that things don't get boring."

"We have an ongoing rivalry with the University of North Carolina."

The 21 fraternities and five sororities attract 11 percent of the men and 14 percent of the women, respectively. The Greek scene provides much of the entertainment, but dorm and suite parties are also popular. Alcohol policies are enforced, and if you're thinking about grabbing a brew, "don't try unless you're 21," warns a senior. Public transportation affords easy access to downtown, with its shops, restaurants, theaters, and nightspots. The university is well integrated into Raleigh, and its proximity to three all-women's colleges helps alleviate the imbalance of the 3-to-2 male/female ratio. Annual events include Wolfstock (a band party) and an All-Nighter in the student center. Many students also like to head to the beach, which is less than two hours away, or to the mountains for skiing, which is about a three-and-a-half-hour trip. Volunteering is popular, too.

With home close by for so many students, the campus does tend to thin out on weekends. Those who stay can cheer on the home teams, which do well in men's tennis, wrestling, gymnastics, and men's and women's cross-country and track and field. But needless to say, basketball reigns supreme—the Wolfpack plays in the high-powered Atlantic Coast Conference. "We have an ongoing rivalry with the University of North Carolina," says a junior. Some crazy NC State fans have stormed nearby Hillsborough Street following game-day victories. The annual State versus Carolina football game always packs the stadium, and the never-ending fight to "Beat Carolina!" permeates the campus year-round. Intramurals also thrive, and a particularly popular event is Big Four Day, when NC State's

Overlaps

UNC at Chapel Hill, East Carolina, Appalachian State, UNC Wilmington, UNC Charlotte

intramural teams compete against their neighbors at Duke, UNC at Chapel Hill, and Wake Forest.

North Carolina State seems to have overcome many of the obstacles associated with large land-grant universities. It has attracted a dedicated and friendly student body independent enough to deal with the inevitable anonymity of a state school, but spirited enough to cheer the Wolfpack to victory. NC State works well for both those who can shoot hoops and those who can calculate the trajectory of the same three-point shot. Says a communications major, "At NCSU, you will be welcomed and able to find your niche easily."

If You Apply To ➤ **NC State:** Early action I: Oct. 15. Early action II: Nov. 1. Regular admissions: Jan. 15. Application fee: $70. No campus or alumni interviews. SATs or ACTs (with writing): required. Subject Tests: optional. Essay question: personal statement.

Northeastern University

360 Huntington Avenue, 526 CP, Boston, MA 02115

Northeastern is synonymous with preprofessional education and hands-on experience. By interspersing co-op jobs with academic study, students can rake in thousands while getting a leg up on the job market—domestic and global. Aided by a huge spike in applications, it is rapidly transforming itself from blue-collar urban into Boston chic. With the city and the rest of the world beckoning, campus life is minimal.

Website: www.northeastern
.edu
Location: City Center
Private
Total Enrollment: 22,091
Undergraduates: 16,685
Male/Female: 50/50
SAT Ranges: CR 630–720,
M 650–740
ACT Ranges: 29–32
Financial Aid: N/A
Expense: Pr $ $
Student Loans: N/A
Average Debt: N/A
Phi Beta Kappa: No
Applicants: 44,208
Accepted: 32%
Enrolled: 19%
Grad in 6 Years: 79%
Returning Freshmen: 96%
Academics: ✏ ✏ ✏
Social: ☎ ☎
Q of L: ★ ★
Admissions: (617) 373-2200

Long known for its co-op program and hands-on learning experiences, Northeastern University has set its sights on becoming one of the region's top-tier institutions. NU is more selective than ever, and there is a push to add new facilities and big-name professors and to foster an atmosphere that encourages students to stick around despite the sometimes impersonal feel on campus. With a strong emphasis on combining liberal arts requirements with up to 18 months of challenging work placements, students come out of this school well rounded, well educated, and ready to take on real-world responsibilities. "We know how to

"Courses are difficult depending on your major."

tailor our undergraduate experiences to increase our professional skills and knowledge," says one psychology major. "It's a really exciting and transformational place to spend these formative years."

Northeastern's 73-acre campus is an oasis located in the heart of Boston, just minutes away from Fenway Park, shopping centers, nightclubs, cafés, Symphony Hall, and the Museum of Fine Arts. The campus's green spaces are interspersed with brick walkways, outdoor art, and a sculpture garden. Older buildings sport utilitarian gray-brick architecture while newer structures are of modern glass and brick design. During inclement weather, students can be found navigating the underground tunnel system that connects many campus buildings. The International Village complex houses approximately 1,200 residents and features a dining area and diverse menu of international cuisines. The building is also home to several state-of-the-art classrooms and administrative offices and Northeastern's first faculty-in-residence. The complex has several green features, including the nation's first university dining service-operated certified Green restaurant located in a LEED Gold building. A visitors center opened in 2012.

Northeastern's general education requirements (known as the NU Core) fall under a series of broad areas, including writing-intensive instruction, mathematical/analytical thinking, comparative understanding of religions and cultures, and knowledge domains. Students must also take part in a first-year learning community, integrated experiential learning, and a capstone experience. An honors program is open to top students and the College of Arts and Sciences has been restructured into three distinct colleges: the College of Arts, Media, and Design; the College of Social Sciences and Humanities; and the College of Science. The creative industries program offers a slew of combined majors, including graphic design and game design, digital art and game design, digital art and interactive media, and computer science and game design. The Northeastern University Scholars Program is limited to 50 students and offers customized global experiences, personalized advising and mentoring, access to university resources, and financial support.

(continued)

Email Address: admissions@ neu.edu

Strongest Programs:
Business/Marketing
Engineering
Health Professions
Social Sciences
Communication/Journalism

"Courses are difficult depending on your major. I've heard that engineering is extremely hard while business is focused on a lot of group projects and working well in teams," says an international business major. "You can certainly feel the tension in the air around finals and midterms," adds a junior. Woven into the Northeastern experience is its co-op education program, which enables students to sample professional careers prior to graduation and see how their classroom studies connect with the real world. Co-op assignments are paid, full-time positions related to the student's major and personal interest. Students complete at least two co-ops, four to six months in length, if they seek to graduate in four years, or three co-ops if they enroll in the university's traditional five-year bachelor's degree program. In an effort to help graduates prepare for the emerging global economy, the co-op program places students in companies around the world, from a soft drink maker in Nigeria to an electronics firm in China, or even at an Antarctic research station. The international business program features an "expat year" in which students spend one semester studying at an overseas university and six months pursuing an international co-op. The Presidential Global Scholars program makes scholarships available to work abroad.

"The students at Northeastern are very global, career-focused, and entrepreneurial."

Undergrads say that most of their teachers are concerned with their needs, and 63 percent of Northeastern's classes have 19 or fewer students. "Most of my teaching has been excellent," says a senior. "Professors and grad students alike have done outstanding jobs. I have also had a handful of bad professors—some of them terrible." Scheduling can be difficult, as students sometimes find that courses they want are offered only when they're scheduled to be away on a job.

"The students at Northeastern are very global, career-focused, and entrepreneurial," says a junior. Northeastern, which was founded as a YMCA educational program, has traditionally served local students from diverse socioeconomic backgrounds. These days, only 29 percent of the students are from Massachusetts. Consistent with Northeastern's efforts to promote a global culture, 15 percent of undergraduates come from overseas, double the proportion of four years ago. "From ethnicity to interest, Northeastern is very diverse," a student says. Besides the money they can earn in co-op programs, outstanding students can compete for merit scholarships. NU's scholarship program evaluates students' potential by considering more than grades and standardized test scores. Instead, the university uses a combination of traditional and nontraditional assessments, including interviews and personality tests. There are more than 250 athletic scholarships—including at least one for each sport.

Fifty-four percent of students live on campus in dorms described as comfortable and roomy. "I've lived on campus for three years and have loved each of my

The Northeastern University Scholars Program is limited to 50 students and offers customized global experiences, personalized advising and mentoring, access to university resources, and financial support.

Scheduling can be difficult, as students sometimes find that courses they want are offered only when they're scheduled to be away on a job.

dorm experiences," a junior says. "They are all very clean and if anything breaks, you just put in a work order and someone will fix it within the week." Getting a room can be a hassle, students say, due to the lottery system that favors seniority. Off-campus options include privately owned apartments or suites located adjacent to the residence halls. The dining halls offer "a lot of options and good food," according to students, who also speak highly of NU Public Safety: "Although Northeastern is right in the middle of Boston, it is a very safe campus. Students have to be swiped in and out of residence halls by a proctor and I always feel safe," says one senior.

When it comes to Northeastern's social scene, "the weekend usually starts on Thursday night, but major parties don't take place until Friday or Saturday," says one student. The co-op program puts a strain on campus social life. There are many clubs and activities, but the continuous flow of students on and off the campus tends to be disruptive. "I may see a friend one quarter in class and then not again for six months. It's hard to stay connected," a student explains. Fraternities and sororities attract 3 percent of NU men and 5 percent of women, respectively. Those who are not in the Greek system find Boston with all its attractions to be a fully acceptable substitute. Boston is the "ultimate college town," according to students, and it

"Northeastern students are a different breed."

offers a seemingly endless array of concerts, museums, clubs, and eateries (not to mention the overabundance of colleges and universities). "My only major complaint is that it's really expensive to live here," one student grumbles. In the winter, students head to the ski slopes of Vermont, and in balmier weather they're off to the beaches of Cape Cod and the North Shore.

Northeastern fields 18 varsity teams (the "Huskies") as part of the Colonial Athletic Association and the Hockey East Association. Competitive teams include women's rowing (CAA champs in 2009, 2011, and 2012), volleyball and soccer, and men's hockey, soccer, and basketball. The biggest sports series of the year is the Beanpot Hockey Tournament, which pits Northeastern against rival teams from Boston College, Boston University, and Harvard. "It is all about bragging rights and pride and the fans from the schools make it fun. It is great to go to the game, cheer for the Huskies, and tear down the other schools," a student says. And the fleet-footed men's and women's track and cross-country teams, who work out in the Bernard Solomon Indoor Track Facility, regularly leave their opponents blinking in the dust. One T-shirt reads, "No—we don't want to B.U.," epitomizing the competitive nature of the sports teams, especially toward those in the Boston area.

Perhaps now, more than ever, a school that truly prepares students to enter the working world is needed. "Northeastern students are a different breed," says a senior. "The typical Northeastern student wears many hats. We are employees at co-op, students in class, friends and roommates in our free time. We balance work and play while still meeting deadlines," explains a student. By the time Northeastern students graduate, they have built up a broad reservoir of experiences that they know will serve them well once they start scouring those job listings—both in the U.S. and around the world.

Overlaps

Boston University, Boston College, NYU, Tufts, Brown, Cornell, University of Massachusetts, University of Pennsylvania

If You Apply To ➤ **Northeastern:** Early action: Nov. 1. Regular admissions: Jan. 15. Application fee: $75. Campus interviews: optional, informational. No alumni interviews. SATs or ACTs: required. Subject Tests: optional. Accepts the Common Application. Essay question.

Northwestern University

1801 Hinman Avenue, P.O. Box 3060, Evanston, IL 60204-3060

The Big Ten is not the Ivy League, and NU has more school spirit than its Eastern counterparts. Much more preprofessional than its nearby rival University of Chicago or any of the Ivies except Penn. More similar to Duke and Stanford. World renowned in journalism. Suburban setting on the shore of Lake Michigan, with quick access to Chicago.

On Sunday nights before finals begin at Northwestern University, students are encouraged to let off steam with a campuswide "primal scream." The ear-shattering event illustrates two big themes at NU: Students work really hard, but they also know how to have some fun. Regarded as the most elite school in the Midwest, this top-tier university, the only private school in the Big Ten, boasts some of the most well-respected preprofessional programs in the country. Plus, Northwestern is ideally located just outside of Chicago. "I love being at a place where I can learn and have a great social life," says one student.

> "Northwestern is definitely a competitive university."

Northwestern is situated on 231 acres about a dozen miles north of the Chicago Loop. An eclectic mix of stone buildings with abundant ivy, the leafy campus is set off from the town of Evanston and runs for a mile along the shore of Lake Michigan. Students migrate between the North Campus (techy) and the South Campus (artsy). The newer buildings are located adjacent to a 14-acre lagoon, part of an 85-acre lakefill addition built in the '60s. This area provides students with a prime location for picnicking, fishing, running, cycling, rollerblading, or just daydreaming. Other notable facilities include the McCormick Tribune Center, a state-of-the-art broadcast and multimedia center; the 84,000-square-foot Center for Nanofabrication and Molecular Self-Assembly; and the Ford Motor Company Engineering Design Center.

Half of Northwestern's undergraduates are enrolled in arts and sciences, while the other half are spread out among five professional schools, all with national reputations. Indeed, students tend to identify more strongly with their school than with Northwestern as a whole. The Medill School of Journalism, the only such program at a top private university, sends student reporters out with iPads and video cameras as well as spiral notebooks. The curriculum integrates multimedia techniques with the study of "audience understanding" and features internships at dozens of top newspapers, magazines, and television stations across the nation. There's also a four-year accelerated B.S.J./M.S.J. program. A dazzling electronic studio centralizes Medill's state-of-the-art broadcast newsroom and the communication school's radio/TV/film department. The McCormick

> "The courses range from challenging to really challenging."

School of Engineering and Applied Science is strong in all aspects of engineering and pairs students with clients with practical problems. Five-year co-op options are available. The School of Music wants students who can combine conservatory-level musicianship with high-level academics. It requires auditions and offers a five-year program from which students emerge with two B.A. degrees. The School of Education and Social Policy is the only school of its kind in the country and competes with Vanderbilt for education majors. Students and faculty members alike are encouraged to range across traditional disciplinary barriers—a policy that has led to the creation of some entirely new fields such as materials science—and students are free to switch schools once they are enrolled.

Website: www.northwestern.edu

Location: Suburban

Private

Total Enrollment: 16,954

Undergraduates: 8,377

Male/Female: 49/51

SAT Ranges: CR 680-760, M 680-780

ACT Ranges: 31-34

Financial Aid: 54%

Expense: Pr $ $ $ $

Student Loans: 42%

Average Debt: $ $

Phi Beta Kappa: Yes

Applicants: 32,060

Accepted: 15%

Enrolled: 41%

Grad in 6 Years: 93%

Returning Freshmen: 97%

Academics: ✐ ✐ ✐ ✐ ✐

Social: ☎ ☎ ☎

Q of L: ★ ★ ★

Admissions: (847) 491-7271

Email Address: ug-admission@northwestern.edu

Strongest Programs:
Chemistry
Engineering
Economics
Journalism
Communication Studies
History
Political Science
Theater
Music

Consistent with this approach, students say the university's best programs include the Integrated Science Program, the Honors Program in Medical Education, and Mathematical Methods in Social Sciences, a selective program that gives students the technical skills to move into various areas of the social sciences. Each of the undergraduate schools determines its own general education requirements, but broad outlines are similar. Each school requires a graduate to have coursework in "the major domains of knowledge"—science, mathematics and technology, individual and social behavior, historical studies, values, the humanities, and the fine arts.

Unlike most schools on a 10-week quarter system, Northwesterners take four (not three) courses each quarter, except in engineering, where five are permitted. "Northwestern is definitely a competitive university," says a freshman. "The courses range from challenging to really challenging," adds an economics major. Students can take a break from the campus through any of the numerous field-study programs and programs abroad. Perhaps one reason students study so hard is the motivation provided by their professors. "The teachers are so approachable," says a freshman. "The quality of teaching is consistently excellent," adds a senior. Virtually all undergraduate courses, including required freshman seminars (of 10 to 15 students) in arts and sciences, are taught by regular faculty members. Introductory courses are larger than most, but the average 100-level class has about 30 students. Strong arts and sciences departments include chemistry, nano sciences, economics, history, and political science. The humanities as a group are less strong.

Finding a social niche can be tough, especially for those who aren't involved in athletics, Greek life, journalism, or theater. Twenty-six percent of students hail from Illinois. Minorities represent a sizable contingent of the student body, with Asian Americans accounting for 19 percent, African Americans 5 percent, and Hispanics 8 percent. Students tend to be very well rounded. NU is a liberal-leaning campus, but the abundance of preprofessionals has added to its image as "young corporate America." Upon graduating, NU students tend to pursue business fields like consulting and finance with technology, education, and communications distant followers. There are no academic merit scholarships, but NU does guarantee to meet the full demonstrated need of every admit, and as a Division I school, it offers a number of scholarships for its athletes. In addition, the university has eliminated loans for families with incomes up to $55,000 a year and capped loans at $5,000 for others.

"The quality of teaching is consistently excellent."

There are a variety of housing options that range from rundown to wonderful, according to students. "The dorms are very comfortable and inviting," one student reports. Most rooms are doubles, but there are also singles, triples, and quadruple rooms as well as suites. Several residential colleges bring students and faculty members together during faculty "firesides" or simply over meals. The newer Slivka Hall houses the engineering residential colleges; there also are special dorms for students in communications, international studies, humanities, commerce and industry, performing arts, and public affairs. Fraternities and sororities also have their own houses. Students can choose to eat at the coffeehouse or at any one of six dining halls on campus. A variety of meal plans are available, including one that provides Sunday brunch and one offering kosher food, and the university staff includes a dietician who consults with and designs nutrition programs for students who have food allergies or other special diet needs. The 35 percent of students who have headed off campus to apartments are mostly juniors and seniors. Students generally feel safe on campus, but crime has been a concern in Evanston, especially after dark.

Upscale Evanston is "the restaurant haven of Chicago's North Shore," says a junior, "very quaint with tons of flowers that bloom every spring." For a night out, of course there is that "toddlin' town," Chicago, right across the border. A short

Half of Northwestern's undergraduates are enrolled in arts and sciences.

The School of Education and Social Policy is the only school of its kind in the country.

stroll off campus brings you to the town's myriad restaurant options, trendy bars, and coffee shops with space to plug in a laptop and study.

Much of the social life on NU's campus is centered on the Greek system, and roughly three-quarters of the students go Greek. For non-Greeks, on-campus entertainment opportunities are numerous, including theater productions, concerts, and movies. The school's alcohol policy is tough, but not always effective, "like the vast majority of campuses nationwide," says a student. The student government and Activities and Organizations Board sponsors an array of campuswide events, such as the very popular 30-hour Dance Marathon and Dillo (Armadillo) Day, an end-of-the-year "festival of music, debauchery, and Greek life," in the words of a journalism major. Another tradition is upheld when representatives of student organizations slip out in the dead of night to paint their colors and slogans on a centrally located rock. Northwestern has the winningest debate team in the country. In all, there are more than 350 student organizations, ranging from an African drum and dance ensemble to Adshop, an advertising agency that lets students hone their marketing skills by promoting local businesses.

Football and tailgate parties are a traditional way of bringing alumni back and rousing the students to support the smallest and only private school in the Big Ten. Although the football team's trip to the 1996 Rose Bowl remains the stuff of legend, the Wildcats tend to be strongest in country club sports. Championship teams in recent years have included men's golf and women's tennis. Other competitive women's teams include volleyball, softball, field hockey, swimming, and NU's newest varsity sport: women's lacrosse. As far as facilities, NU is on par with many schools its size and larger, with the beautiful Norris Aquatics Center/Henry Crown Sports Pavilion and the Nicolet Football and Conference Center, used for conditioning of varsity athletes. The student-sponsored intramural program provides vigorous competition among teams from dorms and rival fraternities.

> "I'm able to have fun in a learning environment."

Northwestern occupies a unique niche in U.S. higher education. It has the academics of the Ivies, the spirited atmosphere of the Big Ten publics, and, along with Duke, Stanford, and perhaps Vanderbilt, combines success in Division I sports with quality instruction. With a strong work ethic and an equally strong desire for play, Northwestern students bask in their school's balance of challenging academics, pre-professional bent, and myriad opportunities to get off campus to learn and let loose. "I'm able to have fun in a learning environment," says a biomedical engineering major.

Each of the undergraduate schools determines its own general education requirements.

Overlaps

Cornell, Duke, University of Michigan, University of Pennsylvania, Stanford

If You Apply To ➤ | **Northwestern:** Early decision: Nov. 1. Regular admissions: Jan. 1. Application fee: $65. Campus and alumni interviews: optional, informational. SATs or ACTs (with writing): required. Subject Tests: recommended. Accepts the Common Application. Essay question: varies every year, pick one of four.

University of Notre Dame

220 Main Building, Notre Dame, IN 46556

The Holy Grail of higher education for many Roman Catholics. ND's heartland location and 82-percent-Catholic enrollment make it a bastion of traditional values. Offers business and engineering in addition to the liberal arts. ND's personality is much closer to Boston College or Holy Cross than Georgetown. Only school ever ranked #1 in both football and graduation rates.

Website: www.nd.edu

Location: Small Town

Private

Total Enrollment: 11,800

Undergraduates: 8,453

Male/Female: 53/47

SAT Ranges: CR 660–750, M 680–770

ACT Ranges: 31–34

Financial Aid: 82%

Expense: Pr $ $ $

Student Loans: 51%

Average Debt: $ $ $

Phi Beta Kappa: No

Applicants: 16,957

Accepted: 23%

Enrolled: 51%

Grad in 6 Years: 95%

Returning Freshmen: 97%

Academics: ✍ ✍ ✍ ✍

Social: ☎ ☎ ☎

Q of L: ★ ★ ★

Admissions: (574) 631-7505

Email Address: admissions@nd.edu

Strongest Programs:
Finance
Psychology
Economics
Political Science
Biological Sciences

The university's endowment is the largest of any of the nation's Roman Catholic colleges and universities.

Founded in 1842 by the French priest Edward Sorin, the University of Notre Dame has come a long way from its fledgling days in a rustic log cabin. While described as "a Catholic academic community of higher learning," its students need not be affiliated with the Roman Catholic Church. Notre Dame takes pride in fostering a culture that values open discussion of religious, spiritual, and social issues—witness the willingness of its president to stick by a controversial decision in 2009 to award President Obama an honorary doctorate even though the President does not share Catholic views on abortion. The school appeals to non-Catholics who are committed to social justice or seek a broadly spiritual dimension to their education. A soft spot for football doesn't hurt either.

"The professors here care a great deal about their students."

With 1,250 acres of rolling hills, twin lakes, and woods, the university offers a peaceful setting for studying. The lofty Golden Dome that rises above the ivy-covered Gothic and modern buildings and the old brick stadium, where in the 1920s Knute Rockne made the Fighting Irish almost synonymous with college football, are national symbols. Newer parts of campus are the Guglielmino Athletics Complex, the Jordan Hall of Science, and a multidisciplinary research building. The university's endowment is the largest of any of the nation's Roman Catholic colleges and universities.

Liberal education is more than just a catchphrase at Notre Dame. No matter what their major, students must take the First Year of Studies, one of the most extensive academic and counseling programs of any university in the nation. The core of the program is a one-semester writing-intensive university seminar limited to 20 students per section. The remainder of each freshman's schedule is reserved for the first of a comprehensive list of general education requirements: one semester each in writing and mathematics and two semesters in natural science, as well as one semester chosen from theology, philosophy, history, social science, and fine arts. It also includes a strong counseling component in which peer advisors are assigned to each student, as are academic advisors and tutors if necessary. Administrators are quick to point out that, due in part to the success of the first-year support program, a whopping 97 percent of freshmen make it through the year and return for sophomore year. Ninety-five percent of freshmen graduate within six years.

"Notre Dame dorm life is extraordinary."

In the College of Arts and Letters, highly regarded departments include English, theology, and philosophy, while physics and chemistry are tops in the College of Science. Within the engineering school, chemical engineering rules. The College of Business Administration's accountancy program is ranked among the nation's best, and the chemistry labs in the Nieuwland Science Hall have first-rate equipment. The academic climate at Notre Dame is said to be fairly rigorous. "The workload is very demanding," says a senior. "It requires the student to have very good time-management skills." And while the atmosphere is competitive, students agree that it is not cut-throat by any measure. Faculty members are praised for being dynamic, personable, knowledgeable, and accessible. "The professors here care a great deal about their students, and it shows," says a biology major. Students report it can be hard to get all the classes they want during a particular semester, but say it's not difficult to graduate in four years.

Notre Dame offers a variety of special academic programs and options. One of the most popular is the Program of Liberal Studies (PLS), in which students study art, philosophy, literature, and the history of Western thought within their Great Books seminars. The Kaneb Center for Teaching and Learning, the university's most recent commitment to teaching, is based in DeBartolo Hall, an 84-classroom complex with state-of-the-art computer and audiovisual equipment. The Arts and Letters Program for Administrators combines a second business major with liberal learning, and the College of Science also gives students the option of pursuing majors in two departments. In addition, Notre Dame offers programs in military and naval science, aerospace studies, and an extensive international study program.

With a predominantly lay board of trustees and faculty, Notre Dame remains committed to "the preservation of a distinctly Catholic community," and it has a more self-consciously Catholic identity than any other major research university, including Boston College and Georgetown. The president and several other top administrators are priests of the Congregation of the Holy Cross, and each dorm has its own chapel with daily masses, though attendance is not required. Nearly 82 percent of the students are Catholic, and students are required to take two theology courses. The main social issues discussed on campus include abortion, gender and racial issues, homosexuality, and faith. Diversity is also a concern and some students feel it is a big problem. But administrators are addressing it, and minority enrollment is growing. African Americans and Hispanics together make up 13 percent of the student body and Asian Americans constitute another 7 percent. Despite its relative cultural homogeneity, Notre Dame recruits from all over the country; 92 percent of the students are from outside Indiana and 1 percent hail from other countries. The university offers competitive academic scholarships to students with outstanding high school records and financial need, and hundreds of athletic scholarships are available.

"The workload is very demanding."

Students report it can be hard to get all the classes they want during a particular semester, but say it's not difficult to graduate in four years.

Eighty percent of ND students choose to live on campus. "Notre Dame dorm life is extraordinary," says a junior. "The dorm rooms are all very well kept and very comfortable." Students are assigned to a dorm for their freshman year, and are encouraged to stay in the same one until graduation. Fraternities are banned, and freshmen are spread out among all campus dorms. The single-sex dorms really become surrogate fraternities and sororities that breed a similar spirit of community and family. Parietal rules (midnight on weekdays, 2 a.m. on weekends) are strictly enforced. Boarders eat in either the North Quad or South Quad cafeterias, and must buy a 19-meal plan. For those who tire of institutional cuisine, the Huddle offers plenty of fast-food options as well as a pay-as-you-go snack bar. Students can also reserve the kitchen to cook their own meals.

Notre Dame has been open to women since 1972, and with a nearly perfect gender split in the undergraduate student body, the ratio is now comparable to many other formerly all-male schools. ND's social life isn't as rambunctious as it once was, thanks to the policy that forbids alcohol at campus social events. The rules relating to alcohol in the dorms are a bit more relaxed. For those who choose not to indulge, there are several groups dedicated to good times without alcohol. Most activities take place on campus and include parties, concerts, and movies. Each dorm holds theme dances about twice a month, and there's always the annual Screw Your Roommate weekend, where students are paired with the blind dates selected by their roomies. Another popular event is the An Tostal Festival, which comes the week before spring finals and guarantees to temporarily relieve academic anxiety with its "childish" games such as pie-eating contests and Jell-O wrestling. The annual Sophomore Literary Festival is entirely student-run and draws prominent writers and poets from across the country. Students are involved in the community through volunteer work—more than 10 percent of grads enter community service positions. The best outlet for culture is nearby Chicago, about 90 minutes away.

"The dorm rooms are all very well kept and very comfortable."

The main social issues discussed on campus include abortion, gender and racial issues, homosexuality, and faith.

With its proud gridiron heritage, there's nothing like Notre Dame football. From Knute Rockne and the Gipper right on down to modern-day greats such as Joe Montana, the spirit of the Fighting Irish reigns supreme and has regained its former glory under head coach Brian Kelly. It wasn't intentional—at least that's what they say—but the giant mosaic of Jesus Christ on the library lifts his hands toward the heavens as if to signal yet another Irish touchdown. Tailgate parties are also celebrated events, occurring before and after the game. Notre Dame offers one of the strongest all-around athletic programs in the country, with several teams—both men's and women's—bringing home Big East titles in recent years. Die-hard jocks who can't make the varsity teams will find plenty of company in ND's very competitive intramural leagues, which attract more than three-quarters of students. The Bookstore Basketball Tournament, the largest hoops tournament in the world with more than 700 teams competing, lasts for a month. ND will soon be moving to the Atlantic Coast Conference for all sports except football and ice hockey.

Although temperatures here can drop below freezing, few dispute that Notre Dame is red-hot. Everyone at the university, from administrators to students, is considered part of the "Notre Dame family." Traditions are held in high esteem. For those looking for high-quality academics, a friendly, caring environment with a Catholic bent, and an excellent athletic scene, ND could be an answer to their prayers.

> **Overlaps**
> **Harvard, Princeton, Duke, Boston College, Stanford**

If You Apply To ➤

ND: Early action: Nov. 1. Regular admissions: Dec. 31. Financial aid: Feb. 15. Application fee: $75. No campus or alumni interviews. SATs or ACTs: required. Subject Tests: optional. Accepts the Common Application. Essay question.

Oberlin College

101 North Professor Street, Carnegie Building, Oberlin, OH 44074-1075

The college that invented nonconformity. From the Underground Railroad and coeducation to the modern peace movement, Obies have long been in the forefront. As at Grinnell and Reed, Oberlin's curriculum is less radical than its students. Oberlin is especially strong in the sciences, and its music conservatory is among the nation's best. The annual Drag Ball is quintessential Oberlin.

Website: www.oberlin.edu
Location: Small Town
Private
Total Enrollment: 2,903
Undergraduates: 2,889
Male/Female: 45/55
SAT Ranges: CR 640–740, M 620–720
ACT Ranges: 28–32
Financial Aid: 83%
Expense: Pr $ $ $ $
Student Loans: 39%
Average Debt: N/A
Phi Beta Kappa: Yes
Applicants: 7,172
Accepted: 31%
Enrolled: 34%

New and contrasting ideas are a way of life at Oberlin College, a liberal arts school where nonconformity is a long tradition. Tucked away in a small Ohio town, Oberlin was the first American college to accept women and minorities, and it was a stop on the Underground Railroad. That pioneering spirit has not faded. With diverse academic challenges ranging from cinema studies to neuroscience, Obies thrive on higher thinking and exploring their myriad talents. A junior says Oberlin appeals to those students "who love to be active, help their communities, challenge themselves, and want to learn."

> **"I've been able to form close relationships with many of my professors."**

Oberlin's attractive campus features a mix of Italian Renaissance buildings (four designed by Cass Gilbert), late 19th- and early 20th-century organic stone structures, and some less interesting 1950s barracks-type dorms. The buildings rise over flatlands typical of the Midwest, which do little to stop brutal winter winds. The Allen Memorial Art Museum, sometimes mentioned in the same breath as Harvard's and Yale's, is one of the loveliest buildings on campus, with a brick-paved, flower-laden courtyard and a fountain. The Oberlin College Science Center offers state-of-the-art classrooms, wireless Internet areas, a science library, and laboratory space. In a nod to environmental concerns, the college produces half of its energy from renewable resources. The Bertram and Judith Kohl Building houses the jazz studies, music history, and music theory programs.

Oberlin has been a leader among liberal arts colleges seeking to promote their science offerings; biology and chemistry are two of the college's strongest departments, and undergraduates may major in interdisciplinary programs like neuroscience and biopsychology. Students also flock to the English, politics, biology, and history departments. Oberlin is one of the few liberal arts colleges to offer a major in creative writing. Other popular majors include East Asian studies and environmental studies; computer science and anthropology attract relatively few majors. Students rave about their faculty. "I've been able to form close relationships with many of my professors—both in my major as well as in other departments—which is extremely valuable," says an English major. Oberlin's conservatory of music holds a well-deserved spot among the nation's most prominent performance schools; the voice, violin, and TIMARA (Technology in Music and Related Arts) programs are especially praised. It is the oldest continuously operating music conservatory in the country, and Oberlin is one of only three liberal arts colleges with a conservatory (the others are Bard and Lawrence). It enrolls about a fifth of Oberlin undergrads, who must audition to gain acceptance. Interdisciplinary and self-created majors, such as African American, Latin American, Russian, Third World, and women's studies, are popular—not surprisingly at such a liberal school. About 86 percent of students study abroad.

"Students are very serious about their work."

Oberlin's students are as serious about their schoolwork as they are about politics, justice, and other social causes. Courses are rigorous; heavy workloads and the occasional Saturday morning class are the norm. "Students are very serious about their work and the academic environment is quite rigorous, but I have never found there to be even the slightest feeling of competition amongst students," says one student. A credit/no-entry policy allows students to take an unlimited number of grade-free courses (if they can get in). Recognizing that students at Oberlin are gifted and want to challenge themselves, most departments offer group and individual independent study opportunities and invite selected students to pursue demanding honors programs, especially during their senior year.

There are no requirements for freshmen at Oberlin, but general education requirements include proficiency in writing and math and nine credit hours in each of the three divisions—arts and humanities, math/natural sciences, and social sciences—plus another nine credit hours in cultural diversity courses, including a foreign language. Students are also required to take one-quarter of the semester hours needed to graduate outside their major's division; those who shy away from math and science can satisfy distribution requirements by taking interdisciplinary courses such as "Chemistry and Crime." Students must also participate in three January terms, during which they pursue month-long projects, traditional or unique, on or off campus. About 40 different first-year seminar classes are available every semester, with enrollment limited to 14 students each, and "it's a great way to make friends," says a student. "It also introduces you to the Oberlin academic experience."

One of Oberlin's more unusual offerings is EXCO, an experimental college that offers students and interested townsfolk the chance to learn together. Most classes are taught by students, and topics can range from fairy tales to knitting to salsa dancing, and much more. Hot spots on campus include the Mudd Library, with more than 2.1 million volumes—a superb facility for research and studying or socializing; the

"Oberlin students care."

famous A-level is the place to be on weeknights. Even more special are the music conservatory's 150 practice rooms, substantial music library, and Steinway pianos—one of the world's largest collections. Each year, 25 to 35 students enter the

(continued)

Grad in 6 Years: 85%
Returning Freshmen: 93%
Academics: ✐ ✐ ✐ ✐ ½
Social: ☎ ☎ ☎
Q of L: ★ ★ ★ ★
Admissions: (440) 775-8411
Email Address: college
.admissions@oberlin.edu

Strongest Programs:
Neuroscience
Environmental Studies
Creative Writing
East Asian Studies
Biology
Chemistry
Politics
Music

Oberlin has been a leader among liberal arts colleges seeking to promote their science offerings.

dual-degree program, which allows them to earn both a B.M. and a B.A. in as little as five years. Dual-degree students must be admitted to both the college and the music conservatory.

"Oberlin students care," says a senior. "They are not only passionate about their studies, but also about their extracurriculars. The arts—music, theater, studio art—and political activism are treated as seriously as academic classes." Eighty-six percent of students are from out of state, primarily from the Mid-Atlantic states. African Americans account for 5 percent of the student body, Asian Americans 4 percent, Hispanics 7 percent, and international students 8 percent. Initiatives to increase diversity at Oberlin include advisors from various ethnic and racial backgrounds and a multicultural resource center with a full-time director. "Though the student body is homogeneously liberal," says a junior, "there are more protests, awareness and advocacy groups, and campaigns here than I can keep track of." A popular annual event is the Drag Ball, in which half the student body comes in full drag. "It's very Oberlin, because it's all about challenging social norms," says a student. Merit scholarships are available to qualified students.

> *Courses are rigorous; heavy workloads and the occasional Saturday morning class are the norm.*

Nearly 90 percent of Oberlin students live on campus in the dorms, including co-ops, several of which focus on foreign languages. Students are required to live on campus for three years—only seniors may move off campus. "The dorms are mixed," a student says. "Upperclassmen get the priority, so they live in the nicer dorms, while the underclassmen dorms are not usually very nice, but build character and provide a bonding experience." Only one dorm is single-sex; all dorms are four-class except Barrows, which is reserved for freshmen. The best dorms are said to be the program houses, including the French House, African Heritage House, Russian House, and Third World House. Students may eat in any of seven dining rooms. Appetizing alternatives to institutional fare can be found at the co-ops that comprise the Oberlin Student Cooperative Association (OSCA), a more than $2-million-a-year corporation run entirely by students. Co-op members plan and prepare their own meals, enjoying everything from homemade bread to whatever's left in the pantry before the next food shipment arrives. "The co-op system is amazing," says a student.

"Everything takes place on campus."

Social life, like so much of the Oberlin experience, is what you make of it, students say. "Everything takes place on campus, and there is a *ton* going on," raves one senior. Even in the middle of the day, "it's hard to walk across campus without becoming distracted by a pick-up game of Frisbee, the construction of a snow fort, or some students dancing contact improvisation on the lawn," says a senior. House parties, plays, movies, and conservatory performances are planned every other night. And since there's no Greek system, nothing is exclusive. As for drinking, underage students can finagle booze, and of-age students are allowed to imbibe in their rooms. "I think the rules work well," a chemistry major says. "Not too many students get into trouble."

> *One of Oberlin's more unusual offerings is EXCO, an experimental college that offers students and interested townsfolk the chance to learn together.*

When the need to wander strikes, Cleveland is only 30 miles away, but students enjoy their small town. "There's only really two square blocks of downtown," says one student, "but within it is basically everything that you need." Another student adds, "Pretty much all of the restaurants downtown are used to working until at least 2 a.m., delivering pizza to hungry late-nighters or having special offers for college students." And Obies are very enthusiastic about giving back to the community through volunteer activities at local schools, hospitals, and nursing homes. "Our motto is 'Think one person can make a difference? So do we!'" says a student.

The Yeomen appear to be building a loyal fan base: The women's cross-country team has brought home multiple Division III North Coast Athletic Conference championships; soccer and women's track and field are competitive as well. As for intramural sports, "as soon as the rain stops in the spring, there are students on every green area between the dorms, playing ultimate Frisbee," says a sophomore. Fencing, Aikido, soccer, and women's rugby also have loyal followings.

Oberlin may be small, but its emphasis on global learning, undergraduate research, and a vibrant liberal arts education helps it burst those statistical seams. Students are more likely to discuss local poverty than the quality of cereal choices in the dining halls, and can be found playing a Steinway or plugging away at astronomy. One Obie sums it up this way: "Oberlin is a place where you can be yourself, but also learn and grow as a person in a diverse environment enhanced by people equally interested in personal growth."

If You Apply To ➤

Oberlin: Early decision I: Nov. 15. Early decision II: Jan. 1. Regular admissions: Jan. 15. Application fee: $35. Campus and alumni interviews: optional, evaluative. SATs or ACTs: required. Subject Tests: recommended. Accepts the Common Application. Essay question.

Occidental College

1600 Campus Road, Los Angeles, CA 90041

Oxy is a streetwise cousin to the more upscale and suburban Claremont Colleges. Plentiful internships and study abroad give Oxy students real-world perspectives. Oxy's innovative diplomacy and world affairs program features an internship at the UN. One of the most diverse liberal arts colleges in the nation.

Occidental College is one of a handful of small colleges located in a big city, in this case Lalaland. But unlike the sprawling and impersonal City of Angels, Oxy emphasizes a strong sense of community and a decidedly diverse student population. Notable alums include Barack Obama, two-time Pulitzer Prize–winning journalist Steve Coll, and two-time Olympic gold medal–winning diver Dr. Sammy Lee. "Students dream big at Oxy," says a senior. "Whether a student wants a career in Hollywood or on Wall Street, everyone knows that it starts in the classroom."

Set against the backdrop of the San Gabriel Mountains, Oxy's self-contained Mediterranean-style campus is a secluded enclave of flowers and trees between Pasadena and Glendale, minutes from downtown Los Angeles. Swan Hall has undergone a $20 million expansion and the student activity center was remodeled to the tune of $2 million.

Inside this urban oasis resides a thriving community of high achievers who don't for a moment believe that the liberal arts are dead, or even wounded. Required first-year cultural studies seminars include topics in human history and culture, with an emphasis on writing skills. Each seminar has 16 students, some of whom **"Students dream big at Oxy."** also share the same residence hall; it's called the Learning Communities Program. In addition, all Oxy students must show proficiency in a foreign language and complete 12 units of world cultures courses, a fine arts course, preindustrial-era coursework, and 12 units of science and math. Many of Occidental's academic departments are excellent, with English, music, chemistry, and an innovative diplomacy and world affairs program among the strongest, and economics the most popular.

Website: www.oxy.edu
Location: City Outskirts
Private
Total Enrollment: 2,178
Undergraduates: 2,176
Male/Female: 44/56
SAT Ranges: CR 600–700, M 600–700
ACT Ranges: 28–32
Financial Aid: 78%
Expense: Pr $ $ $ $
Student Loans: 51%
Average Debt: $ $
Phi Beta Kappa: Yes
Applicants: 6,135
Accepted: 39%
Enrolled: 22%
Grad in 6 Years: 83%
Returning Freshmen: 94%
Academics: ✍ ✍ ✍ ✍
Social: ☎ ☎ ☎
Q of L: ★ ★ ★ ★
Admissions: (800) 825-5262

(continued)

Email Address: admission@
oxy.edu

Strongest Programs:
Diplomacy and World Affairs
Economics
Politics
Science
Urban and Environmental
    Policy
Theater
Art History and Visual Arts

On average, Oxy supports more than 300 student research projects in the sciences, social sciences, and humanities.

Students also broaden their horizons in study abroad programs in nearly 50 countries on five continents.

"Occidental provides an academically challenging environment," says a junior. "I was pleasantly surprised at how much my professors challenged me, pushing me to grow intellectually." Oxy also encourages diverse learning experiences through internships, independent study, and study abroad—including one of only a few undergraduate programs to offer internships with UN-related organizations. On average, Oxy supports more than 300 student research projects in the sciences, social sciences, and humanities. Over the past five years, 150 Occidental students have been invited to present their work at the National Conference on Undergraduate Research. The student-managed Charles R. Blyth Fund allows students to invest about $150,000 of the college's endowment. Upperclassmen on the "O-team" plan freshman orientation, held the week before school starts.

Faculty members are readily available in and out of the classroom, and students say the teaching, in general, is excellent. "Every student is instructed by qualified and worldly professors who really go that extra mile to help students," one sophomore says. The great majority of classes have 25 or fewer students, and as academic advisors are responsible for about four students per class (16 total), personal relationships develop quickly. "I have had in-home lunch, dinner, museum outings, and hour-long office discussions with my professors," explains one senior. Students also broaden their horizons in study abroad programs in nearly 50 countries on five continents; locations include Western Europe, Japan, China, Mexico, Nepal, Hungary, Costa Rica, and Russia. For politicos, there's Oxy-at-the-UN. There are also 3–2 engineering programs with Caltech and Columbia University, an exchange program with Spelman College in Atlanta, and cross-registration privileges with Caltech and Pasadena's Art Center College of Design. Students may also take advantage of a 4–2 biotechnology program with Keck Graduate Institute (of the Claremont Colleges).

"Students are very socially conscious and have a deep passion for diversity," says an economics major. Forty-five percent of the students are from California, and 3 percent hail from foreign nations. African Americans make up 4 percent of the student population, Hispanics 16 percent, and Asian Americans 13 percent. The college's financial aid staff visits local high schools to help families fill out applications, offering sessions in English, Spanish, and Vietnamese. Perhaps not surprisingly, students tend to be liberal and the raging social concerns are "racial and social inequalities, environmentalism, and gender issues," according to one student. Merit scholarships are doled out to qualified students each year—averaging $10,964—but there are no athletic scholarships. Special financial packages are available to low-income students, and Occidental hands out Pell grants to nearly 20 percent of its students (one of the highest percentages in the nation among top-ranked liberal arts colleges).

"I was pleasantly surprised at how much my professors challenged me."

The residence halls are small—almost all house fewer than 150 students—and co-ed by floor or room. Students are jazzed about the newest residence hall, which provides comfortable and modern facilities. Eighty percent of students live on campus, but what you get depends on your luck in the housing lottery. Students from all four classes live together, many in special-interest houses like the Multicultural Hall, the Food Justice House, or the Substance-Free Quad. Freshmen, sophomores, and juniors are required to live on campus and eat in the dining hall (tip from a junior: don't try anything that has an unusual name, like "Mayan tofu"). Campus dining fare is "excellent," says one student.

While the bright lights of L.A. often beckon on weekends, the Oxy campus provides its share of fun, too, whether it be a "basketball game, concert, dance, or party," says one student. Fraternities and sororities, though declining on the Oxy social ladder, attract 10 percent of men and 13 percent of the women, but they are neither selective nor exclusive; students choose which to join, rather than being chosen, and the frats must invite everyone to their functions. As for alcohol, "like most other colleges, there is underage drinking even though this is illegal," says another junior. Dance Production—a 70-year-old tradition in which student dancers perform works by student choreographers—sells out both performances each year. Other big events include Apollo Night (a talent contest) and A Taste of Oxy, a student potluck that showcases the diversity of the Oxy community through food and performance. "Winter Formal is probably my favorite," says a theater major. Here's a tip: Keep your birthday a secret, or on that unhappy day a roaring pack of your more sadistic classmates will carry you out to the middle of campus and mercilessly toss you in the Gilman Fountain. It's a tradition, after all.

A student characterizes the surrounding neighborhood of Eagle Rock as "a quaint little community with an eclectic combination of 'ma and pa' restaurants and plenty of hole-in-the-wall stores." When students become weary of the incestuous social life in the "Oxy fishbowl," they head for the bars, restaurants, museums, and theaters of downtown Los Angeles and Old Pasadena, where, one student notes, "you can find almost anything except snow." But the ski slopes of the San Gabriel Mountains are not far away, and neither is Hollywood nor the beautiful beaches of Southern California. When they tire of California, students try their luck in Las Vegas—or trek south of the border, into Tijuana. A car (your own or someone else's) is practically a necessity, though the college runs a weekend shuttle service to Old Town Pasadena. The weather is warm and sunny, but the air is often thick with that infamous L.A. smog.

> **"Students have a voice at Oxy."**

Oxy's sports teams (the Tigers) compete in Division III and draw a modest following. Football is the most popular, followed by women's basketball (winners of four consecutive conference titles, the latest in 2011) and women's cross-country. Men's rugby is solid, too, and the men's cross-country team brought home the 2011 conference title. And don't forget that L.A. is home to the NBA's Lakers, the NHL's Kings, and baseball's Dodgers. Oxy has a small intramural program; popular club sports include rugby and ultimate Frisbee.

"Students have a voice at Oxy," says a sophomore, "and can easily relay their views to people at the top." Occidental's creative, motivated, and diverse students are not here for the bright lights and beautiful people of Los Angeles; those are just fringe benefits. Instead, students are drawn to this intimate oasis of learning by professors who hate to see anyone waste one whit of intellectual potential. And students here are only too happy to live up to these lofty expectations.

Dance Production—a 70-year-old tradition in which student dancers perform works by student choreographers—sells out both performances each year.

Overlaps
University of Southern California, UC–Berkeley, UCLA, NYU, University of Colorado, Scripps, Pitzer, Whitman

If You Apply To > | **Oxy:** Early decision: Nov. 15. Regular admissions: Jan. 10. Application fee: $60. Campus and alumni interviews: optional, informational. SATs or ACTs: required. Subject Tests: recommended. Accepts the Common Application. Essay question.

Oglethorpe University

4484 Peachtree Road NE, Atlanta, GA 30319

Small wonder that brochures for Oglethorpe trumpet Atlanta as the college's biggest asset. In a region where most liberal arts colleges are in sleepy towns, Oglethorpe has the South's most exciting city at its fingertips. Interdisciplinary core gives shape to the curriculum. Strong Greek system provides the main social life.

Website: www.oglethorpe.edu

Location: Suburban

Private

Total Enrollment: 966

Undergraduates: 956

Male/Female: 42/58

SAT Ranges: CR 530–620,
    M 510–610

ACT Ranges: N/A

Financial Aid: 82%

Expense: Pr $

Student Loans: 89%

Average Debt: $

Phi Beta Kappa: No

Applicants: 2,463

Accepted: 83%

Enrolled: 14%

Grad in 6 Years: 55%

Returning Freshmen: 80%

Academics: ✐ ✐ ✐

Social: ☎ ☎ ☎

Q of L: ★ ★ ★ ★

Admissions: (404) 364-8307

Email Address: admissions@
    oglethorpe.edu

Strongest Programs:

English

Business

Psychology

Social Sciences

The university's guiding principle is the Oglethorpe Idea, which says students should develop academically and as citizens.

Each Christmas, students at Oglethorpe University take part in a unique tradition. The Boar's Head Ceremony celebrates a medieval scholar who halted a stampeding wild boar by ramming his copy of Aristotle down the animal's throat. Though some may find it boorish, students at this small Southern school explain that it fosters a sense of family. "OU is a hidden gem," says one junior. "Although few outside of the Southeast have heard of it, this school provides a top-notch education."

Founded in 1835, the school is named for the idealistic founder of the state of Georgia, James Edward Oglethorpe. Its 118-acre campus is strategically located in Atlanta's inner suburbs, with a picturesque Gothic campus that gives a traditional college feel. The heavily wooded, slightly rolling terrain is perfect territory for walks or long runs, and the beautiful campus has served as the backdrop for several movies and TV shows. Oglethorpe's academic buildings and some residence halls are in the English Gothic style. A new campus center opened in late 2013 and features a dining hall, coffee shop, bookstore, and outdoor patios. The building is also home to campus life offices and serves as the hub of the experiential learning program.

"I have never breezed through a class."

Oglethorpe's strengths are business administration, English, biology, accounting, psychology, and communications. Weaker bets are the fine arts and foreign language departments, though the latter does offer courses in Japanese, German, French, and Spanish. And whatever isn't offered at Oglethorpe can usually be taken through cross-registration at other schools in the Atlanta area. One student offers this assessment: "Many self-proclaimed premed majors change programs within their first semester because of its difficulty. The science departments are particularly demanding."

Aspiring engineers may take advantage of 3–2 dual-degree programs with Auburn, Georgia Tech, the University of Florida, and the University of Southern California. The school also offers courses and additional resources as a member of the Atlanta Regional Council for Higher Education*. Oglethorpe also offers a wide variety of study abroad programs, including a semester at Seigakuin University in Japan and sister-school exchanges in Argentina, the Netherlands, Germany, France, Russia, and Monaco. According to administrators, Oglethorpe "emphasizes the preparation of the humane generalist" and "rejects rigid specialization." That doesn't mean the curriculum is a cakewalk, though. "I have never breezed through a class," says an art history major. "The academics are so rigorous."

The university's guiding principle is the Oglethorpe Idea, which says students should develop academically and as citizens. This philosophy is based on the conviction that education should help students make both a life and a living. All students take the sequenced, interdisciplinary Core Curriculum program at the same point in their college careers, providing them with a model for integrating information and gaining knowledge. In addition to the ability to reason, read, and speak effectively, the core asks students to reflect on and discuss matters fundamental to understanding who they are and what they ought to be. The core requires Narratives of the Self (freshmen), Human Nature and the Social Order (sophomores), Historical Perspectives on the Social Order (juniors), and Science and Human Nature (seniors), plus a fine arts core course in music and culture or art and culture, and coursework in modern mathematics or advanced foreign language.

Oglethorpe's faculty may be demanding, but they're also friendly and helpful. "They really do care for you intellectually and personally," says one junior. Classes are generally small, and most students notice few problems at registration. Advising services are said to be helpful. The library's holdings are minuscule, though—just over 131,000 volumes.

What's an Oglethorpian like? The vast majority are smart, semiconservative offspring of middle- and upper-middle-class Southern families. "We all tend to be open minded, thoughtful, and intellectual," explains one student. Approximately

54 percent ranked in the top quarter of their high school class; most come from public schools and 69 percent are Georgians. "Our campus is pretty small—however, cliques do form. The students are usually extremely personable and cordial." Oglethorpe prides itself on being one of the first Georgia colleges to admit African American students, and today 32 percent of the students are members of minority groups: 21 percent are African American, 3 percent are Asian American, 8 percent are Hispanic, and approximately 3 percent hail from abroad. There's a level of comfort with racial differences, students report.

Oglethorpe's mascot, the Stormy Petrel, is a sea bird that flies in the face of storms. James Oglethorpe was inspired by them on his first visit to Georgia in 1733.

Fifty-seven percent of Oglethorpe's students choose to live on campus—and love it. "The dorms are big and have nice furniture," says an accounting major. Most rooms are suites with private bathrooms, and some singles are available. Some students commute to campus; a quarter live in Atlanta—not a college town, but where the wild life is. "Some weekends, everyone stays around and life is great, and then there are others when campus is deserted," one student explains. Fraternities and sororities, which claim 20 percent of the men and 12 percent of the women, respectively, throw parties that draw big numbers. Officially, the campus is dry, but underage students can find alcohol if they try, students agree. It's rumored that Oglethorpe barflies do more hopping than Georgia bullfrogs, and bars, clubs, and cafés abound within 10 minutes of campus.

Those who tire of the Oglethorpe scene can find excitement on the campuses of the dozen or so other colleges in the area or in downtown Atlanta, which one student describes as "the heart of Atlanta and a few minutes from Buckhead, a party district, and two great malls." Atlanta proper offers everything you can imagine—arts, professional sports (including basketball's Hawks, football's Falcons, and baseball's Braves), and entertainment (ride the Great American Scream Machine at Six Flags). Oglethorpe always has a big contingent going

> **"Some weekends, everyone stays around and life is great, and then there are others when campus is deserted."**

to Savannah for St. Patrick's Day and to New Orleans for Mardi Gras. The campus celebrates its origins once a year during Oglethorpe Day. Students looking for warmer weather, though, head down to sunny Florida.

Oglethorpe's mascot, the Stormy Petrel, is a sea bird that flies in the face of storms. James Oglethorpe was inspired by them on his first visit to Georgia in 1733. Intramurals are important at Oglethorpe, sometimes more so than varsity sports. Perhaps Atlanta's diversions or the relatively small number of students on campus cause varsity sports to be a weak draw. Still, the men's golf team brought home Southern Collegiate Athletic Conference titles in 2009 and 2012, and basketball games against cross-city rival Emory are popular. The Georgia landscape makes possible a plethora of outdoor activities, including hiking at nearby Stone Mountain and boating or swimming in Lake Lanier (named for Georgia poet Sidney Lanier—Oglethorpe Class of 1860).

Though Oglethorpe may lack widespread name recognition, its students get all the attention they need from a caring faculty on a close-knit campus. And being in a large city like Atlanta provides anything else that might be lacking, ranging from great nightlife to internships and postgraduate employment with big-name corporations. In a sea of large Southern state schools, Oglethorpe stands out as a place where students come first.

> ### Overlaps
> **University of Georgia, Emory, Georgia Tech, Mercer**

If You Apply To >

Oglethorpe: Rolling admissions. Application fee: $40. Campus and alumni interviews: optional, evaluative. SATs or ACTs: required. Subject Tests: optional. Accepts the Common Application. Essay question: more about you.

3rd Floor, Lincoln Tower, 1800 Cannon Drive, Columbus, OH 43210

The biggest school in the Big Ten, Ohio State lacks the prestige of a Michigan or a Wisconsin—partly because three major in-state rivals (Cincinnati, Miami, and Ohio U) siphon off many top students. Operates the mother of all college sports programs, recently tainted by the mother of all athletic scandals. Check out the top-notch honors program. Columbus is a major city and the capital of Ohio.

Website: www.osu.edu

Location: City Center

Public

Total Enrollment: 48,776

Undergraduates: 38,708

Male/Female: 52/48

SAT Ranges: CR 540–650, M 610–710

ACT Ranges: 26–30

Financial Aid: 79%

Expense: Pub $ $ $

Student Loans: 59%

Average Debt: $ $ $

Phi Beta Kappa: Yes

Applicants: 25,816

Accepted: 64%

Enrolled: 44%

Grad in 6 Years: 82%

Returning Freshmen: 92%

Academics: ✍ ✍ ✍ ½

Social: 🐿 🐿 🐿 🐿

Q of L: ★ ★ ★

Admissions: (614) 292-3980

Email Address: askabuckeye@osu.edu

Strongest Programs:

Business

Premed

Engineering

Education

Geography

Industrial Design

Linguistics

Psychology

African American Studies

Envision a campus with nearly 50,000 students and too many opportunities to count. What might come to mind is Ohio State University, located in the heart of the state's capital, offering 19 colleges and more than 10,400 courses in 175 undergraduate majors. If those numbers aren't staggering enough, consider the fact that OSU has 39 varsity teams, nearly 50 intramural sports, more than 50 sports clubs, and the third largest campus in the nation. It also has an operating budget larger than that of the state of Rhode Island. While students cite the school's size as both a blessing and a curse, all seem to agree that at OSU, the sky is the limit for those with a desire to sample its academic and other resources. The term "big" might be an understatement. "OSU has something for everyone," says a junior. "You're sure to find what's right for you."

This megauniversity stands on more than 3,000 wooded acres rubbing the edge of downtown Columbus on one side. On the other side, across the Olentangy River,

"OSU has something for everyone."

is farmland associated with the College of Agriculture. OSU's architectural style is anything but consistent, yet it's all tied together in one huge redbrick package. "One part of the campus maintains a nostalgic air while another is relatively modern," observes a student. The grounds are nicely landscaped, and a centrally located lake provides a peaceful setting for contemplation. Other facilities include RPAC—the nation's largest facility dedicated to student fitness, wellness, and recreation—and the Biomed Research Tower. A spate of new construction has added facilities to the campus over the past few years.

Business, education, geography, industrial design, and engineering are among the school's most celebrated departments. OSU bills itself as the place to go for computer graphics and has a supercomputer center to back up its claim. It also boasts the largest and most comprehensive African American studies program anywhere and turns out more African American Ph.D.s than any other university in the nation. Furthermore, the university has the nation's only programs in welding engineering and geodetic science, and the state's only program in medical communications.

The university's fundamental commitment to liberal arts learning means all undergrads must satisfy rigorous general education requirements that include courses in math, writing, foreign language, social science, natural science, and arts and humanities. A selective admissions program has replaced OSU's old open-door policy; applications are read with an emphasis on high school curriculum, grades, and test scores. Cocurricular and work experiences factor in, as do individual circumstances.

"The academic climate is pretty competitive as a whole in the sense that a lot of students take their academics very seriously," says a sophomore. Freshmen experience a variety of class formats and sizes ranging from intimate Freshman Seminars to large lectures. Teaching assistants, not professors, hold smaller recitation sections and deal on a personal level with students. Students find that class sizes are whittled down as they continue in their fields of study. OSU's honors program allows selected students to take classes that are taught by top professors and limited to 25 students each. "The whole system of honors classes, priority scheduling, honors housing, and cocurricular activities really adds to the overall experience at OSU," a biology major says. Internships are required in some programs and optional in others, and possibilities for study abroad include Japan and China. A personalized study program enables students to create their own majors.

Inside Ohio State's ivy-covered halls and modern additions are some of the best up-to-date equipment and facilities, including a "phenomenal" library system with two dozen branches and nearly four million volumes—all coordinated by computer. At such a large institution, the quality of instruction can vary greatly and students report this to be the case. "Overall, the quality of teaching is good," says one student. Freshmen may take advantage of numerous first-year programs, including the First Year Success Series, and pre-enrollment programs like Camp Buckeye and the Leadership Collaborative. Eighty-two percent of Ohio State's students come from Ohio, and the remainder come largely from adjacent states. Every type of background is represented, most in huge numbers, and most seem "friendly and pretty laid-back," according to a freshman. The student body is 7 percent African American; Hispanics and Asian Americans combine for another 9 percent. Merit scholarships averaging $6,261 are available to qualified students; talented athletes vie for 21 scholarships in 21 sports. Several programs are aimed specifically at "enhancing" efforts to attract and retain minority students, including a statewide Young Scholars Program that begins working with students when they start the seventh grade.

"The academic climate is pretty competitive as a whole."

The residence halls that house 25 percent of the Ohio State masses are located in three areas: North, South, and Olentangy (that is, those closest to the Olentangy River). Freshmen—required to live in residence halls unless they are commuting from home—are scattered among each of OSU's 38 residence halls. "The dorms are very good, though they tend to have an industrial feel," says a student. "Most upperclassmen live off campus." When they don't head for off-campus life in Columbus, many find the South campus section among the most desirable (it's more sociable, louder, and full of single rooms). The Towers in the Olentangy section have gained more popularity since their conversion to eight-person suites. All in all, students have a choice of single-sex, co-ed (by floor or by room), or married-couples apartments if they want to live in campus housing. Computer labs are located in each residence area. A system of variable room rates based on frills (air-conditioning, private bath, number of roommates), as well as a choice of four meal-plan options, give students flexibility in determining their housing costs. "The food at OSU is fantastic," chirps one student.

Such a large student market has, of course, produced a strip of bars, fast-food joints, convenience stores, bookstores, vegetarian restaurants, and you-name-its along the edge of the campus on High Street, and downtown Columbus is just a few minutes away. "Columbus is a vibrant town," says a junior. "There are concerts, plays, sporting events, as well as shopping throughout the city." The fine public transportation system carries students not only throughout this capital city but also around the sprawling campus. In addition to the usual shopping centers, restaurants, golf courses, and movie theaters, Columbus boasts a symphony orchestra and ballet, and its central location in the state makes it easily accessible to Cleveland and Cincinnati.

"There are things to do both on and off campus."

Outdoor enthusiasts can ski in nearby Mansfield, canoe and sail on the Olentangy and Scioto rivers, hike around adjacent quarries, or camp in the nearby woods.

OSU is a bustling place on weekends. "Ohio State has a great social life. There are things to do both on and off campus," says one student. Various social events are planned by on-campus housing groups—floors, dorms, or sections of the campus. The student union runs eateries as well as movies and more, and High Street's zillion bars, saloons, restaurants, and discos come to life. Campus policies prohibit

OSU bills itself as the place to go for computer graphics and has a supercomputer center to back up its claim.

Inside Ohio State's ivy-covered halls and modern additions are some of the best up-to-date equipment and facilities.

underage drinking in dorms, but one partier discloses, "I can get served in almost any bar on campus." Still, a junior reports, drinking "is not vital to the OSU experience." Approximately 5 percent of OSU men and 5 percent of the women go Greek. By one account, these students make the Greek system "a way of life and isolate themselves from the rest of the student population."

Ohio State operates the second largest college sports program in the nation—a $127 million operation that lavishes more than $100,000 on each of its athletes—or triple what it spends per undergraduate on education. The Buckeyes field teams in 39 sports, from women's rifle to men's football (a perennial powerhouse that went undefeated in 2012–13). Nonrecruited students should not expect to make any varsity team as walk-ons. Rivalries abound and one student asserts (without a hint of irony), "We party harder, we play harder, and we're more humble [than our rivals]." Recent conference winners include men's baseball, men's and women's basketball, softball, and men's tennis. Many take advantage of an ambitious intramural program that boasts a dozen basketball courts and 26 courts for handball, squash, and racquetball.

OSU's sheer size is sometimes overwhelming to be sure, but students seem to thrive on the challenge and excitement of a big university. For those who really want to be Buckeyes, jump in with both feet and heed advice of one seasoned student: "Get football tickets every year, join a few clubs, use the rec facilities, and learn the bus routes early!"

Overlaps

University of Cincinnati, Miami (OH), Case Western Reserve, Ohio University, University of Michigan, Purdue, Penn State, University of Dayton

If You Apply To ➤

OSU: Rolling admissions. Early action: Nov. 1. Application fee: $60. No campus or alumni interviews. SATs or ACTs: required. Subject Tests: optional. Essay question.

Ohio University

Chubb Hall 120, Athens, OH 45701-2979

Ohio is less than half the size of Ohio State and plays up its homey feel compared to the cast of tens of thousands in Columbus. The Honors Tutorial College is a sure bet for top students who want close contact with faculty. Communications and journalism top the list of prominent programs. Ohio is not in the Big Ten, but the Mid-American Conference has begun to generate more excitement.

Website: www.ohio.edu
Location: Small Town
Public
Total Enrollment: 19,494
Undergraduates: 16,855
Male/Female: 47/53
SAT Ranges: CR 480–590, M 490–610
ACT Ranges: 21–26
Financial Aid: 76%
Expense: Pub $ $
Student Loans: 67%
Average Debt: $ $ $

With top-notch programs in journalism and business, Ohio University has become a competitive public institution without shedding its small-town roots. It has become known as an important research institution, with faculty interests ranging from dinosaur anatomy to rural diabetes rates.

"The climate is laid-back." Students here love to hit the town for fun but are quick to hit the books, too. Those who choose to attend Ohio receive ample returns, says a senior, including "a quality education, lifelong friends, supportive faculty, and a beautiful campus."

Established in 1804 as the first institution of higher learning in the old Northwest Territory, Ohio University is located in Athens, about 75 miles southeast from Columbus, the state capital. Encircled by winding hills, the campus features neo-Georgian architecture, tree-lined redbrick walkways, and white-columned buildings all clustered on "greens," which are like small neighborhoods. Long walks are especially nice during the fall foliage season.

One of the focal points of an Ohio University education, and something that sets the school apart from run-of-the-mill state institutions, is the Honors Tutorial College. Founded in 1972, it's the nation's first multidisciplinary, degree-granting honors program modeled on the tutorial method used in British universities, notably Oxford and Cambridge. It is ranked as one of the best programs on campus, and the most selective: Students must have at least a 1300 on their SAT or a 30 on their ACT, and only about 60 freshmen get in every year. Students take an individualized curriculum in a major field and spend most of their time in one-on-one weekly tutorials with profs. The College of Communication now contains five schools: the schools of journalism, information and telecommunication systems, communication studies, media arts and studies, and visual communication. The Global Learning Community Certificate is an innovative program that prepares students for leadership opportunities in a rapidly changing world.

"My professors have always been willing to work with me."

First-year GLC students work in binational teams with students from universities in Hungary, Ecuador, Thailand, and elsewhere. Students can take an online journalism course, which teaches skills like computer-assisted reporting and Web design.

The academic climate is far from cut-throat, but courses can be demanding. "The climate is laid-back," says one student, "but people do work hard." General education requirements involve a minimum of one course in math or quantitative skills, two courses in English composition, one senior-level interdisciplinary course, plus additional coursework in applied sciences and technology, social sciences, natural sciences, humanities, and cross-cultural perspectives. To lighten the load, you can take electives such as the Language of Rock Music (so you can communicate more effectively with fellow moshers?). Study abroad offers worldwide destinations for anywhere from two weeks to one year; locations include Africa, Asia, Australia, Canada, the Caribbean, Europe, and Latin America. Co-op programs are available for engineering students, and nearly anyone can earn credit for an internship. The university has recently adopted a semester calendar.

Students say most of their professors are top-notch. "My professors have always been willing to work with me and offer out-of-class time to make sure that me and my peers could excel in the courses," a senior says. Freshmen are often taught by full professors with TAs handling study sessions. Classes of 100-plus students do exist, but 37 percent of all classes taken by freshmen have 19 or fewer students. Budget cutbacks have limited access to some classes, and "we need more professors to cut down the class sizes," says a finance major. The university supports learning and residential communities (50 percent of freshmen participate), a common reading experience, and a welcome weekend.

Ohio students are easygoing, yet driven in the classroom. "All of us have a very deep interest in our chosen subject matter," says one student. "I see so much passion amongst my peers for their work." You'll find many classmates from the Buckeye State; 83 percent are Ohioans. Almost everyone at Ohio attended public high school and 16 percent graduated in the top 10th of their class. The student body is overwhelmingly white, although administrators are trying to attract more minority students and have established an Office of Multicultural Programs. Five percent are African American; Hispanics and Asian Americans combine for 3 percent. The Gateway Award Program provides financial aid for outstanding students who show academic excellence, financial need, or a combination of both. Merit awards, averaging $4,136, are available to eligible students, while athletes vie for 233 athletic scholarships in 16 sports.

Campus housing is hit or miss, students report. "The dorms are very old," grumbles a junior. "Since we are running out of space, our university is cramming way too many people into a tiny room." In short, housing is limited and finding a room

(continued)

Phi Beta Kappa: Yes
Applicants: 17,466
Accepted: 78%
Enrolled: 29%
Grad in 6 Years: 65%
Returning Freshmen: 79%
Academics: ✍ ✍ ✍
Social: 🍺 🍺 🍺 🍺
Q of L: ★ ★ ★
Admissions: (740) 593-4100
Email Address: admissions@ ohio.edu

Strongest Programs:
Journalism
Art
Art History
Home Economics
Business
Engineering
Communications
Film

The Global Learning Community Certificate is an innovative program that prepares students for leadership opportunities.

can be stressful. Almost everyone lives on campus for two years then moves into neighboring dwellings. Campus housing includes more than 160 learning communities with more than 2,700 participants. At the "mods," six men and six women occupy separate wings but share a living room and study room. Upperclassmen usually move to fraternity or sorority houses, nearby apartments, or rental houses. Five different meal plans are available at four cafeterias. "The dining facilities are not impressive," grumbles a middle childhood education major. "The food is edible but does not seem very healthy."

The social scene is largely off campus. Uptown Athens is dotted with bars and clubs, campus and community activities such as plays, and guest speakers and performers. Some students also choose to participate in Greek life. Eight percent of men and 12 percent of women join their ranks. "Ohio offers a very cohesive and communal social life," says a sophomore. The administration and some students have tried

"I see so much passion amongst my peers for their work."

to downplay OU's party-school image by strictly enforcing the alcohol policy. Freshmen are required to pass an online alcohol education course; if they don't, they might not be able to register for Ohio classes. But despite these efforts, students say that drinking continues. "Most freshmen drink in their dorm rooms and the bars are almost always crowded," a student explains. Athens's fabled Halloween celebration is a huge block party that draws people from all over the Midwest. Students also look forward to homecoming, International Festival, and block parties like Palmerfest and Millfest. "Athens is its own place," says a senior. "You feel at home. It's beautiful and friendly and like no other." Volunteer opportunities, such as Habitat for Humanity and a local homeless shelter, are available through the Center for Community Service. Students also love to hike and camp at the nearby state parks or trek to Columbus for shopping.

Sports are a big draw at Ohio. Competitive Bobcats teams include men's basketball, field hockey, and football, and women's volleyball. The university also has a nationally ranked forensics program. Seventy intramural and 35 club sports draw 60 percent of freshmen; popular choices include teams for broomball and wallyball (think volleyball using walls).

Students say Ohio University has a lot to offer, from a vibrant social life to quality professors and challenging academics. "I love this school and the city's community," says one student. "I think most students would not regret their decision to come here."

Overlaps

Bowling Green State, Kent State, Miami (OH), Ohio State

If You Apply To ➤

Ohio: Rolling admissions: Sep. 15. Financial aid: Jan. 15. Housing: May 1. Application fee: $45. Campus and alumni interviews: optional, informational. SATs or ACTs: required. Subject Tests: optional. Essay question: optional personal essay.

Ohio Wesleyan University

South Sandusky Street, Delaware, OH 43015

OWU serves up the liberal arts with a popular side dish of business-related programs. In a region of beautiful campuses, Ohio Wesleyan's is nondescript. Like Denison, OWU is working hard to make its fraternities behave. Attracts middle-of-the-road to conservative students with preprofessional aspirations. Offers a variety of programs to raise social awareness, notably Wesleyan in Washington.

Ohio Wesleyan University is a small school with a big commitment to providing its students with a well-rounded education. Affiliated with the Methodist Episcopal Church, OWU hallmarks include strong preparation for graduate and professional school, a solid grounding in the liberal arts, and an emphasis on having fun outside the classroom. Once known for its raucous students, this small university has overcome its hard-partying past and now offers students a rewarding academic experience.

Situated smack in the center of the state and on the outskirts of Columbus, OWU's spacious 200-acre campus is peaceful and quaint, albeit with a highway that runs down the middle. Several buildings are on the National Register of Historic Places. The architecture ranges from Greek Revival to colonial to modern, with ivy-covered brick academic buildings on one side of a busy thoroughfare and dormitories and fraternities on the other side of the highway. Stately University Hall, with its majestic spire and bell tower, is the main campus landmark and houses the president's office and the 1,100-seat Gray Chapel, home to the largest Klais organ in the United States. A new fountain and commons area have been added to the university's main thoroughfare, the JAYwalk.

"The best departments are the natural sciences and psychology."

Preprofessional education has always been Ohio Wesleyan's forte. More than 80 percent of students applying to medical school are accepted. The curriculum includes majors in neuroscience and East Asian studies, and the highly popular zoology and microbiology departments are interesting alternatives to the traditional premed route. The Woltemade Center for Economics, Business, and Entrepreneurship caters to budding entrepreneurs, and the music and fine arts programs offer both professional and liberal arts degrees. "The best departments are the natural sciences and psychology," offers one senior. The Course Connections networks allow students to study a particular topic in depth over a long period of time, selecting courses from disciplines and departments throughout the university. The OWU

"Most Ohio Wesleyan students are super passionate."

Connection program allows students to take cross-departmental courses based on a common theme, such as Crime, Responsibility, and Punishment. Administrators say these courses "help students see the connections between and among disciplines and make them well-rounded experts in a particular topic."

A member of the Great Lakes Colleges Association* consortium, OWU offers numerous curricular programs. The most prominent is the Sagan National Colloquium, a series of lectures, classes, events, and projects around a theme that unites the liberal and civic arts. The honors program offers qualified students one-on-one tutorials and a chance to conduct research with faculty members in areas of mutual interest. The Special Languages program offers the opportunity for self-directed study and tutoring by native speakers in languages such as Arabic, Chinese, Japanese, and Modern Greek. Students may choose to travel throughout the United States and the world on spring break mission trips, or spend a semester in New York City in apprenticeships with working professionals. The school's study abroad offerings are enhanced by Theory-to-Practice Grants that support students in projects ranging from a field dig on the Aegean coast to the study of HIV/AIDS in South Africa and Tanzania. Those interested in government may participate in the Wesleyan in Washington program where they serve internships with senators, representatives, and other government officials.

"The courses are challenging, but nothing that a committed student can't handle," says one junior. Students also point out that peers tend to support one another rather than compete for grades. To graduate, OWU students must take a year of foreign language; three courses each in the social sciences, natural sciences, and humanities; one course in the arts; and one course in cultural diversity. Students must also pass three mandatory writing classes to sharpen their written communication skills, but these aren't burdensome. Students universally laud OWU's faculty for ability

Website: www.owu.edu
Location: Suburban
Private
Total Enrollment: 1,821
Undergraduates: 1,821
Male/Female: 45/55
SAT Ranges: CR 510–620, M 520–640
ACT Ranges: 23–28
Financial Aid: 97%
Expense: Pr $ $
Student Loans: 65%
Average Debt: $ $ $ $
Phi Beta Kappa: Yes
Applicants: 3,835
Accepted: 74%
Enrolled: 19%
Grad in 6 Years: 68%
Returning Freshmen: 83%
Academics: ✐ ✐ ✐ ½
Social: 🐗 🐗 🐗 🐗 🐗
Q of L: ★ ★ ★
Admissions: (800) 922-8953
Email Address: owuadmit@owu.edu

Strongest Programs:
Psychology
Zoology
Economics and Management
Sociology/Anthropology
English
History
Politics and Government
Biology

The Woltemade Center for Economics, Business, and Entrepreneurship caters to budding entrepreneurs.

Those interested
in government
may participate
in the Wesleyan in
Washington program.

and accessibility. "I have only been at OWU for a year, but I have already met some outstanding professors," cheers one international business major. "Our small class sizes mean that there are no TAs and there will be a personal connection with your professor, guaranteed." Also, "the Chaplain's Office is a hidden gem on this campus, and our chaplains are the unsung heroes of Ohio Wesleyan," according to one senior. "Get to know the chaplain's staff while at OWU; they are amazing people who will make your time here phenomenal."

"Most Ohio Wesleyan students are super passionate," a history major says. "They are politically engaged and are in too many clubs." Forty-five percent of students come from Ohio; the student body represents 44 states and 45 nations. Students agree that diversity is valued on campus, but African Americans make up only 5 percent of the student body, Hispanics 3 percent, and Asian Americans 2 percent. Liberals and conservatives are well represented on campus and hot topics include racial, gender, and sexual equality. Presidential, Trustee, and Faculty merit scholarships are offered for full tuition, three-fourths tuition, and half tuition, respectively, and the average financial aid package tops $14,000.

Ninety percent of OWU students live in university-sponsored housing. "The more that the school attempts to become a residential campus, the more trouble there is acquiring a room," grumbles one senior. All but one of the dorms are co-ed, and rooms are mostly apartment-style, four-person suites or doubles. Fraternities, unlike sororities, offer a residential option. "We have a lot of great opportunities on campus. We have small-living units or SLUs, which are essentially themed houses," says a senior. "The members of these houses do house projects every semester for the campus and are an extremely important part of the OWU community." Each meal eaten on the college plan subtracts a certain number of points (far too many in the opinion of most students) from students' accounts, but there are numerous culinary choices, from all-you-can-eat in the three dining halls to pizza and snacks from the college grocery store. "The food is constantly changing and genuinely good. Students also have off-campus food points if they grow tired of on-campus options," says one student.

Among OWU's best-
loved traditions
are Homecoming in
the fall and Alumni
Weekend in the spring.

"One thing you can say about Ohio Wesleyan is that you will never be bored," says one sophomore. "We are in no way a suitcase school," adds another student. "There's always so much going on and there's never enough time to do everything." Does the buttoned-down seriousness of recent years mean that OWU has forsaken its heritage of raucous partying? Administrators certainly hope so. Trying to stamp out drunken binges, OWU slaps fines of up to $150 on all underage students caught drinking and puts them on probation after the fourth offense. One student says, "The campus works to educate students on alcohol and to guide students' decision making." Part of OWU's commitment to mend its partying ways includes dry rush for all fraternities and an armband policy at parties. Greek membership, however, still attracts 40 percent of men and 32 percent of women. Among OWU's best-loved traditions are Homecoming in the fall and Alumni Weekend in the spring, as well as the President's Ball in December.

Delaware, a town of 31,000, is "adorable," says one freshman, and "its main revenue comes from antiquing and its big claim to fame is that it hosts one of the runs for the Kentucky Derby." The Little Brown Jug, one of harness racing's Triple Crown events, takes place each autumn, bringing thousands of people to the city of Delaware. Most students are involved in service, either through mission trips or community service learning in such projects as Habitat for Humanity, Delaware Reads, and the Delaware County Humane Society. "Because of the high amount of volunteering that OWU students do in Delaware, we have a fairly good relationship with the town," one student says. Ohio's capital and largest city, Columbus, is only 30 minutes away by car and offers many job and internship opportunities. Lakes, farms, and even ski slopes are within a few hours' drive.

"We have small-living units or SLUs, which are essentially themed houses."

Overlaps

Denison, Ohio State, Wittenberg, College of Wooster, Miami (OH), Otterbein University, University of Dayton, Ohio Northern

OWU's "Battling Bishops" are a North Coast Athletic Conference powerhouse. Past NCAC champs include men's lacrosse, men's soccer, women's indoor track and field, women's outdoor track and field, men's indoor track and field, men's outdoor track and field, and softball. Sports fever carries over into single-sex and co-ed intramurals (nearly 80 percent of students take part), and a massive annual game of Capture the Flag begins at 11:00 one night and lasts until the wee hours.

Ohio Wesleyan University offers a solid liberal arts education devoid of bells and whistles. "Ohio Wesleyan is a place where the education goes well beyond the classroom," explains one student. "The family atmosphere and the opportunities that the college provides you in a diverse environment enrich the entire college experience."

If You Apply To ⮞	**OWU:** Early decision: Nov. 15. Early action: Jan. 15. Regular admissions and financial aid: Mar. 1. Housing: May 1. Application fee: $35 (paper), free (online). Campus interviews: optional, evaluative. Alumni interviews: optional, informational. SATs or ACTs: required. Subject Tests: optional. Accepts the Common Application. Essay question.

University of Oklahoma

1000 Asp Avenue, Room 127, Norman, OK 73019

Football aside, OU has historically been outclassed by neighbors like the University of Kansas and the University of Texas at Austin. But the signs of improvement are there. Check out the Honors College, which boasts a living/learning option. OU is strong in engineering and geology-related fields.

The University of Oklahoma has more to boast about than its powerhouse football program. President David Boren—a former U.S. senator and Oklahoma governor—has made it a priority to improve both academics and the physical appearance of the state's flagship campus. "There are new buildings everywhere, because President Boren has found the resources to upgrade our university in every way," says a satisfied senior. Couple that with a rigorous honors program and a genuine friendliness among the student body, and it's easy to understand this favorite saying: "Sooner born and Sooner bred, when I die, I'll be Sooner dead!"

Located about 20 miles south of Oklahoma City, OU's 3,500-acre Norman campus features tree-lined streets and predominantly redbrick buildings. Many are historic in nature and built in the Cherokee or prairie Gothic style. The Norman campus houses 16 colleges; six medical and health-related colleges are located on the OU Health Sciences Center campus in Oklahoma City, and programs from colleges on both campuses are also offered at OU's Schusterman Center in Tulsa. In recent years, nearly $1.5 billion in construction projects have been completed, including the $67 million National Weather Research Center, which happens to be the largest weather research center of its kind in the nation. A new, $75 million student housing center opened in late 2013.

> **"The classes at OU are tough but manageable."**

All Oklahoma freshmen start out in University College before choosing among OU's degree-granting institutions, including colleges of architecture, education, and fine arts. The College of Engineering offers aerospace, civil, mechanical, and environmental engineering. In January 2006, the College of Earth and Energy was chartered, consolidating resources related to petroleum and geological engineering, meteorology, geology and geophysics, and geography. OU's petroleum program ranks among

Website: www.ou.edu
Location: Small City
Public
Total Enrollment: 21,114
Undergraduates: 17,953
Male/Female: 50/50
SAT Ranges: CR 510–640, M 540–660
ACT Ranges: 23–29
Financial Aid: 51%
Expense: Pub $ $
Student Loans: 50%
Average Debt: $ $ $
Phi Beta Kappa: Yes
Applicants: 11,650
Accepted: 79%
Enrolled: 45%
Grad in 6 Years: 66%
Returning Freshmen: 84%
Academics: ✏ ✏ ✏
Social: 🎭 🎭 🎭
Q of L: ★ ★ ★
Admissions: (405) 325-2252

(continued)

Email Address: admrec@ ou.edu

Strongest Programs:
Nursing
Petroleum Engineering
Psychology
Health and Exercise Science
Energy Management
Chemistry
Accounting
Meteorology

The Honors College offers small classes with outstanding faculty members and independent study, along with its own dorm.

the best in the nation, and in the College of Arts and Sciences, the natural sciences, notably chemistry, are strong. The Michael F. Price College of Business, named for the superstar investment manager, class of '73, offers a major in entrepreneurship and venture management. Other well-recognized programs at OU include majors in Native American studies and energy management; the OU Native American studies program teaches more Native American languages for college credit than any other institution. The College of Education's rigorous five-year teacher-certification program, Teacher Education Plus (TE-PLUS), incorporates field experience, mentoring, and instruction from 30 full-time professors.

OU's general education requirements consist of three to five courses in symbolic and oral communication, including English composition; two courses in natural science; two courses in social science; four humanities courses; an upper-division general education course outside the major; and a Senior Capstone Experience. The Honors College offers small classes with outstanding faculty members and independent study, along with its own dorm. Top students may also apply for the Scholarship-Leadership Enrichment Program, under which well-known lecturers give seminars at the university for academic credit. A slew of new programs have been added recently, including degrees in world cultural studies and chemical biosciences.

"The classes at OU are tough but manageable," says a senior. "People are competitive about their grades but not to the point that it's overwhelming." OU has made efforts to address large classes and is now one of the nation's few public universities to cap the class size of first-year English comp courses at no more than 19. A junior says, "Class sizes range from 300 in the most basic general education classes to about 20 students in upper division and honors courses." In the past decade, increased private support has helped OU nearly quadruple its endowed faculty positions, helping the school to attract and retain talented professors. "My first semester proved to me that OU values freshmen classes, as all of my professors were engaging, highly qualified, and thoroughly interested in what they were teaching. The professors here are incredible and easy to connect with," says one junior.

"The students at OU are engaged."

"The students at OU are engaged," says one microbiology major. "Whether they are passionate about education or student leadership, I have seen so many of my peers really invest in their work." The student body is primarily homegrown; 66 percent hail from the Sooner state. African Americans, Asian Americans, and Native Americans account for 5 percent each of the student body, while Hispanic students comprise 7 percent. "Students are very informed here," one junior says. "Currently, there is a big push for OU to go green." Qualified students receive scholarships based on academic merit, with awards averaging $2,069. There are also 249 athletic scholarships in a variety of sports, and the Presidential Travel and Study Abroad Scholarships offer $250,000 for students and faculty to study and conduct research around the globe. OU also offers a variety of special aid programs aimed at making the university more affordable for low-income students.

In the past decade, increased private support has helped OU nearly quadruple its endowed faculty positions, helping the school to attract and retain talented professors.

Thirty percent of students live in the university's residence halls, most of which are co-ed by floor. The three tower dorms, the most popular choice for freshmen, are currently undergoing renovations, and many students already benefit from new carpet, new tile in the bathrooms, and modular furniture that can be arranged in a variety of ways. "Housing at OU is about average. The dorms are well maintained, but rooms are small," one student says. Upperclassmen may also choose the OU Traditions Square apartment community. Furnished units in the complex include in-unit washers and dryers and full kitchens, plus high-speed wired and wireless Internet access and access to a fitness area, a pool, sand volleyball courts, and a putting green. According to one student, "Couch Cafeteria has countless options for food and is a favorite of most students at OU." Students say they feel safe on campus. "Campus security is very good and students always feel safe, even when walking back home from the library at two a.m.," says a senior.

"Although Norman is great town, students never have to leave campus in order to de-stress and relax on the weekends," cheers one student. Twenty-two percent of men and 26 percent of women go Greek. Although the dorms and Greek houses are dry, fraternity parties are the highlight of weekends at OU. "Campus Corner provides a lot of the night life with great restaurants and bars located directly across the street from campus," a junior says. The "three strikes" alcohol policy "has greatly cut down on alcohol incidents" on campus, according to one student. The town of Norman, population 100,000, is Oklahoma's third-largest city, and Oklahoma City is just 20 minutes away. Other popular diversions include the annual road trip to Dallas for the OU–Texas game, the Medieval Festival, and the University Sing, a talent show. The Big Event also brings thousands of students into the community for a day of service each year.

> **"Students never have to leave campus in order to de-stress and relax on the weekends."**

The Big Event brings thousands of students into the community for a day of service each year.

OU sports powerhouse athletic teams. Sooner football remains strong under coach Bob Stoops and has brought home the Big 12 Conference title multiple times in recent years. "OU–Texas is insane," says a letters major. "I can't accurately describe it in words. Every football game day, the town swells to over 500,000 people, and I consider game days an all-day festival." The baseball team is competitive and brought home an NCAA tournament title in 2012. Men's golf brought home the national title in 2011. Other recent winners include the men's gymnastics, women's basketball, and women's softball teams. Recreational and intramural programs attract half of the undergraduate population.

"OU offers the classic college experience," says a senior. Indeed, students at Oklahoma have a lot to brag about. "The educational opportunities are top-notch," says one junior, and "a student can come from anywhere and find that they are part of something special." If you're searching for a school with plenty of spirit and a feeling of family, OU may be worth a look—Sooner, rather than later.

Overlaps

Oklahoma State, University of Tulsa, University of Texas, Texas A&M, Texas Tech, Baylor, University of Arkansas, Texas Christian

If You Apply To ➤ | **OU:** Rolling admissions: Apr. 1. Financial aid: Mar. 1. Application fee: $40. Campus interviews: optional, informational. No alumni interviews. SATs or ACTs: required. No Subject Tests. No essay question.

Olin College of Engineering

Olin Way, Needham, MA 02492

Olin opened its doors in 2002 with an innovative project-based curriculum and a commitment to turning out "technologists with soul." Already an elite institution that competes with Caltech and MIT. Every accepted student gets a hefty merit scholarship. Located near Wellesley on the outskirts of Boston.

In the mid-1990s, leaders of the F. W. Olin Foundation began daydreaming about what "state-of-the-art" engineering education for the 21st century would look like. A decade and $470 million later they have their answer: the Franklin W. Olin College of Engineering. This elite engineering school, which graduated its first class and won accreditation in 2006, aims to turn out Steve Jobs–style graduates

Website: www.olin.edu
Location: Suburban
Private
Total Enrollment: 342

(continued)

Undergraduates: 342
Male/Female: 52/48
SAT Ranges: CR 700–775,
  M 725–790
ACT Ranges: 33–34
Financial Aid: 100%
Expense: Pr $ $ $
Student Loans: 18%
Average Debt: $
Phi Beta Kappa: No
Applicants: 781
Accepted: 19%
Enrolled: 54%
Grad in 6 Years: 94%
Returning Freshmen: 96%
Academics: ✑ ✑ ✑ ✑ ✑
Social: ☎ ☎ ☎
Q of L: ★ ★ ★ ★ ★
Admissions: (781) 292-2222
Email Address: info@olin.edu

Strongest Programs:
General Engineering
Electrical and Computer
  Engineering
Mechanical Engineering

who are not only technically competent but who can "come up with innovative ideas and products." The curriculum is project-based, and students become as comfortable in the machine shop as in labs and classrooms. The foundation fathers also decided that, rather than gradually building up the quality and reputation of their new school, they would invest in excellence from the get-go. By offering every admitted student a half-scholarship worth more than $80,000 over four years, Olin has succeeded in luring super-bright students away from Caltech, MIT, and other engineering highfliers. Sure, the college lacks the rich tradition and reputation for research of more established institutions. But that doesn't seem to bother the more than 300 students who have latched on to perhaps the best deal in U.S. higher education. Says one happy denizen, "Olin has quite literally gone from a hole in the ground to a home."

> "Olin has quite literally gone from a hole in the ground to a home."

Olin's 70-acre campus is located adjacent to Babson College in a pleasant suburb less than 20 miles west of Boston. The campus design is an innovative blend of the traditional and futuristic. Five buildings curve around a central green space, creating a sense of community and echoing the design of the traditional New England college. The entire campus is wired for high-tech communications, and designed for easy updating to stay on the cutting edge. The classrooms make use of state-of-the-art instructional media, and there are plenty of meeting and public spaces to encourage the kind of collaboration called for in modern-day engineering. East Hall includes 19 suites and practice rooms, an exercise room, a kitchenette, study rooms, lounges, and bicycle storage.

Olin's innovative curriculum is based on the "Olin Triangle," which emphasizes science and engineering, business and entrepreneurship, and the liberal arts. Students choose from three majors—general engineering, electrical and computer engineering, and mechanical engineering—and a number of concentrations, including bioengineering, computing, materials science, and systems. In addition, students must complete 30 credits of math and science (10 of which must be in math) and 28 credits of arts, humanities, social sciences (AHS), and entrepreneurship, 12 of which must be in AHS. The hands-on nature of the curriculum means that students start out with relatively simple projects such as designing water rockets and progress to more sophisticated challenges like building a wall-climbing gecko—a project that involves analyzing the physics of the natural world and then figuring out how to replicate it mechanically. Concern for "engineering design" is built into every subject. Each student also completes a major yearlong senior capstone project known as SCOPE (Senior Consulting Program for Engineering) in which they work as an engineering consultant for a real live company. Working in teams and across disciplines is the norm for faculty as well as students. "There is a strong emphasis on teamwork," says one student, and "classes are typically pretty intense."

> *The hands-on nature of the curriculum means that students start out with relatively simple projects and progress to more sophisticated challenges.*

Because the academic menu is so narrowly focused, weak programs are virtually nonexistent. While the courses are demanding, students say that the intellectual environment fosters cooperation rather than competition. Grading starts after the first semester. Sixty-three percent of classes have 19 or fewer students, and all are led by professors. Faculty members do not have tenure. Like their students, many of them have been lured from the likes of MIT because they like the challenge of helping to create what one of them termed "the model of engineering for the future."

> "There is a strong emphasis on teamwork."

"Olin professors are amazing," a student says. "They take the time to get to know their students individually and never fail to provide academic or personal advice." The course catalog is thin, especially in liberal arts subjects, but students can and do take courses at nearby Wellesley, Babson, and even Brandeis. The fledgling library is open 24/7, but it is stronger on bytes than books.

First-year students have an opportunity to participate in an interactive weeklong orientation program that includes team-building exercises, meetings, and meals with faculty and advisors, as well as a trip into Boston. The college also encourages students to engage in "Passionate Pursuits," by enabling them to pursue artistic or humanistic interests via nondegree credit projects. A sampling of student projects include Irish dancing, rock climbing, guitar making, marathon training, and Bhangra (Indian folk dancing).

Olin students are indeed "passionate," says a freshman, "and not just about engineering." Only 13 percent hail from Massachusetts, and a whopping 95 percent graduated in the top 10th of their high school class. African Americans comprise 1 percent of the student body, Asian Americans 16 percent, and Hispanics 1 percent. Hot-button issues include environmental awareness, homosexuality, and abortion. "Students are generally liberal," notes a senior. To make sure that it selects students who are a good "fit" for Olin's unique approach to engineering, the admissions office invites 270 applicants to attend one of two "candidates weekends" in the spring where they learn about the school, take part in team projects such as building a weight-bearing bridge out of Styrofoam, and go through a 25-minute interview

When students aren't laboring over the latest engineering project or Structural Biomaterials assignment, they tend to congregate on campus for fun.

"Housing is given on a seniority basis."

with faculty, staff, students, and an alumnus. About 200 of these students are accepted, and about 30 are placed on a waiting list—with admission guaranteed the following fall.

All Olin students live on campus and "housing is given on a seniority basis," says a senior. "The dorms are wonderful," reports one student. "The halls include lounges, kitchens, laundry, and exercise rooms, as well as space dedicated for homework and team study," adds another. The dining hall provides students with a tasty—if repetitive—meal selection that includes "a fresh salad and cold cuts bar, pizza and pasta, and usually two or three entrees for every meal." Olin operates with a student-designed honor system that makes for unlocked rooms and take-home exams. "You can leave your laptop in the lounge, and it won't walk off," said a senior. Campus security is good and "students do feel physically safe," says an engineering design major.

When students aren't laboring over the latest engineering project or Structural Biomaterials assignment, they tend to congregate on campus for fun. "There are parties in the residence halls, and the Student Activities Committee hosts some sort of schoolwide event every weekend," says a junior. There are no Greek organizations, and students say the social scene does not revolve around alcohol. "The campus alcohol policies are quite reasonable," says a student, "relying largely on student responsibility." The student orchestra has no conductor—or, as the joke goes, "not even a semiconductor." When the campus scene grows tiresome, students often travel to nearby Babson (on foot) or Wellesley (by shuttle bus) to

Olin students have watched their school grow up before their eyes.

"It's a small, high-pressure engineering college."

mingle. There are also frequent road trips to Boston, Vermont, or the beaches of Maine. One student concedes, "I wish it were easier to get to Boston. The train station is a mile and a half from campus."

One student describes the surrounding town of Needham as "a quaint bedroom community that tries to be a college town." An engineering major says, "There are good restaurants nearby, but stores in town close early and there isn't much nightlife." Still, students take advantage of volunteer opportunities, and "we also try to have some sort of larger event with the Needham community every month or so," says a student. Such events have included a Halloween labyrinth for local school children and "an event where Olin students auctioned off their skills or services to community members for charity." One junior quips, "At Olin, a tradition is anything that has been done more than two years in a row."

Although Olin does not offer varsity sports, "a number of pick-up leagues have evolved for soccer, Frisbee, football, and basketball," says a junior. "Some students also play on teams at Babson or Wellesley for sports such as lacrosse, rugby, and cross-country." Other popular intramural sports include ultimate Frisbee, soccer, volleyball, and dodgeball.

"Olin is not for everyone," one student warns. "It's a small, high-pressure engineering college." For those who have what it takes, Olin College offers a top-notch engineering degree at a bargain price. Olin students have watched their school grow up before their eyes and blossom into what they and their faculty members believe is the future model for engineering education in this country—one that stresses interdisciplinary project-based instruction and the importance of "learning to learn." It's not at all clear that future employers are ready for the freethinking graduates that Olin is producing, but that's OK. Says one student, "Students who are passionate about things and excited about engineering would do well here."

If You Apply To >

Olin: Regular admissions: Jan. 1. Financial aid: Feb. 15. Application fee: $80. No campus or alumni interviews. SATs or ACTs: required. Subject Tests: required (math, science, and one other). Accepts the Common Application. Essay questions.

University of Oregon

1226 University of Oregon, Eugene, OR 97403-1226

UO may be the best deal in public higher education on the West Coast. Less expensive than the UC system and less selective than the University of Washington, UO is a flagship university of manageable size in a great location. The liberal arts are more than just a slogan, and programs in business and communication are strong.

Blend two vegetarians, one track star, one frat brother, two tree huggers, three hikers, and one conservative. What have you got? Ten UO students. Sure, the joke's hokey, but its offbeat humor is typical of the laid-back, slightly eccentric attitude that prevails here in Eugene, where bicycling is the main form of transportation, recycling is a requirement, and littering is déclassé. As the most accessible of the West Coast flagship universities, the University of Oregon attracts brainy students who are proud of their quirky ways.

UO's buildings date from as early as 1876 and are surrounded by the university's lush 295-acre arboretum-like campus, which boasts 2,000 varieties of dew-kissed trees. Most academic buildings were built before World War II and represent a blend of classical styles, including Georgian, Second Empire, Jacobin, and Lombardic. Residential facilities range from 19th-century colonials to modern high-rises. A $68 million, 185,000-square-foot residence hall opened in 2012 and houses approximately 450 students.

"It is painfully obvious when a professor does not care."

While a liberal arts emphasis underlies Oregon's entire curriculum, general education requirements are not highly structured. The calendar is composed of quarters, and students must take two terms of English composition, two years of foreign language (for a B.A.), one year of math (for a B.S.), and two courses exploring American or international culture, identity, pluralism, and tolerance, plus four courses in each of three areas: arts and letters, social sciences, and natural sciences. Each July, the

Website: www.uoregon.edu
Location: Small City
Public
Total Enrollment: 21,862
Undergraduates: 18,820
Male/Female: 48/52
SAT Ranges: CR 489–608, M 502–616
ACT Ranges: N/A
Financial Aid: 64%
Expense: Pub $ $
Student Loans: 48%
Average Debt: $ $
Phi Beta Kappa: Yes
Applicants: 21,263
Accepted: 74%
Enrolled: 26%
Grad in 6 Years: 68%
Returning Freshmen: 85%
Academics: ✍ ✍ ✍ ½

university offers IntroDUCKtion to new students, featuring opportunities for orientation, registration, and advisement. Freshman seminars introduce students to top professors in small-group settings, and professors have to apply to teach them, a process students applaud. Freshman interest groups help new students develop close working and advising relationships with faculty members and other students.

UO's professional schools—journalism, architecture and allied arts, education, law, business, and music and dance—are highly regarded, and the most popular majors include journalism, business administration, psychology, and biology. The School of Architecture and Allied Arts is the home of Oregon's only accredited degrees in architecture, landscape architecture, and interior architecture. Of the more than 35 departments in the College of Arts and Sciences, students give high marks (and high enrollments) to psychology and biology, and the science departments within this particular college offer many opportunities for research. About 25 percent of undergraduates study abroad during their time at UO and 190 programs are offered in more than 90 countries.

> "The university plays host to a variety of concerts, culture nights, film viewings, guest lecturers, sporting events, and dances."

Highly motivated undergraduates may apply to the Honors College, a small liberal arts college with its own courses. The student-run community internship programs provide credit for community volunteer work, while on-campus internships allow students to earn credit for work with university organizations and academic departments. In keeping with Oregon's eco-friendly reputation, the Green Chemistry Laboratory and Instrumentation Center was the first in the nation to use nontoxic materials in experiments. Pine Mountain Observatory, a field-study resource for astronomy and physics students located high in the Cascade Mountains, and the Oregon Institute of Marine Biology give students a chance for intimate studies in their major.

UO's academic climate "is laid-back and not very competitive," says one senior. Professors are lauded for their skills behind the lectern, although it's not uncommon to find TAs handling some of the teaching duties. "The quality of teaching varies," says one teaching and learning major. "It is painfully obvious when a professor does not care or they simply allow a graduate student to teach the class."

UO students "find what they love and work hard for it," says a journalism major, whether it's "athletics, academics, politics, being Greek, doing research, a campus job, or volunteer work." There is a noticeable contingent of international students, who account for 11 percent of the student body. Asian Americans account for another 5 percent, African Americans 2 percent, and Hispanics 7 percent. "There are a lot of people from California," says a freshman, and "a lot of artsy hipsters." Numerous merit scholarships worth an average of $3,313 and 357 athletic scholarships are awarded to qualified students.

> "Our campus is totally dry by policy."

Twenty percent of UO students choose to live in university housing. "They are pretty small, but I love the cozy feeling," a student says. There are a number of thematic living arrangements—a cross-cultural dorm, an academic-pursuit residence hall, and a music dorm. Students recommend Walton, Carson, and Barnhart Halls. Rooms in the residence halls tend to be small and unimpressive, according to students. "Because the rooms are so small, you don't spend much time in them," one student explains. "There can be a lot of issues getting a room," adds a senior. Any student can sign up for the meal plan in the two main dining halls; restaurants in the student union and off-campus fast food round out the menu. "The dining halls are so good. There are many different choices as well as options for vegan and vegetarian."

(continued)

Social: ☎ ☎ ☎
Q of L: ★ ★ ★ ★
Admissions: (800) 232-3825
Email Address: uoadmit@ uoregon.edu

Strongest Programs:
Architecture
Music
Creative Writing
Business
Chemistry
Journalism and
   Communication

Freshman interest groups help new students develop close working and advising relationships with faculty members and other students.

About 25 percent of undergraduates study abroad during their time at UO and 190 programs are offered in more than 90 countries.

Eugene is "the best college town ever! Everything about Eugene is based around the Ducks!" one student raves. Popular hangouts include Old Taylor's and Rennie's Bar and Grille, and community and public service projects also draw crowds. The one drawback to all this fun is Oregon's weather: It rains and rains. "Eugene gets some sunny days in early fall, late spring, and summer," reports a veteran. Still, the moist climate rarely dampens enthusiasm for the many expeditions available through the university's well-coordinated outdoor program, from rock climbing to skiing. An hour to the west, the rain turns to mist on the Pacific Coast; an hour to the east, it turns to snow in the Cascade Mountains. Students can also escape the weather year-round in the recreation center, complete with a rock climbing wall and juice bar.

Ten percent of UO men and 15 percent of the women join Greek organizations, which provide living space, interesting social diversions, and a wealth of personal development opportunities, such as leadership experience and community service projects. "The university plays host to a variety of concerts, culture nights, film viewings, guest lecturers, sporting events, and dances," one journalism and history double major says. Oregon's 21-year-old drinking age means that alcohol is banned from college-owned dorms, but students claim this rule can be broken. One student explains, "Our campus is totally dry by policy. The only students that are allowed to drink must be of age and do so with their doors closed. Of course, these rules are broken and the Department of Safety does punish students who get caught." Another student concurs, adding, "I feel that this works very well because every staff member goes the extra mile to provide other fun, nonalcoholic events." Major events include the Eugene Celebration, the Oregon Country Fair, the Martin Luther King Jr. Festival, and semiannual street fairs attended by local vendors. University Day, which happens each spring, offers students, faculty, and staff an opportunity to clean up their campus. The Willamette Valley Wine Festival is a fun road trip.

The UO mascot is not just a duck, but Donald Duck. In 1984, Donald Duck was named an "honorary alumnus." Of the Ducks' 19 sports programs, seven finished their respective seasons with a top five ranking, including national titles in women's cross-country and acrobatics and tumbling, and national runners-up finishes in women's track and field and volleyball. UO football appeared in its fourth consecutive BCS bowl game, while the men's golf team placed third at the NCAA championships. When students aren't on the tracks and fields themselves, they're trooping down to the stadium to join the Quacker Backers in cheering on the successful basketball and football teams. The UO debate team brought home two national championships in Spring 2011.

A recent University of Oregon Orientation Week T-shirt sported a picture of a duck and a simple exhortation: "Let your future take flight." UO offers ample opportunities for those with lofty ambitions to succeed. Indeed, UO's caring faculty, excellent academics, and abundance of social activities reveal that UO is all it's quacked up to be.

Overlaps

University of Washington, University of Colorado, Oregon State, Caltech, University of Arizona, UC–Santa Barbara, UC–Santa Cruz, San Diego State

If You Apply To ➢

UO: Early action: Nov. 1. Regular admissions: Jan. 15. Financial aid: Mar. 1. Application fee: $50. No campus or alumni interviews. SATs or ACTs: required. Subject Tests: optional. Essay question.

Oregon State University

Corvallis, OR 97331-2106

The biggest dilemma facing the typical 18-year-old Oregonian is whether to be a Beaver or a Duck. Choose Duck and hang with the ex-hippies in cosmopolitan Eugene. Choose Beaver and get small-town life with professional programs in business, engineering, and life sciences in Corvallis. OSU offers a less-selective option for frustrated UO hopefuls. Strong global emphasis.

With a wide range of academic programs, Oregon State University could very well be the setting of its own movie, titled Planes, Trains, and Submarines. You see, Oregon State is one of just a handful of universities in the country with land-, sea-, and space-grant designations. Though the school might be happy to forget its many years of being called Moo U, that doesn't mean its agriculture department should go unnoticed. In fact, many of the contributions made by Oregon State researchers center on the field of agriculture. Still, there's more to OSU than fruits and vegetables. The most accessible West Coast public university, OSU is strong in many departments, including biotechnology, forestry, and engineering. Says one satisfied freshman, "If you are looking for a college that is close-knit and has a friendly 'college town,' OSU is the place to go!"

Located in the pristine but rainy Willamette Valley, OSU's campus is a mix of older, ivy-covered buildings and more modern structures. In addition to the 500-acre main campus, OSU owns 13,000 acres of forestland near campus and numerous agricultural tracts throughout Oregon. Thousands of azalea and rhododendron bushes welcome springtime on campus with their colorful blooms, and summers are unfailingly sunny. A bevy of newly renovated, LEED-certified facilities have been added over the past few years.

OSU's College of Liberal Arts ranks with Business and Engineering as the largest on campus, but there are many more preprofessionals than poets. With the exceptions of history and English, the liberal arts—including such standard fare as sociology, psychology, economics, and philosophy—play second fiddle to more practical, technical fields. The departments of engineering (with its up-to-date electrical and computer engineering building) and forestry are major drawing cards, and even

"The courses are very rigorous."

though agriculture doesn't lure as many students as it used to, those who do come find excellent programs. Business administration is the most popular major, followed by exercise and sport science, liberal studies, general science, and psychology. The business school offers some of the finest business-related programs in the state, while the health and human performance program—a euphemism for home economics—has expanded its offerings.

OSU's extensive Baccalaureate Core requires courses in a variety of areas, including skills; perspectives; and difference, power, and discrimination. One writing-intensive course is required as well. Perhaps the core's most innovative facet is its "synthesis" requirement, in which upperclassmen take two interdisciplinary courses on global issues in the modern world. The campus's global awareness is also evident in the international degree, which can be coupled with any other course of study. Thus, students can earn a B.S. in forestry and a B.A. in international studies in forestry simultaneously. The level of academic pressure varies by major, but even those in the various honors programs say they don't feel overworked. "The courses are very rigorous, but if you apply yourself you will surely succeed," says a communications major. Most professors are "so captivated by their area of study that they are

Website: www.oregonstate .edu
Location: Small City
Public
Total Enrollment: 20,298
Undergraduates: 17,244
Male/Female: 54/46
SAT Ranges: CR 480–600, M 490–630
ACT Ranges: 21–27
Financial Aid: 75%
Expense: Pub $ $
Student Loans: 63%
Average Debt: $ $
Phi Beta Kappa: No
Applicants: 12,330
Accepted: 79%
Enrolled: 34%
Grad in 6 Years: 61%
Returning Freshmen: 83%
Academics: ✍ ✍ ✍
Social: ☎ ☎ ☎
Q of L: ★ ★ ★
Admissions: (800) 291-4192
Email Address: osuadmit@ oregonstate.edu

Strongest Programs:
Agriculture
Biotechnology
Forestry
Engineering
Business

eager to enlighten others with their knowledge and interests," says a sophomore. Freshmen have full professors for most courses, excluding recitation.

Of particular note is OSU's Experimental College, where undergraduates spice up their semesters with noncredit courses in a range of imaginative subjects—everything from wine tasting to the art of bashing (a medieval war technique). Those who choose a semester abroad may study at universities in England, France, Australia, Mexico, New Zealand, China, and Japan—or participate in individual exchange programs in still more countries. (Oregon State returns the favor, playing host to about 1,500 foreign students from more than 90 nations each year.) The university's small-town location makes it difficult to find much career-oriented part-time employment, and internships are hard to come by. (OSU operates on a quarter system.) Students in almost all majors, however, can participate in the cooperative education program, which allows them to alternate terms of study with several months of work in a relevant job.

> **"The students are a good mixture of city and rural students."**

The business school offers some of the finest business-related programs in the state.

Statistically, Oregon State certainly doesn't offer the most diverse student body. Sixty percent of the students are from Oregon, and the minority population is 1 percent African American, 6 percent Hispanic, and 7 percent Asian American. "The students are a good mixture of city and rural students," says a senior. Big campus issues include abortion and gay/lesbian rights. Most Oregon Staters are conservative and "very all-American—not cowboys and not city slickers, but very middle-of-the-road in all respects," a business major observes. Says an engineering major, "The college has its intelligentsia, its social butterflies, its determined athletes, and any combination of those." Merit scholarships averaging $2,995 are awarded annually, as are more than 250 athletic awards in 12 sports.

The campus's global awareness is also evident in the international degree, which can be coupled with any other course of study.

Freshmen are expected to live in college housing, though fraternity pledges have the option of living in their houses. Co-ed and single-sex options are available in the dorms, which house 21 percent of the students. "The residence halls are comfortable and well maintained, for the most part," says a forestry major. "They also offer many opportunities to get involved and meet new people." In addition to standard rooming situations, a new "wellness" hall offers an exercise room and low-calorie meals. Students can also choose life in one of eight cooperatives or the plentiful off-campus apartments. Foraging for food on your own generally beats so-so dorm food. The better food at frat and sorority houses is one motivation for students to go Greek; 12 percent of the men and 16 percent of the women do so. Alcohol still flows freely at Greek affairs, but crackdowns by the administration and local police have begun to curb the most wanton debauchery.

Cheering for the Beavers' nationally ranked wrestling team, which has had several top 10 national finishes in the past few years, demands a lot of students' time and energy here, as does participation in the well-rounded intramural program. Benny Beaver, the school's former (and somewhat benign) mascot, has been replaced by a more aggressive beaver that students have dubbed the "angry beaver." Other talented varsity squads include women's gymnastics, basketball, and volleyball and men's football and baseball (2013 Pac-12 champs); the basketball team has one of the top-10 winningest programs of all time among NCAA Division I schools. As for rivalries, one student says, "Civil War games between OSU and U of Oregon are a big part of every season."

> **"Civil War games between OSU and U of Oregon are a big part of every season."**

Overlaps

University of Oregon, University of Washington, Washington State, Portland State, University of Portland, Arizona State, Western Oregon, Colorado State

Another popular student activity is complaining about the Willamette Valley weather: "People in the valley don't tan, they rust," warns one native. One reward for this sogginess, however, is the abundance of flowers that bloom in every color and shape each May. Many students consider Corvallis a good-size town; a number of bars and cheap theaters cater to their entertainment needs. Beautifully rugged beaches are less than an hour away, and some of the best skiing in the country can be found in the Cascade Mountains, two hours east. Hiking and rafting are nearby, too, and trips to powwows in the area and camping on the coast provide other good times. Popular campus traditions include the Greeklife Sing (featuring musical numbers staged by fraternity and sorority members) and the annual Fall Festival.

OSU continues to build on its solid reputation as an agricultural institution, marching forward as a faithful part of the state's university system. OSU doesn't scream for attention. Instead, it's content to be a "nice" college, in "a safe and pleasant little town," where professors are "helpful" and, even if everyone doesn't know your name, they'll lend you an umbrella whenever the skies open up.

If You Apply To ➢

Oregon State: Early action: Nov. 1. Regular admissions: Feb. 1. Housing: Jul. 1. Application fee: $60. Campus interviews: optional, informational. No alumni interviews. SATs or ACTs (with writing): required. Subject Tests: optional. No essay question.

University of the Pacific

3601 Pacific Avenue, Stockton, CA 95211

The university's name dates from a time when there were no other universities near the Pacific. Still the only small, independent university in California north of L.A., it offers an eye-popping array of programs for an institution its size, including business, engineering, pharmacy, and education. The student body is equally diverse.

University of the Pacific looks like more than 100 acres of New England plunked down in California wine country. With its stately combination of redbrick and ivy, it could be mistaken for an East Coast liberal arts college. But instead of a blanket of snow, Pacific is surrounded by the lush greenery of the San Joaquin Valley. On campus, this increasingly competitive bastion of learning offers its more than 3,400 undergrads a solid and diverse academic program and scores of things to do when not hitting the books.

With majestic evergreens and flowering trees, Pacific is home to six undergraduate schools and the College of the Pacific, the university's liberal arts and sciences division. There is also a school of law in Sacramento and a superlative school of dentistry in San Francisco. A biological sciences building provides 54,000 square feet of space for the biological sciences program.

Strong departments abound in the schools of engineering, pharmacy, and business (with special programs in the arts/entertainment management and entrepreneurship) as well as the sciences, English, communication, and international studies. Business is the most popular major, followed by biology, engineering, pharmacy, and social sciences. The university-wide general education program has three components: the Pacific seminars, the breadth program, and fundamental skills. All entering students must complete Pacific Seminar I (What Is a Good Society?) and Pacific Seminar II (Topical Seminars on a Good Society) in sequence during their first year and Pacific Seminar III (The Ethics of Family, Work, and Citizenship) in their senior year. In addition to the seminars, students must complete six or nine courses in the breadth

> "Because the class size is small, the students receive a personalized academic experience."

Website: www.pacific.edu
Location: Suburban
Private
Total Enrollment: 5,886
Undergraduates: 3,754
Male/Female: 47/53
SAT Ranges: CR 520–650, M 550–690
ACT Ranges: 23–29
Financial Aid: 73%
Expense: Pr $ $
Student Loans: N/A
Average Debt: N/A
Phi Beta Kappa: Yes
Applicants: 22,972
Accepted: 38%
Enrolled: 10%
Grad in 6 Years: 60%
Returning Freshmen: 83%
Academics: ✐ ✐ ✐
Social: ☎ ☎ ☎
Q of L: ★ ★ ★ ★
Admissions: (209) 946-2211

(continued)

Email Address: admission@
pacific.edu

Strongest Programs:
Business
Pharmacy
Engineering

program and must demonstrate competence in writing, math, and reading. A number of internship and co-op programs are available, and students are guaranteed to have the opportunity for some type of experiential learning. Students may also design their own majors with faculty approval. An extensive study abroad program offers 200 choices in dozens of countries, and international studies majors are required to complete one.

The academic climate varies by department, with students citing the science fields as the most rigorous. Students report that studying accounts for anywhere from 10 to 40 hours a week. The university guarantees graduation in four years (assuming the student follows all university guidelines), or it will pay for the extra schooling. Professors at Pacific get raves for accessibility and personal attention. "The teaching is tremendous, with the experience and care they have for their students," says one senior. "Because the class size is small, the students receive a personalized academic experience." Fifty-three percent of classes taken by freshmen have 19 or fewer students, and TAs teach labs only.

Students may design their own majors with faculty approval.

"Students at Pacific come from a variety of settings and backgrounds. Some can be very studious, but they know how to balance coursework and a personal life very well," says a senior. Eighty-six percent of Pacific students are Californians. Hawaii and Colorado are also strongly represented, while international students make up 5 percent of the student body. As for ethnic diversity, Asian Americans account for 32 percent, while African Americans and Hispanics together make up 22 percent. The school is middle-of-the-road to conservative, though politics in general play a small role on campus. "We're very open to all political, religious, sexual orientations, etc.,"

"The school has a New England feel to it on a West Coast campus."

says a senior. "We have a little bit of everything." Though not unusually expensive by national standards, the university price tag can seem steep when compared to the University of California system. So Pacific has stepped up efforts to compete, using merit scholarships as well as scholarships to athletes in a long list of sports.

Students complain that much social life centers on the Greek scene.

Freshmen and sophomores are required to live on campus, and the few complaints mostly center on aging facilities, some of which have undergone much-needed renovations. Grace Covell Hall, with 350 people, is the largest residence, and two additional suite-style residence halls recently opened. Forty-six percent of undergrads make their home on campus. In terms of quality of life, however, residential life is praised for plentiful social programming. The school occasionally hosts big-name concerts and other campuswide events. Students complain, however, that much social life centers on the Greek scene; 20 percent of men and 19 percent of women go Greek. With three meal plans, two dining halls, and one fast-food-type facility, residents are well fed.

For weekend excitement, Pacific students love to hit the road: Within about two hours, they can be skiing, shopping in San Francisco, or surfing in Monterey. Stockton itself (population 280,000) offers shopping and plenty of fast-food joints, as well as numerous volunteer opportunities. Social opportunities on campus are offered by the Residence Hall Association, intramural and club sports, conservatory and drama/dance programs, Division I athletics, campus movies, sororities and fraternities, and more than 100 student clubs. The school enforces state law, prohibiting all students under 21 from drinking. Students caught violating that policy must take an online course in alcohol education. The majority of Greek houses are designated substance-free, following a trend enforced by their national organizations. "There are opportunities for those who are interested, and our officers are here more to protect the students rather than bust students," notes a senior. Annual campus festivities include Diversity Week, International Spring Festival, the popular Fall Festival, and Greek Week.

Overlaps

UC–Davis, UC–Berkeley, UCLA, Caltech, UC–San Diego, UC–Santa Barbara, University of Southern California, UC–Santa Cruz

The Tigers field a number of competitive Division I teams, including men's and women's basketball and men's golf. The university also fields a solid speech and debate team.

Pitted against the state's immense public university system, Pacific stands out for offering major university opportunities in a small-college setting. The administration is striving to place more focus on its student body, which is becoming more top-notch and diverse. A senior says, "The school has a New England feel to it on a West Coast campus. Even though it's a small institution, it has a lot to offer in terms of academics and extracurricular activities."

If You Apply To > **Pacific:** Early action: Nov. 15. Regular admissions: Jan. 15. Financial aid: Feb. 15. Housing: May 1. Campus interviews: optional, informational. No alumni interviews. SATs or ACTs: required. Subject Tests: recommended. Accepts the Common Application. Essay question.

University of Pennsylvania

I College Hall, Philadelphia, PA 19104-6376

An Ivy League institution in name, Penn has more in common with places like Georgetown and Northwestern—where the liberal arts share center stage with preprofessional programs. At Penn, that means business, engineering, and nursing. Penn has something else other Ivies don't: school spirit. It's a good idea to apply early decision if Penn is your first choice.

Benjamin Franklin would be proud of the way his university has surged in recent years. Once relegated to the bottom of the Ivy League (and confused with Penn State), the University of Pennsylvania is now the first choice for top students who see no conflict between high-level academics and having a life. The undergraduate School of Arts and Sciences—once on the university's back burner—is now central not only to its undergraduates, but also to the remaining three undergraduate schools that tap into its programs and course offerings. Penn established the nation's first medical school, the first business school, the first journalism curriculum, and the first psychology clinic, and is a pioneer in service-learning and service research. In her inaugural address, a former president paid tribute to Franklin as "the ultimate visionary and pragmatist. Franklin thought education should be for the body as well as for the soul—that it should enable a graduate to be a breadwinner as well as a thinker, that it should produce socially conscious citizens as well as conscientious bankers and traders."

> **"Teachers are very accessible and always willing to meet with the students."**

Penn is situated in a tree-shaded, self-contained, 278-acre nest called University City, which is adjacent to downtown Philadelphia. Its 155 buildings range from Victorian Gothic to postmodern. There are very old structures, such as College Hall, and newer ones, such as Wharton's Huntsman Hall and Skirkanich Hall, home to Penn's bioengineering programs. While many students thrive on Philadelphia's cultural abundance, the school is located in the western part of town, once considered to be dangerous. Even so, a senior explains, "there are a wealth of cultural resources at the tip of your fingers, and more and more students are able to find jobs in the Philadelphia area after graduation."

Website: www.upenn.edu
Location: Urban
Private
Total Enrollment: 19,895
Undergraduates: 9,374
Male/Female: 50/50
SAT Ranges: CR 660–760, M 690–780
ACT Ranges: 30–34
Financial Aid: 43%
Expense: Pr $ $ $ $
Student Loans: 38%
Average Debt: $
Phi Beta Kappa: Yes
Applicants: 31,218
Accepted: 13%
Enrolled: 65%
Grad in 6 Years: 96%
Returning Freshmen: 98%
Academics: ✍ ✍ ✍ ✍ ✍
Social: ☎ ☎ ☎
Q of L: ★ ★ ★
Admissions: (215) 898-7507

(continued)

Email Address: Webmaster@
admissions.upenn.edu

Strongest Programs:
Finance
Nursing
Economics
History
Psychology

Penn's reputation is primarily wrapped up with its 12 graduate schools, especially the prestigious Wharton School of Business, the Annenberg School of Communication, and the well-known law, medical, and veterinary schools. Three of four undergraduate schools—engineering, nursing, and the undergraduate division of Wharton—are also professionally oriented and offer an education that's hard to beat anywhere. The undergraduate College of Arts and Sciences (a.k.a. "The College") has come into its own in the past decade or so and provides students with high-quality instruction as well as the chance to run into a Nobel laureate here and there.

Finance is the most popular undergrad major, followed by economics and nursing. Penn's anthropology department ranks with Chicago's as perhaps the best in the country, while programs in management and technology are also outstanding. Penn has earned applause in the field of cognitive and computer sciences because of its special program linking psychology, linguistics, and computers with philosophy. Another popular crème-de-la-crème interdisciplinary major, Biological Basis of Behavior, combines psychology, biology, and anthropology. Students are allowed to design their own individualized majors, and they can hop from school to school—undergraduate or graduate—in doing so. Students in the Vagelos Program in Life Science and Management pursue studies in both the College of Arts and Sciences and the Wharton School, exposing them to research and development, biotech start-ups, managed care, and other related issues.

"Penn is a competitive university."

At the Wharton School, officials have introduced the Joseph Wharton Scholars program, which emphasizes breadth in the arts and sciences. All undergraduates must attain proficiency in one of the 45 foreign languages taught at Penn. Another added plus that comes with a Penn undergraduate education is the opportunity for early entry (submatriculation) into the university's graduate programs. Juniors may apply to any master's program (continuing into the Wharton M.B.A. program is especially popular) and begin completing graduate requirements during their senior year. Penn offers no co-op programs and discourages full-time internships for credit, remaining true to the Ivy League belief that learning should be based in the classroom. Those who want to explore more exotic classrooms may study abroad at Penn's programs in Italy, Scotland, Japan, France, England, China, Nigeria, Spain, Germany, and Russia, among others. Freshmen are encouraged (but not required) to participate in a seminar program that explores various areas of academic interest, and also in the Penn Reading Project, which involves student and faculty discussion of a common text.

While professors at Penn take their research responsibilities seriously, they are surprisingly accessible to freshmen. "Most departments have fantastic professors who are top in their field," says one student, "and have developed a great teaching style." Another student adds, "Teachers are very accessible and always willing to meet with the students." The academic program at Penn is well supplemented by its huge and busy library, which houses more than three million volumes.

Students in the Vagelos Program in Life Science and Management pursue studies in both the College of Arts and Sciences and the Wharton School.

Despite all the preprofessional programs, Penn never lets its undergraduates stray too far from the liberal arts. The general education requirements mandate that students take at least one course in each of seven "sectors": society, history, and tradition; arts and letters; living world; physical world; humanities and social sciences; and natural sciences and mathematics. Students must also complete one course in each of five "skills and methods" areas, including the study of a foreign culture as well as a mandatory writing requirement. Strict academic policies and demanding professors exacerbate the academic pressure. "Penn is a competitive university," says one nursing major, "but is also intellectually stimulating." Each year students evaluate every class themselves and publish their findings in a guide.

Thousands of faculty and students give expression to Benjamin Franklin's adage that service to humanity is "the great aim and end of all learning." To wit, Penn is a national leader in service learning and service research. Students work with local public school students as part of academic coursework in disciplines as diverse as history, anthropology, and mathematics. There are tons of opportunities to volunteer—from tutoring to Big Brothers Big Sisters to the Ronald McDonald House. "Penn students have historically been extremely involved with the local community and have taken the experiences they've had in the neighborhood with them to the real world," an economics and history double major says.

Ninety-four percent of Penn students ranked in the top 10th of their high school class and more than half come from public high school. "There are individuals from all walks of life at this university," one senior says, "each as brilliant as the next." Freshman orientation includes skits that depict students in various situations of possible conflict and include discussions about each situation. "There are all kinds of people with all kinds of personalities, interests, and backgrounds," says a student, "all of which makes Penn a vibrant place to live and study." Seven percent of the student body are African American; Hispanics comprise 9 percent, and Asian Americans account for 19 percent. Penn admits students regardless of need but does not offer any merit, athletic, or academic scholarships. Penn has eliminated loans for eligible undergraduates, regardless of family income, enabling students from a broad range of economic backgrounds to graduate debt-free. The No-Loan initiative expands Penn's commitment to need-blind admissions and is highlighted by an outreach program targeting hundreds of schools and thousands of students from low- and middle-income families.

> *Those who want to explore more exotic classrooms may study abroad at Penn's programs in Italy, Scotland, Japan, France, England, China, Nigeria, Spain, Germany, and Russia, among others.*

Ninety-eight percent of all undergraduates live on campus and enjoy a wide range of living options in Penn's 11 "College Houses." Dorms are co-ed. The Quad, home to three of the 11 houses, seems to be the hot spot, described as "well maintained and incredibly comfortable." Upperclassmen reluctantly move to the high-rises across campus that look like "prefabricated, 24-story monsters" but do offer more space, as well as kitchens. There are living/learning programs in most College Houses for those who are interested in the arts, Asian studies, etc., and want to be surrounded by others with the same interests. Rather than compete in the lottery for rooms, many juniors and seniors simply head off campus—"for the freedom, plus it's a lot cheaper," a junior says. Some end up in nearby renovated three-story houses in the neighborhood. "Off-campus living is just an extension of student neighborhoods, as we tend to stay in large groups," explains a senior. Like

> **"Off-campus living is just an extension of student neighborhoods, as we tend to stay in large groups."**

housing, the meal plans are optional (though strongly recommended freshman year as an important source of social life), and the food isn't all that bad for institutional fare. "The best kept secret on campus is the kosher cafeteria," a finance and management major says.

Undergraduates may work hard during the week, but in contrast to most Ivy League achievers, they leave it behind them on weekends. "Social life at Penn centers around frats," a junior explains. The university prohibits underage drinking, but "parties freely serve alcohol to underage drinkers," says another student. More than two dozen fraternities attract 30 percent of the men and provide "your basic meat-market scene." Similarly, sororities claim 27 percent of the women. The frats' exclusive claim to the houses along Locust Walk, the main artery on campus, has been undone: After some controversy, it was determined that non-Greeks, too, must be able to live at the social nexus of the campus.

Two big annual events at Penn are Spring Fling, a weekend "nothing short of absolutely incredible fun," and Hey Day, when juniors, donning Styrofoam hats, march down Locust Walk to officially become seniors, taking chomps out of each other's hats as they go. Road trips include New York City, Washington, D.C., Atlantic City, and even Maine and Florida. Downtown Philadelphia, only a few minutes away by foot, cab, or public transportation, offers enough social and cultural activities to make up for the less-attractive aspects of city living. "Philly is large and very developed," a sophomore says. Students frequent sporting events, malls, South Street ("a miniature Greenwich Village"), and, of course, myriad bars and dancing joints. "There is a lot of social intermingling among the schools, and university students dominate the nightlife," a student explains.

Penn is more sports-minded than most Ivy schools, and football is the biggie. The team has grown accustomed to sitting on the top of the Ivy League and has sparked a widespread revival of school spirit. Tickets are free for those with a student ID. The Penn–Princeton rivalry is always a crowd pleaser. At the end of the third quarter of each home game, everyone in the stands begins belting out the lyrics of the Penn fight song, and when they get to "Here's a toast to dear old Penn," the students shower the field with burnt toast, "a moment that makes all Penn students proud," gushes a senior. Aside from football, solid Quakers teams include men's basketball and lacrosse, and women's field hockey, basketball, and fencing. A bevy of intramural sports bring thousands of less-seasoned athletes out to play each year, and all types of athletes benefit from the swanky track and weight-lifting facilities. Each spring, Penn hosts the prestigious Penn Relays, a track-and-field extravaganza that attracts the nation's best track athletes.

While its students work hard, Penn lacks the intellectual intensity of some of the other top Ivies, and you can detect preprofessional undercurrents. But most accept it for what it is: a first-rate university where you can live a relatively normal life. Penn is one Ivy League university where no one apologizes for having fun. Says one sophomore: "There is a great balance between academics and social activities, which is rare in such highly competitive institutions."

Ninety-four percent of Penn students ranked in the top 10th of their high school class and more than half come from public high school.

Overlaps

Brown, Columbia, Cornell, Harvard, Stanford, Yale

If You Apply To ➢

Penn: Early decision: Nov. 1. Early action: Dec. 15. Regular admissions: Jan. 1. Application fee: $75. Campus and alumni interviews: optional, evaluative. SATs or ACTs: required. Subject Tests: two required if submitting SATs. Accepts the Common Application. Essay question.

Pennsylvania State University

201 Old Main, University Park, PA 16802

Though scandal has seriously tarnished its image, Penn State remains one of the premier public universities academically. With a student body the size of a small city, the university is strong in fields from meteorology to film and television. The 2,000-student Schreyer Honors College is one of the nation's elite. As for the future of its previously vaunted football program, who knows?

Website: www.psu.edu
Location: Rural
Public
Total Enrollment: 43,379
Undergraduates: 37,619

Once viewed as model of how the values of big-time football and academic excellence could coexist, Penn State is reeling from the conviction of a former assistant football coach as a sexual predator. The scandal, which led to the resignation of the university's president and football coach, made front-page news around the world and tested the legendary school spirit of the 43,000 undergraduate denizens of what sportswriters have long called Happy Valley. Fortunately, that legendary spirit is still alive, as are Penn State's stellar choices in engineering, the sciences, and other fields appropriate to a land grant university.

With an eclectic architectural mix, including white-columned brick, stone, and some modern apartments, this land-grant university continues to experience growth as major renovation and expansion projects continue. New facilities are added every year and renovations and other improvements are constantly underway. "Penn State just keeps growing and improving itself," says one student.

Penn State maintains strong programs in the scientific and technical fields such as earth sciences, engineering, agricultural sciences, and life sciences, as well as nutrition and family studies. The meteorology program boasts alumni worldwide, including the founder of AccuWeather, an internationally renowned private forecasting firm. As a matter of fact, one in every four meteorologists in the United States is a Penn State graduate. The College of Information Sciences and Technology is designed to prepare students for the digital age. The College of Agricultural Sciences has extensive facilities that include huge livestock barns. Its Food Sciences program is one of the best in the nation. Dairy products from the school's cows are sold at an on-campus store, and courses are offered in the production of its famous ice cream. Students can choose from more than 260 baccalaureate programs, and over 160 graduate fields spread over 24 locations statewide, including the College of Medicine and the Dickinson School of Law, both located near Harrisburg. At a school of Penn State's size, there are bound to be some weaknesses, but the curriculum is in a seemingly constant state of change, with programs added and dropped on a regular basis.

> **"Penn State just keeps growing and improving itself."**

Penn State's general education requirements consist of 45 credits that include several communications and quantification courses as well as humanities, arts, natural sciences, social and behavioral sciences, and health and physical education courses. The incorporation of critical thinking skills has been a priority in redesigning the general curriculum. About 2,000 of the university's best and brightest are invited to participate in the Schreyer Honors College, which offers opportunities for independent study and graduate work, as well as honors options in regular courses. According to one student, "The one thing about Penn State is that your academic experience is completely what you make it." Students who are part of the honors college take both honors classes and regular university classes. In addition, undergrads must enroll in "diversity-focused" courses that encourage awareness of minority concerns. One helpful program offered to freshmen is LEAP (Learning Edge Academic Program), which gives new students the benefit of a big university while making it seem small. Students in LEAP take a team approach by taking classes together and living together.

Some of the intro-level lecture courses draw up to 400 students at University Park, yet most of the students seem to agree—classes are excellent and require your full attention. Students report that professors are accessible and engaging—when they are teaching. "I must say I was surprised that I was taught by grad students," says one senior. "For the amount of money I am paying to go here, I would have thought all my classes would be taught by professors." For cramming outside of class, the Penn State library contains approximately 5.1 million volumes. A large number of students study abroad through more than

> **"Your academic experience is completely what you make it."**

180 summer, semester, and full-year programs in more than 45 countries. Combined undergraduate/graduate degree options are available, as are co-op programs in engineering, distance learning, and student-designed majors.

"Penn State students are active, fun, and open minded," says one student. Most undergraduates are residents of Pennsylvania, with 28 percent hailing from out of state and 8 percent hailing from outside the nation. Eighty-four percent ranked in

(continued)

Male/Female: 54/46
SAT Ranges: CR 530–630, M 560–670
ACT Ranges: 25–29
Financial Aid: 51%
Expense: Pub $ $ $ $
Student Loans: 66%
Average Debt: $ $ $ $
Phi Beta Kappa: Yes
Applicants: 47,552
Accepted: 54%
Enrolled: 30%
Grad in 6 Years: 86%
Returning Freshmen: 92%
Academics: ✐ ✐ ✐ ✐ ½
Social: 🏮 🏮 🏮 🏮 🏮
Q of L: ★ ★ ★
Admissions: (814) 865-5471
Email Address: admissions@psu.edu

Strongest Programs:
Earth Sciences
Engineering
Agricultural Sciences
Life Sciences
Nutrition
Family Studies

The curriculum is in a seemingly constant state of change, with programs added and dropped on a regular basis.

the top quarter of their high school class. More than half of Penn State's undergraduates who finish at University Park began their education at one of the university's 19 campuses across the state. Many students note that race and diversity issues can be pronounced on a campus that is still pretty homogeneous for a public university: Asian Americans make up 5 percent of the undergrad population, and African Americans and Hispanics combine for another 10 percent. A whopping 546 athletic scholarships are available, covering all NCAA-approved sports, as are a number of merit awards worth an average of $3,153.

Freshmen must live in the dorms, which students say are comfortable and located near classroom buildings and dining facilities. Thirty-six percent of students live on campus; the balance find a home off campus, often in downtown apartments. "I loved living in the dorms," reports one public relations major. "I think it's part of the whole college experience and I made some great friends along the way." The meal plan operates on a point system where you pay for what you eat.

University Park students take advantage of the picturesque and peaceful locale by engaging in outdoorsy activities, including skiing and snowboarding at a nearby slope, and sailing, canoeing, hiking, and renting cabins in Stone Valley. State College offers cultural events such as symphonies, theatrical shows, and ballets, while the Bryce Jordan Center hosts top-notch performers. The town may be small, but according to a biochem major, "a majority of the students get involved in community service to maintain and constantly improve town relations."

Partying at Penn State is almost as legendary as the football team. "Social life at Penn State is huge," says a freshman. "Most of the parties happen at fraternities, which are both on and off of campus." Students also hit the bars in State College, where "it's very difficult for underage students to be served at the bars," according

"Penn State students are active, fun, and open minded."

to a student. "Students with fake IDs have almost a zero percent chance of gaining admittance." While the administration strives to keep booze out of underage hands on campus, "there are places students can get alcohol, mostly at other people's apartments," says a junior. The HUB (the campus union building) offers nonalcoholic entertainment. The Greeks—which include 14 percent of Penn State men and women—have parties that may or may not include alcohol.

When thousands of alumni converge to cheer on their Nittany Lions in blue and white, the festivities include tailgate parties replete with marshmallow throwing, pregame parties, and postgame revelry. As a member of the Big Ten, Penn State's foes include Michigan and Ohio State, both of which make great road trips, in addition to Philadelphia, Pittsburgh, and New York. Other popular events include the mid-July arts festival, the Dance Marathon, and, of course, homecoming. The Nittany Lions have won more than 60 national titles in a wide variety of sports, including men's and women's volleyball, women's soccer, field hockey, and fencing. There are three large gyms, a competitive-size pool, an indoor ice rink, and an extensive intramural program for the recreational athlete.

For better or for worse, Penn State's reputation for academic excellence has been closely linked in the public mind with the success of its Division I football team and with the personal image of the late Joe Paterno, who was the winningest Division I football coach ever until the NCAA stripped him of many of his victories. The much-beloved Paterno was fired by the university trustees only days after the child sexual abuse scandal involving a former assistant coach erupted, and the university community was thrust into a period of soul-searching about what went wrong. Fortunately, Penn State's sense of pride and community spirit are reasserting themselves. As one proud Lion explains, "Imagine a family of 40,000—the excitement, pride, compassion, and sense of belonging, which is unparalleled at any institution."

Pepperdine University

24255 Pacific Coast Highway, Malibu, CA 90263-4392

Pepperdine has the most beautiful campus setting in America. The buildings are nothing special, but the views of the Pacific Ocean are incomparable. With L.A. nearby, small wonder its popularity is soaring. Students should come to Pepperdine ready to embrace an evangelical Christian emphasis. Pepperdine is not the Stanford of SoCal.

With picturesque surroundings, it's easy to confuse Pepperdine University with its nicknames—Pepperdine Resort and Club Med. Surrounded by the beautiful Southern California seashore, Pepperdine University might seem paradise found for students seeking sunshine rather than studies at this conservative, Christian-affiliated university, though students take their work and their worship seriously. "The philosophy of the school is that God and the academic experience must be married," says a senior telecommunications major. "This creates an intimate learning environment that prides itself on moral integrity and a high academic standard." Business and communications are the blessed programs, though other departments deserve recognition, too. Undergrads praise their educational opportunities, the strength of their school's spiritual community, and the vast sandy beaches beckoning below their hilltop campus.

There's no denying that Pepperdine's location—high in the Santa Monica Mountains, about 25 miles northwest of Los Angeles—is a strong selling point. The 830-acre Malibu campus, to which the school moved in 1972, overlooks the Pacific Ocean and features fountains, hillside gardens, mountain trails, and a 20-minute walk to the beach. Cream-colored, Mediterranean-style buildings topped with red terra cotta roofs dot the landscape. A 125-foot-tall white stucco cross stands near the center of campus, reminding students and faculty of the school's affiliation with the Churches of Christ.

Pepperdine was founded in 1937 by George Pepperdine, a lifelong member of the Churches of Christ who had amassed a fortune through his mail-order auto parts supply company. The church's continued influence on the school pervades many aspects of campus life, from the prohibition of overnight dorm room visits by members of the opposite sex to the requirement that students attend convocation—similar to chapel—14 times each semester. Students at Seaver College, Pepp's undergraduate school, must also take three religion courses. While drinking is officially prohibited on campus, the administration has lifted the ban on dancing and now allows students to choose their own seats at convocation. Though restrictions like this would drive the average kid up a wall, most at Pepperdine like the "highly moral" atmosphere. Says one student: "In comparison to other schools, Pepperdine students generally have a more religious foundation and thus have high standards of moral integrity."

Seaver's academic programs aim to provide students "with a liberal arts education in a Christian environment and relate it to the dynamic qualities of life in the

> "Professors don't accept excuses or laziness."

Website: www.pepperdine.edu

Location: Suburban

Private

Total Enrollment: 5,273

Undergraduates: 3,084

Male/Female: 41/59

SAT Ranges: CR 550–655, M 570–680

ACT Ranges: 25–30

Financial Aid: 85%

Expense: Pr $ $ $

Student Loans: 56%

Average Debt: $ $ $

Phi Beta Kappa: No

Applicants: 8,567

Accepted: 38%

Enrolled: 24%

Grad in 6 Years: 81%

Returning Freshmen: 91%

Academics: ✑ ✑ ✑

Social: ☎ ☎

Q of L: ★ ★ ★

Admissions: (310) 506-4392

Email Address: admission-seaver@pepperdine.edu

Strongest Programs:
Business
Accounting
Communications
Natural Science

21st century." Individual classes are demanding, as is the required General Studies program, which includes a freshman seminar, a physical education course, three courses in Western heritage, two courses each in American heritage and English composition, and one class each in a foreign language and a non-Western culture. However, faculty members are said to be accessible and responsive—not surprising when the average class has 18 students. "The quality of teaching is very personal and exceptional," says an art major. Another student adds, "Because it is a small school, professors don't accept excuses or laziness. They demand a lot from their students and expect a high standard and quality of work."

"Pepperdine tends to shy away from political activism."

The business administration department is unequivocally the strongest and most popular department at Pepperdine, and it tends to set the tone on campus. The communications department, with majors including advertising, public relations, and journalism, is also highly touted, and boasts radio and television broadcasting studios. Biology and computer science are said to be strong, and sports medicine, rare at the undergraduate level, is both popular and well respected. Music studios and a $10 million humanities and visual arts center have been built to enhance the fine arts division. Juniors interested in European culture may spend a year at Pepperdine's own facilities in Heidelberg, London, Florence, or Lausanne. Other study abroad programs are available in Japan and Australia; locations for summer study include East Africa, the Galapagos Islands, Honduras, Madrid, Oxford, and Pepperdine-owned properties.

Back on campus, students trying to complete term papers can use one of the hundreds of public computer terminals and the collections of Pepp's eight-facility library system, which boast more than 400,000 volumes. The well-organized campus Career Center allows students to sign up for job fairs, interviews, and individual and group career-counseling sessions.

One might expect students at this religiously oriented school to be politically conservative, and they most definitely are. Many come from well-to-do California Republican families; there is also a relatively high percentage of wealthy international students. Students joke that there's never a shortage of Porsches and BMWs on campus, but there is a shortage of places to park them. Hispanics account for 17 percent of the students, Asian Americans 14 percent, and African Americans 8 percent. The Republican influence is felt far and wide. Pepperdine has received millions of dollars from conservative Pittsburgh financier Richard Mellon Scaife. One student sums up the political climate gently: "Pepperdine tends to shy away from political activism."

"Parties on weekends are well attended."

Some say flashy student vehicles fit into the small, very wealthy community of Malibu better than the students themselves; the city sees the university as a catalyst for development, and that hurts town/school relations. Because the social scene in Malibu is pretty slack, with a 10 p.m. noise curfew and high price tags for everything, students typically head to L.A., Hollywood, Westwood, and Santa Monica for fun. "For a large proportion of students, academics and their social lives take priority over religious matters," says a public relations major. "Parties on weekends are well attended, and probably draw a larger portion of students than church on Sunday." Eighteen percent of men and 31 percent of women join one of five national fraternities or seven national sororities, which are playing a larger role in social life. Along with student government, they sponsor dances, movies, and other typical college activities, including the occasional illicit drink. "Pepperdine enforces a 'dry' campus, but 'damp' would be a better way of describing the residential community," says one student.

Except for commuters, students are required to live on campus if they are single and under 21. That's a good thing, says one senior, who declares that Pepperdine's

Pepperdine was founded in 1937 by George Pepperdine, a lifelong member of the Churches of Christ who had amassed a fortune through his mail-order auto parts supply company.

Music studios and a $10 million humanities and visual arts center have been built to enhance the fine arts division.

dorms are "comfortable, convenient, and really quite nice." The single-sex dorms and apartments are connected to the campus computer network. Rooms are assigned on a first-come, first-served basis, and the housing stock consists of 22 dorms, a 135-room tower, and a 75-unit apartment complex for juniors and seniors. Freshmen are typically assigned to suites with bathrooms, living rooms, and four double bedrooms. Some consider these arrangements crowded, but a junior says they "connect freshmen instantly to seven suitemates and friends." Despite the above-average cost of living in the Malibu area, many upperclassmen choose to live off campus. The student union serves as the main campus social center, and annual events including Songfest, Family Weekend, and Midnight Madness draw crowds.

Sports receive a lot of attention at Pepperdine, with athletic scholarships offered in multiple sports, and a tennis pavilion and recreation center drawing varsity jocks and weekend warriors alike. The Waves compete in the West Coast Conference. Six teams have brought home conference titles in the last two years, including baseball, women's golf, women's soccer, men's tennis, and women's indoor volleyball. Men's volleyball has won five NCAA championships. Eleven club and intramural sports, including lacrosse, rugby, cycling, surfing, and soccer, keep students busy, as does the physical education department, with classes in everything from surfing to horseback riding.

Pepperdine faces an unusual challenge in trying to marry the Christian focus of a Bible college with the academic rigor of a secular university—all in a location not known for the strength of its moral fiber. Students love to tease their well-manicured university with T-shirts proclaiming, "Pepperdine. 8-month party. 40K cover charge." But most seem to think the solid, values-oriented education they receive is worth the stiff price tag.

> *Despite the above-average cost of living in the Malibu area, many upperclassmen choose to live off campus.*

Overlaps

University of Southern California, UCLA, Loyola Marymount, UC–Santa Barbara, UC–San Diego

If You Apply To ➢ **Pepperdine:** Regular admissions: Jan. 5. Financial aid: Feb. 15. Housing: Jun. 1. Application fee: $65. Campus and alumni interviews: optional, informational. SATs or ACTs: required (SATs preferred). Subject Tests: optional. Accepts the Common Application. Essay question.

University of Pittsburgh

Alumni Hall, 4227 Fifth, Pittsburgh, PA 15260

As its home city has risen in stature, Pitt has become a hot commodity along with next-door neighbor Carnegie Mellon. A state-related university in the mold of the University of Cincinnati—not the state flagship, but strong in a host of mainly preprofessional programs. Curiously, Pitt is among the nation's best in philosophy. Admissions is rolling, so apply early.

With its idled steel-factory stigma a thing of the past, Pittsburgh has joined the ranks of the most livable cities in the United States. The University of Pittsburgh has matured, too, becoming a formidable public research institution. The school offers numerous opportunities for students pursuing business, medical, and engineering careers, but leaves a great deal of room for exploration in the liberal arts. Students are encouraged to be individuals and carve out their own academic niche, either with multiple majors or with certificate programs. Combine this with a satisfying social life, and Pitt has discovered one formula for a rewarding

> **"We've got great academics and a great city at our fingertips."**

Website: www.pitt.edu
Location: City Outskirts
Public
Total Enrollment: 24,901
Undergraduates: 17,223
Male/Female: 50/50
SAT Ranges: CR 570–660, M 600–680

(continued)

ACT Ranges: 26–30
Financial Aid: 55%
Expense: Pub $ $ $ $
Student Loans: 67%
Average Debt: $ $ $ $
Phi Beta Kappa: Yes
Applicants: 24,871
Accepted: 56%
Enrolled: 26%
Grad in 6 Years: 79%
Returning Freshmen: 93%
Academics: ✑ ✑ ✑ ½
Social: ☎ ☎
Q of L: ★ ★
Admissions: (412) 624-7488
Email Address: oafa@pitt.edu

Strongest Programs:
Business Management
Social Sciences
Health Professions
English
Engineering
Philosophy

college experience. "We've got great academics and a great city at our fingertips," says a junior. "It makes for an excellent experience outside of the classroom."

Pitt began as a tiny, private educational academy in the Allegheny Mountains in 1787. Oh, how times have changed. The university, which became state-related in 1966, is adjacent to Carnegie Mellon and is now part of the landscape of shops, parks, museums, galleries, and apartment complexes that make up Oakland, the heart of Pittsburgh's cultural center. Spacious, light-filled, contemporary buildings and generic modern office buildings make up the Pitt campus, but the architectural delight is a 42-story, neo-Gothic academic building, appropriately called the Cathedral of Learning, a national historic landmark. The stately and towering cathedral, with its unique Nationality Rooms, attracts 30,000 visitors annually. And contrary to images you may hold of inner-city Pittsburgh, the campus borders a 456-acre city park. A new residence hall opened in late 2013 and houses 559 freshmen.

"We are willing to help each other succeed."

With nine undergraduate schools and more than 100 baccalaureate programs, Pitt rightfully claims to accommodate students with diverse needs. The academically motivated can take advantage of the excellent University Honors College, which one sophomore gushes is "the best thing at Pitt. It can do so much for students taking a serious interest in their education." It offers "small, intensive classes so students can work with professors and do independent research." Honors students publish the *Pittsburgh Undergraduate Review*, which receives submissions from students nationwide. Pitt's extensive research programs are among its finest assets. The University of Pittsburgh is one of the top 10 institutions in the nation in terms of the annual research support awarded by the National Institutes of Health, and for good reason. Pitt astronomers have made "out of this world" discoveries in recent years, and its physicians were the first to utilize gene therapy on a person with rheumatoid arthritis. The schools of engineering and nursing are excellent and attract high-caliber students. Premed students can even watch transplants at the famed University of Pittsburgh Medical Center, one of the world's leading organ transplant centers. On the arts side, faculty and students in the music department consistently rake in more awards and fellowships than their counterparts at other U.S. universities.

Pitt offers guaranteed admission into graduate programs in physician assistant, business, engineering, communication disorders, dietetics, education, nursing, occupational therapy, social work, public health, public and international affairs, dental medicine, law, medical school, and physical therapy for outstanding freshman applicants. Other solid programs include philosophy, information science, history and philosophy of science, and nursing. The Dietrich School of Arts and Sciences (SAS) has academic requirements that include skill requirements in writing, quantitative and formal reasoning, foreign languages, and distribution requirements in the humanities, social and natural sciences, and foreign cultures. The most popular majors include business, social sciences, English, and engineering.

For undergraduates who want to travel, the university offers hundreds of study abroad options in 65 countries. Closer to home, Pitt is a partner with Carnegie Mellon University and Westinghouse Electric Company in the Pittsburgh Supercomputing Center. There is also the Engineering Co-op, a program in which students alternate terms of study with work experience.

"Students enjoy the academic challenge but are not extremely competitive," a senior says. "We are willing to help each other succeed." Pitt students take advantage of the school's flexible scheduling, which includes a strong evening program and summer sessions, and take on double and even triple majors, ensuring themselves plenty of education and a degree that's well worth the money. First-year students undergo an extensive orientation that includes three days in the summer focused on academics, another five days before the term starts, and a one-credit freshman

With nine undergraduate schools and more than 100 baccalaureate programs, Pitt rightfully claims to accommodate students with diverse needs.

studies seminar. Out of more than 2,000 courses, 60 percent have fewer than 29 students enrolled. Most students agree that professors are very approachable and knowledgeable. "Every professor has been super helpful and willing to meet with me outside of class to get the extra help that I needed to succeed," says a sophomore.

Pitt students are "fun loving, outgoing, well rounded," according to one political science major. "The urban atmosphere pushes students to be involved and work with other organizations and businesses in the area, and that sets us apart from other smaller, more rural colleges in the state," explains a senior. Seventy-three percent of all undergraduates are from Pennsylvania, including a substantial number from the Pittsburgh area. African American students account for 6 percent of the undergraduate student body, Asian Americans 6 percent, and Hispanics 2 percent. Incoming freshmen discuss diversity during orientation; a cultural diversity fair is held at the beginning of the school year and every student must pledge to promote civility on campus. When it comes to political and social issues, "our campus is very vocal," says a senior. Pitt also offers merit awards averaging $11,543 and 252 athletic scholarships are available in 19 varsity sports.

While student housing may have been scarce in the past, Pitt continues to increase the amount of on-campus living space. Forty-four percent of students live in on-campus university housing, which features 20 co-ed and single-sex dorms with liberal visitation hours and all kinds of rooming situations, from singles to seven-person suites. Students say the quality varies greatly: "Our brand-new ones are gorgeous," says a psychology major, "but the oldest ones I wouldn't put my worst enemy in." Another student says, "Living/learning communities are a huge part of our residence life and provide the students an excellent opportunity to live, study, and socialize with other students who share the same interests." Twenty-one dining locations offer plenty of variety, including vegetarian options. Students feel safe on campus, considering the extensive network of campus lighting, emergency phones, the shuttle-bus route, strong police presence, and an on-demand van system.

Pitt's urban location provides a wide variety of social activities. "The city is our campus," says a nursing major. Within minutes of campus are shops, parks, museums, and sporting events. "Social life is wonderful in its diversity, on campus and off," adds a senior. Though only 11 percent of the men and 9 percent of the women belong to the Greek system, the fraternities and sororities play a vital role on campus. Many students say alcohol policies on campus are effective. "Most students go to off-campus parties to drink," one student confides. "However, the penalties are severe when students get caught." A senior notes that underage students caught drinking are referred to the Pittsburgh police department. Pitt students can ride the Port Authority of Pittsburgh bus system for free to nearby neighborhoods to shop and go to coffeehouses, bookstores, or movie theaters. Adjacent Schenley Park offers ice skating, golfing, a pool, jogging trails, and tennis courts. Ski slopes and mountain trails are not far away, and road trips to Penn State and Philadelphia, Boston, and New York City are popular.

In keeping with the university's resurgence, Pitt Panther football has dramatically improved and brought home a share of the Big East title in 2010. Wrestling is solid and men's basketball is also popular. Competition is heated in Big East hoops—and to get Pitt basketball tickets. "Big East athletics are highly competitive," says a sophomore, "so any event involving those is great." However, those Big East rivalries will be a thing of the past, as Pitt (along with Syracuse) has accepted membership into the Atlantic Coast Conference. Approximately 70 percent of undergrads take part in intramurals and club sports.

Pittsburgh boasts innumerable resources and opportunities for its students in the sciences and the arts, and is improving not only in its academics, but also in the

The schools of engineering and nursing are excellent and attract high-caliber students.

"Every professor has been super helpful."

While student housing may have been scarce in the past, Pitt continues to increase the amount of on-campus living space.

Overlaps

Boston University, Carnegie Mellon, Duquesne, NYU, Penn State, Temple, University of Delaware, University of Maryland

caliber of its student body. Pitt is more selective than ever and a solid choice, especially for those seeking strong programs in business, engineering, and health care. That potential for excellence, in the midst of a happening college town, makes for a very happy student body.

If You Apply To ➤

Pitt: Rolling admissions. Financial aid: Mar. 1. Housing: May 1. Application fee: $45. Campus and alumni interviews: optional, informational. SATs or ACTs: required. Subject Tests: optional. Essay question.

Pitzer College: See page 143.

Pomona College: See page 145.

Presbyterian College

503 Broad Street, Clinton, SC 29325

A South Carolina liberal arts college that competes head-to-head with Wofford for students who want their education served up with plenty of personal attention. Programs in business and engineering complement those in the liberal arts. Lacks the urban allure of Furman or Oglethorpe. Nearly two-thirds of PC students are from South Carolina.

Website: www.presby.edu
Location: Small Town
Private
Total Enrollment: 1,355
Undergraduates: 1,124
Male/Female: 45/55
SAT Ranges: CR 480–590, M 495–600
ACT Ranges: 22–27
Financial Aid: 76%
Expense: Pr $
Student Loans: 48%
Average Debt: $ $ $
Phi Beta Kappa: No
Applicants: 1,438
Accepted: 58%
Enrolled: 34%
Grad in 6 Years: 68%
Returning Freshmen: 86%
Academics: ✍ ✍ ✍
Social: ☎ ☎ ☎

Presbyterian College students live up to the motto "While we live, we serve." Approximately 70 percent of students participate in some kind of community service while at PC. And while they're living in the "PC Bubble," they're also learning. Current PC students seem a far cry from the orphans for whom William Plumer Jacobs founded the school way back in 1880. And although today's Presbyterians largely come from stable, economically secure families, they continue to pursue personal, spiritual, and academic growth. "Our students are top-notch in academics and athletics, and practice servitude and Christian love in their daily lives," a senior says. "Only great things are in PC's future!"

"This is obviously not a school for apathetic college students."

The Presbyterian campus sits on 240 acres in the South Carolina piedmont. The redbrick buildings are largely Georgian in style, with tall, white columns and lots of shade trees; many structures are listed on the National Register of Historic Places. The campus resembles Thomas Jefferson's University of Virginia, with buildings grouped around three plazas just perfect for reading, studying, or throwing a Frisbee.

Presbyterian's curriculum emphasizes the traditional liberal arts, combined with requiring freshmen experiences for all students, an electronic portfolio, cross-cultural education, and experiential learning. Course requirements include work on English composition and literature, fine arts, history, math, science, physical education, religion, foreign language, and a social science. Students must also participate in a senior capstone course. The most popular majors are business administration, history, biology, and education. The Confucius Institute, offered in cooperation with the Chinese government, serves to foster a better understanding between the two countries, supports the Chinese language program, and provides students with cultural education.

Academically, PC is rigorous, and students strive to do well, says an education major. "Our college has a very competitive academic atmosphere," offers one junior. "Our courses are extremely rigorous." Presbyterian doesn't use teaching assistants, and students say faculty members are among the school's strongest assets. "Our professors are outstanding in the classroom," says a senior.

Options for off-campus study include programs in France, Austria, Spain, Mexico, Japan, Australia, and New Zealand. Those who can't bear to be away for an entire semester can take part in research and study trips to the Galapagos and Hawaiian Islands dur-

"Students at PC have class."

ing the May "fleximester." The Hansard Society for Parliamentary Government in London offers scholarships to students wishing to study and intern in the UK, while the Russell Program enables those who remain on campus to focus on the media and society, with guest lecturers such as former White House press secretary Dee Dee Myers. The college offers a summerlong program that allows students to complete independent research with faculty members as mentors and guides. The president also works with top academic, full-scholarship students in a small group setting. "All of the [honors] programs are valuable because they allow the top students to share ideas, participate in debates, and learn from other scholars," a biology major says.

PC students are "passionate," observes one student. "This is obviously not a school for apathetic college students. PC students are hard workers." Thirty-four percent of PC students hail from South Carolina, and minorities are a small but increasing presence on campus: African Americans make up 10 percent of the population, and Hispanics and Asian Americans combine for 3 percent. And while you don't have to be Presbyterian to attend PC, it does help, as roughly one-third of the students define themselves as such. "Most students have high Christian morals," a student says. Campus politics tend to be conservative, and some debate centers around religious affiliation, one student says. Merit scholarships are handed out to eligible students, as are 138 athletic awards in 15 sports.

Ninety-seven percent of Presbyterian students live on campus, where all dorms are air-conditioned, and accommodations range from traditional rooms with hall baths to suites and apartments. Where you live is determined by a random lottery, though everyone is guaranteed a bed. "Housing is not too bad," a student says. Another adds, "I really enjoy the dorm life. I believe it allows everyone to stay close and connected." There are two dining halls on campus, both overseen by Sodexho. "Around Thanksgiving and Easter, they serve wonderful meals," says an English major. "The Sunday buffet is awesome—after church, people from the community pay to eat in our cafeteria."

Forty-one percent of PC's men and 47 percent of the women join Greek groups, and "social life is very active," says one student. "Fraternity Court is the popular spot on weekend nights." The school has taken a firm stand against underage drinking, and three violations lead to a two-semester suspension. Students with cars also enjoy heading to Greenville, Columbia, or Spartanburg for a bite to eat or some shopping—or, if there's more time, to Charleston or Atlanta. PC is equidistant from South Carolina's mountains and beaches, providing many opportunities to enjoy the outdoors. "Any road trip is a good road trip," says a junior. Many students join campus clubs, which typically have at least one off-campus retreat each semester.

Owing to PC's aforementioned motto, Student Volunteer Services is the largest organization on campus. The group routinely sends students to local orphanages, nursing homes, schools, and other facilities where their time and talents can be helpful. Favorite annual traditions include Spring Fling, a weekend carnival featuring

(continued)

Q of L: ★ ★ ★ ★
Admissions: (800) 960-7583
Email Address: admissions@ presby.edu

Strongest Programs:
Business Administration
Biology
History
Education
English
Art
Theatre
Christian Education

Options for off-campus study include programs in France, Austria, Spain, Mexico, Japan, Australia, and New Zealand.

Forty-one percent of PC's men and 47 percent of the women join Greek groups.

four or five bands, and the Student Government Association's midnight breakfast, served during exam weeks. Students also look forward to the candlelight Christmas service and to the outdoor graduation ceremony under the oaks, with bagpipes heralding students and faculty in full academic regalia.

PC's 15 varsity sports teams compete in Division I. The college's mascot is the Blue Hose, a reference to the stockings of their Scottish ancestors. (While some students wear kilts during athletic events, most are more conservative, says a junior.) Strong programs include men's baseball and tennis, and women's basketball, softball, and volleyball. All students may take advantage of PC's 31-acre recreational facility, with lighted softball, football, and soccer fields, volleyball courts, a basketball court, a track, and an amphitheater. Recreational sports are divided into three divisions, depending on how competitive you are.

Presbyterian College students take pride in the school's history and traditions, including its very own tartan. PC's church affiliation keeps them focused on service, and on bettering the broader world, giving their classroom experiences added dimension. Says one student, "Students at PC have class. They genuinely care about one another and develop a close sense of family."

Overlaps

Clemson, University of South Carolina, Wofford, Furman, College of Charleston, Davidson, Duke, Erskine

If You Apply To ➤ | **Presbyterian:** Early decision: Nov. 1. Early action: Nov. 15. Regular admissions: Feb. 1. No application fee. Campus interviews: optional, informational. No alumni interviews. SATs or ACTs: required. Subject Tests: optional. Accepts the Common Application. Essay question.

Prescott College

220 Grove Avenue, Prescott, AZ 86301

Not a place where students fresh out of high school typically go. Those who succeed here love the outdoors and are looking for an alternative college experience. Has ready access to northern Arizona and southern Utah, the nation's most exotic outdoor playground. College of the Atlantic is the only remotely comparable college in the *Fiske Guide*. If you loved Outward Bound, consider Prescott.

Website: www.prescott.edu
Location: Small City
Private
Total Enrollment: 703
Undergraduates: 540
Male/Female: 43/57
SAT Ranges: CR 490–640, M 460–590
ACT Ranges: 22–27
Financial Aid: 70%
Expense: Pr $
Student Loans: 68%
Average Debt: $ $
Phi Beta Kappa: No
Applicants: 551
Accepted: 73%

Future *Hunger Games* contestants take note: This tiny outpost in the wilderness of central Arizona is a perfect spot for the nature lover who seeks adventure, wants to learn survival skills, and likes studying outdoors. Where else but Prescott College could you major in adventure education or take courses like Mountain Search and Rescue, Ecopsychology, and Wilderness Rites of Passage? Before any Prescott student sets foot in a classroom, the college sends him or her to the outback for three weeks of hiking and camping. Wilderness Orientation is an introduction to everything Prescott stands for: hands-on experience, personal responsibility, cooperative living, and stewardship of the environment. "We attract a fairly liberal student body that is passionate about the environment and social justice," says one junior.

Founded in 1966, Prescott retains the air of a 1960s commune. Surrounded by national forest, the college's "campus" consists of a two-block-long handful of buildings in the small town of Prescott. The architectural style of the campus ranges from the historic to the modern. The largest of the college's buildings is the Crossroads Center, an all-green building, which houses the library, computer labs, classrooms, conference centers, and the Crossroads Café. The administrative building was once a convent; its chapel is now used for meetings, art shows, and performances.

Prescott bills itself as a college "for the liberal arts and the environment," and most students envision themselves becoming teachers, researchers, park rangers, or wilderness guides. Adventure education, a major including everything from alpine mountaineering to sea kayaking, is a specialty. Also popular is environmental studies, which provides offerings of impressive breadth and depth for such a small school. The major in social and human development—a hodgepodge of sociology, psychology, and New Age mysticism—includes such unorthodox courses as Dreamwork Intensive. Integrative studies has been sep-arated into cultural and regional studies and human development, and is home for core humanities and lib-eral arts areas such as religion, philosophy, and social sciences, as well as an "incuba-tor" for programs such as peace studies. Among the college's few concessions to practicality is the Teacher Education Program, which offers students teaching cre-dentials in elementary, secondary, special, and bilingual education, and English as a second language. Prescott does not offer a comprehensive program in advanced math, chemistry, physics, or foreign languages other than Spanish. The social justice education major emphasizes interdisciplinary competence and is focused on pro-moting full and equitable access to education for all members of society.

> "We attract a fairly liberal student body."

(continued)

Enrolled: 18%
Grad in 6 Years: 45%
Returning Freshmen: 75%
Academics: ✐ ✐ ✐
Social: ☎ ☎
Q of L: ★ ★ ★ ★
Admissions: (877) 350-2100
Email Address: admissions@prescott.edu

Strongest Programs:
Adventure Education
Environmental Studies
Human Development
Cultural and Regional Studies

Prescott's requirements for graduation are characteristically unorthodox. Instead of grades, faculty members give narrative evaluations, although students may elect to receive grades. And rather than accruing credits, students design individualized "degree plans" that outline the competence (major) and breadth (minor) areas they will pursue, and the Senior Project (thesis) they will complete to demonstrate competence (graduate). Students must also obtain two levels of writing certifica-tion (college level and thesis level), and math certification, showing knowledge of college-level algebra.

"People are inspired to work hard because their projects reflect their passions, not because they're worried about getting an A," says one senior. "The courses are as rig-orous as you want to make them." Prescott's calendar is divided into three periods, each with one 10-week quar-ter and one four-week block. During the quarters, stu-dents follow a traditional schedule, studying liberal arts and spending time doing fieldwork and student teaching. During the blocks, students pursue intense immer-sion in one course, most likely in the field, perhaps the backcountry of Baja California, the alpine meadows of Wyoming, or even a local service clinic. Students can even take a one-month rafting trip down the Colorado River for credit. Summers may be spent studying field methods in agroecology at Prescott's 30-acre Wolfberry Farm. Though Prescott does not offer a traditional study abroad program, students are encouraged to take courses at the Kino Bay Center for Cultural and Ecological Studies in Mexico. Back on campus, students may take advantage of majors in creative writ-ing, visual arts, interdisciplinary letters and arts, and environmental studies.

> "People are inspired to work hard."

While Prescott carefully studies the global problems of the environment, it does so in an intimate, localized setting. There's no tenure track at Prescott, so publishing and research take a backseat to teaching. "Because you're not cramming for the next test (I never took one here), you can interact with your coursework in a way that's more meaningful to you," explains one human consciousness major. "Teachers encourage you to follow your passions in your presentations, and it's really inspir-ing to be in an environment where your fellow students are excited to learn."

Instead of grades, faculty members give narrative evaluations.

Environmental issues predominate and one student declares, "Students here are liberal, enthusiastic, and outgoing. They will be the world's future mountaineering guides, peacemakers, and environmentalists." Prescott's unconventional approach entices many well beyond Arizona. Indeed, one-third of students come from the Northeast; only 24 percent are in-staters. The minority population is small, with

African Americans, Hispanics, Native Americans, and Asian Americans making up 13 percent of the total. Twenty-eight percent graduated in the top quarter of their high school class. Prescott offers merit awards averaging $8,232.

Seventeen percent of students call the housing units home. "Our dorms are so amazing we don't even call them dorms," cheers one senior. "The Village is a series of eight-person townhouses. Each townhouse has two single rooms and three double rooms." Those not living on campus fend for themselves in the town of Prescott, a rapidly growing community of approximately 35,000 where almost everything is accessible by bicycle. The college assists with the apartment hunt by providing lists of available properties and by cosigning leases when necessary. As for the towns-folk, students describe them as "a mix of artists, activists, students, locals, retirees, and ranchers." The Prescott meal plan draws praise for being tasty and fresh. "Omnivores, vegetarians, vegans, and gluten-free folk all love the food in the café," cheers one student. "We don't have a formal dining hall, but the freshman dorms do have full kitchens and the café staff offer cooking lessons throughout the semester. There's also free community lunch every Wednesday."

Prescott social life is informal and spontaneous. "There are plenty of social events on campus and the main part of town with bars and restaurants is only a short walk from the school," says an education major. Aside from environmental activities, Prescott offers a nationally recognized literary magazine, *Alligator Juniper*, and a chapter of Amnesty International. Those looking for nightlife can hit Whiskey Row, the town bar scene, or drive to Flagstaff (90 minutes) or Phoenix (two hours).

Though the college offers no athletics, students often participate in city sports leagues. "Our school has bike jousting, juggling, barefoot soccer, ultimate Frisbee, and capoeira—none of which involve competing against other schools," says one student. Prescott's personal touch extends to graduation, a unique experience where a faculty member speaks about each student personally and then the student speaks on his or her own behalf.

Prescott may not have a huge campus or financial resources that are typically associated with larger schools; however, the small classes and interesting programs appeal to a student that would not be interested in your "typical" college. A human development senior explains, "PC students are a unique and self-motivated group of individuals. Our passion and dedication to education springs from a deep and inner desire to effect positive change in the world."

Prescott social life is informal and spontaneous.

Overlaps

Warren Wilson, Evergreen State, Lewis & Clark, College of the Atlantic, Green Mountain, Northern Arizona, University of Vermont, Colorado College

If You Apply To ➤ | **Prescott:** Early decision: Dec. 1. Regular admissions: Aug. 15. Financial aid: Mar. 1. Housing: Apr. 1. No application fee. Campus and alumni interviews: optional, informational. SATs or ACTs: required. Subject Tests: optional. Accepts the Common Application. Apply to particular school or program. Essay question.

Princeton University

110 West College, Princeton, NJ 08540

More conservative than Yale and a third the size of Harvard, Princeton is the smallest of the Ivy League's Big Three. That means more attention from faculty and plenty of opportunity for rigorous independent work. Offers engineering but no business major. The affluent small-town location contrasts with New Haven and Cambridge. Princeton continues to develop residential colleges modeled on Yale's.

Princeton occupies a distinctive niche among America's super-elite universities. It is a major research university with a world-class corps of professors who, in the absence of lots of graduate and professional students, lavish their attention on a relatively modest number of undergraduates. Princeton has an engineering school as well as programs in applied science, architecture and public planning, and public policy, but it is basically an "arts and sciences university." The academic atmosphere across campus is dominated by commitment to the liberal arts—with a carefully structured set of core requirements and a heavy emphasis on independent study, including a mandatory senior thesis. "Many schools brag about great buildings and great professors, but it's really your fellow students that end up making or breaking your college experience," says one sophomore. "What sets Princeton students apart is that they come here not just for an excellent education, but they come to share knowledge with others." For better or worse, Princeton has been known as a bastion of exclusivity although its undergraduates are just as racially and ethnically diverse as any other Ivy League school.

But Princeton is changing. New four-year residential colleges are being established, aimed at broadening the range of social options available to students, and the administration is making major investments in the creative and performing arts and the biological sciences. Sensitive to faculty complaints that Princeton draws too many bright students whose main claim to fame is that they have learned to work the system, the admissions office is on the lookout for more students with demonstrated intellectual curiosity—including more high-ability/low-income students and creative types. The university has also taken the lead in the national war on grade inflation—earning an A is harder than ever. "The courses are very challenging and rigorous," a junior reports, "but perhaps because of that, people are very cooperative. They realize that no one can really succeed alone." With such changes in mind, Princeton is gradually increasing the size of its undergraduate body by 500 students. Princeton has replaced all loans in its financial packages with grants, so just about any qualified student should be able to afford the place (about 75 percent of students graduate debt-free). Princeton's leaders are looking to make the university's particular brand of high-powered undergraduate liberal arts education available to an increasingly diverse group of students.

"The courses are very challenging and rigorous."

Cloistered in a secluded but upscale New Jersey town, Princeton's architectural trademark is Gothic, from the cavernous and ornate university chapel to the four-pronged Cleveland Tower rising majestically above the treetops. Interspersed among the Gothic are examples of colonial architecture, most notably historic Nassau Hall, which served as the temporary home of the Continental Congress in 1783 and has defined elegance in academic architecture ever since. A host of modern structures, some by leading American architects Robert Venturi, Frank Gehry, and I. M. Pei, add variety and distinction to the campus, but the ambiance is still quintessential Ivy League at its best. Princeton's campus is self-contained, but those who venture outside its walls will find the surroundings quite pleasing. One side of the campus abuts quaint Nassau Street, which is dominated by chic (and pricey) boutiques and restaurants, most out of the range of student budgets, although coffee shops and affordable restaurants are becoming more prevalent. The other side of campus ends with a huge man-made lake that was financed by Andrew Carnegie so that Princetonians would not have to forgo crew. The university has recently broken ground on a new arts and transit center, which will house the Lewis Center for the Arts and the Department of Music.

Princeton is distinctive in its scale (among the Ivies, only Dartmouth has a lower total enrollment) and its emphasis on undergraduates. For a major research institution, the university offers its students unparalleled faculty contact. "We have some

Website: www.princeton.edu
Location: Small Town
Private
Total Enrollment: 8,010
Undergraduates: 5,336
Male/Female: 51/49
SAT Ranges: CR 700–790, M 710–800
ACT Ranges: 31–35
Financial Aid: 60%
Expense: Pr $ $
Student Loans: 24%
Average Debt: $
Phi Beta Kappa: Yes
Applicants: 26,664
Accepted: 8%
Enrolled: 65%
Grad in 6 Years: 96%
Returning Freshmen: 98%
Academics: ✍ ✍ ✍ ✍ ✍
Social: ☎ ☎ ☎
Q of L: ★ ★ ★
Admissions: (609) 258-3060
Email Address: uaoffice@ princeton.edu

Strongest Programs:
Physics
Molecular Biology
Public Policy
Economics
Philosophy
Romance Languages
Computer Science
Math
English

of the most brilliant professors in the world here," says a junior. An economics major adds, "I can open the newspaper and read my professor's article or turn on the TV and see him giving a speech, then go to a lecture to hear him speak, then go to his office to speak with him one-on-one." With fewer graduate students to siphon off resources or consume faculty time than at large research universities, undergraduates get the lion's share of both; at last count, 70 percent of Princeton's department heads taught introductory undergraduate courses. Special opportunities to work closely with senior faculty members come with the freshman seminar program, taken by two-thirds of new students, which offers the opportunity to go deep into 65 topics ranging from the Physics of Music to the Search for Life in the Universe. Lovers of literature can study with Joyce Carol Oates, Paul Muldoon, Chang-rae Lee, or Toni Morrison, and nearly every other department has a few stars of its own. Senior professors lead at least one or two of the small discussion groups that accompany each lecture course. Every liberal arts student must fulfill distribution requirements in epistemology and cognition, ethical thought and moral values, historical analysis, literature and the arts, quantitative reasoning, social analysis, and science and technology. Students must also take writing courses. During their junior year, liberal arts students work closely with a faculty member of their choice in completing two junior papers—about 30 pages of independent work each semester in addition to the normal courseload. Princeton is also one of the few colleges in the country to require every graduate to complete a senior thesis—an enterprise that serves as a culmination of their work in their field of concentration. As a result, "seniors develop close personal relationships with their thesis advisors," says one student. Alumni often note the thesis as one of their best experiences at Princeton.

Special opportunities to work closely with senior faculty members come with the freshman seminar program.

As one might expect, Princeton's small size means the number of courses offered is smaller than at other Ivies. But lack of quantity does not beget lack of quality. Princeton's math and philosophy departments are among the best in the nation, and English, physics, economics, molecular biology, public policy, and romance languages are right on their heels. Princeton is one of the few top liberal arts universities with equally strong engineering programs, most notably chemical, mechanical, electrical, and aerospace engineering, and computer sciences (which has its own facilities). In fact, the department of civil engineering and operations research has split into two departments: civil and environmental engineering, and operations research and financial engineering, with the latter becoming one of the most popular majors. One of Princeton's best-known programs is the prestigious Woodrow Wilson School of Public and International Affairs ("Woody Woo" to the students). The university has undertaken a major effort to become a national center in the field of molecular biology, with a laboratory for teaching and research staffed by 28 faculty members.

"We have some of the most brilliant professors in the world here."

Princeton's semester system gives students a two-week reading period before exams in which to catch up, with first-term exams postponed until after New Year's, much to the dismay of many ski buffs and tropical sun worshipers. The university honor code, unique among the Ivies, allows for unproctored exams. The outstanding library facilities embrace five million volumes and provide 500 private study carrels for seniors working on their theses; there are another 700 enclosed carrels in other parts of the campus.

About 10 percent of the student body take advantage of the opportunity to study abroad. Except for students with sufficient advanced standing to complete their degree requirements in three and a half years, leaves of absence must be taken by the year, not the semester, an impediment to "stopping out." The university offers an intriguing five-year program that includes intense language study in an Asian country. There is also a five-year program that leads to a B.S.E. and M.E. in mechanical and aerospace engineering. A limited number of courses can be taken on the pass/fail option and the University Scholars program provides especially qualified students with what the administration calls "maximum freedom in planning programs of study to fulfill individual needs and interests." Although the faculty gets high ratings for its academic advising, students are rather cool on the university's nonacademic counseling programs.

"Our students are tight-knit, extremely hardworking, highly cooperative, and supportive of one another's activities," says an economics major. African Americans account for 7 percent of the student body, Hispanics 7 percent, and Asians 19 percent. While diversity is present, mixing sometimes isn't. "As an African American, I can say that even the African Americans are subdivided based on economics, place of origin, and whether you went to public or private school," explains one senior. And the campus remains socially conservative, with tweed and penny loafers adorning many students. Although students report that there can be a general air of apathy around campus, administrators are quick to point to the 22 political organizations on campus as evidence of students' interest in political and social issues.

> "Seniors develop close personal relationships with their thesis advisors."

Princeton undergraduates are admitted to the university without regard to their financial need, and those who qualify for aid receive generous support. In fact, Princeton was the first major university to replace all loans with grants. Each student's Princeton experience begins with a week of orientation; 800 each year participate in Outdoor Action, a few days of wilderness activities immediately preceding orientation.

In an attempt to improve the quality of life for freshmen and sophomores, Princeton has grouped many of its dorms into residential colleges, each with its own dining hall, faculty residents, and an active social calendar. Under this system, nearly all the freshmen and sophomores live and dine with their residential college unit, alleviating the formerly fragmented social situation. However, by providing a separate social sphere for these students, the system "creates a gulf between underclassmen and upperclassmen." And all too often the upper-level eating clubs steal the thunder from the college's social events. As a result, "the underclassmen spend too much time pining for the day when they, too, can join the closest thing Princeton has to cliques," says one student. Upperclassmen maintain an affiliation to the residential colleges, taking many meals there and even continuing residence there if they prefer.

The university's turn-of-the-century Gothic dorms may look like crosses between cathedrals and castles, and some halls have amenities like living rooms and bay windows. But conditions on the inside are sometimes less glamorous. All dorms are renovated on a rotation schedule, and new dorms have helped ease the housing crunch. Three percent of the students live off campus. The modern and roomy Spelman dorms, which come complete with kitchens, are the best on campus and fill up quickly every year with seniors who do not belong to eating clubs. "The underclassmen live in residential colleges. The rooms are a bit smaller for some of them in the older colleges, but there are laundry rooms, computer clusters, dining halls, and lots of other facilities in each of the residential colleges," a student says.

Princeton's most firmly entrenched bastions of tradition are its famed eating clubs. Run by students and unaffiliated with the school, they line Prospect Avenue, and have, for more than a century, assumed the dual role of weekend fraternity and weekday dining hall. Of the 11, five admit members through an open lottery, but the others still use a controversial selective admissions process called bicker (because of the wrangling over whom to admit), to the chagrin of the administration and most of the students. While many of the clubs opened their doors to women back

During their junior year, liberal arts students work closely with a faculty member of their choice in completing two junior papers.

The university has undertaken a major effort to become a national center in the field of molecular biology, with a laboratory for teaching and research staffed by 28 faculty members.

when Princeton went co-ed, two of the oldest and most exclusive—the Ivy Club and the Tiger Inn—remained all-male until 1991, when a court decision compelled them to admit women. Now, all the clubs are co-ed.

Catering exclusively to upperclassmen, the eating clubs provide a secure sense of community for their members. More than half of all sophomores join one of the clubs at the end of the year, becoming full-fledged members by the fall of their junior year. Annual dues vary; the most expensive is the Ivy Club, which charges its members almost $5,000 a year. Financial aid covers eating costs for those who qualify and want to join. Unfortunately, the social options for those who choose not to join may feel limited. Some opt for life in independent dormitories or join the handful of Greek fraternities and sororities (not sanctioned by the administration) that have sprung up on campus over the past few years and have become feeders to particular eating clubs.

Students rarely venture much farther than New York or Philadelphia, each one hour away (in opposite directions) on the train. "Virtually all social life takes place on campus, both at the eating clubs and at dorm parties," says a sophomore. Few students complain about boredom, and many praise the affluent town of Princeton for the parks, woods, bike trails, and, most important, the quiet and safety it offers students. McCarter Theatre, adjacent to campus, is the nation's seventh-busiest performing arts center and houses Princeton's Triangle Club, which counted Jimmy Stewart and Brooke Shields as members. The roundup of annual campus events includes Communiversity Day, an international festival, and the P Party in the spring, which features a big-name band. Each year about 3,000 students engage in volunteer activities such as tutoring, working in soup kitchens, or helping the elderly.

Princeton has the oldest licensed college radio station in the nation, plenty of journalistic opportunities, a prestigious debating and politics society (Whig-Clio)

"Our students are tight-knit, extremely hardworking, highly cooperative, and supportive of one another."

whose ranks included James Madison and Aaron Burr, and a plethora of arts offerings. Athletics are a big deal at Princeton, both varsity and intramural. Men's football, men's and women's basketball, and women's soccer are the most competitive Tigers teams. Other strong sports programs include men's lacrosse, men's squash, men's and women's crew, and women's softball. The women's rugby club and women's hockey team are also outstanding. Teams from the eating clubs and residential colleges take part in well-attended intramural events ranging from aikido and ballroom dancing to triathlons. Every fall the freshman and sophomore classes square off in Cane Spree, an intramural Olympics that has been a tradition since 1869.

Princeton's unofficial motto is "Princeton in the nation's service and the service of all nations," and the oft-repeated notion that with privilege comes responsibility lives on as part of its culture. It's easy to be humbled at Princeton. Even the most jaded students must be awed and inspired when they think of those who've traversed the campus paths before them, including former U.S. presidents James Madison and Woodrow Wilson. While some may find the ambiance too insular, not many turn down membership in this very rewarding club.

Overlaps

Harvard, Yale, Stanford, MIT

If You Apply To ➤

Princeton: Regular admission: Jan. 1. Single choice early action: Nov. 1. Financial aid: Feb. 1. Application fee: $65. No campus interviews. Alumni interviews: optional, informational. SATs or ACT: required. Subject Tests: required (engineering applicants required to take either physics or chemistry and math I or II). Accepts the Common Application. Essay question: changes every year.

Prin is a tiny college in a tiny town about an hour from St. Louis. All students have ties to Christian Science. Prin is mainly liberal arts, though its most popular program is business administration. More than two-thirds of the students study abroad. Campus tenor is similar to places like Pepperdine (CA) and Wheaton (IL).

Students come to Principia College with a common bond—ties to Christian Science. They shun smoking, drinking, drugs, and sex in favor of God and learning. Prin graduates are culturally, spiritually, and intellectually well rounded, the product of a liberal arts education that promotes critical thinking and a broad worldview. As the only college anywhere for Christian Scientists, Prin attracts a lot of international students. The historic campus is reminiscent of Harry Potter's Hogwarts. But the fictional school of wizardry never had a woolly mammoth to unearth between the dormitories as Prin does. "It's a great place to study," says a junior, "and one gets exposed to a lot of different programs. Above all, we preach that love prevails."

"The housing at Principia is superb."

Principia's 2,600-acre campus, on limestone bluffs above the mighty Mississippi River, was designated a National Historic Landmark in 1993. The dominant architectural influences are colonial American, Tudor, and medieval, and many buildings—including most dormitories—were designed by California architect Bernard Maybeck. A contemporary of Frank Lloyd Wright, Maybeck urged Principia trustees to bring the college to its current spot when they relocated from St. Louis in 1935. The College Chapel, whose bells ring out hymns every evening, is the symbolic center of campus. A 53,000-square-foot indoor athletic facility features a six-lane track and eight-lane pool.

Students say Principia's strongest programs include biology, music, political science, religion, and business. Art students benefit from a 1,000-square-foot studio in the Voney Building for Studio Arts, where they can immerse themselves in painting and drawing. Mass communication majors can hone their craft at the school's working television studio and FM radio station. The science center provides an aviary, a greenhouse, 13 lab rooms, and a computer weather center. In addition to 10 to 12 courses in their major, students must complete one course each in foreign language and the arts, and two courses each in literature; history; religion and philosophy; social science; lab science; and math, computer science, or natural science. Students must also take physical education courses and pass a swimming test.

Academics are challenging, but students can count on each other and their professors for help. "Some classes are far too easy, while others are exceptionally time-consuming and difficult," says a senior. Most of Prin's faculty members receive high marks. "The professors are wonderful at Principia because they are intelligent and able to develop relationships with their students because class sizes are smaller than most colleges," says a junior. Over a given four years, more than two-thirds of Principia students participate in the five or six study abroad programs the school organizes each year. Each program enrolls 18 to 22 students and sites are determined by academic subject and focus. Locations have included France, Germany, Nepal, South Africa, China, and Italy. Others participate in a prairie restoration program,

"The social scene at Prin consists mostly of planned social events and good conversation."

Website: www.principia.edu
Location: Rural
Private
Total Enrollment: 476
Undergraduates: 476
Male/Female: 45/55
SAT Ranges: CR 450–610, M 440–590
ACT Ranges: 20–26
Financial Aid: 96%
Expense: Pr $
Student Loans: 52%
Average Debt: $ $
Phi Beta Kappa: No
Applicants: 195
Accepted: 87%
Enrolled: 68%
Grad in 6 Years: 90%
Returning Freshmen: 92%
Academics: ✍ ✍ ✍
Social: 🏮 🏮 🏮
Q of L: ★ ★ ★ ★
Admissions: (618) 374-5181
Email Address:
collegeadmissions@ principia.edu

Strongest Programs:
Business Administration
Mass Communications
Sociology/Anthropology
Education
Art/Art History

gather data for the study of the Mississippi River's aquatic life, or build solar cars to be entered in races around the world.

"We are all Christian Scientists who strive to be the most moral people we can be," says one junior. "As a community we do our best to hold each other to high standards." The minority population is minuscule—African Americans, Asian Americans, and Hispanics combine for 3 percent of the student body. Still, 15 percent of students arrive from abroad, one of the largest percentages of international students on a college campus in the country. "We might not be in a big city," muses one student, "but Principia has a lot of engaged world citizens." Merit scholarships are available, but no athletic scholarships are offered.

All students live in Prin's dorms, except for the few who are married or live locally with their parents. "The housing at Principia is superb, in the form of large, historical houses rather than the typical dormitory," a senior explains. The rooms are large and comfortable, and those that aren't air-conditioned have ceiling fans. All have new or relatively new furniture. Students are expected not to be in the wings of dorms where the opposite sex lives during "house hours" every night. Freshmen live in two modernized dorms with upperclass resident advisors trained to help new

"Most students are committed to leading lives governed by morality and integrity."

students adjust to college life. "We have comfortable dorms with excellent resident counselors, and we all work together to maintain the community," says one student. In the dining halls, students can submit recipes to the dining service, and in addition to the grill station and a sit-down pub and restaurant, there's always salad, fruit, cereals, and other choices. "Food is typical college cafeteria food," says a student.

"Elsah is not a college town. I think it was established in the 1800s and not much has changed," a junior says. Stores, restaurants, and movie theaters are about 30 minutes away, and St. Louis is about an hour's drive. As Christian Scientists, students eschew alcohol, tobacco, and drugs, and Prin also asks them to sign a pledge of abstention from premarital and extramarital sexual relationships. "Those who sign the contract are committed to those morals for religious reasons," a political science major says. "It's a wonderful thing not to have to deal with alcohol on campus," says one senior. Instead of partying, students keep busy at school-sponsored concerts, movies, dances, or intramural sporting events that pit one dorm against another. "The social scene at Prin consists mostly of planned social events and good conversation," a student explains. "Sure, there are places to go nearby—and some do—but mostly the social scene takes place on campus." Each dorm organizes its own annual celebration, and international students show off their native cuisines at the Whole World Festival. The Public Affairs Conference is the oldest student-run event of its type, bringing in big-name speakers.

Principia's Panthers compete in Division III, and men's and women's soccer and women's tennis are especially competitive. About 60 percent of the student body participates in intramural sports like soccer, basketball, and softball. On sunny afternoons, students can be found playing ultimate Frisbee. Campus athletic facilities include a four-court indoor tennis center, a field house with gym and pool, and outdoor courts and running trails.

Prin students don't mind the conservative environment at their Christian Scientist school. In fact, they seem to revel in it. "Most students are committed to leading lives governed by morality and integrity," a freshman says. Gone are the pressures that take hold of most college students. Prin graduates leave their collegiate bubble ready to take on the world. "There is a commitment to the development of the students academically, socially, morally, and spiritually that is unique," a freshman says.

Principia: Rolling admissions. No application fee. Campus interviews: optional, informational. No alumni interviews. SATs or ACTs: required. Subject Tests: optional (foreign language test). Essay question. Only college in the world that admits only Christian Scientists.

Providence College

Providence, RI 02918

Strong Roman Catholic atmosphere makes Providence more comparable to Notre Dame than to Boston College or Holy Cross. Liberal arts emphasis rooted in required two-year interdisciplinary Western Civilization sequence, though a quarter of students opt for business disciplines. Friars athletic teams do well in small but high-profile Big East Conference. No fraternities or sororities, but Providence is a vibrant college town.

As the nation's only college or university operated by the Dominican Friars, Providence College wears its Roman Catholic and Dominican identities on its sleeve. Three-quarters of students are Catholic, friars in habits walk the campus grounds, crucifixes adorn the walls of classrooms and offices, and St. Dominic's Chapel stands tall in the heart of the campus. The school's mission is grounded in these identities, too, as it aims to "provide an education for the whole person—body, mind, and soul—that bridges the common divides between matter and spirit, God and creation, faith and reason." Students here enjoy solid offerings in the sciences and liberal arts—including a unique and rigorous two-year Western Civ course—and a tight-knit community of like-minded men and women.

Located only an hour's drive from Boston and just a few hours' drive from New York City, Providence College's 105-acre campus is situated in Rhode Island's capital city. The campus boasts open spaces, beautiful lawns, and student-centered facilities. The traditional brick and stone academic buildings, residence halls, and campus chapel coexist with several contemporary structures. Slavin Center—PC's student union—underwent a $6 million addition and renovation in 2009. The expansion includes a two-level glass-enclosed atrium incorporating rooftop photovoltaic cells to harness energy. The Canavan Sports Medicine Center is a 4,000-square-foot facility featuring a 920-square-foot hydrotherapy room and other amenities.

> **"The best departments are the sciences and the business school."**

Providence comprises four schools: the School of Arts and Sciences, the School of Business, the School of Professional Studies, and the School of Continuing Education. Strong programs include biology, chemistry, political science, and psychology. The School of Business, which attracts a quarter of students, offers a number of solid programs, too, including majors in accountancy, finance, management, and marketing. "The best departments are the sciences and the business school," a student says. Another adds, "Although biology is a very popular major here, many seem to complain about the workload. Other programs such as music and psychology seem to receive positive feedback." The Department of Biology offers a combined degree program with the New England College of Optometry, which allows for the completion of the B.A. and doctorate in seven years. Students have ample opportunity for experiential learning through faculty-directed laboratory and field research and internships. The premedical/dental option is designed to prepare students intending

Website: www.providence.edu
Location: City Outskirts
Private
Total Enrollment: 3,965
Undergraduates: 3,800
Male/Female: 43/57
SAT Ranges: CR 520–630, M 530–640
ACT Ranges: 23–28
Financial Aid: 64%
Expense: Pr $ $ $
Student Loans: 70%
Average Debt: $ $ $
Phi Beta Kappa: No
Applicants: 9,652
Accepted: 61%
Enrolled: 17%
Grad in 6 Years: 87%
Returning Freshmen: 90%
Academics: ✍ ✍ ✍
Social: ☎ ☎ ☎
Q of L: ★ ★ ★
Admissions: (401) 865-2535
Email Address: pcadmiss@ providence.edu

Strongest Programs:
Biology
Chemistry
Development of Western
 Civilization
Psychology
Marketing

to pursue careers in medicine and dentistry. All School of Business majors share a common set of core courses to ensure that business graduates have a broad understanding of all major business disciplines. Additional majors include women's studies and creative writing; a certificate in neuroscience is available as well.

A revised core curriculum, effective beginning with the Class of 2016, includes "comprehensive revisions designed to provide students with a liberal arts education responsive to today's complex and rapidly changing global environment," according to administrators. The heart of the curriculum is a sequence of seminar-based classes that comprise the Development of Western Civilization (DWC). This 20-credit course spans students' freshman and sophomore years and introduces them to the seminal ideas and primary texts in history, literature, theology, and philosophy, as well as the music and visual arts that shaped the Western world and other civilizations. Students also pursue studies in theology, philosophy, natural science, social science, quantitative reasoning, and fine arts. The college also requires students to demonstrate proficiency in intensive writing, oral communication, diversity, and civic engagement.

> "The academic climate at Providence College is rigorous but supportive."

The Department of Biology offers a combined degree program with the New England College of Optometry.

"The academic climate at Providence College is rigorous but supportive," says a junior. Nearly all classes have 49 or fewer students and are taught by tenured or junior faculty. "Freshmen are always taught by full professors," says one student. "We do not have TAs here." A Spanish and global studies double major adds, "Professors here go the extra mile for their students. They are enthusiastic, willing, and available to us. They never treat us like we are a number." The Liberal Arts Honors Program offers students of high academic ability and initiative a more in-depth and rigorous version of PC's core curriculum, and honors courses are offered in virtually all areas, including theology, philosophy, social sciences, natural sciences, and fine arts. Small, seminar style classes of 12–15 students allow for extensive one-on-one contact among students and professors. PC's Center for International Studies sends students to locales around the globe, including Argentina, Italy, New Zealand, and South Africa. "Study abroad has a pretty big presence on our campus," confirms an English major.

Only 9 percent of PC's students come from Rhode Island, and the remainder "tend to be mostly from the Northeast," according to one junior. In addition, most students are "preppy, white, Catholic, and generally upper middle class," according to one sophomore. African Americans account for 4 percent of the student body, Hispanics 5 percent, and Asian Americans 1 percent. One percent are foreign nationals. "Most people here are Catholics," says a junior, and many are vocal when it comes to social and political issues. "The most heated debates are generally about religion and race as they are key issues on our campus," a marketing major says. The lack of diversity draws near-universal concern: "I think it is felt very strongly among the minority students that we need more diversity on campus, even with all of our cultural clubs," says a junior. Merit scholarships are available to qualified students and gifted athletes may vie for more than 120 awards in 16 sports.

> "We do not have TAs here."

The Liberal Arts Honors Program offers students of high academic ability and initiative a more in-depth and rigorous version of PC's core curriculum.

Roughly 80 percent of students live in the dorms, where conditions are said to be comfortable if not spacious. "Dorms vary from very comfortable to a tight squeeze," reports one finance major. "They are usually well maintained, and I have never experienced or heard of anyone having trouble getting a room." Options include nine traditional halls, five apartment buildings, and a suite-style residence. Many juniors and seniors move off campus into the surrounding neighborhoods; those that choose to remain on campus have a pick of "great options," according to a junior. Campus dining is "good and constantly getting better," says a global studies major. Campus security is described as sufficient and students report feeling safe on campus. "With the blue light system, Intelliguard system, escort service, and good line of communication between administration and students, I feel as if PC has implemented all that they can to keep students safe," says an English major.

"There is definitely a large social scene at Providence," says one student. A junior adds, "There are an incredible number of opportunities for PC students to explore a range of social events and groups. There are free events for students to attend almost every day of the week, including weekends." Absent a Greek presence, students find other ways to let off steam. Owing to the college's strong Catholic identity, community service and volunteer work are popular pastimes. Annual traditions include a spring concert featuring top national acts and Civ Scream, held at midnight on the eve of Civ finals: "The entire sophomore class circles around the quad and screams to let out their frustration over Civ. People do crazy things and it is always something to remember," says a student. And although the

"Dorms vary from very comfortable to a tight squeeze."

college is located in "kind of a rundown area," students say the city of Providence has much to offer. "Providence is full of opportunities," reports an English major, including a mall, a movie theater, and a cultural district with all sorts of shops and eateries. The city is also home to six other colleges, which greatly enhances opportunities. Popular road trips include treks into Boston and New York City.

The Providence Friars compete at the NCAA Division I level, and 16 of the school's 17 varsity teams compete in the competitive Big East Conference (men's and women's hockey are part of the Hockey East Association). The most competitive teams include men's and women's cross-country and track, men's soccer, women's ice hockey, men's ice hockey, men's and women's basketball, and field hockey. "Basketball and hockey games are very important to PC students because we can show our school spirit," says a sophomore. Students get especially rowdy when rivals UConn, URI, or Syracuse are in town. Intramurals are popular, too, and attract 55 percent of the student body.

Providence College appeals primarily to those students who want to challenge themselves academically without compromising their faith. Despite frequent complaints about the length and rigor of the Western Civ requirement, students here seem content with what the college has to offer and are proud to be part of the PC community. "We are all very similar, which some people might consider a weakness," says one elementary and special education major, "but in the end I feel that everyone here is my friend and that I can relate to them."

Overlaps

Boston College, Fairfield, Fordham, College of the Holy Cross, Loyola (MD), Notre Dame, Villanova

If You Apply To ➤ | **Providence:** Early action: Nov. 1. Early decision: Dec. 1. Regular admissions: Jan. 15. Application fee: $55. Campus interviews: optional, informational. No alumni interviews. SATs or ACTs: optional. Subject Tests: optional. Accepts the Common Application. Essay question.

University of Puget Sound

1500 North Warner, Tacoma, WA 98416

Ask anyone in Tacoma about Puget Sound and they'll tell you that Puget Sound delivers solid liberal arts programs with a touch of business. Within easy reach of the Sound and Mount Rainier, the university specializes in all things Asia, including a nine-month university-sponsored trip. Compare to Whitman and Willamette.

Website: www.pugetsound
.edu

Location: Small City

Private

Total Enrollment: 2,791

Undergraduates: 2,555

Male/Female: 43/57

SAT Ranges: CR 570–688,
M 580–660

ACT Ranges: 26–30

Financial Aid: 94%

Expense: Pr $ $

Student Loans: 58%

Average Debt: $ $ $

Phi Beta Kappa: Yes

Applicants: 4,470

Accepted: 83%

Enrolled: 17%

Grad in 6 Years: 77%

Returning Freshmen: 86%

Academics: ✐ ✐ ✐ ½

Social: ☎ ☎ ☎

Q of L: ★ ★ ★ ★

Admissions: (253) 879-3211

Email Address: admission@
pugetsound.edu

Strongest Programs:

Business Administration

Psychology

English

Politics and Government

Biology

Music

Neuroscience

In all, more than 100 study abroad programs are available in more than 40 nations; 43 percent of students participate.

An ambitious building program and revised core curriculum have raised the profile of the University of Puget Sound, transforming it from a regional liberal arts college in Tacoma to an undergraduate institution with growing national recognition. As part of the new core, students are required to demonstrate foreign language proficiency and pass two freshman seminars and a capstone seminar. What hasn't changed is the school's close-knit community and its emphasis on Asia.

Founded in 1888, Puget Sound is cradled by the Cascade Range and the rugged Olympics, with easy access to the urban energy of Seattle and the natural beauty of Mount Rainier. The 97-acre campus boasts carefully maintained lawns, native fir trees, and plenty of other greenery, thanks to the moist climate. Most buildings, with distinctive arches and porticos, were built in the 1950s and 1960s. Additional facilities include an all-weather track and a 3,850-square-foot Sculpture House, with facilities for welding, woodwork, and painting. A new residence hall opened in 2013 and an expansion to the student center is slated for completion in 2014.

"Puget Sound is strong in the sciences."

Puget Sound students must complete an eight-course core curriculum, which includes a freshman seminar in writing and rhetoric, and another in scholarly and creative inquiry. In their first three years at Puget Sound, students also study five Approaches to Knowing—fine arts, humanities, math, natural sciences, and social sciences. An upper-level integrative course, Connections, challenges traditional disciplinary boundaries and examines the benefits and limits of an interdisciplinary approach to learning. There's also a senior capstone course. Special offerings include a classics-based honors program, the Business Leadership Program, residence-based humanities programs, and the Social Justice Residence Program. "The orientation program is tons of fun and a great way to meet people," says a sophomore.

After navigating Puget Sound's requirements, students may pursue a B.A., B.S., or bachelor of music degree. The most popular majors are business, English, biology, and psychology, followed by international political economy. "Puget Sound is strong in the sciences," says one senior, "especially biology, which is generally one of our most popular majors." The university has also developed a reputation as a jumping-off point to Asia—both literally and figuratively. Its curriculum stresses two of the fastest-growing fields in the region: Asian studies and Pacific Rim economics. Nearly one-third of Puget Sounders take at least one Asian studies course, and once every three years, there's a nine-month school-sponsored trip through Japan, Thailand, Korea, India, China, and Nepal, where participants study native art, architecture, politics, population, and philosophy. In all, more than 100 study abroad programs are available in more than 40 nations; 43 percent of students participate.

Regardless of the department or program, students say the academic climate here is very demanding. "The Puget Sound academic atmosphere is definitely a collaborative one," says a senior. "Coming from an incredibly cut-throat high school magnet program, I wanted to make sure I attended a college where I would be pushed to do strong work without having to sacrifice my other interests." Fifty-five percent of the classes taken by freshmen have 19 students or fewer, and you won't find grad students leading classes here. "The professors here are incredibly compassionate and personable people—I usually go into office hours with a specific question in mind, only to leave 45 minutes later after a discussion of everything from my academic plans to travel recommendations for my upcoming trips," a student says.

While most Puget Sound students come from western states, 23 percent hail from Washington. "People here are friendly, intelligent, engaged," a history major says. "They're also probably nursing various degrees of caffeine addiction, because everyone here is super busy!" African Americans and Hispanics together make up 9 percent of the student body. Asian Americans constitute 7 percent, and an active

Hawaiian student organization sponsors a number of events, including a luau each spring, with "great food and lots of traditional dances." "We have a range of political attitudes on campus," says a junior. "Right now we are focused on fair trade and sustainability." There are no athletic scholarships, but merit awards averaging $12,924 are doled out annually.

Seventy percent of Puget Sound students live on campus, and housing is guaranteed for freshmen, who are sprinkled among the dorms. "The double rooms are above average in size and there is a cleaning service that cleans the dorms five days a week," a student reports, "so they remain nice and fresh." After the first year, students may go Greek and live in chapter housing, pursue a single room in the dorms, or apply for one of 60 university-owned theme houses, which focus on substance-free lifestyles, social justice, or outdoor adventures. Other options include four foreign language houses. Aside from the main campus dining area—which is open from 7 a.m. to 10 p.m. daily and offers Mexican, Chinese, and Italian stations, plus salad and deli bars—students, faculty, and staff can chow down at two campus cafés and the Cellar. "Although the choices can become kind of repetitive toward the end of the school year, there are certain staples like garden tortellini on Fridays that everyone loves, and those looking to break the monotony can eat in the campus pizza parlor or one of two on-campus cafés," reports a senior.

Twenty-one percent of the men and 30 percent of Puget Sound women go Greek.

Twenty-one percent of the men and 30 percent of Puget Sound women go Greek, though fraternities and sororities don't dominate the social scene. "The social life is very casual and takes place in equal parts on and off campus," an international relations major says. Popular school-sponsored activities include the Log Jam BBQ, which kicks off the school year, Midnight Breakfasts, and Foolish Pleasures, a festival of short student-produced films. Students under 21 may not drink, but determined students usually manage to find booze anyway. "Tacoma is incredible!" cheers one English major. "While it embraces the participation of college students, it has such a vibrant culture of its own!" With the mountains and beaches so close—Seattle is 30 minutes away by car, Portland is two hours south, and Vancouver, British Columbia, is three hours north—road trips are *de rigueur*. That's especially true during ski season, and the school rents out all the necessary equipment.

"The social life is very casual and takes place in equal parts on and off campus."

Students are fond of saying that Puget Sound's Division III varsity teams, the Loggers, "Kick Axe." Among the teams that have brought home conference championships in recent years are women's basketball, golf, and swimming, and men's basketball, soccer, and crew. The women's soccer team won its 11th consecutive conference title in 2012–13. The school's archrival is Pacific Lutheran University; "football and basketball games against PLU are a big deal and always packed," says a student-fan.

Don't let the students' slacker-chic casual clothes fool you. Puget Sound means business and serious study for students seeking immersion in the liberal arts and the natural beauty of the outdoors. "The location, student autonomy, quality of education, and size of the student body make this college a wonderful place," says a senior. Those considering Puget Sound may do well to heed one junior's advice: "Be yourself. Let yourself show in your application. Individuality is prized here."

Overlaps

Lewis & Clark, Willamette, University of Washington, University of Oregon, Whitman, Pomona, Kenyon, UC–Davis

If You Apply To ➤

Puget Sound: Early decision: Nov. 15. Regular admissions: Jan. 15. Financial aid: Feb. 1. Housing: May 1. Application fee: $50. Campus and alumni interviews: optional, evaluative. SATs or ACTs: required. No Subject Tests. Accepts the Common Application. Essay question.

Purdue University

1080 Schleman Hall, West Lafayette, IN 47907-1080

Purdue is Indiana's state university for science and technology—with side helpings of business, health professions, and liberal arts. Compare to Kansas State and Big Ten rival Michigan State. Though Purdue is a large university, it does better than most in giving students hands-on opportunities such as internships and co-ops. Flight technology and aerospace are long-time specialties.

Website: www.purdue.edu
Location: Small City
Public
Total Enrollment: 34,851
Undergraduates: 28,717
Male/Female: 58/42
SAT Ranges: CR 510–620,
   M 550–680
ACT Ranges: 24–30
Financial Aid: 57%
Expense: Pub $ $
Student Loans: 54%
Average Debt: $ $ $
Phi Beta Kappa: Yes
Applicants: 30,903
Accepted: 61%
Enrolled: 33%
Grad in 6 Years: 70%
Returning Freshmen: 91%
Academics: ✐ ✐ ✐ ½
Social: ☎ ☎ ☎
Q of L: ★ ★ ★
Admissions: (765) 494-1776
Email Address: admissions@
   purdue.edu

Strongest Programs:
Engineering
Business Management
Pharmacy
International Political Economy
Asian Studies

Successful Indiana colleges have three things in common: a strong agricultural program, a powerhouse basketball team, and a conservative student body. Purdue University has all of these—plus one of the nation's strongest engineering programs, and the distinction of having awarded more bachelor's degrees in the field than any other institution. Purdue is also home to the nation's first computer science department, and its programs in pharmacy, nursing, and management are likewise strong. Budding classicists, dramatists, and vocalists probably should look elsewhere, as liberal arts are not Purdue's forte. But those seeking small-school friendliness with big-school spirit may be very happy here. "There are so many opportunities for a student to get involved," explains a junior.

Purdue is the main attraction in the small industrial town of West Lafayette, where the population triples when students return each fall. The campus features redbrick and limestone buildings arranged around lush shaded courtyards. Recent construction includes Merriott Hall and the France A. Cordova Recreational Sports Center.

Students apply to and enroll in one of Purdue's 10 schools, and academic requirements vary with the school and the major. Typically, they include English, math, a lab science, and perhaps speech or foreign language proficiency. Engineering is the most popular program, followed by biology, management, computer science, and health and kinesiology. Students flock to the five-year engineering co-op program, one of the most competitive on campus, because it marries classroom study with real-world work. Purdue also offers a strong undergraduate program in flight technology, which includes hands-on training at the university's own airport. Purdue has produced more than 20 astronauts, including Neil Armstrong and Gus Grissom. Also strong are programs in veterinary medicine and hospitality and tourism. Study abroad options are available at over 200 sites in more than 50 countries.

> **"Our professors really care and want us to excel so they are very helpful."**

Purdue students are focused on life after graduation; a senior says, "The engineering programs teach tools for problem solving that are directly applicable to skills needed on the job. Plus, there are lots of opportunities for paid research, internships, or cooperative education." And despite the university's size, about half of freshman classes are seminar-style, taught by graduate students and academic advisors who help answer students' questions and provide career advice. "The teaching is great," says a student. "Our professors really care and want us to excel so they are very helpful."

Purdue's student body is fairly homogeneous, with 58 percent from Indiana, 3 percent African American, 5 percent Asian American, and 4 percent Hispanic. Boilermaker pride does stretch across boundaries of race, gender, and socioeconomic background. Thousands of merit scholarships averaging more than $6,342 are awarded annually to qualified students; athletes vie for hundreds of scholarships.

Thirty-five percent of students live in Purdue's dorms; the numbers may be so low because of rules governing male and female visitation hours. (The notion of a "co-ed dorm" here means that both sexes share a dining hall and a lobby.) Almost all freshmen live on campus, though they aren't required to, and Harrison Hall is said to be a good pick for newbies. "The residence halls are very nice," says a student, thanks to "decent room sizes, new furniture, and a great social environment." Most upperclassmen find inexpensive housing just off campus, where walking and riding escorts, blue-light phones, and more than 40 campus police officers help them feel safe. Those with a grumbling stomach are treated to tasty options on campus. "Our food is the best," says an elementary education major.

Alcohol is prohibited in dorms and "people have been kicked out of the residence halls for being caught with alcohol," says a sophomore. Still, underage students get served at the frats, or—as at most schools—when friends over 21 are buying. Those of age may also frequent Harry's Chocolate Shop—a longtime bar, not a candy store. Overall, Greek life draws 18 percent of Purdue men and women and offers many social opportunities. But there are other options, too, says an animal science major, including football, basketball, soccer, and baseball games. "Outside of class, you can do anything from skydiving, paintball, choir, rock climbing, salsa dancing—anything. It's up to you," encourages a senior mechanical engineering major. Purdue's more than 900 organizations range from the BBQ society to professional development clubs.

"This is a college town that has everything you need within walking distance."

As far as college towns go, West Lafayette "would not exist if it weren't for Purdue," one student says. Another adds, "This is a college town that has everything you need within walking distance." As far as community service goes, Purdue students tend to find the "various options very rewarding." "But they should do more," complains one sophomore. Chicago and Indianapolis are favored weekend destinations for students with cars, and each spring, a week of fun and parties leads up to the Grand Prix go-cart races. Students also look forward to the Bug Bowl, an annual celebration sponsored by Purdue's entomology department, including cricket-spitting and cockroach races.

Purdue's athletic facility offers opportunities for weekend warriors and varsity athletes alike. Boilermaker pride manifests itself at Division I games of all types, especially when the opposing team is Indiana University, known derisively as "that school down south," in the annual struggle for the Old Oaken Bucket. Every year, the winner adds a link to a chain on the bucket, in the shape of either an "I" or "P." Women's volleyball and softball and men's and women's basketball are among the most popular sports on campus. The baseball team brought home a Big Ten Conference title in 2012. Thirty-five club sports and 38 intramurals are a big draw for those looking for friendly competition.

A strategic plan developed several years ago has Purdue focused on reaching "the next level of preeminence," through discovery, learning, and engagement—adding more professors and scholarship funding and decreasing the number of teaching assistants. What the happy students here have already discovered is that learning is fun when academics are mixed with a healthy dose of school spirit and general carousing. "The students here are all highly motivated and hard workers," says one senior. "We're also friendly and supportive to each other because there's the feeling that we are all in it together."

Engineering is the most popular program, followed by biology, management, computer science, and health and kinesiology.

Study abroad options are available at over 200 sites in more than 50 countries.

Overlaps

Ball State, Indiana University, Indiana State, University of Illinois, University of Michigan

If You Apply To ➤

Purdue: Regular admissions: Mar. 1. Application fee: $50. No campus or alumni interviews. Apply to particular schools or programs. SATs or ACTs: required. Subject Tests: optional. Essay question.

Queen's University: See page 352.

Quinnipiac University

275 Mount Carmel Avenue, Hamden, CT 06518

For those who can't get into Conn College or Trinity, here comes Quinnipiac University to the rescue. Aggressive expansion of programs and facilities has put it on the map of New England liberal arts colleges with a preprofessional bent. Business and health sciences are big attractions, though Quinnipiac is best known to the public for its political polling. Midway between NYC and Boston.

Website: www.quinnipiac.edu
Location: Suburban
Private
Total Enrollment: 7,469
Undergraduates: 6,231
Male/Female: 38/62
SAT Ranges: CR 500–580, M 510–600
ACT Ranges: 22–26
Financial Aid: 80%
Expense: Pr $ $
Student Loans: 67%
Average Debt: $ $ $ $
Phi Beta Kappa: No
Applicants: 18,825
Accepted: 68%
Enrolled: 14%
Grad in 6 Years: 76%
Returning Freshmen: 86%
Academics: ✑ ✑ ✑
Social: ☎ ☎ ☎
Q of L: ★ ★ ★ ★
Admissions: (203) 582-8600
Email Address: admissions@quinnipiac.edu

Strongest Programs:
Business
Nursing
Health Science Studies
Psychology
Film
Game Design
Interactive Digital Design
Finance

Under the leadership of entrepreneurial president John L. Lahey, Quinnipiac University has experienced a massive growth spurt, including mushrooming enrollment, more than a dozen new graduate programs, a slate of new facilities, and two new campuses. While the expansion has helped to increase the school's national prominence, it hasn't come without some growing pains. Quinnipiac's debt load has quadrupled, elbow room is at a premium, and some complain that class sizes are too large. Still, administrators show no signs of slowing the school's rapid growth. Talented students from around the nation are attracted to the university's solid programs in health, communications, and business, and most seem to take Quinnipiac's explosive expansion in stride. "Quinnipiac has made some unbelievable changes since my freshman year," says a senior. "The campus is constantly evolving for the betterment of student life."

Quinnipiac's 250-acre Mount Carmel campus sits adjacent to Sleeping Giant Mountain State Park, with its 1,700 acres of hiking and walking trails, 90 minutes from New York City and two hours from Boston. The academic, student life, and residence hall buildings are built of traditional New England redbrick, and a large center quad is surrounded by the library, the law school, the student center, the Lender School of Business Center, and the Echlin Center for Health Sciences. The landscape is enhanced by convenient walkways and broad lawns. The three-building College of Arts and Sciences Center features a spacious quad that overlooks Clark's pond and its family of swans. The 250-acre York Hill campus is just across Whitney Avenue. The austere North Haven campus, located four miles from the Mount Carmel Campus, serves as home to the School of Health Sciences, as well as other upper-level and graduate programs. A campus shuttle bus system provides transportation between the campuses as well as to Hamden, New Haven, and North Haven. New construction includes a residence hall and the Frank H. Netter MD School of Medicine.

"Quinnipiac University is a challenging and competitive school."

Quinnipiac offers 56 undergraduate majors and the newest include four flavors of engineering (civil, industrial, software, and mechanical). The most popular majors include nursing, psychology, biology, communications, and management. Physical therapy students enroll in a six-year, combined B.S./D.P.T. program, aspiring physician's assistants may choose a six-year B.S./M.H.S., and there is also a combined B.S./M.O.T. in occupational therapy. Athletic training and nursing are solid choices as well. The Lender School of Business offers strong programs in entrepreneurship and finance, while students in the School of Communications may enroll in the media production program, which emphasizes the technical aspects of digital media pre-production, production, and postproduction. The communications and journalism programs also benefit from several university-owned media outlets, including two radio stations and a television station, and the university is home to the renowned Quinnipiac Polling Institute.

Quinnipiac's liberal arts philosophy is evident in its general education curriculum, which includes three interdisciplinary freshman seminars, freshman composition, and quantitative literacy requirements. There is also a breadth requirement that includes 28 hours of foundational courses in the sciences, social sciences, humanities, and fine arts. "Quinnipiac University is a challenging and competitive school but it is certainly manageable," says a sophomore. All freshmen take part in QU 101, a common reading assignment that explores the role of the individual in the local community. "It gives the student an idea of how he or she fits into the community," a math major says. "It also helps the students adjust to their first year in college." The Arnold Bernhard Library is home to one of the world's largest collections of art commemorating the Great Irish Famine.

"The students who attend Quinnipiac are well rounded."

Forty-eight percent of all classes have 19 or fewer students, and "there are no massive lecture halls," says one journalism major. There are no TAs or graduate assistants, either; all classes are taught by professors, who are praised for their focus on the classroom and the student. "I was surprised by the fact that there are professors who are part-time faculty, who are still working in their field and therefore can give you more real-life advice on what is going on in the real world," says one student. Academically gifted students may enroll in the University Honors Program, which features special seminars, close relationships with professors, and a slew of enrichment and leadership opportunities. Internships and clinical experiences abound: Communications students may elect to spend their summer on production sets or on-air, while political science majors have the opportunity to assist elected officials at the state capital or in Washington, D.C. Study abroad options include jaunts in France, England, Spain, Italy, Canada, and Costa Rica. The semester program in Ireland, at University College Cork, is very popular in both the fall and the spring semesters.

The Lender School of Business offers strong programs in entrepreneurship and finance.

"The school has really changed a lot and it's all been for the better."

Twenty-four percent of Quinnipiac's students come from Connecticut, and 24 percent ranked in the top 10th of their high school class. "The students who attend Quinnipiac are well rounded," says one senior, and "involved in academics, Greek life, clubs, and organizations." The student body is 4 percent African American; Hispanics and Asian Americans make up another 10 percent. Political and social issues aren't a huge concern on campus, students say. Qualified undergraduates receive merit awards averaging $15,000, and gifted athletes vie for 200 athletic scholarships in 21 sports.

Housing is guaranteed for three years for incoming freshmen, and 80 percent of the student body lives on campus in traditional residence halls, suites, townhouses, and apartments. "Housing is comfortable and well maintained," says a mathematics major. Freshmen can expect to live in triples or quads, while sophomores live in suite-style housing. Students are required to purchase a meal plan, and campus dining options include the main dining hall (Café Q) and the Bobcat Den. "There are currently four cafeterias between our three campuses and the food is pretty good," a senior says. Campus security is highly visible and students report feeling safe on campus. "I have never felt unsafe, although I really wish security would have a better action plan for when wild animals come onto campus," says a student. "A skunk thought our campus was home and stayed for many months."

The Quinnipiac social scene is bustling.

The Quinnipiac social scene is bustling. "Although there is a large off-campus social life, the on-campus social life is still very popular," says a junior. The campus hosts a slew of events, including guest speakers, concerts, comedians, and film screenings; there are also more than 100 student clubs to whet the appetite of those seeking a good time. The university sponsors two fraternities and three sororities; 16

percent of the men and 14 percent of the women go Greek. Quinnipiac is a "wet" campus—students 21 or older are allowed to possess alcohol in the dorms—but underage drinkers face stiff penalties. "The alcohol policy works for those who get out of control," a student says. "It obviously doesn't stop all drinking on campus, but it certainly stops things from getting out of hand."

Men's and women's tennis, men's and women's cross-country, and baseball are especially competitive, but nothing brings out the Bobcat faithful like the annual hockey match versus rival Yale.

When students tire of the campus scene, they trek into surrounding towns in search of fun. "I think it's a prime location," says one student. "Hamden has a lot of shops we can take shuttles to or drive to for upperclassmen. New Haven isn't too far and there are so many colleges around there." Hamden does offer the usual mix of chain restaurants, movie theaters, and bowling alleys, although "many students like to take the free shuttle into New Haven to enjoy food, shopping, and the nightlife," says a junior. Many choose to get involved in the local community through volunteer work, including the Quinnipiac Future Teachers Organization and Habitat for Humanity. A student says, "Just about every club or organization has some kind of volunteer program happening every semester."

The Quinnipiac Bobcats field 21 Division I teams and all compete in the Northeast Conference, except for men's and women's ice hockey, which compete in the powerful Eastern College Athletic Conference. In the spring of 2013, they agreed to expand athletic opportunities for women (and keep women's volleyball) to settle a legal battle. Men's and women's basketball and women's lacrosse have each won their respective conference titles in recent years. Men's and women's tennis, men's and women's cross-country, and baseball are especially competitive, but nothing brings out the Bobcat faithful like the annual hockey match versus rival Yale. "That is the biggest game of the year," says a biology major. "Students pack the stadium to show support." Yale also beat Quinnipiac in the 2013 Frozen Four, the national championship. Quinnipiac's "large and very popular intramural sports program" includes competition in basketball, bowling, field hockey, soccer, tennis, volleyball, and dodgeball. The American Marketing Association (AMA) student chapter was a three-time winner at the 2011 International AMA Collegiate Conference.

"The school has really changed a lot and it's all been for the better," cheers one senior. New campuses, expanding academics, and increased selectivity are all part of the university's continuing mission to attract bright students. It's an expensive gamble that administrators and students feel will pay off. "There are more resources here than I can think of," says one satisfied student. "Any student who wants to succeed will succeed."

Overlaps

University of Connecticut, Northeastern, University of Delaware, Fairfield, University of Massachusetts, Marist, Boston University, Ithaca

If You Apply To ➤

Quinnipiac: Rolling admissions: Feb. 1. Early decision: Nov. 1. Application fee: $45. Campus interviews: optional, informational. No alumni interviews. SATs or ACTs: required. No Subject Tests. Accepts the Common Application. Essay question.

Randolph College

2500 Rivermont Avenue, Lynchburg, VA 24503

Co-ed only since 2007, Randolph College has been recast with an international emphasis. Once one of the premier women's colleges in the nation, it still fields strong programs in the liberal and fine arts. Its suburban location on the James River is rich in history, though of limited appeal to those of college age. Still in the early stages of attracting men.

With rich traditions, cozy dorms, and challenging, seminar-based classes, Randolph College has preserved the best elements of its past, while evolving into an institution that remains relevant today. The college, formerly known as Randolph-Macon Women's College, emphasizes a global honors curriculum and offers solid programs in political science, global studies, English, psychology, and dance. It also offers men and women a place to be themselves. "There's a place for everyone: artists, athletes, academics, and everyone in between," says one student.

The college's 100-acre campus sits in the historic neighborhood of Lynchburg (population 80,000), on the banks of the James River. Graceful old buildings are covered with purple wisteria and linked by glass corridors called trolleys; the surrounding trees burst into riotous bloom each spring. Main Hall, dating from 1893, houses dorm rooms, classrooms, and faculty and administrative offices. The Maier Museum of Art has one of the best college collections of American art in the country, but administrators have begun auctioning off many pieces in an effort to raise at least $32 million and reduce financial woes. The school's Riding Center offers indoor and outdoor arenas in the nearby Blue Ridge foothills. The renovated student center features dining, exercise, performance, social, and meeting spaces with state-of-the-art technology, equipment, and furnishings.

> "There's a place for everyone: artists, athletes, academics, and everyone in between."

Randolph's general education requirements are reflected in a matrix of study areas, with artistic expression, cultural inquiry, global issues, gender issues, and quantitative literacy and analysis on one axis, and arts and literature, humanities, natural sciences and math, wellness, and interdisciplinary courses on the other. "It forces you to explore different areas and take classes in almost every department," explains a sophomore. "In your first year you have to take classes in four different departments your first semester and your second semester. I never thought I would major in psychology, but I took a psych class my spring semester and loved it!" All freshmen take the First-Year Seminar, which examines how to maximize academic success. Programs in museum studies and American culture combine classroom study with visits to historic sites; the latter has focused on the Deep South, New England, and the Lewis and Clark expedition, depending on the year. "The academic climate of Randolph is very competitive," says a psychology major. "The professors challenge you and expect a lot from you." The English program has been restructured with minors now available in creative writing, drama, fiction, literature, and poetry. The student-run Honor System has been in effect for over a hundred years.

Biology, psychology, political science, English, and history are some of the most popular majors at Randolph—and among the school's best departments. Since there are no TAs, it's easy for students to form friendships with their professors. "The professors genuinely care that the students learn the material and even have fun doing it," one student says. Students interested in research may compete to assist professors with ongoing projects during an eight-week summer session, and many present their findings at the National Conference on Undergraduate Research. SUPER (Step Up to Physical Science and Engineering at Randolph) is an immersive, residential experience for first-year students that emphasizes math, chemistry, physics, and environmental science. Students take three classes a day as well as enjoy sports, recreation, food, tutoring, organized activities, and field trips.

Though the Randolph community is small, students need not worry about claustrophobia; worldliness is a part of life here. The Visiting International Professor program has brought scholars from China, Nigeria, Croatia, India, and Malaysia to campus. In addition, the school offers $1 million in scholarship money for study abroad, prompting 45 percent of students to study in another country

Website: www.randolph college.edu
Location: Small City
Private
Total Enrollment: 625
Undergraduates: 603
Male/Female: 37/63
SAT Ranges: CR 480–610, M 490–610
ACT Ranges: 20–27
Financial Aid: 99%
Expense: Pr $
Student Loans: 73%
Average Debt: $ $ $ $
Phi Beta Kappa: Yes
Applicants: 892
Accepted: 83%
Enrolled: 24%
Grad in 6 Years: 57%
Returning Freshmen: 80%
Academics: ✍ ✍ ✍
Social: ☎ ☎
Q of L: ★ ★ ★
Admissions: (800) 745-7692
Email Address: admissions@ randolphcollege.edu

Strongest Programs:
Psychology
Chemistry
Biology
English
Environmental Studies
Global Studies
Fine Arts
Classics

All freshmen take the First-Year Seminar, which examines how to maximize academic success.

before graduation. Some programs are thematic in nature, examining peace studies in Nagasaki and Hiroshima, or theater in London and Stratford; others offer Randolph students the option of studying at the University of Reading in England, the Universidad de las Americas in Mexico, or the University of Economics in Prague. The college also participates in the Seven-College Exchange*, the Tri-College Exchange, and in American University's Washington Semester program. Two-thirds of Randolph students secure off-campus internships, with organizations from the Chicago Lyric Opera and London's Imperial College to businesses such as clothing maker Tommy Hilfiger.

> **The student-run Honor System has been in effect for over a hundred years.**

"Students here are kind, welcoming, and very accepting," says one political science major. Fifty-two percent of Randolph students hail from Virginia. Minorities have a sizable presence on campus, with Hispanics comprising 6 percent of the student body, Asian Americans 2 percent, and African Americans 9 percent. The Black Women's Alliance encourages awareness of and respect for differences, and Randolph

"The professors challenge you and expect a lot from you."

is also a member of the International 50, a group of colleges committed to multiculturalism. "Students are very charged and passionate about equal rights," says one student. "Sometimes I feel like I'm in the midst of a socialist movement." Randolph awards merit scholarships each year but there are no athletic awards.

Ninety-one percent of Randolph students live in the dorms, many of which have "high ceilings, carpet or hardwood floors, and large windows with crown molding," according to one history major. Everyone gets a room, eventually, though one student cautions that room draw in the spring can take a long time to sort out. Main Hall, once nicknamed "the Hilton," is the largest dorm, and its central location makes it the most convenient. All rooms are linked to the campus computer network and wired for cable TV. "The food is OK," one student reports. "Chefs are always looking for ways to innovate and make something fun," adds a classmate. Security officers patrol continuously between 4 p.m. and 8 a.m. and take pride in knowing students by name.

> **Two-thirds of Randolph students secure off-campus internships.**

"Social life is vibrant, inclusive, and lively," says one senior. "Everything takes place on campus and I believe students are very appreciative of this fact." The Macon Activities Council makes sure no one is bored by hosting comedians, bands, and other entertainers, as well as talent shows and lip-synch contests. "Other activities include shopping and visiting the dollar theater, or traveling to nearby colleges like Hampden–Sydney and Washington and Lee. Class trips sometimes venture to Washington, D.C., and the Wintergreen ski slopes"—or even as far north as New York City. Charlottesville, Virginia, an hour away, is also home to the University of Virginia, another popular destination for those seeking frat parties and football. Underage drinking is prohibited at Randolph, in accordance with state and federal law (as well as the honor code), and one student reports, "It is looked down upon."

The town of Lynchburg, which hosts two other colleges, has a Walmart, but is otherwise "less than exhilarating," says a biology major. A classics major explains,

"Students are very charged and passionate about equal rights."

"We get along well enough, but the town is not very receptive." Indeed, most clubs in the area are 21 and over, and the restaurants, stores, and movie theaters that do operate are closed by 10 p.m. Thankfully, the college's new coffee bar has opened its doors to satisfy students' caffeine cravings. Students often get involved in the local community via volunteering.

Randolph's Wildcats compete in Division III, and the school's top rival is nearby Sweet Briar. The men's basketball team advanced to the ODAC Tournament finals for the first time in school history in 2010–11, while the men's soccer team won its first ODAC Tournament. The softball team is the most competitive of the women's sports, having made it to the conference championship three consecutive seasons. In 2011, the Wildcat softball squad reached the ODAC Tournament final for the first time. But more than athletic contests, students look forward to Randolph traditions, such as Ring Week (in which a freshman anonymously decorates the door of a junior and leaves her small gifts all week, culminating with a scavenger hunt for her class ring), and the Pumpkin Parade (during which sophomores and seniors, not to be left out, scour campus in search of carved pumpkins). The Never-Ending Weekend each fall includes both a formal and the annual Tacky Party, for which tasteless attire is *de rigueur*.

The students of Randolph aren't shy about their academic goals, career drive, or sense of campus unity. "The college went co-ed years ago and so the population changed," says one student. "But the core dynamic and value system did not. Students still value respect and responsibility."

If You Apply To ➢ | **Randolph:** Early action: Dec. 1. Regular admissions: Mar. 1. Application fee: $35. Campus and alumni interviews: optional, evaluative. SATs or ACTs: required. Subject Tests: optional. Accepts the Common Application. Essay question.

University of Redlands

1200 East Colton, P.O. Box 3080, Redlands, CA 92373-0999

If you like the thought of palm trees against a backdrop of snow-covered peaks, Redlands may be your place. As a "university," Redlands is bigger than Occidental and Whittier. The alternative Johnston Center for Integrative Studies makes an odd contrast to the buttoned-down conservatism of the rest of Redlands.

Amid the dozens of gigantic and well-known universities in the state of California stands the University of Redlands. With its innovative living/learning college and strong preprofessional emphasis, this versatile school is one of higher education's better-kept secrets, and a place where students receive all the personal attention they could want. One student describes it as a "small liberal arts college in sunny Southern California with great financial aid packages."

The University of Redlands' 160-acre campus, covered in majestic oak trees, is designed around "The Quad," a group of dorms that face one another. The two main landmarks are the Memorial Chapel and the administration building. Redlands' facilities are a mixture of older, more historical columned buildings and more modern, renovated ones. The view from the college can only be described as breathtaking. Mountain ranges form the backdrop, and neighboring Big Bear Lake and Arrowhead ski resorts give endless getaway opportunities. Also nearby are the San Gorgonio Wilderness and Joshua Tree National Park. For those looking for big-city adventures, Los Angeles is only an hour away.

Redlands's most distinctive attribute is its experimental living/learning college, where students create their own course of study and are judged by self- and professor evaluations rather than grades. The Johnston Center for Integrative Studies was established in 1969 to function as an "alternative" college within a traditional setting; now that it is a program rather than a separate college, about 10 percent of the students here take advantage of this opportunity. The program offers unusual academic freedom; there are no departments, majors, or distribution requirements. Instead,

Website: www.redlands.edu
Location: Small Town
Private
Total Enrollment: 3,853
Undergraduates: 2,554
Male/Female: 43/57
SAT Ranges: CR 520–620, M 530–620
ACT Ranges: 22–26
Financial Aid: 90%
Expense: Pr $ $
Student Loans: 68%
Average Debt: $ $ $ $
Phi Beta Kappa: Yes
Applicants: 4,501
Accepted: 69%
Enrolled: 24%
Grad in 6 Years: 72%
Returning Freshmen: 91%
Academics: ✐ ✐ ✐
Social: ☎ ☎ ☎

(continued)

Q of L: ★ ★ ★
Admissions: (800) 455-5064
Email Address: admissions@
  redlands.edu

Strongest Programs:
Government
English
Creative Writing
Biology
Chemistry
Music
Environmental Studies

Business is the most popular major, followed by liberal studies, communicative disorders, psychology, and biology.

Redlands has won three recent national championships in women's water polo.

students "contract" with professors for their entire plan of study. At the beginning of each course, students make up the syllabus by consensus and then set their own research and writing goals. Each student develops four-year goals—which are reviewed by a student/faculty board for direction and breadth—within one or more broad areas: the social sciences, behavioral sciences, humanities, and fine and performing arts.

Compared with other Redlands students, Johnston undergrads have higher test scores, with average SATs that are 50 to 75 points above the Redlands median.

> **"[Redlands is a] small liberal arts college in sunny Southern California with great financial aid packages."**

One student explains, "Johnston Center students tend to be independent thinkers, self-motivated, and [don't] take classes just because they have to." Johnston's enrollment declined in the late '70s and '80s as students became very career-oriented and found that alternative education no longer fit their needs. Fortunately, student interests and needs have once again changed, and Johnston is seeing its highest enrollment in nearly two decades.

Aside from Johnston, Redlands is unusual among liberal arts institutions mainly in that it also offers professional programs. The schools of education and music provide strong career training, as does the excellent program in communicative disorders. Business is the most popular major, followed by liberal studies, communicative disorders, psychology, and biology. The environmental studies program consists of courses in natural science, humanities, and social science, focusing on values-based environmental problem solving. Students can receive degrees in environmental studies, environmental science, and environmental management. Redlands has also emerged as a national leader in science curriculum reform.

The liberal arts foundation gives students the fundamental skills essential to effective learning and scholarship by challenging them to examine their own values and the values of society. With its 4–4–1 calendar, Redlands has students take one intensive course each May. Students may also choose from among 100 study abroad options in Europe, Asia, Africa, and Latin America; 35 percent do so. The highly acclaimed freshman seminar program places small groups of first-year students with some of the

> **"The professors are the school's biggest asset."**

school's best professors, while the selective honors program enables outstanding students to work individually with professors, who are very accessible outside of class and occasionally even come by the dorms for "fireside chats." "Freshmen are always taught by full professors," says one sophomore, and a writing major declares that at Redlands, "the professors are the school's biggest asset." Most students agree that Redlands's laid-back academic atmosphere is much appreciated.

Seventy-five percent of the student body comes from within the state, creating a mellow, Southern California atmosphere on campus. The climate is a definite plus, with temperatures rarely below 50 degrees. The typical Redlands student tends to be fairly conservative, although one student reports that the minority of liberals are quite vocal. The racial makeup of the school is diverse, with Hispanics representing 22 percent, Asian Americans 5 percent, and African Americans 3 percent. About a third of the graduating class each year moves on to graduate schools, while 60 percent head into the workforce. Redlands annually awards a variety of merit scholarships averaging $27,088. There are talent awards in art, writing, music, and debate, but there are no athletic scholarships.

Students have nothing but rave reviews for the dormitories, in which 69 percent of the students live. "Each dorm has a personality of its own," exclaims one student. "The dorms are comfortable and complete with Ping-Pong and pool tables," raves a sophomore. Most of the dorms are co-ed, though there is an all-woman dorm. Students agree that freshmen should check out Merriam Hall first. Other housing options include on-campus apartments and student-run co-ops. Students enjoy their food at the Irvine Commons or Plaza Café, part of the Hunsaker University Center. Students can mingle in the "town square" atmosphere of the center's bookstore, café, and student life offices.

The Southern California heat and smog can become unpleasant, and students with wheels often flee Redlands on weekends for healthier pleasure spots along the California coast or in the mountains. But overall, social life is centered on campus activities. Local fraternities and sororities claim 20 percent of the men and 13 percent of the women, respectively, and their parties are open to all—but even these parties are rarely raucous.

"The dorms are comfortable and complete with Ping-Pong and pool tables."

Road trips to Hollywood, Palm Springs, San Francisco, the beach, and even Mexico are common. Despite the school's enforcement efforts, alcohol is accessible. "It is very easy. Students operate bars out of their rooms," reports one student.

The NCAA Division III sports program injects a measure of excitement into the social scene. The Divers compete in the Southern California Intercollegiate Athletic Conference (SCIAC). Men and women compete in basketball, cross-country, golf, soccer, swimming, tennis, track, and water polo. Men also compete in football, while women's teams include lacrosse, softball, and volleyball. In addition, more than 40 percent participate in at least one intramural sport. Redlands has won three recent national championships in women's water polo. Also competitive are football, men's soccer and basketball, and women's soccer and softball.

The University of Redlands is a lot of different things to a lot of different people. With 170 faculty members, it manages to be a preprofessional institute, a liberal arts college, and an alternative school all in one. The Johnston Center is clearly a path to travel for the innovative individualist, but even those who don't join Johnston can probably find what they want and need at Redlands.

Overlaps

Chapman, Loyola Marymount, San Diego State, UC–Santa Barbara, UC–Santa Cruz, UC–San Diego, UCLA, University of San Diego

If You Apply To ➤ | **Redlands:** Early action: Nov. 15. Regular admissions: Jan 15. Financial aid: Mar. 2. Application fee: $30. Campus interviews: optional, informational. No alumni interviews. SATs or ACTs: required. No Subject Tests. Essay question: personal statement.

Reed College

3203 S.E. Woodstock Boulevard, Portland, OR 97202-8199

Reed is a West Coast version of Grinnell or Oberlin, mixing nonconformist students with a traditional and rigorous curriculum. Only 73 percent of first-year students graduate in six years, due to Reed's demands and the fact that its students often live close to the edge. Sends huge numbers of grads on to Ph.D.s. Students who were square pegs in high school often find Reed a square hole.

Reed College is one of the most intellectual colleges in the country. In fact, this hotbed of liberalism has produced 88 Fulbright scholars, 61 Guggenheim Fellowships, 148 National Science Foundation Fellowships, and three winners of the MacArthur Award. It's also the place where the late Steve Jobs—cofounder of Apple—attended for a semester before dropping out to rule the world. Reed is a place where students complain that the library, which closes its doors at midnight on Fridays and Saturdays, shuts down too early. "Reed is the absolute best place for someone who

Website: www.reed.edu
Location: City Outskirts
Private
Total Enrollment: 1,383
Undergraduates: 1,383
Male/Female: 46/54

Although Reed emphasizes personal freedom and responsibility, especially through its Honor Principle, the curriculum and academic requirements are remarkably traditional.

likes to think, to read, to question, and to work," says a student. "It's a community of scholars." Letter grades are de-emphasized as a form of evaluation. Instead, students receive lengthy and detailed commentaries from professors, which fosters continued dialogue and eliminates grade inflation. "Questions and conversations that begin with a professor's prompting, or a question penciled into the margins of an assigned reading, spill over into the rest of student life," says a history major, "and it isn't uncommon to hear a passionate defense of Socrates, or an indictment of neoliberalism or an explanation of organic chemistry on a trail in the middle of the Reed canyon or in the depths of the pool hall."

Located just five miles from downtown Portland, Reed's 115-acre campus boasts rolling lawns, winding lanes, a canyon creek, and protected wetlands. A fish ladder was recently installed to help salmon reach their spawning grounds, and nonnative plants are being removed from the area to protect the natural habitat. In addition to the canyon, the campus hosts 125 different species of trees. Two thousand majestic arbors shade a mix of original campus buildings, constructed of brick, slate, and limestone in the Tudor Gothic style, as well as lodges in the homey Northwest Timber style and some more modern facilities. A new performing arts building opened in 2013. Reed has a tradition of respect for great calligraphy that, among other things, inspired Steve Jobs to build traditional graphics into Apple computers.

"The academic climate of Reed is exciting and intense."

Although Reed emphasizes personal freedom and responsibility, especially through its Honor Principle, the curriculum and academic requirements are remarkably traditional. Freshmen must complete Humanities 110, a yearlong interdisciplinary course focused on society and culture in classical Greece, imperial Rome, and the ancient Mediterranean. The course, which has been taught for more than 50 years, draws on the expertise of 25 professors, including some of Reed's most senior and distinguished faculty. Students must also take courses in four "breadth" areas: literature, philosophy, religion, and the arts; history, social sciences, and psychology; the natural sciences; and mathematics, logic, linguistics, or foreign languages. Seniors must submit a research-based thesis to graduate. On the due date, just after spring classes have ended, seniors march from the library steps to the registrar's office in the Thesis Parade. This marks the beginning of Renn Fayre (originally "Renaissance Fayre"), a weekend-long celebration that involves a bug-eating contest, Glow Opera, and live human chess.

Despite Reed's small size—79 percent of the courses taken by freshmen have 19 or fewer students, and it just gets better from there—the school offers unsurpassed research opportunities in the liberal arts and sciences. Budding physicists and environmental scientists can work with college staff at the 250-kilowatt Triga nuclear reactor, after passing an Atomic Energy Commission examination. "Reed has a fantastic science program for a liberal arts school," says one physics major. "The sciences are an active and thriving branch of inquiry." Fifty-two exchange programs attract 25 percent of each graduating class, taking students to 22 countries, from Germany and China to Ecuador and Russia. Reed also offers domestic exchange programs with Howard, Sarah Lawrence, and the Woods Hole Oceanographic Institute. Dual-degree (3–2) programs include engineering, computer science, and forestry/environmental science.

"Reedies don't take themselves too seriously."

Reed students take full advantage the range of academic options, which often keep them tethered to their computers and study carrels. "The academic climate of Reed is exciting and intense. Students are extremely passionate about learning," says one senior. You'll never find a TA at the lectern here or leading a group discussion, so students rarely attend class unprepared for the lively intellectual banter that typically ensues between inquiring and active minds. "Professors are extremely talented and invested in their students' success," a senior says. Over the years, a quarter of Reed's grads have gone on for Ph.D.s—the highest percentage of any liberal arts college in the country.

While Reed is located in Oregon, its quirky brand of intellectualism means only 9 percent of the students are in-staters. Eight percent are Asian American, 9 percent Hispanic, and 3 percent African American—and 9 percent hail from other nations. "Reedies don't take themselves too seriously despite their commitment to learning and learning well," says one psychology major. "A tongue-in-cheek sense of humor is pervasive throughout the campus." Students define the political climate on campus as liberal and note that while students do get involved in a variety of causes, most are more comfortable talking about issues on an "intellectual or theoretical level."

Sixty-three percent of Reed students live on campus in co-ed housing or in one of the many "theme" dorms, which usually house fewer than 30 people each. Some rooms feature such homey touches as fireplaces or balconies. Freshmen are guaranteed housing, and usually get divided doubles; upperclassmen get singles. Old Dorm Block and Anna Mann are said to be the most popular choices for first-years, and all rooms are connected to the campus computer network. For those who lose out in the housing lottery, or upperclassmen seeking a taste of post-college independence, off-campus houses are cheap and plentiful. "The dorms are comfortable and the staff keeps them clean and in shape," reports one senior. On-campus students must buy the meal plan, and students say outside caterer Bon Appétit does a good job, with salad and sandwich bars and grill and entrée stations available each day at lunch and dinner. "The food is surprisingly good and diverse," one student says, "and the kitchen is happy to help with any particular dietary needs."

"It is an intense environment, both inside and outside the classroom."

"There's so much to do at Reed that students don't leave campus for weeks at a time," says one student. Campus events include movies, game nights, concerts, and lectures. Use of alcohol or drugs is governed by the Honor Principle and a stiff drug and alcohol policy. Students look forward to Paideia (which means "education" in Ancient Greek), a weeklong program of wacky alternative classes before spring semester begins. Paideia's noncredit workshops range from Skittle appreciation and a *South Park* marathon to how to get into law school or make Shrinky Dinks. Each April, students celebrate Nitrogen Day, honoring our atmosphere's most plentiful—and underappreciated—element.

Students say Portland is the perfect college town. "Portland is a college student's dream come true," raves one student. "There is live music every night, a steady stream of literary events, and constant film screenings. Movie tickets usually cost from three to seven dollars in the city's many independent movie theaters, many of which double as breweries and/or pizzerias." Aside from low-key parties and gatherings with friends on and near campus, Reed students love to road-trip—whether to the mammoth Powell's bookstore downtown (about a 15-minute drive) or to Oregon's coastal beaches, mountains, or high desert, all about two hours away. The school also owns a ski cabin on Mount Hood that sleeps 15.

The closest thing Reed has to a school mascot is the Doyle Owl, a 300-pound concrete sculpture that dorms regularly plot to steal from one another. While Reed doesn't have competitive athletics, clubs such as rugby, rowing, and ultimate Frisbee do compete with other clubs in the area. Reedies must also fulfill a three-semester-long physical education requirement. Ballroom dancing, telemark skiing, and juggling are just a few of the many courses offered.

Reed is definitely not for everyone—emblematic items sold in the bookstore bear the unofficial slogan "Atheism, Communism, Free Love." But if you're an

Overlaps

Stanford, Brown, UC–Berkeley, University of Chicago, Lewis & Clark, Yale, Oberlin, Pomona

intellectual who prefers to spend Saturday nights with your nose in a book, this Portland school is definitely worth a look. Reed offers a unique and refreshing mixture of stringent intellectualism with an atmosphere of playfulness and creativity," says a senior. "It is an intense environment, both inside and outside the classroom."

If You Apply To ➤

Reed: Early decision I: Nov. 15. Early decision II: Dec. 20. Regular admissions: Jan. 15. Financial aid: Feb. 1. Housing: Jun. 15. No application fee. Campus and alumni interviews: optional, evaluative. SATs or ACTs: required. Subject Tests: optional. Accepts the Common Application. Essay question.

Rensselaer Polytechnic Institute

110 Eighth Street, Troy, NY 12180-3590

If you can spell Rensselaer, you've already got a leg up on many applicants. RPI is one of the nation's great technical universities—along with Caltech, Harvey Mudd, MIT, and Worcester Polytech—and one of the most innovative. The beauty of RPI is the chance for hands-on learning and synergy between technology and management. Much more selective in admission than it was a few years ago.

Website: www.rpi.edu
Location: Small City
Private
Total Enrollment: 6,459
Undergraduates: 5,298
Male/Female: 71/29
SAT Ranges: CR 610–700, M 660–760
ACT Ranges: 26–31
Financial Aid: 96%
Expense: Pr $ $ $ $
Student Loans: 68%
Average Debt: $ $ $ $
Phi Beta Kappa: Yes
Applicants: 15,222
Accepted: 44%
Enrolled: 20%
Grad in 6 Years: 84%
Returning Freshmen: 94%
Academics: ✎ ✎ ✎ ✎
Social: ☎ ☎ ☎
Q of L: ★ ★ ★
Admissions: (518) 276-6216
Email Address: admissions@rpi.edu

Strongest Programs:
Engineering

It would be an exaggeration to say that technology is God at RPI, though the school's conversion of a Gothic chapel into a computer lab does hint in that direction. Even if it's not deified, technology remains omnipresent at this school, which pioneered the teaching of calculus via computer in the early '90s. Students attend class in fully wired studio classrooms where they work on team projects and collaborate to solve real-world problems. Since 1998, the institute has more than doubled its research funding, and it's one of six original National Science Foundation Nanotechnology Centers in the country. For students who may have been known as geeks in high school, coming to Rensselaer is like coming home.

"The courses are challenging, but not completely overwhelming."

Set high on a bluff overlooking Troy, New York, Rensselaer's 260-acre campus mixes modern research facilities and classical, ivy-covered brick buildings dating to the turn of the century. Almost the entire campus is wireless, allowing students to study and collaborate with each other from anywhere on campus. The East Campus Athletic Village includes a football field, gym, 50-meter pool, and indoor track and field area, as well as indoor and outdoor tennis courts. The university is also home to cutting-edge facilities, including the Center for Biotechnology and Interdisciplinary Studies, which houses more than 400 researchers in biotechnology and related disciplines who work in functional tissue engineering, regenerative medicine, integrated systems biology, bioinformatics, biocatalysis, metabolic engineering, and others.

RPI made its reputation as one of the nation's premier engineering schools, and continues to excel in traditional favorites such as chemical and electrical engineering, as well as newer specialties like environmental and computer systems engineering. Engineering is the most popular major, followed by computer and information sciences, business/marketing, biological sciences, and physical sciences. The nuclear engineering department has its own linear accelerator, while graduate and undergraduate students participate in research at the Center for Industrial Innovation. RPI is a national leader in the study and application of electronic media and offers a B.S. program in electronic arts. The Computational Center for Nanotechnology Innovations (CCNI) is among the world's most powerful university-based supercomputers and is designed to advance semiconductor technology to the nanoscale. Additional majors include cognitive science, Web science, sustainability studies, and the notoriously difficult architecture program.

(continued)

RPI's Lally School of Management and Technology combines elements of a business school with the latest technical applications, and coursework has been redesigned into yearlong classes to capture the complexity of the business world. Entrepreneurship is one of its specialties; budding entrepreneurs may participate in the Rensselaer Business Incubator, a support system for start-up companies run by Rensselaer students and alumni. RPI students are required to take courses in entrepreneurship or have an "entrepreneurial experience" before graduation. The B.S. program in information technology continues to attract top students who often combine it with coursework in e-commerce or the arts. Majors in the humanities and social sci-

"The students at RPI are driven and motivated. They want to get ahead and change the world."

ences are limited, and their quality is directly related to their applicability to technical fields. Still, all students must complete at least 24 credits in these areas, as well as at least 24 credits in physical, life, and engineering sciences, a minimum of 30 credits in their majors, and a writing or writing-intensive course. Additionally, students must complete an international requirement by participating in research or an internship in another country. "The courses are challenging, but not completely overwhelming," says one junior. Still, RPI is more collaborative than competitive due to the heavy amount of teamwork within the classroom.

About two-thirds of Rensselaer students are undergraduates, a high percentage for a top engineering school; because of this, RPI has worked hard to ensure that classes are smaller and more attention is paid to individual needs. Professors are extremely knowledgeable and the quality of teaching is excellent. "The professors are all involved in research and so they bring a personal, applicable perspective to the material they teach," a student says. Juniors and seniors enjoy self-paced courses and occasionally paid positions helping with faculty research. Career counseling is helpful; academic advising has added an "early warning" system to target students who are having trouble.

RPI made its reputation as one of the nation's premier engineering schools.

For students who can't wait to start working, popular co-op programs in more than a dozen fields help them earn both money and credit. Those who already know what field they'll pursue may enter a seven-year dual-degree program in medicine, a six-year program in law, or four- and five-year master's programs in biology, geology, or mathematical science. Although most engineering schools discourage studying abroad, Rensselaer offers exchange programs in more than 15 countries on five continents; 7 percent of undergraduates participate.

Twenty-eight percent of RPI students are New Yorkers, and 95 percent ranked in the top quarter of their high school class. RPI is fairly diverse, with Asian Americans comprising 10 percent of the student body, African Americans 2 percent, and Hispanics 6 percent. Students from scores of countries and nearly every state attend RPI; males

"The freshman dorms are pretty typical but the upper-class residence halls are great."

continue to outnumber females 2 to 1. "The students at RPI are driven and motivated. They want to get ahead and change the world," says one student. RPI is far from a center of political activism; students say they're just too busy. "Politics? Not so much on this campus," says a student. The biggest campus issue may be choosing the Grand Marshal, who oversees a boisterous weeklong carnival celebrating campus elections, during which professors are barred from giving tests. Merit scholarships averaging $13,334 are available, as are 43 athletic scholarships.

Fifty-seven percent of students live in university residence halls; freshmen and sophomores are required to live on campus as part of the student life model known as Clustered Learning Advocacy and Support for Students (CLASS). The program features common living arrangements and a team of faculty and peer advisors with the aim of creating smaller, more tightly knit student communities. "The freshman dorms are pretty typical but the upper-class residence halls are great," one senior reports. Upperclassmen may keep their current room, enter the lottery to get something better, or live in college-owned apartments off campus, widely considered the nicest option. Students report feeling safe on campus. "Security is very good," a business management major says. "Public safety does a great job and they are very underappreciated."

The Computational Center for Nanotechnology Innovations (CCNI) is among the world's most powerful university-based supercomputers.

Social life mostly takes place on campus, but the male/female ratio is a major hassle, forcing lovelorn men to haunt Russell Sage (next door) or Skidmore (40 minutes away) in hopes of finding a mate. A senior says, "There are things to do on campus, but a majority of the social students go to celebrations in the Greek houses and off-campus apartments." Thirty percent of men and 16 percent of women go Greek and, other than Greek parties, weekend options at RPI include

"Hockey at RPI equals insanity." sporting events, live entertainment, concerts, movies, and a half-dozen local pubs—some of which students find easily accept fake IDs. Those under 21 can't have alcohol in the dorms, and fraternities aren't allowed to have "containers of mass distribution" (i.e., kegs) at parties; students say alcohol isn't an issue on campus. Extracurricular clubs, organized around such interests as chess, dance, judo, and skiing, are chartered and funded by a student-managed body that doles out more than $8 million annually.

Free shuttle buses run regularly from campus to downtown Troy, a former industrial revolution town, but there aren't many good reasons to make the trip. "Troy is not a college town," says a senior, "but it does have good places to eat and some beautiful parks." Students and Greek groups do get involved with community service projects, though, and the town offers opportunities for internships. Rensselaer has helped generate economic growth in Troy by investing in the downtown area and providing grants to homebuyers. A six-screen movie theater is within easy reach, and for a taste of bigger-city nightlife, Albany is a half-hour drive. For scenic excursions, the Berkshires, Catskills, Adirondacks, Lake George, Lake Placid, the Saranac Lakes, Montreal, and Boston are popular destinations.

RPI is more collaborative than competitive due to the heavy amount of teamwork within the classroom.

The athletic scene at Rensselaer revolves around hockey, hockey, hockey—the school's only team playing in Division I. One of the biggest weekends of the year is Big Red Freakout, when all festivities center around cheering on the beloved Big Red. "Hockey at RPI equals insanity," one student says. "If you go to one hockey game all season, go to the men's hockey season opener. The place is packed with rowdy RPI students who scream and chant in unison." There are many intramural sports to choose from, but the most popular may be the D-level hockey team (meaning "I really don't know how to play this," says a junior). Other varsity teams play in Division III, and the football, baseball, men's and women's basketball, and women's field hockey teams are most popular. During the 2012–13 season, 21 of RPI's 23 intercollegiate teams had better-than-.500 records.

Computer geeks and video game junkies aren't the only ones who will find a home at Rensselaer. Students who thrive on teamwork and collaboration will also find RPI to their liking. RPI provides cutting-edge technology to students constantly wondering how things work. RPI students work hard—sometimes to the detriment of a social life. "Students at RPI are all a little bit nerdy, and proud of it," a computer engineering major says. "The types of things that might be looked at strangely at other colleges are accepted here."

Overlaps

Carnegie Mellon, Cornell, Georgia Tech, MIT, Worcester Polytechnic

RPI: Early decision: Nov. 15. Regular admissions: Jan. 15. Application fee: $70. No campus or alumni interviews. SATs or ACTs: required. Subject Tests: optional (required for all accelerated program applicants). Accepts the Common Application. Apply to particular programs. Essay question: depends on program.

University of Rhode Island

Kingston, RI 02881

URI is a smallish alternative to UConn and UMass. With Boston, Providence, and vacation hot spot Newport within easy reach, there is plenty to do. Strong programs include engineering, marine science, nursing, and pharmacy. More than a third of URI's students are out-of-staters.

No longer an unabashed party school, the University of Rhode Island has earned a reputation for challenging academics and an emphasis on innovation and interdisciplinary learning. Once ground zero for wild drinking and carousing, the school now provides a culture of learning; the result is an environment in which students engage in service learning, do research with top faculty, and find a much heavier emphasis on alternative styles of learning. "Our college is an amazing place to learn, prosper, and have fun," boasts one sophomore.

URI's 1,200-acre campus is located in the small town of Kingston. Surrounded by farmland and only six miles from the coast, it is also within easy driving distance of cities such as Providence—the Renaissance City and home to Brown, the Rhode Island School of Design, and several other colleges and universities—Boston, and New York. The main academic buildings at URI, a mixture of modern and "old New England granite," surround a central quad on Kingston Hill. At the foot of Kingston Hill lie the athletic buildings and agricultural fields. A new fitness and wellness center opened in 2013 and ground has been broken on a new chemistry building.

New students initially enroll in the University College, which offers academic and career guidance as well as advice on selecting from among required general education courses in communication skills, fine arts and literature, natural and social sciences, letters, mathematics, foreign language, and culture requirements. Undecided or exploratory students are assisted in following their intellectual curiosity to find the perfect fit for a major. All new students take URI 101, a one-credit course intended to acquaint students with support services, cocurricular activities, and academic majors and career options. After a year or two in University College, students choose more specialized colleges, such as the well-regarded College of Pharmacy. The university also offers a marine and environment program, landscape architecture, and African and African American studies. Some majors, such as a professional degree like the doctor of pharmacy, require students to stay for five or six years, but most students graduate in four years. Other notable undergraduate majors include health studies, Chinese, and interdisciplinary studies and dual degrees in medical physics and neuroscience.

Students say the academic climate depends on the program and the professor, and ranges from "laid-back" to "very stressful." "While there are certain programs, such as pharmacy, that are pretty competitive, the university overall is a mellow climate," says one senior. Teaching is a hit-or-miss affair, but freshmen often have full professors. "Some teachers are harder than others, but overall they are all helpful

> "Our campus is dry so almost all social stuff happens off campus."

Website: www.uri.edu
Location: Small Town
Public
Total Enrollment: 13,668
Undergraduates: 11,863
Male/Female: 45/55
SAT Ranges: CR 490–580, M 500–600
ACT Ranges: 21–26
Financial Aid: 66%
Expense: Pub $ $ $
Student Loans: 77%
Average Debt: $ $ $ $
Phi Beta Kappa: Yes
Applicants: 20,637
Accepted: 77%
Enrolled: 21%
Grad in 6 Years: 63%
Returning Freshmen: 81%
Academics: ✍ ✍
Social: 🐦 🐦 🐦 🐦
Q of L: ★ ★ ★
Admissions: (401) 874-7000
Email Address: admission@uri.edu

Strongest Programs:
Nursing
Psychology
Communication Studies
Kinesiology
Human Development and Family Studies
Pharmacy

(continued)

International Engineering Program

Some majors, such as a professional degree like the doctor of pharmacy, require students to stay for five or six years.

and present the information we need to know," says a business management major. The university offers international exchange programs with universities in Australia, England, France, Germany, Japan, Korea, Mexico, Spain, Venezuela, Quebec, and Nova Scotia. Domestic exchange programs are available at more than 175 state colleges and universities. Students can also participate in the international engineering program, spend a year of the five-year program abroad, and major in both engineering and Spanish, German, or French. The Academic Enhancement Center, along with its Writing Center, provides active learning enhancement for all students through peer tutorials, developmental workshops, course-specific collaborative learning projects, supplemental instructional sessions, study groups, and special programs for high-risk students.

Although URI gives preference to in-state students who meet requirements, more than one-third of the entering freshmen are from outside Rhode Island. "Students here are involved and outgoing," one junior says. "They are also full of ideas, which is why we have so many different clubs and activities on campus." Minority enrollment stands at 5 percent African American, 8 percent Hispanic, and 3 percent Asian American. The academic profiles of the incoming class have risen steadily over the past 10 years, in large measure due to the Centennial Scholarship Program for outstanding freshmen. Merit scholarships averaging $5,506 are available, and athletes vie for 194 athletic scholarships in 22 sports.

Though most freshmen live on campus, 56 percent of all undergraduates choose to find off-campus digs. In the past decade, 13 of 19 residence halls have been renovated and 504 bed spaces in apartments and 290 spaces in suites have been added. Still, students find housing to be less than appealing. "If you get a new dorm, then you will be great," says one student. "The older dorms are disgusting." Another adds, "Housing is probably one of the more frustrating things at URI. Some dorms are poorly maintained." Campus dining options earn middling reviews, but students say the food is edible and diverse. Campus security "always roams around," says a student.

"The university overall is a mellow climate."

"Our campus is dry so almost all social stuff happens off campus," a senior reports. "Thursday through Saturday tend to be big party nights, but Sunday through Wednesday are big study nights." The campus coffeehouse hosts open-mic nights, and movie theaters, clubs, and malls beckon just off campus. Greek life attracts 12 percent of the men and 13 percent of the women. The student newspaper that covers it all has one of the most original names anywhere: *The Good 5¢ Cigar* (as in, "what this country needs is"). While the hearty New England winters are invigorating for some students, many wind up catching colds, earning URI the unflattering nickname Upper Respiratory Infection. As for Kingston, it's a sleepy New England college town. "There is nothing in Kingston," complains one student, "but we are 10 minutes from the beach and 30 minutes from Providence." Students get involved in the town through clubs or URI 101, which requires volunteer work. Newport, with its thriving social scene, is just 20 minutes away, and those feeling lucky can get to the Foxwoods Resort and Casino in 45 minutes. Other fun road trips include Boston (90 minutes) and New York City (four hours). Travel is facilitated by the fact that there is an Amtrak stop on campus.

Sports are big at Rhode Island, and basketball games are especially exciting.

Sports are big at Rhode Island, and basketball games are especially exciting. Midnight Madness (the team's first sanctioned practice of the year) is always well attended, and URI fans love it when the Rams defeat archrival Providence College. Men's track and field has brought home the conference title nine times over the last 12 years and women's rowing has captured three of the last five Atlantic 10 championships as well. Another student favorite is oozeball, an April volleyball tournament played in about two feet of mud. As befits the school's locale, sailing draws much

Overlaps

Boston University, University of Connecticut, University of Delaware, University of Massachusetts, Northeastern

interest, and the team regularly produces All-Americans. Students can find unique opportunities running businesses like a flower shop, a sound and lighting group, and a coffeehouse in the Memorial Union under full-time supervision but with a lot of independence.

URI offers students a large-school feel in a small state. Centrally located in dense New England, students benefit from having the ocean at their back door. But instead of spending all their time at the beach or on nearby ski slopes, students work hard to achieve good grades and lay the foundation of lifelong learning.

<table>
<tr><td>If You
Apply
To ➤</td><td>URI: Early action: Dec. 1. Regular admissions: Feb. 1. Financial aid: Mar. 1. Housing: June 1. Application fee: $65. No campus or alumni interviews. SATs or ACTs: required. Subject Tests: optional. Essay question: personal statement (optional).</td></tr>
</table>

Rhode Island School of Design

2 College Street, Providence, RI 02903

The nation's best-known art and design school, RISD sits on a hillside adjacent to Brown. The campus offers easy access to downtown Providence, but it can't match the location of rival Parsons in New York's Greenwich Village. Offers an artsy architecture major in addition to programs in the visual arts. Industrial design is also a specialty.

Founded in the late 19th century to address the country's need for more artisans and craftsmen, the Rhode Island School of Design has grown into a premier arts incubator. It's a place where today's artists and designers gather to share ideas and create tomorrow's masterpieces and architectural icons. RISD grants degrees in virtually every design-related topic, and like the varied curriculum, the students and their creations are as diverse as the colors on an artist's palette. "Students are constantly working to complete projects or produce successful bodies of work," says one student.

Though you might expect an art school like RISD to occupy funky, futuristic buildings, the predominant look here is colonial New England. Set on the upgrade of College Hill, RISD sits at the edge of Providence's beautifully preserved historic district, adjacent to Brown University. Many campus buildings date from the 1700s and early 1800s; the mostly redbrick-and-white-trim group includes converted homes, a bank, and even an old church. The six-story Industrial Design building, designed by faculty member Jim Barnes, occupies the old Roitman furniture company warehouse. Its 50,000 square feet are designed for wood- and metalworking and prototype making. Renovations to the Illustration Studies Building are currently underway.

> **"Students are constantly working to complete projects."**

While RISD looks traditionally New England on the outside, behind its historic walls lies something else entirely. Students give the architecture, graphic design, and industrial design programs top marks, while liberal arts are considered weaker. That said, bachelor's and master's liberal arts concentrations in art history, English and literature, history, philosophy, and social sciences are available, complementing offerings in furniture design and architecture and interior architecture (for grad students). RISD also offers cross-registration at adjacent Brown University for students seeking more diverse courses. The institute's highly specialized library contains

Website: www.risd.edu
Location: Small City
Private
Total Enrollment: 2,386
Undergraduates: 1,971
Male/Female: 33/67
SAT Ranges: CR 550–670, M 570–690
ACT Ranges: N/A
Financial Aid: 66%
Expense: Pr $ $ $
Student Loans: 60%
Average Debt: $ $ $ $
Phi Beta Kappa: No
Applicants: 3,113
Accepted: 25%
Enrolled: 55%
Grad in 6 Years: 87%
Returning Freshmen: 95%
Academics: ✍ ✍ ✍ ✍
Social: ☎ ☎
Q of L: ★ ★ ★ ★
Admissions: (401) 454-6300
Email Address: admissions@risd.edu

(continued)

Strongest Programs:

Illustration

Industrial Design

Architecture

Graphic Design

Painting

662,000 nonbook items (prints, etc.) and 106,000 volumes, and students are likely to be found at their personally assigned studio carrels. Perhaps RISD's most prized facility is its art museum, which boasts more than 85,000 pieces, a superlative collection that includes everything from Roman and Egyptian art to works by Monet, Matisse, and Picasso.

To graduate, students must be in residence for at least two years and must complete a final-year project. They must also finish 126 credit hours—54 in their major, 18 in the Foundation Studies program (an integrated year of "functional and conceptual experiences" that leads to "an understanding of visual language"), 42 in the liberal arts (art and architecture history; English; history, philosophy, social sciences; some electives), and 12 in nonmajor electives. Hands-on studio courses abound, and most classes have fewer than 20 students. Still, a sophomore says, "sometimes classes fill very quickly because they are really interesting, but there are always ample alternatives to choose from." During RISD's winter session, five weeks between the first and second semesters, students are encouraged to take courses outside their major. And each year about 60 juniors and seniors venture to Rome for one of two six-month experiences offered through the European honors program, which provides independent study, projects with critics, and immersion in Italian culture. There is also an international exchange program where students study abroad at approved art institutions.

> "I've been amazed by how a lot of the teachers here are willing to go above and beyond to help out students."

While students at RISD don't "hit the books" in the traditional sense, the in-studio workload is huge. "Our Freshman Foundation program is nicknamed the RISD boot camp," says a senior industrial design student. Students praise faculty members' knowledge and accessibility. "I've been amazed by how a lot of the teachers here are willing to go above and beyond to help out students," cheers one junior, "whether it's staying behind after class to go over work or help them out with internships or their portfolios." Career and academic counseling both get high marks.

RISD students (referred to as "RISDoids" or "Rizdees") come to Providence to form a largely urban mix of styles and personalities. In a word, the school is diverse, and that can create tension. "We are art kids. We act and think like art kids," says a junior. Indeed, only 4 percent of students are native Rhode Islanders, not surprising given the state's small size. Many of the rest are from the vicinity of other East Coast cities, notably New York and Boston. Though highly selective, RISD will often take a chance on students who did not perform well in high school by the usual academic criteria but who make up for that with special artistic talent. The racial makeup of the campus is fairly mixed, with Asian Americans making up 18 percent of the student body, African Americans 2 percent, and Hispanics 7 percent. "We have had many movements towards a greener campus, and towards a greener planet as a whole. Student attitude towards current events is extremely liberal and democratic," says one student. Tuition and fees here are steep; though RISD offers some merit scholarships, athletic scholarships are nonexistent, and the school does not guarantee to meet financial need.

Each year about 60 juniors and seniors venture to Rome for one of two six-month experiences offered through the European honors program.

All noncommuting freshmen must live in co-ed dorms that are comfortable and feature common studio areas and connections to the campus computer network. "All on-campus housing is well maintained, comfortable, and damn luxurious for dorms, with plenty of security," says one film major. "They are all just grossly overpriced." The vast majority of upperclassmen move off campus to nearby apartments, many of which occupy floors of restored homes; RISD also owns an apartment building and some renovated colonial and Victorian houses. All boarders buy the meal plan, which students say has improved as of late. "The food is actually pretty good," admits a senior.

Despite a student body that looks like it could have been plucked from the streets of New York's Greenwich Village, RISD is not the place to come for a wild and funky nightlife. "The social life is mostly centered around friends you work in studio with," explains one sophomore. With three eight-hour studios each week, plus two other classes (and that's just freshman year), "typical social activity is running out for a cup of coffee. If you're desperate, there's always Brown University." Providence also provides some social outlets. The Taproom, shown on the campus map, went dry years ago, and each year, those 21 and over vote on whether to allow drinking in their residences. But underage students can swill. "It is generally easy for underage students to be served," an architecture major says. Though RISD isn't much for traditions, one big annual event is the Artist's Ball, a November formal where dress is "formal or festive, which has been interpreted as everything from chain mail to buck naked," says a senior. When claustrophobia sets in, students can flee to the RISD farm, a 33-acre recreation area on the shores of nearby Narragansett Bay. Boston and New York are one and four hours away by train, respectively.

Though jocks are an endangered species at RISD, recreation opportunities abound. There is no intercollegiate sports program in the ordinary sense, though there is a hockey team, called the Nads (which, of course, leads to RISDoids hollering "Go Nads!"). Students do get involved in intramural sports, ranging from football and baseball to sailing and cycling. There's also a weight room for those who thrive on pumping iron.

Students come to RISD committed to their crafts, and most march to the beat of their own drummers as they rush from studio courses to gallery openings to exhibitions. But this professional preoccupation is not a problem. Students are confident that the endless studio hours are starting them on the path to success. Says a student, "Everyone here is really dedicated to what they are doing, lending a kind of general excitement that I have not seen anywhere else."

Though RISD isn't much for traditions, one big annual event is the Artist's Ball.

Overlaps

Pratt Institute, Maryland Institute College of Art, Parsons School of Design, School of Visual Arts, Cooper Union, Savannah College of Art and Design

If You Apply To ➤

RISD: Early decision: Nov. 1. Regular admissions: Feb. 1. Financial aid: Feb. 15. Application fee: $60. Campus interviews: optional, informational. No alumni interviews. SATs or ACTs: required. No Subject Tests. Essay question: statement of purpose.

Rhodes College

2000 North Parkway, Memphis, TN 38112-1690

Goes head-to-head with Sewanee for the top spot in the pecking order of mid–South liberal arts colleges. Rhodes is the more progressive of the two. While Sewanee has a gorgeous rural campus, Rhodes has Memphis and its red-hot music scene. Economics and international studies head the list of strong programs.

Since 1848, Rhodes College has been instilling the timeless values of truth and honor in Southern sons and daughters, and today increasing numbers of students from the rest of the country are discovering its charms. The school's honor code means exams are not proctored and backpacks are left unattended in the cafeteria. Its small size gives everyone an opportunity to take on leadership roles in campus clubs and organizations, and people are generally "friendly and helpful," says one student. Throw in the college's proximity to Memphis's world-famous Beale Street, barbecue, and

Website: www.rhodes.edu
Location: City Center
Private
Total Enrollment: 1,898
Undergraduates: 1,886
Male/Female: 41/59

(continued)

SAT Ranges: CR 570–690,
   M 580–680

ACT Ranges: 26–31

Financial Aid: 92%

Expense: Pr $ $

Student Loans: 44%

Average Debt: $ $ $

Phi Beta Kappa: Yes

Applicants: 4,138

Accepted: 55%

Enrolled: 25%

Grad in 6 Years: 81%

Returning Freshmen: 92%

Academics: ✐ ✐ ✐ ½

Social: ☎ ☎ ☎

Q of L: ★ ★ ★ ★

Admissions: (800) 844-5969

Email Address: adminfo@
   rhodes.edu

Strongest Programs:

Commerce and Business

Biology

English

Psychology

History

Urban Studies

Archeology

Registration is completed online, and students can get the courses they need to graduate on time.

the blues, and it's clear that Rhodes offers a winning combination. "Rhodes students are generally fun-loving people with passions for academic advancement and community engagement," says a senior.

Rhodes was founded as a Presbyterian school in Clarksville, Tennessee, and it moved to a 100-acre campus in Memphis in 1925. Located in the residential midtown section of the city, Rhodes sits across from a 175-acre park housing the city's largest art museum, a golf course, and the Memphis Zoo, which now has two giant pandas. Whether new or old, all campus buildings are Gothic in style, constructed of Arkansas fieldstone with leaded-glass windows and slate roofs. Thirteen of the original buildings are on the National Register of Historic Places. The $40 million Paul Barret Jr. Library offers Wi-Fi and a coffee shop, along with group study rooms. Recent construction includes a new residence hall to house 140 juniors and seniors.

> "Every professor I've had has been very personable, available, interesting, and invested in the students."

The Rhodes general education curriculum features highly regarded three-course sequences known as Search for Values in the Light of Western History and Religion, and Life: Then and Now. The Search sequence has been part of the Rhodes curriculum for 60 years. To receive a Rhodes degree, students must demonstrate proficiency in 12 areas that form the foundation of the liberal arts. These include being able to critically examine questions of meaning and value, developing excellence in written communication, and understanding how historical forces have shaped human cultures.

Rhodes is especially strong in the natural and social sciences, thanks to labs that have state-of-the-art equipment. A partnership with St. Jude Children's Research Hospital lets students conduct research there in the summers and continue their projects during the next school year. Commerce is the most popular major, followed by biology, English, psychology, and history.

Aside from traditional lecture-style classes, the college offers seminars, honors programs, one-on-one Directed Inquiry tutorials, and interdisciplinary majors. Students who can't find what they want on campus may tap into the Greek and Roman studies program, which offers scholarships for a 24-day travel and study trip to Greece. There's also study abroad in a variety of locations around the world; 63 percent of students participate. The Buckman International Fellows program offers summer internships in Madrid, Hong Kong, and Johannesburg. Rhodes is a member of the Associated Colleges of the South*, and it participates in a second degree program for engineers with Washington University in St. Louis. Rhodes also offers an M.S. in biomedical engineering with the University of Memphis and the University of Tennessee.

The academic climate at Rhodes is "demanding and challenging," according to one student. "Professors expect quality contributions." Nearly all classes taken by freshmen have fewer than 25 students, which means professors are more than talking heads. "Every professor I've had has been very personable, available, interesting, and invested in the students," says a junior and at the end of each semester, students provide anonymous feedback to their profs. Registration is completed online, and though students can get the courses they need to graduate on time, "we often cannot get classes with certain professors until senior year," a junior says.

Like Davidson and Hendrix, Rhodes tends to attract white, Southern, middle- and upper-middle-class students, although minority enrollment is on the rise and students hail from 47 states. "Students tend to be friendly and motivated," a sophomore says. Twenty-seven percent are Tennessee natives; African Americans comprise 6 percent of the student body, Asian Americans 6 percent, and Hispanics add

3 percent. "Representation for minority students is always a hot topic," a student says. Eligible students receive scholarships based on academic merit and the average award tops $16,000. There are no athletic scholarships.

Seventy-one percent of Rhodes students live on campus, where all dorms are air-conditioned and clean. "While expensive, Rhodes dorms are pretty well-maintained," one student says, and most are single sex. Freshmen live in Glassell or Williford, and upperclassmen vie for rooms in the East and West Village apartments during the yearly lottery. "We are in a housing crisis right now, so housing is in chaos," laments one student. "There are too many students and not enough dorms." Students eat in the Refectory or the Lynx Lair; the former has hot food lines for meat eaters and vegetarians, and the latter offers fare such as wraps, sandwiches, and burgers, along with a well-stocked salad bar. "Our two campus dining facilities serve very edible food," reports one student, "and there is typically something for all tastes, preferences, and lifestyles." Students report feeling safe on campus. "Campus security is very friendly and helpful," says one student.

Fraternities draw 37 percent of the men and sororities sign up 54 percent of the women. "Most of Rhodes social life is centered around Greek life, even though only 50 percent of campus is Greek." Chartered buses provide rides to off-campus parties, many of which are sponsored by the Greeks, though independents are welcome to attend. While it's illegal for students under 21 to drink, students say those who are determined can usually find booze—if not at parties, then in other students' rooms. In April, everyone looks forward to the three-day Rites of Spring concert and to the Rites of Play carnival that precedes it, which brings underprivileged kids to campus for a day of food, fun, and games.

> Rhodes fields 10 women's and 10 men's varsity teams, and the Lynx teams compete in Division III.

> **"The entire Rhodes community is incredibly friendly and helpful."**

Lively and energetic Memphis gets so-so marks as a college town, with three other four-year institutions in the area and a number of community colleges as well. There are plenty of clubs and bars, along with live music and arts organizations, volunteer opportunities, and internships. "Service is an integral part of the Rhodes experience," a student says.

Rhodes fields 10 women's and 10 men's varsity teams, and the Lynx teams compete in Division III. The men's and women's basketball, tennis, and cross-country teams, and the women's golf team are among the college's strongest. Half of all students participate in intramurals, where the most popular games are flag football and five-on-five basketball. There are also a number of club sports, including cheerleading, crew, fencing, equestrian, and men's and women's lacrosse. Everyone can use the $22.5 million Bryan Campus Life Center, which boasts squash and racquetball courts and a suspended indoor track.

Rhodes College students adore the school's solid academics and rich Southern tradition. "The entire Rhodes community is incredibly friendly and helpful," says a sophomore. The school's reputation is rising, within and outside the Southeast, leading to what one student calls "explosive growth in enrollment." What hasn't changed is the friendly vibe on campus, and the eagerness of students, faculty, and staff to make sure that you're more than just a number.

Overlaps

Vanderbilt, Tulane, Furman, Washington University in St. Louis, University of the South, Emory, Davidson, Centre

---

If You Apply To >

Rhodes: Early decision: Nov. 1. Early action: Nov. 15. Regular admissions: Jan. 14. Financial aid: Mar. 14. Housing: May 1. Application fee: $45 (paper), free (online). Campus interviews: optional, evaluative. No alumni interviews. SATs or ACTs: required. Subject Tests: optional; required for homeschooled students. Accepts the Common Application. Essay question.

Rice University

6100 Main Street MS-17, Houston, TX 77005-1892

One of the few elite private colleges that keeps tuition relatively affordable. Rice is outstanding in engineering, architecture, and music. With about 3,700 undergraduates, Rice is smaller than many applicants realize. In lieu of frats, Rice has a residential college system like the University of Miami and Yale.

Website: www.rice.edu
Location: City Outskirts
Private
Total Enrollment: 6,484
Undergraduates: 3,848
Male/Female: 51/49
SAT Ranges: CR 660–750,
  M 700–780
ACT Ranges: 30–34
Financial Aid: 64%
Expense: Pr $ $
Student Loans: 25%
Average Debt: $
Phi Beta Kappa: Yes
Applicants: 15,133
Accepted: 17%
Enrolled: 37%
Grad in 6 Years: 92%
Returning Freshmen: 96%
Academics: ✐ ✐ ✐ ✐ ✐
Social: ☎ ☎ ☎
Q of L: ★ ★ ★
Admissions: (713) 348-7423
Email Address: admi@rice
  .edu

Strongest Programs:
Architecture
Biosciences
Engineering
English
History
Music
Nanotechnology
Sociology

Founded nearly a century ago by Texas cotton mogul William Marsh Rice, Rice University has stayed true to its mission of providing unsurpassed programs in science, engineering, the arts, and humanities—with a price tag most families can afford. With its top-notch programs in the liberal arts and sciences and huge endowment (used to keep tuition modest), Rice University is a good deal among top schools. It is the dominant university in the Southwest and second only to Duke in the entire South. Add to that a strong football team, a spirited student body, and an impressive success rate for graduates, and you've got yourself an incredible deal.

Rice was modeled after such disparate institutions as progressive, tuition-free Cooper Union and the more traditional Princeton University. Despite its resemblance to other institutions, Rice maintains distinctive characteristics all its own. The predominant architectural theme of the campus, situated three miles from downtown Houston, is Spanish Mediterranean, and it's surrounded by a row of hedges—the singular buffer between the quiet campus and the sounds of the city. The newest campus addition is the Bio Science Research Collaborative facility.

"Classes are hard."

The students tend to put a lot of pressure on themselves. "Students here are very self-motivated," says a sophomore. "Classes are hard." Science and engineering are the standout programs: Competition in the engineering and premed programs is especially intense, and each year a good number of students who start in these fields retreat to the humanities, which in general are less demanding. In fact, Rice has a long tradition of encouraging double and even triple majors in such seemingly opposite fields as electrical engineering and art history (nearly 40 percent of students earn a double major). Biosciences is the most popular major, followed by psychology, chemical engineering, and mechanical engineering.

Rice has traditionally excelled in the sciences and engineering, and SEs (as these students are called) still dominate the student body. Architecture here is one of the finest undergraduate programs in the nation, and the space physics program works closely with NASA. Under the Mellon Fellow program, selected humanities and social sciences majors may work with a faculty mentor on an academic project that offers a summer research stipend. Under the area-major program, students can draw up proposals for independent interdisciplinary majors. An additional option is the "coherent minor" program, which can replace distribution requirements.

Class size rarely presents a problem; over two-thirds have 19 or fewer students. Faculty members receive high marks, and full professors often teach freshmen. "We have been challenged to think creatively and apply principles," says a student. Everyone operates under the honor system and most exams go unsupervised. There are internships available for engineering and architecture students. The library is stocked with most needed materials and, thanks to a renovation, has become more inviting. Twenty-five percent of students participate in study abroad programs, which are available in 68 countries.

Rice was founded to serve "residents of Houston and the state of Texas," and 46 percent of undergraduates still hail from the Lone Star State. Most of the out-of-staters are transplants from California, Florida, the Northeast, and other Southern states. Rice also ranks below all of its peer institutions except Vanderbilt in its proportion of international students (10 percent). Twenty-two percent of the student body is Asian American, 15 percent is Hispanic, and 7 percent is African American. "You can't really characterize Rice students because there is such a great diversity on campus," says an English major. Because much of the university's $4.6 billion endowment is dedicated to keeping tuition relatively low, Rice costs thousands of dollars less than most other selective, private universities. Rice guarantees to meet the full demonstrated need of every admit. There are merit scholarships available and 210 athletic scholarships are awarded each year. The university has also eliminated loans for students from families with annual incomes below $80,000.

"We have been challenged to think creatively and apply principles."

Fraternities and sororities are forbidden on campus—Rice's founder did not approve of elitist organizations—but their functions are largely assumed by the 11 residential colleges, Rice's version of dorms. Each college has a "faculty master" and houses about 225 students who remain affiliated with it for all four years. Freshmen are randomly assigned to one of the co-ed dorms. Air-conditioning is a standard weapon against Houston's muggy climate, and you may want to keep a can of bug spray handy to ward off mosquitoes during the first few months of the school year. Everyone is guaranteed a room for at least three of the four years, though students go through a lottery. Although two new residential colleges have been added, 25 percent of the students go packing, many seeking quieter surroundings and cheaper rents. Students can eat at any of the college dining halls, where there are plenty of good options. "The food is edible," offers one student, "but there's no getting around the fact that it's cafeteria food."

Under the area-major program, students can draw up proposals for independent interdisciplinary majors.

Houston has a bustling nightlife, but you'd better bring a car to enjoy it. Even though the light rail system makes it easier to get to the city, it's still a challenge to get around—even with free transportation passes. "Houston doesn't have the best public transportation system," says a bioengineering major. Galveston's beaches on the Gulf of Mexico are only 45 minutes away, and heading for New Orleans, especially in February, can make a great weekend trip. "While Rice students can write algorithms and social commentary, they still know how to throw a good party," says one junior. Students don't have time to plan anything more formal on weekends than the traditional TGIF lawn parties on Friday afternoons, but campuswide parties sponsored by one of the residential colleges spring up from time to time. Night of Decadence is Rice's Halloween party, where it is reported that the students appear in "lingerie or less." "The social life is centered around campus parties and pubs," says a student. A classmate adds, "If the themed public parties aren't your thing, you can swing by Willy's Pub for a beer or Lovett Underground for some live music and a cup of coffee." If nothing else, there's always the campus movie.

"The social life is centered around campus parties and pubs."

Ardent football fans abound at Rice; tearing down the goalposts after home victories remains a happy tradition. Other strong Owls programs include baseball (winners of Conference USA titles in 2010 and 2011), men's soccer, women's cross-country, men's indoor track, and both men's and women's tennis. Rice students go really wild for intramurals—the most popular pits the colleges against each other in the Beer-Bike Race, in which co-ed teams of 20 speed around a bicycle track, which gives them a chance to let off academic steam, while onlookers chug beer (or water for those under 21).

Ardent football fans abound at Rice.

"Rice puts a lot of trust and responsibility on its students," a sophomore says. "It's a very maturing experience." As the university grows, it remains to be seen whether it will be able to maintain the close relationships with faculty and the intimate quality of the residential experience that has made it special. When they venture outside the hedges for the last time, students' Rice diplomas open doors to the corporate world. After all, they've had a terrific academic experience and a decent social life for four years, and their wallets haven't been emptied thanks to a relatively modest tuition.

If You Apply To ➤

Rice: Early decision: Nov. 1. Regular admissions: Jan. 1. Financial aid: Mar. 1. Application fee: $75. Campus and alumni interviews: optional, evaluative. SATs or ACTs required. Subject Tests: required (two additional in subjects related to proposed area of study). Accepts the Common Application. Essay question.

University of Richmond

28 Westhampton Way, Richmond, VA 23173

Offers students a preprofessional climate rooted in the liberal arts with touches of the Old South. Though located in the former capital of the Confederacy, there are plenty of Yankee voices on UR's forward-looking campus. Business and a unique school for leadership studies are featured offerings, along with a strong international emphasis. Compare to Bucknell but with urban proximity.

Website: www.richmond.edu
Location: Suburban
Private
Total Enrollment: 3,414
Undergraduates: 2,931
Male/Female: 45/55
SAT Ranges: CR 580–700, M 620–720
ACT Ranges: 28–32
Financial Aid: 69%
Expense: Pr $ $ $ $
Student Loans: 43%
Average Debt: $ $
Phi Beta Kappa: Yes
Applicants: 10,232
Accepted: 30%
Enrolled: 25%
Grad in 6 Years: 83%
Returning Freshmen: 93%
Academics: ✎ ✎ ✎ ½
Social: ☎ ☎ ☎
Q of L: ★ ★ ★
Admissions: (804) 289-8000
Email Address: admissions@richmond.edu

Students at the University of Richmond enjoy a healthy mix of Southern ambience and intellectual rigor that includes small classes, close friendships, and lots of teamwork. A force for progressive liberal arts, UR describes itself as "a private university for the public good." It was a pioneer in leadership studies and continues to expand its international emphasis. Under its unique coordinate system, a holdover from the days of single-sex education, men and women take advantage of separate student governments and traditions. "I've changed here, questioned things I was sure about, and grown so much," says one senior. "Richmond has prepared me for any path I want to follow."

UR's 350-acre campus is nestled amid rolling hills about 15 minutes from downtown Richmond, the state capital. The campus, notable for its stately pines and consistently redbrick collegiate Gothic buildings, wraps around 10-acre Westhampton Lake. The Gottwald Science Center has been expanded and renovated with the latest technology and research equipment. The $20 million Carole Weinstein International Center features an open courtyard with a fountain, surrounded by a cloistered walkway with spiral columns and balconies. A new student activities complex opened in 2013 and contains eight sorority cottages.

> "Study abroad programs are very important here."

All Richmond undergraduates complete general education requirements in communications (including writing and a foreign language) and in six other fields: historical studies, literary studies, natural science, social analysis, symbolic reasoning, and visual and performing arts. Everyone takes a First-Year Seminar in the fall and spring of their first year, with faculty drawn from across the university, on topics ranging from bioethics to art history. Enrollment is capped at 16 students in order to ensure that faculty members can focus on their students' writing. UR is at the forefront of the movement called "digital humanities," and the Digital

Scholarship Lab allows students to mine huge databases in order to look for and generate new knowledge on topics. There is an undergraduate major in philosophy, politics, economics, and law that combines disciplines from the School of Arts & Sciences, Business School, and Law School. Other majors include dance, film studies, and geography. Fifty-seven percent of Richmond students spend at least a summer abroad through one of 55 exchange programs in 75 countries. To encourage globetrotting, the university ponies up the cost of passports. "Study abroad programs are very important here," a student says.

(continued)

Strongest Programs:
Business Administration
International Studies
Leadership Studies
Political Science
Biology

UR boasts the only top 20 undergraduate business school in the nation lodged within a liberal arts institution. Business administration is the most popular major and other popular options include accounting, international studies, political science, and history. The Jepson School of Leadership Studies, founded in 1986 and still unique, draws on the liberal arts to educate students about how they can best serve society. About half of UR students take the foundation leadership course. The Howard Hughes Medical Institutes have given Richmond millions to devise and implement a new freshman-year introductory science course that replaces all the one-semester intro courses in biology, chemistry, and physics—it emphasizes computational science and research methods to speed the top 20 or so of science-oriented freshmen into high-level academic achievement. A new program offers university-paid fellowships for summer research and internships; 300 grants totaling $1.3 million were awarded to undergrads in spring 2013.

"My professors have been absolutely wonderful and inspiring."

Students say competition generally gives way to collaboration in the classroom. "It's a collaborative environment where students learn and experience the benefits of working in teams," says one senior. Richmond students praise the absence of TAs in the classroom. "You often hear horror stories of the huge lecture halls where students buzz in answers and never have contact with their actual professor. Richmond is the exact opposite," a senior says. A classmate adds, "My professors have been absolutely wonderful and inspiring."

A new program offers university-paid fellowships for summer research and internships; 300 grants totaling $1.3 million were awarded to undergrads in spring 2013.

Nearly half of UR students hail from the Northeast, and 19 percent are native Virginians. Foreign students account for 8 percent of the student population. Eight percent of students are African American, 7 percent Asian American, and 7 percent Hispanic. "UR students are the kind of students who wake up in the morning and have a full day scheduled," says one student. "They have classes and meetings and appointments from 8:00 a.m. to 9:00 p.m. They volunteer downtown, they're part of Greek life, they're on a club sport team, and they work on campus. They're pulling As in all their classes and drink entirely too much coffee, but they landed a phenomenal internship for the summer, so it's all worth it." Despite its high sticker price, UR prides itself on being accessible, mainly because it guarantees to meet the demonstrated financial need of all admitted students. The Richmond Scholars program awards 50 full-tuition merit scholarships for every entering class, and student-athletes vie for 170 athletic awards in 16 sports.

Nearly nine out of 10 Richmond students live on campus. "Rooms improve and increase in size as students progress at the University of Richmond," says a student. "There are options for single-sex residence halls, co-ed residence halls (which are suite-style) and apartments (which are built as townhouses). Laundry is included so you never need to search for quarters in order to have clean clothes." The dining hall, or "D-hall," offers hot entrees as well as made-to-order subs, pizza, pasta, burgers, and such. "My favorite option is Mongolian Grill, which is make your own stir-fry," a senior explains. "They also have a gourmet grill cheese bar, a ramen noodle bar, cooked-to-order Angus burgers, and a panini bar. It's an all-you-can-eat facility."

The Richmond Scholars program awards 50 full-tuition merit scholarships for every entering class, and student-athletes vie for 170 athletic awards in 16 sports.

"Traditions are important to Richmond Spiders," says one student. First-year students have Proclamation Night for women and Investiture for men, during which they sign the honor code and write a letter to themselves, which is not opened until senior year. Other regular events range from the Ring Dance, a ball at the elegant Jefferson Hotel where junior women don white gowns and receive their class rings from their fathers, to Festivus, a weekend of carnival games with alumni participating.

"Students are involved in so many clubs and organizations on campus that it fuels social life," says one student. Nonresidential fraternities and sororities attract 13 percent of men and 27 percent of women. For independents or those just tired of the frat-party scene, the Campus Activities Board sponsors movie nights, karaoke, and concerts. The Tyler House Commons has game rooms and a grill and offers video rentals. Although Richmond is more of a small city than a college town, it does have great restaurants, beautiful historic neighborhoods, and plenty of internship opportunities at local corporations and government agencies.

Eager to shed its past image as a "bubble," UR has a strong commitment to the city of Richmond and provides regular transportation downtown. Two-thirds of students are engaged in volunteer programs, donating over 100,000 hours a year. UR is one of the leading college partners of Habitat for Humanity, and students serve at UR's pro bono legal clinic. For those wishing to get away, Williamsburg, Virginia Beach, and Washington, D.C., are not far, and nature buffs also like the river and the nearby backpacking, thanks to the proximity of the Blue Ridge Mountains.

"Traditions are important to Richmond Spiders."

The school's 17 varsity teams (the Spiders) spin their webs in the Division I Atlantic 10 Conference. The men's basketball team made it to the NCAA Sweet 16 in 2011. Women's swimming and diving have won 10 conference titles in the past 11 years, and men's and women's cross-country each brought home a conference title in 2010–11. The football team is a powerhouse as well, and any game against William and Mary draws a crowd for one of the oldest rivalries in Virginia. Fall Saturdays also find throngs of students throwing tailgate parties. Club sports teams are more like fraternities, as members live, eat, and compete together, hosting parties on the side. "They are the way to go!" cheers a senior.

Richmond is working hard to push its vision of preprofessional education shaped by commitments to the liberal arts, leadership, and community involvement. Its students seem to embody the maxim "We work better when we have fun," but a biochemistry major offers this advice: "If you come, plan to work hard."

If You Apply To ➤

Richmond: Early decision: Nov. 15. Regular admissions: Jan. 15. Financial aid: Feb. 15. Housing: May 1. Application fee: $50. Campus and alumni interviews: optional, informational. SATs or ACTs: required. Subject Tests: optional. Accepts the Common Application. Essay question.

Ripon College

300 Seward Street, P.O. Box 248, Ripon, WI 54971

Located where the Republican Party was born in 1854, Ripon is more conservative than Beloit and Lawrence and similar in atmosphere to places like DePauw and Knox. With only about 1,000 students, Ripon is the smallest of the five. Strengths are science, education, and history. About three-fourths of the students are in-staters.

Everything about Ripon College is small, aside from perhaps its academic ambitions. The school is in a tiny Wisconsin town, and there are fewer than 1,000 students, meaning "if you don't go to class, your professor will know," a freshman says. The weather can be a downer, with bitter cold and lots of snow come winter, but the warmth of personal relationships with peers and professors helps to compensate for the frigid temperatures. Says one happy student, "Ripon provides a very comfortable atmosphere where students can really succeed."

Ripon's 250-acre campus sits in a town of 7,000, just off Highway 41 between Fond du Lac and Oshkosh. "The old-fashioned Main Street offers cute shops and restaurants, including a bakery and pizza parlor, and the town's trails and parks are good for recreation," says one student. The college itself features tree-lined walks, wetlands, prairie, and woods, and a mixture of 19th- and 20th-century architecture lends a majestic feel.

"Class grades and projects do not pit students against each other."

Ripon's distribution requirements are arranged around themes: Explore, Select, and Connect. Freshmen take an interdisciplinary seminar and a writing course, as well as one course each in the fine arts, humanities, natural sciences, and social and behavioral sciences. A physical education course is also required, and students must meet a global and cultural studies requirement. Students lay out the rest of their Ripon careers in an individualized learning plan, which may include internships, research, or a senior-year capstone experience. Academics take priority. "While the classes are difficult at Ripon, they are not cut-throat," a senior says. "Class grades and projects do not pit students against each other." There are no teaching assistants, and student-initiated study groups are common. "Professors teach to impart knowledge and foster discussions," a sophomore says, and "professors have office hours for students to come in for extra help."

Ripon's strengths include the sciences, education, and history; students also give high marks to the business curriculum, the arts, communications, and psychology. "From archeological internships in the anthropology department to directing your own plays in the theater department, every program has something unique to offer," says a biology major. Motivated students with AP credits—or just the stamina to take an extra class each term—may finish in three years, thanks to Ripon's accelerated degree program. The forensics team, which dates to 1913 and offers $5,000 scholarships, tests its arguing and advocacy skills in Division I and consistently ranks in the nation's top 20. The Communicating Plus Program emphasizes excellence in written and oral communication and is designed to help students learn to communicate effectively in a variety of life situations.

Ripon students delight in their small classes; 70 percent of those taken by freshmen have 19 or fewer students. Students may take terms away from campus through Ripon programs in Chicago and overseas, or programs sponsored by the Associated Colleges of the Midwest*. An exchange program with Fisk University, a Southern school with mostly African American students, has helped to improve diversity and race relations. In all, students may choose from 25 study abroad programs, which are "phenomenal," according to one student.

"Every program has something unique to offer."

Ripon students are "laid-back, friendly, and positive people," says a student. Three-quarters come from Wisconsin, and most of the rest hail from elsewhere in the Midwest, though a freshman says there are some from as far away as California, Texas, and Hawaii. Most come from middle-class homes, and many are "classic overachievers," says a senior. African Americans comprise 5 percent of the student body, Asian Americans make up 1 percent, and Hispanics add 2 percent. Ripon's claim to fame is its status as the birthplace of the Republican Party, founded on campus on February 28, 1854, to be exact. The school offers merit scholarships averaging

Students lay out the rest of their Ripon careers in an individualized learning plan.

$25,697 but no athletic awards. The Access Ripon College (ARC) program provides no-debt options for qualified students of low-income families. Through a combination of grants and work-study aid, students will have tuition, fees, and room and board covered for four years.

Eighty-eight percent of Ripon students live on campus, since you must petition to live off campus. Freshmen are housed together; students may choose co-ed or single-sex halls, with doubles, singles, or suites. "The dorms are comfortable, clean, and large enough to suit their purpose," offers one student. Ripon has three dining halls—the café-style Terrace; the Pub, with a grill and a la carte options; and the Commons, with a traditional hot-food line. Special tastes are accommodated, but "it remains mass-produced cafeteria food," grumbles one communication major, "which gets tiring after several months."

"Ripon College is not a suitcase school," says one student. "There are many things to do on campus and the college does a great job of bringing in entertainment." Thirty-one percent of the men join fraternities and 28 percent of the women pledge sororities, but the Greeks aren't a major social force. Instead, "alcoholic, non-alcoholic, dance, board game, or movie parties can all be found on a typical night," says a religious studies and history major. Per Wisconsin law, students under 21 aren't permitted to drink, and those caught doing so face fines. The best road trips include nearby Oshkosh and Appleton, or even Milwaukee and Madison. Chicago is a three-hour drive.

Favorite annual traditions include the Springfest concert and carnival and homecoming. At the start of each year, all the churches in Ripon come together to

> **"Ripon College is not a suitcase school."**

host a homemade dinner for students. Though Ripon's winters can be bitterly cold, the college's location in the rugged North Woods means frozen lakes and a blanket of snow are a natural part of the winter landscape. When they tire of their books, students may let off steam with cross-country and downhill skiing, tobogganing, and ice skating—or some fervent cheering for dogsled and iceboat races. And when it's not winter ("for one month during the year," warns one student), nearby Green Lake offers boating, fishing, and other water sports. For those seeking to stay fit and help the environment, Ripon offers the Velorution Project, which provides students with free mountain bikes, painted in Ripon colors, for a year if they pledge to use the bikes as their sole source of wheeled transportation.

Ripon's varsity teams (the Red Hawks) compete in Division III, and matches against Lawrence University usually draw excited crowds, as the Lawrence–Ripon rivalry is one of the oldest in Wisconsin. The football, men's basketball, men's soccer, and softball teams have all ranked highly during recent conference play, and the baseball team brought home Midwest Conference titles in 2012 and 2013. Three-quarters of students participate in intramural sports, which range from basketball and softball to football and inner-tube water polo. "The program is set up into four seasons with two seasons in the fall semester and two in the spring semester. Each sport is also broken up into skill and competitiveness levels," a senior explains.

Ripon College offers a strong grounding in the liberal arts, along with a peaceful, quaint, historical, and friendly community where you'll be much more than a number. "I am on a first-name basis with our dean and president, and it's not because I'm in trouble," a junior says. Though being at such a small place can be stifling, Ripon students aren't complaining. "We are interactive. We are tight-knit. We are a community," one student says. "We are Ripon."

Motivated students with AP credits—or just the stamina to take an extra class each term—may finish in three years.

Overlaps

Carroll, Marquette, St. Norbert, University of Wisconsin–Oshkosh, University of Wisconsin–Madison, University of Wisconsin–La Crosse, Concordia, University of Wisconsin–Whitewater

University of Rochester

Rochester, NY 14627

The name may conjure up a nondescript public university, but Rochester is a quality private university in the orbit of Carnegie Mellon, Case Western Reserve, Johns Hopkins, and Washington University in St. Louis. The university has a scientific bent and a strong reputation for churning out premeds. Has less than half as many undergraduates as neighboring RIT.

The University of Rochester is not afraid of change. This distinguished private university implemented its unique Rochester Renaissance Plan in the mid-1990s, and since then it has never looked back. The plan included reducing class size; making new investments in the library, classrooms, and computer networking facilities; and launching a new curriculum that eliminates entry-level general education courses to allow students to design their own paths.

Founded in 1850, the University of Rochester occupies a snug little 90-acre campus, which nestles up to a bend in the Genesee River. One student acknowledges that the university has "perpetually gray [read: winter] skies," but finds comfort that "it's great for winter sports or studying or even sleeping late on a snowy Saturday." Although a few buildings are modern—the Wilson Commons student center designed by I. M. Pei, for example—most of the older structures come in Greek Revival and Georgian colonial styles. There is an aesthetically pleasing contrast between old and new, and the Eastman Quadrangle, with the library and original academic buildings, adds to Rochester's stately look. Recent construction projects include a new health services building; a five-building, 120-unit dormitory complex; as well as renovations to campus dining facilities and innovative new lab spaces.

> **"Most of the courses will require hours of preparation outside the classroom."**

There are no general education course requirements at Rochester, but all are designed to ensure that students are exposed to the full range of liberal arts. The curriculum—appropriately but unimaginatively known as the Rochester Curriculum—focuses on three classic divisions of learning: humanities and arts; social science; and natural science, mathematics, and engineering. Students choose a major from one of these areas and also complete a cluster of three courses in each of the remaining two divisions. These clusters give students the opportunity for integrated study in diverse fields and the chance to participate in three very different types of learning. Freshmen have the option of taking seminar-style Quest courses, which teach them how to learn and how to make learning a lifetime habit. Quest courses can involve extensive work with original materials, existing and experimental data, and primary texts. Orientation Rochester-style includes a weeklong fall festival called Yellowjacket Weekend designed to help new students "become fully integrated in the university community."

The university's 200 degree programs span the standard fields of study, but Rochester takes special pride in its famed Eastman School of Music. It also excels in

Website: www.rochester.edu
Location: Suburban
Private
Total Enrollment: 8,753
Undergraduates: 5,481
Male/Female: 50/50
SAT Ranges: CR 600–700, M 640–740
ACT Ranges: 28–32
Financial Aid: 83%
Expense: Pr $ $ $ $
Student Loans: 53%
Average Debt: $ $ $
Phi Beta Kappa: Yes
Applicants: 14,987
Accepted: 36%
Enrolled: 23%
Grad in 6 Years: 85%
Returning Freshmen: 96%
Academics: ✍ ✍ ✍ ✍
Social: ☎ ☎ ☎
Q of L: ★ ★ ★
Admissions: (585) 275-3221
Email Address: admit@admissions.rochester.edu

Strongest Programs:
Psychology
Political Science
Financial Economics
Biology
Engineering

the engineering and scientific fields—competition is keen to "beat the mean" among science majors. The Institute of Optics, the nation's first center devoted exclusively to optics, is a leader in basic optical research and theory. Seventy-five percent of students are involved in undergraduate research programs; options include the Research Experience in Physics and Astronomy for Undergraduates (REUs) and the *Journal of Undergraduate Research*. The most popular majors include psychology, political science, and financial economics. Newer programs include American studies, business, optical engineering, audio and music engineering, and digital media studies.

Students say the academic climate at Rochester is challenging. "Most of the courses will require hours of preparation outside the classroom, and attending class is necessary," says a political science and French double major. "Students are challenged intellectually and often must apply theories to real situations and must defend theories in class." Professors are praised for their skills behind the lectern as well as their passion. Rochester's Combined-Admission Programs offer exceptional undergraduates interested in medicine (REMS), engineering (GEAR), or education (GRADE) guaranteed admission to professional or graduate school upon completion of the bachelor's degree. In addition, Rochester's Take Five program offers a tuition-free fifth year that allows students to explore interests outside their major. The Gwen M. Greene Career and Internship Center receives praise for its vigorous preparation of seniors for the job market, and the university sponsors more than 70 foreign study programs, including what one student calls a "chance of a lifetime" British Parliament internship program.

"Students are challenged intellectually."

Thirty-six percent of the students hail from New York State. Many also come from New England, and there's been a large jump in the numbers from Florida, the Midwest, California, and overseas. Asian Americans make up 11 percent of the student body, while African Americans account for 5 percent, and Hispanics another 6 percent. "The students who attend this school are generally laid-back, fun, studious, and kind," says a student. Campus issues include political correctness and anti-sweatshop campaigns, though one student notes political involvement is "lower than might be expected" due to a "lack of free time." Eligible undergraduates receive merit scholarships averaging $13,001. The Rochester Promise initiative offers a $25,000 tuition benefit annually to students who earned their high school diploma in the Rochester City School District and are admitted to the university.

As far as housing is concerned, there's virtually nothing but praise from the 83 percent of students who live on campus all four years. "Dorms are comfortable, modern, high-tech, very generously sized, and well maintained," a senior says. Some of the housing units offer such benefits as computer terminals, telephones with voicemail features, oak floors, and marble trim. All housing offers Internet access. New students are assigned to rooms—usually doubles—and upperclassmen can usually get singles or suites through the lottery. The Susan B. Anthony residence halls come highly recommended. Dormitories are available single-sex, co-ed by floor, and co-ed by room. Though few students choose to live off campus, a new shuttle bus runs to and from the major off-campus living areas. Dormitory students may eat meals in the cafeteria, where a credit system ensures they pay per meal instead of in one lump sum. The fare served in the dining halls receives high ratings from students, especially the a la carte options such as tacos and burritos and the deli bar. The cost, however, draws complaints: "A foot-long Blimpie sub is not worth $10," grouses one student.

Six percent of the men and 9 percent of the women go Greek. Fraternities still contribute heavily to the social life of Greeks and independents alike by sponsoring parties and concerts. UR has its own set of movie theaters, and campus concerts always draw a crowd. "While there are many things to do in the city of Rochester, it seems that most of the social life occurs right on campus," observes one history and psychology double major. Despite the university's best efforts to enforce a stricter alcohol policy, underage drinking still occurs. "This school's policy in no way curtails underage drinking unless students take it upon themselves to obey," one student says. Many students take the free campus shuttle into the greater Rochester area, where they may entertain themselves on the beaches of Lake Ontario, in the International Photography Museum at the George Eastman House, or at the Rochester Philharmonic Orchestra. Favored out-of-town ventures are Niagara Falls, about 70 miles westward, and, for the more venturesome, Toronto, 125 miles farther westward.

Other popular activities include sipping cappuccino at the student union, frequent ski trips, Yellowjacket Weekend, and a spring fling known as Dandelion Day. The Viennese Ball and the Boar's Head Dinner are also popular events. An unofficial Rochester tradition calls for each student to eat a "garbage plate" at the infamous dive called Nick Tahou's before graduating. Wilson Day is an annual day of community service for new and incoming University of Rochester students, and Rochester has been recognized nationally for its high percentage of student volunteers.

> *Fraternities still contribute heavily to the social life of Greeks and independents alike by sponsoring parties and concerts.*

The 23 varsity sports are coming of age at Rochester, and Yellowjacket teams compete in the University Athletic Association. In the last two years, Rochester has captured conference championships in men's basketball, men's and women's swimming and diving, men's squash, men's golf, men's cross-country, and softball. Intramurals are a popular outlet for "ex-jocks from high school who miss their glory days gone by."

> **"Dorms are comfortable, modern, high-tech, very generously sized, and well maintained."**

Even if intramurals aren't your bag, Rochester has an $8 million sports complex, complete with basketball, tennis, squash, and volleyball courts; lighted rooftop tennis courts; a Nautilus fitness center; the Speegle-Wilbraham Aquatic Center with an eight-lane pool; and an indoor track.

In the past, students bemoaned the fact that the school didn't have a wider academic reputation, but that's changing due, in part, to the Rochester Renaissance Plan. Improvements have been made in the curriculum, the facilities, and just about anywhere you look on campus. "Prospective students who are unsure where their academic careers will take them will have no problem finding what excites them intellectually," says a junior. "But more importantly, they will build relationships with others that will last their entire lives." Rochester seems to be winning its battle for a spot among the nation's leading private universities. Now if they could only do something about all that snow.

Overlaps

Cornell, Boston University, SUNY–Binghamton, Brown, Tufts, Washington University in St. Louis, Carnegie Mellon, Yale

---

If You Apply To ➤

Rochester: Early decision: Nov. 1. Regular admissions: Jan. 1. Financial aid: Feb. 15. Application fee: $70 (paper), $35 (online). Campus and alumni interviews: optional, evaluative (required of scholarship candidates). SATs or ACTs: optional. Subject Tests: optional. Musicians apply directly to the Eastman School of Music. Accepts the Common Application. Essay question.

Rochester Institute of Technology

60 Lomb Memorial Drive, Rochester, NY 14623-5604

RIT is the largest of New York's three major technological universities—about double the size of Rensselaer. The school is strong in anything related to computing, art and design, and engineering. In the city built by Kodak (remember them?), photography and imaging are among the tops in the nation. With only a handful of graduate students, RIT is devoted to undergrads.

Website: www.rit.edu
Location: Suburban
Private
Total Enrollment: 14,281
Undergraduates: 12,373
Male/Female: 67/33
SAT Ranges: CR 540–640,
    M 570–680
ACT Ranges: 25–30
Financial Aid: 69%
Expense: Pr $
Student Loans: N/A
Average Debt: N/A
Phi Beta Kappa: No
Applicants: 16,353
Accepted: 58%
Enrolled: 29%
Grad in 6 Years: 63%
Returning Freshmen: 89%
Academics: ✐ ✐ ✐
Social: ☎ ☎ ☎
Q of L: ★ ★ ★
Admissions: (585) 475-6631
Email Address: admissions@
    rit.edu

Strongest Programs:
Photography
Computer Science
Engineering
Biotechnology and
    Bioinformatics
Crafts

The RIT School for American Crafts offers excellent programs in ceramics, woodworking, glass, metalcraft, and jewelry making.

Unlike many liberal arts colleges that prefer that students test the academic waters before deciding on a major or future job plans, RIT focuses on career-oriented and technology-based academics. And unlike many big universities where the academic luminaries shine from research-oriented graduate schools, RIT's spotlight is very definitely on undergraduates. Students seeking up-to-date technological preparation will be at home at RIT. Those who are geared up and ready to "go professional" will be happy to know that the school places more than 3,000 juniors and seniors in full-time paid positions through its co-op program.

While the town of Rochester may sometimes seem like a reluctant host to weekend fun-seekers, it can hardly deny that it is, in fact, a college town; RIT shares the city with six nearby colleges. RIT's main campus, located on 1,300 suburban acres six miles from downtown Rochester, has its own distinctive style—redbrick buildings with sharp, contemporary lines. Additional facilities include the Gordon Field House; the 160,000-square-foot, two-story center includes a 60,000-square-foot field and event venue, an aquatics center for both competition and recreational use, and a fully equipped 16,000-square-foot fitness center.

> **"RIT is known for excelling in photography, engineering, and any computer-related field."**

RIT specializes in carving out niches for itself with unusual programs, and majors are offered in more than 200 fields, from basic electrical and mechanical engineering to packaging science and bioinformatics. Fortunately, applicants narrow the range of choices to a manageable size by applying to one of eight undergraduate colleges: applied science and technology, business, computing and information sciences, engineering, imaging arts and sciences, liberal arts, science, or the National Technical Institute for the Deaf (NTID). As home to NTID, RIT is a leader in providing access services for deaf and hard-of-hearing students.

Predictably, computing and information sciences are among the most popular majors at RIT, as are engineering, photography, engineering technology, and business administration. "RIT is known for excelling in photography, engineering, and any computer-related field," explains a senior, while "any liberal arts majors are less prominent on campus." Academic programs also include aerospace engineering, environmental management, hotel and tourism management, and a physician assistant program. The RIT School for American Crafts offers excellent programs in ceramics, woodworking, glass, metalcraft, and jewelry making, and students have the run of Bevier Gallery, where visiting artists provide firsthand instruction. Other undergraduate programs include chemical engineering, journalism, philosophy, consumer finance, game design and development, public policy, and urban and community studies.

RIT's general education program provides students with more flexibility in meeting requirements. The upshot of this is that the number of required liberal arts credits has been reduced and students may now schedule academic minors—more than 50 have been added within the past few years. Unlike many universities, RIT allows freshmen to schedule significant coursework in their majors early on, and spreads out liberal arts requirements over a more extended period. "You cover a lot of material in a short period of time," says a senior, "leading to a difficult courseload." Undergraduates being the school's top priority, the faculty develops new academic programs to fit career needs. "Professors have a passion for what they teach, and it shows," a biology major says. "The teaching here is outstanding."

Although RIT has its fair share of "typical computer geeks," there are also plenty of outgoing students, especially in the campus clubs and organizations, according to a junior. Forty-six percent of students are from New York State, the remainder coming largely from New Jersey, Pennsylvania, and Connecticut. Five percent of the student body is African American, 6 percent Hispanic, and 5 percent Asian American.

Preprofessionalism is a common bond, but beyond that interests vary. The unique mix of art, engineering, business, and science students, along with the large number of deaf students, creates a diverse atmosphere on campus. Politically, students tend to be aware of global issues and cite war and pollution as hot-button topics. If the men here could change anything, it would likely be the lopsided male/female ratio. RIT admits without regard to student financial need and offers merit scholarships to eligible students, but there are no athletic scholarships.

Fifty-three percent of RIT students live in college dorms and apartments, and students report that getting a room is not that difficult. Freshmen are required to live in the dorms, while upperclassmen can vie for campus apartments on a first-come, first-served basis. But that shouldn't be too tough because, according to the administration, RIT has one of the largest numbers of on-campus apartments in the country. Dorms are highly regarded by most students, are well maintained, and offer a variety of living styles: single-sex, co-ed by room, or co-ed by floor. Special-interest floors range from nonsmoking to "mainstream" (with hearing-impaired students). Vegetarians, vegans, and carnivores will find on-campus meal options to be reasonably diverse. Those who choose to live off campus take advantage of areas serviced by the school shuttle bus. Five percent of men and women choose to go Greek and live and eat in RIT's fraternity and sorority houses. Campus security is "all over campus all of the time," reports one student.

Politically, students tend to be aware of global issues and cite war and pollution as hot-button topics.

"Campus policies on alcohol are very strict," warns a senior, adding, "The policies work because there isn't a lot of partying on campus." The only facilities within walking distance of this sedate suburban campus are a variety of shopping plazas, including one of the largest between New York and Cleveland. Students take road trips to Buffalo, Syracuse, and Canada. For those without transportation, there's always something to do on campus. Drama and other creative arts are less common than parties and movies, but a fine jazz ensemble and a chorus perform regularly. RIT is home to the first ESPN Entertainment Zone area on a U.S. campus as part of student union renovations. Brick City Bash, a favorite way to celebrate the end of a long winter, is held each spring.

"You cover a lot of material in a short period of time."

RIT offers nearly two dozen NCAA Division III athletic teams. The Tigers hockey program competes in Division I and took home the Atlantic Hockey Regular Season Championship title recently. Women's hockey is always at the top of the rankings and the overwhelming sports favorite, a real crowd pleaser that draws even the campus commuters and local residents to the rink. Men's soccer and lacrosse have been recent conference champions. Other sports, such as men's basketball and lacrosse and women's volleyball, have all won ECAC championships in the last two years. Approximately 60 percent of RIT undergrads participate in more than a dozen intramural sports.

Organized and focused, RIT students have their eye on the future. "Students are dedicated and career-oriented, and many go for high degrees," says an imaging science major. And best of all, with all the co-op education opportunities, "we graduate with lots of lab/field/hands-on experience."

Overlaps

Rensselaer Polytechnic, SUNY–Buffalo, Drexel, Clarkson, Worcester Polytechnic, SUNY–Binghamton, Syracuse, Penn State

If You Apply To ➢

RIT: Early decision: Dec. 1. Regular admissions: Feb. 1. Financial aid: Mar. 15. Application fee: $60. Campus and alumni interviews: optional, informational. SATs or ACTs: required. Subject Tests: optional. Accepts the Common Application. Essay question: applicant's choice.

Rollins College

1000 Holt Avenue, Box 2720, Winter Park, FL 32789-4499

Rollins is the marriage of a liberal arts college and a business school that operates under the mantra of "applied liberal arts." A haven for Easterners who want their ticket punched to Florida, Rollins attracts conservative and affluent students and world-class water-skiers. Strong Greek system ensures active, if not diverse, social life. About half the student body comes from outside the Sunshine State.

Website: www.rollins.edu
Location: Small City
Private
Total Enrollment: 2,183
Undergraduates: 1,884
Male/Female: 41/59
SAT Ranges: CR 550–640,
   M 540–640
ACT Ranges: 24–29
Financial Aid: 83%
Expense: Pr $ $
Student Loans: 46%
Average Debt: $ $
Phi Beta Kappa: No
Applicants: 4,542
Accepted: 56%
Enrolled: 20%
Grad in 6 Years: 70%
Returning Freshmen: 84%
Academics: ✍ ✍ ✍
Social: 🍺 🍺 🍺 🍺
Q of L: ★ ★ ★
Admissions: (407) 646-2161
Email Address: admission@
   rollins.edu

Strongest Programs:
Organizational Communication
Psychology
Economics
International Affairs
English

Move over, Mickey Mouse. Stand back, Shamu. You're not the only attractions in central Florida. For students looking to hit the books under the ever-present Florida sunshine, there's also Rollins College. Located in Winter Park, a quiet suburb of Greater Orlando, Rollins offers students plenty of places to have fun when making the grade gets to be too much. "Situated 10 minutes from Orlando and from Disney World, Rollins is close to hundreds of internships and job opportunities just waiting for the next ambitious student," says one satisfied senior.

Rollins's lakefront campus is nationally recognized for its beauty and signature Spanish Mediterranean architecture, featuring stucco buildings, tile roofs, carved woodwork, and decorative balconies. Capitalizing on its location on beautiful Lake Virginia, campus planners have succeeded in combining the natural beauty of the lakeside with consistent architecture. Strong Hall is currently under construction and will accommodate 60 to 80 students in rooms configured as semi-suite residences.

The general education requirements expose Rollins students to various perspectives and areas of knowledge. Students take classes in foreign languages, quantitative reasoning, communication across the curriculum, decision making and valuation, and writing and writing reinforcement. Other requirements include art, Western and non-Western cultures, contemporary American society, and science. For freshmen acclimating to college, the fall-semester Rollins Conference Course eases the transition by placing them into groups of 15 to discuss themes such as imaginary voyages, contemporary ethical issues, and the environment. Each group has a professor-advisor and two upperclassmen peer mentors. Rollins's living/learning communities allow students to live near each other and enroll together in multiple courses; students also have the opportunity to pursue independent research, travel abroad, and take service-learning classes where they earn credit by volunteering in the community.

"It's a great idea to join fraternity and sorority life."

Students give the psychology department their highest marks, and also praise English, education, and international business. The chemistry department turned out a Nobel Prize winner and the Annie Russell Theatre hosts productions staged by the active theater department. An Accelerated Management Program allows qualified freshmen to gain guaranteed admission to the Roy E. Crummer Graduate School of Business when they enter Rollins, leading to B.A. and M.B.A. degrees in five rather than six years.

While the workload at Rollins varies by major, academics are important. "It is a laid-back environment without too much pressure. However, there are opportunities for students to pack on more rigorous courseloads depending on personal preferences," says a music major. Students find there's always help from the professors, with whom they have close relationships. There are no TAs here; teaching is the responsibility of professors, who are said to be "extremely helpful and who only want to see you succeed and find your passion," according to one student. Many students take advantage of Rollins's study abroad program, which offers programs in Australia (a Rollins academic specialty), Germany, and Spain, as well as internships in England, for regular tuition costs. Additional internships and research opportunities are available in Costa Rica, Scotland, Belize, China, Vietnam, and Peru, among others.

"The students at Rollins are either very wealthy and enjoying the campus for the extracurricular activities, Greek Life or entertaining classes," muses one student, "or they are hardworking, receiving academic scholarship and shaping the campus by leading organizations." Forty-three percent of Rollins students are from outside Florida. The student body is 4 percent African American, 13 percent Hispanic, and 3 percent Asian American. While many of the students come from affluent families, adequate financial aid is available, with merit scholarships averaging $18,325 for qualified students and 161 athletic scholarships given to male and female standouts.

Sixty-eight percent of the college's students live on campus in spacious co-ed dorms. "Dorms are really nice," a student says, and feature "big rooms and hardwood floors." For those who prefer to live off campus, "there are plenty of houses and apartments near the campus that can be rented at a reasonable cost," according to one student. Dining facilities are located in the campus center and food is charged on a credit-card system, so students eat when they want and pay only when they eat. One student says, "The food is a little on the pricey side, but it is delicious." And what about safety? "Campus security is top of the line and super friendly," a senior says. Security officers patrol the campus around the clock and call boxes are available throughout the campus.

> **"Students can expect to find a safe haven, a real college experience, and a good escape from the hustle and bustle."**

The high-powered Greek scene claims 29 percent of the men and 35 percent of the women, so there's always a party somewhere. "Social life is big at Rollins," says a recent graduate. "It's a great idea to join fraternity and sorority life: you'll get that social experience, find your own good group of friends, and become more involved on campus." There are movies on Mills Lawn or "dive-in" movies at the pool, lipsynch contests, and live bands in the campus center. "Although there are a great deal of fun activities on campus, the sheer fact that the Disney and Universal theme parks as well as the city of Orlando are so close to the campus means that there is also always something going on off campus as well," says a junior. The administration has clamped down on the social scene, with party monitors checking IDs and a student activity director attending each on-campus party. Underage students caught drinking alcohol will be referred to Rollins's judicial affairs. A senior warns, "If you get caught, you're in major trouble!" Popular road trips include Cocoa Beach, Orlando, Miami, and Tampa.

"Winter Park isn't a typical college town," says one student. "It is one of the oldest cities in Florida, has a charming restaurant and shopping street known as Park Avenue, and is family friendly." Fox Day is "a sacred tradition"—the president cancels classes for the day by placing a fox statue on the front lawn. Students look forward to the tradition every spring and, though they never know exactly which day the president will choose, almost everyone heads for the beach once the day arrives. Many students volunteer with programs such as Habitat for Humanity and tutoring at local schools. Orlando's offerings include entertainment complexes like Downtown Disney and Universal Citywalk, and theme parks such as Walt Disney World, Epcot Center, and Universal Studios.

Sports are an integral part of the Rollins scene. The Tars teams have claimed more than 20 national championships and a plethora of conference titles. Competitive teams include men's and women's soccer, men's basketball, women's basketball (2012 conference champs), women's golf, and softball. Waterski is a perennial powerhouse and men's rowing participated in post-season play recently. Intramural

Forty-three percent of Rollins students are from outside Florida.

The high-powered Greek scene claims 29 percent of the men and 35 percent of the women, so there's always a party somewhere.

Overlaps

University of Florida, University of Central Florida, Florida State, University of Miami, Stetson, College of Charleston, Southern Methodist, Elon

sports are popular, too, with more than 20 leagues and events during the school year. Teams have been formed for table tennis, bowling, and other sports.

Rollins's students enjoy sand and sun, as well as a tough academic climate and a strong sense of history. As the oldest recognized college in the state of Florida, Rollins enjoys the warmth of a blazing sun, a rich legacy, and smooth-as-silk Southern character. Says one senior, "Students can expect to find a safe haven, a real college experience, and a good escape from the hustle and bustle" of the real world.

Rose–Hulman Institute of Technology

5500 Wabash Avenue, Terre Haute, IN 47803

Co-ed since 1995, Rose–Hulman offers the rare combination of technical education and personal attention. Only Caltech, Clarkson, and Harvey Mudd offer comparable intimacy and a technical academic environment. Nearby Indiana State and St. Mary's of the Woods help mitigate the skewed gender ratio. RHIT is among the few engineering schools with significant study abroad offerings.

Website: www.rose-hulman.edu

Location: Suburban

Private

Total Enrollment: 2,158

Undergraduates: 2,093

Male/Female: 79/21

SAT Ranges: CR 560–670, M 630–730

ACT Ranges: 27–32

Financial Aid: 98%

Expense: Pr $ $ $

Student Loans: 71%

Average Debt: $ $ $ $

Phi Beta Kappa: No

Applicants: 4,469

Accepted: 66%

Enrolled: 21%

Grad in 6 Years: 82%

Returning Freshmen: 94%

Academics: ✍ ✍ ✍

Social: ☎

Q of L: ★ ★

Admissions: (812) 877-8213

Email Address: admissions@rose-hulman.edu

The Rose–Hulman Institute of Technology may not be as well known as Caltech, MIT, or even Carnegie Mellon, but it was the first private college to offer an undergraduate degree in chemical engineering, and it continues to innovate today. If you can stomach the lopsided male/female ratio and the limited list of majors (all in engineering and the sciences), Rose offers an outstanding technical background and bright prospects for future employment. Students are smart, motivated, and highly competitive, and love using their computers for work and play. "We are all dorks," says a senior. "Some of us just hide it better than others."

"We are all dorks."

Established in 1874, Rose–Hulman is the oldest private engineering school west of the Alleghenies. Its benefactors were Chauncey Rose, an entrepreneur who brought the railroad to Indiana, and the Hulman family, owners of the Indianapolis Speedway, who gave their fortune to the institution in 1970. (A Hulman family member is the person who says, "Ladies and gentlemen, start your engines" every year before the race.) The 200-acre campus includes numerous trees, two small lakes, and a student apartment complex. Lakeside Residence Hall opened in 2012.

General education requirements at Rose include math, physics, chemistry, and humanities and social sciences. Humanities professors "are very eager to educate and expose science- and engineering-oriented people to a different way of thinking," an applied biology major says. In the first quarter, freshmen must take a life skills course that covers such topics as time management and study skills.

Students in every program except math must work in a team and complete a project for an outside company. Rose–Hulman Ventures is a business incubator program that allows students to gain experience in product development, while Fast-Track Calculus compresses three quarters of calculus into five intense weeks before the start of freshman year. For those in need of new vistas, there are opportunities to study abroad in a bevy of international locales, including Italy, Norway, South

Korea, Russia, and Turkey; 4 percent of students participate. In addition, students may apply to study abroad with a non-RHIT program and receive credit toward their degree. The Home for Environmentally Responsible Engineering (HERE) program aims to integrate residential learning with a specialized pilot curriculum in which sustainability is incorporated into special sections of required courses.

"The courses at Rose are very challenging and demanding," says one sophomore, "and most people who come here want to do very well academically." Regardless of which discipline you choose, odds are you'll find faculty members eager to help, plus plenty of free tutoring if you need it. "Our professors love to teach," one student explains. "Research and side projects come in as a distant second to teaching." Thirty-three percent of classes have 19 or fewer students. "There is no such thing as a teaching assistant at Rose," a software engineering major says.

The typical Rose–Hulman student is "very motivated and curious," says a senior. "We have everything from multisport athletes to introverted gamers," adds a junior, "but since we're all engineers it kind of keeps everyone together." African Americans comprise 3 percent of the student body, and Asian Americans make up 4 percent, while Hispanics add 3 percent. Hot issues tend to center on campus issues rather than those of global concern. "Students are conservative but don't really get involved politically," one senior explains. Merit scholarships are available, averaging $10,527, but there are no athletic awards.

Sixty-two percent of students live on campus. Freshmen are guaranteed rooms in the dorms, as are any sophomores who want them. The residence halls boast weekly maid service, and "we're allowed to do almost anything to the rooms, like add lofts or decks to gain space," says a civil engineering major. (At an engineering school, would you expect anything less?) All but two dorms have air-conditioning. Most upperclassmen move into Greek houses or find other off-campus digs, students say. There's a traditional cafeteria, as well as a restaurant-style dining facility, and students say you won't go hungry, as there are typically at least five entrée choices at each meal plus fresh fruit, and steak and seafood on Friday nights. "They certainly make provisions for vegans, vegetarians, and students who are allergic to certain types of food, and will even make sack lunches if you are unable to attend lunch during the day," a senior says. As for safety, "there is essentially zero crime on campus," according to one student.

The town of Terre Haute has some restaurants, a mall, a Starbucks, and two movie theaters, but generally, it's "sleepy and lacking in nightlife, so we create our own," says a physics major. Various groups, including the Greek organizations and Habitat for Humanity, help the town out with various service projects. There are eight fraternities and three sororities, which draw 26 percent of the men and 23 percent of the women, respectively. "The girl/guy ratio here definitely hurts social life," confides a student, "but overall it's not bad." When it comes to alcohol, the Rose–Hulman campus is officially dry, but the unofficial policy is "out of sight, out of mind," says a senior. "As long as you aren't doing anything stupid or being disruptive, you will be left alone." Students say the best weekend activities are usually road trips to Chicago, Cincinnati, Indianapolis, or St. Louis, all within a few hours' drive. Everyone looks forward to the homecoming bonfire, and to basketball games against DePauw. "Homecoming is very big," says a sophomore. "Freshmen build up and guard the bonfire the week preceding homecoming while upperclassmen try to sabotage it," explains a junior.

Varsity teams (the "Engineers") play in Division III, and the baseball, softball, and men's and women's soccer teams are the most competitive; men's soccer, baseball, women's volleyball, and men's and women's tennis each brought home conference titles in recent seasons. If you're envisioning Rose–Hulman students as

> "Students are conservative but don't really get involved politically."

The HERE program aims to integrate residential learning with a specialized pilot curriculum in which sustainability is incorporated into special sections of required courses.

If you're envisioning Rose–Hulman students as pasty-faced lab dwellers, you're sorely misinformed.

Overlaps

Purdue, University of Illinois, Colorado School of Mines, Rensselaer Polytechnic, Indiana University, Rochester Institute of Technology, Worcester Polytechnic, Ohio State

pasty-faced lab dwellers, you're sorely misinformed. Sixty-two percent of students participate in intramurals, with softball, basketball, and volleyball the most popular, and the Indianapolis Colts even use Rose's facilities for monthlong summer camps.

Students committed to careers in engineering or the sciences will find a top-flight education at this Midwestern technical school. While Rose "doesn't have that big-school pride" so common in this part of the country, students appreciate the feel created by the small classes and school's small size. "Our community atmosphere makes us different from anywhere else," a junior says. "Where else do you know the dean of students by his first name? Or talk to your professors while you are working out?"

If You Apply To > **Rose–Hulman:** Rolling admissions. Application fee: $40 (paper), free (online). Campus and alumni interviews: optional, informational. SATs or ACTs: required. Subject Tests: optional. Accepts the Common Application. No essay question.

Rutgers–The State University of New Jersey

65 Davidson Road, Piscataway, NJ 08854-8097

Rutgers is a huge institution spread over three regional campuses and 29 colleges or schools. Rutgers College on the New Brunswick campus is the most prominent. Everything is available: engineering, business, pharmacy, the arts, and the nation's largest women's college (Douglass College in New Brunswick). Recent arrival of big-time football is a mixed blessing.

Website: www.rutgers.edu
Location: Small City
Public
Total Enrollment: 48,070
Undergraduates: 39,966
Male/Female: 50/50
SAT Ranges: CR 500–620, M 540–670
ACT Ranges: N/A
Financial Aid: 53%
Expense: Pub $ $ $ $
Student Loans: 57%
Average Debt: $ $ $
Phi Beta Kappa: No
Applicants: 46,184
Accepted: 60%
Enrolled: 28%
Grad in 6 Years: 75%
Returning Freshmen: 91%
Academics: ✍ ✍ ✍ ✍
Social: ☎ ☎ ☎
Q of L: ★ ★ ★
Admissions: (732) 932-4636

Life at Rutgers University is all about choice. Choices between the more than 100 undergraduate majors and 4,000 courses offered among its campuses in New Brunswick, Newark, and Camden. Choices about which of the more than 400 student organizations to join. Even choices about which library to visit, as there are 18 branches with holdings of more than three million volumes university-wide. "Rutgers's best quality is its wide variety of majors, classes, and social activities," says one junior.

Rutgers University has three regional campuses (Camden, Newark, and New Brunswick/Piscataway). Rutgers–New Brunswick/Piscataway, which has the largest concentration of students, is composed of five smaller campuses located along the Raritan River. The campuses are connected by a free university bus system and students travel among campuses to take classes. Rutgers–Newark is in a downtown section of Newark, giving the campus neighborhood a collegiate feel. The smallest campus in the Rutgers system is in Camden, located one stop away from the shopping and cultural offerings of downtown Philadelphia. For those seeking a broad-based education, the university has eight liberal arts schools spread out among its campuses. Seven colleges cater to the needs of students wanting a preprofessional school (business, nursing, life and environmental studies, fine and performing arts, engineering, and pharmacy).

"I completely revere most of my professors."

Among the nearly 100 majors, the most popular include psychology, biological sciences, and accounting. Especially strong academic programs include accounting, history, political science, and chemistry. The workload is steady for most students; science majors and pharmacy students can expect the heaviest load. "The courses here require a great deal of thought and outside preparation if you want to be successful," says a political science major. Other majors include cell biology and neuroscience, genetics and microbiology, biomedical engineering, evolutionary anthropology, and allied health technology. As at any big state university, registration can sometimes be a headache, but the advent of online registration has helped.

In an effort to reverse the traditional exodus of New Jersey high school superstars from the state, Rutgers offers a variety of honors programs, including special seminars, internships, independent projects, and research opportunities with the faculty. Rutgers also provides its undergraduates with a chance to study abroad in Great Britain, Costa Rica, France, Germany, India, Ireland, Israel, Italy, Mexico, Switzerland, and Spain. Biology students have the run of the 370-acre Rutgers Ecological Preserve and Natural Teaching Area. In addition, Rutgers is home to more than 100 specialized research centers and institutes dedicated to the study of topics ranging from ancient Roman art to mountain gorillas. Professors generally get high marks. "I completely revere most of my professors," says a junior. "They are intelligent, well respected in their fields, and present dynamic lectures."

Although the administration has been attempting to increase the number of out-of-staters, 95 percent of Rutgers students hail from New Jersey. Nevertheless, the student population is as diverse as that of the state, with a good proportion of students from cities, suburbs, farms, and seaside communities. Minorities account for nearly half the students: 11 percent are African American, 15 percent are Hispanic, and 25 percent are Asian American. "I feel I've grown so much here and learned so much about being a member of a rich and diverse community," explains one senior. The school's administration takes pride in its Committee to Advance Our Common Purpose, for students who want to reduce prejudice and promote diversity on campus. In the past, the committee developed a webpage for multicultural resources and submitted a proposal for the creation of an Intercultural Relations Study Group. The school does not guarantee to meet the full demonstrated need of every admit. About 400 students receive athletic scholarships in a wide range of sports, and more than 6,500 receive merit awards.

On-campus housing in New Brunswick accommodates approximately 41 percent of full-time students. "There has been a big push recently to renovate the dorms, so most of them are really nice," says a history major. Another student says, "With the exception of a few mediocre dorms for freshmen, most are extremely large and have air-conditioning; some have free cable TV; and a good number are hardwired for Internet access." On-campus housing options include conventional dorms, special-interest areas, and apartment complexes with kitchens and living rooms. The university also offers a special dormitory for students who are trying to overcome addictions to drugs and alcohol.

The city of New Brunswick is an attractive place to go for a drink or dinner on the town. Just don't stray too far from the campus. Rutgers has its own police department that possesses the same training and powers as the New Jersey State Police. "I personally don't feel safe in New Brunswick, so I restrict my outings to on-campus locations," one student admits. For those who want to hit the road for fun, New York City and Philadelphia are each only about an hour's drive or train ride, and students flood the Jersey Shore in springtime. The Rutgers College Program Council offers trips ranging from white-water rafting to mountain climbing to skiing. "The variety of activities at Rutgers provides you with the opportunity to have fun any way you desire," says one student. "There are lots of on-campus social activities," a senior explains, including "movies, coffeehouses, local and bigger bands, lectures, and parties. Off-campus activities include frat parties and bars." Over a recent five-year period, students enrolled in the Citizenship and Service Education Program at Rutgers contributed more than 90,000 hours of service to communities across New

(continued)

Email Address: admissions@
ugadm.rutgers.edu

Strongest Programs:
Accounting
History
Pharmacy
Biological Sciences
Political Science
Psychology
Engineering
Chemistry

As at any big state university, registration can sometimes be a headache.

"I feel I've grown so much here."

The Greek system, which attracts only a small percentage of men and women, is entirely off campus.

Jersey. "Students definitely get involved in the surrounding community and do a lot of volunteer work," says a senior.

The Greek system, which attracts only a small percentage of men and women, is entirely off campus. While the school neither owns nor administers any of the Greek organizations, it does have a university office for Greek affairs, which oversees the welfare of those belonging to fraternities and sororities. Students say a lot of the nightlife for the New Brunswick campus takes place at the Greek houses. Reportedly, it is "difficult to drink in dorms," but underage students drink if they really want to.

"The variety of activities at Rutgers provides you with the opportunity to have fun any way you desire."

Each college has its own student center with pinball machines, pool tables, bowling alleys, and a snack bar. Major social events include Reggae Day at Livingston, Agricultural Field Day at Cook, and Oktoberfest for the campus as a whole. Pioneer Pride Night is Camden's big party. During homecoming, tailgate parties are held in the stadium parking lot, featuring tons of food (including roast pigs and whole sides of beef), continuous music, and thousands of revelers.

Varsity, intramural, and club sports fill whatever gap is left by the social scene. In fact, the university fields more than 1,000 athletes—among the most of any university in the nation. The Rutgers baseball team is competitive, as are many other Scarlet Knights teams, including football, tennis, lacrosse, soccer, and track. Women's basketball, fencing, soccer, softball, field hockey, tennis, and track teams are also strong. Rutgers is eliminating seven sports, including men's and women's swimming and men's cross-country. The firing of the men's basketball coach for his abusing of players attracted unwanted publicity and allegations that the administration's ambitions for athletic success were getting out of hand. A member of the Big East in football, Rutgers has experienced a regular season resurgence in recent years.

Rutgers has a plethora of people and programs characteristic of a large state university. It also offers a lot more, including loyal support from the state's legislature and private sector and tuition that is relatively affordable. Says one satisfied student: "From the diversity of its majors and courses to the hundreds of student organizations on campus, Rutgers gives me a chance to explore a world of options."

Overlaps

Montclair, College of New Jersey, NYU, Penn State, Rowan University

If You Apply To >

Rutgers: Regular admissions: Dec. 1. Application fee: $65. No campus or alumni interviews. SATs or ACTs: required. No Subject Tests. No essay. Apply to particular school.

University of St. Andrews: See page 367.

College of St. Benedict and St. John's University

P.O. Box 7155, Collegeville, MN 56321-7155

The College of St. Benedict (CSB) and St. John's University (SJU) are throwbacks to the way colleges were 50 years ago: men and women on separate campuses and copious amounts of school spirit. Roman Catholics comprise about 58 percent of the students, and monastic communities are very active on both campuses. Nearly 80 percent of the students are from Minnesota.

Remember when women's colleges had nearby brother schools, when dorms were single-sex, and when visitors of the opposite gender were only welcome at certain times? No? Well, you might ask your grandparents. Or you could visit the College of St. Benedict and St. John's University. These two single-sex campuses are five miles apart and have their own presidents, but they share a common heritage and mission: Students and faculty join together in a shared liberal arts education, guided by principles of their Benedictine founders. The schools' small sizes and strong sense of tradition give rise to a tight-knit community. "Everyone smiles or says hello to one another and opens doors for each other, even if they don't know them," says a junior economics major. "There is a great sense of community, and everyone is so warm and welcoming."

Owned and operated by the largest men's Benedictine monastery in the world, St. John's occupies 2,500 pristine acres in rural Minnesota, an area filled with forests, lakes, and the wide-open spaces perfect for outdoorsy types. The two colleges are connected by a free and frequent shuttle bus. Alongside a 130-year-old quadrangle erected by monks is a strikingly modern church designed by Marcel Breuer. St. Benedict is a cohesive 800-acre campus comprised of redbrick buildings and cobblestone walks. Together, the colleges have invested millions in facilities in recent years. Centennial Commons opened in 2012 and houses 124 upperclassmen; enhancements to the athletic facilities are underway.

St. Benedict and St. John's share a joint academic program through which students take classes together on both campuses. The core curriculum requires a first-year seminar and the Ethics Common Seminar, and students must fulfill requirements in a number of areas, including the humanities, natural sciences, social sciences, fine arts, theology, and foreign language. An honors program serves exceptional freshmen, and upper-class students may also apply. The global business leadership program capitalizes on the school's international ethos and programming. Students give high marks to science programs such as premed, chemistry, and the environmental studies major, as well as to education. The environmental studies program is one of the few in the country that is interdisciplinary, and it benefits from access to the area's natural resources and the largest solar farm in the upper Midwest. Undergraduate research is becoming more prevalent, and there is an endowed summer research program in the health and medical areas. The theology program benefits from abundant resources, including the Hill Museum & Manuscript Library, one of the foremost microfilm collections of centuries-old handwritten manuscripts.

> "There is a great sense of community."

"While the coursework may be more strenuous than a typical school, the emphasis on small student-to-faculty ratios provides a sort of guiding hand through challenging studies," says one English major. Very few classes have more than 30 students, and some fill up fast. The small classes encourage strong student/faculty ties. "My professors have always been very helpful and knowledgeable. I have never been disappointed in the quality of education I am receiving from them," says a senior. Members of the monastic communities make up under 5 percent of the CSB/SJU faculty. For those who tire of the Minnesota winters, which can start in October and run until April, faculty-led international study programs are offered in 14 countries on six continents, including new programs in Guatemala and India. Each program is limited to about 30 students, and more than half of CSB/SJU students take part. Numerous shorter trips are offered during semester break and summer break.

Known as "Bennies" or "Johnies," CSB/SJU students "tend to be honest, fun, hardworking, and—most importantly—loyal and respectful," according to a junior. Fifty-eight percent of students are Roman Catholic, 78 percent are from Minnesota, and most are white. African Americans and Hispanics constitute 6 percent of the student body, and Asian Americans add another 5 percent. International students

Website: www.csbsju.edu
Location: Small City
Private
Total Enrollment: 3,920
Undergraduates: 3,860
Male/Female: 47/53
SAT Ranges: CR 480–590, M 480–610
ACT Ranges: 23–28
Financial Aid: 94%
Expense: Pr $ $
Student Loans: 72%
Average Debt: $ $ $ $
Phi Beta Kappa: No
Applicants: 3,533
Accepted: 76%
Enrolled: 35%
Grad in 6 Years: 79%
Returning Freshmen: 89%
Academics: ✑ ✑ ✑
Social: ☎ ☎ ☎
Q of L: ★ ★ ★
Admissions: (800) 544-1489
Email Address: admissions@csbsju.edu

Strongest Programs:
Biology
Chemistry
Economics
Music
Psychology
Education
Nursing
Management

Undergraduate research is becoming more prevalent, and there is an endowed summer research program in the health and medical areas.

account for 6 percent of the student population. Politically, "we encompass all viewpoints," a junior says, "from ultraconservative to ultraliberal," and hot topics include gender issues, homosexuality, and abortion. Merit scholarships averaging $13,569 are available, although there are no athletic scholarships.

Through a four-year residential program, 85 percent of students live on campus. The residence halls are staffed partly by members of the monastic communities, but students aren't made to feel like a nun is watching their every move. "Housing is very comfortable and clean," says one Hispanic studies major. "All students can get a room without any problem." Each room has a sink, plus wireless Internet connection for each student. One thing they don't have is overnight visits from members of the opposite sex. Other options include on-campus apartments, such as Flynntown, an independent living area for upperclass students that features a number of different options and has a central student center. Students can choose from four dining halls on either campus and most report the fare to be tasty and diverse. Students report feeling safe on campus. "Campus security is good and does make me feel safe," says one student.

Since there are no fraternities or sororities here, students have learned to make their own fun. SJU's Stephen B. Humphrey Fine Arts Theater and CSB's Benedicta Arts Center host a wide variety of cultural events. "We have a thriving social life at college off campus and on campus," reports one senior. "We have a club called JEC (Joint Events Council) that plans a lot of on-campus events and activities at least every week." Says a sophomore. "Off campus, there are many things to do in St. Cloud and also in St. Joseph, such as parties, coffee shops, restaurants, shopping, and movies." Alcohol is available to those over the age of 21, but students report that underage drinkers face stiff penalties if caught imbibing.

"Housing is very comfortable and clean."

The activities of St. Cloud (metro population nearly 200,000) are less than 10 minutes away by car, and the Twin Cities are about an hour away. Each year, students look forward to the Festival of Cultures, Fruit-at-the-Finish Triathlon, the Senior Farewell, and spring break trips involving community service. Also popular is the annual Pines music festival, which welcomes the spring with a day of concerts featuring popular national acts.

The football team is a perennial Division III powerhouse, and its rivalry with St. Thomas is as strong as ever. Curiously enough, a team of guys known as the Rat Pack gets students psyched up for games. The St. Benedict basketball team is a regular conference champion. Men's lacrosse have made seven consecutive trips to the Division II national championships. Men's track and field and cross-country and men's soccer and volleyball also brought home conference championships recently. Nonvarsity students can participate in a variety of club and intramural sports. CSB/SJU students can enjoy such activities as kayaking and indoor rock climbing through the Outdoor Leadership Center, and St. Benedict women can go on outdoor recreation trips with the Women's Expedition program.

Students at these two Catholic schools "are genuinely friendly, relaxed, motivated, and outgoing," a junior says. Those who attend CSB/SJU revel in the schools' small-town setting, their traditions, and the grounding that comes from their shared Benedictine values. "Our school is welcoming," a sophomore says. "The campus is beautiful, but the people make it what it is."

Overlaps

University of St. Thomas, University of Minnesota–Twin Cities, Gustavus Adolphus, University of Minnesota–Duluth, St. Olaf, St. Cloud State, Minnesota State, University of Wisconsin–Madison

If You Apply To ➤

St. Benedict and St. John's: Early action: Nov. 15. Regular admissions: Jan. 15. Financial aid: Mar. 15. Housing: May 15. No application fee. Campus and alumni interviews: optional, informational. SATs or ACTs: required. Accepts the Common Application. Essay question.

St. John's College

Annapolis Campus: P.O. Box 2800, Annapolis, MD 21404-2800
Santa Fe Campus: 1160 Camino Cruz Blanca, Santa Fe, NM 87505-4599

Books, books, and more books is what you'll get at St. John's—from Thucydides to Tolstoy, Euclid to Einstein. St. John's attracts smart, intellectual, and nonconformist students who like to talk (and argue) about books. Easy to get in, not so easy to graduate. One of the few institutions with two coequal campuses. Students admitted to one can spend time at the other.

With no traditional professors, departments, or majors, few lectures, and a combined total of just over 1,000 students on its two campuses, St. John's College is about as far from the typical postsecondary experience as you can get. Or maybe it's much closer to what college used to be—after all, the Annapolis campus traces its roots to King William's School—the Maryland colony's "free" school—founded in 1696. More than two centuries later, in 1964, St. John's opened a second campus in Santa Fe, New Mexico, to facilitate a doubling of enrollment and offer its super-serious students a change of scenery. While the campuses may be a thousand miles apart, the Johnnies who populate them share an all-consuming quest for knowledge in the classical tradition. Their true teachers are the Great Books, about 150 of the most influential works of Western civilization. "One of the beautiful things about the St. John's program and its focus on the unchanging questions of mankind is that it changes very little," says a student. "I appreciate the sense that I am studying something permanent and real."

> "There is a real sense of community."

Physically, the two St. John's campuses are more than just two time zones from one another. The colonial brick structures of the small urban campus in Annapolis, where the central classroom building dates from 1742, are squeezed into the city's historic district. With the Maryland state capitol and the U.S. Naval Academy in the neighborhood, this campus exudes old-world charm, and its location at the confluence of the Severn River and the Chesapeake Bay allows students to participate in sailing, crew, and individual sculling. The Santa Fe campus sits on 250 acres on the outskirts of the sun-drenched capital of New Mexico. The adobe-style buildings reflect Spanish and Native American traditions, and their perch in the Sangre de Cristo Mountains offers beautiful views of the city below. Students at St. John's in Santa Fe can get back to nature in several nearby national parks, which offer hiking, mountain biking, snowboarding, and skiing. Students may attend both campuses during their academic careers, and about a quarter do so.

> "The small-scale discussion format of our classes really makes St. John's a community where students help one another."

The St. John's curriculum, known as "the program," has every student read the Great Books in roughly chronological order. All students major in liberal arts, discussing the books in seminars, writing papers about them, and debating the riddles of human existence they raise. Classes are led by tutors, who would be tenured professors anywhere else, but here are just the most advanced students. Each tutor is required to teach any subject within the curriculum (resisting the general trend in American academia toward more and more specialization). As a group, the tutors help students divine wisdom from each other and from great philosophers and thinkers, from Thucydides and Tolstoy to Euclid and Einstein. Both campuses follow a curriculum that would have delighted poet and educator Matthew Arnold, who argued that the goal of education is "to know the best which has been thought and said in the world."

Annapolis
Website: www.stjohnscollege .edu
Location: City Outskirts
Private
Total Enrollment: 590
Undergraduates: 449
Male/Female: 55/45
SAT Ranges: CR 640–730, M 570–680
ACT Ranges: 25–30
Financial Aid: 71%
Expense: Pr $ $ $ $
Student Loans: 74%
Average Debt: N/A
Phi Beta Kappa: No
Applicants: 378
Accepted: 82%
Enrolled: 38%
Grad in 6 Years: 67%
Returning Freshmen: 81%
Academics: ✍ ✍ ✍ ✍ ½
Social: ☎ ☎ ☎
Q of L: ★ ★ ★ ★
Admissions: (800) 727-9238
Email Address: admissions@ sjca.edu

Strongest Programs:
The Great Books Program

Santa Fe
Website: www.stjohnscollege .edu
Location: City Outskirts
Private
Total Enrollment: 429
Undergraduates: 349
Male/Female: 57/43

(continued)

SAT Ranges: CR 640–730,
   M 570–690
ACT Ranges: 25–30
Financial Aid: 79%
Expense: Pr $ $ $ $
Student Loans: 64%
Average Debt: N/A
Phi Beta Kappa: No
Applicants: 251
Accepted: 84%
Enrolled: 47%
Grad in 6 Years: 58%
Returning Freshmen: 72%
Academics: ✍ ✍ ✍ ✍ ½
Social: ☎ ☎ ☎
Q of L: ★ ★ ★ ★
Admissions: (505) 984-6060
Email Address: admissions@
   sjcsf.edu

Strongest Programs:
The Great Books Program

The St. John's curriculum, known as "the program," has every student read the Great Books in roughly chronological order.

There are no registration or scheduling hassles at St. John's; the daily course of study is mapped out before students set foot on campus. The curriculum includes four years of mathematics, two years of ancient Greek and French, three years of laboratory science, a year of music, and, of course, four years of Great Books seminars. Freshmen study the Greeks, sophomores advance through the Romans and the Renaissance, juniors cover the 17th and 18th centuries, and seniors do the 19th and 20th centuries. Readings are from primary sources only: math from Euclid and Ptolemy, physics from Einstein, psychology from Freud, and so on. For about seven weeks in the junior and senior years, seminars are suspended and students study a book or topic one-on-one with a tutor. The assumption is that the Great Books can stand on their own, representing the highest achievements of human intellect. "There is a real sense of community and a collaborative feel to all of the academic work we do," says one sophomore. "Our class conversations carry over into the dining hall, the quad, the common rooms, and coffee shop."

> "Students here feel comfortable with one another."

Students say the junior year, with its advanced curriculum in math and the natural sciences, is the most challenging. Still, the climate is anything but cut-throat. "The small-scale discussion format of our classes really makes St. John's a community where students help one another," says a junior. While there are no multiple-choice tests and no formal exams, since everyone's doing the same thing, there's a lot of peer pressure not to slack off. "Bonding over readings in Plato or Euclid is inevitable," says one student. Many St. John's students find they need a year off between the sophomore and junior years to decompress; some switch from Annapolis to Santa Fe or vice versa, and about 30 percent of students take more than six years to graduate. Unlike traditional liberal arts colleges, St. John's doesn't allow students to earn credit for study abroad; all eight semesters must be completed in residence.

Admission of qualified students to St. John's is first come, first served, and when the campuses are full, admissions begin for the following semester. A fifth of the students are transfers from more conventional colleges—a true act of devotion, since St. John's requires everyone to begin as freshmen. Minorities represent 16 percent of the student body in Santa Fe and 11 percent in Annapolis. Though the reasons students choose St. John's are never simple, the common thread is a fierce love of learning. "Johnnies tend to be inquisitive, active learners, bright, curious, and great conversationalists," says one student. There are no merit or athletic awards, but qualified international students may take advantage of special financial aid packages.

Roughly two-thirds of students in Annapolis and three-quarters of those in Santa Fe live on campus in the co-ed dorms; freshmen are guaranteed a room. In Annapolis, the six "historic" residence halls are arranged around a central quad, while the two modern halls face College Creek. (Students warn that "historic" is code for "old," and complain about "schizophrenic heating and cooling" and a lack of hot water for morning showers.) In Santa Fe, the dorms are small modern units clustered around courtyards. Most students get singles or divided double rooms. Upperclassmen typically live off campus in apartments and group houses; those who stay in the dorms usually get single rooms. There are no fraternities or sororities.

> "The liberal arts/classics thing is pretty well preserved."

"Students here feel comfortable with one another," says one student, "and the intramural program, school parties, dance parties, and other social events are a great way to meet members of other classes." Drinking is a favored release for Johnnies, who have, of course, read Plato's Symposium and are familiar with the likes of François Rabelais ("Drink constantly. You will never die."). Still, hard liquor is not allowed on campus, and parties and kegs must be registered. And although no one under 21 may be legally served at college-sponsored events, which are patrolled to prevent underage drinking, youngsters tip their share of brew at smaller gatherings and in their rooms. Only students who are extremely rowdy or disruptive are reported to the dean's office to face penalties. "Campus security really only makes it an issue if you do first," one student explains.

Santa Fe undergraduates plunge into the outdoorsy activities made possible by their mountaintop location, while Annapolis students limit their adventures to intramural teams with names like the Druids and the Furies. Road trips to Washington, D.C., Baltimore, New York, and Assateague State Park are options for students with cars; the annual spring break trip to the Santa Fe campus is popular as well, and known as Wagons West. In Santa Fe, some students venture south of the border on weekends, while others head for Taos Ski Valley or Ski Santa Fe. Nearby blues and jazz clubs are also popular, though one student cautions that town shuts down around 9 p.m. Santa Fe also tends to be pricey, especially for students on a budget.

Popular annual events on both campuses include Lola's, a casino night sponsored by the junior class to raise money for Reality, a three-day festival of food, games, and general debauchery thrown for the seniors the weekend before commencement. There's Melee, the club where "combatants" fight epic battles with foam weapons of their own creation, and Tuesday Nite Fites, where students vote for line-ups like Funk versus Dinosaurs and then debate the winner. There's also Fasching, a 1930s-style formal dance; the Ark party, held to celebrate the sophomores' completion of the Old Testament; and Oktoberfest. Senior Prank is a day-long surprise party for the whole college community. Intramural sports in Annapolis include flag football (with rules like you'll see nowhere else), basketball, soccer, team handball, and softball. Participation is voluntary, but anyone who wants to play is included. There are also intercollegiate club teams in crew, fencing, croquet, and women's soccer. In fact, the Johnnies hold more national croquet titles than any other college and the match against The Naval Academy each spring is the occasion for a genteel lawn party. In Santa Fe, the nearby Rio Grande and Chama rivers offer excellent white-water canoeing, kayaking, and rafting, while the Hueco Tanks area offers rock climbing and bouldering; the Outdoor Programs Office organizes trips and makes athletic equipment available for use.

Students at St. John's are as passionate about learning as their peers at other schools are about basketball rivalries or blowout parties. And while those larger colleges and universities try desperately to grow and change, St. John's cherishes its tradition—including the mandate that seniors wear formal academic dress to their oral examinations, which are open to the public. "I don't know if you could have another college where life was as determined by what takes place in class," muses a junior. "The liberal arts/classics thing is pretty well preserved, so apart from new dorms and the yoga craze at the gym, it's the same St. John's as always, and most likely will be five years from now, too."

Students say the junior year, with its advanced curriculum in math and the natural sciences, is the most challenging.

In fact, the Johnnies hold more national croquet titles than any other college.

Overlaps

Brown, University of Chicago, Goucher, Oberlin, Sarah Lawrence, Swarthmore, University of Virginia, Wellesley

If You Apply To ➢ **St. John's:** Rolling admissions. No application fee. Campus interviews: recommended, evaluative. Alumni interviews: optional, informational. SATs and ACTs: optional. Subject Tests: optional. Essay questions.

St. John's University and College of St. Benedict: See page 610.

St. Lawrence University

Canton, NY 13617

St. Lawrence is perched far back in the north country, closer to Ottawa and Montreal than to Syracuse. Isolation breeds camaraderie, and SLU students have a special bond similar to that at places like Dartmouth and Whitman. Environmental studies is the crown jewel. Compare to Allegheny and Hobart and William Smith.

Website: www.stlawu.edu
Location: City Outskirts
Private
Total Enrollment: 2,488
Undergraduates: 2,398
Male/Female: 45/55
SAT Ranges: CR 560–650,
   M 570–660
ACT Ranges: 25–29
Financial Aid: 90%
Expense: Pr $ $ $ $
Student Loans: 61%
Average Debt: $ $
Phi Beta Kappa: Yes
Applicants: 4,067
Accepted: 48%
Enrolled: 33%
Grad in 6 Years: 80%
Returning Freshmen: 93%
Academics: ✐ ✐ ✐
Social: ☎ ☎ ☎
Q of L: ★ ★ ★
Admissions: (800) 285-1856
Email Address: admissions@
   stlawu.edu

Strongest Programs:
Biology
Economics
English
Psychology
Environmental Studies
Mathematics
Government

St. Lawrence University seeks snow lovers who place equal value on their experiences inside and outside the classroom. Its upstate New York location offers quick access to both pristine ski slopes and rugged hiking trails—and to the bright lights of Ottawa and Montreal. Classes are small and there are no TAs, meaning it's as easy to form friendships with faculty members as it is with fellow students. A flood of new facilities has helped to make the campus almost as breathtaking as the natural beauty that surrounds it. "Everyone at St. Lawrence smiles," quips one senior. "This is easy, as everyone's so good-looking."

> **"Everyone's so good-looking."**

Hiking trails, a river, and a golf course surround SLU's 30 buildings, which sit on a 1,000-acre tract; facilities are clustered, so even the most distant buildings are only 10 minutes from one another. Many buildings date from the late 19th century, and though their exteriors have been preserved, their interiors are fully modernized. In all, the school has invested $200 million to beautify and better its campus over the past decade. The LEED Gold–certified Johnson Hall of Science supports the biology, chemistry, biochemistry, neuroscience, and psychology programs. A 155-bed residence hall is under construction and will be powered by geothermal energy.

St. Lawrence offers a classical liberal arts education, placing a premium on small classes and team teaching. General education requirements include courses in the following areas: The Human Experience and the Natural World; Human Diversity: Culture and Communication; Quantitative/Logical Reasoning; Environmental Literacy; and Integrated Learning. Everyone also participates in the two-semester First-Year Program, which emphasizes critical thinking, communications, and interdisciplinary content. "Students are separated into first-year 'colleges' for housing, and each college is enrolled together in a unique course," an economics major explains. There are more than a dozen "residential colleges," each with 30 to 45 students, and FYP professors also serve as academic advisors. "Some of my best friends on campus are from my FYP," explains a student, "and normally these tight-knit communities tend to stay close all four years at SLU."

Economics and psychology are the most popular majors, followed by biology, government, and environmental studies. In an effort "to make the world our classroom," St. Lawrence encourages students to spend time away from campus. More than half do so, and while some participate in one of the

> **"Some of my best friends on campus are from my FYP."**

school's 18 international programs, others choose the nearby "Adirondack semester" at Saranac Lake, or programs in Canada and Washington, D.C. The Sullivan University Fellows Program offers 25 to 30 students housing and $3,500 stipends for summer research. The university has added a plethora of programs, including a sustainability semester and an international program in Jordan.

The academic climate demands students pay attention and keep up with coursework, but competition is hardly a concern. "The courses can be challenging," says one student, "but the best part about the challenges is that they are often rewarding." Since there are no teaching assistants, full professors teach even the introductory courses; more than two-thirds of the courses taken by freshmen have 19 students or fewer. "Teachers value the input of each student, and oftentimes a significant part of the overall class grade is based on participation," says a junior.

"Students who do well at SLU are those who are outgoing," confides one senior, adding that "someone who isn't afraid to try new things and wants to be involved" is likely to enjoy the SLU experience. Forty-one percent of the students at St. Lawrence are New Yorkers; two-thirds graduated from public high school, 3 percent are African American, 4 percent are Hispanic, and 2 percent are Asian American. "Politics can be important" on campus, says one student, "although peripherally for most students." Nineteen percent of freshmen are eligible for Pell Grants, and the university awards merit scholarships to top students. The school also hands out athletic scholarships for Division I men's and women's ice hockey. (Other SLU teams compete in Division III.)

Virtually all SLU students live in the dorms, and seniors definitely have it best, with access to "new and spacious townhouses that sit along the golf course," says a sophomore. Everyone else makes do in the "adequate" residence halls, which have mostly double rooms featuring wireless Internet access, cable TV, computer and

"We do not live in a college town at all."

study lounges, vending machines, laundry rooms, and kitchens. In the dining halls there are themed dinners once a month, as well as ethnic foods, vegetarian options, and even organic items. Other options include the pub and convenience store, both in the student center, and a café in the physical education building. In addition, 9 percent of the men and 16 percent of the women go Greek; fraternity and sorority members may live and eat in their chapter houses.

SLU's social scene takes place mainly on campus. "St. Lawrence can't outsource our fun to the surrounding city because there is none," says a government major. "Instead, we learn to make our own fun, building a vibrant, involved community as we do so." University-sponsored activities include a campus nightclub, four different first-run movies each week, and the campus coffeehouse—a great place to hear a live band, acoustic guitarist, or comedian. Still, students say, the most popular pastimes include skiing, hiking, and road trips to Ottawa and Montreal, where there's better shopping and dining, and the drinking age is lower, too. On campus, students under 21 aren't permitted to drink, per New York State law. That said, "people still do it, because they think they can get away with it," says a senior. "Not all do," and those who are caught are required to complete counseling and educational programs.

The "charming" town of Canton is "a speck on the state map," says one student. "We are surrounded by farmland, then by forest and mountains. We do not live in a college town at all." Still, Canton does have everything from bagels to handmade jewelry to bars and restaurants, and Potsdam, 10 minutes away, offers more. Favorite annual traditions include Winterfest, a two-week celebration of the season, and Peak Weekend, during which the SLU Outing Club tries to "put St. Lawrence students on every peak in the Adirondacks."

In varsity sports, the Division I Skating Saints are the top draw, especially when the opponent is archrival Clarkson, and men's basketball and field hockey are recent conference champs. The equestrian team brought home the 2012 and 2013 IHSA national titles. Most St. Lawrence students enjoy sports; the school's fine athletic facilities include two field houses, one with 10 squash courts and a second with five indoor tennis courts, a pool, a three-story climbing wall, and a ropes course. The school's golf course doubles as a running route in warmer weather and a cross-country ski trail during the winter. Hiking and rock climbing are also popular, as is canoeing down the St. Lawrence River (when it's not frozen over). Over 90 percent of all students participate in intramurals at some point; available sports range from basketball and broomball to ruckus and Wiffle ball.

Overlaps

Colby, Hamilton, Hobart and William Smith, Colgate, University of Vermont

St. Lawrence makes up for frigid winters with the warmth of a close-knit, caring community. As the frenzied pace of construction winds down and academic standards are ratcheted up, SLU is a school on the rise, especially for those wanting to get back to nature.

If You Apply To ➤

St. Lawrence: Early decision: Nov.1. Regular admissions and financial aid: Feb. 1. Application fee: $60. Campus interviews: recommended, evaluative. Alumni interviews: optional, informational. SATs or ACTs: optional. Subject Tests: optional. Accepts the Common Application. Essay question: Common Application questions.

Saint Louis University

221 North Grand Boulevard, St. Louis, MO 63103

This is not your father's SLU. The campus and surrounding neighborhood have been spiffed up in the past two decades, and SLU's campus is a pleasant oasis in the bustle of midtown St. Louis. In addition to strengths in premed and communications, SLU has an unusual specialty in aviation science. Competes with Loyola Chicago and Marquette for bragging rights among Midwestern Jesuit institutions.

Website: www.slu.edu
Location: City Outskirts
Private
Total Enrollment: 11,148
Undergraduates: 7,730
Male/Female: 41/59
SAT Ranges: CR 530–660, M 540–670
ACT Ranges: 25–30
Financial Aid: 89%
Expense: Pr $
Student Loans: 63%
Average Debt: $ $ $ $
Phi Beta Kappa: Yes
Applicants: 13,060
Accepted: 64%
Enrolled: 20%
Grad in 6 Years: 71%
Returning Freshmen: 88%
Academics: ✍ ✍ ✍
Social: ☎ ☎
Q of L: ★ ★ ★
Admissions: (314) 977-2500
Email Address: admitme@slu.edu

Strongest Programs:
Aerospace Engineering
Aviation Science

Within sight of St. Louis's famed Gateway Arch, the historical gateway to the American West, sits Saint Louis University, the first university established west of the Mississippi River. The school's academic atmosphere is shaped by its Jesuit tradition; administrators ensure that each student receives personal care and attention and expect graduates to contribute to society and lead efforts for social change. In return, students find an atmosphere where their faith is encouraged. SLU offers students many nationally recognized programs, from premed to aviation and, of course, theology. "SLU is the type of university that prepares the whole person to go out into the world," says a freshman.

Since 1987, the SLU campus has undergone an $840 million renovation and features pedestrian walkways, lush greenery, fountains, and sculptures, as well as the signature Saint Louis University gates at all entrances. Cupples House, a beautiful old mansion in the middle of campus, houses 19th-century furniture and an art gallery—and is just a short walk from a new, modern focal point on campus, the Busch Student Center. The center is home to a bookstore, copy center, eateries, lounges, and conference facilities. Numerous renovations and additions have been completed over the last few years, including the John and Lucy Cook Hall, which doubled the size of the business school facilities; the Saint Louis University Museum of Art (SLUMA); and the Salus Center, which houses the School of Public Health.

"I think this school sets high standards for its students."

In keeping with its strong Jesuit commitment to education in the broadest sense, all SLU undergrads must complete distribution requirements in cultural diversity, world history, fine arts, literature, science, social science, mathematics, languages, and foundations of discourse. Additionally, students must take philosophy and theology courses, such as SLUVision, which integrates community service with the philosophy and theology component. The most popular majors are biology, nursing, business administration, psychology, and physical therapy. Premed, philosophy, and theology are also outstanding programs. SLU attracts scholars from around the globe with one of the world's most complete microfilm collections of Vatican documents. Parks College, America's first certified college of aviation, offers degree programs in aviation science and is a legacy of the days when St. Louis was a flying hub. (Remember Charles Lindbergh's "Spirit of St. Louis"?) The College of Arts and Science's meteorology program provides students with an opportunity to study with specialists in satellite, radar, and mesoscale meteorology. The College of Public Service offers majors in communication disorders, educational studies, and urban affairs, which encourage students to put research into action.

The academic climate at SLU is "very competitive," according to one junior. "I think this school sets high standards for its students," adds a classmate, "thereby creating opportunities for a good learning environment." The quality of teaching varies greatly according to professor, students say. "I have had horrible professors and wonderful professors," a sophomore says. Seventy-one percent of SLU freshmen come from the top quarter of their high school class. More than 300 SLU students currently study outside of the United States. In Madrid, Spain, SLU has one of the largest and most charming American campuses in Europe. The Micah House Program is a living/learning program integrated around themes of peace and justice—it takes its name from the biblical prophet Micah, who spoke out against social injustice in ancient Israel. The Manresa Program offers interdisciplinary and integrated study in the intellectual and social traditions of the Church from the New Testament period to the present.

SLU students tend to be "friendly and pretty laid-back," says a senior, but "most take school seriously." Many students come from private, religiously affiliated high schools, and 31 percent hail from the Show-Me State; the balance represents all 50 states and more than 70 foreign countries. African Americans comprise 7 percent of the student body, Asian Americans 8 percent, and Hispanics 4 percent. Because SLU is a Jesuit insti-

"The dorms are sufficient."

tution, human rights and abortion are prominent debates. The residential life department trains diversity advocates who serve as programmers and facilitators for the dorms; they get in-depth training about diversity, racism, and oppression. Billiken World Festival is a weeklong celebration of diversity that includes a citywide festival of African and Caribbean culture and music. The school offers 118 athletic scholarships, along with merit scholarships worth an average of $14,283.

Just over half of students live on campus. Upperclassmen can move into spacious courtyard-style apartments, but many opt for less expensive apartments off campus. "The dorms are sufficient," one student says. "They're nothing to brag about." The dining options are tasty, but students complain about the lack of healthy options. "The campus isn't really vegetarian/vegan friendly," laments one sophomore. Students say they feel safe on campus thanks to an active public safety department and the continuing improvement of surrounding neighborhoods.

Social life at SLU includes campus events, such as movies in the Quad, dances, and Greek parties, and the plethora of restaurants and coffee shops in St. Louis, as well as movie theaters, museums, bars, sporting events, and nightlife. A student says, "The social life is very active. Students know how to juggle personal lives with academic lives." Greek life at SLU—highly unusual for a Jesuit institution—claims 19 percent of the men and 18 percent of the women. Students say most parties take place in off-campus apartments or at an off-campus fraternity house, and despite the rules limiting alcohol on campus, it's common in the apartments. Spring Fever and Fall Homecoming, both annual events, feature bands, club-sponsored booths, and vendors. True to tradition, Sunday evening Mass is usually packed with students of all beliefs, and "practically everyone" participates in community service and outreach projects. Road trips to Kansas City, Chicago, and nearby schools like the University of Illinois and Indiana University are also popular.

SLU has no varsity football team, but Billiken squads more than compensate for this deficit. (A billiken was a common good-luck charm in the early 1900s. A popular

(continued)

Biology
Communication
Nursing
Philosophy
Theology
Pharmacy

The most popular majors are biology, nursing, business administration, psychology, and physical therapy.

Billiken World Festival is a weeklong celebration of diversity that includes a citywide festival of African and Caribbean culture and music.

Overlaps

University of Missouri, Marquette, University of Illinois, Washington University in St. Louis, Loyola (IL), Truman State, Creighton, Indiana University

sportswriter of the time said the charm resembled the then-football coach, and the name stuck.) Men's and women's basketball have been highly successful (the men's team advanced to the NCAA Tournament for the first time since 1999–2000), along with women's volleyball and soccer. The SLU Division I men's soccer team routinely wins the Conference USA championships and has been in the NCAA quarterfinals multiple times. The most popular intramural sports include flag football, dodgeball, basketball, softball, and soccer. For weekend warriors, the Simon Recreation Center boasts a 40-meter pool, six racquetball courts, and loads of equipment.

Saint Louis University is winning students' devotion and increasing its national visibility by offering a slew of strong programs. The Jesuit education prepares students to work for a more just and humane world. "SLU is a good choice for its relatively moderate-sized classrooms, its dedication toward a Jesuit mission, and its enjoyable learning environment," says a senior. "I am very happy that I chose SLU."

If You Apply To ➤

SLU: Rolling admissions: Financial aid: Mar. 1. Housing: May 1. No application fee. Campus and alumni interviews: optional, informational. SATs or ACTs: required. No Subject Tests. Apply to particular programs. Accepts the Common Application. Essay question.

St. Mary's College of Maryland

St. Mary's City, MD 20686

A public liberal arts institution of the same breed as Mary Washington, UNC Asheville, and much larger William and Mary. St. Mary's historic but sleepy environs are 90 minutes from D.C. and Baltimore on Maryland's western shore. With the Chesapeake Bay close at hand, St. Mary's is a haven for sailors. Maryland's public "honors college" is a well-kept secret beyond Maryland's borders; less than 20 percent of the students come from out of state.

Website: www.smcm.edu
Location: Rural
Public
Total Enrollment: 1,855
Undergraduates: 1,824
Male/Female: 40/60
SAT Ranges: CR 570–670, M 540–650
ACT Ranges: 25–30
Financial Aid: 75%
Expense: Pub $ $ $ $
Student Loans: 54%
Average Debt: $ $
Phi Beta Kappa: Yes
Applicants: 1,985
Accepted: 72%
Enrolled: 29%
Grad in 6 Years: 81%
Returning Freshmen: 87%

Twenty-five years ago, St. Mary's College of Maryland was just another public college, albeit one with a gorgeous waterfront campus in the oldest continuously inhabited English settlement in the New World. In 1992, the state of Maryland decided to make St. Mary's its public "honors college"—and the rest, as they say around there, is history. With a student/faculty ratio of 12 to 1, students here can easily design their own majors, undertake independent research projects, or work closely with professors to investigate whatever interests them. "This is truly a home away from home," says a biology major. "This place will allow you to try new things, understand yourself better, and open your eyes to the world."

St. Mary's has never been owned by any religious denomination and takes its name from its founding in 1846 in St. Mary's City, the original capital of Maryland.

"Most of our professors expect a lot from us and the students are well aware of this expectation."

It began as a boarding school for women, intended as a monument to the colonial birthplace of the state. The campus sits on a peninsula in southern Maryland where the Potomac River meets the Chesapeake Bay. Not surprisingly, it has an excellent center for estuary research, as well as a strong working relationship with the Chesapeake Biological Laboratory; the school even has its own marina right on the St. Mary's River, with a shoreline that gets beautiful sunset views. Architectural styles range from colonial to modern buildings, though the land on which the campus is built belongs to a 1,100-acre national historic landmark, commemorating Maryland's first colonial settlement. For that reason, students may step over archeological digs as they stroll to class.

The cornerstone of a St. Mary's education is the First Year Seminar. These small, discussion-focused classes are taught by professors from every discipline at the college, and introduce students to intellectual inquiry in a setting of active learning. Students may choose from dozens of topics—ranging from "A Softer Energy Footprint" to "Math, Music, and the Mind"—in order to cultivate an area of particular interest while building critical thinking, researching, writing, and speaking skills. St. Mary's core curriculum also mandates that students complete a senior capstone project, and complete coursework in arts, cultural perspectives, humanistic foundations, mathematics, natural sciences, and social sciences. They must also demonstrate foreign language proficiency and fulfill a minimum of four credits to complete the Experiencing the Liberal Arts in the World requirement. Biology is among the most popular majors, and also one of the more difficult programs; students can spend time on the college's research boat when they tire of the lab. Students also sign up in droves for psychology, English, economics, and political science. The strong music department includes prize-winning pianist Brian Ganz, and aside from the 22 established majors, plus the self-designed major, and seven cross-disciplinary study areas, more freethinking types may design their own programs. Science majors benefit from a state-of-the-art facility, with 55,000 square feet of classrooms, labs, and research space. An applied physics major has been added and the human studies major has been dropped.

"Courses are rather hard," observes one junior. "Most of our professors expect a lot from us and the students are well aware of this expectation." Students with exceptional academic potential may participate in the Nitze Scholars Program, which offers special seminars and opportunities for the study of foreign culture. St. Mary's also offers study programs at Oxford's Center for Medieval and Renaissance Studies, the University of Heidelberg in Germany, China's Fudan University, and the Institute for the Study of Politics in Paris. St. Mary's offers study programs in the Gambia, Argentina, Thailand, Costa Rica, India, and more. There are also short-term study tours to the Gambia, Belize, India, Greece, Peru, and England, among others. Additionally, the college partners with the National Student Exchange to further expand the opportunities available to St. Mary's students.

Eighty-seven percent of St. Mary's students come from Maryland, which helps give the campus a homegrown feel. The student body is a "mix of hippies and sailors and academics and the nicest people you will ever meet," according to one junior. Thirty-two percent of students are from the top 10th of their high school class and more minority students are finding their way to the peninsula: African Americans account for 7 percent of the student body, Hispanics 5 percent, and Asian Americans 2 percent. The prevailing issue on campus seems to be the environment. "One of the reasons I think this is so important on campus is because our school has such a deep history and connection with the surrounding area," says a junior. St. Mary's is more expensive than other publics in Maryland but less expensive than the private liberal arts colleges with which it also competes. Qualified students receive merit scholarships, worth an average of $3,990. There are no athletic awards, since teams compete in Division III.

Campus housing is "comfortable and popular among students," according to a student. "Since almost all students are on campus, and everyone is guaranteed housing for four years, there is a large intermixing of different kinds of people," notes one psychology student. Eighty-six percent of full-time students live on campus,

"We have a river, a great social community, and rigorous academics."

(continued)

Academics: ✎ ✎ ✎ ✎
Social: ☎ ☎ ☎
Q of L: ★ ★ ★ ★
Admissions: (800) 492-7181
Email Address: admissions@smcm.edu

Strongest Programs:
English
Psychology
Economics
Political Science
Biology

St. Mary's has never been owned by any religious denomination and takes its name from its founding in 1846 in St. Mary's City.

Students with exceptional academic potential may participate in the Nitze Scholars Program.

and most residence halls are co-ed. Apartments and townhouses with kitchens are reserved for upperclassmen, and students select rooms based on the number of credits they have. Older students get preference if they decide to retain a room or want a different one nearby; there are some choices off campus, too, including old farmhouses and riverside cottages for rent. Students report that food in the dining hall, known as the Great Room, is quite good and diverse. Those who tire of the food line may join the vegetarian co-op.

St. Mary's doesn't have fraternities or sororities, and its secluded location—about two hours from Washington, D.C., Annapolis, and Baltimore—means there's little nightlife off campus. "People have a lot of parties," explains an economics major, "but there's also stuff to do for people who don't want to drink," including movies, comedians, and open-mic nights. Students say they don't mind the isolation: "Point Lookout is only 10 or 15 minutes away," one explains. "If you love the water, this is the place to be," with sailing and other pursuits close at hand. "It's virtually impossible to graduate without knowing how to sail," says one student. The waterfront also becomes the focus of campuswide activities, including the cardboard boat race held each fall, Earth Day in April, and the end-of-year World Carnival. For the culture-hungry, there are also theaters, an art gallery, lectures, and films on campus.

> **"The student body is a mix of hippies and sailors and academics and the nicest people you will ever meet."**

St. Mary's fields a number of competitive Seahawks teams. Men's basketball has made four appearances in the NCAA Division III Championship Tournament, including advancing to the Elite 8 in 2011. For six consecutive seasons, women's swimming has had three Seahawks qualify for the NCAA Division III Championships. The sailing program has brought home 15 national titles since 1993 and has had more than 150 of its student-athletes recognized as All-Americans in that time. Overall, about a third of the students at St. Mary's take part in intramurals; floor hockey, badminton, and basketball are the most popular.

St. Mary's has worked hard to establish itself as one of the nation's premier public liberal arts colleges. Though its small size and remote location can be stifling, students leave with a solid grounding in the liberal arts—and the close bonds that they forge with friends during peaceful days on Chesapeake Bay. "We have a river, a great social community, and rigorous academics," says a mathematics major. For those looking to be part of an intellectual community in a small-town setting, St. Mary's just might be a place to set sail.

St. Mary's doesn't have fraternities or sororities.

Overlaps

University of Maryland, University of Maryland Baltimore County, College of William and Mary, Towson, Salisbury, Washington College, James Madison, American

If You Apply To ➢

St. Mary's: Early decision I: Nov. 1. Early decision II: Dec. 1 Regular admissions: Jan. 31. Financial aid: Feb. 28. Application fee: $50. Campus interviews: recommended, evaluative. No alumni interviews. SATs or ACTs: required. Subject Tests: optional. Essay question.

Saint Michael's College

One Winooski Park, Colchester, VT 05439

Roman Catholic liberal arts college located in a top college town with breathtaking views of the Adirondack and Green mountains. Cheerful academic community with most students being New Englanders. Proximity to UVM makes for vibrant social scene. Easy access to Montreal and to some of the best skiing in the East.

Saint Michael's College carries the distinction of being the only Edmundite institution of higher learning in the world. The college was established by the Society of Saint Edmund, a group of Roman Catholic country priests who took Saint Edmund, Archbishop of Canterbury, as their patron and spiritual inspiration. The Society of Saint Edmund maintains an on-campus presence to this day, and the influence of Saint Edmund can be found in the college's dedication to meaningful residential experiences, comprehensive liberal arts, and social justice. "There is something special to St. Mike's which is hard to put into words," says one sophomore. A junior adds, "Saint Michael's teaches students to go out into the world and work to make it a better place."

"There is something special to St. Mike's."

Founded in 1904, Saint Michael's College sits on 440 acres overlooking Vermont's breathtaking Green Mountains and the winding Winooski River. Just five minutes from Burlington, the campus features three-story redbrick architecture and a central tree-lined rectangular green, anchored on one end by the glass-front library and the other by the chapel. To the east, Mount Mansfield—Vermont's tallest peak—provides a spectacular backdrop. The $2 million Pomerleau Alumni Center is the first LEED-certified facility on campus. The two-story center includes offices, a multifunction meeting room, the Trinity Conference Room, and a spacious living area. Recent construction includes the Quad Commons, featuring a new student center and residential hall, which opened in late 2013.

Saint Michael's offers a plethora of solid programs, including biology, chemistry, English, history, religious studies, mathematics, and psychology. The elementary education and business programs are top draws, too. "There are a lot of business and education majors on campus," a political science major says. "Our education department does an incredible job of preparing us for our licensure and to be passionate, socially just educators with lots of tricks up our sleeves," adds one junior. A popular 3–2 program with the University of Vermont allows students to earn an engineering degree, and there are hybrid summer courses, including an art history course based partly at the Metropolitan Museum in New York City. Students may also take advantage of cross-registration options with Champlain College and Burlington College.

"There isn't a strong sense of competitiveness among the students."

Regardless of major, students agree that courses are demanding. "While many of the courses offered here are challenging, there isn't a strong sense of competitiveness among the students. Everyone here is really supportive of each other," says one freshman. The general education curriculum includes a writing- and research-intensive First Year Seminar, and other requirements that fall into the categories of Foundations in Faith, Values, and Thought (courses in philosophy, religious studies, and ethical decision making); Pathways to Understanding the World (including courses in literary and historical studies, quantitative reasoning, global issues that impact the common good, scientific reasoning, and second-language acquisition); and Participatory Learning and Competencies, which includes an experiential learning requirement for all students. "Competition between students is minimal, but professors expect a high level of commitment and hard work from students," says one sophomore. Nearly 68 percent of Saint Michael's students take part in undergraduate research, and many receive stipends for full-time work as research partners with faculty. Study abroad options include international study trips to such far-flung locales as Ghana, Guyana, Tanzania, France, Italy, Brazil, and Costa Rica; 40 percent of undergraduates participate.

Back on campus, students praise professors for their knowledge and willingness to make themselves accessible. "It is crazy to see how passionate every teacher is about the topic they are teaching and how passionate they are about each student

---

Website: www.smcvt.edu
Location: Small City
Private
Total Enrollment: 1,989
Undergraduates: 1,925
Male/Female: 48/52
SAT Ranges: CR 530–630, M 520–620
ACT Ranges: 23–28
Financial Aid: 98%
Expense: Pr $ $
Student Loans: 71%
Average Debt: $ $ $ $
Phi Beta Kappa: Yes
Applicants: 4,474
Accepted: 78%
Enrolled: 15%
Grad in 6 Years: 79%
Returning Freshmen: 89%
Academics: ✍ ✍ ✍
Social: 🕿 🕿 🕿 🕿
Q of L: ★ ★ ★
Admissions: (800) 762-8000
Email Address: admission@smcvt.edu

Strongest Programs:
Biology
Chemistry
English
History
Religious Studies
Mathematics
Psychology
Accounting

A popular 3–2 program with the University of Vermont allows students to earn an engineering degree.

learning the material well," says a freshman. Sixty-three percent of classes taken by freshmen have 19 or fewer students and "freshmen are taught by full professors," according to a sophomore.

"Students at St. Mike's are genuine and happy," says one student. Sixty percent identify as Catholic and "most of the Catholicism you see on campus comes in the form of service, with the Edmundite influence being reflected in the very active MOVE program, our community service organization," a freshman explains. African Americans account for only 2 percent of the student body, Hispanics 4 percent, and Asian Americans 2 percent. Twenty-one percent come from Vermont and 27 percent ranked in the top 10th of their high school class. Campus politics lean left, students say, although conservatives are well represented too. "Students are engaged and active on campus and in our greater community," a junior says, and hot-button issues include sustainability, social justice, and homosexuality. The college offers merit awards to qualified students, and student-athletes vie for 20 basketball scholarships.

Students are required to spend all four years on campus in the residence halls. "The first-year residence halls are aging and could use some renovation, but housing options for upperclassmen are excellent," says a student. There are a number of housing options, including substance-free, international, and honors halls. Residence halls include traditional dorms with double and single rooms; townhouses with single bedrooms, kitchens, dining areas, and living rooms; and suites with single bedrooms and shared living spaces. Campus dining options include an unlimited meal plan at the Green Mountain Dining Room, which serves a variety of fare, including entrees, pizza, salads, soups, and vegetarian/vegan dishes. "In addition to offering tasty dishes," says one student, "the dining hall is healthy." Students report feeling safe on campus and laud the student-run Fire & Rescue Squad, which provides professional emergency services to the campus and a large segment of the surrounding county.

"Students at St. Mike's are genuine and happy."

Despite the lack of a Greek scene, "the social life is outstanding," raves one student. "Because SMC is 100 percent residential, almost all the social life takes place on campus, which is great for building a close community," adds a sophomore. The Residential Initiative Program delivers a slew of weekend programs designed to engage students and provide an alternative to the typical party scene. Campuswide activities include comedians, coffeehouse music and poetry performances, and talent shows. Every Friday night, the college hosts the Weekend Grilling Program, which provides free food (hamburgers, hot dogs, or pizza) between 11 p.m. and 1 a.m. Apart from senior housing, the campus is dry and students report that underage drinking is dealt with swiftly; those who want to imbibe travel off campus to take part in Burlington's bar scene. Popular road trips "are to downtown Burlington or to the mountains and great outdoors like Mount Mansfield or Camel's Hump," says one student. Montreal is a popular weekend trip.

Burlington (population 40,000) is "a great college town as it contains three other colleges: UVM, Champlain, and Vermont Community College," a sophomore says. "The area consists of young people and entrepreneurs, offering a fun atmosphere to eat, shop, and go out in." Saint Michael's students receive a free bus pass that will take them downtown, and they can often be found volunteering in the surrounding community. "Volunteering is a huge aspect of life at Saint Michael's," confirms one student. The Mobilization of Volunteer Efforts (MOVE) program was named the United Way's Hometown Hero for 2009—the first time an entire organization received the honor—and 70 percent of students get involved in at least one service program over the course of their college careers.

Saint Michael's fields a number of Division II sports and competes in the Northeast-10 Conference. Competitive Purple Knights teams include men's and women's tennis, men's lacrosse and hockey, and women's field hockey, soccer, and basketball. Recreational and intramural programs are popular, too, and include the Wilderness Program, which provides access to sea kayaking, rock and ice climbing, white-water rafting, and other outdoor activities. Students cite P-Day ("centered around coming together as a school to have fun, participate in competitions, and listen to music") and the MLK Talent Show ("always a packed house") as popular annual events.

Saint Michael's attracts students who want to use their education for the betterment of the world and who appreciate the unique vision inspired by Saint Edmund so many years ago. "College is not just about obtaining a degree," says a junior, "but about learning who you are as a person and deciding what path you want to take in life. Saint Michael's College offers students the opportunities to do so."

If You Apply To ➤

St. Michael's: Early action: Dec. 1. Regular admissions: Feb. 1. Financial aid: Feb. 15. Housing: May 1. Application fee: $50. Campus interviews: optional, evaluative. Alumni interviews: optional, informational. SATs or ACTs: optional. No Subject Tests. Accepts the Common Application. Essay question: Common Application.

St. Olaf College

1520 St. Olaf Avenue, Northfield, MN 55057-1098

The well-scrubbed undergraduates at St. Olaf are a stark contrast to the grunge of crosstown rival Carleton. The music program is world famous, and two-thirds of students study abroad. Daily chapel is not mandatory, but many students go. With over 3,000 students, St. Olaf is on the big side of small.

Northfield, Minnesota, which bills itself as the city of "Cows, Colleges, and Contentment," is home to St. Olaf College. Founded by Norwegian Lutheran immigrants and affiliated with the Evangelical Lutheran Church in America, St. Olaf provides a solid liberal arts education and plenty of opportunities to study abroad. One Olie describes her peers at St. Olaf as "Minnesota nice," adding, "I feel personally valued and supported by the faculty and administrators. I felt at home here from day one."

St. Olaf's meticulously landscaped 350-acre campus, featured in several architectural journals, is located on Manitou Heights, overlooking the Cannon River valley and Northfield. More than 10,000 trees, native prairie, and a wetlands wildlife area surround the 34 native limestone buildings that form the campus. The student union, the Buntrock Commons, offers dining and food services, a bookstore, a post office, conference and banquet facilities, a movie theater, and a game room. Regents Hall of Natural and Mathematical Sciences, a 200,000-square-foot science center, is the largest and most complex academic facility in the nation to earn the prestigious LEED Platinum rating.

> **"I felt at home here from day one."**

All students at St. Olaf complete a general education requirement that covers three areas: foundation studies, core studies, and integrative study. Typically, 14 to 16 courses satisfy the general education requirements; some courses may fulfill requirements in more than one area.

Biology, mathematics, economics, chemistry, and psychology are hailed as the best programs. The music department draws high praise; it offers many performance opportunities with eight school choirs and seven instrumental ensembles. The

Website: www.stolaf.edu
Location: Small Town
Private
Total Enrollment: 3,115
Undergraduates: 3,115
Male/Female: 44/56
SAT Ranges: CR 580–700,
 M 580–700
ACT Ranges: 28–31
Financial Aid: 90%
Expense: Pr $ $
Student Loans: 61%
Average Debt: $ $ $
Phi Beta Kappa: Yes
Applicants: 3,937
Accepted: 60%
Enrolled: 36%
Grad in 6 Years: 85%
Returning Freshmen: 93%
Academics: ✍ ✍ ✍ ✍
Social: ☎ ☎ ☎
Q of L: ★ ★ ★ ★

(continued)

Admissions: (507) 786-2222
Email Address: admissions@
stolaf.edu

Strongest Programs:
Chemistry
Biology
Psychology
Economics
English
Mathematics
Music

choirs perform in major venues around the nation, and can be heard singing with the Minnesota Orchestra. In the last quarter-century, the college has cultivated an international agenda for its students and faculty, and has created the largest international studies program in the country among liberal arts colleges. More than 100 programs are available in 46 countries, including China, Japan, Scotland, and India, and some are offered through membership in the Associated Colleges of the Midwest* consortium. There are also several opportunities to spend a semester studying elsewhere in the country. Research is available in the sciences and psychology—41 percent of students take advantage of it—and the Center for Integrative Studies allows students to form their own majors. The Science Conversation is a yearlong program for sophomores that brings together students and faculty with a broad range of academic interests for a critical exploration of science within its historical, cultural, and social contexts.

> **"Professors will get to know your name."**

Faculty members are highly praised by students. "Professors will get to know your name and expect you to be actively involved during class," says a junior. Further, they are "readily available outside of class for additional help, as they are committed to students' success." Instructors participate in and out of the classroom, reportedly having as many as 10 hours of open-office time a week. Still, just because professors want to see them succeed doesn't mean students don't have their work cut out for them. "I consider it very rigorous," admits one junior. "I know that I need to make a point each semester to enroll in at least one level-100 course because I will be overwhelmed by the challenges brought forth by most upper-level classes." There's also an annual study break where professors serve their stressed-out pupils ice cream.

Forty-five percent of students hail from Minnesota. "We are a hardworking, caring group that likes to see others do well," says a sophomore. "Typically, most of us are active in many things such as sports, intramurals, student government, and clubs on campus." Asian Americans make up 5 percent, Hispanics 4 percent, and African Americans 2 percent. Most students are high achievers from Midwestern public schools, drawn in part by hundreds of merit scholarships.

Ninety-one percent of undergrads live in on-campus housing, with college-owned houses available off campus. "Dorms are comfortable and usually well maintained, but outdated," a student reports. Dorms are co-ed by floor, and each has its own personality. Rooms are selected by lottery, and it can be difficult to get a room at times. Students eat in a large modern cafeteria, where the food is considered above average for college fare. "St. Olaf's dining facilities are about as good as they can get. With nine lines of fresh and always changing food, their is something for everyone," reasons a student. The campus is described as "very safe" thanks to security, and students feel confident in the public safety department.

> **"We are a hardworking, caring group."**

St. Olaf's social life takes place mostly on campus, and weekend activities include a nightclub called Lion's Pause and a coffeehouse, the Alley. "The Pause, an entirely student-run organization complete with TVs, hangout areas, food, and a main stage, is the place to go for entertainment," says a junior. The fine arts department provides many music, theater, and dance performances. "Most social life is defined by small dorm parties," adds a sophomore. The campus is officially dry, and there are no fraternities or sororities at St. Olaf, but that doesn't mean students don't imbibe. Alcohol is available to those determined enough to seek it out, students report, and can also be found at local bars. The Student Activities Committee sponsors frequent dances, speakers, and cultural events, covered by student fees and at-the-door ticket sales. Daily chapel services, though not mandatory, are heavily attended.

Northfield is "friendly and intimate," but there is little of social interest for St. Olaf students aside from neighboring Carleton. Each September, the locals re-enact

More than 100 programs are available in 46 countries, including China, Japan, Scotland, and India.

the failed 1876 attempt by Jesse James to rob the local bank. The most talked-about annual event, which has been running for more than 100 years, is the four-day Christmas Festival, during which five choirs and the St. Olaf Orchestra combine in televised concerts celebrating Christmas. A fall concert has featured such performers as Motion City Soundtrack and Ben Folds. Many students volunteer in Northfield and report a friendly rapport with the community. "Students are actively involved in community mentor, volunteer, and outreach programs," one student says. For those with wanderlust, buses leave regularly for the twin cities of Minneapolis and St. Paul, less than an hour's drive, where one can experience a shopper's paradise at the huge Mall of America.

St. Olaf has outstanding Division III athletic programs. Men's ice hockey is strong, while Ole baseball has won nearly 30 conference championships. Men's swimming and diving and women's golf are also competitive. There is also an extensive intramural program, and broomball—ice hockey played with brooms instead of sticks, and shoes rather than skates—is the sport of choice in the winter. The St. Olaf football team competes against Carleton for the honor of having the statue in the town's square face the winning campus. The game, called the Cereal Bowl, is sponsored by Malt-O-Meal, which has a factory in town. The chorus of St. Olaf's fight song is "Um Ya Ya," which has become a popular chant on campus.

For those yearning for a school where spirituality and scholarship exist on the same exalted plane, St. Olaf could be the right place to spend four years. It's a school where students work hard, are encouraged by good teachers, toughened by Minnesota winters, and nourished by strong moral values—in addition to hearty Scandinavian food. Says one satisfied senior: "It is an experience that will change your life and challenge you in ways you never thought possible."

> *There's an annual study break where professors serve their stressed-out pupils ice cream.*

Overlaps
University of Minnesota, Gustavus Adolphus, Carleton, Luther, University of Wisconsin, Macalester, Northwestern, Lawrence

If You Apply To ➤ **St. Olaf:** Early decision: Nov. 15. Regular admissions: Jan. 15. Application fee: $40 (paper), free (online). Campus interviews: optional, informational. No alumni interviews. SATs or ACTs: required. Subject Tests: optional. Accepts the Common Application. Essay question: describe your interest in St. Olaf.

University of San Diego

5998 Alcala Park, San Diego, CA 92110

With a panoramic view of the Pacific Ocean, USD is riding a wave of popularity due to its sun-drenched location. Not to be confused with its UC counterpart across town, USD is now often preferred to Roman Catholic counterparts the University of San Francisco and Santa Clara. Strong in business and engineering.

Students at the University of San Diego have many reasons to cheer: a beatific oceanside campus. A rich Roman Catholic heritage centered around ethical conduct and compassionate service. And an array of superb academics, including solid programs in business and engineering. "USD is becoming more and more competitive and the academic programs continue to get better," says one freshman. "There has never been a better time to come to USD than right now."

Founded in 1949, the USD campus occupies 180 acres on a mesa overlooking San Diego's Mission Bay and is only two miles north of downtown San Diego. The buildings are designed in 16th-century Spanish Renaissance architectural style in a nod to San Diego's Catholic heritage and the Universidad de Alcalá in Spain. At one end of

Website: www.sandiego.edu
Location: City Center
Private
Total Enrollment: 6,784
Undergraduates: 5,211
Male/Female: 45/55
SAT Ranges: CR 550–650, M 570–670
ACT Ranges: 25–30

Those who overdose on Southern California's ubiquitous blue skies and sunshine may take part in USD's robust study abroad program.

campus is the Joan Kroc (of McDonald's fame) Center for Peace and Justice; at the other end is the Jenny Craig Athletic Center, where you can work off your Big Macs. The four-story, 50,000-square-foot Student Life Pavilion features student lounges, seminar and conference rooms, the USD radio and television studios, and the United Front Multicultural Center. A new, state-of-the-art baseball facility opened in spring 2013.

USD offers more than 60 degree programs across six schools: the School of Business Administration, the School of Leadership and Education Sciences, the School of Law, the School of Nursing & Health Science, the College of Arts & Sciences, and the Joan B. Kroc School of Peace Studies. The most popular undergraduate majors include business, communication studies, accountancy, finance, and marketing. The mathematics and theology departments tend to be avoided: "Unless students are super interested in those topics, math and religious classes have the stereotype of being extremely difficult and boring," says an accountancy major. Additional majors include biophysics, behavioral neuroscience, and Italian studies.

"Social life at USD is rather diverse."

Core curriculum requirements are grouped into three clusters: indispensable competencies (written literacy, mathematical competency, logic, second language); traditions (theology and religious studies, philosophy); and horizons (humanities and fine arts, natural sciences, social sciences, diversity of human experience). "Despite the fact that most students are heavily involved all over campus as well, academics take the priority in most cases," says one sociology major. Professors are said to be knowledgeable and accessible, if not always adaptable. "For the most part, the quality of teaching is fantastic," says one student. "Some professors seem to be stuck in their ways, however, having trouble helping students with different learning styles." Freshman take part in USD's First Year Experience, which features small preceptorial classes taught by faculty advisors. Students are also assigned a Preceptorial Assistant to serve as a mentor and are required to live on campus. The Honors Program offers small classes and a core curriculum of innovative courses to qualified students. Those who overdose on Southern California's ubiquitous blue skies and sunshine may take part in USD's robust study abroad program, which sends students to live and study in over 35 countries for a year, semester, summer, or intersession; 87 percent of students participate.

"The students at USD, for the most part, are intelligent and work hard," says a senior. "But, since we are close to the beach, the majority of them are laid-back and not overachievers." Fifty-six percent hail from the Golden State and 6 percent are international students. USD has a considerable minority population: African Americans account for 3 percent of the student body, Hispanics 18 percent, and Asian Americans 6 percent. Despite its Roman Catholic heritage, students say the campus atmosphere skews liberal. "I would say the biggest social issue is diversity and tolerance," says one freshman. "The university is making a big push toward acceptance and understanding of all people and beliefs." The school offers merit awards (averaging $13,277) to qualified students and there are 113 athletic awards in 15 sports.

Forty-five percent of students live in campus housing and freshman are required to do so. "The dorms rock!" cheers one succinct student. Most rooms are triples or quadruples; upperclassmen tend to move off campus to nearby apartments along the beach. When the dinner bell rings, students have plenty to cheer about. "Dining facilities are top-notch," says one freshman. "In our cafeteria alone, we have 12 different types of food options, from Chinese to pizza to Vietnamese and even a cereal bar. Then there are three other dining locations on campus, each with their own type of dining experience." Campus security is excellent, students say. "We only have three entrances into USD and there is always someone at the gate making sure everything is going well," a business administration major explains.

And how about the campus social scene? "Social life at USD is rather diverse. Activities range from sports games, concerts and comedy shows, to house parties,

Greek life events, and study sessions," a finance major says. For those who choose to eschew the sand and waves in favor of campus fun, USD offers a slate of on-campus activities, including movies, concerts, and Mass (lest you forget, USD is a Catholic university). The Greek scene attracts 20 percent of the men and 32 percent of the women. Alcohol is allowed only in designated areas by those students of legal age, and "this policy is heavily enforced by the RAs," says a marketing major. Downtown San Diego has plenty to offer, including a bevy of bars, eateries, and shopping centers. Popular road trips include Las Vegas and Big Bear. Back on campus, students enjoy annual festivals such as International Week and Greek Week, internship and career fairs, the Alcalá Bazaar, and Homecoming.

USD sponsors nearly 20 NCAA Division I intercollegiate teams and is a member of the West Coast Conference for all sports except football, which competes in the Pioneer League (and which brought home the 2011 conference title). The Toreros have earned a record-setting five consecutive WCC Commissioner's Cups, an all-sports award

presented at the end of each academic year to the league's top performing school in conference play. Students are especially rowdy when the USD basketball team takes on rival Gonzaga. Sixteen sports and recreational clubs are available to students; among the most popular are basketball, football, inner-tube polo, kickball, soccer, and tennis.

Despite the common student complaints about the lack of parking and the sky-rocketing cost of tuition, USD students seem to understand that they are living out their college careers in one of the most beautiful spots in the country. "The great thing about USD is you can get a great education in a challenging academic environment and in one of the most beautiful cities in the nation," says a sophomore. "The USD experience can't be beat."

Overlaps

University of Southern California, Loyola Marymount, Santa Clara, UC–Santa Barbara, UCLA, UC–San Diego

If You Apply To ➢

USD: Regular admissions: Dec. 15. Application fee: $55. No campus or alumni interviews. SATs or ACTs: required. Subject Tests: optional. Accepts the Common Application. Essay question.

University of San Francisco

2130 Fulton Street, San Francisco, CA 94117-1080

Talk about prime real estate: USF is next door to the legendary Haight-Ashbury district, down the street from Golden Gate Park, and within five miles of the Pacific Ocean. Though USF is a Jesuit institution, only about half of its students are Roman Catholic. Pacific Rim studies is a standout. Over 40 percent of the students are from out of state.

In the heart of one of the nation's most liberal cities is a thriving Jesuit university that has become an integral part of its community. Instead of shunning the city's reputation, the University of San Francisco embraces it. With an incredibly diverse student body and an emphasis on programs such as nursing and business, students encounter a broad set of cultures, academic challenges in a liberal arts setting, and the chance to put all that experience to good use.

USF's 55 well-kept acres, spotted with beautiful basilica-type buildings and modern facilities, are, as one student puts it, "wedged into the heart of San Francisco." The campus stands atop one of San Francisco's seven hills, adjacent to Golden Gate Park,

Website: www.usfca.edu
Location: City Center
Private
Total Enrollment: 9,152
Undergraduates: 6,033
Male/Female: 37/63
SAT Ranges: CR 510–620, M 530–630

(continued)

ACT Ranges: 22–27
Financial Aid: 60%
Expense: Pr $ $
Student Loans: 65%
Average Debt: $ $ $ $
Phi Beta Kappa: No
Applicants: 11,223
Accepted: 69%
Enrolled: 17%
Grad in 6 Years: 67%
Returning Freshmen: 88%
Academics: ✐ ✐ ✐
Social: ☎ ☎ ☎
Q of L: ★ ★ ★ ★
Admissions: (415) 422-6563
Email Address: admission@
usfca.edu

Strongest Programs:
Business Administration
Hospitality Management
Psychology
Communication
Nursing
Biology
Pacific Rim Studies

overlooking San Francisco Bay and the city skyline. The One Stop Services Office combines registrar, financial aid, and payment services in one convenient location. The newest campus addition is the John Lo Schiavo, S.J. Center for Science and Innovation.

Although liberal arts programs draw the most majors, there is also a strong emphasis on preprofessional programs, especially nursing, health studies, communications, and business. The Center for the Pacific Rim allows students to do interdisciplinary majors with an Asian focus, as does the Asian studies program. The 44-unit core curriculum requires students to take courses in six major categories: foundation of communication; math and sciences; humanities; philosophy, theology, and ethics; social sciences; and visual and performing arts. The St. Ignatius Institute program offers an integrated four-year curriculum based on the great books of Western civilization presented in an unusual seminar/lecture combination. The program is not restricted to top students, and participants can spend their junior year studying in Oxford, Rome, or Budapest.

> "USF is not an extremely competitive school."

Some of the preprofessional majors are demanding, and students say that competition is common, but not cut-throat. "USF is not an extremely competitive school," says one junior, "but at the same time it's not all fun and games." Extensive and mandatory academic advising ensures that students' courseloads are manageable. Forty-five percent of classes taken by freshmen have 19 or fewer students and more than 90 percent of the faculty hold terminal degrees in their academic discipline. "All of my professors are approachable and more than willing to help," a student says. Another adds, "The teachers interact with the students."

The university operates on the basis of fall and spring semesters, with optional three-week courses during the five-week winter break. There's also a joint B.A./B.S.-J.D. program. The visual arts program provides courses in art education, graphic and fine art, drawing, painting, art history, and museum studies. Five computer labs are available to students, and every residence hall is equipped with high-speed Internet connections. Community-minded students take advantage of volunteer programs, mostly through University Ministries. USF is also the official host of the Human Rights Watch Festival, which is integrated into the curriculum. A three-part series of success courses emphasizes study skills, critical thinking, and career and major exploration, and aims to create successful college students. "The freshman seminars are worthwhile," says a computer science major. "They offer a lot of information and it helps get first-time students used to being away from home."

> "This place can be dead sometimes."

A three-part series of success courses emphasizes study skills, critical thinking, and career and major exploration, and aims to create successful college students.

Sixty-four percent of the students are from California, and nearly half attended private or parochial high schools. Asian Americans account for 23 percent of the population, African Americans 4 percent, and Hispanics 19 percent. One of the university's missions is to "prepare men and women to shape a multicultural world with creativity, generosity, and compassion." Admissions are need-blind, and USF offers merit scholarships as well as more than 150 athletic scholarships in eight Division I sports.

On-campus housing is guaranteed for the first two years and 32 percent of undergrads choose to live in student housing. After that, at least half the students brave San Francisco's budget-busting rental market. "Rooms are small and in decent shape," says a junior. On-campus students say the dining facilities offer a range of vegetarian and other choices. Campus security is visible and students report feeling safe despite being located in a major metropolitan area. "USF and the surrounding area are patrolled heavily by the SFPD and USF's Public Safety Department," says one student, adding, "I have always felt safe on campus."

"This place can be dead sometimes," a student laments. "Most of the social life takes place off campus." Campus activities include the Hawaiian Club's annual luau and the Barrio Festival held by the Filipino American Club. The College Players is the oldest continuously performing college theater group in the West. Fraternities and sororities attract 1 percent of men and women, although they don't have houses. Though underage drinking is officially prohibited, students find ways to skirt the policy. USF's greatest asset is undoubtedly its location. San Francisco is a cosmopolitan city where students can take advantage of reliable public transportation, including the famous cable cars, to get to a variety of cultural attractions, ranging from Chinatown to the symphony. Nightlife is great for those who want to dance at the clubs or meet in the bars.

Varsity athletics provide a popular diversion, and the USF Dons tout a conference-winning national powerhouse in soccer. Women's cross-country won its fourth straight West Coast Conference Championship in 2012; basketball and baseball are among the most popular sports for male athletes, while the women have formed strong volleyball and basketball teams. Athletes are pleased with the health and recreation center, which touts an Olympic-size swimming pool, exercise rooms, and courts.

The core mission of USF is to use the Jesuit tradition, which views "faith and reason as complementary resources in the search for truth and authentic human development," as the backdrop for a solid liberal arts and preprofessional education. Students take advantage of the cosmopolitan setting to get involved and make the most of their time here. "There is so much to do, not only at the school, but in the city as well," says one student, "which is a big part of the learning experience."

Varsity athletics provide a popular diversion, and the USF Dons tout a conference-winning national powerhouse in soccer.

Overlaps
Loyola Marymount, San Francisco State, Santa Clara, UC–Santa Barbara, UC–Santa Cruz, UCLA, UC–Berkeley

If You Apply To ➢

USF: Early Decision and early action: Nov. 15. Regular admissions: Jan. 15. Financial aid: Feb. 1. Housing: May 1. Application fee: $55. Campus and alumni interviews: optional, informational. SATs or ACTs: required. ACT optional writing test required for placement only. Accepts the Common Application. Essay question.

Santa Clara University

500 El Camino Real, Santa Clara, CA 95053-1500

Santa Clara is one of the few midsized universities in California that is not impossible to get into. Gorgeous Silicon Valley campus is within easy reach of San Francisco and the large endowment also contributes to an air of prosperity. A well-developed core curriculum keeps students focused on the basics. Santa Clara offers engineering and business in addition to the liberal arts.

Steeped in history and tradition, Santa Clara University was founded with a Jesuit mission that emphasizes a commitment to academics and the community. Classes stay small and intimate, while the revised curriculum focuses on an expanding global society. The class schedule is based on quarters (10 weeks), and classes are challenging, but not too competitive. According to one senior, the environment and school "promote group work and learning as a community."

SCU's old-world charm includes 106 acres complete with lush green lawns, palm trees, and luscious rose gardens, accented by authentic Spanish architecture. The Mission Gardens, with many olive trees, are a beautiful escape from the pressures of school. The famous classic mission church was rebuilt in 1926 in the design of the six previous churches that were destroyed by disasters ranging from fires to floods. A student activities center opened in 2010, and the Benson

Website: www.scu.edu
Location: Small City
Private
Total Enrollment: 6,818
Undergraduates: 5,104
Male/Female: 50/50
SAT Ranges: CR 590–680, M 610–700
ACT Ranges: 27–31
Financial Aid: 84%
Expense: Pr $ $ $

Memorial Center has been remodeled and features a meditation room and a variety of dining options.

The core curriculum, with the theme Community and Leadership for a Global Society, is meant to give the students broad knowledge in three main areas: community, global societies, and leadership. Courses include composition, Western culture, world culture, the United States, ethics, religious studies, mathematics and the natural sciences, technology, social sciences, and foreign language. There is also an emphasis on preprofessional programs like engineering and business. Students can opt for the 3–2 engineering program, which allows them to get a bachelor's and master's degree in five years, and the Leavey School of Business is renowned along the West Coast, with accounting, agribusiness, and retail management being particularly strong. In the College of Arts and Sciences, psychology remains popular, as do biology, communications, and English. Other notable majors include bioengineering, Web design and engineering, public health sciences, and environmental studies.

> **"Communications is the most popular major."**

For those students looking for more of a challenge, the honors program places 45 to 50 selected freshmen in special classes, and an endowed scholarship sponsors one student's junior year at Mansfield College, Oxford University. Also, an extensive study abroad program, in which approximately one-third of the students participate, allows travel and study in Europe, Central and South America, the Caribbean, Canada, Africa, Asia, New Zealand, and Australia.

As at any small school, resources and facilities are limited. Students complain that finding a seat in some of the classes is a challenge. "Communications is the most popular major and therefore they are the hardest classes to get into," says one student. But a senior explains that if your first choice isn't available, "there is always a required course available to take instead." Bottom line: Stay flexible and you'll likely graduate on time.

Small classes taught by full professors mean "the quality of teaching is good and professors are really there to help the students rather than do research," says a senior. "They have a passion for students and want to see us succeed," adds a sophomore. The academic climate is described as challenging. "The academic climate at SCU is more competitive than most. Classes are challenging and really require extra work and independent thinking," says a sophomore.

> **As at any small school, resources and facilities are limited.**

More than half the students are Roman Catholic, and religion, while not intrusive, is a factor in many aspects of campus life. Campus ministry provides counseling and opportunities for spiritual development, and many students are active in local volunteer organizations. "Most SCU students are white, upper-class prep school kids from California," says a junior. Sixty-two percent of the student body is comprised of undergraduates from California, and the rest are from the West Coast or at least the West—Oregon, Hawaii, Washington, and Arizona. Split fairly evenly between parochial and public schools, 81 percent of the students are from the top quarter of their graduating class. The diversity on campus is impressive; 14 percent of the students are Asian American, 3 percent are African American, and 18 percent are Hispanic. A variety of academic and athletic scholarships are available to those who qualify.

> **"There's a great social life both on and off campus."**

Almost all freshmen and sophomores live on campus, but soon they are packing up and heading for apartments. Most residence halls are co-ed by floor. "Housing here is good because it caters to the partiers, the studiers, and everyone in between," says one student. The Freshman Residential Learning Community program gives incoming students the opportunity to room with students who share similar academic or social interests. All students, including commuters and those living off campus, belong to RLCs and take courses with other members of the group. In all, there are nine RLC programs with emphases such as Italian arts and culture, environmental sustainability, diversity, and social justice. "Dining facilities are wonderful," cheers one student. "The food is very edible, healthy, and emphasizes sustainability."

Greek organizations no longer exist at Santa Clara, but don't let this fool you: Social activity is alive and well. With such beautiful weather and great California locations and events nearby, how could anyone resist partying and road trips? "There's a great social life both on and off campus and over a hundred clubs and programs to get involved in," says one student. Only 20 miles away is Santa Cruz, for those who want to bask in the sun. San Francisco is 45 minutes away and other short road trips to popular hot spots include Napa Valley, Monterey, and Palo Alto. Those who choose to party on or near campus can take advantage of the school's attempt at enforcing "no drinking and driving" by providing the students with transportation called the Bronco Bus. "Underage drinking is not tolerated," warns an accounting major. Alternate forms of leisure activities include a fitness center that is open for long hours and The Bronco, a sports and recreation bar where students over 21 can drink beer or wine.

The Santa Clara Broncos compete in Division I and competitive programs include women's volleyball, cross-country, and basketball, and men's golf and soccer. Intramural sports are big here, too, drawing nearly 4,000 students. The university also offers 18 club sports.

Santa Clara University is a warm place—in every sense of the word—and a comfortable and beautiful setting where morality and ethics are infused into the curriculum of strong academics. It's this blend of traditional values and progressive academics that turns out people who want to make a difference in the world.

> *Greek organizations no longer exist at Santa Clara, but don't let this fool you: Social activity is alive and well.*

Overlaps

Caltech, Loyola Marymount, UC–Berkeley, UC–Davis, University of San Diego

If You Apply To ➤

SCU: Early decision and early action: Nov. 1. Regular admissions: Jan. 7. Housing: May 1. Application fee: $55. No campus or alumni interviews. SATs or ACTs: required (SATs preferred). Subject Tests: optional. Accepts the Common Application. Essay question.

Sarah Lawrence College

1 Mead Way, Bronxville, NY 10708-5999

A pricey and free-spirited sister of East Coast alternative institutions like Bard and Bennington. Though SLC is co-ed, women outnumber men nearly 3 to 1. Strong in the humanities and fine arts with a specialty in creative writing. Full of quirky, headstrong intellectuals who hop the train to New York City every chance they get.

Sarah Lawrence College attracts creative, highly motivated individuals who are both critical thinkers and devotees of independent learning. They love literature and the fine arts and take pride in their academic prowess. Indeed, freedom and exploration are valued more highly than any tradition here, save perhaps May Fair. And although some students lament SLC's move toward the mainstream (including more sports teams than ever), they also appreciate the things that haven't changed on campus, such as the emphasis on small classes and one-on-one conferences with professors. "This place can be a safe haven for you if you are creative and independent," says one senior. Those looking for "a standard experience (frats and football)" might want to look elsewhere.

Website: www.sarahlawrence.edu
Location: Suburban
Private
Total Enrollment: 1,576
Undergraduates: 1,318
Male/Female: 27/73
SAT Ranges: N/A
ACT Ranges: N/A

(continued)

Financial Aid: 67%

Expense: Pr $ $ $ $

Student Loans: 61%

Average Debt: $

Phi Beta Kappa: Yes

Applicants: 2,165

Accepted: 62%

Enrolled: 26%

Grad in 6 Years: 77%

Returning Freshmen: 90%

Academics: ✍ ✍ ✍ ✍

Social: ☎ ☎

Q of L: ★ ★ ★

Admissions: (800) 888-2858

Email Address: slcadmit@
    sarahlawrence.edu

Strongest Programs:

History

Literature

Psychology

Writing

Visual and Performing Arts

*It's tough to find
two Sarah Lawrence
students studying
the same thing.*

Founded in 1926, Sarah Lawrence sits on a quaint, 404-acre tract in the city of Yonkers, a wealthy Westchester County community, where even the public library boasts Oriental rugs and fireplaces. Bronxville is a "quiet, wealthy, conservative little town where almost everything shuts down after 8:00 p.m.," according to one senior. On campus, the prevailing architectural theme is English Tudor, including mansions from converted estates, but more modern structures are present as well. The landscape is hilly and green, with more than a hundred types of trees and abundant rock outcroppings. Because the school's founders believed that there should be as little physical separation as possible between life and work, many classrooms, dormitory suites, and faculty offices are all housed in the same ivy-covered buildings.

General education requirements at Sarah Lawrence include credits in at least three of four academic areas, leaving lots of room for students to dabble in whatever strikes their fancy. In fact, it's tough to find two Sarah Lawrence students studying the same thing, because every student designs his or her own program of study, and almost no subject is out of bounds. And, since there are no mandatory or required courses, competition is virtually nonexistent, says a senior: "Professors are idealistic and brilliant—and they provide students with a challenging courseload." Though there are formal grades, more important is the student's portfolio of work, accompanied by in-depth, written evaluations from professors, filed twice a year. Not surprisingly, SLC no longer considers SAT scores as part of the admissions process.

> "This place can be a safe haven for you if you are creative and independent."

Regardless of what they focus on, all students become intimately acquainted with the written word; writing begins in the first year at SLC, and continues relentlessly "across the curriculum" for the next three. Courses at Sarah Lawrence "are generally demanding," says a student studying computer science. That's because everyone takes only three courses per semester. Still, professors meet with their students weekly or biweekly, in a system modeled after Oxford University's tutorials, so there's no time to slack off—or fall behind. To ease the transition to college, all first-years take a First-Year Studies seminar. Typically, more than 30 subjects are available, and "you pick the topic before school starts," says one student. Courses can last just one semester or for the full year.

Perhaps because of SLC's emphasis on personal relationships with professors, even the registration process requires deep thought: Students interview teachers to ensure that courses fit into their academic plans, and to confirm the instructor is someone they respect and want to study with. And although getting into popular classes can be a problem, administrators guarantee students at least two of their first three choices each semester. "The quality of teaching is simply extraordinary," says one student, and "teaching assistants do not exist." Study abroad programs are offered in Florence, Catania, Paris, Oxford, London, and Havana; 50 percent of students participate.

The most popular concentrations at Sarah Lawrence include visual arts, writing, literature, history, and psychology. Aspiring psychologists—also a significant group on campus—may participate in fieldwork at the college's Early Childhood Center. Students benefit both from the college's proximity to New York City and from expanded offerings in filmmaking and film history. Weaker departments include Russian, Japanese, and German, administrators say, since each has only one professor. The premed program, more structured than other offerings, places nearly all eligible graduates into medical school. Though students concentrating in the sciences are few and far between, those who focus on biology, chemistry, and physics have access to a science center, with 22,500 square feet of classrooms, lab benches,

> "Professors are idealistic and brilliant."

and computer technology. Though its holdings are small—just 224,000 volumes—the charming library takes the sting out of studying, with an area for eating and a pillow room for occasional naps.

The typical Sarah Lawrence student is hardworking and passionate about learning. "To characterize a typical Sarah Lawrence student is folly," sighs one student. "In fact, most of us will say that there is no typical Sarah Lawrence student." A classmate gives it a shot, nevertheless: "Most students at Sarah Lawrence are left-leaning, progressive, and supportive of the LGBT community." Twenty percent are natives of New York State—the bulk from nearby New York City—and minorities account for 24 percent of the student body: 8 percent African American, 7 percent Asian American, 9 percent Hispanic, and 1 percent Native American. Students report that political and social issues attract much attention, and debates have included the presidential campaign and environmental concerns. There are no merit or athletic scholarships.

Seventy-seven percent of Sarah Lawrence students live on campus, where "dorms are excellent for everyone who is not a freshman," says a sophomore. A senior adds, "Housing is not created equal here. There are many different kinds, from actual houses, to a traditional college-style dormitory, to converted Tudor mansions (one of which I proudly call home)." Upperclassmen

> **"To characterize a typical Sarah Lawrence student is folly."**

may get to live in one of three townhouse complexes. Students on a budget often commute from Westchester County's lower-rent districts, or from their parents' homes in New York City. Dining services cater to the quarter of SLC students who are vegetarians, but the meal plan is "ridiculously overpriced," students say. The student center's greasy spoon is also an option, and most dorms have their own kitchens as well. Security is "easygoing and omnipresent," says a student.

When the weekend comes, SLC has a modicum of social life—free dances and movies, plays, poetry readings, guest lectures, and tea and coffeehouses—but most students head south to New York City, just a half hour away by train. Theater fans and aspiring actors flock to discounted Broadway shows, and clubs, bars, museums, and concert halls also beckon. "Parties, drinking, and debauchery are common on weekends, but can be avoided just the same," says one student. Campus policies require hosts that serve alcohol to register. Although alcohol policies are "rigorous," students report they are not effective at curbing underage drinking. Favorite traditions include May Fair, the "actually interesting" sex education program called Sleaze Week, and midnight breakfast, served during the last week of each semester.

The Sarah Lawrence Gryphons compete in the Division III Hudson Valley Conference, and the women's swimming and tennis teams have brought home conference titles in recent years. The intramural program revolves around invitational events—road races, basketball and squash tournaments, fitness challenges—rather than league play. The men's basketball and women's equestrian teams attract the most fans. And if you can't find the team or activity you want? "The school is so generous with money," says one student. "Start a club, propose it to Student Senate, and you'll get $2,000 for whatever project you choose."

Sarah Lawrence offers a close-knit community for writers and artists, in a lush setting just outside the hustle and bustle of Manhattan. "If you want an intensely creative, small liberal arts college with amazing professors and opportunities, and you're OK without a large party scene, then this is very likely the best place for you," explains a junior. One caveat, though—all that personal attention doesn't come cheap, and admissions at SLC are need-aware. "Assume your financial aid will decrease, and the tuition will increase, by at least a few thousand dollars each year," a student says.

Students interview teachers to ensure that courses fit into their academic plans.

Students report that political and social issues attract much attention.

Overlaps

Bard, NYU, Hampshire, Emerson, Bennington, Boston University, Lewis & Clark, Oberlin

Scripps College: See page 147.

Seattle University

Seattle, WA 98122-1090

Unlike the University of Washington, Seattle U is a stone's throw from downtown and within walking distance of the waterfront. Jesuit tradition guarantees student growth both academically and in community service. Transitioning to a national institution and Division I athletics, but remains true to its humble roots. Out-of-staters are drawn as much by the city of Seattle as by the university itself.

Website: www.seattleu.edu
Location: City Center
Private
Total Enrollment: 5,757
Undergraduates: 4,351
Male/Female: 41/59
SAT Ranges: CR 530–640,
  M 540–640
ACT Ranges: 24–29
Financial Aid: 87%
Expense: Pr $
Student Loans: 73%
Average Debt: $ $ $
Phi Beta Kappa: No
Applicants: 6,862
Accepted: 72%
Enrolled: 19%
Grad in 6 Years: 77%
Returning Freshmen: 87%
Academics: ✍ ✍ ✍
Social: ☎ ☎ ☎
Q of L: ★ ★ ★ ★
Admissions: (206) 296-6000
Email Address: admissions@
  seattleu.edu

Strongest Programs:
Nursing
Finance
Marketing

Although Seattle has cultivated a reputation based largely on software, Starbucks, and perpetually gray skies, the city is also home to Seattle University, a vibrant Jesuit institution that attracts nearly 6,000 students to its urban campus. With strong preprofessional programs and a commitment to social and spiritual engagement, SU continues to express its mission to empower leaders for a just and humane world. "I have found that we often care more about how we can help other people around us," says one student, "rather than trying to make millions of dollars to buy huge houses and nice cars."

SU's campus is a 45-acre urban sanctuary in the heart of Seattle. Bordered by busy city streets, the diverse campus buildings are united by a recurring theme of redbrick and light-filled atriums. The Chapel of St. Ignatius is a prize-winning building designed by Steven Holl around the concept of a "gathering of different lights." New buildings are designed to meet environmentally friendly standards, and energy efficiency and sustainability are top priorities for renovations. Campus grounds have long been pesticide-free, and special areas like the Ethnobotanical Garden and Japanese American Remembrance Garden highlight native plants and local history. The James Tower Clinical Nursing Lab is a state-of-the-art training facility for nursing students. In late 2011 the university opened a 21,000-square-foot fitness center featuring the latest in strength training and cardio equipment.

> **"We often care more about how we can help other people around us."**

The new, 60-credit University Core Curriculum introduces all students to the "unique tradition of Jesuit liberal education" and aims to develop the whole person for a life of service, provide a foundation for questioning and learning in any major or profession throughout one's entire life, and give a common intellectual experience to all SU students. The core features seminars in writing, quantitative reasoning and creative expression, humanities, social sciences and natural sciences, as well as coursework in philosophy and theology. Freshmen complete a first-year seminar built around a central theme or problem (enrollment is limited to 19 students), and seniors must complete a capstone course or project. In addition, SU has implemented a writing-across-the-curriculum initiative that requires all sophomores to submit a writing sample for assessment.

SU students choose from more than 60 undergraduate degree programs, and popular majors include nursing, management, psychology, English, and finance. Chemistry and biology are solid choices, and motivated students may enroll in the University Honors program, which offers three concurrent classes in every term. The program focuses on the humanities from the dawn of civilization to the present age and makes extensive use of the seminar format. "Many of the courses at SU require the student to think in unconventional ways and to explore theories and questions that may not have an easy answer," reports one junior. "Those who struggle with classes are helped by others, and those who are excelling are happy to help others," adds a senior. Fifty-one percent of classes have 19 or fewer students and professors are accessible. "Because of our small class sizes, professors really know who their students are and care about their academic endeavors," says a junior. Additional programs include undergraduate degrees in public affairs, cell and molecular biology, and marine and conservation biology.

"Those who struggle with classes are helped by others."

When students want to escape Seattle's gray skies and near-constant drizzle, they can take part in the university's study abroad program. Overall, more than 500 students pack their bags each year for locations around the world, including Austria, Cambodia, China, France, Japan, and Uganda. SU also sends approximately 20 students to the National Conference for Undergraduate Research each year as part of a robust undergraduate research program.

"Everyone at Seattle U has a passion and is willing to embrace it," says a mechanical engineering major. Forty-seven percent of SU students hail from Washington and 10 percent are from other nations. African Americans comprise 4 percent of the student body, Asian Americans account for 17 percent, and Hispanics add another 9 percent. Despite its religious ties, "Seattle University is a very liberal and progressive institution," states one junior. "I think that students are aware and active in the social and environmental justice issues that plague the world today," adds a history major. Merit scholarships are awarded annually, and student athletes vie for 30 scholarships in 11 sports.

Forty-one percent of SU students live in university housing. "The dorms are well maintained, and the maintenance staff is quick to respond to requests," a senior says. Bellarmine Hall features student lounges complete with cable TV, a kitchen, and a state-of-the-art education center complete with computer lab, study lounge, and private study rooms. Campion Hall is on the south side of campus and offers spectacular views of Seattle, while students in Xavier Hall share a sincere interest in global studies, cross-cultural education, and a desire to live in a culturally diverse and enriching learning community. Chardin Hall houses approximately 150 freshmen, sophomores, and juniors in four-person suites that include two double rooms adjoined by a private bathroom. The university offers 12 residential communities, including options for those interested in eco-awareness, global affairs, wellness, outdoor adventure and leadership, and the arts. Dining gets high marks: "Our food is awesome!" cheers one student. "We have local, seasonal, organic, and sustainable food whenever possible. Made-to-order sushi at lunch, pasta, wok, soup, sandwiches, pizza, salad bar, and Mexican station. Tons of vegetarian and vegan and celiac-friendly options."

"There is always something to do on campus," says a sophomore, including more than 80 student clubs and organizations. Consistent with Jesuit traditions, there are no fraternities or sororities, and "not a whole lot of drinking occurs on campus," according to one student. Instead, students head off campus to enjoy Seattle's vibrant nightlife. "The campus overlooks the urban center of Seattle," explains a student, "and it's a 10-minute walk to the heart of downtown." Once there, students

(continued)
Accounting
Management
Criminal Justice
Digital Design
Computer Science

Programs include undergraduate degrees in public affairs, cell and molecular biology, and marine and conservation biology.

Successful Redhawks programs include women's soccer, volleyball, and basketball, and men's baseball and basketball.

Overlaps

University of Washington, University of Portland, Western Washington, Gonzaga, Seattle Pacific, University of San Francisco, Washington State, University of Oregon

can take advantage of the city's ubiquitous coffeehouses, eateries, and shops, or engage in volunteer work and service-learning opportunities.

SU competes in the Western Athletic Conference (and Division I). Successful Redhawks programs include women's soccer, volleyball, and basketball, and men's baseball and basketball. "There has always been a rivalry between Seattle University and Seattle Pacific University," a political science major says. Intramural and recreational sports draw 75 percent of students.

With its emphasis on the liberal arts, civic engagement, and Jesuit principles, SU affords students an experience "which focuses on educating the entire person," according to one junior. For those students who are not averse to hard work and overcast skies, Seattle University might be an inspired choice—just be sure to pack a parka.

<table>
<tr><td>If You Apply To ≫</td><td>Seattle: Early action: Nov. 15. Regular admissions: Jan. 15. Financial aid: Feb. 1. Application fee: $55. Campus interviews: optional, informational. No alumni interviews. SATs or ACTs: required. No Subject Tests. Accepts the Common Application. Essay question.</td></tr>
</table>

Skidmore College

815 North Broadway, Saratoga Springs, NY 12866

Founded in 1903 as the Young Women's Industrial Club of Saratoga, co-ed Skidmore College still excels in the fine and performing arts that were then deemed proper for young ladies. Little else remains the same. Compare to Connecticut College, Vassar, and Wheaton (MA), all institutions that made the successful transition to coeducation. Unique wooded campus gives the feel of living in a forest.

Skidmore College serves up solid academics with a decidedly nontraditional flair. Although these politically liberal and free-spirited students complain about the cold weather and frosty relations with the conservative locals, Skidmore students are a happy lot. Classes are small, faculty members are available, and "the college has a charm, sort of like a summer camp," says a junior. And thanks to an emphasis on interdisciplinary learning, students can "have diverse interests and are able to dabble in anything," a senior says.

In 1961, as enrollment surpassed 1,300 and Skidmore's turn-of-the-century Victorian buildings grew obsolete, Skidmore traded its campus in the heart of Saratoga Springs for 750 acres on the northwest edge of town. Since then, the campus has grown to more than 50 buildings on 890 acres, and the student body has doubled in size (men were welcomed in 1971). While contemporary in style, the new buildings on Skidmore's Jonsson campus reflect the Victorian heritage of the school's original Scribner campus. Covered walkways connect the residential, academic, and social centers, and the prevailing views are of surrounding mountains, woods, and fields. The Zankel Music Center opened in 2010 and features a 600-seat performance hall. A bevy of apartment-style student residences have added 238 beds.

> "Skidmore's academics are definitely challenging; they push you to become better thinkers."

The most popular majors at Skidmore are business, psychology, English, art, and government. Not coincidentally, students say these are some of the college's

Website: www.skidmore.edu
Location: Small City
Private
Total Enrollment: 2,614
Undergraduates: 2,614
Male/Female: 40/60
SAT Ranges: CR 560–670, M 560–670
ACT Ranges: 26–30
Financial Aid: 56%
Expense: Pr $ $ $ $
Student Loans: 42%
Average Debt: $ $
Phi Beta Kappa: Yes
Applicants: 5,702
Accepted: 42%
Enrolled: 27%
Grad in 6 Years: 88%
Returning Freshmen: 92%
Academics: ✏ ✏ ✏ ✏
Social: ☎ ☎ ☎

best programs as well. Biology, environmental studies, and geoscience majors may conduct fieldwork in the college's 300-acre North Woods, a natural laboratory. Through the Hudson-Mohawk Association of Colleges and Universities, students may take courses at most other colleges nearby. There are also cooperative programs in engineering with Dartmouth and Clarkson; a Washington semester with American University*; a semester at the Marine Biological Laboratory in Woods Hole, Massachusetts; a master of arts in teaching with Union University; M.B.A. programs with Clarkson, Rochester Institute of Technology, and Union; and cooperative nursing and physical/occupational therapy programs with NYU and the Sage Colleges, respectively. The college has also established the Skidmore Analytical Interdisciplinary Laboratory (SAIL), an integrated research instrumentation cluster that enables faculty and students in biology, chemistry, environmental studies, and anthropology to engage in research that links molecular composition to the structure and function of biological, chemical, environmental, and anthropological systems.

(continued)

Q of L: ★ ★ ★
Admissions: (800) 867-6007
Email Address: admissions@ skidmore.edu

Strongest Programs:
Social Sciences
Visual and Performing Arts
Business/Marketing
Psychology
English

Most students agree that coursework is challenging but not competitive. "Skidmore's academics are definitely challenging; they push you to become better thinkers, writers, and overall better students. Each class I have taken has taught me something new and I find myself enjoying the work," says a junior. Skidmore augments liberal arts and sciences offerings with preprofessional majors in management and business, education, exercise science, and social work. Art majors and other non-majors frequently enroll in a popular introductory business class, where they make

"With no Greek life, Skidmore puts a ton of money toward the 100 clubs and organizations."

presentations to corporate executives. Another much-praised option is off-campus study, especially through Skidmore-run programs in France, England, Spain, or China, in addition to domestic programs at other colleges and universities. Some 57 percent of students spend at least one semester off campus. Skidmore's Summer Faculty-Student Research Program provides students an opportunity to work individually with faculty mentors on original research in disciplines ranging from biology to management and business. Students spend five to 10 weeks in the lab or the classroom immersed in research. Professors are lauded for their accessibility and knowledge. "There are some professors who have just blown me away with their lectures," a junior says, and "because they know their material so well and are truly interested in what they are teaching, the students get more from their classes."

Skidmore's First Year Experience includes a classwide summer reading project and a choice from among 50 Scribner seminars. Each seminar is capped at 15 students, and taught by a professor who also becomes the mentor and advisor for that group. Seminar topics are broad and varied, in keeping with Skidmore's nearly 50 majors. They range from Molecular Frontier to Post-Wall German Cinema to Hard Times in the Big Easy. Students in each seminar live near one another along with an upper-class peer mentor, and themes raised in the summer reading crop up again during the year in campuswide programming.

Skidmore's First Year Experience includes a classwide summer reading project and a choice from among 50 Scribner seminars.

"There is a stereotype that we are all 'artsy hipsters' and I wouldn't deny that some of us definitely are, but we often forget about the other students, who make up so much of the population here," says a junior. Given Skidmore's hefty price tag—more than Harvard's—many students are well-off; they hail primarily from New York, New Jersey, and New England. Asian Americans constitute 6 percent of the student body, Hispanics 8 percent, and African Americans 6 percent. Awards for academic merit—four annually in music ($48,000 over four years) and five annually in math and science ($60,000 over four years)—are available, although there are no athletic scholarships. And recently, grant-funded science scholarships for economically disadvantaged students were instituted. More than 40 percent of students take advantage of the college's $39 million dollars in financial aid.

Eighty-six percent of Skidmore students live in the dorms, and most students get singles after freshman year. Dorms are integrated by class and co-ed by floor or suite, with kitchenettes and lounges on every floor. "The dorms are incredibly comfortable, spacious, and clean," says a student. Most buildings have carpet, air-conditioning, and cozy window seats. Juniors and seniors typically get single rooms in the centrally located residence halls or move to apartments—whether on campus in Northwoods Village Apartments, off campus in Saratoga Springs, or in Skidmore's new Hillside apartments. The Murray-Aikins dining center provides students with fresh food choices in a state-of-the-art facility. "I have friends come and visit me from other schools and demand to be sneaked into our dining hall," says a freshman.

Students reach out to the community through BenefAction, a volunteer group connected to several local agencies and schools.

"With no Greek life, Skidmore puts a ton of money toward the 100 clubs and organizations. With over 3,000 events every year, the question is not what will you do on the weekend, it's what you won't have time to do," says one senior. The school's three-strikes policy means fines don't kick in until the third time an underage student is busted with alcohol, causing some students to call the policy "a joke." The best road trips include Albany, New York City, Boston—and especially Montreal, where you don't need a fake ID to drink at 19. Every year there are also two or three formal dances, often in the elegant and formal Hall of Springs, plus Fun Day in the spring, with games and an inflatable obstacle course on the college green.

The nearby Adirondacks and Green Mountains make Skidmore a haven for backpackers, skiers, and members of the popular Outdoors Club, while the old resort town of Saratoga Springs, with its healing waters and antique shops, offers plenty of culture, including the Saratoga Performing Arts Center and the country's oldest thoroughbred racetrack. Saratoga is also the summer home of the New York City Ballet, the Lake George Opera, and the Philadelphia Orchestra. Students reach out to the community through BenefAction, a volunteer group connected to several local agencies and schools. Skidmore's more traditional activities, which have continued even after a quarter-century of coeducation, include Junior Ring Week, when juniors receive their class rings and a dance is held in honor of their initiation.

Skidmore's men's and women's varsity teams (the "Thoroughbreds") compete in NCAA Division III; men's baseball, basketball, tennis, and golf teams have claimed league championships in recent years, as has volleyball, and women's tennis. The riding program won the Intercollegiate Horse Show Association national championship in 2013. Varsity athletes and weekend warriors alike enjoy the 400-meter, all-weather track and the athletic center, which includes a fitness center and locker rooms.

Skidmore continues to win the hearts of motivated students with gorgeous scenery, caring faculty, and its flexibility, openness, and receptivity to change and growth. Students here are also a bit quirky, says a sophomore, "wearing shorts in the winter, for example." They're more likely to cheer on the fall of a foreign dictator than a goal by the lacrosse team. The point is, there's room for—and encouragement of—all types of students. Says a women's studies major, "The campus is beautiful, and the professors and students actually create bonds that last a lifetime."

Overlaps
Boston University, Brown, Colgate, Connecticut College, Dartmouth, NYU, Vassar, Wesleyan

If You Apply To ➤ **Skidmore:** Early decision: Nov. 15. Regular admissions: Jan. 15. Financial aid: Feb. 1. Housing: May 1. Application fee: $65. Campus and alumni interviews: optional, evaluative. SATs or ACTs: required. Subject Tests: recommended. Accepts the Common Application. Essay question: Common Application.

Smith College

College Lane, Northampton, MA 01063

The furthest left-leaning of the nation's leading women's colleges. Liberal Northampton provides sophisticated social life, and the Five College Consortium* adds depth and breadth all around. With a total enrollment of about 3,100, Smith is the biggest of the top women's colleges, and the first to offer engineering. Compare to Bryn Mawr.

Heaven only knows what Sophia Smith would think of the women's college she founded in 1871 with the hope it would be "pervaded by the Spirit of Evangelical Christian Religion." There are still Evangelicals at Smith, but today they join the rest of their schoolmates in crusading against racism, classism, sexism, and homophobia. Though the all-female school remains strongly committed to its liberal arts mission, it is also focused on placing women at the forefront of science and technology. Students here have the opportunity to become leaders in the male-dominated field of engineering, or pursue interdisciplinary fields such as landscape studies. "Smith has an open curriculum, a great college town, and a very strong science program," says one sophomore.

Smith is in the small city of Northampton, an artsy oasis within an hour's drive of the Berkshire Mountains. The 147-acre campus resembles a medieval fortress from the front gate, but inside it sparkles with many gardens, Paradise Pond, and a plant house. Buildings cover a range of styles from late 18th century to modern, and the college has successfully retained its historic atmosphere while keeping facilities up-to-date. The college's science and engineering building, Ford Hall, has earned LEED Gold certification.

Be ready to hit the books with your newfound sisters at Smith. Coursework is described as "very intense and very difficult," although the atmosphere is "not too competitive because we all want to grow together," according to one student. Smith's student-run honor system, which covers everything from exams to library checkout, is widely praised and enforced. Students generally refrain from discussing grades, choosing instead to focus on helping one another.

Government is among the most popular majors on campus, followed by psychology, economics, English, and biological sciences. One in four Smith women majors in science and thereby enjoys numerous opportunities to assist professors with their research. The STRIDE program allows freshmen and sophomores to become paid research assistants to professors. Science students also benefit from a spacious, state-of-the-art science center. Two electron microscopes are available for

> "Smith students are women who know what they want and know how to get things done."

student use, and, through the Five College Consortium*, students have access to one of the best radio astronomy facilities in the world. Smith's art history department is among the best in the nation and enjoys access to the college's superb museum.

With the exception of at least one writing course, Smith women have unusual freedom to plan a course of study. They must take half of their credits outside of their major, and first-year students can take small seminars on topics such as Biography in African History. Qualified students may enter the Smith Scholars program and embark on one or two years of independent or extra college research for full credit. About 100 older students are enrolled in the Ada Comstock Scholars program for women going back to college. The Picker Program in Engineering and Technology is the first of its kind at a women's college and offers students the

Website: www.smith.edu
Location: Suburban
Private
Total Enrollment: 3,125
Undergraduates: 2,643
Male/Female: 0/100
SAT Ranges: CR 610–720, M 600–710
ACT Ranges: 27–31
Financial Aid: 71%
Expense: Pr $ $ $
Student Loans: 67%
Average Debt: $ $
Phi Beta Kappa: Yes
Applicants: 4,341
Accepted: 42%
Enrolled: 35%
Grad in 6 Years: 85%
Returning Freshmen: 93%
Academics: ✍ ✍ ✍ ✍ ½
Social: ☎ ☎ ☎
Q of L: ★ ★ ★ ★
Admissions: (413) 585-2500
Email Address: admissions@smith.edu

Strongest Programs:
Government
Art
Psychology
Biological Sciences
Economics
Engineering

opportunity to pursue an ambitious engineering program taught within the full depth and breadth of the liberal arts. Those who complete it are among the most sought after graduates of any U.S. college, and administrators hope the curriculum

"My professors have all been accessible and supportive."

will lead to greater gender parity in engineering. Members of the first graduating class headed to prestigious graduate programs at Cornell, Harvard, MIT, Princeton, and other colleges, and two received highly competitive National Science Foundation fellowships; others were quickly commandeered by employers. Newer offerings include landscape studies, which focuses on the relationship between humans and natural and built environments; it's the only such program in the country.

All courses are taught by full professors, and students seem to be pleased with the quality of teaching and their access to the professors. "My professors have all been accessible and supportive as well as open minded and articulate," says a sophomore. Smith's four libraries have almost 2 million holdings among them, making it one of the largest collections of any liberal arts college in the country. Students can study for a semester or two at one of 12 well-known New England colleges through the Twelve College Exchange Program*, or take advantage of the innovative Maritime Studies Program*. Students are also enthusiastic about the opportunity to take part in Smith's well-known study abroad program, which usually sends half the junior class abroad for at least a semester in a number of countries. The Praxis program allows each student to participate in at least one summer internship funded by the college.

Smith students are "women who know what they want and know how to get things done," says a government major. Sixty-eight percent of Smith first-years ranked in the top 10th of their high school class. Less than 20 percent hail from Massachusetts. African Americans account for 5 percent of the student body, Asian Americans 12 percent, Hispanics 9 percent, and Native Americans less than 1 percent. Nobody disputes that Smith is a liberal place, with social issues of the day

"The house system builds strong community."

dominating conversations, though some students are surprised to find themselves in such a free-wheeling atmosphere. With an endowment of more than a billion dollars, Smith has deeper pockets than many of its competitors. And though it's got a hefty price tag, the school manages to recruit a diverse group of women who aren't afraid to say what they think. Need-based grants are handed out annually.

Housing at Smith, which consists of houses, not dorms, is unabashedly adored, and home to 95 percent of students. "The house system builds strong community and each house has its own traditions," a student explains. Students note that they often eat breakfast in their pajamas and that the bathrooms are probably much cleaner than if there were men around. Each of the 36 houses, accommodating from 10 to 100 students, is a self-governing unit, responsible for everything from visiting hours to weekend parties and concerts. Accoutrements in each house include a living room, a TV room, and a study room, many with a fireplace and a grand piano. The head resident, selected by the administration, is the leader of the house, but the elected house council runs day-to-day affairs.

The atmosphere is less that of a sorority than of an extended family. Except for one senior house, classes are mixed in each house, and first-year students easily mingle with seniors. Incoming students can indicate a preference for size and location of their first house, and changes are possible by entering a lottery. All undergraduates except for Ada Comstock scholars must live on campus—a bone of contention among some juniors and seniors. Two alternatives offered are a vegetarian cooperative and an apartment complex. A house system is also used for the dining halls,

With the exception of at least one writing course, Smith women have unusual freedom to plan a course of study.

Students can study for a semester or two at one of 12 well-known New England colleges through the Twelve College Exchange Program.*

and the food is highly praised. There are 15 dining halls on campus open for specific times for breakfast, lunch, and dinner on the weekdays and brunch and dinner on the weekends. Some houses even have family-style Thursday dinners to which students invite faculty members.

You will not be greeted with a rocking social scene at Smith, but there are plenty of parties to be had and great places to visit. "The student organizations on campus are pretty good at organizing events like movie nights and sundae parties," says a senior. Meeting men (or non-Smith women) is made easier by the five-college system. In addition, each house throws an average of two parties a semester. For special weekends, a whole fraternity may be invited from Dartmouth or another nearby college, an arrangement that is only slightly more civilized than the typical college bar scene. Students must be 21 to drink alcohol at campus parties; IDs are checked and hands are stamped. Students say the alcohol policies are getting stricter. There is a free bus service to the other four members of the consortium, which offer a broad range of social and cultural opportunities.

Northampton, known as NoHo after New York City's SoHo neighborhood, is a college town of about 30,000 that is known for funky bohemianism. The town is home to multiple subcultures, and is generally tolerant of everyone. "Northampton is one of my favorite places," says a senior. "It's small and artsy, has multiple venues for music and dance, a dance club, bowling alley, and a lot of great restaurants. There is never a lack of nightlife." The Community Service Office (CSO) arranges for students to volunteer in about 600 placements in Northampton, the surrounding communities, and on campus. Smith also offers time-honored traditions like Mountain Day, when the president cancels class for a day of hiking and female bonding, complete with brown-bag lunches. The New England countryside has numerous special charms, including ski slopes only an hour away. The best road trips are to Boston (two hours) or New York City (three hours).

> **"The student organizations on campus are pretty good at organizing events like movie nights and sundae parties."**

Smith has a long tradition of success in Division III athletics; the college was the first women's college to join the NCAA, and still places a premium on recruiting scholar-athletes. Top teams include crew, basketball, soccer, and equestrian. The rowing and volleyball teams have brought home recent championships. Smith's multimillion-dollar sports complex includes indoor tennis and track facilities, a six-lane swimming pool, and a riding ring. Inter-house competitions include everything from kickball to inner-tube water polo to rugby.

"Smith isn't for everyone," acknowledges one senior. "It can be hard to adapt to the environment of a women's college. But it's been the most valuable thing I've ever done." The strict evangelism is gone, and today's Smith women are far from Sophia Smith wannabes. But her namesake and spirit live on at this eclectic, open-minded institution where women don lab coats, power suits, combat boots, and even white dresses at graduation. This "community of close, intelligent, interesting, and compassionate women" readies them to be and do just about anything.

Housing at Smith, which consists of houses, not dorms, is unabashedly adored, and home to 95 percent of students.

Overlaps

Barnard, Brown, Bryn Mawr, Mount Holyoke, Oberlin, Scripps, Wellesley

If You Apply To ➤ **Smith:** Early decision I: Nov. 15. Early decision II: Jan. 1. Regular admissions: Jan. 15. No application fee. Campus and alumnae interviews: recommended, evaluative. SATs or ACTs: optional. Subject Tests: optional. Accepts the Common Application. Essay question: Common Application questions.

Sewanee is like a little bit of Britain's Oxford plunked down in the highlands of Tennessee. More conservative than Davidson and Rhodes, Sewanee is a guardian of the tried and true. Affiliated with the Episcopal Church, Sewanee still draws heavily from old-line Southern families. Jackets, ties, and academic gowns are still seen frequently.

Website: www.sewanee.edu

Location: Rural

Private

Total Enrollment: 1,524

Undergraduates: 1,450

Male/Female: 48/52

SAT Ranges: CR 590–690, M 580–660

ACT Ranges: 26–30

Financial Aid: 85%

Expense: Pr $

Student Loans: 40%

Average Debt: $ $

Phi Beta Kappa: Yes

Applicants: 3,369

Accepted: 59%

Enrolled: 23%

Grad in 6 Years: 78%

Returning Freshmen: 86%

Academics: ✑ ✑ ✑ ✑

Social: ☎ ☎ ☎

Q of L: ★ ★ ★ ★

Admissions: (800) 522-2234

Email Address: admiss@ sewanee.edu

Strongest Programs:

English

Economics

History

International and Global
  Studies

Psychology

Environmental Studies

Theatre

Art and Art History

Tradition is revered at University of the South, known simply as Sewanee after the school-owned village where it's located. Leonidas Polk, an Episcopal bishop and later a Confederate general, founded the school in 1857, envisioning it as a distinguished center of learning in the region. When Sewanee's cornerstone was destroyed during the Civil War, Anglican parishes in England gave money to restart the school, and Oxford and Cambridge donated the library's first volumes. Sewanee opened again in 1868, with nine students and four professors. Though there are many traditions that remain alive and well, students say the school is modernizing and some traditions are disappearing as the school emphasizes a broader national appeal. "This is a great academic college that will provide you with fun and unique experiences that will be burned into your mind for the rest of time," says one junior.

> **"This is a great academic college that will provide you with fun and unique experiences."**

Sewanee is located atop Tennessee's Cumberland Plateau, between Chattanooga and Nashville. The atmosphere is like "attending Oxford in England," a freshman says, "only with mountains!" Stately English Gothic buildings are carved from beige-and-pink sandstone native to the region, and each has plenty of space, as the school spreads out over a 13,000-acre plot fondly known as "the Domain." Particularly noteworthy structures are St. Luke's and All Saints Chapel, and Convocation Hall, built in 1886. The campus has strong ties to the Episcopal Church, even calling its semesters Advent and Easter, and the student body is overwhelmingly Christian. Gailor Hall, once a dorm and dining facility, is now a center for languages and literature, with offices for the *Sewanee Review*—the oldest continuously published literary quarterly in the United States—and the Sewanee Writers' Conference.

To graduate, all Sewanee students must take at least 32 courses, achieve a GPA of at least 2.0, and spend at least four semesters in residence, including both semesters of the final year. Students pursue six learning objectives in their first two years: Reading Closely; Understanding the Arts; Seeking Meaning; Exploring Past and Present; Observing and Experimenting; and Cross-Cultural Comprehension. In addition to pre-orientation, a new "Finding Your Place" program enhances the first-year experience with academic, social, and geographical exploration, including outdoor and community-based studies. In keeping with European tradition, Sewanee seniors must also pass comprehensive exams in their majors to earn their diplomas. While students are tested, friends decorate their cars to celebrate.

> **"The intimate nature of the school makes people who don't belong very obvious."**

Sewanee's English department is nationally recognized, thanks in part to a bequest from playwright Tennessee Williams. The sciences are also strong, especially variations on environmental studies. The school's unique natural resources department focuses on geology and forestry, and offers a cooperative master's program with Duke and Yale. Premed and preprofessional programs are also highly regarded; about nine of every 10 students applying to medical, dental, and veterinary schools in the last decade have been admitted. The international and global studies major replaces several former programs, and weaker departments include Russian and Japanese, as each has only two professors. One side note about pets on campus: The dogs and cats you may see running around are said to be the reincarnated souls of deceased professors.

Speaking of those professors, most wear black academic gowns when they teach, as do members of Sewanee's signature honor society, the Order of the Gownsmen. Administrators say students and professors voluntarily observe these traditions to demonstrate their commitment to teaching and learning. "The professors are brilliant and, on top of that, they care deeply about their students," says a cultural anthropology major. Typically, women wear dresses or skirts to class, and men wear jackets and ties. Sewanee also takes its honor code very seriously. Violations—such as lying, cheating, or stealing—usually result in expulsion. Sewanee is "steeped in tradition that almost all students abide by, no matter how archaic," a sophomore says. Classwork is taken seriously, too. "The courses can be quite challenging," says a junior. "They are the perfect fit for the hardworking, motivated, intelligent, and articulate students that Sewanee tends to attract."

Sewanee students are not simply a "large group of privileged preps," argues one senior. Rather, they are "personable, intelligent, motivated, honest, and friendly," says an art major. Twenty-six percent of Sewanee's students are Tennessee natives, though many of the rest come from the Southeast. Southern culture is strong here and the atmosphere can be quite familial—more than a quarter of entering freshmen are legacies. Minorities have a small but growing presence on campus, with African Americans making up 4 percent of the student body, Asian Americans 2 percent, and Hispanics 4 percent. Sewanee is attempting to boost diversity with financial aid packages and merit awards, including the Tutu Scholars program for students from South Africa. The university has made serious efforts to keep its cost down and in 2011 actually lowered its tuition by 10 percent. Each year, the school hands out academic scholarships but no athletic awards. Students who maintain a 3.0 cumulative GPA may have the loan portion of their financial aid award replaced with grant money.

Ninety-six percent of Sewanee students live in the dorms, and the most sought-after bunk is Humphreys Hall, which houses 119 students from all classes in singles, doubles, and suites—and is air-conditioned. "Most of the dorms are really wonderful," says a student. Language houses are also available. McClurg Dining Hall serves a wide variety of food and accommodates students' requests, students say. Life on the mountain is peaceful and "students most always feel safe and secure," according to one junior. "The intimate nature of the school makes people who don't belong very obvious," adds another.

Greek life is a huge deal here, with approximately 70 percent of the men and women signing up. "Social life takes place mainly on campus," a student reports. "Greek life rules the social scene but university-funded programs help keep life from becoming one long frat-a-thon." Still, drinking is a fact of life, even though it's against the law for anyone under 21. "Alcohol policies are enforced in the dorms and glass bottles are a huge no-no," says a senior. Annual Fall and Spring Party Weekends draw alumni and friends back to campus, and students also enjoy the Shakespeare Festival and blues fest. Popular road trips include Atlanta, Nashville, and Chattanooga, so it helps to have a car. Nearby lakes, waterfalls, and caverns also offer rafting, hiking, camping, and other active day trips.

Sports are popular at Sewanee, where virtually no one gets cut from varsity squads because they compete in Division III. The most popular Tigers sport on campus is probably football—not so much because the team is any good, but because games are

Sewanee opened again in 1868, with nine students and four professors.

"The courses can be quite challenging."

Sewanee's English department is nationally recognized, thanks in part to a bequest from playwright Tennessee Williams.

Overlaps

Rhodes, University of Georgia, University of Tennessee, University of Virginia, Washington and Lee, Furman, UNC at Chapel Hill, Wofford

important social events, where everyone shows up in coats, ties, and dresses (presumably, not all at once). And then there's the cheer: "Sewanee, Sewanee, leave 'em in the lurch. Down with the heathens and up with the Church. Yea, Sewanee's right." Men's and women's lacrosse is strong and the equestrian team has reached nationals multiple times in recent years (most recently in 2012). Swimming, diving, and tennis teams are also competitive. About 60 percent of students participate in intramural sports, ranging from tennis and touch football to handball, Ping-Pong, and pool.

Sewanee's small size means it offers students plenty of opportunity to really make a difference. And the rich traditions tap into the university's long history and give the campus a life and personality all its own. "The [Sewanee] community ebbs and flows like all communities tend to do," says a student, "but its sentiment remains the same: It is and will always be home."

If You Apply To > **Sewanee:** Early decision: Nov. 15. Early action: Dec. 1. Regular admissions: Feb. 1. Financial aid: Mar. 1. Application fee: $45 (paper), free (online). Campus and alumni interviews: optional, evaluative. SATs or ACTs: optional. No Subject Tests. Accepts the Common Application. Essay question.

University of South Carolina

Columbia, SC 29208

In the state that started the Civil War, USC struggles against the image of being one giant step behind UNC at Chapel Hill. The university has paid big money to attract star professors and boasts one of the top international business programs in the nation. Criminal justice is also a specialty. In contrast to Clemson, USC is in a major city. Check out the Honors College.

Whether it's football or international business, students at the University of South Carolina are game—after all, they're the Gamecocks and, like their mascot, they've got plenty of fighting spirit. Students love to cheer on the school's football and basketball teams, especially if the opponent is longtime rival Clemson. And while 75 percent of the student body comes from within the state, South Carolina is working hard to give its campus a more global feel through programs such as SEED, which stands for Students Educating and Empowering for Diversity. "Diversity and loyalty are two words to describe Gamecock students," says a chemical engineering major.

South Carolina's mostly modern campus is located in the heart of Columbia (population 450,000), which also happens to be the state capital. Government buildings and downtown businesses are within an easy walk, allowing students to secure internships or even part-time jobs during the school year. The old section of the campus, which dates to the school's 1801 founding, includes the glorious oak-lined Horseshoe; 10 of its 19th-century buildings are now listed in the National Register of Historic Places. The $250 million Innovista complex integrates public and private sector research in high-tech facilities. The Dodie Anderson Academic Enrichment Center provides 40,500 square feet of computer labs, seminar and tutor rooms, and an array of nutritionists, psychologists, tutors, and learning specialists to assist students.

South Carolina offers a slew of undergraduate degree programs; biological sciences is popular, as is experimental psychology, nursing, exercise science, and hotel,

> **"Diversity and loyalty are two words to describe Gamecock students."**

Website: www.sc.edu
Location: City Center
Public
Total Enrollment: 26,574
Undergraduates: 21,527
Male/Female: 46/54
SAT Ranges: CR 540–640, M 560–650
ACT Ranges: 24–29
Financial Aid: 87%
Expense: Pub $ $ $ $
Student Loans: 46%
Average Debt: $ $
Phi Beta Kappa: Yes
Applicants: 23,429
Accepted: 61%
Enrolled: 33%
Grad in 6 Years: 72%
Returning Freshmen: 87%
Academics: ✐ ✐ ✐
Social: ☎ ☎ ☎

restaurant, and tourism. "For the most part, the courses are challenging and the environment is laid-back," says one senior. A classmate adds, "Students share notes, study together, and help out others." Students in the journalism and mass communications program benefit from an excellent film library right on campus, while budding marine scientists may study and do research at a 17,000-acre facility about three hours away. Because South Carolina's coastal economy depends on foreign trade, the university has also developed a top-notch international business program. Art students, neglected at many universities, here have access to the latest cameras, editing stations, and computers, as well as pottery kilns and other necessary equipment. Musicians benefit from a four-level building with classrooms, a music and performance library, rehearsal rooms, recording studios, and a 250-seat lecture hall. An unusual minor in medical humanities gives doctors-to-be an introduction to the ethical, cultural, legal, economic, and political factors that affect medical practice today. Top students may want to set their sights on the acclaimed Honors College, which accommodates 1,260 undergrads and offers, as one denizen put it, "all of the attention and faculty interaction you would get at a small college," plus "a lot of research opportunities."

> "Students share notes, study together, and help out others."

(continued)

Q of L: ★ ★ ★
Admissions: (803) 777-7700
Email Address: admissions-ugrad@sc.edu

Strongest Programs:
Experimental Psychology
Integrated IT
Biological Sciences
Exercise Science
Nursing
International Business
Marine Science
Engineering

Regardless of the program in which they enroll, students must complete the Carolina Core, a series of distribution requirements that includes courses in problem solving, writing, global citizenship and multicultural understanding, and scientific literacy (among others). Foreign language proficiency is required for graduation, as is the three-hour University 101 seminar, designed to help freshmen adjust to college. To build community, there's the Freshman Reading Experience, in which entering students read the same book before coming to campus then discuss it in small groups upon arrival. Thirty-six percent of the classes taken by freshmen have 19 or fewer students, and the quality of teaching is reportedly a mixed bag: "Just like any school, you will have motivational, inspirational, life-changing professors and you will have the occasional professor who should consider a career change," one student says. The English program benefits from sizable collections of research material on F. Scott Fitzgerald and Ernest Hemingway, both held in the on-campus library.

Regardless of the program in which they enroll, students must complete the Carolina Core.

USC draws students from all 50 states and from more than 100 countries and also has the highest number of minority students of any public university in the state; 10 percent are African American, 3 percent are Asian American, and 4 percent are Hispanic. "Our students are quite adventurous and do seek out opportunities to be involved both on campus and in the community," says one student. Another says hot-button issues include education funding, gay rights, and marijuana laws, but since there are about 300 religious, social, athletic, and professional clubs on campus, you'll probably be able to find a niche, no matter where you fall on the political spectrum. The university awards more than 100 merit scholarships, as well as 22 athletic awards in 14 sports, including cheerleading and diving. The Gamecock Guarantee promises that each eligible student's undergraduate tuition and technology fee will be covered for up to four years if the student meets the program's academic, financial, and participation criteria.

An unusual minor in medical humanities gives doctors-to-be an introduction to the ethical, cultural, legal, economic, and political factors that affect medical practice today.

Only 36 percent of USC students live on campus, because housing can be expensive and difficult to get, students say. "I loved living on campus," says one junior. "It was so easy to walk to class from my residence hall. I never had to worry about parking or being late to class as long as my alarm went off in time!" The best rooms in the stately old Horseshoe section of campus, for example, cost considerably more than traditional double rooms with hall baths located elsewhere. The best advice? Apply early, since the system is first come, first served, and freshmen compete with upperclassmen for space. The surest way to beat the housing system? Get into the Honors College, which entitles you to some of the best rooms. Dining options range from fast-food stands (Chick-fil-A, Einstein Bros. Bagels, Burger King) to all-you-can-eat lines, with plenty of vegetarian and healthy choices—and of course, some junk food, too. "You will never go hungry," promises one student. Students report feeling safe while roaming campus. In addition to a full-time police presence, "there are over 160 emergency call boxes located throughout campus," notes one junior.

"Social life is bustling," a student says, with "a lot to do on campus and in the city." Thirteen percent of South Carolina's men and 28 percent of the women go Greek, and their chapters provide much of the weekend social life on campus. While students under 21 may not legally drink, some "sneak it in, and are not bothered if they behave themselves," says a speech major. Still, administrators have become more concerned about binge and underage drinking, and funding for alternative activities during high-risk times for alcohol has recently tripled. Those activities include films, dance performances, theatrical productions, concerts, and comedy shows. Downtown Columbia offers more theaters, a comedy club, a performing arts center, and Five Points, a strip boasting six different bars. Outdoorsy types will appreciate Myrtle Beach, just three hours away, and the mountain ranges four hours north, for hiking, skiing, and camping.

"Our students are quite adventurous and do seek out opportunities to be involved both on campus and in the community."

Fall football weekends are always a big deal at South Carolina, and recent successes with coach Steve Spurrier have given fans lots of reasons to cheer. The enduring USC–Clemson rivalry is one of the oldest and most colorful in college sports, with festivities beginning weeks in advance; aside from the Tigerburn parade and bonfire and the all-night tailgating parties, the schools compete in a blood drive. The baseball team won two consecutive national titles in 2010 and 2011. Winter weekends welcome another of USC's strong sports, basketball, played in the 342,000-square-foot Colonial Center. All students may dip into the indoor and outdoor pools at the Strom Thurmond Fitness and Wellness Center, which also features an indoor track, volleyball and basketball courts, a climbing wall, and racquetball courts.

The pace of change is picking up at South Carolina's flagship university. With a campus beautification initiative underway, along with scholarships and small, seminar-style courses working to draw more capable students, it seems that no place could be finer, indeed.

Overlaps

Clemson, College of Charleston, Furman, University of Georgia, UNC at Chapel Hill

If You Apply To ➤ | **South Carolina:** Early action: Oct. 15. Regular admissions: Dec. 1. Application fee: $50. No campus or alumni interviews. SATs or ACTs: required. No Subject Tests. Essay question: optional personal statement.

University of Southern California

University Park, Los Angeles, CA 90098

USC's old handle: "The University of Spoiled Children." USC's new handle: highly selective West Coast university with preeminent programs in arts and media and business. The difference: a deluge in applications of historic proportions as students flock to the region's only major private university that just happens to have one of the nation's best football teams. L.A.'s answer to SMU on the one hand and NYU on the other.

Once dismissed as little more than an academic bastion of privilege, the University of Southern California has come into its own as a West Coast destination for students seeking the advantages of study in a center for the arts, technology, communication, and international trade. The school's lush campus and prime Los Angeles location has led to a flood of applicants, making it continually tougher to win admission. Students cheer on national championship teams, solid engineering, cinematic arts, business, and communications programs, and give high marks to the Trojan alumni network as well. Sometimes accused of being elitist, USC is nevertheless turning out the next generation of Los Angeles business leaders.

> **"When you are at USC, you feel like you're at the beach."**

USC's University Park campus has an unmistakably upscale vibe and offers a mix of traditional ivy-covered and modern structures, arranged around fountains and reflecting pools, well shaded from the Southern California sun. Sitting on 226 parklike acres, just minutes from downtown Los Angeles, USC is a veritable urban oasis. Some nearby areas are pretty rough, but thanks to USC's police department, most students say they've never felt unsafe. "When you are at USC, you feel like you're at the beach: hot girls tanning in the quad, people playing Frisbee," says a sophomore. The 193,000-square-foot Ronald Tutor Campus Center features meeting rooms, lounges, a ballroom, department offices, and dining options.

USC's Core Curriculum requires nine courses: six general education, two intensive writing, and one diversity. Together, administrators say, they "provide a coherent approach to fundamental areas of learning, and give students the tools to think critically, communicate clearly, and locate themselves in history." Students with high GPAs and test scores may choose the Thematic Option—a.k.a. the "Traumatic Option"—in place of regular general education courses. The 200 or so who do get smaller classes with some of the university's best teachers and a handpicked group of writing instructors. Freshmen may also join one of the school's Learning Communities, groups of 20 students with common academic interests, such

> **"I have come across professors who seemed to care more about research than the students."**

as business, medicine, technology, or languages. Each community takes four common courses during the first year and meets with a dedicated faculty mentor and staff advisor three to six times a semester. The progressive degree program allows students to apply to a master's-level program during their junior year; depending on the field, one can earn a bachelor's and master's degree in as little as 10 semesters.

The academic climate is challenging and new students "often have to adjust because either they are not the best in their class anymore or they have to work harder to be the best," says a senior. Aside from a strong alumni network, USC offers undergraduates the chance to pursue degrees not only in the College of Letters, Arts, and Sciences, but also at any of its 17 professional schools and schools of the arts. In fact, USC strongly encourages students to pursue double majors or a combination of majors and minors in unrelated academic fields. This means business majors may minor in bioethics or Russian, that international relations majors may double major in urban planning or international urban development, and art history majors may study cinema and television, the music industry, or business, too. The Renaissance Scholars program recognizes those who excel in two or more disparate areas of study by finishing their majors and minors in no more than five years and achieving a GPA of 3.5 or higher in those disciplines. Additionally, the Discovery Scholars program honors original research and creativity among undergraduates, and the Global Scholars program singles out students who excel both at home and abroad. The quality of teaching varies, especially in some introductory courses for freshmen, which can be huge. "I have come across professors who

---

Website: www.usc.edu
Location: City Center
Private
Total Enrollment: 34,236
Undergraduates: 17,497
Male/Female: 49/51
SAT Ranges: CR 620–720, M 650–760
ACT Ranges: 29–33
Financial Aid: 66%
Expense: Pr $ $
Student Loans: 45%
Average Debt: $ $ $
Phi Beta Kappa: Yes
Applicants: 46,104
Accepted: 20%
Enrolled: 33%
Grad in 6 Years: 90%
Returning Freshmen: 97%
Academics: ✐ ✐ ✐ ½
Social: ☎ ☎ ☎
Q of L: ★ ★ ★
Admissions: (213) 740-1111
Email Address: admitusc@usc.edu

Strongest Programs:
Business
Cinema/Television
Engineering
Communications
Art

Freshmen may join one of the school's Learning Communities.

seemed to care more about research than the students," says an accounting major, but, overall, "the professors are truly amazing."

USC students are a healthy mix of "artistic brilliance and ambitious drive," says one senior. Twenty-eight percent of USC undergrads come from out of state, and the majority went to public high schools, though the university consistently boasts one of the highest proportions of foreign students in the country. Even aside from this international presence, this campus is one of the most diverse in the U.S., with African Americans making up 5 percent of the student body, Hispanics adding 14 percent, and Asian Americans contributing 23 percent. Regardless of their nationality, most students here are "outgoing and friendly," says a music industry major—and most pride themselves on their ability to multitask, maintaining decent grades along with an active social life. Hundreds of merit scholarships are awarded each year (averaging $16,668), as are 353 athletic awards.

Freshmen are guaranteed university housing, and students say dorm rooms, which come with microwaves and refrigerators, are comfortable.

Freshmen are guaranteed university housing, and students say dorm rooms, which come with microwaves and refrigerators, are comfortable. Halls are co-ed, and, "New 1 North is definitely the social dorm that everyone in surrounding residence halls wishes they lived in," says a sophomore. Since swimming pools, tennis courts, carpeting, and air-conditioning are just some of the luxuries to be found in USC dorms, it's no wonder more upperclassmen would like to stay on campus. But because there isn't enough space for everyone, sophomores, juniors, and seniors typically move to fraternity and sorority houses or apartments, which are just a short walk away. (Twenty-five percent of the men and 21 percent of the women go Greek.) Dining halls offer plenty of options, including an international buffet in the Parkside complex, burgers at Carl's Jr., and glazed doughnuts at Krispy Kreme. Blue-light phones, tram and taxi services, and escorts from the campus police mean most students don't worry too much about crime.

"We are drawing an academically competitive and involved student body."

Though Los Angeles is hardly a "college town" in the traditional sense, "it does allow you to experience a wide variety of cultures," says an accounting major. Whether you're looking for an internship at a law firm or a movie studio, you want to learn to surf, or you're eager to check out a new band before they get signed to a major label, L.A. delivers. Famous Venice Beach is just a few miles from USC's campus, and in the winter months, students can reach the San Gabriel Mountains (and its ski resorts) in less than an hour (by car, not by skis). USC students are also active in the community, tutoring in 10 local schools through the Joint Educational Project.

On campus, sports are pretty much the biggest thing going.

On campus, sports are pretty much the biggest thing going. Football mania reached a fever pitch several seasons ago when the Trojans brought home two consecutive national titles and played for a third, and the team hopes to recapture some of that glory under its new head coach. The men's and women's water polo and women's volleyball teams are also championship-caliber. Indeed, two of USC's biggest schoolwide traditions revolve around the ol' pigskin. The first is Troy Week—the week leading up to the UCLA game—which culminates with a pep rally and concert in the middle of campus. Then there's the Weekender, when USC students take off en masse for northern California to see their beloved Trojans face off against Stanford or Berkeley. Throngs of USC undergrads, alumni, and fans gather in San Francisco's Union Square for a huge pep rally, featuring the band, cheerleaders, and university personalities. Overall, the men's and women's athletic teams have brought home more than 100 national titles.

USC is a university on the move. Students here enjoy solid academics, a thriving social scene, and enough sunshine to craft the perfect tan. "We are drawing an academically competitive and involved student body," says a geography and communications major. "We have received major donations. And USC athletics are back

Overlaps

UCLA, UC–Berkeley, Stanford, NYU, Boston University, University of Michigan, Northwestern, Cornell

on par." Pack your sunscreen, flip-flops, and some assertiveness, and you'll fit right in. Shrinking violets, on the other hand, should probably look elsewhere.

Southern Methodist University

P.O. Box 750181, Dallas, TX 75275-0181

SMU is all but the official alma mater of the Dallas business and professional elite. The university is best known for business, performing arts, and upscale conservatism. Though tuition is moderate by national standards, SMU is pricey compared to rivals Rice and Texas Christian. Opulent campus adds to the atmosphere of affluence.

Southern Methodist University is a training ground for the business elite of Dallas, and for those who may want to lead the state of Texas someday. With admissions standards on the rise, both for entering freshmen and for current students who want to transfer into the Cox School of Business and SMU's other top programs, "the stereotypical fraternity or sorority member can't just breeze by," says a senior. "I have seen a shift from social to studious since arriving."

SMU's lush, well-landscaped campus is located in the affluent suburb of University Park, "five minutes from downtown Dallas and within 30 minutes of everything else," according to one student. Flower beds, fountains, and neatly trimmed lawns surround stately brick buildings, most in the collegiate Georgian style. Dallas Hall, with its four-story rotunda, is the centerpiece. The Dedman Center for Lifetime Sports opened in 2006, as did the Embrey Engineering Building, one of the first academic buildings in the nation to be designed and constructed to

"I hold SMU professors in the highest esteem."

LEED Gold standards of environmental design. The George W. Bush Presidential Center, to include library, museum, and independent institute, opened in 2013.

SMU's University Curriculum (UC) includes a variety of coursework within four distinct areas: Foundation (written and oral communication); Pillars (course sequences in pure and applied science, historical contexts, philosophical and religious inquiry and ethics, institutions and cultures, and creativity and aesthetics); Proficiencies and Experiences (credit-bearing courses and noncredit activities that address writing, quantitative reasoning, information literacy, oral communication, community engagement, human diversity, global engagement, and a second language); and a three-hour Capstone requirement.

The most popular field of study at SMU is economics, followed by finance, psychology, accounting, and political science. Engineers have access to an extensive co-op program, thanks to the proximity of more than 800 high-tech companies, including Nokia and Texas Instruments, which have facilities in the Dallas suburbs. The John Goodwin Tower Center for Political Studies, named for the former senator, focuses on international relations and comparative politics, while the on-campus Tate Forums provide informal question-and-answer sessions with national and international figures. The Meadows School of the Arts shines just as brightly. Its facilities include the Bob Hope and Greer Garson theaters, funded by their eponymous

Website: www.smu.edu
Location: City Center
Private
Total Enrollment: 7,648
Undergraduates: 5,992
Male/Female: 49/51
SAT Ranges: CR 590–680, M 600–690
ACT Ranges: 27–31
Financial Aid: 71%
Expense: Pr $ $ $
Student Loans: 35%
Average Debt: $ $ $ $
Phi Beta Kappa: Yes
Applicants: 11,217
Accepted: 54%
Enrolled: 24%
Grad in 6 Years: 75%
Returning Freshmen: 91%
Academics: ✍ ✍ ✍
Social: 🕿 🕿 🕿 🕿
Q of L: ★ ★ ★ ★
Admissions: (214) 768-2058
Email Address: ugadmission@smu.edu

Strongest Programs:
History
Anthropology
Political Science
Business
Natural Sciences/Premed

performers, and the Meadows Museum, which houses one of the finest collections of Spanish art outside of Spain. The Bobby B. Lyle School of Engineering is the first engineering school in the nation to host a Lockheed Martin Skunk Works Lab for intense and rapid innovations. The lab is modeled after the iconic California research facility established to solve complex technology problems.

SMU's humanities programs are notable, too, with English and history particularly strong. SMU publishes *Southwest Review*, one of the four oldest continuously published literary quarterlies in the nation. The Annette Caldwell Simmons School of Education and Human Development offers undergraduate and graduate teaching certifications, as well as a slate of graduate degrees. Students praise professors for the quality of their instruction and their willingness to make themselves accessible. "I hold SMU professors in the highest esteem," says a junior. "They go above and beyond to make learning experiences relevant and meaningful." SMU prides itself on small classes; 60 percent of the courses taken by freshmen have 19 or fewer students. Teaching assistants are available for extra help, students say, but they never teach classes. Freshmen have a variety of special programs available to them, including "orientation programs like AARO and Mustang Corral (an off-campus retreat)," says one student. They "help students to gain experience and knowledge about the university and its programs."

"I would say there is a bit of competition."

Southern Methodist University is a training ground for the business elite of Dallas.

"The academic climate at SMU is pretty challenging," says one junior. "I would say there is a bit of competition but for the most part it is an extremely collaborative and nurturing environment." The Honors Program enables about 850 students to take seminars on topics not offered broadly, with enrollment in each course capped at 15 to 20 students. Nearly 150 study abroad programs take students to 50 nations; 30 percent of all undergraduates participate each year. SMU also operates a second campus near Taos, New Mexico, on the grounds of historic Fort Burgwin, a mid-19th-century army outpost, and an excavated 13th-century pueblo. Each year, about 25 exceptional students are named President's Scholars; they get full-tuition scholarships, plus opportunities to study abroad and attend a retreat in Taos, being matched with corporate mentors, and meeting with the world leaders who visit campus for the Tate Distinguished Lecture Series.

Although it was founded by what is now the United Methodist Church, SMU is nondenominational and welcomes students of all faiths. Just over half of SMU students are Texans, and politically, they lean right. "Our students are smart," says a journalism major. "The average student who doesn't get involved on campus might have issues fitting in." Hispanics account for 12 percent of the student body, while Asian Americans comprise 7 percent and African Americans 6 percent. SMU offers a loan program for middle-income families, as well as nearly 350 athletic scholarships.

"Social life at SMU is really fun."

The Bobby B. Lyle School of Engineering is the first engineering school in the nation to host a Lockheed Martin Skunk Works Lab.

Thirty-two percent of SMU undergrads live on campus, and freshmen are required to do so. "After freshman year it is hard to get in a dorm, and most people move off campus unless they live in a sorority or fraternity house," a student says. All residence halls are co-ed by floor, and theme floors are also available, focused on honors, wellness, community service, multiculturalism, or the arts. Options include single and double rooms, some with their own bathrooms. The Academic–Community Engagement house allows students to live and provide community service in East Dallas, a struggling section of the city. SMU's two dining halls offer hot entrees, salad and sandwich bars, and plenty of desserts. The traditional, all-you-can-eat meal plans also include dining dollars that can be used at the on-campus Subway and Chick-fil-A outposts. "The dining facilities at SMU are top-notch," cheers one student.

When the weekend comes, nearly 200 student groups sponsor speakers and other diversions. "Social life at SMU is really fun," says a journalism major, "especially since we are in a first-class city." With Dallas so close and the campus officially dry—except on football game days—much social life takes place off campus. (Regardless of their age, students say it's easy to find beer at the fraternity houses. Those under 21 and caught drinking are referred to the Judicial Council, but "if you act like a responsible adult, you will be treated like one," says a senior.) Forty-seven percent of the women join sororities and 34 percent of the men pledge fraternities. Highlights of the campus calendar include the Mane Event, honoring the Mustang mascot, and the Celebration of Lights, when students gather to enjoy holiday lights and carols at Dallas Hall. Formals and other Greek parties are by invitation only, and students are often bused to them. SMU's neighborhood is "very nice and safe," says one student, noting that museums, amusement parks, big-league sports, entertainment, and shopping are all within a quick drive. Cars are necessary for road trips to New Orleans (for Mardi Gras), Shreveport (for gambling), and Austin (where the Sixth Street bars and music halls stay open until the wee hours).

Football games are a big deal here—after all, this is Texas—and SMU students get riled up for the annual battle against Texas Christian University. When the Mustangs play at home, there's tailgating on the Boulevard, with tents, family activities, music, and food on the main quad. SMU is a member of Conference USA; men's golf, men's and women's soccer, and men's and women's swimming and diving are especially competitive and frequent conference champs. Intramural options attract roughly one-third of undergrads and include water polo, billiards, dodgeball, and even tug-of-war.

"The quality of life for students at SMU is great," a sophomore cheers. "It is an environment that fosters success." Although known for its beautiful people and striking campus, SMU offers solid preprofessional training along with an active social life, and provides students the opportunity to give back to the city of Dallas—with more than just their bar tabs.

Overlaps

University of Southern California, University of Texas, Texas Christian, Trinity, Tulane, Vanderbilt

If You Apply To ➤

Southern Methodist: Rolling admissions: Mar. 15. Early action: Nov. 1. Housing: May 1. Application fee: $60. No campus or alumni interviews. SATs or ACTs: required. Subject Tests: optional. Accepts the Common Application. Essay question.

Southwestern University

1001 E. University Avenue, Georgetown, TX 78626

Southwestern is one of the top liberal arts colleges in Texas. Compare to Austin and Trinity. Southwestern is about half the size of the latter and prides itself on individual attention and down-to-earth friendliness. Academic strengths include psychology, fine arts, and inquiry-based sciences. Offers an unusually rich array of interdisciplinary and student-centered learning.

In a state known for political conservatism, and for the prevailing view that bigger is better, Southwestern University stands out. "I was initially drawn in by the beautiful campus," admits one senior, "but I stayed because of the opportunities to form strong relationships with both professors and friends, the ability to get involved and make a difference, and the challenging academics."

The Southwestern campus sits on 700 acres at the edge of the rolling Texas Hill Country, although the city of Austin has spread northward and swallowed

Website: www.southwestern .edu
Location: Suburban
Private
Total Enrollment: 1,368
Undergraduates: 1,368

(continued)

Male/Female: 39/61

SAT Ranges: CR 530–660,
  M 550–650

ACT Ranges: 24–29

Financial Aid: 96%

Expense: Pr $

Student Loans: 57%

Average Debt: $ $ $ $

Phi Beta Kappa: Yes

Applicants: 2,795

Accepted: 61%

Enrolled: 21%

Grad in 6 Years: 75%

Returning Freshmen: 86%

Academics: ✐ ✐ ✐ ½

Social: ☎ ☎ ☎

Q of L: ★ ★ ★

Admissions: (512) 863-1200

Email Address: admission@
  southwestern.edu

Strongest Programs:
Business
Biological Sciences
Communication
Psychology
Education
Computer Science
Physics
International Studies

*The Paideia Program
allows students to
take seminars in
small groups with one
professor for three
years and participate
in related out-of-the-
classroom experiences.*

Georgetown. The limestone buildings, built in the Romanesque style, date from the early 20th century, and there are plenty of open spaces and new athletic facilities, including two soccer fields, a softball diamond, a football field house, and a track facility. The Prothro Center for Lifelong Learning brings together key student services and programs in one location, including career, counseling, and health services.

To graduate, Southwestern students must complete First-Year Seminar, one math or computer science course, one natural science course with lab, and two each in humanities, social sciences, fine arts, and fitness and recreational activities. Students must also demonstrate proficiency in a foreign language and satisfy requirements around intercultural perspectives, social justice, and a capstone experience.

"Students go out of their way to help each other succeed."

SU encourages undergraduate research, and each year holds a symposium to showcase students' scholarly endeavors. The King Creativity Fund, established by an alumnus, supports up to 20 "innovative and visionary projects" each academic year, with grants of up to $1,500 each. Starting this year all students will participate in the Paideia Program, whereby they pursue a particular theme, such as world health or gender identity, in multiple courses and thus come to see how the various disciplines are interconnected.

"The academic climate of Southwestern is rigorous but not competitive. While the courses are very challenging, students go out of their way to help each other succeed," says one junior. Eighty percent of classes have 19 students or fewer, and professors are praised for their willingness to help students succeed. "The quality of teaching is fantastic," cheers one communication studies major. "I'm a transfer student from a big state school, and I'm amazed at how wonderful these small discussion courses are. When you put passionate professors in an intimate teaching environment, the educational opportunities are endless." The most popular majors include biology, psychology, business, English, and communication studies. Half of Southwestern's students choose to study abroad, and each year, SU hosts faculty-led programs in London, Mexico, Germany, and Honduras, plus a service-learning program in Jamaica. Internships are available, too, offering the chance to study politics, foreign policy, journalism, or architecture in Washington, D.C., or to apprentice with professional artists, designers, actors, and filmmakers in New York. Southwestern is also affiliated with the United Methodist Church and is a member of the Associated Colleges of the South*.

"Like other schools, students vary," says one sociology major, "from the lacrosse jocks, the liberal atheists, the band and chorus members, the environmental activists, the sorority girls, and the art majors who live in the painting studio." Eighty-eight percent of Southwestern students come from Texas. Hispanics are the largest minority group at SU, comprising 18 percent of the student body; African Americans add 3 percent and Asian Americans 4 percent. "There's a broad spectrum of views, but only a few perspectives are represented when it comes to activism and speaking out," says a political science and Spanish major. SU's tuition is markedly less than at institutions of similar quality elsewhere in the United States. In addition, eligible students receive scholarships based on academic performance; talent awards are also available for fine arts majors, though there are no athletic scholarships.

Seventy-eight percent of SU students live in the residence halls, where options improve as you get older—juniors and seniors usually get apartment-style facilities with their own bedrooms, bathrooms, and kitchens. "First-year dorms weren't glamorous," says one student, "but I loved everyone on my hall, including the RAs. We were a little family!" Most rooms are suite-style, with housekeepers cleaning up several times a week. Dining halls are all-you-can-eat, and also serve Sunday brunch. "The dining facilities are pretty good. It can get a little boring sometimes, but it's never bad," reasons one student. Students report feeling safe on campus. "It is an incredibly secure and comfortable environment," says an anthropology major.

"Almost all social life takes place on campus. Wednesday, Friday, and Saturday nights are the main party nights, but there is always something going on," says one political science major. Southwestern has a strong Greek system, drawing 29 percent of the men and 20 percent of the women, "but you do not have to be Greek to have a fabulous social life," says a sociology major. SU is officially a dry campus—no kegs are allowed, and anyone under 21 caught imbibing is fined "something like $75," says a sophomore. Traditions have a big impact on the social scene, too. "Between the annual musical festival, Clusterfest, Pirate training during first year orientation, Late Night Breakfast (an event where faculty and staff serve students breakfast during finals week while karaoke and other fun stuff happens!) and hoping to find the secret senior society around campus during high energy weeks of campus, Southwestern has some great things to attend," cheers a senior.

> The school belongs to the Southern Collegiate Athletic Conference and football has returned after a 63-year absence.

Georgetown itself is "the perfect college town," according to a freshman, but also caters to families and retirees. Things are changing thanks to the mall, two new movie theaters, and several restaurants. The bars and clubs of Austin's Sixth Street are just a half hour away, and San Antonio, College Station, and Houston aren't that much further. The Blue Hole, popular for swimming, is within walking distance of campus as well. And the Pirate Bike Program has

> **"It is an incredibly secure and comfortable environment."**

made 30 new yellow bicycles available, for free, to students, faculty, and staff—riders simply pick up a bike when they need one, then leave it for the next rider when they reach their destination.

The Southwestern Pirates offer 20 Division III varsity sports, including men's and women's lacrosse, rare in Texas. The school belongs to the Southern Collegiate Athletic Conference and football has returned after a 63-year absence. Men's basketball and soccer are the most popular sports for spectators, especially games against archrival Trinity University in San Antonio. A professional sports specialist and eight undergraduate assistants oversee 26 intramural leagues and tournaments each year. Teams and individuals compete in everything from tennis and bowling to dodgeball, soccer, and inner-tube water polo.

"SU allows you to continue to grow and challenge yourself in a safe and accepting atmosphere," says a freshman. A sociology major adds: "There are so many differing views here, yet everyone is accepting and so nice." Couple that feeling of friendliness with "phenomenal" professors and a campus full of natural beauty, and the attraction of this Hill Country college becomes clear. In a state where things tend to be huge and overwhelming, Southwestern University proves that good things can come in small packages.

Overlaps

Trinity University, University of Texas at Austin, Baylor, Austin College, Texas A&M, Rice, Texas Christian, Hendrix

If You Apply To ➤ **Southwestern:** Early action: Nov. 15. Regular admissions: Feb. 1. Financial aid: Mar. 1. Housing: May 1. No application fee. Campus interviews: optional, evaluative. No alumni interviews. SATs or ACTs: required. No Subject Tests. Accepts the Common Application. Essay question.

Spelman College: See page 34.

Stanford University

Stanford, CA 94305-3005

If you're looking for an Eastern counterpart to Stanford, think Duke with a touch of MIT mixed in. Stanford's big-time athletics, preprofessional feel, and laid-back atmosphere set it apart from Ivy League competitors. In contrast to the hurly-burly of Bay Area rival Berkeley, Stanford's aura is upscale, spacious, and green. Bring your bike and a pair of sunglasses.

Website: www.stanford.edu
Location: City Outskirts
Private
Total Enrollment: 15,431
Undergraduates: 6,999
Male/Female: 52/48
SAT Ranges: CR 680–780,
  M 700–790
ACT Ranges: 31–34
Financial Aid: 82%
Expense: Pr $ $ $
Student Loans: 25%
Average Debt: $
Phi Beta Kappa: Yes
Applicants: 36,632
Accepted: 7%
Enrolled: 73%
Grad in 6 Years: 95%
Returning Freshmen: 98%
Academics: ✏ ✏ ✏ ✏ ✏
Social: 🐵 🐵 🐵 🐵
Q of L: ★ ★ ★ ★ ★
Admissions: (650) 723-2091
Email Address: admission@
  stanford.edu

Strongest Programs:
Biology
Computer Science
International Relations
Engineering
Political Science
Economics

You might think the only difference between Stanford and the Ivy League is a couple hundred extra sunny days each year. You'd be wrong. From the red-tiled roofs to the lush greenery and California vibe, Stanford is a world away from the Gothic intellectual culture of the Ivies. Virtually all the great Eastern universities began as places to ponder human existence and the meaning of life, using European institutions as their models. Stanford, by contrast, built its academic reputation around science and engineering, fields characterized by American ingenuity, and only later cultivated excellence in the humanities and social sciences. Stanford is, without a doubt, the nation's first great "American" university.

"The atmosphere is very collaborative."

The differences between Stanford and other institutions it competes against for the country's top high school seniors are evident everywhere, from the architecture to the curriculum. The school's mission-style buildings look outward to the world at large, rather than inward to ivy-covered courtyards. And unlike Yale and Princeton, Stanford—founded in 1885 by Leland and Jane Stanford in honor of their son Leland Jr.—has been co-ed from the beginning. During its centennial, the school became the first U.S. university to successfully launch a billion-dollar capital campaign; today Stanford's endowment is $17 billion. Some architectural critics say the campus looks like the world's biggest Mexican restaurant, even though Frederick Law Olmsted, designer of New York City's Central Park, planned many of the buildings. The campus stretches from the foothills of the Santa Cruz Mountains to the edge of Palo Alto in the heart of Silicon Valley, smack in the middle of earthquake country. The campus is nationally recognized as "bicycle friendly" and the university operates free bike repair stations. Recent buildings include the Hasso Plattner Institute of Design, the Center for Nanoscale Science and Engineering, and the Big Concert Hall.

Biology and human biology, the quintessential premed preparation, are the most popular programs on campus, followed by economics and international relations. Stanford has also developed a particularly interesting set of interdisciplinary programs. For students who are inclined to study abroad, programs are offered in locations around the globe, including Australia, Japan, Chile, England, China, Germany, Italy, Spain, Russia, and France. In fact, 40 percent of each graduating class takes advantage of these programs. Closer to home, the Stanford-in-Washington program allows 60 students to live, study, and intern in the nation's capital each quarter. The Haas Center for Public Service offers 50 or so service-learning courses in a wide range of disciplines, while the communications department sponsors the Rebele internship, which offers paid positions at various California newspapers. The Stanford Hopkins Marine Station is located on a mile of coastland in Pacific Grove, next to the Monterey Bay Aquarium, and offers courses in marine and biological sciences.

"The professors are incredibly impressive and highly acclaimed."

Stanford has changed its general education requirements and now requires students to complete a course in "creative expressions," as well as one called Thinking

Matters. This new course aims to facilitate students' transition from high school to college by focusing on the development of the qualities of mind and the critical and analytical skills necessary for university-level investigation and discovery. Stanford has also instituted new breadth requirements for the baccalaureate degree. Called Ways of Thinking, Ways of Doing, the new requirement includes two courses in aesthetic and interpretive inquiry, two courses in social inquiry, two courses in scientific analysis, one course in formal reasoning, one course in quantitative reasoning, one course in engaging difference, one course in moral and ethical reasoning, and one course in creative expression. During the sophomore year, the course includes oral, visual, and digital communication. The Schwab Learning Center—named after alum Charles Schwab—offers services for students with learning disabilities and Attention Deficit Hyperactivity Disorder. There's also Summer Research College, designed to create community among undergraduates engaged in full-time summer research on campus, and three honors programs.

Biology and human biology, the quintessential premed preparation, are the most popular programs on campus.

Don't let Stanford's California location fool you into thinking studying is optional—it's more like a full-time job. "The atmosphere is very collaborative, I would not have been able to get through a lot of my harder classes without the study groups I formed," one student says. Another believes students are like ducks: "They look peaceful on the surface, but they're paddling like mad underneath." Stanford's faculty ranks among the best in the nation, with most departments boasting a nationally known name or two. Professors are considered outstanding scholars with outstanding credentials, and 95 percent of classes are

"The diversity of students at Stanford is second to none."

taught by faculty, as opposed to graduate students. "The teaching quality obviously varies between classes, but overall I would say the quality is excellent and the professors are incredibly impressive and highly acclaimed," a human biology major says. Eighty-seven percent of classes have 49 or fewer students. Befitting its location in Silicon Valley, Stanford is pioneering in the use of mobile technologies, including replacing paper textbooks with tablet-based digital ones.

"The diversity of students at Stanford is second to none," boasts one student. "You come across not only Olympic champions and future Rhodes scholars, but also world champion speed skaters, unicyclists, prized researchers, and concert musicians, among others." A senior describes her peers as "humble, amazing, and just a little bit weird." Fifty-eight percent attended public high school; 94 percent of a recent freshman class graduated in the top 10th of their class. Forty percent of students are from California, while international students account for 7 percent of the student population. Minority enrollment is far above average, with Asian Americans accounting for 19 percent of the student body, Hispanics 17 percent, African Americans 6 percent, and Native Americans 1 percent. Political debates don't dominate campus life, but students are socially aware. "We are not as politically active as Cal, but we are not apathetic," a senior says. "Stanford is the sunny, palm tree-laced, Spanish-inspired Ivy of the West," boasts a communications major. "Just being in California provides a lax attitude."

Don't let Stanford's California location fool you into thinking studying is optional—it's more like a full-time job.

About 3 percent of Stanford's students take advantage of its stop-out policy, which lets students take some time off along the way, rather than staying in school for four straight years. Admissions are need-blind, and the university guarantees to meet the full demonstrated financial need of every domestic admit. While there are no merit scholarships, 82 percent of students receive some sort of internal or external financial aid; the university also awards some 300 athletic scholarships annually in 34 sports.

Freshmen must live on campus, and Stanford guarantees housing for four years; 91 percent of students stay on campus, with most of the others attending Stanford-in-Washington or other off-campus study programs. One percent of students commute from home, in part because of the lack of affordable off-campus options in the extraordinarily expensive Silicon Valley. "The campus is so big that it would be a hassle to commute to and from campus," explains one junior, "and since most students live on campus, I think you would feel left out if you didn't." As students gain seniority, a lottery system decides where they'll live. "Junior year I lived in an old faculty mansion for 30 students that had a Thai chef," one student says. The multimillion-dollar Governor's Corner complex includes all-oak fixtures, homey rooms with views of the foothills, microwave ovens in the kitchenettes, and Italian leather sofas in the lounges. Dorm dwellers must sign up for a meal plan. Campus security is good, students say, and includes an escort service. "Students feel incredibly safe," says a human-biology major.

When academic pressures become too great, students seek refuge in the outdoors. Nearby hills are perfect for jogging and biking, and Palo Alto "has a few fun hangouts and is slightly overpriced," a political science major says. Trips to the Sierra Nevada mountains (four hours away) or to the Pacific coast (45 minutes) are popular, as are jaunts to San Francisco, Los Angeles, or the Napa Valley.

Like most things at Stanford, activities and social life vary a great deal, although most take place on campus.

Like most things at Stanford, activities and social life vary a great deal, although most take place on campus. "Apart from all-campus parties, there are always concerts from different groups, dance performances, plays, comedy shows, and in-dorm activities planned by staff members," a student says. As tradition goes, freshmen aren't "true Stanford students" until they've been kissed at midnight in the quad by a senior. Full Moon on the Quad occurs at the first full moon, and features a bevy of first-year students eager to receive their initiation (courtesy of a well-timed entrance by upperclassmen). Greek organizations claim 24 percent of the men and 28 percent of the women, and provide their share of happy hours and weekend bashes, which are open to all. Underage drinking happens, but is kept under control, students say. "The RAs are not required to report instances of drinking, so it's safe and open," a senior says.

"Since most students live on campus, I think you would feel left out if you didn't."

Another Stanford tradition is the Viennese Ball, a February event that may make you wish you'd taken ballroom dancing lessons. Halloween finds students partying at the Mausoleum, the Stanfords' final resting place.

Stanford has a proud athletic tradition and recently celebrated its 100th NCAA championship. Cardinal teams recently won their 18th Director's Cup, which recognizes the best overall collegiate athletic program in the country. Women's sports have brought home the Capital Cup, signifying the best women's sports program nationally, while men's basketball won the National Invitation Tournament in 2012. The baseball team has been to the College World Series and the football team has become a powerhouse. The annual contest against archrival Cal (Berkeley) is dubbed the "Big Game." The Leland Stanford Junior University Marching Band proudly revels in its raucous irreverence, to the delight of students and the dismay of conservative types. For those not inclined to varsity play, Stanford offers a full slate of intramurals, and its vast sports complex includes 26 tennis courts, two gymnasiums, a stadium, an 18-hole golf course, and four swimming pools. The equestrian team is housed at the newly renovated Red Barn, where horseback-riding lessons are also offered.

"Stanford is the whole package," boasts one senior. The university's sunny demeanor and infectious West Coast optimism offer an appealing alternative to the gloom and gray weather that seem to hang over some of its East Coast counterparts, with the same high-caliber academics and deep athletic traditions that have made them great. "The unique combination of top-tier academics, beautiful weather, championship athletics, fascinating people, and self-deprecating humor—you won't find that anywhere else," one student says.

Overlaps

Harvard, Yale, Princeton, MIT, Brown, Columbia, Duke, University of Pennsylvania

State University of New York

As the largest university system in the world, the State University of New York provides more than 438,000 students with a vast landscape of educational opportunities—both figuratively and literally. Encompassing 64 widely dispersed campuses and 21,000 acres of property, SUNY's staggering physical presence is exceeded only by the scope of its academic offerings. Although it has faced the same budget troubles as other state university systems—with predictable effects on program offerings—SUNY universities remain among the most affordable of public universities, including for out-of-state students.

The statistics of SUNY (pronounced "SOOney") are awesome. The university has an annual operating budget of billions, greater than the gross national product of many countries and larger than the budget of more than a dozen American states. It has more than 430,000 students, 4,000 academic programs, and 24,500 faculty members, and maintains more than 2,200 buildings. Every year it awards approximately 65,000 degrees, from associate to Ph.D., in thousands of different academic fields. And—you're not going to believe this one—it has more than one million living graduates.

Such figures are all the more remarkable considering that until 1948, New York had no state university at all. That year, the legislature created the State University around a cluster of 32 existing public institutions, the best of which focused on the training of teachers, to handle the flow of returning World War II veterans. But a "gentleman's agreement" not to compete with the state's private colleges (which for generations had enjoyed a monopoly on higher education in New York) hindered SUNY's movement into the liberal arts. Not until Nelson A. Rockefeller became governor in 1960 and made the expansion of the university his major priority did SUNY begin its dramatic growth.

SUNY has now ripened into a network of four research-oriented "university centers," 13 arts and sciences colleges, six agricultural and technical colleges, five "statutory" colleges, four specialized colleges, 30 locally sponsored community colleges, and four health science centers. Annual costs at institutions like SUNY–Albany have traditionally been well below those at such hoary and prestigious publicly supported flagship campuses as California at Berkeley and the University of Michigan, but they are now slightly above the national average.

Prospective students apply directly to the SUNY unit they seek to attend. Forty-six of the colleges, though, use a "common form" application that enables a prospective student to apply to as many as four SUNY campuses at the same time. The central administration runs a SUNY Admissions Assistance Service that helps rejected students find places at other campuses. Students who earn associate degrees at community or other two-year colleges are guaranteed the chance to continue their education at a four-year institution, though not necessarily at their first choice. The level of selectivity varies widely. Most community colleges guarantee admission to any local high school student, but the university centers, as well as some specialized colleges, are among the most competitive public institutions in the nation. As part of a recent "standards revolution," SUNY trustees voted to adopt a new budgeting model designed to financially reward campuses that increase enrollment. Undergraduates at all liberal arts colleges and university centers pay the same tuition, but the rates at community colleges vary (and are lower). Out-of-state students, who make up only 4 percent of SUNY students, pay about double the amount of in-state tuition.

Mainly for political reasons, the State University of New York chose not to follow the model of other states and build a single flagship campus the likes of an Ann Arbor, Madison, or Chapel Hill. Instead, it created the four university centers with undergraduate, graduate, and professional schools and research facilities in each corner of the state. When they were created in the 1960s, each one hoped to become fully comprehensive, but there has been a certain degree of specialization from the beginning. They also decided not to establish a Division I football program, something that has lowered their visibility to out-of-state students, as has the lack of prestigious Ph.D. programs.

Albany is strongest in education and public policy, Binghamton is best known for undergraduate arts and sciences, and Stony Brook is noted for its hard sciences. Buffalo, formerly a private university, maintains a strong reputation in the life sciences and geography and comes the closest of any of the four to being a fully comprehensive university. Critics of the system say that the decision to forgo a flagship campus guarantees a lack of national prominence, and the lack of big-time football or other sports programs has affected SUNY's reputation as well. Still, many insist that somewhere in the labs and libraries of these four university centers are lurking the Nobel Prize winners of this century. To these supporters, it's only a matter of time before SUNY achieves excellence in depth as well as breadth.

The 13 colleges of arts and sciences likewise vary widely in size and character. They range from the 26,000-student University at Buffalo, whose 125-acre campus reflects the urban flavor of the state's second-largest city, to the rural and highly selective College at Geneseo, where the student body is nearly twice the size of the village population. Still others are suburban campuses, such as Purchase, which specializes in the performing arts, and Old Westbury, which was started as an experimental institution to serve minority students, older women, and others who have been "bypassed" by more traditional institutions.

With the exception of Purchase and Old Westbury, which were started from scratch, the four-year colleges are all former teachers' colleges that have, for the most part, successfully made the transition into liberal arts colleges on the small, private New England model. Now they face a new problem: the growing desire of students to study business, computer science, and other more technically oriented subjects. Some have adjusted to these demands well; others are trying to resist the trend.

SUNY's technical and specialized colleges, while not enjoying the prominence of the colleges of arts and sciences, serve the demand for vocational training in a variety of two- and four-year programs. Five of the six agricultural and technical colleges—Alfred, Canton, Cobleskill, Delhi, and Morrisville—are concerned primarily with agriculture, but also have programs in engineering, nursing, medical technology, data processing, and business administration. The sixth, Farmingdale, offers the widest range of programs, from ornamental horticulture to aerospace technology. A new upper-division technical campus at Utica–Rome now provides graduates of these two-year institutions with an opportunity to finish their education in SUNY instead of having to head for the University of Massachusetts, Ohio State, Penn State University, or destinations in other directions.

Four of the five statutory schools are at Cornell University—agriculture and life sciences, human ecology, industrial and labor relations, and veterinary medicine—while the internationally known College of Ceramics is housed at Alfred University, another private university. In addition to Utica–Rome, the specialized colleges consist of the College of Environmental Sciences and Forestry at Syracuse, the Maritime College at Fort Schuyler in the Bronx, the College of Optometry in New York City, and the Fashion Institute of Technology, whose graduates are gobbled up as fast as they emerge by employers in the Manhattan Garment District.

The 29 community colleges have traditionally been the stepchildren of the system, but the combination of rampant vocationalism and the rising cost of education elsewhere is rapidly turning them into the most robust members of the family. Students once looked to the community colleges for terminal degrees that could be readily applied in the marketplace. Now, with the cost of college soaring, a growing number of students who otherwise would have been packed off to a four-year college are saving money by staying home for the first two years and then transferring to a four-year college—or even a university center—to get their bachelor's degrees.

Following are full-length descriptions of SUNY–Purchase, which is the liberal arts institution best known beyond New York's borders, SUNY–Geneseo, and the four university centers.

SUNY–University at Albany

1400 Washington Avenue, Albany, NY 12222

Like the rest of the SUNY system, Albany is much better than its relative anonymity would suggest. Strong in anything related to politics, public policy, and criminal justice. Study abroad programs in Europe and Asia are also strengths. Only 10 percent of undergrads are from out of state. Campus is a living testament to just how bad 1960s architecture could be.

Founded in 1844 to train teachers, SUNY–Albany offers a bevy of outstanding programs in arts and sciences, business administration, and preprofessional programs. Study abroad is solid, too, but it's the university's politics-related programs that truly shine.

Designed by Edward Durrell Stone, who also designed the Kennedy Center and Lincoln Center, SUNY–Albany's campus is stark, modern, and suburban. Almost all the academic buildings are clustered in the center of the campus, while students are housed in symmetrically situated quads so similar in appearance that it usually takes a semester to

"I think there's a lot of importance placed on academic achievement."

figure out which one is yours. (Hint: The quads are named for periods in New York history—Indian, Dutch, Colonial, State, and Freedom—and progress clockwise around the campus.) Recent additions include buildings for the School of Business and for life sciences research.

Most of the preprofessional programs are among the best of any SUNY branch. Students in the public administration and social welfare programs may take advantage of their proximity to the state government to participate in internships. Biology, physics, sociology, and psychology are other notable majors, and undergrads are clamoring for admittance to the university's business administration program, which is especially strong in accounting. The New York State Writers' Institute is the least traditional of Albany's offerings, and with William Kennedy as head of the institute, the university's dream of becoming distinguished for its creative writing is well on its way. The College of Nanoscale Science and Engineering is the first college in the world devoted exclusively to the study of nanoscale science. Although the university motto is "the world within reach," budget cuts have led to a suspension of majors in all languages except Spanish.

The university is currently undergoing a three-year general education transition, but for the time being all undergraduates must fulfill Albany's 30-credit general education program, which includes courses in disciplinary perspectives, national and international perspectives, mathematics and statistics, pluralism and diversity, communication and reasoning competencies, and foreign language. If this liberal arts exposure whets your appetite for interdisciplinary study, try your hand at human biology, information science, or urban studies. The more career-minded can sign up for one of 40 B.A./M.A. programs or opt for a law degree, with the bachelor's in only six years in conjunction with Albany Law School. Many students take advantage of SUNY–Albany's superior offerings in foreign study. The university was one of the first in the nation to develop exchange programs with Russia (and China, for that matter). In all, Albany sponsors more than 65 programs in 35 countries.

Project Renaissance brings together groups of 300 freshmen with a team of instructors in a shared academic and living community. Participants engage in a yearlong, unified course of study covering 12 hours of the university's general education requirements, and have access to special perks including housing and

faculty mentors. Qualified students can take part in the Honors College, which allows freshmen and sophomores to enroll in up to six introductory courses that have been designed by distin-

"There are some superstar professors and a bad apple here and there."

guished faculty. The courses emphasize research, service learning, and a creative component. Senior honors students design and complete a yearlong research or creative project.

The academic climate is challenging and courses tend to be demanding. "I think there's a lot of importance placed on academic achievement," says one junior. "In certain classes—especially the honors classes—there is a competitive climate."

Website: www.albany.edu
Location: City Outskirts
Public
Total Enrollment: 14,168
Undergraduates: 12,004
Male/Female: 52/48
SAT Ranges: CR 490–580, M 520–610
ACT Ranges: 22–26
Financial Aid: 78%
Expense: Pub $ $
Student Loans: 68%
Average Debt: $ $
Phi Beta Kappa: Yes
Applicants: 21,178
Accepted: 55%
Enrolled: 22%
Grad in 6 Years: 63%
Returning Freshmen: 83%
Academics: ✍ ✍ ✍ ✍
Social: ☎ ☎ ☎
Q of L: ★ ★ ★
Admissions: (518) 442-5435
Email Address: ugadmissions@albany.edu

Strongest Programs:
Criminal Justice
Atmospheric Science
Physics
Accounting
Business
Political Science
Social Welfare
Computer Science

Students form study groups to help one another through the coursework, and professors are always available to offer support. "The quality of teaching is excellent overall," a physics major says. "There are some superstar professors and a bad apple here and there, but usually very good instructors."

The student body comprises "bits and pieces of every Long Island high school and a dash of upstate, topped off with a Big Apple or two," according to one student. Another adds, "There are a handful that I think made it into UAlbany by some kind of miracle. Most of the students I interact with, though, are the opposite." All but 12 percent of the students are native New Yorkers. African American and Hispanic enrollment now stands at 25 percent combined, while Asian Americans make up another 7 percent. Fifty-three percent of the students are from the top quarter of their high school class. SUNY–Albany makes available merit scholarships and more than 250 athletic scholarships are offered in 16 sports. Low-income students may qualify for the Equal Opportunity Program, which offers additional academic and financial support.

Fifty-eight percent of students live in university housing; freshmen and sophomores are required to live in dorms. "Dorms are sometimes small," says one student, "but you get used to it." Others report that the co-ed quads are exceptionally friendly, surprisingly quiet, and comfortable. Each floor is divided into four- to six-person suites. But the word from most students is that the best dorms are in the Alumni Quad on the downtown campus. "Alumni has much more attractive rooms and ambiance overall," says a business major. Many students move off campus because "the transportation system to and from campus is convenient and the cost of apartments is as cheap (or cheaper) than living on campus," says a junior. Students on the main campus take their meals at any of the four dorms or at the campus center that includes a food court and bookstore, while downtowners haunt the cheap local eateries as well as their own cafeterias.

"You can spend months without leaving campus."

"You can spend months without leaving campus," says one student. "It's relatively large and there's always something going on." While most people are serious about their work, a SUNY–Albany weekend starts on Thursday night for many. Students go to parties or go barhopping about town. Students warn that alcohol policies forbidding underage drinking are strict and well enforced. "You can get into a lot of trouble if you're caught on campus with alcohol," says a student. Fraternities and sororities attract 1 percent of the men and 2 percent of the women respectively, and have become the main party-throwers on campus. Albany students tend to be traditional, but rites-of-spring festivals, mandatory after enduring the miserable upstate winters, have produced Guinness records for the largest games of Simon Says, Twister, and Musical Chairs, as well as the all-school pillow fight. Fountain Day brings thousands of students together for the spring turn-on of the infamous podium fountain. Mayfest is a huge all-school concert party that brings in well-known as well as up-and-coming bands. The natural resources of the upstate region keep students busy skiing and hiking. Treks to Montreal and Saratoga are popular. Plus, the student association owns and operates Dippikill, a wilderness retreat described as Albany's "own little Walden" in the Adirondacks.

Men's football, basketball, and lacrosse, and women's softball, volleyball, and track and field are strong, and the Great Danes are members of the Division I America East Conference. Recent conference champs include men's basketball (2012–13), women's basketball (2012–13), men's cross-country, football, women's track and field, and men's lacrosse. Meanwhile, intramurals engender a great deal of student enthusiasm, and participation numbers in the thousands.

SUNY–Albany is not the concrete, sterile diploma mill it may appear to be. It's a place of opportunity for those willing to put in the hours and hard work. As one veteran warns, "You can find an outlet here for even the most obscure interest, but this is not a school that will educate you when you're not looking."

SUNY–Binghamton University

P.O. Box 6001, Binghamton, NY 13902-6000

If 100,000 screaming fans on a Saturday afternoon tickles your fancy, head 200 miles southwest to Penn State. Binghamton has become one of the premier public universities in the Northeast because of its outstanding academics and commitment to undergraduates. It is writing the rules on how to integrate global awareness and international experiences into undergraduate study.

Binghamton University offers a private-school experience at a public-school price, even for out-of-staters. With more than 130 clubs, over 450 study abroad opportunities, and an emphasis on small classes—84 percent of those taken by undergraduates have fewer than 50 students—it's no wonder that students who apply here are also considering schools such as Cornell and NYU. Binghamton offers an intellectually challenging environment with an emphasis on global experiences, including study abroad opportunities in more than 50 countries, area studies programs that focus on specific regions of the world and the unique Languages Across the Curriculum program.

Binghamton's campus sits on 930 acres of open grassy space, and includes a nature preserve, trails, fountains, and a pond. The oldest buildings date from 1958, so the prevailing architectural style is modern and "functional." Some students say that, from the air, the circular campus bears a striking resemblance to the human brain, but administrators say that's merely a coincidence. Four additional residence halls were completed in 2013, as was a Center for Excellence building.

Binghamton students apply to one of the university's five schools with undergraduate programs: the Decker School of Nursing, the Harpur College of Arts and Sciences, the College of Community and Public Affairs, the School of Management, and the Thomas J. Watson School of Engineering and Applied Science, named for the founder of IBM. A sixth unit, the School of Graduate Education, offers only graduate-level degrees. Regardless of the school they choose, students face the same general education requirements, which span five thematic areas: language and communication, creating a global vision, sciences and mathematics, aesthetics and humanities, and physical activity and wellness. All Binghamton undergraduates must complete one of the global interdependence (or "G") courses offered in all departments as part of the effort to equip students with "a basic understanding of the complex dimensions of contemporary global issues." Individual schools have developed their own international programs, such as a global management concentration in the School of Management. Management is a popular major, and qualified students may submatriculate into Binghamton's M.B.A. program to earn undergraduate and graduate degrees in five years. "Binghamton has an extraordinary school of

> "The dining halls are actually pretty good."

Website: www.binghamton.edu
Location: Suburban
Public
Total Enrollment: 13,535
Undergraduates: 11,877
Male/Female: 53/47
SAT Ranges: CR 590–675, M 630–710
ACT Ranges: 27–30
Financial Aid: 70%
Expense: Pub $ $
Student Loans: 53%
Average Debt: $ $
Phi Beta Kappa: Yes
Applicants: 28,232
Accepted: 43%
Enrolled: 21%
Grad in 6 Years: 79%
Returning Freshmen: 91%
Academics: ✎ ✎ ✎ ✎ ½
Social: ☎ ☎ ☎
Q of L: ★ ★ ★ ★
Admissions: (607) 777-2171
Email Address: admit@binghamton.edu

Strongest Programs:
Psychology
Engineering
Biology

management. It's currently the most competitive school within the university, and students that are accepted into the program are almost always guaranteed a job upon graduation," says one student. Other popular choices include psychology, English, biology, and engineering.

Binghamton's academic reputation is enhanced by a tough grading policy, which includes plusses and minuses as well as straight letter grades, and Fs on the transcripts of failing students rather than no credit. "Students are usually self-motivated and cooperative," says a sophomore. "Beating the test is usually more important than beating other students." Professors receive high marks for classroom presentations and accessibility. "I've never taken a class with a professor that didn't truly care about my progress as a student," a student says. Faculty-supervised independent research, often culminating in a senior honors thesis, is common in Harpur College. Binghamton operates student exchanges with universities around the world and directly sponsors more than 30 study abroad programs in locations as diverse as the United Kingdom, the Netherlands, Germany, Spain, Turkey, Costa Rica, India, Morocco, China, Austria, Korea, Ghana, and Australia. "Study abroad at Binghamton is huge!" says an English major.

The Binghamton Scholars Program offers financial aid, special seminars, and leadership training to exceptional students, along with opportunities for experiential learning and junior- and senior-year capstone projects. The Evolutionary Studies and Global Studies integrated curricula allow students to supplement their major coursework with interdisciplinary exploration. And programs in global and international affairs, information systems, and management bring more than 300 students a year to Binghamton from four of Turkey's most prestigious universities. Binghamton administrators hope the programs will also encourage more of their students to travel to Turkey and the Middle East. Students also have the option to design their own majors via the Individualized Major Program in Harpur College. Newer majors include Chinese studies, Japanese studies, and Korean studies.

Annual campus traditions include the Passing of the Vegetables, to welcome winter, and Jumping on the Coat during the Spring Fling carnival, to celebrate the arrival of warm weather.

Students at Binghamton come from all walks of life, says a senior. "Students here are not only very smart, but also very diverse in their interests and very compassionate," adds another student. Although Binghamton offers a top-notch liberal arts and sciences education, word of its excellence has been slow to cross state lines: Only 11 percent of students come from outside of the Empire State. By other measures, though, Binghamton's student body is rather diverse: African Americans make up 5 percent of the total, while Hispanics add 10 percent and Asian Americans 14 percent. Hot political issues range from the global to the local (state funding for campus programs). Binghamton offers merit scholarships worth an average of $6,709, as well as 330 full or partial athletic scholarships in 21 sports.

"I've made lifelong friends, gotten a top education, and grown as a person."

Sixty-one percent of Binghamton's students live in the dorms, where options range from traditional double rooms with bathrooms down the hall to suites and apartments. "The new dorms are really nice, but the older dorms tend to be more relaxed and social," says one sophomore. A classmate adds, "We have a community-style dorm system, where there are five neighborhoods or communities, each with four to six buildings. This makes connecting with others easy, and much more intimate." Dining halls have plenty of options, including sushi. "The dining halls are actually pretty good. They are clean, and the staff is always very helpful," one student says. Students report feeling safe while trekking around the university grounds. "There has never been a time when I felt unsafe walking on campus," says one student.

Binghamton students apply to one of the university's five schools with undergraduate programs.

When the weekend comes, Binghamton students know how to let off steam. "There is no need to leave campus for entertainment," says one student. "The new bowling alley and pool hall—as well as early movies—is great on weekends, and clubs provide more opportunities than any one person could possibly have time for." Aside from the usual concerts and plays, a program called Late Night Binghamton brings free movies, games, a coffee bar, and other nonalcoholic fun to campus, from 10 p.m. until 2 a.m. every Friday and Saturday. "Social life on campus is very active. Few people go home for the weekends," a junior says. Frat parties also occur off campus; 12 percent of the men and 10 percent of the women go Greek. While some underage students do manage to find alcohol, any caught violating the policy "will be taken care of accordingly," says a senior.

Binghamton itself is "far from the most exciting place on earth, but the community is still alive and has its own distinct pulse," according to a bioengineering major. "The nearest Walmart is infested with students no matter what time of day," adds a senior. The downtown area offers some restaurants and bars, and "many students volunteer with local groups, such as food drives and mentoring children," says a nursing major. Students also get involved in Special Olympics and various fund-raising walks, and "there is even a co-ed service fraternity." Popular road trips include Ithaca, for parties at Ithaca College and Cornell, and Syracuse, for the Carousel Mall, as well as Cortland and Oneonta, about an hour away by car. The toughest part about going away may be finding a parking space when you return, as permits currently outnumber spaces by about three to one. Annual campus traditions include the Passing of the Vegetables, to welcome winter, and Jumping on the Coat during the Spring Fling carnival, to celebrate the arrival of warm weather. Picnic in the Park is the annual senior barbecue.

Binghamton teams compete in Division I, but the school doesn't field a football squad. As a result, some of the most significant rivalries are with Cornell in men's lacrosse and co-rec football, where teams have three men and three women and always a female quarterback. In 2011, men's tennis earned its eighth NCAA Championship berth in the last 10 years; other recent America East Conference champs include men's baseball, volleyball, wrestling, and cross-country. The basketball team brought home its first NCAA championship tournament berth in 2009 but sparked a huge and embarrassing scandal over allegations of misconduct and academic deficiencies on the part of its players. Given the weather in this part of New York, a popular winter pastime is "traying," or downhill sledding on cafeteria trays. Intramurals attract more than 80 percent of the student body.

With a four-year graduation rate that is among the highest of any public university, Binghamton has a reputation for an excellent education at a reasonable price that continues to draw smart New Yorkers to its vibrant and growing campus. "Binghamton helps students meet the two ultimate goals that anyone should have when they graduate: relatively little debt and strong job or grad school prospects," says a sophomore. Despite the hubbub of city life, the university maintains a cozy feel. Says a human development major, "I've made lifelong friends, gotten a top education, and grown as a person."

Binghamton's academic reputation is enhanced by a tough grading policy, which includes plusses and minuses.

Overlaps

Cornell, NYU, Boston University, SUNY–Stony Brook, SUNY–Geneseo, Rutgers, University of Delaware, Penn State

If You Apply To ➤ **SUNY–Binghamton:** Rolling admissions: Feb. 1. Early action: Nov. 15. Housing: May 1. Application fee: $50. No campus or alumni interviews. SATs or ACTs: required. Subject Tests: optional. Accepts the Common Application. Essay question.

Glamorous it is not, but the University at Buffalo offers solid programs in everything from business and engineering to geography and English. The majority of students come from western New York and a high percentage commute from home. The largest of the SUNY campuses, it is trying to build its reputation with big-time sports, to mixed success.

Website: www.buffalo.edu
Location: Suburban
Public
Total Enrollment: 23,741
Undergraduates: 17,604
Male/Female: 55/45
SAT Ranges: CR 500–600,
   M 550–650
ACT Ranges: 23–28
Financial Aid: 63%
Expense: Pub $
Student Loans: 45%
Average Debt: $
Phi Beta Kappa: Yes
Applicants: 22,009
Accepted: 57%
Enrolled: 29%
Grad in 6 Years: 70%
Returning Freshmen: 87%
Academics: ✐ ✐ ✐ ✐
Social: ☎ ☎
Q of L: ★ ★
Admissions: (716) 645-6900
Email Address:
   ub-admissions@buffalo.edu

Strongest Programs:
Business Administration
Engineering
Psychology
Architecture
Communications
English
Computer and Information
   Sciences

Although part of the mammoth State University of New York system, the University at Buffalo takes steps to ensure it doesn't get overlooked. Very few universities share its strength in medicine, engineering, and computer science, and UB is one of the world's leading supercomputer sites. Its resources are large enough to warrant two campuses, North and South. In addition to the sciences, the former private university is strong in the arts, humanities, and professional schools. Students interested in pharmacy and architecture find Buffalo has the only schools in the SUNY system. "As large as we are, we are a very diverse and welcoming atmosphere," says a senior. Notable alums include CNN senior anchor Wolf Blitzer, entertainment mogul Harvey Weinstein, and Millard Drexler, chairman and CEO of J. Crew.

> "The climate is very competitive."

The North campus of the University at Buffalo, home to most undergraduate programs, stretches across 1,100 acres in the suburbs just outside the city line and boasts buildings designed by world-renowned architects such as I. M. Pei. Meanwhile, the South campus, along Main Street, favors collegiate ivy-covered buildings and the schools of architecture and health sciences, including the highly rated programs in medicine and dentistry. The university provides connecting bus service—known as the UB Stampede—between the North and South campuses. The university continues building and renovating at a steady pace as part of a master plan to grow by 10,000 students, 750 faculty, and 600 staff members by 2020.

"The climate is very competitive," says one exercise science major. "Many general sciences are based on a curve, but are also used to weed out the students who won't be able to handle the harder courses." The engineering and business management schools are nationally prominent, and architecture is solid. Occupational and physical therapy programs are also quite good, while the English department is notable for its emphasis on poetry. Well-known poets visit the campus frequently, and students not only compose and read poetry, but study the art of performing it as well. French, physiology, geography, and music are highly regarded, but other humanities vary in quality.

General education requirements are standardized and include courses such as writing skills, math sciences, natural sciences, foreign language, world civilizations, and American pluralism. The university offers combined programs in economics (B.A./M.S.) and informatics (B.A./B.S.), as well as programs for adult health, geriatric, and acute care nursing. UB has a multitude of special programs, joint degrees (such as a five-year B.S./M.B.A.), and interdisciplinary majors, as well as opportunities for self-designed majors and study abroad. Students accepted into the honors program enjoy smaller classes, priority in class registration, individual faculty mentors, and special scholarships regardless of financial need. Freshmen are encouraged to take University Experience 101, which orients students to UB's academic life, general social experience, and resources. About two-thirds of students do so. "First-year seminars and classes help make the college transition a successful and enjoyable one,"

> "The quality of teaching varies."

says a sociology major. More than $2.2 million in merit scholarships are available through the Honors and University Scholars programs.

Class size can be a problem, especially for freshmen. Scheduling conflicts are not unusual, and required courses are often the most difficult to get into. But registration is available online or by phone. Students seem to accept that some degree of faculty unavailability is the necessary trade-off for having professors who are experts in their fields at a school where graduate education and research get lots of the attention. "The quality of teaching varies. With my general education courses, I disliked most of my professors as it seemed like they cared more about their research than my education. However, as my courses got more specific to my major, I found most of my professors to be inspiring and truly great at what they do," a senior says. The academically oriented student body spends plenty of time in UB's six main libraries or one of the several branches, which are, for the most part, comfortable and well stocked at three million volumes.

French, physiology, geography, and music are highly regarded, but other humanities vary in quality.

Sixty-three percent of UB students ranked in the top quarter of their high school class and more than 80 percent hail from New York. African Americans and Hispanics combined account for 14 percent of the student body, and Asian Americans represent another 13 percent. UB's considerable efforts in increasing awareness of diversity include a Committee on Campus Tolerance, Office of Student Multicultural Affairs, and Multicultural Leadership Council. Students report that campus politics tend to lean left and current issues include environmental sustainability, the economy, and LGBT concerns. "Students feel as though they have a forum to speak their minds," says a senior. Merit scholarships are available for qualified students; student-athletes vie for nearly 400 athletic awards in 12 sports.

Thirty-five percent of students live on campus; the rest commute from home or find apartments near the Main Street campus. Students warn that potential renters should shuffle off to Buffalo a couple of months early to secure a place. "The dorms are a lot better than some schools I have seen," says an electrical engineering major. "The apartments are excellent but are quickly becoming more pricier than more elegant and affordable off-campus housing." UB has added several apartment-style complexes over the last few years for upperclassmen who wish to live on campus. Those complexes feature cable, high-speed Internet connections, and central air-conditioning. Most of the on-campus dwellers are housed on the Amherst campus. Governors is known as the nicest, smallest, and quietest dorm on campus, while social butterflies prefer Ellicott. The Main Street campus dorms are smaller, older, and of a more traditional collegiate design, which upperclassmen tend to prefer. Three all-freshmen dorms house extremely sociable freshmen. Security on campus is adequate, with a full-time police station and emergency call lights all around. The quality of cafeteria fare falls somewhere between "OK" and "decent," according to students, and there are options for those with special dietary concerns.

"The dorms are a lot better than some schools I have seen."

Freshmen are encouraged to take University Experience 101.

One senior says students "have to be involved in something in order to feel a part of the school. There are so many sports teams, club teams, frats, sororities, and student life activity clubs; there's something for everyone." The Greek scene is small; 2 percent of UB men and women participate. Drinking is banned in the "dry" dorms, but students over 21 are allowed to drink in the "wet" dorms. Underage drinkers face "severe punishments" if caught, a junior reports. Activities during the week are mostly on campus, but students tend to gravitate to downtown Buffalo on the weekends. Friday night happy hour centers on beer and the chicken wings that spread the fame of Buffalo cuisine. Also popular are the Albright-Knox Art Gallery, with its world-renowned collection of modern art, and the Triple-A baseball Bisons, who play downtown. The two major pro teams, the Buffalo Bills in football and the Sabres in hockey, are both top draws. Although most students are content to stay in Buffalo, those who want a change of scene can drive to Niagara Falls, Toronto, Rochester, or Cleveland. "The best road trip is 10 minutes to Canada," says an anthropology and geology double major.

Having a car might be a good idea, though parking can be a problem on campus. Students without cars can get trapped when the intercampus bus stops running after 2:00 a.m. on weekends. The winters are cold in Buffalo, but students can take refuge inside a series of tunnels that connect the buildings. The flip side is that the outlying areas of the city offer great skiing, skating, and snowmobiling—and the ski club even offers free rides to the slopes. UB supports more than 500 other student organizations ranging from jugglers to math enthusiasts. Students can preview their honeymoons by darting over to Niagara Falls, just a few minutes away, or flee the country altogether by driving to Canada, where the drinking age is lower.

"The on-campus events revolve around football and basketball," says a senior. UB is the only major SUNY unit to field a Division I-A football team. The baseball team won the MAC regular season title and the women's rowing team has won several Dad Vail Regattas. The university also sent nearly a dozen athletes to the Olympic trials. School spirit is sometimes generated at the student union and UB's impressive sports complex, which boasts the fourth-largest pool in the world, a 10,000-seat arena, squash and racquetball courts, and other amenities. Intramural sports are popular, and earthy types appreciate the annual Oozefest—a mud-volleyball tournament.

UB students love the size of their school, with its huge range of academic programs, social events, and people to meet. Yes, students are exposed to the long Buffalo winter, but they also get exposed to some top-notch professors. And they get to meet a diverse mix of native New Yorkers, other East Coast residents, and international students drawn to the university's outstanding science programs.

If You Apply To ➤

University at Buffalo: Rolling admissions: Feb. 1. Early decision: Nov. 1. Financial aid: Mar. 1. Housing: May 1. Application fee: $50. No campus or alumni interviews. SATs or ACTs: required. Accepts the Common Application. No essay question.

SUNY–College at Geneseo

1 College Circle, Geneseo, NY 14454

Geneseo is a preferred option for New Yorkers who want the feel of a private college at a public-university price. It is similar in scale to Mary Washington and William and Mary in Virginia, smaller than Miami of Ohio. Offers business and education in addition to the liberal arts. Less than 5 percent of the students are from out of state.

The SUNY–College at Geneseo offers a seriously academic environment at a state-school price. This public institution attracts high achievers from around the nation. Students here "tend to be friendly, liberal, and hardworking, and most like to have fun on the weekends," says a junior. Responsive, attentive professors help compensate for the long winters and somewhat isolated location. And excellent preprofessional programs in disciplines such as education and business have been making it harder to win admission to this most bucolic campus of the New York State university system.

Geneseo sits in the scenic Genesee Valley of western New York. Campus architecture ranges from Gothic to modern, and the surrounding community has been designated a National Historic Landmark Community by the U.S. Department of the Interior. An elementary education major calls the town "small and inviting" and says the historic buildings and nearby forests and mountains make for "lots of beautiful scenery."

Biology is the most popular major at Geneseo, followed by psychology, childhood education/special education, English, and business administration. Regardless of their course of study, all students must demonstrate foreign language proficiency. General education requirements also include

"The students here are friendly, intelligent, and driven."

two courses each in the natural sciences, social sciences, and fine arts; a two-semester sequence in Western humanities; and one course each in non-Western traditions, U.S. history, and numeric and symbolic reasoning. During freshman year, all students take a seminar in critical writing and reading in a small class focusing on a unique topic related to the instructor's discipline. Students may also enroll in a one-credit First Year Seminar focused on a topic such as genealogy, Chinese medicine, or Frederick Douglass. Cooperative programs with other SUNY campuses in dentistry, optometry, business, physical therapy, and other disciplines allow students to finish their graduate degrees a year ahead of schedule.

"The courses at Geneseo are difficult and academically challenging, but the professors are extremely helpful and accessible, so their high expectations are achievable," says a junior. One benefit of Geneseo's size: "You will never have a TA, except in labs," says a freshman. And even then, "labs are overseen by a professor." Twenty students from each class are invited to join the prestigious Honors Program; membership includes a $1,400 annual scholarship and five courses designed specifically for the program, plus a thesis during the senior year. The Geneseo Opportunities for Leadership Development (GOLD) program seeks to prepare students for college and community leadership roles via workshops and conferences. The college offers 50 study abroad programs in 24 nations; through other SUNY campuses, students have access to 600 programs in 60 nations. New living/learning communities have been launched for a small group of physics and biology majors.

Ninety-five percent of Geneseo students are from New York State, and the vast majority attended public high school. "The students here are friendly, intelligent, and driven," says a history major. "Everyone here was at the top of their high school classes, so you are surrounded by people who are very similar to yourself." Asian Americans make up 7 percent of the student body, while Hispanic students comprise

"You will never have a TA, except in labs."

6 percent and African Americans make up 2 percent. "Students are really involved," says a student. Admissions are not need-blind; Geneseo offers merit scholarships averaging $2,000 each, but no athletic awards.

Fifty-four percent of Geneseo students live in the dorms, and rooms are guaranteed for four years. "The dorms are well maintained and cleaned before you move in," notes one student. Students say they feel safe at Geneseo, and while campus food can't compare to mom's home cooking, "it has improved over the years," says a senior. "Now it's actually pretty good." Provisions are made for vegans and vegetarians, and special meals are served on holidays.

Fraternities draw 16 percent of the men and sororities claim 24 percent of the women; if Greek parties don't appeal, students can hit the campus dance club (the Knight Spot) or partake in school-sponsored late-night activities at the College Union. "I really enjoy Geneseo Late Knight, which are weekend events. They have performances, arts and crafts, contests, and other activities," says one freshman. Some dorms are dry; even in those that aren't, only students over 21 are permitted to have or consume alcohol, and they may not do either in the presence of underage students. Still, this is college, says a sophomore: "Rules are made to be broken."

(continued)

Financial Aid: 63%
Expense: Pub $
Student Loans: 67%
Average Debt: $
Phi Beta Kappa: Yes
Applicants: 9,164
Accepted: 46%
Enrolled: 25%
Grad in 6 Years: 79%
Returning Freshmen: 90%
Academics: ✍ ✍ ✍ ½
Social: ☎ ☎ ☎
Q of L: ★ ★ ★ ★
Admissions: (585) 245-5571
Email Address: admissions@geneseo.edu

Strongest Programs:
Business
Communicative Disorders and
    Sciences
Education
English
Psychology
Music
Biology
Natural Sciences

Students may also enroll in a one-credit First Year Seminar focused on a topic such as genealogy, Chinese medicine, or Frederick Douglass.

Circle K and Alpha Phi Omega, the co-ed service fraternity, allow students to make a difference in the community. In addition, there are nearly 200 other student-run organizations, including a newspaper and radio and television stations. "One of the most unique organizations we have on campus is called Upstate Escapes. They provide students with a way to get off campus and do any number of activities for a great price," cheers one student.

The "gorgeous small town" of Geneseo "really caters to college students," says an education major. There's a supermarket and a Walmart, and restaurants and shops on Main Street. Outdoorsy types will appreciate the nearby mountain ranges, which offer plenty of opportunities to hike and ski; boaters will enjoy beautiful Conesus Lake, only a 10-minute drive from campus. Popular road trips include Rochester, 30 miles north, and Buffalo, 60 miles west; don't forget your hat, mittens, and parka!

Half of Geneseo students participate in intramural sports, and "broomball is the most popular," says a sophomore. Basketball and volleyball are also very popular. Geneseo's varsity teams compete in NCAA Division III, and the men's and women's cross-country, outdoor track, and swimming teams are competitive. But hockey stirs up the most school spirit. "Hockey is huge here," says a senior. Students also look forward to Spring Fest and MidKnight Madness, the pep rally that precedes the basketball season.

The SUNY–College at Geneseo gives students the best of two worlds. Given its size, professors can provide the kind of personal attention normally seen only at private liberal arts colleges; because of its public status, that attention comes at bargain-basement cost. Those factors have made it more and more difficult to get in—and, it turns out, getting in is only half the battle. "Students are very serious about their education," says a sophomore. "Once you are here, you must work hard."

Overlaps

Colgate, Cornell University, Hamilton, Boston College, Skidmore, NYU, SUNY–Buffalo, University of Rochester

If You Apply To ➤ **SUNY–Geneseo:** Early decision: Nov. 15. Regular admissions: Jan. 1. Financial aid: Feb. 15. Housing: May 1. Application fee: $50. No campus or alumni interviews. SATs or ACTs: required. Subject Tests: optional. Accepts the Common Application. Essay question.

SUNY–Purchase College

735 Anderson Hill Road, Purchase, NY 10577-1400

One of the few public institutions that is also an arts specialty school. The visual and performing arts are signature programs, though Purchase has developed some liberal arts specialties in areas like environmental science. Percentage-wise, the most selective institution in the SUNY system. Limited campus life because students head for the city.

Website: www.purchase.edu
Location: Suburban
Public
Total Enrollment: 3,760
Undergraduates: 3,659
Male/Female: 44/56
SAT Ranges: CR 500–610, M 480–570

SUNY–Purchase College is a dream come true for aspiring artists of all kinds—an academic environment that provides a strong sense of community and support, yet celebrates individuals for their unique talents and contributions. It's OK to be an individual here. A literature major says, "There's a raw energy that exists on campus—in the students and professors—that I don't think many other colleges have."

Set on a 500-acre wooded estate in an area of Westchester's most scenic suburbia, Purchase has a campus described by one student as "sleek, modern, ominous, and brick." The college has earned a national reputation for its instruction in music, dance, visual arts, theater, and film. Almost all the faculty members in the School of the Arts are professionals who perform or exhibit regularly in the New York metropolitan area, and the spacious, dazzling facilities rank among the best in the world. Purchase College boasts of the Neuberger Museum, the sixth-largest public college museum. The four-theater Performing Arts Center is huge, and dance students, whose building contains a dozen studios, whirlpool rooms, and a "body-correction" facility, may never again work in such splendid and well-equipped surroundings.

Mingling with highly motivated and talented performers and artists can make some students in the liberal arts and sciences feel a little drab and out of place. "Dancers, actors, visual artists, and music students pull the most weight as far as campus life is concerned," says a student. Still, Purchase is a fine place to study humanities and the natural sciences, particularly literature, psychology, art history, environmental studies, and biology. Most of the shaky liberal arts and sciences programs are confined to some majors in the social sciences and language and culture, where "there are not a lot of class options," according to one junior.

"Housing is very limited."

Students in the liberal arts and sciences spend one-third of their time at Purchase fulfilling the general education requirements, which include 10 knowledge areas. Students take mathematics, natural sciences, social science, American history, Western civilization, other world civilizations, the arts, humanities, foreign language, and basic communications. In addition to these core requirements, they also must take critical thinking and information management as skill areas, and everyone must complete a senior project. Students in the arts divisions usually have many more required courses, culminating in a senior recital or show. There are two separate sets of degree requirements, one for the liberal arts and sciences and one for the performing and visual arts. B.F.A. students in the performing and visual arts are required to sample the liberal arts; B.A. and B.S. students in the liberal arts and sciences are required to sample fine arts courses. Additional programs include a B.S. in visual arts, a B.A. in biochemistry, and a B.A. in sociology.

The atmosphere at Purchase varies between programs. "The courses are very generic in the liberal arts and quite heavy and rigorous in the conservatories," reports a music major. Students tend to be serious about their own personal achievements and professors are said to be accessible and friendly. "The professors are engaged, extremely qualified, and very interested in our education," says a student.

Purchase is comprised of "all the students from high school who weren't the cheerleaders and football players," says one student, describing classmates as "artsy, creative, hippies, gay, vegans, and open-minded, liberal activists." Roughly three-quarters of the student body are from New York State, most from New York City and Westchester County. Others are from Long Island, New Jersey, and Connecticut, but all are different and very political (that means very liberal). African Americans account for 8 percent of the student body, Hispanics 17 percent, and Asian Americans 2 percent. "Our student body is full of scholars and artists, most of whom are heavily driven by our politically active campus," says a women's studies/sociology major. Indeed, the largest student organization on this politically active campus is the gay and lesbian union. "We are diverse, but politically, we are a very liberal college," says a senior. "We believe strongly in animal rights, civil rights, women's rights, etc." In addition to need-based aid, merit scholarships are awarded each year on the basis of academic achievements, auditions, and portfolios.

"The courses are very generic in the liberal arts."

Approximately one-third of the student body commutes from nearby communities, though housing in the surrounding suburbs is expensive and hard to find.

(continued)

ACT Ranges: 21–27
Financial Aid: 74%
Expense: Pub $
Student Loans: 60%
Average Debt: $ $ $
Phi Beta Kappa: No
Applicants: 8,907
Accepted: 33%
Enrolled: 23%
Grad in 6 Years: 63%
Returning Freshmen: 83%
Academics: ✍ ✍ ✍ ½
Social: ☎ ☎ ☎
Q of L: ★ ★ ★
Admissions: (914) 251-6300
Email Address: admissions@ purchase.edu

Strongest Programs:
Acting
Art History
Dance
Environmental Studies
Film
Liberal Studies
Music
Women's Studies

Approximately one-third of the student body commutes from nearby communities.

"Housing is very limited," confides one student. "There are older and newer dorms and their condition definitely reflects their age." The two eating facilities offer decent fare, and for those who tire of institutional cuisine, there is a student-run co-op that specializes in health food.

The campus is a neighbor to the world headquarters of IBM, Texaco, AMF, General Foods, and Pepsico. No college town exists per se at Purchase. "Because so many students are from New York, the weekends are pretty dead," complains one student. Still, the Big Apple provides a regular weekend distraction that inhibits the formation of a tight campus community. Since the campus shuttle bus runs only once on the weekend, students started their own van service, which goes into Manhattan three times a day. Still, "a car is a definite must at Purchase," counsels one student. The Performing Arts Center is host to at least two student or faculty performances every weekend, and there is a constant flow of New York artists and celebrities. Notes a music major, "Campus is very quiet but the student center always has something going on," and the over-21 crowd often frequents the Pub. Fraternities and sororities are definitely out. "The closest we come to Greek are the two guys from Athens who go here," quips a staunch independent. Besides, as one artist explains, "individuality is far more important to the artist than being part of a group." Despite the unconventional aura of the place, Purchase is not without its traditions, including Fall Ball ("a big dance where everyone dresses in drag"), Fall Fest, Zombie Prom, Culture Shock, and Purchase Prom.

Purchase athletes compete in Division III, and the few competitive Panthers teams include men's basketball, women's volleyball, and women's soccer. Men's basketball and the women's swim team have won the Skyline Conference championship in recent years. Intramural programs draw 30 percent of students, but informal Frisbee-tossing remains more popular than organized sports. Says a student: "Our 'teams' are our dancers, our vocalists, our musicians, and our theater companies."

Despite a conspicuous lack of a college-town atmosphere, Purchase is a perfect place to study the arts and still be able to indulge in academics of all kinds, or vice versa. "It's a great place to come and devote yourself to your craft," says a senior. Those willing to put up with what a student calls "an isolated campus full of ugly architecture" may find that Purchase offers the opportunity for a personalized, diverse education unique within the SUNY system.

Purchase athletes compete in Division III.

Overlaps

Ithaca, NYU, SUNY–Albany, SUNY–Binghamton, SUNY–New Paltz, SUNY–Stony Brook

If You Apply To > **SUNY–Purchase College:** Rolling admissions. Application fee: $50. Campus interviews: recommended, evaluative (required of theater design/technology and film program applicants). No alumni interviews. SATs or ACTs: required. Subject Tests: optional. Essay question. Apply to particular school or program. Auditions held for acting, dance, and music.

SUNY–Stony Brook University

118 Administration Building, Stony Brook, NY 11794-1901

Strategically located 90 minutes from New York City, Stony Brook has risen a few notches in the SUNY pecking order. The natural sciences, engineering, and health fields are the major drawing cards. Situated in the lap of Long Island luxury, Stony Brook offers easy access to beachfront playlands. Still caters mainly to students from the New York tristate area.

Stony Brook, one of the academic leaders in the SUNY system, aims to be the model of a student-centered research university. The six undergraduate colleges provide a small college community experience with all the assets of a leading research university. The public university has made a name for itself with its top-notch programs in the hard sciences. It has also become known for its highly competitive learning environment and the high quality of its professors. In short, "Stony Brook is the complete package," boasts one senior.

"Stony Brook is a competitive academic school."

The school's location on Long Island's plush North Shore (Gatsby's stomping grounds) is a wonderful drawing point. Sitting on about 1,000 wooded acres just outside of the small, picturesque village of Stony Brook, and only 90 minutes from New York City and half an hour from the beaches of the South Shore, the campus is a conglomeration of redbrick Federal-style buildings interspersed with several modern brick and concrete designs. Campus beautification is a priority, and grass and trees have replaced much of the uninspiring campus concrete.

Coming of age in the high-tech era, Stony Brook quickly became known and respected for its science departments. Facilities are extensive, and the science faculty includes a number of internationally known researchers. The comprehensive university hospital and research center make health sciences strong, especially physical therapy. The hospital, which has been ranked among the nation's best for teaching, attracts grants to the campus and offers a lot of opportunities for various research programs for undergrads as well as graduate students. Engineering is also strong, along with business administration and psychology. The school's arts program benefits from a fine arts center, complete with studios and a reference library. The center complements Stony Brook's beautiful five-theater Staller Center for the Arts. The music department faculty boasts the American pianist Gilbert Kalish.

"Stony Brook's students are by far one of the most diverse of all student bodies on Long Island."

Students spend a lot of time studying. "Stony Brook is a competitive academic school and the classes are challenging," a junior says. Although professors spend much time with their own research projects, they make time for their students. "Most are great teachers and explain the material clearly," says one student. TAs aren't as common as full professors, but "often the TAs can be better teachers," asserts a physics major. Freshmen are the last to register, so they sometimes have to wait a semester or two to get into the most popular electives.

Stony Brook's Diversified Education Curriculum requires students to demonstrate competency in math, communication, and critical thinking. Students must also show an understanding of natural and social sciences, and knowledge of American history, Western civilization, other world civilizations, the humanities, and the arts. Students in the College of Arts and Sciences, the College of Business, and some within the School of Health Technology and Management are required to demonstrate basic foreign language proficiency, and must know how to use computers. Freshmen participate in theme-based academic and cocurricular programs, which include two small seminar courses. The first course is an introduction to the university; the second is up to the faculty member teaching it to decide. Its purpose is to introduce students to what the faculty is studying and researching. Other notable majors are offered in sustainability studies, ecosystems and human impact, coastal environmental studies and environmental design, and policy and planning.

An Undergraduate Research and Creative Activities program (URECA) offers undergraduates the opportunity to work on research projects with faculty members from the time they are freshmen until they graduate. Women in Science and Engineering (WISE) is a multifaceted program for women who show promise in math, science, or engineering. All freshmen—residents and commuters alike—enter

Some students take advantage of one of Stony Brook's wonderful travel programs (France, England, Italy, Japan, and Tanzania are just some of the possibilities).

the university as members of one of six undergraduate colleges. Each college has its own faculty director, as well as both academic and residential advisors. Some students take advantage of one of Stony Brook's wonderful travel programs (France, England, Italy, Japan, and Tanzania are just some of the possibilities), while others choose established internships in the fields of policy analysis, political science, psychology, foreign language, or social welfare. Combined B.A./M.A. or B.S./M.S. programs are available in engineering, the teaching of math, and management and policy.

Seventy-eight percent of Stony Brook students hail from New York, and about half commute from Long Island homes. "In addition to being extremely bright and high-achieving, Stony Brook's students are by far one of the most diverse of all student bodies on Long Island," a senior says. Nearly three-quarters graduated in the top quarter of their high school class, and 30 percent of Stony Brook's graduates go on to graduate and professional schools. The student body is 7 percent African American, 10 percent Hispanic, and 26 percent Asian American. The university has a Campus Relations Team, composed of university police officers who educate the community on topics ranging from personal safety to rape prevention to drug and alcohol awareness. Students are also required to take classes focusing on different cultures. Merit scholarships are given out each year, in addition to several hundred athletic scholarships.

Stony Brook, which has one of the largest residential facilities in the SUNY system, has a slew of robust facilities that provide students access to state-of-the-art fitness centers, computing facilities, Internet, and widescreen TVs. Fifty-nine percent of undergrads live in university housing. "The dorms are nice," says one student. While residential freshmen must take a meal plan, upperclassmen who live on campus either opt for a flexible food-service plan or pay a nominal fee to cook for themselves. The suites come equipped with dishwashers and ranges, and each hall has a lounge and kitchen area, all of which, students say, could be kept a lot cleaner. Kosher and vegetarian food co-ops keep interested students well supplied with cheap eats.

"Loads of kids go home on the weekends."

Even though "loads of kids go home on the weekends," most activities take place on campus, since there isn't too much to do in Stony Brook. "Social life on campus is very organized," says one student. "There are major events held every few weeks." The university has fairly strict policies on alcohol consumption, and "the policies are as effective as possible with young students in college," a senior reports. The longtime ban on fraternities and sororities has been lifted, so a fledgling Greek system is another option and draws 1 percent of Stony Brook men and women. Current and classic movies are screened during the week, and other entertainment is available in the form of frequent concerts, plays, and other performances. Annual festivals in the fall and spring and the football game with Hofstra are among the biggest social events of the year. Because many students go home on the weekends, Thursday is the big party night.

The students who remain on the weekends often go beachcombing on the nearby North Shore or the Atlantic Ocean shore of Long Island, or head into New York City. "You absolutely need a car if you want to get around the town at all," says a junior. Still, many students make do with trains, and a station is conveniently located at the edge of campus. "Stony Brook is a wealthy residential town that cannot be categorized as a 'college town,'" one student says. "It doesn't appreciate the large campus located within its limits." Nearby Port Jefferson offers small shops and interesting restaurants.

Sports facilities have been upgraded, and all 20 varsity Seawolves teams compete in Division I. The men's soccer team has won the America East championship, while the football team has won the Big South championship. Intramurals provide one of the school's greatest rallying points, and competition in oozeball (a mud-caked variant of volleyball) is especially fierce. In all, 28 sports and recreational activities are available.

Though Stony Brook is not old enough to have ivy-covered walls, it does offer some of the best academic opportunities in the SUNY system. Students have to maneuver around lots of rough spots, including increasing class sizes and decreasing course offerings. Yet despite these budget crisis–induced problems, students share in the promise of Stony Brook's future. In the meantime, they boast of their school's diversity and creativity as well as the feeling of hospitality that pervades campus life.

If You Apply To ➤

SUNY–Stony Brook: Regular admissions: Jan. 15. Application fee: $50. Campus interviews: optional, informational. No alumni interviews. SATs or ACTs: required. Subject Tests: recommended. Accepts the Common Application. Essay question: personal statement.

Stetson University

421 N. Woodland Boulevard, DeLand, FL 32723

The oldest private college in Florida, Stetson keeps company with the likes of Baylor and Furman among prominent Deep South institutions with historic ties to the Baptist Church. The common thread is conservatism, and business is easily the most popular program. Stetson is also strong in music and has a specialty in sport and integrative health sciences. More like a small college than a university.

Stetson University, named for the maker of the famed 10-gallon hat, draws students from around the Southeast with its small size and emphasis on the liberal arts. Long a bastion of conservatism, students say the school has become more liberal since cutting ties with the Southern Baptists. With top-notch business courses and surprising strengths in music and Russian studies, this Florida university continues to attract students who aren't afraid to wear a variety of hats during their stay.

Located halfway between Walt Disney World and Daytona Beach, Stetson's 170-acre campus features mainly brick structures in styles from Gothic to Moorish to Southern colonial. While some modern wood buildings are scattered about, the theme is decidedly old-fashioned, complete with royal palms and oak trees. A $12.6 million renovation brought high-resolution cameras, new computers, and state-of-the-art sound and projection systems to class-

> **"Faculty seem passionate about their areas and coursework."**

rooms in the LEED-certified Lynn Business Center, along with a high-tech 144-seat auditorium. The science center is a 22,000-square-foot expansion to the existing science building, Sage Hall.

Stetson has three undergraduate colleges—music, business administration, and arts and sciences—and its general education requirements apply to all of them. General education requirements are divided into three categories: Foundations, Knowledge of Human Cultures and the Natural World, and Personal and Social Responsibility. All entering students take a First Year Seminar (FSEM), which allows students to work closely with Stetson faculty to ease the transition to college. All freshmen who are undecided on a major participate in the Discovery program, and all students take a Junior seminar that focuses on personal and social responsibility.

Website: www.stetson.edu
Location: Small City
Private
Total Enrollment: 3,671
Undergraduates: 2,469
Male/Female: 44/56
SAT Ranges: CR 530–630, M 525–630
ACT Ranges: 23–28
Financial Aid: 98%
Expense: Pr $ $
Student Loans: 77%
Average Debt: $ $ $ $
Phi Beta Kappa: Yes
Applicants: 4,862
Accepted: 60%
Enrolled: 28%
Grad in 6 Years: 64%
Returning Freshmen: 79%
Academics: ✐ ✐ ✐
Social: ☎ ☎ ☎
Q of L: ★ ★ ★
Admissions: (386) 822-7100

(continued)

Email Address: admissions@
stetson.edu

Strongest Programs:
Business Administration
Psychology
Finance
Political Science
Marketing

Business is Stetson's most popular program, and would-be money managers benefit from the award-winning Roland George Investments program, where they oversee a cash portfolio worth nearly $3 million. Students who hope to work for themselves can tap into the Prince Entrepreneurial Program, which connects them with successful business owners, while the Family Enterprise Center was one of the first in the nation in educating students for work in family businesses. Education is also popular and has received national acclaim for its research on single-gender classrooms and its impact on performance in public schools. Stetson's music school is notable (ahem) for its programs in brass instruments, organ, and voice.

Classes are "challenging but not impossible," says a senior. Students in the college of arts and sciences benefit from the Sullivan Writing Program and the Lawson Program in Philosophy. They also complete a research project before graduation; those who choose to do so in the summer may get funding from the Stetson Undergraduate Research Experience (SURE) program. Professors are always willing to help; a management major says many have worked in the field they are teaching before stepping in front of the lectern. "The quality of teaching I have received has been exceptional," says one senior. "Faculty seem passionate about their areas and coursework and care about individual student success." Fifty-six percent of classes have 19 or fewer students. Students with wanderlust may study abroad in France, Germany, Hong Kong, Mexico, Russia, Spain, and Oxford in the United Kingdom; Stetson's honors program incorporates international study, community service, and a senior colloquium, and also allows students to create their own majors. In addition, there are internship opportunities in Germany, England, and Latin America, and each year, professors lead study trips to places such as Turkey, Greece, and the Czech Republic.

> **"There is ample social life on campus, one need only to search for it."**

Three-quarters of Stetson "Hatters" are native Floridians; they tend to be white, wealthy, and friendly, a sociology major says. A junior describes Hatters as "very approachable and ready to have a conversation about anything." African Americans constitute 7 percent of the student body, Hispanics make up 15 percent, and Asian Americans add 2 percent. Students report little interest in political or social issues such as campus diversity. Ninety-eight percent of Stetson students receive financial aid and scholarships based on academic merit, rather than need, and Stetson also hands out athletic scholarships in baseball, basketball, golf, soccer, tennis, softball, cross-country, and volleyball.

Sixty-seven percent of Stetson students live in the school's dorms and many report that housing has gone from terrible to top-notch. "The housing department has done a complete turnaround," says one senior. "The staff is friendly, helpful, and constantly working to improve the residential experience of students." Students say Emily Hall, Chaudoin, Stetson, and Conrad are in the best shape, but they add that more people would probably move off campus if the school didn't cut financial aid awards for doing so. Stetson's traditional cafeteria is known as the Commons, and features a made-to-order deli sandwich line, a pizza bar, and a grill serving burgers and fries. There's also the Hat Rack food court, with a bagel stand, a smoothie shop, and another fast-food grill. "The food is edible if you like bricks and diverse if you like pasta," quips a junior. Campus security receives mixed reviews. "I always feel safe on the central part of campus, but avoid the outer parts of campus at night because there seems to be less patrolling there," says one student.

Students with wanderlust may study abroad in France, Germany, Hong Kong, Mexico, Russia, Spain, and Oxford in the United Kingdom.

"There is ample social life on campus, one need only to search for it," says a student. Social life at Stetson occurs mainly off campus, where students usually drift to local bars or seek entertainment further abroad. Fraternities attract 28 percent of the men and sororities draw 24 percent of the women, but Greek parties don't get too raucous. The Council for Student Activities brings in big-name acts and music majors also stage concerts. Students look forward to annual events such as Greenfeather, aimed at promoting community service, and Greek Week, when sorority and fraternity chapters compete in a lip-synch contest and other events to raise money for charity. When your birthday rolls around, don't forget to wear your bathing suit—it's a tradition for fellow students to toss you into the midcampus Holler Fountain.

As for the "adorable, small Southern town" of DeLand, it boasts "shops, galleries, and cafés," but only three bars, so students often head to Orlando (40 minutes from campus) or Daytona Beach (20 minutes) to eat out, shop, or dance the night away. In addition to the omnipresent beaches, Blue Spring and DeLeon Springs offer canoeing and nature watching. Popular road trips include Miami for clubbing, the Keys for camping, and Gainesville, to see the University of Florida Gators play.

Stetson's teams compete in NCAA Division I, and a football team took the field in August 2013 for the first time in 58 years. The Hatters are a perennial powerhouse in baseball, and the team competes regularly in the NCAA Regionals. Women's golf and basketball are strong, as are softball and tennis. For those not up to intercollegiate competition, the Hollis Wellness Center includes a field house, outdoor pool, game room, dance studio, and exercise room. In addition, 48 percent of students participate in club and intramural sports, ranging from bowling and flag football to Ping-Pong, inner-tube water polo, and sand volleyball is becoming a popular spectator sport.

Stetson students savor the one-on-one attention freely given at this small Sunshine State university. After four years spent enjoying great weather and forming close friendships with peers and professors, they emerge with solid academic foundations for future work or study.

Overlaps

University of Florida, Florida State, University of Central Florida, Rollins, Jacksonville University, University of Miami (FL), University of Tampa, Elon

If You Apply To ➤

Stetson: Rolling admissions. Application fee: $50. Campus interviews: optional, evaluative. No alumni interviews. SATs or ACTs: optional. No Subject Tests. Accepts the Common Application. Essay question.

Stevens Institute of Technology

Castle Point on the Hudson, Hoboken, NJ 07030

Stevens ranks with Clarkson and Worcester Polytechnic among East Coast technical institutes that offer intimacy and personalized education. Youth-oriented Hoboken is a major plus and a quicker commute to Manhattan than most places in Brooklyn.

At Stevens Institute of Technology, students accept intense classwork, all-nighters, and trips to the Big Apple as givens. The school is located just across the Hudson River from Manhattan, which means that students have the cultural, athletic, and gastronomic resources of the Big Apple at their fingertips. The problem is finding time to take advantage of everything New York City offers. (This is the city that never sleeps; nor, it seems, do students at Stevens.) "The workload is a love-hate relationship," sighs a freshman. "We hate it while we do it, but it benefits us in the end." Engineering and the sciences dominate campus life, but students seem prepared to take on the challenge of balancing work and play. "Stevens is a great place to embrace one's inner nerd and party too," says one satisfied student.

"Stevens is a tough school."

Website: www.stevens.edu
Location: Small City
Private
Total Enrollment: 3,925
Undergraduates: 2,519
Male/Female: 73/27
SAT Ranges: CR 570–670, M 640–720
ACT Ranges: 27–32
Financial Aid: 92%

Professional practice is an important part of the Stevens environment, with nearly all students participating in cooperative education, internships, or mature research projects.

There's an eclectic mix of architectural styles on Stevens's 55-acre campus. Many of the residence halls and administrative buildings are redbrick; classroom and lab facilities range from traditional, ivy-covered brownstones to modern glass-and-steel structures. The Kenneth J. Altorfer Academic Complex offers 13,500 square feet of modern spaces dedicated to classrooms and a graduate student research center.

Stevens is organized into four schools—the Charles V. Schaefer Jr. School of Engineering and Science, the Wesley J. Howe School of Technology Management, the College of Arts and Letters, and the School of Systems and Enterprises—and offers 34 majors. Engineering has long been king of the hill at Stevens; programs in biomedical, chemical, civil, electrical, environmental, naval, and computer engineering are all highly regarded, as is the major in mechanical engineering, not surprising since Stevens was the first school to award a degree in the field. "Stevens is a tough school," says a junior. "Students get thrown into very difficult courses and are expected to catch on."

Each major at Stevens has its own requirements, but most programs require calculus, chemistry, physics, humanities courses, and physical education. In the engineering school, the core curriculum is followed by technical electives that culminate in a senior design project. Two five-year programs are also available; one allows students to incorporate internships into their studies, and the other enables students to take fewer courses per term, without extra tuition charges, to make the workload a little more manageable. All entering students are now required to participate in the Freshman Experience, which is a sequence of two common courses: Writing and Communications Seminar and Humanities Colloquium. Other notable programs

"Stevens students are generally really hardworking and have a full schedule."

include cybersecurity, music and technology, information systems, science communications, and naval engineering. Study abroad opportunities include exchange programs with universities in Australia, Scotland, and Turkey, a chemical ecology program in the Dominican Republic, and programs run by the International Student Exchange. Stevens also has an active on-campus recruiting program with major corporations, start-up firms, and the government. The university offers the only undergraduate quantitative finance degree in the nation. Graduates of the program are prepared for such roles as trading assistants, risk managers, or analysts. Professional practice is an important part of the Stevens environment, with nearly all students participating in cooperative education, internships, or mature research projects.

"Stevens students are generally really hardworking and have a full schedule," says one chemical biology major. "They somehow balance school work with involvement in school organizations including professional societies, media outlets, ethnic organizations, and many other activities." Sixty-one percent of the students at Stevens are from New Jersey; another third come from the greater New York City portion of New York State. Ten percent of the student body is Asian American, 9 percent is Hispanic, and 2 percent is African American. Women comprise only 27 percent of the student body. Politics doesn't receive a lot of attention on campus, although the Stevens Political Awareness Committee can be quite active. Admissions officers look more closely at high school grades, especially in math and science, than at test scores; evaluative, on-campus interviews are also highly encouraged of local applicants. Interviews are required for international applicants and for those applying to the university's accelerated programs. In addition to need-based financial aid, 15 percent of students at Stevens receive scholarships based on academic merit, averaging $14,882 per year.

Campus housing is guaranteed for a student's entire four- or five-year stay at Stevens, which is fortunate because the Hoboken housing market is almost as tight—and expensive—as the one in Manhattan. Sixty-six percent of Stevens students live on campus. "As Stevens accepts more students each year, it gets harder to get an on-campus dorm or apartment from the lottery," reports a student. In addition to standard dorms, there are fraternities, old brownstones off campus, and "very nice" university-leased apartments. Students say that the dining hall has improved greatly in recent years. "I enjoy the campus food, and there are many options off campus that are part of the meal plan," says a junior. Another student says, "Campus security is great. The open campus is patrolled by Stevens police who couldn't be more friendly."

Twenty-eight percent of Stevens men join fraternities, and 30 percent of the women pledge sororities, so Greek groups control much of the social life on campus. That is changing, though, with the formation of an Entertainment Committee that plans weekly events, from comedy nights to hypnotists and musical guests. "Social life at Stevens is great. There is a great Greek community, and Hoboken has a immense amount of bars and clubs," says a senior. Greenwich Village, Times Square, and the bright lights of Broadway are just 15 minutes away on the PATH train. There is also Hoboken, which offers popular pubs and clubs right next to campus. Road trips, often taken by train, include Yankee Stadium in the Bronx and Six Flags Great Adventure, a New Jersey amusement park. Beaches and ski slopes are both within a 90-minute drive.

Students cheer enthusiastically when the Stevens Ducks are competing. Men's and women's swimming each brought home national titles in the past two years and Stevens teams have won conference titles in field hockey, women's basketball, men's and women's soccer, men's and women's lacrosse, men's tennis, and women's fencing. Men's basketball has won 20 games each of the last two years as well. For those without the time or talent to play at the varsity level, there are intramurals in everything from basketball, soccer, and football to dodgeball and even bowling.

With its lopsided male/female ratio and its emphasis on technical disciplines, Stevens isn't for everyone. But that doesn't mean it's not worth a look. Graduates go on to make a dent in the world; notable alums include Frederick Reines, who detected the subatomic world of the neutrino and was honored as Nobel Laureate for his achievement; Frederick Winslow Taylor, father of scientific management; and Alfred W. Fielding, inventor of Bubble Wrap. "You'll work hard at Stevens," admits one sophomore, "but there are plenty of ways to enjoy yourself." Stevens's urban location and relatively small size can make for fun times once the studying is done.

Students cheer enthusiastically when the Stevens Ducks are competing.

Overlaps
Rensselaer, Worcester Polytechnic, Lehigh, Drexel, Carnegie Mellon, Rutgers, Johns Hopkins, College of New Jersey

If You Apply To ➤

Stevens: Early decision I: Nov. 15. Early decision II: Jan. 15. Regular admissions: Feb. 1. Financial aid: Feb. 15. Housing: Jun. 1. No application fee. Campus interviews: highly encouraged for local applicants, evaluative; required for international applicants and students applying to accelerated programs. No alumni interviews. SATs or ACTs: required. Subject Tests: optional. Accepts the Common Application. Essay question: personal statement.

Susquehanna University

Selinsgrove, PA 17870

Susquehanna offers welcome relief from the plodding, unimaginative education at many small-scale universities. Its innovative core curriculum includes personal development and transition skills (e.g., computer proficiency) in addition to more conventional topics. Best known for its business program. A more down-to-earth atmosphere than at upscale competitors like Bucknell and Dickinson.

Website: www.susqu.edu

Location: Small Town

Private

Total Enrollment: 2,132

Undergraduates: 2,132

Male/Female: 46/54

SAT Ranges: CR 510–610, M 510–600

ACT Ranges: 23–28

Financial Aid: 96%

Expense: Pr $ $

Student Loans: 76%

Average Debt: $ $ $ $

Phi Beta Kappa: No

Applicants: 3,458

Accepted: 76%

Enrolled: 24%

Grad in 6 Years: 77%

Returning Freshmen: 84%

Academics: ✍ ✍ ✍

Social: ☎ ☎ ☎

Q of L: ★ ★ ★ ★

Admissions: (800) 326-9672

Email Address: suadmiss@susqu.edu

Strongest Programs:

Business Administration

Communications

Psychology

Creative Writing

Biology

Fall Weekend, homecoming, and Spring Weekend are the big annual events.

"Susquewho?" That's the question many students ask when they're first introduced to this undergraduate institution. While it may not be a household name, Susquehanna University is earning a reputation as an innovator. Friendly faculty, personal attention, and an increasing emphasis on community make SU a good place to expand your mind and indulge your senses. "The institution cares about the students, and the campus is well maintained and has a lot to offer," says a senior. "SU truly feels like home."

Susquehanna's campus is beautiful, set on 325 lush acres in the small town of Selinsgrove on the Susquehanna River. Most of the 60 buildings on campus are brick, with Georgian the predominant architectural style. Selinsgrove Hall, built in 1858, and Seibert Hall, built in 1901, are on the National Register of Historic Places. The campus is compact and serene. The 18th Street Commons opened in 2012 and provides townhouse living for upperclass students on the edge of campus.

"Social life at Susquehanna is very active."

SU's best academic programs include business, the sciences, creative writing, music, graphic design, and psychology. The Sigmund Weis School of Business is not only one of the most striking buildings on campus, but is also a prestigious business program that attracts the most Susquehanna students. The Weis School also sponsors a semester in London exclusively for its junior business majors. The business school, along with the other majors, encourages Susquehanna students to take summer internships as a crucial part of their education and future job searches. Susquehanna is becoming increasingly recognized for its science programs, especially biology (another popular major), biochemistry, and environmental science. The most recent additions to the curriculum include a major in Italian and minors in strategic studies and editing and publishing.

Susquehanna's Central Curriculum consists of 56 credits and emphasizes coursework in five areas: Richness of Thought (fine arts and math); Scientific Explanations; Human Interactions (history, sociology, ethics, and language); Intellectual Skills (writing, oral presentation, and teamwork); and Connections (an off-campus cross-cultural experience matched with diversity classes). All freshmen must take a writing seminar (or its honors equivalent) that involves small-group readings and discussion of a particular author. Reading centers on a common contemporary work, with the author often visiting campus to partake in the seminar. An "unbelievably helpful" seven-week orientation experience is offered to first-year students; topics include study skills, stress management, and interpersonal communication. Freshmen also have access to Leadership Passport, a series of workshops and mentoring to help students develop their leadership potential. Through the Global Opportunities (GO) Program, all students are guaranteed an opportunity to study away from campus for as little as two weeks or as long as a semester.

For about a 10th of each class, the academic experience is defined by the Susquehanna Honors Program. Unlike other programs in schools of similar size, SU's program does not separate its students from the rest of the campus. Instead, it allows students to take most of their classes with the general student body, thus creating a balance between freedom of choice and a challenging education. "The honors program significantly widens the range of classes open to students and allows them to fulfill their core requirements in creative ways," says a participant. Honors students or not, most agree that SU offers a moderately demanding academic climate. "The courses, whether major or elective, are tough," offers one senior.

Student/faculty interaction is one of Susquehanna's strong points, and students have high praise for their professors. "The quality of teaching is exceptional. All Susquehanna students are taught by full professors and most of these professors hold a doctorate or the highest degree possible in their field," says one student.

SU students may also take classes at nearby Bucknell University. An assistantship program for outstanding first-year students combines a $16,000 scholarship with hands-on work with a professor or staff member (10 hours per week). Past positions have included academic research, university publications, the Writers' Institute, and marketing research.

Forty-eight percent of SU students are from Pennsylvania, and the majority attended public high school. "SU students are genuine and truly care about making a difference in the community and the world," says one student. Five percent of the student population is African American, 5 percent Hispanic, and 1 percent Asian American. A communications major explains, "Diversity and multiculturalism are big issues. The university wants the student body to be more diverse." To wit, the Chief Diversity Officer and the Center for Diversity and Social Justice focus on educating students on issues of diversity, including "invisible differences" such as socioeconomic status, religion, and sexual orientation. Merit scholarships averaging $13,726 are available for resident Einsteins, but there are no athletic scholarships.

Seventy-seven percent of Susquehanna students reside on campus. "For the most part, the dorm and housing situation is very good," says a biology major. Students must get permission to live off campus, and those who have that privilege—mostly seniors—are selected by lottery. Campus vittles are described as "not bad" to "very good" and campus security is good, according to most, and includes well-lit walkways and emergency call boxes.

"Social life at Susquehanna is very active and gatherings occur throughout the week," explains a student, "typically on campus." Sixteen percent of the men and 14 percent of the women belong to fraternities or sororities, respectively. Fall Weekend, homecoming, and Spring Weekend are the big annual events. Favorite campus traditions include a candlelight Christmas service and a Thanksgiving dinner at which faculty members serve students "the best meal of the year."

> **"The courses, whether major or elective, are tough."**

Outside the university, Selinsgrove is "small and quaint" with several restaurants and stores. In the surrounding countryside, "it's not uncommon to see an Amish family go by in their horse and buggy or for them to come to your off-campus house selling home-baked goods," says a student. For those with cars, it's a short drive to additional shopping and entertainment options. Penn State is an hour's drive. SU began by preparing students for the ministry, and the university's commitment to the community has remained strong. Each year, two-thirds of the student population volunteer on significant community service projects.

Sports are popular among Susquehanna students and 25 percent of students are varsity athletes. Men's and women's cross-country, men's soccer, and men's track are recent conference champs, and other solid teams include men's and women's basketball, women's volleyball, and men's golf. Intramural sports are very popular (45 percent of undergraduates participate), with more than two dozen programs offered.

At Susquehanna, "the professors care about their students," a biochemistry major says. A classmate adds that the "personal atmosphere, great faculty/student relationships, and beautiful campus" make Susquehanna worthwhile—and a name worth learning. In short, says a junior, "the possibilities here are endless."

For about a 10th of each class, the academic experience is defined by the Susquehanna Honors Program.

Overlaps

University of Delaware, Elizabethtown, Gettysburg, Juniata, Penn State, University of Scranton

If You Apply To ➤

Susquehanna: Early decision: Dec. 15. Regular admissions: Mar. 1. Financial aid: May 1. Application fee: $25 (paper), free (online). Campus and alumni interviews: optional, informational. SATs or ACTs: optional; students may submit two graded writing samples instead. Subject Tests: optional. Accepts the Common Application. Essay question.

Swarthmore College

500 College Avenue, Swarthmore, PA 19081-1397

Don't mistake Swarthmore for a miniature version of an Ivy League school. Swat is more intellectual (and liberal) than its counterparts in New Haven and Cambridge. The college's honors program gives hardy souls a taste of graduate school, which is where many Swatties invariably end up. Geekier than Wesleyan, more grounded than Reed, more serious than just about anywhere.

Website: www.swarthmore
.edu
Location: City Outskirts
Private
Total Enrollment: 1,532
Undergraduates: 1,532
Male/Female: 49/51
SAT Ranges: CR 680–780,
M 670–770
ACT Ranges: 30–33
Financial Aid: 51%
Expense: Pr $ $ $
Student Loans: 34%
Average Debt: $
Phi Beta Kappa: Yes
Applicants: 6,589
Accepted: 14%
Enrolled: 40%
Grad in 6 Years: 92%
Returning Freshmen: 97%
Academics: ✐ ✐ ✐ ✐ ✐
Social: ☎ ☎ ☎
Q of L: ★ ★ ★ ★
Admissions: (610) 328-8300
Email Address: admissions@
swarthmore.edu

Strongest Programs:
Economics
Biology
Political Science
English Literature
History
Sociology and Anthropology

Swarthmore College's leafy green campus may be just 11 miles from Philadelphia, but students often don't have the time or the inclination to make the jaunt. That's because they have opted for one of the country's most self-consciously intellectual undergraduate environments. Swatties are bright, hardworking, and eclectic in their interests, and campus life is fabled for its intensity. But the intensity doesn't come from huge amounts of coursework (à la Yale) as much as the self-imposed drive of talented students who want to do lots of things simultaneously—from academics to social protest to rugby—and do them well. "Swat is a truly intellectual place where people love ideas with all of their hearts," a senior philosophy major says. "But that doesn't prevent them from having an eye for activism and a knack for partying hard."

> **"Swat is a truly intellectual place where people love ideas."**

Swarthmore's 425-acre campus is a nationally registered arboretum, distinguished by rolling wooded hills. Multistory buildings with natural stone exteriors from local quarries, shaped roofs, and cornices are the norm, fostering a quiet, collegiate atmosphere. Two residence halls feature loft-style rooms and environmentally friendly "green" roofs, while the Wister Education Center and Greenhouse is LEED Gold certified and includes classrooms, exhibit areas, and greenhouse space. The Worth Health Center underwent extensive renovations in 2012, including new exam rooms and central air-conditioning.

Students are required to take three courses in each of its three divisions—humanities, natural sciences and engineering (unusual for a liberal arts college), and social sciences—and at least two of the three must be in different departments. Students must also complete 20 courses outside their majors, demonstrate foreign language competency, and fulfill a physical education requirement, which includes a swimming test. Students fulfill the writing requirement by taking three writing courses from at least two divisions. Freshman seminars emphasize close interaction with faculty members in a seminar format; about 86 percent of students participate. The acclaimed honors program features small seminars or independent study, collegial relationships between students and professors, and written and oral examinations by external reviewers at the end of the senior year, accompanied by festive banquets. About a third of Swat's juniors and seniors take the honors option, after demonstrating—through their academic records—that they can handle the work.

The college has boosted the number of departments in which students may pursue honors to include studio and performing arts, as well as study abroad. Forty percent of Swarthmore students study abroad in countries such as France, Japan, Poland, and Spain, and the Off-Campus Study Office helps arrange programs in other countries. Cross-registration is also offered with nearby Bryn Mawr, Haverford, and Penn, and a semester exchange program includes Harvey Mudd, Middlebury, Mills, Pomona, and Tufts.

While the academic climate at Swarthmore is intense, it is not competitive. There is no class rank or dean's list, and there is a big emphasis on group projects. A freshman explains, "While the courses are generally very challenging, the environment of Swat is not competitive at all. You will often see students reminding each other of assignments, giving each other tips on how to succeed, and studying in the library together." Indeed, the administration has encouraged a spirit of collegiality by sprinkling small lounges and cappuccino bars around the dorms and academic spaces. "The school does not have a graduate program, so all the professors have basically chosen to work with undergrads and seem to enjoy that experience," one German studies major says. Aside from teaching, Swarthmore professors also serve as advisors, each helping a small group of students choose their classes each semester. Students are likewise assigned to Student Academic Mentors, who shepherd them through the transition to college and the first year on campus.

"While the courses are generally very challenging, the environment of Swat is not competitive at all."

"Ultimately, we are all nerds here," a history major says. "Each of us in our own way has found a place where our passionate, geekiest interests are validated, appreciated, and celebrated by our fellow Swatties." Swarthmore is home to a diverse student body; 2 percent are native Pennsylvanians. The student body is 6 percent African American, 14 percent Asian American, and 13 percent Hispanic. Consistent with their school's Quaker roots, the student body at Swarthmore pays huge attention to social and political issues, and the Eugene Lang Center for Civic and Social Responsibility has made Swarthmore a national force in the area of service learning. "Swarthmore is characterized by a genuine will to do good in the world," a senior engineering major says. The school encourages students to be as educated as possible on issues of cultural, racial, and socioeconomic pluralism, and the entire community is brought into decisions on issues such as socially responsible investments and pay scale of campus workers. In an effort to reduce the loan burden for students, the college has replaced loans with grants.

Swatties are bright, hardworking, and eclectic in their interests, and campus life is fabled for its intensity.

Ninety-three percent of undergraduates live on campus, and residence halls are "a nice living experience," says one student. "The dorms each have their own personality," adds a senior, "and for the most part they are quite comfortable and well maintained." Housing is guaranteed for all four years, although upperclassmen tend to gravitate toward off-campus housing. Dining options are described as better than typical college fare. "There are tons of options at every single meal," says a student. "When I'm at school, I eat much healthier than at home. I wouldn't even consider going off of the meal plan." "The town of Swarthmore is incredibly safe, so it cuts down on the possibility of crime to begin with," says one junior. "In addition, we have a great campus safety program that is quick to respond in any circumstance."

"Swarthmore is characterized by a genuine will to do good in the world."

Most social life at Swarthmore takes place on campus, and it often begins late, since students hit the books until 10 or 11 p.m. and then head out for fun. "Most of the social life takes place on campus in the dorms and at campuswide open parties," says an economics major. "In order to receive funding from the Social Affairs Committee (SAC), an event has to be open to all members of campus. Because of this regulation, you don't have to worry about getting in to a party or having to pay for most events." Annual activities include Primal Scream, a tradition where everyone screams at midnight the night before exams; the Mile Run, where everyone decorates the McCabe Library with toilet paper around shelves (the founder of Scott Tissue is an alumnus and contributor); and last, but certainly not least, Screw Your Roommate, in which roommates pair each other with other roommates and are forced to meet each other in "really crazy" manners. There's also a student-run café and Pub Night every Thursday. "Most people stay on campus on the weekends, but Philadelphia is just a train ride away," one student says.

Aside from teaching, Swarthmore professors also serve as advisors, each helping a small group of students choose their classes each semester.

When it comes to alcohol, Swarthmore follows Pennsylvania law, which states that you must be 21 to drink. "Campus police are not disciplinarians," a student says. "They want students to be safe." Swarthmore's two fraternities attract just over 14 percent of the men; a newly formed sorority launched in 2012–13. The Greeks and other campus groups volunteer in both Philadelphia and the nearby smaller city of Chester. "Almost everyone is involved in some way," explains a junior.

Students' biggest complaints include lack of sleep and too much work. If they're not studying, Swatties are volunteering or out pursuing a personal whim. "Swatties are quirky," says a junior honors history major. "We're passionate about what we do—whether that's mini-golf, [or] studying endangered languages in Alaska, or dissent from the 17th century Anglican Church in Virginia. Swatties don't just do their academic work for the grades or to be first in the class, but because they want to." The village of Swarthmore, known as the "'Ville," has some stores,

"Almost everyone is involved in some way."

a pizza parlor, and a Chinese restaurant. The environment fosters a feeling of safety and security, but students say there's not much in the way of off-campus social activity. For that, students hop from the on-campus station into Philadelphia, where many temptations await, including concerts, dance clubs, museums, and four professional sports teams. The King of Prussia mall, with a movie theater and department stores, isn't far, either.

With Swarthmore's focus on academics, athletics aren't a high priority. The school scrapped its football program because the need to recruit enough males to remain competitive in the increasingly intense Division III environment was undermining efforts to recruit students with other interests and talents. Men's soccer won the 2012 Eastern Collegiate Athletic Conference (ECAC) championship and the women's soccer team advanced to the 2012 Centennial Conference finals. Other competitive Garnet teams include men's and women's tennis, badminton, men's lacrosse, volleyball, softball, and men's and women's swimming. Any victory over archrival Haverford will have Swatties swelling with pride. Intramurals are also popular, with the rugby team's Dash for Cash fund-raiser a favored annual event. Players streak through the halls of the main administration building, where spectators—including faculty and administrators—hold out money for them to grab. In the Crum Regatta, student-made boats float in nearby Crum Creek—Swarthmore's answer to the America's Cup.

Swarthmore is an institution where the administration supports the student body completely and students are given a voice in a variety of issues ranging from faculty-hiring decisions to making campuswide policies. Students who want to take an active role in their education beyond the classroom door may find the right fit here. "Swarthmore will show you just how much you can take on and accomplish," says a student. "By your second year, you'll probably be running some organization or sitting on a college committee."

The environment fosters a feeling of safety and security, but students say there's not much in the way of off-campus social activity.

Overlaps

Brown, Harvard, Yale, Princeton, Stanford

If You Apply To ➢

Swarthmore: Early decision: Nov. 15. Regular admissions: Jan. 1. Application fee: $60. Campus and alumni interviews: optional, evaluative. SAT and two Subject Tests, ACT with writing section, or SAT and ACT with or without writing section: required. Accepts the Common Application. Essay question.

Sweet Briar College

Box B, Sweet Briar, VA 24595

Sweet Briar offers the pure women's college experience—served up with plenty of tradition and gift-wrapped in one of the nation's most beautiful campuses. SBC is the country girl next to in-state rivals Hollins and Randolph, both in nearby cities. Academic standouts include English and the life sciences, and it now offers engineering.

Indiana Fletcher Williams, who founded Sweet Briar College in 1901, envisioned a school that would educate young women "to be useful members of society." These days, the college—in the heart of beautiful, rural Virginia—produces more career women than homemakers, and a few men even make an appearance as nondegree or exchange students. But this remains a place where, in the words of a popular bumper sticker, "Women are leaders and men are guests."

Set on 3,250 acres of rolling green hills, dotted with small lakes, and at the foothills of the Blue Ridge Mountains, Sweet Briar's campus of early 20th-century red-brick charmers is a picture of pastoral beauty. Sweet Briar House, now the president's residence, was once the 19th-century home of the college's founder and is listed on the National Register of Historic Places. The Florence Elston Inn and Conference Center includes high-tech meeting rooms, and the school's old dairy farms have been converted into facilities for the studio arts programs. Additional facilities include the Fitness and Athletic Center (FAC), featuring a theater, a racquetball/squash court, three indoor tennis courts and a suspended running track, and the eco-friendly Green Village student housing.

> **"Women are leaders and men are guests."**

Sweet Briar's general education program has four components: an English course called Thought and Expression, Skills Requirements (oral and written communication, and quantitative reasoning), Experience Requirements (self-assessment, physical activity, and a major), and Knowledge Area Requirements (various courses, including Western and non-Western culture, foreign language, the arts, economics, politics, and law). Seniors must pass a culminating exercise in their majors, which may include comprehensive exams. Students give high marks to Sweet Briar's science programs, which benefit from state-of-the-art equipment such as a digital scanning electron microscope, modular laser lab, gas chromatograph/mass spectrograph, and a nuclear magnetic resonance spectrometer. Students may take science-related classes at nearby Lynchburg College and Randolph College. The college is only one of two women's colleges in the nation (the other is Smith) to offer an ABET-accredited undergraduate engineering degree. Undergraduate research is valued here; recent student-faculty projects have included investigating the causes of dying coral, studying drama and rhetoric in ancient Rome, and working with the campus's resident colony of 100-plus live sharks.

> **"We deserve a better academic reputation than we get."**

"I think frankly we deserve a better academic reputation than we get," says one sophomore. "Some semesters, I've found myself reading well over 300 pages of material per week, a good chunk of that in languages other than English, and doing 15 to 20 papers of varying lengths over the course of the semester." Professors are rated highly, according to one student. "I have never had a bad professor at Sweet Briar. Even those professors whose classes I struggled in were more than happy to meet with me, oftentimes outside of their office hours, to help me understand the

---

Website: www.sbc.edu

Location: Rural

Private

Total Enrollment: 574

Undergraduates: 561

Male/Female: 0/100

SAT Ranges: CR 490–610, M 450–570

ACT Ranges: 22–27

Financial Aid: 98%

Expense: Pr $

Student Loans: 63%

Average Debt: $ $

Phi Beta Kappa: Yes

Applicants: 763

Accepted: 79%

Enrolled: 29%

Grad in 6 Years: 62%

Returning Freshmen: 74%

Academics: ✏ ✏ ✏

Social: ☎ ☎

Q of L: ★ ★ ★ ★

Admissions: (800) 381-6142

Email Address: admissions@sbc.edu

Strongest Programs:

Psychology
Biology
Chemistry
Government
English/Creative Writing
History
International Affairs
Business

material and provide me with resources to get better." The Sweet Briar Honor Pledge, which states that "Sweet Briar women do not lie, cheat, steal, or violate the rights of others," makes possible self-scheduled exams and take-home tests. An honors program and self-designed majors allow some students to further challenge themselves. "All Sweet Briar women can be trusted to carry themselves honorably," says a student. Sweet Briar's unique academic advising program utilizes a team of advisors, put together by the student, who help each student choose courses and a course of study that fits with her interests after college, as well as internships, study abroad experiences, and/or job opportunities.

Sweet Briar's Junior Year in France is the oldest and best known of its study abroad programs. And the younger Junior Year in Spain program is gaining in popularity, as are exchanges with Germany's Heidelberg University and Oxford University in the UK. It's also common for faculty to offer short courses abroad during semester breaks, such as a theater course in London or an antiquities course in Italy. Students can also spend time on other campuses through the Seven-College Exchange, the Tri-College Exchange, or 3–2 liberal arts and engineering programs. Classes end in early May, providing ample opportunity for internships. Sweet Briar's unusually strong alumnae network is helpful in arranging positions and housing in cities across the country.

Students may take science-related classes at nearby Lynchburg College and Randolph College.

"The students at Sweet Briar are strong, motivated, independent women," says an economics major. Forty-eight percent of Sweet Briar's student body hail from Virginia and 53 percent graduated in the top quarter of their high school class. Nine percent are African American, 6 percent Hispanic, and 3 percent Asian American. An increasing number of older "turning point" students also contribute a valued perspective. Common campus complaints include the lack of parking and budget constraints. "Right now, everyone is feeling budget cuts," says a sophomore. "Departments are shrinking or being cut altogether and it's tough to see. Humanities majors in particular are feeling the squeeze." Various merit scholarships ease the financial burden for some and are available for up to $14,466 each.

The Sweet Briar Honor Pledge states that "Sweet Briar women do not lie, cheat, steal, or violate the rights of others."

Ninety-three percent of Sweet Briar's students live in the college's vintage dorms, which are more like stately antebellum homes with sweeping wooden staircases, fireplaces, and furnished parlors. "I love that all of our dorms aren't modern monstrosities," says a history major. Thanks to lots of attention from the college, they have aged gracefully, with "hardwood floors and functioning ceiling fans," adds a senior. With a few exceptions, students are required to live on campus all four years.

"Right now, everyone is feeling budget cuts." Student leaders are given the first shot at singles, and upperclassmen choose rooms in a lottery. All residents may eat in the common dining hall or may choose to eat at the short-order-type restaurant called the Houston Bistro. "The food here is delicious and diverse," a student reports. Security receives high marks, too: "Campus security is excellent; I have never felt unsafe," says a student.

When the weekend rolls around, the Campus Event Organization's annual fee is put to good use, covering mixers with other schools, theatrical performances, formal dances, and yearbooks. "On campus, we have movie nights, game nights, boathouse parties, and just generally hang out with each other," says a senior. A classmate adds, "The weekends are what you make them, and have the possibility to become anything you wish." Campus events attract men "like flies," one student says—and if students don't like the ones who show up, frat parties beckon at Washington and Lee, Hampden–Sydney and the University of Virginia (an hour away). Other popular road trips include Washington, D.C., and Virginia's beaches (three hours). Campus alcohol policies are "very strict," a sophomore says, and heavy drinking is rare. SBC students volunteer at local schools and with Habitat for Humanity. And the Sweet Briar Outdoor Program has introduced hundreds of girls to the joys of backpacking,

Ninety-three percent of Sweet Briar's students live in the college's vintage dorms.

canoeing, and white-water rafting with weekly expeditions. Students also lovingly nurture traditions such as Founder's Day, lantern bearing, step singing, and "tapping" for clubs: "Tap Clubs are a huge tradition," says a sophomore. "They are similar to sororities but students do not rush for them and are chosen based on common interest. The doings of Tap Clubs are secret, but it isn't uncommon to see someone running around in costume in the middle of the night."

SBC's Vixens compete in Division III. Field hockey, lacrosse, soccer, softball, swimming, and tennis offer ample opportunities for the athlete to excel. The equestrienne team finished the 2012 ODAC Equestrian Championships in first place. In 2011, Sweet Briar students won the Virginia Foundation for Independent Colleges' Ethics Bowl, an annual debate competition in applied ethics.

Women come here for a well-balanced mix of academics, friendliness, and career preparation. "This school is not for the immature students who think college is about drinking beer and going out," asserts an English major. "This place will give you an education with a capital 'E.'" While some complain about the remoteness of the school's rural location, most say the beauty of the campus and the sense of family that prevails are more than satisfactory compensation.

If You Apply To ➤ **Sweet Briar:** Rolling admissions. Application fee: $40. Campus interviews: optional, evaluative. Alumnae interviews: optional, informational. SATs or ACTs: required. Subject Tests: optional. Accepts the Common Application. Essay question.

Syracuse University

201 Tolley Administration Building, Syracuse, NY 13244-1140

Syracuse has redefined itself as a research university that takes undergraduates seriously and believes that academic quality can go hand in hand with student diversity. Offerings such as the Gateway program provide small classes for first-year students. World famous in communications, Syracuse is also strong in engineering and public affairs. Basketball provides solace during long winter nights.

Anyone who has watched college sports on TV is familiar with the bright orange color associated with Syracuse University. They have seen the screaming fans and the stadiums overflowing with cheering hordes. Beyond all the athletic fanfare is passion of another sort: Syracuse has set out to become a student-centered research university. By fostering close relationships between students and faculty, expanding course offerings, and pouring loads of money into facility upgrades, Syracuse's reputation as an academic assembly line with killer sports teams is rapidly changing.

The Syracuse campus is located on a hill overlooking the town of Syracuse in central New York State. The character and mixture of architectural styles depict a continuously changing campus, which is grassy, full of trees, and bordered by residential neighborhoods. Fifteen of SU's 140 buildings are listed in the National Register of Historic Places. Many schools and colleges have restructured facilities to accommodate more faculty/student research, as well as social interaction between the two groups. A new library will house approximately 1.6 million volumes in a heat- and humidity-controlled environment.

Syracuse has a diverse set of academic offerings. The Newhouse School of Public Communications is undoubtedly Syracuse's flagship and offers a dual program

Website: www.syr.edu
Location: Small City
Private
Total Enrollment: 18,547
Undergraduates: 13,925
Male/Female: 45/55
SAT Ranges: CR 510–620, M 540–650
ACT Ranges: 23–28
Financial Aid: 75%
Expense: Pr $ $
Student Loans: 61%
Average Debt: $ $ $ $
Phi Beta Kappa: Yes
Applicants: 25,790
Accepted: 51%

(continued)

Enrolled: 26%

Grad in 6 Years: 82%

Returning Freshmen: 92%

Academics: ✏ ✏ ✏

Social: ☎ ☎ ☎

Q of L: ★ ★ ★

Admissions: (315) 443-3611

Email Address: orange@syr
.edu

Strongest Programs:

Aerospace Engineering

Architecture

Entrepreneurship

Information Management and
Technology

Inclusive Education

Political Science

Policy Studies

The College of Arts and Sciences is the largest college at Syracuse and offers recognized programs in creative writing, philosophy, geography, and chemistry.

where students can major in any one of the eight Newhouse majors and have a dual major in information management and technology. Also well known is the Maxwell School of Citizenship and Public Affairs, whose faculty members teach sought-after undergraduate economics, history, geography, political science, and social sciences. Teaming with NASA, the school has a $3 million virtual aerospace engineering facility—one of three in the nation—where students have helped design a reusable space launch vehicle. SU students have also participated in NASA's reduced-gravity student flight programs. The College of Arts and Sciences is the largest college at Syracuse and offers recognized programs in creative writing, philosophy, geography, and chemistry. Students participate in undergraduate research and 38 percent study abroad. The most popular majors are psychology, information management and technology, architecture, biology, and communication and rhetorical studies.

> **"The competition between students is certainly palpable."**

General education requirements vary, but all Syracuse students are expected to take writing courses. Several schools and colleges subscribe to the Arts and Sciences core requirements, which include coursework in the sciences, math, social sciences, humanities, and contemporary issues. Entering freshmen must complete a writing seminar, and each school and college offers a small-group experience course, known as the Freshman Forum, to share common first-year experiences and stimulate discussion of academic and personal issues. The Gateway program allows freshmen to take introductory classes with senior faculty members in a small classroom setting. For upperclassmen, Syracuse offers a strong honors program based on seminars and independent research.

Students at Syracuse can expect challenging courses and competitive peers. "The competition between students is certainly palpable," says one senior. Despite the school's large size, students say professors are friendly and accessible. "Even with larger lecture classes, I feel that my professors have gone above and beyond to make themselves available for students," a bioengineering major says. Classes are usually small (fewer than 25 students) and registration can be easy. "Students do not have difficulty getting into the course they would like to or are required to take," assures one junior.

Admissions standards differ among the various schools and are most rigorous in the professional schools, especially architecture, communications, and engineering. Thirty-eight percent of Syracuse's undergraduates come from the top 10th of their high school class, and 68 percent attended public high school. "Students are involved, active, friendly, and spirited," says a senior. The number of students of color has been steadily increasing and the university has taken measures to recruit low-income students. African Americans comprise 9 percent of the student body, Asian Americans 8 percent, and Hispanics 10 percent. Forty-two percent of the students are from New York State, and most of those hail from New York City and Long Island. A quarter of students qualify for Pell Grants. There are hundreds of athletic scholarships in sports ranging from football and basketball to rowing and lacrosse. Merit scholarships are also available.

> **"I feel that my professors have gone above and beyond to make themselves available for students."**

Seventy-five percent of the undergraduates live in university housing, which is described as clean and comfortable. Syracuse is continually upgrading dorm facilities, and students appreciate the efforts. Freshmen and sophomores are required to live in the dorms, and should check out Brewster-Boland, Day, and Flint halls. Living and dining in fraternity or sorority houses is another option because 21 percent of the men and 26 percent of the women go Greek. As for campus safety, SU has emergency alarms throughout the campus, a card-key access system in all dorms, and bus service for students studying late on campus. "Public safety officers are constantly on patrol," notes a student.

The social life tends to stay on campus for freshmen and sophomores and move off campus for upperclassmen. "Syracuse offers tons of things to do," says a senior, thanks to "over 300 clubs on campus." There are always activities available such as movies, bowling, skating, and dancing. Students over 21 spend many an evening barhopping on Marshall Street, a lively strip near campus. For underage students, there is a campus club where student bands play and nonalcoholic drinks and snacks are free. Drama productions are frequent on the weekends, and popular road trips include Ithaca, Niagara Falls, Montreal, and Rochester.

Classes are usually small (fewer than 25 students) and registration can be easy.

Students generally enjoy the town of Syracuse, which offers a variety of off-campus retreats. "Everything you need is within walking distance," a junior says. Many students are involved in the community through internships in the corporations and SU education students give more than 40,000 hours in

"Public safety officers are constantly on patrol."

community service in Syracuse. Downtown is within easy reach on foot or by convenient public transportation. Once there, opportunities include an excellent art museum, a resident opera company, a symphony, and a string of movie theaters and restaurants. If you tire of the city life, several quaint country towns, complete with orchards, lakes, and waterfalls, are nearby, as are several ski resorts. The Turning Stone casino is a big draw. The six-story Carousel Mall, about 10 minutes away, has an 18-theater cinema. Erie Boulevard is home to big chain stores, and the city's Armory Square is flanked with coffee shops, upscale boutiques, clubs, and eateries.

The Syracuse athletic program was rocked in the fall of 2011 when a longtime associate basketball coach was fired over allegations that he molested several men when they were boys. The incident prompted much discussion on campus regarding the values inherent in big-time sports and their role in the Academy. Nevertheless, amid the soul-searching, the spacious Carrier Dome continues to rock. Football games against Miami and a basketball rivalry with Georgetown make for great fun and much enthusiasm during the year and the excitement is sure to continue as the university moves to the Atlantic Coast Conference. SU's men's basketball, football, cross-country, rowing, and boxing teams have won conference titles. The "painters" are famous at SU—they are the students who paint each letter of the school's name on their bare chests and run through rain, sleet, or snow to each home game in the Carrier Dome. Though the Dome seats 33,000 for basketball—enough to shatter NCAA attendance records—tickets must still be parceled out by a lottery, to the disdain of some. About 1,200 students participate in 20 intramural sports.

Though the Dome seats 33,000 for basketball—enough to shatter NCAA attendance records— tickets must still be parceled out by a lottery.

Administrators say that the Syracuse mission can be summed up as "scholarship in action." From special partnerships with NASA to opportunities to study abroad or help out right at home, students at Syracuse know they've got something unique. The place itself can be enough to inspire school spirit. The wintry climate is problematic, but a senior says, "SU has given me every opportunity imaginable. I'd come back here any day for a chance to do it all again."

Overlaps
Boston University, Cornell, NYU, Northeastern, Penn State

If You Apply To ➤

Syracuse: Early decision: Nov. 15. Regular admissions: Jan. 1. Financial aid: Feb. 1. Housing: May 1. Application fee: $70. Campus and alumni interviews: optional, evaluative. SATs or ACTs: required. No Subject Tests. Apply to particular program; can apply to single, dual, or combined programs. Accepts the Common Application. Essay question.

University of Tennessee Knoxville

Knoxville, TN 37996-0230

UT is in the middle of the pack among its Southeastern rivals—behind Florida, U of Georgia, and UNC; ahead of Alabama, Arkansas, and Ole Miss. As the only major public university in Tennessee, UT comes close to being all things to all students. Strong in business, engineering, and communications. One of the few Southern flagship universities located in a major city.

Website: www.utk.edu
Location: City Center
Public
Total Enrollment: 25,935
Undergraduates: 19,480
Male/Female: 51/49
SAT Ranges: CR 530–640, M 530–650
ACT Ranges: 24–29
Financial Aid: 59%
Expense: Pub $ $ $
Student Loans: 49%
Average Debt: $ $
Phi Beta Kappa: Yes
Applicants: 14,398
Accepted: 67%
Enrolled: 43%
Grad in 6 Years: 66%
Returning Freshmen: 85%
Academics: ✍ ✍ ✍
Social: ☎ ☎ ☎ ☎
Q of L: ★ ★ ★
Admissions: (865) 974-2184
Email Address: admissions@utk.edu

Strongest Programs:
Psychology
Political Science
Logistics and Transportation
Biological Sciences
English

Students at the University of Tennessee put a premium on school spirit, athletics, and academics—usually in that order. In the fall, more than 100,000 boisterous fans pack into one of the nation's largest on-campus football stadiums to watch the Volunteers play against national powerhouses like Alabama, Arkansas, and Florida. Also competitive are the SEC-dominating women's basketball and soccer teams and men's baseball teams. Amid this excitement, it's easy to forget that UT also prides itself on having a strong academic program. "Bleeding orange is the only way to go!" cheers one happy volunteer.

Set in the foothills of the Great Smoky Mountains, UT is in the heart of east Tennessee's urban hub and only a few miles away from Oak Ridge, Tennessee, home to the prominent Oak Ridge National Laboratory. The 560-acre campus has an array of architectural styles ranging from Gothic to Georgian to modern. Particularly noteworthy is the John C. Hodges Library—the largest one in the state—built in the shape of a ziggurat. Other campus additions include the Howard Baker Jr. Center for Public Policy and the Haslam Business Building, a state-of-the-art facility that houses the College of Business. A new student center is slated to open in 2016 and will include a 50,000-square-foot bookstore.

Many strong academic programs are in preprofessional fields, most notably business, architecture, accounting, and engineering. On the liberal arts side, psychology and communications are popular majors. Several majors in French, German, and Spanish incorporate a concentration in international business. UT is the managing partner of Oak Ridge National Laboratory—the federal government's largest nonweapons lab—which bolsters science and technology offerings, and involves more than 400 students and faculty in majors as diverse as English and physics. UT established the Haslam Scholars program for 15 of the nation's top students. Selection criteria include scholastic achievement, leadership potential, maturity, seriousness of purpose, and special talents. Haslam scholars enjoy intimate study groups mentored by top UT faculty, and benefits include a $1,500 laptop computer,

"Some classes are harder than anything I could imagine."

study abroad experience, and up to $5,500 to support a senior research thesis and travel to present their work. Haslam scholars also receive the Chancellor's Scholarship, which covers tuition and fees, room and board, and other expenses. Students who participate in the Whittle Scholars Program are encouraged to pursue their leadership skills through campus and community organizations, and are given the opportunity to travel to a variety of different countries including Argentina, Australia, France, Mexico, and the Netherlands. In all, UT offers programs in 54 countries on six continents.

Academic competition varies, depending on the class, as does course difficulty. "Some classes are harder than anything I could imagine and some require little effort," says one junior. UT faculty get a generally positive rating. "I have had some really good professors and some mediocre ones as well," a logistics major says. Students report occasional problems with registration because preference is given to seniors, but none that would extend a four-year stay. "During the past two years, courses were difficult to get into because there were too many students attending UT," says a senior. Advising also gets mixed reviews, depending on the field of study, and students are expected to meet with their advisors each semester before registering. UT's general education requirements are fairly extensive and include courses in written and oral communications, quantitative reasoning, arts and humanities, culture and civilizations, social sciences, and natural sciences, plus intermediate proficiency in a foreign language or multicultural studies. Business majors are immersed in a broad liberal arts program, including a foreign language requirement, during their first two years of study.

The social calendar is dotted with numerous major events, including River Fest on the nearby Tennessee River.

UT students are "levelheaded but tend to get a little crazy on the weekends," says a student. Ninety-two percent of the student body is made up of homegrown Tennesseans, and 50 percent of the freshman class graduated in the top 10th of their high school class. Minority enrollment remains steady; African Americans account for 7 percent of the students, while Asian Americans and Hispanics each account for 3 percent. Students also warn that the campus's size can lead to a phenomenon called the "Big Orange Screw," in which the impersonal bureaucratic system makes stu-

"Alabama is a four-letter word."

dents' lives miserable. Financial aid opportunities have been generous, with lots of merit scholarships available, but these recently took a big hit when the athletic department reneged on plans to contribute $18 million over the next two years for scholarships and fellowships because it had to finance a $9 million buyout of a fired football coach and his staff.

Thirty-seven percent of UT students live on campus. "The dorms are OK," says one junior. "Some of them are very old and need renovating." The dorms are for the most part comfortable and well maintained, and about the only hitch is that some don't have air-conditioning (which can be brutal if you're there in August). Each of the dorms has a residence hall association, which for a token fee provides checkout of sports equipment, games, cooking utensils, and other useful items. The university goes out of its way to ensure the security of the campus and the students. To this end, UT has installed remote alarm units that allow students to report a crime from anywhere on campus. "There are cops everywhere," a junior says. "As long as you're not stupid, you're fine."

The RecSports program attracts 27 percent of undergraduates and features (among others) flag football, volleyball, intramurals, and fitness programs.

Students say that the social life is "very important" and active both on and off campus. The social calendar is dotted with numerous major events, including River Fest on the nearby Tennessee River, Saturday Night on the Town, and the Dogwood Arts Festival. Greek life is growing more popular—13 percent of the men and 21 percent of the women go Greek. Alcohol flows freely, even for underage students. But nothing compares to the sea of orange that engulfs the campus on Saturday afternoons in the fall. More than 100,000 people jam the football stadium to see the Volunteers (a term dating to the Mexican War) take on Southeast Conference rivals ("'Alabama' is a four-letter word" in these parts). Denizens liken football to religion in Knoxville. UT has claimed more than 120 men's SEC regular-season and tournament titles and nearly 70 women's team titles, as well as national titles in a variety of sports. The RecSports program attracts 27 percent of undergraduates and features (among others) flag football, volleyball, intramurals, and fitness programs.

The University of Tennessee is well known for its athletics, and administrators and students are hoping that it can develop the same reputation for academics. Though the oft-sluggish bureaucracy may turn some off, many will find the myriad opportunities here at the "Big Orange" to be well worth the squeezing. In fact, one senior says, "it is very easy to get involved and succeed at UT."

Overlaps

East Tennessee State, Middle Tennessee State, Tennessee Tech, University of Georgia, University of Tennessee Chattanooga

University of Texas at Austin

John Hargis Hall, Austin, Texas 78712-1157

UT is on anybody's list of the top 10 public universities in the nation. The Plan II liberal arts honors program is one of the nation's most renowned. Though it is also the capital of Texas, Austin ranks among the nation's best college towns while being a progressive enclave in a conservative state. Boot camp for aspiring political types in the Lone Star State and beyond.

Website: www.utexas.edu
Location: City Center
Public
Total Enrollment: 47,630
Undergraduates: 36,724
Male/Female: 48/52
SAT Ranges: CR 550–670, M 580–710
ACT Ranges: 25–31
Financial Aid: 61%
Expense: Pub $ $
Student Loans: 50%
Average Debt: $ $ $
Phi Beta Kappa: Yes
Applicants: 35,431
Accepted: 47%
Enrolled: 49%
Grad in 6 Years: 79%
Returning Freshmen: 93%
Academics: ✎ ✎ ✎ ✎ ½
Social: ☎ ☎ ☎ ☎
Q of L: ★ ★ ★ ★
Admissions: (512) 475-7399
Email Address: N/A

Strongest Programs:
Engineering
Business
Law
Education
Pharmacy

The University of Texas at Austin has come a long way from where it began in 1883 as a small school with only one building, eight teachers, two departments, and 221 students. Today, the UT campus is Texas-sized home to more than 46,000 students. From its extensive academic programs to its powerful athletic teams to its location in one of the nation's ultimate college towns, the University of Texas has everything a Longhorn could ask for. "Our university is a diverse community with amazing opportunities for success," says a junior.

A 400-acre oasis near downtown Austin, replete with rolling hills, trees, creeks, and fountains, the campus features buildings ranging from "old, distinguished" limestone structures to contemporary Southwest architecture. Statues of famous Texans line the mall, and the fabled UT Tower is adorned with a large clock and chimes (a lifesaver for the disorganized). From the steps of the tower, one can see the verdant Austin hills and the state capitol. The outstanding library system at the University of Texas has more than seven million volumes located in 19 different libraries across campus, and is the sixth-largest academic library system in the United States.

Many UT classes are extremely large, and smaller sections fill up quickly. UT is a research-oriented institution, so the professors are often busy in the laboratories or the library. They do, however, have office hours. "My professors are above and beyond my expectations," says a psychology major.

"My professors are above and beyond my expectations."

"Their own interest in their topics is obvious and the determination to aid the students is admirable."

The list of academic strengths at University of Texas is impressive for such a large school. Undergraduate offerings in accounting, architecture, botany, biology, business, foreign languages, and history are first-rate. The engineering and computer science departments are excellent and continue to expand. The English department is huge (nearly 100 tenure-track professors) and students give it high marks, but the art/photography department is said to need improvement. The prestigious Institute for Fusion Studies boasts one of the world's largest telescopes.

The Plan II liberal arts honors program, a national model, is one of the oldest honors programs in the country and one of the best academic deals anywhere. It offers qualified students a flexible curriculum, top-notch professors, small seminar courses, and individualized counseling, and provides them with all of the advantages of a large university in a small-college atmosphere. Business and natural sciences honors programs are also available. Engineering majors can alternate work and study in the co-op program, while education and health majors hold term-time internships. Being in the capital city should have its advantages, and it does. Almost 200 UT undergrads work for lawmakers in the Texas State House, only a 20-minute walk from campus. A strong Reading and Study Skills Lab services students in need of remedial help. Study abroad options are available in more than 80 countries and UT sends roughly 2,500 students to foreign locales annually.

Students say the academic climate is competitive and demanding. "There are many rigorous majors that have accelerated courses or competitive programs," says a student. Freshmen can take University 101, which covers everything from major requirements to healthy lifestyle choices and cultural diversity. In addition, the colleges within the university have established basic requirements for all majors: four English courses, with two writing intensives; five courses in social sciences; five courses in natural sciences and math; and one course in the fine arts or humanities. Entering freshmen are also expected to complete a "Signature Course" within their first year of attendance. Signature courses introduce undergraduates to academic discussion and analysis of issues from an interdisciplinary perspective.

UT students are "intelligent, involved, and proactive in their education," says a senior. Eighty percent of UT students are Texans. Students say there is no dominant political pattern on campus—despite the fact that historically UT has been integral in the careers of big-time (conservative) Texas politicians. The liberals are anything but hiding out on this huge campus. Political issues, such as human rights, gun control, and abortion, can get students pretty riled up on one side or the other here. Hispanics account for 22 percent of students, Asian Americans 19 percent, and African Americans 5 percent. Caucasians account for 52 percent of total enrollment and, for the first time in the university's history, less than half of freshmen. The university offers special "welcome programs" for African American and Hispanic students, with social and educational events and peer mentoring. The university also provides thousands of merit scholarships based on academic performance, as well as hundreds of athletic scholarships in 16 sports.

University housing accommodates only 19 percent of students and it ranges from functional to plush. Dormies have a variety of living options based on common social and educational interests. "Most of the dorms are old," says a student, "but they have nice facilities." Most students live off campus; apartments and condos close to campus are lovely—and very expensive. More reasonably priced digs can be found in other parts of town, a free shuttle ride away. But be forewarned: With 110 buildings, UT life requires lots of walking, especially for commuters, though bus stops and parking lots are scattered about. As for food, there is a wide variety of options, including healthy, vegetarian, kosher, and vegan fare. What's more, "other cafés and convenience stores on campus offer even more selection," says one student. Security is a concern (Austin is an urban area, after all) but students report feeling safe on campus, thanks to an active and highly visible security department.

As the state capital, Austin is not a typical college town, but it is one of the best ones. "I love it," exclaims a junior. "It was really the deciding factor on going to UT. It has a great live music scene and is beautiful." Nightlife centers on nearby Sixth Street, full of pubs and restaurants of all types, and the well-known music scene that features everything from jazz to rock to blues to folk. Austin is also known as "Bat City" after the colony of Mexican free-tailed bats that live under the Congress Avenue Bridge in the spring and summer. It's the largest urban bat colony in North America. Along with live music, bat-catching is one of Austin's most popular activities. Halloween

Engineering majors can alternate work and study in the co-op program, while education and health majors hold term-time internships.

"There are many rigorous majors that have accelerated courses or competitive programs."

Students say the academic climate is competitive and demanding.

"Most of the dorms are old."

draws an estimated 80,000 costumed revelers to Sixth Street (and sometimes up its lampposts). Annual festivals include 40 Acres, a sprawling carnival of all the campus organizations, and Eeyore's birthday party, where students pay homage to the A. A. Milne character with food and live music. Two pep rallies get students psyched before the Longhorns play Texas A&M or Oklahoma, their biggest rivals. And Texas Independence Day provides an occasion for celebration in March.

On campus, the Texas Union sponsors movies and social events and boasts the world's only collection of orange-top pool tables. For those more interested in octaves than eight balls, the Performing Arts Center has two concert halls that attract nationally known performers. There are also more than 950 student organizations from which to choose. Students hang out at the union's coffee shop or café, and the on-campus pub draws top local talent to the stage (but you must be 21 to drink). When the weather gets too muggy (quite often in spring and summer), students head for off-campus campgrounds, lakes, and parks. The most popular road trips are to San Antonio or Dallas. For Spring Break, the students travel to Padre Island, if not New Orleans. Although only 3 percent of the men and 5 percent of the women go Greek, members of fraternities and sororities are "probably highest on the social totem pole," says one student. The chapters tend to be choosy, have high visibility, and have increased in size dramatically over the past year.

Athletics are as vital as oxygen to most Texans. In fact, the UT Tower is lit in Longhorn orange whenever any school team wins. The athletic department has a budget in excess of $100 million and spends more than $150,000 a year on nutritional supplements such as Gatorade and Power Bars. The students look forward to the annual Texas–Oklahoma football game played in the Cotton Bowl in Dallas, and the

> **"Football games pull the student body together and give us a chance to show our school spirit."**

Texas A&M–UT game is an incredibly noisy experience you have to see to believe. "Football games pull the student body together and give us a chance to show our school spirit," says one student. Bevo XIV, the famed UT mascot, is the latest in a long line of longhorn mascots who have at various times been known to bolt loose from their handlers, rip their shirts, and, on one occasion, lie down in the end zone during a football game. Basketball is also popular, and the men's and women's teams regularly reach their respective NCAA tournaments. The baseball program has many alumni in the major leagues, and the annual spring game between UT's baseball alumni and the current college squad is quite a contest. The men's golf, swimming, baseball, and outdoor track and field teams have each brought home conference championships, as have women's golf, swimming and diving, softball, basketball, and indoor and outdoor track and field teams. The chess team is a perennial power-house, too. UT's intramural program draws 90 percent of the students and is the largest in the nation. It offers weekend athletes access to the same great facilities that the big-time jocks use.

The University of Texas may seem overwhelming because of its imposing size, but students say the school spirit and sense of community found here make it feel smaller. UT prides itself in having one of the most reasonably priced tuitions in the country. It offers one of the best all-around educational experiences a student could ask for, especially if you make it into Plan II.

Overlaps

Baylor, Duke, University of Houston, MIT, NYU, Rice, Texas A&M, Vanderbilt

If You Apply To ➤ **UT–Austin:** Rolling admissions: Dec. 1. Financial aid: Mar. 15. Application fee: $75. No campus or alumni interviews. SATs or ACTs (with writing): required. Subject Tests: not used for admissions decisions (may be used for placement purposes). Apply either to institution as a whole or particular program. Essay question.

University of Texas at Dallas

Richardson, TX 75080

A rising star in the Lone Star State, UTD is now the most selective of the regional campuses of the UT system. Has put on a full-court press to attract top students in science and technology. Good living conditions and a serious honors program. Football here is of the flag variety. Has a lower acceptance rate and a higher percentage of out-of-staters than either Texas A&M or Texas Tech.

Founded in 1961 as a graduate research center, the University of Texas at Dallas did not begin awarding undergraduate degrees until 1975. It wasn't until 1990 that UT Dallas admitted its first freshman class. Since that time, the university has continued to grow and hone its chops as a four-year university with an emphasis on engineering, mathematics, the sciences, and the management of new technologies. "UTD is a young, vibrant, and promising institution," raves one senior. "Even freshmen have the chance to create new organizations and traditions, work in real labs with full professors, and be in contact with top administrators." Although the university may not fit the typical Texas "frats and football" mold, students here still find plenty of reasons to cheer.

> "Even freshmen have the chance to create new organizations and traditions."

Situated on 500 rolling acres in the Dallas suburb of Richardson, UT Dallas has the feel of a large corporate campus. Most buildings are positioned around an interior mall that features a variety of blooming trees, low flower beds, and fountains. The predominant architectural style is 1970s tilt wall concrete, and many buildings are interconnected by a series of glass sky bridges. The Natural Science and Engineering Research Laboratory provides 192,000 square feet of state-of-the-art labs, including "class 1000" clean rooms that have highly controlled environments to prevent contamination. The building is playfully referred to as the "mermaid building" for its iridescent blue, green, and magenta shingles, which resemble fish scales. A slew of new facilities have opened recently, including two new residence halls, a 28,000-square-foot dining hall, and a new university bookstore and visitors center. The ATEC Building opened in 2013 and features classrooms for game design, visual arts, drawing and painting studios, and photography labs.

To graduate, UT Dallas students must complete a general education curriculum consisting of 42 credit hours across eight disciplines: communication, mathematics, natural science, humanities, fine arts, Texas and American history, government, and social and behavioral sciences. Freshmen are expected to take a first-year rhetoric class, which is a small group seminar designed to teach college survival skills and to ensure that students receive appropriate advising. Qualified first-year students may also enroll in Collegium V, an honors program that grants students access to special social and academic opportunities. The program is valuable because it "gets smaller groups together to form real communities and resource networks," according to one junior.

> "Lower-level courses are generally more laid-back."

UTD offers budding scientists an especially solid choice of majors, including highly respected programs in audiology, neurology, and nanotechnology. In fact, all of the hard sciences draw praise, and students flock to the engineering and computer science programs, which are among the school's most popular majors. Students say the academic climate is collaborative, but courses can be grueling. "Lower-level courses are generally more laid-back," says a senior, while "core and upper-level

Website: www.utdallas.edu
Location: Suburban
Public
Total Enrollment: 14,120
Undergraduates: 9,385
Male/Female: 57/43
SAT Ranges: CR 560–680, M 600–710
ACT Ranges: 26–31
Financial Aid: 75%
Expense: Pub $ $ $
Student Loans: 36%
Average Debt: $
Phi Beta Kappa: Yes
Applicants: 7,079
Accepted: 51%
Enrolled: 42%
Grad in 6 Years: 64%
Returning Freshmen: 85%
Academics: ✐ ✐ ✐
Social: ☎ ☎ ☎
Q of L: ★ ★ ★
Admissions: (972) 883-2270
Email Address: interest@ utdallas.edu

Strongest Programs:
Biology
Accounting
Business Administration
Computer Science
Art and Technology
Mechanical Engineering

courses are very challenging." Those seeking to add a pinch of the humanities to their science may opt for the innovative arts and technology program, which unites art and engineering. Newer degrees include marketing, management information systems, and global business.

Seventy-five percent of classes have 49 or fewer students, and "freshmen are usually taught by full professors," says a senior. A finance major adds, "Though some classes are big, students are always given a chance to voice their opinions. The professors are also willing to help outside of class." The Undergraduate Research Program offers students stipends specifically to pursue short-term research proposals, and the university recently opened the state's first Confucius Institute, which promotes a better understanding of Chinese language and business through classes and travel. The McDermott Scholars program offers a full ride plus stipends for international travel, field trips, and other benefits; approximately 20 freshmen are selected every year.

"Students at UTD are of a different breed," says a sophomore. "We tend to be a bit on the nerdy side and have a notorious reputation for not being very social." Ninety-two percent hail from the Lone Star State. Seventy-three percent ranked in the top quarter of their high school class, and many favor academics and research over sports, says a sophomore. African Americans account for 6 percent of the student body, Asian Americans add 25 percent, and Hispanics comprise 16 percent. When it comes to political and social issues, students don't show much concern. "Ha!" scoffs one computer science major. "UTD is pretty apathetic toward social and political issues," says one student. "Whenever an event is put on with candidates in upcoming elections, or information about current political topics, attendance tends to be pretty low." The university hands out merit scholarships averaging $10,478 each year, but no athletic scholarships. Students whose annual family income is less than $25,000 are eligible for the Tuition Promise program, which provides tuition and fees. Academic Bridge takes 30 to 40 local students whose academic credentials are not quite high enough to meet UTD standards and pays them to attend an intensive summer prep experience, including classes and off-campus trips. Those who perform well are admitted to the university.

"The social life at UTD is bland."

Twenty-five percent of the students live on campus in apartment-style residence villages. "The apartments are comfortable," a freshman reports, "and maintenance comes when there are problems." Freshmen participate in a living/learning community; options include arts and technology, computer science, engineering and management. LLC students live in the same apartment building, attend classes together, and participate in various group activities. On-campus dining is somewhat limited and the meal plan is expensive, according to students. "The food on campus is edible but not really diverse," says one junior. Students hope that options improve now that a new dining hall has opened. Security gets a definite "thumbs-up" from students thanks to good lighting, emergency call boxes, and an active security staff.

"The social life at UTD is bland," grumbles one student. The only spice is the growing Greek life program. There are frequent concerts, dinners, movies, and dances, and the aforementioned Greek scene, which attracts 3 percent of UTD men and 2 percent of the women. Alcohol policies prohibit underage drinking and the university is "fairly strict" when it comes to enforcing the rules. Popular traditions include homecoming, the Cometville Carnival, and the oozeball tournament (that's mud volleyball, for the uninitiated). "We're still young and traditions are still forming," says a sophomore.

Richardson is "definitely not a college town, but the surrounding community is pleasant and relaxed," says a senior. Students frequent the neighborhood grocery stores and restaurants and get involved with the locals through volunteering and community service projects. When it's time for off-campus fun, many head into downtown Dallas, which is "lively, artsy, and sophisticated," according to a molecular biology major.

UTD may be one of the few places in Texas where football isn't considered to be as vital to life as oxygen. In fact, you won't find football listed among the university's varsity teams, which compete in the Division III American Southwest Conference. Almost every Comets program is a perennial conference contender, but especially competitive teams include men's basketball, women's volleyball, men's and women's soccer, and men's baseball. The chess team is a powerhouse as well, having made 13 consecutive appearances in the Final Four of College Chess. Approximately 50 percent of the student body takes part in recreational or club sports, and the most popular activities include flag football, basketball, and soccer. Students also enjoy a wide array of individual and group fitness programs.

UTD appeals to those students seeking a business-centric curriculum, access to undergraduate research and top-notch facilities, and administrators who value their input. "Students actually matter here," says a junior. Thanks to UTD's relative youth, "undergraduates see a lot more lab time. Students can get involved across programs. Non-theater majors can participate in university productions, non-prelaw students are on the mock trial team, science majors participate in model UN, and the list goes on," says a freshman. Indeed, students here aren't bound by tradition—they're creating it.

If You Apply To >

UT Dallas: Rolling admissions: Jul. 1. Financial aid: Mar. 31. Housing: May 1. Application fee: $50. No campus or alumni interviews. SATs or ACTs (with writing): required. Subject Tests: optional. Essay question: personal statement (optional).

Texas A&M University

College Station, TX 77843-0100

Coming to A&M is like joining a fraternity with 50,000 members. In addition to fanatical school spirit, Texas A&M offers leading programs in the natural sciences, business, and engineering. To succeed in this mass of humanity, students must find their academic niche. The student body is 95 percent Texan, and out-of-staters should be prepared for major culture shock.

Since its inception as a military academy, Texas A&M University has become known for its top-notch engineering program and its unsurpassed school spirit. This school of more than 40,000 undergrads boasts a massive endowment and more traditions than Vatican City. When they're not studying for rigorous technical classes, Aggies are likely to be found at "yell practice" before each home football game or yelling—the administration says sternly, "Aggies don't cheer, they yell!"—for their teams at other high-energy athletic events.

Texas A&M is now the largest university campus in the country, in terms of acreage—something made obvious to students every time they walk to class. The A&M campus combines historic brick buildings from the turn of the century with newer structures in more modern styles, and is pulled together by a heavy cover of live oak trees. The campus is in a constant state of flux, as renovations and new construction take place on a regular basis.

Texas A&M is best known for its agriculture and engineering colleges, and for veterinary medicine, although the university is cultivating a strong liberal arts

Website: www.tamu.edu
Location: Small City
Public
Total Enrollment: 44,179
Undergraduates: 36,215
Male/Female: 52/48
SAT Ranges: CR 520–640, M 560–670
ACT Ranges: 24–30
Financial Aid: 68%
Expense: Pub $ $
Student Loans: 46%
Average Debt: $ $
Phi Beta Kappa: Yes

(continued)

Applicants: 27,798
Accepted: 67%
Enrolled: 44%
Grad in 6 Years: 80%
Returning Freshmen: 92%
Academics: ✏ ✏ ✏ ✏
Social: ☎ ☎ ☎
Q of L: ★ ★ ★
Admissions: (979) 845-3741
Email Address: admissions@ tamu.edu

Strongest Programs:
Engineering
Business
Veterinary Medicine
Agriculture
Architecture
Biomedical Sciences

The Academy for Future International Leaders trains 15 students per year in international business and cultural issues, followed by a summer international internship.

program and an even stronger business school. Aggies also stand by science programs, especially chemistry and physics. Technical programs of virtually all kinds are heartily supported at A&M, especially nuclear, space, and biotechnical research. A&M has become a sea-grant college due to its outstanding research in oceanography, and is also a space-grant college. Add that to the college's land-grant status, and the whole universe seems covered by A&M. Coursework sometimes takes students

"Aggies don't cheer, they yell!" far from Aggieland. Participants in the Nautical Archaeology Program conduct research all over the world. The Academy for Future International Leaders trains 15 students per year in international business and cultural issues, followed by a summer international internship.

Incoming Aggies can expect some heavy coursework in general education requirements, which consist of communications, math, natural sciences, humanities, social/behavioral sciences, kinesiology, visual/performing arts, and U.S. history/political science. They are also expected to have at least two years of a foreign language, complete a cultural diversity requirement, and demonstrate computer literacy. Students generally agree that academics are taken seriously at A&M. "It's competitive in a laid-back way," says one senior. "My classes are difficult—I can't just breeze through them—but I don't get so stressed out about them that I can't have a life outside of school." Professors receive rave reviews, although TAs and grad students are often behind the lectern. "Texas A&M has many dedicated, involved professors that truly care about imparting knowledge," a student reports. Because of the school's size, it's sometimes hard to enroll in a required class. "You just have to go to the professor and get forced in," one student advises. The administration hopes to alleviate the situation by adding nearly 450 faculty members over the next few years as a part of the "faculty reinvestment program."

Ninety-five percent of students are from Texas and the political climate is decidedly conservative. "Students at Texas A&M have a drive and passion to give back. Whether it is giving back to Texas A&M or the Bryan/College Station community, Aggies take to heart our core value of selfless service," muses one junior. The school's departments of Multicultural Services and Student Life offer numerous programs to enhance minority student recruitment and retention. African Americans comprise 4 percent of the student body, Asian Americans 5 percent, and Hispanics 20 percent. "The biggest issues are probably hunger, abortion, and the right to carry a concealed weapon," says a history major. Athletes compete for the 424 scholarships parceled out each year, while scholars vie for thousands of merit awards averaging more than $5,600 each.

A&M's single-sex and co-ed dorms range from cheap and not-so-comfortable to expensive and cushy (with air-conditioning and private bathrooms). "Apply for housing as quickly as you can to ensure you get a residence hall, because not many students have the opportunity to live on campus," a sophomore says. Most upperclassmen live in the numerous apartments and houses in College Station or its twin city, Bryan. But they needn't fear being cut off from campus life, as the entire town is filled with Aggies, and the university offers a shuttle bus to and from scores of

"My classes are difficult—I can't just breeze through them." apartment complexes throughout the community. Several meal plans are offered in the dining halls, and snack shops are all over campus. "The major issue right now is that the student union is under construction and its eateries have been relocated until it reopens next spring," a student explains. Campus security is lauded, but the school is not incident-free.

"Social life takes place both on and off campus," says one senior. "There are plenty of organizations to get involved in and a lot of these organizations have meetings and activities on campus. That being said, there are a lot of parties that take place off campus as well." Although College Station may appear uninspiring at first glance, most students fall in love with it. "College Station is a model college town," a senior explains. "Every restaurant has an 'Aggie special,' and the radio stations play our 'war hymn' at times throughout the day." And when the school empties out for a holiday, the town does too. Students are actively involved in the community, including the largest single-day service project in the nation annually, the Big Event. Although the Texas Alcoholic Beverage Commission is stationed in town, "those who choose to drink have no problem getting alcohol." Those with more sophisticated tastes can drive an hour and a half to either Houston or Austin or three hours to Dallas. Greeks draw 6 percent of the men and 12 percent of the women, and students say Greek life is less important than at other schools. More than 700 organizations are available to meet everyone's interests.

Athletics, whether on the varsity level or for recreation, are tops on anyone's list here. The school began competing in the uber-competitive Southeastern Conference in 2012 and made an impressive debut by racking up several conference wins and defeating top-ranked Alabama in the process.

"Aggies take to heart our core value of selfless service."

Football fans rock Kyle Field with cries of "Gig 'em, Aggies," or "Hump it, Ags." After touchdowns are scored, Aggie fans kiss their dates, and the annual game against the University of Texas stirs up the Aggies and their fans all season long. Men's baseball routinely fields outstanding teams, and the women's golf and soccer teams have brought home a few championships of their own. The women's gymnastics club has won multiple national titles. The well-organized and extensive intramural program includes hundreds of softball teams. Tennis has become a popular sport as well, along with flag football, basketball, and soccer. Aggie jokes abound, much to the chagrin of A&M students, who don't take too kindly to being the object of ridicule. Example: "How do you get a one-armed Aggie out of a tree?" "Wave."

Favorite traditions include "Twelfth Man," in which all students stand for the entirety of every football game as a symbol of their loyalty and readiness to take part, and the Aggie Muster, a memorial service for A&M alumni around the world who died within the year. There's also the 300-plus member Fightin' Texas Aggie Band and the senior "boot line" at the end of the halftime show. The treasured Corps of Cadets, one of the largest military training programs in the country, is structured like a military unit; students lead other cadets. While less than 10 percent of the school belong to the Corps, it remains the single most important conservator of the spirit and tradition in Aggieland. Yet another ritual: Thousands of seniors join hands and meander through the campus visiting favorite spots for the last time. The ritual, known as the Elephant Walk, takes its name from elephants who wander away from their herds before they die.

While extremely large, Texas A&M is uniquely familial. Being a student here is being a part of something seemingly so much bigger, which is what the Aggie spirit embodies. Students get the best of two intense worlds at A&M—a large school with tons of people surrounded by a small community. A&M's no longer just a military school; it's a potpourri of varied educational opportunities worth cheering. Boasts one senior, "We have the same traditions as were created years ago and, young or old, Aggies know them all."

Overlaps

University of Texas, Texas Tech, Baylor, Texas State, Texas Christian, University of Houston

If You Apply To ➢

Texas A&M: Rolling admissions: Dec. 1. Application fee: $60. No campus or alumni interviews. SATs or ACTs: required. Subject Tests: optional. Essay question. Apply to particular schools or programs. Primarily committed to state residents.

Texas Christian University

TCU Box 297013, Fort Worth, TX 76129

The personalized private alternative to Texas-sized state universities. Tuition is less, and the student body less affluent, than that at archrival SMU. Though affiliated with the Disciples of Christ, TCU goes lighter on religion than, say, Baylor. Strengths include the fine arts, business, and communications. Riding the wave of popularity due partly to recent exploits of the football team.

Website: www.tcu.edu
Location: City Outskirts
Private
Total Enrollment: 8,643
Undergraduates: 8,124
Male/Female: 40/60
SAT Ranges: CR 530–630,
    M 550–650
ACT Ranges: 25–30
Financial Aid: 73%
Expense: Pr $
Student Loans: 41%
Average Debt: $ $ $ $
Phi Beta Kappa: Yes
Applicants: 19,335
Accepted: 41%
Enrolled: 23%
Grad in 6 Years: 75%
Returning Freshmen: 90%
Academics: ✍ ✍ ✍
Social: ☎ ☎ ☎
Q of L: ★ ★ ★
Admissions: (817) 257-7490
Email Address: frogmail@
    tcu.edu

Strongest Programs:
Business
Nursing
Communications
Fine Arts
Engineering
Premed

You know a school has spirit when its students paint themselves purple to cheer raucously for a horny frog. Although outsiders might be baffled by such a display, Texans know these folks are TCU fans cheering for the home team (known officially as the Texas Christian University Horned Frogs) at a Saturday afternoon football game. There's a true sense of solidarity and school spirit here. "TCU is welcoming," says a senior. "That's why I came as a freshman and stayed until graduation."

The spacious 275-acre campus is kept in almost perfect condition and features tree-lined walkways and grassy areas. Nearby is a lovely residential neighborhood not too far from the shops and restaurants of downtown Fort Worth. The campus features an eclectic mix of architecture, ranging from neo-Georgian to contemporary. Facilities also include the Campus Recreation Center and the Walsh Center for Performing Arts, a 56,000-square-foot performance hall and theater complex. The 2012–13 football season opened to a newly renovated stadium.

Students choose their majors from 110 disciplines, with the core curriculum embodying the base of the liberal arts education. The core emphasizes critical thinking and is divided into three areas: essential competencies; human experience and endeavors; and heritage, mission, vision, and values. There are freshman seminar courses, along with a student orientation and Frog Camp (an optional summer camp that emphasizes team building and school spirit).

TCU's standout programs are business, nursing, communications, engineering, and fine arts. In the Neeley School of Business, some students manage a $1.5 million investment portfolio that is one of the largest student-run investment funds in the nation. The university also offers an innovative dance program with a ballet major, a strong theater internship program, and a major in ranch management. The communications program offers hands-on experience in various areas including broadcast news, reporting, and advertising/public relations. The campus also features a geological center for remote sensing, a nuclear magnetic resonance facility, and an art gallery, along with a state-of-the-art electrical engineering lab.

The academic climate at TCU is challenging, but not overwhelming. "TCU students are definitely concerned about academics and grades, but there is also a feeling of support and open cooperation between students," says an English major.

"TCU should be called PCU." Professors are well liked and respected. "The quality of teaching is unbeatable," enthuses one student. Academic advising receives high marks, too. "My advisor is so eager to help," says a student. "I think he really enjoys giving me advice." The university offers more than 175 study abroad programs in over 40 countries around the world, including Europe, South America, Asia, Africa, and Australia.

TCU's student body is fairly homogeneous; 63 percent are from Texas, many from affluent, conservative families. Forty-three percent graduated in the top 10th of their high school class and 62 percent attended public high school. African Americans account for 5 percent of the student body, Hispanics 11 percent, and Asian Americans 2 percent. TCU is affiliated with the Christian Church (Disciples of Christ), but the atmosphere is not overtly religious. This is hardly an activist campus, but it is definitely correct to be politically correct. In fact, "TCU should be called PCU," says a junior. TCU offers merit scholarships and hundreds of athletic scholarships.

Forty-seven percent of the student body lives on campus and dorm life is a good experience. Cable and free Internet access are available in all rooms. Students describe them as comfortable and clean. An evening transportation service, Froggy Five-O, takes you wherever you want to go on campus. "There are also plenty of lights and emergency phones," one freshman says, "so students feel physically safe." Many juniors and seniors move off campus, and fraternity and sorority members may live in their Greek houses after freshman year. Dorm residents must take the meal plan, which does not receive high marks. A variety of other dining options are offered at various locations around campus.

Greek life is important at TCU; 42 percent of the men and 51 percent of the women join Greek organizations. They party in the esprit de corps tradition, but there's plenty of fun left in Fort Worth and on campus to keep the non-Greek Frogs hopping. The alcohol rules on campus are fairly strict

There are freshman seminar courses, along with a student orientation and Frog Camp (an optional summer camp that emphasizes team building and school spirit).

"We all really love our school and what it stands for."

for minors: Resident advisors even perform occasional "fridge checks" looking for alcohol in students' rooms. "Alcohol violations are a big deal," one student says.

"Fort Worth is cultured and has plenty of things to do," says a senior. "Downtown has tons of bars, clubs, theaters, and comedy shows and is safe to walk around in. The stockyards let you get in touch with the inner country in you, and no one should miss a visit to Billy Bob's, the world's largest honky tonk." Dallas is only 45 minutes to the east. Parents' Weekend, Siblings' Weekend, homecoming, and the traditional lighting of the Christmas tree are all special events. Road trips include Austin, San Antonio, the Gulf Coast, and Shreveport, Louisiana.

This is hardly an activist campus, but it is definitely correct to be politically correct.

TCU athletics entered a new era in 2012 with its membership in the Big 12. The Horned Frog football program has made 14 bowl appearances in the last 15 seasons, including a 2011 Rose Bowl championship. TCU has had success across the board with its athletics program. Over the last few years, 16 of 20 sports have been represented in NCAA postseason play with 12 teams nationally ranked. Nine sports have won conference titles. TCU baseball reached the College World Series in 2010, while the rifle program won the 2010 and 2012 NCAA national championships. On-campus sports facilities feature two indoor pools, weight rooms, a track, and tennis, basketball, sand volleyball, and racquetball courts.

Those seeking a personalized college experience that's heavy on the academics and light on the religious influence may want to consider TCU. "We all really love our school and what it stands for," says one student. Like the beloved Horned Frog, TCU graduates have taken a giant leap toward their futures.

Overlaps

Baylor, University of Texas at Austin, Southern Methodist, Texas A&M, University of Southern California, University of North Texas, Texas Tech, Vanderbilt

If You Apply To ➤ | **TCU:** Early decision and early action: Nov. 1. Regular admissions: Feb. 15. Financial aid: Mar. 15. Housing: May 1. Application fee: $40. Campus interviews: optional, informational. No alumni interviews. SATs or ACTs: required. Subject Tests: optional. Accepts the Common Application. No essay question.

A child of the remote West Texas plains, Texas Tech is finally emerging from the shadow of Texas A&M as one of the state's top research universities. It takes big-time sports to be on the map in Texas, and the Red Raiders are making a name for themselves. Bills itself as smaller and more personal than UT or A&M.

Website: www.ttu.edu
Location: City Center
Public
Total Enrollment: 27,381
Undergraduates: 23,562
Male/Female: 55/45
SAT Ranges: CR 500–590,
    M 520–620
ACT Ranges: 22–27
Financial Aid: 62%
Expense: Pub $ $
Student Loans: 44%
Average Debt: $
Phi Beta Kappa: Yes
Applicants: 18,027
Accepted: 64%
Enrolled: 39%
Grad in 6 Years: 61%
Returning Freshmen: 81%
Academics: ✍ ✍ ✍
Social: ☎ ☎ ☎
Q of L: ★ ★ ★
Admissions: (806) 742-1480
Email Address: admissions@ttu.edu

Strongest Programs:
Exercise and Sports Science
University Studies
Psychology
Biology
Mechanical Engineering
Environmental Toxicology
Technical Communication

Texas Tech University has come a long way from its humble beginnings. First proposed in 1923 in the West Texas city of Lubbock, Tech opened its doors two years later as an independent institution, with fewer than 1,000 students, and courses in the liberal arts, agriculture, engineering, and home economics. Today, Tech hosts more than 27,000 students, about 400 student organizations, hundreds of undergraduate programs, and schools of medicine and law.

Tech's 1,839-acre campus features expansive lawns, impressive landscaping, and Spanish Renaissance–style red-tile-roofed buildings. The school has completed more than $1 billion in construction projects in recent years, including the Boston Avenue Residence Hall and Jerry S. Rawls College of Business Administration. Tech also has a slew of other facilities around Texas, such as a 16,000-acre agricultural facility and research farm.

The university's 10 undergraduate colleges and schools boast more than 150 degree programs. Tech's general education requirements span all of the colleges and schools, and include courses in written and oral communication, math, natural science, humanities, visual and performing arts, social and behavioral sciences, and multiculturalism.

Despite Tech's massive size, 76 percent of the classes taken by freshmen have 49 or fewer students. "The academic climate is very strong," says one senior. "Each year that I have been here, the classes have gotten harder and the professors more experienced." Those professors "have changed my life and made me think for myself," explains a communication studies major. Graduate assistants may lead discussion sections or labs, but they aren't the main force at the lectern. A one-credit freshman seminar helps with the transition from high school to college (80 percent participate), and learning communities provide students with ample service-learning opportunities.

"'Techsans' are truly down to earth and friendly."

The College of Agricultural Sciences and Natural Resources "has the strongest financial foothold on campus, with the largest endowment," says an economics major. "Within the College of Human Sciences lies the department of personal and family financial planning, the best of its type in the country." Outstanding students may enroll in Tech's Honors College, where they sit on committees, help with recruiting, make decisions about course content, and evaluate faculty. They can also work on research projects, either independently (with a professor's guidance) or as part of a student/faculty team. Tech invested $2 million in undergraduate research in one recent year, and about 2,500 students participated, investigating topics such as pain management, wind engineering, and sick-building syndrome. Those yearning to leave the hardscrabble plains of Texas may study abroad in over 80 countries; Tech also has its own campus in Seville, Spain, where courses are taught by Tech professors (in English and Spanish) and students live with local families.

The Tech student body is largely homegrown; only 6 percent of students hail from outside the Lone Star State. "'Techsans' are truly down to earth and friendly," says one student. "We come from small, West Texas towns and some of the largest cities in the

United States." Asian Americans account for 3 percent of the total student population, African Americans 6 percent, Hispanics 19 percent, and nonresident aliens 3 percent. Diversity and the role of Greek life on campus are among the hottest political and social issues. Tech offers merit scholarships worth an average of $2,323, as well as 300 athletic awards in 17 varsity sports. Elite chess players can vie for a handful of scholarships as well. The Red Raider Guarantee offers free tuition and fees to qualified freshmen who are Texas residents and whose families earn less than $40,000.

Only 25 percent of the students at Tech live in the dorms and freshmen are required to do so. "The dorms are the ultimate college experience," says one senior. Co-ed, single-sex, and quiet study dorms are available. Most students do move off campus by their sophomore year. Blue-light emergency phones and a safe-ride shuttle service help students feel safe, and dining options are plentiful. "Whether you're a vegetarian or on a protein diet, you'll eat well here," says a junior. About 50 restaurants in the area also take the university's Tech Express debit card, and many have student specials one night a week.

Tech is officially dry and "punishments are quite harsh" for those who attempt to skirt the university's alcohol policies, a senior warns. Since so many students live off campus, that's where most of the weekend action is. Still, for those on campus who wish to participate, there are more than 400 student organizations from which to choose. Three percent of the men pledge fraternities, and 6 percent of the women join sororities, so a sizable contingent heads to the parties at Greek Circle, where students say it's fairly easy for the underage to be served. The Depot District is also a popular destination, as most bars and clubs admit anyone 18 and over.

> "We have a good mix of 'small-town' students and 'big-town' students."

The city of Lubbock (population 200,000) offers many opportunities to get involved with the community, through work with the Boys and Girls Clubs, Habitat for Humanity, animal shelters, or Bible study at local churches. Annual traditions include homecoming, complete with a chili cook-off; the Carol of Lights during the first weekend in December; and Arbor Day, when hundreds of students fan out across campus to plant flowers and trees for the spring. Popular road trips include any of the four nearby lakes (for picnicking, boating, or camping), skiing in New Mexico (four hours away), and anywhere the Red Raiders are playing, especially if it's against the University of Texas Longhorns.

The Division I Red Raiders compete in the Big 12 Conference, and the football, baseball, and men's track and field teams are among the school's best. When players take the field, the Masked Rider, replete with red and black cape and cowboy hat, motivates the crowd by galloping up and down the sidelines. Women's cross-country is strong, having brought home the Mountain Region championship recently. Intramural sports, which about half of the undergraduates take part in, include everything from the typical soccer and flag football to mud volleyball, table tennis, dodge ball, and inner-tube water polo.

Texas Tech has come a long way in a short time and over the past 90 years the school has done much to carve out its own niche. "We have a good mix of 'small-town' students and 'big-town' students," says a communications major. If you can stand the heat and relative isolation of the West Texas Plains, and the effort it takes to be more than a number at a school of this size, Texas Tech may be worth a look.

A one-credit freshman seminar helps with the transition from high school to college (80 percent participate), and learning communities provide students with ample service-learning opportunities.

The Red Raider Guarantee offers free tuition and fees to qualified freshmen who are Texas residents and whose families earn less than $40,000.

Overlaps

Texas A&M, University of Texas, Texas State, University of Houston, University of North Texas, Baylor, Stephen F. Austin State

If You Apply To >

Texas Tech: Rolling admissions: Mar. 1. Financial aid: Mar. 15. Application fee: $60. No campus or alumni interviews. SATs or ACTs (with writing): required. Subject Tests: optional. Essay question.

University of Toronto: See page 354.

Trinity College

300 Summit Street, Hartford, CT 06106

While many small colleges have been treading water, Trinity has had a notable increase in applications and selectivity in recent years. It is taking imaginative advantage of its urban setting through a $175 million community revitalization initiative. Trinity joins Lafayette, Smith, Swarthmore, and Union as a small liberal arts college that offers engineering.

Website: www.trincoll.edu
Location: City Center
Private
Total Enrollment: 2,196
Undergraduates: 2,195
Male/Female: 52/48
SAT Ranges: CR 590–690, M 600–700
ACT Ranges: 26–30
Financial Aid: 41%
Expense: Pr $ $ $ $
Student Loans: 41%
Average Debt: $
Phi Beta Kappa: Yes
Applicants: 7,720
Accepted: 34%
Enrolled: 23%
Grad in 6 Years: 83%
Returning Freshmen: 88%
Academics: ✍ ✍ ✍ ✍
Social: 🏰 🏰 🏰 🏰
Q of L: ★ ★ ★
Admissions: (860) 297-2180
Email Address: admissions.office@trincoll.edu

Strongest Programs:
Economics
Political Science
History
Biology
Chemistry
Engineering
Modern Languages

For students at Trinity College, the learning experience doesn't stop at the campus borders. At first glance, the small liberal arts college and the large, gritty city of Hartford, Connecticut, seem like an uneasy match. But instead of insulating itself from outside problems, Trinity takes advantage of its surroundings by using Hartford as its classroom. The centerpiece of the college's community revitalization effort is the Learning Corridor, an eclectic mix of 16 schools in the neighborhood surrounding the campus. On campus, academic standards continue to rise, and students graduate with a strong liberal arts background. "Students are the priority here," says one senior. "The personal attention I found at Trinity is unrivaled."

> **"The personal attention I found at Trinity is unrivaled."**

Splendid Gothic-style stone buildings behind wrought-iron fences decorate Trinity's 100-acre campus. The large, grassy quadrangle is home to pickup games of hackeysack and lazy relaxation on warm spring and fall afternoons. Along with revitalizing the neighborhood that surrounds it, Trinity's campus is undergoing its own revitalization. Recent renovations include restoration and modernization of the "Long Walk" dormitory and classroom facilities in some of the college's original buildings.

Trinity's general education requirements include one course each in the arts, humanities, natural sciences, numerical and symbolic reasoning, and social sciences. Students must also demonstrate proficiency in writing and mathematics and fulfill a foreign language requirement. The First-Year Program includes a seminar emphasizing writing, speaking, and critical thinking; the seminar instructor serves as students' academic advisor. Freshmen may also choose one of three guided-studies programs in the humanities; natural sciences; or the history, culture, and future of cities, which one student calls "phenomenal—very challenging and rewarding." A global engagement requirement can be completed by coursework or study abroad.

Students give rave reviews to Trinity's English, economics, and computer science departments, and say the school's small but accredited engineering program is likewise strong. That department sponsors the Fire-Fighting Home Robot Contest, the largest public robotics competition in the U.S., open to entrants of any age, ability, and experience. Through the BEACON program, biomedical engineering students can take courses at UConn, the UConn Health Center, and the University of Hartford while conducting research at three area health centers. Trinity's close ties to the community also are apparent in the curriculum; students can take courses on urban development and the history of the city of Hartford. Thirty Community Learning courses are offered each year that provide an out-of-classroom learning experience.

Faculty/student collaboration is a tradition at Trinity. Two-thirds of a recent graduating class worked with professors on research and scholarly papers, and many students join their mentors to present findings at symposia. "The academic climate is rigorous but not overly competitive," says a senior. Students say that professors have high expectations of students and most go the extra mile to provide support. "The quality of teaching is truly outstanding," says a student. "Most professors are distinguished as authorities in their fields."

Nearly two-thirds of the students seek internships with businesses and government agencies in Hartford (the insurance capital of the world), and some also take terms at other schools through the Twelve College Exchange*. The Global Sites program enables students to study with Trinity professors in six exotic locations, from South Africa and Trinidad to Chile, Nepal, and China. Other enticing choices include the Mystic Seaport term* for marine biology enthusiasts, studying Italian language and art history at Trinity's campus in Rome, or learning Spanish at the University of Cordoba. Back on campus, the Department of Theater and Dance offers an unusual integrated major, and sponsors a study-away program with LaMaMa in New York City and Europe. Administrators caution that the educational studies department offers students a richer understanding of the field, but that to get teacher certification, students must tap into the Hartford higher education consortium.

> "The academic climate is rigorous but not overly competitive."

Seventeen percent of Trinity students are Connecticut natives; many of the rest hail from Massachusetts and other nearby states. On the whole, they are "prep school students from privileged families," according to a sophomore. Asian Americans account for 5 percent of the student body, Hispanics constitute 7 percent, and African Americans comprise 6 percent. Although no one would mistake the campus for a political hot zone, students remain aware of global issues and local concerns. The college offers no athletic scholarships, but does provide special financial packages to replace student loans for financially needy students. In addition, the majority of admissions decisions are made without regard to financial considerations, and the college guarantees it will meet the full demonstrated need for four years.

> *A global engagement requirement can be completed by coursework or study abroad.*

Eighty-nine percent of Trinity's students live in the co-ed dorms. The best bets for freshmen are said to be Jones or Jarvis because of their central location on the quad. "Some dorms are much nicer than others," says a student, "but most dorms are average." After freshman year, rooms are assigned by lottery; seniors pick first, then juniors and sophomores, though everyone is guaranteed a bed. Options include singles, doubles, quads, units with kitchens, and theme houses for those interested in music, community service, wellness, art, and quiet. Freshmen must eat in Trinity's dining hall; the Bistro, an upscale but reasonable café, is another choice for students on the meal plan. Others hibernate in the Cave, which offers sandwiches and grilled fare. Overall, students report the campus dining options to be edible and adequate.

> "Most dorms are average."

Speaking of options, when it comes to Trinity's social scene, there are plenty. "The social life revolves around on-campus activity," a sophomore says. Some students praise the Trinity College Activities Council, which brings in comedians and musical performers and organizes parties, study breaks, and community service days. "The campus dances are very popular with the entire student body," says a senior. The Underground Coffeehouse and the Bistro's weekly comedy nights are also popular. A college-sponsored "culture van" takes students to downtown Hartford to catch a show at the Busnell or visit the Wadsworth Atheneum, the nation's oldest public art museum. But the action on Thursday, Friday, and Saturday nights is mostly on campus and mostly at the co-ed Greek houses (20 percent of men and 16 percent of women join up). Alcohol is not hard to come by, but "the campus policies on alcohol are fairly severe on underage drinkers and abusers," says a student. Spring Weekend brings bands to campus for a three-day party outdoors.

> *Students give rave reviews to Trinity's English, economics, and computer science departments.*

Popular road trips include Montreal, Boston, New York City, and the beaches and mountains of Maine.

Students describe surrounding Hartford as "scary" and "a terrible college town," but admit that things are improving. "Hartford has a terrific assortment of restaurants, ranging from cheap but delicious ethnic fare to upscale, parent-friendly places," says a philosophy major. Hartford also "offers unique opportunities for internships, mentoring, and community service," adds a sophomore. The $175 million community revitalization campaign includes a $5.1 million grant from the W.K. Kellogg Foundation and draws on existing community resources. The Office of Community Service and Civic Engagement offers opportunities for students to work and learn in the city. Students have created and run organizations that provide housing, tutoring, meals, and other services to youth, families, and senior citizens.

Trinity's Bantams compete in Division III, and thanks to its international recruits, both men's and women's squash are powerhouses (the men's program has brought home 13 consecutive national titles). Recent conference championship teams include men's and women's golf and men's rowing. Homecoming typically brings Wesleyan or Amherst to campus for a football game, which gets underway after Trinity students burn the opposing school's letter on the quad. Fifty percent of students take part in the intramural and club sports programs.

Trinity is ahead of the curve in liberal arts education, and, a sophomore says, "you can appreciate it much better if you are interested in more than one subject." Even more importantly, Trinity students have taken their civic responsibility to heart. "Our average student is self-motivated and active, whether it be in sports or in clubs or community service," a senior says. "It's a place where everyone can have their voice heard."

Although no one would mistake the campus for a political hot zone, students remain aware of global issues and local concerns.

Overlaps

Boston College, Boston University, Brown, Dartmouth, Yale, Wesleyan, Middlebury, Bowdoin

If You Apply To ➤

Trinity College: Early decision: Nov. 15. Regular admissions: Jan. 1. Application fee: $60. Campus and alumni interviews: optional, informational. SATs, ACTs, or three Subject Tests: required. Accepts the Common Application. Essay question.

Trinity College Dublin: See page 370.

Trinity College Dublin: See page 370.

Trinity University

One Trinity Place, San Antonio, TX 78212-7200

One of the few quality Southwestern liberal arts colleges in a major city. Trinity is twice as big as nearby rivals Austin and Southwestern and offers a diverse curriculum that includes business, education, and engineering in addition to the liberal arts. Upscale and conservative. San Antonio runs neck and neck with Austin as the most desirable city in Texas.

Website: www.trinity.edu
Location: City Center
Private
Total Enrollment: 2,422

Trinity University is a small school with big bucks. Thanks to that liquid that gushes out of the Texas soil, Trinity has one of the nation's largest educational endowments at a school its size. The wealth is used unashamedly to lure capable students with bargain tuition rates and to entice talented professors with Texas-sized salaries. The result? A student body comprised of smart, ambitious men and women, and a stellar faculty. Students here enjoy challenges, but still manage a laid-back Texas attitude. "It's friendly, warm, personal, engaged, and academically stimulating," a senior says.

Trinity was founded in a small central Texas town just after the end of the Civil War. In 1952, the school moved to its current location, a residential area about three miles from downtown San Antonio, one of the most beautiful cities in the Southwest. The 117-acre campus, filled with the Southern archi-tecture of O'Neill Ford, is located on what was once a rock quarry. Everything fits the school's somewhat well-to-do image, from the uniform redbrick buildings to the stately pathways that wind along gorgeous green lawns and through immaculate gardens spotted with Henry Moore sculptures. Trinity's most dominant landmark is Murchison Tower, which rises in the center of campus and is visible from numerous vantage points throughout San Antonio. A state-of-the-art center for sciences and innovation opened recently.

"The people are smart and competitive."

The school makes a concerted effort to maintain its admissions standards, keep-ing a small enrollment, tightening the grading system, and recruiting high achievers with greater energy than is possible from larger universities. The university has set its sights on becoming the premier small liberal arts school in the Southwest. Students report that the academics are rigorous, but the climate is not competitive. "The courses can be rigorous and thought provoking, challenging and inspiring," says a junior. Another student adds, "The people are smart and competitive, but they are also willing to help one another and are generally modest about their level of intelligence." The classes at Trinity are small; 58 percent have 19 or fewer stu-dents, and freshmen are assigned to mentor groups of 10 to 15 students for aca-demic and guidance counseling, as well as peer tutoring from upperclassmen.

The professors at Trinity are "available, brilliant, and helpful," according to a junior. "They always hold office hours for students to come in and talk or ask ques-tions." Trinity has a highly praised education department, with a five-year M.A.T. program and a good premed program. Other strong departments include econom-ics, business, and engineering and chemistry. The communications department offers students hands-on training with television equipment or the chance to pro-duce a newscast. Accounting majors are offered a chance to serve an internship with the big four accounting firms in San Antonio, Houston, Dallas, or Austin while earn-ing a salary and receiving college credit.

Trinity's approach to general education requirements takes the form of the Common Curriculum, under which students must take courses from five areas: cul-tural heritage, art and literature, human social interaction, quantitative reasoning, and science and technology. Students must also have proficiency in a foreign language and computer skills, although those require-ments can be fulfilled in high school. First-year students must take a topical seminar and a writing workshop, or an intensive, six-credit, one-semester Readings from Western Culture. As a member of the Associated Colleges of the South*, Trinity approves a number of study abroad programs and encourages premed and prelaw students, as well as history and English majors, to take advantage of them. Another feature of Trinity's curriculum is an opportunity for students to participate in research projects with faculty mentors. Trinity has one of the fastest-growing Chinese language programs in the country, and the Languages Across the Curriculum program features classes such as religion and anthropology taught in languages including German, Spanish, and Russian.

"The professors at Trinity are available, brilliant, and helpful."

Sixty-six percent of Trinity students are Texans. The school is fairly diverse; Hispanics alone account for 15 percent, Asian Americans another 7 percent, and African Americans 4 percent. As with most universities, there is some attention paid

(continued)

Undergraduates: 2,311
Male/Female: 46/54
SAT Ranges: CR 570–680, M 580–670
ACT Ranges: 26–31
Financial Aid: 86%
Expense: Pr $
Student Loans: 46%
Average Debt: $ $ $ $
Phi Beta Kappa: Yes
Applicants: 4,402
Accepted: 64%
Enrolled: 21%
Grad in 6 Years: 80%
Returning Freshmen: 89%
Academics: ✏️ ✏️ ✏️
Social: ☎ ☎ ☎
Q of L: ★ ★ ★
Admissions: (800) 874-6489
Email Address: admissions@trinity.edu

Strongest Programs:
Business Administration
Modern Languages and
    Literature
English
Political Science
Communications
Economics
History

The university has set its sights on becoming the premier small liberal arts school in the Southwest.

to social and political issues. Merit scholarships averaging $13,039 are available to academically gifted students; there are no athletic scholarships.

Trinity requires students to live on campus until their junior year. In fact, 75 percent of the students live in the residence halls, which one student describes as "fantastic, with walk-in closets, private balconies, suite-style rooms, and a cleaning service." Dorms are co-ed, with one single-sex residence hall that is off-limits to freshmen; all dorms are wired for cable and the Internet. "We are spoiled!" boasts one junior. Most seniors move off campus so they can have single rooms. Campus dining is "delicious," according to a student. "I've been eating on campus for four years and I'm still not sick of the food."

San Antonio, with its famed River Walk, receives a well-deserved "thumbs-up" from students. "San Antonio is a great place to be, because there are so many things to do. That being said, you need a car to get almost anywhere." says one student. And it doesn't hurt that the city is home to several colleges. All those "young people" frequent the many outdoor shops and cafés at the River Walk, as well as touristy hangouts such as Sea World. There are also many cultural and musical attractions. Students get involved in city life through the Trinity University Volunteer Action Center.

"Most of the social life occurs on campus," says a philosophy major. "There are over 100 student organizations that put events on every weekend. You more often than not have to choose which event you are going to attend as opposed to whether or not to attend an event." Most of the parties are within walking distance of the school and are primarily hosted by the fraternities and sororities—but open to all students. Thirteen percent of the men and 12 percent of the women in the student body join the local fraternity and sorority organizations. Country line dancing is also a popular activity, and the university sponsors an excellent lecture series that brings notable politicians and public figures to campus. Alcohol may be consumed on Trinity's campus by those of legal age in any of the upper-class dorms, except for designated substance-free floors.

"There are over 100 student organizations that put events on every weekend."

The beautiful, warm weather of San Antonio provides plenty of activities for the students year-round, but there are also plenty of fun road trips that the students enjoy. The funky state capital of Austin is 90 miles north, and students can also road-trip internationally to nearby Mexico. An annual event most students look forward to is Fiesta, a weeklong celebration of San Antonio's mixed culture that features bands, dancing, food, and drink. They also anticipate the Tigerfest dance and parade on homecoming weekend and the Chili Cook-Off that pits Greek and other clubs against one another. The school year kicks off with a party at the school's bell tower, which students can climb to get a knockout view of San Antonio.

Sports are another popular activity at Trinity, where they compete in the Division III and SCAC Championships. Trinity has won several national championships and captured approximately a dozen Southern Collegiate Athletic Conference (SCAC) President's Trophies, which are awarded to the school with the best overall athletic program. In fact, one student brags, "there are no rivalries in sports since we win at everything." Successful sports include football, baseball, men's and women's soccer, basketball, tennis, and women's volleyball. Sixty-five percent of students take advantage of the intramural program, and flag football is the most popular sport.

A big state and big money give students at this small university many of the advantages of a larger school. If you are looking for a small community feel with quality professors, look no further than Trinity. "It is a very nice campus, students hold a lot of school pride, and the teachers are very welcoming," one satisfied student says.

<table>
<tr><td>

If You Apply To ➤

</td><td>

Trinity University: Early decision: Nov. 1. Early action: Jan. 1. Regular admissions: Feb. 1. Financial aid: Feb. 15. Housing: May 1. Application fee: $50 (paper), free (online). Campus and alumni interviews: optional, informational. SATs or ACTs: required. Subject Tests: optional. Accepts the Common Application. Essay question: Common application personal statement.

</td></tr>
</table>

Truman State University

100 East Normal, Kirksville, MO 63501

Truman has more in common with private institutions than with nondescript regional publics. Looking for a public ivy niche like Miami of Ohio and William and Mary. Rural setting encourages strong focus on academics. Nearly a quarter of the students are from out of state, mainly from Illinois.

Truman State University, Missouri's only public liberal arts college, attracts overachievers from across the Show-Me State. Indeed, since 1985—when the school shifted to a statewide liberal arts and sciences mission—Truman has worked to become a "public ivy" on the order of Miami University (OH) or the College of William and Mary. True, the small town of Kirksville, Missouri, is no Williamsburg, Virginia—or even Oxford, Ohio. But the school's relative isolation makes it easier to focus on academics. One happy senior says, "Truman is the best option for highly motivated students looking for a supportive and friendly learning environment."

Truman is located in the northeastern corner of Missouri, about 200 miles from both Kansas City and St. Louis. Founded in 1967 as a regional teacher training institution, the school became a statewide university in 1985 and 10 years later took the name of the only Missourian to serve as a president of the United States. The flower-laden campus includes approximately 40 buildings on 140 acres, many of which are Georgian in style—in fact, the oldest portion of the campus, dating to 1873, is modeled on Thomas Jefferson's University of Virginia. A health sciences building opened recently and residence hall renovations continue.

The most popular major is biology; business administration, psychology, English, and exercise science round out the list of programs with the highest enrollment. An interdisciplinary major allows students to combine coursework from two or more disciplines to create a specialized major. There are also five-year programs for students interested in education or accounting, which culminate in the awarding of bachelor's and master's degrees. Newer majors include a B.F.A. in creative writing and a B.A. in romance languages.

"The courses are rigorous, but there are so many resources students can take advantage of in order to succeed," says one senior. Truman's general education requirements revolve around the liberal arts and sciences. The Liberal Studies Program forms the core of all academic majors; students must complete six "Modes of Inquiry" which include courses in fine arts, math, science, philosophy/religion, humanities, foreign language, and social science. In the junior year, students complete an interdisciplinary, writing-enhanced seminar. All first-year students are required to participate in a one-day orientation session during the summer as well as Truman Week, which is designed to help freshmen adjust to college life.

Nearly all classes taken by freshmen have fewer than 50 students, which makes access to professors the norm. "The quality of teaching is incredible," says one

> **"[Professors] give their best effort to present the information in an interesting and efficient way."**

Website: www.truman.edu
Location: Small City
Public
Total Enrollment: 5,461
Undergraduates: 5,301
Male/Female: 40/60
SAT Ranges: CR 550–710, M 550–650
ACT Ranges: 24–29
Financial Aid: 51%
Expense: Pub $
Student Loans: 52%
Average Debt: $ $
Phi Beta Kappa: Yes
Applicants: 4,445
Accepted: 74%
Enrolled: 39%
Grad in 6 Years: 74%
Returning Freshmen: 89%
Academics: ✍ ✍ ✍
Social: ☎ ☎ ☎
Q of L: ★ ★ ★
Admissions: (660) 785-4114
Email Address: admissions@truman.edu

Strongest Programs:
Biology
Business Administration
Psychology
English
Classical and Modern Languages
Political Science
Exercise Science

chemistry major. "When the professors walk into class, they will give their best effort to present the information in an interesting and efficient way." Approximately 25 percent of the student body go abroad annually, visiting 63 countries through the College Consortium for International Studies, Australearn, International Exchange Program, and the Council on International Educational Exchange. All students conduct independent research or collaborate with faculty members on research projects. In 2011, the Office of Student Research at Truman State University provided funding for 25 undergraduate students to present their research, scholarship, and creative activities at the 25th National Conference on Undergraduate Research at Ithaca College in New York. Typically, Truman State University sends one of the largest delegations of undergraduates to the conference on a yearly basis.

All students conduct independent research or collaborate with faculty members on research projects.

"Truman students are passionate about very different things, and are united in their love for pursuing those passions," says one senior. Seventy-seven percent of Truman students hail from Missouri and 79 percent ranked in the top quarter of their high school class. Hispanics comprise 2 percent and Asian Americans 2 percent of the Truman student body; African Americans add 4 percent. Merit scholarships are available to qualified students; the average award is $5,334. The school also hands out 279 athletic scholarships in 20 sports. The Truman Access Grant provides funding of $1,000 to a limited number of students who have unmet need after their federal financial aid and Truman scholarship award has been packaged.

"There is stuff happening on campus constantly, seven days a week."

Forty-five percent of Truman students live on campus in the residence halls, and "each hallway is decorated so they have more of a warm feeling—not like the feel of a prison," a junior says. Most of the dorms have been completely renovated within the last four years, and they are air-conditioned, comfortable, and well furnished, students say. Dining-hall menus are on a five-week rotation, and students describe campus fare as "average" and "tolerable." Students report feeling safe while on campus. "I have never felt unsafe on Truman's campus," says one student. "There are round-the-clock campus security guards, as well as an emergency system that is in place to ensure the safety of the Truman community."

"There is stuff happening on campus constantly, seven days a week," cheers one senior. "Between sports, plays, music performances, art shows, and live entertainment, students are generally enjoying themselves on Truman's campus all the time." The Greek system plays an integral part in Truman's social life; 25 percent of men and 17 percent of women sign up. Other diversions are provided by the Student Activities Board, which brings in comedians, bands, movies, and plays. Students also venture out on popular road trips to St. Louis, Kansas City, various destinations in Iowa, and Quincy, Illinois. Everyone looks forward to homecoming in the fall and the Final Blowout carnival in the spring, with wacky games, inflatables, free food, and fireworks. Other enjoyable traditions include snowball fights in the winter and "late-night runs to Pancake City after playing Capture the Flag."

Truman's SERVE Center keeps a list of projects seeking volunteers, and the Big Event is a campuswide day of service that sends vast numbers of Truman students out to better the community.

The town of Kirksville (population 17,000) leaves much to be desired but grows on you, say students. "All of the essentials of a college town are present, including a Walmart, a bowling alley, a good movie theater, and a beautiful state park," a business administration major says. Students take advantage of various opportunities to get involved on campus and in the Kirksville community. Truman's SERVE Center keeps a list of projects seeking volunteers, and the Big Event is a campuswide day of service that sends vast numbers of Truman students out to better the community.

When not competing academically, Truman's Bulldogs (now members of the Great Lakes Valley Conference) are succeeding on the playing field and in the pool. The men's and women's swim teams have won multiple NCAA Division II titles

Overlaps

University of Missouri, Missouri State, Saint Louis University, Rockhurst University, Missouri University of Science and Technology, University of Central Missouri

and the women's volleyball team is highly competitive. Truman's Forensics Team has brought home the state title for 10 consecutive years. Intramural sports here began in the 1920s and include everything from table tennis to basketball, ultimate Frisbee, and running; 40 percent of students participate.

Truman State offers a winning combination of challenging academics and a close-knit community. Though Truman's rural Missouri location isn't for everyone, its bargain-basement price is certainly worth considering. "Be ready to work," advises a junior, "and be ready to meet people who will impact the rest of your life."

Tufts University

Bendetson Hall, Medford, MA 02155

Tufts will always be a second banana to Harvard in the Boston area, but given the Hub's runaway popularity among college students, second is not so bad. Has more in common with Brown than any other Ivy. Best known for international relations, Tufts is also strong in engineering and health-related fields. In the Experimental College, students can take off-the-wall courses for credit.

Some academic superstars used to consider Tufts University a safety school, a respectable place to go if you didn't get into Cornell or Penn. But Tufts isn't so safe anymore, at least not when it comes to admissions. Applications are up dramatically, propelling Tufts into the ranks of the more selective schools in the country. "It has become more competitive," says one sophomore. With its strong academics, high-achieving student body, and attractive setting, some might say that not all that much more separates Tufts University from its illustrious neighbors, Harvard and MIT, than a few stops on the T. Says one junior, "At Tufts it is cool to be smart."

Tufts's 150-acre, tree-lined hilltop campus overlooks the heart of nearby Boston and is a striking scene. The main campus, with its brick and stone buildings, sits on the Medford/Somerville boundary. Medford, the fifth-oldest city in the country, was a powerful shipbuilding center during the 19th century. Somerville lies adjacent to the Tufts campus, and in 1776, the first American flag was raised on its Prospect Hill.

"At Tufts it is cool to be smart."

For years, Tufts has devoted resources to traditional areas of graduate strength—medicine, dentistry, veterinary, and diplomacy—as well as new ventures, such as a Nutrition Research Center. Such additions had only a peripheral impact on the liberal arts and engineering colleges, but Tufts has made a noticeable commitment to facilities that primarily benefit undergraduates.

Undergraduate teaching is what attracts students to Tufts. They get highly personalized attention from faculty, and they enjoy wide freedom to pursue independent study, and complete research and internships for credit. "The course material is known to be very challenging, but the academic climate here is supportive, rather than cut-throat," a student says. Strong departments include international relations, political science, biology, engineering, drama, and languages, and there is an excellent child-study program. The most popular major is international relations,

Website: www.tufts.edu
Location: City Outskirts
Private
Total Enrollment: 9,955
Undergraduates: 5,148
Male/Female: 49/51
SAT Ranges: CR 670–760, M 680–760
ACT Ranges: 30–33
Financial Aid: 45%
Expense: Pr $ $
Student Loans: 37%
Average Debt: $ $
Phi Beta Kappa: Yes
Applicants: 16,369
Accepted: 21%
Enrolled: 37%
Grad in 6 Years: 90%
Returning Freshmen: 97%
Academics: ✍ ✍ ✍ ✍ ½
Social: ☎ ☎ ☎
Q of L: ★ ★ ★ ★
Admissions: (617) 627-5256
Email Address: admissions .inquiry@ase.tufts.edu

(continued)

followed by biology, economics, political science, and psychology. While upper-level courses are reasonably sized (with an average of about 25 students), intro lectures can be quite large.

Tufts has two popular programs in which students who need a break from being students can develop and teach courses: the Experimental College, which annually offers more than 100 nontraditional, full-credit courses taught by students, faculty, and outside lecturers; and the Freshman Explorations seminars, each taught by two upperclassmen and a faculty member to between 10 and 15 students. With topics ranging from media and politics to juggling, Exploration courses are a way for freshmen to get to know each other and ease into the college experience, since the teachers double as advisors. The Curricular Advising Program enrolls freshmen in their faculty advisor's course during the first semester; recent courses include Biotechnology Engineering, Sex and Gender in Society, and Aspects of the Sephardic Tradition. The Institute for Global Leadership includes the popular, interdisciplinary EPIIC (Education for Public Inquiry and International Citizenship) program, which prepares young people to play active roles in their communities at the local, national, or global level. The yearlong intensive experience revolves around a theme and includes a weekly colloquium, international symposium, and a research project or internship. EPIIC's 2012–2013 theme was "Global Health and Security."

> "The academic climate here is supportive rather than cut-throat."

Tufts students also get a healthy diet of traditional academic fare. For liberal arts students, distribution requirements include a World Civilization course in addition to art, English and foreign languages, social sciences, humanities, natural sciences, and math. Engineers must take six courses in the arts, humanities, and social sciences, with one of those fulfilling a writing requirement. Full professors, who are praised for their knowledge, teach most courses. "Within a year, I have found a very specific interest in a wide academic field, and I attribute that to our passionate professors," says a student. Tufts offers the Washington Semester*, the Mystic Seaport program*, an exchange with Swarthmore, and cross-registration at a number of Boston schools. Tufts is among the top 10 research universities for the percentage of undergrads who study abroad and frequently ranks as one of the top Peace Corps suppliers.

Undergraduate teaching is what attracts students to Tufts.

"Students enjoy being here," says a psychology major. "They are excited about learning, they work hard, and they also like to have a good time. Tufts students are laid-back, humble, but also incredibly intelligent." Sixteen percent of students hail from Massachusetts; New Jersey, New York, and California are also well represented. The university's reputation in international relations attracts a substantial number of international students (7 percent) and Americans living abroad. Asian Americans make up 10 percent of the population, Hispanics 7 percent, and African Americans 4 percent. Active citizenship is the biggest issue on campus, according to one student: "Tufts teaches students to be leaders and wants students to actively contribute their knowledge to the world." No merit or athletic scholarships are available, but several prepayment and loan options are, and in the past the school has met the full demonstrated need of all admits. There are additional financial incentives for students from low-income families.

> "Tufts students are laid-back, humble, but also incredibly intelligent."

Sixty-four percent of students live on campus. Accommodations in the Uphill and Downhill (the two quads joined by a great expanse of grass and trees) campus dorms vary from long hallways of double rooms to apartment-like suites, old houses, and co-ops. "The nice thing about our dorms is that they're very sizeable and don't usually feel crowded," says one student. "Our bathrooms are well maintained and some dorms even offer ones used by one person at a time!" A good-natured rivalry exists between the two areas; freshmen and sophomores must live on campus in the dorms, while upperclassmen compete in a lottery. "After your freshman year, you have the opportunity to live in one of the regular dorms or in one of the specialty or language houses as well as sorority or fraternity houses (if you decide to pledge)," a student explains. Apartments are plentiful and, according to at least one student, affordable. All but one of the dorms are co-ed by floor, suite, or alternating rooms. All first-years are required to have the unlimited meal plan; other meal plans average 2–3, 5, 6–7, 10, and 13–14 meals per week. "The food at Tufts is probably my favorite thing. We are incredibly lucky to have diverse options and a dining staff that is committed to the happiness of students," cheers one freshman.

While suburban Medford is not very exciting for those of the college class, the T metro system extends to the Tufts campus, so it's easy to make a quick jaunt to "student city" (a.k.a. Boston) for work or play. Davis Square is even nearer and provides plenty of restaurants, nightlife, and music stores. Tufts has earned a national reputation for its programs to promote the "responsible" use of alcohol. Besides, "there is very little pressure to drink," according to an engineering major.

A small band of fraternities and sororities provides many of the on-campus weekend parties; 19 percent of the men and 11 percent of the women join the Greek system. University-sponsored activities include concerts, plays (there are 15 to 20 productions each year at Aidekman Arts Center), and parties, and there are two-dollar movies on Wednesday and weekend nights. "There's always something to do at Tufts," says one student. "Almost every weekend, we have numerous concerts, sporting events, performances, and lectures that Tufts students can (and do) attend." Major campus events in the fall include homecoming and Halloween on the Hill, the latter of which is a carnival for children in the community. Of all student activities, the largest by far, with more than 500 students, is the Leonard Carmichael Society, the umbrella group for all volunteer activities. The students are involved in programs of adult literacy, blood drives, elderly outreach, teaching English as a second language, hunger projects, tutoring, low-income housing construction, and active work with the homeless and with battered women.

Tufts students take athletics seriously and the varsity athletic programs had a string of successes in the 2012–13 season. Men's cross-country won their fourth NESCAC Championship and went on to place seventh at the NCAA National Championships, while the women's field hockey team won the NCAA National Championship, the first ever women's national title in school history. The co-ed sailing team won their first ever Intercollegiate Sailing Association (ICSA) Match Racing National Championship and the women's basketball team made it to the NCAA Sweet 16 for the second straight year. Men's lacrosse won their fourth straight NESCAC title and advanced to the NCAA Quarterfinals. Other teams qualifying for NCAA Championship play for the 2012–13 season were the men's soccer, men's and women's swimming, and women's tennis. The intramural and recreational programs serve nearly half the student body via 14 intramural sports and 11 club sports. "Participation is pretty popular among the student body," a student says.

Tufts is in the midst of a modern-day renaissance, or what many universities know as a capital campaign. Money raised already is allowing Tufts to improve campus facilities and financial aid for students. This, along with a swelling applicant pool, makes Tufts a much hotter school than it was just a few years ago. And its proximity to Boston, an intellectual and educational mecca, makes it even more attractive. "Tufts students are proud to be here and strive to make the most of these four years that pass all too fast," says one student. Tufts gives every indication that it's going to keep scaling the university ranks until it reaches the summit—and that's not too far from Walnut Hill.

The Curricular Advising Program enrolls freshmen in their faculty advisor's course during the first semester.

"Tufts students are proud to be here."

A small band of fraternities and sororities provides many of the on-campus weekend parties.

Overlaps

Brown, Boston University, Boston College, Cornell, University of Pennsylvania, Harvard, Columbia, Northeastern

Tulane University

6823 St. Charles Avenue, New Orleans, LA 70118

The map may say that Tulane is in the South, but Tulane has the temperament of an East Coast institution. The university is trying to shoehorn its way into the front rank of Southeastern universities, though it still trails Emory and Vanderbilt. Post–Katrina, Tulane has developed a strong emphasis on community service. High achievers should shoot for the Tulane Scholars program.

Website: www.tulane.edu

Location: City Center

Private

Total Enrollment: 10,835

Undergraduates: 6,443

Male/Female: 42/58

SAT Ranges: CR 630–720, M 620–710

ACT Ranges: 29–32

Financial Aid: 40%

Expense: Pr $ $ $ $

Student Loans: 40%

Average Debt: $ $ $ $

Phi Beta Kappa: Yes

Applicants: 30,080

Accepted: 27%

Enrolled: 20%

Grad in 6 Years: 75%

Returning Freshmen: 89%

Academics: ✑ ✑ ✑ ½

Social: 🏮 🏮 🏮 🏮

Q of L: ★ ★ ★

Admissions: (504) 865-5260

Email Address: undergrad_admissions@tulane.edu

Strongest Programs:
Premed
Prelaw
Political Economy
Biomedical Engineering
Business
Anthropology
Latin American Studies

Once a staid, genteel choice for students seeking a traditional education, Tulane University has rebranded itself with an emphasis on community service and now attracts service-minded students from around the nation who choose from more than 130 service-learning opportunities, many of them existing courses that were revamped to include a service-learning component after Hurricane Katrina. Indeed, Tulane promises a solid education to those who are willing to take up residence in the Big Easy.

The school's 110-acre campus is located in an attractive residential area of uptown New Orleans, about 15 minutes from the French Quarter and the business district. Tulane's administration building, Gibson Hall, faces St. Charles Avenue, where one of the nation's last streetcar lines still clatters past mansions. Across the street is Audubon Park, a 385-acre spread where students jog, walk, study, or feed the ducks in the lagoon. The buildings of gray limestone and pillared brick, separated by live southern oak trees, are modeled after the neocollegiate/Creole mixture indigenous to Louisiana institutional-type structures. One particular point of pride is the university's 13 Tiffany windows, one of the largest collections in existence.

Tulane remains committed to its mission as a major research university that emphasizes undergraduate opportunities. Tulane's strength lies in the natural sciences, environmental sciences, and the humanities; international studies in general and Latin American studies in particular are especially strong. The Stone Center for Latin American studies includes the 200,000-volume Latin American Library and offers more than 150 courses taught by 80 faculty members. An interdisciplinary program in political economy (economics, political science, and philosophy) stands out among the social sciences and is very

"There is a large Northeastern constituency here."

popular with prelaw students. The School of Science and Engineering is comprised of five distinct divisions: biological sciences and engineering; chemical sciences and engineering; physical and material sciences; earth and environmental sciences; and mathematics and computational science. Environmental studies majors benefit from the Tulane/Xavier Center for Bioenvironmental Research, where faculty members and students work together on research projects that include hazardous-waste remediation and the ecological effects of environmental contaminants.

Tulane offers study abroad programs in 81 nations, including one-semester programs to locations such as Japan to study sociology and culture, Mexico City to delve into the language, and London to study liberal arts. In addition, the Tulane/

Newcomb Junior Year Abroad program is one of the country's oldest and most prestigious programs, in which the student is fully immersed in the language and culture of the particular country. Several programs help freshmen make the transition from high school to college. One is TIDES, where students can join groups on such topics as Understanding Your Classmates, World Religions, and Cultures. Another offering for freshmen is the First Year Experience, one-credit courses on such subjects as Metacognition (Thinking about Thinking), Campus Life, and Women and Leadership.

Most classes have 30 or fewer students, making it sometimes difficult for students to get into the classes of their choice. Although the majority of those classes are taught by full professors, graduate instructors are most likely to teach the beginning-level classes in English, foreign languages, and math. Overall, students praise Tulane's faculty, and the academic atmosphere can be very intense, depending on the class. All Tulane liberal arts majors must complete a rigorous set of general education and distribution requirements that include a service-learning course as well as a service-learning project, such as doing urban archeology or teaching in a local school. In the process of satisfying the requirements, students must take at least one course in Western and non-Western civilization and complete a public service component, as well as a writing-intensive class, although freshmen with high SATs can place out of some classes.

Environmental studies majors benefit from the Tulane/Xavier Center for Bioenvironmental Research.

"If you're a Northerner, it's impossible to escape the Southern influence."

Each year the university's highly acclaimed honors program invites about 700 outstanding students, known as Tulane Scholars, to partake in accelerated courses taught by top professors. These select scholars also have the opportunity to design their own major and spend their junior year abroad.

Tulane has a somewhat Southern feel and is a sophisticated and cosmopolitan institution. Says one student, "There is a large Northeastern constituency here who have brought their Type-A personalities and racial tolerance down to a Southern city. If you're a Northerner, it's impossible to escape the Southern influence of the city, and if you're a Southerner, it's impossible to escape the Northern influence that exists on campus." The student body is 10 percent African American, 6 percent Hispanic, and 4 percent Asian American. Students are drawn to service opportunities, and volunteering is encouraged and common. Tulane awards hundreds of merit scholarships, averaging $21,157, and 188 athletic scholarships in six sports.

Each year the university's highly acclaimed honors program invites about 700 outstanding students.

Forty-four percent of students live on campus; nonlocal freshmen must do so. After freshman year, housing is by lottery, and choices include Stadium Place, a student apartment complex. Many students opt to move off campus, claiming that it's much cheaper than university housing, but others are concerned about the safety factor of living in New Orleans. Some men live in their fraternity houses, but sororities only have social halls due to an old New Orleans law that makes it illegal to have more than four unrelated women living in one house. Freshmen have to stomach the cost of Tulane's meal plan, but alternatives exist at the University Center food court.

Social life at Tulane goes almost without saying. "New Orleans itself never stops partying!" boasts a junior. Fraternities and sororities are a presence—26 percent of the men and 40 percent of the women join—but do not dominate the social life. Though you're supposed to be 21 to buy alcohol or enjoy the bar scene in the cafés and clubs that dot the French Quarter, a sophomore explains that "alcohol is accessible." Mardi Gras is such a celebration that classes are suspended for two days and students from all over the country pour in to celebrate. An annual Jazzfest in the spring also draws wide participation. Road-trip destinations include the Gulf Coast, Mississippi, Houston, Atlanta, and Memphis.

While schoolwork is taken seriously at Tulane, so are sports. The campuswide acclaim for men's basketball borders on hysteria, and the women's basketball team

Overlaps

Washington University in St. Louis, Vanderbilt, University of Michigan, Louisiana State, Emory, Georgetown, University of Miami (FL), University of South Carolina

is solid, too. The university fields 16 Green Waves teams that compete in Conference USA. Club sports are big, and students can also opt for weight work, squash, or swimming among other options at the Reily Recreational Center.

While Tulane is rich in Southern tradition, it is a forward-looking school where the possibilities seem endless. And like its hometown, it is a diverse, energetic melting pot of interests and activity. Those seeking a dynamic, service-oriented education in a vibrant city need look no further. *C'est si bon!*

<table>
<tr><td>If You Apply To ➤</td><td>Tulane: Early action: Nov. 15. Regular admissions: Jan. 15. Financial aid: Feb. 15. Housing: May 1. No application fee. Campus interviews: optional, informational. No alumni interviews. SATs or ACTs: required. Subject Tests: optional (homeschooled applicants only).</td></tr>
</table>

University of Tulsa

600 South College Avenue, Tulsa, OK 74104

Tulsa is a notch smaller than Texas Christian and Washington U, but bigger than most liberal arts colleges. The university has a technical orientation rooted in Oklahoma oil, but it has a much more diverse curriculum than Colorado School of Mines and offers engineering with a personal touch. Tulsa has an innovative program allowing undergraduates to do research beginning their first semester. Modern English literature a strength.

Website: www.utulsa.edu
Location: Small City
Private
Total Enrollment: 3,825
Undergraduates: 2,989
Male/Female: 57/43
SAT Ranges: CR 570–710, M 590–700
ACT Ranges: 25–31
Financial Aid: 88%
Expense: Pr $
Student Loans: 45%
Average Debt: $ $ $ $
Phi Beta Kappa: Yes
Applicants: 6,984
Accepted: 41%
Enrolled: 24%
Grad in 6 Years: 66%
Returning Freshmen: 86%
Academics: ✍ ✍ ✍
Social: ☎ ☎ ☎
Q of L: ★ ★
Admissions: (908) 631-2307
Email Address: admission@utulsa.edu

The University of Tulsa is a small, private liberal arts school with a growing international reputation. Known for its engineering programs, including petroleum and geosciences, it attracts students from around the world. With an emphasis on undergraduate research, hands-on work experience, and a diverse array of course offerings, TU has found its niche. "The second I walked on campus, I felt at home," says one happy student. "I know that sounds cheesy, but every single person I met was genuine, friendly, and really wanted to get to know me."

TU's 210-acre campus is just three miles from downtown Tulsa, and there's a striking view of the city's skyline from the steps of the neo-Gothic McFarlin Library. The university's more than 70 buildings run the architectural gamut from 1930s-vintage neo-Gothic to contemporary, all variations on a theme of yellow Tennessee limestone dubbed "TU stone." A 12,000-square-foot addition to the McFarlin Library consolidates the library's computing and technology resources into one location. The Roxana Rozsa and Robert Eugene Lorton Performance Center is TU's showcase facility for the musical and performance arts and includes a full performance stage with ballet floor, a hydraulic orchestra pit, theatrical lighting, and acoustical control booths. The J. Newton Rayzor Hall houses the Computer Science and Electrical Engineering department and boasts 37,616 square feet of space.

> "The second I walked on campus, I felt at home."

In addition to its well-established and internationally recognized petroleum and geosciences engineering programs, TU offers solid majors in computer science, the natural sciences, and many social sciences. The rapidly growing English department has some impressive resources at its disposal in McFarlin Library's special collections. The collections boast original works by 19th- and 20th-century American and British authors, including books, letters, manuscripts, a stained necktie that once belonged to James Joyce, and more than 50,000 items representing Nobel laureate V. S. Naipaul's life and work from the 1950s to the present.

In accordance with the Tulsa Curriculum, the cornerstone of the school's emphasis on liberal arts, all undergraduates take two writing courses, at least one mathematics course, and one or two years of foreign language, depending on the degree. In addition, each student completes at least 25 credit hours of general curriculum classes in aesthetic inquiry and creative experience, historical and social interpretation, and scientific investigation. "Most students are high achievers who push themselves," says one student. "For this reason, the climate can be very competitive." Professors generally receive high marks from students. "What makes TU's quality of teaching especially outstanding is the one-on-one interaction with professors," a student says. Another adds, "I have really enjoyed my professors. All have seemed very knowledgeable and helpful when it came to mastering the material."

Honors students take exclusive seminars, complete a thesis or advanced project, and can live together in a computer-equipped house. The Tulsa Undergraduate Research Challenge offers outstanding opportunities for cutting-edge scientific research, and has produced 57 Goldwater Scholarship winners, 50 National Science Foundation Graduate Fellowships, 11 Truman Scholarships, and 15 Fulbright Grants (among others). The University allows students with significant advanced placement credits in history, chemistry, or applied mathematics to complete a baccalaureate and master's program in a total of five years. Twenty-two percent travel abroad for programs including language immersion in Spain, studio art in Italy, business integration in Germany, and environmental study in Costa Rica. Tulsa is also one of 20 schools in the nation that train America's Cyber Corps, the first line of defense against computer hackers and terrorists. The exercise science degree has received national accreditation for teacher certification.

TU students are "dedicated, intelligent, competitive, and accepting," muses a management major. A junior adds, "While students like to have fun, there is a certain professional vibe in the air." Forty-five percent of Tulsa's students are from Oklahoma; most others are from the Midwest and Southwest, with many hailing from Dallas and St. Louis. Twenty-two percent are foreign, coming from the Middle East, East Asia, and Scandinavia. The student body is 5 percent African American, 3 percent Asian American, and 4 percent Hispanic. Students say all political views are represented on campus, and hot topics include environmental sustainability and the war in Iraq. Athletes compete for 354 scholarships in 18 sports. TU also offers merit scholarships, averaging $14,920, and the university has embarked on a campaign to raise scholarship funds in an effort to decrease student loan levels.

At Tulsa, freshmen and sophomores are required to live on campus. "Dorms are dorms—sufficiently clean, not as nice as possible, a necessity for underclassmen," says one junior. Seventy-four percent of the students use campus housing and they have plenty of options, including dorms, fraternity and sorority houses, and campus apartments. The single-sex dorms are quieter and more attractive to upperclassmen. Dining choices receive a passing grade, although the fare varies in quality. "The dining facilities are probably TU's biggest downfall," a junior laments. Students report feeling safe on campus. "Campus security is one of the highest priorities at TU," says a junior. "They are very visible and take their jobs seriously. I have never felt unsafe on campus."

The social life at TU is surprisingly robust, thanks to hundreds of student organizations and a healthy Greek life. There are scheduled events and students enjoy simply hanging with friends at small parties, too. "Our students are incredibly smart, but also very sociable," says a junior. The Bricktown section of Oklahoma City and nearby casinos (for those 21 and older), along with more distant Dallas, St. Louis, and Kansas

(continued)

Strongest Programs:
Petroleum Engineering
Management
Energy Management
Finance
Mechanical Engineering
English

Honors students take exclusive seminars, complete a thesis or advanced project, and can live together in a computer-equipped house.

"Most students are high achievers who push themselves."

Twenty-two percent travel abroad for programs including language immersion in Spain, studio art in Italy, business integration in Germany, and environmental study in Costa Rica.

City, are popular road trips. The Greek organizations claim 21 percent of TU men and 23 percent of the women, and the frats host campuswide house parties. Student-initiated policies govern drinking on campus. Administrators say this self-policing has led to responsible imbibing. "There is always a party happening somewhere on campus," says one student, "but there are also activities for students who do not drink."

Campus traditions include the ringing of the college bell in the Alumni Center cupola by each senior after his or her last class and during Springfest. Other big events include Reggaefest, homecoming, and Greek events such as the Kappa Sigma Olympics, the Sigma Chi Derby Days, and the Delta Gamma Anchor Splash. Nearby parks, lakes, and a huge recreational water park please outdoor enthusiasts. Downtown Tulsa offers symphony, ballet, opera, and an annual Oktoberfest. Students are very active in community service. "Students can get involved in a variety of community organizations such as churches, Habitat for Humanity, Big Brothers Big Sisters, and Tulsa's Day Center for the Homeless," says one student.

> "While students like to have fun, there is a certain professional vibe in the air."

Here in Oklahoma, sports are important (very, *very* important!). Students get riled up when the football team is pitted against rivals Oklahoma and Oklahoma State, and when the basketball team suits up against Arkansas and OSU. The Golden Hurricanes compete in Conference USA, and 2012–13 conference champs include women's volleyball and basketball, and men's cross-country and soccer. The football team brought home a conference title and won the 2012 Liberty Bowl. At least 80 percent of undergrads participate in at least one of the 30 intramural sports; the most popular by far is flag football.

TU is trying to do some things differently: be a small liberal arts school in a part of the country most known for sprawling public universities, and incorporate professional preparation with an emphasis on broad intellectual challenges. Those considering the University of Tulsa might do well to heed the advice of this junior: "Get involved! It'll make or break the experience."

Overlaps

Southern Methodist, Texas Christian, Washington University in St. Louis, University of Oklahoma, Oklahoma State, University of Texas

If You Apply To ➢

Tulsa: Rolling admissions. Application fee: $50. Campus interviews: recommended, evaluative. No alumni interviews. SATs or ACTs: required. No Subject Tests. Accepts the Common Application. Essay question.

Union College

807 Union Street, Schenectady, NY 12308

Union is split down the middle between liberal arts and engineering. That means its center of gravity is more toward the technical side than places like Lafayette, Trinity, and Tufts, but less so than Clarkson and Rensselaer. Schenectady is less than exciting, but there are outdoor getaways in all directions. Relatively anonymous because it does not fit into conventional categories.

Website: www.union.edu
Location: Small City
Private
Total Enrollment: 2,183

Founded in 1795, Union College is one of the oldest nondenominational colleges in the country. Its name reflects the founders' desire to create a welcoming, unifying academic community open to the region's diverse religious and national groups. More than 200 years later, this independent liberal arts college is known for its interdisciplinary studies and its study abroad programs. At Union, engineering and the arts go hand-in-hand. Undergraduate research has deep roots at Union, starting in the 20th century when a chemistry professor began involving students in his colloid chemistry investigations. Today, "Union is constantly thinking of ways to better the students' experience," says one satisfied freshman.

Union's 100-acre campus, designed in 1813 by French architect and landscaper Joseph Jacques Ramée, sits on a hill overlooking Schenectady. Ramée's vision took shape in brownstone and redbrick, with plenty of white arches, pilasters, and lacy green trees; the campus plan also includes eight acres of formal gardens and woodlands. The 16-sided Nott Memorial, a National Historic Landmark, is a meet-

"It's a little competitive but mostly laid-back."

ing, study, and exhibition center—and the site of a naked run each year. Parcels of land adjacent to College Park Hall, a hotel-turned-dorm, have become soccer fields for college and community use. Butterfield Hall provides state-of-the-art bioengineering facilities, including a mechanical testing lab and a clean room. The Henle Dance Pavilion is the newest addition to campus and features a 2,200-square-foot dance studio, classrooms, a costume shop, office, meeting rooms, and a gallery.

Union's general education requirements "provide the sort of education that will allow students to flourish in a rapidly changing world by analyzing and integrating knowledge from a wide variety of areas," according to administrators. Students must take two core courses in their first and second years that promote reading, writing, and analytical skills. They also must take three interdisciplinary courses in an approved cluster and eight courses spread among social science, humanities, linguistic and cultural competency, quantitative and mathematical reasoning, and natural and applied science or engineering. The $22 million Peter Irving Wold Science and Engineering Center is home for interdisciplinary study across departments, with programs in biochemistry, environmental studies, music, and electrical engineering. The state-of-the-art facility includes a high performance computing lab, music production studio, and a rooftop renewable energy lab.

Among Union's most popular majors are biology, psychology, and political science. Students also flock to economics and history; the latter department is home to Union's most esteemed lecturer, Stephen Berk, whose course on the Holocaust and Twentieth-Century Europe is a hot ticket. Each year, about 50 incoming freshmen are named Union Scholars. The designation extends the First-Year Preceptorial to two terms from one, allows students to work on independent study projects, and gives them access to departmental honors programs and expanded study abroad options. Each spring, Union cancels classes one afternoon for the Charles Steinmetz Symposium, so that students can present scholarly projects to their peers and professors in a professional conference atmosphere.

Interdisciplinary study is the norm at Union, with established programs in biochemistry, bioengineering, Latin American and Caribbean studies, law and public policy, neuroscience, Russian and Eastern European studies, and women's and gender studies, to name a few. The Educational Studies program allows aspiring teachers to complete courses and fieldwork required for secondary school certification in a variety of subjects, along with a strong liberal arts grounding. The Leadership in Medicine program, a joint program with the Graduate College of Union University and Albany Medical College, gives students the opportunity to earn a bachelor's degree, a master of science in

"The housing lottery can be somewhat confusing and stressful."

health management or master of business administration in health systems administration, and a medical degree in eight years. Newer programs include an undergraduate degree in Africana studies and minors in Greek studies and Jewish studies.

"It's a little competitive but mostly laid-back," says a sophomore. Students give the faculty high marks. "The professors are great. They're informed and enthusiastic

(continued)

Undergraduates: 2,183
Male/Female: 54/46
SAT Ranges: CR 590–680, M 620–700
ACT Ranges: 28–32
Financial Aid: 74%
Expense: Pr $ $ $ $
Student Loans: 58%
Average Debt: $ $ $
Phi Beta Kappa: Yes
Applicants: 5,565
Accepted: 38%
Enrolled: 28%
Grad in 6 Years: 83%
Returning Freshmen: 94%
Academics: ✐ ✐ ✐ ✐
Social: ☎ ☎ ☎
Q of L: ★ ★ ★
Admissions: (518) 388-6112
Email Address: admissions@union.edu

Strongest Programs:
Political Science
Mathematics
Mechanical Engineering
Chemistry
Philosophy
Psychology
Modern Languages

Each year, about 50 incoming freshmen are named Union Scholars.

about their subjects," says a student. Sixty-eight percent of all freshmen classes have 19 or fewer students, and students can expect to see full professors at the lecterns rather than TAs. Union operates on a trimester system, which means thrice-a-year exams and a late start to summer jobs—but also the opportunity to concentrate on just three courses a term. More terms also means more opportunities for independent study and internships, either in the state capital of Albany, 20 minutes away, or in Washington, D.C. By the time graduation rolls around, over half of each class has studied abroad.

Forty percent of Union students are New Yorkers, and 64 percent went to public high schools. A neuroscience major describes fellow students as "very preppy and conservative." Four percent of the student body is African American, another 7 percent is Hispanic, and 6 percent is Asian American. The school has been working to boost these numbers through its membership in the Consortium for High Achievement and Success and the establishment of the President's Commission on Diversity. Union offers a number of merit scholarships averaging $10,000, but no athletic scholarships.

Eighty-nine percent of Union students live in the dorms. The Minerva house system (named after the Roman goddess of wisdom) is aimed at getting students and faculty members to contribute to Union's social, residential, and intellectual life—

"The social life at Union has really made my college experience."

and, students say, at decreasing the influence of the Greek system, which draws 38 percent of the men and women. Union's dorms "have singles, doubles, triples, and suites (quads)," says a student. Students recommend West, which is co-ed by room and thus very social, as well as Fox and Davidson, where freshmen and sophomores live in suites: two double bedrooms and a "huge" common room. "The housing lottery can be somewhat confusing and stressful," a freshman laments, "but otherwise it's a fair process." Dining options consist of four main eating areas and "the food is not too bad," according to one student.

"The social life at Union has really made my college experience," says one chemistry major. "Union does a phenomenal job of balancing a challenging and rewarding academic life with a fulfilling and diverse social life." There are a variety of campus events, including comedians, concerts, and speakers. The administration has established a committee of students, staff, and faculty members to oversee programming about alcohol abuse. Favorite annual traditions include the lobster bake (each student gets his or her own crustacean) and Springfest, a huge concert. An unofficial graduation requirement is to do a lap around the Nott Memorial—sans clothing.

Off campus, Schenectady is an old-line industrial city that's a decent—if not great—college town, according to a freshman. Says a sophomore, "There are essentially no college-town amenities—like bookstores—in walking distance. You need a car." What Schenectady lacks can be found in Saratoga Springs, which boasts restaurants, jazz clubs, horse racing, and Skidmore College, or in the nearby Adirondacks and Catskills. Popular road trips include Boston, Montreal, New York, and the ski slopes of nearby Vermont. And students are trying to help Schenectady rebound, through tutoring programs in local schools and work with Big Brothers Big Sisters. There's also a service project during freshman orientation. "My group had to paint one of the bridges in Schenectady," says one student. "It was actually a good time."

Union's athletic teams compete in Division III, aside from men's and women's ice hockey, both of which are Division I. The former emerged as national champions at the 2014 Frozen Four. Men's soccer and football and women's lacrosse, softball, soccer, and swimming have recently brought home league championships. There's a full-time director of intramural sports, which include teams in everything from tennis and volleyball to broomball and lacrosse. Rugby and ultimate Frisbee enjoy club status, and about 60 percent of students participate in intramural or club athletics.

Union's mission is constantly evolving, as the college struggles to meet the needs and interests of students and faculty. It retains its commitment to a strong core liberal arts curriculum while acknowledging the increasing effect of globalization and technology. Union College has plenty to offer—a small, friendly place full of eager intellectual exchange. You just have to seek it out.

<table>
<tr><td>If You Apply To ➤</td><td>Union: Early decision: Nov. 15. Regular admissions: Jan. 15. Financial aid: Feb. 1. Application fee: $50 (paper), free (online). Campus and alumni interviews: optional, evaluative. SATs or ACTs: optional (required for combined programs). Subject Tests: required if neither SAT nor ACT is submitted (writing and two others). Accepts the Common Application. Essay question.</td></tr>
</table>

Ursinus College

Box 1000, Collegeville, PA 19426

Ursinus is the smallest of the cohort of eastern Pennsylvania liberal arts colleges that includes Franklin and Marshall, Layfayette, and Muhlenberg. The plus side is more attention from faculty and more emphasis on independent learning. Although Philly is within arm's reach, the setting is quiet.

Ursinus College takes its name from a 16th-century German Calvinist, Zacharias Ursinus, who directed that students should "examine all things and keep what is good." So, for many years, the school focused on training in practical fields ranging from business administration to sports science. Recently, though, Ursinus has returned to its liberal arts roots—even expanding its offerings and restructuring its core curriculum to emphasize the philosophical underpinnings of modern thought. What hasn't changed is the close-knit feel of the school. "At Ursinus you can truly make a name for yourself," says one sophomore.

Ursinus is located in Collegeville, about 40 minutes west of Philadelphia, and 10 miles from the green, rolling hills of Valley Forge National Park. Buildings on the 170-acre campus are mostly constructed of Pennsylvania fieldstone; many have had their interiors upgraded and their exteriors preserved and restored. Actors and dancers benefit from rehearsal and exhibition space in the Kaleidoscope performing arts center. An athletic field has been added recently.

General education requirements at Ursinus fall under the college's Plan for Liberal Studies, and they are grounded in the assumption that while individuals have intrinsic value, they also live in a community. Therefore, the core includes two semesters of the Common Intellectual Experience—a course that explores topics from Plato to Buddhist scripture to Nietzsche—as well as requirements in science, culture, and history. Students also choose one of 28 majors and engage in at least one Independent Learning Experience—a research project, an internship, study abroad, or student teaching—before graduation. For honors students, the requirements are more stringent; their independent projects are evaluated by outside examiners. And up to 30 percent of rising seniors get fellowships from the school to fund full-time summer research projects with a faculty member. The library has 400,000 volumes, and the school is connected to OCLC, a consortium of more than 18,000 libraries; most books requested through the system are accessible within a few days. Ursinus students may also use the Penn libraries.

> "At Ursinus you can truly make a name for yourself."

Website: www.ursinus.edu
Location: Suburban
Private
Total Enrollment: 1,651
Undergraduates: 1,651
Male/Female: 49/51
SAT Ranges: CR 540–650, M 540–660
ACT Ranges: 24–28
Financial Aid: 69%
Expense: Pr $ $ $
Student Loans: 60%
Average Debt: $ $ $
Phi Beta Kappa: Yes
Applicants: 3,518
Accepted: 70%
Enrolled: 19%
Grad in 6 Years: 80%
Returning Freshmen: 90%
Academics: ✏ ✏ ✏
Social: ☎ ☎ ☎
Q of L: ★ ★ ★
Admissions: (610) 409-3200
Email Address: admissions@ursinus.edu

Strongest Programs:
Biology
Chemistry

The most popular majors here include biology, business and economics, psychology, exercise and sport science, and English. The college also offers strong programs in politics and international relations; the latter is led by Joe Melrose, former U.S. ambassador to Sierra Leone. The academic climate is largely dependent on the course of study. "The students are all incredibly talented and impressive, making classes competitive," says one senior. "However, there is not a cut-throat competitive climate here." Professors draw praise for their skills in the classroom. "The quality of teaching is excellent," says one student. "The professors are always available to meet with students outside of the classroom to provide additional help." Classes are small—79 percent have 19 or fewer students—and students say they are pleased with the quality of teaching, especially since there are no TAs. Study abroad is available around the globe, thanks to the college's membership in the Bradley University Consortium. Ursinus also offers programs with its own faculty in Japan, Mexico, Spain, Italy, England, Costa Rica, and Germany. Finally, students can take a term at other U.S. universities, such as Howard and American in Washington, D.C., while prospective engineers may choose 3–2 programs at Columbia University and elsewhere.

"There is not a cut-throat competitive climate here."

"A significant number of students have two majors and are involved in multiple clubs on campus," says one politics major. Fifty-three percent are from Pennsylvania, with most others hailing from New York, New Jersey, and other Mid-Atlantic and New England states. African Americans make up 6 percent of the student body, Asian Americans 5 percent, and Hispanics 5 percent, and students report little tension among the groups. Race relations, sexual harassment, and physical safety are covered in peer education programs included in freshman orientation. The gay and lesbian organization on campus is very active, but otherwise, students aren't politically active. There are merit scholarships available each year, but no athletic scholarships are offered.

Ninety-six percent of students at Ursinus live in the dorms, which adds to the feeling of community. Upperclassmen quickly grab the Main Street houses, a string of Victorian-era homes across the street from campus, while freshmen are clustered in the Quad and BWC, short for Brodbeck-Wilkinson-Curtis, which have generously sized rooms. "The dorms are decent," says a student, "although they are not really anything to write home about." There are four meal plans—19, 14, or 10 meals per week, or 220 meals per semester—and all of them give students access to the main dining room and to Zack's, a snack bar. "The food can be repetitive after your first year," says one student, but "the options are generally good."

"The dorms are decent."

The most popular majors here include biology, business and economics, psychology, exercise and sport science, and English.

The town of Collegeville is just 10 blocks long—and Ursinus takes up five of those. "Collegeville is not a college town," grumbles one student. "There is very little to do off campus unless you are looking to go out to eat." Still, the town is growing, and is adding the amenities that students want and need, such as a sushi restaurant, a sports bar, an ice cream and coffee shop, four pizza parlors—and, most importantly, late-night pizza delivery. On campus, Greek life draws 10 percent of the men and 15 percent of the women, and fraternity parties are a popular weekend diversion. "Social life is pretty much centered around the athletic teams and the Greeks," says one freshman. Registered on-campus parties are monitored by student "social hosts" who check IDs and make sure things don't get out of hand. "We have a zero-tolerance policy on underage drinking, period, and any drinking in the freshman centers," explains one student. Other options include free movies, lectures, and dances—or the shops and restaurants of central Philadelphia, less than an hour away. Many students with cars escape to the Jersey shore during warmer months, and each spring, students look forward to Airband, "a big charity lip-synching and

Ursinus students love sports, and 60 percent play on a Division III varsity or an intramural team.

performing event," says an English major. Finally, there are four mega-malls within a 20-minute drive of the campus, including the King of Prussia complex, the second-largest mall in the country.

Ursinus students love sports, and 60 percent play on a Division III varsity or an intramural team. And for women seeking post-collegiate careers in coaching, Ursinus is a well-known stepping stone to those posts; more than 50 colleges have hired Ursinus alumnae. The Bears field hockey team is a perennial contender for the national championship, and the women's lacrosse team is also strong. Recent conference champions include the men's and women's basketball teams and the wrestling squad. Among other contributions in the world of sports, Ursinus is mentioned in Trivial Pursuit for having a tree in the end zone of its football field.

Ursinus is on the rise. It may not be in the center of a big metropolitan area, and it doesn't offer big-time sports, but the college compensates for its lack of size with the feeling that students, faculty, and staff are one big family. New majors and facilities for aspiring artists are helping to diversify the student population, while development in the town of Collegeville is adding excitement to life outside the classroom. "Ursinus allows students to be themselves and appreciates them for their uniqueness and diversity of passions and interests."

> ### Overlaps
> **Muhlenberg, Gettysburg, Penn State, Franklin and Marshall, Dickinson, Temple, Ithaca, College of New Jersey**

If You Apply To ➤ **Ursinus:** Early action: Dec. 1. Early decision: Jan. 15. Regular admissions and Financial aid: Feb. 15. Application fee: $50 (paper), free (online). Campus interviews: optional, evaluative. No alumni interviews. SATs or ACTs: required (optional for those in top 10 percent). Subject Tests: considered if submitted. Accepts the Common Application. Essay question.

University of Utah

250 SSB, Salt Lake City, UT 84112

With the true-blue Mormons typically heading for BYU, University of Utah attracts a diverse crowd that is drawn to the region's only major city. The majority of Utah students hail from the Salt Lake City region, and many commute from home. Science and professional programs such as business and engineering are the most popular.

In addition to being the flagship institution of the public Utah System of Higher Education, the University of Utah is a major national scientific research center. Founded in 1850, the university is unusual in its ability to offer students the advantages of living in a city while at the same time maintaining a connection with nature. "We have the school spirit, the drive to transform the world, and the resources and connections needed for students to succeed," cheers one senior. Under a state-government-backed program called UStar, the university has begun poaching star faculty members from other U.S. and foreign universities in fields that align with the state's existing economic strengths, such as medical devices and computer gaming.

Set in the foothills of the Wasatch Mountains near the shores of the Great Salt Lake, the university enjoys a picturesque location a half-hour drive from "the greatest snow on earth." Occupying 1,500 well-landscaped acres with nearly as many different kinds of trees as undergraduates, the campus is the state's arboretum. The architectural style of the university's structures ranges from 19th-century, ivy-covered buildings to state-of-the-art athletic facilities. The lake, snow, and beautiful

"We have the drive to transform the world."

Website: www.utah.edu	
Location: City Center	
Public	
Total Enrollment: 23,042	
Undergraduates: 17,297	
Male/Female: 55/45	
SAT Ranges: CR 510–620, M 510–650	
ACT Ranges: 21–27	
Financial Aid: 52%	
Expense: Pub $	
Student Loans: 50%	
Average Debt: $	
Phi Beta Kappa: No	
Applicants: 11,118	
Accepted: 83%	

*The Learning
Engagement
Achievement Progress
(LEAP) program is
a yearlong learning
community committed
to the principles
of civic awareness
and service.*

mountain location are among the reasons why this city was chosen to host the 2002 Winter Olympics.

Utah students choose from a comprehensive academic menu, including more than 100 undergraduate majors. While the professional degrees are quite popular, the U does not skimp on general education requirements. Students must fulfill classes in writing, American institutions, math, statistics, and intellectual explorations, which includes two courses in the humanities,

"Much of the social life is recreational."

sciences, social sciences, or fine arts, as well as an international course requirement. There are also bachelor's degree requirements, which include upper-division writing, a course in diversity, and either foreign language or quantitative courses. Renowned for its research in biomedical engineering, Utah hosted the first mechanical heart transplant. The Undergraduate Research Opportunities Program offers semester grants to students who join faculty members in scholarly pursuits. Study abroad programs are available in more than 50 countries around the globe. The My Utah Signature Experience (MUSE) Program seeks to provide every student with a unique experience via community engagement, global learning, innovation, leadership, internships, and research and learning communities.

The academic climate can be challenging, but the rigor varies by class, program, and professor. "The courses are challenging but you learn a lot!" a mass communication major says. Introductory courses often enroll hundreds of students, and freshmen often find themselves in very large lectures with smaller discussion sections led by graduate student teaching assistants. Utah's professors generally receive high marks from the students. "I think the majority of professors care about teaching and researching and learning, and want to share that love with their students," says a materials science and engineering student. The Learning Engagement Achievement Progress (LEAP) program is a yearlong learning community committed to the principles of civic awareness and service. LEAP features dedicated faculty and peer advisors who mentor new students and challenge them academically through a two-semester sequence of seminars; 8 percent of freshmen participate.

Utah's students are a mostly middle-class, fairly homogeneous lot; of the 73 percent who are from Utah, nearly all attended public schools. "We have a very liberal campus in comparison to much of Utah and Salt Lake City," a junior says. African American and Native American students together make up 2 percent of the student population, Asian Americans account for 6 percent, and Hispanics 9 percent. There is an active student government and most students agree that students here are less conservative than those found at rival BYU. "Diversity and religion are probably the biggest issues on campus," says one student. Utah offers a handful of scholarships for academic achievement (averaging $5,652) and 247 athletic scholarships in 16 sports.

Only 14 percent of students live on campus, but those who do seem to be pleased with the accommodations. "New facilities were built for the 2002 Olympics so our rooms are bigger, more comfortable, and well maintained throughout the year," one student reports. Students are also generally satisfied with the food, though edibility varies based on which campus eatery you choose. "There are always vegetarian options," says a senior. Students also report feeling safe on campus, thanks to emergency call boxes and a visible security presence.

Social life is low-key, due in large part to the high number of commuters. A mere 3 percent of the men and 4 percent of women go Greek. Still, "there is something happening every day on campus and there is not enough time to enjoy all the activities," says one student. "From lectures, concerts, dance performances, and late-night Crimson Nights parties, there is something for everyone." What's more, Utah is located close to the mountains, "so much of the social life is recreational," according to one junior. Favorite road trips take students to Las Vegas, Lake Powell, and nearby ski resorts (with slopeside bus service available from the school).

Salt Lake City isn't exactly a college town, but a junior says, "the nightlife in SLC downtown is great if you are over 21." Some students get very involved in community service or political activities. Adjacent to campus, the Latter Day Saints Institute of Religion sponsors dances and other social activities with a decidedly conservative bent. Cultural activities include the respected Utah Symphony, several dance companies, opera, and, of course, the Mormon Tabernacle Choir. For basketball fans, there's the Utah Jazz.

Football and basketball bring students together in the MUSS—Mighty Utah Student Section—where the cheering is loudest in games against rival BYU. "Our rivalry with BYU is known as 'the holy war,'" explains one sophomore. The football team has won the 2011 Sun Bowl and the skiing team were runners-up for the 2011, 2012, and 2013 NCAA titles. Other competitive Utes teams include women's soccer, volleyball, and swimming, and men's tennis. In addition to the university's dozens of intramurals and club sports, the Outdoor Recreation Program offers backpacking, river running, canoeing, mountain biking, and skiing trips.

Students say that diversity and academic quality are both on the rise at Utah. "The best thing about students at the U is that they are friendly to all, supportive of each other, and you can do whatever you want," says a computer animation major. It's also one of the few places where you can find nationally recognized professional programs within easy reach of nationally recognized skiing.

> *The My Utah Signature Experience (MUSE) Program seeks to provide every student with a unique experience.*

Overlaps

BYU, Utah State, Utah Valley, Weber State, Southern Utah, Westminster, University of Colorado

---

If You Apply To ➤

University of Utah: Regular admissions: Feb. 1. Financial aid: Apr. 1. Application fee: $45. Campus and alumni interviews: optional, informational. SATs or ACTs: required. Subject Tests: optional. No essay question.

Vanderbilt University

2305 West End Avenue, Nashville, TN 37240

More "Southern" than Duke or Emory, Vandy has traditionally been a preferred choice for residents of the Deep South suburbs of Atlanta and Birmingham. Along with Tulane, it is the only leading Southern private institution with both business and engineering. Strong music program complements Nashville's vibrant music scene. Neck and neck with Emory in selectivity, a step behind Duke academically.

Once a quiet, conservative school in the heart of the South, Vanderbilt University has made a serious effort to diversify its student body and bring a more cosmopolitan atmosphere to campus. Sure, football games here continue to require coats, ties, pearls, and dates (though presumably not all at once), but the university has succeeded in marrying Old South gentility with modern attitudes. The result is a relaxed, friendly culture that makes the rigorous academic environment easier to handle. "Students looking for a balance between great academics and a solid social life need to look at Vandy," says a history major.

Founded in 1873 by Cornelius Vanderbilt, the university's 330-acre tract in Nashville was named a national arboretum in the late 1980s and includes Peabody

> **"Everyone is very high-achieving and the course content is difficult."**

Website: www.vanderbilt.edu
Location: City Center
Private
Total Enrollment: 11,854
Undergraduates: 6,712
Male/Female: 50/50
SAT Ranges: CR 690–770, M 710–790
ACT Ranges: 32–34
Financial Aid: 48%
Expense: Pr $ $ $

(continued)

Student Loans: 34%

Average Debt: $

Phi Beta Kappa: Yes

Applicants: 28,348

Accepted: 14%

Enrolled: 40%

Grad in 6 Years: 92%

Returning Freshmen: 96%

Academics: 🖉 🖉 🖉 🖉

Social: ☎ ☎ ☎ ☎

Q of L: ★ ★ ★ ★

Admissions: (615) 322-2561

Email Address: admissions@
vanderbilt.edu

Strongest Programs:

Music and Arts

Education

English

Social Sciences

Engineering

Popular majors include economics, human and organizational development, political science, interdisciplinary studies, and psychology.

College, the central section of which is listed on the National Register of Historic Places. On the main campus, art and sculptures dot the landscape, and architectural styles range from Gothic to modern glass and brick. In the past few years, the school has added the Ben Schulman Center for Jewish Life, a 48,000-square-foot studio arts center, and the Bishop Joseph Johnson Black Cultural Center. The Sarratt Student Center remains a center of student life, with a movie theater, Rand Dining Hall, a pub, and offices for the student-run newspaper, radio station, and other student organizations. The student recreation center is currently being renovated.

Undergraduates choose one of four schools—College of Arts and Science, School of Engineering, Blair School of Music, or Peabody College of Education and Human Development—but everyone takes their core liberal arts courses in the College of Arts and Science, where the writing program is a standout. Freshman seminars allow students to explore various topics in small groups with close faculty interaction;

"I truly feel like professors care."

recent seminars have included everything from "New York, New York: Film and Literature" to "Americans in Paris" and "Ethics of Life and Death." Popular majors include economics, human and organizational development, political science, interdisciplinary studies, and psychology. Education majors, who enroll at Vanderbilt's Peabody College, are required to double major, usually in a liberal arts field. They also have the opportunity to spend a summer at England's Cambridge University while teaching at a British school. Many students interested in financial careers declare an economics major and pursue a managerial studies minor; there's also a 3–2 program with Vandy's Owen Graduate School of Business, which lets talented undergraduates save a year on the path to their M.B.A.s. Additional programs include a major and an honors program in women's studies, a minor in Italian studies, and a concentration in collaborative arts for pianists.

"The academic climate of Vanderbilt is competitive," a psychology major says. "Everyone is very high-achieving and the course content is difficult." In the classroom, Vanderbilt students are governed by the school's honor system, which dates from 1875. The system governs all aspects of academic conduct, and makes it possible for Vandy to give unproctored exams. Students rave about the faculty. "The quality of teaching is unmatched," a junior raves. "I truly feel like professors care about educating students in and out of the classroom, as many professors go out of their way to encourage students to get involved with research and internship opportunities."

Vanderbilt's study abroad program attracts 41 percent of students and offers the chance to spend a summer, a semester, or a year on one of six continents via 130 programs. The optional May session allows students to spend four weeks on a single project, helpful for double majors, or those who'd like to spend some time in a foreign country but can't commit to being away for an entire term. During the "Maymester," drama classes may tour London theaters while archeology students work on digs. The state-of-the-art library also has one of the country's best archives of network evening newscasts, a boon for historians and political scientists. The

"An outsider might be struck by how homogeneously Southern, blond, and beautiful the students are."

ENGAGE program offers select incoming undergraduates the opportunity to receive conditional admission to the Vanderbilt graduate or professional school of their choice at the same time they are admitted as freshmen. Students from all four undergraduate schools participate in research and many copublish articles. The campus is home to more than 120 research centers.

"An outsider might be struck by how homogeneously Southern, blond, and beautiful the students are," says a history major. "While this misses some nuances, it's generally true." Vanderbilt students are split more or less down the middle politically between conservatives and liberals. "Our student body is pretty apathetic about political issues," says one senior. "The faculty is more liberal than the student body but both are fairly mixed, ideologically speaking." Asian Americans account for 8 percent of the student body, African Americans 8 percent, and Hispanics 8 percent. In addition to need-based financial aid, Vanderbilt offers merit scholarships averaging $24,788 and 240 athletic awards in 15 sports. The university is one of only a handful in the nation that both consider applications on a need-blind basis and meet full demonstrated need.

Eighty-three percent of Vanderbilt undergraduates live in the dorms and all first-year students come together on one of the most historic areas of campus. Known as the Commons, the initiative is designed to foster a sense of community among the university's freshmen. "Housing is absolutely amazing," a senior says. Students have opportunities to meet and to personally know the faculty who live in the houses and to take part in a yearlong core program that brings together freshmen, peer mentors, and faculty advisors to discuss the challenges and opportunities of the college experience. Older students may choose 10-person townhouses, six-room suites, theme dorms, and school-owned apartments. Seniors may move off campus but must obtain a special waiver. Vanderbilt has more than a dozen dining facilities, and freshmen are required to buy a dinner plan. "The food is pretty good," observes one student. Students report feeling safe on campus, thanks to an active security department. "Campus security is wonderful," says another student. "Vanderbilt has its own police force and they are there solely to watch out for Vanderbilt students and keep us safe."

Fifty-five percent of the women and 30 percent of the men join the Greek system; while many Greek parties are open to the entire campus, the effort to encourage mixing between the groups is not always successful. "Fraternities and sororities start the social scene," a senior says, "but certainly don't encompass all aspects of Vanderbilt's social life." Dating is big; the most coveted invitation is the Accolade formal that precedes homecoming, tickets to which are both expensive and limited. (Funds from the Accolade benefit scholarships for minority students.) Another favorite Vanderbilt tradition is the Rites of Spring festival, a music festival that takes place on the main lawn. Though Vanderbilt students seem to drink just as much as those at any other school, they have to work to get their hands on booze, since open containers are banned in public and kegs are also taboo. As at many colleges, though, "underage students can find loopholes," says one student.

Vanderbilt's proximity to Music City USA provides plenty to do. "Nashville is so much fun," cheers one senior. "The list of excellent restaurants, bars, shopping, and live music venues is endless." Country music fans shouldn't miss the Hall of Fame. Beyond Nashville's borders are the Great Smoky Mountains, and state parks with picnic facilities, beautiful lakes, and skiing in the winter. The best road trips are to Memphis (home of Elvis!), New Orleans (for Mardi Gras), Louisville (for the Kentucky Derby), and Atlanta. Students also engage in the local community through a variety of service-oriented programs.

Vanderbilt is the smallest—and the only private—institution in the competitive and football-crazy Southeastern Conference. Former Vandy chancellor E. Gordon Gee reconfigured the athletic program in an effort to cut costs. Instead of losing ground (as many feared), the programs thrived and recently added a $30 million practice facility for football. Still, the university struggles to convince fans to fill the stadium for home games. The men's and women's basketball squads are perennial contenders and the baseball team earned its first berth in the College World Series in 2011. The women's bowling team brought home the university's first NCAA championship in 2007 and were runners-up in 2011. The debate team

Vanderbilt's study abroad program attracts 41 percent of students.

"Fraternities and sororities start the social scene."

Eighty-three percent of Vanderbilt undergraduates live in the dorms and all first-year students come together on one of the most historic areas of campus.

is competitive, too, winning the 2010 American Debate Association National Championship. There are 40 club sports for weekend jocks, as well as more than 40 intramural sports.

Vanderbilt is no longer simply a regional powerhouse. The school is capitalizing on its unique blend of Southern charm and scholarly achievement to attract students from around the country. Four years here do carry a steep price tag; witness a tongue-in-cheek campus slogan, "Vanderbilt: It Even Sounds Expensive." But for many, investing in a Vanderbilt education is money well spent.

If You Apply To ➤

Vanderbilt: Early decision: Nov. 1. Regular admissions: Jan. 3. Application fee: $50. No campus interviews. Alumni interviews: optional, informational. SATs or ACTs: required. Subject Tests: optional. Apply to particular school or program. Accepts the Common Application. Essay question: Common Application questions.

Vassar College

Poughkeepsie, NY 12604

It is hard to imagine that Vassar once considered picking up and moving to Yale in the 1960s rather than become a co-ed institution. Thirty-five years after admitting men, still on its ancient and picturesque campus, Vassar is a thriving, highly selective, avant-garde institution with an accent on the fine arts and humanities.

Are you a scientist who composes music in your spare time? Or perhaps an actor who also enjoys dissecting Plato and Aristotle? If so, you may feel at home at Vassar, a small liberal arts college just 70 miles north of New York City. Once known as the most liberal of the Seven Sisters, and still a bastion of the left, Vassar prides itself on curricular flexibility, tolerance, and diversity. "We range from jocks to hippies, musicians to activists," says a senior. A junior adds, "What ties us together is our intellectual curiosity and general respect for the world."

> **"Professors are engaged and care about their students."**

The college's 1,000-acre campus, just outside Poughkeepsie, New York, includes two lakes and plenty of trees. Daffodils bloom in the spring, and foliage is omnipresent in the fall. Encircled by a fieldstone wall, the campus also boasts an astronomical observatory with one of the largest telescopes in the Northeast, a state-of-the-art chemistry building, a farm with an ecological field station, and an art center with 13,500 works, from Ancient Egyptian to modern times. The architecture is predominantly neo-Gothic, with buildings also designed by notables such as Marcel Breuer, Eero Saarinen, and James Renwick.

Vassar has no core curriculum, and no general education or distribution requirements. Indeed, academic flexibility is paramount. That said, all students must take a Freshman Course, a small seminar emphasizing oral and written expression, as well as one course that requires significant quantitative analysis. Students must also demonstrate intermediate-level proficiency in a foreign language by studying one of the 18 languages taught at Vassar, or through a satisfactory score on an AP or SAT II test. Since Vassar has no graduate students or research-only faculty, all classes are taught by professors. "Professors are engaged and care about their students," a senior says. Small classes and tutorials are the norm, and exams are given under an honor system.

The most popular majors include English, psychology, political science, economics, and biological sciences. Regardless of their course of study, students find the

Website: www.vassar.edu
Location: Suburban
Private
Total Enrollment: 2,355
Undergraduates: 2,355
Male/Female: 44/56
SAT Ranges: CR 660–750, M 650–740
ACT Ranges: 29–32
Financial Aid: 63%
Expense: Pr $ $ $ $
Student Loans: 48%
Average Debt: $
Phi Beta Kappa: Yes
Applicants: 7,908
Accepted: 23%
Enrolled: 36%
Grad in 6 Years: 91%
Returning Freshmen: 96%
Academics: ✎ ✎ ✎ ✎ ½
Social: ☎ ☎ ☎
Q of L: ★ ★ ★ ★
Admissions: (845) 437-7300
Email Address: admission@vassar.edu

academic climate cooperative rather than competitive. "Vassar's academic environment is supportive and focused on group work," a physics major says. The biology building houses two electron microscopes, while music students are spoiled by a grand collection of Steinway pianos spread across the campus. Each year, 45 percent of students study abroad via 300 approved programs in 60 countries. Vassar is also one of a rapidly dwindling number of colleges that allow students to use their financial aid packages to support study away from campus.

Back in the United States, Vassar students interested in urban education benefit from the school's agreement with New York's Bank Street College. In addition, there are programs with the other 11 members of the Twelve College Exchange* and at four historically black colleges, as well as a drama program at the Eugene O'Neill Theater and a maritime

> "Vassar students tend to be self-motivated, accepting, and opinionated."

studies program at the Mystic Seaport*, both in Connecticut. Also highly regarded is the college's Undergraduate Research Summer Institute (URSI), which offers stipends for students to work one-on-one with faculty members on scientific projects, either at Vassar or off campus. Finally, the Ford Scholars program offers opportunities for student/faculty collaboration in the humanities and social sciences.

Other than the obvious change, coeducation has little impact on the type of student attracted to Vassar. Seventy percent of Vassar students were in the top 10th of their high school classes; 26 percent are native New Yorkers. "Vassar students tend to be self-motivated, accepting, and opinionated," explains one senior. Minorities account for a substantial subset of the student population, with Asian Americans making up 9 percent, African Americans 6 percent, and Hispanics 11 percent. The school's ALANA Center supports and recognizes students of color and other ethnic and cultural groups. Hot-button political issues include war, immigration, and race, one student says. The college offers need-blind admissions for all first-year applicants and loan reductions are made available to qualified low-income students.

Housing is guaranteed for four years and 94 percent of students live on campus, where there's an eclectic mix of nine dorms. All but one are co-ed. "Some dorms are really modern and sparkling," says a junior. "Others have a vintage college feel, with traditional wood paneling, trim, and floors." The word is that Lathrop is the best dorm for freshmen, but no halls are reserved strictly for first-

> "We take the time to enjoy college for what it is."

year students. Juniors and seniors favor the college-owned townhouses (five-person suites), and the four-person Terrace Apartments, both with kitchens and living rooms. "Dorm spirit is pretty big here," confides a junior. When those hunger pangs strike, students take advantage of two dining facilities that provide a wide assortment of vittles. "It's not my mom's cooking," one student confides, "but it's still good and edible."

Vassar doesn't have a Greek system, so social life revolves around films, lectures, parties, concerts, and the like. "There are more than 1,000 events registered on the campus every year," a senior reports, "which is nearly 40 events a week." Students who are 21 or older can party at the on-campus dance club Matthew's Mug, named for school founder Matthew Vassar. Those not old enough to legally imbibe can drop by the college's coffeehouse. And while alcohol is permitted on campus, "underage drinking and open containers are not," says a political science major. Poughkeepsie itself is an old industrial town—not too exciting after dark, but with plenty of opportunities for fieldwork and internships for academic credit with local politicians, businesses, and community organizations. Restaurants and shops are within walking distance of campus, and malls and movie theaters aren't much farther away. In warmer weather, Mohonk State Park offers hiking and other outdoor diversions. Also close by are Franklin Roosevelt's Hyde Park (for history) and the Culinary Institute of

The Ford Scholars program offers opportunities for student/faculty collaboration in the humanities and social sciences.

The school's ALANA Center supports and recognizes students of color and other ethnic and cultural groups.

America (for cheap gourmet meals prepared by fellow students). Popular road trips include New York City and Boston, both easily reached by train.

Owing to its heritage as one of the Seven Sisters, traditions are big at Vassar. "The year starts with Serenading—a time when the freshmen pay tribute to the seniors by singing them songs," one student explains. "The day ends with fireworks over the lake, and a trophy is presented to the dorm with the best song." On Founder's Day in May, the entire community celebrates Matthew Vassar's birthday with music, carnival rides, food, and a day out on the grass. Fireworks and a movie cap off the festivities. "It's basically a big carnival for everyone at Vassar," says a junior. Students can still unwind after a hard day of classes with afternoon tea in the Rose Parlor of historic Main Building. And the number of a cappella singing groups has now reached double digits, one student says.

Vassar's varsity squads (the "Brewers") compete in the Liberty League, and the women's basketball team were Liberty League champs in 2010–11. Women's rugby is solid, too, as are men's and women's tennis. Intramural sports are offered at two levels, competitive and recreational, and roughly half the student body participates. Teams face off in everything from basketball and softball to billiards, golf, Frisbee, Ping-Pong, and water polo.

While Vassar continues to offer a menu of high-quality liberal arts courses emphasizing interdisciplinary connections, the college has also embraced technology and diversity. "Vassar is a vibrant community where students, faculty, administration, and staff all take an interest in each other," says a senior. "People are happy and optimistic," a junior adds. "We take the time to enjoy college for what it is—a serious, but not too serious, time of life for learning and development."

Owing to its heritage as one of the Seven Sisters, traditions are big at Vassar.

Overlaps
Brown, Columbia, Cornell, Wesleyan, Williams, Yale

If You Apply To ➤

Vassar: Early decision I: Nov. 15. Early decision II: Jan. 1. Regular admissions: Jan. 1. Application fee: $70. No campus interviews. Alumni interviews: optional, informational. SAT and two Subject Tests or ACT (with writing): required. Accepts the Common Application. Essay question: Common Application and personal statement.

University of Vermont

194 South Prospect Street, Burlington, VT 05401

For an out-of-stater sizing up public universities, there could hardly be a more appealing place than UVM. The size is manageable, Burlington is a fabulous college town, and Lake Champlain and the Green Mountains are on your doorstep. UVM feels like a private university, but, alas, it is also priced like one. Attracts a mix of party animals and serious types.

Website: www.uvm.edu
Location: Small City
Public
Total Enrollment: 11,097
Undergraduates: 9,803
Male/Female: 44/56
SAT Ranges: CR 540–640, M 550–650
ACT Ranges: 24–29

With its beautiful setting, wide academic offerings, and abundance of clubs and cocurricular pursuits, the University of Vermont draws students from around the country. And, says a math major, they're not all granola types with a penchant for soy milk and snowboarding: "From hippies to preppies, UVM has it all, and they all coexist." While it's a public school, UVM's academics, research opportunities, and price tag are more akin to those of a private institution. Generous financial aid packages and growth plans are helping to ensure that Vermont remains both affordable and relevant, amid increasing competition with schools of both types.

Chartered in 1791, UVM was established as the fifth college in New England. UVM's picturesque campus sits on the shores of Lake Champlain in Burlington, virtually a stone's throw from the Canadian border. Architectural styles range from colonial to high Victorian Gothic and functional modern; the oldest structures, in the center of the campus, are recognized on the National Registry of Historic Places. The 164,000-square-foot Dudley H. Davis student center provides a bistro and space for entertainment, multiple dining options, and meeting space. James M. Jeffords Hall offers state-of-the-art teaching labs and classrooms for students in biology, anatomy, biochemistry, botany, and other life sciences.

The product of a merger of a private college and public university, UVM attained quasi-public status in 1862 with the passage of the Morrill Land Grant College Act. Today, the university blends the traditions of both a private and public university. UVM's seven undergraduate colleges and schools set their own curricula and general education requirements, but administrators say most students need to take at least 30 credits—or 10 courses—in the arts, humanities, social sciences, languages, literature, math, and physical sciences. Also mandatory is a credit-bearing course in Race and Culture or a course that explores race relations and ethnic diversity in the United States. A three-credit foundational writing and information literacy requirement for all first-time, first-year students goes into effect in late 2014. The most popular majors are business administration, biology, psychology, English, and environmental studies; students also give high marks to the engineering program.

> "By and large, the professors are a fantastic group of people."

Premed, nursing, and prevet students benefit from the research and teaching capabilities of Vermont's fine medical school, as well as from a seven-year program with the vet school at Tufts. Additional majors include neuroscience and linguistics. A life skills program for athletes emphasizes health and wellness, academic skills, and moral and ethical reasoning.

How tough is the academic environment? "It really depends on what coursework you're following," says one student. "I know that some majors are infamously more rigorous than others, like the nursing, premed, and animal science majors." Professors are praised for their engaging style and accessibility. "By and large, the professors are a fantastic group of people," says a junior. "They care a lot about the students and have unbelievable knowledge and experiences, which they pass along." Special programs for first-years include the five-day TREK programs, in which students go hiking or biking, do community service, or take a leadership skills development course before classes start. It's led by upper-class student mentors. Students are especially enthused about the Teacher Advisor Program (TAP), in which groups of 10 to 15 first-years participate in a writing-intensive, discussion-oriented seminar taught by a professor who is also each student's advisor. Through the Vermont Legislative Research Service, undergraduate public policy students provide state legislators with policy briefs on current issues. Each year, about one-third of all undergrads go abroad; UVM offers 900 programs in 60 countries.

UVM students are "incredibly passionate, friendly, and outgoing," says a senior. A sophomore adds, "Everyone is always doing something, whether it be school-related or a club or just being able to explore all of Vermont's natural assets." Thirty-six percent of UVM students are native Vermonters and 71 percent graduated in the top quarter of their high school class. Hispanics comprise 4 percent of the student body, Asian Americans 2 percent, and African Americans 1 percent. Despite the low minority representation, "students are very passionate about issues of social justice," says a senior. Liberals outnumber conservatives, if only slightly, and "the school is big on social justice," explains a junior. UVM offers merit scholarships and 241 athletic awards in 23 sports.

First-years and sophomores must live on campus. "Living in the res hall is a ton of fun and it's an awesome environment to meet new people," says an animal

---

(continued)

Financial Aid: 86%
Expense: Pub $ $ $ $
Student Loans: 59%
Average Debt: $ $ $
Phi Beta Kappa: Yes
Applicants: 21,808
Accepted: 77%
Enrolled: 14%
Grad in 6 Years: 76%
Returning Freshmen: 85%
Academics: ✑ ✑ ✑ ½
Social: ☎ ☎ ☎ ☎ ☎
Q of L: ★ ★ ★ ★ ★
Admissions: (802) 656-3370
Email Address: admissions@uvm.edu

Strongest Programs:
Business Administration
Psychology
Biology
Environmental Studies
English
Nutrition and Food Sciences
Neuroscience
Music and Dance

A three-credit foundational writing and information literacy requirement for all first-time, first-year students goes into effect in late 2014.

science major. Most juniors and seniors move off campus, "which creates a great UVM community in downtown Burlington," says a student, but the new residence halls for upperclassmen encourage more of them to stay on campus. The administration has also declared all residence halls alcohol-free. UVM has more than a dozen dining halls, and they buy two-thirds of their food from local farmers. "There are so many options it's nuts! Vegan, vegetarian, sushi, Indian, gluten free, and local food every day," cheers one student. Security is good, too, according to students: "We have the blue-light emergency system, our own police force, and a card control access system for every building on campus," a student explains.

Men's basketball has brought home numerous conference titles.

"The social life at UVM is a great experience," says one student. "There are multiple organizations on campus that organize different events for students on campus such as bands, comedians, pub quiz night, and karaoke." Just 7 percent of UVM men and 6 percent of the women join Greek groups, so when the weekend comes, college-sponsored movies, dances, bars, and coffeehouses are big draws. Much of the fun also happens on nearby ski slopes and in Burlington itself, where the music scene draws top talent and is always bustling. A popular campus T-shirt warns: "If you want to party, come to UVM. If you want to stay, study!" Per Vermont law, students under 21 may not drink, so the most popular road trip is Montreal—90 minutes away—with even bigger concerts and a drinking age of 18.

"Burlington is the quintessential college town," says one senior. "There are tons of coffee shops and music venues, and the bar/club scene is great." Indeed, the energetic downtown boasts symphonies, art galleries, chic shopping, and lively bars and restaurants, plus there's Lake Champlain only five minutes away, not to mention the mountains and ski slopes. As much as they love their little city, students also look forward to getting out of town. The Outing Club is one of UVM's most popular student organizations, as the nearby Green Mountains, White Mountains, and Adirondacks offer prime hiking, backpacking, and rock climbing. Students are also actively engaged with the local community through volunteer opportunities. "UVM is a very socially conscious school," says a student.

"We value hands-on experience to give depth to our education."

UVM fields a number of highly competitive Catamount ("cat of the mountains") teams. Vermont's ice hockey team is the school's pride and joy, having ranked as high as second nationally. Students get access to tickets before the general public, a nice perk since games are always sold out. Soccer draws crowds in the fall, since there is no football team. Men's basketball has brought home numerous conference titles, and the school has earned seven America East Academic Cups for the best overall combined GPA among its student athletes. The ski team is a perennial powerhouse (and 2012 national title holders) and the lacrosse team and men's and women's soccer are also very competitive. Most students participate in at least one intramural sport, with broomball being most popular. Joystick jocks can sign up for intramural video game tournaments.

Students at UVM may be laid-back, but they're also curious, caring, open minded, active, and willing to work hard. "We value hands-on experience to give depth to our education," says a junior. They enjoy giving their all, both in the classroom and outside, viewing extracurricular involvement as critical to the undergraduate experience. One happy junior sums up UVM this way: "We are the real deal."

Overlaps

University of New Hampshire, University of Massachusetts, Northeastern, University of Connecticut, Boston University, Boston College, Cornell, Dartmouth

If You Apply To ➤

UVM: Early action: Nov. 1. Regular admissions: Jan. 15. Financial aid: Feb. 10. Application fee: $55. No campus or alumni interviews. SATs or ACTs (with writing): required. No Subject Tests. Apply to individual schools or programs. Accepts the Common Application. Essay questions: Common Application.

Villanova University

800 Lancaster Avenue, Villanova, PA 19085-1672

Set in an upscale suburb, Villanova is gaining popularity as Philadelphia's answer to Boston College. As at BC, about 80 percent of the students are Roman Catholic (compared with about half at Georgetown). The troika of business, engineering, and nursing are popular at 'Nova. Downtown Philadelphia is a quick hop away by train.

Villanova University takes pride in its Augustinian roots, even basing its admissions essay on one of St. Augustine's teachings about transforming "hearts and minds." The school has all the trappings of a typical Roman Catholic university, from strong academics to deeply rooted traditions and rivalries, and students firmly dedicated to their faith. Says one junior, "There are times I walk out of a class at Villanova and just have to stop for a second to take it all in and appreciate what an amazing opportunity I've been afforded."

Founded in 1842 by the community-focused Order of Saint Augustine, Villanova's lush campus of more than 260 acres is situated along Philadelphia's suburban Main Line. The campus continues to keep some of its historical roots with ivy-covered buildings, well-kept lawns, and secluded, tree-lined walkways. The university is currently undertaking an initiative to transform the current campus landscape. The transformation includes the building of new residence halls, renovating existing residence halls to be more sustainable, renewing and expanding current academic space, and improving the campus landscape and accessibility.

Nursing, finance, and engineering are especially popular at Villanova, as are the political science and communication programs. Undergraduates may enroll in the College of Liberal Arts and Sciences, the Villanova School of Business, the College of Engineering, or the College of Nursing. General education requirements vary by school, but all students take the two-semester Augustine and Culture Seminar (ACS). In the first semester, students read works from the ancient, medieval, and Renaissance periods—ranging from the Greeks and Saint Augustine to the Middle Ages and Shakespeare. In the second semester, students explore works from the Early Modern, Enlightenment, Romantic, Modernist, and Contemporary eras.

> "The students who attend Villanova are passionate and devoted."

"The courses are rigorous and are often discussion-oriented and reading- and writing-intensive," says one communication major. Another student says, "Villanova professors go the extra mile for their students through office hours, research, and personal conversations." An honors program is available to about 200 students, by invitation only. But even outside the honors program, a biology major says that in recent years, "the academics have become more demanding, and the admissions process has become more competitive." Additional undergraduate majors include Latin American studies, gender and women's studies, and Arab and Islamic studies.

"The students who attend Villanova are passionate and devoted," says a sophomore. "They care about their work, but, more importantly, they care about their community." Many are from the East Coast, and 25 percent hail from Pennsylvania. African Americans account for 5 percent of the student body, Hispanics comprise 8 percent, and Asian Americans contribute 6 percent. "We're not an extremely political campus," one student muses, "although social justice issues like poverty, hunger, and homelessness are all big issues." Merit scholarships are available, as are more than 200 athletic scholarships in a variety of sports.

Website: www.villanova.edu
Location: Suburban
Private
Total Enrollment: 8,620
Undergraduates: 6,576
Male/Female: 49/51
SAT Ranges: CR 590–680, M 610–710
ACT Ranges: 28–31
Financial Aid: 75%
Expense: Pr $ $ $
Student Loans: 53%
Average Debt: $ $ $ $
Phi Beta Kappa: Yes
Applicants: 14,901
Accepted: 46%
Enrolled: 24%
Grad in 6 Years: 88%
Returning Freshmen: 94%
Academics: ✍ ✍ ✍
Social: ☎ ☎ ☎
Q of L: ★ ★ ★
Admissions: (610) 519-4000
Email Address: gotovu@villanova.edu

Strongest Programs:
Business
Marketing
Nursing
Social Science
Engineering

Housing on campus is guaranteed for three years and 70 percent of the student population calls the dorms home. "Rooms are great at Villanova," says one senior. "My first and second year I had a sink in my room so I didn't have to walk down the hall to wash my face or brush my teeth. You can get all the premium channels you want and even DVR." Freshmen live primarily on the South Campus Circle, while upperclassmen take their chances in the lottery system. Most seniors move to houses and apartments in the surrounding towns. The meal plan offers more than a dozen campus eateries, which serve everything from pizza to Chinese food, wraps, and vegetarian and vegan menus. "Food at Villanova is delicious," says a student: "Tons of variety with so many options I sometimes don't know which one to choose."

"I have never had a dull weekend at Villanova because there is always something going on. If you are looking to party, you can. If you are looking to just chill, you can do that, too," a student explains. Weekend social life centers around cam-

"Rooms are great at Villanova." pus events and parties, some sponsored by Greek groups, which claim 17 percent of the men and 34 percent of the women. If you are under 21 and caught drinking on campus, "you see the Dean and a fine is given," says a junior. On Fridays and Saturdays there is something called "Late Night at Villanova" where comedians, bands, open mic, and dance parties provide an opportunity for students to get together with friends at the Student Center. Despite the tough courses, students take pride in finding the time to socialize and stay involved in the community. "Students don't have to have any prior experience to do Habitat for Humanity," says a junior, "nor do they have to be Catholic to go on a retreat. We send about 400 people away for a week in the fall and another 400 in the spring for Habitat or mission trips." Each fall, Villanova hosts the largest student-run Special Olympics, which draws people from the local community as well as the campus. Juniors and seniors tend to spend evenings at bars along the local Main Line or in Philadelphia, just 12 minutes away by train. The city's entertainment and cultural opportunities include museums and pro sports, as well as events at numerous other colleges and universities, from La Salle and Temple to Drexel, Penn, and St. Joseph's.

When they're not out socializing, Villanova students are cheering for their Wildcats, "unleashing the Wildcat within" against their rivals. Solid teams include men's basketball and women's cross-country. The university has also produced nearly 60 Olympians in its history, and Villanovans have participated in every Summer Olympics since 1948. The school's fitness complex has a swimming center and an indoor track, and 75 percent of students participate in intramural sports.

Despite the changes in the world around it, Villanova continues to be a Catholic university devoted to its students, community, and strong traditions, both spiritually and academically. The administration has launched a $600 million fund-raising drive aimed at making it one of the premier Roman Catholic institutions alongside Notre Dame, Georgetown, and Boston College. "Everyone works hard, plays hard, and still finds time to give back to the community," says a senior. While the school takes pride in tradition, it recognizes the technology improvements, continuing upgrades to facilities, and changing and improving educational programs will help its students remain competitive in the workplace and the world beyond.

If You Apply To ➤ **Villanova:** Early action: Nov. 1. Regular admissions: Jan. 15. Application fee: $80. No campus interviews. Alumni interviews: optional, informational. SATs or ACTs (with writing): required. Subject Tests: optional. Apply to a particular school or program. Accepts the Common Application. Essay question.

University of Virginia

P.O. Box 400160, Charlottesville, VA 22904

Is it Thomas Jefferson? The Romanesque architecture? The Charlottesville air? Whatever it is, students nationwide go ga-ga for UVA, where competition for out-of-state admission has hit the Ivy League level. Relatively small for a top-notch public flagship, UVA combines old-line conservatism with a touch of rowdy frat boy. Charlottesville is a big small town with plenty of culture, just over two hours from D.C.

Easily one of the most prestigious public schools in the nation, the University of Virginia is known to all in Charlottesville as Mr. Jefferson's University. Not just any Mr. Jefferson, mind you, but *the* Mr. Jefferson, author of the Declaration of Independence. Though he passed away more nearly two centuries ago, he is referred to here as if he ran down to the apothecary shop for a bit of snuff and will be back in a moment. Of all his accomplishments, Jefferson was arguably proudest of UVA—he even asked that his epitaph speak to his role in creating the university rather than his presidency of the United States. UVA attracted national attention in mid-2012 when a rogue board summarily fired the president, Teresa Sullivan, only to be forced to rehire her in the face of outrage from students, faculty, and much of the national higher education community. The ostensible issue was the pace of institutional change, especially in the area of online education, but, consistent with UVA's genetic reverence for tradition, the incident will be chewed over for a long time to come.

Located just east of the Blue Ridge Mountains in central Virginia, UVA's campus is dotted with historic buildings designed by Jefferson himself and still in use today. At the core is Jefferson's "academical village," with majestic white pillars, serpentine walls, and extensive brickwork. The village rises around a rectangular terraced green, known as the Lawn, which is flanked by two rows of identical one-story rooms reserved for undergraduate student leaders. Five pavilions, each in a different style, are arranged on either side of the Lawn; all of them open onto a colonnaded walkway. Behind the buildings are public gardens, while the Rotunda, a half-scale model of the Roman Pantheon, overlooks the Lawn.

UVA isn't just an elite public school; this university holds its own against the best private schools as well. The most popular majors are commerce, psychology, biology, foreign affairs, and history. Foreign languages and politics also get high marks, but that's a double-edged sword: "Spanish, economics, and politics have university-provided waitlists because their class sizes never accommodate the demand of students wanting to enroll," says a senior. Sociology and the life sciences draw praise as well, but students caution that math and other quantitative disciplines can be rough—and not just because of the subject matter. "Half of the professors in statistics don't speak English," gripes a junior. Most students matriculate into the College of Arts and Sciences, but undergraduates may also enroll in the schools of Engineering, Nursing, or Architecture. After their second year, about 320 external transfer students and students from other UVA schools transfer into the McIntire School of Commerce, UVA's undergraduate business school. Not surprisingly, competition for these spots is tough. "The academic climate is definitely competitive, which can be good because it pushes people to their best, but it can create a very stressful and unpleasant atmosphere," says a senior. A classmate adds, "I think students go out of their way to help each other and be collaborative so we all succeed."

> **"The academic climate is definitely competitive, which can be good because it pushes people to their best."**

Website: www.virginia.edu
Location: Small City
Public
Total Enrollment: 20,027
Undergraduates: 14,137
Male/Female: 45/55
SAT Ranges: CR 620–720, M 640–740
ACT Ranges: 28–32
Financial Aid: 43%
Expense: Pub $ $ $
Student Loans: 36%
Average Debt: $ $
Phi Beta Kappa: Yes
Applicants: 27,193
Accepted: 30%
Enrolled: 42%
Grad in 6 Years: 93%
Returning Freshmen: 97%
Academics: ✍ ✍ ✍ ✍ ✍
Social: 🐦 🐦 🐦 🐦
Q of L: ★ ★ ★ ★ ★
Admissions: (434) 982-3200
Email Address: undergrad admission@virginia.edu

Strongest Programs:
English
Spanish and Portuguese
Religious Studies
German
Physiology

Virginia requires students in the College of Arts and Sciences and the McIntire School to master a foreign language before graduation. Arts and Sciences students must also take courses in English composition, humanities and fine arts, social science, natural sciences and mathematics, non-Western studies, and composition. Special programs for freshmen include University Seminars, designed to develop critical thinking skills in an environment that encourages interactive learning and intensive discussion, and are limited to 20 students each. "These classes are based on interesting, current topics that provide somewhat of a break from your rigorous, everyday class," says a sociology major. They're also taught by some of the university's best faculty. A five-year program for aspiring teachers yields a B.A. from the College of Arts and Sciences and a Master of Teaching degree from UVA's Curry School of Education. An intensive two-week January term provides additional opportunities for study abroad, research seminars, and interdisciplinary coursework. The Batten School of Leadership and Public Policy trains students for public service careers in both domestic and international arenas and offers a five-year bachelor/master of public policy.

"The quality of teaching is incredibly high."

Highly capable students may win admission to the Echols Scholars program, which allows about 200 top-entering freshmen the chance to pursue academic exploration without the constraints of distribution or major-field requirements. Echols students also live together for their first year. The Rodman Scholars program in the School of Engineering and Applied Science selects its members based on financial need, leadership, and scholarship. Students who qualify for the Distinguished Majors program may pursue independent study during their third and fourth years. "The quality of teaching is incredibly high, not just from the quality of lectures but also from the experiences that our professors bring to the classroom," says a senior. "One professor I had taught a politics course on the Middle East, centered around the Camp David negotiations. As it turns out, he was at the negotiations and shared first-hand anecdotes of playing chess with Sadat."

Students instituted Virginia's notable honor system in 1842, after no one owned up to shooting a professor on the Lawn. The residence halls, student council, and Judiciary Committee remain student-run to this day—and they really put the brakes on lying, cheating, or stealing. And don't take the policies lightly—breaching the codes means a swift dismissal from campus. After a number of controversial cases recently, discussions continue about the appropriateness of the single-sanction system. But rest assured, some form of the honor code will remain a way of life here, as many students say the policies keep them feeling comfortable leaving backpacks and laptops unattended.

UVA students are described as "accomplished and humble." Says one classics major, "Students maintain high standards of themselves and others, while also being defined by the values of honor and integrity. Our honor code is more than just some words scribbled on paper—it's a way of life and a bond of trust between you, your peers, and faculty." Sixty-three percent of students are Virginians; admission for out-of-staters gets tougher every year, and many of those students come from New York, New Jersey, Pennsylvania, and Maryland. Seven percent of UVA students are African American, 12 percent are Asian American, and 6 percent are Hispanic. The school hands out hundreds of athletic scholarships each year, along with merit awards, including 25 to 30 highly prized Jefferson Scholarships, given annually by the alumni association and good for full tuition, room, and board. The Access UVA program, which used to eliminate loans for students from low-income families, has now been sharply curtailed.

"Students maintain high standards of themselves and others."

After their second year, about 320 external transfer students and students from other UVA schools transfer into the McIntire School of Commerce, UVA's undergraduate business school.

Forty-one percent of students at Virginia live on campus, including 1,100 who bunk in the three residential colleges: Brown College at Monroe Hill, Hereford College, and International Residential College. Hereford's contemporary architecture has been described by the *New York Times* as "proudly, almost defiantly modern," in contrast to most of the other campus buildings. There are foreign language houses for students who want to work on their Russian, Spanish, French, or German—and one house where students can find groups of peers speaking Arabic, Chinese, Hindi-Urdu, Italian, Japanese, or Persian. "UVA has been building beautiful new dorms with AC and everything else you can imagine for first-year students. [We] call them McMansions since they are so nice," quips one senior. Fifty-four top students win the honor of living in spartan rooms along the lawn, and there is the option of #13, which was occupied for a semester by Edgar Allan Poe in 1826 before he was suspended for nonpayment of tuition. For upperclassmen, getting a decent on-campus apartment is slightly more difficult, prompting many students to move off campus. Meal plans are required for first-years and campus fare receives decent reviews. "What I love about our dining hall is its a fixed price (or swipe) for all the campus food," says one student. "This means that I can eat whatever I want, without having to worry about whether I will having dining dollars left over at the end of the semester." Upperclassmen either cook for themselves or take meals at the Greek houses; fraternities draw 21 percent of Virginia's men, and sororities sign up 22 percent of the women.

Mr. Jefferson founded UVA as a place where students could come together to "drink from the cup of knowledge," and now that fraternity rush is dry and parties must have guest lists, there's a lot less quaffing of other brews going on. Still, determined Virginians haven't stopped metamorphosing into Rowdy Wahoos when the sun goes down—the nickname comes from a school cheer about a fish that can drink twice its weight. Alcohol policies "are geared toward education, rather than punishment," says one student. "That seems to work. As long as students understand that there is no pressure to drink and that there are consequences to their actions, then they will be safe." For nondrinkers and those under 21, the student-run University Union and more than 500 clubs and other organizations offer movies, concerts, social hours, and other booze-free options. "The social life at UVA is pretty lively," says one senior. "Students turn out en masse for sporting events, but at night they tend to hang out."

As for Charlottesville, it's "the perfect college town," says an anthropology major. "Malls and historical places are located close by. The community is rather affluent, safe, and extremely friendly," adds another student. There are amazing restaurants, gorgeous vineyards and wineries, and plenty of bars, shops, theaters, and other cultural attractions. Students also tend to immerse themselves in community service in the area; UVA's nationally recognized Madison House coordinates the activities of a host of volunteer groups. Outdoorsy folks can hike, bike, ski, and sightsee in the nearby Blue Ridge Mountains, or simply daydream while strolling Skyline Drive. Popular road trips include Washington, D.C., Richmond, and anywhere the Cavaliers are playing football, basketball, or soccer.

While big-time Atlantic Coast Conference basketball has long been an integral part of UVA life, the Cavaliers field a number of competitive teams, including men's and women's swimming and diving, men's tennis, women's rowing, and men's baseball. There are also more than a dozen intramural sports leagues or tournaments, in everything from flag football to inner-tube water polo, and more than 65 club sports. Favorite traditions include Foxfield each April, in which students dress up and host catered parties prior to attending a steeplechase horse race; jackets and ties also come out for football games, a relic of when UVA was all male and gridiron

A five-year program for aspiring teachers yields a B.A. from the College of Arts and Sciences and a Master of Teaching degree from UVA's Curry School of Education.

"Students turn out en masse for sporting events."

The school hands out hundreds of athletic scholarships each year, along with merit awards, including 25 to 30 highly prized Jefferson Scholarships.

Overlaps

Duke, James Madison, University of Pennsylvania, Princeton, College of William and Mary, Virginia Tech

contests were an opportunity to meet women; and May brings Beach Week. We could tell you more about the various secret societies, but we won't—they're secret, after all!

UVA offers a top-notch education at a bargain-basement price, at least for in-state students. "If you really want to blaze your own trail," says a senior, "UVA is the place." The social life is rowdy, the academics are rigorous, and the friendships that are formed here last far beyond the college years—much as Mr. Jefferson's legacy continues to be felt on campus, years after his death.

Virginia Tech

Blacksburg, VA 24061

Offers a unique blend of high tech and Southern hospitality. Engineering has always been its calling card, but business and architecture are popular. Blacksburg is a nice college town, but is far from the population centers near the coast. Hokie Nation loves its football team. Compare to Clemson, Georgia Tech, and Purdue.

Website: www.vt.edu
Location: Rural
Public
Total Enrollment: 31,087
Undergraduates: 23,364
Male/Female: 59/41
SAT Ranges: CR 540–640, M 570–680
ACT Ranges: N/A
Financial Aid: 60%
Expense: Pub $ $ $
Student Loans: 54%
Average Debt: $ $ $
Phi Beta Kappa: Yes
Applicants: 20,191
Accepted: 70%
Enrolled: 39%
Grad in 6 Years: 83%
Returning Freshmen: 93%
Academics: ✑ ✑ ✑
Social: ☎ ☎ ☎
Q of L: ★ ★ ★ ★
Admissions: (540) 231-6267
Email Address: vtadmiss@vt.edu

Officially known as the Virginia Polytechnic Institute and State University, Virginia Tech is a former land-grant university that now offers a slate of solid academic programs, competitive Division I athletics, and storied traditions. Engineering, business, and architecture attract top students from around the country who are proud to be part of the "Hokie Nation."

Its campus, set on a plateau in the scenic Blue Ridge Mountains, occupies 3,000 acres and comes complete with a duck pond, hiking trails, and a 200-year-old plantation that is a local landmark. Students enjoy unlimited outdoor recreation thanks to the proximity of the Jefferson National Forest, the Appalachian Trail, the scenic Blue Ridge Parkway, and the majestic old New River. The campus buildings are an attractive mix of gray limestone structures, colonial-style brick, and modern cement buildings. The campus continues to undergo renovations and additions, including a state-of-the-art dining facility.

Virginia Tech is best known for its first-rate technical and professional training. For undergrads with an appetite for engineering, Tech has programs for every taste, including aerospace, ocean, biological systems, civil, chemical, computer, electrical, industrial systems, materials, mechanical (the most popular), and mining. The Pamplin College of Business is also prominent, and the five-year architecture program is considered one of the nation's best. Though no longer Tech's centerpiece, the College of Agriculture and Life Sciences remains strong, especially in animal science. Students in the College of Natural Resources can choose from such concentrations as environmental conservation, fisheries science, forestry, and wildlife management. They may also select a major in environmental resource management.

> **"Freshmen are taught by professors and grad students."**

Students in the sciences reap the benefits of their high-tech environment; other disciplines do not fare so well. The humanities have been hard-hit by budget cuts.

In particular, "religious studies, foreign languages, and philosophy are dwindling away," says a senior. One bright spot is internationally known poet Nikki Giovanni, who teaches creative writing and advanced poetry. The university also has a tradition of excellence in the performing arts, and the school's theater group has received more awards from the American College Theater Arts Festival than any other college in the Southeast.

Introductory class size tends to be large—sometimes well into the hundreds—and the budget axe has only made matters worse. Most of the big lecture classes are taught by full-time faculty, though discussions and grading are generally handled by TAs. Nevertheless, a communications major says her professors "keep you on the edge of your seat." An accounting major adds, "Freshmen are taught by professors and grad students." All students are required to take courses in English, math, humanities, and social and natural science. There is also a foreign language requirement, though high school coursework may cover this. The 1,500 or so students who participate in the university honors program are guaranteed access to top faculty and research opportunities.

Each year, more than 1,000 students take advantage of Tech's co-op opportunities available in almost all majors. The nationally acclaimed Small Business Institute program enables faculty-led groups of business majors to work with local merchants, analyze their problems, and make suggestions on how to increase profits. The Corps of Cadets, a tradition once on the verge of extinction, has made a comeback. Cadets earn a minor in leadership and can choose from three tracks: military/ROTC, civic professions, or a combination of the two. For those who want to study abroad, Tech offers more than 200 programs in 60 nations around the globe.

Students looking at pricey Northeastern technical schools will find Tech a real bargain. Not surprisingly, the admissions office is inundated with out-of-state applicants, which means stiff competition for the slots available to non-Virginians. Tech's relative isolation from major cities is a drag on minority recruitment: African Americans and Hispanics combine for 9 percent of the student body; Asian Americans account for another 9 percent. Eighty-four percent of students graduated in the top quarter of their high school class. Students with financial need who apply for aid before the deadline receive priority consideration; those who apply later are likely to be out of luck. Tech hands out a few hundred athletic scholarships, and there are merit scholarships available to qualified students. The "Funds for the Future" program aims to provide additional aid to low-income undergraduates.

> "Most students go downtown to shoot pool, dance, or go to a bar."

Tech housing is nothing to write home about, but adequate to meet the needs of most students. "Rooms are on the small side, but they provide all you need to live," says a freshman. Some 25 undergraduate dorms serve 8,400 students; 38 percent of the student body lives on campus, though only freshmen and the Corps of Cadets are required to. Most upperclassmen live off campus in nearby apartment complexes. Dietrick's Depot, the largest dining hall on campus, was recently renovated. Three specialty lines supplement the standard dining-hall fare to create an intimate, café-style atmosphere. Students who are committed to a healthy lifestyle can opt to reside in the WELL (Wellness Environment for Living and Learning), which will provide them with a substance-free atmosphere, includes special healthy-living courses, and is overseen by a specially trained wellness staff.

Leisure-time favorites include school-sponsored plays, jazz concerts, arts and crafts fairs, and dances. The nearby Cascades National Park is an especially popular retreat for lovers and camping jocks alike, and tubing down the New River is a ritual for summer students. Thirteen percent of the men and 24 percent of the women join fraternities and sororities, which set the tone of the social life. If going

(continued)

Strongest Programs:
Engineering
Architecture and Urban
    Studies
Business
Sciences
Human Resources and
    Education
Mathematics
Forestry and Wildlife Services

The university also has a tradition of excellence in the performing arts.

Leisure-time favorites include school-sponsored plays, jazz concerts, arts and crafts fairs, and dances.

Greek isn't for you, don't worry. As one student says, "Most students go downtown to shoot pool, dance, or go to a bar." The most important annual events are the Ring Dance (when the juniors receive their school rings), the German Club's Midwinter's Dance, and the Corps of Cadets military ball. Blacksburg offers the usual city fare and one student says the town "revolves around Tech." For real big-city action, Washington, D.C., and Richmond are four and three hours away by car, respectively.

Virginia Tech competes in the Atlantic Coast Conference and the football team's multiple appearances in postseason bowl games have cheered alumni and hiked applications by several thousand. The annual big game pits the Hokies against the Cavaliers of the University of Virginia. Tech has one of the nation's most extensive intramural programs, with everything from football to horseshoes and underwater hockey—a recent rage—and more than 400 softball teams each spring, many of them co-ed. Weekend athletes benefit from the addition of a fitness center.

The Virginia Tech website encourages students to "invent the future," and that's just what today's citizens of the Hokie Nation aim to do. By taking advantage of Tech's particular blend of high-tech learning and Southern hospitality, students have countless opportunities to conduct research, travel abroad, and spend four years with like-minded men and women.

If You Apply To >

Tech: Early decision: Nov. 1. Regular admissions: Jan. 15. Financial aid: Feb. 15. Application fee: $60. No campus or alumni interviews. SATs: required. Subject Tests: optional (required for applicants from non-accredited schools). No essay question.

Wabash College

301 West Wabash, Crawfordsville, IN 47933

Wabash and Hampden–Sydney in Virginia are the last of the all-male breed. With steady enrollment and plenty of money in the bank, Wabash shows no signs of changing. Intense bonding is an important part of the Wabash experience, and few co-ed schools can match the loyalty of Wabash alumni. The Gentleman's Rule says it all.

Wabash was founded in Indiana in 1832 by transplanted Ivy Leaguers who shared the Enlightenment's optimistic view of human nature and envisioned a "classical and English high school rising into a college as soon as the wants of the country demand." Their vision proved to be on target. All-male Wabash has not only prospered but also remained true to its conservative academic and social traditions. "We have a code of self-responsibility," says one senior. "Wabash only has one rule, the Gentleman's Rule. It clearly states that Wabash men are to be responsible citizens on and off campus." Gentlemen or not, Wabash alumni have strong emotional and social ties to their alma mater.

"Wabash only has one rule, the Gentleman's Rule."

The Wabash campus is characterized by redbrick, white-pillared, Federal-style buildings (three are originals from the 1830s). Located in the heart of Crawfordsville, a small town of about 15,000, Wabash is surrounded by grass and tall trees that are part of the gorgeous Fuller Arboretum.

The Wabash educational program has certainly proved itself over the years. This small college has amassed an impressive list of alumni: executives of major corporations, doctors, lawyers, and a large number of Ph.D.s. Wabash alumni are typically faithful to their school in the form of generous donations. On a per-capita basis, the school's $320 million endowment makes it one of the wealthiest in the nation. This financial security enables Wabash to refuse any federal aid, with the exception of Pell Grants, which go directly to students.

Biology and modern languages draw the most majors at Wabash, and the highest accolades go to the biology (premed) and chemistry departments, which are among the most challenging and produce many successful grads. Wabash has an electron microscope and a laser spectrometer, a 180-acre biological field station, and a cell culture lab. Political science and the psychology department are also popular, but students say the "[rhetoric] department is not as academically stringent as others." A 42,600-square-foot fine arts center provides studio space and practice rooms and is a pleasant addition to the music and art departments. Wabash emphasizes its mission as a liberal arts college and the traditional programs have been augmented with cross-cultural immersion learning courses with travel components—at no cost—during spring break or at the end of the semesters to countries such as Peru, Turkey, and Kenya.

> "Professors keep students involved in the class."

General education requirements include courses from a wide variety of fields—natural and behavioral sciences, literature and fine arts, mathematics, language studies, and a course on cultures and traditions. In addition, a freshman tutorial is designed to focus students on reading, writing, and class participation and is followed by new course entitled "Enduring Questions." A special writing center is available for all Wabash students who demonstrate a weakness in written communication skills. Juniors are encouraged to study on continents throughout the world or in various domestic programs through the Great Lakes College Association*. Those who can't satisfy their high-tech interests at Wabash can opt for a 3–2 program in engineering with Columbia University or Washington University in St. Louis, or a dual degree in engineering with Purdue University. Wabash also offers a tuition-free semester after graduation to train students to become teachers. "Professors expect a lot out of their students and peers challenge each other in the classroom, oftentimes in intense class discussions," says one senior. "Students at Wabash are very competitive." Professors are described as engaging and ready to assist. "Professors keep students involved in the class, whether that be through discussion or through meetings during their office hours. They are extremely knowledgeable and very accessible," says one student.

> *Professors are described as engaging and ready to assist.*

Most of Wabash's students come from public high schools in Indiana, and 70 percent were in the top quarter of their high school class. The campus is mostly conservative, though both Republican and Democratic student organizations are strong. One political science major says, "While the all-male nature of Wabash can sometimes lead to a hypermasculine environment, faculty have worked hard to provide opportunities for students to think seriously about gender issues, which leads many students to be even more thoughtful about not only our environment here, but also dynamics that exist outside of Wabash." African Americans comprise 6 percent of the student body, Hispanics 5 percent, Asian Americans 1 percent, and international students 7 percent. Merit scholarships are available to qualified students.

> "Social life is most robust during the fall because of football season."

Residential life for the temporary denizens of small-town Crawfordsville revolves around the nine fraternities, each with its own house. Fifty-one percent of the students join up, and many end up living with their brothers. As an alternative to Greek life, there are three modern dorms, two of which have all single rooms. Dorm residents must eat in the dining hall and food is described as "very diverse and

(continued)

Accepted: 67%
Enrolled: 28%
Grad in 6 Years: 73%
Returning Freshmen: 86%
Academics: ✍ ✍ ✍ ½
Social: ☎ ☎
Q of L: ★ ★ ★
Admissions: (765) 361-6225
Email Address: admissions@ wabash.edu

Strongest Programs:
Prebusiness
Economics
Biology
Chemistry
Premed

edible." Those living in the dorms (and the 13 percent who live off campus) may feel excluded from what there is of campus social life because the fraternities "ship in" sorority members from Butler, DePauw, Indiana, and Purdue for parties. Campus security gets mixed reviews. "I would say that Wabash has a lot of work to do here," says one student. "Campus security is incredibly limited, and the laid-back nature of residential life at Wabash seems to exacerbate this."

The surrounding town of Crawfordsville leaves much to be desired, and students say most (if not all) social life takes place on campus. "The lack of any individuals without a Y chromosome" is a constant complaint, according to one senior. As for drinking on campus, students agree that policies are loose. "There is one rule on campus—act as a gentleman at all times—and this applies to alcohol consumption as well," says a student. Significant campus events include the Monon-Keg rugby game and homecoming. Another popular, though less sweaty, event is Chapel Sing, where all the freshmen sing the lengthy school song in unison. "Social life is most robust during the fall because of football season," says a senior. "That draws a lot of friends from colleges around the state."

The football team has brought home five NCAC championships in the past eight years.

The Little Giants (so named because the 1904 football team was performing above its weight) take their athletics seriously and field a number of solid programs. The football team has brought home five NCAC championships in the past eight years, and track and field has won three consecutive conference titles. Baseball and cross-country are solid, too. When they're not studying or partying, students are likely to be found working out in the gym or running. Eighty percent of students participate in intramurals, which encompass 20 sports, including flag football and softball. School spirit is abundant, especially when the opponent is long-standing rival DePauw and the Monan Bell is at stake.

Traditions have not changed much since the school's founding in the 1830s and still play an important part in the lives of the men at Wabash. Some students complain about the lack of women and culture in the surrounding area, but many are happy with the education they have received. The college prides itself on intensive and rigorous programs. It's a boys club and the students know they will be able to focus on their classes without female distractions during the school week. Says one junior, "Men who are looking to be taken seriously and who want to be challenged and trained on *how* to think rather than *what* to think should choose Wabash."

Overlaps
Indiana University, Purdue, Butler, DePauw, Hanover, Franklin

If You Apply To ➤

Wabash: Early decision: Nov. 15. Early action: Dec. 1. Regular admissions: Jan. 15. Financial aid: Mar. 1. Housing: Jun. 2. Application fee: $40. Campus and alumni interviews: optional, informational. SATs or ACTs: required. Accepts the Common Application. Essay question.

Wake Forest University

Winston-Salem, NC 27109

Wake Forest's Baptist heritage and Winston-Salem location give it a more down-home flavor than Duke or Emory. With just under 4,800 undergraduates, Wake Forest is small compared with its ACC rivals but bigger than most liberal arts colleges. The strong Greek system dominates the social scene. Holds its own in the Atlantic Coast Conference with universities more than five times its size.

Already one of the top private schools in the Southeast, Wake Forest is working to transform its regional recognition into a national reputation. Long known for basketball—at least half the student body attends every home game, one junior says—Wake Forest's solid academics are worthy of a look as well. Students work hard, hence the nickname "Work Forest," but the university's size and strong Greek system means it's also easy to establish close friendships. "Wake Forest is the best of both worlds," says a political science major. "Academics are challenging and you're surrounded by motivated and intelligent peers. At the same time, students pride themselves on being social."

> **"Most students manage an active social calendar, multiple extracurriculars, and a demanding courseload."**

Located in the Central Piedmont region of North Carolina, Wake Forest's 340-acre campus features flowers, wooded trails, and stately magnolias. There are more than 40 Georgian-style buildings constructed of old Virginia brick with granite trim. That new mortar and stone complements the school's lush surroundings, including the 148-acre Reynolda Gardens annex, with a formal garden and greenhouses. The garden features one of the first collections of Japanese cherry trees in the U.S. In 2011, the university opened a new, 23,000-square-foot welcome center featuring public meeting spaces, staff offices, and a 260-seat auditorium. Two new residence halls opened in 2013.

To graduate from Wake Forest, students must complete two courses in health and exercise science, one foreign language course, a writing seminar, and a first-year seminar. In addition, students must take two courses in history, religion, or philosophy; one in literature; one in fine arts; two in the social and behavioral sciences; and two in the natural sciences, math, and computer science. Students must also satisfy quantitative reasoning and cultural diversity requirements. Popular programs include business, communication, political science, biology, and psychology.

A junior says the academic environment is "a competitive climate that encourages students to retain a professional and intellectually serious approach to academics." The Institute for Public Engagement allows students to put their skills and knowledge to work helping the community; the center takes its name from the school's motto, which means "In Service to Humanity." Exceptionally able students may qualify for the "Honors in Arts and Sciences" distinction by taking three or more honors seminars during their first three years. Faculty members get high marks; graduate assistants may teach labs, but professors are at the lectern during larger classes and at the head of the table in many seminars. "The teachers at Wake Forest are dedicated to not only challenging students through innovative and rigorous assignments, but also by allowing them to explore the ideas brought up in the classroom through interactive lessons, as well as through individual exploration in the real world," says one communications major. Richter Fellowships fund collaborative research between students and faculty members. And for those who get claustrophobic in Winston-Salem, Wake Forest's own residential study centers on the Grand Canal in Venice and in London and Vienna beckon. Sixty percent of the student body studies abroad and there are programs available in 200 cities in more than 70 countries worldwide.

"Students at Wake Forest pride themselves at being multifaceted and diversely talented," says a history major. "Most students manage an active social calendar, multiple extracurriculars, and a demanding courseload." While Wake Forest students travel the globe sampling foreign cultures, life on campus is fairly homogeneous. Twenty-three percent of the student body hails from North Carolina; many others come from nearby Southern states. African Americans make up 8 percent of the university's student population, Asian Americans add 5 percent, and Hispanics contribute 6 percent, though Wake Forest's efforts to boost diversity continue. "We are not a politically active school," a senior explains. "Students tend to be very

Website: www.wfu.edu
Location: Suburban
Private
Total Enrollment: 7,253
Undergraduates: 4,741
Male/Female: 48/52
SAT Ranges: CR 620–700, M 630–710
ACT Ranges: 29–31
Financial Aid: 56%
Expense: Pr $ $ $
Student Loans: 38%
Average Debt: $ $ $ $
Phi Beta Kappa: Yes
Applicants: 11,407
Accepted: 34%
Enrolled: 32%
Grad in 6 Years: 88%
Returning Freshmen: 94%
Academics: ✍ ✍ ✍ ✍
Social: ☎ ☎ ☎
Q of L: ★ ★ ★
Admissions: (336) 758-5201
Email Address: admissions@wfu.edu

Strongest Programs:
Business and Enterprise Management
Psychology
Political Science
Communication
Finance

Sixty percent of the student body studies abroad and there are programs available in 200 cities in more than 70 countries worldwide.

conservative," adds a sophomore. Qualified students receive scholarships based on academic merit, and the average award is approximately $11,739. There are also several hundred athletic scholarships.

Sixty-eight percent of students live on campus; freshmen are required to do so, and everyone else is guaranteed housing, unless they move off campus and later decide to return. "As at any college, there is a vast range of quality of dorms. Those built last year are inevitably nicer than those built in the 1970s. However, all dorms and apartments are comfortable," a freshman reports. Dining options continue to draw jeers from students. "The cafeteria food sucks," gripes one particularly blunt student. "The other dining options on campus are acceptable—but barely." On the other hand, students say campus security is excellent. "Only minor instances of crime are reported," a junior says.

"The social life at Wake Forest is extremely vibrant and constantly moving, you just have to know what you're looking for," says a junior. Thirty-eight percent of men and 52 percent of women go Greek; fraternities have open parties on and off campus, and sororities have date functions and other invite-only events. "The social life at Wake Forest is heavily dominated by the Greek system," says a student. "However, other organizations, such as Student Union, make a huge effort to bring other social options, such as concerts, movies, and events, to campus." Underage students find it difficult to obtain alcohol at campus parties, so many venture off campus to imbibe. The school's honor code helps to keep rowdy behavior in check; as one student says, "If you are caught with alcohol, and you are under 21, there are strict consequences." Everyone enjoys the annual homecoming festivities, and after the Demon Deacons score a victory on the basketball court, students roll the quad in toilet paper to celebrate. Other favorite events include a midnight concert by the school orchestra every Halloween, with members in full costume, and the Lilting Banshees comedy troupe, which helps students laugh off their stressful workloads. Popular road trips are to the beach or the mountains; Chapel Hill, Durham, and Raleigh are each 100 miles away, and Atlanta and the Washington/Baltimore areas are about five hours' drive.

> "The social life at Wake Forest is extremely vibrant and constantly moving, you just have to know what you're looking for."

The city of Winston-Salem is rich in culture, with a symphony, a Christmastime "Moravian love feast," and the well-known Carolina School of the Arts. It's also home to the corporate headquarters of Krispy Kreme Doughnuts. "Winston is a very suburban town with a lot of young families and a Southern feel," a student says. In addition to Wake's on-campus Museum of Anthropology, a number of art museums—Reynolda House, the Museum of American Art, and Southeastern Center for Contemporary Art—are within three miles of campus. The town also has a strong music scene, with live bands playing at Ziggy's and the Garage. Popular volunteer activities include Project Pumpkin, a trick-or-treat night on campus for underprivileged children.

When it comes to sports, basketball is the undisputed king at Wake Forest. The men's team competes in the incredibly tough Atlantic Coast Conference and is perennially strong. Other solid teams include baseball, men's and women's golf, men's and women's tennis, and men's and women's soccer. Of course, virtually any contest against in-state rival UNC at Chapel Hill is guaranteed to get students excited. Intramural and club sports are also offered; the most popular intramurals include soccer, basketball, and flag football, though volleyball, water polo, and bowling are available, too. "Fun supersedes talent," a senior says. "Students are rarely left out of a particular game if they express interest in participating."

That spirit of involvement and dedication to the community pervades the Wake Forest experience. Whether students are serving the less fortunate or chipping away at their heavy workloads, they benefit from motivated peers, dedicated faculty, and

Overlaps

University of North Carolina, University of Virginia, Vanderbilt, Emory, Duke, University of Notre Dame, Davidson, Boston College

gorgeous surroundings. "Learning to work under pressure and time constraints is pivotal to your future success," one student explains. "Wake students receive not only the advantage of small classes, but also the benefits of a big-name school for the next step in their lives."

<table>
<tr><td>If You Apply To ➤</td><td>Wake Forest: Early decision: Nov. 15. Regular admissions: Jan. 1. Application fee: $50. Campus and alumni interviews: optional, evaluative. SATs or ACTs (with writing): optional. Subject Tests: optional. Accepts the Common Application. Essay question.</td></tr>
</table>

Warren Wilson College

P.O. Box 9000, Asheville, NC 28815-9000

Among a handful of schools where students combine academics, community service, and on-campus work that helps keep tuition down. Roots in the culture of Appalachia combine with a strong international and environmental orientation to give Warren Wilson its unique flavor. Setting in the mountains of western North Carolina is tough to beat. Campus atmosphere ranges from liberal to alternative.

Warren Wilson, a small liberal arts college, is flush with engaging little quirks. It promotes global perspectives, puts students to work on the campus farm, and makes service learning a central part of the educational experience. The school is also at the forefront of the "green" movement and has partnered with the city of Asheville to purchase offsets for 100 percent of its carbon emission. And at what other college is white-water paddling considered a leading intercollegiate sport? "Probably the most notable thing about Warren Wilson students is that we are a very expressive group," says a senior. "We wear the clothes that we want to wear, we dance and sing and play music, we talk about whatever comes to mind. This is a place where you can be whoever you want and you don't get judged for it. "

Founded by the Presbyterian Church in 1894 as the Asheville Farm School, Warren Wilson College initially provided formal schooling for "mountain boys." In 1967, it evolved into a four-year, co-ed liberal arts college that, while still maintaining its Presbyterian ties, welcomes students of all backgrounds. WWC is located 15 minutes from downtown Asheville in the lush Swannanoa Valley of the Blue Ridge Mountains. Its 1,132-acre campus features formal gardens, fruit and vegetable gardens, a 300-acre farm, and a myriad of hiking trails. Consistent with campus culture, the wood and stone buildings are small in scale and done in an architectural style that emphasizes natural earth tones accented by extensive stonework by traditional Appalachian stonemasons. The campus is home to one of the most important Cherokee archeological sites in the Southern Appalachian Mountains, dating from as early as 5,000 B.C. WWC is also home to North Carolina Outward Bound, an organization with which it has close ties, and the Mountain Area Child and Family Center, which serves as a laboratory school for students of education, psychology, and social work.

The signature feature of the WWC curriculum is its unique Triad Education Program, which combines liberal arts coursework, community service, and campus work. Students may choose from 40 majors and concentrations and 27 minors. The most popular majors are environmental studies, biology, English/creative writing,

"Classes are mostly informal with lots of discussion based learning."

Website: www.warren-wilson.edu
Location: City Outskirts
Private
Total Enrollment: 913
Undergraduates: 841
Male/Female: 39/61
SAT Ranges: CR 500–650, M 480–590
ACT Ranges: 23–28
Financial Aid: 92%
Expense: Pr $
Student Loans: 59%
Average Debt: $ $
Phi Beta Kappa: No
Applicants: 955
Accepted: 72%
Enrolled: 22%
Grad in 6 Years: 57%
Returning Freshmen: 68%
Academics: ✐ ✐ ✐ ½
Social: ☎ ☎ ☎
Q of L: ★ ★ ★ ★ ★
Admissions: (800) 934-3536
Email Address: admit@warren-wilson.edu

Strongest Programs:
Art

Warren Wilson College initially provided formal schooling for "mountain boys."

history/political science, and global studies. To graduate, students have to perform at least 100 hours of service learning through organizations such as Habitat for Humanity or environmental organizations. Warren Wilson is also one of only a half dozen four-year colleges in the nation that requires all residential students to work on campus. To fulfill their weekly 15-hour work requirement, students do electrical work, plumbing, and landscaping; clean the dorms; tend the farm animals; and maintain the campus gardens.

To meet general education requirements, WWC students take at least one class within each of the school's eight liberal arts areas: language and global issues, literature, history and political science, natural science, mathematics, social science, philosophy and religion, and artistic expression. They must also take two college composition courses. The First-Year Experience Program lays a foundation for academic success by introducing students to the study-serve-work trinity through small, interactive group activities. All first-year students enroll in the First-Year Seminar, which includes field experience and/or a service-learning component that takes students and faculty off campus for a day or a weekend.

Fifty-five percent of students study abroad during their time at WWC. Juniors take a semester-long course and then spend several weeks on an international "field experience"—with the cost partly built into their regular tuition—and qualified students may also study for a semester or two in countries such as Guatemala, Costa Rica, Italy, Scotland, Greece, and Vietnam. The college offers honors programs in biology, chemistry, English, environmental studies, math, and computer science; 5 percent of students enroll. Internship opportunities are available in most undergraduate programs, and there are dual-degree programs in pre-environmental management, preforestry, and applied science. The Appalachian Studies program serves as a catalyst for local cultural activities, including numerous musical groups. The integrative studies major allows students to develop and complete individually designed majors. And where else does the music department offer you the choice of "finger-picking" or "flat-picking" guitar?

Students say hard work is the norm, but the atmosphere is relaxed. "Classes are mostly informal with lots of discussion-based learning, especially in the upper-level classes," says a history major. "However, this does not mean that classes are easy. In fact, the amount of homework can be overwhelming sometimes." Creative writing and the natural sciences receive high marks from students, but music and physics could use improvement. Seventy-one percent of classes have 19 or fewer students, and students say the quality of teaching is generally good, thanks to experienced teachers. "The teaching quality, except for a few anomalies, is of the highest caliber," says a senior.

"The typical Warren Wilson student is passionate, outspoken, and willing to work hard. Many are very open minded and embrace alternative ways of looking at the world," says a global studies major. A sophomore adds, "There are people here who hate being outside, and there are people here who never want to be inside. There are gamers, farmers, writers, and everything in between. I guess if there's one

"The typical Warren Wilson student is passionate, outspoken, and willing to work hard."

thing that is common is that we are all pretty open to new ideas and like engaging in open, intellectual conversations about the world." Upon graduation, most go into service professions such as teaching or working for environmental or other nongovernmental organizations. The first step for many is into the Peace Corps. Eighty percent of the student body hail from out of state and approximately three-quarters attended public school. African Americans and Hispanics account for 4 percent and 2 percent, respectively, while Asian Americans account for 1 percent. The campus is a "hive of activism," a freshman says, and hot campus issues include diversity, sexual assault, and climate change. Merit scholarships averaging $3,000 are available, but there are no athletic scholarships.

Ninety percent of students live in dorms. "Generally the quality of the dorm that you live in depends on seniority, because that is how rooms are selected," explains a student. "The freshmen dorms are no great shakes, but if you preservere things will get better." The 36-bed EcoDorm—the first building on a college campus to achieve LEED Platinum certification in the category of Existing Buildings—incorporates solar heating and natural ventilation, and is made of hardwoods milled on campus. Overall, housing is plentiful and well maintained (unless the student workforce slacks off). Dining is a treat, and there are plenty of edible options, including vegetarian and vegan meals. The student-run Cow Pie Café serves mostly foods grown on campus. "The menu in the cafeteria is like clockwork—very predictable," says a student. Security is said to be adequate. "Public Safety makes me feel safe within the community," says a junior.

> "Public Safety makes me feel safe."

Social life is "centered on campus," according to one student. Another adds, "Ninety percent of students live on the campus, so dorm parties and other social gatherings are a weekend staple. However, most students are not involved in the party scene, and I would say that the primary way in which people socialize is by dropping by someone else's dorm room to hang out." Despite the absence of Greek organizations, students find plenty of ways to have fun and blow off steam. The outing club is the largest on campus and sponsors weekly hiking, skiing, or other excursions. Students of legal drinking age are allowed to imbibe indoors, and students say it's very easy for underage students to obtain alcohol. "The unofficial policy is that if you are being respectful and responsible, no one is going to question your actions," says one student. Popular events include Mayhem (a parade in May) and homecoming, which features live bluegrass music, a barbecue, hay rides, and dancing.

Asheville is "definitely not a traditional college town, but it has tons to offer," says an elementary education major. Museums, cafés, theaters, music clubs, and the symphony are only 15 minutes away. "The downtown scene is amazing for the relative small size of the town," says a student. Thanks to the college's service requirement, students take an active role in the community through volunteer work. WWC sponsors short-term service projects during vacation breaks, and students camp out overnight in order to qualify for the annual trip to Cumberland Island off the coast of Georgia. Popular road trips include Atlanta and the beaches of South Carolina, but the best excursions "are to protests and political events or camping and backpacking trips," according to a political science major.

> "There are no big sports teams or other rivalries."

The signature feature of the WWC curriculum is its unique Triad Education Program.

Students say hard work is the norm, but the atmosphere is relaxed.

In a state famed for its rabid sports fans, Warren Wilson students are decidedly laid-back about athletics. "There are no big sports teams or other rivalries," says a freshman. "Students come here largely because they don't like those rivalries. There is a great sense of school spirit, nonetheless." The Fighting Owls are members of the Collegiate Athletic Association and competitive sports include men's basketball (2013 conference champions), mountain biking (with 10 consecutive top four finishes), road cycling, basketball, cross-country, soccer, and swimming. Thirty percent of WWC students participate in intramural or recreational sports, which range from rock climbing to tennis to basketball. Students have access to myriad facilities, including soccer fields, basketball courts, an indoor pool, and a fitness center.

Success at Warren Wilson is measured not only by grades, but by community service and a sense of stewardship. "It's a pretty self-selecting school," a junior advises. "If you aren't attracted to the ideals we hold dear here, don't come." Those who aren't afraid to get their hands dirty will see this small liberal arts college as a valuable place that combines the notion of thinking globally with acting locally.

Overlaps

Hampshire, Earlham, UNC Asheville, Guilford, Appalachian State, Evergreen, Lewis & Clark, Reed

University of Washington

1410 N.E. Campus Parkway, Seattle, WA 98195

UDub wows visitors with its sprawling parklike campus in hugely popular Seattle. Washington is tougher than University of Oregon for out-of-state admission but not as hard as UC heavyweights Berkeley or UCLA. Location near the coast and mountains makes for strong marine and environmental studies programs. Has recently increased its percentage of out-of-staters in an effort to balance the budget.

Website: www.washington
.edu

Location: Urban

Public

Total Enrollment: 36,905

Undergraduates: 25,995

Male/Female: 48/52

SAT Ranges: CR 520–650,
M 580–700

ACT Ranges: 24–30

Financial Aid: 44%

Expense: Pub $ $ $

Student Loans: 49%

Average Debt: $

Phi Beta Kappa: Yes

Applicants: 26,138

Accepted: 59%

Enrolled: 39%

Grad in 6 Years: 80%

Returning Freshmen: 93%

Academics: ✏ ✏ ✏ ✏ ½

Social: ☎ ☎ ☎

Q of L: ★ ★ ★

Admissions: (206) 543-9686

Email Address: info@uwb
.edu

Strongest Programs:

Business

English

Psychology

Drama

Engineering

Computer Science

Washington has cemented its reputation as a solid research institution. In fact, UW has been the number one public university in federal research funding since 1974.

"Housing is almost always full." Students here understand that anonymity and size are the prices that must be paid for the wealth of opportunities that await them. Those looking for an extra-personal touch might want to investigate the school's two branch campuses in Tacoma and Bothell, where class sizes average 25 students. But if the Seattle campus is your focus, one senior hints, just "learn to work the system."

Washington's Seattle campus blends Gothic architecture and the lush, green landscape of the Pacific Northwest. It features a number of distinctive landmarks. Red Square sits atop the Central Plaza parking garage and features the Broken Obelisk, a 26-foot-high steel sculpture gifted to the university by the Virginia Wright Fund. All of the university's energy comes from renewable resources (including, of course, hydropower) and, despite campus growth, UW has reduced its overall energy use.

Many of Washington's diverse undergraduate strengths correspond with its excellent graduate programs. The competitive business major, for example, benefits from the university's highly regarded business school and is the most popular undergraduate major, followed by biology, art, and English. Similarly, students majoring in public health, community medicine, pharmacy, and nursing profit from access to facilities and faculty at the medical school, an international leader in cancer and heart research, cell biology, and organ transplants. Also recommended for undergraduates are biological and life sciences and most engineering programs, especially computer science, computer engineering, and bioengineering. Reflecting the focus on natural resources in Washington's economy, the program in fisheries is excellent, as are earth and atmospheric sciences, including oceanography.

"All of the teachers I've had have been passionate about the courses they teach."

Undergraduates in both professional and liberal arts programs must take five credits in English composition, seven credits in writing beyond composition, and one course in quantitative and symbolic reasoning. Students must also fulfill 40 credits in general education requirements, including the arts, individuals and societies, and the natural world. Schools and colleges also have their own requirements that must be met. Many Washington professors are tops in their field, but students may have to be patient about seeing professors after class. Like other major state universities, UW faces budget difficulties, resulting in larger classes and limited course selection. Still, students say they rarely have trouble getting into desired classes. Approximately one-third of the classes have 19 or fewer students. "The faculty is top-notch," raves one sophomore. "All of the teachers I've had have been passionate about the courses they teach."

For those interested in skirting the masses, UW sports an honors program that offers small classes on interesting subjects taught by fine professors. The academic environment at UW is "fairly competitive and students have to work hard to do well," according to an international studies major. "Classes can be challenging." And if students get the itch to see some different scenery, there are 70 different study abroad programs offered in 20 countries, including China, Denmark, and Russia. A program in experiential learning encourages students to find internships and participate in community service. This fits in with a variety of classes that give students the opportunity to volunteer as part of their coursework. A senior says, "There's simply no better way to learn than by combining challenging courses with real-world experience. When you're learning in the classroom, you can't always apply it. Experience adds to your learning, and it helps you remember it." Freshmen are given special attention via the Freshman Interest Group (FIG) program, which offers freshmen a chance to meet, discuss, and study with other freshmen who have similar interests. Each FIG consists of 20 to 24 students who share a cluster of classes (which meet graduation requirements), and includes a weekly seminar led by a junior or senior peer advisor. Also of interest to freshmen are General Studies 101, an optional two-credit course designed to help students meet the demands and expectations of college life, and Freshman Seminars, one-credit courses with 10 or 12 other freshmen.

Part of the reason for UW's national anonymity is the fact that it turns away large numbers of out-of-state applicants, preferring to keep its focus on the home folks. Students tend to "come from all walks of life and from all over the world," says a senior. "They are go-getters and active in the world around them." Sixty-seven percent of undergraduates are state residents, and an unusually large proportion are over the age of 25. The student body is 14 percent Asian American, with Hispanics, Native Americans, and African Americans combining for another 5 percent. Students say the school strives for diversity by offering Valuing Diversity workshops to foster increased awareness of and sensitivity to individual differences. Merit scholarships averaging more than $4,000 are awarded to Washington residents with good high school records and test scores. Athletic scholarships are awarded to men and women in 21 sports, including swimming, women's gymnastics, golf, tennis, and track and field.

> "The dorms and fraternities seem to contain the most social activity."

Two-thirds of freshmen live in the school's eight co-ed dorms. "Students who choose to live on campus have to apply for housing well in advance as so many students apply to live in the dorms," says one student. "Housing is almost always full." Hagget provides a comfortable setting for freshmen, and McMahon is recommended for those inclined to party. Housing is also available for married students, and the fraternity and sorority organizations are home to 6 percent of the men and 5 percent of the women. The rest live off campus in Seattle or other parts of King County. Each dorm has its own cafeteria and fast-food line based on a debit card system. The Husky Union Building also offers a dining hall, espresso bar (don't forget, this is Seattle!), writing center, sun deck, and lounges. "The food is decent," reports a junior. "It is restaurant style, so there are lots of choices."

Given the large number of commuters, it's no surprise that most of Washington's social life takes place away from campus, except for the Greeks (members of a combined total of 48 fraternities and sororities). "The dorms and fraternities seem to

(continued)
Architecture
Biology

UW sports an honors program that offers small classes on interesting subjects taught by fine professors.

Part of the reason for UW's national anonymity is the fact that it turns away large numbers of out-of-state applicants.

contain the most social activity, and what they lack is made up for by the proximity to downtown Seattle," says one student. A junior adds, "On campus there are over 550 registered student organizations, so you can pretty much guarantee that there is a group for you." Neither dormies nor Greeks are supposed to drink if they're under 21. Sooner or later most students hit "the Ave," University Way, where shops and restaurants await them. A 10-minute bus ride connects students to a full array of urban offerings in Seattle. The Seattle Center and other venues host outstanding operas, symphonies, and touring shows, while Qwest Field houses the NFL's Seahawks and Safeco Field the MLB Mariners. But who needs pro sports with Washington's Huskies around? Husky Fever breaks out on every football weekend, and the stands are always packed for UW's team, especially when Washington State comes to town to vie for the coveted Apple Cup. Other strong UW teams include women's basketball, crew, cross-country, and tennis, and men's crew, basketball, baseball, soccer, and tennis.

More than anything else, the great outdoors defines the University of Washington. The campus offers breathtaking views of Lake Washington and the Olympic Mountains. Outdoor pastimes for students include boating, hiking, camping, and skiing, all found nearby, and Canada is close enough for road trips to Vancouver. The weather is consistently temperate, and natives insist that the city's reputation for rain is undeserved. Then again, the sports stadium has an overhang to protect spectators from showers.

While some students will not appreciate the no-nonsense and occasionally impersonal academic programs and the lack of a centralized social life, many students can overlook these obstacles for the big picture of the up-and-coming University of Washington—one that takes in more than just the beautiful scenery.

Overlaps

UC–Berkeley, UCLA, University of Oregon, University of Southern California, Washington State, Western Washington

If You Apply To ➤

Washington: Rolling admissions: Dec. 1. Application fee: $60. No campus or alumni interviews. SATs or ACTs (with writing): required. Subject Tests: optional. Essay question: personal statement. Primarily committed to state residents.

Washington and Jefferson College

60 South Lincoln Street, Washington, PA 15301

Premed Central would be as good a name as any for W&J, which has one of the nation's highest proportions of students who go on to medical school. Law school and business school are also popular destinations. The tenor of life is conservative and the Greek system dominates the social life. Smaller and less national than Allegheny; a notch above Hiram and Westminster.

Website: www.washjeff.edu
Location: Small Town
Private
Total Enrollment: 1,387
Undergraduates: 1,387
Male/Female: 49/51
SAT Ranges: CR 520–610, M 520–620

Wannabe doctors and lawyers would be well-advised to give Washington and Jefferson College a look. This small Pennsylvania college is renowned for its prepro-fessional programs and graduates are almost guaranteed acceptance into medical or health-related graduate programs. Classes remain small here and, despite the some-what rural location, students enjoy an active social life thanks to a hearty Greek scene and the nearby city of Pittsburgh. "W&J is unique in that it's like a mullet," explains one sophomore: "Business up front with a party in the back."

The campus, like the student body, is tight-knit: More than 50 buildings sit on 60 acres in a small town about 30 miles outside of Pittsburgh. W&J is the

11th-oldest college in the country and houses the eighth-oldest college building, which was built in 1793. Famous songwriter Stephen Foster was a student here—at least until he was kicked out. The prevailing architectural style is traditional colonial/Georgian, though modern structures have been added at a rapid pace during the past two decades. The four-story Howard J. Burnett Center houses the economics, business and accounting, modern languages, education, and entrepreneurial studies departments, and the Office of Lifelong Learning. The Technology Center includes computer labs and a video-conferencing center. The $33 million John A. Swanson Science Center is home to the physical sciences, including physics, chemistry, and biochemistry.

Graduation requirements call for students to complete 32 full-semester courses and two intercession courses. They must also demonstrate proficiency in writing, speaking, reading, quantitative reasoning, foreign language, and use of information technology. Students must take credits in culture and intellectual tradition, fine arts, language and literature, science and mathematics, and social sciences. Students must satisfy language, cultural diversity, and physical education and wellness requirements. A thematic major allows students to design their own course of study, while double majors produce such types as a biologist well versed in literature. Rare among liberal arts colleges are the 3–4 programs with the Pennsylvania Colleges of Optometry and Podiatry. More technically minded students can take advantage of the 3–2 engineering programs with Case Western Reserve and Washington University in St. Louis. Business administration, psychology, English, political science, and biology are the most popular majors. The Magellan Project enables participating students to put their liberal arts education to work through study abroad, domestic and international internships, and undergraduate research.

> "The classes are competitive and challenging."

W&J's formula for success starts with individual attention in small classes; 70 percent of freshman classes have 19 students or fewer. "The academics are rigorous, and I spend most or all of my weekends studying, reading, or doing homework," says one junior. Fifty-seven percent of students ranked in the top quarter of their high school class, and most agree the academic climate at W&J is tough, especially for those on the premed and prelaw tracks. "The classes are competitive and challenging, but not impossible," a student confirms. Full professors teach most classes. "I have been taught by dedicated professors who really care about what I learn," a student says.

During the January intersession, students find brief apprenticeships in prospective career areas, take a school tour abroad (locations include the Bahamas, Australia, London, Russia, China, Africa, Brazil, and Eastern Europe), or engage in nontraditional coursework. There is also a semester- or year-abroad option in Germany, Moscow, Russia, or Bogotá, Colombia. Other study abroad opportunities are also available in Australia, Europe, Asia, and Latin America.

"The students are really upper- to middle-class white kids," says one student. Indeed, diversity is not W&J's strong suit: 70 percent of the students hail from Pennsylvania and many are from neighboring states in the Northeast. Three percent of students are African American, 3 percent Hispanic, and 2 percent Asian American. "The students are well educated, critical thinkers, and very active (whether in the community, Greek, student

> "The students are really upper- to middle-class white kids."

organizations, theater/arts, and so on)," says a psychology major. Students get a bargain at this somewhat pricey school if they win one of the several hundred academic scholarships that average $13,170. There are no athletic scholarships, and the school doesn't guarantee to meet students' full demonstrated need, but the

(continued)

ACT Ranges: 23–28
Financial Aid: 99%
Expense: Pr $ $
Student Loans: 78%
Average Debt: N/A
Phi Beta Kappa: Yes
Applicants: 6,504
Accepted: 41%
Enrolled: 14%
Grad in 6 Years: 74%
Returning Freshmen: 83%
Academics: ✏️ ✏️ ✏️
Social: ☎ ☎ ☎
Q of L: ★ ★
Admissions: (724) 223-6025
Email Address: admission@ washjeff.edu

Strongest Programs:
Premed
Prelaw
Business Administration
Biology
English

W&J's formula for success starts with individual attention in small classes.

same package is promised for a student's four years at the college. The Give It Forward Together (GIFT) program raises funds specifically to help in-need students remain in school.

Students can live in either co-ed or single-sex dorms, and 91 percent of students live on campus. Housing is guaranteed for four years and dorms are described as comfortable and well maintained. "The dorms are quite well taken care of and the maintenance staff works hard to ensure that everything works as it needs to," says one student. Students also say the freshman dorms are fair, but the choices get better with academic rank, and on-campus apartments are available based on GPA, activities, and need. Campus vittles are reportedly "very edible" and diverse.

The Greek scene is active and draws 37 percent of the men and 43 percent of the women. A crackdown on alcohol and noise violations has somewhat dampened the school's tradition of enormous parties, but the Student Activity Board has begun filling the gap with more on-campus events, such as free movies, and a student-run coffeehouse provides another nonfrat option. "W&J provides plenty of social options," says a junior. "We have the HUB with flat-screen televisions, Wii, Netflix, pool tables, a Ping-Pong table, and a café where students get free food and milkshakes every weekend!" A nonalcoholic pub called George & Tom's has become quite a popular diversion with comedy, musical, and novelty/variety acts. During the course of the year, the Spring Street Fair and Spring Concert are the most popular events. "Social life is nice because the college is small and you have a chance to build close friendships," a freshman says.

"Intramurals are huge on campus."

Students can also head home on the weekends or explore dating opportunities at nearby colleges, most notably Penn State and the University of Pittsburgh. One of the most popular excursions is a 30-minute commute to Pittsburgh. Still, not all students share the administration's appreciation for "the unique characteristics of the western Pennsylvania milieu." Many complain that there is nothing to do in this former steel/mining town, now hit by hard times. "Washington doesn't have much to offer in the way of entertainment," says a student. "Most people just take the drive to Pittsburgh," adds another. Townies tend to be a bit resentful of dressy W&J undergrads, but students try to assuage this attitude by actively volunteering in the community.

Just about anyone has a shot at varsity sports where the teams are known, naturally, as the Presidents. Competitive teams include men's football, baseball, and golf and women's basketball, golf, and soccer. Forty-one percent of students participate in intramural and recreational sports, with flag football, basketball, and bowling attracting the most interest. "Intramurals are huge on campus. People can get very competitive and it becomes a big deal," a student says. There are also numerous clubs to join, from the equestrian club to the student theater company.

With state-of-the-art facilities, and expanding academic options, the leadership at W&J is opening more and more doors for students. Students praise the education they receive, the professors who give it to them, and the climate in which they receive it. "My experience here is unforgettable," a senior says. "I have made lifelong friends and gained so much."

Overlaps

Penn State, University of Pittsburgh, Allegheny, Westminster, Saint Vincent, Duquesne, Robert Morris, College of Wooster

If You Apply To ➤

W&J: Early decision: Dec. 1. Early action: Jan. 15. Regular admissions: Mar. 3. Financial aid: Feb. 15. Application fee: $25 (paper), free (online). Campus interviews: optional, evaluative. No alumni interviews. SATs or ACTs: optional. Subject Tests: optional. Accepts the Common Application. Essay question.

Washington and Lee University

Lexington, VA 24450

Coeducation came to tradition-bound W&L, and the pillars of the Colonnade did not come tumbling down. Twenty-eight years after women were admitted, W&L is the most selective small college in the South, rivaled only by Davidson. W&L supplements the liberal arts with strong programs in business and journalism. Picture-postcard campus is three hours from Washington, D.C.

Washington and Lee University, which shares the town of Lexington, Virginia, with the Virginia Military Institute, has always epitomized Southern gentility. The Fancy Dress Ball is a highlight of each year, and "the Speaking Tradition," tracing its roots to Robert E. Lee, results in at least casual communication between members of the W&L community when they pass one another on the well-manicured grounds. But this is not your grandfather's W&L. Women have been on the scene for nearly three decades, and today's atmosphere is a little less 19th-century and a little more 21st-century—as befits one of the South's leading liberal arts colleges. Says one junior, "W&L feels like a college should."

W&L's wooded campus sits atop a hill of lush green lawns, sweeping from one national landmark to another. Redbrick buildings feature white Doric columns and the prevailing architectural style is Greek Revival, although the physical face is changing. The school boasts the John W. Elrod University Commons, which contains a dining hall, movie theater, and bookstore. The Hillel House features a café and conference rooms, and renovations continue on the historic Colonnade. The chapel is the burial site of Robert E. Lee.

Although a standard liberal arts program remains the foundation of W&L's curriculum, the university offers excellent preprofessional programs, particularly business, economics, and accounting, through the Williams School of Commerce, Economics, and Politics. Journalism and mass communications are popular, as are history and English. W&L also has bachelor's degree programs in fields as diverse as Russian area studies and East Asian languages and literature, engineering, and neuroscience. Typically, 51 percent of all students spend time abroad and options include more than 50 destination countries. The Spring Term has been transformed into a single, four-week experience intended to offer students and faculty more innovative approaches to teaching and learning.

> "W&L feels like a college should."

General education requirements account for one-third of a student's coursework. Distribution requirements at W&L include courses in literature, fine arts, history, philosophy, and religion; one course in science and math; social science courses; four terms of physical education; proficiency in swimming; and two years of a foreign language.

"Classes are quite competitive, but this is balanced out by a strong community of help including both professors and other students," a freshman says. Classes tend to be small—71 percent have 19 or fewer students—and freshmen can count on getting professors; there are no teaching assistants. Says one student, "Professors are all extremely qualified and many have been published and are well-known names in their field." The famous Honor System ("The foundation of all areas of the school," according to one student) lends a relaxed feeling to the otherwise rigorous academic climate. Tests and final exams are taken without faculty supervision; doors remain unlocked, laptops stay on desks, and library stacks are open 24 hours a day. Well-qualified students can apply for the Robert E. Lee Undergraduate Research Program,

Website: www.wlu.edu
Location: Small Town
Private
Total Enrollment: 2,291
Undergraduates: 1,834
Male/Female: 51/49
SAT Ranges: CR 650–740, M 650–740
ACT Ranges: 29–32
Financial Aid: 49%
Expense: Pr $ $ $
Student Loans: 31%
Average Debt: $ $
Phi Beta Kappa: Yes
Applicants: 5,972
Accepted: 19%
Enrolled: 41%
Grad in 6 Years: 90%
Returning Freshmen: 95%
Academics: ✎ ✎ ✎ ✎ ½
Social: ☎ ☎ ☎
Q of L: ★ ★ ★ ★
Admissions: (540) 458-8710
Email Address: admissions@wlu.edu

Strongest Programs:
Business
History
Politics
English
Journalism
Economics

which offers students paid fellowships for assisting professors in research or doing their own.

"Generally, the students here fit into the classic Southern prep school image," says one student. "They, however, are among the most honorable, generous, and friendly people I have ever met." Although students can be cliquish, on the whole this is a friendly campus. Though the atmosphere is still more traditional than at most leading liberal arts colleges, the days of rock-ribbed conservatism are gone. Middle-of-the-road is perhaps the best way to describe the political leanings of today's W&L student body. African Americans account for a modest 3 percent of the student body, though the school insists that it is strongly committed to recruiting African American students; Hispanics make up 3 percent, and Asian Americans 3 percent. Fourteen percent of students are native Virginians, but students northeast of D.C. are well represented, making up more than 30 percent of the student body. The number of applications continues to rise dramatically, as do the median SAT scores of each freshman class, and the acceptance rate is below 20 percent. Washington and Lee offers merit-based awards averaging $31,000.

Fifty-nine percent of students reside on campus. Students spend their first year at W&L in co-ed dorms which are "definitely not five-star accommodations," according to one student. Still, "many students see the freshman living experience as a rite

"Professors are all extremely qualified."

of passage." Upperclassmen dorms and apartments are available, and many students move into country houses when they are juniors or seniors. Freshmen must purchase a meal plan and "dining is good for freshmen," says one student, "although most eat in fraternity/sorority houses in subsequent years." The Honor System and campus security contribute to the students' feelings of safety on campus. "It's a very safe town and campus," says an economics major.

"The Greek system dominates the social life," a student says. Eighty-one percent of the men join fraternities; sororities claim 82 percent of the women. Greek bashes often feature live bands, although the Fancy Dress Ball, or "$100,000 prom," also draws raves. A lot of creative energy goes into fraternity parties and W&L's mock political convention for the party out of power, held every four years, has predicted past presidential nominees with uncanny accuracy. Underage drinking is banned in the dorms, but students insist "students like to party and drink." The Foxfield races near Charlottesville and the Kentucky Derby are popular road-trip destinations. Washington, D.C., Richmond, and Roanoke are easily reached by car for weekend trips, but because there is seldom a dull moment, most students like to stay on campus during weekends.

With its scenic location in the midst of the Appalachian Mountains, the university provides an abundance of activities for nature lovers, including hunting, fishing, camping, mountain biking, skiing, and tubing on the rivers. Lexington is "charming and historical," says one Middle East studies major. Lexington, a "quiet, friendly town that has much history to offer," also offers a few bars, two movie theaters, and several restaurants. "Dominated by the beauty of surrounding Shenandoah Valley and the Blue Ridge Mountains, Lex is small, but has everything one might need," a senior says.

Washington and Lee offers more than 20 varsity sports at the NCAA Division III level, and most Generals teams participate in the Old Dominion Athletic Conference. Recent conference champs include football, women's cross-country, men's and women's tennis (2013), women's lacrosse and women's swimming. The university sponsors approximately 25 intramural sports, ranging from waffle ball to flag football; three-quarters of the student body participate.

Despite giving in to coeducation several decades ago, a sense of history still pervades the campus. So too does the energy of one of the nation's ablest student bodies. "Washington and Lee students are proud to be W&L students and this is evident in their happiness and commitment to pursue their academics," concludes a sophomore.

Washington College

300 Washington Avenue, Chestertown, MD 21620

Washington College is the oldest school in the country that hardly anyone has ever heard of. Small liberal arts college with strengths in creative writing, American history, and environmental studies. The college has George Washington rather than Thomas Jefferson as its *éminence grise*. Chestertown is dullsville, so students make their own fun. Though the college is not very selective, it is best known for the annual Sophie Kerr Prize—worth over $60,000 to a lucky graduating senior.

Washington College was founded in 1782, making it the 10th oldest college in the country. The fact that it still has fewer than 1,500 students makes one wonder what administrators were thinking over the last couple of centuries, but hey, not everyone is Bill Gates. Fortunately, this small liberal arts college on Chesapeake Bay now finds itself in a century to its liking. The school is now on the move with upgraded facilities, an expanding student body, and innovative offerings in creative writing, American history, and environmental studies.

Chartered in 1782 in the closing days of the American Revolution, Washington College was the first college to be established in the newly independent United States, and the first to adopt a thoroughly secular mission: educating citizens, patriots, and leaders for the new democracy. It takes its name from George Washington, who never slept in any of its dorms but who did make a modest founding grant of 50 guineas and served as a trustee. His spirit looms over the campus as strongly as that of "Mr. Jefferson" at UVA. One of the first things freshmen do upon arrival is to make a pilgrimage to Mount Vernon to sign the Honor Code (WC students cannot tell lies).

Washington College sits on 112 acres adjacent to downtown Chestertown, a quiet community of 5,200 on the Chester River on the eastern shore of Chesapeake Bay. Most of the 50 buildings are redbrick, Georgian-style structures connected by old brick walkways and enhanced by large shade trees. The historic heart of the campus is the green where commencement is held and where a bronze statue of You Know Who keeps watch. The oldest buildings, the Hill Dorms, were built in the mid-19th century on the footprints of earlier structures. The college has recently invested more than $80 million in its physical plant, including new dorms, a makeover of Miller Library, and a newly renovated fitness center. The new Gibson Center of the Arts, the Toll Science Center, and the Hodson Commons mix large expanses of glass with traditional redbrick. Thirteen newer residence halls occupy what students call the "Western Shore" overlooking the main athletic field.

> "Students come to the school simply for the English and creative writing program."

Website: www.washcoll.edu
Location: Small Town
Private
Total Enrollment: 1,444
Undergraduates: 1,444
Male/Female: 42/58
SAT Ranges: CR 540–630, M 530–620
ACT Ranges: 23–27
Financial Aid: 90%
Expense: Pr $ $
Student Loans: 66%
Average Debt: $ $ $ $
Phi Beta Kappa: Yes
Applicants: 4,484
Accepted: 66%
Enrolled: 14%
Grad in 6 Years: 73%
Returning Freshmen: 85%
Academics: ✍ ✍ ✍
Social: ☎ ☎ ☎
Q of L: ★ ★ ★
Admissions: (410) 778-7700
Email Address: wc_admissions@washcoll.edu

Strongest Programs:
Creative Writing
Business Management

(continued)

First-year students begin their studies with a required Global Perspectives: Research and Writing (GRW) course in which they consider problems and issues from an international perspective. There are also standard distribution requirements. In order to graduate, students must also complete a Senior Capstone Experience that, depending on their major field, can take the form of a comprehensive exam, thesis, scientific research project, theatrical production, or portfolio of writing or artwork.

While the most popular majors include business management, economics, psychology, and biology, everyone agrees that the college's signature academic strengths are English literature and creative writing. Regardless of their disciplines, all students are expected to develop writing proficiency, and the college offers a four-year integrated approach to nurturing good writers. "Students come to the school simply for the English and creative writing program, and no wonder," gushes one English major. "We have an incredibly talented and qualified teaching staff." The school has a long-standing tradition of bringing writers such as Edward Albee, Toni Morrison, Joyce Carol Oates, and Jane Smiley to campus. The Rose O'Neill Literary House is a cultural hub where students can discuss poetry and literature over a cup of tea and freshly baked cookies. Seniors from all disciplines may submit writing portfolios to vie for the Sophie Kerr Prize. Named after a popular American writer of the early 20th century, it is the largest undergraduate literary prize in the country and inevitably gives the school its annual 15 minutes of fame in the national media. The 2013 winner took home a check for $61,192.

"The quality of teaching is superb."

Consistent with its location, Washington is a wonderful place to study American history. The C.V. Starr Center for the Study of the American Experience, located in the old Custom House on the Chester River, helps students study the culture of the Native Americans who once populated the area, trace the Revolutionary War campaigns in the Chesapeake region, and explore the area's maritime heritage from aboard Sultana, a reproduction 18th-century schooner. The center also offers Quill & Compass Scholarships for first-year students, and invites scholars working on books or other projects to live in a restored colonial house and share their expertise with the campus community.

Regardless of their disciplines, all students are expected to develop writing proficiency.

WC also takes advantage of its rural setting and nearby waterways to offer a strong program in environmental studies. The Center for Environment & Society promotes interdisciplinary research and learning revolving around stewardship of the area's natural resources, including a Chesapeake Semester that offers hands-on experience in the watershed and a trip to Peru for comparative study. A major new CES project called the Chester River Watershed Observatory seeks to make the Chester "the most studied, measured, mapped, and monitored body of water in North America, if not the world." Other special academic programs include the Douglass Cater Society of Junior Fellows, which offers competitive grants to support undergraduate research anywhere in the world to about 50 of the school's top students, and the Presidential Fellows Program, which offers special academic opportunities to the top 10 percent of entering freshmen. The college offers roughly 30 study abroad programs in two dozen countries as well as six short-term travel/study programs. One of the most popular is a three-week trek each June through the literary landscapes of England, Ireland, and Scotland to explore what inspired the likes of Wordsworth, Coleridge, and Shelley. Environmental science students can apply for summer study programs in Bermuda, Ecuador, and coastal Maine.

"Being in a small school allows us to really get involved."

With the exception of a few introductory classes, students report that all of their instruction comes from full professors. "The quality of teaching is superb," raves one student. "I have been so impressed with the knowledge and consideration that our professors give us." WC operates on a four-credits-per-course basis, with three hours of classes and students expected to work on their own for the fourth. A clinical counseling major describes the academic climate as "competitive but in a supportive way." A political science major adds, "Most students pick challenging courses, but it is certainly possible to avoid them." Students sense that Washington is becoming more rigorous. "The GPA cutoff for Dean's List is becoming more competitive," says an English major. "Students are being encouraged more to step out of their comfort zones and push themselves." Every freshman is assigned to a Peer Mentor, an older students who is trained to help them adjust to the academic and other sides of college life.

"So many students participate in clubs, organizations, athletics, and other school student groups," says one sophomore. "Being in a small school allows us to really get involved and create a positive environment." Forty-two percent of students at Washington are from Maryland, with 4 percent from other countries. Sixty-eight percent of undergraduates graduated from public schools, with 35 percent ranking in the top 10th of their high school classes. Students at Washington College are overwhelmingly Caucasian (82 percent), with 2 percent African American, 4 percent Hispanic, and 2 percent Asian American. Despite this seeming homogeneity, a drama major suggests that "students are really diverse in terms of interests and passions." Washington College's sticker price is high, but 90 percent of students receive some sort of financial aid, with an average award of $15,000. There are no athletic scholarships, and financial aid is available to international students.

All students are guaranteed on-campus housing for all four years, and 85 percent take up the offer. Washington offers three co-ed theme houses in the historic Hill Dorms complex—international, creative arts, and science—and language suites are available to advanced students of French, German, Japanese, and Spanish. The Wellness Living section of one residence hall opened last fall to stress good health—emotional, social, intellectual, and spiritual, as well as physical. Rooms are assigned through a lottery with numbers based on class year. A sophomore reports that "not all dorms are created equal, but none of them are completely unacceptable." The two newest dorms, Chester and Sassafrass, are among the choicest. A senior complains that "the recent influx of incoming class populations has made overcrowding a problem," with some lounges now converted into rooms. Students take their meals at the newly renovated dining hall, and reviews of the quality and variety of food are generally high. "The dining hall does spoil us sometimes," says an environmental studies major. "We had crab at dinner the other week, a Maryland specialty." After-hours venues sell sandwiches and such, and the recent library makeover added a café for late-night snacks and coffee. Students also say they feel safe on campus and that security is good. "Whether you're locked out of your room or there is a larger issue, Public Safety is always there," says one student.

The sleepy nature of Chestertown means that most social life takes place on campus. "Chestertown is, to put it bluntly, boring," says a senior. But a sophomore adds, "The social life is different because of our location and our environment. It is all about hanging out with your friends and your peers. It helps to encourage strong relationships." Greek life is strong at Washington, with one-sixth of the men belonging to fraternities and one-third of women to sororities. The Crab Feast, put on by the frères of Phi Delta Theta, is popular, as is the May Day celebration, which gives students an excuse to strip to their birthday suits at midnight and scamper around the quad. By far the biggest social event of the year is the Birthday Ball in February in honor of you-know-who's birthday. "We love our namesake," says an English major. "The ball is a formal event for students, faculty, and staff to celebrate school spirit, dress up, and have a great time." Every first-year student is required to

Consistent with its location, Washington is a wonderful place to study American history.

"Chestertown is, to put it bluntly, boring."

The college offers roughly 30 study abroad programs in two dozen countries as well as six short-term travel/study programs.

complete the online course AlcoholEdu for College. The school operates a Safe Ride service for students who want a ride home after a weekend night out on the town. "In the event that someone needs medical assistance, they and the person who calls for help will not be penalized," says a sophomore. Students with wanderlust can head for Annapolis, Baltimore, Philadelphia, or Washington, D.C.

WC's Shoremen and Shorewomen compete in the Division III Centennial Conference. The school has a long tradition of success in men's lacrosse and men's tennis, and it has produced numerous All-Americans in women's swimming. The men's and women's rowing and the co-ed sailing teams have recently become nationally competitive. Students turn out in huge numbers for the annual War on the Shore, when the men's lacrosse team takes on its biggest rival, Salisbury University. Sixty percent of students participate in the more than 16 intramural and club sports, with soccer being the most popular. "While intramural sports are casual, they can get competitive," says a history major.

After being around for more than 200 years without making much of a stir beyond Chesapeake Bay, Washington College now seems bent on carving out a niche for itself in academic areas where it has a comparative advantage, especially creative writing, American history, and the environment. Students describe WC as a "small, tight-knit community" bound by the classic values of a small liberal arts college. George would probably approve.

If You Apply To ➤

Washington College: Early decision: Nov. 15. Early action: Dec. 1. Regular admissions: Mar. 15. Financial aid: Mar. 1. Housing: Jun. 1. Application fee: $55. Campus interviews: optional, evaluative. Alumni interviews: optional, informational. SATs or ACTs: required. Subject Tests: optional. Accepts the Common Application.

Washington University in St. Louis

Campus Box 1089, One Brookings, St. Louis, MO 63130-4899

No longer simply a backup to the Ivies, Washington U has emerged as a nationally competitive university with a wholesome Midwestern feel. Core strength in the biological sciences, but strong across the disciplines. Maintains low acceptance rate by favoring early decision and denying top applicants who it thinks will enroll elsewhere. The result is a higher ranking in *U.S.News & World Report*.

Washington University has made a name for itself as one of higher education's rising stars. Though it's always been well recognized regionally, Washington U long ago established itself as a truly national institution—with a relaxed Midwestern feel that differentiates it from the high-strung Eastern Ivies. Applications have skyrocketed, and with a hefty endowment, strong preprofessional programs, and an emphasis on research, it's not hard to see why. "It's the campus community and life that really makes Washington U so special," says a junior. "It's a place to grow and learn while having an unbelievably fun time."

The school's 169-acre campus adjoins Forest Park, one of the nation's three largest urban parks. Buildings are constructed in the collegiate Gothic style, mostly in red Missouri granite and white limestone, with plenty of climbing ivy, gargoyles, and arches. Eliot Residence Hall, South 40 College Hall, and Brauer Hall, which serves as the home for the Department of Energy, Environmental & Chemical Engineering, were each completed in recent years.

Undergraduates enroll in one or more of Washington U's five schools—arts and sciences, architecture, art, business, or engineering. Double and interdisciplinary majors, such as environmental studies, are encouraged and easily arranged—so easily arranged, in fact, that about 60 percent of students earn either a major and minor or more than one major, and sometimes more than one degree. General education requirements vary by school and program. For liberal arts students, they include courses in quantitative reasoning, physical and life sciences, social or behavioral sciences, minority or gender studies, language or the arts, and English composition.

"It's the campus community and life that really makes Washington U so special."

Washington U's offerings in the natural sciences, especially biology and chemistry, have long been notable, especially among premeds. The outstanding medical school runs a faculty exchange program with the undergraduate biology department, which affords bio majors significant opportunities to conduct advanced laboratory research. The University Scholars Program allows students to apply for undergraduate and graduate admission before entering college. If accepted, students can begin exploring their chosen career path earlier—though they aren't obligated to follow through if their interests change.

The freshman FOCUS program helps balance the preprofessional bent of some of Washington U's best programs with the school's desire to provide a broad and deep educational experience and a smaller class size. In FOCUS, students use a weekly seminar to explore topics of contemporary significance, such as law and society. The program lets first-year students work closely with professors—including at least one Nobel Prize winner—and sample offerings from various departments. Other notable options include one-, two-, and four-year interdisciplinary programs such as Text and Tradition; International Leadership Program; and Mind, Brain, and Behavior. Students also have the opportunity to study in more than 50 different countries and are able to incorporate international study into their undergraduate program. In recent years, select groups of students have studied with faculty in summer programs in Ecuador, France, India, Italy, Mexico, Spain, and the United Kingdom. The university was an early adopter of the "strategic partner" model, where a select number of universities around the world are chosen to develop relationships ranging from research to faculty and student exchanges. It now has 28 such partnerships in Asian cities such as Beijing, Hong Kong, New Delhi, and Tokyo as well as ties in Barcelona, Helsinki, and other European destinations.

As Washington U's applicant pool has gotten bigger, the admissions committee has become more selective—and classes have gotten tougher, students report. "I've found the academic climate to be reassuring, open, and inclusive. Everyone wants to do well, but never at the expense of someone else," says one chemical engineering major. Those who are struggling will

"I've found the academic climate to be reassuring, open, and inclusive."

find plenty of help from teaching assistants who conduct help sessions or study groups with their peers. What really sets Washington U's quality of teaching apart is that undergrads have access to one-on-one mentoring relationships with the top faculty. "This year alone, one of my classes was a 150-person lecture class and another was a 12-person seminar. Yet what makes the quality of Washington U's teaching so remarkable is that, despite these disparate class sizes, I was on a first-name basis with both of the professors," one student says.

"We don't take ourselves too seriously and aren't afraid to have fun and experience new things," says an anthropology major. "Students tend to be way over-involved and passionate about the things they do and enjoy sharing their passions with friends." The school's population is relatively heterogeneous, with African Americans comprising 6 percent, Hispanics 5 percent, Asian Americans 17 percent,

(continued)

Phi Beta Kappa: Yes
Applicants: 27,265
Accepted: 18%
Enrolled: 34%
Grad in 6 Years: 94%
Returning Freshmen: 96%
Academics: ✐ ✐ ✐ ✐ ½
Social: 🍷 🍷 🍷 🍷
Q of L: ★ ★ ★ ★
Admissions: (800) 638-0700
Email Address: admissions@ wustl.edu

Strongest Programs:
Biology and Natural Sciences
Premed
Psychology
Foreign Languages
English
Accounting and Business
Political Science
Earth and Planetary Sciences

The University Scholars Program allows students to apply for undergraduate and graduate admission before entering college.

and international students 9 percent. "Some kids are very active with outside world and U.S. politics," says one student, "but the school tends to get more riled up over campus issues." There's also a large contingent from Eastern states like New York and New Jersey, many of whom are Jewish, leading to much debate about the Arab-Israeli conflict. Organizations such as STAR (Students Together Against Racism) and ADHOC (Against Discrimination and Hatred on Campus) also help enlighten students. Fifty-two percent of all undergraduates receive some form of financial aid, but there are no athletic scholarships.

Seventy-nine percent of Washington U students live in the school's dormitories, known as residential colleges. "The Office of Residential Life and the First Year Center have a serious talent for making incoming students feel right at home," cheers one junior. "Honestly, I was paired with a roommate who quickly became my best friend." All dorms are co-ed and air-conditioned, and some have suites for six to eight students of the same gender. Freshmen are guaranteed rooms, and students who stay in the dorms after that are promised rooms for the following year, says a junior. Upperclassmen may live in university-owned apartments, and there's always an argument as to which dorm is better. Some juniors and seniors do choose true off-campus digs in the nearby neighborhoods of University City and Clayton, where apartments are reasonably priced. Dorm dwellers and others who buy the meal plan may use their credits in any of the dining centers. "Dining facilities, like the housing, are unbelievable," raves one freshman. Campus security is praised, too. "In addition to the blue light system, the school offers something called Bear Patrol where a student can get a ride anywhere on campus if he or she does not feel safe," reports one marketing major. "However, in my two years at the university, I have never felt unsafe, nor have I known anyone who has felt unsafe."

"We don't take ourselves too seriously."

Washington U students pride themselves on being able to balance work and play, and on weekends, movies, fraternity parties, and concerts tear them away from their books. "Social life at Washington U is pretty centered around Greek life, but the Greek system is very inclusive of both Greeks and non-Greeks," says one sophomore. Every spring, the whole campus turns out for the century-old Thurtene Carnival, the oldest student-run philanthropic festival in the country. Diwali, a Hindu festival, draws huge crowds. Student groups—especially fraternities and sororities, which attract 25 percent of the men and women—build booths, sell food, and put on plays; profits are donated to a children's charity. Another big event is Walk In, Lay Down (WILD), held at the beginning and end of the academic year. Everyone brings a blanket to the main quad, assumes a horizontal position, and listens to live bands. Alcohol policies emphasize responsible drinking, though students younger than 21 aren't supposed to drink at all per Missouri law. "I think the policies are very effective and students are happy with what is in place," an environmental studies major explains.

Aside from an active campus social life, Washington U offers incredible recreational options because of its location abutting Forest Park: A golf course, an ice-skating rink, a zoo, a lake with boat rentals, art and history museums, an outdoor theater, and a science center are all within a short walk. The St. Louis Rams, Blues, and Cardinals attract pro football, hockey, and baseball fans, and the city is also home to the addictive Ted Drewes frozen custard. The school runs a free shuttle service to parts of St. Louis not within walking distance, and community service programs such as "Each One Teach One," in partnership with the city's schools, attract a sizable number of students. "We are just seven miles from downtown St. Louis," says a senior. Another adds, "It is a wonderful place to be a student. It features the benefits of a major metropolitan

"The Office of Residential Life and the First Year Center have a serious talent for making incoming students feel right at home."

area but retains a strong sense of neighborhood. It is very accessible to students—most major cultural institutions are either free or very cheap." The best road trips include Chicago; Nashville and Memphis, Tennessee; Lake of the Ozarks; and Columbia, Missouri—home of the University of Missouri.

The Washington U Bears compete in Division III; women's basketball is a powerhouse, having brought home NCAA championships multiple times. Other strong programs include women's volleyball, men's and women's soccer, men's and women's cross-country, men's tennis, and football. Intramural sports range from badminton, arm wrestling, and floor hockey to pocket billiards and ultimate Frisbee.

With demanding courses and excellent programs in the sciences and other fields, Washington U is no longer a sleepy little Midwestern school. The joke among high school guidance counselors is that no one gets admitted to selectivity-conscious Washington U through regular admissions—you are either locked in through early admissions or cherry-picked off the waitlist. But however they get there, students find Washington U both academically challenging and personally supportive. "The atmosphere is not only about learning academically, but growing as a person," says one senior. "My experiences have taught me to live life to the fullest."

> ### Overlaps
>
> **Northwestern, Duke, Yale, Harvard, Stanford, Vanderbilt, Brown, University of Pennsylvania**

If You Apply To ➢

Washington U: Early decision: Nov. 15. Regular admissions: Jan. 15. Financial aid: Feb. 1. Application fee: $75. Campus and alumni interviews: optional, evaluative. SATs or ACTs: required. Subject Tests: optional. Apply to one of five undergraduate schools. Accepts the Common Application. Essay question: personal statement.

Wellesley College

Wellesley, MA 02481

There is no better recipe for popularity than a postcard-perfect campus on the outskirts of Boston. That formula keeps Wellesley near the top of the women's college pecking order—along with superb programs in economics and the natural sciences. Among leading women's colleges, only Barnard accepts a lower percentage. Nearly a quarter of the students are Asian American, the highest proportion in the East.

Wellesley is not just the best women's college in the nation—it's one of the best colleges in the nation, period. With an alumnae roster that includes Hillary Rodham Clinton, Madame Chiang Kai-shek, Madeleine Albright, and Diane Sawyer, Wellesley College should be at the top of the list for high achievers who are seeking the benefits of an all-women's college. Wellesley women excel in whatever field they choose, including traditional male bastions like economics and the sciences. "Wellesley creates strong, smart, confident women," says an English major.

"Wellesley creates strong, smart, confident women."

Nestled in a Boston suburb, the Wellesley campus, one of the most beautiful anywhere, occupies 500 rolling acres of cultivated and natural areas, including Lake Waban. Campus buildings range in architectural style from Gothic (with stone towers and brick quadrangles) to state-of-the-art science, arts, and sports facilities. A 22-acre arboretum and botanical garden features a wide variety of trees and plants. The college recently reopened The Diana Chapman Walsh Alumnae Hall, which houses the Theatre Studies Department, a 1,300-seat auditorium, a black box theater, and a ballroom.

Website: www.wellesley.edu
Location: Suburban
Private
Total Enrollment: 2,352
Undergraduates: 2,352
Male/Female: 0/100
SAT Ranges: CR 650–740, M 640–740
ACT Ranges: 29–32
Financial Aid: 60%
Expense: Pr $ $ $
Student Loans: 54%
Average Debt: $
Phi Beta Kappa: No
Applicants: 4,478
Accepted: 30%

(continued)

Enrolled: 43%

Grad in 6 Years: 92%

Returning Freshmen: 97%

Academics: ✍ ✍ ✍ ✍ ✍

Social: ☎ ☎ ☎

Q of L: ★ ★ ★ ★

Admissions: (781) 283-2270

Email Address: admission@
wellesley.edu

Strongest Programs:

Economics

Political Science

Psychology

English

International Relations

Neuroscience

The five libraries sport a computerized catalog system that is accessible from on or off campus.

With its hefty endowment (the largest among the nation's all-female colleges and universities) and lavish facilities, Wellesley offers a top-of-the-line educational experience. The most popular majors are economics, political science, psychology, English, and biological sciences, and economics is known as the powerhouse. In fact, Wellesley has produced virtually all of the country's high-ranking female economists. Students in molecular biology work with faculty on DNA research, and a high-tech science center houses two electron microscopes, two NMR spectrometers, ultracentrifuges, two lasers, and other such equipment. "It is hard to say which department is the best," a psychology major muses, "because I believe that each department has a lot to offer."

The Ruth Nagel Jones Theater provides performance space for experimental theater and main stage productions. The Davis Museum and Cultural Center houses 11 galleries, a cinema, and a café. The students at Wellesley will find an academic art museum to their benefit, along with more than a million volumes in the campus libraries. The five libraries sport a computerized catalog system that is accessible from on or off campus. Anything Wellesley women find lacking in their facilities or curriculum can probably be found at MIT, where they have full cross-registration privileges. Wellesley students can also take courses at Babson College, Brandeis University, and nearby Olin College of Engineering, or participate in exchange programs with Spelman College in Atlanta or Mills College in Oakland, California.

> **"Each department has a lot to offer."**

Wellesley has distribution requirements that include three units drawn from language and literature and visual arts, music, theater, film, and video; one unit from social and behavioral analysis; a unit each from two of the following: epistemology and cognition; religion, ethics, and moral philosophy; and historical studies; and three units from natural and physical science and mathematical modeling and problem solving. In addition, students must take a first-year writing class, a foreign language, and a course on multiculturalism. Academics are taken very seriously at Wellesley. "Courses are challenging, but overall I've found classes and the academic climate manageable," one student explains. Professors are highly respected and make themselves available through email, voicemail, office hours, and by appointment. "The quality of teaching is always excellent," one student says. Another adds, "The professors care about the students and their needs."

Grants from private foundations have allowed Wellesley to add other innovative programs, including independent research tutorials for advanced science students and fellowship funding for joint student/faculty projects. Students can participate in the Twelve College Exchange*, including the National Theater Institute and the Maritime Studies Program*, or they can travel and study abroad through one of Wellesley's recently expanded international programs, including the summer internship program in Washington, D.C.

Under the honor system, students may take their finals, unsupervised, at any time during exam week. Class sizes are almost always small (they average 18 to 23 students per class). First-years (as they are exclusively called here) and upperclasswomen alike have faculty advisors. First-years also have a dean of first-year students to offer additional advice on courses and other academic matters. "There are good counseling resources available, but students must seek them out," explains a sophomore.

> **"The professors care about the students and their needs."**

"Students here are conscientious workers with a history of high achievement," says a sophomore. "They expect a lot of themselves." Although the Northeast is the best represented geographical area (though only 16 percent are from Massachusetts), students come from every state and more than 75 countries. Seventy-eight percent ranked in the top 10th of their high school class. Six percent of Wellesley women are African American, 21 percent are Asian American, and 10 percent are Hispanic. Whatever their background, most students share an "intellectual curiosity and a willingness to expand their current knowledge," says a music major. "Wellesley is a very liberal campus and students tend to have strong opinions about current issues, and they are not afraid to speak out about them," adds a sophomore. Wellesley has eliminated loans for families with incomes below $60,000 a year and capped loans for others.

Residence life at Wellesley is a step ahead of most institutions, to say the least. Virtually every student lives on campus, in rooms that are described as "immaculate." Residence halls feature high-ceilinged living rooms, hardwood floors, fireplaces, computers and laser printers, television annexes, walk-in closets, kitchenettes with microwaves, and even grand pianos. The halls are renovated every five years or so and all are well maintained, students say. "The dorms are comfortable and cleaned often," says one student. "There have been housing crunches, but all students are accommodated." All residence halls are smoke-free. There are no halls specifically for first-years—all classes live on all floors. Peer tutors

"There are good counseling resources available."

also live in each hall. These students, called APT advisors, are trained to tutor in specific subjects and in study skills and time management. Juniors and seniors are generally granted single rooms. Two co-ops, one with a feminist bent, present an educational housing option. Meal cards are valid in all six dining halls and at the campus snack bar, which is stocked with everything from milk and flour to Twinkies. "The food is fairly decent," says a student.

When it comes to weekend fun, Wellesley is in a prime location. Not even half an hour away, Boston is the place where Wellesley women can mingle with lots of other students—specifically male—from Harvard and MIT. Cambridge—with Harvard Square, MIT frat parties, and lots of jazz clubs—is accessible by an hourly school shuttle that runs on weekdays and weekends. There is also a commuter rail station located a short walk from school. "Social life on campus is relatively quiet," says a psychology major. Cape Cod, Providence, and the Vermont and New Hampshire ski slopes are close by car.

The town of Wellesley is an upper-crust Boston suburb without many amenities for students. "Be forewarned," cautions a student, "Wellesley is a snobby town of rich people." Wellesley is also a dry town, but there is a student-run pub in the campus center. When alcohol is served, campus police check IDs. The Lulu Chow Wang Campus Center, referred to affectionately as "the Lulu," is a hub of activity day and night. Students enjoy going to the student-run Café Hoop, the campus coffeehouse, to sip tea or share a fro-yo or a chocolate croissant. The closest thing Wellesley has to sororities are nonresidential societies for arts and music, literature, Shakespeare, and general lectures. These societies also sometimes hold parties.

Wellesley is chock-full of traditions, but the most endearing ones include Flower Sunday, step-singing (an all-campus sing-along on the chapel steps), the sophomore class planting a tree, a junior class variety show, Spring Weekend (with a big-name band and comedian), and a hoop-rolling contest by seniors in their graduation robes. The winner of this contest will supposedly be the first in her class to achieve her goals, whatever they may be, and she gets off to a flying start when her classmates toss her in the lake. Speaking of the lake, students mention their unofficial campus event, Lake Day, where students take breaks between (or from) classes to enjoy a festival held on the lawn near the lake.

Many students balance their academic schedule with athletics and club sports. Lacrosse, swimming, softball, volleyball, and tennis are among the top Blue varsity teams. The sports center, named the Nannerl Keohane Sports Center in honor of Wellesley's 11th president (who went on to run Duke), offers an Olympic-size pool; squash, racquetball, and tennis courts; dance studios; a weight room; and an indoor track. Harvard's Head of the Charles crew race and the Boston Marathon—Wellesley's "Scream Tunnel" is legendary among runners worldwide—share honors as the most popular spectator sports of the year. The big athletic rival is Smith College, another of the Seven Sisters group of great women's colleges.

When it comes to academics, Wellesley women are serious. Their school is competitive with all but the top three Ivies. Many of them enjoy the traditions of the school and appreciate the idyllic atmosphere for contemplation, but know they are poised to dominate whatever field they enter. As one contented senior says, "It's a wonderful place to grow as individuals, as students, and as women."

If You Apply To ➤ **Wellesley:** Early decision: Nov. 1. Regular admissions and financial aid: Jan. 15. Application fee: $50 (paper), free (online). Campus and alumnae interviews: optional, evaluative. SATs and Subject Tests (writing and two others) or ACTs: required. Accepts the Common Application. Essay question. Students participate on admissions board.

Wells College

Aurora, NY 13026

Recently passed the nine-year mark as a co-ed institution, with men now comprising about one-third of the students. A family atmosphere is the hallmark of Wells, right down to the dinner bell that calls everyone to the evening meal. Wells is big on interdisciplinary study and internships during the January term. Needs to increase enrollment to put itself on solid ground.

Website: www.wells.edu
Location: Rural
Private
Total Enrollment: 532
Undergraduates: 532
Male/Female: 33/67
SAT Ranges: CR 480–600, M 470–590
ACT Ranges: 21–28
Financial Aid: 94%
Expense: Pr $
Student Loans: 82%
Average Debt: $ $ $ $
Phi Beta Kappa: Yes
Applicants: 1,803
Accepted: 45%
Enrolled: 25%
Grad in 6 Years: 57%
Returning Freshmen: 70%
Academics: ✐ ✐ ✐
Social: ☎ ☎
Q of L: ★ ★ ★ ★
Admissions: (315) 364-3264

Faced with a lingering cash crunch and declining appeal of single-sex education, Wells College opened its doors to men in 2005 for the first time since its founding in 1868. More students means more money to help fix old buildings, boost financial aid packages, and improve faculty salaries, or at least replace professors who retire. Still, the school hasn't abandoned its storied history. Whether it's riding to graduation in an old Wells Fargo stagecoach or showing off in the annual Odd-Even basketball game between freshmen and sophomores, the tradition of Wells is apparent at every turn. With only about 530 students, anonymity is nonexistent, and close relationships with professors and peers come with the territory.

Wells's 365-acre campus sits on the shores of Cayuga Lake—and on the National Register of Historic Places. Most buildings are old, massive, and covered with ivy—the way college should look, you might say. The lakeside location affords beautiful sunsets as well as boating and fishing opportunities—a welcome relief from the sometimes arduous studying that also goes on here. The Schwartz Athletic Center has received extensive renovations, and a 45,000-square-foot science facility is open for business. The facility includes classrooms, labs, offices, and a 92-seat lecture hall.

"All of my professors are highly qualified."

Wells aims to give students a solid grounding in the liberal arts. To that end, general education requirements include two courses in a foreign language, one course in formal reasoning, three courses in the arts and humanities (with at least one in each area), three courses in the natural or social sciences (with at least one lab), and four courses in physical education, including one semester of swimming and one focused on wellness. Students are also required to complete a senior thesis.

Wells 101, a core course required for all first-years, covers the basics of college writing, speaking, and analytical thinking.

The most popular majors include English, biology, psychology, sociology and anthropology, and history; students also give high marks to education and women's studies. There's an unusual minor in bookbinding, while a minor in indigenous studies and first nations has been added. Regardless of major, "the courses are quite challenging and rigorous," says a junior, "but students are not competitive with each other." Fortunately, professors are available and eager to help students. "All of my professors are highly qualified, extremely intelligent, and very caring," a psychology major says. Business majors may concentrate in entrepreneurship, social justice, art and art gallery management, or hospitality.

Students with broad interests may choose one of Wells's integrated majors, such as American studies, which require coursework across traditional disciplinary boundaries. Individualized majors are available for students whose needs are not met by established programs. There are also dual-degree programs in community health and business administration with the University of Rochester; in veterinary medicine with Cornell University; and in engineering with Case Western Reserve, Clarkson, Columbia, and Cornell. For a change of pace, students may take one non-major course each semester on a pass/fail basis. They may also cross-register for up to four courses each at Cornell and at Ithaca College.

Wells uses a semester calendar with elements of the 4–1–4 plan, with internships, research, and study abroad taking place in January. Though the school doesn't focus on business and other professional fields, there is a corporate-affiliate program aimed at preparing women to work in the financial world through special courses and lectures, and portfolio-management experience. Ninety percent of Wells students participate in at least one internship; foreign study is available, too, and flagship programs include Italy, Spain, and France. Almost all courses taken by freshmen have 25 students or fewer, and most are discussion-based, with

"[We] aren't afraid to be our genuine selves."

the professor present to moderate and focus the conversation. The student-run collegiate association enforces the honor system, and take-home and self-scheduled tests are the rule rather than the exception.

Wells students "aren't afraid to be our genuine selves," says one English major. "We're all a little odd and that's OK." Sixty percent of Wells students are state residents; Asian Americans make up 2 percent of the student body, African Americans 11 percent, and Hispanics 5 percent. Courses, workshops, and a support network for new students help to educate the campus on the importance of multiculturalism. The campus is very liberal, and women's rights, feminism, and homosexuality are key topics of discussion. There are numerous merit scholarships, averaging just over $19,000 each, but no athletic awards.

All students are guaranteed college housing, and 90 percent do live in the dorms, since only seniors are permitted to move off campus. There are plenty of single rooms, though first-years are typically assigned to doubles. Aside from complaints that the heat is too high during the winter, students rave about their residences, some of which have bay windows and winding staircases, and all of which offer lake views. "Leach and Dodge tend to be more social dorms, while Weld is more of a study dorm," a senior explains. "Main and Weld both offer a healthy lifestyle floor, and GP is our all-women's dorm for upperclasswomen." The food gets decidedly less stellar reviews— "OK" to "not great"—but at least it's served in a magnificent Tudor-style dining hall, with two working fireplaces. Security is "extremely reliable," says one student.

Though there are no Greek organizations at Wells, the school doesn't need them, given its bevy of other traditions. For example, bells are rung every evening to announce dinner, and also to celebrate the first snowfall of the season. Additionally,

(continued)

Email Address: admissions@wells.edu

Strongest Programs:
Psychology
Biological and Chemical
    Sciences
English
Performing Arts
Education

Wells 101, a core course required for all first-years, covers the basics of college writing, speaking, and analytical thinking.

Business majors may concentrate in entrepreneurship, social justice, art and art gallery management, or hospitality.

tea and coffee are served every weekday afternoon. Though the long dresses and china cups have long since disappeared, tea is still a great time to hang out with friends, faculty members, and staff, as well as a welcome break from long afternoon seminars. On the last day of classes, there's a celebration around the sycamore tree, where sophomores present roses to seniors. Then, the president of the college and her staff serve breakfast to the graduating class.

"Most students stay on campus to socialize," says a sociology major. The Student Activities Club sponsors comedians, dances, movie and spa nights, guest speakers, and poetry slams, but if you want to party, head to Cornell or Ithaca College in the Wells van. "We like to venture off campus since Aurora is so small," a visual arts major says. Underage students can get alcohol, and no one seems to bother them if they're drinking, as long as they're not bothering anyone else—and frankly, drinking isn't much of a focus here, anyway.

The town of Aurora has a pizza parlor, ice cream shop, bar, and hotel—and that's about it. "It's a small village, not a college town at all," says a sociology major, but the

"Leach and Dodge tend to be more social dorms, while Weld is more of a study dorm."

residents are friendly and on good terms with students. As a result, students enjoy getting out and about, whether they head to Auburn and Syracuse for shopping, or to New York City and Montreal for shows and other big-city perks. Given the beautiful, hilly terrain, Wells students also enjoy camping in the warmer months, and cross-country or downhill skiing in the winter, especially with the slopes of Greek Peak less than an hour away.

Varsity teams at Wells compete in Division III, and the soccer, tennis, and field hockey squads are the strongest Express teams. Also popular are swimming, lacrosse, and softball—and since the college is so small, "everyone that I know of has been able to play," says a psychology major. Anyone may use the golf course and the college's tennis and paddle-tennis courts, while the field house offers a pool and other exercise equipment.

Wells students aren't ones to shy away from a challenge, so odds are they'll weather the school's co-ed status. As for the men, well, they'll be hard-pressed to change the "liberal, progressive, feminist, and independent" spirit of this place, but that suits most students just fine. "I believe the classes are good, the community is wonderful, and Wells really prepares you for life," says a student. "I already feel more independent having studied at Wells."

Overlaps

Ithaca, Le Moyne, SUNY–Albany, Elmira, Hobart and William Smith, Rochester Institute of Technology, Sarah Lawrence, Hartwick

If You Apply To ➤

Wells: Early action and early decision: Dec. 15. Regular admissions: Mar. 1. Financial aid: Mar. 15. Housing: Jul. 15. Campus and alumni interviews: optional, informational. Application fee: $40. SATs or ACTs: required. No Subject Tests. Accepts the Common Application. Essay question.

Wesleyan University

45 Wyllys Avenue, Middletown, CT 06459

Usually compared to Amherst or Williams, Wesleyan is really more like Swarthmore. The key differences: Wesleyan is twice as big and a little more streetwise. Wes students are progressive, politically minded, and fiercely independent. Exotic specialties like ethnomusicology and East Asian studies add spice to the scene. New York and Boston are both two hours away but not easily accessible on public transportation.

Whether they're engrossed in academics, debating and demonstrating over various issues, or engaged in community service, Wesleyan students seem to do things with a passion and intensity that helps set this school apart from tamer institutions. "Wes students take an in-your-face approach to life," says a government major. "There's an energy on this campus; for me, it's a spirit of creativity and political energy," a sophomore explains. In recent years, a significant number of Wesleyan alumni have gone on to make their mark in the entertainment industry and the high-tech world on the West Coast.

"Wes students take an in-your-face approach to life."

It begins with the Wesleyan campus architecture, which is as diverse as the student body. The nucleus of this stately university is a century-old row of lovely brownstones that look out over the football field. The rest of the buildings can be described as "eclectic" and range from mod-looking dorms of the '50s and '60s to the beautiful and modern Center for the Arts. The Wesleyan-owned student residences look freshly plucked from Main Street, USA. The new Wesleyan Career center is situated in the heart of the campus and features a multipurpose career commons with a broadcast suite.

"Wesleyan is very collaborative. The academic climate of the school encourages students to work together, whether it is through studying together for exams, having conversations about their writing, or working as a team to accomplish a community service project outside the classroom," a senior says. Wesleyan has used its wealth to attract highly rated faculty members who are expected to be scholar-teachers: academic superstars who juggle groundbreaking research, enthusiastic lectures, and personal student attention at the same time—and they seem to pull it off. "The professors here are all extremely knowledgeable about their field and very enthusiastic to teach," says a government major. Among Wesleyan's strongest departments are music, astronomy, economics, molecular biology and biochemistry, American studies, earth and environmental sciences, and English. But even the smaller departments attract attention. Ethnomusicology, including African drumming and dance, is a particular specialty; students can be found reclining on the wide, carpeted bleachers at the World Music Hall or watching a dozen musicians play the Indonesian gamelan. The film department is first-rate and has a national reputation. The East Asian Studies Center has both a strong program and an authentic Japanese tea room. The math department emphasizes problem solving in small groups rather than interminable lectures dedicated to theory. Undergraduates in the sciences work alongside faculty in their research laboratories and frequently earn the opportunity to publish in scientific journals. The fastest-growing major is the interdisciplinary neuroscience-and-behavior program.

Wesleyan's curriculum renewal program ensures the relevance of liberal arts education in the 21st century by offering seminars for first-year students, clustering courses to help students reach their academic goals, and requiring an electronic portfolio from each student that allows students to compile their work and set goals with their advisors. Students are expected in their first two years to take a minimum of two courses in each of three areas—humanities and the arts, social and behavioral sciences, and natural sciences and mathematics. During their second two years, students must take one course in each of the three areas. At the end of their freshman year, Wesleyan students can apply to major in one of three competitive, interdisciplinary seminar colleges: the College of Letters (literature, politics, and history), the College of Social Studies (politics, economics, history), and the Science in Society program (concerned with the humane use of scientific knowledge, à la Buckminster Fuller). The College of the Environment opened in 2009 and seeks to "develop informed citizens who can discuss environmental issues from a variety of disciplinary perspectives, understand their connections to social or political issues, and derive well-formulated, independent conclusions,"

"Wesleyan students are proud to work creatively outside the box."

Website: www.wesleyan.edu
Location: Small City
Private
Total Enrollment: 3,113
Undergraduates: 2,924
Male/Female: 48/52
SAT Ranges: CR 640–740, M 660–740
ACT Ranges: 29–33
Financial Aid: 50%
Expense: Pr $ $ $ $
Student Loans: 45%
Average Debt: $
Phi Beta Kappa: Yes
Applicants: 10,046
Accepted: 21%
Enrolled: 36%
Grad in 6 Years: 91%
Returning Freshmen: 95%
Academics: ✍ ✍ ✍ ✍ ✍
Social: ☎ ☎ ☎
Q of L: ★ ★ ★
Admissions: (860) 685-3000
Email Address: admissions@ wesleyan.edu

Strongest Programs:
Astronomy
Classical Studies
East Asian Studies
Earth and Environmental Sciences
Economics
English/Creative Writing
Molecular Biology and Biochemistry
Music
Film

according to administrators. The College of Film and Moving Image opened recently as well. The university implements a Web-based course selection and registration system and a preregistration system allocating course slots according to student preferences, class year, and major requirements. In addition to the nearly 50 majors available, Wesleyan also offers a number of certificate programs, including environmental studies and molecular biophysics.

"Where many of Wesleyan's rivals attract straight-thinking, by-the-book individuals, Wesleyan students are proud to work creatively outside the box and search for less commonly explored answers," says one student. It is hands down an activist campus. One sophomore lists rallies and protests alongside parties and concerts as part of the campus social life. The politics generally take a leftist bent. "Students are usually on the more liberal side of issues," says a Romance studies major. But students level their smarts against topics close to home, mostly the university administration.

> The film department is first-rate and has a national reputation.

Wesleyan strives to keep its classes small, and 68 percent of the courses have 19 or fewer students. Some students claim they sometimes have trouble getting into the "hot" courses. "With popular classes, you have to be persistent, but you can get in," a history major says. If beseeching is not your style, studying abroad may be a temporary tonic to registration headaches. Programs are available in Israel, Germany, Africa, Japan, Latin America, France, Spain, and China. Students can also study at Mystic Seaport* or take a semester at another Twelve College Exchange* school. Internships are popular, and students can also take advantage of 3–2 engineering programs with Dartmouth, Caltech, and Columbia.

Wesleyan likes to describe itself as "a small college with university resources." The libraries have more than a million volumes, practically unheard of at a school this size. Students claim that whenever you happen to walk past the brightly lit, glass-walled study room of Sci-Li (the science library), you're apt to see numerous students huddled over their books. Wesleyan's excellent reputation and strong recruiting network attract students from all over, ensuring the clash of viewpoints that makes it such a vital place. "Three things best describe Wesleyan students: creative, socially aware, and passionate," says one

> "With popular classes, you have to be persistent, but you can get in."

senior. "Students here are excited to learn in order to become creative thinkers that will contribute something original to their field, whatever their interest may be." The student body is 7 percent African American, 10 percent Hispanic, and 9 percent Asian American. Students report that diversity is cherished at Wes. "Wes students are tolerant because there's an open dialogue both in and outside of the classroom that creates a high level of awareness and acceptance," says a student. Sixty-nine percent graduated in the top 10th of their high school class. The university will admit 90 percent of freshmen on the traditional need-blind basis but admits the rest with an eye on their ability to pay. There is also a policy waiving any loan obligation for families worth up to $40,000 per year. Freshman orientation, which gets rave reviews, consists of a week of standard preregistration fare, plus comedy nights, movies, and square dancing.

For housing, most freshmen are consigned to singles or doubles in the campus dorms. Popular opinion indicates that the Butterfield complex is the choice for quiet study, while Clark Hall is where the party people go. Housing is guaranteed for four years. Juniors and seniors enjoy numerous housing options: townhouses for four or five students, fraternities, college-owned houses and apartments, or special-interest houses organized around concerns such as ecology, feminism, or minority student unity. Upperclassmen who want to live off campus must apply for permission. Accommodations are "comfortable and very large," says a Romance studies major. Those who move off have the option of eating at home, in the school grill, or at the fraternity eating clubs. "Vegetarians love Wesleyan and so do meat eaters. There is an option for everyone," one student says. Everyone else takes meals in the university center.

> The College of Film and Moving Image opened recently as well.

Middletown is a small city within easy driving distance of Hartford and New Haven, but it is off the beaten track of steady public transportation. It has undergone a renaissance in recent years, and students love the myriad of ethnic restaurants available. "Middletown isn't a bad place for college," says a student. "There are bars on Main Street that cater to a college crowd. Plus, there is a diverse collection of restaurants, which is great for when the family comes to visit." Wes students contribute a great deal of time to community service and help maintain a peaceful, beneficial relationship with the town. And Wesleyan's rural surroundings afford the much-appreciated opportunity to jog through the countryside, swim at nearby Wadsworth Falls, or pick apples in the local orchards. Good road trips include New York and Boston, each two hours away, and decent ski areas and beaches just under an hour away.

Although two former fraternities have turned into co-ed literary societies, Greek life at the remaining three is a jock preserve. Only 4 percent of the men and less than 1 percent of the women go Greek. Wesleyan's enforcement of the 21-year-old drinking age is moderate compared with most schools. Consistent with the university's encouragement of independence, students bear a large part of the responsibility for policing themselves. "To the university's credit, they are really

"Most of Wesleyan's social life happens on campus."

stressing alcohol awareness, so to speak," says a neuroscience and behavioral studies major. Students who throw a party for 75 or more people must attend a workshop that stresses safe drinking. Still, most students concur that it is quite easy for the underaged to imbibe. "You can get alcohol if you want to," notes a sophomore. It seems, however, that drinking alcohol is a minor event when compared to the multitude of other things happening on campus. Activities abound from comedy performances to a cappella groups, films, plays, bands, lectures, parties, and events planned by the more than 200 student groups. "Most of Wesleyan's social life happens on campus," says one senior. "There's always something going on during the weekends or even throughout the week, so there's no great need to leave the campus to have a good time." Major events on the social calendar include Spring Fling and Fall Ball—two outdoor festivals—and Uncle Duke Day and Zonker Harris Day, two similar events with a more psychedelic, 1960s flavor, in which students pay tribute to the infamous Doonesbury characters.

The Wesleyan Cardinals compete in the New England Small College Athletic Conference (NESCAC) and field 29 varsity teams. There are also 11 club sports teams and nine intramural sports. Annual encounters with "Little Three" rivals Williams and Amherst get even the most bookwormish student out of the library and into the heat of the action. The ultimate Frisbee club (the "Nietzsche Factor," named after a former star player's dog, not the philosopher) almost always whips challengers, and intramurals are extremely popular. Athletics are enhanced by a complex that comes complete with a 200-meter indoor track, a fitness center, and a 50-meter pool.

The key to Wesleyan's success seems to be the fostering of an intellectual milieu where independent thinking and an appreciation of differences are omnipresent. This New England college offers more academic and extracurricular options than almost any school its size, and the Wesleyan experience means liberal learning in a climate of individual freedom. The freedom at Wesleyan requires motivated students who stay on task despite the laid-back atmosphere. There are abundant opportunities open to students willing to take advantage of them, which is precisely what these doers do.

Programs are available in Israel, Germany, Africa, Japan, Latin America, France, Spain, and China.

Overlaps

Brown, Yale, Amherst, Vassar, University of Chicago, Pomona, Tufts, NYU

If You Apply To ➤

Wesleyan: Early decision I: Nov. 15. Early decision II and regular admissions: Jan. 1. Application fee: $55. Campus and alumni interviews: optional, evaluative. SAT and two SAT Subject Tests or ACT: required. Accepts the Common Application. Essay question: Common Application.

West Virginia University

P.O. Box 6009, Morgantown, WV 26506-6009

Surrounded by the likes of Ohio, Pennsylvania, and Virginia, West Virginia has traditionally exported its best students to other states for college. But WVU also attracts its share of out-of-staters, some drawn to its one-of-a-kind forensics program. The honors program is a must for top students, and the university has solid programs in professional fields ranging from journalism to engineering.

West Virginia University earned the right to be the state's flagship land-grant college by being the only one in the state to offer research and doctoral-degree programs. With more than 193 degree programs, approximately 350 student organizations, and 17 intercollegiate varsity athletic programs, it's no wonder students flock to this large university. With strong academic programs and student organizations, the school has become a solid choice for scholars, researchers, and athletes, as well as party animals.

WVU is situated in the picturesque mountains of north-central West Virginia, a few miles from the Pennsylvania border and overlooking the Monongahela River. A driverless rail system bridges the school's two campuses—the older Morgantown and the more modern Evansdale, which are a mile and a half apart. Ten of the ivy-covered Morgantown buildings, dating mainly from the 19th century, are listed on the National Register of Historic Places; many of their interiors have been restored or renovated. Campus construction is booming with $300 million invested in new classrooms, labs, and student wellness facilities.

West Virginia's degree programs span 14 schools, the best of which are engineering (particularly energy-related) and the allied health sciences (medical technology, physical therapy, nursing, and occupational therapy). The most popular majors are business, engineering, journalism, biology, and the health fields. Regardless of major, students must complete the General Education Curriculum (GEC), designed to ensure all students have a foundation of skills and knowledge necessary to reason clearly, communicate effectively, and contribute to society. Graduates are expected to possess knowledge and experience in nine objective areas—communication, math and science, issues of contemporary society, history, artistic expression, the individual in society, American culture, non-Western culture, and Western culture. Additional programs include undergraduate majors in management information systems, business for foreign languages, art history, music, and theater.

> **"The overall academic climate is generally laid-back."**

While WVU is a big school, administrators say that roughly three-quarters of classes taken by freshmen have 50 or fewer students. Students say the difficulty of WVU academics depends largely on the classes they take. "The overall academic climate is generally laid-back," says a senior, "but certain classes and a segment of the student population create a competitive climate." The First-Year Experience helps students adjust to college with New Student Convocation, dorm-based Freshman Interest Groups, and Resident Faculty Leaders, who live next door to the dorms and serve as mentors and friends. A one-credit course, University 101—First Year Experience, also helps students understand the academic, social, and emotional expectations of the college experience, covering study skills, university and community support services, goal setting, and career planning. On the other end of the spectrum, an honors program offers small classes, special housing, and early registration to the top 5 percent of WVU students.

Website: www.wvu.edu
Location: Small City
Public
Total Enrollment: 25,895
Undergraduates: 21,118
Male/Female: 55/45
SAT Ranges: CR 460–560, M 470–580
ACT Ranges: 21–26
Financial Aid: 63%
Expense: Pub $
Student Loans: 54%
Average Debt: $ $ $
Phi Beta Kappa: Yes
Applicants: 16,521
Accepted: 85%
Enrolled: 36%
Grad in 6 Years: 56%
Returning Freshmen: 77%
Academics: ✍ ✍
Social: 🐦 🐦 🐦 🐦
Q of L: ★ ★ ★
Admissions: (304) 293-2121
Email Address: go2wvu@mail.wvu.edu

Strongest Programs:
Forensic and Investigative Science
Biometric Systems
Engineering
Political Science
Pharmacy
Psychology
Allied Health

Though WVU attracts students from all U.S. states and nearly 90 countries, it is primarily regional. Fifty-six percent of undergrads are in-staters, and a sizable contingent arrives from western Pennsylvania and southern New Jersey—so many that the university has been dubbed "New Jersey University: West Virginia campus." Says one student: "WVU has a unique conglomerate of students, ranging from Appalachian natives to a lot of inner-city NYC kids and New Jersey natives." African Americans comprise 5 percent of the student body, and Hispanics and Asian Americans combine for 5 percent. The university offers merit scholarships and nearly 250 athletic scholarships.

An honors program offers small classes, special housing, and early registration to the top 5 percent of WVU students.

Twenty-five percent of WVU's undergraduates live on campus, where dorms are mediocre but fill up fast because of the increase in students flocking to the university. Most are co-ed; the older ones are known for their character, while the newer residential complexes on the Evansdale campus have larger rooms and luxuries like air-conditioning. Many upperclassmen opt for nearby apartments. Seven percent of the men and women go Greek and may live in their respective chapter houses. Each dorm has its own cafeteria, and students may buy meal plans regardless of where they live. Fraternities and sororities have their own cooks. The biggest complaint is the lack of parking—the campus is so large students say they need cars to get around, but there isn't any place to park. Students can ride the Morgantown Mountain Line buses for free from 10 p.m. to 3 a.m. Thursday through Saturday. They stop at all university housing.

"Every football game is a festival in some way."

Morgantown is a small city with a college-town feel and plenty of community service opportunities, students say. "This town revolves around the university and provides so much for the students," says a senior. The school has worked hard to curtail underage drinking, banning alcohol in the dorms and limiting each frat to three social events per semester with 300 members and guests. Students report that it's now nearly impossible for those under 21 to be served on campus and say off-campus bars have also cracked down. That said, social life is still centered on campus, often focused on the free food, movies, bands, and comedians offered Thursday through Saturday by the school-sponsored Up All Night program. Spring Fest and Fall Fest provide stress relief each semester, and Mountaineer Week showcases the customs of Appalachia. For those with cars, road trips to Columbus, Washington, D.C., or Pittsburgh are quick and easy. Football rivalries with Syracuse, Maryland, and Pittsburgh (the "Backyard Brawl") take students farther afield. "Every football game is a festival in some way," says a senior.

Social life is still centered on campus, often focused on the free food, movies, bands, and comedians offered Thursday through Saturday.

Aside from Mountaineer football, which has achieved national prominence, West Virginia fields competitive women's soccer, riflery, gymnastics, and basketball teams, and men's soccer, basketball, rowing, and wrestling. There are hundreds of intramural teams, the most popular being basketball, flag football, dodgeball, and indoor soccer.

As WVU grows, the university continues to be dedicated to research that will improve the lives of citizens not only in West Virginia, but across the globe. At the same time, WVU's mission is changing to be more student-centered. And the campus is forever growing and changing. "WVU is a school," says a senior, "that won't look the same for very long."

Overlaps

Marshall, University of Maryland, Ohio State, Penn State, University of Pittsburgh, Virginia Tech

If You Apply To ➤ **West Virginia:** Rolling admissions. Application fee: $30 (in state), $60 (out of state). Campus and alumni interviews: optional, informational. SATs or ACTs: required. No Subject Tests. No essay question.

Wheaton College (IL)

501 College Avenue, Wheaton, IL 60187

Wheaton is at the top of the heap in Evangelical education, rivaled only by Pepperdine (with its Malibu digs) and traditional competitors such as Calvin and Hope. Students pledge to live a Christian life. Wheaton's low tuition makes it relatively affordable. The worldly temptations of Chicago are less than an hour away.

Website: www.wheaton.edu
Location: Suburban
Private
Total Enrollment: 2,701
Undergraduates: 2,433
Male/Female: 49/51
SAT Ranges: CR 600–720, M 610–700
ACT Ranges: 27–32
Financial Aid: 73%
Expense: Pr $
Student Loans: 59%
Average Debt: $ $
Phi Beta Kappa: No
Applicants: 1,959
Accepted: 69%
Enrolled: 44%
Grad in 6 Years: 90%
Returning Freshmen: 95%
Academics: ✍ ✍ ✍
Social: ☎ ☎ ☎
Q of L: ★ ★ ★ ★
Admissions: (800) 222-2419
Email Address: admissions@wheaton.edu

Strongest Programs:
Biology
Business/Economics
English
Music
Bible
International Relations
Political Science
Psychology

Wheaton College combines academic rigor and Evangelical orthodoxy with a firm commitment to the liberal arts, preparing students "to help build the church and improve society worldwide For Christ and His Kingdom." The Community Covenant prohibits the use of alcohol, tobacco, or drugs; professors are allowed to drink and smoke, but are discouraged from doing so, especially in front of students. Though most adolescents would chafe under such restrictions, Wheaties take it all in stride. A happy junior says, "Wheaton offers a unique balance of academic excellence, extracurricular activity, and Christian community that simply cannot be found anywhere else."

> **"Study abroad programs are quite common."**

Wheaton is nondenominational and its verdant, 80-acre campus is an oasis of sorts, in the midst of one of Chicago's oldest and most established suburbs. The castle-like Blanchard Hall, built in the last century, keeps watch over the community from atop the front campus hill; when couples get engaged, they climb to the top of the tower to share their news by ringing the bell. Nearby is the $13.5 million Billy Graham Center, a museum and library that has become a hub for research on American Evangelicalism. (Graham is a Wheaton alumnus.) An $80 million science center opened in late 2010 and provides 135,000 square feet of research, teaching, and exhibit space.

General education requirements at Wheaton include intermediate-level foreign language study; proficiency in quantitative skills, writing, and oral communication; and varying amounts of credit hours in nine thematic areas: wellness, philosophy, Biblical studies, world history, social science, lab science, natural science, literature, and art and music. In the classroom, there's an emphasis on teamwork, though classes can be demanding. "Since the majority of students are high achievers, classes are rigorous and challenging," says a junior. "Students have high expectations for their classes and professors." The quality of teaching varies, but students get "the benefit of Christian professors who provide a stimulating intellectual experience in light of the Christian faith," according to one junior.

Sporting the largest endowment among the nation's Evangelical schools, Wheaton offers students a generous bevy of programs and facilities. Business is Wheaton's most popular major, followed by music, English, applied health science, and communication. Students have the opportunity to perform research at Argonne National Laboratory, just down the road, and for those seeking a truly global experience, there's study abroad in East Asia, England, France, Germany, Spain, Russia, Latin America, and Israel; 49 percent of students do so. "Study abroad programs are quite common to the Wheaton experience," a student says, and are described as "superb and life-changing."

> **"Wheaton students are high-achieving."**

Those concerned with social justice, a definite focus at Wheaton, may be interested in the Human Needs and Global Resources (HNGR) program, which sends students to Third World countries for six months of work on development projects such as building roads and schools. Wheaties may also spend a semester at one of the 12 other Evangelical schools that belong to the Council for Christian Colleges and Universities*. Motivated students may opt for 3–2 programs that allow them to combine an undergraduate degree in the liberal arts with a master's in nursing or engineering, saving a year in the process. Summer study in astronomy, meteorology, biology, chemistry, geology, and environmental science is available at the Black Hills Science Station, while leadership training takes place at Honey Rock, Wheaton's campus in the Wisconsin North Woods. For incoming freshmen, the 18-day Wheaton Passage wilderness trek provides "an experience in team building, self-discovery, and physical challenge that should not be missed," says a sophomore.

"Wheaton students are high-achieving, both academically and in other areas of life," says one junior. "They are, for the most part, serious about their Christian faith, and excited about working it out in their various areas of interest." Twenty-five percent of Wheaton students hail from Illinois, and 84 percent graduated in the top quarter of their high school class, a fact that adds to both the intellectual energy and the academic pressure on campus. African Americans comprise 2 percent of the student body, Hispanics make up 4 percent, and Asian Americans add 8 percent. Important social and political issues find their way into campus conversation. "The student attitudes vary pretty widely: Some are conservative, while some are liberal, though nearly all will fall somewhere within the spectrum of distinctively Christian responses," says one student. Many students lead church youth groups, and others get involved in the community through tutoring or volunteer work at homeless shelters, prisons, or hospitals. Merit awards averaging $5,493 are awarded to qualified students. There are no athletic scholarships.

Ninety percent of Wheaton students live in the single-sex dorms, and accommodations range from traditional double rooms with bathrooms down the hall to college-owned houses and apartments. "Housing is very comfortable and well kept. Not luxurious, but entirely sufficient for college students," says one junior. Opposite-sex visitation is limited to certain hours on certain days, though "each semester, dorms are allowed two 'raids' to their opposite

"Most of the social life at Wheaton happens on campus."

floor," says an education major. Everyone eats in Anderson Commons, where an outside vendor called Bon Appétit does the cooking. "They offer such diversity—Cajun, Asian, Italian, pizza, sandwiches," says a sophomore. "Everything is still made from scratch!" a senior adds. Students report feeling safe on campus: "Campus security is excellent," says a business major. "They are a phone call away."

Since Wheaton lacks fraternities and sororities, and because students agree to abstain from alcohol, drugs, and tobacco, the social life revolves around other pursuits. "Most of the social life at Wheaton happens on campus," says a psychology major. "We have a lot of fun here, but all alcohol-free fun. We have tons of fun events on campus and through student clubs or college union. Plus, there's always just hanging out with friends or having Nerf battles in their apartments." A commuter train near campus whisks students to downtown Chicago in 45 minutes, where restaurants, blues clubs, theaters, museums, shopping, and professional sports are in abundance. Favorite traditions include Missions in Focus week, which brings missionary organizations and Christian speakers to campus, and the individual dorm floors' own traditions, one of which includes an annual root beer kegger.

Wheaton's teams compete in Division III, and competitive Thunder teams include men's and women's soccer, men's and women's basketball, and men's and women's cross-country. Football, basketball, and soccer games "are always exciting and well attended," says one student, especially if the opponent is Augustana. The debate and chess teams are competitive, too. And while it's not an athletic competition per se, juniors and seniors do get excited about decorating "the Bench," a reinforced concrete slab that is the subject of an ongoing and often rough-and-tumble

Sporting the largest endowment among the nation's Evangelical schools, Wheaton offers students a generous bevy of programs and facilities.

Ninety percent of Wheaton students live in the single-sex dorms.

game of keep-away. For recreational players, the sports center boasts basketball courts, a climbing wall, and a weight-lifting facility.

"Wheaton has a reputation for being a rigorously academic school with intelligent, committed students," says one junior. Even after more than 140 years, Wheaton remains "committed to the principle that truth is revealed by God through Christ, in whom is hidden all the treasures of wisdom and knowledge." While this kind of education isn't for everyone, students believe their school's dedication to Christianity only strengthens the bonds they develop with one another—and their understanding of the broader world.

If You Apply To ➤ **Wheaton (IL):** Early action: Nov. 1. Regular admissions: Jan. 10. Application fee: $50. Campus interviews: optional, evaluative. No alumni interviews. SATs or ACTs (with writing): required. Subject Tests: optional. Essay question.

Wheaton College (MA)

Norton, MA 02766

Although its address says it's in Massachusetts, Wheaton is actually closer to Providence than to Boston. But getting to either by train is quick and easy. One of the few nationally known institutions in the area that is not impossible to get into. Curriculum includes interdisciplinary, hands-on, and project-based work in addition to traditional courses. Smaller than Skidmore, comparable to Connecticut College.

Wheaton College offers students plenty of opportunities to make their academic marks. Since 2000, more than 161 Wheaton students have received national fellowships, including 3 Rhodes scholars and 4 Marshall scholars. The college remains among the top 10 liberal arts colleges for Fulbright scholars as well. When students aren't hitting the books, they can be found socializing or taking part in extracurricular activities. "There is a distinct profile for the successful Wheaton student," offers one senior: "A self-motivated, creative, and active person. Students do well at Wheaton if they are open and willing to immerse themselves in campus initiatives and clubs as well as their studies."

Wheaton's rural location offers few distractions from intellectual pursuits. Its 400-acre campus blends Georgian brick buildings and modern structures set among beautiful lawns and shade trees. The two halves of the campus are separated by Peacock Pond, which probably qualifies as the only heated duck pond on any American campus. Newest additions to the campus include the $42 million Mars Center for Science and Technology.

> **"I would highly recommend the science departments."**

Students say Wheaton's best programs include psychology, political science, religion, international relations, economics, and history. "I would highly recommend the science departments," says a junior. "They have produced a great number of scholars and have the most readily available opportunities for student/professor research." Programs in the arts are well recognized, impressive given the school's small size, and the chemistry department is also strong. The major in Hispanic studies benefits from its affiliation with a study abroad program in Cordoba, and a Mellon Foundation grant supports native speakers in Spanish and other languages. Those interested in interdisciplinary or cross-disciplinary work may design

Website: www.wheaton
college.edu
Location: Suburban
Private
Total Enrollment: 1,613
Undergraduates: 1,613
Male/Female: 36/64
SAT Ranges: CR 560–670,
M 560–650
ACT Ranges: 25–30
Financial Aid: 81%
Expense: Pr $ $ $ $
Student Loans: 61%
Average Debt: $ $ $
Phi Beta Kappa: Yes
Applicants: 4,046
Accepted: 64%
Enrolled: 18%
Grad in 6 Years: 82%
Returning Freshmen: 86%
Academics: ✍ ✍ ✍
Social: ☎ ☎ ☎
Q of L: ★ ★ ★ ★
Admissions: (508) 286-8251

an independent major or add classes taken at other schools in the Twelve College Exchange Program*. Students may also take classes not offered at Wheaton at nearby Brown University. For those tired of studying on land, Wheaton offers the Maritime Studies Program*. Dual-degree programs offer motivated students the chance to earn a bachelor's degree in engineering or graduate degrees in business, communication, religion, or optometry in conjunction. Wheaton offers more than 75 study abroad programs in far-flung locales such as Peru, Japan, Samoa, and Botswana.

Wheaton's curriculum shows students how to make linkages between disciplines. Rather than simply checking off required courses, all Wheaton students study across the major academic fields, developing a fully dimensional view of the world. In practical terms, this means that every student must take a series of courses on a single **"The students are eclectic."** topic from various departments. The curriculum links experiential learning to each department and requires a capstone senior project. Core classes include English, quantitative skills, foreign language, natural science, and non-Western history. Students also choose a first-year seminar from among 25 sections, each focused on "controversies" that have generated debate or heralded changes in how they experience or understand the world.

"Classes are challenging and directed at pushing students to think in new ways," says one senior. "I think that the climate is such that students are individually competitive, in that they are driving themselves to be better, but not aggressive or cutthroat towards one another." Wheaton's small classes encourage close ties between students and faculty. "The relationships that you develop with professors here are unparalleled," a psychology major cheers. Aside from a faculty advisor, students get a staff mentor and two peer advisors, known as preceptors. The Filene Center for Academic Advising and Career Services gets high marks from students seeking internships—and jobs after graduation.

About a third of Wheaton's students come from Massachusetts, and 62 percent went to public high schools. "The students are eclectic," says one junior. "I'd say that there are almost no loners at Wheaton. Everybody tends to find a peer group, make friends, and enjoy themselves. There's a tremendous amount of academic and social diversity on campus." The student body is largely white; African Americans account for 5 percent, Hispanics 7 percent, and Asian Americans 3 percent. Students are friendly and open to differing views. Politically, liberals and conservatives are both well represented on campus. The administration has undertaken a massive capital campaign, using some of the proceeds to hire more minority scholars—and recruit more minority students. Merit awards averaging $11,915 are available, but there are no athletic awards.

As might be expected on this small, suburban campus, virtually everyone (95 percent) lives in one of Wheaton's dorms or houses. Gebbie Hall regularly hosts panels, presentations, and colloquia on gender issues. All students are guaranteed housing for four years; freshmen live in doubles, triples, or quads, and upperclassmen try their luck in the lottery system. "The rooms are generously sized and equipped with all the necessities," says a history major. The bright and spacious dining halls offer unlimited food, and the biggest winners of all are the ducks, which thrive on the leftover bread students toss into Peacock Pond. "The food is getting better," says one junior. "There's a big push for local, fresh, and organic produce." Students also say they feel safe on campus and that security is visible and active. "They patrol 24 hours a day to ensure things are OK," says a sophomore.

Social life at Wheaton includes dances, concerts, lectures, and parties on campus, or road trips. "We're 20 minutes from Providence, and 40 minutes from Boston. If you can't find something to do on the weekend, you're just looking for something to complain about," a student says. The town of Norton, just outside campus,

(continued)

Email Address: admission@ wheatoncollege.edu

Strongest Programs:
Psychology
English
Economics
Political Science
Biology
Humanities
Italian
French
Mathematics

Those interested in interdisciplinary or cross-disciplinary work may design an independent major or add classes taken at other schools in the Twelve College Exchange Program.*

The Filene Center for Academic Advising and Career Services gets high marks from students seeking internships—and jobs after graduation.

draws some students with a Big Brother Big Sister program, hospital visits, and opportunities to tutor and mentor children, but there's little to do otherwise, students say. "It's a very quiet town, and most students stay on campus rather than venture off into Norton," says a student. "But there are different restaurants, stores,

"If you can't find something to do on the weekend, you're just looking for something to complain about."

malls, recreational activities, and concerts that are located in the surrounding towns." Students head to the college's student center, which offers a café, dance studio, and sun deck for afternoon study breaks. There are no sororities and fraternities here, which helps cut down on underage drinking, though students say that, as on most campuses, "drinking and partying does occur."

When they're not immersed in classwork, Wheaton students love to put on their dancing shoes—whether for the Boston Bash party on a boat in Boston Harbor, for the Valentine's Dance, or for any number of events at Rosecliff, a mansion in Newport, Rhode Island. Spring Weekend features the Head of the Peacock boat race, where students build ships and race them across the pond, as well as live bands and outdoor barbecues. When it rains, students get dirty as they slide around the craters on Wheaton's lawns, an activity known as "dimple diving."

The Wheaton Lyons compete in Division III. The Lyons nickname goes back to Wheaton's days as an all-female school, and it honors Mary Lyons, the 19th-century educational pioneer who founded Mount Holyoke. The strongest teams include men's and women's soccer—both of which have won numerous championships. Recent conference champs also include men's baseball, women's basketball, and women's track and field. The athletic facility boasts an eight-lane swimming pool, a field house, and an 850-seat arena for basketball or volleyball. Almost 50 percent of the student body participates in intramural sports.

Students at Wheaton take an active role and are involved in campus planning and college operations, as well as in their community. "We don't just have coffee in the café," says a political science major. "We text with deans, have lunch with professors, coffee with advisors, a beer with our favorite professor. These kinds of relationships are the Wheaton way. They supplement the intellectual energy and debate that takes place among students." Indeed, students here take pride in their achievements inside and outside the classroom, while striving to preserve the school's friendly, small-town feel.

Social life at Wheaton includes dances, concerts, lectures, and parties on campus, or road trips.

Overlaps

Bates, Connecticut College, Hamilton, Skidmore, University of Vermont, Boston University, Brandeis, Clark

If You Apply To ➤ **Wheaton (MA):** Early decision and early action: Nov. 15. Regular admissions: Jan. 15. Financial aid: Feb. 1. Application fee: $50. Campus and alumni interviews: optional, evaluative. SATs or ACTs: optional. Subject Tests: optional. Accepts the Common Application. Essay question.

Whitman College

345 Boyer Avenue, Walla Walla, WA 99362-2083

Whitman has quietly established itself as one of the West's leading liberal arts colleges. Don't bother with the umbrella: Walla Walla is in arid eastern Washington. Whitman's isolation breeds community spirit and alumni loyalty. True to its liberal arts heritage, Whitman has no business program. Combines outdoorsy camaraderie with the slower pace of life in the rural Northwest.

You don't have to own a Frisbee to succeed at Whitman, but if you've got one, bring it along—you'll find a campus full of students eager to toss it back to you. Though it isn't well known outside the Pacific Northwest, Whitman offers a top-notch liberal arts education, along with plenty of fun for outdoorsy types. Students are down to earth and friendly and feel a deep loyalty to one another—and to their school. "The Whitman community is more supportive and inspiring than I would have thought possible," says a senior. "Here you can grow and excel to your absolute potential."

Whitman was founded in 1882 and named in honor of Marcus and Narcissa Whitman, who served the Cayuse Indians and immigrants on the Oregon Trail. Even today, everything important is within walking distance of campus, including the main drag of Walla Walla ("Walla Squared"), which once won a national Best Main Street award. The 117-acre campus, where colonial buildings and modern facilities sport New England ivy, sits at the foot of the Blue Mountains, surrounded by golden wheat fields and vineyards. Beyond Walla Walla (which means "many waters" in the Cayuse Indian language) are gorgeous mountains, rivers, and forests.

All Whitman students complete the General Studies Program, which includes both a first-year core and distribution requirements in various disciplines. The first-year program revolves around a seminar called Encounters that emphasizes analytical reading of texts—such as Plato's *Symposium*,

"Here you can grow and excel to your absolute potential."

Homer's *Odyssey*, the Bible, and Mary Shelley's *Frankenstein*—as well as effective writing. Students then take at least six credits in social sciences, humanities, fine arts, and science, as well as three or more credits in quantitative analysis, and two courses that focus on alternative voices. Seniors must pass comprehensive written and oral exams in their major; Whitman is the first U.S. college or university to require seniors to do so.

"Classes are generally difficult, but in a way that encourages cooperation among students rather than a malicious competition where grades and rank are most important," says a sophomore. A freshman adds, "Everyone works together to do well. I bounce paper ideas off of my peers all the time and because of their collective input, I turn in much better work than I would on my own." Biology, English, psychology, and politics are some of the best (and most popular) departments at Whitman; the school also boasts an astronomy program, unusual among small colleges. Though Whitman lacks a business program, its alumni include John Stanton, a cell phone pioneer who made millions of dollars building and selling VoiceStream and then Western Wireless. Whitman also has an extensive Asian art collection, and additional coursework in Chinese language and Asian studies is offered through a summer program in China. One unusual offering is the Parents Core, which allows parents to do the same readings as their children in core classes, join in online discussions, and get together twice a year for face-to-face meetings. Additional programs include global studies and film and media studies.

Whitman has 3–2 or 3–3 programs in engineering and computer science (with Caltech, Columbia, Duke, the University of Washington, and Washington University in St. Louis), international studies and international business (Monterey Institute of International Studies), computer science and oceanography (University of Washington), forestry or environmental management (Duke), and law (Columbia). Students may also pursue teacher certification through partnerships with the University of Puget Sound. Foreign study is available in countries ranging from Japan and Sri Lanka to England, Italy, Ireland, and Egypt, and students may take

"Classes are generally difficult."

terms within the U.S. at the Chicago Urban Studies Program, the Philadelphia Center, the Washington Semester, and Biosphere 2. "Semester in the West is the biggest up-and-coming program," adds a psychology major. "Students travel for one

Website: www.whitman.edu
Location: Small City
Private
Total Enrollment: 1,508
Undergraduates: 1,508
Male/Female: 43/57
SAT Ranges: CR 610–740, M 610–700
ACT Ranges: 29–32
Financial Aid: 76%
Expense: Pr $ $ $
Student Loans: 48%
Average Debt: $
Phi Beta Kappa: Yes
Applicants: 2,854
Accepted: 49%
Enrolled: 28%
Grad in 6 Years: 86%
Returning Freshmen: 94%
Academics: ✍ ✍ ✍ ✍
Social: ☎ ☎ ☎
Q of L: ★ ★ ★ ★
Admissions: (509) 527-5176
Email Address: admission@whitman.edu

Strongest Programs:
Politics
English
Psychology
History
Biology

Seniors must pass comprehensive written and oral exams in their major.

semester along the West Coast, learning from different professors in variable environments." An environmental studies major says, "Professors are extremely knowledgeable in their fields and are excited to get to know their students."

"No matter how different they may be, most Whitties seem to absolutely love the school," a junior says. "Students are very passionate about what they study, whether it's social justice or poetry." Thirty-five percent of Whitties are from Washington State, and many of the rest hail from the suburbs of Western cities, notably San Francisco and Portland. Ten percent of the student body is Asian American, 6 percent is Hispanic, and 2 percent is African American. Political issues don't dominate campus conversation. "There's a handful of super-vocal students and then a sea of apathy surrounding them," says a freshman. There are numerous merit scholarships averaging $10,000 but no athletic awards.

Sixty-seven percent of students live in campus housing; freshmen and sophomores are required to do so. "Dorms are very comfortable, especially compared to dorms I have seen at other schools," says one student, "and the maintenance staff is friendly and does a great job." Prentiss Hall and Lyman House, both built in 1926, have received multimillion-dollar facelifts; theme houses are available for students interested in foreign languages, fine arts, writing, community service, Asian studies,

"Professors are extremely knowledgeable."

environmental studies, multiculturalism, and the outdoors. "ResLife does a great job of matching people up with roommates," adds a freshman, "and the living options are diverse and spread out across campus." Dining halls are run by Bon Appétit, and students say the company is responsive to special requests. "The food is very good, especially at the beginning of the semester, although it is hard not to get sick of it by the end," says a sophomore. Students report feeling safe on campus and "the worst problem is bike theft," according to one Spanish major.

The social life at Whitman revolves around fraternity parties—40 percent of the men and 37 percent of the women go Greek—and other on-campus events, such as theatrical productions and the spring Renaissance Faire. "Students at Whitman are very social," says one sophomore. "Most large parties take place either in one of the four fraternity houses or in off-campus houses. Smaller get-togethers and parties are also popular in personal rooms in the residence halls." The close-knit campus fosters a community vibe, but can be a hassle, too. "Dating here is insane because everyone knows everyone's business," says a freshman. "Prepare for celibacy if you're an average human being." The town of Walla Walla supports a symphony, community playhouse, art galleries, two rodeos, and a hot-air balloon festival. "Walla Walla is small, but full of culture," says one student. Annual traditions include Duckfest, in which students create ducks, place them all over campus, and then design a map indicating where they are, so that peers, professors, and community members can take a walking tour—and college president George Bridges can rank the best efforts. Dragfest is a popular dance party, and the end of the year brings "the Beer Mile, where students celebrate on Ankeny Field, and the administration is thankful we're safe," says a junior.

Outdoor pursuits are important in this part of the country, where autumn is gorgeous, winter sporadically snowy, and spring delightfully warm. Walla Walla (population 30,000) is located in the center of agricultural southeastern Washington, in an arid valley. Hiking, biking, and backpacking are minutes away, and white-water rafting and rock climbing are popular on weekends.

"Most Whitties seem to absolutely love the school."

Two ski centers and other recreational areas are within an hour's drive, and Seattle (260 miles) and Portland (235 miles) offer a welcome change of scenery.

Whitman scrapped varsity football in the late 1970s, but the Missionaries maintain an active interest in physical activity. At the varsity level, teams compete

Whitman also has an extensive Asian art collection, and additional coursework in Chinese language and Asian studies is offered through a summer program in China.

The social life at Whitman revolves around fraternity parties—40 percent of the men and 37 percent of the women go Greek.

in Division III; competitive teams include men's and women's tennis (both 2013 conference champs) and women's golf. Women's basketball is solid, too, having advanced to the Elite 8 in 2013. Club lacrosse and rugby tournaments draw crowds, as does "Onionfest," the ultimate Frisbee competition, and "Anchor Smash," the spring intramural football tournament. Rock climbers can challenge themselves on two walls.

"If you're choosing a liberal arts school in the Northwest," says a student, "choose Whitman!" Indeed, students seeking a solid liberal arts education with a healthy dose of outdoor fun would do well to heed this enthusiastic Whittie's advice. Professors here know their stuff and care about teaching and their students. Combine the college's beautiful campus with the close friendships nurtured by its small size, and it's easy to see why Whitties remain loyal to each other—and their school—long after they've left campus.

> ## Overlaps
> **Lewis & Clark, Willamette, Pomona, Stanford, Carleton, Middlebury, University of Puget Sound, University of Washington**

If You Apply To ➤

Whitman: Early decision: Nov. 15. Regular admissions: Jan. 15. Application fee: $50. Campus interviews: optional, evaluative. No alumni interviews. SATs or ACTs: required. Subject Tests: optional. Accepts the Common Application. Essay question.

Whittier College

13406 East Philadelphia, P.O. Box 634, Whittier, CA 90608-4413

Whittier's Quaker heritage brings a touch of the East to suburban L.A. Less selective than Occidental and the Claremont Colleges, Whittier lures top students with a bevy of academic scholarships. Whittier's functional campus lacks the opulence of the Claremonts and the panache of Pepperdine.

Founded in 1887 by members of the Society of Friends, Whittier College is fast becoming a global training ground. Whittier students can be found all around the world, studying in 30 foreign countries. And when they return to the Whittier campus, they have access to caring faculty and a close-knit friendly environment.

Located just 18 miles away from downtown Los Angeles, the college is perched on a hill overlooking the town of Whittier, California, with the San Gabriel Mountains rising up from the horizon. The 73-acre campus is a pleasant mixture of modern buildings tucked between the red-roofed, white-walled Spanish traditionals. Its landmark building, Deihl Hall, has been updated to include a digital audio/video computer lab for languages. Renovation and expansion of the Bonnie Bell Wardman Library is complete. A four-foot-high granite monument stands on the north campus lawn, honoring Whittier's most famous alum, former president Richard Nixon.

"For the most part, the quality of the teaching has been very intense."

Whittier offers its students two major programs: the liberal education program and the Whittier Scholars Program. About 80 percent of the students take the revised liberal education track, in which they fulfill distribution requirements in writing skills, mathematics, natural sciences, global perspectives, comparative knowledge, and creative and kinesthetic performance. The emphasis of the liberal education program is on an interdisciplinary focus, globalism, and critical and quantitative thinking. These liberally educated Whittierans next choose a major from among 26 departments, the strongest and most popular of which include English, biology,

Website: www.whittier.edu
Location: Suburban
Private
Total Enrollment: 2,123
Undergraduates: 1,626
Male/Female: 47/53
SAT Ranges: CR 460–580, M 480–590
ACT Ranges: 20–25
Financial Aid: 95%
Expense: Pr $ $
Student Loans: 77%
Average Debt: $ $ $ $
Phi Beta Kappa: No
Applicants: 4,123
Accepted: 64%
Enrolled: 16%
Grad in 6 Years: 67%
Returning Freshmen: 86%
Academics: ✍ ✍ ✍
Social: ☎ ☎ ☎

(continued)

Q of L: ★ ★ ★ ★
Admissions: (562) 907-4238
Email Address: admission@
  whittier.edu

Strongest Programs:
Child Development
Education
Social Work
Psychology
Business
Biology
Political Science
English

The emphasis of the liberal education program is on an interdisciplinary focus, globalism, and critical and quantitative thinking.

psychology, political science, and business administration, and programs that focus on teaching certification.

Whittier officially ended its affiliation with the Quakers in the 1940s, but the prevailing spirit of community hearkens back to their traditions. The academic climate can be challenging, but students report competition to be rare among classmates. One senior says, "The academic climate is competitive and rigorous, but definitely manageable." Freshmen are taught by full professors, most of whom "have been excellent," a kinesiology major says. "For the most part, the quality of the teaching has been very intense, but very rewarding," adds another student. "Whittier students tend to be open and friendly," says a student majoring in comparative cultures. "You aren't afraid to sit with someone you haven't met before."

"We have a hippie vibe."

Whittier's signature program is the Whittier Scholars Program, a path taken by 20 percent of the undergraduates who choose to bypass the traditional liberal education program. They are relieved of most general requirements and start from square one with an "educational design" process. With the help of an academic advisor, the scholars carve their majors out of standard offerings by taking a bit of this and a bit of that. Majors have included such names as symbol systems, visual studies and business, and dynamics of politics and urban life. The program is highly regarded because of the more active role it allows students to play and the freedom it affords them in pursuing their interests. All students, no matter which curriculum they choose, must fulfill a yearlong freshman writing requirement. In an attempt to help freshmen develop both their critical thinking skills and their ability to communicate clearly in writing, Whittier lets students choose their preferences from a variety of seminars. They are also encouraged to take an additional writing course, mathematics, and lab science during their freshman year. First-years also must attend a series of speakers who discuss topics relevant to student coursework and must take part in the Exploring Los Angeles series, which includes trips to museums and cultural events. Study abroad options include programs in Denmark, India, Mexico, and Asia, and undergraduates may also take foreign study tours during the January interim.

"We have a hippie vibe," says an international business major, and the campus is "very liberal." More than three-quarters of the students come from California, and the rest are from all over the United States and the world. Diversity plays a major role on this campus. While African Americans make up 6 percent of the students, Hispanic enrollment is an impressive 37 percent, and Asian Americans constitute 11 percent. The Black Student Union and Hispanic Student Association are vocal on campus. An on-campus cultural center focuses on diversity programming and resources. "Tolerance is a big watchword on campus," a junior says. "You can get severely disciplined or expelled for being intolerant." In addition to need-based aid, the college grants merit scholarships averaging $17,928.

Just over half of Whittier students seek off-campus housing, but the Turner Residence Hall entices many students to stay on campus and vie for a chance to get a room with a panoramic view of Los Angeles. Most freshmen are assigned rooms, while Whittier scholars, athletes, and members of Whittier's social societies tend to cluster in selected dorms and houses. "The price for on-campus housing is unreasonably high," complains one student. "Dorms have old furniture and many do not have air-conditioning." As part of the meal plan, all campus residents must take at least 10 meals at the Campus Inn dining hall, where the food is said to be typical college fare. "Food is diverse and edible," a sophomore says. The Spot (Whittier's popular campus coffeehouse) includes a state-of-the-art nightclub called—what else?—the Club.

"Everybody knows everybody."

Nine social societies (they're not called fraternities or sororities here) attract 10 percent of the men and 13 percent of the women but hardly dominate the social scene. However, their dances, which frequently feature live entertainment, are welcomed by all. For many, entertainment takes the form of road trips, everywhere from Disneyland to the California beaches. Other common destinations include Las Vegas, Mexico, Joshua Tree, Hollywood, San Diego, and northern California. Whittier itself is a spot for community-minded students to get involved. "Whittier is a friendly town," one junior says. "The college is involved a lot with the community."

Whittier has a fairly strict alcohol policy and students say it's difficult for underage drinkers to get served at campus events. "Underage students are not allowed to even be in the same proximity as alcohol," a senior says. Popular annual events include a Spring Sing talent show, the football game against archrival Occidental College—dubbed the Battle of the Shoes—and Sportsfest, which is a campuswide competition in which dorms compete in a variety of athletic, intellectual, and wacky games and events. A favorite among students is Mona Kai, a Hawaiian party put on by the Lancer Society, when tons of sand are shipped in for the event. Also favored is the Midnight Breakfast served by professors during second-semester finals. The most important campus landmark is the Rock, which sits near the front of campus and is given a fresh coat of paint by countless aspiring artists. The beach is a frequent destination, and for nightlife, Los Angeles looms large. The local community, known as Uptown Whittier, offers quaint shops, restaurants, and cobblestone sidewalks, but little in the way of entertainment.

Men's lacrosse is the most successful Poets team on campus. Men's football and soccer and women's soccer, softball, and track are the most popular. Intramurals are a big draw, too. "The most popular are inner-tube water polo and volleyball," says one freshman. Facilities have gotten an upgrade, including a new football field and a fully equipped fitness center.

The students at Whittier have created a supportive, intimate environment where people work together and celebrate their diversity. "It's a small, friendly place where everybody knows everybody," a junior math major says. With the opportunity to design their own majors, students are active in their own education.

Study abroad options include programs in Denmark, India, Mexico, and Asia.

Overlaps

UC–Irvine, UCLA, Cal State Fullerton, Chapman, University of La Verne, Loyola Marymount, Occidental, University of Redlands

If You Apply To ➤ | **Whittier:** Early action: Nov. 15. Regular admissions: Feb. 1. Application fee: $50. Campus interviews: optional, evaluative. No alumni interviews. SATs or ACTs: required. Subject Tests: optional. Accepts the Common Application. Essay question.

Willamette University

900 State Street, Salem, OR 97301

Willamette is strategically located next door to the Oregon state capitol and 40 minutes from Portland. Bigger than Whitman, smaller than U of Puget Sound, and more traditional than Lewis & Clark, Willamette offers extensive study abroad enhanced by ties to Asia. Well-known in the West but has yet to develop a national reputation to equal that of competitors such as Lewis & Clark.

Willamette University, founded in 1842, was the first university in the Pacific Northwest. Students can take advantage of their proximity to the state's legislative offices and a nearby hospital for internships, jobs, or off-campus learning experiences, including a comprehensive study abroad program that carries students to destinations around the globe. On campus, students find a more personal

Website: www.willamette.edu
Location: City Center
Private
Total Enrollment: 2,725

(continued)

Undergraduates: 1,968

Male/Female: 45/55

SAT Ranges: CR 560–680,
  M 560–660

ACT Ranges: 25–30

Financial Aid: 96%

Expense: Pr $ $ $

Student Loans: 64%

Average Debt: $ $ $

Phi Beta Kappa: Yes

Applicants: 8,887

Accepted: 60%

Enrolled: 10%

Grad in 6 Years: 77%

Returning Freshmen: 86%

Academics: ✎ ✎ ✎ ½

Social: ☎ ☎ ☎

Q of L: ★ ★ ★ ★

Admissions: (877) LIBARTS

Email Address: libarts@
  willamette.edu

Strongest Programs:
Politics
Biology
English
Economics

atmosphere than larger universities nearby and appreciate the low-key yet challenging academic milieu. "Here at Willamette we look at the big picture and focus on quality of life," muses one sophomore, "because there is so much more to college than books and parties."

The 61-acre campus lies across the street from the Oregon state capitol building and the state Supreme Court, providing a perfect avenue for student internships and political involvement. Willamette is home to full trees (thanks to Oregon's omnipresent rain), small wildlife, and occasionally steelhead salmon, which splash around in the Mill Stream that runs between WU's redbrick academic buildings. Zena Farm and Forest is a 300-acre outdoor laboratory used by hundreds of students each term. Ford Hall is a LEED Gold–certified building featuring large, collaborative learning spaces and faculty offices.

> **"We look at the big picture and focus on quality of life."**

Willamette (pronounced "Will-AM-it") offers bachelor of arts and bachelor of music degrees, and the most popular majors are economics, politics, Spanish, psychology, and history. Students say other good bets include biology and chemistry. All students complete the freshman College Colloquium seminar, four writing-centered courses, two courses in quantitative and analytical reasoning, study in a language other than English, and coursework in six modes of inquiry—the natural world; the arts; arguments, reasons, and values; thinking historically; interpreting texts; and understanding society. Students also take capstone senior seminars, often culminating in research or thesis projects. Fifty-five percent of the student body participates in a robust study abroad program that sends them to nearly 40 nations, and Willamette also benefits from its proximity to the United States campus of Tokyo International University.

Classes are small; 72 percent of those taken by freshmen have 19 or fewer on the roster. Students work hard but don't compete for grades. "People work hard, but are always willing to help each other out. Study groups form spontaneously, and I've never heard of anyone worried about ruining the curve by studying with others," says a senior. Outside the classroom, the computerized card catalog and spacious study lounges in the Mark O. Hatfield Library (named for the former U.S. senator) make it easier to shoulder the workload. If students aren't reading or writing papers, numerous undergraduate research opportunities beckon. Support has more than doubled with the creation of the Carson Undergraduate Research Awards, the Science Collaborative Research Program, and a humanities center. Notable majors include archaeology, Chinese studies, American ethnic studies, contemporary music improvisation, and combined mathematics and economics.

Students give Willamette's professors high marks for being "amazing, engaging, and supportive." Without a doubt, the low student/faculty ratio helps foster this personal atmosphere. If the college is suffering budget cutbacks, students haven't taken notice. "In fact, we've been in a state of expansion," says a senior.

Classes are small; 72 percent of those taken by freshmen have 19 or fewer on the roster.

"The typical Willamette student is hard to describe, because there are students who express their individuality through purple hair and bare feet, students who dress in suits most days because they have internships in the Governor's office, students who are passionate and dedicated musicians, students who like to party, and everything in between," says one psychology major. Twenty-six percent of WU students are native Oregonians, and much of the remainder comes from Western states, notably California and Washington. African Americans make up 5 percent of the student body, Hispanics 10 percent, and Asian Americans 10 percent. Women's issues and race relations spark discussion on campus. "There are always rallies being formed," says a sophomore. "Willamette tends to be very involved in state and city political issues." Willamette offers talent and academic merit scholarships each year averaging $15,128; there are no athletic awards.

Seventy-eight percent of Willamette students live in campus housing, which is social and convenient to classes and parties; doing so is required for freshmen and sophomores. "Housing is a great introduction to the Willamette community," an anthropology major says. All housing is co-ed, and theme wings or floors are available, focused on community service, the outdoors, wellness, or substance-free living. "Willamette's wellness floors are very popular and build very strong relationships," says a politics major. The student-owned and operated Bistro offers a coffeehouse atmosphere and is a popular alternative to cafeteria fare. "I like the food at Willamette a lot," says a history major. "I think that people complain about the food just because it is a normal thing to do, but, really, it is good food." When it comes to security, students feel very safe on campus, although "some of the neighborhoods around campus can be problematic," according to one chemistry major.

Most of WU's social life takes place on campus.

Most of WU's social life takes place on campus, whether it's free movies and lectures, open-mic nights at the Bistro, dance parties (salsa or swing), or performances by the music and theater departments. "There are events happening on campus virtually every night, but there are also parties off campus if you want to find them," says a student. Eighteen percent of the Willamette men and 20 percent of the women go Greek. The Ram Brewery draws big crowds on Thursdays. Annual social highlights include the spring Wulapalooza, celebrating art and music, and the Hawaiian Club Luau, where students chow down on spit-roasted pig. Each fall, students from Tokyo International organize the Harvest Festival. Other wacky traditions include being Mill-Streamed—dumped into the campus

"The typical Willamette student is hard to describe."

brook on your birthday. When it comes to drinking, Willamette abides by state law, which says no one under 21 can imbibe—but students say anyone who wants booze can find and consume it behind closed doors.

Downtown Salem is a short walk from campus, and while students say it's no college town, it does have movies, shopping, restaurants, and coffeehouses. Also nearby are the Cascade Mountains and rugged beaches of Lincoln City and Coos Bay (an hour's drive), skiing and snowboarding on Mount Hood or in the high desert town of Bend (three hours), and the cosmopolitan cities of Portland (40 minutes) and Seattle (about four hours north). San Francisco is an eight- to nine-hour drive. Willamette students remain true to the school motto, "Not unto ourselves alone are we born," when they go "Into the Streets" for a day of service each fall.

The Willamette Bearcats compete in Division III, and football, men's basketball, and women's softball are strong. The men's and women's cross-country teams have won numerous West Region Championships in recent years. The annual football game against Pacific Lutheran usually has conference championship implications, and games against Linfield are also well attended.

Willamette may be the best little school you've never heard of, especially if you're from outside the California-Oregon-Washington corridor. "Community is what sets Willamette apart. Many of the Pacific Northwest schools look similar on paper, but once you step foot on campus it is clear how warm and caring students, staff, and faculty are," says a senior. The school's close-knit community is strengthened by its emphasis on service and by warm, supportive faculty members who push students to achieve.

Overlaps

Lewis & Clark, University of Puget Sound, University of Portland, UC–Davis, University of Oregon, UC–Berkeley, University of Washington, Whitman

If You Apply To ➤

Willamette: Early action: Nov. 15. Regular admissions and financial aid: Feb. 1. Housing: Jun. 7. Application fee: $50. Campus interviews: optional, informational. No alumni interviews. SATs or ACTs: required. Subject Tests: optional. Accepts the Common Application. Essay question.

College of William and Mary

P.O. Box 8795, Williamsburg, VA 23187-8795

Founded in 1693 as a private university, William and Mary is the original public Ivy. History, government, and international studies are among the strongest departments. With more than 6,000 undergraduates, larger than Mary Washington and Richmond, and smaller but more intellectual than the University of Virginia. Has recently raised its quota of out-of-staters to help cope with a funding squeeze.

Website: www.wm.edu

Location: Small City

Public

Total Enrollment: 7,761

Undergraduates: 6,091

Male/Female: 45/55

SAT Ranges: CR 630–740, M 620–720

ACT Ranges: 28–32

Financial Aid: 33%

Expense: Pub $ $ $ $

Student Loans: 41%

Average Debt: $ $

Phi Beta Kappa: Yes

Applicants: 13,660

Accepted: 32%

Enrolled: 33%

Grad in 6 Years: 90%

Returning Freshmen: 96%

Academics: ✎ ✎ ✎ ✎ ✎

Social: ☎ ☎ ☎

Q of L: ★ ★ ★

Admissions: (757) 221-4223

Email Address: admission@wm.edu

Strongest Programs:
Business
Government
History
Psychology
English
Biology

Though the physical campus might seem stuck in a time warp, students say everything about William and Mary—from the amazing faculty to the picturesque grounds—is up to date. Traditions abound, yet this historic university—the second oldest in the nation after Harvard—continues to evolve in its pursuit of academic excellence. "Students at William and Mary choose to attend the college for its intense academic rigor, strong sense of community, rich history, and legacy of traditions," says one senior. It has graduated three former United States presidents—Thomas Jefferson, James Monroe, and John Tyler. Rival UVA prides itself on being "Mr. Jefferson's" university, but W&M has the distinction of having educated Mr. Jefferson in the first place.

> "I would rate the quality of teaching as extraordinary."

A profusion of azaleas and crape myrtle adds splashes of color to William and Mary's finely manicured campus, located about 150 miles southeast of Washington, D.C. The campus is divided into three sections and includes Lake Matoaka, the oldest human-made lake in Virginia, and a wooded wildlife preserve, which is filled with trails and widely used by the science departments. The Ancient Campus is a grouping of three colonial structures, the oldest being the Sir Christopher Wren Building, which was constructed between 1695 and 1700 and is the oldest college building and arguably one of the loveliest in the country that remains in use. The Old Campus, where the buildings date from the '20s and '30s, recently added a 390-room residence hall. New Campus, where ground was first broken in the '60s, includes an Integrated Science Center, a recreation center, and the 95,000-square-foot Sadler center. The W&M campus boasts one of the most romantic spots of any in the nation: Crim Dell, a wooded area with a small pond spanned by an old-style wooden bridge. A spate of new construction includes 11 new fraternity houses and a significant renovation of Tucker Hall.

William and Mary, which was founded as a private college and did not go public until 1906, created Phi Beta Kappa in December of 1776. The honor code, established by Thomas Jefferson in 1779, demands much from the college's students. Fittingly, the history department, which cosponsors the Omohundro Institute for Early American History and Culture with Colonial Williamsburg, is a signature program at William and Mary. Business, government, psychology, English, and biology are among the most popular majors. The accounting program ranks in the top 20 nationwide; employers seek out graduates from the program. There are summer and yearlong study abroad programs around the globe, from Europe to China, South Africa, Russia, and Mexico, and summer field schools in archeology. Another program allows students to spend two years in Williamsburg and two at St. Andrews in Scotland and end up with degrees from both institutions. Approximately 46 percent of W&M's graduating class receive credit for studying abroad. The top 7 percent of freshmen are designated Monroe scholars and receive summer research stipends to support independent projects, typically used after their sophomore or junior year.

> "Students are a little dorky, but incredibly nice, bright, and giving."

The academic climate is rigorous, students say, but cooperation among peers is the norm. "There have been many times when I had to miss a class and all I had to do was send an email to fellow students before my email inbox was full of helpful notes. This type of setting makes the classes more fun, easier, and productive," says one history major. Nearly half of all classes have 19 or fewer students, although a few introductory lectures may have a couple hundred. Virtually every class is taught by a full professor, and TAs are used for grading or lab purposes only. The college established freshman seminars, limited to 15 students each, which provide even closer faculty interaction. "I would rate the quality of teaching as extraordinary," says a senior. "The professors here have their own ways of teaching, but also opening up a platform for students to freely discuss topics and learn from one another's experiences."

W&M graduation requirements are thorough and include proficiency in a foreign language, writing, and computing (major-specific). More specific general education requirements include a course in mathematics and quantitative reasoning; two courses in the natural sciences; two in the social sciences; one each in literature and history of the arts and creative and performing arts; and one course in philosophical, religious, and social thought. The Center for Honors and Interdisciplinary Studies allows outstanding students four semesters of intensive liberal arts seminars, with lectures by top scholars from around the country, and facilitates interdisciplinary majors like American studies, environmental science, and women's studies.

William and Mary students are "a little dorky, but incredibly nice, bright, and giving," according to one student. Another adds, "Students are generally very hard-working and diverse in talents and convictions." Because William and Mary is a state-supported university, roughly two-thirds of its students are Virginians.

"Freshman dorms are freshman dorms."

Competition for the nonresident spots—mostly taken by students from the mid-Atlantic and farther north—is stiff. Ninety-seven percent of freshmen ranked in the top quarter of their high school class. The college has made a major effort to recruit and retain more minorities; Asian Americans now account for 6 percent of the students, Hispanics make up 9 percent, and African Americans contribute 7 percent. An ongoing series of programs in the residence halls addresses safety issues as well as diversity and gender communication. "Students are incredibly well informed regarding current issues," says an English major. W&M has its share of eagerly recruited athletes; 288 athletic scholarships are offered annually. Merit scholarships are doled out to qualified undergrads.

Seventy-two percent of the undergraduates live on campus in mostly co-ed dorms that range from stately old halls with high ceilings to modern buildings equipped with air-conditioning. All freshmen are guaranteed a room on campus (with cable, wireless, and Internet connections), but after that students try their luck with the infamous room selection process ("stressful but efficient"). "Freshman dorms are freshman dorms," says one senior. "They are nice, clean, and livable, but by no means paradise." Special-interest housing is available—there are seven language houses and an International Studies hall, Africa House, Community Scholars House, and a Mosaic House—and life in a fraternity or sorority house is also an option. Students give the three campus cafeterias less-than-stellar reviews, but all freshmen must purchase a meal plan. Others have a variety of options, including cooking in the dorms and dinner plans in sorority and fraternity houses. "The food is just OK and I'm not always a fan of what is available," observes a senior. Campus security is regarded as tight, although crime is not a big issue.

W&M isn't known as a social school, but there's always something to do on campus. "Social events take place on and off campus, with recent years trending

The accounting program ranks in the top 20 nationwide; employers seek out graduates from the program.

Each year, more than 500 Tribe student-athletes compete on 23 Division I teams.

more off campus," observes a public policy major. "Greek life makes up much of the off-campus social life, whereas clubs and organizations operate mostly on campus." On any given weekend, students can enjoy the soothing voices of one of the many a cappella groups, dance the night away at fraternity parties, grab a midnight snack at the Sadler Center, or watch the latest dance or theater performance at Phi Beta Kappa Theater. Twenty-five percent of the men and 30 percent of the women join Greek organizations, which host most of the on-campus parties. The few local bars pick up the rest. The college has strict policies against underage drinking, but students say as long as they are safe, they stay out of trouble. The Office of Student Activities sponsors mixers, bands, and a film series.

Anyone who gets restless can always step across the street to Colonial Williamsburg to picnic in the restored area, walk or jog down Duke of Gloucester Street (called "Dog Street"), or study in one of the beautiful gardens. "Eventually, you don't raise an eyebrow when Colonial reenactors are behind you at the grocery store buying beer," quips one senior. Its appeal to tourists notwithstanding, Williamsburg leaves much to be desired as a college town. Nightlife is a hit-or-miss affair (mostly miss), although volunteer opportunities abound and many students participate. Richmond and Norfolk, each an hour's drive, are top road trips; the University of Virginia, although an archrival, is also popular; and Virginia Beach, a favorite springtime mecca, is a little farther away.

Traditions are the stuff of which William and Mary is made, and perhaps the most cherished is the annual Yule Log Ceremony in the Wren Building, where students sing carols and hear the president, dressed in a Santa Claus outfit, read the Dr. Seuss story *How the Grinch Stole Christmas*. Grand Illumination is a great Christmas fireworks display in nearby Colonial Williamsburg, and on Charter Day, bells chime and students celebrate the distinguished history of their 300-year-old institution. Each year, freshmen walk through the Wren Building for Opening Convocation, where they're greeted by cheering upperclassmen and faculty. Four years later, as they graduate, they walk through the Wren in the other direction. Romantics will be happy to learn that any couple who kisses at the top of Crim Dell Bridge will eventually be married. The Seven Society, a secret society of students dedicated to the college, is among the most revered on campus. "William and Mary has four centuries' worth of traditions, legends, and mysteries," says one senior. Each year, more than 500 Tribe student-athletes compete on 23 Division I teams. Twenty-one intramurals and clubs such as softball and ultimate Frisbee attract a large percentage of the student body. The recreational athletic complex serves the health and fitness needs of students and faculty.

"William and Mary has four centuries' worth of traditions, legends, and mysteries."

From Thomas Jefferson to Jon Stewart, William and Mary has educated some of the nation's most famous and infamous. William and Mary's traditions stretch back to the dawn of this nation, and its grand old campus and stirring history make it a distinguished and cherished part of many students' lives. "Students learn so much from amazing peers and find great mentors in the faculty and administration," says a senior. "At the end of their time here, students feel they have learned a lot as students, but have grown as people."

If You Apply To ➤ **William and Mary:** Early decision: Nov. 1. Regular admissions: Jan. 1. Application fee: $70. Campus interviews: optional, evaluative. No alumni interviews. SATs or ACTs: required. Subject Tests: optional. Accepts the Common Application. Essay question: personal statement.

Williamstown, MA 01267

Running neck and neck with Amherst on the selectivity chart, Williams occupies a campus of surpassing beauty in the foothills of the Berkshires. Has shaken the preppy image, but still attracts plenty of well-toned, all-around jock-intellectuals who will one day be corporate CEOs. The splendid isolation of Williamstown is either a blessing or a curse.

Williams College vies with rival Amherst for possession of both the color purple—they each use it on team uniforms and in their logos—and the title of most selective liberal arts college in the United States. While both schools have large numbers of "preppy, white, rich kids," students at Williams tend to be more "athletic, well-rounded, driven, friendly, and liberal," says a junior. At this isolated hamlet in the Berkshires, school spirit abounds, and the stunning natural backdrop helps keep everyone in a good mood. When not gazing at the purple mountains' majesty, students at Williams are digging into their studies with fervor.

The college's buildings constitute a virtual omnium-gatherum of architectural styles, from the elegantly simple Federal design of the original West College to contemporary structures by Charles Moore and William Rawn. The brick and gray stone buildings are arranged in loosely organized quads, which are both enclosed and open to nature. Students may take advantage of WCMA (the Williams College Museum of Art), the Clark Art Institute, and MASS MoCA, a nearby center for contemporary visual, performing, and media arts.

The Williams curriculum emphasizes interdisciplinary studies and personalized teaching. The majority of courses taken by freshmen enroll 25 students or fewer. Distribution requirements include at least three courses in each of the school's three divisions, languages and arts, social studies, and sciences and mathematics; two must be completed by the end of the sophomore year. Students must also fulfill requirements in writing and in quantitative and formal reasoning, pick a major from more than 30 options, pass four quarters of phys ed, and spend at least six semesters in residence. The optional First-Year Residential Seminars allow one group of students taking a common course to live in the same hall, helping to integrate the social and intellectual aspects of college life. Williams has increased the number of its courses taught in the Oxford tutorial format: Two students and a faculty member meet each week, with the students alternating who has to write a paper and who gets to critique it. Students also must complete

"There is little sense of competition between students."

four winter study projects or courses during the January Winter Study. Students with wanderlust may accompany faculty members on relatively inexpensive study tours, to exotic locales such as India, the former Soviet Union, and West Africa during Winter Study.

In addition, in January, the Free University, designed by students, is in operation and students may sign up for enrichment courses in which they teach each other everything from how to make wontons to how to do the jitterbug. If the walls of campus threaten to close in, especially during the bitter and blustery winter, take a term away, through the college's study away office, the Twelve College Exchange*, or the Williams at Mystic Seaport* program. There's also an innovative program organized with Oxford's Exeter College in England, as well as the Africa programs. One of Williams's greatest strengths is art history, which benefits from one of the finest college art museums in America, along with economics, psychology, political science,

Website: www.williams.edu
Location: Small Town
Private
Total Enrollment: 2,065
Undergraduates: 2,011
Male/Female: 48/52
SAT Ranges: CR 670–780, M 660–780
ACT Ranges: 30–34
Financial Aid: 53%
Expense: Pr $ $ $ $
Student Loans: 31%
Average Debt: $
Phi Beta Kappa: Yes
Applicants: 7,069
Accepted: 17%
Enrolled: 45%
Grad in 6 Years: 96%
Returning Freshmen: 96%
Academics: ✍ ✍ ✍ ✍ ✍
Social: ☎ ☎ ☎
Q of L: ★ ★ ★
Admissions: (413) 597-2211
Email Address: admission@williams.edu

Strongest Programs:
Economics
Psychology
History
Political Science
Biology
Art History
English

math, and history, students say. Students in the environmental program can perform fieldwork in 2,000-acre, college-owned Hopkins Forest. The college's ample resources are made possible by its hefty endowment, the largest of any small liberal arts college.

"Courses are rigorous and most professors are very demanding both in terms of workload and critical engagement," says one senior, "but there is little sense of competition between students." There are only two small graduate programs at Williams—in art history and in development economics—so graduate students are few and far between and you'll never find them at the lectern. "Professors insist on having a personal connection with the students and always help if needed," a student explains. "The quality of teaching is excellent." Faculty members are quick to return email, says a sophomore, and may invite students over for informal get-togethers and home-cooked meals. The college also provides a stipend for advisors to take their charges out for a bite to eat.

Students with wanderlust may accompany faculty members on relatively inexpensive study tours, to exotic locales such as India, the former Soviet Union, and West Africa during Winter Study.

The typical Williams student is bright, enthusiastic, energetic, and well informed about current events. "Williams students are amazing," says one student. "I know people who can read *Harry Potter* in Latin, translate rap songs into Arabic, and sight-read 'Rocket Man' perfectly on the piano." African Americans make up 11 percent of the student body, while Asian Americans add 14 percent, and Hispanics comprise 10 percent. Politically, Williams is mostly liberal, says a student, and "there are students who are passionate about politics and social issues, but they are not a majority." There are no merit or athletic scholarships, and the school's program to eliminate all loans from financial aid packages has been scrapped due to the recession.

Most students remain in the dorms for all four years because they're guaranteed a bed—and because only seniors are eligible to move out. Some freshmen luck into large single rooms in one of the school's dorms. "All the dorms at Williams are good," says one student. "You can't go wrong with any housing here." First-years live in groups of about 20 students each (known as "entries") along with junior advisors, who serve as big siblings, mentors, and sounding boards. After the first year, students have an affiliation with one of four upperclassmen residential neighborhoods and enter their housing draw. Small co-ops are available for seniors who want to cook and simulate a more off-campus living experience. Campus dining receives mixed reviews: "They make a big effort, but the results are unpredictable," says one student.

"The school brings in a lot of speakers, comedians, and musical groups."

Fraternities and sororities were abolished long ago, but that hasn't stopped Williams students from partying. "Social life is mostly on campus because there really isn't anything to do in Williamstown," says one student. Another adds, "The school brings in a lot of speakers, comedians, and musical groups, but for the most part, the social life revolves around parties in dorms." Drinking is a popular pastime on weekends, but most students report no pressure to imbibe. The college has taken steps to make sure that whatever drinking does go on happens safely by offering a first-year education program at the beginning of the school year, outlawing drinking games, requiring registration of parties over a certain size, mandating availability of food and nonalcoholic beverages whenever alcohol is present, and regulating tailgating. Further measures are under review by a faculty/student committee. Films and concerts abound on most weekends, while favorite traditions include Winter Carnival, Spring Fling, the Harvest Dinner, and Mountain Day, one of the first three Fridays in October. Which day it will be is a well-kept secret, broken only when the college president sends out an email canceling classes, and church bells begin tolling at 8 a.m. Students hike to the top of Mount Greylock, where hot cider and donuts are waiting on the summit.

The typical Williams student is bright, enthusiastic, energetic, and well informed about current events.

The small village of Williamstown is "sort of the quintessential New England town," says a student. When students aren't holed up in the library, nearby slopes and trails beckon, offering skiing, cycling, and backpacking. The main street in town boasts "several strange clothing stores that I've never been in, a bunch of overpriced antique shops and pharmacies, and three ethnic restaurants," says a political science major. The Clark Art Institute, within walking distance of campus, possesses one of the finest collections of Renoir and Degas in the nation, as well as a great library. The modern college music center attracts top classical musicians, and the college theater is home to the Williamstown Theatre Festival, which often features Broadway stars. There's a Walmart 15 minutes away and a Stop and Shop grocery store even closer, and civilization—in the form of Albany, New York—is just an hour's drive. Other popular destinations include New York City (three hours by car).

Sports are more like a religion here than an extracurricular activity. The Williams Ephs are a perennial winner of the Division III Directors Cup, awarded annually to the school with the strongest overall athletic program and athletes have an edge in admission (as long as they are also smart). Any contest with archrival Amherst ensures a big crowd. After all, Amherst was founded in 1821 by a breakaway group of Williams students, along with the school's then-president. The men's and women's swim teams are nationally ranked, and the men's tennis, basketball, and track and field teams are among the many that have brought home conference titles. Softball and field hockey are likewise strong, and the squash and ski teams are so good they compete in Division I.

It takes a special kind of student to be happy at Williams. Those who delight in the life of the mind, who can take or leave the creature comforts found at more urban schools, will no doubt bleed purple by the time they leave. "You feel safe here—isolated, yet shielded from the outside world," says a Chinese major. Certainly, what's warm and fuzzy for some is claustrophobic for others. Generally, though, among students who stick it out, "complaints are few and far between," reports a recent graduate. "We love it!"

Overlaps

Amherst, Brown, Dartmouth, Harvard, Middlebury, Princeton, Stanford, Yale

If You Apply To ➤ **Williams:** Early decision: Nov. 10. Regular admissions: Jan. 1. Application fee: $65. Campus interviews: optional, informational. No alumni interviews. SATs or ACTs: required. Subject Tests: required (any two). Accepts the Common Application. Essay question.

University of Wisconsin–Madison

BEST BUY

702 W. Johnson Street, Suite 1101, Madison, WI 53706-1481

Madison draws a third of its students from out of state, the highest proportion among leading Midwestern public universities. Why brave the cold? Reasons include top programs in an array of professional fields and several innovative living/learning programs. There's also the pleasure of life in Madison, a combination state capital/ college town in the mold of Austin, Texas.

At the University of Wisconsin–Madison, nearly 30,000 undergraduates take advantage of world-class academics and a rich array of resources. Professional programs are strong and you'll need a strong desire to learn—and a very warm coat—to succeed here.

Described by one Madison student as "architecturally olden with a modern touch," the mainly brick campus is distinctive. It spreads out over 936 hilly, tree-covered acres and across an isthmus between two glacial lakes, Mendota and

Website: www.wisc.edu
Location: City Center
Public
Total Enrollment: 37,726
Undergraduates: 27,883
Male/Female: 48/52

(continued)

SAT Ranges: CR 530–650,
M 630–750

ACT Ranges: 26–30

Financial Aid: 63%

Expense: Pub $ $

Student Loans: 49%

Average Debt: $ $

Phi Beta Kappa: Yes

Applicants: 29,034

Accepted: 55%

Enrolled: 40%

Grad in 6 Years: 83%

Returning Freshmen: 95%

Academics: ✑ ✑ ✑ ✑ ½

Social: ☎ ☎ ☎ ☎

Q of L: ★ ★ ★ ★

Admissions: (608) 262-3961

Email Address:
onwisconsin@admissions
.wisc.edu

Strongest Programs:
Political Science
Psychology
English
Economics
History

For students who prefer the academic road less traveled, options include the Integrated Liberal Studies (ILS).

Monona, named by prehistoric Native Americans who once lived along their shores. From atop Bascom Hill, the center of campus, you look east past the statue of Lincoln and the liberal arts buildings, down to a library mall that was the scene of many a political demonstration during the '60s. Farther east you see rows of State Street pubs and restaurants and the bleached dome of the Wisconsin state capitol. On the other side of the hill, another part of campus, dedicated to the agricultural and health sciences, twists along Lake Mendota. But students from both sides of the hill congregate in the old student union, the Rathskeller, where political arguments and backgammon games can rage all night. Outside on the union's veranda, students can look out at the sailboats in summer or iceboats in winter.

"It's easy to get lost in the crowd here."

Madison's academic climate is demanding. Predictably, grading is tough and inflexible and often figured on a strict curve. "There are a lot of smart people studying here," notes one student. A list of first-rate academic programs at Madison would constitute a college catalog elsewhere. There are 70 programs considered in the top 10 nationally. Some highlights include education, agriculture, communications, biological sciences, and social studies. The most popular majors are political science, biology, economics, history, and psychology. Due to overcrowding, some popular fields, such as engineering and business, have had to restrict entry to their majors by requiring high GPAs.

Distribution requirements vary among the different schools and academic departments, but they are uniformly rigorous, with science and math courses required for B.A. students, and a foreign language for virtually everyone. All students must fulfill a three-part graduation requirement in quantitative reasoning, communication, and ethnic studies. For students who prefer the academic road less traveled, options include the Integrated Liberal Studies (ILS), which consists of related courses introducing the achievements of Western culture. A variety of internships are available, as are study abroad programs all over the world, including Europe, Brazil, India, Israel, and Thailand.

Professors at Madison are certainly among the nation's best, with Nobel laureates, National Academy of Science members, and Guggenheim fellows scattered liberally among the departments. While the university's size can be daunting, harried freshmen aren't left to fend for themselves. The university offers a number of first-year programs designed to ease the transition into college life. A first-year seminar encourages students to examine learning strategies, connect with faculty, staff, and peers, and become familiar with campus resources. First-Year Interest Groups consist of 20 first-year students who may live in the same residence hall or "residential neighborhood" and who also enroll in a cluster of three classes together. Each FIG cluster of courses has a central theme; the central or "synthesizing" course integrates content from the other two classes.

"Frat parties are a very popular break from the bar scene."

If there is one common characteristic among Madison undergraduates, it is assertiveness. "It's easy to get lost in the crowd here, so you have to be fairly strong and confident," declares one student. "No one holds your hand." The flip side is that "anyone can fit in, you just have to find your own niche." Just less than two-thirds of the students are from Wisconsin. The school is a heartland of progressive politics, and Madison's reputation as a haven for liberals remains intact. "Students here are called liberal because they are eager and willing to change and are continually looking for newer and better ideas," explains an activist. African Americans and Hispanics currently make up 7 percent of the student body, while Asian Americans constitute another 6 percent. Academic merit scholarships are awarded each year, and most of the sports on campus offer full scholarships. The Madison Initiative for Undergraduates raises funds for need-based institutional aid for needy undergraduates.

Twenty-five percent of undergrads reside in university housing. Dorms are either co-ed or single sex and come equipped with laundry facilities, game rooms, and lounges. Most also have a cafeteria. The student union also offers two meal plans, and there are plenty of restaurants and fast-food places nearby. Campus safety is always an issue, but the school offers a variety of services for those on campus. There are escort services for those walking and those needing a ride, and a free shuttle system that operates seven days a week. Madison (a.k.a. Madtown) has been the stomping ground for many fine rock 'n' roll or blues bands on the road to fame.

There are more film clubs than anyone can follow, and everyone has a favorite bar. Nine percent of the men and 8 percent of the women go Greek. "Frat parties are a very popular break from the bar scene," reports one expert on both options. One old standby that is still as popular as ever is the student union, which hosts bands, shows, and so forth and provides a great atmosphere in which to hang out. Volunteering is another popular option; for a decade the university has provided the Peace Corps with the most entrants of any college or university in the nation. Nature enthusiasts can lose themselves in the university's 12,000-acre nature preserve or hit nearby ski slopes.

The students at this Big Ten school show "tons of interest" in sports, especially hockey and football, and especially when the Badgers try to rout the University of Michigan's Wolverines. Bucky Badger apparel, emblazoned with slogans ranging from the urbane to the decidedly uncouth, is ubiquitous. However, the much-acclaimed marching band may outdo all the teams in popularity. The Badgers are recent Big Ten champions in a number of sports, notably men's cross-country, men's basketball, men's indoor and outdoor track, and women's hockey. Intramurals are also popular.

One of the best and most well-rounded state schools anywhere, Madison is a school that students sum up as "diverse, intellectual, fashionable, and moderately hedonistic." And these are the qualities that attract bright and energetic students from everywhere. "You feel you're accepted for who you are no matter what," says one student. "It's so nice to just be yourself."

Volunteering is another popular option; for a decade the university has provided the Peace Corps with the most entrants of any college or university in the nation.

Overlaps

Boston University, University of Illinois, Indiana, University of Michigan, Northwestern

If You Apply To ➤

Wisconsin: Rolling admissions: Feb. 3. Housing: May 1. Application fee: $44. No campus or alumni interviews. SATs or ACTs (with writing): required. No Subject Tests. Essay question. Special consideration given to students from disadvantaged backgrounds.

Wittenberg University

P.O. Box 720, Springfield, OH 45501

Wittenberg is an outpost of cozy Midwestern friendliness. Less national than Denison or Wooster, Witt has plenty of old-fashioned school spirit and powerhouse Division III athletic teams. Top students should aim for the honors and fellows programs, the latter providing a chance for undergraduate research. Witt doles out plenty of merit scholarships to better-than-average students.

Founded in 1845 by German Lutherans, Wittenberg University remains true to its faith by emphasizing strong student/faculty relationships—and making sure that students don't become too comfortable in the campus bubble. In fact, before granting their diplomas, Wittenberg requires students to complete 30 hours of community service in the surrounding town of Springfield (population 65,000). Students

Website: www.wittenberg.edu
Location: Small City
Private
Total Enrollment: 1,714

(continued)

Undergraduates: 1,714
Male/Female: 45/55
SAT Ranges: CR 500–600,
 M 500–620
ACT Ranges: 23–28
Financial Aid: 95%
Expense: Pr $ $
Student Loans: 71%
Average Debt: $ $ $ $
Phi Beta Kappa: Yes
Applicants: 4,887
Accepted: 91%
Enrolled: 11%
Grad in 6 Years: 65%
Returning Freshmen: 78%
Academics: ✍ ✍ ✍
Social: ☎ ☎ ☎
Q of L: ★ ★ ★
Admissions: (877) 206-0332
Email Address: admission@
 wittenberg.edu

Strongest Programs:
Education
Biology
Management
Psychology
English

Professors are roundly praised for their teaching styles and willingness to make themselves available outside the classroom.

at Wittenberg work hard at their studies, but they are also actively engaged in more than 120 student organizations, performing arts groups, and intramurals. "The campus is beautiful, it's a great school, and it's so obvious how much everyone here loves it," gushes an education major. "It already feels like home."

The Wittenberg campus is classic Midwestern collegiate, with a mixture of 1800s and Gothic-inspired buildings on 100 rolling acres in southwestern Ohio. The red-brick Myers residence hall, with picturesque white pillars and an open-air dome dating from the 19th century, stands at the center. Blair Hall—which houses the university's education department—includes more than 21,000 square feet of combined classroom and laboratory space. Students also appreciate the campus locale. "Our proximity to quaint country living and the abundance of opportunity in the city makes for an ideal location," says a junior.

"It's a great school, and it's so obvious how much everyone here loves it."

Wittenberg's general education requirements emphasize a solid liberal arts background. The school's Wittenberg Plan includes 17 learning goals, ranging from experience with writing and research to exposure to the natural sciences and foreign languages. Students select courses from a variety of disciplines to meet the goals, and also must fulfill requirements in religion or philosophy, non-Western cultures, and physical education. Wittenberg has comprehensive First-Year Programs for new students, which include a leadership development program and academic and social support services. There is also a University Honors Program that enrolls 25 percent of all students, and ample opportunities to work on research with faculty members.

Wittenberg students give high marks to the school's education department; other strong programs include biology, English, and business—so perhaps it's not surprising that the most popular majors on campus are in those fields. Other strong programs include East Asian studies, Russian and Central Eurasian studies, and theater and dance. The academic climate is described as "challenging but friendly," and study groups are common, according to one junior. Professors are roundly praised for their teaching styles and willingness to make themselves available outside the classroom. "Students take advantage of having professors who are extremely knowledgeable by getting help with class problems or even career advice," one senior says.

Despite Wittenberg's small size, students say they have no trouble registering for needed courses and graduating in four years. So long as students declare their major on time and complete all courses with a C or better, the college guarantees a degree in four years—and will pay for any additional necessary courses. Wittenberg also encourages students to take a semester or a year away from campus, either in the U.S. or abroad, and 25 percent do so. Options include the International Student Exchange Program, field study in the Bahamas, work with the National Institutes of Health in Washington, D.C., or a summer in Wittenberg's Local Government Management Internship Program. Wittenberg also offers 3–2 engineering programs with Columbia University and Case Western Reserve. Minors include health science, international studies, financial economics, and sports management.

"Witt students are proactive," says a junior. "We are constantly championing new causes, whether through community service or fund-raising. We are always on the go!" Seventy-one percent of Wittenberg students are native Ohioans and 2 percent hail from other countries. Many others are from nearby states like Indiana, Michigan, and Pennsylvania. African Americans comprise 7 percent of the student body, and Hispanics and Asian Americans together account for 4 percent. The school's multicultural affairs director looks to boost those modest numbers through changes in

"Students take advantage of having professors who are extremely knowledgeable."

minority recruiting and advising. Students say the campus is fairly evenly split between conservatives and liberals, and both groups are vocal. "Everyone is open to different opinions," a biology major says. Wittenberg offers merit scholarships but no athletic scholarships. The Wittenberg College Access Program (WittCAP) provides special financial aid packages to academically talented students from low-income families.

Eighty-three percent of all Wittenburg students reside on campus; freshmen and sophomores are required to do so. After that, most choose nearby houses and apartments owned by the school. "Dorms are spacious and air-conditioned," a student says, "with options for all-girls, honors, and substance-free housing." Sophomore students have first dibs on rooms, and then the freshmen are assigned to the remaining rooms, so almost everyone gets a double when he or she first comes to campus. Greek groups draw 30 percent of the men and 33 percent of the women; members may live in chapter houses. For those in need of sustenance (perhaps to fuel those all-night study sessions), there is a variety of dining options. "The food doesn't taste the best, but is acceptable," says one sophomore. There is also a salad bar, and vegetarian and low-fat options do exist.

When the weekend rolls around, social life centers on parties in houses, dorm rooms, and apartments on or near campus. "There is always something to do," says a junior. Greek groups, the Union Board, and the Residence Hall Association also bring in guest speakers, movies, comedians, and concerts.

> **"We are constantly championing new causes."**

Favorite annual events include Greek Week, homecoming ("the alumni involvement is incredible"), and Wittfest in May, a music festival with games, food, prizes, and socializing before finals. "It is open to the community, but all the students go," a senior says. "It resembles a carnival, and at night there's a big concert on the lawn." There's also W Day, a day during the week preceding Wittfest in which many students skip classes to party outside. Springfield has movie theaters, a mall, restaurants, and a $15 million performing arts center. Popular road trips include Dayton (30 minutes), Columbus (45 minutes), and Cincinnati (90 minutes), and for those with more time, Washington, D.C., New York City, and Chicago. Nearby state parks also offer swimming, camping, biking trails, and picnics in the warmer months, and skiing in the winter.

Wittenberg's athletic teams (the "Tigers") are competitive in Division III, especially in the major sports. Recent championship teams include men's football and basketball (each with the most victories in NCAA Division III history), and women's volleyball, soccer, and basketball. Rivalries with Allegheny, Wabash, and The College of Wooster really get students riled up. Intramurals and club sports are a huge draw, too, with sports such as crew, ice hockey, and rugby. Weekend warriors may take advantage of the Bill Edwards Athletic and Recreational Complex, which boasts a stadium and eight-lane track, football and soccer fields, 12 lighted tennis courts, a state-of-the-art fitness center and weight room, plus a pool and racquetball courts.

While not as well known as many of its bigger Midwestern brethren, Wittenberg has plenty to offer those students who decide to attend, including solid honors and fellows programs, an active Greek scene, and serious Division III athletics.

Recent championship teams include men's football and basketball (each with the most victories in NCAA Division III history).

Overlaps

Miami (OH), Ohio State, Ohio Wesleyan, Denison, University of Dayton, College of Wooster, Capital, Otterbein

If You Apply To ➢

Wittenberg: Rolling admissions. Early decision: Nov. 15. Early action: Dec. 2. Application fee: $40 (paper), free (online). Campus interviews: recommended, evaluative. Alumni interviews: optional, informational. SATs or ACTs: optional. Subject Tests: optional. Accepts the Common Application. Essay question.

Wofford College

429 North Church Street, Spartanburg, SC 29303-3663

Wofford is about one-third as large as Furman and roughly the same size as Presbyterian. With more than a few gentleman jocks, Wofford is one of the smallest institutions to compete in Division I football. Fraternities and sororities dominate the traditional social scene. Among the few small colleges with more men than women.

Website: www.wofford.edu
Location: Small City
Private
Total Enrollment: 1,588
Undergraduates: 1,588
Male/Female: 51/49
SAT Ranges: CR 570–670,
   M 590–680
ACT Ranges: 23–28
Financial Aid: 90%
Expense: Pr $
Student Loans: 50%
Average Debt: $ $
Phi Beta Kappa: Yes
Applicants: 3,197
Accepted: 63%
Enrolled: 22%
Grad in 6 Years: 84%
Returning Freshmen: 89%
Academics: ✍ ✍ ✍
Social: ☎ ☎
Q of L: ★ ★ ★
Admissions: (864) 597-4130
Email Address: admission@
   wofford.edu

Strongest Programs:
Life Sciences
Prelaw
Business
English
Computer Science
Economics

Wofford students take pride in the Wofford Way, combining a well-rounded curriculum built on traditional strengths in the STEM disciplines with career-related internships and study abroad. The college has taken bold steps to increase enrollment while lowering the student/faculty ratio. Students study hard under the "eyes of Old Main" and often visit their professors' homes for dinner, forming lasting friendships with peers and faculty members. Wofford "is a world of its own and it holds a special place in every student's heart," says a sophomore.

> **"My courses have been incredibly challenging."**

Wofford is near the heart of Spartanburg, a midsize city in the northwest corner of South Carolina. Founded in 1854, it's one of fewer than 200 existing American colleges that opened before the Civil War—and it still operates on its original campus. Azaleas, magnolias, and dogwoods surround the distinctive, twin-towered Main Building and four original faculty homes on the 150-acre campus, which has been designated an arboretum. Nearly 4,500 trees have been planted since 1992. Recent construction includes a new organize chemistry laboratory and a new center for choral and instrumental music.

Traditionally, Wofford's strongest and most attractive programs have been in the life sciences, which account for more than one-third of its graduates and a large share of its Phi Beta Kappas. Business programs, especially when combined with a second major in foreign languages, and English, with its emphasis on creative writing, are solid and getting better. Students rave about Wofford's programs in biology and economics. Nearly two dozen of the school's 260 graduates go on to graduate medical or dental programs within two years of graduation; another two dozen go on to prestigious law schools. For aspiring entrepreneurs, Wofford's alumni network has clout: More than 1,200 of its 15,000 living graduates serve as heads or owners of corporations or organizations. Prospective engineers may apply for 3–2 programs with Clemson or New York's Columbia University. Religion, English, foreign language, and study abroad programs also get high marks, especially for the one lucky junior chosen as the Presidential International Scholar. This student is sent around the world, all expenses paid, to study an issue of global importance for a year. Students in the Creative Writing Sequence end by writing a novella, the best of which is given the Benjamin Wofford Prize and is published in paperback.

"My courses have been incredibly challenging and academically enriching," a senior says. Dozens of new courses and interdisciplinary course sequences have been added to the curriculum in the past decade. Courses are required in English, fine arts, foreign languages, humanities, science, history, philosophy, cultural perspectives, math, and physical education. Wofford also boasts a unique program called the Novel Experience, part of the first-year orientation.

> **"Students tend to be fairly conservative."**

The program consists of a common reading, which is then discussed during a meeting of 22 humanities classes at different restaurants throughout Spartanburg. The Presidential Seminar brings together 20 outstanding graduating seniors representing different majors for selected readings from classical and contemporary essays. The seminar participants and invited guests come together once a week for a three-hour class in which they discuss philosophy, politics, and the complexities of human nature.

"Professors get to know students on a personal level and encourage students to come visit their office about both class and personal concerns," says a psychology major "Many help students secure research positions, internships, and other opportunities." The Wofford College Success Initiative is a scholarship-based learning community that complements the curriculum. While not for academic credit, it reinforces traditional liberal arts concepts such as critical thinking and communications through intellectual explorations and experiences. Students take one exploration each fall semester and propose an independent or small-group exploration that could form the basis of team projects. Recent programs include learning American Sign Language with faculty and students at the South Carolina School for the Deaf and Blind.

Sixty-five percent of the student body graduated from public high school—55 percent in the top 10th of their class. "I would say students who attend Wofford are very bright, driven, and wealthy. Many were at the top of their classes in high schools," says a senior. "Students tend to be fairly conservative and very Southern—you'll see a whole lot of polo shirts and khakis," adds another. African Americans comprise 8 percent of the student population, Asian Americans 3 percent, and Hispanics 2 percent. Politically, the campus is fairly conservative but all viewpoints are represented, students say. "There tends to be a small but vocal liberal minority challenging standards of tradition," says a junior. Merit scholarships averaging $14,769 are available to qualified students, and especially needy students may be eligible for the Bonner Scholars program. There are also more than 110 athletic scholarships available in 19 sports.

Ninety-three percent of Wofford's students live in the dorms, where first-year women get doubles in Greene Hall, and their male counterparts have similar digs in Marsh Hall. "Each year that you are at Wofford, the housing situation gets better and better," says a biology major, "culminating in the Village—a fantastic apartment community for the seniors." Students give so-so marks to the college cafeteria. "The food lacks diversity and there is a blandness to the taste," says one student. Campus security is also said to be less than stellar. "We feel as if our Campus Safety officers are not properly trained to handle dangerous situations," one senior says.

The Greek system is a huge force in Wofford's social life, with fraternities attracting 43 percent of the men and 55 percent of the women. Each fraternity has a house and most host parties every Friday and Saturday—with some kicking off the weekend on Thursday. "The social life at Wofford College is exciting and fun," says one student. "Most social activities do take place on campus, although Spartanburg and Greenville also have a lot to offer." The campus is dry, except for certain events, like Spring Weekend, where alcohol for those of age is allowed on Fraternity Row, a student says. The Student Affairs Committee offers campuswide events like comedians and music for those uninterested in the Greek system.

"Most social activities do take place on campus."

Off campus, Spartanburg is home to Converse College and a few other schools. Students say it's not a great college town, but that is changing with the addition of coffee shops and other fun hangouts. Students can head to Greenville, Atlanta, and Charlotte. And almost every Wofford student participates in some type of volunteer work. Terrier Play Day brings kids from the community to campus for a fair with booths and games. Bid Day, when the fraternities tap their new members, is another annual tradition, involving lots of mud, and then a bath in the college fountain. Every year before finals, student musicians and readers perform a Festival of Nine Lessons and Carols, perhaps praying as well for luck on their exams. "Spring Weekend is another event that is always a much anticipated time of the year at Wofford, as there are bands, cookouts, shaving cream fights, and a beach volleyball tournament," says a student.

The Presidential Seminar brings together 20 outstanding graduating seniors representing different majors for selected readings from classical and contemporary essays.

The campus is dry, except for certain events, like Spring Weekend.

The Wofford Terriers have gotten the best of former rival The Citadel in football in recent seasons.

The Wofford Terriers have gotten the best of former rival The Citadel in football in recent seasons and won Southern Conference titles in 2011 and 2012. Men and women compete side by side on Wofford's riflery team and the school fields a team in the Southeastern Air Rifle Conference. Other solid programs include men's basketball (2009 and 2010 conference champs) and soccer.

Wofford's former chaplain was fond of saying, "You don't come to Wofford—you join it." And students say that's true, citing the close-knit community and intimate student/faculty relationships fostered by the school's small size. "I've often said that there is a close community at Wofford, but it is really more of a family," says a senior. "Administrators are not merely the authority but are real friends to students. Wofford is a family of seekers with learning as its focus."

If You Apply To ➤

Wofford: Early decision: Nov. 1. Early action: Nov. 15. Regular admissions: Feb. 11. Financial aid: Mar. 1. Housing: May 1. Application fee: $35. Campus and alumni interviews: optional, informational. SATs or ACTs: required. Subject Tests: optional. Accepts the Common Application. Essay question.

The College of Wooster

Wooster, OH 44691

Though not well-known to the general public, Wooster is renowned in academic circles around the world. Getting in is not difficult, but graduating takes work. All students complete an independent study project in their last two years. More intellectually serious than competitors such as Denison. Prides itself on turning above-average students into real scholars.

Instead of teaching students what to think, The College of Wooster focuses on teaching students how to do so. From the first courses of the freshman-year seminar to the final day when seniors hand in their theses, the college paves each student's path to independence. The emphasis here is on global perspectives and the heritage that stems from its origin as a college founded by Presbyterians. The one-to-one attention from faculty makes Wooster an intellectual refuge in the rural countryside of Ohio. A senior says Wooster most appeals to students who "enjoy academic challenges, a strong and friendly community, and hands-on learning experiences."

Located in the city of Wooster, Ohio, COW's hilltop campus is spread over 240 acres, many campus buildings designed in the English–collegiate Gothic style and constructed of cream-colored brick. More recent buildings are trimmed in Indiana limestone or Ohio sandstone. The central arch and two towers of Kauke Hall, the central building in Quinby Quadrangle, the square around which the college grew, make it stand out. The Gault Library for Independent Study offers a private carrel for each senior in the humanities and social sciences. Scot Center, a 123,000-square-foot student recreation center, opened in early 2012 and features four indoor courts for basketball, volleyball, and tennis; a 200-meter track; a fitness center; and new locker rooms, meeting rooms, and athletic department offices.

What goes on behind the facades of Wooster's attractive buildings is more impressive than the structures themselves. The required first-year seminar in critical inquiry, limited to 15 students per section, invites students to engage in issues, questions, or ideas around a variety of topics. Recent examples include The History of the Future; The Psychology and Persuasion of Advertising; and Oil, Terror and

Political Islam in West Africa: Should We Be Very Afraid? "The climate is collaborative," says one student, and "the research skills you develop are second to none."

Wooster's curriculum is built around the required Independent Study, which lets students explore subjects they're passionate about with one-on-one faculty guidance. Independent Study has become such a part of COW that each year seniors celebrate IS Monday—the day they turn in their projects—with a campuswide parade. "We are led around campus by the bagpipers," says a senior. "The whole campus

"The climate is collaborative."

shows up." Completion of the IS earns you a Tootsie Roll, to eat or keep for posterity next to your diploma. "It's a day all Wooster graduates will always remember!" a senior says. The college even awards almost $100,000 each year for student research, travel, or materials to support thesis work.

In addition to the critical inquiry seminar, three semesters of Independent Study, and six cross-discipline courses, Wooster mandates courses in writing, global and cultural perspectives, religious perspectives, and quantitative reasoning; foreign language proficiency; and seven to nine courses in the student's major. Students praise faculty members for their devotion to teaching and mentoring; only a few introductory courses have teaching assistants, who run review sessions and offer extra help. "The professors are freakin' awesome," gushes a freshman. "They are so concerned for the students and the topic they are teaching, and are willing to put in hours and hours of extra time and effort to make sure the students succeed." It's not uncommon for science majors to coauthor faculty papers, while students in the Jenny Investment Club manage a million-dollar portion of the college's assets, with professors serving as advisors.

"Wooster is not an easy school. It has rigorous academic programs with high, but accessible standards," says one English major. The most popular majors at Wooster are English, history, psychology, biology, and political science. The foreign language departments are small but provide individual attention to each student. Students in the biochemistry/molecular biology program take a foundation of core science courses and can choose between upper-level chemistry and/or biology classes along with their Independent Study. Wooster also sponsors overseas programs on five continents, by itself and through the Great Lakes Colleges Association*.

"The students here are openhearted, hardworking, honest, and well rounded," a freshman says. And as the college's reputation spreads, it's becoming more selective, with acceptance rates falling and freshman-retention rates improving. African Americans constitute 9 percent of the student body, Asian Americans 3 percent, and Hispanics 4 percent. Wooster has a strong international flavor—7 percent of students hail from foreign nations. Thirty-five percent of the students are from Ohio. Merit awards averaging $18,000 are available and over $42 million in aid takes the form of merit scholarships and need-based grants offered to students without repayment obligation.

Ninety-nine percent of students live on Wooster's smoke-free campus in 12 co-ed and one single-sex dorm, where rooms are small but comfortable. "They are not the newest buildings but they definitely get the job done," says a mathematics major. Students stay connected with the community through the Wooster Volunteer Network. Students seriously committed to service may apply to live in one of the college's 29 residential program houses, each of which is affiliated with a community

"The professors are freakin' awesome."

group. Food in the two campus dining halls is getting better, more parking has been added, and all dorms are now wired for cable television. Given Wooster's location "in the middle of corn fields," security isn't an issue, students say, although emergency phones are strategically located just in case. "Campus security is very involved and accessible," one student says.

(continued)

Admissions: (800) 877-9905
Email Address: admissions@ wooster.edu

Strongest Programs:
Biology
Economics
English
Communication
Political Science
Psychology
History
Sociology and Anthropology

Wooster's curriculum is built around the required Independent Study.

Wooster social life is campus-based, thanks in large part to the school's isolated location. "The vast majority of social life takes place on campus," says a senior. "Most students go out on Wednesday and Saturday nights, and Wooster students know how to party." As for alcohol, "it is getting harder and harder for underage students to be served" on campus, says a senior. The college has no national Greek organizations, but local "sections" draw 14 percent of men and "clubs" attract 20 percent of women. One major weekend hangout is the Underground, a bar and dance club that hosts well-known bands, as well as the campus's bowling alley, pool hall, and game room. The school's Scottish heritage can be seen in its bagpipe band, which naturally performs in kilts, and in its Scottish dancers, who trot on stage during the fall's Scot Spirit Day. "The Scot Bagpipers playing 'Amazing Grace' is beyond compare," says a junior. Other annual traditions include the outdoor Party on the Green, a fall concert, and the formal Winter Gala, where students, faculty, and staff dance the night away to the sounds of a swing band. When it snows—which it does quite often in Wooster—the student body descends upon the central arch and fills it with snow.

> **Wooster social life is campus-based, thanks in large part to the school's isolated location.**

> **"The students here are openhearted, hardworking, honest, and well rounded."**

Wooster fields a number of competitive Division III teams. Fighting Scots basketball is a spectator favorite and other competitive programs include women's lacrosse and field hockey, and men's baseball. Any match versus rival Wittenberg usually brings out the fan in Wooster students (you have to get the free tickets well ahead of time), and men's and women's soccer, men's and women's swimming, and women's lacrosse have been strong in recent years.

The College of Wooster is nationally recognized for its commitment to independent study and its international focus. Wooster students are proud to be "fighting Scots" and independent thinkers. They make do during the long, cold winters by immersing themselves in study and finding ways to have a good time. A senior has only one complaint about his time at Wooster: "It goes too fast!"

Overlaps
Denison, Ohio State, Kenyon, Ohio Wesleyan, Allegheny, Oberlin, Miami (OH), DePauw

If You Apply To ➤

Wooster: Early decision and early action: Nov. 15. Regular admissions: Feb. 15. Application fee: $40 (paper), free (online). Campus and alumni interviews: optional, evaluative. SATs or ACTs: required. No Subject Tests. Accepts the Common Application. Essay question: personal statement.

Worcester Polytechnic Institute

100 Institute Road, Worcester, MA 01609-2280

Small, innovative, and undergraduate-oriented, WPI is anything but a stodgy technical institute. The WPI Plan is hands-on and project-based and takes a humanistic view of engineering. Emphasizes teamwork instead of competition. Global emphasis unusual for an engineering school. The only test-optional techie school, WPI is half the size of Rensselaer and a third as big as MIT.

Website: www.wpi.edu
Location: Small City
Private
Total Enrollment: 4,384

As a pioneer in engineering education, Worcester Polytechnic Institute has built a solid reputation. But with its ever-expanding academic curriculum, surprising devotion to music and theater, and dedication to hands-on undergraduate experiences, WPI has expanded the definition of what it means to be a techie haven. Students must complete several extensive projects, endure seven-week semesters, and engage in real-world experiences. But it's WPI's humanistic approach to engineering that really sets it apart.

WPI is the third-oldest independent science and engineering school in the nation. Its compact 80-acre campus is set atop one of Worcester's "seven hills" on the residential outskirts of town and borders two parks and the historic Highland Street District, where local merchants and students come together to form the neighborhood community. Old English stone buildings complete with creeping ivy are focal points of the architecture, but modern facilities have moved in to claim their own space on the immaculately kept grounds. A 145,000-square-foot sports and recreation center was completed on 2012 and includes fitness space, a four-court gymnasium, swimming pool, jogging track, and other amenities.

"WPI is a very competitive atmosphere."

The intent of WPI's unique grading system and educational philosophy is to polish social skills, build self-confidence, produce well-rounded students, and nurture young people interested in using their knowledge to improve the world. WPI focuses especially on developing teamwork. The curriculum remains remarkably flexible for a high-powered technological university. Standard course distribution requirements vary by major but include courses in engineering, math, and science. Every WPI student must also complete a humanities and arts requirement. To promote cooperation and cohesiveness, the only recorded grades are A, B, C, or No Record. Failing grades do not appear on transcripts, and the school does not compute GPAs or class ranks.

There are four terms per academic year at WPI, each lasting seven weeks, which students say changes the climate. "WPI is a very competitive atmosphere," says one student. The Interactive Qualifying Project has students apply technical knowledge to one of society's problems and the Major Qualifying Project represents a student's first chance to work on a truly professional-level problem. Courses provide the information students need to complete their projects, reemphasizing WPI's curriculum as one driven by knowledge and not credit. When students are not completing projects, they take three courses per term. Some say it's difficult to graduate in four years in majors such as chemical engineering.

The most popular programs are mechanical engineering, electrical and computer engineering, civil engineering, chemical engineering, biomedical engineering, and robotics engineering. There are also a number of interdisciplinary programs such as prelaw, bioinformatics and computational biology, and international studies. The school has launched the nation's first undergraduate program focusing on robotic engineering, which emphasizes mechanical, electrical, and computer engineering knowledge and has grown to include M.S. and Ph.D. programs,

"The quality of teaching is very high."

making it the first university to offer all three levels. A major in Interactive Media and Game Development requires coursework in computer science and the humanities and arts. Many biomedical engineering majors do their projects at UMass Medical and Tufts Veterinary, as well as at local hospitals. WPI has a joint Ph.D. Program with UMass medical school. WPI also offers a rare fire protection engineering program and a system dynamics major and minor. Math and science types can pick up middle or high school teaching credentials on the way through the university's new STEM education center. The theater technology major requires projects in set, lighting, or audio design, which means school shows often highlight cutting-edge production techniques. Well over 300 students participate in 22 musical and theatrical groups; WPI has one of the largest music programs among technological universities. Professors are praised for their availability and willingness to establish relationships. "The quality of teaching is very high at WPI," says a biotechnology

(continued)

Undergraduates: 3,730
Male/Female: 68/32
SAT Ranges: CR 560–670, M 640–720
ACT Ranges: 27–32
Financial Aid: 99%
Expense: Pr $ $ $
Student Loans: N/A
Average Debt: N/A
Phi Beta Kappa: No
Applicants: 7,585
Accepted: 53%
Enrolled: 24%
Grad in 6 Years: 84%
Returning Freshmen: 96%
Academics: ✎ ✎ ✎ ½
Social: ☎ ☎ ☎
Q of L: ★ ★ ★
Admissions: (508) 831-5286
Email Address: admissions@wpi.edu

Strongest Programs:
Computer Science
Mechanical/Electrical and Computer Engineering
Biology/Biotechnology
Biomedical Engineering

To promote cooperation and cohesiveness, the only recorded grades are A, B, C, or No Record.

major. "All of the professors have a Ph.D. or the terminal degree in their field and they are at WPI because they want to teach undergraduates."

In light of an increasingly interdependent global economy, WPI offers a unique Global Perspectives Program that spans more than 30 project centers on six continents. More than 50 percent of WPI students visit locations including France, South Africa, Argentina, Australia, Costa Rica, Hong Kong, and Namibia. The school's residential project centers in New York, Silicon Valley, Washington, D.C., England, Denmark, Italy, Puerto Rico, and Thailand provide students with the opportunity to tackle current problems for a sponsor and spend the term working independently on a specific sociotechnical assignment under the direction of one or more faculty members. The co-op program offers upperclassmen two eight-month work experiences and adds an extra half or full year to the degree program.

"One unifying characteristic of WPI students is their high level of involvement in campus and community activities, many of which are unrelated to science/engineering fields," explains one aerospace engineering major. Ninety-two percent of students ranked in the top quarter of their high school class. African Americans and Hispanics together account for 10 percent of the students, and Asian Americans

"There is an abundance of on-campus programming."

represent an additional 5 percent. International students comprise 13 percent of the student body. Politics doesn't factor too much into campus debates, though students are aware of current events. Typical complaints include the lack of parking, the need for better recreational facilities, and the dearth of females on campus. Merit scholarships averaging $15,584 are doled out annually, but there are no athletic scholarships. The Marshall/Chavez/Means Scholarship recognizes the academic achievements of African American, Latino, and American Indian students, and awards typically range from $12,500 to $25,000.

Only first-year students are guaranteed spots in the university residence halls; however, the room-assignment process usually allows upperclassmen their first, second, or third choice. There are 12 co-ed halls, including a spacious 230-bed residence hall that houses students in suites of four or six, on-campus apartments, and smaller houses for more homelike living. "WPI recently opened a new state-of-the-art residence hall which includes student-suggested amenities such as air-conditioning, technology suites, and dedicated music practice rooms," notes a senior. Fifty-three percent of the students live on campus, and they can choose from the multiple meal plans of the dining halls. "The dining facilities are very good and diverse. We have a main dining hall, a food court, and a restaurant so there is something for everyone," a senior says.

Twenty-eight percent of the men join fraternities and 41 percent of the women enter sororities. "Students can stay busy and entertained for the entire year with just the events on campus," says one senior. Of-age students may have alcohol, provided it is kept in their rooms, but underage students find a way to imbibe. In addition to Greek parties, there are student-organized coffeehouses, board game nights, laser tag, concerts, poetry readings, movies, and pub shows. "There is an abundance of on-campus programming including movies on weekends, monthly musicians and comedians, intramural sporting events, clubs activities, and much more," says a student. Nearby colleges such as Assumption, Clark University, and Holy Cross are linked to WPI through shuttle buses, which provide even more social and academic opportunities. Boston and Hartford are both an hour's drive, as are ski resorts and beaches.

A notable campus tradition is the Goat's Head Rivalry, a grudge match between the freshman and sophomore classes that includes the Pennant Rush, a rope pull next to Institute Pond, and a WPI trivia competition. The prize? A 100-year-old bronze goat's head trophy (the winning class's year is engraved on it). There is also

Overlaps

Rensselaer Polytechnic Institute, Northeastern, MIT, University of Massachusetts, Rochester Institute of Technology, Cornell, Boston University, Carnegie Mellon

an annual festival of international culture and QuadFest, complete with carnival rides. Students say the campus center encourages cohesiveness across the campus and offers a viable alternative to the Greek domination of the social scene.

While not particularly scenic (to say the least), Worcester does offer a large number of clubs and restaurants and an art museum. A large multipurpose arena is host to frequent concerts and occasional visits from Boston's Bruins and Celtics and a minor-league hockey team. The WPI Engineers compete in NCAA Division III sports and fields a number of competitive teams, including men's basketball (sporting 10 consecutive seasons with 20 or more wins) and baseball. More than half of the student body participates in intramural and recreational sports.

One of WPI's chants is fittingly mathematic: "E to the x, d-y, d-x, e to the x, d-x; cosine, secant, tangent, sine; 3.14159; e^i, radical, pi; fight 'em fight 'em WPI!" If you know what any of that stuff means, you'll fit right in.

If You Apply To ➤ | **WPI:** Early action: Jan. 1. Regular admissions and financial aid: Feb. 1. Application fee: $60. Campus interviews: optional, evaluative. No alumni interviews. SATs or ACTs: optional. Subject Tests: optional. Accepts the Common Application. Essay questions: personal choice.

Xavier University of Louisiana

BEST BUY

1 Drexel Drive, New Orleans, LA 70125

Xavier's strategic location in New Orleans is its biggest drawing card. XU is bigger than a small college, but smaller than most universities. Competes with other leading historically black institutions such as Howard, Morehouse, and Spelman. About one-fourth of the students are Roman Catholic, and a like number are of an ethnicity other than African American. Strong in pharmacy and other sciences.

As the nation's only historically African American Roman Catholic college, Xavier University remains committed to "the promotion of a more just and humane society." This small New Orleans university prepares students for their chosen careers while providing a strong foundation in the liberal arts. With its stellar reputation for graduating a wealth of scientists, Xavier has much to offer. Says one English major: "Xavier is where future leaders are made."

The school was founded in 1915 by Katharine Drexel, a former Philadelphia socialite who devoted her life to the education of African Americans and Native Americans. Drexel was canonized in 2000 by Pope John Paul II. Xavier is located near the heart of New Orleans in a quiet neighborhood dotted with bungalows. The focal point of the campus is the Library Resource Center, which, with its green roof and stately neo-Gothic architectural style, has become a landmark for those traveling by car from the New Orleans airport to the French Quarter. A closed campus green mutes the urban feel of the encroaching city, and yellow brick buildings have been erected among the older limestone structures. Xavier was hard-hit in 2005 by Hurricane Katrina, which left the entire campus underwater. The university shut down for the fall semester, and more than 500 students, mainly freshman, did not return. Since then, however, enrollments have been returning to normal and, thanks in part to hurricane relief funds, Xavier has gone on a $65 million renovation and building spree that includes the

"If you want to go into medicine, I would recommend Xavier."

Website: www.xula.edu
Location: City Center
Private
Total Enrollment: 2,976
Undergraduates: 2,396
Male/Female: 29/71
SAT Ranges: CR 430–560, M 440–550
ACT Ranges: 19–25
Financial Aid: 92%
Expense: Pr $
Student Loans: N/A
Average Debt: N/A
Phi Beta Kappa: No
Applicants: 3,987
Accepted: 64%
Enrolled: 26%
Grad in 6 Years: 47%
Returning Freshmen: 65%
Academics: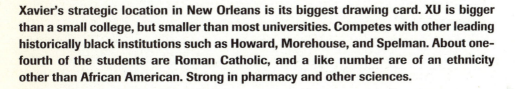

(continued)

Social: ☎ ☎ ☎

Q of L: ★ ★ ★

Admissions: (504) 520-7388

Email Address: apply@xula
.edu

Strongest Programs:
Biology
Chemistry
English
Psychology
Art

The university maintains its reputation as one of the most effective teaching institutions anywhere.

When students tire of microscopes and Mass, they can trek into the Crescent City.

state-of-the-art Qatar Pharmacy Pavilion (donated by the Persian Gulf country), a new sports complex, and the stunning St. Katharine Drexel Chapel designed by renowned Argentine architect Cesar Pelli.

The university maintains its reputation as one of the most effective teaching institutions anywhere; the National Science Foundation has designated it as one of only a few Model Institutions for Excellence. Political science is a small but good department, and the psychology and education departments have been traditional strengths. "If you want to go into medicine, I would recommend Xavier," explains a student. "They have one of, if not the best, premed programs for minority students." Nearly two-thirds of the student body majors in a science-related field. Xavier has frequently led the nation in the number of undergraduate physical science degrees awarded to African Americans, as well as the number of African Americans placed into medical school. Xavier is also credited with educating 25 percent of all African American pharmacists nationally. In addition to the many internships available, Xavier offers cooperative education programs in all fields and study abroad programs throughout Europe; Africa; Japan; and North, Central, and South America. The Center for the Advancement of Teaching works to improve pedagogy across the curriculum and encourages African American students to become teachers and researchers, especially in the sciences.

Xavier's undergraduate curriculum is centered on the liberal arts. All students are required to take a core of prescribed courses in theology and philosophy, the arts and humanities, communications, history and the social sciences, mathematics and the natural sciences. Freshmen also take a mandatory seminar to help them adjust to college life. "The academic climate is very competitive," says one chemistry major. "The courses are not a cakewalk and the teachers are here to help, but nothing is given." Priests and nuns teach and help run the school, though the multiracial faculty and staff are composed of laypeople. "Teaching has been excellent due to small class sizes," says a sophomore. "Students are able to interact closely with teachers and each other." Academic and career advising are well received, and registration doesn't present any major concerns. Public health is now available as an undergraduate major.

There is a strong emphasis on community service, which is required with some on-campus organizations. Students are also concerned about social issues outside of the university. "Many information sessions or forums are developed so that Xavier students can be kept abreast of the current events of the world that affect us," a senior says. For a historically African American college, Xavier's student body is quite diverse. Twenty percent of the students come from public schools and 82 percent are African American. Students come mostly from the Deep South; 58 percent are from Louisiana, and a high percentage are second- or third-generation Xavierites. "The students are very goal-oriented," says a student. "They know exactly what they want and go after it." Xavier has achieved a national reputation for its programs to reach out to local high schools to identify and nurture talented minority students. Sixty percent of Xavier students graduated in the top quarter of their high school class. There are athletic and talent awards available to qualified students.

"The students are very goal-oriented."

Forty-seven percent of Xavier students live in the residence halls. "Housing is great," says a student. Three of the four contemporary-looking residence halls are single sex. Though the housing situation is far from perfect, students admit that dorm rooms are comfortable and well kept. New Orleans is a major city with a fair share of crime, so campus security is always an issue. Although Xavier's campus security is highly visible, it "definitely needs to be tightened up," says a chemistry major.

When students tire of microscopes and Mass, they can trek into the Crescent City. Back on campus, fraternities and sororities play a leading role in extracurricular and social life, though only 3 percent of the men and 6 percent of the women go

Greek. Popular events include Bayou Classic and Spring Fest. But don't get caught drinking—Xavier is a dry campus. "They do room inspections and confiscate prohibited items," explains a sophomore. Underage drinkers return to the city where nearly anything goes. When it comes to road trips, students head to Baton Rouge, Shreveport, Tallahassee, Houston, and Miami.

Varsity sports include men's and women's basketball, tennis, and cross-country (all recent conference champs), and the teams are enthusiastically supported, especially when the opponent is rival Dillard. Intramural sports are also offered with high participation from men in basketball, tennis, cross-country, and flag football.

Students at Xavier focus on their studies, community service, and school spirit for basketball. With a mind for the future, Xavier stays true to its beginnings as a historically black and Catholic university and to a mission of preparing students for a future that will "promote a more just and humane society."

Overlaps

Dillard, Florida A&M, Hampton, Howard, Louisiana State, University of New Orleans, Spelman

If You Apply To ➤ **Xavier:** Early action: Jan. 15. Regular admissions: Mar. 1. Application fee: $25. Campus and alumni interviews: optional, informational. Recommendations are very important. SATs or ACTs: required. Subject Tests: optional. Accepts the Common Application. No essay.

Yale University

38 Hillhouse Avenue, New Haven, CT 06511

Yale is the middle-sized member of the Ivy League's big three: bigger than Princeton, smaller than Harvard. Its widely imitated residential-college system helps Yale strike a balance between being a research university and an undergraduate college. New Haven isn't New York, but it has been spruced up in recent years. Plan to work hard.

Founded in 1701 by Connecticut Congregationalists concerned about "backsliding" among their counterparts at a certain school in Cambridge, Massachusetts, Yale has long been recognized as one of the nation's—and the world's—finest private universities, and one of the handful of Ivy League schools focused on undergraduates. Students here remain as focused on their studies and as humble of their achievements as ever. And thanks to Yale's residential college system, this huge research university feels like more of a home for its students. "Yale students are truly happy to be here," says a sophomore. "Everyone has a massive crush on Yale and that makes all the difference in living and working here for four years."

> "Yale students are truly happy to be here."

Yale's campus looks like the traditional archetype—magnificent courtyards, imposing quadrangles, Gothic buildings designed by James Gamble Rogers, and Harkness Tower, a 201-foot spire once washed with acid to create its aged, stately look. All the residential colleges, some of which date back to the 1930s, have been renovated, thanks to a $300 million effort. Yale also has committed $500 million to promote its basic science, engineering, and biomedical research programs. The Malone Engineering Center offers state-of-the-art facilities for undergraduate research. Kroon Hall is a LEED-certified building that houses the environmental studies program—the building uses less than 50 percent of the energy of a similarly sized conventional building.

Inside Yale's wrought-iron gates, academic programs are superb across the board. Arts and humanities programs are especially outstanding. The prominence

Website: www.yale.edu
Location: Urban
Private
Total Enrollment: 11,740
Undergraduates: 5,393
Male/Female: 50/50
SAT Ranges: CR 700–800, M 710–790
ACT Ranges: 32–35
Financial Aid: 52%
Expense: Pr $ $ $
Student Loans: 23%
Average Debt: $
Phi Beta Kappa: Yes
Applicants: 28,977
Accepted: 7%
Enrolled: 68%
Grad in 6 Years: 96%
Returning Freshmen: 99%
Academics: ✎ ✎ ✎ ✎ ✎
Social: ☎ ☎ ☎

(continued)

Q of L: ★ ★ ★

Admissions: (203) 432-9316

Email Address: student.
questions@yale.edu

Strongest Programs:

Art and Architecture

History

English

Biology

Economics

Political Science

Psychology

Music

Drama

of the arts makes for an interesting juxtaposition: While tradition is ever-present on campus, today's Yale attracts one of the most liberal and forward-thinking student bodies in the Ivy League. Still, the Puritan work ethic remains. Graduating from Yale requires 36 credits, or nine courses a year, rather than the 32 courses required at most other colleges. Students agree that hard work is the norm here and collaboration is one of the keys to success. "The academic climate is rigorous, but very doable," says one sophomore. "Students at Yale are all hard workers and bright individuals, and thus classes have a high level of discussion and academic rigor."

Although Yale has 10 professional schools and a Graduate School of Arts and Sciences, Yale College—the undergraduate arts and sciences division—remains the university's heart. Virtually all professors teach undergraduates, and the professional schools' resources—especially architecture, fine arts, drama, and music—are available to them as well. Yale's superb history department offers the most popular undergraduate major, followed by political science, biology, English, and economics. History offers one of the most demanding programs, including a mandatory 30- to 50-page senior essay. The English department is routinely at the vanguard of literary theory, while an outstanding interdisciplinary humanities major includes the study of the medieval, Renaissance, and modern periods. While some science majors grumble about the walk up Science Hill, where most labs and science classrooms are, they agree it's worth the trip. The biological science department is excellent, where student interests range from biomedical engineering research to preparation for medical school. "Students devoted to the sciences find their departments have top-notch professors and unparalleled emphasis on the undergraduate education," a sophomore says. Architecture and modern languages, especially French and Chinese, are first-rate, and the school's Center for the Study of Globalization is renowned as well. Elite students with a particularly strong appetite for the humanities can enroll in Directed Studies, which examines the literature, philosophy, history, and politics of Western tradition. Prospective DSers should be prepared for some serious bonding with their books—they don't call it "Directed Suicide" for nothing. Freshmen with strong science backgrounds can enroll in Perspectives on Science, their version of DS.

> **"Students at Yale are all hard workers and bright individuals."**

Despite its reverence for tradition, Yale doesn't require any specific courses for graduation, and it doesn't have a core curriculum. Instead, students must take two classes in humanities and arts, social sciences, and natural sciences and math, along with two courses that emphasize writing and another two that emphasize quantitative reasoning. Instead of preregistering, students spend two weeks "shopping" at the beginning of each term, sampling morsels of the various offerings before finalizing their schedules. Yale also mandates intermediate-level mastery of a foreign language, and students must study a language for one to three semesters, depending on their proficiency. Although Yale has historically discouraged study abroad (why would anyone ever want to leave New Haven?), this is changing somewhat. Each year, about 100 juniors participate in the Junior Term/Year Abroad program, while others study abroad during the summer, on a leave of absence, or after graduation. Yale also sponsors the Yale World Fellowships, in which burgeoning world leaders spend a semester in a new global leadership program.

The English department is routinely at the vanguard of literary theory.

Introductory-level classes at Yale are usually large lectures, accompanied by small recitation and discussion sections, typically led by graduate teaching assistants. Some of the most popular courses, such as John Gaddis's Cold War history class, seem more like performances, students say. Upper-level seminars are small and plentiful, and underclassmen can usually get into the ones that interest them. Of the 1,000 classes offered each semester, nearly 80 percent have 19 or fewer students.

"The quality of teaching is spectacular. Professors teach almost every single class, and TAs only teach sections of larger lectures. Yale has a policy that requires all of their professors teach undergraduates, so even a freshman may be taking classes from a Nobel laureate," one economics major says. Freshman seminars allow first-year students to interact with professors and peers in small groups.

"The students at Yale wow me everyday," gushes one American studies major. "Yale is a top university, so obviously the kids are bright and hardworking. Above all, though, they are passionate people, not only in that they have hobbies that they enjoy, but activities and pursuits that they believe in." Eighty-eight percent of the student body is from out of state; a large majority of the student body hails from the Northeast. Yale is also consistently more popular with women than many of its rivals, most notably Princeton; the student body is evenly split along gender lines. Most traditions unique to Yale—all-male singing groups like the Whiffenpoofs, drinking at "the tables down at Mory's"—have female counterparts, like Whim 'n Rhythm, if they haven't gone co-ed. African Americans make up 7 percent of students, Hispanics 10 percent, and Asian Americans 16 percent. Foreign students account for 13 percent of the student body. Its best-known alumnus notwithstanding, Yalies are less conservative than their counterparts at Harvard and Princeton, and they aren't shy about expressing their opinions. "Yale students are incredibly active politically and socially and are very conscious of world issues," one history major says. Yale strives to make an education accessible to everyone, shifting focus to attract more students from low-income families; families making less than $60,000 a year don't pay any portion of the cost of their child's education.

The residential colleges that serve as Yale's dorms—and as the focal points for undergraduate social life—are "one of the greatest attractions in a Yale education," says one student. "The residential college is a smaller community among the larger Yale community and is like a family away from home," adds a junior. Endowed by Yale graduate Edward S. Harkness (who also began the house system at Harvard) and modeled on those at Oxford and Cambridge, Yale's colleges provide intimate living/learning communities, creating the atmosphere of a small liberal arts college within a large research university. Each college has a library, dining hall, and special facilities such as photography darkrooms or tree swings— one is even said to have an endowment used solely for whipped cream. Dining halls serve great food,

"The quality of teaching is spectacular."

students say, and one has a completely organic menu. "Dining has been a pleasant surprise. The food varies from day to day, but is usually delicious and diverse," says a student. All colleges also have their own dean and affiliated faculty members, a few of whom live in the college, who can help undergraduates struggling to adapt to the rigors of college life. Residential college masters organize social and cultural events, including master's teas, where prominent public figures meet with groups of students. College-sponsored seminars, along with plays, concerts, lectures, and other events, add to the cultural life of the university as a whole.

Much of each residential college's distinctive identity comes from its architecture. "The dorms are like castles!" says one student. Indeed, some buildings are fashioned in a craggy, fortress-like Gothic style, while others are done in the more open colonial style, with redbrick and green shutters as the prevailing motif. All colleges have their own special nooks and crannies with cryptic inscriptions paying tribute to illustrious Yalies of generations past. Most freshmen live together in the Old Campus, the historic 19th-century quadrangle, before moving into their colleges as sophomores, who, along with juniors, generally live in suites of single and double rooms. Many seniors get singles. Some upperclassmen move into New Haven, although 88 percent choose to stay on campus all four years. "Housing at Yale is unrivaled," insists one student.

Each year, about 100 juniors participate in the Junior Term/Year Abroad program, while others study abroad during the summer, on a leave of absence, or after graduation.

In addition to identifying with their colleges, many Yale students identify strongly with extracurricular groups, clubs, and organizations, spending most of their waking hours outside class at the newspaper, radio station, or computer center. Particularly clubby are the a cappella singing groups, whose members do everything from drinking together on certain weeknights to touring together during spring break. Many of Yale's mysterious secret societies, such as Skull and Bones (which counts President George W. Bush and former presidential candidate John Kerry as members), have their own mausoleum-like clubhouses and issue invitations to those with the right qualifications. There are also the Yale Anti-Gravity Society and improv comedy groups.

Though studying takes the lion's share of their time, students here also find ways to unwind. "Most social activities happen on campus," explains one sophomore. "There are parties but also tons of other events, like movie screenings, club events, and performances. There is never a dull moment." The university doesn't have a strict policy on alcohol, students say. "It's nice that the administration trusts students and I think for the most part students respond really well to that trust," says a junior. Still, the drinking age of 21 is enforced at larger, university-sponsored bashes, pushing most socializing to private parties in the colleges or off-campus apartments. A handful of Greek organizations have yet to make their mark. For the artistically inclined, local film societies offer numerous weekend screenings and York Square Cinemas show indie films, foreign films, and the occasional blockbuster. The Palace Theater and the Shubert Performing Arts Center host touring Broadway musicals, dance companies, musicians, and popular singers. The Tony Award–winning Yale Repertory Theater is an excellent, innovative professional company that depends heavily on graduate school talent but always brings in a few top stage stars each season. "On the weekends, the life stays on campus as there is so much going on," says a junior. Natural history and art museums on and near campus, especially the British Art Center, are excellent. For those who want more excitement, the typical Yalie refrain on New Haven—"It's halfway between New York and Boston"—tells it all. Metro North trains run almost hourly to New York, and visiting Boston is nearly as easy. Storrs, Connecticut, home of UConn, is also a popular road trip.

> **"The residential college is a smaller community among the larger Yale community."**

Once-gritty New Haven is now "the perfect college town," students say, because of its size and location and proliferation of new restaurants and other gathering places. "New Haven itself has amazing restaurants offering every possible type of cuisine and venues to attract shows, concerts, and movies," cheers one student. A summer jazz festival brings thousands to the historic town green, and there are outdoor ethnic food fairs and theatrical performances. The city's long-standing theatrical tradition—it was once the place to try out plays headed for Broadway—has been revived with the reopening of two grand old theater and concert halls a block from campus. Locals will swear that Pepe's on Wooster Street was the first (and best!) pizza parlor in the country, while Louis's Lunch was the first true hamburger joint. On Saturdays, "all roads lead to Toads," a popular dance club. Relations between students and locals are improving, and more than two-thirds of Yale undergrads do volunteer work in town through Dwight Hall, the largest college community service organization in the country.

Yale fields a full complement of athletic teams (the Bulldogs), which play in the Division I. More than half the student body takes part in intramural competition among the residential colleges; the winning college gets the coveted Tying Cup. The annual Harvard–Yale football game is the hottest event on campus. The men's ice hockey team won the national Division I championship in 2013.

Yale is one of America's oldest institutions of higher learning, and students and graduates here take seriously the intonation, "For God, for country, and for Yale."

In addition to identifying with their colleges, many Yale students identify strongly with extracurricular groups, clubs, and organizations.

For proof, just remember that among its alumni, Yale counts the presidents or former presidents of about 70 other colleges and universities, as well as three recent presidents of the United States. As the university passes its three hundredth anniversary, its past and former students continue to make their marks on the world. "Yale offers a collegial and relaxed atmosphere that makes your four years here some of the most enjoyable times of your life," says one senior. "Oh, and then there's that world-renowned education you're receiving while you're here."

Overlaps

Harvard, Stanford, Princeton

If You Apply To ➤

Yale: Early action: Nov. 1. Regular admissions: Dec. 31. Financial aid: Mar. 14. Application fee: $75. Campus and alumni interviews: optional, evaluative. SATs or ACTs: required. Subject Tests: required. Accepts the Common Application. Essay question: Common Application and supplement.

Consortia

Students who feel that attending a small college might limit their college experiences should realize that many of these schools have banded together to offer unusual programs that they could not support on their own. Offerings range from exchange programs—trading places with a student on another campus—to a semester or two anywhere in the world on one of the seven continents or somewhere out at sea.

The following is a list of some of the largest and oldest of these programs, some sponsored by groups of colleges and others by independent agencies. An asterisk (*) after the name of a college indicates that the institution is the subject of a write-up in the *Fiske Guide*.

The **Associated Colleges of the Midwest** (www.acm.edu) comprises 14 institutions in five states: Beloit*, Lawrence*, and Ripon* in Wisconsin; Carleton*, Macalester*, and St. Olaf* in Minnesota; Knox*, Lake Forest*, and Monmouth in Illinois; Coe, Cornell*, Grinnell*, and Luther College in Iowa; and Colorado College*.

The consortium offers its students semester-long programs to study art in London and Florence, culture and society in Florence, ecology and human origins in Tanzania, university immersion in Botswana, culture and tradition in India, liberal arts or environmental science in Brazil (Brazil programs are taught in Portuguese and restricted to ACM students), language and culture in Costa Rica, and tropical field research in Costa Rica. Students can stay in Japan for either a term or an academic year with a host family. During the summer, students can also travel to Pune, India, or Mexico City, Mexico, for service learning programs.

The Arts of London and the Florence program are the most popular with students. Language study is a component of all the ACM overseas programs. Prior language study is required for the programs in Costa Rica, Japan, and Mexico. Domestic off-campus programs include Humanities at the Newberry Library (an in-depth research project) or a semester in Chicago in the arts, business, entrepreneurship and society, urban education, or urban studies. Scientists can study at the Oak Ridge National Laboratory in Tennessee.

Living arrangements vary with the program and region. Students in Chicago programs live in apartments and residential hotels. Oak Ridge scientists live in an apartment complex. There are no comprehensive costs for any of the ACM programs, domestic or foreign, and tuition is based on the home school's standard fees. The programs are open to sophomores, juniors, and seniors majoring in all fields. The only programs that tend to be especially strict with admissions are the Oak Ridge, Newberry, and Brazil arrangements.

The **Associated Colleges of the South** (www.colleges.org), incorporated in 1991, is composed of 16 Southern schools (Birmingham–Southern*, Centenary, Centre*, Davidson*, Millsaps*, Rhodes*, Rollins*, University of the South (Sewanee)*, Furman University*, Hendrix College*, Morehouse College*, Southwestern University*, Spelman*, Trinity University*, the University of Richmond*, and Washington and Lee*). Established to strengthen liberal education in the South, the consortium focuses on academic program development (with attention to international programs) and faculty, staff, and student development. Overseas courses are offered year-round. Affiliated and ACS-managed programs offer students several international opportunities: They can trace the transformation of Central Europe through study based in Hungary, explore field biology and sustainable development in Costa Rica, or participate in service learning in Honduras. Students can also study at Oxford and the University of Sydney.

The **Atlanta Regional Council for Higher Education** (www.atlantahighered.org) comprises 20 public and private colleges and universities in the Atlanta area, as well as several specialized institutions of higher education. Members are Agnes Scott College*, Brenau University, Clark Atlanta University, Clayton College and State University, Columbia Theological Seminary, Emory University*, Georgia Gwinnett College, Georgia Institute of Technology*, Georgia State University, Interdenominational Theological Center, Kennesaw State University, Mercer University, Morehouse College*, Morehouse School of Medicine, Oglethorpe University*, Savannah College of Art and Design, Southern Polytechnic State University, Spelman College*, the University of Georgia*, and the University of West Georgia.

Students from member colleges and universities may register for approved courses at any of the other institutions, including those with highly specialized courses. The consortium's interlibrary lending program uses a daily truck delivery service to put more than 10 million books and other resources at students' disposal.

The **Christian College Consortium** (www.ccconsortium.org) comprises 13 of the nation's top evangelical liberal arts schools that collectively enroll 25,000 undergraduates and 7,500 graduates: Asbury, Bethel (MN), George Fox, Gordon*, Greenville, Houghton*, Malone, Messiah, Seattle Pacific, Taylor, Trinity (IL), Westmont, and Wheaton (IL)*.

The consortium offers a "student visitors program" whereby students can spend a semester—with little paper pushing—at any of the member schools. Each school sets the GPA requirement for its off-campus options, which include sustainable tropical agriculture in Haiti, Chinese economic development, and Christian service learning in Guatemala.

More than 100 students (not including freshmen) participate each year, and the cost is strictly the home school's regular fees. Other than a reasonably good grade average, there are no special requirements. Consortium schools share a wide array of international programs on a space-available basis.

The **Five College Consortium** (www.fivecolleges.edu) is a nonprofit organization that comprises Amherst*, Hampshire*, the University of Massachusetts Amherst*, Mount Holyoke*, and Smith* and is designed to enhance the social and cultural life of the 30,000 students attending these Pioneer Valley colleges. Legally known as Five Colleges, Inc., this cooperative arrangement allows any undergraduate at the four private liberal arts colleges and UMass to take any of the 5,300 courses offered by the 2,200-member faculty for credit and use the library facilities of any of the other four schools. A free bus service shuttles students between the schools.

The consortium sponsors joint departments in dance and astronomy, as well as a number of interdisciplinary programs, including African American/black studies, East Asian languages, coastal and marine sciences, Near Eastern studies, and peace and world security studies. Certificate programs are available in Asian studies, African studies, Buddhist studies, coastal and marine sciences (not open to Amherst College), cognitive neuroscience (closed to both Amherst College and UMass Amherst), culture, health, and science, ethnomusicology (pending approval at UMass Amherst), international relations, Latin American studies, logic, Middle Eastern studies, American Indian studies, Russian studies, East European studies, and Eurasian studies. There are five college centers for American studies, East Asian studies, women's studies research, and world languages. Additionally, the consortium offers a major in film studies.

Students from the four smaller colleges benefit from the large number of course choices available at the university. The undergrads from UMass, in turn, take advantage of the small-college atmosphere as well as particularly strong departments such as art at Smith, sculpture at Mount Holyoke, and film and photography at Hampshire. There is also a Five College Orchestra and an open theater auditions policy that allows students to audition for parts in productions at any of the colleges. The social and cultural aspects of the Five College Consortium are more informal than the academic structure. The consortium puts out a calendar listing art shows, lectures, concerts, and films at the five schools, as well as the bus schedules. In addition, student-sponsored parties are advertised on all campuses, and there is a good deal of informal meeting of students from the various schools.

For those students taking courses on other campuses, one's home-school meal ticket is valid on any of the five member campuses for lunch. Dinners are available with special permission. Taking classes at other schools is encouraged, but not usually for first-semester freshmen. The consortium is a big drawing card for all schools involved.

The **Great Lakes Colleges Association** (www.glca.org) comprises 13 independent liberal arts institutions in four states. In Michigan: Albion*, Hope*, and Kalamazoo*. In Indiana: DePauw University*, Earlham College*, and Wabash College*. In Ohio: Antioch, Denison*, Kenyon*, Oberlin*, Ohio Wesleyan*, and The College of Wooster*. And, in Pennsylvania: Allegheny College*. The GLCA offers students off-campus opportunities both in the U.S. and overseas. Domestic programs include a liberal arts urban-study semester in Philadelphia; a New York City arts program; a Newberry Library humanities program in Chicago; and scientific study at Oak Ridge National Laboratory in Tennessee (see the Associated Colleges of the Midwest description for further detail). International offerings include a Japan program based at Waseda University and the Border Studies Program, a hybrid domestic/international program focusing on immigration and other border issues in Tucson, Arizona, and Mexico. The ACM, a similar consortium, collaborates with the GLCA on the Oak Ridge Sciences, Newberry Library, and Japan Study programs. Primarily juniors participate, but the programs are open to sophomores and seniors. The domestic programs in New York and Philadelphia are popular domestic choices for American as well as international students.

The **Lehigh Valley Association of Independent Colleges** (www.lvaic.org) is a 42-year-old cooperative effort between six colleges in the same area of Pennsylvania: Cedar Crest, Desales, Lafayette*, Lehigh*, Moravian, and Muhlenburg*.

Approximately 400 students each year cross-register at member campuses, although the bulk of the activity occurs between schools that are closest to each other. LVAIC facilitates occasional conferences at member colleges on women's studies, ecology and evolution, mathematics, social justice, and medieval studies. A Jewish studies program, headquartered at Lehigh, draws on the faculties of Lehigh, Lafayette, and Muhlenberg. Faculty members travel from college to college in order to offer students a variety of courses in this field. The association's Consortium Professors program puts faculty on two other member campuses each year to teach unusual or special-interest courses. Several members exchange courses by video conferences. Special seminars are arranged at central locations for selected students, with transportation provided. Students at each college are eligible for reduced-rate tickets to plays and other events on campuses of association schools. But the most frequently used service of the association is its interlibrary loan program, which permits students at one institution to use the research facilities of the others. Summer study abroad programs take students to Germany, Spain, and Italy.

The **Maritime Studies Program** (www.williams.edu/williamsmystic) of Williams College and Mystic Seaport Museum is an interdisciplinary semester designed for about 20 undergraduates (primarily juniors, but some second-semester sophomores and seniors) who are eager to augment liberal arts education with an in-depth study of the sea. Participants take four Williams College courses (maritime history, literature of the sea, marine policy, and oceanography or marine ecology). Classes are taught with an emphasis on independent research in the setting of the Mystic Seaport Museum. Classroom lectures are enhanced by hands-on experience in celestial navigation, board building, sailing, blacksmithing, and other historic crafts. Students spend two weeks offshore in deep-sea oceanographic research aboard a traditionally rigged schooner highlighting the purpose of the program: to understand our relationship with the sea—past, present, and future.

Most students are drawn from 20 affiliate colleges: Amherst*, Bates*, Bowdoin*, Colby*, Colgate*, Connecticut*, Dartmouth*, Hamilton*, Middlebury*, Mount Holyoke*, Oberlin*, Smith*, Trinity College*, Tufts*, Union*, Vassar*, Wellesley*, Wesleyan*, Wheaton (MA)*, and Williams*. Credit is granted through Williams College, and financial aid is transferable. Students are evenly split between scientific and humanities backgrounds, and those from all four-year liberal arts colleges are encouraged to apply.

Sea Semester (www.sea.edu, not to be confused with Semester at Sea) is a similar venture for water lovers, but it is designed for students geared more toward the theoretical and practical applications of the subject. Each year, two 12-week voyages are offered in both the fall and spring, as is an eight-week summer trip. Each expedition is thematic and prerequisites vary accordingly. For example, Ocean Voyages is open to students from any major, while Documenting Change in the Caribbean and Oceans and Climate are designed for students from the social sciences and sciences, respectively. Depending on the program, 25 or 48 students are in each session. All majors are considered as long as students are in good academic standing, submit transcripts and recommendations, and have an interview with an alumnus in their area.

Students spend the first half of the term living on Sea's campus in the Woods Hole area and immersing themselves in oceanography and maritime and nautical studies. Independent-study projects begun ashore are completed during the sea component aboard either a schooner or a brigantine, which cruises along the eastern seaboard and out into the Atlantic, North Atlantic, or Caribbean, depending on the season. Recent Pacific programs include San Francisco to Honolulu, Honolulu to the Midway Islands, and Mexico to Tahiti. Six weeks on the ocean is when theory becomes reality, and the usual mission consists of enough navigation, oceanographic data collection, and record keeping to keep even Columbus on the right course.

Students from affiliated colleges (Barnard College*, Boston University*, Carleton College*, College of Charleston*, Colgate*, Connecticut College*, Cornell*, Dartmouth*, University of Denver*, DePauw University*, Drexel*, Eckerd*, The Evergreen State College*, Franklin and Marshall College*, The George Washington University*, Hamilton College*, Ithaca College*, Jacksonville University, Lafayette College*, Lawrence University*, University of Massachusetts Amherst*, University of New Hampshire*, University of North Carolina at Chapel Hill*, University of Northern Colorado, Northeastern University*, Oberlin College*, Oregon State University*, University of Pennsylvania*, Purdue University*, Reed College*, University of Rhode Island*, Rice University*, Ripon College*, Rochester Institute of Technology*, Roger Williams University, Rowan University, Salve Regina University, University of San Diego*, Syracuse University*, Ursinus College*, and Villanova University*) receive a semester's worth of credit directly through their school. Students from other schools must receive credit through Boston University.

Semester at Sea (www.semesteratsea.com) takes qualified students from any college and whisks them around the globe on a study/cruise odyssey. Based at the University of Virginia, this program is administered by the non-profit Institute for Shipboard Education, established in 1976 to promote global education and understanding. It takes around 600 students each term (from second-semester freshmen to grads) and puts them on a ship bound for almost everywhere. The vessel itself is a college campus in its own right. Seventy-five courses are taught by 39 professors in subjects ranging from anthropology to marketing, and usually stressing the international scene as well as the sea itself. What's more, over 50 student organizations, including art, theater, music, service, journalism, and student government, can be found on board. When students aren't at sea, they're in port in any of 12 foreign countries in Europe, the Middle East, Asia, Africa, and South America, and it's not uncommon for leaders and diplomats to meet them along the way.

The program requires a cumulative GPA of 2.75 or higher. Limited financial aid is available in the form of a range of merit scholarships based on demonstrated leadership and GPA. Work study and the usual federal grants and loans can help to defray the cost. Credits are awarded by UVA. Most colleges do recognize the Semester at Sea program and will provide participating students with a full term's worth of credits.

The **Twelve-College Exchange Program** comprises 11 selective schools in the Northeast: Amherst*, Bowdoin*, Connecticut College*, Dartmouth*, Mount Holyoke*, Smith*, Trinity (CT)*, Vassar*, Wellesley*, Wesleyan*, and Wheaton (MA)*. In addition, the Williams-Mystic maritime program is open to exchange students.

The program means that students enrolled in any of these schools can visit for a semester or two (usually the latter) with a minimum of red tape. Approximately 300 students utilize the opportunity each year; most of them are juniors. Placement is determined mainly by available space, but students must also display good academic standing. While the home college arranges the exchange, students must meet the fees and standards of the host school. Financial-aid holders can usually carry their packages with them. Study at the Eugene O'Neill National Theater Institute is also available through the consortium.

The **Washington Semester of American University** (www.american.edu/washingtonsemester) takes about 750 students each year from hundreds of colleges across the country (who meet the minimum academic qualification of a 2.75 GPA) and gives them unbeatable academic and political opportunities in the nation's capital. The program is the oldest of its kind in Washington.

Students take part in a semester of seminars with policymakers and lobbyists, an internship, and a choice between an elective course at the university or a self-designed, in-depth research project. Recent seminar topics include Peace and Conflict Studies with travel to Serbia, Croatia, and Bosnia; an International Environment and Development practicum based in Ghana; and an American Politics seminar that brought notables such as Justice Scalia and Sy Hersh to campus. Students live in dorms on the campus and are guided by a staff of 21 American University professors.

Ninety percent of the students are drawn from 240 affiliated schools. Each semester, approximately 100 students from nonaffiliated schools participate. Although admissions competition depends on the home school and how many it chooses to nominate, the average GPA hovers around a 3.3. Most who participate are juniors, but second-semester sophomores and seniors get equal consideration. The cost is either American University's tuition, room, board, and fees or that of the home school. Just over a third of the affiliated colleges are profiled in the *Fiske Guide*.

Index

Acknowledgments

FISKE GUIDE TO COLLEGES STAFF

Editor: Edward B. Fiske
Managing Editor: Shawn Logue
Contributing Editor: Bruce G. Hammond
Production Coordinator: Julia Fiske Hogan

The *Fiske Guide to Colleges* reflects the talents, energy, and ideas of many people. Chief among them are Shawn Logue, the managing editor, and Julia Fiske Hogan, the production coordinator. I am also grateful for the continuing valuable contributions of Bruce G. Hammond, my coauthor on the *Fiske Guide to Getting Into the Right College* and other resources in the field of college admissions. We continue to marvel at the dedicated, formidable editorial assistance of Dominique Raccah, Todd Stocke, Suzanna Bainbridge, Michelle Lecuyer, Katherine Pidde, and Rachel Kahn. Others who made important contributions were Holly Bahn, Sarah Cardillo, Michael DeCarlo, Liz Kelsch, Bob Lessard, Heather Moore, Sean Murray, Chris Norton, Paul O'Neill, Darren Orange, and Jessica Zulli.

In the final analysis, the *Fiske Guide* is dependent on the contributions of the thousands of students and college administrators who took the time to answer detailed and demanding questionnaires. Their candor and cooperation are deeply appreciated; and while I, of course, accept full responsibility for the final product, the quality and usefulness of the book is a testimony to their thoughtful reflections on their colleges and universities.

Edward B. Fiske
Durham, NC
May 2014

EDITORIAL ADVISORY GROUP

Richard Avitabile, Westport, CT
Nancy Beane, Atlanta, GA
Sam Bigelow, Wallingford, CT
Eileen Blattner, Shaker Heights, OH
Angela Connor, Raleigh, NC
Carol Gill, Dobbs Ferry, NY
Peggy Hoch, Palo Alto, CA
Marsha Irwin, San Francisco, CA
Gerimae Kleinman, Delray Beach, FL
Katrin Muir Lao, Houston, TX

Frank Leana, St. Louis Park, MN
David Miller, Pebble Beach, CA
Judy Muir, Houston, TX
Susan Moriarty Paton, New Haven, CT
Gay S. Pepper, Fairfield, CT
Jan Russell, Walnut Creek, CA
Rod Skinner, Milton, MA
Geoff Smith, San Francisco, CA
Chris Teare, U.S. Virgin Islands

COLLEGE COUNSELORS ADVISORY GROUP

Marilyn Albarelli, Moravian Academy (PA)

Scott Anderson, St. George's Independent School (TN)

Christine Asmussen, St. Andrew's–Sewanee School (TN)

Bruce Bailey, Lakeside School (WA)

Amy E. Belstra, Cherry Creek H.S. (CO)

Greg Birk, American School in Switzerland, Montagnola (CH)

Susan T. Bisson, Advocates for Human Potential (MA)

Francine E. Block, American College Admissions Consultants (PA)

Robin Boren, Education Consultant (CO)

Clarice Boring, Cody H.S. (WY)

John B. Boshoven, Community High School & Jewish Academy of Metro Detroit (MI)

Mimi Bradley, St. Andrew's Episcopal School (MS)

Claire Cafaro, Clear Directions (NJ)

Nancy Caine, St. Augustine H.S. (CA)

Jane M. Catanzaro, College Advising Services (CT)

Mary Chapman, St. Catherine's School (VA)

Kathy Cleaver, Durham Academy (NC)

Jimmie Lee Cogburn, Independent Counselor (GA)

Alison Cotten, Cypress Falls H.S. (TX)

Alice Cotti, Polytechnic School (CA)

Rod Cox, St. Johns Country Day School (FL)

Kim Crockard, Crockard College Counseling (AL)

Carroll K. Davis, North Central H.S. (IN)

Mary Jo Dawson, Academy of the Sacred Heart (MI)

Lexi Eagles, Greensboro Day School (NC)

Dan Feldhaus, Iolani School (HI)

Ralph S. Figueroa, Albuquerque Academy (NM)

Emily E. FitzHugh, The Gunnery (CT)

Larry Fletcher, Salesianum School (DE)

Nancy Fomby, Episcopal School of Dallas (TX)

Daniel Franklin, Education Consultant (CO)

Laura Johnson Frey, Vermont Academy (VT)

Phyllis Gill, Providence Day School (NC)

H. Scotte Gordon, Moses Brown School (RI)

Freida Gottsegen, Education Consultant (GA)

Molly Gotwals, Suffield Academy (CT)

Kathleen Barnes Grant, The Catlin Gabel School (OR)

Madelyn Gray, John Burroughs School (MO)

Amy Grieger, Northfield Mount Hermon School (MA)

Mimi Grossman, St. Mary's Episcopal School (TN)

Elizabeth Hall, Education Consulting Services (TX)

Andrea L. Hays, Education Consultant (GA)

Darnell Heywood, Columbus Academy (OH)

Bruce Hunter, Rowland Hall–St. Mark's School (UT)

Deanna L. Hunter, Shawnee Mission East H.S. (KS)

Linda King, College Connections (NY)

Sharon Koenings, Brookfield Academy (WI)

Joan Jacobson, Shawnee Mission South H.S. (KS)

Diane Johnson, Lawrence Public Schools (NY)

Gerimae Kleinman, Delray Beach (FL)

Laurie Leftwich, Brother Martin High School (LA)

MaryJane London, Los Angeles Center for Enriched Studies (CA)

Martha Lyman, Deerfield Academy (MA)

Brad MacGowan, Newton North H.S. (MA)

Robert S. MacLellan Jr., Hebron Academy (ME)

Susan Marrs, The Seven Hills School (OH)

Karen A. Mason, Germantown Academy (PA)

Lynne McConnell, Rumson–Fair Haven Regional H.S. (NJ)

Lisa Micele, University of Illinois Laboratory H.S. (IL)

Corky Miller-Strong, The Culver Academies (IN)

Janet Miranda, Prestonwood Christian Academy (TX)

Joyce Vining Morgan, White Mountain School (NH)

Gunnar W. Olson, Indian Springs School (AL)

Stuart Oremus, Wellington School (OH)

Deborah Robinson, Mandarin H.S. (FL)

Julie Rollins, Episcopal H.S. (TX)

Heidi Rose, Crystal Springs Uplands School (CA)

William C. Rowe, Thomas Jefferson School (MO)

Bruce Scher, Chicagoland Jewish H.S. (IL)

David Schindel, Sandia Preparatory School (NM)

Kathy Z. Schmidt, St. Mary's Hall (TX)

Barbara Simmons, Notre Dame High School (CA)

Joe Stehno, Bishop Brady H.S. (NH)

Bruce Stempien, Weston H.S. (CT)

Paul M. Stoneham, The Key School (MD)

Ted de Villafranca, Peddie School (NJ)

Scott White, Montclair H.S. (NJ)

Linda Zimring, Los Angeles United School District (CA)

About the Authors

In 1980, when he was education editor of the *New York Times*, **Edward B. Fiske** sensed that college-bound students and their families needed better information on which to base their educational choices. Thus was born the *Fiske Guide to Colleges*. A graduate of Wesleyan University, Fiske did graduate work at Columbia University and assorted other bastions of higher learning. He left the *Times* in 1991 to pursue a variety of educational and journalistic interests, including a book on school reform, *Smart Schools, Smart Kids*. When not visiting colleges, he can be found playing tennis, sailing, or doing research on the educational problems of South Africa and other Third World countries for UNESCO and other international organizations. Fiske lives in Durham, North Carolina, near the campus of Duke University, where his wife, Helen Ladd, is a member of the faculty. They are coauthors of *When Schools Compete: A Cautionary Tale, Elusive Equity: Education Reform in Post-Apartheid South Africa*, and *Handbook of Research in Education Finance and Policy*.

Shawn Logue has served on the *Fiske Guide to Colleges* staff since 1995, first as a staff writer and subsequently in his current position as managing editor. He has written extensively for the corporate and educational marketplace. His professional background includes leadership experience in the private, public, and nonprofit sectors, including roles in educational administration, corporate communications, organizational training and coaching, and Web development. Mr. Logue is also the owner and principal consultant of Clariti Consulting, LLC (www.ClaritiConsulting.com), a content and business strategy consultancy located in Connecticut.

Invitation to Readers

The *Fiske Guide to Colleges* welcomes comments from readers on the write-ups contained in the guide, as well as suggestions regarding ways that we could better serve our readers. Please send your comments to:

Fiske Guide to Colleges
Fax: (630) 835-7859
Email: editor@fiskeguide.com

Thanks for your interest in the *Fiske Guide*.

Off to college with the complete line of Fiske books!

"The best college guide you can buy."—*USA Today*

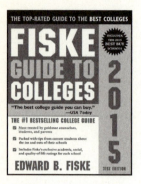

978-1-4022-6065-0 • $23.99

The #1 bestselling college guide

For more than 30 years, the *Fiske Guide to Colleges* has been the bestselling and most trusted college guide used by students, parents, and counselors across the country! The guide includes an in-depth look at more than 320 colleges and universities in the U.S., Canada, Great Britain, and Ireland. It rates each school on a scale of 1 to 5 on academics, social life, and quality of life. It also describes campus culture, lists each school's best programs, and provides average SAT and ACT scores. *Fiske Guide to Colleges* is unequaled at capturing the true essence of each school while providing all the necessary statistics.

978-1-4022-9576-8 • $14.99

Learn how to write the essay that gets you accepted

From the most trusted name in college admissions resources comes the first application-essay book designed for those who need it most: bright students who aren't natural writers. This all-inclusive guide to tackling the application essay provides more than 100 real sample essays, as well as tips and tools for editing from first draft to final submission.

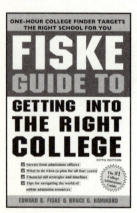

978-1-4022-9579-9 • $16.99

Understand the admissions process and where you fit in best

Fiske Guide to Getting Into the Right College takes students and parents step-by-step through the college admissions process, including selecting your top choices, interviewing, getting letters of recommendation, understanding how admissions offices work, and getting the most financial aid you can. The expert advice and tips will help you get accepted at a challenging school that fits your personality and learning style.

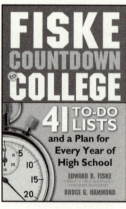

978-1-4022-1897-2 • $9.99

Every year counts

Fiske Countdown to College breaks down the entire college-prep process into dozens of simple checklists that will keep everyone calm and on schedule. From freshman year to the day you leave home, the most trusted name in college admissions keeps you informed of the dos and don'ts that will help you find and fit into your perfect college. Includes quotes and advice from students, parents, and counselors.

College Countdown brings you the complete line of Fiske books
Available at your local or online bookseller
Visit www.collegecountdown.com for more information

Get the Fiske college-prep advantage for all four years of high school!

978-1-4022-6081-0 • $12.99

Matriculate with confidence

Here are the 250 most important words students need to know to be successful in college and beyond, from the former education editor of the *New York Times* and a leading authority on college admissions. Each entry contains information on the word origin, a complete definition, and example sentences, making this book both the perfect gift for high school graduation and an effective tool for expanding a student's vocabulary, increasing word comprehension, and honing writing skills.

978-1-4022-0653-5 • $13.99

Learn—don't just memorize—more than 1,000 words

This amazing new system for building your vocabulary will teach students and word lovers alike to learn—not just memorize—essential words. Readers will learn thousands of new terms in weeks. *Fiske WordPower* includes more than 1,000 words and definitions, example sentences, origins and roots, plus quizzes to determine comprehension.

978-1-4022-6078-0 • $12.99

Discover the words you need to succeed

Starting off with a powerful vocabulary is the best way to prepare for a successful, stress-free time in high school. *Fiske 250 Words Every High School Freshman Needs to Know* will give you the tools to sharpen your writing skills and use language evocatively. Nail your English essays, the SAT and ACT writing tests, and all of your college and scholarship applications.

FISKE'S
College Admission Pledge
for Students

I have accepted the fact that my parents are clueless. I am serene. I will betray not a tremor when they offer opinions or advice, no matter how laughable. My soul will be light as a feather when my mother elbows her way to the front of my college tour and talks the guide's ear off. I am serene.

Going to college is a stressful time for my parents, even though they are not the ones going. I recognize that neurosis is beyond anyone's control. Each week, I will calmly reassure them that I am working on my essays, have registered for my tests, am finishing my applications, have scheduled my interviews, am aware of all deadlines, and will have everything done in plenty of time. I will smile good-naturedly as my parent asks four follow-up questions at College Night.

I will try not to say "no" simply because my parents say "yes," and I will remain open to the possibility, however improbable, that they may have a point. I may not be fully conscious of my anxieties about the college search—the fear of being judged and the fear of leaving home are both strong. I don't really want to get out of here as much as I say I do, and it is easier to put off thinking about the college search than to get it done. My parents are right about the importance of being proactive, even if they do get carried away.

Though the college search belongs to me, I will listen to my parents. They know me better than anyone else, and they are the ones who will pay most of the bills. Their ideas about what will be best for me are based on years of experience in the real world. I will seriously consider what they say as I form my own opinions.

I must take charge of the college search. If I do, the nagging will stop, and everyone's anxiety will go down. My parents have given me a remarkable gift—the ability to think and do for myself. I know I can do it with a little help from Mom and Dad.

FISKE'S

College Admission Pledge
for Parents

I am resigned to the fact that my child's college search will end in disaster. I am serene. Deadlines will be missed and scholarships will be lost as my child lounges under pulsating headphones or stares transfixed at an Xbox. I am a parent and I know nothing. I am serene.

Confronted with endless procrastination, my impulse is to take control—to register for tests, plan visits, schedule interviews, and get applications. It was I who asked those four follow-up questions at College Night—I couldn't help myself. And yet I know that everything will be fine if I can summon the fortitude to relax. My child is smart, capable, and perhaps a little too accustomed to me jumping in and fixing things. I will hold back. I will drop hints and encourage, then back off. I will facilitate rather than dominate. The college search won't happen on my schedule, but it will happen.

I will not get too high or low about any facet of the college search. By doing so, I give it more importance than it really has. My child's self-worth may already be too wrapped up in getting an acceptance letter. I will attempt to lessen the fear rather than heighten it.

I will try not to say "no" simply because my son or daughter says "yes," and I will remain open to the possibility, however improbable, that my child has the most important things under control. I understand that my anxiety comes partly from a sense of impending loss. I can feel my child slipping away. Sometimes I hold on too tightly or let social acceptability cloud the issue of what is best.

I realize that my child is almost ready to go and that a little rebellion at this time of life can be a good thing. I will respect and encourage independence, even if some of it is expressed as resentment toward me. I will make suggestions with care and try to avoid unnecessary confrontation.

Paying for college is my responsibility. I will take a major role in the search for financial aid and scholarships and speak honestly to my child about the financial realities we face.

I must help my son or daughter take charge of the college search. I will try to support without smothering, encourage without annoying, and consult without controlling. The college search is too big to be handled alone—I will be there every step of the way.

Notes

Notes

Notes